Lecture Notes in Artificial Intelligence   3641

Edited by J. G. Carbonell and J. Siekmann

Subseries of Lecture Notes in Computer Science

Dominik Ślęzak Guoyin Wang
Marcin Szczuka Ivo Düntsch
Yiyu Yao (Eds.)

Rough Sets, Fuzzy Sets, Data Mining, and Granular Computing

10th International Conference, RSFDGrC 2005
Regina, Canada, August 31 – September 3, 2005
Proceedings, Part I

 Springer

Series Editors

Jaime G. Carbonell, Carnegie Mellon University, Pittsburgh, PA, USA
Jörg Siekmann, University of Saarland, Saarbrücken, Germany

Volume Editors

Dominik Ślęzak
Yiyu Yao
University of Regina, Department of Computer Science
3737 Wascana Parkway, Regina, SK S4S 0A2, Canada
E-mail: {slezak, yyao}@cs.uregina.ca

Guoyin Wang
Chongqing University of Posts and Telecommunications
Institute of Computer Science and Technology
Chongqing, 400065, P.R. China
E-mail: wanggy@ieee.org

Marcin Szczuka
Warsaw University, Institute of Mathematics
Banacha 2, 02-097, Warsaw, Poland
E-mail: szczuka@mimuw.edu.pl

Ivo Düntsch
Brock University, Computer Science Department
St. Catharines, Ontario L2S 3A1, Canada
E-mail: duentsch@brocku.ca

Library of Congress Control Number: 2005931253

CR Subject Classification (1998): I.2, H.2.4, H.3, F.4.1, F.1, I.5, H.4

ISSN   0302-9743
ISBN-10   3-540-28653-5 Springer Berlin Heidelberg New York
ISBN-13   978-3-540-28653-0 Springer Berlin Heidelberg New York

Springer is a part of Springer Science+Business Media

springeronline.com

© Springer-Verlag Berlin Heidelberg 2005
Printed in Germany

Typesetting: Camera-ready by author, data conversion by Scientific Publishing Services, Chennai, India
Printed on acid-free paper   SPIN: 11548669   06/3142   5 4 3 2 1 0

Preface

This volume contains the papers selected for presentation at the 10th International Conference on Rough Sets, Fuzzy Sets, Data Mining, and Granular Computing, RSFDGrC 2005, organized at the University of Regina, August 31st–September 3rd, 2005. This conference followed in the footsteps of international events devoted to the subject of rough sets, held so far in Canada, China, Japan, Poland, Sweden, and the USA. RSFDGrC achieved the status of biennial international conference, starting from 2003 in Chongqing, China.

The theory of rough sets, proposed by Zdzisław Pawlak in 1982, is a model of approximate reasoning. The main idea is based on indiscernibility relations that describe indistinguishability of objects. Concepts are represented by approximations. In applications, rough set methodology focuses on approximate representation of knowledge derivable from data. It leads to significant results in many areas such as finance, industry, multimedia, and medicine.

The RSFDGrC conferences put an emphasis on connections between rough sets and fuzzy sets, granular computing, and knowledge discovery and data mining, both at the level of theoretical foundations and real-life applications. In the case of this event, additional effort was made to establish a linkage towards a broader range of applications. We achieved it by including in the conference program the workshops on bioinformatics, security engineering, and embedded systems, as well as tutorials and sessions related to other application areas.

Revision Process

There were 277 submissions, excluding the invited, workshop, and special session papers. Every paper was examined by at least three reviewers. Out of the papers initially selected, some were approved subject to major revision and then additionally evaluated by the Advisory Board and Program Committee members; 119 papers were finally accepted, this gives an acceptance ratio equal to 43.0%.

In the case of workshops, 22 out of 130 submissions were finally approved to be published in the proceedings; this gives an acceptance ratio equal to 16.9%.

The reviewing process for the special session included in the proceedings was conducted independently by its organizers; 5 papers were finally accepted.

Final versions of all invited, regular, workshop, and special session papers were thoroughly revised by the editors, often with several iterations of corrections.

Layout of Proceedings

The regular, invited, workshop, and special session papers are published within 30 chapters, grouped with respect to their topics. The conference materials are split into two volumes (LNAI 3641 and 3642), both consisting of 15 chapters.

This volume contains 75 papers. Three invited papers are gathered in Chap. 1. The remaining 72 regular papers are gathered in Chaps. 2–15, related to rough set approximations, rough-algebraic foundations, feature selection and reduction, reasoning in information tables, rough-probabilistic approaches, rough-fuzzy hybridization, fuzzy methods in data analysis, evolutionary computing, machine learning, approximate and uncertain reasoning, probabilistic network models, spatial and temporal reasoning, non-standard logics, and granular computing.

Acknowledgements

We wish to thank Zdzisław Pawlak and Lotfi A. Zadeh for acting as honorary chairs of the conference. We are also very grateful to the scientists who kindly agreed to give the keynote, plenary, and tutorial lectures: Vladimir Vapnik and Ronald Yager; Salvatore Greco, Hung Son Nguyen, Witold Pedrycz, Dimiter Vakarelov, Julio Valdés, and Ning Zhong; and Andrzej Czyżewski, Stéphane Demri, Igor Jurisica, Bożena Kostek, Ewa Orłowska, and Piotr Wasilewski.

Our special thanks go to Andrzej Skowron for presenting the keynote lecture on behalf of Zdzisław Pawlak, James F. Peters and René V. Mayorga for organizing the special session, and Jiman Hong, Tai-hoon Kim, and Sung Y. Shin for organizing three workshops at RSFDGrC 2005.

We are grateful for support given by the University of Regina, Faculty of Science, and Department of Computer Science. We would like to express our gratitude to all the people who helped in the organization of the conference in Regina: Brien Maguire and Lois Adams for coordinating all the arrangements, as well as Donalda Kozlowski, Connie Novitski, and Janice Savoie for support at various stages of conference preparations; Cory Butz for serving as a publicity chair; Robert Cowles and Peng Yao for administrating and improving the conference software systems; Hong Yao for launching the conference homepage, and Shan Hua for its updating and taking care of email correspondence; all other students of Computer Science who helped during the conference preparations.

We would like to thank the authors who contributed to this volume. We are very grateful to the chairs, Advisory Board, and Program Committee members who helped in the revision process. We also acknowledge all the reviewers not listed in the conference committee. Their names are listed on a separate page, including also those who evaluated the workshop paper submissions.

Last but not least, we are grateful to Alfred Hofmann and Anna Kramer at Springer for support and cooperation during preparation of this volume.

June 2005

Dominik Ślęzak
Guoyin Wang
Marcin Szczuka
Ivo Düntsch
Yiyu Yao

RSFDGrC 2005 Conference Committee

Honorary Chairs	Zdzisław Pawlak, Lotfi A. Zadeh
Conference Chairs	Wojciech Ziarko, Yiyu Yao, Xiaohua Hu
Program Chair	Dominik Ślęzak
Program Co-chairs	Ivo Düntsch, James F. Peters, Guoyin Wang
Workshop Chair	JingTao Yao
Tutorial Chair	Marcin Szczuka
Publicity Chair	Cory Butz
Local Organizing Chair	Brien Maguire
Conference Secretary	Lois Adams

Advisory Board

Nick Cercone	Stan Matwin	Roman Słowiński
Salvatore Greco	Ewa Orłowska	Zbigniew Suraj
Jerzy Grzymała-Busse	Sankar K. Pal	Shusaku Tsumoto
Masahiro Inuiguchi	Witold Pedrycz	Julio Valdes
Jan Komorowski	Lech Polkowski	Jue Wang
Tsau Young Lin	Zbigniew Raś	Bo Zhang
Qing Liu	Andrzej Skowron	Ning Zhong

Program Committee

Mohua Banerjee	Jiye Liang	Henryk Rybiński
Jan Bazan	Churn-Jung Liau	Hiroshi Sakai
Malcolm Beynon	Pawan Lingras	Zhongzhi Shi
Hans-Dieter Burkhard	Chunnian Liu	Arul Siromoney
Gianpiero Cattaneo	Benedetto Matarazzo	Jerzy Stefanowski
Chien-Chung Chan	Ernestina Menasalvas-Ruiz	Jarosław Stepaniuk
Juan-Carlos Cubero	Duoqian Miao	Roman Świniarski
Andrzej Czyżewski	Sadaaki Miyamoto	Piotr Synak
Jitender S. Deogun	John Mordeson	Gwo-Hshiung Tzeng
Didier Dubois	Mikhail Moshkov	Dimiter Vakarelov
Maria C. Fernandez-Baizan	Hiroshi Motoda	Alicja Wakulicz-Deja
Günther Gediga	Tetsuya Murai	Hui Wang
Anna Gomolińska	Michinori Nakata	Lipo Wang
Shoji Hirano	Hung Son Nguyen	Paul P. Wang
Ryszard Janicki	Sinh Hoa Nguyen	Anita Wasilewska
Jouni Jarvinen	Piero Pagliani	Jakub Wróblewski
Licheng Jiao	Frederick Petry	Keming Xie
Janusz Kacprzyk	Henri Prade	Zongben Xu
Jacek Koronacki	Mohamed Quafafou	Wen-Xiu Zhang
Bożena Kostek	Vijay Raghavan	Yanqing Zhang
Marzena Kryszkiewicz	Sheela Ramanna	Zhi-Hua Zhou

Non-committee Reviewers

Adam Ameur
Robin Andersson
Ryan Benton
Steffen Bickel
Fuyuan Cao
Jesus Cardenosa
Yoojin Chung
Piotr Dałka
Agnieszka Dardzińska
Anca Doloc-Mihu
Isabel Drost
Eugene Eberbach
Santiago Eibe Garcia
Stefan Enroth
František Franek
Alicja Gruźdź
Junyoung Heo
Jiman Hong
Piotr Hońko
Torgeir Hvidsten
Aleksandra Ihnatowicz
Gangil Jeon
Guang Jiang
Bo Jin

Andrzej Kaczmarek
Wolfram Kahl
Katarzyna Kierzkowska
Hanil Kim
Jung-Yeop Kim
Sung-Ryul Kim
Tai-hoon Kim
Maciej Koutny
Sangjun Lee
Jiye Li
Gabriela Lindemann
Krzysztof Marasek
Óscar Marbán
René V. Mayorga
Dagmar Monett Díaz
Lalita Narupiyakul
Jose Negrete Martinez
Phu Chien Nguyen
Atorn Nuntiyagul
Kouzou Ohara
J. Orzechowski-Westholm
Tianjie Pang
Puntip Pattaraintakorn
Jiming Peng

Concepción Pérez Llera
Skip Poehlman
Yuhua Qian
Kenneth Revett
Tobias Scheffer
Kay Schröter
Biren Shah
Charlie Shim
Sung Y. Shin
Chang O. Sung
Robert Susmaga
Piotr Szczuko
Yu Tang
Yuchun Tang
Alexandre Termier
Tinko Tinchev
Uma Maheswari V.
Junhong Wang
Haibin Wang
Ying Xie
Sangho Yi
Yan Zhao
Marta Zorrilla
Włodek Zuberek

Table of Contents

Feature Selection and Reduction

Reasoning in Information Systems

Rough-Probabilistic Approaches

Rough-Fuzzy Hybridization

Fuzzy Methods in Data Analysis

Evolutionary Computing

Machine Learning

Approximate and Uncertain Reasoning

Probabilistic Network Models

Spatial and Temporal Reasoning

Non-standard Logics

Granular Computing

Rough Sets and Flow Graphs

Zdzisław Pawlak

Institute for Theoretical and Applied Informatics,
Polish Academy of Sciences,
ul. Bałtycka 5, 44-100 Gliwice, Poland
Warsaw School of Information Technology,
ul. Newelska 6, 01-447 Warsaw, Poland
zpw@ii.pw.edu.pl

Abstract. This paper concerns the relationship between rough sets and flow graphs. It is shown that flow graph can be used both as formal language for computing approximations of sets in the sense of rough set theory, and as description tool for data structure. This description is employed next for finding patterns in data. To this end decision algorithm induced by the flow graph is defined and studied.

Keywords: rough sets; flow graphs; decision algorithms.

1 Introduction

We study in this paper the relationship between rough sets and flow graphs. It is revealed that flow graph can be used as a formal language for rough set theory and can be also used for decision algorithm simplification. Flow graphs introduced in this paper are different from those proposed by Ford and Fulkerson for optimal flow analysis [1].

Flow graphs can be used for approximate reasoning modeling based on the flow principle. In particular, it is shown in this paper that if we interpret nodes of flow graphs as subsets of a finite universe, such that for any branch (x,y) of the flow graph (x is an input of y) we have $x \cap y \neq \emptyset$, then the union of all inputs x of y is the upper approximation of y. Similarly, the union of all inputs x of y, such that $x \subseteq y$, is the lower approximation of y, provided that all inputs of y are mutually disjoint.

Besides, independency and dependency (statistical) of conditions and decisions of decision rules are defined and discussed.

This paper is a continuation of the author's ideas presented in [7,8] (see also [2,3]).

2 Rough Sets

In this section we recall briefly after [6] basic concept of rough set theory.

A starting point of rough set based data analysis is a data set, called an information system.

D. Ślęzak et al. (Eds.): RSFDGrC 2005, LNAI 3641, pp. 1–11, 2005.

Formally, by an *information system* we will understand a pair S = (U, A), where U and A, are finite, nonempty sets called the *universe*, and the set of *attributes*, respectively. With every attribute a ∈ A we associate a set V_a of its *values*, called the *domain* of a. Any subset B of A determines a binary relation I(B) on U, called an *indiscernibility relation*, and defined as follows: (x, y) ∈ I(B) if and only if a(x) = a(y) for every a ∈ A, where a(x) denotes the value of attribute a for element x.

Obviously I(B) is an equivalence relation. The family of all equivalence classes of I(B), i.e., a partition determined by B, will be denoted by U/I(B), or simply by U/B. An equivalence class of I(B), i.e., block of the partition U/B, containing x will be denoted by B(x).

If (x, y) belongs to I(B), we will say that x and y are B-*indiscernible* (*indiscernible with respect to* B). Equivalence classes of the relation I(B) (or blocks of the partition U/B) are referred to as B-*elementary sets* or B-*granules*.

If we distinguish in an information system two disjoint classes of attributes, called *condition* and *decision attributes*, respectively, then the system will be called a *decision system*, denoted by S = (U, C, D), where C and D are disjoint sets of condition and decision attributes, respectively.

Suppose we are given an information system S = (U, A), X ⊆ U, and B ⊆ A. Our task is to describe the set X in terms of attribute values from B. To this end we define two operations assigning to every X ⊆ U two sets $B_*(X)$ and $B^*(X)$ called the B-*lower* and the B-*upper approximation* of X, respectively, and defined as follows:

$$B_*(X) = \bigcup_{x \in U} \{B(x) : B(x) \subseteq X\} \tag{1}$$

$$B^*(X) = \bigcup_{x \in U} \{B(x) : B(x) \cap X \neq \emptyset\} \tag{2}$$

Hence, the B-lower approximation of a set X is the union of all B-granules that are included in X, whereas its B-upper approximation is the union of all B-granules that have a nonempty intersection with X. The set

$$BN_B(X) = B^*(X) - B_*(X) \tag{3}$$

will be referred to as to the B-*boundary region* of X.

If the boundary region of X is the empty set, i.e., $BN_B(X) = \emptyset$, then X is *crisp* (*exact*) with respect to B. In the opposite case, i.e., if $BN_B(X) \neq \emptyset$, then X is referred to as to *rough* (*inexact*) with respect to B.

3   Flow Graphs

In this section we recall after [7] basic definitions and properties of flow graphs.

Flow graphs can be considered as a special kind of databases, where instead of data about individual objects some statistical features of objects are presented in terms of information flow distribution. It turns out that such data representation gives a new insight into data structures and leads to new methods of intelligent data analysis.

A flow graph is a *directed acyclic finite* graph $G = (N, \mathcal{B}, \varphi)$, where N is a set of *nodes*, $\mathcal{B} \subseteq N \times N$ is a set of *directed branches*, $\varphi : \mathcal{B} \to R^+$ is a *flow function*, and R^+ is the set of non-negative reals. We list basic concepts of flow graphs:

- If $(x, y) \in \mathcal{B}$ then x is an *input* of y and y is an *output* of x.
- If $x \in N$ then $I(x)$ and $O(x)$ denote the sets of all x's inputs and outputs.
- *Input* and *output* of a graph G are defined, respectively, as

$$I(G) = \{x \in N : I(x) = \emptyset\} \text{ and } O(G) = \{x \in N : O(x) = \emptyset\}$$

- Inputs and outputs of G are its *external nodes*; other nodes are *internal*.
- If $(x, y) \in \mathcal{B}$ then $\varphi(x, y)$ is a *throughflow* from x to y;
  We will assume in what follows that $\varphi(x, y) \neq 0$ for every $(x, y) \in \mathcal{B}$.

With every node x of a flow graph G we associate its *inflow*

$$\varphi_+(x) = \sum_{y \in I(x)} \varphi(y, x) \tag{4}$$

and *outflow*

$$\varphi_-(x) = \sum_{y \in O(x)} \varphi(x, y) \tag{5}$$

Similarly, we define an inflow and an outflow for the whole flow graph G:

$$\varphi_+(G) = \sum_{x \in I(G)} \varphi_-(x) \tag{6}$$

$$\varphi_-(G) = \sum_{x \in O(G)} \varphi_+(x) \tag{7}$$

We assume that for any internal node x, $\varphi_+(x) = \varphi_-(x) = \varphi(x)$, where $\varphi(x)$ is the throughflow of node x.

Obviously, $\varphi_+(G) = \varphi_-(G) = \varphi(G)$, where $\varphi(G)$ is the throughflow of G.

The above formulas can be considered as *flow conservation equations* [2].

Example: Assume that there are 100 play blocks in the collection; 60 are triangular, 40 are square, 70 are blue, 10 are red, 20 are green, 10 are small and 90 are large. Flow graph for the set of play blocks is presented in Fig. 1. We see that there are 45 triangular and blue play blocks, etc. Thus the flow gives clear picture of the relationship between different features of play blocks.   □

If we replace flow by relative flow with respect to total flow, we obtain a *normalized flow graph* – a *directed acyclic finite* graph $G = (N, \mathcal{B}, \sigma)$, where, as before,

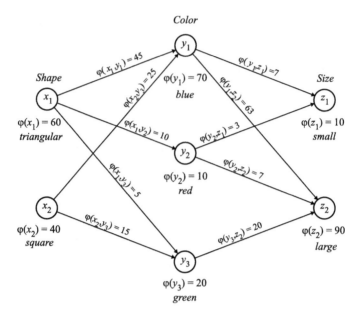

Fig. 1. Flow graph

N is a set of *nodes*, $\mathcal{B} \subseteq N \times N$ is a set of *directed branches*, but instead of $\varphi : \mathcal{B} \to R^+$ we have a *normalized flow* defined by

$$\sigma(x, y) = \frac{\varphi(x, y)}{\varphi(G)} \tag{8}$$

for any $(x, y) \in \mathcal{B}$.

The value of $\sigma(x, y)$ is called the *strength* of (x, y). Obviously, $0 \le \sigma(x, y) \le 1$. The strength of the branch expresses simply the ratio of throughflow of the branch to the total flow.

Normalized graphs have interesting properties which are discussed next. In what follows we will use normalized flow graphs only, therefore by flow graphs we will understand normalized flow graphs, unless stated otherwise.

For the sake of further study, if we invert all arrows in a flow graph the new resulting flow graph will be called *inverse*.

With every node x of a flow graph G we associate its *normalized inflow*

$$\sigma_+(x) = \frac{\varphi_+(x)}{\varphi(G)} = \sum_{y \in I(x)} \sigma(y, x) \tag{9}$$

and *normalized outflow*

$$\sigma_-(x) = \frac{\varphi_-(x)}{\varphi(G)} = \sum_{y \in O(x)} \sigma(x, y) \tag{10}$$

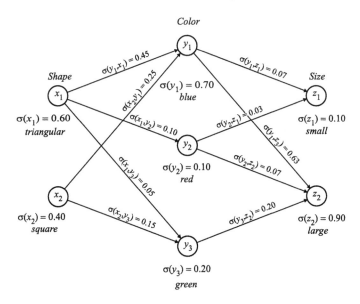

Fig. 2. Normalized flow graph

Obviously, for any internal node x, we have $\sigma_+(x) = \sigma_-(x) = \sigma(x)$, where $\sigma(x)$ is a *normalized throughflow* of x. Moreover, let

$$\sigma_+(G) = \frac{\varphi_+(G)}{\varphi(G)} = \sum_{x \in I(G)} \sigma_-(x) \tag{11}$$

$$\sigma_-(G) = \frac{\varphi_-(G)}{\varphi(G)} = \sum_{x \in O(G)} \sigma_+(x) \tag{12}$$

Obviously, $\sigma_+(G) = \sigma_-(G) = \sigma(G) = 1$.

A (*directed*) *path* from x to y, $x \neq y$, in G is a sequence of nodes $x_1, \ldots, x_n$ such that $x_1 = x$, $x_n = y$ and $(x_i, x_{i+1}) \in \mathcal{B}$ for every i, $1 \leq i \leq n-1$. A path from x to y is denoted by $[x \ldots y]$ and $n-1$ is called *length* of the path.

A flow graph is *linear* if all paths from node x to node y have the same length, for every pair of nodes x, y.

A set of nodes of a linear flow graph is called a k-*layer* if it consists of all nodes of this graph linked by a path of the length k with some input node.

The set of all inputs will be called the *input layer* of the flow graph, whereas the set of all outputs is the *output layer* of the flow graph. For any input node x and output node y of a linear graph, the length of $[x \ldots y]$ is the same. The layers different than input and output layers will be referred to as to *hidden layers*.

Example (cont.): Fig. 2 shows normalized flow graph for the play blocks. We have three layers $\{x_1, x_2\}$, $\{y_1, y_2, y_3\}$ and $\{z_1, z_2\}$, where $\{x_1, x_2\}$ is the input layer, $\{z_1, z_2\}$ is the output layer and $\{y_1, y_2, y_3\}$ is the hidden layer.   □

4   Certainty and Coverage Factors

With every branch (x, y) of a flow graph G we associate the *certainty factor*

$$\text{cer}(x, y) = \frac{\sigma(x, y)}{\sigma(x)} \tag{13}$$

and the *coverage factor*

$$\text{cov}(x, y) = \frac{\sigma(x, y)}{\sigma(y)} \tag{14}$$

where $\sigma(x) \neq 0$ and $\sigma(y) \neq 0$.

These coefficients are widely used in data mining (see, e.g., [5,11,12]) but they can be traced back to Lukasiewicz [4], who used them first in connection with his research on logic and probability.

If we interpret nodes of a flow graph as subsets of a fixed set U (the universe), then $\text{cer}(x, y)$ can be understood as the degree of inclusion of x in y [9], while $\text{cov}(x, y)$ – as the degree of inclusion of y in x, for any sets x, y, where:

$$\text{cer}(X, Y) = \begin{cases} \frac{|X \cap Y|}{|X|} & \text{if } X \neq \emptyset \\ 1 & \text{if } X = \emptyset \end{cases}$$

$cov(X, Y) = cer(Y, X)$, and $|x|$ denotes the cardinality of set x.

Observe that by x, y we denote both nodes of the flow graph and subsets of the universe U. However, it does not lead to confusion, because it is always clear from the context when we speak about nodes or sets.

Assume that if $\{x_1, \ldots, x_n\}$ is a layer then $x_i \cap x_j = \emptyset$ for any $x_i \neq x_j$, and $\sum_{i=1}^{n} x_i = U$, i.e., every layer is a partition of the universe.

Consequently, the union of all inputs x of y can be understood as the upper approximation of y and the union of all inputs x of y such that $\text{cer}(x, y) = 1$ as the lower approximation of y.

In what follows, we will interpret layers as attributes in information systems, input and hidden layers are interpreted as condition attributes, whereas output layer is interpreted as the decision attribute.

Example (cont.): Fig. 3 illustrates certainty and coverage factors for previously considered example. Here, the input layer represents condition attribute *shape*, the hidden layer – the condition attribute *color*, whereas the output layer – the decision attribute *size*. We can see from the graph that the lower approximation of z_1 is the empty set, whereas the upper approximation of z_1 is $y_1 \cup y_2$. The lower approximation of z_2 is y_3, whereas the upper approximation is $y_1 \cup y_2 \cup y_3$. The lower approximation of y_1 is the empty set, and the upper approximation is $x_1 \cup x_2$. For the set y_2 both approximations are equal x_1, etc.

From the inverse flow graph we get, e.g., that the lower approximation of x_2 is the empty set, the upper approximation is the set $y_1 \cup y_3$, and the lower and upper approximations of y_3 are both equal to z_2.   □

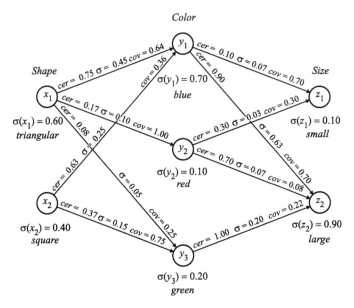

Fig. 3. Certainty and coverage factors

The following properties are immediate consequences of definitions given above:

$$\sum_{y \in O(x)} cer(x, y) = 1 \tag{15}$$

$$\sum_{x \in I(y)} cov(x, y) = 1 \tag{16}$$

$$\sigma(x) = \sum_{y \in O(x)} cer(x, y)\sigma(x) = \sum_{y \in O(x)} \sigma(x, y) \tag{17}$$

$$\sigma(y) = \sum_{x \in I(y)} cov(x, y)\sigma(y) = \sum_{x \in I(y)} \sigma(x, y) \tag{18}$$

$$cer(x, y) = \frac{cov(x, y)\sigma(y)}{\sigma(x)} \tag{19}$$

$$cov(x, y) = \frac{cer(x, y)\sigma(x)}{\sigma(y)} \tag{20}$$

The above properties have a probabilistic flavor, e.g., equations (17) and (18) have a form of total probability theorem, whereas formulas (19) and (20) are

Bayes' rules [10]. However, in our approach, these properties are interpreted in a deterministic way and they describe flow distribution among branches in the network.

The *certainty*, *coverage*, and *strength* of the path $[x_1 \ldots x_n]$ are defined as

$$\mathrm{cer}[x_1 \ldots x_n] = \prod_{i=1}^{n-1} \mathrm{cer}(x_i, x_{i+1}) \tag{21}$$

$$\mathrm{cov}[x_1 \ldots x_n] = \prod_{i=1}^{n-1} \mathrm{cov}(x_i, x_{i+1}) \tag{22}$$

$$\sigma[x \ldots y] = \sigma(x)\mathrm{cer}[x \ldots y] = \sigma(y)\mathrm{cov}[x \ldots y] \tag{23}$$

respectively.

5   Flow Graph and Decision Algorithms

Flow graphs can be interpreted as decision algorithms [7].

Let us assume that the set of nodes of a flow graph is interpreted as a set of logical formulas. The formulas are understood as propositional functions and if x is a formula, then $\sigma(x)$ is to be interpreted as a truth value of the formula. Let us observe that the truth values are numbers from the closed interval $< 0, 1 >$, i.e., $0 \leq \sigma(x) \leq 1$.

According to [4] these truth values can be also interpreted as probabilities. Thus $\sigma(x)$ can be understood as flow distribution ratio (percentage), truth value or probability. We will stick to the first interpretation.

With every branch (x, y) we associate a decision rule $x \rightarrow y$, read *if* x *then* y; x will be referred to as to *condition*, whereas y – *decision* of the rule. Such a rule is characterized by three numbers: $\sigma(x, y)$, $\mathrm{cer}(x, y)$, and $\mathrm{cov}(x, y)$.

Table 1. Decision algorithm

	certainty	coverage	strength
$x_1, y_1 \rightarrow z_1$	0.10	0.45	0.05
$x_1, y_1 \rightarrow z_2$	0.90	0.45	0.41
$x_1, y_2 \rightarrow z_1$	0.30	0.30	0.03
$x_1, y_2 \rightarrow z_2$	0.70	0.08	0.07
$x_1, y_3 \rightarrow z_2$	1.00	0.06	0.05
$x_2, y_1 \rightarrow z_1$	0.10	0.25	0.02
$x_2, y_1 \rightarrow z_2$	0.90	0.25	0.23
$x_2, y_3 \rightarrow z_2$	1.00	0.17	0.15

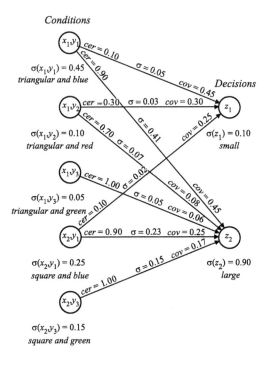

Fig. 4. Flow graph of the decision algorithm

Thus every path $[x_1 \ldots x_n]$ determines a sequence of decision rules $x_1 \rightarrow x_2$, $x_2 \rightarrow x_3, \ldots, x_{n-1} \rightarrow x_n$. From previous considerations it follows that such sequence can be interpreted as a single decision rule $x_1 x_2 \ldots x_{n-1} \rightarrow x_n$, in short $x^* \rightarrow x_n$, where $x^* = x_1 x_2 \ldots x_{n-1}$, characterized by

$$\mathrm{cer}(x^*, x_n) = \frac{\sigma(x^*, x_n)}{\sigma(x^*)} \tag{24}$$

$$\mathrm{cov}(x^*, x_n) = \frac{\sigma(x^*, x_n)}{\sigma(x_n)} \tag{25}$$

where

$$\sigma(x^*, x_n) = \sigma[x_1, \ldots, x_{n-1}, x_n] \quad \text{and} \quad \sigma(x^*) = \sigma[x_1, \ldots, x_{n-1}] \tag{26}$$

The set of all decision rules $x_{i_1} x_{i_2} \ldots x_{i_{n-1}} \rightarrow x_{i_n}$ associated with paths $[x_{i_1} \ldots x_{i_n}]$, such that x_{i_1} and x_{i_n} are input and output of the flow graph, respectively, will be called a *decision algorithm* induced by the flow graph.

Example (cont.): Decision algorithm induced by the flow graph given in Fig. 3 is shown in Table 1. With the decision algorithm we can associate a flow graph as shown in Fig. 4. Observe that the values of coefficients in Fig. 4 may not satisfy exactly formulas (15)-(18) due to the round off errors in the computations.

One can see that the lower approximation of set z_1 is the empty set and the upper approximation of z_1 is $(x_1 \cap y_1) \cup (x_1 \cap y_2) \cup (x_2 \cap y_1)$. The lower approximation of z_2 is $(x_1 \cap y_3) \cup (x_2 \cap y_3)$ and its upper approximation is equal to $(x_1 \cap y_1) \cup (x_1 \cap y_2) \cup (x_1 \cap y_3) \cup (x_2 \cap y_1) \cup (x_2 \cap y_3)$. □

6   Conclusion

We have shown in this paper that approximations, basic operations in rough set theory, which are in fact topological interior and closure operations defined in algebraic terms, can be also defined in terms of flow intensity in a flow graph. If we associate with every node of a flow graph a subset of a fixed universe then the flow graph induces a relational structure such that two nodes connected by a branch may be interpreted as partial inclusion of the corresponding subsets.

In particular, if X is included in Y then X belongs to the lower approximation of Y and if X is partially included in Y then X belongs to the upper approximation of Y. Thus, the flow graph can be interpreted as family of lower and upper approximations of subsets associated its nodes. This leads to a very simple method of computing approximations without involving set theoretical operations but employing only certainty and coverage coefficients.

This can be specially useful when data are given in a form of a decision table, and the associated flow graph can be easily used to compute approximations and consequently – decision rules (sure and possible).

This idea can be also formulated simpler by defining approximation of nodes in a flow graph – instead of approximation of sets associated with nodes of the flow graph. However, we have not consider this idea in this paper.

Finally, we would like to present some research topics related to flow graphs:

1. *Extracting relevant flow graphs from data.* Flow graphs derived from data tables can be treated as a form of knowledge representation encoded in these tables. Reasoning based on flow graphs can be much more efficient than reasoning performed directly from data tables. However, one should develop algorithms for extracting from data flow graphs that make it possible to perform such reasoning with the satisfactory quality.
2. *Developing case-based reasoning methods for cases with decisions represented by flow graphs.* In particular, this includes developing methods for incremental learning with flow graphs as compound decisions.
3. *Reasoning about changes of flow graphs.* Flow graphs can also be used in reasoning about changes. This will require developing algorithms for inducing rules predicting changes of flow graphs from properties of changing data.

Acknowledgments

Thanks are due to Prof. Andrzej Skowron and Dr. Dominik Ślęzak for critical remarks.

References

1. Ford, L.R., Fulkerson, D.R.: Flows in Networks. Princeton University Press, Princeton. New Jersey (1962)
2. Greco, S., Pawlak, Z., Słowiński, R.: Generalized decision algorithms, rough inference rules and flow graphs. In: J.J. Alpigini, J.F. Peters, A. Skowron, N. Zhong (eds.), Rough Sets and Current Trends in Computing. Lecture Notes in Artificial Intelligence 2475, Springer-Verlag, Berlin (2002) 93-104
3. Greco, S., Pawlak, Z., Słowiński, R.: Bayesian confirmation measures within rough set approach. In: S. Tsumoto, R. Słowiński, J. Komorowski, J. Grzymała-Busse (eds.), Rough Sets and Current Trends in Computing (RSCTC 2004). Lecture Notes in Artificial Intelligence 3066, Springer Verlag, Berlin (2004) 261-270
4. Łukasiewicz, J.: Die logishen Grundlagen der Wahrscheinilchkeitsrechnung. Kraków (1913). In: L. Borkowski (ed.), Jan Łukasiewicz – Selected Works. North Holland Publishing Company, Amsterdam, London, Polish Scientific Publishers, Warsaw (1970) 16-63
5. E. Kloesgen, J. Żytkow (eds.): Handbook of Knowledge Discovery and Data Mining. Oxford University Press, Oxford, UK (2002)
6. Pawlak, Z.: Rough Sets: Theoretical Aspects of Reasoning about Data. System Theory, Knowledge Engineering and Problem Solving 9, Kluwer Academic Publishers, Dordrecht (1991)
7. Pawlak, Z.: Rough sets, decision algorithms and Bayes' theorem. European Journal of Operational Research, 136 (2002) 181-189
8. Pawlak, Z.: Flow graphs and decision algorithms. In: G. Wang, Y. Yao, A. Skowron (eds.), Rough Sets, Fuzzy Sets, Data Mining and Granular Computing (RSFDGrC 2003). Lecture Notes in Artificial Intelligence, 2639, Springer Verlag, Berlin (2003) 1-10
9. Polkowski, L., Skowron, A.: Rough mereology: A new paradigm for approximation reasoning. International Journal of Approximate Reasoning, 15(4) (1996) 333-365
10. Swinburne, R. (ed.): Bayes's Theorem. In: Proceedings of the British Academy, 113, Oxford University Press (2002)
11. Tsumoto, S.: Modelling medical diagnostic rules based on rough sets. In: L. Polkowski, A. Skowron (eds.), Rough Sets and Current Trends in Computing (RSCTC'98). Lecture Notes in Artificial Intelligence 1424, Springer Verlag, Berlin (1998) 475-482
12. Wong, S.K.M., Ziarko, W.: Algorithm for inductive learning. Bull. Polish Academy of Sciences 34(5-6) (1986) 271-276

A Modal Characterization of Indiscernibility and Similarity Relations in Pawlak's Information Systems*

Dimiter Vakarelov

Department of Mathematical Logic with Laboratory for Applied Logic,
Faculty of Mathematics and Computer Science,
Sofia University blvd James Bouchier 5,
1126 Sofia, Bulgaria
dvak@fmi.uni-sofia.bg

Abstract. In this paper we present a modal logic **IND** for Pawlak's information systems giving a modal characterization of 9 informational relations: strong indiscernibility, as well as weak and strong versions of forward and backward informational inclusion, as well as positive and negative similarities. **IND** extends the logic **INF** introduced in [4] by adding a modality corresponding to strong indiscernibility relation. The main problem in the modal treating of strong indiscernibility is that its definition is not modally definable. This requires special copying techniques, which in the presence of many interacting modalities presents complications. One of the main aims of the paper is to demonstrate such techniques and to present an information logic complete in the intended semantics and containing almost all natural information relations. It is proved that **IND** possesses finite model property and hence is decidable.

1   Introduction

This paper is in the field of information logics, initiated by Orlowska and Pawlak [3]. For more information, motivation and references for this area of research the reader is invited to consult the book by Demri and Orlowska [2] and also [5]. The present paper extends some results from [4] where modal logic **INF** for Pawlak's information systems was introduced and studied. **INF** is one of the first systems based on a large list of modal operations corresponding to various kinds of informational relations considered in their weak and strong versions: forward and backward informational inclusion, as well as positive and negative similarity relations. We add to the above list one more relation – strong indiscernibility, which leads to a new modal logic **IND**. If we denote the strong forward inclusion by $\leq$ then the strong indiscernibility $\equiv$ has the following definition:

$(\equiv)$ $x \equiv y$ iff $x \leq y$ and $y \leq x$.

---

* The work is carried out in the framework of COST Action 274 TARSKI on Theory and Applications of Relational Structures as Knowledge Instruments.

D. Ślęzak et al. (Eds.): RSFDGrC 2005, LNAI 3641, pp. 12–22, 2005.

It is well known in modal logic that the condition ($\equiv$) is not modally definable, which presents serious difficulties in its modal axiomatization. Normally in such situations we proceed as follows. We find "sufficiently enough" modally definable consequences from ($\equiv$) and the characteristic axioms for the other informational relations which can be characterized by modal axioms. In this way we obtain a logic which is complete in a class of models which are not desirable, that is why they are called *nonstandard*. Then it is proved that the logic based on the class of nonstandard models coincides with the logic based on the standard models – this is done by special copying techniques. This technique, however, is not universal and depends on a specific case. The main difficulty is to see how much modally definable consequences from ($\equiv$) are "sufficiently enough" in order the copying construction to work. In the present case the difficulty arises by great number of other informational relations, interacting in many different ways.

The second important problem is decidability of the obtained system. We apply for that purpose filtration – a known modal logic technique. As copying, filtration construction is not a universal one and is also quite case sensitive. So the second aim of the paper is to present a filtration construction for **IND**.

The paper is organized as follows. In Section 1 we give the relevant definitions for the Pawlak's information system and information relations included in **IND**. Section 2 is devoted to the syntax and semantics for **IND**. Here we introduce abstract, standard and non-standard models for **IND**. In Section 3 we introduce the copying construction for **IND** and prove that different semantics define one and the same logic. In Section 4 we propose a Hilbert type axiomatization of **IND** and prove a completeness theorem. In Section 5 we give the filtration construction for **IND** and prove that **IND** possesses finite model property and is decidable. Section 6 is for some open problems and concluding remarks.

2 Information Systems and Informational Relations

We adopt the Pawlak's information systems, named attribute systems in [4]:

Definition 1. A-systems. *By an attribute system, A-system for short, we mean any system of the form $S = (Ob, At, \{Val(a) : a \in At\}, f)$, where:*

- *$Ob \neq \varnothing$ is a set whose elements are called objects,*
- *At is a set whose elements are called attributes,*
- *For each $a \in At$, $Val(a)$ is a set with elements called values of attribute a,*
- *f is a two-argument total function, called information function, which assigns to each object $x \in Ob$ and attribute $a \in At$ a subset $f(x, a) \subseteq Val(a)$, called information of x according to a. The components of an A-system will be written with subscript S: Ob_S, At_S, $Val_S(a)$ and f_S.*

Definition 2. Some informational relations in A-systems. *Let S be an A-system, and let $x, y \in Ob_S$. We introduce the following informational relations in S (we use abbreviation inf. inc. for informational inclusion):*

strong indiscernibility	$x \equiv y$ iff $(\forall a \in At)(f(x,a) = f(y,a))$
strong forward inf. inc.	$x \leq y$ iff $(\forall a \in At)(f(x,a) \subseteq f(y,a))$
weak forward inf. inc.	$x \preceq y$ iff $(\exists a \in At)(f(x,a) \subseteq f(y,a))$
strong backward inf. inc.	$x \geq y$ iff $(\forall a \in At)(f(x,a) \supseteq f(y,a))$
weak backward inf. inc.	$x \succeq y$ iff $(\exists a \in At)(f(x,a) \supseteq f(y,a))$
strong positive similarity	$x \, \sigma \, y$ iff $(\forall a \in At)(f(x,a) \cap f(y,a) \neq \varnothing)$
weak positive similarity	$x \, \Sigma \, y$ iff $(\exists a \in At)(f(x,a) \cap f(y,a) \neq \varnothing)$
strong negative similarity	$x \, \nu \, y$ iff $(\forall a \in At)(\overline{f(x,a)} \cap \overline{f(y,a)} \neq \varnothing)$
weak negative similarity	$x \, N \, y$ iff $(\exists a \in At)(\overline{f(x,a)} \cap \overline{f(y,a)} \neq \varnothing)$

Lemma 1. *([4]) The following first-order conditions are true for any $x, y, z \in Ob_S$ (the script S is omitted):*

S1 $x \leq x$

S2 $x \leq y$ and $y \leq z \to x \leq z$

S3 $x \Sigma y \to y \Sigma x$

S4 $x \Sigma y \to x \Sigma x$

S5 $x \Sigma y$ and $y \leq z \to x \Sigma z$

S6 $x \Sigma x$ or $x \leq y$

S7 $x N y \to y N x$

S8 $x N y \to x N x$

S9 $x \leq y$ and $y N z \to x N z$

S10 $y N y$ or $x \leq y$

S11 $x N z$ or $y \Sigma z$ or $x \leq y$

S12 $x \preceq x$

S13 $x \leq y$ and $y \preceq z \to x \preceq z$

S14 $x \preceq y$ and $y \leq z \to x \preceq z$

S15 $x \sigma y \to y \sigma x$

S16 $x \sigma y \to x \sigma x$

S17 $x \sigma y$ and $y \leq z \to x \sigma z$

S18 $x \sigma x$ or $x \preceq y$

S19 $x \sigma y$ and $y \preceq z \to x \Sigma z$

S20 $x \sigma z$ or $y N z$ or $x \preceq y$

S21 $x \nu y \to y \nu x$

S22 $x \nu y \to x \nu x$

S23 $x \leq y$ and $y \nu z \to x \nu z$

S24 $y \nu y$ or $x \preceq y$

S25 $x \preceq y$ and $y \nu z \to x N z$

S26 $x \Sigma z$ or $y \nu z$ or $x \preceq y$

$(\geq)$ $x \geq y$ iff $y \leq x$

$(\succeq)$ $x \succeq y$ iff $y \preceq x$

$(\equiv)$ $x \equiv y$ iff $x \leq y$ and $y \leq x$

Lemma 1 suggests the following definition.

Definition 3. *Let $\underline{W} = (W, \leq, \preceq, \geq, \succeq, \sigma, \Sigma, \nu, N)$ be a relational system.*

- *$\underline{W}$ is called a bi-similarity structure if it satisfies the conditions S1-S26, $(\geq)$ and $(\succeq)$ from Lemma 1.*
- *The system $\underline{W} = (W, \leq, \preceq, \geq, \succeq, \sigma, \Sigma, \nu, N, \equiv)$ is called an Ind-structure if it satisfies the conditions S1-S26, $(\geq)$, $(\succeq)$ and $(\equiv)$ from Lemma 1.*
- *If S is an A-system then $W(S) = (Ob_S, \leq_S, \preceq_S, \geq_S, \succeq_S, \sigma_S, \Sigma_S, \nu_S, N_S, \equiv_S)$ is called standard Ind-structure over S.*

Note that each Ind-structure is a bi-similarity structure; Each bi-similarity structure can be considered as an Ind-structure defining $x \equiv y$ iff $x \leq y$ and $y \leq x$.

Theorem 1. *Each Ind-structure is a standard Ind-structure.*

Proof. Let $\underline{W} = (W, \leq, \preceq, \sigma, \Sigma, \nu, N, \equiv)$ be an Ind-structure. Then $\underline{W}$ is a bi-similarity structure. By lemma 2.5 from [4] each bi-similarity structure is a standard one, and by axiom $(\equiv)$ this implies that $\underline{W}$ is a standard Ind-structure. ∎

3   The Information Logic IND

Now we introduce a modal logic **IND** based on the informational relations $\leq, \preceq$ $, \geq, \succeq, \sigma, \Sigma, \nu, N, \equiv$. It extends the logic **INF** introduced in [4] by the modality $[\equiv]$ corresponding to the indiscernibility relation $\equiv$.

Syntax of IND. Language of **IND** contains the following primitive symbols:

- VAR - a denumerable set of propositional variables,
- $\neg, \wedge, \vee$ – the classical Boolean connectives,
- Modal operators: $[U]$ – the universal modality, and $[R]$ – the informational modality, for each $R \in \{\leq, \preceq, \geq, \succeq, \sigma, \Sigma, \nu, N, \equiv\}$,
- $(,)$ – parentheses.

The notion of a formula is standard. We will use also standard definitions for implication $\Rightarrow$, equivalence $\Leftrightarrow$, 1 and diamond modality $< R > A = \neg[R]\neg A$.

Semantics of IND. We interpret the language of **IND** in relational structures of the form $\underline{W} = (W, \leq, \preceq, \geq, \succeq, \sigma, \Sigma, \nu, N, \equiv)$. A function $v : VAR \rightarrow 2^W$ is called a valuation, it assigns to each variable $p \in VAR$ a subset $v(p) \subseteq W$. The pair $M = (\underline{W}, v)$ is called a model. The satisfiability relation $x \Vdash_v A$ (the formula A is true in a point $x \in W$ at the valuation v) is defined inductively according to the standard Kripke semantics:

- $x \Vdash_v p$ iff $x \in v(p)$, $p \in VAR$.
- $x \Vdash_v \neg A$ iff $x \not\Vdash_v A$,
- $x \Vdash_v A \wedge B$ iff $x \Vdash_v A$ and $x \Vdash_v B$,
- $x \Vdash_v A \vee B$ iff $x \Vdash_v A$ or $x \Vdash_v B$,
- $x \Vdash [R]A$ iff $(\forall y \in W)(xRy \rightarrow y \Vdash_v A)$, $R \in \{\leq, \preceq, \geq, \succeq, \sigma, \Sigma, \nu, N, \equiv\}$,
- $x \Vdash [U]A$ iff $(\forall y \in W)(y \Vdash_v A)$.

We say that the formula A is true in the model M if for any $x \in W$ we have $x \Vdash_v A$; A is true in the structure $\underline{W}$ if it is true in all models over $\underline{W}$; A is true in a class Σ of structures if it is true in any member of Σ.

Because of modal undefinability of the condition $(\equiv)$ we introduce the notion of a non-standard Ind-structure.

Definition 4. Non-standard Ind-structures. *By a non-standard Ind-structure we mean any structure of the type* $\underline{W} = (W, \leq, \preceq, \geq, \succeq, \sigma, \Sigma, \nu, N, \equiv)$ *satisfying S1-S26, $(\geq)$, $(\succeq)$ and the following seven conditions instead of $(\equiv)$:*

$(\equiv_1)$	$x\overline{\Sigma}x$ *and* $y \leq x \rightarrow x \equiv y$,
$(\equiv_2)$	$x\overline{N}x$ *and* $x \leq y \rightarrow x \leq y$,
$(\equiv_3)$	$x\overline{\Sigma}z$ *and* $x\overline{N}z$ *and* $y \leq x \rightarrow x \equiv y$,
$(\equiv_4)$	$x \equiv x$,
$(\equiv_5)$	$x \equiv y \rightarrow y \equiv x$,
$(\equiv_6)$	$x \equiv y$ *and* $y \equiv z \rightarrow x \equiv z$,
$(\equiv_7)$	$x \equiv y \rightarrow x \leq y$.

Note that all of the conditions ($\equiv_i$), $i = 1 - 7$ are true in any Ind-structure. Any non-standard Ind-structure is an Ind-structure, if it satisfies condition

($*$) $x \le y$ and $y \le x \rightarrow x \equiv y$

Let $\underline{W}$ be a non-standard Ind-structure. Define the equivalence relation:

($\cong$) $x \cong y$ iff $x \le y$ and $y \le x$.

Equivalence classes with respect to $\equiv$ and $\cong$ will be called $\equiv$-clusters and $\cong$-clusters, denoted by $\equiv(x)$ and $\cong(x)$ respectively. By axiom ($\equiv_7$) we obtain that $x \equiv y \rightarrow x \cong y$, so each $\equiv$-cluster is contained in some $\cong$-cluster. In other words, each $\cong$-cluster is an union of $\equiv$-clusters.

Definition 5. Normal $\cong$-clusters. *A $\cong$-cluster α is called normal if α is itself an $\equiv$-cluster.*

Lemma 2. *The following properties hold:*

(i) *If $x\overline{\Sigma}x$ then $\cong(x)$ is a normal $\cong$-cluster. If $x\overline{\Sigma}x$ and $y\overline{\Sigma}y$, then $\cong(x) = \cong(y)$.*
(ii) *If $x\overline{N}x$ then $\cong(x)$ is normal $\cong$-cluster. If $x\overline{N}x$ and $y\overline{N}y$ then $\cong(x) = \cong(y)$.*
(iii) *Let $x\overline{\Sigma}z$ and $y\overline{N}z$. Let an $\cong$-cluster α contain x and y. Then α is normal.*

Proof. (i) Suppose $x\overline{\Sigma}x$. To show that $\cong(x)$ is a normal $\cong$-cluster we will prove that $\cong(x) = \equiv(x)$. Obviously $\equiv(x) \subseteq \cong(x)$. For the converse inclusion suppose that $z \in \cong(x)$. Then $z \cong x$, $z \le x$ and by axiom ($\equiv_1$) we obtain $x \equiv z$ and consequently $z \in \equiv(x)$. For the second claim in (i) suppose that $x\overline{\Sigma}x$ and $y\overline{\Sigma}y$ hold. By axiom S6 we obtain $y \le x$ and by axiom ($\equiv_1$) we get $x \equiv y$. This implies $x \cong y$ and consequently $\cong(x) = \cong(y)$. (ii), (iii) can be shown similarly.∎

We will use three classes of structures for the language of **IND**: $\Sigma(Ind)$ – the class of all Ind-structures; $\Sigma(standard.Ind)$ – the class of all standard Ind-structures; $\Sigma(nonstandard.Ind)$ – the class of non-standard structures. $\Sigma(Ind)$ forms the abstract semantics of **IND**; $\Sigma(standard.Ind)$ forms the standard semantics of **IND**; $\Sigma(nonstandard.Ind)$ forms the non-standard semantics of **IND**. In the next section we prove that three kinds of semantics of **IND** are equivalent. Standard semantics is the intended one for **IND**. Taking some analogy from programming languages containing abstract data types: Abstract semantics considers the information relations as *abstract data types*, while standard semantics can be considered as their *procedural semantics*. Non-standard semantics is a generalization of the abstract one and extracts from the latter the modal definability part. It is suitable for axiomatization and for the decidability proof.

4   Equivalence of the Abstract, Standard and Non-standard Semantics of IND

Let Σ be a class of structures of the type $\underline{W} = (W, \le, \preceq, \ge, \succeq, \sigma, \Sigma, \nu, N, \equiv)$ and let $\mathcal{L}(\Sigma) = \{A : A \text{ is true in } \Sigma\}$. The set $\mathcal{L}(\Sigma)$ is called the logic of Σ. This is a semantic definition of a logic. We will consider three logics based on the three kinds of semantic structures for **IND**. Proving that the corresponding logics coincide means the equivalence of the three semantics.

Proposition 1. $\mathcal{L}(\Sigma(Ind)) = \mathcal{L}(\Sigma(standard.Ind))$

Proof. – By Theorem 1.   ∎

Our next aim is to prove that the logics $\mathcal{L}(\Sigma(Ind))$ and $\mathcal{L}(\Sigma(nonstandard.Ind))$ coincide. For that purpose we need the notion of copying (see e.g. [5]).

Definition 6. Copying construction. *Let $\underline{W} = (W, \{R_k : k \in K\})$, and $\underline{W'} = (W', \{R'_k : k \in K\})$, be two relational systems of the same type and $M = (\underline{W}, v)$ and $M' = (\underline{W'}, v')$ be models over $\underline{W}$ and $\underline{W'}$ respectively. Let I be a non-empty set of mappings from W into W' and let for any $i \in I$ the application of i to $x \in W$ be denoted by x_i. We say that I is a copying from $\underline{W}$ to $\underline{W'}$ if the following conditions are satisfied:*

(CoI1) $W' = \bigcup_{i \in I} W_i$, *where* $W_i = \{x_i : x \in W \text{ and } i \in I\}$.
(CoI2) *For any* $x, y \in W$ *and* $i, j \in I$: *if* $x_i = y_j$ *then* $x = y$.
(CoR1) *For any* $R \in \{R_k : k \in K\}$ *and* $i \in I$: *if* xRy *then* $(\exists j \in I)(x_i R' y_j)$.
(CoR2) *For any* $x \in W$, $y' \in W'$ *and* $i \in I$ *we have:*
$\qquad$ *if* $x_i R' y'$ *then* $(\exists y \in W)(\exists j \in I)(y_j = y' \text{ and } xRy)$.
(CoV) *We say that* I *is a copying from the model* M *to the model* M' *if for any* $p \in VAR$, $x \in W$ *and* $i \in I$ *we have:* $x \in v(p)$ *iff* $x_i \in v'(p)$.

Lemma 3. Copying lemma.

(i) *Let $\underline{W}$ and $\underline{W'}$ be two structures, v be a valuation in W and I be a copying from $\underline{W}$ to $\underline{W'}$. Then there exist a valuation v' in W' such that I is a copying from the model $M = (\underline{W}, v)$ to the model $M' = (\underline{W'}, v')$.*
(ii) *The following is true for any formula A, $x \in W$, $i \in I$: $x \Vdash_v A$ iff $x_i \Vdash_{v'} A$.*

Proof. (i) Define $v'(p) = \{x' \in W' : (\exists x \in W)(\exists i \in I)(x' = x_i)\}$.
$\qquad$ (ii) The proof goes by induction on the complexity of the formula A.   ∎

Proposition 2. *Let $\underline{W}$ be a non-standard Ind-structure. Then there exists an Ind-structure $\underline{W'}$ and a copying I from $\underline{W}$ to $\underline{W'}$.*

Proof. Let $\underline{W} = (W, \leq, \preceq, \geq, \succeq, \sigma, \Sigma, \nu, N, \equiv)$ be a non-standard Ind-structure and $I = Z = \{0, \pm 1, \pm 2, \ldots\}$ be the set of integers. We will consider the elements of I as mappings over W as follows: for $x \in W$ and $i \in I$ define:

$$x_i = \begin{cases} x & \text{if } \cong (x) \text{ is a normal } \cong\text{-cluster} \\ (x, i) & \text{otherwise.} \end{cases}$$

Denote by $W' = \{x_i : x \in W, i \in I\}$. Then the mappings from I are mappings from W into W'. It remains to define relations in $\underline{W'}$. For the relations $R' \in \{\preceq' , \succeq', \sigma', \Sigma', \nu', N'\}$ we put $x_i R' y_j$ iff xRy. For the relation $\leq'$ let $\ll$ be a well ordering of the set of all clusters $\equiv (x)$ of W (guaranteed by the axiom of choice). We consider two cases:

Case 1: At least one of the following three conditions holds: **(1)** $\cong (x)$ is a normal $\cong$-cluster; **(2)** $\cong (y)$ is a normal cluster; **(3)** the relation $x \cong y$ does not hold. In this case we put $x_i \leq' y_j$ iff $x \leq y$.

Case 2: The opposite, i.e. neither of the conditions (1), (2), (3) hold. Then $x_i = (x, i)$, $y_j = (y, j)$, $\cong (x) = \cong (y)$ and the $\cong$-cluster $\alpha = \cong (x) = \cong (y)$ is not normal and contains the $\equiv$-clusters $\equiv (x)$ and $\equiv (y)$. In this case we define:

$$x_i \leq' y_j \text{ iff } x \leq y \text{ and } (i < j \text{ or } (i = j \text{ and } \equiv (x) \ll \equiv (y)))$$

Now the relations $\geq'$ and $\equiv'$ we define by means of $\leq'$ as follows:

$$x_i \geq' y_j \text{ iff } y_j \leq' x_i, \qquad x_i \equiv' y_j \text{ iff } x_i \leq' y_j \text{ and } x_i \geq' y_j$$

First we will show that the conditions of copying are satisfied. For $(CoI1)$ and $(CoI2)$ this follows from the definition of I as a set of mappings and from the definition of W'. Condition $(CoR2)$ (except for the case $(Co \equiv 2)$) follows directly from the definition of the corresponding relation R'. Conditions $(CoR1)$ for the cases $R \in \{\preceq, \succeq, \sigma, \Sigma, \nu, N\}$ are also straightforward.

For the condition $(Co \leq 1)$ suppose $x \leq y$ and $i \in I$ and proceed to prove that $(\exists j \in I)(x_i \leq' y_j)$. For the case 1 of the definition of $\leq'$ j is arbitrary. For the case 2 take $j = i$, if $\equiv (x) \ll \equiv (y)$, and $j > i$, if not $\equiv (x) \ll \equiv (y)$. In a similar way one can verify the condition $(Co \geq)$.

For $(Co \equiv 1)$ suppose $x \equiv y$ and $i \in I$. We have to find $j \in I$ such that $x_i \leq' y_j$ and $x_i \geq' y_j$. From $x \equiv y$ by axiom $(\equiv_7)$ we get $x \cong y$, so $\cong (x) = \cong (y) = \alpha$.

Case 1: α is normal. Then any $j \in I$ will do the job.

Case 2: α is not normal. From $x \equiv y$ we obtain $\equiv (x) = \equiv (y)$, so $\equiv (x) \ll \equiv (y)$ and $\equiv (y) \ll \equiv (x)$. In this case $j = i$ will do the job.

For the condition $(Co \equiv 2)$ suppose $x_i \equiv' y_j$ (i.e. $x_i \leq' y_j$ and $y_j \leq' x_i$) and proceed to show $x \equiv y$. By $(Co \leq 2)$ we have $x \leq y$ and $y \leq x$, consequently $x \cong y$. This implies $\cong (x) = \cong (y) = \alpha$ and $x, y \in \alpha$.

Case 1: α is normal. Then $x \equiv y$.

Case 2: α is not normal. Then we obtain:

(*) $(i < j$ or $(i = j$ and $(\equiv (x) \ll \equiv (y)))$ and

(**) $(j < i$ or $(j = i$ and $(\equiv (y) \ll \equiv (x)))$.

From (*) and (**) we obtain $\equiv (x) \ll \equiv (y)$ and $\equiv (y) \ll \equiv (x)$. Since $\ll$ is an antisymmetric relation we obtain $\equiv (x) = \equiv (y)$ and consequently $x \equiv y$.

Now it remains to show that W' is an Ind-structure. Special attention need the conditions $S2$, $S6$, $S10$ and $S11$, the other conditions are straightforward. We shall give proofs for $S2$ and $S6$, the proofs for $S10$ and $S11$ are similar.

Axiom S2. Suppose $x_i \leq' y_j$ and $y_j \leq' z_k$ and proceed to show $x_i \leq' z_k$. By $Co \leq 2$ we obtain $x \leq y$, $y \leq z$ and consequently $x \leq z$. If the case 1 of the definition of $\leq'$ is fulfilled for the pair x, z then we have $x_i \leq' z_k$. For the case 2 of the definition of $\leq'$ we have: $\cong (x)$ is not normal, $\cong (z)$ is not normal and $x \cong z$, consequently $x \leq z$, $z \leq x$ and $\cong (x) = \cong (z)$. From here and $x \leq y$ and $y \leq z$ we obtain $z \leq y$ and $y \leq z$, which yields $z \cong y$. So we have $\cong (x) = \cong (y) = \cong (z) = \alpha$ and α is not a normal $\cong$-cluster. Then from $x_i \leq' y_j$ and $y_j \leq' z_k$ we obtain:

(#) $i < j$ or $(i = j$ and $\equiv (x) \ll \equiv (y))$, and

(##) $j < k$ or $(j = k$ and $\equiv (y) \ll \equiv (z))$.

From (#) and (##) we obtain $i < k$ or $(i = k$ and $\equiv (x) \ll \equiv (z))$. This together with $x \leq z$ implies $x_i \leq' z_k$, which completes the proof of $S2$.

Axiom S6. Suppose $x_i \overline{\Sigma} x_i$ and proceed to show $x_i \leq' y_j$. From $x_i \overline{\Sigma} x_i$ we obtain $x \overline{\Sigma} x$ then by axiom $S6$ for W we obtain $x \leq y$. By lemma 2 we obtain that $\cong (x)$ is a normal $\cong$-cluster. Then by the case 2 of the definition of $\leq'$ we obtain $x_i \leq' y_j$. ∎

Proposition 3. $\mathcal{L}(\Sigma(Ind)) = \mathcal{L}(\Sigma(nonstandard.Ind))$.

Proof. Obviously $\mathcal{L}(\Sigma(nonstandard.Ind)) \subseteq \mathcal{L}(\Sigma(Ind))$. Suppose that the converse inclusion does not hold. Then there exists a formula $A \in \mathcal{L}(\Sigma(Ind))$ and $A \notin \mathcal{L}(\Sigma(nonstandard.Ind))$. This implies that there is a nonstandard Ind-structure $\underline{W}$, valuation v and a point $x \in W$ such that $x \not\Vdash_v A$. By proposition 2 there exists an Ind-structure $\underline{W}'$ and a copying I from $\underline{W}$ to $\underline{W}'$. By the copying lemma there exists a valuation v' in $\underline{W}'$ such that for any $i \in I$ $x_i \not\Vdash_{v'} A$, so A is not true in $\underline{W}'$ and consequently $A \notin \mathcal{L}(\Sigma(Ind))$ – a contradiction. ∎

5   A Complete Axiomatization of IND

We propose the following axiomatization of **IND**. In the following A, B, C are arbitrary formulas and $R \in \{\leq, \preceq, \geq, \succeq, \sigma, \Sigma, \nu, N, \equiv, U\}$.

Axiom schemes:

(**Bool**) All or enough Boolean tautologies   (**K**) $[R](A \Rightarrow B) \Rightarrow ([R]A \Rightarrow [R]B)$

(**A** $\geq$) $<\leq> [\geq]A \Rightarrow A$, $<\geq> [\leq]A \Rightarrow A$ (**A** $\succeq$) $<\preceq> [\succeq]A \Rightarrow A$, $<\succeq> [\preceq]A \Rightarrow A$

(**AU**) $[U]A \Rightarrow A$, $[U]A \Rightarrow [U][U]A$, $<U> [U]A \Rightarrow A$, $[U]A \Rightarrow [R]A$

(**Ax1**) $[\leq]A \Rightarrow A$ (**Ax2**) $[\leq]A \Rightarrow [\leq][\leq]A$

(**Ax3**) $<\Sigma> [\Sigma]A \Rightarrow A$ (**Ax4**) $<\Sigma>1 \Rightarrow ([\Sigma]A \Rightarrow A)$

(**Ax5**) $[\Sigma]A \Rightarrow [\Sigma][\leq]A$ (**Ax6**) $[\leq]A \Rightarrow ([U]A \vee ([\Sigma]B \Rightarrow B))$

(**Ax7**) $<N> [N]A \Rightarrow A$ (**Ax8**) $<N>1 \Rightarrow ([N]A \rightarrow A)$

(**Ax9**) $[N]A \Rightarrow [N][\leq]A$ (**Ax10**) $[\geq]A \Rightarrow ([U]A \vee ([N]B \Rightarrow B))$

(**Ax11**) $[\geq]A \wedge [\Sigma]B \Rightarrow ([U]B \vee [U]([N]B \Rightarrow A))$ (**Ax12**) $[\preceq]A \Rightarrow A$

(**Ax13**) $[\preceq]A \Rightarrow [\leq][\preceq]A$ (**Ax14**) $[\preceq]A \Rightarrow [\preceq][\leq]A$

(**Ax15**) $<\sigma> [\sigma]A \Rightarrow A$ (**Ax16**) $<\sigma>1 \Rightarrow ([\sigma]A \Rightarrow A)$

(**Ax17**) $[\sigma][\leq]A$ (**Ax18**) $[\preceq]A \Rightarrow ([U]A \vee ([\sigma]B \Rightarrow B))$

(**Ax19**) $[\sigma]A \Rightarrow [\sigma][\preceq]A$ (**Ax20**) $[\preceq]A \wedge [\sigma]B \Rightarrow ([U]B \vee ([N]B \Rightarrow A))$

(**Ax21**) $<\nu> [\nu]A \Rightarrow A$ (**Ax22**) $<\nu>1 \Rightarrow ([\nu]A \Rightarrow A)$

(**Ax23**) $[\nu]A \Rightarrow [\nu][\geq]A$ (**Ax24**) $[\nu]A \Rightarrow ([U]A \vee ([\nu]B \Rightarrow B))$

(**Ax25**) $[N]A \Rightarrow ([U]A \vee ([\nu]B \Rightarrow B))$ (**Ax26**) $[\preceq]A \wedge [\Sigma]B \Rightarrow ([U]B \vee [U]([\nu]B \Rightarrow A))$

(**Ax $\equiv_1$**) $[\leq]([\equiv]B \Rightarrow ([\Sigma]A \Rightarrow A)) \vee B$ (**Ax $\equiv_2$**) $[\geq]([\equiv]B \Rightarrow ([N]A \Rightarrow A)) \vee B$

(**Ax $\equiv_3$**) $[U]A \vee ([\equiv]B \wedge [\Sigma]A \Rightarrow [\geq]([N]A \Rightarrow B))$ (**Ax $\equiv_4$**) $[\equiv]A \Rightarrow A$

(**Ax $\equiv_5$**) $A \Rightarrow [\equiv] <\equiv> A$ (**Ax $\equiv_6$**) $[\equiv]A \Rightarrow [\equiv][\equiv]A$ (**Ax $\equiv_7$**) $[\leq]A \Rightarrow [\equiv]A$

Inference rules: (**MP**) Modus Ponens $\frac{A, \, A \Rightarrow B}{B}$ (**N**) Necessitation $\frac{A}{[R]A}$

Theorem 2. Completeness Theorem for IND. *The following conditions are equivalent for any formula A of* **IND***:*

(i) A *is a theorem of* **IND***,*
(ii) A *is true in all non-standard Ind-structures,*
(iii) A *is true in all Ind-structures,*
(iv) A *is true in all standard Ind-structures.*

Proof. Equivalence of (ii), (iii) and (iv) follows from Propositions 1 and 3. Implication $(i) \rightarrow (ii)$ is by a routine verification that all axioms are true in nonstandard structures and that inference rules preserve validity. Since we have in our language the universal modality $[U]$, implication $(ii) \rightarrow (i)$ is proved by using generated canonical model construction. Namely, let W be the set of all maximal consistent sets of the logic **IND**. For any $R \in \{\leq, \preceq, \geq, \succeq, \sigma, \Sigma, \nu, N, \equiv, U\}$ define $[R]x = \{A : [R]A \in x\}$. It is easy to show that U is an equivalence relation in W containing all other relations R. For any $a \in W$ let $W_a = \{x \in W : xUa\}$ and let R_a be the restrictions of relations R to the set W_a. Using the fact that U is an equivalence relation in U, U_a is the universal relation in W_a. Then applying the axioms of the logic one can prove that $\underline{W}_a = (W_a, \{R_a\})$ is a nonstandard Ind-structure, called the canonical structure generated by a. Define the canonical valuation $v(p) = \{x \in W_a : p \in x\}$. Then one can prove by induction that for any formula A, $x \Vdash_v A$ iff $A \in x$. Now, to prove $(ii) \rightarrow (i)$ suppose that A is not a theorem of **IND**. Then there exists a maximal consistent set a such that $A \notin a$. Consider canonical model $(\underline{W}_a, v)$ generated by a. Then $a \not\Vdash_v A$. ∎

6   Decidability of IND

We shall show that **IND** is decidable proving that the logic possesses the finite model property by means of the method of filtration.

Definition 7. Filtration. *Let* $\underline{W} = (W, \leq, \preceq, \geq, \succeq, \sigma, \Sigma, \nu, N, \equiv)$ *be a nonstandard Ind-structure and* $M = (\underline{W}, v)$ *be a model over* $\underline{W}$ *and let* Γ *be a finite set of formulas closed under subformulas. Define an equivalence relation* $\simeq$ *in* W *as follows:* $x \simeq y$ *iff* $(\forall A \in \Gamma)(x \Vdash_v A \leftrightarrow y \Vdash_v A)$. *Let for* $x \in W$ *and* $p \in VAR$, $|x| = \{y \in W : x \simeq y\}$ *and* $W' = \{|x| : x \in W\}$, $v'(p) = \{|x| : x \in v(p)\}$ *and let* $\underline{W}' = (W', \leq', \preceq', \geq', \succeq', \sigma', \Sigma', \nu', N', \equiv')$ *be a nonstandard Ind-structure. We say that the model* $M' = (\underline{W}', v')$ *is a filtration of* M *through* Γ *if the following conditions are satisfied for any relation* $R \in \{\leq, \preceq, \geq, \succeq, \sigma, \Sigma, \nu, N, \equiv, U\}$:

(R1) *If* xRy *then* $|x|R'|y|$,
(R2) *If* $|x|R'|y|$ *then* $(\forall [R]A \in \Gamma)(x \Vdash_v [R]A \rightarrow\Vdash y \Vdash_v A)$.

Lemma 4. Filtration lemma. *The following two conditions are true:*

(i) *The set* W' *has at most* 2^n *elements where* n *is a number of elements of* Γ.
(ii) *For any formula* $A \in \Gamma$ *and* $x \in W$: $x \Vdash_v A$ *iff* $|x| \Vdash v'A$.

The proof of this lemma is standard and can be find for instance in [1,2].

Proposition 4. Filtration for IND. *Let* $\underline{W} = (W, \leq, \preceq, \geq, \succeq, \sigma, \Sigma, \nu, N, \equiv, v)$ *be a model over a non-standard structure and B be a modal formula. Then there exist a finite set of formulas Γ closed under subformulas with a cardinality $\leq$ $9.n + 4$, where n is the number of subformulas of B and a filtration $\underline{W}' = (W', \leq'$ $, \preceq', \geq', \succeq', \sigma', \Sigma', \nu', N', \equiv')$ of $\underline{W}$ through Γ.*

Proof. Let Γ be the smallest set of formulas closed under subformulas and satisfying the following two conditions:

($\Gamma 1$) $< R > 1 \in \Gamma$ for $R \in \{\Sigma, \sigma, N, \nu\}$,
($\Gamma 2$)   For any formula A and $R \in \{\leq, \preceq, \geq, \succeq, \sigma, \Sigma, \nu, N, \equiv, U\}$:
             If for some R, $[R]A \in \Gamma$, then for all R, $[R]A \in \Gamma$.

Obviously Γ is a finite set of formulas containing no more than $9.n + 4$ elements, where n is the number of the subformulas of B. Define W' and v' as in the definition of filtration. For $|x|, |y| \in W'$ define:

(1) $|x| \leq' |y|$ iff $(\forall [\leq]A \in \Gamma)...$

$(x \Vdash_v [\leq]A \to y \Vdash_v [\leq]A)$ & $(y \Vdash_v [\geq]A \to x \Vdash_v [\geq]A)$ &
$(y \Vdash_v [\Sigma]A \to x \Vdash_v [\Sigma]A)$ & $(x \Vdash_v [N]A \to y \Vdash_v [N]A)$ &
$(x \Vdash_v [\preceq]A \to y \Vdash_v [\preceq]A)$ & $(y \Vdash_v [\succeq]A \to x \Vdash_v [\succeq]A)$ &
$(y \Vdash_v [\sigma]A \to x \Vdash_v [\sigma]A)$ & $(x \Vdash_v [\nu]A \to y \Vdash_v [\nu]A)$ &
$(x \Vdash_v < \Sigma > 1 \to y \Vdash_v < \Sigma > 1)$ & $(y \Vdash_v < N > 1 \to x \Vdash_v < N > 1)$ &
$(x \Vdash_v < \sigma > 1 \to y \Vdash_v < \sigma > 1)$ & $(y \Vdash_v < \nu > 1 \to x \Vdash_v < \nu > 1)$

(2) $|x| \geq' |y|$ iff $|y| \leq' |x|$

(3) $|x| \Sigma' |y|$ iff $(\forall [\Sigma]A \in \Gamma)...$

$(x \Vdash_v [\Sigma]A \to y \Vdash_v [\leq]A)$ & $(y \Vdash_v [\Sigma]A \to x \Vdash_v [\leq]A)$ &
$(x \Vdash_v < \Sigma > 1$ & $y \Vdash_v < \Sigma > 1)$

(4) $|x| N' |y|$ iff $(\forall [\Sigma]A \in \Gamma)...$

$(x \Vdash_v [N]A \to y \Vdash_v [\geq]A)$ & $(y \Vdash_v [N]A \to x \Vdash_v [\geq]A)$ &
$(x \Vdash_v < N > 1$ & $y \Vdash_v < N > 1)$

(5) $|x| \prec' |y|$ iff $(\forall [\preceq]A \in \Gamma)...$

$(x \Vdash_v [\preceq]A \to y \Vdash_v [\leq]A)$ & $(y \Vdash_v [\succeq]A \to x \Vdash_v [\geq]A)$ &
$(y \Vdash_v [\Sigma]A \to x \Vdash_v [\sigma]A)$ & $(x \Vdash_v [N]A \to y \Vdash_v [\nu]A)$ &
$(x \Vdash_v < \sigma > 1 \to y \Vdash_v < \Sigma > 1)$ & $(y \Vdash_v < \nu > 1 \to x \Vdash_v < N > 1)$

(6) $|x| \succeq' |y|$ iff $|y| \preceq' |x|$

(7) $|x| \sigma' |y|$ iff $(\forall [\sigma]A \in \Gamma)...$

$(x \Vdash_v [\sigma]A \to y \Vdash_v [\leq]A)$ & $(y \Vdash_v [\sigma]A \to x \Vdash_v [\leq]A)$ &
$(x \Vdash_v [\Sigma]A \to y \Vdash_v [\preceq]A)$ & $(y \Vdash_v [\Sigma]A \to x \Vdash_v [\preceq]A)$ &
$(x \Vdash_v < \sigma > 1$ & $y \Vdash_v < \sigma > 1)$

(8) $|x| \nu' |y|$ iff $(\forall [\nu]A \in \Gamma)...$

$(x \Vdash_v [\nu]A \to y \Vdash_v [\geq]A)$ & $(y \Vdash_v [\nu]A \to x \Vdash_v [\geq]A)$ &
$(x \Vdash_v [N]A \to y \Vdash_v [\succeq]A)$ & $(y \Vdash_v [N]A \to x \Vdash_v [\succeq]A)$ &
$(x \Vdash_v < \nu > 1$ & $y \Vdash_v < \nu > 1)$

(9) $|x| \equiv' |y|$ iff $|x| \leq' |y|$ & $|x| \geq' |y|$

The required model is $M' = (\underline{W'}, v')$. The proof that the conditions of filtration are satisfied and that $\underline{W}$ is a nonstandard Ind-structure is long but easy and routine and is left to the reader.   ∎

As a corollary from Proposition 4 we obtain the following theorem.

Theorem 3. Finite model property and decidability of IND.

(i) *For any formula A which is not theorem of* **IND**, *there exists a nonstandard model $M = (\underline{W}, v)$ such that $Card(W) \leq 2^{9 \cdot n + 4}$ in which A is not true.*
(ii) **IND** *is decidable.*

7   Open Problems and Concluding Remarks

One open problem is to estimate the exact complexity of **IND**. It is proved in [2] that the satisfiability problem for the logic **NIL**, which is a quite small sublogic of **IND**, based only on the information relations $\leq, \geq, \sigma$, is **PSPACE** complete. The proof is quite long and complicated and it will be interesting to see if it can be extended for such a complex system like **IND**.

Another problem is to find the minimal basis for the two-place informational relations in A-systems and to characterize them by first-order axioms. Note that this problem is solved for the simpler notion of P-systems in [5]. If we adopt the definition of information relation in A-systems given in [5], the following 11 informational relations form a basis for all two-place informational relations: the 6 relations $\leq, \preceq, \Sigma, \sigma, N, \nu$ from section 1 and the following 5 additional informational relations (we use abbreviation w. m. ext. emp. and uni. for weak mixed extreme emptiness and universality):

weak indiscernibility	$x \cong y$ iff $(\exists a \in At)(f(x,a) = f(y,a))$
weak complementarity	$x \, C \, y$ iff $(\exists a \in At)(f(x,a) = -f(y,a))$
weak extreme emptiness	$x \, E \, y$ iff $(\exists a \in At)(f(x,a) = \varnothing \ \& \ f(y,a) = \varnothing)$
weak extreme universality	$x \, U \, y$ iff $(\exists a \in At)(f(x,a) = Val_a \ \& \ f(y,a) = Val_a)$
w. m. ext. emp. and uni.	$x \, EU \, y$ iff $(\exists a \in At)(f(x,a) = \varnothing \ \& \ f(y,a) = Val_a)$

References

1. Blackburn, P., de Rijke, M., Venema, Y.: Modal Logic. Cambridge University Press, Cambridge Tracts in Theoretical Computer Science, 53 (2001)
2. Demri, S., Orlowska, E.: Incomplete information: Structure, Inference, Complexity. Springer-Verlag Berlin Heidelberg (2002)
3. Orlowska, E., Pawlak, Z.: Representation of nondeterministic information. Theoretical Computer Science, 29 (1984) 27-39
4. Vakarelov, D.: A Duality Between Pawlak's Knowledge Representation Systems and Bi-consequence Systems. Studia Logica, 55 (1995) 205-228
5. Vakarelov, D.: Information systems, similarity relations and modal logics. In: E. Orlowska (ed.): Incomplete information: Rough Set Analysis. Studies in Fuzziness and Soft Computing, 13, Phisica, Heidelberg (1998)

Granular Computing with Shadowed Sets

Witold Pedrycz

Department of Electrical & Computer Engineering,
University of Alberta,
Edmonton AB T6R 2G7 Canada
Systems Research Institute, Polish Academy of Sciences,
Warsaw, Poland

Abstract. In this study, we discuss a concept of shadowed sets and elaborate on their applications. To establish some sound compromise between the qualitative Boolean (two-valued) description of data and quantitative membership grades, we introduce an interpretation framework of shadowed sets. Shadowed sets are discussed as three-valued constructs induced by fuzzy sets assuming three values (that could be interpreted as full membership, full exclusion, and uncertain). The algorithm of converting membership functions into this quantification is a result of a certain optimization problem guided by the principle of uncertainty localization. With the shadowed sets of clusters in place, discussed are various ideas of relational calculus on such constructs. We demonstrate how shadowed sets help in problems in data interpretation in fuzzy clustering by leading to the three-valued quantification of data structure that consists of core, shadowed, and uncertain structure.

Keywords: shadowed sets, three-valued logic, fuzzy sets, principle of uncertainty localization, relational equations, data interpretation, fuzzy clustering, outliers, cores of clusters.

1 Introductory Comments

Fuzzy sets offer a wealth of detailed numeric information conveyed by their detailed numeric membership grades (membership functions). This very detailed conceptualization of information granules may act as a two-edge sword. On one hand we may enjoy a very detailed quantification of elements to a given concept (fuzzy set). On the other hand, those membership grades could be somewhat overwhelming and introduce some burden when it comes to a general interpretation. It is also worth noting that numeric processing of membership grades comes with some computing overhead. In order to get a better insight into the matter, let us refer to data analysis and data interpretation. Here, clustering is regarded as a fundamental conceptual and computational framework of data analysis [1] [7]. The discovered structure emerging in the form of clusters is essential to numerous tasks of understanding and reasoning about the nature of data. The description of the structure of patterns may involve various activities such as assigning meaning to the groups, identifying possible outliers or highlighting groups of patterns that require special attention, revealing

D. Ślęzak et al. (Eds.): RSFDGrC 2005, LNAI 3641, pp. 23–32, 2005.

dependencies between the groups, etc. With the advent of fuzzy clustering and its various applications, cf. [2][3][5][8][9][10][13][14], we arrived at the important and qualitatively different view at data analysis. Instead of generating a binary (yes-no) allocation of patterns to clusters, which could be quite restrictive in many cases, the notion of partial membership helps quantify the aspect of belongingness in a far greater detail. The degree of membership is quite a tangible and intuitively convincing structural indicator, which one could use to gauge a level of typicality of a given pattern to the cluster. The lower the membership degree, the less likely the pattern could be treated as belonging to the cluster. No doubt that the departure from the yes-no (1-0) binary quantification is a useful enhancement of the clustering techniques. By the same token, the continuity of the gradation of membership in some applications could be too detailed in cases we are interested in capturing the essence of the clusters. For instance, some practical questions might arise under different circumstances. Is pattern typical to the cluster? Is it of borderline character? Should it be excluded from the cluster? Does it need more attention and should be flagged to the user for detailed considerations? To handle these problems, we argue that the membership functions describing the patterns could be subject to some threshold operation associated with a simple decision rule: accept the pattern to be typical if its membership grade is not lower than some predefined threshold α, $\alpha \in [0,1]$. The result of this thresholding is a so-called α-cut of the fuzzy set leading to the obvious binary rule as shown above. While this rule (referred to as a "hardening" mechanism of fuzzy sets) seems to be sound and quite acceptable, it comes with a major obstacle. We are not clear as to the choice of the critical value of α.

Given these issues, we discuss the concept of shadowed sets [11][12]. Shadowed sets are information granules induced by fuzzy sets so that they capture the essence of fuzzy sets at the same time reducing the numeric burden because of their limited three-valued characterization of shadowed sets. This non-numeric character of shadowed sets is also of particular interest when dealing with their interpretation abilities.

The study is organized into 5 sections. We start with a closer look at shadowed sets introducing the idea in great detail (Section 2) and in Section 3 discuss their ensuing design that is inherently induced by fuzzy sets. Further extensions into the realm of relational calculus and relational equations are covered in Section 4. The three-valued interpretation abilities offered by shadowed sets are discussed in fuzzy clusters. To facilitate interpretation of fuzzy clusters we introduce the notions of core, shadowed and uncertain structure of data. Concluding comments are offered in Section 6.

2 Shadowed Sets as a Symbolic Manifestation of Fuzzy Sets

In this section, we briefly recall the concept of shadowed sets [12] (see also [4][6]) and elaborate on the main motivation behind their inception and highlight further developments and applications. Formally speaking, a shadowed set A is a set-valued mapping coming in the following form

$$A : \mathbf{X} \rightarrow \{ 0, [0,1], 1 \} \tag{1}$$

where X is a given universe of discourse (space).The co-domain of A consists of three components that is 0, 1, and the unit interval [0,1]. They can be treated as degrees of membership of elements to A. These three quantification levels come with an apparent interpretation. All elements for which A(x) assume 1 are called a core of the shadowed set -- they embrace all elements that are fully compatible with the concept conveyed by A. The elements of X for which A(x) attains zero are excluded from A. The elements of X for which we have assigned the unit interval are completely uncertain -- we are not at position to allocate any numeric membership grade. Therefore we allow the usage of the unit interval, which reflects uncertainty meaning that any numeric value could be permitted here. In essence, such element could be excluded (we pick up the lowest possible value from the unit interval), exhibit partial membership (any number within the range from 0 and 1) or could be fully allocated to A. Given this extreme level of uncertainty (nothing is known and all values are allowed), we call these elements shadows and hence the name of the shadowed set. An illustration of a shadowed set is included in Figure 1.

Fig. 1. An example of a shadowed set A; note shadows formed around the cores of the construct

One can view this mapping (shadowed set) as an example of a three-valued logic as encountered in the classic model introduced by Lukasiewicz. Having this in mind, we can think of shadowed sets as a symbolic representation of numeric fuzzy sets. Obviously, the elements of co-domain of A could be labeled using symbols (say, certain, shadow, excluded; or a, b, c and alike) endowed with some well-defined semantics.

The operations on shadowed Table 1, sets are isomorphic with those encountered in the three-valued logic.

Table 1. Logic operations (*and*, *or*, and *complement*) on shadowed sets; here a shadow is denoted by S (= [0,1])

A∩B	0	S	1
0	0	0	0
S	0	S	S
1	0	S	1

A∪B	0	S	1
0	0	S	1
S	S	S	1
1	1	1	1

$\overline{A}$	
0	1
S	S
1	0

These logic operations are conceptually convincing; we observe an effect of preservation of uncertainty. In the case of the *or* operation, we note that combining a single numeric value of exclusion (0) with the shadow, we arrive at the shadow (as nothing specific could be stated about the result of this logic aggregation). Similar effect occurs for the *and* operator when being applied to the shadow and the logic value of 1.

The simplicity of shadowed sets becomes their obvious advantage. Dealing with three logic values simplifies not only the interpretation but it is advantageous in all computing, especially when such calculations are contrasted with the calculations completed for fuzzy sets involving detailed numeric membership grades. Let us note that logic operators that are typically realized by means of some t- and s-norms require computing of the numeric values of the membership grades. In contrast those realized on shadowed sets are based on comparison operations and therefore are far less demanding.

While shadowed sets could be sought as new and standalone constructs, our objective is to treat them as information granules induced by some fuzzy sets. The bottom line of our approach is straightforward – considering fuzzy sets (or fuzzy relations) as the point of departure and acknowledging computing overhead associated with them, we regard shadowed sets as constructs that capture the essence of fuzzy sets while help reducing the overall computing effort and simplifying ensuing interpretation. In the next section, we concentrate on the development of shadowed sets for given fuzzy sets.

3 The Development of Shadowed Sets

Accepting the point of view that shadowed sets are algorithmically implied (induced) by some fuzzy sets, we are interested in the transformation mechanisms translating fuzzy sets into the corresponding shadowed sets. The underlying concept is the one of uncertainty condensation or "localization". While in fuzzy sets we encounter intermediate membership grades located in-between 0 and 1 and distributed practically across the entire space, in shadowed sets we "localize" the uncertainty effect by building constrained and fairly compact shadows. By doing so we could remove (or better to say, re-distribute) uncertainty from the rest of the universe of discourse by bringing the corresponding low and high membership grades to zero and one and then compensating these changes by allowing for the emergence of uncertainty regions. This transformation could lead to a certain optimization process in which we complete a total balance of uncertainty.

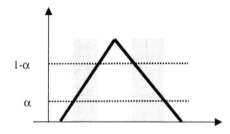

Fig. 2. The concept of a shadowed set induced by some fuzzy set; note the range of membership grades (located between α and $1-\alpha$) generating a shadow

To illustrate this optimization, let us start with a continuous, symmetric, unimodal, and normal membership function A. In this case we can split the problem into two tasks by considering separately the increasing and decreasing portion of the membership function, Figure 2.

For the increasing portion of the membership function, we reduce low membership grades to zero, elevate high membership grades to one and compensate these changes (which in essence lead to an elimination of partial membership grades) by allowing for a region of the shadow where there are no specific membership values assigned but we admit the entire unit interval as feasible membership grades. Computationally, we form the following balance of uncertainty preservation that could be symbolically expressed as

$$\text{Reduction of membership} + \text{Elevation of membership} = \text{shadow} \qquad (2)$$

Again referring to Figure 2 and given the membership grades below α and above $1-\alpha$, $\alpha \in (0, \frac{1}{2})$, we express the components of the above relationship in the form (we assume that all integrals do exist).

Reduction of membership (low membership grades are reduced to zero)

$$\int_{x:A(x)\leq\alpha} A(x)dx$$

Elevation of membership (high membership grades elevated to 1)

$$\int_{x:A(x)\geq 1-\alpha} (1 - A(x))dx$$

Shadow

$$\int_{x:\alpha<A(x)<1-\alpha} dx$$

The minimization of the absolute difference

$$V(\alpha) = |\ \int_{x:A(x)\leq\alpha} A(x)dx + \int_{x:A(x)\geq 1-\alpha} (1 - A(x))dx - \int_{x:\alpha<A(x)<1-\alpha} dx\ | \qquad (3)$$

completed with respect to α is given in the form of the following optimization problem

$$\alpha_{opt} = \arg\min_{\alpha} V(\alpha) \qquad (4)$$

where $\alpha \in (0, \frac{1}{2})$. For instance, when dealing with triangular membership function (and it appears that the result does not require the symmetry requirement), the optimal value of α is equal to $\sqrt{2} - 1 \approx 0.4142$ [11]. For the parabolic membership functions, the optimization leads to the value of α equal to 0.405.

Let us move on to the most general case in which we do not impose any assumptions as to the form of the membership function. We consider discrete membership values $u_1, u_2, \ldots u_N$. Denote the minimal and maximal value in this set by u_{min} and u_{max}, respectively. The overall reduction of lower membership grades is expressed in the form of the following sum $\sum_{k\in\Omega} u_k$ where $\Omega = \{k|\ u_k \leq \alpha\}$. The elevation of higher membership grades to one leads to the expression $\sum_{k\in\Phi}(1 - u_k)$ with $\Phi = \{k|\ u_k \geq u_{max} - \alpha\ \}$. For the shadows we consider the cardinality of the set $\Delta = \{k|\ u_k \in (\ \alpha,\ u_{max} - \alpha)\}$. Then the above conditions translate into the following optimization problem

$$V(\alpha) = |\sum_{k\in\Omega} u_k + \sum_{k\in\Phi}(1 - u_k)\ -\ card(\Delta)| \rightarrow \text{minimize with respect to } \alpha \qquad (5)$$

where the range of feasible values of α is given as $[u_{min},\ \dfrac{u_{min} + u_{max}}{2}\ ]$.

Once optimized, the resulting shadowed set can be treated as a concise descriptor of the fuzzy cluster. For the original fuzzy set A (fuzzy cluster), we denote by core(A), shadow(A), respectively the core and shadow of the shadowed set induced by A.

The above design process could be generalized in such a way that we introduce a continuous and increasing functional γ (u): $[0,1] \rightarrow [0,1]$ that helps quantify the original values of the membership grades when taken into consideration in the balance captured by (2). When reducing membership grades we use the expression

$$\int_{x:A(x)\leq\alpha} \gamma(A(x))dx \qquad (6)$$

while the elevation of membership is guided by the form

$$\int_{x:A(x)\geq 1-\alpha} (1 - \gamma(A(x)))dx \qquad (7)$$

The typical form of the functional would be a polynomial $\gamma(u) = u^p$, $p > 0$.

4   Relational Calculus with Shadowed Sets and Relational Equations

So far we have introduced basic logic operations on shadowed sets. These in turn can be combined together in building transformations between shadowed sets defined in different spaces (universes of discourse) X and Y.

In analogy with shadowed sets, we can introduce a concept of a shadowed relation. For instance, given a Cartesian product of two spaces X and Y, a shadowed relation R is regarded as a mapping

$$R : \mathbf{X} \times \mathbf{Y} \rightarrow \{\ 0,\ 1,\ [0,1]\} \qquad (8)$$

where the individual elements of R denote a degree of strength of relationships between the individual pairs of elements of this Cartesian product.

Shadowed sets and shadowed relations give rise to a concept of shadowed relational calculus and shadowed relational equations. The fundamental transformations come in the form of max-min and min-max compositions. Given a shadow set X and some shadowed relation R defined in finite spaces X and X $\times$ Y, respectively, the max-min composition of X and   R, denoted as X $\circ$ R, yields a shadowed set Y in Y whose characterization is provided in the following form

$$Y(y_j) = \max_{i=1,2,...,n} [\, \min(X(x_i), R(x_i, y_j))] \qquad (9)$$

j=1,2...,m. Card($\mathbf{X}$) = n, Card($\mathbf{Y}$) =m. Here the max and min operations are defined by the union and intersection operators discussed in Section 2. In the min-max composition we reverse the order the operators in comparison with the arrangements shown above.

These two composition operators are used in the description of shadowed relational systems where X is treated as an inputs, R captures the input-output relationships and Y is the resulting output. Various analysis and synthesis problems in such systems can be represented and solved in the framework of shadowed relational equations. The two main categories of problems can be distinguished: (a) synthesis (estimation) in which we are provided with X and Y and R has to be determined (the more general statement involves a collection of input-output shadowed sets (X_k, Y_k), k=1, 2, ...,N) and (b) inverse problem in which Y and R are given while X has to be determined.

The solutions to these problems dwell on the use of an implication operator whose definition in given in the tabular form shown below

Table 2. Logic operation of *implication* on shadowed sets

A→B	0	S	1
0	1	1	1
S	0	S	1
1	0	S	1

Furthermore we require to introduce an order relation (greater than, $\lhd$) in the family of shadowed sets by admitting the following 0 $\lhd$ S $\lhd$ 1. Not going into details, we recall the fundamental result concerning the synthesis problem.

Theorem. If the solution set to X $\circ$ R = Y for X and Y given is nonempty, then its greatest solution (in the sense of the above stated order) is provided in the form

$$\hat{R} = X \rightarrow Y \qquad (10)$$

with the implication operator applied pointwise to the pairs of the elements of X and Y.

5   Taxonomy of Data in Structure Description

It is well known that fuzzy clusters being the result of fuzzy clustering are described by membership functions A_1, A_2,..., A_c. Given objective function-based fuzzy clustering (such as e.g., Fuzzy C-Means; FCM for short), we note that they constitute the rows of the resulting partition matrix. Each of them gives rise to the corresponding shadowed set. Given this collection of shadowed sets, each pattern could be interpreted on a basis of its categorization to the induced shadowed sets. The three-valued evaluation is useful with this regard and its interpretability is worth emphasizing. In what follows, we will be referring to Ai as a shadowed set (which in essence does not lead to any misunderstanding as it has been induced by the corresponding fuzzy sets). We introduce the following sets of patterns based on their allocation to the components of the shadowed sets of the clusters.

Core data structure – Those are the patterns that belong to a core of at least one or more shadowed sets

$$\text{Core data structure} = \{ \, \mathbf{x} \mid \exists_i \, \mathbf{x} \in \text{core} \, (A_i) \, \} \tag{11}$$

The core is composed are the data points that form the backbone of the structure revealed through the clustering mechanisms. They clearly belong to a single cluster or could be shared between several clusters (in the case they overlap).

Shadowed data structure – This structure is formed by patterns that do not belong to core of any of the shadowed sets but fall within the shadow of one or more shadowed sets. Formally, we write this down in the form

$$\text{Shadowed data structure} = \{\mathbf{x} \mid \exists_i \, \mathbf{x} \in \text{shadow} \, (A_i) \, \text{ and } \forall_i \mathbf{x} \notin \text{core}(A_i) \} \tag{12}$$

Noticeably, this structure embraces patterns that raise some hesitation as to their possible interpretation. The pattern falling within this region requires more attention as to its possible membership and final quantification

Uncertain data structure – The patterns belonging to this structure are those that are left out from all shadows meaning that

$$\text{Uncertain data structure} = \{ \, \mathbf{x} \mid \forall_i \, \mathbf{x} \notin \text{shadow} \, (A_i) \, \text{ and } \forall_i \mathbf{x} \notin \text{core}(A_i) \} \tag{13}$$

This structure consists of patterns that could be practically regarded as peripheral to the clusters revealed in the data set. It is likely that most of them could be the outliers or highly atypical data points quite distinct from the primary structure (that is the core and shadowed structure) that require more attention. In this sense we have formed a mechanism attracting attention to those patterns that may trigger some action.

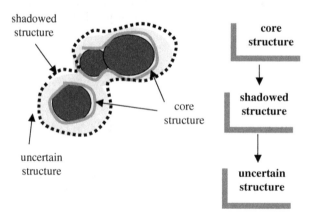

Fig. 4. Interpretation of data structure revealed in the clustering process along with the hierarchy of concepts describing the data

The illustration of these three concepts describing the data structure is included in Figure 4. It is worth noting that such data categorization forms an obvious hierarchy of structures revealed by the clustering procedure. We start with the core data structure (which is the most central to the structure description), move down to the shadowed structure and finally flag the uncertain structure.

6   Conclusions

We have introduced and discuss a role of shadowed sets regarded as one of possible vehicles of granular computing. Given the three valued logic character of the underlying construct, it can be regarded as a concise and operationally appealing vehicle of processing fuzzy sets where the detailed membership grades inherent to any fuzzy set are transformed into the regions of inclusion, exclusion and uncertainty. We have indicated that the shadowed sets lead to a full-fledged calculus of such information granules including relational calculus on shadowed sets.

It is beneficial to point out that while fuzzy sets deliver very detailed information about structure (which is regarded to be superior to any Boolean character of structure description with set-based formalism of cluster characterization), the approach based on shadowed sets are positioned somewhere in-between. In this sense, it could be regarded as a standalone interpretation mechanism or we can use it in conjunction with the detailed membership information. The use of it to data clustering and interpretation is another convincing example of the use of shadowed sets.

References

1. Bezdek, J.C., Keller, J., Krishnapuram, R., Pal, N.R.: Fuzzy Models and Algorithms for Pattern Recognition and Image Processing, Kluwer Academic Publishers, Boston (1999)
2. Bhanu, B., Dong,A.: Concepts learning with fuzzy clustering and relevance feedback, *Engineering Applications of Artificial Intelligence,* 15 (2001) 123-138
3. Castellano, G., Castiello, C., Fanelli, A.M., Mencar C.:, Knowledge discovery by a neuro-fuzzy modeling framework, Fuzzy Sets and Systems, 149 (2005) 187-207
4. Cattaneo, G., Ciucci, D.: An algebraic approach to shadowed sets, In: Electronic Notes in Theoretical Computer Science, Vol. 82. Springer-Verlag, Berlin Heidelberg New York (2001) 1-12
5. Crespo, F. Weber, R.: A methodology for dynamic data mining based on fuzzy clustering, Fuzzy Sets and Systems 150 (205) 267-284
6. Gürkan, E., Erkmen, I., Erkmen, A.M.: Two-way fuzzy adaptive identification and control of a flexible-joint robot arm, Information Sciences, 145 (2004) 13-43
7. Hoppner, F., Klawonn, F., Kruse, R., Runkler, T.:Fuzzy Cluster Analysis: Methods for Classification, Data Analysis and Image Recognition, John Wiley New York, (1999)
8. Liu, H., Huang, S.T.: Evolutionary semi-supervised fuzzy clustering, Pattern Recognition Letters 24 (2003) 3105-3113)
9. Ménard, M. Eboueya, M.: Extreme physical information and objective function in fuzzy clustering, Fuzzy Sets and Systems, 128 (2002) 285-303
10. Ong, S.H., Zhao, X.: On post-clustering evaluation and modification, Pattern Recognition Letters, 21 (2000) 365- 373

11. Pedrycz, W.: Shadowed sets: representing and processing fuzzy sets, IEEE Trans. on Systems, Man, and Cybernetics, part B, 28 (1998) 103-109
12. Pedrycz, W.: Shadowed sets: bridging fuzzy and rough sets, In: Pal, S.K Skowron, A. (eds): Rough Fuzzy Hybridization. A New Trend in Decision-Making, Springer-Verlag, Singapore, (1999) 179-199
13. Pedrycz, W.: Fuzzy clustering with a knowledge-based guidance, Pattern Recognition Letters, 25 (2004) 469-480
14. Tsekouras, G., Sarimveis, H., Kavakli, E., Bafas, G.: A hierarchical fuzzy-clustering approach to fuzzy modeling, Fuzzy Sets and Systems, 150 (2005) 245-266

Rough Sets and Higher Order Vagueness

Andrzej Skowron[1] and Roman Swiniarski[2,3]

[1] Institute of Mathematics, Warsaw University,
Banacha 2, 02-097 Warsaw, Poland
skowron@mimuw.edu.pl
[2] Institute of Computer Science, Polish Academy of Sciences,
Ordona 21, 01-237 Warsaw, Poland
[3] Department of Mathematical and Computer Sciences,
San Diego State University,
5500 Campanile Drive San Diego, CA 92182, USA
rswiniar@sciences.sdsu.edu

Abstract. We present a rough set approach to vague concept approximation within the adaptive learning framework. In particular, the role of extensions of approximation spaces in searching for concept approximation is emphasized. Boundary regions of approximated concepts within the adaptive learning framework are satisfying the higher order vagueness condition, i.e., the boundary regions of vague concepts are not crisp. There are important consequences of the presented framework for research on adaptive approximation of vague concepts and reasoning about approximated concepts. An illustrative example is included showing the application of Boolean reasoning in adaptive learning.

Keywords: vagueness, rough sets, higher order vagueness, adaptive learning.

1 Introduction

There is a long debate in philosophy on vague concepts [2]. Nowadays, computer scientists are also interested in vague (imprecise) concepts. Lotfi Zadeh [20] introduced a very successful approach to vagueness. In this approach, sets are defined by partial membership in contrast to crisp membership used in the classical definition of a set. Rough set theory [4] expresses vagueness not by means of membership but by employing the boundary region of a set. If the boundary region of a set is empty it means that a particular set is crisp, otherwise the set is rough (inexact). The non-empty boundary region of the set means that our knowledge about the set is not sufficient to define the set precisely. A discussion on vagueness in the context of fuzzy sets and rough sets can be found in [8]. In this paper some consequences on understanding of vague concepts caused by inductive extensions of approximation spaces and adaptive concept learning are outlined. This paper is an extension of [10]. In particular, we discuss a problem of adaptive learning of concept approximation assuming that learning is performed in a dynamic environment with many concepts that are linked by vague dependencies.

D. Ślęzak et al. (Eds.): RSFDGrC 2005, LNAI 3641, pp. 33–42, 2005.

2   Approximation Spaces and Their Inductive Extensions

In [4] any approximation space is defined as a pair (U, R), where U is a universe of objects and $R \subseteq U \times U$ is an indiscernibility relation defined by an attribute set.

The lower approximation, the upper approximation and the boundary region are defined as crisp sets. It means that the higher order vagueness condition is not satisfied [2]. We will return to this issue in Section 3.

We use the definition of approximation space introduced in [11]. Any approximation space is a tuple $AS = (U, I, \nu)$, where U is the universe of objects, I is an uncertainty function, and ν is a measure of inclusion called the inclusion function, generalized in rough mereology to the rough inclusion [11,13].

In this section, we consider the problem of approximation of concepts over a universe U^*, i.e., subsets of U^*. We assume that the concepts are perceived only through some subsets of U^*, called samples. This is a typical situation in machine learning, pattern recognition, or data mining [1]. In this section we explain the rough set approach to induction of concept approximations. The approach is based on inductive extension of approximation spaces.

Let $U \subseteq U^*$ be a finite sample and let $C_U = C \cap U$ for any concept $C \subseteq U^*$. Let $AS = (U, I, \nu)$ be an approximation space over the sample U. The problem we consider is how to extend the approximations of C_U defined by AS to approximation of C over U^*. We show that the problem can be described as searching for an extension $AS^* = (U^*, I^*, \nu^*)$ of the approximation space AS relevant for approximation of C. This requires showing how to induce values of the extended inclusion function to relevant subsets of U^* that are suitable for the approximation of C. Observe that for the approximation of C, it is enough to induce the necessary values of the inclusion function ν^* without knowing the exact value of $I^*(x) \subseteq U^*$ for $x \in U^*$.

We consider an example for rule-based classifiers. However, the analogous considerations for k-NN classifiers, feed-forward neural networks, and hierarchical classifiers [1]) show that their construction is based on the inductive inclusion extension [13,10].

Let AS be a given approximation space for C_U and let us consider a language L in which the neighborhood $I(x) \subseteq U$ is expressible by a formula $pat(x)$, for any $x \in U$. It means that $I(x) = \|pat(x)\|_U \subseteq U$, where $\|pat(x)\|_U$ denotes the meaning of $pat(x)$ restricted to the sample U. In the case of rule-based classifiers, patterns of the form $pat(x)$ are defined by feature value vectors.

We assume that for any new object $x \in U^* \setminus U$, we can obtain (e.g., as a result of a sensor measurement) a pattern $pat(x) \in L$ with semantics $\|pat(x)\|_{U^*} \subseteq U^*$. However, the relationships between information granules over U^*, e.g., $\|pat(x)\|_{U^*}$ and $\|pat(y)\|_{U^*}$, for different $x, y \in U^*$, are known only to a degree estimated by using relationships between the restrictions of these sets to the sample U, i.e., between sets $\|pat(x)\|_{U^*} \cap U$ and $\|pat(y)\|_{U^*} \cap U$.

The set of patterns $\{pat(x) : x \in U\}$ is usually not relevant for approximation of the concept $C \subseteq U^*$. Such patterns can be too specific or not general enough, and can directly be applied only to a very limited number of new sample elements. However, by using some generalization strategies, one can search in a family of patterns definable from $\{pat(x) : x \in U\}$ in L, for such new patterns that are relevant for approximation of concepts over U^*. Let us consider a subset $PATTERNS(AS, L, C) \subseteq L$ chosen as a set of pattern candidates for relevant approximation of a given concept C. For rule based classifiers one can search for such candidate patterns among sets definable by subsequences of feature value vectors corresponding to objects from the sample U. The set $PATTERNS(AS, L, C)$ can be selected using some quality measures evaluated on meanings (semantics) of patterns from this set restricted to the sample U (like the numbers of examples from the concept C_U and its complement that support a given pattern). Then, on the basis of properties of sets definable by these patterns over U, we induce approximate values of the inclusion function $\nu^*(X, C)$ on subsets of $X \subseteq U^*$ definable by any such pattern and the concept C. Next, we induce the value of ν^* on pairs (X, Y) where $X \subseteq U^*$ is definable by a pattern from $\{pat(x) : x \in U^*\}$ and $Y \subseteq U^*$ is definable by a pattern from $PATTERNS(AS, L, C)$.

Finally, for any object $x \in U^* \setminus U$ we induce the degree $\nu^*(\|pat(x)\|_{U^*}, C)$ applying a conflict resolution strategy $Conflict\_res$ (e.g, a voting strategy) to two families of degrees:

$$\{\nu^*(\|pat(x)\|_{U^*}, \|pat\|_{U^*}) : pat \in PATTERNS(AS, L, C)\}, \qquad (1)$$

$$\{\nu^*(\|pat\|_{U^*}, C) : pat \in PATTERNS(AS, L, C)\}. \qquad (2)$$

Values of the inclusion function for the remaining subsets of U^* can be chosen in any way – they do not have any impact on the approximations of C. Moreover, observe that for the approximation of C we do not need to know the exact values of uncertainty function I^* – it is enough to induce the values of the inclusion function ν^*. The defined extension ν^* of ν to some subsets of U^* makes it possible to define an approximation of the concept C in a new approximation space AS^*.

Observe, that the value $\nu^*(I^*(x), C)$ of the induced inclusion function for any object $x \in U^* - U$ is based on collected arguments *for* and *against* belonging of x to C. In this way, the approximation of concepts over U^* can be explained as a process of searching for relevant approximation spaces, in particular inducing relevant approximation spaces.

3   Approximate Reasoning About Vague Concepts Based on Adaptive Learning and Reasoning

We have recognized that for a given concept $C \subseteq U^*$ and any object $x \in U^*$, instead of crisp decision about the relationship of $I^*(x)$ and C, we can gather some arguments *for* and *against* it only. Next, it is necessary to induce from such arguments the value $\nu^*(I(x), C)$ using some strategies making it possible to resolve conflicts between those arguments [1,12]. Usually some general principles are used such as the minimal length principle [1] in searching for algorithms computing an extension $\nu^*(I(x), C)$. However, often the approximated concept over $U^* - U$ is too compound to be induced directly from $\nu(I(x), C)$. This is the reason that the existing learning methods can be not satisfactory for inducing high quality concept approximations in case of complex concepts [17]. There have been several attempts trying to omit this drawback. One of them is the incremental learning used in machine learning and also by the rough set community (see, e.g., [18]). In this case, an increasing sequence of samples $U_1 \subseteq \ldots \subseteq U_k \subseteq \ldots$ is considered and the task is to induce the extensions $\nu^{(1)}, \ldots, \nu^{(k)}, \ldots$ of inclusion functions. Still we know rather very little about relevant strategies for inducing such extensions. Some other approaches are based on hierarchical (layered) learning [14] or reinforcement learning [16]. However, there are several issues, important for learning that are not within the scope of these approaches. For example, the target concept can gradually change over time and this concept drift is a natural extension for incremental learning systems toward adaptive systems. In adaptive learning it is important not only what we learn but also how we learn, how we measure changes in a distributed environment and induce from them adaptive changes of constructed concept approximations. The adaptive learning for autonomous systems became a challenge for machine learning, robotics, complex systems, and multiagent systems. It is becoming also a very attractive research area for the rough set approach.

In general, from given information about the approximated concept C, the approximation space AS related to this information is constructed and next an extension AS^* of AS is induced. The induced approximations are only temporary, usually not matching exactly the approximated concept (even if we assume that the concept can be defined but its definition is unknown during learning). This means that the approximations will be necessary to change if some new arguments *for* and *against* will be gathered and an information or knowledge about the approximated concept will be updated. Hence, we should express a risk in prediction of decisions on the basis of the induced classification algorithms (classifiers) based on AS^* rather than exact decisions only. Such risk depends on negotiation strategies between arguments *for* and *against*, searching strategies for relevant patterns used for concept approximation, etc. This aspect is related to the higher order of vagueness [2]. Its consequence is that lower approximations, upper approximations, and boundary regions for vague concepts are not crisp.

Let us consider now some examples of adaptive concept approximation schemes.

Example 1. In Figure 1 we present an example of adaptive concept approximation scheme Sch. By $Inf(C)$ and $Inf'(C)$ we denote information about the approximated concept (e.g., decision table for C or training sample) in different (relevant) moments of time[1]. ENV denotes an environment, DS is an operation constructing an approximation space $AS_{Inf(C)}$ from a given sample $Inf(C)$. IN is an extension operation transforming the approximation space $AS_{Inf(C)}$ to an approximation space AS^* for the concept C; Q denotes a quality measure for the

---

[1] For simplicity, in Figure 1 we do not present time constraints.

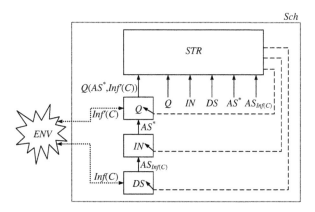

Fig. 1. An example of adaptive concept approximation scheme

induced approximation space AS^* on a new sample $Inf'(C)$. STR is a strategy that adaptively changes the approximation of C by modifying Q, IN, and DS.

The scheme Sch describes an adaptive strategy ST modifying the induced approximation space AS^* with respect to the changing information about the concept C. To explain this in more detail, let us first assume that a procedure $new_C(ENV, u)$ is given returning from the environment ENV and current information u about the concept C a new piece of information about this concept (e.g., an extension of a sample u of C). In particular, $Inf^{(0)}(C) = new_C(ENV, \emptyset)$ and $Inf^{(k+1)}(C) = new_C(ENV, Inf^{(k)}(C))$ for $k = 0, \ldots$. In Figure 1 $Inf'(C) = Inf^{(1)}(C)$. Next, assuming that operations $Q^{(0)} = Q$, $DS^{(0)} = DS$, $IN^{(0)} = IN$ are given, we define $Q^{(k+1)}$, $DS^{(k+1)}$, $IN^{(k+1)}$, $DS^{(k+1)}(Inf^{(k+1)}(C))$, and $AS^{*(k+1)}$ for $k = 0, \ldots,$ by

$$(Q^{(k+1)}, DS^{(k+1)}, IN^{(k+1)}) = \qquad\qquad\qquad\qquad (3)$$
$$= STR(Q^{(k)}(AS^{*(k)}, Inf^{(k+1)}(C)), Q^{(k)}, IN^{(k)}, DS^{(k)}, AS^{*(k)}, AS^{(k)}_{Inf^{(k)}(C)})$$
$$AS^{(k+1)}_{Inf^{(k+1)}(C)} = DS^{(k+1)}(Inf^{(k+1)}(C)); \quad AS^{*(k+1)} = IN^{(k+1)}(AS^{(k+1)}_{Inf^{(k+1)}(C)}).$$

One can see that the concept of approximation space considered so far should be substituted by a more complex one represented by the scheme Sch making it possible to generate a sequence of approximation spaces $AS^{*(k)}$ for $k = 1, \ldots$ derived in an adaptive process of approximation of the concept C. One can also treat the scheme Sch as a complex information granule [12].

One can easily derive more complex adaptive schemes with metastrategies that make it possible to modify also strategies.

Example 2. In Figure 2 there is presented an idea of a scheme where a metastrategy MS can change adaptively also strategies STR_i in schemes Sch_i for $i = 1, \ldots, n$ where n is the number of schemes. The metastrategy MS can be, e.g., a fusion strategy for classifiers corresponding to different regions of the concept C. Even more compound scheme can be obtained by considering strategies

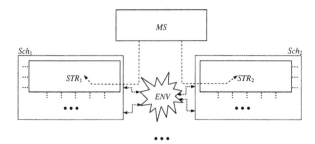

Fig. 2. An example of metastrategy in adaptive concept approximation

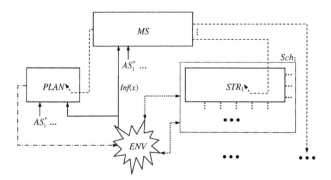

Fig. 3. An example of adaptive plan scheme

based on cooperation among the schemes for obtaining concept approximations of high quality. In Figure 3 an adaptive scheme for plan modification is presented. $PLAN$ is modified by a metastrategy MS that adaptively changes strategies in schemes Sch_i where $i = 1, \ldots, n$. This is performed on the basis of the derived approximation spaces AS_i^* induced for concepts that are guards of plan instructions and on the basis of information $Inf(x)$ about the state x of the environment ENV. The generated approximation spaces together with the plan structure are adaptively adjusted to make it possible to achieve plan goals.

The above examples are showing that the context in which sequences of approximation spaces are generated can have complex structure represented by relevant adaptive schemes.

There are some important consequences of our considerations for research on approximate reasoning about vague concepts. It is not possible to base such reasoning only on *static* models of the concepts (i.e., approximations of given concepts [4] or membership functions [20] induced from a sample available at a given moment) and on multi-valued logics widely used for reasoning about rough sets or fuzzy sets (see, e.g., [6,20,3,21]). Instead of this we need evolving systems of logics that in open and changing environments will make it possible to gradually acquire knowledge about approximated concepts and reason about them. Along this line an important research perspective arises. Among interesting topics are strategies for modeling of networks supporting such approximate reasoning (e.g.,

AR schemes and networks [12] can be considered as a step toward developing such strategies), strategies for adaptive revision of such networks, foundations for autonomous systems based on vague concepts.

Some recently reported results on rough sets seem to be important for developing foundations for adaptive systems. In particular, we would like to mention approximate reasoning in distributed environments based on rough mereological and granular approaches (see, e.g., [7,12]) and investigations on reasoning about changes based on rough sets and granular computing.

4   An Example: Inducing Concept Descriptions Consistent with Constraints Specified by Experts

From our considerations it follows that adaptive learning should be performed in a dynamic environment in which different vague concepts are approximated and it is necessary to preserve constraints among them. In this section we consider an illustrative example that can be treated as a starting point to further investigations on adaptive learning.

We consider together with facts, which can be represented using decision tables, some dependencies between concept approximations. These dependencies are specified by experts and represent their domain knowledge. An example of such dependency is "if road is slippery and the speed of the car is high then there is a high chance that the accident will appear". A question arises how to induce the concept approximations using together the facts represented in data tables and such dependencies. One can develop strategies for inducing decision rules preserving the dependencies between approximated concepts or for tuning the generated decision rules to preserve such dependencies. We apply another approach based on some ideas of non-monotonic reasoning. We assume that together with data tables there is given expert knowledge specified by constraints or dependencies between approximated concepts. For example, let us consider for three decisions d_1, d_2, d_3 the following constraint:

- **if** d_1 =*high* **and** d_2 =*medium* **then** $d_3 = 1$; or
- **if** *with certainty* d_1 =*high* **and** *one can not exclude* d_2 =*medium* **then** *with certainty* $d_3 = 1$.

We propose a method based on Boolean reasoning for tuning the induced from data table sets of rules (received by rough set and Boolean reasoning methods, e.g., in the form of so called minimal rules) so that the new induced concept approximations will satisfy the additional constraints specified by experts. These constraints are in the form of dependencies between approximated concepts (e.g., decision classes) or their (lower, upper) approximations or boundary regions. Let us observe that the phrase *with certainty* can be expressed by the lower approximation; and the phrase *it can not be excluded that* the upper approximation of concepts. Here, we would like to explain the main idea by example.

Example 3. Let us consider a decision table presented in Table 1. We have the following minimal decision rules of the decision table:

Table 1. Decision Table DT

	a	b	c	d
x_1	0	1	2	0
x_2	0	2	1	0
x_3	0	1	1	0
x_4	1	2	0	1
x_5	2	1	0	1
x_6	1	1	0	1

$r_1 : a = 0 \rightarrow d = 0;$ $r_2 : c = 2 \rightarrow d = 0;$ $r_3 : c = 1 \rightarrow d = 0;$
$r_4 : c = 0 \rightarrow d = 1;$ $r_5 : a = 1 \rightarrow d = 1;$ $r_6 : a = 2 \rightarrow d = 1;$

Let us consider the following constraint: $non(d = 0 \wedge d = 1)$. One can see that it is necessary to resolve conflict between left hand sides of the following pairs of rules: r_1, r_4; r_2, r_5; r_2, r_6; r_3, r_5 and r_3, r_6. These conflicts arise because conjunctions of left hand sides of listed pairs of rules are consistent (i.e., they do not include subformulas of the form $a = v \wedge a \neq v$). Hence, a new object can be matched by such rules and they will vote for different decisions 0 and 1, respectively. Let us consider the following propositional variables: $[i : a \neq v]$, $[i : a = v]$ with the intended meaning *left hand side of the rule r_i must be extended by $a \neq v$, $a = v$, respectively*. The conflicts can be encoded by the following propositional formula:

$$([1 : c \neq 0] \vee [4 : a \neq 0]) \wedge ([2 : a \neq 1] \vee [5 : c \neq 2]) \wedge ([2 : a \neq 2] \vee [6 : c \neq 2]) \wedge$$
$$([3 : a \neq 1] \vee [5 : c \neq 1]) \wedge ([3 : a \neq 2] \vee [6 : c \neq 1])$$

For example, the first part of the above formula describes a fact that the conflict between rules r_1, r_4 can be resolved by extending the left hand side of the rule r_1 by $c \neq 0$ or by extending the left hand side of the rule r_4 by $a \neq 0$. By computing (prime) implicants of this formula one can obtain all possible solutions, i.e., pairs of rule sets (approximating decision classes corresponding to $d = 0$ and $d = 1$) with resolved conflicts. In particular, let us consider the following implicant of the formula: $[1 : c \neq 0] \wedge [2 : a \neq 1] \wedge [2 : a \neq 2] \wedge [3 : a \neq 1] \wedge [3 : a \neq 2]$. Hence, after a simplification, we obtain the following solution, i.e., a pair of rule sets:

$r_{1'} : a = 0 \wedge c = 1 \rightarrow d = 0;$ $r_{2'} : a = 0 \wedge c = 2 \rightarrow d = 0;$ and
$r_4 : c = 0 \rightarrow d = 1;$ $r_5 : a = 1 \rightarrow d = 1;$ $r_6 : a = 2 \rightarrow d = 1.$

From example it follows that we can obtain different sets of rules resolving conflicts. One can look for pruning some solutions for conflict resolution using some criteria such as the rule support or descriptor occurrence frequencies on the left hand sides of the rules. Next, one can construct classifiers over such sets of rules and use them for classifying new objects using some fusion strategy. Another solution can start from generation of a sample of possible solutions (a family of sets of rules with eliminated conflicts) and next use strategies for conflict resolving between the sets of rules from the family.

A more advanced case of adaptive learning of a family of concepts is when the concepts are learned in a distributed environment consisting of distributed data tables and an additional data table with examples of "global" states, i.e., condition attribute value vectors over all data tables (see, e.g. [15]). Such vectors represent constraints for coexistence of condition attribute value vectors of data tables for different concepts. From the data table for global states one can induce rules representing constraints for local coexistence of attribute vector values from different data tables. These dependencies can be used as constraints for adaptive tuning of decision rules induced for different concepts.

For real-life data the formulas for conflict resolving can be large and efficient heuristics are necessary for solution construction. One can apply some strategies that have been developed using Boolean reasoning and rough sets [9]. Another approach can be based on decomposition of formulas using domain knowledge.

5   Conclusions

There are several conclusions from our discussion. Among them are:

1. Recognition of the importance of the inclusion function, generalized in rough mereology to rough inclusion (see, e.g., [7]). This has been used in investigations of information granule calculi, in particular those based on rough mereology (see, e.g., [12,7]) and approximation spaces based on information granules (see, e.g., [13]).
2. Observation that vague concepts cannot be approximated with satisfactory quality by *static* constructs such as induced membership inclusion functions, approximations or models derived, e.g., from a sample. Understanding of vague concepts can be only realized in a process in which the induced models are adaptively matching the concepts in a dynamically changing environment. This conclusion seems to have important consequences for further development of rough set theory in combination with fuzzy sets and other soft computing paradigms for adaptive approximate reasoning.

Acknowledgment

The research has been supported by the grant 3 T11C 002 26 from Ministry of Scientific Research and Information Technology of the Republic of Poland.

References

1. J. Friedman, T. Hastie, R. Tibshirani (2001). *The Elements of Statistical Learning: Data Mining, Inference, and Prediction.* Springer-Verlag, Heidelberg.
2. R. Keefe (2000). *Theories of Vagueness.* Cambridge Studies in Philosophy, Cambridge, UK.
3. J. Pavelka (1979). On Fuzzy Logic I-III. *Zeit. Math Logik Grund. Math.* **25**, 45–52, 119-134, 447-464.

4. Z. Pawlak (1991). *Rough Sets: Theoretical Aspects of Reasoning about Data.* System Theory, Knowledge Engineering and Problem Solving **9**, Kluwer Academic Publishers, Dordrecht.
5. Z. Pawlak, A. Skowron (1994). Rough Membership Functions. In R. R. Yager, M. Fedrizzi, J. Kacprzyk (eds.), *Advances in the Dempster-Schafer Theory of Evidence*, John Wiley and Sons, New York, 251–271.
6. L. Polkowski (2002). *Rough Sets: Mathematical Foundations.* Physica-Verlag, Heidelberg.
7. L. Polkowski, A. Skowron (1996). Rough Mereology: A New Paradigm for Approximate Reasoning. *International Journal of Approximate Reasoning* **15**, 333–365.
8. S. Read (1995). *Thinking about Logic. An Introduction to the Philosophy of Logic.* Oxford University Press, Oxford, New York.
9. A. Skowron (2000) Rough Sets in KDD. *16-th World Computer Congress* (IFIP'2000), Beijing, August 19-25, 2000, In: Zhongzhi Shi, Boi Faltings, Mark Musen (Eds.) Proceedings of Conference on Intelligent Information Processing (IIP2000), Publishing House of Electronic Industry, Beijing, 2000, 1–17.
10. A. Skowron (2005). Rough Sets and Vague Concepts. *Fundamenta Informaticae* **4(1-4)**, 417–431.
11. A. Skowron, J. Stepaniuk (1996). Tolerance Approximation Spaces. *Fundamenta Informaticae* **27**, 245–253.
12. A. Skowron, J. Stepaniuk (2004). Information Granules and Rough-Neural Computing. In S.K. Pal, L. Polkowski, A. Skowron (eds.), *Rough-Neural Computing: Techniques for Computing with Words*, Cognitive Technologies, Springer-Verlag, Heidelberg, 43–84.
13. A. Skowron, R. Swiniarski, P. Synak (2004). Approximation Spaces and Information Granulation. LNAI **3066**, Springer, Heidelberg, 114–123.
14. P. Stone (2000). *Layered Learning in Multi-Agent Systems: A Winning Approach to Robotic Soccer.* The MIT Press, Cambridge, MA.
15. Z. Suraj (1998). The synthesis problem of concurrent systems specified by dynamic information systems. In Polkowski, L., Skowron, A. (eds.), *Rough Sets in Knowledge Discovery 2: Applications, Case Studies and Software Systems*, Physica-Verlag, Heidelberg, 418–448.
16. R.S. Sutton, A.G. Barto (1998). *Reinforcement Learning: An Introduction.* MIT Press, Cambridge, MA.
17. V. Vapnik (1998). *Statistical Learning Theory.* John Wiley & Sons, New York, NY.
18. A. Wojna (2001). Constraint Based Incremental Learning of Classification Rules. LNAI **2005**, 428-435, Springer-Verlag, Heidelberg.
19. W. Ziarko (1993). Variable Precision Rough Set Model. *Journal of Computer and System Sciences* **46**, 39–59.
20. L.A. Zadeh (1965). Fuzzy sets. *Information and Control* **8**, 333–353.
21. L.A. Zadeh (1996). Fuzzy Logic = Computing with Words. *IEEE Transactions on Fuzzy Systems* **2**, 103–111.

Approximation in Formal Concept Analysis

Ming-Wen Shao[1,2] and Wen-Xiu Zhang[1]

[1] Faculty of Science, Institute for Information and System Sciences,
Xi'an Jiaotong University, Xi'an, Shaan'xi 710049, P. R. China
shaomingwen1837@163.com, wxzhang@xjtu.edu.cn
[2] School of Information Technology, Jiangxi University of Finance & Economics,
Nanchang, Jiangxi 330013, P. R. China

Abstract. We introduce a pair of rough set approximations in formal concept analysis. The proposed approximation operators are defined based on both lattice-theoretic and set-theoretic operators. The properties of the approximation operators are examined. Algorithms for attribute reduction and object reduction in concept lattices are presented.

1 Introduction

The theory of rough sets, proposed by Pawlak [1], provides a method of set approximation and a tool for data mining and data analysis. The basic operators in rough set theory are approximations. Using the concepts of lower and upper approximations, knowledge hidden in information tables may be unravelled and expressed in the form of decision rules [2,3,4,5]. In the classical rough set model, the lower and upper approximation operators are defined based on an equivalence relation on a universe of objects. The equivalence relation, however, seems to be a very stringent condition that may limit the application domain of the rough set model. In recent years, the notion of approximation operators has been generalized by using non-equivalence binary relations [3,4,6,7,8,9,10].

Formal concept analysis has been proposed and used for conceptual data analysis and knowledge processing [11,12]. A formal concept is defined by an (objects, attributes) pair. The set of objects is referred to as the extension, and the set of attributes as the intension, of the formal concept. They uniquely determine each other [11,12]. Generalizations of formal concept analysis can also be found in the literatures [13,14,15,16,17].

The combination of formal concept analysis and rough set theory provides new approaches for data analysis. The notions of formal concept and formal concept lattice can be introduced into rough set theory by constructing different types of formal concepts [15,16,17]. For example, the object oriented concepts [15] and the attribute oriented concepts [16] have been introduced. Rough set approximation operators can be introduced into formal concept analysis by considering different types of definability [24]. Many efforts have been made to compare and combine the two theories [15,16,17,18,19,20,21].

Based on the notions of the object oriented concepts [15] and the attribute oriented concepts [16], we define a pair of rough set approximation operators

D. Ślęzak et al. (Eds.): RSFDGrC 2005, LNAI 3641, pp. 43–53, 2005.

within formal contexts and discuss their properties. We give the sufficient and necessary conditions for classifying an attribute and an object as dispensable or indispensable, and present algorithms for attribute reduction and object reduction for concept lattices. By adopting the notions of discernibility matrix and discernibility function [3,23], we study all attribute reducts and all object reducts.

2   Formal Contexts and Rough Approximation Operators

A formal context is a triplet (U, A, R), where U is a non-empty finite set of objects and A is a non-empty finite set of attributes, and R is a relation between U and A, which is a subset of the Cartesian product $U \times A$. A formal context is in fact a binary information table in rough set theory.

In a formal context (U, A, R), for a pair of elements $x \in U$ and $y \in A$, if $(x, y) \in R$, we write xRy and read it as "the object x has the attribute y", or "the attribute y is possessed by object x". We can associate a set of attributes with an object $x \in U$ and a set of objects with an attribute $y \in A$, respectively, as follows [15,17]:

$$xR = \{y \in A \mid xRy\} \subseteq A, \quad Ry = \{x \in U \mid xRy\} \subseteq U.$$

They can be extended to subsets of objects and attributes, respectively, as [15]:

$$XR = \bigcup_{x \in X} xR, \quad RB = \bigcup_{y \in B} Ry.$$

Example 2.1. Table 1 is an example of a formal context with $U = \{1, 2, 3, 4, 5, 6\}$ and $A = \{a, b, c, d, e, f\}$. In Table 1, object 1 has attributes a, d and f; attribute a is possessed by objects 1, 2 and 5.

Let (U, A, R) be a formal context, a pair of approximation operators, $^\square, ^\diamond :$ $2^U \to 2^A$ are defined by (see [15,17]):

$$X^\square = \{y \in A \mid Ry \subseteq X\}, \ X^\diamond = \{y \in A \mid Ry \cap X \neq \emptyset\} = \bigcup_{x \in X} xR = XR.$$

Table 1. A formal context (U, A, R)

	a	b	c	d	e	f
1	1	0	0	1	0	1
2	1	1	0	1	1	1
3	0	0	0	1	0	0
4	0	0	1	0	1	0
5	1	1	0	1	1	1
6	0	0	1	0	1	0

Similarly, a pair of approximation operators, $\square, \diamond : 2^A \to 2^U$ are defined by (see [15,17]):

$$B^\square = \{x \in U \mid xR \subseteq B\}, \ B^\diamond = \{x \in U \mid xR \cap B \neq \emptyset\} = \bigcup_{y \in B} Ry = RB.$$

They are in fact dual operators related by:

$$\sim (\sim X)^\square = X^\diamond, \quad \sim (\sim X)^\diamond = X^\square, \quad \sim (\sim B)^\square = B^\diamond, \quad \sim (\sim B)^\diamond = B^\square,$$

where $\sim$ denotes the complement of a set.

Let (U, A, R) be a formal context, $X, X_1, X_2 \subseteq U$ and $B, B_1, B_2 \subseteq A$, the pair of approximation operators satisfy the followings properties (see [15,16,17]):

(i) $\quad X_1 \subseteq X_2 \Longrightarrow X_1^\square \subseteq X_2^\square, \ X_1^\diamond \subseteq X_2^\diamond,$
$\qquad B_1 \subseteq B_2 \Longrightarrow B_1^\square \subseteq B_2^\square, \ B_1^\diamond \subseteq B_2^\diamond;$

(ii) $\quad X^{\square\diamond} \subseteq X \subseteq X^{\diamond\square}, \ B^{\square\diamond} \subseteq B \subseteq B^{\diamond\square};$

(iii) $\quad X^{\diamond\square\diamond} = X^\diamond, \ X^{\square\diamond\square} = X^\square, \ B^{\diamond\square\diamond} = B^\diamond, \ B^{\square\diamond\square} = B^\square;$

(iv) $\quad (X_1 \cap X_2)^\square = X_1^\square \cap X_2^\square, \ (X_1 \cup X_2)^\diamond = X_1^\diamond \cup X_2^\diamond,$
$\qquad (B_1 \cap B_2)^\square = B_1^\square \cap B_2^\square, \ (B_1 \cup B_2)^\diamond = B_1^\diamond \cup B_2^\diamond.$

Definition 2.1. Let (U, A, R) be a formal context. For any set $X \subseteq U$, a pair of lower and upper approximations, $apr(X)$ and $\overline{apr}(X)$, is defined by

$$apr(X) = X^{\square\diamond}, \quad \overline{apr}(X) = X^{\diamond\square}.$$

Operators, $\square\diamond, \diamond\square : 2^U \longrightarrow 2^U$, are referred to as the lower and upper approximation operators, and the pair $(apr(X), \overline{apr}(X))$ is referred to as a generalized rough set.

Theorem 2.1. Let (U, A, R) be a formal context. The lower and upper approximation satisfy the following properties: for any $X, Y \subseteq U$,

$(L_1) \qquad apr(X) =\sim (\overline{apr}(\sim X)),$
$(U_1) \qquad \overline{apr}(X) =\sim (apr(\sim X));$
$(L_2) \qquad apr(\emptyset) = \overline{apr}(\emptyset) = \emptyset,$
$(U_2) \qquad \overline{apr}(U) = apr(U) = U;$
$(L_3) \qquad apr(X \cap Y) \subseteq apr(X) \cap apr(Y),$
$(U_3) \qquad \overline{apr}(X \cup Y) \supseteq \overline{apr}(X) \cup \overline{apr}(Y);$
$(L_4) \qquad X \subseteq Y \Longrightarrow apr(X) \subseteq apr(Y),$
$(U_4) \qquad X \subseteq Y \Longrightarrow \overline{apr}(X) \subseteq \overline{apr}(Y);$
$(L_5) \qquad apr(X \cup Y) \supseteq apr(X) \cup apr(Y),$
$(U_5) \qquad \overline{apr}(X \cap Y) \subseteq \overline{apr}(X) \cap \overline{apr}(Y);$
$(L_6) \qquad apr(apr(X)) = apr(X),$
$(U_6) \qquad \overline{apr}(\overline{apr}(X)) = \overline{apr}(X).$

Proof: Properties (L_1) and (U_1) show that approximation operators apr and $\overline{apr}$ are dual to each other. Properties with the same number may be regarded as dual properties. Thus, we only need to prove one of them.

For any $X \subseteq U$, we have

$$
\begin{aligned}
\sim (\overline{apr}(\sim X)) &=\sim (\sim X)^{\Diamond\Box} =\sim ((\sim (X)^{\Diamond})^{\Box}) \\
&=\sim (\sim (\sim (\sim X)^{\Diamond})^{\Diamond}) = (\sim (\sim X)^{\Diamond})^{\Diamond} \\
&= X^{\Box\Diamond} = \underline{apr}(X),
\end{aligned}
$$

from which (L_1) follows. (U_1) can be directly induced by (L_1). (L_2) follows immediately from the definition of lower approximation. For any $X, Y \subseteq U$,

$$
\begin{aligned}
\underline{apr}(X \cap Y) = (X \cap Y)^{\Box\Diamond} &= (X^{\Box} \cap Y^{\Box})^{\Diamond} \\
&= R(X^{\Box} \cap Y^{\Box}) \subseteq R(X^{\Box}) \cap R(Y^{\Box}) = (X)^{\Box\Diamond} \cap (Y)^{\Box\Diamond} \\
&= \underline{apr}(X) \cap \underline{apr}(Y),
\end{aligned}
$$

which implies (L_3). Properties (L_4) follows directly from Property (i). Since $\underline{apr}(X) \cup \underline{apr}(Y) = X^{\Box\Diamond} \cup Y^{\Box\Diamond} = (X^{\Box} \cup Y^{\Box})^{\Diamond} \subseteq (X \cup Y)^{\Box\Diamond} = \underline{apr}(X \cup Y)$, Property (L_5) holds. Since $\underline{apr}(\underline{apr}(X)) = (X^{\Box\Diamond})^{\Box\Diamond} = X^{\Box\Diamond\Box\Diamond}$, by Property (iii) we conclude that (L_6) holds. $\qquad\square$

Definition 2.2. Let (U, A, R) be a formal context. For any set $B \subseteq A$, a pair of lower and upper approximations, $\underline{apr}(B)$ and $\overline{apr}(B)$, is defined by

$$
\underline{apr}(B) = B^{\Box\Diamond}, \quad \overline{apr}(B) = B^{\Diamond\Box}.
$$

Operators, $^{\Box\Diamond}$, $^{\Diamond\Box} : 2^A \longrightarrow 2^A$, are referred to as the lower and upper approximation operators, and the pair $(\underline{apr}(B), \overline{apr}(B))$ is referred to as a generalized rough set.

Theorem 2.2. Let (U, A, R) be a formal context. The lower and upper approximation satisfy the following properties: for all $B, C \subseteq A$,

$$
\begin{array}{ll}
(L'_1) & \underline{apr}(B) =\sim (\overline{apr}(\sim B)), \\
(U'_1) & \overline{apr}(B) =\sim (\underline{apr}(\sim B)); \\
(L'_2) & \underline{apr}(\emptyset) = \overline{apr}(\emptyset) = \emptyset), \\
(U'_2) & \overline{apr}(A) = \underline{apr}(A) = A; \\
(L'_3) & \underline{apr}(B \cap C) \subseteq \underline{apr}(B) \cap \underline{apr}(C), \\
(U'_3) & \overline{apr}(B \cup C) \supseteq \overline{apr}(B) \cup \overline{apr}(C); \\
(L'_4) & B \subseteq C \Longrightarrow \underline{apr}(B) \subseteq \underline{apr}(C), \\
(U'_4) & B \subseteq C \Longrightarrow \overline{apr}(B) \subseteq \overline{apr}(C); \\
(L'_5) & \underline{apr}(B \cup C) \supseteq \underline{apr}(B) \cup \underline{apr}(C), \\
(U'_5) & \overline{apr}(B \cap C) \subseteq \overline{apr}(B) \cap \overline{apr}(C); \\
(L'_6) & \underline{apr}(\underline{apr}(B)) = \underline{apr}(B), \\
(U'_6) & \overline{apr}(\overline{apr}(B)) = \overline{apr}(B).
\end{array}
$$

These properties can be proved in a way similar to Theorem 2.1.

Based on a formal context, different types of concept lattices can be defined. For example, Yao introduced the object oriented concept lattice [15,17], Duntsch and Gediga introduced the attribute oriented concept lattice [16].

Let (U, A, R) be a formal context. A pair (X, Y), $X \subseteq U, Y \subseteq A$, is called an object oriented concept if $X = Y^\diamond$ and $Y = X^\square$ [15,17]. A pair (X, Y), $X \subseteq U, Y \subseteq A$, is called an attribute oriented concept if $X = Y^\square$ and $Y = X^\diamond$ [16,17]. The set of objects X is referred to as the extension of the concept, and the set of attributes Y is referred to as the intension of the concept. For two formal concepts (X_1, Y_1) and (X_2, Y_2), (X_1, Y_1) is a sub-concept of (X_2, Y_2) provided that $X_1 \subseteq X_2$ (which is equivalent to $Y_1 \subseteq Y_2$), and write as $(X_1, Y_1) \leq (X_2, Y_2)$. The relation $\leq$ is the hierarchical order of the concepts.

The set of all object oriented concepts forms a complete lattice which is denoted by $L_1(U, A, R)$. The meet and join of the concepts are given by:

$$(X_1, Y_1) \vee (X_2, Y_2) = (X_1 \cup X_2, (X_1 \cup X_2)^\square) = (X_1 \cup X_2, (Y_1 \cup Y_2)^{\diamond\square}),$$
$$(X_1, Y_1) \wedge (X_2, Y_2) = ((Y_1 \cap Y_2)^\diamond, Y_1 \cap Y_2) = ((X_1 \cap X_2)^{\square\diamond}, Y_1 \cap Y_2).$$

The set of all attribute oriented concepts forms a complete lattice which is denoted by $L_2(U, A, R)$ with meet and join defined by:

$$(X_1, Y_1) \vee (X_2, Y_2) = ((Y_1 \cup Y_2)^\square, Y_1 \cup Y_2) = ((X_1 \cup X_2)^{\diamond\square}, Y_1 \cup Y_2),$$
$$(X_1, Y_1) \wedge (X_2, Y_2) = (X_1 \cap X_2, (X_1 \cap X_2)^\diamond) = (X_1 \cap X_2, (Y_1 \cap Y_2)^{\square\diamond}).$$

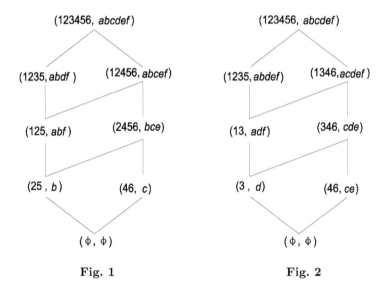

Fig. 1   Fig. 2

Fig. 1 gives the object oriented concept lattice, and Fig. 2 gives the attribute oriented concept lattice defined by the formal context of Example 2.1.

Let (U, A, R) be a formal context, $X \subseteq U, B \subseteq A$, since $(X^{\square\diamond})^\square = X^\square$, $(B^{\diamond\square})^\diamond = B^\diamond$, $(X^{\square\diamond}, X^\square)$ and $(B^\diamond, B^{\diamond\square})$ are object oriented concepts; on the other hand, since $(X^{\diamond\square})^\diamond = X^\diamond$, $(B^{\square\diamond})^\square = B^\square$, $(X^{\diamond\square}, X^\diamond)$ and $(B^\square, B^{\square\diamond})$ are attribute oriented concepts. By the definition of $apr(X)$ and $\overline{apr}(X)$, $apr(X)$ is the extent of the object oriented concept derived from X, and $\overline{apr}(X)$ is the extent of the attribute oriented concept derived from X. Similarity, $apr(B)$ is the intent of the attribute oriented concept derived from B, and $\overline{apr}(B)$ is the intent of the object oriented concept derived from B.

Example 2.2. In Example 2.1, let $X = \{1, 4, 6\}$ and $B = \{a, d\}$. From the Figure 1 and Figure 2, we have that

$$apr(X) = X^{\square\diamond} = \{4, 6\}, \quad \overline{apr}(X) = X^{\diamond\square} = \{1, 3, 4, 6\},$$
$$\underline{apr}(B) = B^{\square\diamond} = \{d\}, \quad \overline{apr}(B) = B^{\diamond\square} = \{a, b, d, f\}.$$

Theorem 2.3. Let (U, A, R) be a formal context and $X \subseteq U$, then
  (1) $apr(X) = X$ iff X is the extent of an object oriented concept;
  (2) $\overline{apr}(X) = X$ iff X is the extent of an attribute oriented concept.

Proof : Straightforward.   □

Theorem 2.4. Let (U, A, R) be a formal context and $B \subseteq A$, then
  (1) $apr(B) = B$ iff A is the extent of an attribute oriented concept;
  (2) $\overline{apr}(B) = B$ iff A is the extent of an object oriented concept.

Proof : Straightforward.   □

3   Attribute Reduction in Concept Lattices

In this section, we discuss the attribute reduction for concept lattices.

Definition 3.1. Let $L_i(U, A_1, R_1)$ and $L_i(U, A_2, R_2)$ $(i = 1, 2)$ be two object oriented concept lattices $(i = 1)$ and attribute oriented concept lattices $(i = 2)$. We say that $L_i(U, A_2, R_2)$ is extension coarser than $L_i(U, A_1, R_1)$, if for any $(X, B) \in L_i(U, A_2, R_2)$, there exist $(X, B^{'}) \in L_i(U, A_1, R_1)$, and denoted by

$$L_i(U, A_1, R_1) \leq L_i(U, A_2, R_2), \ (i = 1, 2).$$

If $L_i(U, A_1, R_1) \leq L_i(U, A_2, R_2)$ and $L_i(U, A_2, R_2) \leq L_i(U, A_1, R_1)$, we say that $L_i(U, A_1, R_1)$ and $L_i(U, A_2, R_2)$ are isomorphic, and denoted by

$$L_i(U, A_1, R_1) \cong L_i(U, A_2, R_2), \ (i = 1, 2).$$

Theorem 3.1. Let (U, A, R) be a formal context, $A_1, A_2 \subseteq A$, then

$$L_1(U, A_1, R_1) \cong L_1(U, A_2, R_2) \Longleftrightarrow L_2(U, A_1, R_1) \cong L_2(U, A_2, R_2).$$

Proof : For any $(X, B) \in L_1(U, A_1, R_1)$, we have $(X^{\sim}, B^{\sim}) \in L_2(U, A_1, R_1)$ (see [15,17]). Thus,

$$L_1(U, A_1, R_1) \leq L_1(U, A_2, R_2) \Longleftrightarrow$$
$$\forall (X, B) \in L_1(U, A_2, R_2), \exists (X, B^{'}) \in L_1(U, A_1, R_1) \Longleftrightarrow$$
$$\forall (X^{\sim}, B^{\sim}) \in L_2(U, A_2, R_2), \exists (X^{\sim}, (B^{'})^{\sim}) \in L_2(U, A_1, R_1) \Longleftrightarrow$$
$$L_2(U, A_1, R_1) \leq L_2(U, A_2, R_2).$$

By the similar proof, we have

$$L_1(U, A_2, R_2) \leq L_1(U, A_1, R_1) \Longleftrightarrow L_2(U, A_2, R_2) \leq L_2(U, A_1, R_1). \qquad \square$$

Let (U, A, R) be a formal context and $D \subseteq A$. We denote $R_D = R \cap (U \times D)$.

Theorem 3.2. Let (U, A, R) be a formal context, then $\forall\, D \subseteq A\ (D \neq \emptyset)$, $L_i(U, A, R) \leq L_i(U, D, R_D)\ (i = 1, 2)$.

Proof : For any $(X, B) \in L_1(U, D, R_D)$, we have $(X^{\square\diamond}, X^{\square}) \in L_1(U, A, R)$. We need to prove $X^{\square\diamond} = X$. By property (ii), we have $X^{\square\diamond} \subseteq X$. On the other hand, since $B = X^{\square} \cap D \subseteq X^{\square}$, $X = B^{\diamond} \subseteq X^{\square\diamond}$, i.e., $X^{\square\diamond} = X$. Thus, $L_1(U, A, R) \leq L_1(U, D, R_D)$. $L_2(U, A, R) \leq L_2(U, D, R_D)$ follows immediately from Theorem 3.1. $\qquad \square$

Definition 3.2. Let (U, A, R) be a formal context and $a \in A$. We say that a is dispensable in $L_i(U, A, R)$, if $L_i(U, A, R) \cong L_i(U, A\backslash\{a\}, R_{A\backslash\{a\}})$; otherwise, a is indispensable $(i = 1, 2)$.

Theorem 3.3. Let (U, A, R) be a formal context and $a \in A$, then a is dispensable in $L_i(U, A, R)$ iff $\exists\, C \subseteq A\backslash\{a\}$, such that $a^{\diamond} = C^{\diamond}\ (i = 1, 2)$.

Proof : We prove for the case of $i = 1$.
($\Leftarrow$) We need to prove $L_1(U, A, R) \cong L_1(U, A\backslash\{a\}, R_{A\backslash\{a\}})$. From Theorem 3.2 we have $L_1(U, A, R) \leq L_1(U, A\backslash\{a\}, R_{A\backslash\{a\}})$. Then, we only need to prove $L_1(U, A\backslash\{a\}, R_{A\backslash\{a\}}) \leq L_1(U, A, R)$, i.e., $\forall\, (X, B) \in L_1(U, A, R)$. In turn, we need to prove $(X, B\backslash\{a\}) \in L_1(U, A\backslash\{a\}, R_{A\backslash\{a\}})$. If $a \notin B$, it is clear that $(X, B) \in L_1(U, A\backslash\{a\}, R_{A\backslash\{a\}})$. Assume that $a \in B$. Since $X = B^{\diamond}$ and $a^{\diamond} = C^{\diamond}$, we have $C \subseteq X^{\square} = B$. Thus, $(B\backslash\{a\})^{\diamond} = X$. Therefore, $(X, B\backslash\{a\}) = ((B\backslash\{a\})^{\diamond}, X^{\square}) \in L_1(U, A\backslash\{a\}, R_{A\backslash\{a\}})$.
($\Rightarrow$) It is easy to see that $(a^{\diamond}, a^{\diamond\square}) \in L_1(U, A, R)$. Since a is dispensable, $(a^{\diamond}, a^{\diamond\square}\backslash\{a\}) \in L_1(U, A\backslash\{a\}, R_{A\backslash\{a\}})$. Therefore, $(a^{\diamond\square}\backslash\{a\})^{\diamond} = a^{\diamond}$, denoted by $C = a^{\diamond\square}\backslash\{a\}$. It follows that $C^{\diamond} = a^{\diamond}$. $\qquad \square$

Proposition 3.1. Let (U, A, R) be a formal context and $a \in A$, then a is indispensable in $L_i(U, A, R)$ iff $a^{\diamond} \neq C^{\diamond}$ for any $C \subseteq A\backslash\{a\}\ (i = 1, 2)$.

Proof : It immediately follows from Theorem 3.3. $\qquad \square$

Definition 3.3. Let (U, A, R) be a formal context, $D \subseteq A$. We say that D is a consistent set of $L_i(U, A, R)$, if $L_i(U, A, R) \cong L_i(U, D, R_D)\ (i = 1, 2)$. If D is a consistent set, and for any $b \in D$, $L_i(U, A, R) \not\cong L_i(U, D\backslash\{b\}, R_{D\backslash\{b\}})$, then D is referred to as an attribute reduct of $L_i(U, A, R)\ (i = 1, 2)$.

Proposition 3.2. Let (U, A, R) be a formal context, $D \subseteq A\ (D \neq \emptyset)$, D is a consistent set of $L_i(U, A, R) \Longleftrightarrow L_i(U, D, R_D) \leq L_i(U, A, R)\ (i = 1, 2)$.

Proof : It immediately follows from Theorem 3.2. $\qquad \square$
From the Theorem 3.1, we have:

D is an attribute reduct of $L_1(U, A, R) \Longleftrightarrow D$ is an attribute educt of $L_2(U, A, R)$.

Theorem 3.4. Let (U, A, R) be a formal context, and $D \subseteq A$, then D is an attribute reduct of $L_i(U, A, R)$ $(i = 1, 2)$ iff $\exists\, C \subseteq D$, such that $a^\diamond = C^\diamond$ for all $a \in A \backslash D$ and $\nexists\, E \subseteq D \backslash \{b\}$, such that $b^\diamond = E^\diamond$ for all $b \in D$.

Proof : It immediately follows from Theorem 3.3 and Proposition 3.1.   □

Definition 3.4. Let (U, A, R) be a formal context. Given $(X_l, B_l)_i, (X_j, B_j)_i \in L_i(U, A, I)$, we define:

$$DA_i((X_l, B_l)_i, (X_j, B_j)_i) = B_l \cup B_j - B_l \cap B_j, \quad (i = 1, 2).$$

$DA_i((X_l, B_l)_i, (X_j, B_j)_i (i = 1, 2)$ are called object oriented concept lattices and attribute oriented concept lattices discernibility attribute set, respectively. Moreover,

$$\mathcal{DA}_i = (DA_i((X_l, B_l)_i, (X_j, B_j)_i), (X_l, B_l)_i, (X_j, B_j)_i \in L_i(U, A, I)), (i = 1, 2)$$

are called object oriented concept lattices and attribute oriented concept lattices discernibility attribute matrix, respectively.

Let $\mathcal{DA}_i$ be the discernibility attribute matrices of $L_i(U, A, I)$ $(i = 1, 2)$. We define:

$$MA_i = \wedge\{\vee\{a : a \in DA_i((X_l, B_l)_i, (X_j, B_j)_i)\} : (X_l, B_l)_i, (X_j, B_j)_i \in L_i(U, A, I)\}.$$

MA_i $(i = 1, 2)$ are referred to, respectively, as the discernibility attribute function of $L_1(U, A, I)$, and the discernibility attribute function of $L_2(U, A, I)$. The minimal disjunctive normal form of each discernibility attribute function determine all attribute reducts uniquely [22].

Theorem 3.5. Let (U, A, R) be a formal context and $X \subseteq U$. Suppose $D \subseteq A$ is an attribute reduct of $L_i(U, A, R)$ $(i = 1, 2)$, and $\underline{apr}_D(X)$ and $\overline{apr}_D(X)$ are the lower and upper approximation of X in formal context (U, D, R_D). Then

$$\underline{apr}_D(X) = \underline{apr}(X), \quad \overline{apr}_D(X) = \overline{apr}(X).$$

Proof : For any $X \subseteq U$, we that $(X^{\square\diamond}, X^\square) \in L_1(U, A, R)$. Since D is a reduct of $L_1(U, A, R)$, $(X^{\square\diamond}, X^\square \cap D) \in L_1(U, D, R_D)$. Thus, $\underline{apr}_D(X) = \underline{apr}(X)$. Similarly we can prove $\overline{apr}_D(X) = \overline{apr}(X)$.   □

4   Object Reduction in Concept Lattices

Object reduction for concept lattices is similar to the attribute reduction. We therefore only present the main results without giving any details.

Definition 4.1. Let $L_i(U_1, A, R_1)$ and $L_i(U_2, A, R_2)$ be two object oriented concept lattices $(i = 1)$ and attribute oriented concept lattices $(i = 2)$. We say that $L_i(U_2, A, R_2)$ is intension coarser than $L_i(U_1, A, R_1)$, if for any $(X, B) \in L_i(U_2, A, R_2)$, there exist $(X', B) \in L_i(U_1, A, R_1)$, and denoted by

$$L_i(U_1, A, R_1) \leq L_i(U_2, A, R_2), \quad (i = 1, 2).$$

If $L_i(U_1, A, R_1) \leq L_i(U_2, A, R_2)$ and $L_i(U_2, A, R_2) \leq L_i(U_1, A, R_1)$, we say that $L_i(U_1, A, R_1)$ and $L_i(U_2, A, R_2)$ are isomorphic, and denoted by

$$L_i(U_1, A, R_1) \cong L_i(U_2, A, R_2), \; (i = 1, 2).$$

Theorem 4.1. Let (U, A, R) be a formal context, $U_1, U_2 \subseteq U$, then

$$L_1(U_1, A, R_1) \cong L_1(U_2, A, R_2) \Longleftrightarrow L_2(U_1, A, R_1) \cong L_2(U_2, A, R_2).$$

Let (U, A, R) be a formal context and $V \subseteq U$. For $V \subseteq U$, we denote $R_V = R \cap (V \times A)$.

Theorem 4.2. Let (U, A, R) be a formal context, then $\forall \; V \subseteq U \; (V \neq \emptyset)$, $L_i(U, A, R) \leq L_i(V, A, R_V), \; (i = 1, 2)$.

Definition 4.2. Let (U, A, R) be a formal context and $u \in U$. We say u is dispensable in $L_i(U, A, R)$, if $L_i(U, A, R) \cong L_i(U \backslash \{u\}, A, R_{U \backslash \{u\}})$; otherwise, u is indispensable, $(i = 1, 2)$.

Theorem 4.3. Let (U, A, R) be a formal context and $x \in U$, then x is dispensable in $L_i(U, A, R)$ iff $\exists \; V \subseteq U \backslash \{x\}$, such that $x^{\Diamond} = V^{\Diamond} \; (i = 1, 2)$.

Proposition 4.1. Let (U, A, R) be a formal context and $u \in U$, then U is indispensable in $L_i(U, A, R)$ iff $u^{\Diamond} \neq V^{\Diamond}$ for any $V \subseteq U \backslash \{u\}$, $(i = 1, 2)$.

Definition 4.3. Let (U, A, R) be a formal context, $V \subseteq U$. A subset of objects V is a consistent set of $L_i(U, A, R)$, if $L_i(U, A, R) \cong L_i(V, A, R_V)$. If V is a consistent set, and for any $v \in V, L_i(U, A, R) \ncong L_i(V \backslash \{v\}, A, R_{V \backslash \{v\}})$, then V is referred to as an object reduct of $L_i(U, A, R)$, $(i = 1, 2)$.

Proposition 4.2. Let (U, A, R) be a formal context, $V \subseteq U \; (V \neq \emptyset)$, then V is a consistent set of $L_i(U, A, R) \Longleftrightarrow L_i(V, A, R_V) \leq L_i(U, A, R), \; (i = 1, 2)$.

From Theorem 4.1, it is easy to see that

V is an object reduct of $L_1(U, A, R) \Longleftrightarrow V$ is an object reduct of $L_2(U, A, R)$.

Theorem 4.4. Let (U, A, R) be a formal context, and $V \subseteq U$, then V is an object reduct of $L_i(U, A, R)$ iff $\exists \; V_1 \subseteq V$, such that $x^{\Diamond} = V_1^{\Diamond}$ for all $x \in U \backslash V$ and $\nexists \; V_2 \subseteq V \backslash \{v\}$, such that $v^{\Diamond} = V_2^{\Diamond}$ for all $v \in V$.

Definition 4.4. Let (U, A, R) be a formal context. For $(X_l, B_l)_i, (X_j, B_j)_i \in L_i(U, A, R)$, we define:

$$DO_i((X_l, B_l)_i, (X_j, B_j)_i) = X_l \cup X_j - X_l \cap X_j.$$

They are called object oriented concept lattices and attribute oriented concept lattices discernibility object set, respectively. Moreover,

$$\mathcal{DO}_i = (DO_i((X_i, B_i)_i, (X_j, B_j)_i), (X_i, B_i)_i, (X_j, B_j)_i \in L_i(U, A, R)), \; (i = 1, 2)$$

are called object oriented concept lattices and attribute oriented concept lattices discernibility object matrix, respectively.

Let $\mathcal{DO}_i$ be the discernibility object matrices of $L_i(U, A, R)$ $(i = 1, 2)$. Then

$$MO_i = \wedge\{\vee\{x : x \in DO_i((X_i, B_i)_i, (X_j, B_j)_i)\} : (X_l, B_l)_i, (X_j, B_j)_i \in L_i(U, A, R)\},$$

are referred to as the discernibility object function of $L_i(U, A, R)$. The minimal disjunctive normal form of each discernibility object function determine all object reducts uniquely [22].

Theorem 4.5. Let (U, A, R) be a formal context and $B \subseteq A$. $V \subseteq U$, is an object reduct of $L_i(U, A, R)$, $\underline{apr}_V(B)$ and $\overline{apr}_V(B)$ denote the lower and upper approximation of B in formal context (V, A, R_V). Then

$$\underline{apr}_V(B) = \underline{apr}(B), \quad \overline{apr}_V(B) = \overline{apr}(B).$$

5   Conclusions

The approximation of sets and knowledge reduction are two important issues in rough set theory. Based on the notions of the attribute oriented concepts and the object oriented concepts, we defined a pair of rough set approximations using formal contexts. Similar to rough set reduction, we give approaches for attribute reduction and object reduction in concept lattices. By the proposed method, we can remove the attributes and objects that are not essential to the proposed approximation operators. The relationships between the attribute reduction of concept lattices and the attribute reduction of rough set need to further attention.

Acknowledgments

This paper was supported by the National 973 Program of China (no.2002CB 312206) and the National Natural Science Foundation of China (no. 60373078).

References

1. Pawlak, Z.: Rough sets. International Journal of Computer and Information Science, 11 (1982) 341–356.
2. Pawlak, Z.: Rough Sets Theory and It's Application to Data Analysis [J]. Cybernetics Systems, An International Journal, 29 (1998) 661–688.
3. Kryszkiewicz, M.: Rough set approach to incomplete systems. Information Sciences, 112 (1998) 39–49.
4. Ziarko, W.: Variable precision rough set model. Journal of Computer and System Sciences, 46 (1993) 39–59.
5. Tsumoto, S.: Automated extraction of medical expert system rules from clinical databases based on rough set theory. Information Sciences, 112 (1998) 67–84.
6. Greco, S., Matarazzo, B., Slowinski, R.: A New Rough Set Approach to Multicriteria and Multiattribute Classification. In: Polkowski, L., Skowron, A. (Eds.): Rough sets and Current Trends in Computing (RSTCTC'98). Lecture Notes in Artificial Intelligence 1424, Springer, Berlin (1998) 60–67.

7. Lin, T.Y., Liu, Q.: Rough approximate operators: axiomatic rough set theory. In: Ziarko, W. (Ed.): Rough Sets, Fuzzy Sets and Knowledge Discovery. Springer, Berlin (1994) 256–260.
8. Quafafou, M.: α-RST: a generalization of rough set theory. Information Science, 124 (2000) 301–316.
9. Slowinski, R., Vanderpooten, D.: Similarity relation as a basis for rough approximations. In: Paul P. Wang (Ed.): Advances in Machine Intelligence and Soft-Computing. Department of Electrical Engineering, Duke University, Durham, NC, USA (1997) 17–33.
10. Yao, Y.Y., Lin, T.Y.: Generalization of rough sets using modal logic. Intelligent Automation and Soft Computing, An International Journal, 2 (1996) 103–120.
11. Wille, R.: Restructuring lattice theory: an approach based on hierarchies of concepts. In: Rival, I. (Ed.): Ordered Sets. Reidel, Dordrecht-Boston (1982) 445–470.
12. Gediga, G., Wille, R.: Formal Concept Analysis. Mathematic Foundations. Springer, Berlin (1999).
13. Chaudron, L., Maille, N.: Generalized formal concept analysis. In: The Eighth International Conference on Conceptual Structures (ICCS 2000), Darmstadt, Germany. Lecture Notes in Artificial Intelligence 1867, Springer, Berlin (2000) 357–370.
14. Deogun, J.S., Saqer, J.: Monotone concepts for formal concept analysis,. Discrete Applied Mathematics, 144 (2004) 70–78.
15. Yao, Y.Y.: Concept lattices in rough set theory. In: Proceedings of 2004 Annual Meeting of the North American Fuzzy Information Processing Society (2004) 796–801.
16. Gediga, G., Duentsch, I.: Modal-style operators in qualitative data analysis. Rroceedings of the 2002 IEEE International Conference on Data Mining (2002) 155–162.
17. Yao, Y.Y.: A comparative study of formal concept analysis and rough set theory in Data analysis. Rough Sets and Current Trends in Computing, Proceedings of 3rd International Conference, RSCTC'04 (2004).
18. Hu, K., Sui, Y., Lu, Y., Wang, J., Shi, C.: Concept approximation in concept lattice. Knowledge Discovery and Data Mining, Proceedings of the 5th Pacific-Asia Conference, PAKDD 2001. Lecture Notes in Computer Science 2035, Springer, Berlin (2001) 167–173.
19. Kent, R.E.: Rough concept analysis: a synthesis of rough sets and formal concept analysis. Fundamenta Informaticae, 27 (1996) 169–181.
20. Saquer, J., Deogun, J.S.: Formal rough concept analysis. New directions in Rough Sets, Data Mining, and Granular-Soft Computing. Lecture Notes in Computer Science 1711, Springer, Berlin (1999) 91–99.
21. Wolff, K.E.: A conceptual view of knowledge bases in rough set theory. Rough Sets and Current Trends in Computing, Second International Conference, RSCTC 2000. Lecture Notes in Computer Science 2005, Springer, Berlin (2001) 220–228.
22. Shao, M.-W., Zhang, W.-X.: The reduction of concept lattices in rough set theory. Manuscript (2004).
23. Skowron, A., Rauszer, C.: The discernibility matrices and functions in information systems. In: Slowinski, R. (Ed.), Intelligent Decision Support: Handbook of Applications and Advances of Rough Sets Theory. Kluwer Academic Publishers, Dordrecht (1992) 331–362.
24. Yao, Y.Y., Chen, Y.: Rough set approximations in formal concept analysis. In: Proceedings of 2004 Annual Meeting of the North American Fuzzy Information Processing Society (2004) 73–78.

Second-Order Rough Approximations in Multi-criteria Classification with Imprecise Evaluations and Assignments

Krzysztof Dembczyński[1], Salvatore Greco[2], and Roman Słowiński[1,3]

[1] Institute of Computing Science,
Poznań University of Technology, 60-965 Poznań, Poland
{kdembczynski, rslowinski}@cs.put.poznan.pl
[2] Faculty of Economics, University of Catania, 95129 Catania, Italy
salgreco@unict.it
[3] Institute for Systems Research,
Polish Academy of Sciences, 01-447 Warsaw, Poland

Abstract. The rough approximations are considered in the context of multi-criteria classification problem where evaluations of objects on particular criteria and their assignments to decision classes are imprecise and given in the form of intervals of possible values. Within Dominance-based Rough Set Approach (DRSA), the lower and upper approximations reflect the inconsistencies with respect to dominance principle. In the considered case, also the interval assignments have to be taken into account. This requires a new formulation of the dominance principle. A possible solution to the problem consists in introducing the second-order rough approximations. The methodology based on these approximations preserves well-known properties of rough approximations, such as rough inclusion, complementarity, identity of boundaries and monotonicity.

1 Introduction

In this paper, we consider an instance of the multi-criteria classification problem, in which objects are described and assigned *imprecisely*. We assume that the assignments and the evaluations on criteria are represented by *intervals*. The non-univocal (interval) assignment of an object is defined through the lowest and the highest class to which an object could belong. The interval evaluation is defined similarly, through the highest and the lowest value that an object may obtain on a given criterion.

In the multi-criteria classification problems, assignment of objects to decision classes may be inconsistent with respect to the *dominance principle*. It requires that any object x, having not worse evaluations than some object y on the considered set of criteria, cannot be assigned to a worse class than y. Greco, Matarazzo and Słowiński [4,5,6,7,9] have introduced Dominance-based Rough Set Approach (DRSA) that is able to handle these inconsistencies. According to the DRSA methodology, some selected reference objects are assigned by the Decision Maker (DM) to pre-defined decision classes, which are completely ordered

D. Ślęzak et al. (Eds.): RSFDGrC 2005, LNAI 3641, pp. 54–63, 2005.
© Springer-Verlag Berlin Heidelberg 2005

by preference. The assignment of reference objects to decision classes constitutes preference information from which the preference model is induced. The DRSA allows to get lower and upper (rough) approximations of unions of decision classes that reflect the inconsistencies with the dominance principle. The rough approximations are then used in induction of decision rules representing, respectively, certain and possible patterns of DM's preferences. The preference model in the form of decision rules explains a decision policy of the DM and permits to classify new objects in line with the DM's preferences. Taking into account the interval evaluations and assignments requires, however, the dominance principle to be revised and the DRSA methodology to be adapted adequately. A possible solution to the problem consists in introducing the *second-order rough approximations* that result from both, the imprecision of interval assignments and the inconsistencies with respect to the dominance principle. These approximations satisfy the usual properties considered in rough set theory such as *rough inclusion, complementarity, identity of boundaries* and *monotonicity*.

Let us remark that the classification problem with interval evaluations and assignments is a generalization of the classification problem with missing values considered within DRSA [5]. Indeed, an interval evaluation on a criterion could be seen as a "partially missing value" because a non-univocal evaluation, spanned over an interval is like a value partially unknown. In the extreme case, an interval equal to the whole domain of a criterion is a completely missing value. A similar, but less general problem of approximating univocal assignments with interval orders has been already considered by the authors in the context of hierarchical multi-attribute and multi-criteria classification [1]. Some elements of the present generalization have been also already reported in [2].

The article is organized in the following way. Section 2 contains problem statement and basic definitions. Section 3 describes several types of dominance relations used further in definitions of rough approximations. In Section 4, the dominance principle is extended for the considered case. Sections 5 presents definitions of decision and condition granules. The main results, i.e. the generalization of DRSA into second-order rough approximations, are described in Section 6. The last section presents conclusions.

2   Problem Statement

Multi-criteria classification consists in an assignment of objects from a set A to pre-defined *decision classes* Cl_t, $t \in T = \{1, \ldots, n\}$. It is assumed that the classes are preference-ordered according to an increasing order of class indices, i.e. for all $r, s \in T$, such that $r > s$, the objects from Cl_r are strictly preferred to the objects from Cl_s. The objects are described by *condition criteria*, i.e. attributes with preference-ordered domains.

In order to support multi-criteria classification, one must construct a preference model. One possible way is to induce this model from a set of exemplary decisions (assignments of objects to decision classes) made on a set of selected objects called *reference objects* $U \subseteq A$. The reference objects are relatively well-known to the DM, who can easily assign them to pre-defined classes.

The reference objects and their descriptions are often presented in a *decision table* $S = \langle U, C, D \rangle$, where $U \subseteq A$ is a finite, non-empty set of reference objects. C represents a set of condition criteria, and D represents a set of decision criteria that describe assignments of objects to decision classes. D is often a singleton $(D = \{d\})$, where d is shortly called *decision*. C and D are disjoint, finite and non-empty sets that jointly constitute a set of all criteria Q. It is assumed, without loss of generality, that the domain of each criterion $q \in Q$, denoted by V_q, is numerically coded with an increasing order of preference. The domains of criteria may correspond to cardinal or ordinal scales, however, we are exploiting the ordinal information (the weakest) only, whatever is the scale. The domain of decision d is a finite set $(T = \{1, \ldots, n\})$ due to a finite number of decision classes.

The imprecise (interval) evaluations and assignments of objects on any criterion $(q \in Q)$ are defined by an *information function* $\hat{f}(x, q) = \langle l(x, q), u(x, q) \rangle$, where $l, u : U \times Q \rightarrow V_q$ and $u(x, q) \geq l(x, q)$. $\langle l(x, q), u(x, q) \rangle$ is a subset of V_q referred to as an *interval evaluation* (or *assignment*, if q refers to d) of x on criterion q; $l(x, q)$ and $u(x, q)$ are the *lower* and the *upper boundary* of the interval, respectively. Observe that if these two values are equal, then the interval boils down to a single, precise value (it will be denoted by $f(x, q) = l(x, q) = u(x, q)$). Let us notice, that a missing evaluation could be also presented as an interval, such that $l(x, q)$ is the smallest value and $u(x, q)$ is the highest value from a domain of criterion q. It will be denoted by $\hat{f}(x, q) = \langle min(V_q), max(V_q) \rangle$.

An interval $\langle l(x, q), u(x, q) \rangle$ has the following interpretation. The precise evaluation (or assignment) of x on criterion q, denoted by $f(x, q)$, is presently unknown, but a range of this value is known and restricted by lower and upper boundary, i.e. $l(x, q)$ and $u(x, q)$, respectively. In the following, we assume that $f(x, q)$ is any value from $\langle l(x, q), u(x, q) \rangle$ with the same possibility. In other words, any interval evaluation defines the *highest* and the *lowest* value which an object could obtain on criterion $q \in C$. The non-univocal assignment of an object defines the *lowest* and the *highest* decision class to which an object could belong.

An example of decision table containing interval evaluations and assignments is presented in Table 1. It contains two condition criteria q_1 and q_2, decision criterion d and ten reference objects $U = \{x_1, \ldots, x_{10}\}$. Objects are assigned, not necessarily univocally, to four decision classes (Cl_1, Cl_2, Cl_3, Cl_4).

3   Dominance Relations

Within the basic DRSA, the notions of *weak preference* (or *outranking*) relation $\succeq_q$ and P-dominance relation D_P are defined as follows. For any $x, y \in U$ and $q \in Q$, $x \succeq_q y$ means that x is at least as good as (*is weakly preferred to*) y with respect to criterion q. Moreover, taking into account more than one criterion, we say that x dominates y with respect to $P \subseteq Q$ (shortly x P-dominates

Table 1. Decision table containing interval evaluations and assignments

U	q_1	q_2	d	U	q_1	q_2	d
x_1	$\langle 46, 50\rangle$	$\langle 48, 52\rangle$	4	x_6	24	10	$\langle 2, 3\rangle$
x_2	$\langle 44, 48\rangle$	$\langle 48, 50\rangle$	4	x_7	$\langle 6, 8\rangle$	$\langle 14, 20\rangle$	$\langle 1, 2\rangle$
x_3	$\langle 49, 52\rangle$	44	3	x_8	$\langle 9, 10\rangle$	$\langle 16, 20\rangle$	$\langle 1, 2\rangle$
x_4	26	$\langle 28, 35\rangle$	3	x_9	8	11	1
x_5	30	$\langle 26, 32\rangle$	2	x_{10}	$\langle 15, 27\rangle$	11	1

y), if $x \succeq_q y$ for all $q \in P$. The weak preference relation $\succeq_q$ is supposed to be a complete pre-order and, therefore, the P-dominance relation D_P, being the intersection of complete pre-orders $\succeq_q$, $q \in P$, is a partial pre-order in the set of reference objects.

When generalizing DRSA to the case of imprecise evaluations and assignments, the following weak preference relations with respect to $q \in Q$ can be considered:

- *possible weak preference relation:* $x \overline{\succeq}_q y \Leftrightarrow u(x, q) \geq l(y, q)$,
- *lower-end weak preference relation:* $x \succeq_q^l y \Leftrightarrow l(x, q) \geq l(y, q)$,
- *upper-end weak preference relation:* $x \succeq_q^u y \Leftrightarrow u(x, q) \geq u(y, q)$.

For the above defined weak preference relations one can easily get the corresponding P-dominance relations, where $P \subseteq Q$:

- *possible $\overline{P}$-dominance relation:* $x \overline{D}_P y \Leftrightarrow x \overline{\succeq}_q y$, for all $q \in P$,
- *P-lower-end dominance relation:* $x D_P^l y \Leftrightarrow x \succeq_q^l y$, for all $q \in P$,
- *P-upper-end dominance relation:* $x D_P^u y \Leftrightarrow x \succeq_q^u y$, for all $q \in P$.

Let us notice that the possible weak preference relation $\overline{\succeq}_q$ is an interval order [3] which is strongly complete and Ferrers transitive. It is easy to see [2], however, that the possible $\overline{P}$-dominance relation $\overline{D}_P$ based on interval orders is only reflexive - it is neither Ferrers transitive nor partial interval order in the sense of Roubens and Vincke [8]. The P-lower-end relation D_P^l and the P-upper-end relation D_P^u are reflexive and transitive.

Let us show, for example, that the following relations hold in Table 1, for $P = \{q_1, q_2\}$:

- $x_1 \overline{D}_P x_2$, because $u(x_1, q_1) = 50 \geq l(x_2, q_1) = 44$ and $u(x_1, q_2) = 52 \geq l(x_2, q_2) = 48$,
- $x_1 D_P^l x_2$, because $l(x_1, q_1) = 46 \geq l(x_2, q_1) = 44$ and $l(x_1, q_2) = 48 \geq l(x_2, q_2) = 48$,
- $x_1 D_P^u x_2$, because $u(x_1, q_1) = 50 \geq u(x_2, q_1) = 48$ and $u(x_1, q_2) = 52 \geq u(x_2, q_2) = 50$,
- and, $x_5 \overline{D}_P x_4$, because $u(x_5, q_1) = l(x_5, q_1) = 30 \geq u(x_4, q_1) = l(x_4, q_1) = 26$ and $u(x_5, q_2) = 32 \geq l(x_4, q_2) = 28$ (it may be remarked that, in spite of this dominance, x_5 is assigned to a worse class than x_4).

The dominance relations are not complete. For example, any dominance relation does not hold between x_2 and x_3.

4   Dominance Principle

In decision analysis, the *dominance principle* requires that an object having not worse evaluations on condition criteria than another object is assigned to a class not worse than the other object. More formally, the dominance principle can be expressed as follows:

$$xD_Py \Rightarrow xD_{\{d\}}y, \text{ for any } P \subseteq C.$$

In other words, it could be said that if x P-dominates y (x is not worse than y with respect to all criteria from P), then the assignment of x to a decision class should be not worse than the assignment of y. It could also be said that the assignment of y should be not better than the assignment of x. Any violation of the above principle is called *inconsistency*.

Taking into account imprecise evaluations and assignments, the above has to be revised. Let us express the dominance principle in the following way:

$$x\overline{D}_Py \Rightarrow xD^l_{\{d\}}y \wedge xD^u_{\{d\}}y, \text{ for any } P \subseteq C.$$

Its interpretation is the following: if x possibly dominates y, then the assignment of x should be not worse than the worst assignment of y and the assignment of y should be not better than the best assignment of x. This formulation is an extension of the former dominance principle, so that for univocal evaluations and assignments, it boils down to the former one. In the following, we refer to the latter formulation only.

The main reason for such a formulation is that an additional information that makes finer evaluations of reference objects should not increase the number of inconsistencies among these objects. Let us consider two objects that are inconsistent after getting finer evaluations (the interval assignments are just smaller, not displaced, i.e. they are subintervals of the original intervals). These two objects had have to be inconsistent also before the new information comes. This is concordant with the rough set philosophy which requires that if we knew more about objects, then we would obtain more consistent knowledge.

Let us illustrate the inconsistencies using the example introduced in Section 2. Objects x_4 and x_5 are inconsistent, because $x_5\overline{D}_Px_4$, but x_5 is assigned to a worse class than x_4. It may be remarked that the new (finer) information about intervals describing these objects may eliminate this inconsistency (for example, if $u(x_5, q_2) = 30$ and $l(x_4, q_2) = 31$). Objects x_2 and x_3 are consistent, in turn, and any new (finer) information describing these objects will not cause any new inconsistency. Observe, finally, that according to the extended formulation of the dominance principle, objects x_7 and x_8 are not inconsistent because of the interval assignments.

Let us also notice that a finer interval assignment of an object may introduce a new inconsistency with respect to the dominance principle. For example, if assignment of x_7 changed from $\langle 1, 2 \rangle$ to 2, then x_7 and x_8 would be inconsistent. In this case, however, the interval assignment is equivalent to inconsistency with the dominance principle. As we will see in the next sections, due to introduction of the second-order rough approximations, this situation does not introduce any new inconsistency into final results of analysis (see discussion following definitions of rough approximations in Section 6).

5   Decision and Condition Granules

The rough approximations concern granules resulting from information carried out by the decision criterion. The approximation is made using granules resulting from information carried out by condition criteria. The granules are called *decision* and *condition* granules, respectively.

The decision granules are defined using P-lower-end and P-upper-end dominance relations:

$$D_{\{d\}}^{l+}(x) = \{y \in U : yD_{\{d\}}^{l}x\}, \quad D_{\{d\}}^{u-}(x) = \{y \in U : xD_{\{d\}}^{u}y\},$$
$$\overline{D}_{\{d\}}^{+}(x) = \{y \in U : y\overline{D}_{\{d\}}x\}, \quad \overline{D}_{\{d\}}^{-}(x) = \{y \in U : x\overline{D}_{\{d\}}y\},$$

and are referred to as d-dominating sets, d-dominated sets, $\overline{d}$-dominating sets and $\overline{d}$-dominated sets, respectively.

If in the definition of the above granules one would use a class index $t \in T$ (value t on decision criterion d) instead of an object x, then they would boil down to the specific approximations of upward and downward unions of decision classes:

$$\underline{Cl}_t^{\geq} = \{y \in U : l(y,d) \geq t\}, \quad \underline{Cl}_t^{\leq} = \{y \in U : u(y,d) \leq t\},$$
$$\overline{Cl}_t^{\geq} = \{y \in U : u(y,d) \geq t\}, \quad \overline{Cl}_t^{\leq} = \{y \in U : l(y,d) \leq t\}.$$

The statement $x \in \underline{Cl}_t^{\geq}$ ($x \in \underline{Cl}_t^{\leq}$) means "$x$ belongs to at least (at most) class Cl_t", while the statement $x \in \overline{Cl}_t^{\geq}$ ($x \in \overline{Cl}_t^{\leq}$) means "$x$ could belong to at least (at most) class Cl_t". Let us remark that in comparison with original DRSA, the upward union of decision classes $Cl_t^{\geq}$ is replaced here by two upward unions $\underline{Cl}_t^{\geq}$ and $\overline{Cl}_t^{\geq}$ representing sets of objects with *sure* and *unsure* assignment, respectively. Similarly, the downward union of decision classes $Cl_t^{\leq}$ is replaced by two downward unions $\underline{Cl}_t^{\leq}$ and $\overline{Cl}_t^{\leq}$. In fact, the upward and downward unions of decision classes ($Cl_t^{\geq}$ and $Cl_t^{\leq}$) become *rough sets* in the considered case. The lower and upper approximations of $Cl_t^{\geq}$ ($Cl_t^{\leq}$) are $\underline{Cl}_t^{\geq}$ and $\overline{Cl}_t^{\geq}$ ($\underline{Cl}_t^{\leq}$ and $\overline{Cl}_t^{\leq}$), respectively. Let us explain this correspondence in the case of $Cl_t^{\geq}$.

Let us remind, that $Cl_t^{\geq}$ is defined as $Cl_t^{\geq} = \{x \in U : f(x,d) \geq t\}$, where $f(x,d)$ is a precise value representing an univocal assignment. Let us define $S_t^{\geq} = \{s \in T : s \geq t\}$ and rewrite the above definition to: $Cl_t^{\geq} = \{x \in U : f(x,d) \in S_t^{\geq}\}$ (or in equivalent way: $Cl_t^{\geq} = \{x \in U : \{f(x,d)\} \subseteq S_t^{\geq}\}$). In the case of interval assignments, $f(x,d)$ has to be replaced by $\widehat{f}(x,d)$, that is a subset of T, which may be completely included in or overlap with $S_t^{\geq}$. Therefore, it is not possible to represent $Cl_t^{\geq}$ exactly in terms of interval assignments $\widehat{f}(x,d)$, so

$Cl_t^{\geq}$ may be expressed as a rough set through its lower and upper approximation defined as:

$$\underline{Cl_t^{\geq}} = \{x \in U : \widehat{f}(x, d) \subseteq S_t^{\geq}\}, \quad \overline{Cl_t^{\geq}} = \{x \in U : \widehat{f}(x, d) \cap S_t^{\geq} \neq \emptyset\}.$$

Note that $\widehat{f}(x, d) \subseteq S_t^{\geq}$ is equivalent to $l(x, d) \geq t$ and $\widehat{f}(x, d) \cap S_t^{\geq} \neq \emptyset$ is equivalent to $u(x, d) \geq t$.

Let us consider objects x_6, x_7 and x_8 from Table 1. The corresponding information functions $\widehat{f}(x, d)$ returns the following subsets: $\widehat{f}(x_6, d) = \{2, 3\}$, $\widehat{f}(x_7, d) = \widehat{f}(x_8, d) = \{1, 2\}$. It is obvious that $Cl_2^{\geq}$ cannot be expressed using these objects and the lower and the upper approximation of this set has to be computed. They are: $\underline{Cl_2^{\geq}} = \{x_6\}$, because $\widehat{f}(x_6, d) \subseteq S_2^{\geq}$ (i.e. $l(x_6, d) \geq 2$) and, $\overline{Cl_2^{\geq}} = \{x_6, x_7, x_8\}$, because additionally $\widehat{f}(x_7, d) \cap S_2^{\geq} \neq \emptyset$ (i.e. $u(x_7, d) \geq 2$) and $\widehat{f}(x_8, d) \cap S_2^{\geq} \neq \emptyset$ (i.e. $u(x_8, d) \geq 2$).

There are two types of condition granules that are useful in the following considerations. They are $\overline{P}$-dominating sets and $\overline{P}$-dominated sets defined, respectively, as:

$$\overline{D}_P^+(x) = \{y \in U : y\overline{D}_P x\}, \quad \overline{D}_P^-(x) = \{y \in U : x\overline{D}_P y\}.$$

Let us illustrate these definitions by computing these sets for object x_4: $\overline{D}_P^+(x_4) = \{x_1, x_2, x_3, x_4, x_5\}$, $\overline{D}_P^-(x_4) = \{x_4, x_6, x_7, x_8, x_9, x_{10}\}$.

Let us remark that both decision and condition granules are cones in decision and condition spaces, respectively. The origin of a decision cone is a class index $t \in T$, while the origin of a condition cone is an object $x \in U$. The dominating cones are open towards increasing preferences, and the dominated cones are open towards decreasing preferences.

6   Dominance-Based Rough Approximations

Before we define the rough approximations taking into account imprecise evaluations and assignments, consider the following definition of P-generalized decision for an object $x \in U$:

$$\delta_P(x) = \langle l_P(x), u_P(x) \rangle,$$

where

$$l_P(x) = min\{l(y, d) : y\overline{D}_P x, y \in U\}, \quad u_P(x) = max\{u(y, d) : x\overline{D}_P y, y \in U\}.$$

In other words, the P-generalized decision reflects an imprecision of interval assignment of object x and inconsistencies with the dominance principle caused by this object. $l_P(x)$ is the lowest decision class, to which objects $\overline{P}$-dominating x may belong; $u_P(x)$ is the highest decision class, to which objects $\overline{P}$-dominated by x may belong. If $l_P(x) = u_P(x)$, then it means that object x is univocally assigned and P-consistent with respect to the dominance principle.

Let us compute the P-generalized decision for x_1 and x_6. Remark that x_1 does not cause any inconsistency and, therefore, $\delta_P(x_1) = \langle 4, 4 \rangle$. Object x_6

is assigned imprecisely to classes 2 and 3 and, moreover, it is dominated by x_{10} that is assigned to worse class than the worst assignment of x_6. Therefore, $\delta_P(x_6) = \langle 1, 3 \rangle$.

We will use the concept of rough approximation to express the interval assignment of objects to decision classes and inconsistencies with respect to the dominance principle, taking into account criteria from subset $P \subseteq C$. The lower approximation should correspond to a certain assignment, while the upper approximation to a possible assignment. Consequently, it will be reasonable to consider P-lower approximation of a sure assignment ($\underline{Cl_t^{\geq}}$ or $\underline{Cl_t^{\leq}}$) and P-upper approximation of an unsure assignment ($\overline{Cl_t^{\geq}}$ or $\overline{Cl_t^{\leq}}$) - they will just correspond to certain and possible assignments expressed in terms of criteria from $P \subseteq C$. In this way, we obtain the following *second-order rough approximations*:

$$\underline{P}(\underline{Cl_t^{\geq}}) = \{x \in U : \overline{D}_P^+(x) \subseteq \underline{Cl_t^{\geq}}\}, \quad \overline{P}(\overline{Cl_t^{\geq}}) = \{x \in U : \overline{D}_P^-(x) \cap \overline{Cl_t^{\geq}} \neq \emptyset\},$$

$$\underline{P}(\underline{Cl_t^{\leq}}) = \{x \in U : \overline{D}_P^-(x) \subseteq \underline{Cl_t^{\leq}}\}, \quad \overline{P}(\overline{Cl_t^{\leq}}) = \{x \in U : \overline{D}_P^+(x) \cap \overline{Cl_t^{\leq}} \neq \emptyset\},$$

where $t \in T$. They are referred to as P-lower approximation of $\underline{Cl_t^{\geq}}$, P-upper approximation of $\overline{Cl_t^{\geq}}$, P-lower approximation of $\underline{Cl_t^{\leq}}$ and P-upper approximation of $\overline{Cl_t^{\geq}}$, respectively.

Let us remark that these approximations may be expressed using P-generalized decision. For example, for $t \in T$, we have:

$$\underline{P}(\underline{Cl_t^{\geq}}) = \{x \in U : \overline{D}_P^+(x) \subseteq \underline{Cl_t^{\geq}}\} =$$
$$= \{x \in U : \forall y \in U, y\overline{D}_P x \Rightarrow l(y,d) \geq t\} =$$
$$= \{x \in U : min\{l(y,d) : y\overline{D}_P x, y \in U\} \geq t\} = \{x \in U : l_P(x) \geq t\},$$

and similarly, for $t \in T$:

$$\overline{P}(\overline{Cl_t^{\geq}}) = \{x \in U : \overline{D}_P^-(x) \cap \overline{Cl_t^{\geq}} \neq \emptyset\} =$$
$$= \{x \in U : \exists y \in U \text{ such that } x\overline{D}_P y \wedge u(y,d) \geq t\} =$$
$$= \{x \in U : max\{u(y,d) : x\overline{D}_P y, y \in U\} \geq t\} = \{x \in U : u_P(x) \geq t\}.$$

The remaining definitions may be formulated in the same way, i.e.:

$$\underline{P}(\underline{Cl_t^{\leq}}) = \{x \in U : u_P(x) \leq t\} \text{ and } \overline{P}(\overline{Cl_t^{\leq}}) = \{x \in U : l_P(x) \leq t\}, \text{ for } t \in T.$$

Let us compute these approximations for our example:

$$\underline{P}(\underline{Cl_4^{\geq}}) = \{x_1, x_2\}, \qquad \overline{P}(\overline{Cl_4^{\geq}}) = \{x_1, x_2\},$$
$$\underline{P}(\underline{Cl_3^{\geq}}) = \{x_1, x_2, x_3\}, \qquad \overline{P}(\overline{Cl_3^{\geq}}) = \{x_1, \ldots, x_6, x_{10}\},$$
$$\underline{P}(\underline{Cl_2^{\geq}}) = \{x_1, \ldots, x_5\}, \qquad \overline{P}(\overline{Cl_2^{\geq}}) = \{x_1, \ldots, x_8, x_{10}\},$$
$$\underline{P}(\underline{Cl_3^{\leq}}) = \{x_3, \ldots, x_{10}\}, \qquad \overline{P}(\overline{Cl_3^{\leq}}) = \{x_3, \ldots, x_{10}\},$$
$$\underline{P}(\underline{Cl_2^{\leq}}) = \{x_7, x_8, x_9\}, \qquad \overline{P}(\overline{Cl_2^{\leq}}) = \{x_4, \ldots, x_{10}\},$$
$$\underline{P}(\underline{Cl_1^{\leq}}) = \{x_9\}, \qquad \overline{P}(\overline{Cl_1^{\leq}}) = \{x_6, x_7, x_8, x_9, x_{10}\},$$
$$\underline{P}(\underline{Cl_1^{\geq}}) = \overline{P}(\overline{Cl_1^{\geq}}) = \underline{P}(\underline{Cl_4^{\leq}}) = \overline{P}(\overline{Cl_4^{\leq}}) = U,$$

where "..." denotes consecutive objects. It is easy to see that the inconsistencies with respect to the dominance principle and the imprecise assignments are taken into account in the above computations. It may be remarked, for example, that:

- x_4 and x_5 belong to $\underline{P}(Cl_3^{\leq})$ and to $\underline{P}(Cl_2^{\geq})$,
- x_6 and x_{10} belong to $\underline{P}(Cl_3^{\leq})$ and to $\underline{P}(Cl_1^{\geq})$,
- x_7 and x_8 belong to $\underline{P}(Cl_2^{\leq})$ and to $\underline{P}(Cl_1^{\geq})$,

where the presented approximations are the extreme ones, i.e. a lower approximation of the lowest $\underline{Cl_t^{\leq}}$ and a lower approximation of the highest $\underline{Cl_t^{\geq}}$, to which an object belongs. In other words, these approximations reflect the P-generalized decisions (see, for example, results for x_6). Let us come back for a while to the discussion from the last paragraph of section 4 concerning objects x_7 and x_8. Note that the computed rough approximations are the same, independently of the fact whether x_7 has been assigned to $\langle 1, 2 \rangle$ or to 2.

The following theorems ensure that the above definitions maintain the main properties of rough approximations. These are: *rough inclusion, complementarity, identity of boundaries* and *monotonicity*.

Theorem 1 (Rough Inclusion). *For any $t \in T$ and for any $P \subseteq C$, there hold:*

$$\underline{P}(Cl_t^{\geq}) \subseteq Cl_t^{\geq} \subseteq \overline{Cl_t^{\geq}} \subseteq \overline{P}(\overline{Cl_t^{\geq}}), \quad \underline{P}(Cl_t^{\leq}) \subseteq Cl_t^{\leq} \subseteq \overline{Cl_t^{\leq}} \subseteq \overline{P}(\overline{Cl_t^{\leq}}).$$

Theorem 2 (Complementarity). *For any $P \in C$, there hold:*

$$\underline{P}(Cl_t^{\geq}) = U - \overline{P}(\overline{Cl_{t-1}^{\leq}}), \quad t = 2, \ldots, n,$$
$$\underline{P}(Cl_t^{\leq}) = U - \overline{P}(\overline{Cl_{t+1}^{\geq}}), \quad t = 1, \ldots, n - 1.$$

Let us define the boundary regions as differences between the P-upper and the P-lower approximations, i.e. as sets including all inconsistent objects with respect to sure and unsure assignments:

$$Bn_P^{\geq t} = \overline{P}(\overline{Cl_t^{\geq}}) - \underline{P}(Cl_t^{\geq}), \quad Bn_P^{\leq t} = \overline{P}(\overline{Cl_t^{\leq}}) - \underline{P}(Cl_t^{\leq}).$$

Theorem 3 (Identity of Boundaries). *For any $t = 2, \ldots, n$ and for any $P \subseteq C$, it holds:*

$$Bn_P^{\geq t} = Bn_P^{\leq t-1}$$

Theorem 4 (Monotonicity). *For any $t \in T$ and for any $P \subseteq R \subseteq C$, there hold:*

$$\underline{P}(Cl_t^{\geq}) \subseteq \underline{R}(Cl_t^{\geq}), \quad \underline{P}(Cl_t^{\leq}) \subseteq \underline{R}(Cl_t^{\leq})$$
$$\overline{P}(\overline{Cl_t^{\geq}}) \supseteq \overline{R}(\overline{Cl_t^{\geq}}), \quad \overline{P}(\overline{Cl_t^{\leq}}) \supseteq \overline{R}(\overline{Cl_t^{\leq}})$$
$$Bn_P^{\geq t} \supseteq Bn_R^{\geq t}, \quad Bn_P^{\leq t} \supseteq Bn_R^{\leq t}.$$

The proofs of theorems are straightforward and are not included because of the lack of space.

7   Conclusions

The presented results extend the original DRSA and allow analyzing decision tables with interval evaluations on particular criteria as well as interval assignments to decision classes. To solve this problem, we introduced specific definitions of dominance relations and we revised adequately the dominance principle. This led us to a definition of new decision and condition granules used for second-order rough approximations. It is worth underlining that the definitions of second-order rough approximations satisfy all the usual properties of rough approximations: inclusion, complementarity, identity of boundaries and monotonicity. In a further paper, some other elements of the theory will be presented, together with decision rule induction and classification procedures.

Acknowledgements. The first and the third author wish to acknowledge financial support from the State Committee for Scientific Research (KBN grant no. 3T11F 02127). The research of the second author has been supported by Italian Ministry of Education, University and Scientific Research (MIUR).

References

1. Dembczyński, K., Greco, S., Słowiński, R.: Methodology of rough-set-based classification and sorting with hierarchical structure of attributes and criteria. Control & Cybernetics, **31** 4 (2003) 891–920
2. Dembczyński, K., Greco, S., Słowiński, R.: Dominance-based Rough Set Approach to Multicriteria Classification with Interval Evaluations and Assignments. Proceedings of the Third International Conferences on Decision Support for Telecomunications and Information Society, Warsaw (2003) 73–84
3. Fishburn, P. C.: Interval Orders and Interval Graphs. J. Wiley, New York (1985)
4. Greco S., Matarazzo, B., Słowiński, R.: Rough approximation of a preference relation by dominance relations. European Journal of Operational Research, **117** (1999) 63–83
5. Greco S., Matarazzo, B., Słowiński, R.: Dealing with missing data in rough set analysis of multi-attribute and multi-criteria decision problems. [In]: Zanakis, S. H., Doukidis, G., Zopounidis, C. (eds.): Decision Making: Recent Developments and Worldwide Applications. Kluwer Academic Publishers, Dordrecht (2000) 295–316
6. Greco S., Matarazzo, B., Słowiński, R.: Rough sets theory for multicriteria decision analysis. European Journal of Operational Research, **129** 1 (2001) 1–47
7. Greco S., Matarazzo, B., Słowiński, R.: Rough sets methodology for sorting problems in presence of multiple attributes and criteria. European Journal of Operational Research, **238** (2002) 247–259
8. Roubens, M., Vincke, Ph.: Preference Modelling. Springer Verlag, Berlin (1985)
9. Słowiński, R., Greco S., Matarazzo, B.: Rough Set Based Decision Support. Chapter 16 [in]: Burke, E., Kendall, G. (eds.): Introductory Tutorials on Optimization, Search and Decision Support Methodologies. Springer-Verlag, Boston (2005)

New Approach for Basic Rough Set Concepts

A.A. Allam, M.Y. Bakeir, and E.A. Abo-Tabl

Mathematics Department, Faculty of Science,
Assiut University, 71516 Assiut, Egypt

Abstract. The standard rough set theory has been introduced in 1982
[5]. In this paper we use a topological concepts to investigate a new definitions for the lower and upper approximation operators. This approach
is a generalization for Pawlak approach and the generalizations in [2,
7, 10, 12, 13, 14, 15, 16]. Properties of the suggested concepts are obtained. Also comparison between our approach and previous approaches
are given. In this case, we show that the generalized approximation space
is a topological space for any reflexive relation.

Keywords: Approximation operators, similarity relations, rough sets,
topological space.

1 Introduction

Rough set theory [5] is a recent approach for reasoning about data. It has
achieved a large amount of applications in various real-life fields, like medicine,
pharmacology, banking, market research, engineering, speech recognition, material science, information analysis, data analysis, data mining, control and linguistics (see the bibliography of [6] and [17, 18]).

The main idea of rough sets corresponds to the lower and upper set approximations. These two approximations are exactly the interior and the closure
of the set with respect to a certain topology τ on a collection U of imprecise
data acquired from any real-life field. The base of the topology τ is formed by
equivalence classes of an equivalence relation E defined on U using the available
information about data.

Following the connection between rough set concepts and topological notions,
we investigate new definitions of the lower and upper approximation operators
for similarity relation R. The equivalence class may be replaced by an element
of the base $\{<p>R|p \in U\}$ of the topology τ. It generalizes Pawlak's approach
and other extensions [2, 7, 10, 12, 13, 14, 15, 16]. It can be also compared with
other similarity-based generalizations of rough sets, like e.g. that reported by
Slowinski and Vanderpooten in [9].

The paper is organized as follows: In Section 2, we include the foundations of
rough sets, together with some generalizations known from literature. In Section
3, we present our approach and show a number of its mathematical properties.
In particular, the proposed generalized approximation space (U, R) is a topological space for any reflexive relation R. Comparison between our approach and

D. Ślęzak et al. (Eds.): RSFDGrC 2005, LNAI 3641, pp. 64–73, 2005.

previous models is given as well. The paper is concluded with final remarks in Section 4.

2 Standard and Generalized Rough Sets

The notion of approximation spaces is one of the fundamental concepts in the theory of rough sets. This section presents a review of the Pawlak approximation space constructed from an equivalence relation and its generalization using any binary relations.

Suppose U is a finite and nonempty set called the universe. Let $E \subset U \times U$ be an equivalence relation on U. The pair (U, E) is called an approximation space [5, 6]. Let $[x]_E$ denote the class of x such that $[x]_E = \{y \in U : xEy\}$. Then the lower and upper approximation of a subset X of U are defined as

$$\underline{E}(X) = \{x \in U : [x]_E \subset X\}$$

$$\overline{E}(X) = \{x \in U : [x]_E \cap X \neq \phi\}$$

A rough set is the pair $(\underline{E}(X), \overline{E}(X))$. Obviously, we have $\underline{E}(X) \subset X \subset \overline{E}(X)$. The lower approximation of X contains the elements x such that all the elements that are indistinguishable from x are in X. The upper approximation of X contains the elements x such that at least one element that is indistinguishable from x belongs to X.

This definition can be extended to any relation R, leading to the notion of generalized approximate space [11]. let xR be the right neighborhoods defined as

$$xR = \{y \in U : xRy\}$$

The lower and upper approximations of X according to R are then defined as

$$\underline{R}(X) = \{x \in U : xR \subset X\}$$

$$\overline{R}(X) = \{x \in U : xR \cap X \neq \phi\}$$

Obviously, if R is an equivalence relation, $xR = [x]_R$ and these definitions are equivalent to the original Pawlak's definitions.

We list the properties that are of interest in the theory of rough sets.

L1. $\underline{R}(X) = [\overline{R}(X^c)]^c$, where X^c denotes the complementation of X in U.
L2. $\underline{R}(U) = U$.
L3. $\underline{R}(X \cap Y) = \underline{R}(X) \cap \underline{R}(Y)$.
L4. $\underline{R}(X \cup Y) \supset \underline{R}(X) \cup \underline{R}(Y)$.
L5. $X \subset Y \Rightarrow \underline{R}(X) \subset \underline{R}(Y)$.
L6. $\underline{R}(\phi) = \phi$.
L7. $\underline{R}(X) \subset X$.
L8. $X \subset \underline{R}(\overline{R}(X))$.
L9. $\underline{R}(X) \subset \underline{R}(\underline{R}(X))$.
L10. $\overline{R}(X) \subset \underline{R}(\overline{R}(X))$.

$U1.$ $\overline{R}(X) = [\underline{R}(X^c)]^c$.
$U2.$ $\overline{R}(\phi) = \phi$.
$U3.$ $\overline{R}(X \cup Y) = \overline{R}(X) \cup \overline{R}(Y)$.
$U4.$ $\overline{R}(X \cap Y) \subset \overline{R}(X) \cap \overline{R}(Y)$.
$U5.$ $X \subset Y \Rightarrow \overline{R}(X) \subset \overline{R}(Y)$.
$U6.$ $\overline{R}(U) = U$.
$U7.$ $X \subset \overline{R}(X)$.
$U8.$ $\overline{R}(\underline{R}(X)) \subset X$.
$U9.$ $\overline{R}(\overline{R}(X)) \subset \overline{R}(X)$.
$U10.$ $\overline{R}(\underline{R}(X)) \subset \underline{R}(X)$.
$K.$ $\underline{R}(X^c \cup Y) \subset \underline{R}(X)^c \cup \underline{R}(Y)$.
$LU.$ $\underline{R}(X) \subset \overline{R}(X)$.

Properties $L1$ and $U1$ state that two approximations are dual to each other. Hence, Properties with the same numbers may be regarded as dual properties. Properties $L9$, $L10$, $U9$ and $U10$ are expressed in terms of set inclusion. The standard version using set equality can be derived from $L1L10$ and $U1U10$. For example, it follows from $L7$ and $L9$ that $\underline{R}(X) \subset \underline{R}(\underline{R}(X))$. It should also be noted that these properties are not independent.

With respect to any subset $X \subseteq U$, the universe can be divided into three disjoint regions using the lower and upper approximations:

$$BN(X) = \overline{R}(X) - \underline{R}(X),$$

$$POS(X) = \underline{R}(X),$$

$$NEG(X) = U - \overline{R}(X).$$

An element of the negative region $NEG(X)$ definitely does not belong to X, an element of the positive region $POS(X)$ definitely belongs to X, and an element of the boundary region $BND(X)$ only possibly belongs to X.

In Table 1 [3] we follow the properties that are satisfied by the different definitions above of rough sets.

A topological space can be described by using a pair of interior and closure operators [7]. There may exist some relationships between a topological space and rough set. In fact, the lower and upper approximation operators in a Pawlak approximation space can be interpreted as a pair of interior and closure operators in a topological space (U, τ).

Definition 1. [8] Let (U, τ) be a topological space, a closure (resp. interior) operator $cl : U \to 2^U$ (resp. $int : U \to \tau$) satisfy the Kuratowski axioms iff for every $X, Y \in U$ the following hold:

(1) $cl(\phi) = \phi$ (resp. $int(U) = U$,
(2) $cl(X \cup Y) = cl(X) \cup cl(Y)$ (resp. $int(X \cap Y) = int(X) \cap int(Y)$),
(3) $X \subseteq cl(X)$ (resp. $int(X) \subseteq X$),
(4) $cl(cl(X)) = cl(X)$ (resp. $int(X) = int(int(X)))$.

In general, a pair of interior and closure operators characterized by Kuratowski axioms may not satisfy all properties of the Pawlak rough set. The following

Table 1. Comparison between the properties of rough sets depending the properties of R. A cross ($\times$) indicates that property is satisfied. The first column contains the list of properties of rough sets. The next five columns are for rough sets, defined for any relation, reflexive relation, tolerance (reflexive and symmetric) relation, dominance (reflexive and transitive) relation and equivalence relation respectively.

Property	Any relation	Reflexive	Tolerance	Dominance	Equivalence
L1	$\times$	$\times$	$\times$	$\times$	$\times$
L2	$\times$	$\times$	$\times$	$\times$	$\times$
L3	$\times$	$\times$	$\times$	$\times$	$\times$
L4	$\times$	$\times$	$\times$	$\times$	$\times$
L5	$\times$	$\times$	$\times$	$\times$	$\times$
L6		$\times$	$\times$	$\times$	$\times$
L7		$\times$	$\times$	$\times$	$\times$
L8			$\times$		$\times$
L9				$\times$	$\times$
L10					$\times$
U1	$\times$	$\times$	$\times$	$\times$	$\times$
U2	$\times$	$\times$	$\times$	$\times$	$\times$
U3	$\times$	$\times$	$\times$	$\times$	$\times$
U4	$\times$	$\times$	$\times$	$\times$	$\times$
U5	$\times$	$\times$	$\times$	$\times$	$\times$
U6		$\times$	$\times$	$\times$	$\times$
U7		$\times$	$\times$	$\times$	$\times$
U8			$\times$		$\times$
U9				$\times$	$\times$
U10					$\times$
K	$\times$	$\times$	$\times$	$\times$	$\times$
LU		$\times$	$\times$	$\times$	$\times$

theorem states that a reflexive and transitive relation is sufficient for the approximation operators to be interior and closure operators [4].

Theorem 1. Suppose R is a reflexive and transitive relation on U. The pair of lower and upper approximations is a pair of interior and closure operators satisfying Kuratowski axioms.

3   New Approach for Rough Sets

If we consider the finite intersections of right neighborhoods as granule, the set of granules form a classical topology (in other words, right neighborhood is a sub-base). But we will take "complete intersections" as a granule and study its approximation. This section presents a study about a new definitions of lower and upper approximation operators for similarity relation R (reflexive or tolerance or dominance) and a comparison between this definitions and the definitions of generalized approximation operators in [11].

Definition 2. [1] Let R be any binary relation on U, a set $< p > R$ is the intersection of all right neighborhoods containing p, i.e., $< p > R = \bigcap_{p \in xR}(xR)$.

Definition 3. Let R be any binary relation on U, The lower and upper approximations of X according to R are then defined as

$$\underline{R}(X) = \{x \in U :< x > R \subset X\}$$
$$\overline{R}(X) = \{x \in U :< x > R \cap X \neq \phi\}$$

Proposition 1. For any binary relation R on a nonempty set U the following conditions hold for every $X \subset U$.

(i) $\underline{R}(X) = [\overline{R}(X^c)]^c$.
(ii) $\underline{R}(U) = U$.
(iii) $\underline{R}(X \cap Y) = \underline{R}(X) \cap \underline{R}(Y)$.
(iv) $X \subset Y \Rightarrow \underline{R}(X) \subset \underline{R}(Y)$.
(v) $\underline{R}(X \cup Y) \supset \underline{R}(X) \cup \underline{R}(Y)$.
(vi) $\underline{R}(X) \subset \underline{R}(\underline{R}(X))$.

Proof. (i)

$$[\overline{R}(X^c)]^c = \{x \in U :< x > R \cap X^c \neq \phi\}^c$$
$$= \{x \in U :< x > R \cap X^c = \phi\}$$
$$= \{x \in U :< x > R \subset X\}$$
$$= \underline{R}(X).$$

(ii) Since for every $x \in U$, $< x > R \subset U$ hence, $x \in \underline{R}(U)$. Then $U \subset \underline{R}(U)$. Also since $\underline{R}(U) \subset U$. Thus, $\underline{R}(U) = U$.

(iii)

$$\underline{R}(X \cap Y) = \{x \in U :< x > R \subset X \cap Y\}$$
$$= \{x \in U :< x > R \subset X \wedge < x > R \subset Y\}$$
$$= \{x \in U :< x > R \subset X\} \cap \{x \in U :< x > R \subset Y\}$$
$$= \underline{R}(X) \cap \underline{R}(Y).$$

(iv) Let $X \subset Y$ and $x \in \underline{R}(X)$, then $< x > R \subset X$ and so $< x > R \subset Y$, hence $x \in \underline{R}(Y)$. Thus $\underline{R}(X) \subset \underline{R}(Y)$.

(v) Since $X \subset X \cup Y$ then $\underline{R}(X) \subset \underline{R}(X \cup Y)$ also, $Y \subset X \cup Y$ then $\underline{R}(Y) \subset \underline{R}(X \cup Y)$, hence $\underline{R}(X \cup Y) \supset \underline{R}(X) \cup \underline{R}(Y)$.

(vi) Let $x \in \underline{R}(X)$, we want to show that $x \in (\underline{R}(X))$, i.e., $< x > R \subset \underline{R}(X)$ or for all $y \in < x > R \Rightarrow < y > R \subset X$. Since $x \in \underline{R}(X)$, then $< x > R \subset X$. Let $y \in < x > R$ then $< y > R \subset < x > R$ for all $y \in < x > R$, hence $< y > R \subset X$ for all $y \in < x > R$. Thus $y \in \underline{R}(X)$ for all $y \in < x > R$ and so $< x > R \subset \underline{R}(X)$, i.e., $x \in \underline{R}(\underline{R}(X))$. Hence, $\underline{R}(X) \subset \underline{R}(\underline{R}(X))$.

We can introduce an example to prove that the inverse in (v) in proposition 1. is not true in general.

Example 1. Let $R = \{(a, a), (a, b), (b, c), (c, a), (b, d), (d, e), (e, e), (e, b)\}$ be any binary relation on a nonempty set $U = \{a, b, c, d, e\}$. Then, $< a > R = \{a\}$,

$< b > R = \{b\}$, $< c > R = < d > R = \{c, d\}$ and $< e > R = \{e\}$. If $X = \{a, c\}$ and $Y = \{b, d\}$, then $\underline{R}(X) = \{a\}$ and $\underline{R}(Y) = \{b\}$ hence, $\underline{R}(X) \cup \underline{R}(Y) = \{a, b\}$ but $\underline{R}(X \cup Y) = \{a, b, c, d\}$, i.e., $\underline{R}(X \cup Y) \neq \underline{R}(X) \cup \underline{R}(Y)$.

Proposition 2. If a binary relation R on U is a reflexive relation, then the following conditions hold.

(i) $\underline{R}(\phi) = \phi$.
(ii) $\underline{R}(X) \subset X$.

Proof. (i) Since R is a reflexive relation on U, then $x \in < x > R$ for all $x \in U$, also there is no $x \in U$ such that $< x > R \subset \phi$ hence $\underline{R}(\phi) = \phi$.

(ii) Assume that $x \in \underline{R}(X)$, then $< x > R \subset X$. Since R is a reflexive relation on U, then $x \in < x > R$ for all $x \in U$ and there is no $y \in U - X$ such that $< y > R \subset X$. Thus $x \in X$ and so $\underline{R}(X) \subset X$.

We can give an example to show that the inverse in (ii) in proposition 2. is not true in general.

Example 2. Let $R = \{(a, a), (b, b), (c, c), (d, d),\ (a, b), (b, c), (c, a), (d, a)\}$ be any binary reflexive relation on a nonempty set $U = \{a, b, c, d\}$. Then, $< a > R = \{a\}$, $< b > R = \{b\}$, $< c > R = \{c\}$ and $< d > R = \{a, d\}$. If $X = \{b, c, d\}$, then $\underline{R}(X) = \{b, c\}$, thus $\underline{R}(X) \neq X$.

Proposition 3. Let R be an equivalence relation on a nonempty set U, then the following conditions hold.

(i) $X \subset \underline{R}(\overline{R}(X))$.
(ii) $\overline{R}(X) \subset \underline{R}(\overline{R}(X))$.

Proof. (i) Let $x \in X$, we want to show that $x \in \underline{R}(\overline{R}(X))$, i.e., $< x > R \subset \overline{R}(X)$ or $< y > R \cap X \neq \phi$ for all $y \in < x > R$. Since R is an equivalence relation, then $< x > R = < Y > R$ or $< x > R \cap < y > R = \phi$ for all $x, y \in U$, then for all $x \in X$ and $y \in < x > R$, $< y > R \cap X \neq \phi$, i.e., $y \in \overline{R}(X)$ for all $y \in < x > R$, then $< x > R \subset \overline{R}(X)$, thus $x \in \underline{R}(\overline{R}(X))$ and so $X \subset \underline{R}(\overline{R}(X))$.

(ii) Let $x \in \overline{R}(X)$, we want to show that $x \in \underline{R}(\overline{R}(X))$, since $x \in \overline{R}(X)$, then $< x > R \cap X \neq \phi$, also R is an equivalence relation hence, $< y > R \cap X \neq \phi$ for all $y \in < x > R$, then $y \in \overline{R}(X)$ for all $y \in < x > R$, i.e., $< x > R \subset \overline{R}(X)$ thus, $x \in \underline{R}(\overline{R}(X))$. Hence, $\overline{R}(X) \subset \underline{R}(\overline{R}(X))$.

The following example show that the inverse in (i) in proposition 3. is not true in general.

Example 3. Let $R = \{(a, a), (b, b), (c, c), (d, d), (a, b), (b, a), (b, c), (c, b), (a, c), (c, a)\}$ be an equivalence relation on a nonempty set $U = \{a, b, c, d\}$. Then $< a > R = < b > R = < c > R = \{a, b, c\}$ and $< d > R = \{d\}$. If $X = \{c, d\}$, then $\overline{R}(X) = \{a, b, c, d\}$ and $\underline{R}(\overline{R}(X)) = \{a, b, c, d\}$, hence $X \neq \underline{R}(\overline{R}(X))$.

The following example prove that the first condition in proposition 3. is not hold if the relation R is tolerance relation.

Example 4. Let $R = \{(a, a), (b, b), (c, c), (d, d), (a, b), (b, a), (b, c), (c, b)\}$ be a tolerance relation on a nonempty set $U = \{a, b, c, d\}$. Then $< a > R = \{a, b\}$, $< b > R = \{b\}$, $< c > R = \{b, c\}$ and $< d > R = \{d\}$. If $X = \{a, c\}$, then $\overline{R}(X) = \{a, c\}$ and $\underline{R}(\overline{R}(X)) = \phi$, hence $X \not\subseteq \underline{R}(\overline{R}(X))$.

We can prove that the following lemma from proposition 2. and proposition 3.

Lemma 1. If R is an equivalence relation on a nonempty set U, then $\overline{R}(X) = \underline{R}(\overline{R}(X))$.

Lemma 2. If R is a binary irreflexive, symmetric and transitive relation on a nonempty set U, then $X \subset \underline{R}(\overline{R}(X))$ for all $X \subset U$.

Proof. Let R be an irreflexive, symmetric and transitive relation on a nonempty set U, i.e., $< x > R = \{x\}$ or ϕ for all $x \in U$ and let $x \in X$, then there are two cases: the first is $< x > R = \phi$ and hence $< x > R \subset \overline{R}(X)$, then $x \in \underline{R}(\overline{R}(X))$. The second is $< x > R = \{x\}$ and so $< x > R \cap X \neq \phi$, then $x \in \overline{R}(X)$, i.e., $< x > R \subset \overline{R}(X)$, hence $x \in \underline{R}(\overline{R}(X))$. Thus $X \subset \underline{R}(\overline{R}(X))$.

The following example prove that the inverse in lemma 2. is not true in general.

Example 5. Let $R = \{(a, b), (b, a), (b, c), (c, b), (a, c), (c, a)\}$ be an irreflexive, symmetric and transitive relation on a nonempty set $U = \{a, b, c, d\}$. Then $< a > R = \{a\}$, $< b > R = \{b\}$, $< c > R = \{c\}$ and $< d > R = \phi$. If $X = \{a, b\}$, then $\overline{R}(X) = \{a, b\}$ and $\underline{R}(\overline{R}(X)) = \{a, b, d\}$, hence $X \neq \underline{R}(\overline{R}(X))$.

Proposition 4. For any binary relation R on a nonempty set U the following conditions hold for every $X \subset U$.
(i) $\overline{R}(X) = [\underline{R}(X^c)]^c$.
(ii) $\overline{R}(\phi) = \phi$.
(iii) $\overline{R}(X \cup Y) = \overline{R}(X) \cap \overline{R}(Y)$.
(iv) $X \subset Y \Rightarrow \overline{R}(X) \subset \overline{R}(Y)$.
(v) $\overline{R}(X \cap Y) \subset \overline{R}(X) \cap \overline{R}(Y)$.
(vi) $\overline{R}(\overline{R}(X)) \subset \overline{R}(X)$.

Proof. The proof is the same as for proposition 1.

Proposition 5. If a binary relation R on U is a reflexive relation, then the following conditions hold.
(i) $\overline{R}(U) = U$.
(ii) $X \subset \overline{R}(X)$.

Proof. The proof is the same as for proposition 2.

Proposition 6. Let R be an equivalence relation on a nonempty set U, then the following conditions hold.
(i) $\overline{R}(\underline{R}(X)) \subset X$.
(ii) $\overline{R}(\underline{R}(X)) \subset \underline{R}(X)$.

Proof. The proof is the same as for proposition 3.

Table 2. Comparison between the properties of rough sets depending the properties of R. A cross ($\times$) indicates that property is satisfied. The first column contains the list of properties of rough sets. The next five columns are for rough sets, defined for any relation, reflexive relation, tolerance, dominance and equivalence relation respectively.

Property	Any relation	Reflexive	Tolerance	dominance	Equivalence
L1	$\times$	$\times$	$\times$	$\times$	$\times$
L2	$\times$	$\times$	$\times$	$\times$	$\times$
L3	$\times$	$\times$	$\times$	$\times$	$\times$
L4	$\times$	$\times$	$\times$	$\times$	$\times$
L5	$\times$	$\times$	$\times$	$\times$	$\times$
L6		$\times$	$\times$	$\times$	$\times$
L7		$\times$	$\times$	$\times$	$\times$
L8					$\times$
L9	$\times$	$\times$	$\times$	$\times$	$\times$
L10					$\times$
U1	$\times$	$\times$	$\times$	$\times$	$\times$
U2	$\times$	$\times$	$\times$	$\times$	$\times$
U3	$\times$	$\times$	$\times$	$\times$	$\times$
U4	$\times$	$\times$	$\times$	$\times$	$\times$
U5	$\times$	$\times$	$\times$	$\times$	$\times$
U6		$\times$	$\times$	$\times$	$\times$
U7		$\times$	$\times$	$\times$	$\times$
U8					$\times$
U9	$\times$	$\times$	$\times$	$\times$	$\times$
U10					$\times$
K	$\times$	$\times$	$\times$	$\times$	$\times$
LU		$\times$	$\times$	$\times$	$\times$

From proposition 5. and proposition 6. we have:

Lemma 3. If R is an equivalence relation on a nonempty set U, then $\overline{R}(\underline{R}(X)) = \underline{R}(X)$.

Lemma 4. If R is a binary irreflexive, symmetric and transitive relation on a nonempty set U, then $\overline{R}(\underline{R}(X)) \subset X$ for all $X \subset U$.

Proof. The proof is the same as for lemma 2.

From proposition 2. and proposition 5. we can prove the following lemma.

Lemma 5. If a binary relation R on a nonempty set U is a reflexive relation, then $\underline{R}(X) \subset X \subset \overline{R}(X)$.

Lemma 6. If R is any binary relation on a nonempty set U, then $\underline{R}(X^c \cup Y) \subset \underline{R}(X)^c \cup \underline{R}(Y)$ for all $X, Y \subset U$.

Proof. Let $x \notin \underline{R}(X)^c \cup \underline{R}(Y)$, then $x \notin \underline{R}(X)^c$ and $x \notin \underline{R}(Y)$ hence, $x \in \underline{R}(X)$ and $x \notin \underline{R}(Y)$, i.e., $< x > R \subset X$ and $< x > R \notin Y$, then $< x > R \nsubseteq X^c$

and $< x > R \not\subseteq Y$, hence $< x > R \not\subseteq X^c \cup Y$, thus $x \notin \underline{R}(X^c \cup Y)$, i.e., $\underline{R}(X^c \cup Y) \subset \underline{R}(X)^c \cup \underline{R}(Y)$.

The following example prove that the inverse in lemma 6. is not true in general.

Example 6. In Example 1., if $X = \{a, c\}$ and $Y = \{b, d\}$, then $\underline{R}(X^c \cup Y) = \{b, e\}$, $\underline{R}(Y) = \{b\}$, $\underline{R}(X) = \{a\}$ and $\underline{R}(X)^c = \{b, c, d, e\}$, then $\underline{R}(X)^c \cup \underline{R}(Y) = \{b, c, d, e\}$. Thus $\underline{R}(X^c \cup Y) \neq \underline{R}(X)^c \cup \underline{R}(Y)$.

In Table 2 we summarize the previous results with the properties of R, derived using new definitions of the lower and upper approximation operators.

The following theorem states that a reflexive relation is sufficient for the approximation operators in definition 3. to be interior and closure operators.

Theorem 2. Suppose R is a reflexive relation on U. The pair of lower and upper approximations in definition 3. is a pair of interior and closure operators satisfying Kuratowski axioms.

Proof. The proof follows from definition 1. and propositions 1., 2., 4. and 5.

4   Conclusion

In this paper, we used the base $\{< p > R | p \in U\}$ of a topology τ on U generated by any binary relation R, to investigate new definitions for the lower and upper approximation operators. In this case the generalized approximation space (U, R) is a topological space for any reflexive relation R. Topology τ, constructed from a relation on a real-life data U, may help in formalizing many applications. For example, if U is a collection of symptoms and diseases and R is a binary expert-driven relation on U, topology τ generated by R is not only an abstract mathematical structure but also a knowledge base for U. In particular, if $X \subseteq U$, then X is a strong indication for any disease $p \in int(X)$.

References

1. Allam, A.A., Bakeir, M.Y., Abo-Tabl, E.A.: A relational view to some basic topological concepts. Submitted.
2. Kim, D.: Data classification based on tolerant rough set. Pattern Recognition, 34 (2001) 1613-1624
3. Bloch, I.: On links between mathematical morphology and rough sets. Pattern Recognition, 33 (2000) 1487-1496
4. Kortelainen, J.: On relationship between modified sets, topological spaces and rough sets. Fuzzy sets and systems, 61 (1994) 91-95
5. Pawlak, Z.: Rough sets. International Journal of Information and Computer Sciences, 11 (1982) 341-356
6. Pawlak, Z.: Rough sets. Theoretical Aspects of Reasoning about Data. Kluwer Academic Publishers (1991)
7. Pomykala, J.A.: Approximation operations in approximation space. Bulletin of the Polish Academy of Sciences, Mathematics, 35 (1987) 653-662

8. Rasiowa, H.: An algebraic approach to non-classical logics. North-Holland, Amsterdam (1974)
9. Slowinski, R., Vanderpooten, D.: A Generalized Definition of Rough Approximations Based on Similarity. IEEE Transactions on Knowledge and Data Engineering, 12(2) (2000) 331-336
10. Wybraniec-Skardowska, U.: On a generalization of approximation space. Bulletin of the Polish Academy of Sciences, Mathematics, 37 (1989) 51-61
11. Yao, Y.Y.: Two views of the theory of rough sets in finite universes. International Journal of Approximation Reasoning, 15 (1996) 291-317
12. Yao, Y.Y.: Constructive and algebraic methods of the theory of rough sets. Information Sciences, 109 (1998) 21-47
13. Yao, Y.Y.: Generalized rough set models. In: Rough Sets in Knowledge Discovery, Polkowski, L. and Skowron, A. (Eds.). Physica-Verlag, Heidelberg (1998) 286-318
14. Yao, Y.Y.: Relational interpretations of neighborhood operators and rough set approximation operators. Information Sciences, 111 (1998) 239-259
15. Yao, Y.Y., Lin, T.Y.: Generalized of rough sets using model logic. Intelligent Automation and Soft Computing, 2 (1996) 103-120
16. Yao, Y.Y., Wong, S.K.M., Lin, T.Y.: A review of rough set models. In: Rough Sets and Data Mining: Analysis for Imprecise Data, Lin, T.Y. and Cercone, N. (Eds). Kluwer Academic Publishers, Boston, (1997) 47-75
17. Electronic Bulletin of Rough Set Community http://www.cs.uregina.ca/~roughset
18. Rough Set Database System http://rsds.wsiz.rzeszow.pl/rsds.php

A Partitional View of Concept Lattice

Jian-Jun Qi[1], Ling Wei[2], and Zeng-Zhi Li[1]

[1] Institute of Computer Architecture and Network, Xi'an Jiaotong University,
Xi'an, 710049, PR China
qjjwv@nwu.edu.cn
[2] Department of Mathematics, Northwest University, Xi'an, 710069, PR China

Abstract. Formal concept analysis and rough set theory are two different methods for knowledge representation and knowledge discovery, and
both have been successfully applied to various fields. The basis of rough
set theory is an equivalence relation on a universe of objects, and that of
formal concept analysis is an ordered hierarchical structure — concept
lattice. This paper discusses the basic connection between formal concept
analysis and rough set theory, and also analyzes the relationship between
a concept lattice and the power set of a partition. Finally, it is proved
that a concept lattice can be transformed into a partition and vice versa,
and transformation algorithms and examples are given.

1 Introduction

Formal concept analysis (FCA) is proposed by Wille R. in 1982 [1,2], and rough
set theory (RST) is proposed by Pawlak Z. [3,4] in the same year. FCA and RST
are two different approaches to analyze data, they study and represent implicit
knowledge in data from different aspects. The basis of RST is an equivalence
relation induced by attributes over a set of objects. This relation divides the
object set into equivalence classes, which form a partition of the set. The basis
of FCA are formal concepts which are induced by a binary relation between a
set of objects and a set of attributes, and concept lattices which are ordered
hierarchical structures of formal concepts. Although RST and FCA are different
theories, they have much in common, in terms of both goals and methodologies
[5]. There is a need for systematically studying the relationships and interconnections between FCA and RST. This paper presents our results on the topic.

Most of the researches on the relationships between FCA and RST
[5,6,7,8,9,10] focus on introducing the notion of approximation operators into
FCA. Literature [11] explains that the intension of each concept defines an equivalence relation, which partitions the object set into two equivalence classes: one
consists of the extension of the concept, and the other consists of all of the other
objects. Our paper emphasizes the transformation between a concept lattice and
a partition. In our paper, the "partition" is determined by the relation defined by
all attributes. Literature [2] gives a mapping, which establishes the correspondence from each object to a concept (object concept). Our paper analyzes the
relationship between a concept lattice and the power set of a partition, gives the
transformation methods between a partition and a concept lattice.

D. Ślęzak et al. (Eds.): RSFDGrC 2005, LNAI 3641, pp. 74–83, 2005.

The paper is organized as follows. Section 2 recalls basic definitions both in FCA and in RST, and discusses the basic connections between FCA and RST. Section 3 analyzes the relationship between a concept lattice and the power set of a partition. Section 4 proves that a concept lattice can be transformed into a partition and vice versa. Section 5 gives transformation examples. Finally, Section 6 concludes the paper.

2   Preliminaries

First, to make this paper self-contained, the involved notions both in FCA and in RST are introduced [2,12]. At the same time, the basic connections between FCA and RST are discussed.

2.1   Basic Definitions in Formal Concept Analysis

Definition 1. *A triple (U, A, I) is called a formal context, if U and A are sets and $I \subseteq U \times A$ is a binary relation between U and A. $U = \{x_1, \ldots, x_n\}$, each $x_i(i \leq n)$ is called an object. $A = \{a_1, \ldots, a_m\}$, each $a_j(j \leq m)$ is called an attribute.*

In a formal context (U, A, I), if $(x, a) \in I$, also written as xIa, we say that the object x has the attribute a, or that a is fulfilled by x. In this paper, $(x, a) \in I$ is denoted by 1, and $(x, a) \notin I$ is denoted by 0. Thus, a formal context can be represented by a table only with 0 and 1.

With respect to a formal context (U, A, I), we define a pair of dual operators for $X \subseteq U$ and $B \subseteq A$ by:

$$X^* = \{a \in A | (x, a) \in I \text{ for all } x \in X\}, \tag{1}$$

$$B^* = \{x \in U | (x, a) \in I \text{ for all } a \in B\}. \tag{2}$$

X^* is the set of all the attributes shared by all the objects in X, and B^* is the set of all the objects that fulfill all the attributes in B. The two operators have the following properties: for all $X_1, X_2, X \subseteq U$ and all $B_1, B_2, B \subseteq A$,

1. $X_1 \subseteq X_2 \Rightarrow X_2^* \subseteq X_1^*$, $B_1 \subseteq B_2 \Rightarrow B_2^* \subseteq B_1^*$.
2. $X \subseteq X^{**}$, $B \subseteq B^{**}$.
3. $X^* = X^{***}$, $B^* = B^{***}$.
4. $X \subseteq B^* \Leftrightarrow B \subseteq X^*$.
5. $(X_1 \cup X_2)^* = X_1^* \cap X_2^*$, $(B_1 \cup B_2)^* = B_1^* \cap B_2^*$.
6. $(X_1 \cap X_2)^* \supseteq X_1^* \cup X_2^*$, $(B_1 \cap B_2)^* \supseteq B_1^* \cup B_2^*$.

We write $\{x\}^*$ as x^* for $x \in U$, and write $\{a\}^*$ as a^* for $a \in A$. A formal context (U, A, I) is canonical if $\forall x \in U$, $x^* \neq \emptyset$, $x^* \neq A$, and $\forall a \in A$, $a^* \neq \emptyset$, $a^* \neq U$. In general, the formal contexts in this paper are canonical.

Definition 2. *Let (U, A, I) be a formal context. A pair (X, B) is called a formal concept, for short, a concept, of (U, A, I), if and only if $X \subseteq U$, $B \subseteq A$, $X^* = B$ and $X = B^*$. X is called the extension and B is called the intension of (X, B).*

The concepts of a formal context (U, A, I) are ordered by

$$(X_1, B_1) \leq (X_2, B_2) \Leftrightarrow X_1 \subseteq X_2 (\Leftrightarrow B_1 \supseteq B_2) . \tag{3}$$

Where (X_1, B_1) and (X_2, B_2) are concepts. (X_1, B_1) is called a sub-concept of (X_2, B_2), and (X_2, B_2) is called a super-concept of (X_1, B_1). The notation $(X_1, B_1) < (X_2, B_2)$ denotes the fact that $(X_1, B_1) \leq (X_2, B_2)$ and $(X_1, B_1) \neq (X_2, B_2)$. If $(X_1, B_1) < (X_2, B_2)$ and there does not exist a concept (Y, C) such that $(X_1, B_1) < (Y, C) < (X_2, B_2)$, then (X_1, B_1) is called a child-concept (immediate sub-concept) of (X_2, B_2) and (X_2, B_2) is called a parent-concept (immediate super-concept) of (X_1, B_1), this is denoted by $(X_1, B_1) \prec (X_2, B_2)$.

All the concepts form a complete lattice that is called the concept lattice of (U, A, I) and denoted by $L(U, A, I)$. The infimum and supremum are given by:

$$(X_1, B_1) \wedge (X_2, B_2) = (X_1 \cap X_2, (B_1 \cup B_2)^{**}) , \tag{4}$$

$$(X_1, B_1) \vee (X_2, B_2) = ((X_1 \cup X_2)^{**}, B_1 \cap B_2) . \tag{5}$$

2.2   Basic Definitions in Rough Set Theory

Definition 3. *A triple (U, A, F) is called an information system, if U and A are sets and F is a set of relation between U and A. $U = \{x_1, \ldots, x_n\}$, each $x_i (i \leq n)$ is called an object. $A = \{a_1, \ldots, a_m\}$, each $a_j (j \leq m)$ is called an attribute. $F = \{f_j | j \leq m\}$, where $f_j = f_{a_j} : U \to V_j (j \leq m)$ and V_j is the domain of the attribute a_j.*

Let (U, A, F) be an information system. For $B \subseteq A$, we define a binary relation $R_B = \{(x_i, x_j) | f_l(x_i) = f_l(x_j)$ for all $a_l \in B\}$. R_B is an equivalence relation on U, and it determines a partition $U/R_B = \{[x_i]_{R_B} | x_i \in U\}$, where $[x_i]_{R_B} = \{x_j | (x_i, x_j) \in R_B\} = \{x_j | f_l(x_j) = f_l(x_i)$ for all $a_l \in B\}$. For simplicity, we write $[x_i]_B$ instead of $[x_i]_{R_B}$, $[x_i]_b$ instead of $[x_i]_{R_{\{b\}}}$.

2.3   Basic Connection Between FCA and RST

A data set is represented by an information system (U, A, F) in RST, and by a formal context (U, A, I) in FCA. We describe (U, A, I) as a table only with 1 and 0. Such representation implies: $\forall x \in U, \forall a \in A$, if $(x, a) \in I$, then the value of the attribute a with respect to the object x is 1; otherwise, the value is 0. Namely, $(x, a) \in I \Leftrightarrow f_a(x) = 1$, $(x, a) \notin I \Leftrightarrow f_a(x) = 0$. Thus, a formal context can be taken as a special information system, in which every attribute value of every object is either 0 or 1. In addition, an information system in RST is a multi-valued context in FCA, it can be transformed into a formal context [2].

Based on the above representations, we can analyze a formal context not only by RST but also by FCA. From the point of view of RST, both equivalence class and partition are used to describe objects (and to describe attributes implicitly). Similarly, from the point of view of FCA, both formal concept and concept lattice are used to describe objects and attributes. Hence, in a formal context, we can study the relationship between formal concept and equivalence class, and the relationship between concept lattice and partition to understand the connection between RST and FCA, and to further combine them.

3   Relationship Between Concept Lattice and the Power Set of Partition

In a formal context (U, A, I), each equivalence class $[x_i]_A$ corresponds to a pair $([x_i]_A, B_i)$, where $B_i = [x_i]_A^*$, and $\forall x \in [x_i]_A, x^* = B_i$; $\forall x \notin [x_i]_A, x^* \neq B_i$. The set of all such pairs is denoted by $\Delta = \{([x_i]_A, B_i)|[x_i]_A \in U/R_A, B_i = [x_i]_A^*\}$.

Theorem 1. *Let (U, A, I) be a formal context, U/R_A be the partition on it. Put*

$$\sigma(U/R_A) = \{\bigcup_{Y \in P} Y | P \subseteq U/R_A\} \ . \tag{6}$$

Then, for all $(X, B) \in L(U, A, I)$, $X \in \sigma(U/R_A)$.

Proof. Let $(X, B) \in L(U, A, I)$, $P = \{[x_i]_A|[x_i]_A \in U/R_A, [x_i]_A \cap X \neq \emptyset\}$. Then we have $P \subseteq U/R_A$, $\bigcup_{Y \in P} Y \in \sigma(U/R_A)$, and $\bigcup_{Y \in P} Y \supseteq X$. On the other hand, $\forall x \in [x_i]_A$, it is clear that $x^* = [x_i]_A^*$. So, if $[x_i]_A \cap X \neq \emptyset$, then $[x_i]_A \subseteq X$. It follows that $\bigcup_{Y \in P} Y \subseteq X$. Thus we have $X = \bigcup_{Y \in P} Y \in \sigma(U/R_A)$.

Theorem 2. *Let (U, A, I) be a formal context. Put*

$$L(U/R_A) = \{(Y, C)|Y \in \sigma(U/R_A), C = Y^*\} \ . \tag{7}$$

Then, for all $(X, B) \in L(U, A, I)$, the following 2 conclusions hold:

1. *$(X, B) \in L(U/R_A)$.*
2. *For all $(X_i, B) \in L(U/R_A)$, $X_i \subseteq X$.*

Proof. 1. This is a direct consequence of Theorem 1 and $B = X^*$.
   2. $\forall (X_i, B) \in L(U/R_A)$, $X_i^* = B$. So, $X_i \subseteq X_i^{**} = B^* = X$.

Corollary 1. *Let (U, A, I) be a formal context. Then,*

$$L(U, A, I) = \{(X, B)|(X, B) \in L(U/R_A), and \ X = \bigcup_{(X_i, B) \in L(U/R_A)} X_i\} \ . \tag{8}$$

Theorem 1, 2 and Corollary 1 give the relationship between a concept lattice and the power set of a partition. On the one hand, we know that the power set of U/R_A is a lattice. On the other hand, according to the definitions, the set of all Y for (Y, C) in $L(U/R_A)$ is equal to $\sigma(U/R_A)$, there is a one-to-one correspondence between the elements in $\sigma(U/R_A)$ and the ones in the power set of U/R_A. Therefore, $L(U/R_A)$ is also a lattice (ordered by inclusion relation between Y), these two lattices are isomorphic. Theorem 1 shows that the extension of each concept of (U, A, I) is an element in $\sigma(U/R_A)$, i.e., the union of all the elements that belong to an element in the power set of U/R_A. Theorem 2 and Corollary 1 further show that each concept (X, B) of (U, A, I) is the maximum one among the pairs (Y, C) satisfying $C = B$ in $L(U/R_A)$, and vice versa.

From the above analysis, we can get a method for constructing a concept lattice from a partition. At first, $L(U/R_A)$ is formed based on U/R_A. Then, we gather together all the pairs (Y, C) in $L(U/R_A)$ with the same C. Finally, all the maximum pairs of each class in $L(U/R_A)$ constitute $L(U, A, I)$.

Corollary 2. *Let* (U, A, I) *be a formal context. Then for all* $([x_i]_A, B_i) \in \Delta$, $(\bigcup_{k \in \tau} [x_k]_A, B_i) \in L(U, A, I)$, *where* $([x_k]_A, B_k) \in \Delta$, $B_k \supseteq B_i$, $k \in \tau (\tau$ *is an index set).*

Proof. Clearly, $([x_i]_A, B_i)$ is some $([x_k]_A, B_k)$, from which, we have $[x_i]_A \subseteq \bigcup_{k \in \tau} [x_k]_A$, and then $(\bigcup_{k \in \tau} [x_k]_A)^* = B_i$. So, $(\bigcup_{k \in \tau} [x_k]_A, B_i) \in L(U/R_A)$, and $\bigcup_{k \in \tau} [x_k]_A \supseteq Y$ for any $(Y, B_i) \in L(U/R_A)$. Thus $(\bigcup_{k \in \tau} [x_k]_A, B_i) \in L(U, A, I)$.

4   Transformation Between Concept Lattice and Partition

Theorem 3 (Transformation theorem from a concept lattice to a partition). *Let* (U, A, I) *be a formal context. For any* $(X, B) \in L(U, A, I)$, *the set* $\{(X_t, B_t) | (X_t, B_t) \in L(U, A, I), (X_t, B_t) \prec (X, B), t \in \tau\}$ *includes all of the child-concepts of* (X, B). *Then,*

$$U/R_A = \{X - \bigcup_{t \in \tau} X_t\} - \{\emptyset\} \ . \tag{9}$$

Proof. By proving the following three assertions, we can conclude this theorem.

1. $(X_1 - \bigcup_{i \in \tau_1} X_{1i}) \cap (X_2 - \bigcup_{j \in \tau_2} X_{2j}) = \emptyset$, where $(X_1, B_1) \neq (X_2, B_2) \in L(U, A, I)$,
   $(X_{1i}, B_{1i}) \in L(U, A, I)$ such that $(X_{1i}, B_{1i}) \prec (X_1, B_1)$ for all $i \in \tau_1$,
   $(X_{2j}, B_{2j}) \in L(U, A, I)$ such that $(X_{2j}, B_{2j}) \prec (X_2, B_2)$ for all $j \in \tau_2$.
2. $\bigcup_{(X,B) \in L(U,A,I)} (X - \bigcup_{t \in \tau} X_t) = U$.
3. If $X - \bigcup_{t \in \tau} X_t \neq \emptyset$, then $(x, y) \in R_A$ for all $x, y \in X - \bigcup_{t \in \tau} X_t$.

Suppose $(X_1 - \bigcup_{i \in \tau_1} X_{1i}) \cap (X_2 - \bigcup_{j \in \tau_2} X_{2j}) \neq \emptyset$. Then there exists an object x which satisfies $x \in X_1 \cap X_2$, $x \notin \bigcup_{i \in \tau_1} X_{1i}$, $x \notin \bigcup_{j \in \tau_2} X_{2j}$. However, because $X_1 \cap X_2$ is the extension of $(Y, C) = (X_1, B_1) \wedge (X_2, B_2)$ and $(X_1, B_1) \neq (X_2, B_2)$, we have $(Y, C) < (X_1, B_1)$ or $(Y, C) < (X_2, B_2)$. Suppose $(Y, C) < (X_1, B_1)$, then there exists $(X_{1l}, B_{1l}) \prec (X_1, B_1)(l \in \tau_1)$ such that $X_1 \cap X_2 = Y \subseteq X_{1l} \subseteq \bigcup_{i \in \tau_1} X_{1i}$. Thus, $x \in \bigcup_{i \in \tau_1} X_{1i}$, which is contradictory to the previous result. So 1) follows.

It is easy to see that $\bigcup_{(X,B) \in L(U,A,I)} (X - \bigcup_{t \in \tau} X_t) \subseteq U$. On the other hand, $\forall x \in U$, there exists a concept (X, B) such that $x \in X$. Let $(X_t, B_t) \prec (X, B)$, $t \in \tau$. Then, either $x \in X - \bigcup_{t \in \tau} X_t$ or $x \in \bigcup_{t \in \tau} X_t$. If $x \in \bigcup_{t \in \tau} X_t$, there exists $(X_l, B_l) \prec (X, B) (l \in \tau)$ such that $x \in X_l$. Taking (X_l, B_l) as (X, B) and repeating the above reasoning, we obtain either that $x \in X - \bigcup_{t \in \tau} X_t$ holds, or that $(\emptyset, A)$ is finally the only one child-concept of (X, B) (the formal context is canonical), which implies $x \in X = X - \emptyset = X - \bigcup_{t \in \tau} X_t$. So, $\forall x \in U$, there exists a concept

(X, B) such that $x \in (X - \bigcup_{t \in \tau} X_t)$. Therefore $\bigcup_{(X,B) \in L(U,A,I)} (X - \bigcup_{t \in \tau} X_t) \supseteq U$.
Thus, 2) holds.

Suppose $X - \bigcup_{t \in \tau} X_t \neq \emptyset$. For any $x, y \in X - \bigcup_{t \in \tau} X_t$, we have $x, y \in X$ and $x, y \notin \bigcup_{t \in \tau} X_t$. Since $x, y \in X$, it follows that $f_b(x) = f_b(y) = 1 (\forall b \in B)$. Meanwhile, $x, y \notin \bigcup_{t \in \tau} X_t$ implies that $f_c(x) = f_c(y) = 0 (\forall c \in A - B)$. So, $f_a(x) = f_a(y) (\forall a \in A)$, i.e., $(x, y) \in R_A$. Such result means that the partition given by (9) is certainly the one defined by R_A.

Theorem 3 shows that the partition defined by R_A can be obtained from the concept lattice of (U, A, I). For a concept (X, B), $X - \bigcup_{t \in \tau} X_t \neq \emptyset$ is an equivalence class. For each object in this class, the attributes in B have value 1 and the ones in $A - B$ have value 0. In addition, we can easily see that any equivalence class cannot be obtained from $(\emptyset, A)$, but that the extension of every parent-concept of $(\emptyset, A)$ is an equivalence class. Thus, we can deduce the following algorithm.

Algorithm 1 (Transformation algorithm from a concept lattice to a partition). Let $L(U, A, I)$ be a concept lattice, and P be a set.

1. Mark $(\emptyset, A)$, and set $P = \emptyset$.
2. For each parent-concept of $(\emptyset, A)$, mark it and put its extension into P.
3. For each unmarked concept (X, B), mark it and find out all its child-concepts $(X_t, B_t)(t \in \tau)$ to compute $Y = X - \bigcup_{t \in \tau} X_t$. If $Y \neq \emptyset$, put Y into P.
4. P is the partition defined by R_A after all the concepts are marked.

Lemma 1. *Let (U, A, I) be a formal context, $(X, B), (Y, C) \in L(U, A, I)$ and $(X, B) \prec (Y, C)$. For any $([x_i]_A, B_i) \in \Delta$ such that $[x_i]_A \subseteq Y - X$, $B_i \cap B = C$.*

Proof. Suppose $([x_j]_A, B_j) \in \Delta$ such that $[x_j]_A \subseteq Y - X$ but $B_j \cap B \neq C$. Since $(X, B) \prec (Y, C)$, we have $B \supset C$. And we obtain that $B_j \supset C$ and $B_j \cap B \neq B$ from $[x_j]_A \subseteq Y - X$. So, $B \supset B_j \cap B \supset C$. In addition, it is easy to see that $X, [x_j]_A \subseteq (B_j \cap B)^*$. Let $X' = (B_j \cap B)^* - (X \cup [x_j]_A)$, then $X'^* \supseteq B_j \cap B$. Hence, $(B_j \cap B)^{**} = (X' \cup X \cup [x_j]_A)^* = X'^* \cap B \cap B_j = B_j \cap B$. So, $((B_j \cap B)^*, B_j \cap B)$ is a concept. Therefore, $(X, B) < ((B_j \cap B)^*, B_j \cap B) < (Y, C)$. This result is contrary to that $(X, B) \prec (Y, C)$. Thus, the assertion of this lemma holds.

Theorem 4 (Transformation theorem from a partition to a concept lattice). *Let (U, A, I) be a formal context. Then for any $(X, B) \in L(U, A, I)$ satisfying $X \neq U$, the set of all its parent-concepts is*

$$\{(\bigcup_{k \in \tau_i} [x_k]_A \cup X, B_i \cap B) | i \in \tau\} , \tag{10}$$

where $([x_i]_A, B_i) \in \Delta$ satisfies $[x_i]_A \cap X = \emptyset$ and $B_i \cap B \not\subset B_j \cap B$ for each $([x_j]_A, B_j) \in \Delta$ such that $[x_j]_A \cap X = \emptyset$, $([x_k]_A, B_k) \in \Delta (k \in \tau_i)$ satisfies $[x_k]_A \cap X = \emptyset$ and $B_k \supseteq B_i \cap B$.

Proof. We need to prove the following two aspects.

1. All the elements in the set described as (10) are concepts, furthermore, they are parent-concepts of (X, B).
2. Any parent-concept of (X, B) can be described in the form of the element in the set shown as (10).

1). Clearly, $(B_i \cap B)^* = \bigcup_{k \in \tau_i} [x_k]_A \cup X$. In addition, since $([x_i]_A, B_i)$ is some $([x_k]_A, B_k)$, we have $(\bigcup_{k \in \tau_i} [x_k]_A \cup X)^* = \bigcap_{k \in \tau_i} B_k \cap B = \bigcap_{k \in \tau_i} B_k \cap B_i \cap B = B_i \cap B$. So $(Y, C) = (\bigcup_{k \in \tau_i} [x_k]_A \cup X, B_i \cap B)$ is a concept, and $(X, B) < (Y, C)$.

On the other hand, suppose $(X, B) \not\prec (Y, C)$. Then there exists a concept (X', B') such that $(X, B) < (X', B') < (Y, C)$. So $X \subset X' \subset Y$, $B \supset B' \supset C$. By Lemma 1, there exists $([x_j]_A, B_j) \in \Delta$ satisfying $[x_j]_A \subseteq X' - X \subset Y - X$ and $B_j \cap B = B' \supset C = B_i \cap B$. This is contradictory to $B_i \cap B \not\subset B_j \cap B$. Therefore, (Y, C) is a parent-concept of (X, B).

2). Suppose (X_t, B_t) is a parent-concept of (X, B). Then $X_t \supset X$, $B_t \subset B$. Let $X' = \bigcup_{k \in \tau_t} [x_k]_A$, where $([x_k]_A, B_k) \in \Delta (k \in \tau_t)$ satisfying $[x_k]_A \cap X = \emptyset$ and $B_k \supseteq B_t$. Thus, $X_t = B_t^* = X' \cup X = \bigcup_{k \in \tau_t} [x_k]_A \cup X$.

On the other hand, for any $([x_j]_A, B_j) \in \Delta$ such that $[x_j]_A \cap X = \emptyset$, there are two cases as follows:

If $[x_j]_A \cap X_t \neq \emptyset$, then $[x_j]_A \subseteq X_t - X$, $B_j \cap B = B_t$. Because $X_t - X \neq \emptyset$, there exists $([x_i]_A, B_i) \in \Delta$ such that $[x_i]_A \cap X = \emptyset$ and $B_t = B_i \cap B$. So, $B_j \cap B = B_t = B_i \cap B$. From which, $B_i \cap B \not\subset B_j \cap B$ follows.

If $[x_j]_A \cap X_t = \emptyset$, then $B_j \cap B \not\supseteq B_t$. Therefore, $B_i \cap B = B_t \not\subset B_j \cap B$.

Thus, there exists $([x_i]_A, B_i) \in \Delta$ such that $[x_i]_A \cap X = \emptyset$, $B_t = B_i \cap B$, and $B_i \cap B \not\subset B_j \cap B$ for each $([x_j]_A, B_j) \in \Delta$ which satisfies $[x_j]_A \cap X = \emptyset$.

As a result, we obtain that any parent-concept of (X, B) can be described in the form of the element shown in (10).

Theorem 4 shows that the whole concept lattice can be constructed from bottom to top based on the partition. The algorithm is as follows.

Algorithm 2 (Transformation algorithm from a partition to a concept lattice). Let (U, A, I) be a formal context, C and P be sets, L be a lattice.

1. Put $(\emptyset, A)$ into L, $(\emptyset, A)$ is the minimum concept. Set $C = \{(\emptyset, A)\}$, $P = \emptyset$.
2. For each concept (X, B) in C, find out all the pairs $([x_i]_A, B_i)$ in Δ which satisfy the conditions of Theorem 4. Every such pair in Δ determines a parent-concept of (X, B), put this parent-concept into L and P, and connect it with (X, B) in L.
3. Set $C = P$, $P = \emptyset$. Repeat the step 2 until C has only one concept whose extension is U.

Table 1. A formal context (U, A, I)

	a	b	c	d	e
1	1	1	0	1	1
2	1	1	1	0	0
3	0	0	0	1	0
4	1	1	1	0	0

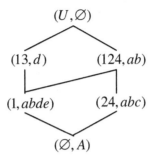

Fig. 1. The concept lattice of (U, A, I)

5 Example

Example 1 (Transformation from a concept lattice to a partition). We consider a formal context (U, A, I) shown as Table 1, its concept lattice is shown as Figure 1.

We can get the partition by Algorithm 1.

Since the parent-concepts of $(\emptyset, A)$ are $(\{1\}, \{a, b, d, e\})$ and $(\{2, 4\}, \{a, b, c\})$, $\{1\}$ and $\{2, 4\}$ are equivalence classes. Then we consider the other concepts.

The child-concepts of $(U, \emptyset)$ are $(\{1, 3\}, \{d\})$ and $(\{1, 2, 4\}, \{a, b\})$. So $Y = \emptyset$.

The child-concept of $(\{1, 3\}, \{d\})$ is $(\{1\}, \{a, b, d, e\})$. So $Y = \{3\}$. Thus, $\{3\}$ is an equivalence class.

The child-concepts of $(\{1, 2, 4\}, \{a, b\})$ are $(\{1\}, \{a, b, d, e\})$, $(\{2, 4\}, \{a, b, c\})$. So $Y = \emptyset$.

The mapping between each concept and its corresponding Y is shown as Table 2.

Finally, we get the partition of Table 1: $U/R_A = \{\{1\}, \{2, 4\}, \{3\}\}$.

Table 2. Mapping from concept to equivalence class

Concept	$(\emptyset, A)$	$(1, abde)$	$(24, abc)$	$(13, d)$	$(124, ab)$	$(U, \emptyset)$
Y	$\emptyset$	1	24	3	$\emptyset$	$\emptyset$

Example 2 (Transformation from a partition to a concept lattice). We still consider the formal context (U, A, I) shown in Table 1. It is known that

$$U/R_A = \{\{1\}, \{2, 4\}, \{3\}\} \ ,$$

$$\Delta = \{(\{1\}, \{a, b, d, e\}), (\{2, 4\}, \{a, b, c\}), (\{3\}, \{d\})\} \ .$$

Now, we construct the concept lattice by Algorithm 2.

1. $(\emptyset, A)$ is the minimum concept. Set $C = \{(\emptyset, A)\}$.
2. For the concept $(\emptyset, A)$, the pairs $([x_i]_A, B_i)$ in Δ which satisfy the conditions of Theorem 4 are $(\{1\}, \{a, b, d, e\})$ and $(\{2, 4\}, \{a, b, c\})$. The parent-concept of $(\emptyset, A)$ decided by $(\{1\}, \{a, b, d, e\})$ is $(\{1\}, \{a, b, d, e\})$, and the one decided by $(\{2, 4\}, \{a, b, c\})$ is $(\{2, 4\}, \{a, b, c\})$. Connect these parent-concepts with $(\emptyset, A)$.

   Now, $C = \{(\{1\}, \{a, b, d, e\}), (\{2, 4\}, \{a, b, c\})\}$.
3. For the concept $(\{1\}, \{a, b, d, e\})$, the pairs $([x_i]_A, B_i)$ in Δ which satisfy the conditions of Theorem 4 are $(\{2, 4\}, \{a, b, c\})$ and $(\{3\}, \{d\})$. The parent-concept of $(\{1\}, \{a, b, d, e\})$ decided by $(\{2, 4\}, \{a, b, c\})$ is $(\{1, 2, 4\}, \{a, b\})$, and the one decided by $(\{3\}, \{d\})$ is $(\{1, 3\}, \{d\})$. Connect these parent-concepts with $(\{1\}, \{a, b, d, e\})$.

   For the concept $(\{2, 4\}, \{a, b, c\})$, in Δ, there is only $(\{1\}, \{a, b, d, e\})$ satisfying the conditions of Theorem 4. The parent-concept of $(\{2, 4\}, \{a, b, c\})$ decided by $(\{1\}, \{a, b, d, e\})$ is $(\{1, 2, 4\}, \{a, b\})$. Connect this parent-concept with $(\{2, 4\}, \{a, b, c\})$.

   Now, $C = \{(\{1, 3\}, \{d\}), (\{1, 2, 4\}, \{a, b\})\}$.
4. For the concept $(\{1, 3\}, \{d\})$, there is only one pair in Δ satisfying the requests, it is $(\{2, 4\}, \{a, b, c\})$. The parent-concept of $(\{1, 3\}, \{d\})$ decided by $(\{2, 4\}, \{a, b, c\})$ is $(U, \emptyset)$. Connect $(U, \emptyset)$ with $(\{1, 3\}, \{d\})$.

   For the concept $(\{1, 2, 4\}, \{a, b\})$, there also is only one pair in Δ satisfying the requests, it is $(\{3\}, \{d\})$. The parent-concept of $(\{1, 2, 4\}, \{a, b\})$ decided by $(\{3\}, \{d\})$ also is $(U, \emptyset)$. Connect $(U, \emptyset)$ with $(\{1, 2, 4\}, \{a, b\})$.

   Now, $C = \{(U, \emptyset)\}$.

The final concept lattice obtained is shown as Figure 1.

6   Conclusions

FCA and RST are two different approaches to analyze data, and they study and represent implicit knowledge in data from different aspects. Both of them have been successfully applied to various fields. By studying the relationship between these two theories and combining them, we can further analyze and understand data. The relationship between FCA and RST can be studied from different viewpoint, and this paper focuses on the concept lattice and the partition that are the basis of FCA and RST respectively. In this paper, we discussed the basic connection between the two theories, and emphatically analyzed the relationship between formal concept and equivalence class, and the relationship between concept lattice and partition. We proved that a concept lattice can be transformed into a partition and vice versa, and also gave the transformation examples.

Acknowledgements

The authors gratefully acknowledge Professor Wen-Xiu Zhang because of his discussions in the seminar. The authors gratefully acknowledge the suggestions of the reviewers and the hard work of the RSFDGrC 2005 Program Committee.

The authors also gratefully acknowledge the support of the Natural Scientific Research Project of the Education Department of Shaanxi Province in China (No.04JK131), and of the National Natural Science Foundation of China (No.60173059).

References

1. Wille, R.: Restructuring Lattice Theory: an Approach Based on Hierarchies of Concepts. In: Rival, I. (ed.): Ordered Sets. Reidel Publishing Company, Dordrecht-Boston (1982) 445-470
2. Ganter, B., Wille, R.: Formal Concept Analysis, Mathematical Foundations. Springer-Verlag, Berlin Heidelberg (1999)
3. Pawlak, Z.: Rough Sets. International Journal of Computer and Information Sciences. 11 (1982) 341-356
4. Pawlak, Z.: Rough Sets, Theoretical Aspects of Reasoning about Data. Kluwer Academic Publishers, Dordrecht (1991)
5. Kent, R.E.: Rough Concept Analysis: a Synthesis of Rough Rets and Formal Concept Analysis. Fundamenta Informaticae. 27 (1996) 169-181
6. Yao, Y.Y., Chen, Y.H.: Rough Set Approximations in Formal Concept Analysis. In: Dick, S., Kurgan, L., Pedrycz, W., Reformat, M. (eds.): Proceedings of 2004 Annual Meeting of the North American Fuzzy Information Processing Society. IEEE (2004) 73-78
7. Hu, K., Sui, Y., Lu, Y., Wang, J., Shi, C.: Concept Approximation in Concept Lattice. In: Cheung, D., Williams, G.J., Li, Q. (eds.): Proceedings of the 5th Pacific-Asia Conference on Knowledge Discovery and Data Mining. Lecture Notes in Computer Science, Vol. 2035. Springer-Verlag, Berlin Heidelberg (2001) 167-173
8. Saquer, J., Deogun, J.S.: Concept Approximations Based on Rough Sets and Similarity Measures. Int. J. Appl. Math. Comput. Sci. 11 (2001) 655-674
9. Ho, T.B.: Acquiring Concept Approximations in the Framework of Rough Concept Analysis. In: Kangassalo, H., Charrel, P.-J. (eds.): Preprint of the 7th European-Japanese Conference on Information Modelling and Knowledge Bases. Toulouse, France (1997) 186-195
10. Pagliani, P.: From Concept Lattices to Approximation Spaces: Algebraic Structures of some Spaces of Partial Objects. Fundamenta Informaticae. 18 (1993) 1-25
11. Hu, K.Y., Lu, Y.C., Sh, C.Y.: Advances in Concept Lattice and its Application. Journal of Tsinghua University (Sci & Tech). 40 (2000) 77-81
12. Zhang, W.X., Leung, Y., Wu, W.Z.: Information System and Knowledge Discovery. Science Publishing Company, Beijing (2003)

Characterizations of Attributes in Generalized Approximation Representation Spaces

Guo-Fang Qiu[1], Wen-Xiu Zhang[2], and Wei-Zhi Wu[3]

[1] The College of Management, Zhejiang University,
Hangzhou, Zhejiang 310027, P. R. China
qiugf@zju.edu.cn
[2] Faculty of Science, Institute for Information and System Sciences,
Xi'an Jiaotong University, Xi'an, Shaanxi 710049, PR China
wxzhang@mail.xjtu.edu.cn
[3] Information College, Zhejiang Ocean University,
Zhoushan, Zhejiang 316004, P. R. China
wuwz@zjou.net.cn

Abstract. We discuss characterizations of three important types of attribute sets in generalized approximation representation spaces, in which binary relations on the universe are reflexive. Many information tables, such as consistent or inconsistent decision tables, variable precision rough set models, consistent decision tables with ordered valued domains and with continuous valued domains, and decision tables with fuzzy decisions, can be unified to generalized approximation representation spaces. A general approach to knowledge reduction based on rough set theory is proposed.

1 Introduction

Rough set theory, proposed by Pawlak [8] in 1980s, deals problems with inexact, uncertain or vague information. The theory has been applied in the fields, such as machine learning, pattern recognition, decision analysis, process control, knowledge discovery in databases, and expert systems.

One fundamental aspect of rough set theory involves a search for particular subsets of condition attributes that provide the same information for classification purposes as the entire set of attributes. Such subsets are called attribute reducts. Reduct and core are two important concepts in the study of rough set theory. Many types of knowledge reducts have been proposed in the area of rough sets, each of the reducts aimed at some basic requirements [1, 4-7, 9, 10, 13, 14, 16, 17]. In [12], Skowron and Rauszer introduced the notion of discernibility matrix which became a major tool for searching reducts and core in information systems. Using the similar idea, Mi *et al.* [6] and Zhang *et al.* [16] discussed approaches to knowledge reduction in inconsistent and incomplete information systems, respectively. In [17], Zhang and Wu presented theorems that characterize consistent sets, and approaches for knowledge reduction in information

D. Ślęzak et al. (Eds.): RSFDGrC 2005, LNAI 3641, pp. 84–93, 2005.

systems with fuzzy decisions. Yao and Greco [2, 15] studied a generalized decision logic language to treat dominance relations and discovered ordering rules for a particular types of binary relations.

In this paper, we first introduce the concept of generalized approximation representation space in Section 2. In Section 3, we demonstrate that many special information systems such as consistent or inconsistent decision tables [9, 16], variable precision rough set models [6, 18], consistent decision tables with ordered valued domains and with continuous valued domains [2, 3, 11, 15], and decision tables with fuzzy decisions [17] can be unified under the framework of approximation representation space theory. By analyzing the consistent attribute set and the reduction set of a consistent generalized approximation representation space, we give characterizations of three important types of attribute sets, and provide the conditions for determining the necessary and unnecessary attribute sets. We then present concluding remarks in Section 4.

2 Consistent Generalized Approximation Representation Spaces

Definition 1. *Let (U, A) be an approximation space, where $U = \{x_1, x_2, \ldots, x_n\}$ is a finite set of objects called the universe of discourse, $A = \{a_1, a_2, \ldots, a_m\}$ is a finite set of attributes,*

$$\mathcal{R} = \{R_a \subseteq U \times U : a \in A\} \tag{1}$$

is a family of reflexive binary relations on U, and R' is a reflexive binary relation on U. The quadruple $(U, A, \mathcal{R}, R')$ is called a generalized approximation representation space.

Definition 2. *Let $S = (U, A, \mathcal{R}, R')$ be a generalized approximation representation space. With a subset of attributes $B \subseteq A$, a binary relation on U is given by:*

$$R_B = \bigcap_{a \in B} R_a. \tag{2}$$

The system S is called a consistent generalized approximation representation space if $R_A \subseteq R'$. If $R_B \subseteq R'$ ($B \subseteq A$), then B is called a consistent attribute set of S. If B is a consistent attribute set of S and no proper subset of B is a consistent attribute set of S, then B is a reduct set of S.

Consider an information table (U, A, F), where $F = \{f_l : U \to V_l \ (l \leq m)\}$, V_l is the domain of the attribute a_l. Based on the equality relation on attribute values, we can define equivalence relations as follows [9]:

$$R_a = \{(x_i, x_j) : f_a(x_i) = f_a(x_j)\} \ (a \in A), \tag{3}$$

$$\mathcal{R} = \{R_a \subseteq U \times U : a \in A\}, \tag{4}$$

$$R_A = \{(x_i, x_j) : f_l(x_i) = f_l(x_j) \ (a_l \in A)\} \quad (l \leq m). \tag{5}$$

We obtain a consistent generalized approximation representation space $S = (U, A, \mathcal{R}, R_A)$. In general, Yao and Wong [15] suggested that arbitrary binary relations on the attribute values can be used. The binary relations in turn induce binary relations on U. This can be easily done by replacing the equality relation "=" with an arbitrary binary relation in the above equations.

For a consistent decision table (U, A, F, d), where d is a decision attribute, $S = (U, A, \mathcal{R}, R_d)$ is a consistent generalized approximation representation space, where

$$R_d = \{(x_i, x_j) : \ d(x_i) = d(x_j)\}. \tag{6}$$

The reason is that we have $R_A \subseteq R_d$ from a consistent decision table.

By definition, if we can choose a proper reflexive relation R', any information table may be expressed a generalized approximation representation space.

If (U, A, F, d) is an inconsistent decision table, we define

$$U/R_d = \{D_j : \ j \leq r\},$$

$$D(D_j/[x_i]_B) = \frac{|D_j \cap [x_i]_B|}{|[x_i]_B|},$$

$$\mu_B(x_i) = (D(D_1/[x_i]_B), D(D_2/[x_i]_B), \ldots, D(D_r/[x_i]_B)),$$

$$\eta_B(x_i) = \{D_j : \ D(D_j/[x_i]_B) = \max_{k \leq r} D(D_k/[x_i]_B)\},$$

where U/R_d is a classification of the universe U with respect to R_d, $D(./.)$ is an inclusion degree [16], $[x_i]_B$ is an equivalence class containing x_i with respect to the attribute set B, $|X|$ is the cardinality of the set X.

Theorem 1. *Let (U, A, F, d) be an inconsistent decision table, then $S = (U, A, \mathcal{R}, R_\mu)$ is a consistent generalized approximation representation space, and $B \subseteq A$ is a consistent attribute set of S if and only if (iff)*

$$\mu_B(x_i) = \mu_A(x_i) \ (x_i \in U), \tag{7}$$

where

$$R_\mu = \{(x_i, x_j) : \ \mu_A(x_i) = \mu_A(x_j)\}. \tag{8}$$

Proof. Since R_μ is an equivalence relation on U, $(x_i, x_j) \in R_A$ implies $[x_i]_A = [x_j]_A$, that is, $\mu_A(x_i) = \mu_A(x_j)$, thus $(x_i, x_j) \in R_\mu$, i.e. $R_A \subseteq R_\mu$. Hence $(U, A, \mathcal{R}, R_\mu)$ is a consistent generalized approximation representation space.

If B is a consistent set of S, then $R_B \subseteq R_\mu$, that is $(x_i, x_j) \in R_B$ implies $(x_i, x_j) \in R_\mu$, i.e. $x_j \in [x_i]_B$ implies $\mu_A(x_j) = \mu_A(x_i)$. It follows:

$$D(D_k/[x_j]_A) = D(D_k/[x_i]_A) \quad (k \leq r, x_j \in [x_i]_B).$$

Thus we have

$$\begin{aligned}
D(D_k/[x_i]_B) &= \frac{|D_k \cap [x_i]_B|}{|[x_i]_B|} \\
&= \sum \{D(D_k/[x_j]_A) \frac{|[x_j]_A|}{|[x_i]_B|} : [x_j]_A \subseteq [x_i]_B\} \\
&= D(D_k/[x_i]_A) \quad (k \leq r, x_i \in U),
\end{aligned}$$

from which we have $\mu_B(x_i) = \mu_A(x_i) \ (x_i \in U)$.

Conversely, suppose $\mu_B(x_i) = \mu_A(x_i)(x_i \in U)$. If $(x_i, x_j) \in R_B$, i.e., $[x_i]_B = [x_j]_B$, then $\mu_B(x_i) = \mu_B(x_j)$, hence $\mu_A(x_i) = \mu_A(x_j)$, that is, $(x_i, x_j) \in R_\mu$. Thus, we conclude that $R_B \subseteq R_\mu$.

Similarly, $S = (U, A, \mathcal{R}, R_\eta)$ is a consistent generalized approximation representation space, where

$$R_\eta = \{(x_i, x_j) : \ \eta_A(x_i) = \eta_A(x_j)\}. \tag{9}$$

The set B is a consistent attribute set of S iff

$$\eta_B(x_i) = \eta_A(x_i) \ (x_i \in U). \tag{10}$$

Now we consider a variable precision rough set model [19]. Let (U, A, F, d) be a decision table, for any $\beta > 0.5, B \subseteq A$, we define:

$$\underline{R}_B^\beta(D_k) = \{x_i \in U : \ D(D_k/[x_i]_B) \geq \beta)\} \ (k \leq r),$$
$$\overline{R}_B^\beta(D_k) = \{x_i \in U : \ D(D_k/[x_i]_B) > 1 - \beta\} \ (k \leq r),$$
$$\underline{R}_B^\beta = (\underline{R}_B^\beta(D_1), \underline{R}_B^\beta(D_2), \ldots, \underline{R}_B^\beta(D_r)),$$
$$\overline{R}_B^\beta = (\overline{R}_B^\beta(D_1), \overline{R}_B^\beta(D_2), \ldots, \overline{R}_B^\beta(D_r)).$$

Theorem 2. *Let (U, A, F, d) be a decision table, for any $\beta > 0.5, B \subseteq A$, we have:*

(1) $S_1 = (U, A, \mathcal{R}, \underline{R}^\beta)$ is a consistent generalized approximation representation space, and $B \subseteq A$ is a consistent attribute set of S_1 iff $\underline{R}_B^\beta = \underline{R}_A^\beta$, where

$$\underline{R}^\beta = \{(x_i, x_j) : \ x_i \in \underline{R}_A^\beta(D_k) \Longleftrightarrow x_j \in \underline{R}_A^\beta(D_k) \ (k \leq r)\}. \tag{11}$$

(2) $S_2 = (U, A, \mathcal{R}, \overline{R}^\beta)$ is a consistent generalized approximation representation space, and $B \subseteq A$ is a consistent attribute set of S_2 iff $\overline{R}_B^\beta = \overline{R}_A^\beta$, where

$$\overline{R}^\beta = \{(x_i, x_j) : \ x_i \in \overline{R}_A^\beta(D_k) \Longleftrightarrow x_j \in \overline{R}_A^\beta(D_k) \ (k \leq r)\}. \tag{12}$$

Proof. (1) Since $\underline{R}^\beta$ is an equivalence relation on U, and $R_A \subseteq \underline{R}^\beta$, we conclude that $(U, A, \mathcal{R}, \underline{R}^\beta)$ is a consistent generalized approximation representation space. We only need to prove that

$$R_B \subseteq \underline{R}^\beta \Longleftrightarrow \underline{R}_B^\beta = \underline{R}_A^\beta.$$

If $\underline{R}_B^\beta = \underline{R}_A^\beta$, then $\underline{R}_B^\beta(D_k) = \underline{R}_A^\beta(D_k) \ (k \leq r)$. If $(x_i, x_j) \in R_B$, that is, $[x_i]_B = [x_j]_B$, then

$$x_i \in \underline{R}_B^\beta(D_k) \Longleftrightarrow x_j \in \underline{R}_B^\beta(D_k) \ (k \leq r).$$

Hence,

$$x_i \in \underline{R}_A^\beta(D_k) \Longleftrightarrow x_j \in \underline{R}_A^\beta(D_k) \ (k \leq r).$$

Thus $(x_i, x_j) \in \underline{R}^\beta$, from which we have $R_B \subseteq \underline{R}^\beta$.

Conversely, if $R_B \subseteq \underline{R}^\beta$, i.e., $[x_i]_B = [x_j]_B$, then

$$x_i \in \underline{R}_A^\beta(D_k) \Longleftrightarrow x_j \in \underline{R}_A^\beta(D_k) \quad (k \leq r).$$

Similar to Theorem 1, we can prove that

$$x_i \in \underline{R}_A^\beta(D_k) \Longleftrightarrow x_i \in \underline{R}_B^\beta(D_k) \quad (k \leq r).$$

Thus, $\underline{R}_B^\beta(D_k) = \underline{R}_A^\beta(D_k)(k \leq r)$, i.e., $\underline{R}_B^\beta = \underline{R}_A^\beta$.

(2) It is similar to the proof of (1).

We have shown that an information table, a consistent or an inconsistent decision table and a variable precision rough set model can be expressed as a consistent generalized approximation representation space by defining a suitable R', respectively. In what follows we will show that a decision table with ordered or continuous valued domains can also be changed into a generalized approximation space.

Theorem 3. *Let (U, A, F, d) be a decision table with ordered valued domains, then $S = (U, A, \mathcal{R}, R_d^\leq)$ is a generalized approximation representation space, where*

$$R_a^\leq = \{(x_i, x_j) : f_a(x_i) \leq f_a(x_j)\}, \tag{13}$$
$$\mathcal{R} = \{R_a^\leq : a \in A\}, \tag{14}$$
$$R_d^\leq = \{(x_i, x_j) : d(x_i) \leq d(x_j)\}. \tag{15}$$

Proof. Since $(x_i, x_j) \in R_a^\leq$ iff $f_a(x_i) \leq f_a(x_j)$, and $d(x_i) \leq d(x_j)$ iff $(x_i, x_j) \in R_d^\leq$, $R_a^\leq$ and $R_d^\leq$ are reflexive relations. Therefore $S = (U, A, \mathcal{R}, R_d^\leq)$ is a generalized approximation representation space.

Similarly, $S = (U, A, \mathcal{R}, R_d^\geq)$ is a generalized approximation representation space, where

$$R_a^\geq = \{(x_i, x_j) : f_a(x_i) \geq f_a(x_j)\}, \tag{16}$$
$$\mathcal{R}' = \{R_a^\geq : a \in A\}, \tag{17}$$
$$R_d^\geq = \{(x_i, x_j) : d(x_i) \geq d(x_j)\}. \tag{18}$$

If $R_A^\leq \subseteq R_d^\leq$, then $S = (U, A, \mathcal{R}, R_d^\leq)$ is a consistent generalized approximation representation space. Similarly, $R_A^\geq \subseteq R_d^\geq$ implies that $S = (U, A, \mathcal{R}', R_d^\geq)$ is a consistent generalized approximation representation space.

Theorem 4. *Let (U, A, F, d) be a decision table with continuous valued domains, then $S = (U, A, \mathcal{R}, R_d^\varepsilon)$ is a generalized approximation representation space, where*

$$R_a^\varepsilon = \{(x_i, x_j) : |f_a(x_i) - f_a(x_j)| \leq \varepsilon\}, \tag{19}$$
$$\mathcal{R} = \{R_a^\varepsilon : a \in A\}, \tag{20}$$
$$R_d^\varepsilon = \{(x_i, x_j) : |d(x_i) - d(x_j)| \leq \varepsilon\}. \tag{21}$$

Proof. It is similar to the proof of Theorem 3.

If $R_A^\varepsilon \subseteq R_d^\varepsilon$, then $S = (U, A, \mathcal{R}, R_d^\varepsilon)$ is a consistent generalized approximation representation space.

Theorem 5. *Let* $(U, A, F, \mathcal{D})$ *be a decision table with fuzzy decisions, where* $\mathcal{D} = \{D_p : U \to [0, 1] \ (p \le v)\}$,

$$R_a = \{(x_i, x_j) : f_a(x_i) = f_a(x_j)\},$$
$$\underline{R}_B(D_j)(x_i) = \min\{D_j(x) : x \in [x_i]_B\} \ (B \subseteq A),$$
$$\underline{M}_B(x_i) = \{D_k : \underline{R}_B(D_k)(x_i) = \max_{j \le r} \underline{R}_B(D_j)(x_i)\} \ (B \subseteq A),$$
$$\underline{M}_A = \{(x_i, x_j) : \underline{M}_A(x_i) = \underline{M}_A(x_j)\}.$$

Then $(U, A, \mathcal{R}, \underline{M}_A)$ *is a consistent generalized approximation representation space, and* B *is a consistent attribute set of* S *iff*

$$\underline{M}_B(x_i) = \underline{M}_A(x_i) \ (x_i \in U). \tag{22}$$

Proof. It is similar to the proof of Theorem 1.

Similarly, $S = (U, A, \mathcal{R}, \overline{M}_A)$ is a consistent generalized approximation representation space, where

$$\overline{R}_B(D_j)(x_i) = \max\{D_j(x) : x \in [x_i]_B\} \ (B \subseteq A),$$
$$\overline{M}_B(x_i) = \{D_k : \overline{R}_B(D_k)(x_i) = \min_{j \le r} \overline{R}_B(D_j)(x_i)\} \ (B \subseteq A),$$
$$\overline{M}_A = \{(x_i, x_j) : \overline{M}_A(x_i) = \overline{M}_A(x_j)\}.$$

The set B is a consistent attribute set of S iff

$$\overline{M}_B(x_i) = \overline{M}_A(x_i) \ (x_i \in U). \tag{23}$$

3   Characterizations of Attributes in Consistent Generalized Approximation Representation Spaces

From Section 2, we can see that an information table in which binary relations are reflexive can be unified into a generalized approximation representation space. Many special information tables can also be changed into consistent generalized approximation representation spaces. Thus we only discuss the characterization of attributes in an approximation representation space, from which characterizations of attributes in the above mentioned information tables easily follow.

Definition 3. *Let* $S = (U, A, \mathcal{R}, R')$ *be a generalized approximation representation space and*

$$D_{R'}(x_i, x_j) = \begin{cases} \{a \in A : (x_i, x_j) \notin R_a\}, & (x_i, x_j) \notin R', \\ \emptyset, & (x_i, x_j) \in R'. \end{cases}$$

Then $D_{R'}(x_i, x_j)$ *is called the discernibility set of objects* x_i *and* x_j*, and* $\mathcal{D}_{R'} = \{D_{R'}(x_i, x_j) \neq \emptyset : x_i, x_j \in U\}$ *is all nonempty discernibility sets of the generalized approximation representation space* S.

If $S = (U, A, \mathcal{R}, R')$ is a consistent generalized approximation representation space, then we have $D_{R'}(x_i, x_j) \neq \emptyset$ for all $(x_i, x_j) \notin R'$. In fact, since $R_A \subseteq R'$, that is, $(x_i, x_j) \notin R'$ implies $(x_i, x_j) \notin R_A = \bigcap_{a \in A} R_a$, there exists $a \in A$ such that $(x_i, x_j) \notin R_a$, i.e. $(x_i, x_j) \notin R'$ implies $D_{R'}(x_i, x_j) \neq \emptyset$.

Theorem 6. *Let $S = (U, A, \mathcal{R}, R')$ be a consistent generalized approximation representation space, then $B \subseteq A$ is a consistent attribute set of S iff*

$$D_{R'}(x_i, x_j) \neq \emptyset \Longrightarrow B \cap D_{R'}(x_i, x_j) \neq \emptyset. \tag{24}$$

Proof. B is a consistent attribute set of S, or equivalently $R_B \subseteq R'$ iff

$$(x_i, x_j) \notin R' \Longrightarrow (x_i, x_j) \notin R_B.$$

Then $B \subseteq A$ is a consistent attribute set of S iff $D'_R(x_i, x_j) \neq \emptyset$ implies that there exists $a \in B$ such that $(x_i, x_j) \notin R_a$. Hence $B \cap D'_R(x_i, x_j) \neq \emptyset$.

Definition 4. *Let $S = (U, A, \mathcal{R}, R')$ be a consistent generalized approximation representation space and $\{B_k : k \leq l\}$ be the set of all reducts of S. The sets of attributes defined by*

$$C = \bigcap_{k \leq l} B_k, \quad K = \bigcup_{k \leq l} B_k - C, \quad I = A - (K \cup C).$$

are called the core, the relative necessary attribute, and the unnecessary attribute set of S, respectively.

Theorem 7. *Let $S = (U, A, \mathcal{R}, R')$ be a consistent generalized approximation representation space, then the following assertions are equivalent:*
  (1) *a is an element of the core of S,*
  (2) *There exists $x_i, x_j \in U$ such that $D_{R'}(x_i, x_j) = \{a\}$,*
  (3) *$R_{A-\{a\}} \nsubseteq R'$.*

Proof. $(1) \Rightarrow (2)$. Suppose that there are at least two attributes in any discernibility set including a, let

$$B = \bigcup_{i,j} (D_{R'}(x_i, x_j) - \{a\}).$$

Then

$$B \cap D_{R'}(x_i, x_j) \neq \emptyset \quad (x_i, x_j \notin R').$$

By Theorem 6, we know that B is a consistent attribute set of S, and $a \notin B$, thus there exists a reduct B' such that $a \notin B'$, which contradicts that a is an element of the core of S.

$(2) \Rightarrow (3)$. Let $D_{R'}(x_i, x_j) = \{a\}$, that is, $(x_i, x_j) \notin R', (x_i, x_j) \notin R_a$, and $(x_i, x_j) \in R_b (b \neq a)$, that is, $(x_i, x_j) \notin R'$ and $(x_i, x_j) \in R_{A-\{a\}}$, hence $R_{A-\{a\}} \nsubseteq R'$.

$(3) \Rightarrow (1)$. If a is not an element of the core of S, then there exists a reduct B such that $a \notin B$, in turn, $B \subseteq A - \{a\}$, thus $R_{A-\{a\}} \subseteq R_B \subseteq R'$, which contradicts $R_{A-\{a\}} \nsubseteq R'$.

Theorem 8. *Let* $S = (U, A, \mathcal{R}, R')$ *be a consistent generalized approximation representation space, then* $a \in A$ *is an unnecessary attribute of S iff*

$$R(a) \subseteq R' \cup R_a, \tag{25}$$

where

$$R(a) = \cup\{R_{B-\{a\}} : \ R_B \subseteq R', B \subseteq A\}. \tag{26}$$

Proof. Necessity. If a is an element of the unnecessary attribute set of S, then a doesn't exist in any attribute reduction set, thus for any $R_B \subseteq R'(B \subseteq A)$, we have $R_{B-\{a\}} \subseteq R'$, consequently $R(a) \subseteq R' \cup R_a$.

Sufficiency. If $R(a) \subseteq R' \cup R_a$, then for any $B \subseteq A, R_B \subseteq R'$, we have $R_{B-\{a\}} \subseteq R' \cup R_a$, i.e. $R_{B-\{a\}} \cap R_a^c \subseteq R'$, thus $R_{B-\{a\}} = R_B \cup (R_{B-\{a\}} \cap R_a^c) \subseteq R'$. Consequently, a doesn't exist any attribute reduction set, i.e. a is an element of the unnecessary attribute set.

Let C be a core of S, if $R_C \subseteq R' \cup R_a$, we have $R(a) \subseteq R' \cup R_a$. Thus $R_C \subseteq R' \cup R_a$ is the sufficient condition when a is an element of the unnecessary attribute set of S. However, this is a simple method for applications.

Theorem 9. *Let* $S = (U, A, \mathcal{R}, R')$ *be a consistent generalized approximation representation space, then*
  (1) *a is an element of the core of S iff* $R_{A-\{a\}} \not\subseteq R'$.
  (2) *a is an unnecessary attribute of S iff* $R(a) \subseteq R' \cup R_a$.
  (3) *a is a relative necessary attribute of S iff* $R_{A-\{a\}} \subseteq R'$ *and* $R(a) \not\subseteq R' \cup R_a$.

Example 1. Given an information table (U, A, F) (Table 1), where

$$U = \{x_1, x_2, x_3, x_4, x_5, x_6, x_7, x_8\},$$
$$A = \{a_1, a_2, a_3, a_4\}.$$

For any $a \in A$, denote $\mathcal{R} = \{R_a : \ a \in A\}$, where

$$R_a = \{(x_i, x_j) \in U \times U : \ f_a(x_i) = f_a(x_j)\}.$$

It can be calculated that

$$U/R_{a_1} = \{\{x_2\}, \{x_1, x_3, x_4, x_5, x_6, x_7, x_8\}\},$$
$$U/R_{a_2} = \{\{x_1, x_2, x_3\}, \{x_4, x_5, x_6, x_7, x_8\}\},$$
$$U/R_{a_3} = \{\{x_1, x_3\}, \{x_2, x_4, x_5, x_7\}, \{x_6, x_8\}\},$$
$$U/R_{a_4} = \{\{x_1, x_3\}, \{x_2, x_4, x_5, x_6, x_7, x_8\}\}.$$

$S = (U, A, \mathcal{R}, R_A)$ is a consistent generalized approximation representation space, where $R_A = \bigcap_{a \in A} R_a$. We can obtain:

$$D_{R_A} = \{\{a_3\}, \{a_1, a_2\}, \{a_1, a_2, a_3\}, \{a_1, a_3, a_4\}, \{a_2, a_3, a_4\}, A\}.$$

Table 1. An Information Table

U	a_1	a_2	a_3	a_4
x_1	1	1	3	2
x_2	2	1	2	1
x_3	1	1	3	2
x_4	1	2	2	1
x_5	1	2	2	1
x_6	1	2	1	1
x_7	1	2	2	1
x_8	1	2	1	1

Thus there are two reducts of S: $B_1 = \{a_1, a_3\}, B_2 = \{a_2, a_3\}$. Therefore

$$C = \{a_3\}, \quad K = \{a_1, a_2\}, \quad I = \{a_4\}.$$

Obviously, $\{a_3\}$ is the core of S.

We can see that $R_{a_3} \subseteq R_{a_4}, R_{a_3} \not\subseteq R_{a_1}, R_{a_3} \not\subseteq R_{a_2}$, and $R_{A-\{a_k\}} \subseteq R_A (k \neq 3)$. Thus a_4 is an unnecessary attribute and $\{a_1, a_2\}$ is the relative necessary attribute set of S.

4   Conclusions

We have introduced the concept of generalized approximation representation space and established knowledge reduction theorems. We have also examined characterizations of three important types of attribute sets on this space. Since many information tables, such as consistent and inconsistent decision tables, variable precision rough set models, consistent decision tables with ordered valued domains and consistent decision tables with continuous valued domains, and decision tables with fuzzy decisions, can be unified under the framework of generalized approximation representation space theory, their knowledge discovery theory can be unified.

Acknowledgements

This work is supported by a grant from the Major State Basic Research Development Program of China (973 Program No.2002CB312200) and a grant from the National Natural Science Foundation of China (No.60373078).

References

1. Beynon, M.: Reducts within the variable precision rough sets model: A further inverstigation. European Journal of Operational Research **134**(2001) 592–605
2. Greco, S., Matarazzo, B., Slowinski, R.: Rough approximation of a preference relation by dominance relations. European Journal of Operational Research **117**(1999) 63–83

3. Iwinski, T.B.: Ordinal information system, I. Bulletin of the Polish Academy of Sciences, Mathematics **36**(1988) 467–475
4. Kryszkiewicz, M.: Comparative study of alternative types of knowledge reduction in insistent systems. International Journal of Intelligent Systems **16**(2001) 105–120
5. Leung, Y., Wu, W.-Z., Zhang, W.-X.: Knowledge acquisition in incomplete information systens: a rough set approach. European Journal of Operational Research **168**(2006) 164–180
6. Mi, J.-S., Wu, W.-Z., Zhang, W.-X.: Approaches to knowledge reduction based on variable precision rough set model. Information Sciences **159**(2004) 255–272
7. Nguyen, H.S., Slezak, D.: Approximation reducts and association rules correspondence and complexity results. in: Zhong, N., Skowron, A., Oshuga, S., Eds. New Directions in Rough Sets, Data Mining, and Granular-Soft Computing, LNAI 1711, Springer, Berlin, 1999, pp.137–145
8. Pawlak, Z.: Rough sets. International Journal of Computer and Information Sciences **11**(1982) 341–356
9. Pawlak, Z.: Rough Sets—Theoretical Aspects of Reasoning about Data. Dordrecht, Kluwer Academic Publishers, 1991
10. Qiu, G.-F., Li, H.-Z., Xu, L.D., Zhang, W.-X.: A knowledge processing method for intelligent systems based on inclusion degree. Expert Systems **4**(2003) 187–195
11. Sai, Y., Yao, Y.Y., Zhong, N.: Data analysis and mining in ordered information tables. Proceedings of the 2001 IEEE International Conference on Data Mining, 2001, pp. 497–504
12. Skowron, A., Rauszer, C.: The discernibility matrices and functions in information systems. In: Slowinski, R., ed. Intelligent Decision Support: Handbook of Applications and Advances of the Rough Set Theory. Kluwer Academic Publishers, Dordrecht, 1992, pp.331–36
13. Slezak, D.: Searching for dynamic reducts in inconsistent decision tables. in: Proceedings of IPMU'98, Paris, France, Vol.2, 1998, pp.1362–1369
14. Wu, W.-Z., Zhang, M., Li, H.-Z., Mi, J.-S.: Knowledge reduction in random information systems via Dempster-Shafer theory of evidence. Information Sciences (to appear)
15. Yao, Y.Y., Wong, S.K.M.: Generalization of rough sets using relationships between attribute values, *Proceedings of the 2nd Annual Joint Conference on Information Sciences*, 1995, pp. 30–33
16. Zhang, W.-X., Leung, Y., Wu, W.-Z.: Information Systems and Knowledge Discovery. Beijing, Science Press, 2003
17. Zhang, M., Wu, W.-Z.: Knowledge reduction in information systems with fuzzy decisions. Chinese Journal of Engineering Mathematics **20**(2003) 53–58
18. Ziarko, W.: Variable precision rough set model. Journal of Computer and System Sciences **46**(1993) 39–59

Proximity Spaces of Exact Sets

Peter John Apostoli and Akira Kanda

Department of Philosophy, The University of Pretoria,
0002, Pretoria, South Africa

Abstract. [4] placed an approximation space $(U, \equiv)$ in a type-lowering
retraction with its power set 2^U such that the $\equiv$-exact subsets of U comprise the kernel of the retraction, where $\equiv$ is the equivalence relation of
set-theoretic indiscernibility within the resulting universe of exact sets.
Since a concept thus forms a set just in case it is $\equiv$-exact, set-theoretic
comprehension in $(U, \equiv)$ is governed by the method of upper and lower
approximations of Rough Set Theory. Some central features of this universe were informally axiomatized in [3] in terms of the notion of a Proximal Frege Structure and its associated modal Boolean algebra of exact
sets. The present essay generalizes the axiomatic notion of a PFS to
tolerance (reflexive, symmetric) relations, where the universe of exact
sets forms a modal ortho-lattice. An example of this general notion is
provided by the tolerance relation of "matching" over U.

1   Introduction

Kripkean semantics [21] for modal logic extends the theory of points sets with
modal operators induced by a binary "accessibility" relation on a universe of
points. Abstract set theory also extends the theory of point sets, with the addition of a type-lowering corresepondence between a universe and its power set.
Ever since the rapid development of modal logic [12] in the 1960's, philosophers
have sought a unification of the concepts of modal logic with those of abstract
set theory. Typically, e.g., [14,24,25], this is attempted by basing axiomatic set
theory upon modal quantifier logic instead of standard first order logic. These
approaches regard axiomatic set theory to be an unproblematic starting point
for the investigation of modal set theory, and the extension of the language of
set theory by modal operators as analogous to the extension of quantifier logic
by modal operators.

However, one limitation of this approach stems from the thorny fact that
the consistency of axiomatic set theory is still an open mathematical question.
What if modal notions *underlie* set theoretic comprehension? In that case, the
difficulty in finding a model for Zermelo and Fraenkel's axioms is naturally to
be expected. [4] explored this question and proposed an alternative marriage of
modal logic and abstract set theory based upon Rough Set Theory [23,26].

By placing an approximation space $(U, \equiv)$ in a type-lowering retraction with
its power set 2^U, [4] showed that a concept forms a set just in case it is $\equiv$-
exact. Set-theoretic comprehension in $(U, \equiv)$ is thus governed by the method of

D. Ślęzak et al. (Eds.): RSFDGrC 2005, LNAI 3641, pp. 94–103, 2005.

upper and lower approximations of RST. Thus, modal concepts indeed underlie abstract set theory, raising serious questions regarding the philosophical motivation for the standard approaches to "modal set theory". The naive extention of the language of axiomatic set theory to modal quantifier logic ignores the conceptual priority of modality in abstract set theory.

This paper is organized as follows. Section one introduces the notion of a proximity (or tolerance) space and its associated ortho-lattice of parts, providing some motivating examples from, e.g., mathematics and physics. Then, generalizing the developments of [3], section two introduces axiomatically the general notion of a Proximal Frege Structure and its associated modal ortho-latice of exact sets. Model constructions [4] ensuring the consistency of these notions are then summarized. Some key properties of these models which are independent of the basic axioms of PFS are discussed and an open question regarding the tolerance relation of "matching" is raised. The paper concludes by airing the task of axiomatizing abstract set theory as formalizations of the general notion of a PFS.

2 Proximity Structures

Let $U \neq \emptyset$ and $\sim \subseteq U \times U$ be a tolerance (reflexive, symmetric) relation on U. The pair $(U, \sim)$ is called a *proximity structure*. When in addition $\sim$ is an equivalence relation, $(U, \sim)$ is called an *approximation structure*.[1] For each point $u \in U$, let $[u]_\sim$ denote the class of successors of u under $\sim$, i.e.,

$$[u]_\sim =_{df} \{x \in U \mid u \sim x\}$$

$\sim$-classes $[u]_\sim$ are called ($\sim$-) *granules*, or *elementary* subsets, of U. Let $A \subseteq U$;

$$Int_\sim(A) =_{df} \bigcup\{[u]_\sim \mid [u]_\sim \subseteq A\},$$
$$Cl_\sim(A) =_{df} \bigcup\{[u]_\sim \mid [u]_\sim \cap A \neq \emptyset\},$$

are called the *lower* and *upper approximations* of A, respectively (in contexts where $\sim$ is given, the subscripted " $\sim$ " is usually suppressed). A is called $\sim$-*exact* iff it is the union of a family of $\sim$-granules, i.e., iff

$$A = \bigcup_{u \in X} [u]_\sim$$

for some $X \subseteq U$. Note that if $\sim$ is an equivalence relation, then A is $\sim$-exact iff $Cl(A) = A = Int(A)$. It is natural to regard $\sim$-exact subsets of U as the *parts* of U and elementary subsets as the *atomic parts* of U. $\mathcal{C}(\sim)$ denotes the family of $\sim$-exact subsets of U. Then $(U, \mathcal{C}(\sim))$ is called a *proximity space*.[2] When $\sim$ is

---

[1] As indicated in the above Introduction, the symbol "$\equiv$" is often used to denote tolerance relations which are also equivalence relations.

[2] Proximity structures and spaces, also known as *tolerance approximation spaces, generalized approximation spaces* or *parameterized approximation spaces*, are studied in [30,31].

an equivalence relation, $(U, \mathcal{C}(\sim))$ is called an *approximation space*. A reason for using the term "proximity" here is, as we shall see, it is helpful to think of $x \sim y$ as meaning "x is near y".

Let $S = (U, \mathcal{C}(\sim))$ be a proximity space and $A, B \subseteq U$. Following [7], define

$$A \bigvee_S B =_{df} A \cup B,$$
$$A \bigwedge_S B =_{df} Int(A \cap B),$$
$$A^c =_{df} Cl(U - A).$$

I.e., the *join of A and B* is their set theoretic union, their *meet* is the *interior* of their intersection and the *complement* A^c of A is the exterior of $U - A$. Then

$$(\mathcal{C}(\sim), \bigvee_S, \bigwedge_S, {}^c, \emptyset, U) \tag{1}$$

is a complete ortholattice [6,7,9] of exact subsets. That is, for any $A, B \in \mathcal{C}(\sim)$,

1. $(A^c)^c = A$,
2. $A \bigvee_S A^c = U$,
3. $A \bigwedge_S A^c = \emptyset$,
4. $A \subseteq B \Rightarrow B^c \subseteq A^c$.

Any discrete space is a proximity space in which $\sim$ is the identity relation. More generally, a proximity space S is a topological space if and only if its proximity relation is transitive, and in that case S is almost (quasi) discrete in the sense that its lattice of parts is isomorphic to the lattice of parts of a discrete space.

Proximity spaces admit of several interpretations which serve to reveal their significance. Quoting directly from [7]:

(a) S may be viewed as a space or field of perception, its points as locations in it, the relation $\sim$ as representing *the indiscernibility of locations*, the quantum at a given location as the *minimum perceptibilium* at that location, and the parts of S as the perceptibly specifiable subregions of S. This idea is best illustrated by assigning the set U a metric δ, choosing a fixed $\varepsilon > 0$ and then defining $x \sim y \Leftrightarrow \delta(x, y) \leq \varepsilon$.

(b) S may be thought of as the set of *outcomes of an experiment* and $\sim$ as the relation of equality *up to the limits of experimental error*. The quantum at an outcome is then "the outcome within a specified margin of error" of experimental practice.

(c) S may be taken to be the set of states of a quantum system and $s \sim t$ as the relation: "a measurement of the system in a state s has a non zero probability of leaving the system in state t, or vice-versa." More precisely, we take a Hilbert space H, put $S = H - \{0\}$, and define the proximity relation $\sim$ on S by $s \sim t \Leftrightarrow \langle s, t \rangle \neq 0$ (s is not orthogonal to t). It is then readily shown that the lattice of parts of S is isomorphic to the ortholattice of closed subspaces of H. Consequently, *[complemented] lattices of parts of proximity spaces include the [complemented] lattices of closed subspaces of Hilbert spaces — the lattices associated with Birkhoff and von Neumann's "quantum logic"*.

(d) S may be taken to be the set of *hyperreal numbers* in a model of Robinson's nonstandard analysis (see, e.g., Bell and Machover [5]) and $\sim$ is the relation of infinitesimal nearness. In this case $\sim$ is *transitive*.

(e) S may be taken to be the *affine line* in a model of synthetic differential geometry (see Kock [20]). In this case there exist many square zero infinitesimals in S, i.e., elements $\varepsilon \neq 0$ such that $\varepsilon^2 = 0$, and we take $x \sim y$ to mean that the difference $x - y$ is such an infinitesimal, i.e., $(x - y)^2 = 0$. Unlike the situation in (d), the relation $\sim$ here is *not* generally transitive.

3   Proximal Frege Structures

According to the principle of comprehension in set theory, every "admissible" concept forms an element of the universe called a "set". Frege represented this principle by postulating the existence of an "extension function" assigning objects to concepts. Models of set theory which establish a type-lowering correspondence between a universe and its power set are thus called "Frege structures" [1,8]. [3,4] considered the idea of basing a Frege structure upon an approximation space so that the admissible concepts are precisely the exact subsets of the universe. This section generalizes the development of the resulting "Proximal Frege Structure" to arbitrary tolerance relations. Most of the results of [3] hold in this more general setting and so are not given special mention.

Let $(U, \sim)$ be a proximity structure and $\ulcorner \cdot \urcorner : 2^U \to U, \llcorner \cdot \lrcorner : U \to 2^U$ be functions, called *down* and *up* (for type-lowering and type-raising), respectively. Assume that:

1. $(\ulcorner \cdot \urcorner, \llcorner \cdot \lrcorner)$ is a retraction pair, i.e., $\ulcorner \llcorner u \lrcorner \urcorner = u$ (i.e., $\ulcorner \cdot \urcorner \circ \llcorner \cdot \lrcorner = 1_U$); thus $\ulcorner \cdot \urcorner$ is a retraction and $\llcorner \cdot \lrcorner$ is the adjoining section.

2. The operator $\llcorner \cdot \lrcorner \circ \ulcorner \cdot \urcorner$ is the operator $Cl_\sim$ over 2^U. This is that for every $X \subseteq U, \llcorner \ulcorner X \urcorner \lrcorner$ is $\sim$-exact and

$$\llcorner \ulcorner X \urcorner \lrcorner = Cl(X).$$

3. The $\sim$-exact subsets of U are precisely the $X \subseteq U$ for which $\llcorner \ulcorner X \urcorner \lrcorner = X$. They are fixed-point of the operator $\llcorner \cdot \lrcorner \circ \ulcorner \cdot \urcorner$.

Then $\mathfrak{F} = (U, \sim, \ulcorner \cdot \urcorner, \llcorner \cdot \lrcorner)$ is called a *(generalized) PFS*. Elements of U are $\mathfrak{F}$-*sets*.

The family $\mathcal{C}(\sim)$ of $\sim$-exact subsets of U is precisely the image of U under $\llcorner \cdot \lrcorner$. In algebraic terms $\mathcal{C}(\sim)$ is the kernel of the retraction mapping. Further we have the isomorphism $\mathcal{C}(\sim) \approx U$ given by:

$$i : \mathcal{C}(\sim) \to U : X \mapsto \ulcorner X \urcorner, j : U \to \mathcal{C}(\sim) : u \mapsto \llcorner u \lrcorner.$$

In summary: $\mathcal{C}(\sim) \approx U \lhd 2^U$, where $U \lhd 2^U$ asserts the existence of a retraction pair holding between 2^U and U.

As a simple example of a PFS, we offer the following two point structure

$$(U, \sim, \ulcorner \cdot \urcorner, \llcorner \cdot \lrcorner),$$

where $U = \{0,1\}, \sim = U \times U, \ulcorner \emptyset \urcorner = 0, \ulcorner X \urcorner = 1 \ (X \subseteq U, X \neq \emptyset), \llcorner 0 \lrcorner = \emptyset$ and $\llcorner 1 \lrcorner = U$. A less trivial example [4] of a PFS based upon an equvalence relation, $\mathfrak{G}$, is described in the sequel.

Let $\mathfrak{F} = (U, \sim, \ulcorner \cdot \urcorner, \llcorner \cdot \lrcorner)$ be a generalized PFS. Writing "$u_1 \in_{\mathfrak{F}} u_2$" for "$u_1 \in \llcorner u_2 \lrcorner$", U is thus interpreted [3] as a universe of $\mathfrak{F}$-sets; $\llcorner \cdot \lrcorner$ supports the relation of set membership holding between $\mathfrak{F}$-sets (elements of U). Writing "$\{u : X(u)\}$" to denote $\ulcorner X \urcorner$, $\mathfrak{F}$ thus validates the Principle of Naive Comprehension

$$(\forall u)(u \in_{\mathfrak{F}} \{u : X(u)\} \leftrightarrow X(u)) \tag{2}$$

for $\sim$-exact subsets X of U. Further, let $x, y \in U$; then,

$$(\forall u)(u \in_{\mathfrak{F}} x \leftrightarrow u \in_{\mathfrak{F}} y) \leftrightarrow x = y,$$

i.e., the principle of extensionality holds for $\mathfrak{F}$-sets.

Let $x, y \in U$. Define x to be set-theoretically *indiscernible* from y, symbolically, $x \equiv_{\mathfrak{F}} y$, iff x and y are elements of precisely the same $\mathfrak{F}$-sets:

$$x \equiv_{\mathfrak{F}} y \Leftrightarrow_{df} (\forall u)(x \in_{\mathfrak{F}} u \leftrightarrow y \in_{\mathfrak{F}} u).$$

Set-theoretic indiscernibiltity is thus an equivalence relation on U and a congruence for the $\sim$-exact subsets of U. Further, define

$$x \equiv_{\sim} y \Leftrightarrow_{df} [x]_{\sim} = [y]_{\sim}.$$

Note that since $\sim$ is a tolerance relation on U, all $\sim$-exact subsets of U are relationally closed under $\equiv_{\sim}$. Indeed, $x \equiv_{\mathfrak{F}} y$ iff $x \equiv_{\sim} y$, i.e., $\equiv_{\sim}$ is just set-theoretic indiscernibility. Also,

$$x \equiv_{\mathfrak{F}} y \Rightarrow x \sim y \quad (x, y \in U)$$

holds generally but the converse principle

$$x \sim y \Rightarrow x \equiv_{\mathfrak{F}} y \quad (x, y \in U)$$

holds just in case $\sim$ is an equivalence relation. Thus, when $\sim$ is an equivalence relation, it may always be interpreted as set-theoretic indiscernibility.

3.1   Ortholattice of Exact Sets

Let $\mathfrak{F} = (U, \sim, \ulcorner \cdot \urcorner, \llcorner \cdot \lrcorner)$ be a PFS based upon a tolerance relation $\sim$. Since elements of U represent exact subsets of U, the complete ortholattice given (defined) by 1 is isomorphic to

$$(U, \ulcorner \vee \urcorner, \ulcorner \wedge \urcorner, \ulcorner c \urcorner, \ulcorner \emptyset \urcorner, \ulcorner U \urcorner) \tag{3}$$

under the restriction $\ulcorner \cdot \urcorner \upharpoonright \mathcal{C}(\sim)$ of the type-lowering retraction to $\sim$-exact subsets of U. Here, $\ulcorner \vee \urcorner, \ulcorner \wedge \urcorner, \ulcorner c \urcorner$, denote the definitions of join and meet natural to $\mathfrak{F}$-sets, e.g.,

$$u_1 \ulcorner \vee \urcorner u_2 =_{df} \ulcorner \llcorner u_1 \lrcorner \bigvee_S \llcorner u_1 \lrcorner \urcorner = \ulcorner \llcorner u_1 \lrcorner \cup \llcorner u_1 \lrcorner \urcorner$$
$$u_1 \ulcorner \wedge \urcorner u_2 =_{df} \ulcorner \llcorner u_1 \lrcorner \bigwedge_S \llcorner u_1 \lrcorner \urcorner$$
$$u \ulcorner c \urcorner =_{df} \ulcorner \llcorner u \lrcorner^c \urcorner.$$

We define "$u_1 \ulcorner \subseteq \urcorner u_2$" to be "$\llcorner u_1 \lrcorner \subseteq \llcorner u_2 \lrcorner$", i.e., *inclusion* is the partial ordering naturally associated with the ortholattice of $\mathfrak{F}$-sets given in 3. Usually, the corner quotes are suppressed in naming these operations.

Let $a \in U$. Since unions of $\sim$-exact subsets are $\sim$-exact,

$$\{x \in U \mid (\exists y \in U)(a \sim y \wedge x \in_{\mathfrak{F}} y)\}$$

is an exact subset of U. Thus we define the *outer penumbra* of a, symbolically, $\Diamond a$, to be the $\mathfrak{F}$-set $\bigvee[a]_\sim$. Similarly, since closures of intersections of $\sim$-exact subsets are $\sim$-exact,

$$Cl(\{x \in U \mid (\forall y \in U)(a \sim y \rightarrow x \in_{\mathfrak{F}} y)\})$$

is an exact subset of U. Define the *inner penumbra*, $\Box a$, to be the $\mathfrak{F}$-set $\bigwedge[a]_\sim$. These operations, called the *penumbral modalities*, were interpreted in [3,4] using David Lewis' counterpart semantics for modal logic [22]. Given $\mathfrak{F}$-sets a and b, we call b a *counterpart* of a whenever $a \sim b$. Then $\Box a$ ($\Diamond a$) represents the set of $\mathfrak{F}$-sets that belong to all (some) counterparts of a. In this sense, we can say that an $\mathfrak{F}$-set x *necessarily* (*possibly*) belongs to a just in case x belongs to $\Box a$ ($\Diamond a$).

When augmented by the penumbral modal operators, the complete ortholattice of $\mathfrak{F}$-sets given by 3 forms an extensive, idempotent modal ortholattice

$$(U, \ulcorner \vee \urcorner, \ulcorner \wedge \urcorner, \ulcorner c \urcorner, \ulcorner \emptyset \urcorner, \ulcorner U \urcorner, \Diamond, \Box), \tag{4}$$

which fails, however, to satisfy the principle of monotonicity characteristic of Kripkean modal logic. Curiously, in addition,

$$\Box \Diamond u \subseteq \Box u \quad (u \in U).$$

When $\sim$ is an equivalence relation, the lattice given by 4 is a modal Boolean algebra (called the "penumbral" modal algebra [3,4]), an example of "abstract" approximation space in the sense of [11] and "generalized" approximation space in the sense of [34].

3.2   Models of PFS

An example of a PFS

$$\mathfrak{G} = (M_{max}, \equiv, \ulcorner \cdot \urcorner, \llcorner \cdot \lrcorner)$$

based upon the equivalence relation $\equiv$ of set theoretic indiscernibility was constructed in [4] with the theory of Sequences of Finite Projections (SFP) objects, a branch of Domain Theory [29] which studies the asymptotic behaviour of ω-sequences of monotone (order preserving) projections between finite partial orders. [3] First, a complete partial order (cpo) D_∞ satisfying

$$D_\infty \approx_{CSFP} [D_\infty \rightarrow T]_C$$

---

[3] See also [2] for the details of this construction.

is constructed [29] as the inverse limit of a recursively defined sequence of projections of finite partial orders, where $\approx_{CSFP}$ is continuous (limit preserving) order isomorphism of cpo's in the category $CSFP$ of SFP objects and continuous functions, $[D_\infty \to T]_C$ is the cpo of all continuous (limit preserving) functions from D_∞ to T under the information order associated with the nesting of partial characteristic functions and T is the domain of three-valued truth

$$
\begin{array}{cc}
true & false \\
\diagdown & \diagup \\
 & \perp
\end{array}
$$

under the information ordering $\leq_k$ (where $\perp$ represents a truth-value gap as in partial logic [10,13,19]). Then [4], since D_∞ is an SFP object, each monotone function $f : D_\infty \to T$ is maximally approximated by a unique continuous function c_f in $[D_\infty \to T]_C$, whence c_f in D_∞ under representation. Then, the complete partial order M of monotone functions from D_∞ to T is constructed as a solution for the reflexive equation

$$ M \approx_{\mathcal{M}} \prec M \to T \succ $$

where $\approx_{\mathcal{M}}$ is order isomorphism of cpo's in the category $\mathcal{M}$ of cpos's and montotone functions, and $\prec M \to X \succ$ is the set of all "hyper-continuous" functions from M to T. A monotone function $f : M \to T$ is said to be *hyper-continuous* iff for every $m \in M, f(m) = f(c_m)$. In words, *hyper-continuous functions are those monotone functions which can not distinguish m from c_m.* Note that a monotone function $f : M \to T$ is hyper-continuous just in case

$$ c_x = c_y \Rightarrow f(x) = f(y) \quad (x, y \in M). $$

I.e., over M, the equivalence relation of sharing a common maximal continuous approximation is a congruence for all hyper-continuous functions.

Writing "$x \in y$" for $y(x) = true$ and '$x \notin y$" for $y(x) = false$, M may be interpreted as a universe of partial sets-in-extension. Finally, let M_{max} be the set of maximal elements of M. Then [4] we have

$$ (\forall x, y \in M_{max})[x \in y \vee x \notin y]. $$

M_{max} is thus a classical (bivalent) subuniverse of M. Let $\equiv$ be the relation of set-theoretic indiscernibility, defined for $x, y \in M_{max}$ by

$$ x \equiv y \Leftrightarrow_{df} (\forall z \in M_{max})[x \in z \leftrightarrow y \in z]. $$

Then we have the fundamental result [4] that set-theoretic indiscernibility over M_{max} is the relation of sharing a common maximal continuous approximation.

A natural example of a PFS based upon a non-transitive tolerance relation on M_{max} can now be given. Let $x, y \in M_{max}$. x *matches* y iff there is a $m \in M$ such that $c_x, c_y \leq m$. Matching is thus a tolerance relation over M_{max} which expresses the compatibility of the maximal continuous approximations of $\mathfrak{G}$-sets:

two elements of M_{max} match iff their respective maximal continuous approximations yield, for any given argument, $\leq_k$-comparable truth values, i.e., they agree on the *classical* (non-$\perp$) truth values they take for a given argument. Since matching is "hyper-continuous" (a congruence for $\equiv$) in both x and y, all subsets of M_{max} which are exact with respect to matching are $\equiv$-exact, whence they may be comprehended as $\mathfrak{G}$-sets. Thus M_{max} forms a generalized PFS under the tolerance relation of matching.

On the Discernibility of the Disjoint: The above axioms for PFS's based upon an equivalence relation fall short of articulating all of the important structure of $\mathfrak{G}$. For example, distinct disjoint $\mathfrak{G}$-sets are discernible; in particular, the empty $\mathfrak{G}$-set is a "singularity" in having no counterparts other than itself [4]. Further, since the complements of indiscernible $\mathfrak{G}$-sets are indiscernible, it follows that the universal $\mathfrak{G}$-set is also a singularity in this sense. These properties are logically independent of the basic axioms and may be falsified on the two-point PFS presented above. For example, the "discernibility of the disjoint" asserts the existence of infinitely many pairwise distinct granules of $\mathfrak{F}$-sets and its adoption as an additional axiom of PFS's entails Peano's axioms for second order arithmetic [4].

Plenitude: Another important property of $\mathfrak{G}$ established in [4] is the following principle of Plenitude. Let $\mathfrak{F} = (U, \equiv, \ulcorner \cdot \urcorner, \llcorner \cdot \lrcorner)$ be a PFS based upon an equivalence relation $\equiv$. In [3], $\mathfrak{F}$ was say to be a *plenum* iff the following two conditions hold for all $a, b \in U$: (A) $\Box a \equiv \Diamond a$ and (B) $a \subseteq b$ and $a \equiv b$ entails for all $c \in U$,

$$a \subseteq c \subseteq b \Rightarrow c \equiv b.$$

[4] showed that $\mathfrak{G}$ is a plenum and, further, if $\mathfrak{F}$ is a plenum, then

$$([a]_\equiv, \ulcorner \vee \urcorner, \ulcorner \wedge \urcorner, \ulcorner c \urcorner, \Box a, \Diamond a)$$

is a complete Boolean algebra with the least (greatest) element $\Box a$ ($\Diamond a$). Thus, the universe of a plenum factors into a family of granules $[a]_\equiv$, each of which is a complete Boolean algebra[4]. We conclude by asking a question: does M_{max} satisfy conditions (A) and (B) – thus forming a "generalized plenum" whose granules are complete ortho-lattices – under the non-transitive tolerance relation of matching?

4   Conclusion

Our development of the notion of a generalized PFS has been axiomatic and informal. The model construction of [4] ensures the consistency of these informal axioms. It further provides a natural example of a PFS based upon the non-transitive tolerance relation of "matching". The task of presenting various axiomatic set theories as consistent "formalizations" of generalized PFS's is a

---

[4] E.g., though M_{max} has hyper-continuum many elements, it factors into continuum many such granules.

task aired here for future research. E.g., the Principle of Naive Comprehension for exact concepts given in 2 may be symbolized by both effective and noneffective axiom schemes in L. Characterizing the proof theoretic strength of theories which adjoin various comprehension schemes for exact concepts to the first order theory of a tolerance (or equivalence) relation remains an open problem in the foundations of mathematics.

References

1. Aczel, P.: Frege Structure and the Notions of Proposition, Truth and Set. In: Barwise, J., Keisler, H., Kunen, K. (eds.), The Kleene Symposium. North-Holland (1980) 31-59
2. Apostoli, P., Kanda, A., Polkowski, L.: First Steps Towards Computably Infinite Information Systems. In: Dubois, D., Grzymala-Busse, J., Inuiguchi M., Polkowski, L. (eds.), Rough Sets and Fuzzy Sets. Transactions in Rough Sets, Vol. 2. Lecture Notes in Computer Science, Springer-Verlag, Berlin Heidelberg New York (2004) 161-198
3. Apostoli, P., A., Kanda, A.: Approximation Spaces of Type-Free Sets. In: Ziarko, W., Yao, Y.Y. (eds.): Proc. of Rough Sets and Current Trends in Computing 2000. Lecture Notes in Artificial Intelligence 2005, Springer-Verlag, Berlin Heidelberg New York (2000) 98-105
4. Apostoli, P., Kanda, A.: Parts of the Continuum: towards a modern ontology of science. Forthcoming in: Nowak, L. (ed.), Poznan Studies in the Philosophy of Science and the Humanities (2005)
5. Bell, J.L., Machover, M.: A Course in Mathematical Logic. North Holland (1977)
6. Bell, J.L.: Orthologic, Forcing and the Manifestation of Attributes. In: Proc. of the Southeast Asian Conference on Logic. Studies in Logic, Vol. III, North Holland (1983)
7. Bell, J.L.: A new Approach to Quantum Logic. Brit. J. Phil. Sci., 37 (1986) 83-99
8. Bell, J.L.: Set and Classes as Many. J. of Philosophical Logic, 29 (6) (2000) 595-681
9. Birkhoff, G.: Lattice Theory. 3rd edition. Amer. Math. Colloq. Publs., XXV (1960)
10. Blamey, S.: Partial Logic. In: Gabbay, D., Guenthner, F. (eds.), Handbook of Philosophical Logic. D. Reidel Publishing Company, III (1986) 1-70
11. Cattaneo, G.: Abstract Approximation Spaces for Rough Theories. In: Polkowski, L., Skowron, A. (eds.), Rough Sets in Knowledge Discovery: Methodology and Applications. Springer-Verlag, Berlin Heidelberg New York (1998)
12. Chellas, B.F.: An Introduction to Modal Logic. Cambridge University Press, Cambridge (1980)
13. Feferman, S.: Towards Useful Type-free Theories I. Journal of Symbolic Logic, 49 (1984) 75-111
14. Fine, K.: First-Order Modal Theories, I-Sets. Nous, 15 (1981) 177-205
15. Frege, G.: Die Grundlagen der Arithmetik. Eine logisch mathematische Untersachung uber den Begridd der Zahl. Breslau, William Koebner. English translation by J. L. Austin, The Foundations of Arihmetic. Oxford, Basil Blackwell (1950)
16. Frege, G.: Grundgesetze der Arithmetik. Vols. 1, 2. Jena, Verlag Hermann Pohle. Reprinted at Hildesheim. Vol. 1 is partially translated in [17]. Vol. 2 is translated in part in [18] (1893, 1903)
17. Frege, G.: Translations from the Philosophical Writings of Gottlob Frege. Edited and translated by Peter Geach and Max Black. Oxford, Basil Blackwell (1960)

18. Furth, M.: The Basic Laws of Arithmetic: Exposititon of the system. Berkeley, University of California Press (1964)
19. Gilmore, P.C.: Natural Deduction Based Set Theories: A New Resolution of the Old Paradoxes. J. of Symbolic Logic., 51. (1986) 394-411
20. Kock, A.: Synthetic Differential Geometry. London Math. Soc. Lecture Notes, 51, Cambridge University Press (1981)
21. Kripke, S.: Semantical Analysis of Modal Logic I. Normal Modal Propositional Calculi. Zeitschrift f. Math. Logik und Grundlagen d. Math., 9 (1963)
22. Lewis, D.: Counterpart Theory and Quantified Modal Logic. J. of Philosophy, 65 (1968) 113-26. Reprinted in Michael J. Loux (ed), The Possible and the Actual. Cornell, U.P. (1979)
23. Orlowska, E.: Semantics of Vague Concepts. In: Foundations of Logic and Linguistics, Problems and Their Solutions. Dorn, G. and Weingartner, P. (eds.), Plenum Press, NewYork (1985)
24. Parsons, C.: What is the iterative conception of set? In: R.E. Butts and J. Hintikka (eds.), Logic, Foundation of Mathematics, and Computability Theory. D. Reidel (1977) 335-67. Reprinted in P. Benacerraf, P., Putnam, H. (eds.), Philosophy of Mathematics: Selected Readings. 2nd ed. Cambridge University Press. (1983) 503-529. Also reprinted in Mathematics in Philosophy, Selected Essays, Cornell University Press.
25. Parsons, C.: Modal Set Theories. Journal of Symbolic Logic, 46. (1981) 683-4
26. Pawlak, Z.: Rough Sets, Algebraic and Topological Approaches. In: International Journal of Computer and Information Sciences, 11 (1982) 341-356
27. Plotkin, G.: A Power Domain Construction. SIAM Journal on Computing, 5 (1976) 452-487
28. Scott, D.: Continuous lattices. Lecture Notes in Math, 274, Springer, Berlin (1971) 97-136
29. Scott, D.: Data Types as Lattices. SIAM Journal on Computing, 5. (1976) 522-587
30. Skowron, A., Stepaniuk, J.: Generalized Approximation Spaces. In: Proc. 3rd Int. Workshop on Rough Sets and Soft Computing. San Jose, USA, Nov. 10-12 (1994)
31. Skowron, A., Stepaniuk, J.: Tolerance Approximation Spaces. Fundamenta Informaticae, 27. (1996) 245-253
32. Smyth, M.: Power Domains. Journal of Computer and Systems Science, 16 (1978) 23-36
33. Smyth, M., Plotkin, G.: The Categorical Solutions of Recursive Domain Equations. In: Proc. of the 18th FOCS Conference (1977)
34. Yao, Y.Y.: On Generalizing Pawlak Approximation Operators. In: Polkowski, L., Skowron, A. (eds.), Rough Sets and Current Trends in Computing 1998. Lecture Notes in Artificial Intelligence 1414, Springer-Verlag (1998) 289-307

Rough Group, Rough Subgroup and Their Properties

Duoqian Miao[1], Suqing Han[2], Daoguo Li[1], and Lijun Sun[1]

[1] Department of Computer Science and Technology, Tongji University,
Shanghai 200092, P.R.China
miaoduoqian@163.com
[2] Institute of Automation, Chinese Academy of Sciences,
Beijing 100080, P.R.China
sqhan@sina.com

Abstract. The theory of rough sets is an extension of the set theory, for the study of intelligent systems characterized by insufficient and incomplete information. Since proposed by Pawlak, rough sets have evoked a lot of research. Theoretic study has included algebra aspect of rough sets. In paper [1] the concept of rough group and rough subgroup was introduced, but with some deficiencies remaining. In this paper, we intend to make up for these shortages, improve definitions of rough group and rough subgroup, and prove their new properties.

1 Introduction

Pawlak proposed the rough set theory in 1982. In recent years, there has been a fast growing interest in this new emerging theory – ranging from work in pure theory, such as e.g. topological and algebraic foundations [4], [5], [6], [7], to diverse areas of applications.

In [2], based on Pawlak's definition of rough equality, as well as the works by Orlowska [8] and Banerjee and Chakraborty [9], the algebraic technique was used to give a deep mathematical meaning to the rough set theory. The concepts of topological Boolean algebra, rough algebra, quasi-Boolean algebra, topological quasi-Boolean algebra and topological rough algebra, etc., were introduced. Furthermore, it was proved that rough algebra is not a Boolean algebra, but a quasi-Boolean algebra. In [3], based on the lattice theoretical approach suggested by Iwinski [10], it was proved that the original family of rough sets $\Re^{\circ}$, as well as $\Re$ and the rough approximation space $\Re^*$ with corresponding operations, are stone algebras. However, for groups, rings and fields, little work has been done.

In [1], the concepts of rough group and rough subgroup have been introduced, but there are some parts that remain irrational. First, the definition of rough group based on G, if G is a rough set, $\forall x, y \in G$, $x * y \in G$, is vague. Second, in the definition of second property of rough group, there are some items which are unreasonable as concerning rough group G: (1) the range in which the association law holds is G; (2) the set e with the binary operation defined on U is trivial rough subgroup of G; (3) the intersection of two rough subgroups of a rough

D. Ślęzak et al. (Eds.): RSFDGrC 2005, LNAI 3641, pp. 104–113, 2005.

group is still a rough subgroup. The main work of this paper is to improve the parts that mentioned above, then, to prove some properties of rough group and rough subgroup. In section 2, a short overview of the work by Pawlak that relates to this paper is given; in section 3, new definitions of rough group and rough subgroup are introduced; in section 4, rough right cosets and rough left cosets are defined and some properties of rough cosets are proved; in section 5, the definition of rough invariant sets is given and some of its properties are proved; in section 6, the homomorphism and isomorphism of rough group are introduced; in section 7, some examples for rough group, rough subgroup and their properties are given; and in the last, further study need to be done in this field and the significance of this research work are given in the conclusion part.

2   The Basic Theory of Rough Sets

Definition 1. *Let U be a finite non-empty set called universe and R be a family equivalence relation on U. The pair (U, R) is called an approximation space, denoted by $K = (U, R)$.*

Definition 2. *Let U be a universe, C be a family of subsets of U, $C = \{X_1, X_2, \ldots, X_n\}$. C is called a classification of U if the following properties are satisfied:*

(1) $X_1 \cup X_2 \cup \ldots \cup X_n = U$;
(2) $X_i \cap X_j = (i \neq j)$.

Definition 3. *Let U be a universe and R be an equivalence relation on U. We denote the equivalence class of object x in R by $[x]_R$. The set $\{[x]_R | x \in U\}$ is called a classification of U induced by R.*

Definition 4. *Let (U, R) be an approximation space and X be a subset of U. The sets*

(1) $\overline{X} = \{x | [x]_R \cap X \neq \}$;
(2) $\underline{X} = \{x | [x]_R \subseteq X\}$;
(3) $BN(X) = \overline{X} - \underline{X}$

are called upper approximation, lower approximation, and boundary region of X in K, respectively.

Property 1. Let $X, Y \subset U$, where U is a universe. The following properties hold:

(1) $\underline{X} \subset X \subset \overline{X}$
(2) $\underline{\,} = \overline{\,} = , \underline{U} = \overline{U} = U$
(3) $\underline{X \cap Y} = \underline{X} \cap \underline{Y}$
(4) $\overline{X \cap Y} \subset \overline{X} \cap \overline{Y}$
(5) $\underline{X \cup Y} \subset \underline{X} \cup \underline{Y}$
(6) $\overline{X \cup Y} = \overline{X} \cup \overline{Y}$
(7) $X \subset Y$ if and only if $\underline{X} \subset \underline{Y}, \overline{X} \subset \overline{Y}$

3   Rough Group and Rough Subgroup

Definition 5. *Let* $K = (U, R)$ *be an approximation space and* $*$ *be a binary operation defined on* U. *A subset* G *of universe* U *is called a rough group if the following properties are satisfied:*

(1) $\forall x, y \in G, x * y \in \overline{G}$;
(2) Association property holds in $\overline{G}$;
(3) $\exists e \in \overline{G}$ *such that* $\forall x \in G, x * e = e * x = x$; e *is called the rough identity element of rough group* G;
(4) $\forall x \in G, \exists y \in G$ *such that* $x * y = y * x = e$; y *is called the rough inverse element of* x *in* G.

Property 2. (1) There is one and only one identity element in rough group G.
(2) $\forall x \in G$, there is only one y such that $x * y = y * x = e$; we denote it by x^{-1}.

Property 3. (1) $(x^{-1})^{-1} = x$.
(2) $(x * y)^{-1} = y^{-1} * x^{-1}$.

Property 4. Elimination law holds in G, i.e. $\forall a, x, x', y, y' \in G$,

(1) if $a * x = a * x'$ then $x = x'$.
(2) if $y * a = y' * a$ then $y = y'$.

Definition 6. *A non-empty subset* H *of rough group* G *is called its rough subgroup, if it is a rough group itself with respect to operation* $*$.

There is only one guaranteed trivial rough subgroup of rough group G, i.e. G itself. A necessary and sufficient condition for $\{e\}$ to be a trivial rough subgroup of rough group G is $e \in G$.

Theorem 1. *A necessary and sufficient condition for a subset* H *of a rough group* G *to be a rough subgroup is that:*

(1) $\forall x, y \in H, x * y \in \overline{H}$;
(2) $\forall x \in H, x^{-1} \in H$.

Proof. The necessary condition is obvious. We prove only the sufficient condition. By (1) we have $\forall x, y \in H, x * y \in \overline{H}$, by (2) we have $\forall x \in H, x^{-1 \in H}$, by (1) and (2) we have $\forall x \in H, x * x^{-1} = e \in \overline{H}$, because association holds in $\overline{G}$, so it holds in $\overline{H}$. Hence the theorem is proved.

Another difference between rough group and group is the following:

Theorem 2. *Let* H_1 *and* H_2 *be two rough subgroups of the rough group* G. *A sufficient condition for intersection of two rough subgroups of a rough group to be a rough subgroup is* $\overline{H_1} \cap \overline{H_2} = \overline{H_1 \cap H_2}$.

Proof. Suppose H_1 and H_2 are two rough subgroups of G. It is obvious that $H_1 \cap H_2 \subset G$. Consider $x, y \in H_1 \cap H_2$. Because H_1 and H_2 are rough subgroups, we have $x * y \in \overline{H_1}$, $x * y \in \overline{H_2}$, and $x^{-1} \in H_1, x^{-1} \in H_2$, i.e. $x * y \in \overline{H_1} \cap \overline{H_2}$ and $x^{-1} \in H_1 \cap H_2$. Assuming $\overline{H_1} \cap \overline{H_2} = \overline{H_1 \cap H_2}$, we have $x * y \in \overline{H_1 \cap H_2}$ and $x^{-1} \in H_1 \cap H_2$. Thus $H_1 \cap H_2$ is a rough subgroup of G.

Definition 7. *A rough group is called a commutative rough group if for every* $x, y \in G$, *we have* $x * y = y * x$.

4   Rough Coset

Let (U, R) be a universe, $G \subset U$ be a rough group and H be a rough subgroup of G. Let us define a relationship of elements of rough group G as follows:
   $\sim: a \sim b$ if and only if $a * b^{-1} \in H \cup \{e\}$.

Theorem 3. *"$\sim$" is a compatible relation over elements of rough group G.*

Proof. $\forall a \in G$, since G is a rough group, $a^{-1} \in G$. Since $a * a^{-1} = e$, we have $a \sim a$. Further, $\forall a, b \in G$, if $a \sim b$, then $a * b^{-1} \in H \cup \{e\}$ i.e. $a * b^{-1} \in H$ or $a * b^{-1} \in \{e\}$. If $a * b^{-1} \in H$, then, since H is a rough subgroup of G, we have $(a * b^{-1})^{-1} = b * a^{-1} \in H$, thus $b \sim a$. If $a * b^{-1} \in \{e\}$, then $a * b^{-1} = e$. That means $b * a^{-1} = (a * b^{-1})^{-1} = e^{-1} = e$, thus $b \sim a$. Hence, "$\sim$" is compatible.

Definition 8. *Compatible category defined by relation "$\sim$" is called rough right coset. Rough right coset that contains element a is denoted by $H * a$, i.e.*
   $H * a = \{h * a | h \in H, a \in G, h * a \in G\} \cup \{a\}$.

Let (U, R) be an approximation space, $G \subset U$ be a rough group and H be its rough subgroup. Consider relation of elements of G defined as follows:
   $\sim': a \sim' b$ if and only if $a^{-1} * b \in H \cup \{e\}$.

Theorem 4. *"$\sim'$" is a compatible relation over elements of rough group G.*

Definition 9. *Compatible category defined by relation "$\sim'$" is called rough left coset. Rough left coset that contains element a is denoted by $a * H$, i.e.*
   $a * H = \{a * h | h \in H, a \in G, a * h \in G\} \cup \{a\}$.

Remark: Generally speaking, the binary operation of rough group dissatisfies commutative law, so the compatible relations "$\sim$" and "$\sim'$" are different. As a result, the rough left and right cosets are also different.

Theorem 5. *The rough left cosets and rough right cosets are equal in number.*

Proof. Denote by S_1, S_2 the families of rough right and left cosets, respectively. Define $\varphi : S_1 \to S_2$ such that $\varphi(H * a) = a^{-1} * H$. We prove that φ is bijection.

1. If $H * a = H * b \ (a \neq b)$, then $a * b^{-1} \in H$. Because H is a rough subgroup, we have $b * a^{-1} \in H$, that means $a^{-1} \in b^{-1} * H$, i.e. $a^{-1} * H = b^{-1} * H$. Hence, φ is a mapping.
2. Any element $a * H$ of S_2 is the image of $H * a^{-1}$ – the element of S_1. Hence, φ is onto mapping.
3. If $H * a \neq H * b$, then $a * b^{-1} \notin H$, i.e. $a^{-1} * H \neq b^{-1} * H$. Hence, φ is a one-to-one mapping.

Thus the rough left cosets and rough right cosets are equal in number.

Definition 10. *The number of both rough left cosets and rough right cosets is called index of subgroup H in G.*

5   Rough Invariant Subgroup

Definition 11. *A rough subgroup N of rough group G is called a rough invariant subgroup, if $\forall a \in G, a * N = N * a$.*

Theorem 6. *A necessary and sufficient condition for a rough subgroup N of rough group G to be a rough invariant subgroup is that $\forall a \in G, a * N * a^{-1} = N$.*

Proof. Suppose N is a rough invariant subgroup of G. By definition, $\forall a \in G$, we have $a * N = N * a$. Because G is a rough group, we have
$$(a * N) * a^{-1} = (N * a) * a^{-1}$$
$$a * N * a^{-1} = N * (a * a^{-1})$$
i.e. $a * N * a^{-1} = N$.
Suppose N is a rough subgroup of G and $\forall a \in G, a * N * a^{-1} = N$. Then
$$(a * N * a^{-1}) * a = N * a$$
i.e. $a * N = N * a$.
Thus N is a rough invariant subgroup of G.

Theorem 7. *A necessary and sufficient condition for a rough subgroup N of G to be a rough invariant subgroup is that $\forall a \in G$ and $n \in N$, $a * n * a^{-1} \in N$.*

Proof. Suppose N is a rough invariant subgroup of rough group G. We have
$$\forall a \in G, a * N * a^{-1} = N.$$
For any $n \in N$, we therefore have
$$a * n * a^{-1} \in N.$$
Suppose N is a rough subgroup of rough group G. Suppose $\forall a \in G$, $n \in N$, $a * n * a^{-1} \in N$. We have
$$a * N * a^{-1} \subset N$$
Because $a^{-1} \in G$, we further have
$$a^{-1} * N * a \subset N$$
It follows that
$$a * (a^{-1} * N * a) * a^{-1} \subset a * N * a^{-1}$$
i.e. $N \subset a * N * a^{-1}$
Since $a * N * a^{-1} \subset N$ and $N \subset a * N * a^{-1}$, we have $a * N * a^{-1} = N$. Thus N is a rough invariant subgroup.

6   Homomorphism and Isomorphism of Rough Group

Let $(U_1, R_1), (U_2, R_2)$ be two approximation spaces, and $*, \overline{\ast}$ be binary operations over universes U_1 and U_2, respectively.

Definition 12. *Let $G_1 \subset U_1, G_2 \subset U_2$. G_1, G_2 are called rough homomorphism sets if there exists a surjection $\varphi : \overline{G_1} \to \overline{G_2}$ such that*
$$\forall x, y \in \overline{G_1}, \varphi(x * y) = \varphi(x) \overline{\ast} \varphi(y).$$

Theorem 8. *Let G_1 and G_2 be rough homomorphism sets. If $*$ satisfies commutative law, then $\overline{\ast}$ also satisfies it.*

Proof. Consider G_1, G_2, and φ such that $\forall x, y \in \overline{G_1}, \varphi(x * y) = \varphi(x) \overline{*} \varphi(y)$. For every $\varphi(x), \varphi(y) \in \overline{G_2}$, since φ is surjection, there exist $x, y \in \overline{G_1}$ such that $x \to \varphi(x), y \to \varphi(y)$. Thus $\varphi(x * y) = \varphi(x) \overline{*} \varphi(y)$, and $\varphi(y * x) = \varphi(y) \overline{*} \varphi(x)$. Now, assuming $x * y = y * x$, we obtain $\varphi(x) \overline{*} \varphi(y) = \varphi(y) \overline{*} \varphi(x)$. That means that $*$ satisfies commutative law.

Theorem 9. *Let $G_1 \subset U_1, G_2 \subset U_2$ be rough groups that are rough homomorphism and let $\overline{\varphi(G_1)} = \overline{G_2}$. Then $\varphi(G_1)$ is also a rough group.*

Proof.
1. $\forall x', y' \in \varphi(G_1)$, consider $x, y \in G_1$ such that $x \to x', y \to y'$. We have $\varphi(x * y) = \varphi(x) \overline{*} \varphi(y) \in \overline{G_2} = \overline{\varphi(G_1)}$, that is $x' \overline{*} y' \in \varphi(G_1)$.
2. Since $e \in \overline{G_1}$, $\varphi(e) \in \overline{G_2}$ and $\forall \varphi(x) \in \varphi(G_1), \varphi(e) \overline{*} \varphi(x) = \varphi(x * e) = \varphi(x)$
3. G_1 is a rough group, so $\forall x, y, z \in G_1, x * (y * z) = (x * y) * z$. Hence:
   $\varphi(x * (y * z)) = \varphi(x) \overline{*} \varphi(y * z) = \varphi(x) \overline{*} (\varphi(y) \overline{*} \varphi(z))$
   $\varphi((x * y) * z)) = \varphi(x * y) \overline{*} \varphi(z) = (\varphi(x) \overline{*} \varphi(y)) \overline{*} \varphi(z)$
   i.e. $(\varphi(x) \overline{*} \varphi(y)) \overline{*} \varphi(z) \varphi(x) \overline{*} (\varphi(y) \overline{*} \varphi(z))$.
4. $\forall x' \in \varphi(G_1)$, consider $x \in G_1$ such that $x \to x'$. Since G_1 is a rough group, $x^{-1} \in G_1$. Hence $\varphi(x^{-1}) \in \varphi(G_1)$ and $\varphi(x) \overline{*} \varphi(x^{-1}) = \varphi(x^{-1}) \overline{*} \varphi(x) = \varphi(e)$. Therefore, we can put $(x')^{-1} = \varphi(x^{-1})$. Consequently, we can conclude that $\varphi(G_1)$ is a rough group.

Theorem 10. *Let $G_1 \subset U_1, G_2 \subset U_2$ be rough groups that are rough homomorphism. Let e and $\overline{e}$ be rough identity elements of G_1 and G_2 respectively. Then $\varphi(e) = \overline{e}$ and $\varphi(a^{-1}) = \varphi(a)^{-1}$.*

Definition 13. *Let $G_1 \subset U_1, G_2 \subset U_2$ be rough groups that are rough homomorphism. Let e and $\overline{e}$ be rough identity elements of G_1 and G_2 respectively. The set $\{x | \varphi(x) = \overline{e}, x \in G_1\}$ is called rough homomorphism kernel, denoted by N.*

Theorem 11. *Let $G_1 \subset U_1, G_2 \subset U_2$ be rough groups that are rough homomorphism. Rough homomorphism kernel N is a rough invariant subgroup of G_1.*

Proof. Let φ be onto mapping from $\overline{G_1}$ to $\overline{G_2}$. $\forall x, y \in N$ we have $\varphi(x) = \overline{e}, \varphi(y) = \overline{e}$. Thus $\varphi(x * y) = \varphi(x) \overline{*} \varphi(y) = \overline{e} \overline{*} \overline{e} = \overline{e}$, i.e. $x * y \in N$. Moreover, $\forall x \in N$, we have $\varphi(x) = \overline{e}$. Because $\varphi(x^{-1}) = \varphi(y)^{-1} = \overline{e}^{-1} = \overline{e}$, we get $x^{-1} \in N$. We can conclude that N is a rough invariant subgroup of G_1.

Theorem 12. *Let $G_1 \subset U_1, G_2 \subset U_2$ be rough groups that are rough homomorphism. Let H_1, N_1 be rough subgroup and rough invariant subgroup of G_1, respectively. Then:*

(1) $\varphi(H_1)$ is rough subgroup of G_2 if $\varphi(\overline{H_1}) = \overline{\varphi(H_1)}$;
(2) $\varphi(N_1)$ is rough invariant subgroup of G_2 if $\varphi(G_1) = G_2$ & $\varphi(\overline{N_1}) = \overline{\varphi(N_1)}$.

Proof. (1):
Consider an onto mapping φ from $\overline{G_1}$ to $\overline{G_2}$ such that
   $\forall x, y \in \overline{G_1}, \varphi(x * y) = \varphi(x) \overline{*} \varphi(y)$.
$\forall \varphi(x), \varphi(y) \in \varphi(H_1)$, by the definition of φ, there exists $x, y \in H_1$ such that
   $x \to \varphi(x)$ and $\varphi(x) \overline{*} \varphi(y) = \varphi(x * y) \in \varphi(\overline{H_1})$.

Because $\varphi(\overline{H_1}) = \overline{\varphi(H_1)}$, we have
$$\varphi(x)\overline{*}\varphi(y) \in \varphi(\overline{H_1}).$$
Further, $\forall \varphi(x) \in \varphi(H_1)$, by the definition of φ, there exists $x \in H_1$ such that
$$x \to \varphi(x), y \to \varphi(y).$$
Because H_1 is a rough subgroup of G_1, we have
$$x^{-1} \in H_1.$$
Thus
$$\varphi(a)^{-1} = \varphi(a^{-1}) \in \varphi(H_1).$$
We can conclude that $\varphi(H_1)$ is a rough subgroup of G_2.

Proof. (2):
By (1), it is easy to see that $\varphi(N_1)$ is a rough subgroup of G_2 if
$$\varphi(\overline{N_1}) = \overline{\varphi(N_1)}.$$
$\forall \varphi(x) \in G_2$, because $\varphi(G_1) = G_2$, we have
$$\varphi(x) \in \varphi(G_1).$$
Thus
$$x \in G_1, \ x^{-1} \in G_1 \text{ and } \varphi(x^{-1}) \in \varphi(G_1) = G_2.$$
Because $\forall \varphi(x) \in G_2, \varphi(n) \in \varphi(N_1)$ there is
$$\varphi(x)\overline{*}\varphi(n)\overline{*}\varphi(x^{-1}) = \varphi(x * n * x^{-1})$$
and N_1 is rough invariant subgroup of G_1, we have
$$x * n * x^{-1} \in N_1.$$
Hence
$$\varphi(x)\overline{*}\varphi(n)\overline{*}\varphi(x^{-1}) \in \varphi(N_1).$$
We can conclude that $\varphi(N_1)$ is a rough invariant subgroup of G_1.

Theorem 13. *Let $G_1 \subset U_1, G_2 \subset U_2$ be rough groups that are rough homomorphism. Let H_2, N_2 be rough subgroup and rough invariant subgroup of G_2 respectively. Then*

(1) H_1 which is the inverse image of H_2 is rough subgroup of G_1 if $\varphi(\overline{H_1}) = \overline{H_2}$
(2) N_1 which is the inverse image of N_2 is rough invariant subgroup of G_1 if $\varphi(G_1) = G_2 \ \& \ \varphi(\overline{N_1}) = \overline{N_2}$.

Proof. (2):
Because H_1 is the inverse image of H_2, we have
$$\varphi(H_1) = H_2.$$
That is, $\forall x, y \in H_1$, we have
$$\varphi(x), \varphi(y) \in H_2.$$
Because H_2 is a rough subgroup of G_2, we have
$$\varphi(x * y) = \varphi(x)\overline{*}\varphi(y) \in \overline{H_2} = \varphi(\overline{H_1}).$$
Thus
$$x * y \in \overline{H_1}.$$
$\forall x \in H_1$, we have
$$\varphi(x) \in H_2.$$
Because H_2 is a rough subgroup of G_2, we have
$$\varphi(x)^{-1} = \varphi(x^{-1}) \in H_2.$$
Thus $x^{-1} \in H_1$.

Proof. (2):

By (1), it is easy to know that N_1 is a rough subgroup of G_2 if
$$\varphi(\overline{N_1}) = \overline{\varphi(N_1)}.$$
$\forall x \in G_1, n \in N_1$, we have
$$\varphi(x) \in \varphi(G_1) = G_2, \varphi(x)^{-1} = \varphi(x^{-1}) \in \varphi(G_1) = G_2, \varphi(n) \in N_2$$
Because N_2 is a rough invariant subgroup of G_2, we have
$$\varphi(x) \overline{*} \varphi(n) \overline{*} \varphi(x^{-1}) = \varphi(x * n * x^{-1}) \in N_2.$$
Thus
$$x * n * x^{-1} \in N_1.$$
Hence N_1 which is the inverse image of N_2 is a rough invariant subgroup of G_1 if $\varphi(G_1) = G_2$ and $\varphi(\overline{N_1}) = \overline{N_2}$.

7   Examples

Example 1. Let U be the set of all permutation of S_4 and $*$ be the multiplication operation of permutation. A classification of U is $U/R = \{E_1, E_2, E_3, E_4\}$, where
$$E_1 = \{(1), (12), (13), (14), (23), (24), (34)\},$$
$$E_2 = \{(123), (132), (124), (142), (134), (143), (234), (243)\},$$
$$E_3 = \{(1234), (1243), (1324), (1342), (1423), (1432)\},$$
$$E_4 = \{(12)(34), (13)(24), (14)(23)\},$$
Let $X_1 = \{(1), (12), (13)\}$, then
$$\overline{X_1} = \{(1), (12), (13), (14), (23), (24), (34)\}.$$
Because $(12) * (13) = (123) \notin \overline{X_1}$, we have X_1 is not a rough group.
Let $X_2 = \{(12), (123), (132)\}$, then
$$\overline{X_2} = E_1 \cup E_2.$$
Because

(1) $\forall x, y \in X_2, x * y \in \overline{X_2}$;
(2) $(12) * (12) = (1) \in \overline{X_2}$;
(3) Association property holds in $\overline{X_2}$;
(4) $(12)^{-1} = (12) \in X_2, (123)^{-1} = 132 \in X_2, (132)^{-1} = (123) \in X_2$.

Thus we have that X_2 is a rough group.
Let $X_3 = \{(1), (123), (132)\}$, then $\overline{X_3} = E_1 \cup E_2$.
Because

(1) $X_3 \subset X_2$;
(2) $\forall x, y \in X_3, x * y \in \overline{X_3}$;
(3) $(1)^{-1} = (1) \in X_3, (123)^{-1} = (132) \in X_3, (13)^{-1} = (13) \in X_3$;

Thus we have that X_3 is a rough subgroup of rough group X_2¡£

Example 2. Let $U = \{[0], [1], [2], [3], [4], [5], [6], [7], [8], [9]\}$ be a set of surplus class with respect to module 9 and $*$ be the plus of surplus class. A classification of U is $U/R = \{E_1, E_2, E_3\}$, where $E_1 = \{[0], [1], [2]\}$, $E_2 = \{[3], [4], [5]\}$, $E_3 = \{[6], [7], [8]\}$,
Let $X_1 = \{[2], [7], [8], [1]\}$, then $\overline{X_1} = E_1 \cup E_2$. Because $[2] * [1] = [3] \notin \overline{X_1}$, thus we have X_1 is not a rough group.

Let $X_2 = \{[2], [7], [5], [4]\}$, then $\overline{X_2} = E_1 \cup E_2 \cup E_3 = U$. Because

(1) $\forall x, y \in X_2, x * y \in \overline{X_2}$;
(2) Association property holds in $\overline{X_2}$;
(3) $[2] * [7] = 0 \in \overline{X_2}$;
(4) $[2]^{-1} = [7] \in X_2, [7]^{-1} = [2] \in X_2, [5]^{-1} = [4] \in X_2, [4]^{-1} = [5] \in X_2$;

We have that X_2 is a rough group.
　　Let $X_3 = \{[2], [3], [6], [7]\}$, then $\overline{X_3} = E_1 \cup E_2 \cup E_3 = U$.
Because

(1) $\forall x, y \in X_3, x * y \in \overline{X_3}$;
(2) Association property holds in $\overline{X_3}$;
(3) $[0] \in \overline{X_3}$
(4) $[2]^{-1} = [7] \in X_3, [7]^{-1} = [2] \in X_3, [3]^{-1} = [6] \in X_3, [6]^{-1} = [3] \in X_3$;

We have that X_3 is a rough group.
　　Let $X_4 = X_2 \cap X_3 = \{[2], [7]\}$ then $\overline{X_4} = E_1 \cup E_3$
Because $[2] * [2] = [4] \notin X_4$, we have X_4 is not a rough subgroup of rough group X_2 or rough group X_3.

Example 3. Let U be the set of all permutation of S_4 and $*$ be the multiplication operation of permutation. A classification of U is $U/R = \{E_1, E_2, E_3, E_4, E_5\}$, where

$\quad E_1 = \{(1), (123), (132)\}$,
$\quad E_2 = \{(12), (13), (23), (14), (24), (34)\}$,
$\quad E_3 = \{(124), (142), (134), (143), (234), (243)\}$,
$\quad E_4 = \{(1234), (1243), (1324), (1342), (1423), (1432)\}$,
$\quad E_5 = \{(12)(34), (13)(24), (14)(23)\}$,
Let $G = \{(12), (13), (123), (132)\}$, $N = (123), (132)$, then
$\quad \overline{G} = (1), (123), (132), (12), (13), (23), (14), (24), (34) \ \overline{N} = (1), (123), (132)$
It is easy to prove that G is a rough group and N is a rough subgroup of rough group G. Because

$\quad (12) * N = (13), (23) = N * (12) = (23), (13)$
$\quad (13) * N = (23), (12) = N * (13) = (12), (23)$
$\quad (123) * N = (132), (1) = N * (123) = (132), (1)$
$\quad (132) * N = (1), (123) = N * (132) = (1), (123)$
We have N is a rough invariant subgroup.

8   Conclusion

In this paper we have shown that the theory of rough sets can be applied to the algebra systems – groups. We have also improved some deficiencies of the approach proposed in [1], and proved some new properties of rough groups and rough subgroups. Following this, a lot of work should be still done continually, such as e.g. an extension of theory of rough sets to rough rings and rough fields. Further studies in this direction will enable to understand better the connections between relatively novel ideas of the theory of rough sets and already well-known algebraic approaches.

Acknowledgments

This research has been supported by grant No. 60175016 and 60475019 from the National Natural Science Foundation of China.

References

1. Biswas, R., Nanda, S.: Rough Groups and Rough Subgroups. Bull. Pol. AC.: Math., 42 (1994) 251-254
2. Lin, T.Y.: Topological and Fuzzy Rough Sets. In: Intelligent Decision Support. Kluwer Academic Publishers, Boston/London/Dordrecht (1992) 287-304
3. Pomykala, J., Pomykala, J.A.: The Stone Algebra of Rough Sets. Bull. Pol. AC.: Math., 36 (1988) 495-507
4. Pawlak, Z.: Rough Sets – Theoretical Aspects of Reasoning about Data. Kluwer Academic Publishers, Boston/London/Dordrecht (1991)
5. Yao, Y.Y.: On generalizing Pawlak approximation operators. Lecture Notes in Artificial Intelligence, 1424 (1998) 298-307
6. Yao, Y.Y., Wong, S.K.M., Lin, T.Y.: A Review of Rough Set Models. In: Rough Set and Data Mining. Kluwer Academic Publishers, Boston/London/Dordrecht (1997) 47-71
7. Miao, D.Q., Wang, J.: An Information Representation of Concepts and Operations in Rough Sets. Journal of Software, 10(2) (1999) 113-116
8. Duentsch, I., Orlowska, E., Wang, H.: Algebras of Approximating Regions. Fundam. Inform., 46(1-2) (2001) 78-82
9. Banerjee, M.H., Chakraborty, M.K.: Rough Sets Through Algebraic Logic. Fundam. Inform., 28(3-4) (1996) 211-221
10. Iwinski, T.B.: An Algebraic Approach to Rough Sets. Bull. Pol. AC.: Math., 35 (1987) 673-683

Concept Lattices vs. Approximation Spaces*

Piotr Wasilewski

Warsaw University, Faculty of Psychology,
Stawki 5/7, 00-183 Warsaw, Poland
piotr@psych.uw.edu.pl

Abstract. The aim of this paper is to compare concept lattices and approximation spaces. For this purpose general approximation spaces are introduced. It is shown that formal contexts and information systems on one hand and general approximation spaces on the other could be mutually represented e.g. for every information system exists a general approximation space such that both structures determines the same indiscernibility relation. A close relationship between Pawlak's approximation spaces and general approximation spaces also holds: for each approximation space exists a general approximation space such that both spaces determine the same definable sets. It is shown on the basis of these relationships that an extent of the every formal concept is a definable set in some Pawlak's approximation space. The problem when concept lattices are isomorphic to algebras of definable sets in approximation spaces is also investigated.

1 Introduction

Formal Concept Analysis (FCA) and Rough Set Theory (RST) are significant theories in the field of data mining. They represent information in similar way, as descriptions of objects over families of attributes. However, both theories use different algebraic structures within information analysis. FCA uses concept lattices which are, up to isomorphism, complete lattices, while RST uses algebras of definable sets and algebras of rough sets connected with approximation spaces. These algebras are complete, atomic Boolean and Stone algebras respectively. Thus represented information is analyzed in different ways by FCA and RST. The aim of this paper is to compare these different ways of analysis through the comparison of their main tools, namely concept lattices and approximation spaces. For this purpose general approximation spaces will be introduced.

---

* This paper presents results of research, which was done by the author during his Ph.D. studies in the Department of Logic, Jagiellonian University, Kraków, Poland. Research project was supported by the Polish Ministry of Science and Information Society Technologies under grant no. 2 H01A 025 23.

D. Ślęzak et al. (Eds.): RSFDGrC 2005, LNAI 3641, pp. 114–123, 2005.
© Springer-Verlag Berlin Heidelberg 2005

2   Information Structures

Concept lattices and approximation spaces are based on formal contexts and deterministic information systems which are closely connected to single valued information systems. These information structures are drafted in this section.

2.1   Single-Valued Information Systems

Single-valued information systems are basic information structures within the "object - attribute" approach to the representation of information (Düntsch, Gediga, Orłowska, [2]).

A *single-valued information system* is a structure

$$\langle OB, AT, \{V_a : a \in AT\}\rangle,$$

where OB is a finite set of *objects*, AT is a finite set of mappings $a : OB \longrightarrow V_a$; each $a \in AT$ is called an *attribute* and V_a is the set of *attribute values* of attribute a.

Single valued information systems are formal treatments of one of the oldest and main operationalizations of data (Düntsch, Gediga, Orłowska, [2]). Formal contexts and deterministic information systems are other operationalizations of data closely connected to single valued inforation systems. In fact both could be seen as transformations of single valued information systems preserving distinguishability between objects with respect to attributes.

2.2   Formal Contexts and Concept Lattices

Concept lattices were introduced by Rudolph Wille ([7]). Construction of concept lattices is based on some Galois connections determined by *formal contexts*. For a detailed presentation of FCA see (Ganter, Wille [3]).

A *formal context* is a structure of the form

$$\langle G, M, I\rangle,$$

where G and M are sets of *objects* and *attributes* respectively, and $I \subseteq G \times M$ is a binary relation. If $g \in G$, $m \in M$ and $(g, m) \in I$, then the object g is said to have the attribute m, in this case we write also gIm.

For a single-valued information system $\langle OB, AT, \{V_a : a \in AT\}\rangle$ one can construct a family of binary attributes $Q_{AT} := \{Q_a^v : v \in V_a\}$, where for all $x \in OB$, $Q_a^v(x) = 1 \Leftrightarrow a(x) = v$, otherwise $Q_a^v(x) = 0$. The context relation I_{AT} is constructed as follows: $(x, Q_a^v) \in I_{AT} \Leftrightarrow Q_a^v(x) = 1$. Thus $\langle OB, Q_{AT}, I_{AT}\rangle$ is a formal context such that $a(x) = v \Leftrightarrow (x, Q_a^v) \in I_{AT}$. This construction presents a transformation single valued systems into formal contexts and it is quite analogous to *nominalizations of multivalued contexts* (Ganter, Wille [3]).

For any formal context we define two functions $i : \mathcal{P}(G) \longrightarrow \mathcal{P}(M)$ and $e : \mathcal{P}(M) \longrightarrow \mathcal{P}(G)$, as follows:

$$X^i = \{m \in M : (g, m) \in I, \forall\, g \in X\}, \text{ where } X^i = i(X) \text{ for } X \subseteq G,$$
$$Y^e = \{g \in G : (g, m) \in I, \forall\, m \in Y\}, \text{ where } Y^e = e(Y) \text{ for } Y \subseteq M.$$

Note that operators ^{i} and ^{e} creates a Galois connection (see Ganter, Wille [3]).

A set m^e, for each attribute $m \in M$, one can interpret as an extent of the attribute m, instead of m^e we will write $/m/$. Let $\Gamma \subseteq M$, then $/\Gamma/$ denotes the family of extents of attributes from the family Γ i.e. $/\Gamma/ := \{ /m/ : m \in \Gamma \}$.

For any formal context $\langle G, M, I \rangle$ we define an *indiscernibility relation* $\simeq_M$ as follows: for all $x, y \in G$,

$$(x, y) \in \simeq_M :\Leftrightarrow (x, m) \in I \Leftrightarrow (y, m) \in I \ for\ each\ m \in M.$$

A formal concept of the context $\langle G, M, I \rangle$ is a pair (A, B) with $A \subseteq G$, $B \subseteq M$, $A^i = B$ and $B^e = A$. A is called the *extent* and B is called the *intent* of the concept (A, B). $\underline{\mathcal{B}}(G, M, I)$ denotes the set of all concepts of the context $\langle G, M, I \rangle$. Let $(A_1, B_1), (A_2, B_2) \in \underline{\mathcal{B}}(G, M, I)$. (A_1, B_1) is a *subconcept* of (A_2, B_2), if $A_1 \subseteq A_2$ (one can prove that this is equivalent to $B_2 \subseteq B_1$) and we write $(A_1, B_1) \leq (A_2, B_2)$. Relation $\leq$ is a partial order on the family of all concepts of the context $\langle G, M, I \rangle$. Moreover, partially ordered set $\langle \underline{\mathcal{B}}(G, M, I), \leq \rangle$ is a complete lattice, this lattice we will also denote by $\underline{\mathcal{B}}(G, M, I)$. The family of extents of all formal concepts of the context $\underline{\mathcal{B}}(G, M, I)$ is denoted by $\underline{\mathcal{B}}_M(G, I)$. Let us note, that $\langle \underline{\mathcal{B}}_M(G, I), \subseteq \rangle$ is a lattice isomorphic to the concept lattice $\underline{\mathcal{B}}(G, M, I)$.

2.3   Information Systems and Approximation Spaces

Deterministic information systems (see Pawlak [4]) slightly differ from one-valued information systems: Attributes in the deterministic information systems are not functions but arguments of one function which assigns each pair of an object and an attribute, a value of that attribute.

A *deterministic information system* is a structure of the form

$$\langle OB, AT, \{V_a : a \in AT\}, f \rangle,$$

where OB is a non-empty set of *objects*, AT is a non-empty set of *attributes*, V_a is a non-empty set of *values* of the attribute a, and f is a function $OB \times AT \longrightarrow \bigcup_{a \in AT} V_a$ such that for every $(x, a) \in OB \times AT$, $f(x, a) \in V_a$. In this paper we deal with deterministic information systems only, so in the sequel the adjective "deterministic" is skipped. Let us note that for any single-valued information system $\langle OB, AT, \{V_a : a \in AT\} \rangle$ there is an information system $\langle OB, AT, \{V_a : a \in AT\}, f \rangle$ such that $f(x, a) = v \Leftrightarrow a(x) = v$ for all $x \in OB$ and $a \in AT$.

For any information system $\langle OB, AT, \{V_a : a \in AT\}, f \rangle$, and for any set of attributes $A \subseteq AT$ we define the *indiscernibility relation* $ind(A)$ for all $x, y \in OB$ as follows

$$(x, y) \in ind(A) :\Leftrightarrow f(x, a) = f(y, a) \ for\ all\ a \in A.$$

An ordered pair (U, R) is called an *approximation space*, where U is non empty set and R is an equivalence relation on U. Equivalence classes of the relation R are called *atoms* of an approximation spaces (U, R) (shortly R-atoms).

We assume that $\emptyset$ is also R-atom. A set X is called *definable in* an approximation space (U, R), if X is a union of R-atoms. The family of all sets definable in the space (U, R) is denoted by $\mathrm{Com}_R(U)$.

For any $X \subseteq U$ we define a *lower approximation* and an *upper approximation* of X in (U, R) respectively:

$$\underline{R}(X) = \bigcup \{Y \in U_{/R} : Y \subseteq X\},$$

$$\overline{R}(X) = \bigcup \{Y \in U_{/R} : Y \cap X \neq \emptyset\}.$$

In case it will not lead to misunderstanding we will use expressions "atom" and "definable set" instead of expressions "R-atom" and "R-definable set".

It is possible to show that $X \in Com_R(U)$ iff $X = \underline{R}(X)$ iff $X = \overline{R}(X)$.

3   General Approximation Spaces

In this paragraph we introduce *general approximation spaces*. We outline some connections between general approximation spaces, complete algebras of sets and indiscernibility relations determined by families of sets. We show that general approximation spaces are equivalent to the classical Pawlak's approximation spaces. A detailed exposition and proofs can be found in (Wasilewski [6]).

Complete algebras of sets are, by definitions, algebras of sets closed under arbitrary unions and intersections, where Boolean operations are finite union, finite intersection and set complementation respectively. Set complementation we denote by "'": let $\mathcal{A}$ be a complete algebra of sets on a set U and $A \in \mathcal{A}$, $A' := U \setminus A$.

Let $\mathcal{C} \subseteq \mathcal{P}(U)$. $Sg^c(\mathcal{C})$ denotes the least complete algebra of sets on U containing the family $\mathcal{C}$. If $\mathcal{A}$ is an algebra of sets then $At(\mathcal{A})$ denotes the family of atoms of $\mathcal{A}$.

Definition 1. *Let U be any nonempty set and $\mathcal{C} \subseteq \mathcal{P}(U)$. An ordered pair $(U, \mathcal{C})$ we call a general approximation space. We define two operators on the set U: for any $X \subseteq U$:*

$$\underline{\mathcal{C}}(X) := \bigcup \{A \in Sg^c(\mathcal{C}) : A \subseteq X\},$$

$$\overline{\mathcal{C}}(X) := \bigcap \{A \in Sg^c(\mathcal{C}) : X \subseteq A\}.$$

Elements of the complete algebra of sets $Sg^c(\mathcal{C})$ are called sets definable in $(U, \mathcal{C})$. The algebra $Sg^c(\mathcal{C})$ is denoted by $Com_{\mathcal{C}}(U)$ and called the algebra of definable sets in the approximation space $(U, \mathcal{C})$. Operators $\underline{\mathcal{C}}$, $\overline{\mathcal{C}}$ are called a lower and an upper approximation respectively.

Any general approximation space determine an indiscernibility relation with respect to sets and families of sets:

Definition 2. *Let U be a nonempty set. For any set $C \in \mathcal{P}(U)$ we define an indiscernibility relation with respect to C as follows:*

$$x \approx_C y \iff_{def} x \in C \iff y \in C$$

For any family of sets $\mathcal{C} \subseteq \mathcal{P}(U)$ we define an indiscernibility relation with respect to family $\mathcal{C}$:

$$(x, y) \in \approx_{\mathcal{C}} \Leftrightarrow_{def} (x, y) \in \bigcap_{C \in \mathcal{C}} \approx_C$$

Observe that $\approx_C$ and $\approx_{\mathcal{C}}$ are equivalence relations on U.

There is the following connections between indiscernibility relations with respect to families of sets and complete algebras of sets (Wasilewski [6]):

Proposition 1. *Let U be a non-empty set, $\mathcal{C} \subseteq \mathcal{P}(U)$ and $\mathcal{A} = Sg^c(\mathcal{C})$, then*

$$At(\mathcal{A}) = U_{/\approx_{\mathcal{C}}}.$$

Let us recall that any complete algebra of sets is atomic. It is easy to show that each set from complete algebra of sets is a union of its atoms. Thus the following holds:

Proposition 2. *Let U be a non-empty set, $\mathcal{C} \subseteq \mathcal{P}(U)$ and $\mathcal{A} = Sg^c(\mathcal{C})$. Each set $B \in \mathcal{A}$ is a union of equivalence classes of the indiscernibility relation $\approx_{\mathcal{C}}$.*

For each approximation space (U, R) there is a family of sets $\mathcal{C} \subseteq \mathcal{P}(U)$ such that $R = \approx_{\mathcal{C}}$. It is enough to consider $U_{/R}$, since $R = \approx_{U_{/R}}$. Obviously, the partition $U_{/R}$ is not a unique family determining the relation R. Two different families of sets can determine the same indiscernibility relation. The following theorem shows a necessary and sufficient condition for it:

Theorem 1. *Let U be any nonempty set and $\mathcal{C}, \mathcal{D} \subseteq \mathcal{P}(U)$, then:*

$$\approx_{\mathcal{C}} = \approx_{\mathcal{D}} \Leftrightarrow Sg^c(\mathcal{C}) = Sg^c(\mathcal{D}).$$

We can represent any approximation space by some general approximation space in the following sense:

Theorem 2. *For any approximation space (U, R) there is a general approximation space $(U, \mathcal{C})$ such that $Com_R(U) = Com_{\mathcal{C}}(U)$, i.e. both spaces determine the same definable sets.*

Proof. Let (U, R) be an approximation space. Let us choose a family $\mathcal{C} \subseteq \mathcal{P}(U)$ such that $R = \approx_{\mathcal{C}}$ (one can take the family $U_{/R}$, other families, which are not partitions, also can be taken). Thus $(U, \mathcal{C})$ is a general approximation space. Since $R = \approx_{U_{/R}}$, then $\approx_{U_{/R}} = \approx_{\mathcal{C}}$. Thus $Sg^c(U_{/R}) = Sg^c(\mathcal{C})$, by theorem 1. Let us note that $U_{\approx_{U_{/R}}} = U_{/R}$. We obtain from proposition 1: $At(Sg^c(U_{/R})) = U_{\approx_{U_{/R}}}$, thus $At(Sg^c(U_{/R})) = U_{/R}$. Proposition 2 implies that any set $B \in Sg^c(U_{/R})$ is a union of equivalence classes of the relation $\approx_{U_{/R}}$, thus any set $B \in Sg^c(U_{/R})$ is a union of equivalence classes of the relation R. Therefore $Sg^c(U_{/R}) \subseteq Com_R(U)$, i.e. all elements of $Sg^c(U_{/R})$ are definable sets in the approximation space (U, R). Since $Sg^c(U_{/R})$ is closed under unions of all subfamilies of $Sg^c(U_{/R})$, then the reverse inclusion also holds. Thus $Com_R(U) = Sg^c(U_{/R})$. We have shown that $Sg^c(U_{/R}) = Sg^c(\mathcal{C})$, therefore $Com_R(U) = Sg^c(\mathcal{C})$ and $Com_R(U) = Com_\mathcal{C}(U)$. Thus the approximation space (U, R) and the general approximation space $(U, \mathcal{C})$ determine the same definable sets.

Theorem 3. *Let (U, R) be an approximation space and $(U, \mathcal{C})$ be a general approximation space. For any set $X \subseteq U$ the following conditions are equivalent:*

(1) $\underline{R}(X) = \underline{\mathcal{C}}(X)$ and $\overline{R}(X) = \overline{\mathcal{C}}(X)$,
(2) $\approx_\mathcal{C} \; = \; R$.

Thus general approximation spaces are equivalent to Pawlak's approximation spaces.

Proof. Let (U, R) be an approximation space and $(U, \mathcal{C})$ be a general approximation space.

($\Leftarrow$) Let $\approx_\mathcal{C} = R$. Consequently, as in the proof of theorem 2, we obtain that $Com_R(U) = Sg^c(U_{/R}) = Sg^c(\mathcal{C}) = Com_\mathcal{C}(U)$. Since $Com_R(U) = Sg^c(\mathcal{C})$, then it follows from definitions that for all $X \subseteq U$, $\underline{R}(X) = \underline{\mathcal{C}}(X)$.

Let $Y \subseteq U$. Note that $\overline{R}(Y) \in Com_R(U)$, then $\overline{R}(Y) \in Sg^c(\mathcal{C})$. Therefore $\overline{R}(Y) \in \{A \in Sg^c(\mathcal{C}) : X \subseteq A\}$, now then $\bigcap\{A \in Sg^c(\mathcal{C}) : X \subseteq A\} \subseteq \overline{R}(Y)$. Thus $\overline{\mathcal{C}}(Y) \subseteq \overline{R}(Y)$.

Note that $Y \subseteq \overline{\mathcal{C}}(Y)$. It follows from the definition of the operator $\overline{R}$ that $\overline{R}(Y) \subseteq \overline{R}(\overline{\mathcal{C}}(Y))$. Note that $\overline{\mathcal{C}}(Y) \in Sg^c(\mathcal{C})$. Since $Com_R(U) = Sg^c(\mathcal{C})$, then from the fact that $X \in Com_R(U) \Leftrightarrow \overline{R}(X) = X$ we obtain that $\overline{R}(\overline{\mathcal{C}}(Y)) = \overline{\mathcal{C}}(Y)$. We have shown that $\overline{R}(Y) \subseteq \overline{R}(\overline{\mathcal{C}}(Y))$. Thus $\overline{R}(Y) \subseteq \overline{\mathcal{C}}(Y)$. Since the set $Y \subseteq U$ was chosen arbitrarily, then for any set $X \subseteq U$, $\overline{R}(X) = \overline{\mathcal{C}}(X)$.

($\Rightarrow$) Let $X \in Com_R(U)$, thus $X = \overline{R}(X)$. Since $\overline{R}(X) = \overline{\mathcal{C}}(X)$, then $X = \overline{\mathcal{C}}(X) = \bigcap\{A \in Sg^c(\mathcal{C}) : X \subseteq A\}$. Note that $\bigcap\{A \in Sg^c(\mathcal{C}) : X \subseteq A\} \in Sg^c(\mathcal{C})$, since $Sg^c(\mathcal{C})$ is a complete algebra of sets. Thus $X \in Sg^c(\mathcal{C})$, therefore $Com_R(U) \subseteq Sg^c(\mathcal{C})$.

Let $X \in Sg^c(\mathcal{C})$, then $X \in \{A \in Sg^c(\mathcal{C}) : X \subseteq A\}$. Thus $\bigcap\{A \in Sg^c(\mathcal{C}) : X \subseteq A\} \subseteq X$, and $\overline{\mathcal{C}}(X) \subseteq X$. Reverse inclusion follows directly from the definition of the operator $\overline{\mathcal{C}}$. Thus $X = \overline{\mathcal{C}}(X)$. Since $\overline{\mathcal{C}}(X) = \overline{R}(X)$, then $X = \overline{R}(X)$. Consequently, we obtain that $X \in Com_R(U)$. Therefore $Sg^c(\mathcal{C}) \subseteq Com_R(U)$. Thus $Com_R(U) = Sg^c(\mathcal{C})$. We have shown in the proof of the theorem 2 that $Com_R(U) = Sg^c(U_{/R})$. Thus $Sg^c(U_{/R}) = Sg^c(\mathcal{C})$. It follows from theorem 1 that $\approx_{U_{/R}} \; = \; \approx_\mathcal{C}$. Since $R = \approx_{U_{/R}}$, then $R = \approx_\mathcal{C}$.

4   Representations

It is well known that Wille's formal contexts and Pawlak's information systems are closely connected: Each formal context can be viewed as a deterministic information system and every information system determines a formal context such that both structures provide the same information about the underlying objects (e.g. see Demri, Orłowska [1]).

Proposition 3. *For any formal context $\langle G, M, I \rangle$ there is a general approxima-tion space $(U, \mathcal{C})$ such that $\simeq_M = \approx_{\mathcal{C}}$.*

Proof. Let $\langle G, M, I \rangle$ be a formal context. Choose the family $/M/ \subseteq \mathcal{P}(G)$, and note that for all $x, y \in G$ and for any $m \in M$, $x \in /M/ \Leftrightarrow (x, m) \in I$. Thus $(x, m) \in I \Leftrightarrow (y, m) \in I$ iff $x \in /m/ \Leftrightarrow y \in /m/$ for all $m \in M$ and consequently $\simeq_M = \approx_{/M/}$. Therefore $(G, /M/)$ is a general approximation space such that $\simeq_M = \approx_{/M/}$.

Proposition 4. *For any general approximation space $(U, \mathcal{C})$ there is a formal context $\langle G, M, I \rangle$ such that $\approx_{\mathcal{C}} = \simeq_M$.*

Proof. Let $(U, \mathcal{C})$ be a general approximation space. It is enough to note that $\langle U, \mathcal{C}, \in \rangle$ is a formal context and, obviously, $\approx_{\mathcal{C}} = \simeq_{\mathcal{C}}$.

Proposition 5. *For any information system $\langle OB, AT, \{V_a : a \in AT\}, f \rangle$ there is a general approximation space $(U, \mathcal{C})$ such that $ind(AT) = \approx_{\mathcal{C}}$.*

Proof. Let $\langle OB, AT, \{V_a : a \in AT\}, f \rangle$ be an information system. For all $a \in AT$ and $v \in V_a$ we define a family $C_a^v := \{x \in OB : f(x, a) = v\}$. Let a family $\mathcal{C}_{AT}$ be defined as follows: $\mathcal{C}_{AT} := \{C_a^v : a \in AT, v \in V_a\}$. Thus $(OB, \mathcal{C}_{AT})$ is a general approximation space. Assume that $(x, y) \in ind(AT)$. The following steps are equivalent:

$$a(x) = a(y), \ \forall a \in AT$$
$$x \in a^{-1}(v) \Leftrightarrow y \in a^{-1}(v), \ \forall v \in V_a \forall a \in AT$$
$$x \in C \Leftrightarrow y \in C, \ \forall C \in \mathcal{C}_{AT}$$
$$(x, y) \in \approx_{\mathcal{C}_{AT}}.$$

Thus $(OB, \mathcal{C}_{AT})$ is a general approximation space such that $ind(AT) = \approx_{\mathcal{C}_{AT}}$.

Proposition 6. *For any general approximation space $(U, \mathcal{C})$ there is an infor-mation system $\langle OB, AT, \{V_a : a \in AT\}, f \rangle$ such that $\approx_{\mathcal{C}} = ind(AT)$.*

Proof. Let $(U, \mathcal{C})$ be a general approximation space. Consider an information system $\langle U, \mathcal{C}, \{V_C : C \in \mathcal{C}\}, f \rangle$, where $V_C = \{0, 1\}$ for each $C \in \mathcal{C}$ and a function f assigns each pair (a, C) the value of the characteristic function χ_C for the object a. Assume that $(x, y) \in \approx_{\mathcal{C}}$. The following steps are equivalent:

$$x \in C \Leftrightarrow y \in C, \ \forall C \in \mathcal{C}$$
$$\chi_C(x) = \chi_C(y), \ \forall C \in \mathcal{C}$$
$$f(x, C) = f(x, C), \ \forall C \in \mathcal{C}$$
$$(x, y) \in ind(AT).$$

Thus $\langle U, \mathcal{C}, \{V_C : C \in \mathcal{C}\}, f \rangle$ is an information system such that $\approx_{\mathcal{C}} = ind(AT)$.

5   Concept Lattices and Approximation Spaces

In this section we show that extents of formal concepts of any concept lattice are definable sets in some approximation space.

Definition 3. *Let U be any set, $\mathcal{C} \subseteq \mathcal{P}(U)$. We define the following operator $D_\mathcal{C} : \mathcal{P}(U) \longrightarrow \mathcal{P}(U)$ on the set U:*

$$D_\mathcal{C}(A) := \bigcap \{C \in \mathcal{C} : A \subseteq C\}.$$

Proposition 7. *Let U be any set, $\mathcal{C} \subseteq \mathcal{P}(U)$, then the operator $D_\mathcal{C}$ is closure operator on the set U, such that closed subsets of $D_\mathcal{C}$ are exactly definable sets in the general approximation space $(U, \mathcal{C})$.*

Proof. $A \subseteq D_\mathcal{C}(A)$ follows directly from definition. Observe that for all $C \in \mathcal{C}$, $\{C \in \mathcal{C} : D_\mathcal{C}(A) \subseteq C\} = \{C \in \mathcal{C} : A \subseteq C\}$ and so $\bigcap \{C \in \mathcal{C} : D_\mathcal{C}(A) \subseteq C\} = \bigcap \{C \in \mathcal{C} : A \subseteq C\}$. Thus $D_\mathcal{C}(D_\mathcal{C}(A)) = D_\mathcal{C}(A)$. If $A \subseteq B$, then $\{C \in \mathcal{C} : B \subseteq C\} \subseteq \{C \in \mathcal{C} : A \subseteq C\}$, and so $\bigcap \{C \in \mathcal{C} : A \subseteq C\} \subseteq \bigcap \{C \in \mathcal{C} : B \subseteq C\}$. Therefore $D_\mathcal{C}(A) \subseteq D_\mathcal{C}(B)$. Let $X = D_\mathcal{C}(X)$. Since $D_\mathcal{C}(X) = \bigcap \{C \in \mathcal{C} : X \subseteq C\} \in Sg^c(\mathcal{C})$, then the closed subset X is definable in the general approximation space $(U, \mathcal{C})$. Let $Y \in Sg^c(\mathcal{C})$, then $Y \in \{C \in \mathcal{C} : Y \subseteq C\}$. Therefore $D_\mathcal{C}(Y) \subseteq Y$ and $Y = D_\mathcal{C}(Y)$ Because set $A, B, X, Y \subseteq U$ where chosen arbitrarily, then $D_\mathcal{C}$ is a closure operator on the set U such that its closed subsets are exactly definable sets in the general approximation space $(U, \mathcal{C})$.

Lemma 1. *Let $\langle G, M, I \rangle$ be a context, $A \subseteq G$, $\Gamma \subseteq M$ and $\psi \in M$, then:*

(1) $\Gamma^e = \bigcap /\Gamma/$,
(2) $A^i = \{m \in M : A \subseteq /m/\}$,
(3) $D_{/M/}(A) = \bigcap \{/m/ \in /M/ : A \subseteq /m/\} = \{m \in M : A \subseteq /m/\}^e = A^{ie}$.

Theorem 4. *The extents of the formal concepts of the any formal context are definable sets in some approximation space and general approximation space.*

Proof. Let $\langle G, M, I \rangle$ be a formal context. Observe that $(G, /M/)$ is a general approximation space. Choose $(A, B) \in \underline{\mathcal{B}}(G, M, I)$, thus $A = B^e$ and from lemma 1.1 we get $A = B^e = \bigcap /B/$, where $/B/ \subseteq /M/$. Thus $A = D_{/M/}(A)$. It follows from the proposition 7 that A is a definable set in the general approximation space $(G, /M/)$. Note that $A = /M/(A)$. We have shown, proving Proposition 5, that $\simeq_M = \approx_{/M/}$. Thus from theorem 5 we get $\simeq_M(A)$. Therefore A is a definable set in the approximation space $(G, \simeq_M)$. Since the concept $(A, B) \in \underline{\mathcal{B}}(G, M, I)$ was chosen arbitrarily, then an extent of the each concept of formal context $\langle G, M, I \rangle$ is a definable set in the approximation space $(G, \simeq_M)$ and in the general approximation space $(G, /M/)$.

Definition 4. *A formal context $\langle G, M, I \rangle$ is:*

complemented[2] iff for any $m \in M$ there is $m_0 \in M$ such that $/m_0/ = /m/'$,
closed under intersections iff for any $\Gamma \subseteq M$ there is $m_0 \in M$ such that $\bigcap /\Gamma/ = /m_0/$,
closed under unions iff for any $\Gamma \subseteq M$ there is $m_0 \in M$ such that $\bigcup /\Gamma/ = /m_0/$,
Boolean iff $\langle G, M, I \rangle$ is complemented, closed under unions and intersections.

---

[2] Complemented contexts usually are called dichotomic contexts.

Lemma 2. *For a context $\langle G, M, I \rangle$ the following conditions are equivalent:*

(1) $\langle G, M, I \rangle$ *is Boolean.*
(2) $\langle G, M, I \rangle$ *is complemented and closed under intersections.*
(3) $\langle G, M, I \rangle$ *is complemented and closed under unions.*

Theorem 5. *For any Boolean context $\langle G, M, I \rangle$ the following conditions hold:*

(1) $Sg^c(/M/) = /M/$.
(2) $Sg^c(/M/) = \underline{\mathcal{B}}_M(G, I)$.
(3) *The concept lattice $\underline{\mathcal{B}}(G, M, I)$ is isomorphic to $Com_{/M/}(U)$ - algebra of definable sets in the general approximation space $(U, /M/)$.*

Proof. Let $\langle G, M, I \rangle$ be a Boolean context, i.e. $\langle G, M, I \rangle$ is complemented, closed under unions and intersections.

(1) Assume that $A \in Sg^c(/M/)$, then, by the proposition 7, $A = D_{/M/}(A)$. Thus from lemma 1.3 we have $A = D_{/M/}(A) = \{m \in M : A \subseteq /m/\}^e = \bigcap\{/m/ \in M : A \subseteq /m/\}$. Note that $\{m \in M : A \subseteq /m/\} \subseteq M$ and $/\{m \in M : A \subseteq /m/\}/ = \{/m/ \in M : A \subseteq /m/\}$. Since the context $\langle G, M, I \rangle$ is closed under intersections, then there is $m_0 \in M$ such that $\bigcap\{/m/ \in M : A \subseteq /m/\} = /m_0/$. Thus $A = /m_0/$ and $A \in /M/$. Therefore $A \in /M/$, and $Sg^c(/M/) \subseteq /M/$. Reverse inclusion is obvious, then consequently $Sg^c(/M/) = /M/$.

(2) Let $A \in Sg^c(/M/)$, then $A = D_{/M/}(A)$, by the proposition 7. Lemma 1.3 implies that $A = D_{/M/}(A) = \{m \in M : A \subseteq /m/\}^e$. Let $B := \{m \in M : A \subseteq /m/\}$, therefore $A = B^e$ and by lemma 1.2 $A^i = \{m \in M : A \subseteq /m/\} = B$. Thus $(A, B) \in \underline{\mathcal{B}}(G, M, I)$, now then $Sg^c(/M/) \subseteq \underline{\mathcal{B}}_M(G, I)$.

Assume that $A \in \underline{\mathcal{B}}_M(G, I)$, then there is $B \subseteq M$ such that $(A, B) \in \underline{\mathcal{B}}(G, M, I)$. Thus $A = B^e$ and by lemma 1.1 $A = \bigcap /B/$. Since $/B/ \subseteq /M/ \subseteq Sg^c(/M/)$, then $\bigcap /B/ \in Sg^c(/M/)$, now then $A \in Sg^c(/M/)$. Thus $\underline{\mathcal{B}}_M(G, I) \subseteq Sg^c(/M/)$. Therefore $Sg^c(/M/) = \underline{\mathcal{B}}_M(G, I)$.

(3) Remind that $Sg^c(/M/) = Com_{/M/}(U)$. Since $Sg^c(/M/) = \underline{\mathcal{B}}_M(G, I)$, then $\underline{\mathcal{B}}_M(G, I)$ is a complete algebra of sets and so $\underline{\mathcal{B}}_M(G, I)$ is a complete, atomic Boolean algebra. The concept lattice $\underline{\mathcal{B}}(G, M, I)$, as a lattice, is isomorphic to the extent lattice $\underline{\mathcal{B}}_M(G, I)$. Thus $\underline{\mathcal{B}}(G, M, I)$ is a distributive, complemented lattice with the complement operation induced from $\underline{\mathcal{B}}_M(G, I)$. Therefore the concept lattice is a complete, atomic Boolean algebra isomorphic to $Com_{/M/}(U)$ - algebra of definable sets in the general approximation space $(U, /M/)$.

Theorem 6. *Let a context $\langle G, M, I \rangle$ be closed under intersections and let the family of attribute M is finite. Then the following conditions are equivalent:*

(1) $\langle G, M, I \rangle$ *is a Boolean context.*
(2) $Sg^c(/M/) = \underline{\mathcal{B}}_M(G, I)$.
(3) *The concept lattice $\underline{\mathcal{B}}(G, M, I)$ is isomorphic to $Com_{/M/}(G)$ - algebra of definable sets in the general approximation space $(G, /M/)$.*

Proof. Let $\langle G, M, I \rangle$ be a formal context closed under intersection such that $|M| < \aleph_0$. The implication $(1) \Rightarrow (3)$ comes from theorem 5.3.

$(3) \Rightarrow (2)$ Assume that $\underline{\mathcal{B}}(G, M, I)$ is isomorphic to $Com_{/M/}(U)$ - algebra of definable sets in the general approximation space $(G, /M/)$. Thus the extent lattice $\underline{\mathcal{B}}_M(G, I)$ is isomorphic to $Com_{/M/}(U)$. Since $Com_{/M/}(U) = Sg^c(/M/)$, then there is a bijection $f : \underline{\mathcal{B}}_M(G, I) \longrightarrow Sg^c(/M/)$. Since $|M| < \aleph_0$, then $|\underline{\mathcal{B}}_M(G, I)| = |Sg^c(/M/)| < \aleph_0$. Therefore $Sg^c(/M/) \subseteq \underline{\mathcal{B}}_M(G, I)$. If not, then should be $B \in Sg^c(/M/)$ such that $B \notin \underline{\mathcal{B}}_M(G, I)$, and so $|\underline{\mathcal{B}}_M(G, I)| \neq |Sg^c(/M/)|$. It was shown in the proof of the theorem 4 that $\underline{\mathcal{B}}_M(G, I) \subseteq Com_{/M/}(U)$, thus $\underline{\mathcal{B}}_M(G, I) \subseteq Sg^c(/M/)$. Therefore $Sg^c(/M/) = \underline{\mathcal{B}}_M(G, I)$.

$(2) \Rightarrow (1)$ $\underline{\mathcal{B}}_M(G, I) = Sg^c(/M/)$. Let $m \in M$, then $/m/ \in Sg^c(/M/)$. Since $/m/' \in Sg^c(/M/)$, $/m/' \in \underline{\mathcal{B}}_M(G, I)$. Thus there is a family $\Gamma \subseteq M$ such that $/m/' = \bigcap /\Gamma/$. Because the context $\langle G, M, I \rangle$ is closed under intersection, then there is a property $m_0 \in M$ such that $/m_0/ = \bigcap /\Gamma/ = /M/'$, so $/m_0/ = /m/'$. Since $m \in M$ was chosen arbitrarily, then the context $\langle G, M, I \rangle$ is complemented. Because $\langle G, M, I \rangle$ is closed under intersections, then from lemma 2 we obtain that the context $\langle G, M, I \rangle$ is Boolean.

The question of necessary conditions for the extents of formal concepts of a context $\langle G, M, I \rangle$ to be exactly the definable sets in some approximation space (U, R) is still open.

References

1. Demri, S., Orłowska, E.: Incomplete Information: Structure, Inference, Complexity. Springer 2002.
2. Düntsch, I., Gediga, G., Orłowska, E.: Relational attribute systems. International Journal of Human-Computer Studies. **55** (2001) 293–309
3. Ganter, B., Wille, R.: Formal Concept Analysis: Mathematical Foundation. Springer 1999.
4. Pawlak, Z.: Rough sets. International Journal of Computing and Information Sciences. **18** (1982) 341–356
5. Pawlak, Z.: Rough sets. Theoretical Aspects of Reasoning About Data. Kluwer Academic Publisher 1991
6. Wasilewski, P.: On Selected Similarity Relations and their Applications into Cognitive Science. Ph.D. thesis, Jagiellonian University, Cracow, Poland 2004 (*in polish*)
7. Wille, R.: Restructuring lattice theory. In Rival, I., editor, Ordered Sets. Reidel, Dodrecht. (1982) 445–470

Rough Sets over the Boolean Algebras

Gui-Long Liu

School of Information Sciences,
Beijing Language and Culture University, Beijing, 100083, P.R. China
liuguilong@blcu.edu.cn

Abstract. This paper studies some matrix properties of rough sets over an arbitrary Boolean algebra, and their comparison with the corresponding ones of Pawlak's rough sets, a tool for data mining. The matrix representation of the lower and upper approximation operators of rough sets is given. Matrix approach provides an explicit formula for computing lower and upper approximations. The lower and upper approximation operators of column vector over an arbitrary Boolean algebra are defined. Finally, a set of axioms is constructed to characterize the upper approximation operator of column vector.

1 Introduction

The rough set theory, proposed by Zdzislaw Pawlak [1,2] in early eighties, is an extension of the classical set theory. The main purpose of this theory is the automated transformation of data into knowledge. It has a wide range of uses, such as machine learning, pattern recognition, and data mining. Rough set is especially helpful in dealing with vagueness and uncertainty in decision situations. It has emerged as another major mathematical tool for modelling the vagueness present in human classification mechanism.

Since rough set theory was proposed, many proposals have been made for generalizing and interpreting rough sets [3,4,5]. Extensive studies have been carried out to compare the rough set theory and its generalization.

This paper studies some matrix properties of rough sets over an arbitrary Boolean algebra. we propose a matrix view of the theory of rough sets. Under such a view, lower and upper approximations of rough set and generalized rough set are related to the matrix operator. We can easily to give an explicit formula for computing lower and upper approximations according to this matrix view.

The paper is organized as follows. In section 2, we provide some definitions of rough sets. In section 3, we give the matrix characterization of the lower and upper approximation operators of rough set. In section 4, we define the lower and upper approximation operators of a column vector over an arbitrary Boolean algebra, and extend the results of section 3 to the case of an arbitrary Boolean algebra. In section 5, a set of axioms is constructed to characterize the upper approximation operator of column vector.

D. Ślęzak et al. (Eds.): RSFDGrC 2005, LNAI 3641, pp. 124–131, 2005.

2   Preliminaries

In this section we recall some basic definitions of set approximations as well as some generalizations of these definitions for similarity (tolerance) relations.

Let U be a nonempty finite set of objects called the universe. Let R be an equivalence relation on U. We use U/R to denote the family of all equivalence classes of R (or classifications of U), and we use $[x]$ to denote an equivalence class in R containing an element $x \in U$. The pair (U, R) is called an approximation space. For any $X \subseteq U$ one can define the lower approximation and the upper approximation of X [1] by

$$\underline{R}X = \{x \in U | [x] \subseteq X\}, \text{ and } \overline{R}X = \{x \in U | [x] \cap X \neq \emptyset\}.$$

respectively. The pair $(\underline{R}X, \overline{R}X)$ is referred to as the rough set of X. The rough set $(\underline{R}X, \overline{R}X)$ denote the description of X under the present knowledge, i.e., the classification of U.

Several authors [5,10] point out a necessity to introduce a more general approach by considering a similarity (i.e. reflexive and symmetric) relation (or even arbitrary binary relation) $R \subseteq U \times U$ in the set U of objects instead of equivalence relation. By taking a similarity class $R(x) = \{y \in U | xRy\}$ instead of the equivalence class one can obtain a generalization of the definitions of the lower approximation and the upper approximation of X by $\underline{R}X = \{x \in U | R(x) \subseteq X\}$ and $\overline{R}X = \{x \in U | R(x) \cap X \neq \emptyset\}$ [3], respectively.

3   Matrices Representations of Rough Sets

In this section we will give the matrix representations of the lower approximation and upper approximation.

When U is a finite universe set, say $U = \{u_1, u_2, \ldots, u_n\}$, and X is a subset of U. Then the characteristic function of X is assigns 1 to an element that belong to X and 0 to an element that does not belong to X. Thus subset X can be represented by an n- tuple $X = (x_1, x_2, \ldots, x_n)^T$ (i.e., X is a column Boolean vector), where T denote the transpose operation and

$$x_i = \begin{cases} 1, u_i \in X \\ 0, u_i \notin X \end{cases}$$

We do not distinguish the subset X of U and its corresponding column Boolean vector $X = (x_1, x_2, \ldots, x_n)^T$. For example, if $U = \{u_1, u_2, u_3\}, X = \{u_1, u_3\}$, then we write $X = (1, 0, 1)^T$. Let R be an arbitrary binary relation on U, and let $M_R = (a_{ij})$ be the corresponding $n \times n$ matrix representing R. That is.

$$a_{ij} = \begin{cases} 1, u_i R u_j \\ 0, u_i \overline{R} u_j \end{cases}$$

For any $X \subseteq U$ the lower approximation and the upper approximation of X can be computed from M_R and X. That is, the lower and upper approximation operators of rough sets can be redefined using the matrix representation.

Theorem 1. *Let $U = \{u_1, u_2, \ldots, u_n\}$ be the universe set, R an arbitrary binary relation on U, M_R the $n \times n$ matrix representing R, and X a subset of U, then*

(a) $\overline{R}X = M_R X$, where $M_R X$ is the Boolean product of $n \times n$ (Boolean) matrix M_R and column Boolean vector X.

(b) $\underline{R}X = -(M_R(-X))$, where $-X$ denote the complementary set of X.

Proof. Note that the characteristic function of X is still denoted by X. $\wedge, \vee$ denote minimum and maximum operations, respectively. Let $M_R = (a_{ij})$.

(a) If $u_i \in \overline{R}X$, then $R(u_i) \cap X \neq \emptyset$, and at least a $u_j \in R(u_i), u_j \in X$, that is to say $u_i R u_j$ and $u_j \in X$. Thus $a_{ij} = 1, X(u_j) = 1$, and

$$(M_R X(u_i)) = \vee_{k=1}^n (a_{ik} \wedge X(u_k)) = a_{ij} \wedge X(u_j) = 1$$

Hence $\overline{R}X \subseteq M_R X$. Similarly $M_R X \subseteq \overline{R}X$ and $M_R X = \overline{R}X$.

(b) Since

$$x \in \underline{R}(-X) \Leftrightarrow R(x) \subseteq -X \Leftrightarrow R(X) \cap X \neq \emptyset \Leftrightarrow x \notin \overline{R}X \Leftrightarrow x \in -\overline{R}X.$$

Therefore, $\underline{R}X = -(\overline{R}(-X)) = -(M_R(-X))$.

Example 1. Consider a universe $U = \{u_1, u_2, u_3\}$. Let R be a binary relation on U:

$$R = \{(u_1, u_1), (u_1, u_3), (u_2, u_1), (u_3, u_2), (u_3, u_3)\}$$

Suppose $X = \{u_1, u_3\} = (1, 0, 1)^T$, then $M_R = \begin{pmatrix} 1 & 0 & 1 \\ 1 & 0 & 0 \\ 0 & 1 & 1 \end{pmatrix}$,

$$\overline{R}X = M_R X = \begin{pmatrix} 1 & 0 & 1 \\ 1 & 0 & 0 \\ 0 & 1 & 1 \end{pmatrix} \begin{pmatrix} 1 \\ 0 \\ 1 \end{pmatrix} = \begin{pmatrix} 1 \\ 1 \\ 1 \end{pmatrix} = U,$$

and

$$\underline{R}X = -M_R(-X) = -\begin{pmatrix} 1 & 0 & 1 \\ 1 & 0 & 0 \\ 0 & 1 & 1 \end{pmatrix} \begin{pmatrix} 0 \\ 1 \\ 0 \end{pmatrix} = -\begin{pmatrix} 0 \\ 0 \\ 1 \end{pmatrix} = \begin{pmatrix} 1 \\ 1 \\ 0 \end{pmatrix} = \{u_1, u_2\}.$$

Immediately from Theorem 1, we can derive the following conclusion:

Proposition 1. *Let $U = \{u_1, u_2, \ldots, u_n\}$ be the universe set, R an arbitrary binary relation on U, and X a subset of U, then for all $X \subseteq U$*

(a)$X \subseteq \overline{R}X$ if and only if R is a reflexive.

(b)$\overline{R}(\overline{R}X) \subseteq \overline{R}X$ if and only if R is a transitive.

Proof. (a) For singleton subset $X = \{u_i\}$ of U, we have $X \subseteq \overline{R}X$. Using theorem 1, it follows $\{u_i\} \subseteq \overline{R}\{u_i\}$, that is, $1 = \vee_{j=1}^n (a_{ij} \wedge X(u_j)) = a_{ii} \wedge 1 = a_{ii}$, Thus, R is a reflexive.

Conversely, if R is a reflexive and $u_i \in X$, then $(\overline{R}X)(u_i) = \vee_{j=1}^n (a_{ij} \wedge X(u_j)) \geq a_{ii} \wedge X(u_i) = 1$, namely, $u_i \in \overline{R}X$, that is $X \subseteq \overline{R}X$.

(b) $\overline{R}(\overline{R}X) \subseteq \overline{R}X$, using theorem 1, if and only if $(M_R)^2 X \subseteq M_R X$ for all subset $X \subseteq U$. We know that $(M_R)^2 X \subseteq M_R X$ if and only if $(M_R)^2 \subseteq M_R$, namely, $R^2 \subseteq R$. Thus $\overline{R}(\overline{R}X) \subseteq \overline{R}X$ if and only if R is a transitive.

4   Approximation Operators in Boolean Algebras

Yao [4] has proposed generalized notion of approximation operators in the finite Boolean algebras. The Boolean matrix is the special case of matrix over a Boolean algebra. In this section, using the matrix approaches, we will give the another generalized approximation operators in Boolean algebras.

Let $(L, \wedge, \vee, -, 0, 1)$ be a Boolean algebra, and let $L^{n \times n}$ be the set of all $n \times n$ matrices over L. Suppose that $A = (a_{ij})$ and $B = (b_{ij})$ are two $n \times n$ matrices over L, we define $A \vee B = (a_{ij} \vee b_{ij})$, $AB = (\vee_{k=1}^{n} a_{ik} \wedge b_{kj})$, $-A = (-a_{ij})$, and $A^k = A^{k-1}A, (k = 1, 2, \ldots)$. Similarly, we can define the product MX of a $n \times n$ matrix $M = (a_{ij})$ over L and a n-column vector $X = (x_1, x_2, \ldots, x_n)^T$ over L, where T denote the transpose.

Let L^n be the set of all n-column vector over L. Scalar multiplication in L^n is defined as follows: $c(x_1, x_2, \ldots, x_n)^T = (c \wedge x_1, c \wedge x_2, \ldots, c \wedge x_n)$ for all $c \in L$ and $(x_1, x_2, \ldots, x_n)^T \in L^n$. If we denote the n unit column vectors $e_1 = (1, 0, \ldots, 0)^T, e_2 = (0, 1, \ldots, 0)^T, \ldots, e_n = (0, 0, \ldots, 1)^T$, then any n-column vector of L^n is a linear combination of these, because $(x_1, x_2, \ldots, x_n)^T = x_1 e_1 \vee x_2 e_2 \vee \ldots \vee x_n e_n$. Suppose $X = (x_1, x_2, \ldots, x_n)^T, Y = (y_1, y_2, \ldots, y_n)^T \in L^n$, if we define $X \leq Y$ if and only if $x_i \leq y_i$ for all $1 \leq i, j \leq n$, then $(L^n, \leq)$ is a partially ordered set.

Definition 1. *Let $(L, \wedge, \vee, -, 0, 1)$ be a Boolean algebra, and $M = (a_{ij})$ a $n \times n$ matrix over L. M is said to be*

1. *reflexive, if $a_{ii} = 1$ for all $1 \leq i \leq n$;*
2. *symmetric, if $a_{ij} = a_{ji}$ for all $1 \leq i, j \leq n$;*
3. *transitive, if $A^2 \leq A$;*
4. *and equivalence matrix, if it is reflexive, symmetric, and transitive.*

Using the theorem 1, the approximation operators of a vector over an arbitrary Boolean algebras can be generalized as follows.

Definition 2. *Let $(L, \wedge, \vee, -, 0, 1)$ be a Boolean algebra, $M = (a_{ij})$ a $n \times n$ matrix over L, and $X = (x_1, x_2, \ldots, x_n)^T$ a n-column vector over L. The lower and upper approximations of the n-column vector X, denote by $\underline{M}X$ and $\overline{M}X$, respectively, are defined as*

$$\overline{M}X = MX, \text{ and } \underline{M}X = -M(-X)$$

Since $L = \{0, 1\}$ is a Boolean algebra. The n-Boolean column vector represents a subset of universe, the above definition coincides with the lower and upper approximation operators of Pawlak's rough set if $L = \{0, 1\}$.

Example 2. Consider Boolean algebra D_{30} of all positive integer divisors of 30 under the partial order of divisibility. The join and meet of a, b are their least common multiple and greatest common divisor, respectively. That is,

$$a \vee b = LCM(a, b), a \wedge b = GCD(a, b)$$

Let $M = \begin{pmatrix} 15\ 2\ 3 \\ 6\ \ 1\ 5 \\ 3\ 1\ 6 \end{pmatrix}$, then for vector $X = \begin{pmatrix} 2 \\ 3 \\ 5 \end{pmatrix}$,

$$\overline{M}X = \begin{pmatrix} 15\ 2\ 3 \\ 6\ \ 1\ 5 \\ 3\ \ 1\ 6 \end{pmatrix} \begin{pmatrix} 2 \\ 3 \\ 5 \end{pmatrix} = \begin{pmatrix} 1 \\ 10 \\ 1 \end{pmatrix}$$

and

$$\underline{M}X = - \begin{pmatrix} 15\ 2\ 3 \\ 6\ \ 1\ 5 \\ 3\ \ 1\ 6 \end{pmatrix} \begin{pmatrix} -2 \\ -3 \\ -5 \end{pmatrix} = - \begin{pmatrix} 15\ 2\ 3 \\ 6\ \ 1\ 5 \\ 3\ \ 1\ 6 \end{pmatrix} \begin{pmatrix} 15 \\ 10 \\ 6 \end{pmatrix} = - \begin{pmatrix} 30 \\ 3 \\ 6 \end{pmatrix} = \begin{pmatrix} 1 \\ 10 \\ 5 \end{pmatrix}$$

The lower and upper approximations satisfy the following properties:

Theorem 2. Let $(L, \wedge, \vee, -, 0, 1)$ be a Boolean algebra, and $M = (a_{ij})$ a $n \times n$ matrix over L. Then

(1) $X \leq \overline{M}X \Leftrightarrow \underline{M}X \leq X \Leftrightarrow M$ is a reflexive matrix;
(2) $\overline{M}(\overline{M}X) \leq \overline{M}X \Leftrightarrow \underline{M}X \leq \underline{M}(\underline{M}X) \Leftrightarrow M$ is a transitive matrix.

Proof. (1) if $X \leq \overline{M}X$, then for n-unit vectors $e_i \in L^n, 1 \leq i \leq n$, Using Definition 2, we have $e_i \leq \overline{M}e_i$, that is,

$$1 \leq \vee_{j=1}^n (a_{ij} \wedge e_j) = a_{ii} \wedge 1 = a_{ii}$$

Thus, $a_{ii} = 1$ and M is a reflexive.
Conversely, if M is a reflexive matrix and $X = (x_1, x_2, \ldots, x_n)^T$, then

$$\vee_{j=1}^n (a_{ij} \wedge x_j) \geq a_{ii} \wedge x_i = 1 \wedge x_i = x_i$$

namely, $X \leq \overline{M}X$. Similarly, $X \leq \overline{M}X \Leftrightarrow \underline{M}X \leq X$ can be proved by the duality of $\overline{M}$ and $\underline{M}$.

(2) Using Definition 2, $\overline{M}(\overline{M}X) \leq \overline{M}X$, if and only if $(M)^2 X \leq MX$ for all $X \in L^n$. We also know that $(M)^2 X \leq MX$ if and only if $(M)^2 \leq M$. Thus $\overline{M}(\overline{M}X) \leq \overline{M}X$ if and only if M is a transitive. By the duality of $\overline{M}$ and $\underline{M}$, it follows: $\overline{M}(\overline{M}X) \leq \overline{M}X$ if and only if $\underline{M}X \leq \underline{M}(\underline{M}X)$.

From definition 2 we list some results about rough set of the vector over L:

Theorem 3. Let $(L, \wedge, \vee, -, 0, 1)$ be a Boolean algebra, and $M = (a_{ij})$ a $n \times n$ equivalence matrix over L. Then for all n-column vectors X, Y over L,

(1) $\overline{M}(0, 0, \ldots, 0)^T = (0, 0, \ldots, 0)^T, \underline{M}(1, 1, \ldots, 1)^T = (1, 1, \ldots, 1)^T$;
(2) $\overline{M}(X \vee Y) = \overline{M}X \vee \overline{M}Y, \underline{M}(X \wedge Y) = \underline{M}X \wedge \underline{M}Y$;
(3) if $X \leq Y$, then $\overline{M}X \leq \overline{M}Y$ and $\underline{M}Y \leq \underline{M}X$;
(4) $\overline{M}(X \wedge Y) \leq \overline{M}X \wedge \overline{M}Y$ and $\underline{M}X \vee \underline{M}Y \leq \underline{M}(X \vee Y)$;
(5) $X \leq \overline{M}X, \underline{M}X \leq X$;
(6) $\overline{M}(\overline{M}X) = \overline{M}X; \underline{M}(\underline{M}X) = \underline{M}X$,
(7) $\overline{M}(aX \vee bY) = a\overline{M}X \vee b\overline{M}Y$ for all $a, b \in L$.

Proof. (1) Clearly, By Definition 2,

$$\overline{M}(0,0,\ldots,0)^T = M(0,0,\ldots,0)^T = (0,0,\ldots,0)^T$$

and

$$\underline{M}(1,1,\ldots,1)^T = -\overline{M}(-(1,1,\ldots,1)^T)$$
$$= -\overline{M}(0,0,\ldots,0)^T = -(0,0,\ldots,0)^T = (1,1,\ldots,1)^T$$

(2) By Definition 2,

$$\overline{M}(X \vee Y) = M(X \vee Y) = MX \vee MY = \overline{M}X \vee \overline{M}Y$$

and

$$\underline{M}(X \wedge Y) = -\overline{M}(-(X \wedge Y)) = -\overline{M}(-X \vee -Y)$$
$$= -(\overline{M}(-X) \vee \overline{M}(-Y)) = -M(-X) \wedge -M(-Y) = \underline{M}X \wedge \underline{M}Y$$

(3) If $X \leq Y$, then $MX \leq MY$. That is, $\overline{M}X \leq \overline{M}Y$. By duality, $\underline{M}X \leq \underline{M}Y$.

(4) From (3), $\overline{M}(X \wedge Y) \leq \overline{M}X$, and $\overline{M}(X \wedge Y) \leq \overline{M}Y$, hence, $\overline{M}(X \wedge Y) \leq \overline{M}X \wedge \overline{M}Y$. Similarly, $\underline{M}X \vee \underline{M}Y \leq \underline{M}(X \vee Y)$.

(5) By the reflexive property of matrix M, $X \leq \overline{M}X$. By the duality of $\overline{M}$ and $\underline{M}$, $\underline{M}X \leq X$.

(6) Since M is an equivalence matrix, we have $M^2 = M$, thus $\overline{M}(\overline{M}X) = M(MX) = M^2X = MX = \overline{M}X$, and $\underline{M}(\underline{M}X) = -\overline{M}\overline{M}(-X) = -\overline{M}(-X) = \underline{M}X$.

(7) By Definition 2, $\overline{M}(aX \vee bY) = M(aX \vee bY) = M(aX) \vee M(bY) = aMX \vee bMY = a\overline{M}X \vee b\overline{M}Y$ for all $a, b \in L$.

5   Rough Set Algebras

Pawlak's lower and upper approximation operators have been axiomized. Now, we want to know which are the characteristic properties for the upper approximation operator over a Boolean algebra. In this section, we take an axiomatic approach by starting explicitly properties on upper approximation operator. One of main objectives is to investigate the conditions on approximation operators, so that they characterize the rough set defined by a matrix over an arbitrary Boolean algebra.

Theorem 4. *Let L be a Boolean algebra. Suppose $s, S : L^n \to L^n$ is a pair of dual operators, i.e., for all n-column vector X over $L, s(X) = -S(-X)$. If S satisfies the following axiom:*

$$S(aX \vee bY) = aS(X) \vee bS(Y),$$

for all $X, Y \in L^n$ and $a, b \in L$, then there exists a matrix $M = (a_{ij})$ over L such that for all $X \in L^n, s(X) = \underline{M}X$ and $S(X) = \overline{M}X$.

Proof. Suppose operator S obey $S(aX \vee bY) = aS(X) \vee bS(Y)$. We can construct a matrix $M = (a_{ij})$ as follows:

$$a_{ij} = e_i^T S e_j, 1 \leq i, j \leq n,$$

then $S(e_j) = \begin{pmatrix} a_{1j} \\ a_{2j} \\ \vdots \\ a_{nj} \end{pmatrix}$, and for all $X = (x_1, x_2, \ldots, x_n)^T \in L^n$

$$MX = (a_{ij}) \begin{pmatrix} x_1 \\ x_2 \\ \vdots \\ x_n \end{pmatrix} = (a_{ij})(x_1 \wedge e_1 \vee x_2 \wedge e_2 \vee \ldots \vee x_n \wedge e_n)$$

$$= (a_{ij})(x_1 \wedge e_1) \vee (a_{ij})(x_2 \wedge e_2) \vee \ldots \vee (a_{ij})(x_n \wedge e_n)$$

$$= \begin{pmatrix} a_{11} \wedge x_1 \\ a_{21} \wedge x_2 \\ \vdots \\ a_{n1} \wedge x_n \end{pmatrix} \vee \begin{pmatrix} a_{12} \wedge x_1 \\ a_{22} \wedge x_2 \\ \vdots \\ a_{n2} \wedge x_n \end{pmatrix} \vee \ldots \vee \begin{pmatrix} a_{1n} \wedge x_1 \\ a_{2n} \wedge x_2 \\ \vdots \\ a_{nn} \wedge x_n \end{pmatrix}$$

$$= x_1 \begin{pmatrix} a_{11} \\ a_{21} \\ \vdots \\ a_{n1} \end{pmatrix} \vee x_2 \begin{pmatrix} a_{12} \\ a_{22} \\ \vdots \\ a_{n2} \end{pmatrix} \vee \ldots \vee x_n \begin{pmatrix} a_{1n} \\ a_{2n} \\ \vdots \\ a_{nn} \end{pmatrix}$$

$$= x_1 S(e_1) \vee x_2 S(e_2) \vee \ldots \vee x_n S(e_n)$$
$$= S(x_1 e_1 \vee x_2 e_2 \vee \ldots \vee x_n e_n) = SX.$$

From Theorem 2 and Theorem 4, we have

Theorem 5. *Let L be a Boolean algebra. Suppose $s, S : L^n \to L^n$ is a pair of dual operators, i.e., for all n-column vector X over L, $s(X) = -S(-X)$, S satisfies $S(aX \vee bY) = aS(X) \vee bS(Y)$, for all $X, Y \in L^n$. Then there exists*

(1) a reflexive matrix $M = (a_{ij})$ over L,
(2) a transitive matrix $M = (a_{ij})$ over L,

such that $sX = \underline{M}X$ and $SX = \overline{M}X$ for all $X \in L^n$, if and only if S satisfies

(1) $X \leq S(X)$;
(2) $S(SX) \leq SX$.

Proof. By Theorem 4, there exists a matrix M over L such that $S(X) = \overline{M}X = MX$ for all $X \in L^n$. Thus

(1) Matrix M is a reflexive if and only if $X \leq MX$, if and only if $X \leq S(X)$.
(2) Matrix M is a transitive if and only if $M^2 \leq M$, if and only if $S(S(X)) \leq S(X)$.

6   Conclusions

This paper presents a matrix view of the theory of rough sets. The traditional views interpret rough set theory as an extension of set theory with two additional unary operators and focus on the characterization of members of rough sets. Under matrix view, it is easy to extend the lower and upper approximations of a set to that of a vector over an arbitrary Boolean algebra. A set of axioms is constructed to characterize the upper approximation operator of column vector using matrix view.

Acknowledgements. The author expresses his sincere thanks to the anonymous referees for their careful reading, and for the helpful suggestions which greatly improved the exposition of the paper.

References

1. Pawlak, Z.: Rough sets, International Journal of Computer and Information Sciences **11** (1982) 341-356.
2. Pawlak, Z.: Rough sets-theoretical aspects of reasoning about data, Kluwer Academic Publishers, Boston, MA, 1991.
3. Yao, Y.Y.: Two views of the theory of rough sets in finite universes, International Journal of Approximation Reasoning, **15** (1996) 291-317.
4. Yao, Y.Y.: On generalizing pawlak approximation operators, Procedings of the First International Conference, RSCTC' 98, LNAI 1424, 1998, 298-307.
5. Yao, Y.Y.: Constructive and algebraic methods of the rough sets,Information Sciences, **109** (1998) 21-47.
6. Give'on, Y.: Lattice matrices, Information and Control,**7** (1964) 477-484.
7. Baets, B.D., Meyer, H.D.: On the existence and construction of T-transitive closure, Information Sciences **152** (2003) 167-179.
8. Jarvinen, J.: On the structure of rough approximations, Fundamenta Informaticae **53** (2002) 135-153.
9. Grassmann, W.K., Tremblay, J.P.: Logic and discrete mathematics, a computer science perspective, Prentice Hall, 1996.
10. Banerjee, M., Pal, S.K.: Roughness of a fuzzy set, Information Sciences **93** (1996) 235-246.

Algebraic Approach to Generalized Rough Sets

Michiro Kondo

School of Information Environment,
Tokyo Denki University, Inzai, 270-1382, Japan
kondo@sie.dendai.ac.jp

Abstract. In this paper, we introduce the notion of generalized algebraic lower (upper) approximation operator and give its characterization theorem. That is, for any atomic complete Boolean algebra $\mathcal{B}$ with the set $\mathcal{A}(\mathcal{B})$ of atoms, a map $L : \mathcal{B} \to \mathcal{B}$ is an algebraic lower approximation operator if and only if there exists a binary relation R on $\mathcal{A}(\mathcal{B})$ such that $L = R_-$, where R_- is the lower approximation defined by the binary relation R. This generalizes the results given by Yao.

1   Introduction

The connections between modal logics and rough sets have been considered by many authors [3,11,14,17]. They enable us to have a full understanding of the rough set theory from the view point of modal logic. More importantly, results from modal logic can be used to enrich the study of rough sets [3,17]. In this paper, we attempt to make a further contribution.

Based on the results from modal logic, we consider a generalized rough lower (upper) approximation operator and study its algebraic properties in the sense of Yao [15,16]. Specifically, we prove more general and fundamental properties of approximation spaces of generalized rough sets. They are in fact the generalizations of the results presented in [15,16] and others.

Many papers on rough sets deal with a finite universe of approximation spaces. For example, all theorems in [15] are based on the assumption of a finite universe. Consider the following theorem (one of the main theorems in [16]):

A map $L : \mathcal{P}(X) \to \mathcal{P}(X)$ satisfies the conditions
- (a) $LX = X$,
- (b) $L(A \cap B) = LA \cap LB$,

if and only if there exists a binary relation R on X such that $L = R_-$, where R_- is defined by $R_-(A) = \{x \in X \mid \forall y(xRy \to y \in A)\}$ for each subset $A \subseteq X$.

The theorem holds only for a finite universe X. In fact, there exists a counter example for the infinite case. Let X be the set of all real numbers with usual topology. We define a map $L : \mathcal{P}(X) \to \mathcal{P}(X)$ by: for $A \in \mathcal{P}(X)$,

LA is the interior of A, that is, the largest open set contained in A.

It is clear that

D. Ślęzak et al. (Eds.): RSFDGrC 2005, LNAI 3641, pp. 132–140, 2005.

(a) $LX = X$ and
(b) $L(A \cap B) = LA \cap LB$.

If the theorem above holds in this case, then there exists a binary relation R on X such that $L = R_-$. For each family $\{A_\lambda\}$ of subsets of X, it holds that

$$R_-\left(\bigcap A_\lambda\right) = \bigcap R_-(A_\lambda).$$

By taking

$$A_n = \left(-\frac{1}{n}, 1 + \frac{1}{n}\right) \quad (n \in N),$$

we have

$$\bigcap A_n = [0, 1],$$

and

$$L\left(\bigcap A_n\right) = (0, 1).$$

On the other hand, if $L = R_-$, since

$$R_-\left(\bigcap A_n\right) = \bigcap R_-(A_n) = \bigcap LA_n = \bigcap A_n,$$

we have

$$L\left(\bigcap A_n\right) = (0, 1) \neq [0, 1] = R_-\left(\bigcap A_n\right).$$

This is a contradiction. Thus, the theorem above does not hold for the infinite set X. As a consequence, the results following from this theorem in Yao's paper hold only for a finite X.

We extend the theorem to without any restriction on the cardinality of X and show the general results. It perhaps should be pointed out that although some of the results are known to researchers in modal logics, they are not so well known to researchers in rough sets. A further exploration of such results may serve the purpose of bringing more insights into rough sets.

2   Preliminaries

Let X be a non-empty set and R a binary relation on X. A structure (X, R) is called an approximation space [12]. We define a map $R_- : P(X) \to P(X)$ based on R as follows: for $A \in P(X)$,

$$R_-(A) = \{x \in X \mid \forall y \, (xRy \to y \in A)\}.$$

From definition the following holds. (cf. [5,12,13])

Proposition 1.
(1) $A \subseteq B \implies R_-(A) \subseteq R_-(B)$
(2) $R_-\left(\bigcap_\lambda A_\lambda\right) = \bigcap_\lambda R_-(A_\lambda)$
(3) $\bigcup_\lambda R_-(A_\lambda) \subseteq R_-\left(\bigcup_\lambda A_\lambda\right)$

A map $L : \mathcal{P}(X) \to \mathcal{P}(X)$ satisfying

(a) $LX = X$
(b) $L(\bigcap A_\lambda) = \bigcap LA_\lambda$ $(\forall A_\lambda \in \mathcal{P}(X))$

is called a *lower approximation operator* and a map $H : \mathcal{P}(X) \to \mathcal{P}(X)$ defined by: for $A \in \mathcal{P}(X)$,

$$HA = (L(A^c))^c,$$

is called a *upper approximation operator*. The two operators L and H are dual to each other. We only need to treat the operator L. In case of X being finite, the map L defined here is identical to the map L defined by Yao [15,16].

Lemma 1. *For each $A \in \mathcal{P}(X)$,*

$$A = \bigcap \{\{y\}^c \mid y \notin A\}.$$

Proof. Suppose that $a \in \bigcap\{\{y\}^c \mid y \notin A\}$. For all $y \notin A$, we have

$$a \in \{y\}^c.$$

If $a \notin A$, then $a \in \{a\}^c$ by the assumption. But this is a contradiction. Thus $a \in A$, that is,

$$\bigcap\{\{y\}^c \mid y \notin A\} \subseteq A.$$

Conversely, since $A \subseteq \{y\}^c$ for all $y \notin A$, it is clear that

$$A \subseteq \bigcap\{\{y\}^c \mid y \notin A\}.$$

Thus we have

$$A = \bigcap\{\{y\}^c \mid y \notin A\}.$$

From this lemma, we can easily obtain the next result, which generalizes the theorem given by Yao [15,16].

Theorem 1. *For any map $L : \mathcal{P}(X) \to \mathcal{P}(X)$, L is a lower approximation operator if and only if there exists a binary relation R on X such that $L = R_-$.*

Proof. ($\Longleftarrow$) It is obvious.
($\Longrightarrow$) We define a relation R on X by

$$xRy \iff x \notin L(\{y\}^c).$$

From definition of R we can show that $LA = R_-(A)$ for any $A \subseteq X$. Indeed, if $x \notin R_-(A)$ then there exists y such that xRy but $y \notin A$. Since $y \in A^c$, we have $\{y\} \subseteq A^c$ and hence $A \subseteq \{y\}^c$. This implies that $LA \subseteq L(\{y\}^c)$. On the other hand xRy yields $x \notin L(\{y\}^c)$. Thus we have $x \notin LA$ and hence

$$LA \subseteq R_-(A).$$

Conversely, if $x \notin LA$, since $A = \bigcap\{\{y\}^c \mid y \notin A\}$ by the lemma above, then we have

$$x \notin LA = L\left(\bigcap\{\{y\}^c \mid y \notin A\}\right) = \bigcap\{L(\{y\}^c) \mid y \notin A\}.$$

Since there exists $y \notin A$ such that $x \notin L(\{y\}^c)$, it follows from definition of R that xRy and $y \notin A$. Thus $x \notin R_-(A)$, that is,

$$R_-(A) \subseteq LA.$$

Hence we have

$$LA = R_-(A) \quad (\forall A \subseteq X).$$

3   The General Case

By extending the results of last section, we can get algebraically general results. For any non-empty set X, the set $\mathcal{P}(X)$ of all subsets of X can be considered as a *complete Boolean algebra* under the usual operations $\cup, \cap$ and ^{c}. Moreover, by identifying an element $a \in X$ with the singleton set $\{a\} \in \mathcal{P}(X)$, the Boolean algebra $\mathcal{P}(X)$ is *atomic* with the set X of atoms. This enables us to give a general definition of lower (upper) approximation operator (cf. [7,8,10]).

Let $\mathcal{B}$ be an *atomic complete Boolean algebra* with the set $\mathcal{A}(\mathcal{B})$ of atoms and R a relation on $\mathcal{A}(\mathcal{B})$. For all element $a \in \mathcal{A}(\mathcal{B})$ and $x \in \mathcal{B}$, we define maps $r : \mathcal{A}(\mathcal{B}) \to \mathcal{B}$ and $R_- : \mathcal{B} \to \mathcal{B}$ by

$$r(a) = \bigvee\{b_\lambda \in \mathcal{A}(\mathcal{B}) \mid aRb_\lambda\}$$
$$R_-(x) = \bigvee\{a \in \mathcal{A}(\mathcal{B}) \mid r(a) \leq x\}.$$

If we take $\mathcal{B} = \mathcal{P}(X)$ and $\mathcal{A}(\mathcal{B}) = X$, then the definition of R_- coincides with the operator L in Yao's papers [15,16].

A map $L : \mathcal{B} \to \mathcal{B}$ satisfying the condition $(*)$

$$(*) \qquad L(\bigcap x_\lambda) = \bigcap Lx_\lambda \quad (\forall x_\lambda \in \mathcal{B})$$

is called an *algebraic lower approximation operator*. We note that if we take the index set Λ to be empty then we have $L1 = 1$. We can show the following results, which are generalization of Yao's ones.

> **Main Theorem.** A map $L : \mathcal{B} \to \mathcal{B}$ is an algebraic lower approximation operator if and only if there exists a relation R on $\mathcal{A}(\mathcal{B})$ such that $L = R_-$.

We prepare some lemmas to prove the theorem.

Lemma 2. *For all $a \in \mathcal{A}(\mathcal{B})$ and $x \in \mathcal{B}$, we have*

$$a \leq R_-(x) \iff r(a) \leq x.$$

Proof. Suppose that $a \le R_-(x) = \bigvee \{b_\lambda \in \mathcal{A}(\mathcal{B}) \mid r(b_\lambda) \le x\}$. Since

$$a = a \wedge \bigvee \{b_\lambda \in \mathcal{A}(\mathcal{B}) \mid r(b_\lambda) \le x\}$$
$$= \bigvee \{a \wedge b_\lambda \mid r(b_\lambda) \le x, a, b_\lambda \in \mathcal{A}(\mathcal{B})\},$$

it follows from $a \in \mathcal{A}(\mathcal{B})$ that there exists $b_\lambda \in \mathcal{A}(\mathcal{B})$ such that $a = a \wedge b_\lambda$ and $r(b_\lambda) \le x$. Thus we have $a = b_\lambda$ and $r(a) \le x$.

Conversely, assume that $r(a) \le x$. From definition of R_-, it follows that $a \le R_-(x)$ and hence

$$a \le R_-(x) \iff r(a) \le x.$$

Lemma 3. *For $a, b \in \mathcal{A}(\mathcal{B})$, we have*

$$b \le r(a) \iff aRb.$$

Proof. If $b \le r(a)$, since $r(a) = \bigvee \{b_\lambda \in \mathcal{A}(\mathcal{B}) \mid aRb_\lambda\}$, then we have

$$b = b \wedge r(a)$$
$$= b \wedge \bigvee \{b_\lambda \in \mathcal{A}(\mathcal{B}) \mid aRb_\lambda\}$$
$$= \bigvee \{b \wedge b_\lambda \mid aRb_\lambda, b, b_\lambda \in \mathcal{A}(\mathcal{B})\}.$$

There exists $b_\lambda \in \mathcal{A}(\mathcal{B})$ such that $b = b \wedge b_\lambda$ and aRb_λ. This means that $b = b_\lambda$ and aRb.

Conversely, if aRb and $b \in \mathcal{A}(\mathcal{B})$ then $b \le r(a)$. Thus,

$$b \le r(a) \iff aRb.$$

Lemma 4. *For all $x \in \mathcal{B}$,*

$$x = \bigwedge \{b_\lambda' \mid b_\lambda \not\le x\}.$$

Proof. If $b_\lambda \not\le x$, $(b_\lambda \in \mathcal{A}(\mathcal{B}))$, since $b_\lambda \wedge x' \ne 0$, then there is an atom $a \in \mathcal{A}(\mathcal{B})$ such that $a \le b_\lambda \wedge x'$. Then $a = b_\lambda$ and $a \le x'$. This implies that $b_\lambda \le x'$, that is, $x \le b_\lambda'$. Hence we have

$$x \le \bigwedge \{b_\lambda' \mid b_\lambda \not\le x\}.$$

Conversely, suppose that $a \le \bigwedge \{b_\lambda' \mid b_\lambda \not\le x\}$ for $a \in \mathcal{A}(\mathcal{B})$. In this case we have $a \le b_\lambda'$ for all $b_\lambda \not\le x$. If $a \not\le x$, then it follows from assumption that $a \le a'$ and hence $a = 0$. But this is a contradiction. Hence we get

$$a \le x,$$

that is, for all $a \in \mathcal{A}(\mathcal{B})$,

$$a \le \bigwedge \{b_\lambda' \mid b_\lambda \not\le x\} \implies a \le x.$$

Since $\mathcal{B}$ is atomic,

$$\bigwedge \{b'_\lambda \mid b_\lambda \not\leq x\} \leq x.$$

Therefore,

$$x = \bigwedge \{b'_\lambda \mid b_\lambda \not\leq x\}.$$

From these lemmas we can obtain additional results.

Theorem 2. *A map $L : \mathcal{B} \to \mathcal{B}$ is an algebraic lower approximation operator if and only if there exists a relation R on $\mathcal{A}(\mathcal{B})$ such that $L = R_-$.*

Proof. ($\Longleftarrow$) It is obvious.

($\Longrightarrow$) At first we shall show that $Lx \leq R_-(x)$. For all $a \in \mathcal{A}(\mathcal{B})$, assume that $a \not\leq R_-(x)$. Since $r(a) \not\leq x$ and hence $r(a) \wedge x' \neq 0$, there is an atom $b \in \mathcal{A}(\mathcal{B})$ such that $b \leq r(a) \wedge x'$. Since $b \leq x'$, we also have $x \leq b'$ and $Lx \leq Lb'$. On the other hand, since $b \leq r(a)$, it follows that aRb and $a \not\leq Lb'$ by definition of R. Thus

$$a \not\leq Lx.$$

That is, for all $a \in \mathcal{A}(\mathcal{B})$, $a \not\leq R_-(x)$ implies $a \not\leq Lx$. This yields

$$Lx \leq R_-(x).$$

Conversely, suppose that $a \not\leq Lx$ for all $a \in \mathcal{A}(\mathcal{B})$. Since $x = \bigwedge \{b'_\lambda \mid b_\lambda \not\leq x\}$, we get that

$$a \not\leq Lx = L \left(\bigwedge \{b'_\lambda \mid b_\lambda \not\leq x\} \right) = \bigwedge \{L(b'_\lambda) \mid b_\lambda \not\leq x\}.$$

Hence there are $b_\lambda \in \mathcal{A}(\mathcal{B})$ such that $a \not\leq L(b'_\lambda)$ and $b_\lambda \not\leq x$. It follows from definition of R that aRb_λ. Since $b_\lambda \leq r(a)$, there exists $b_\lambda \in \mathcal{A}(\mathcal{B})$ such that $b_\lambda \leq r(a)$ and $b_\lambda \not\leq x$. That is, $r(a) \not\leq x$. This implies $a \not\leq R_-(x)$. Thus for all $a \in \mathcal{A}(\mathcal{B})$, we have

$$a \not\leq Lx \implies a \not\leq R_-(x).$$

From $R_-(x) \leq Lx$ it follows $Lx = R_-(x)$.

For $\varphi : \mathcal{A}(\mathcal{B}) \to \mathcal{B}$, three kinds of maps are defined in [7,8]:

$$\varphi : \text{extensive} \iff x \leq \varphi(x)$$
$$\varphi : \text{symmetric} \iff x \leq \varphi(y) \text{ implies } y \leq \varphi(x)$$
$$\varphi : \text{closed} \iff y \leq \varphi(x) \text{ implies } \varphi(y) \leq \varphi(x)$$

Since x and y are atoms, we see that a symmetric map φ can be represented by

$$\varphi : \text{symmetric} \iff x \wedge \varphi(y) = 0 \text{ iff } y \wedge \varphi(x) = 0.$$

That is, φ is *self-conjugate* in the sense of [1]. Considering the relation between R and the properties of map φ corresponding to the *possibility operator* in modal logics, if we define R by

$$(x, y) \in R \iff y \leq \varphi(x),$$

then it can be proved that

$$\varphi : \text{extensive} \iff R : \text{reflexive}$$
$$\varphi : \text{symmetric} \iff R : \text{symmetric}$$
$$\varphi : \text{closed} \iff R : \text{transitive}$$

For example, in the case of φ being closed, suppose that φ is closed and xRy and yRz. Since $y \leq \varphi(x)$ and $z \leq \varphi(y)$, we have $\varphi(y) \leq \varphi(x)$ by closedness of φ and hence $z \leq \varphi(y) \leq \varphi(x)$. Thus we have $z \leq \varphi(x)$ and so xRz. This means that R is transitive. Conversely, assume that R is transitive and $y \leq \varphi(x)$, that is, xRy. For every $u \in \mathcal{A}(\mathcal{B})$ such that $u \leq \varphi(y)$, since yRu and xRy, it follows that xRu and $u \leq \varphi(x)$. Thus we have for every $u \in \mathcal{A}(\mathcal{B})$, if $u \leq \varphi(y)$ then $u \leq \varphi(x)$. This concludes that $\varphi(y) \leq \varphi(x)$, that is, φ is closed.

We note that we do not use the extra assumption of R at all in the proof of the theorem. This means that if we add the condition to the relation R then we can prove the corresponding theorem similarly. For example if we want a theorem in case of a reflexive relation R, then we add the *extensive* condition to the operator L. By considering the completeness theorem of modal logics, we have the following result ([4,9]).

Theorem 3. *A map $L : \mathcal{B} \to \mathcal{B}$ satisfying the conditions, respectively,*

(L-ext) L : extensive
(L-sym) L : symmetric
(L-clo) L : closed

is an algebraic lower approximation operator if and only if there exists a relation R on $\mathcal{A}(\mathcal{B})$ such that $L = R_-$ with the corresponding conditions

(ref) R is reflexive
(sym) R is symmetric
(trans) R is transitive

4   Other Properties

In this last section, we consider problems about the operator R_-:

(Q1) When is it *finitary* ?
(Q2) When does it preserve $\bigvee$?

In general an operator ξ on X is called *finitary* (cf. [1,2]) if

$$\xi(A) = \bigcup \{\xi(F) \mid F \text{ is a finite subset of } A\}.$$

As to (Q1), we give a definition of the relation R to be locally finite. Let X be a non-empty set. A relation R on X is called *locally finite* if $R(x) = \{y \in X \mid xRy\}$ is a finite subset of X for every $x \in X$. Then we have an answer to (Q1).

Theorem 4. R *is locally finite if and only if R_- is a finitary operator.*

Proof. Suppose that R is locally finite. Since R_- is order preserving, it is sufficient to show that

$$R_-(A) \subseteq \bigcup \{R_-(B) \mid B \text{ is a finite subset of } A\}.$$

Let $x \in R_-(A)$. If we take $B = R(x)$, then we have $x \in R_-(B)$ and B is the finite subset of A. This implies that $R_-(A) \subseteq \bigcup \{R_-(B) \mid B$ is a finite subset of $A\}$.

Conversely, we assume that R_- is finitary. Since $X = R_-(X)$, we have $x \in R_-(X)$ for any $x \in X$. There is a finite subset A_x of X such that $x \in R_-(A_x)$ and hence $R(x) \subseteq A_x$. Since A_x is finite, $R(x)$ is also finite for every $x \in X$. This means that R is locally finite.

It is easy to show that if R is reflexive and transitive then we have

$$R_-(\bigcup R_-(A_\lambda)) = \bigcup R_-(A_\lambda).$$

But in general, we do not have the property

$$(\alpha): \quad R_-(\bigcup A_\lambda) = \bigcup R_-(A_\lambda).$$

Therefore, it is important to study when the equality holds. This is the question (Q2). As to the problem we have

Theorem 5. (α) *holds if and only if $|R(x)| = 1$ for every $x \in X$, that is, R is a function.*

Proof. We assume that (α) holds. If xRy and xRz, since $x \in R_-(\{y, z\}) = R_-(y) \cup R_-(z)$, we have $x \in R_-(y)$ or $x \in R_-(z)$. If $x \in R_-(y)$, since xRz, then we have $z \in \{y\}$, that is, $z = y$. The other case is similar. Thus we have $y = z$. This implies that R is the function.

Conversely, we suppose that R is the function. In this case we have

$$R_-(\bigcup A_\lambda) \subseteq \bigcup R_-(A_\lambda).$$

Otherwise, there is an element $x \in R_-(\bigcup A_\lambda)$ but $x \notin \bigcup R_-(A_\lambda)$. Thus, for every $\lambda \in \Lambda$, there is an element y_λ such that

$$xRy_\lambda \text{ and } y_\lambda \notin A_\lambda.$$

By assumption, we can choose an element t which is independent of $\lambda \in \Lambda$ such that

$$xRt \text{ but } t \notin A_\lambda \text{ for every } \lambda \in \Lambda.$$

Hence, for the element t, we have xRt but $t \notin \bigcup A_\lambda$ and

$$x \notin R_-(\bigcup A_\lambda).$$

This is a contradiction. Thus, we can conclude that $R_-(\bigcup A_\lambda) \subseteq \bigcup R_-(A_\lambda)$. The converse inclusion is obvious, so we get that

$$(\alpha): \quad R_-(\bigcup A_\lambda) = \bigcup R_-(A_\lambda).$$

5 Conclusion

In this paper, we introduce the notion of generalized algebraic lower (upper) approximation operator and give its characterization theorem. It is shown that for any atomic complete Boolean algebra $\mathcal{B}$ with the set $\mathcal{A}(\mathcal{B})$ of atoms, a map $L : \mathcal{B} \to \mathcal{B}$ is an algebraic lower approximation operator if and only if there exists a binary relation R on $\mathcal{A}(\mathcal{B})$ such that $L = R_-$. Moreover we consider the relationships between modal logic and algebraic lower approximation operator with additional properties. Final, we give answers to the questions (1) when is the operator R_- finitary? and (2) when does it preserve *sup*?

The results presented in this paper would provide more insights into and a full understanding of approximation operators in rough set theory.

References

1. Birkhoff, G.: Lattice Theory. AMS, Providence Rhode Island (1995)
2. Davey, B.A., Priestly, H.A.: Introduction to Lattices and Order. Cambridge University Press (2002)
3. Gediga, G., Düntsch, I.: Modal-style operators in qualitative data analysis. In: Proceedings of the 2002 IEEE International Conference on Data Mining (2002) 155-162
4. Hughes, G.E., Cresswell, M.J.: A companion to modal logic. Methuen (1984)
5. Iwinski, T.B.: Algebraic approach to rough sets. Bull. Pol. Ac. Math., 35 (1987) 673-683
6. Jonsson, B., Tarski, A.: Boolean algebras with operators. Part I. American Jour. of Math., 73 (1951) 891-939
7. Jarvinen, J.: Knowledge representation and rough sets. TUCS Dissertations 14, Turku Center for Computer Science, Turku, Finland (1999)
8. Jarvinen, J.: On the structure of rough approximations. TUCS Technical report 447, Turku Center for Computer Science, Turku, Finland (2002)
9. Goldblatt, R.: Logics of time and computation. CSLI Lecture Notes 7 (1987)
10. Kondo, M.: On the structure of generalized rough sets. To appear in Information Sciences
11. Orlowska, E.: Rough set semantics for non-classical logics. In: W. Ziarko (Ed.), Rough Sets, Fuzzy Sets and Knowledge Discovery. Springer-Verlag (1994) 143-148
12. Pawlak, Z.: Rough sets. Int. J.Inform. Comp.Sci., 11 (1982) 341-356
13. Polkowski, L.: Rough Sets: Mathematical Foundations. Physica-Verlag, Springer (2002)
14. Vakarelov, D.: Modal logics for knowledge representation systems. Theoretical Computer Science, 90 (1991) 433-456
15. Yao, Y.Y.: Two views of the theory of rough sets in finite universes. Int. J. Approximate Reasoning, 15 (1996) 291-317
16. Yao, Y.Y.: Constructive and algebraic methods of the theory of rough sets. Information Sciences, 109 (1998) 21-47
17. Yao, Y.Y., Lin, T.Y.: Generalization of rough sets using modal logic. Intelligent Automation and Soft Computing, An International Journal, 2 (1996) 103-120

Logic for Rough Sets with Rough Double Stone Algebraic Semantics

Jian-Hua Dai

Institute of Artificial Intelligence,
Zhejiang University, Hangzhou 310012, P.R. China
jhdai@126.com

Abstract. Many researchers study rough sets from the point of view of description of the rough set pairs(a rough set pair is also called a rough set), i.e. <lower approximation set, upper approximation set>. An important result is that the collection of rough sets of an approximation space can be made into a regular double Stone algebra. In this paper, a logic for rough sets, i.e., the sequent calculus corresponding to rough double Stone algebra, is proposed. The syntax and semantics are defined. The soundless and completeness are proved.

1 Introduction

Rough set theory was introduced by Pawlak [12] to account for the definability of a concept with an approximation in an approximation space (U, R), where U is a set, and R is an equivalence relation on U. It captures and formalizes the basic phenomenon of information granulation. The finer the granulation is, the more concepts are definable in it. For those concepts not definable in an approximation space, their lower and upper approximations can be defined.

Lin and Liu [9] replaced equivalence relation with arbitrary binary relation, and the equivalence classes are replaced by neighborhood at the same time. By means of the two replacements, they defined more general approximation operators. Yao [16] interpreted Rough set theory as an extension of set theory with two additional unary set-theoretic operators referred to as approximation operators. Such an interpretation is consistent with interpreting modal logic as an extension of classical two-valued logic with two added unary operators. Based on atomic Boolean lattice, Jarvinen [8] proposed a more general framework for the study of approximation. Dai [3]introduced molecular lattices into the research on rough sets and constructed structure of rough approximations based on molecular lattices.

At the same time, researchers also study rough sets from the point of view of description of the rough set pairs, i.e. <lower approximation set, upper approximation set>. Iwiński [7] suggested a lattice theoretical approach. Iwiński's aim, which was extended by J. Pomykala and J. A. Pomykala [13] later, was to endow the rough seubsets of U with a natural algebraic structure. In [5], Gehrke and Walker extended J. Pomykala and J. A. Pomykala's work in [13] by proposing

D. Ślęzak et al. (Eds.): RSFDGrC 2005, LNAI 3641, pp. 141–148, 2005.

a precise structure theorem for the Stone algebra of rough sets which is in a setting more general than that in [13]. J. Pomykala and J. A. Pomykala's work was also improved by Comer [2] who noticed that the collection of rough sets of an approximation space is in fact a regular double Stone algebra when one introduced another unary operator, i.e. the dual pseudo-complement operator. In [10], Pagliani investigated rough set systems within the framework Nelson algebras under the assumption of a finite universe. Banerjee and Chakraborty [1] used pre-rough algebras adding some structure topological quasi-Boolean algebras. In [6], Iturrioz presented some strong relations between rough sets and 3-valued Lukasiewicz algebras.Under some conditions, rough sets of an approximation can be interpreted as 3-valued Post algebras. Pagliani also studied the relations between rough sets and 3-valued structures in [11] based on the assumption of finite universe. In fact, a regular double Stone algebra is a 3-valued Lukasiewicz algebra, a semi-simple Nelson algebra or a co-Heyting algebra. So, the work of Comer [2] are found to be quite significant in the studies of Rough set theory.

The algebras mentioned above all have rough sets as their models. They can be called rough algebras. The search for relationship between logic and algebra goes back to the inventions of Boole and his follows [14]. Those investigations yielded what we now call Boolean algebra. The close links between classical logic and the theory of Boolean algebras has been known for a long time. Consequently, a question naturally arose: what are the logics that correspond to rough algebras? Düntsch [4] presents a logic corresponding to regular double Stone algebras. The interconnections between the logic and regular double Stone algebras was discussed, but the logic itself including axioms, inference rules, soundness and completeness were not discussed. More important, the logic is Hilbert-type. Banerjee and Chakraborty [1] presented a logical system corresponding pre-rough algebra. The logic is Hilbert-type formulations with axioms and rules of inference. Sen and Chakraborty [15] proposed sequent calculi for topological quasi-Boolean algebras and pre-rough algebras.

In this paper, we intend to study the logical system for rough sets as double Stone algebraic semantics. Based on the work of Comer [2], the collection of all the rough sets for a given approximation space can be made into a regular double Stone algebra, called rough double Stone algebra in this paper. In the present work, a logic for rough sets, i.e., the sequent calculus corresponding to rough double Stone algebra, is proposed and studied. The language, axioms and rules are presented. The soundness and completeness of the logic are proved.

2   Definitions and Notations

Let (U, R) be an approximation space, where U is the universe and R is an equivalence relation on U. With each approximation space (U, R), two operators on $\mathcal{P}(U)$ can be defined. For any $X \subseteq U$, then the lower approximation of X and the upper approximation of X are defined as:

$$R_-(X) = \bigcup \{[X]_R | [X]_R \subseteq X\} \tag{1}$$

$$R^-(X) = \bigcup\{[X]_R | [X]_R \cap X \neq \emptyset\} \tag{2}$$

The pair $< R_-(X), R^-(X) >$ is called a rough set. X is termed definable set(also termed exact set) in approximation space (U, R) if and only if $R_-(X) = R^-(X)$. For the sake of simplicity, the lower approximation and upper approximation are also denoted as $\underline{X}$ and $\overline{X}$ respectively. In this paper, we denote the collection of all rough sets of an approximation (U, R) as $\mathcal{RS}(U)$.

Definition 1. *A structure* $(L, \vee, \wedge,^*,^+, 0, 1)$ *is a regular double Stone algebra if*

1. $(L, \vee, \wedge,^*,^+ 0, 1)$ *is a lattice with least element 0 and greatest element 1;*
2. $\forall x \in L$ *there is an element* x^*, *for any* $y \in L$ *satisfying*

$$x \wedge y = 0 \; iff \; y \leq x^*;$$

3. $\forall x \in L$ *there is an element* x, *for any* $y \in L$ *satisfying*

$$x \vee y = 1 \; iff \; x^+ \leq y;$$

4. $\forall x \in L, x^* \vee x^{**} = 1, x^+ \wedge x^{++} = 0;$
5. $x^* = y^*$ *and* $x^+ = y^+$ *imply* $x = y$.

The element x^* *is termed pseudo-complement of* x, x^+ *is termed dual pseudo-complement of* x. *The structure* L *satisfying the conditions 1-4 is called a double Stone algebra. It is called regular, if it additionally satisfies the condition 5. In fact,the condition 5 is equivalent to*

$$x \wedge x^+ \leq x \vee x^*.$$

It was shown by J. Pomykala and J. A. Pomykala [13] that the collection of all rough sets of (U, R), denoted as $\mathcal{RS}(U)$, can be made into a Stone algebra expressed as $(\mathcal{RS}(U), \oplus, \otimes,^*, < \emptyset, \emptyset >, < U, U >)$. The work of J. Pomykala and J. A. Pomykala was improved by Comer [2] who noticed that $\mathcal{RS}(U)$ is in fact a regular double Stone algebra expressed as:

$$(\mathcal{RS}(U), \oplus, \otimes,^*,^+, < \emptyset, \emptyset >, < U, U >),$$

where $< \emptyset, \emptyset >$ is the least element and $< U, U >$ is the greatest element. The union operator $\oplus$, join operator $\otimes$, pseudo-complement operator * and the dual pseudo-complement operator $^+$ are defined as following:

$$< \underline{X}, \overline{X} > \oplus < \underline{Y}, \overline{Y} > = < \underline{X} \cup \underline{Y}, \overline{X} \cup \overline{Y} > \tag{3}$$

$$< \underline{X}, \overline{X} > \otimes < \underline{Y}, \overline{Y} > = < \underline{X} \cap \underline{Y}, \overline{X} \cap \overline{Y} > \tag{4}$$

$$< \underline{X}, \overline{X} >^* = < U - \overline{X}, U - \overline{X} > = < (\overline{X})^c, (\overline{X})^c > \tag{5}$$

$$< \underline{X}, \overline{X} >^+ = < U - \underline{X}, U - \underline{X} > = < (\underline{X})^c, (\underline{X})^c > \tag{6}$$

Proposition 1. [2] *A rough double Stone algebra* $(\mathcal{RS}(U), \oplus, \otimes,^*,^+, < \emptyset, \emptyset >, < U, U >)$ *is a regular double Stone algebra. Conversely, each regular double Stone algebra is isomorphic to subalgebra of* $\mathcal{RS}(U)$ *for some approximation space* (U, R).

3   Logic with Rough Double Stone Algebraic Semantics

Motivated by the background described in the preceding section, we propose here a **L**ogic for **R**ough sets with **D**ouble **S**tone algebraic semantics, i.e., the sequent calculus corresponding to rough double Stone algebra. We denote this logic as **RDSL**.

Expressions of the language of the logic **RDSL** are built from the symbols of the following disjoint sets:

- VAR: prepositional variables $p, q, !`!`$
- Connectives: two binary connectives $\vee, \wedge$, which represent join and union; two unary connectives $\sim, \neg$, which represent pseudo-negation and dual pseudo-negation.
- Constants: $\top, \bot$ mean true and false.
- Brackets: (,)

The set WFF of all wffs of **RDSL** is defined by the familiar method.

The semantics of the logic is defined as follows:

Definition 2. *A rough double Stone algebra model or r2S model is a rough double Stone algebra equipped with a meaning function m based on $v : VAR \to \mathcal{P}(U)$, called the valuation function, for which for all $p \in VAR$,*

$$v(p) = < A, B > \in \mathcal{RS}(U) \tag{7}$$

The meaning function $m : WFF \to \mathcal{P}(U)$ extends the evaluation v to arbitrary wffs as follows:
a) $m(\bot) = < \emptyset, \emptyset >$
b) $m(\top) = < U, U >$
For each $p \in VAR$, we get
c) $m(p) = v(p)$
For $p, q \in WFF$, we have
d) $m(p \wedge q) = m(p) \otimes (q)$
e) $m(p \vee q) = m(p) \oplus (q)$
f) $m(\sim p) = m(p)^*$
g) $m(\neg p) = m(p)^+$

Definition 3. *By a sequent we mean an expression of the form $\Gamma \Rightarrow \Delta$, where Γ and Δ are multisets of formulas.*

Definition 4. *Let Γ is $p_1, p_2, \ldots\ldots, p_m$ and Δ is $q_1, q_2, \ldots\ldots, q_n$, then sequent $\Gamma \Rightarrow \Delta$ is said to be valid in a r2S model $\mathbf{M}$, denoted as $\models_M \Gamma \Rightarrow \Delta$, if and only if*

$$m(p_1) \otimes \ldots \otimes m(p_m) \leq m(q_1) \oplus \ldots \oplus m(q_n)$$

which can be written as $m(\Gamma) \leq m(\Delta)$. $\Gamma \Rightarrow \Delta$ is said to be valid, denoted as $\models \Gamma \Rightarrow \Delta$, if $\Gamma \Rightarrow \Delta$ is valid in every r2S model $\mathbf{M}$.

Lemma 1. *Let $p, q \in WFF, m(p) =< A, B >, m(q) =< C, D >$, then the sequent $p \Rightarrow q$ is valid if and only if $A \subseteq C$ and $B \subseteq D$.*

Now, we state the axioms and rules of **RDSL** in the following.

Axiom schemes:

(A1)$p \Rightarrow p$

(A2)$p \Rightarrow \sim\sim p$

(A3)$\sim p \Rightarrow \sim\sim\sim p$

(A4)$\neg\neg p \Rightarrow p$

(A5)$\neg\neg\neg p \Rightarrow \neg p$

We should notice that $\sim$ and $\neg$ are not standard negation connectives. They can be called pseudo-negation connective and dual pseudo-negation connective respectively.

Rules of inference:

$$(\text{Cut}) \frac{\Gamma \Rightarrow p, \Delta \quad \Gamma', p \Rightarrow \Delta'}{\Gamma, \Gamma' \Rightarrow \Delta, \Delta'}$$

$$(\text{Rule}\sim) \frac{\Gamma \Rightarrow \Delta}{\sim \Delta \Rightarrow \sim \Gamma}$$

$$(\text{Rule}\neg) \frac{\Gamma \Rightarrow \Delta}{\neg \Delta \Rightarrow \neg \Gamma}$$

$$(\text{LW}) \frac{\Gamma \Rightarrow \Delta}{\Gamma, p \Rightarrow \Delta}$$

$$(\text{RW}) \frac{\Gamma \Rightarrow \Delta}{\Gamma \Rightarrow p, \Delta}$$

$$(\text{LC}) \frac{\Gamma, p, p \Rightarrow \Delta}{\Gamma, p \Rightarrow \Delta}$$

$$(\text{RC}) \frac{\Gamma \Rightarrow p, p, \Delta}{\Gamma \Rightarrow p, \Delta}$$

$$(\text{L}\vee) \frac{\Gamma, p \Rightarrow \Delta \quad \Gamma', q \Rightarrow \Delta'}{\Gamma, \Gamma', p \vee q \Rightarrow \Delta, \Delta'}$$

$$(\text{R}\vee) \frac{\Gamma \Rightarrow p, q, \Delta}{\Gamma \Rightarrow p \vee q, \Delta}$$

$$(\text{L}\wedge) \frac{\Gamma, p, q \Rightarrow \Delta}{\Gamma, p \wedge q \Rightarrow \Delta}$$

$$(\text{R}\wedge) \frac{\Gamma \Rightarrow p, \Delta \quad \Gamma' \Rightarrow q, \Delta'}{\Gamma, \Gamma' \Rightarrow p \wedge q, \Delta, \Delta'}$$

$$(\text{L}\bot) \Gamma, \bot \Rightarrow \Delta$$

$$(\text{R}\top) \Gamma \Rightarrow \top, \Delta$$

$\sim \Gamma$ is $\sim p_1, \sim p_2, \cdot, p_m$ when Γ is $p_1, p_2, \cdot, p_m$. A similar convention is adopted for$\sim \Delta$. $\neg \Gamma$ is $\neg p_1, \neg p_2, \cdot, p_m$ when Γ is $p_1, p_2, \cdot, p_m$. A similar convention is adopted for $\neg \Delta$.

Remark 1. $\vdash_{RDSL} \Gamma \Rightarrow \Delta$ will denote that $\Gamma \Rightarrow \Delta$ is a theorem of **RDSL**. If there is no risk of confusion,$\vdash_{RDSL} \Gamma \Rightarrow \Delta$ is written as $\vdash \Gamma \Rightarrow \Delta$.

Theorem 1 (Soundness). *If $\vdash \Gamma \Rightarrow \Delta$ in **RDSL**, then $\Gamma \Rightarrow \Delta$ is valid in every r2S-model, i.e. $\models_M \Gamma \Rightarrow \Delta$.*

Proof. In order to prove the soundness of a logical system, it is necessary to prove validity of the axioms and that the rules preserve validity. Here, we just prove the validity of Axioms (A2),(A4) and that the rules (Cut),(Rule¬),(L∨) preserve validity. Other axioms and rules can be proved similarly.

(A2). Let $m(p) = < A, B >$, then we can get the following by definition of meaning function $m(\sim \sim p) = < A, B >^{**} = < B, B >$.For $A \subseteq B$, (A2) is straightforwardly obtained from Lemma 1.

(A4). Let $m(p) = < A, B >$, then we can get the following by definition of meaning function $m(\neg \neg p) = < A, B >^{++} = < A, A >$.For $A \subseteq B$, (A4) is also straightforwardly obtained from Lemma 1.

(Cut). Let $\Gamma \Rightarrow p, \Delta$ and $\Gamma', p \Rightarrow \Delta'$ be valid. The validity of $\Gamma \Rightarrow p, \Delta$ means $m(\Gamma) \leq m(\Delta) \oplus m(p)$. Let $m(p) = < A, B >, m(\Gamma) = < E, F >, m(\Delta) = < G, H >, m(\Gamma') = < I, J >, m(\Delta') = < P, Q >$, then we know $E \subseteq A \cup G$. It means

$$E \cap I \subseteq (I \cap A) \cup (G \cap I) \tag{8}$$

From the validity of $\Gamma' \Rightarrow \Delta'$, we can get

$$I \cap A \subseteq P \tag{9}$$

From (8) and (9), we get $E \cap I \subseteq G \cup P$. Similarly, we can prove $F \cap J \subseteq H \cup Q$. Consequently, $m(\Gamma) \otimes m(\Gamma') \leq m(\Delta) \oplus m(\Delta')$, which means $\Gamma, \Gamma' \Rightarrow \Delta, \Delta'$

(Rule¬). Let $\Gamma \Rightarrow \Delta$ be valid. The validity of $\Gamma \Rightarrow \Delta$ means $m(\Gamma) \leq m(\Delta)$. Let $m(\Gamma) = < E, F >, m(\Delta) = < G, H >$. By hypothesis, $E \subseteq G$. It is obvious that $G^c \subseteq E^c$. Consequently, $m(\neg \Delta) \leq m(\neg \Gamma)$, which means $\neg \Delta \Rightarrow \Gamma$.

(L∨). Let $\Gamma, p \Rightarrow \Delta$ and $\Gamma', q \Rightarrow \Delta'$ be valid. That mean $m(\Gamma) \otimes m(p) \leq m(\Delta)$ and $m(\Gamma') \otimes m(q) \leq m(\Delta')$. Let $m(p) = < A, B >, m(q) = < C, D >, m(\Gamma) = < E, F >, m(\Delta) = < G, H >, m(\Gamma') = < I, J >, m(\Delta') = < P, Q >$, then we know

$$A \cap E \subseteq G \tag{10}$$

$$I \cap C \subseteq P \tag{11}$$

From (10), we know $A \cap E \cap I \subseteq G \cap I$. From (11), we get $I \cap C \cap E \subseteq P \cap E$. Consequently,

$$(A \cap E \cap I) \cup (I \cap C \cap E) \subseteq (G \cap I) \cup (P \cap E) \subseteq G \cup P$$

Then we get

$$E \cap I \cap (A \cup C) \subseteq G \cup P \tag{12}$$

Similarly, we can get

$$F \cap J \cap (B \cup D) \subseteq H \cup Q \tag{13}$$

From (12),(13) we know $m(\Gamma) \otimes m(\Gamma') \otimes m(p \vee q) \leq m(\Delta) \oplus m(\Delta')$, which means $\Gamma, \Gamma', p \vee q \Rightarrow \Delta, \Delta'$.

By the validity of axioms and preserving validity of rules, mathematical induction is used on the depth of derivation of the sequent, then the soundness can be proved. $\square$

Theorem 2 (Completeness). *If $\Gamma \Rightarrow \Delta$ is valid in every r2S-model, i.e.,$\models_M$ $\Gamma \Rightarrow \Delta$, then $\vdash \Gamma \Rightarrow \Delta$ in **RDSL**.*

Proof. In order to prove completeness of a system, we first construct the corresponding Lindenbaum algebra. A relation $\approx$ is defined on the set WFF by the following:

$$p \approx q \text{ if and only if } \vdash p \Rightarrow q \text{ and } \vdash q \Rightarrow p$$

We can prove that $\approx$ is a congruence relation. The quotient algebra is then formed in the usual way with the equivalence class $[p]$ for each well-formed formula p. Moreover, the relation $\leq$ on $WFF/_{\approx}$ defined by the equivalence

$$[p] \leq [q] \text{ if and only if } \vdash p \Rightarrow q \text{ in } \textbf{RDSL}$$

is an partial order on $WFF/_{\approx}$.

Then it is shown that the Lindenbaum algebra along with the canonical valuation is a model for **RDSL**. This proves completeness, since if $\models \Gamma \Rightarrow \Delta$, it holds in $(WFF/_{\approx}, \leq)$ with the canonical valuation. Thus $[\Gamma] \leq [\Delta]$ which implies $\vdash \Gamma \Rightarrow \Delta$ in **RDSL**. $\square$

4   Conclusion

In this paper, we propose a logic **RDSL** for rough sets, i.e., the sequent calculus corresponding to rough double Stone algebra. The syntax and semantics are defined. The soundless and completeness are proved. A rough double Stone algebra is in fact a regular double Stone algebra. Conversely, Comer [2] has proved that any regular double Stone algebra is isomorphic to a subalgebra of some rough double Stone algebra. As well known, a regular double Stone algebra is equivalent to a 3-valued Łukasiewicz algebra. So, we suppose that **RDSL** is equivalent to the calculus with 3-valued Łukasiewicz algebra models. In our future work, we will check this suppose.

Acknowledgements

The work is supported by the 973 National Key Basic Research and Development Program of China(No.2002CB312106), the China Postdoctoral Science

Foundation(No.2004035715), and the Science&Technology Program of Zhejiang Province in China (No.2004C31098).

The author is grateful to the anonymous reviewers for their valuable comments and suggestions when reading the manuscript.

References

1. Banerjee, M., Chakraborty, M.K.: Rough sets through algebraic logic. Fundamenta Informaticae, **28**, (1996)211-221.
2. Comer, S.: On connections between information systems, rough sets and algebraic logic. In: Algebraic methods in logic and computer science. Banach Center Publications (1993)117-124.
3. Dai, J.H.: Structure of rough approximations based on molecular lattices. Proceedings of 4th International Conference on Rough Sets and Current Trends in Computing (RSCTC2004), LNAI 3066, Springer-Verlag, Berlin (2004)69-77.
4. Düntsch, I.: A logic for rough sets. Theoretical Computer Science, (1997)427-436
5. Gehrke, M., Walker, E.: On the structure of rough sets. Bulletin of the Polish Academy of Sciences: Mathematics, **40**, (1992)235-255.
6. Iturrioz, L.: Rough sets and 3-valued structures. In: Orlowska, E. (eds.): Logic at work. Springer-Verlag, Herdberg (1998)596-603.
7. Iwiński, T.B.: Algebraic approach to rough sets. Bulletin of the Polish Academy of Sci-ences: Mathematics, **35**, (1987)673-683.
8. Jarvinen, J.: On the structure of rough approximations. Proceedings of 3rd International Conference on Rough Sets and Current Trends in Computing (RSCTC2002), LNAI 2475, Springer-Verlag, Berlin (2002)123-130.
9. Lin, T.Y., Liu, Q.: Rough approximate operators: Axiomatic rough set theory. In: Ziarko, W. P. (eds.): Rough Sets, Fuzzy Sets and Knowledge Discovery. Springer-Verlag, Berlin (1994)256-260.
10. Pagliani, P.: Rough sets and Nelson algebras. Fundamenta Informaticae, **27**, (1996)205-219.
11. Pagliani, P.: Rough set theory and logic-algebraic structures. In: Orlowska, E. (eds.): Incomplete information: Rough set analysis,Physica-Verlag, Herdberg (1998)109-190.
12. Pawlak, Z.: Rough Sets-Theoretical Aspects of Reasoning about Data. Kluwer Academic Publishers, Dordrecht (1991).
13. Pomykala, J., Pomykala, J.A.: The Stone algebra of rough sets. Bulletin of the Polish Academy of Sciences: Mathematics, **36**, (1988)495-508.
14. Rasiowa, H.: An algebraic approach to non-classical logics. North Holland, Amsterdam, (1974).
15. Sen, J., Chakraborty, M.K.: A study of interconnections between rough and 3-valued Lukasiewicz logics. Fundamenta Informaticae, **51**, (2002)311-324.
16. Yao, Y.Y.: Constructive and algebraic methods of the theory of rough sets. Information Sciences, **109**, (1998)21-47.

On Partial Tests and Partial Reducts for Decision Tables

Mikhail Ju. Moshkov[1] and Marcin Piliszczuk[2]

[1] Institute of Computer Science, University of Silesia,
39, Będzińska St., Sosnowiec, 41-200, Poland
[2] Institute of Computer Science, University of Silesia,
39, Będzińska St., Sosnowiec, 41-200, Poland
{moshkov, piliszcz}@us.edu.pl

Abstract. In the paper a greedy algorithm for construction of partial tests is considered. Bounds on minimal cardinality of partial reducts are obtained. Results of experiments with software implementation of the greedy algorithm are described.

Keywords: partial cover, partial test, partial reduct, greedy algorithm.

1 Introduction

Let T be a decision table in which each column is labeled by an attribute and each row is labeled by a decision. It is possible that equal rows have different decisions. So we consider not only crisp but also rough decision tables [5].

A test is a subset of the set of attributes (columns) of the table which separate all pairs of different rows with different decisions. A reduct is a test such that each proper subset of this test is not a test.

A partial test is an arbitrary subset U of the set of attributes. Let a be the number of unordered pairs of different rows from T with different decisions, and b be the number of unordered pairs of different rows with different decisions which can be separated by attributes from U. The number $\gamma(U) = 1 - b/a$ is called the inaccuracy of the partial test U. A partial test U is called a partial reduct if for each proper subset V of the set U the inequality $\gamma(V) > \gamma(U)$ holds. It is clear that for each partial test U there exists a partial reduct V such that $V \subseteq U$ and $\gamma(V) = \gamma(U)$. So if we have a partial test U then it is not difficult to construct (by removal of some attributes from U) a partial reduct V such that $\gamma(V) = \gamma(U)$ and $|V| \leq |U|$.

The consideration of partial reducts and tests is justified in the case when the aim of decision table investigation is the discovery of new knowledge [6]. If a given decision table contains a noise then the construction of an exact reduct may be excessive. On the other hand, if we will try to discover knowledge based on obtained set of attributes, it will be more convenient for us to work with smaller set.

The notions of partial test and partial reduct, considered in this paper, are very close to the notion of approximate reduct introduced by Z. Pawlak in [5],

D. Ślęzak et al. (Eds.): RSFDGrC 2005, LNAI 3641, pp. 149–155, 2005.
© Springer-Verlag Berlin Heidelberg 2005

where he wrote that "the idea of an approximate reduct can be useful in cases when a smaller number of condition attributes is preferred over accuracy of classification".

H.S. Nguyen and D. Ślęzak in [4] proved that for each α, $0 \leq \alpha < 1$, the problem of construction of a partial reduct with minimal cardinality, which inaccuracy is at most α, is NP-hard (see full proof in [9]). Similar result for partial covers was obtained by D. Ślęzak in [8].

In [3] we have considered a greedy algorithm for partial test and reduct construction for crisp decision tables, and some bounds on minimal cardinality of partial reducts. In this paper we generalize results from [3] on the case of rough decision tables and obtain two new lower bounds.

We consider a greedy algorithm that for a given decision table and a given α, $0 \leq \alpha < 1$, constructs a partial test which inaccuracy is at most α. Denote by $R_{min}(\alpha)$ the minimal cardinality of a partial test which inaccuracy is at most α. It is clear that $R_{min}(\alpha)$ is the minimal cardinality of a partial reduct which inaccuracy is at most α. Denote by $R_{greedy}(\alpha)$ the cardinality of the partial test constructed by greedy algorithm. Denote by P the number of unordered pairs of different rows with different decisions.

The considered greedy algorithm allows obtain not only upper bound on the value $R_{min}(\alpha)$ of the kind $R_{min}(\alpha) \leq R_{greedy}(\alpha)$ but also some lower bounds on the value $R_{min}(\alpha)$.

Based on results of P. Slavík from [6] we conclude that if $\lceil P(1 - \alpha) \rceil \geq 2$ then

$$R_{greedy}(\alpha) < R_{min}(\alpha) \left(\ln \lceil P(1 - \alpha) \rceil - \ln \ln \lceil P(1 - \alpha) \rceil + 0.78 \right) .$$

We can use this inequality to obtain a lower bound on $R_{min}(\alpha)$ (see Proposition 10 in Sect. 3). For example, if $R_{greedy}(0.1) = 90$ and $P = 100$ then $R_{min}(0.1) \geq 24$. Unfortunately, the considered bound depends on the value P. If $R_{greedy}(0.1) = 90$ and $P = 1000$ then we obtain the bound $R_{min}(0.1) \geq 16$ only.

Based on results from [2] we conclude that for any β, $0 < \beta \leq \alpha < 1$, the inequality

$$R_{greedy}(\alpha) \leq R_{min}(\alpha - \beta) \ln \beta^{-1} + 1$$

holds. We can use this inequality to obtain a lower bound on $R_{min}(\alpha - \beta)$ which will not depend on P (see Proposition 11 in Sect. 3). For example, if $R_{greedy}(0.1) = 90$ then $R_{min}(0.05) \geq 30$.

The third type of lower bounds, considered in this paper, can be found in Sect. 3 (see Proposition 12).

The paper consists of four sections and conclusion. In the second section we consider greedy algorithm for partial cover construction, some results from [1,2,3,6] and two further lower bounds on minimal cardinality of partial cover. Based on these results, in the third section we study greedy algorithm for partial test construction. In the fourth section we describe results of some experiments with software implementation of greedy algorithm for partial test construction.

2   Greedy Algorithm for Partial Cover Construction

Let A be a nonempty finite set and S be a family of subsets of A such that $\bigcup_{B \in S} B = A$. Let $Q = \{B_1, \ldots, B_t\}$ be a subfamily of S. Denote $\gamma(Q) = 1 - |B_1 \cup \ldots \cup B_t| / |A|$. The subfamily Q will be called a *partial cover* of the set A, and the number $\gamma(Q)$ will be called the *inaccuracy* of this partial cover. The number t will be called the *cardinality* of the partial cover Q.

Let α be a real number and $0 \le \alpha < 1$. Denote by $C_{\min}(\alpha)$ the minimal cardinality of a partial cover which inaccuracy is at most α.

Consider greedy algorithm constructing a partial cover which inaccuracy is at most α. In the family S we choose a set B_1 with maximal cardinality, and include the set B_1 into originating partial cover. If $\gamma(\{B_1\}) \le \alpha$ then we finish the work of our algorithm. Otherwise, in the family S we choose a set B_2 such that the cardinality of $B_2 \setminus B_1$ is maximal, and include the set B_2 into originating partial cover. If $\gamma(\{B_1, B_2\}) \le \alpha$ then we finish the work of our algorithm. Otherwise, in the family S we choose a set B_3 such that the cardinality of $B_3 \setminus (B_1 \cup B_2)$ is maximal, and include the set B_3 into originating partial cover, etc.

Denote by $C_{\text{greedy}}(\alpha)$ the cardinality of the partial cover constructed by the considered algorithm. It is clear that the inaccuracy of this partial cover is at most α. Denote by N the cardinality of the set A.

The following statement was obtained by P. Slavík in [7].

Proposition 1. *Let α be a real number, $0 \le \alpha < 1$ and $\lceil N(1 - \alpha) \rceil \ge 2$. Then*

$$C_{\text{greedy}}(\alpha) < C_{\min}(\alpha) \left(\ln \lceil N(1 - \alpha) \rceil - \ln \ln \lceil N(1 - \alpha) \rceil + 0.78 \right) \ .$$

In [1] it was proved that $C_{\text{greedy}}(\alpha) < C_{\min}(0) \ln \alpha^{-1} + 1$ if $C_{\text{greedy}}(\alpha) > 1$. The following statement was obtained in [2].

Proposition 2. *Let β be a real number and $0 < \beta \le \alpha < 1$. Then*

$$C_{\text{greedy}}(\alpha) \le C_{\min}(\alpha - \beta) \ln \beta^{-1} + 1 \ .$$

It is possible to use the considered greedy algorithm not only for partial cover construction but also for obtaining of lower and upper bounds on the value $C_{\min}(\alpha)$.

Let us apply the greedy algorithm with parameter $\alpha = 0$ to the set A and the family S. This algorithm will choose sequentially subsets $B_1, \ldots, B_m$ from S such that $\gamma(\{B_1, \ldots, B_m\}) = 0$. Denote $Q_0 = \emptyset$ and for $i = 1, \ldots, m$ denote $Q_i = \{B_1, \ldots, B_i\}$. For $i = 0, \ldots, m$ denote $\gamma_i = \gamma(Q_i)$. It is clear that

$$0 = \gamma_m < \gamma_{m-1} < \ldots < \gamma_0 = 1 \ .$$

The following upper bound on $C_{\min}(\alpha)$ is obvious and was mentioned in [3].

Proposition 3. *Let α be a real number, $0 \le \alpha < 1$, and k be the number from $\{1, \ldots, m\}$ such that $\gamma_k \le \alpha < \gamma_{k-1}$. Then*

$$C_{\min}(\alpha) \le k \ .$$

The next lower bound on $C_{\min}(\alpha)$ follows from Proposition 1.

Proposition 4. *Let α be a real number, $0 \leq \alpha < 1$, $\lceil N(1-\alpha) \rceil \geq 2$ and k be the number from $\{1, \ldots, m\}$ such that $\gamma_k \leq \alpha < \gamma_{k-1}$. Then*

$$C_{\min}(\alpha) > k/(\ln \lceil N(1-\alpha) \rceil - \ln\ln \lceil N(1-\alpha) \rceil + 0.78) .$$

The following lower bound on $C_{\min}(\alpha)$ was proved in [3].

Proposition 5. *Let α be a real number, $0 \leq \alpha < 1$, k be the number from $\{1, \ldots, m\}$ such that $\gamma_k \leq \alpha < \gamma_{k-1}$ and $k \geq 3$. Then*

$$C_{\min}(\alpha) \geq \max\left\{(j-1)/\ln(\gamma_j - \alpha)^{-1} : j = k-1, \ldots, 2\right\} .$$

Let us prove one more lower bound on $C_{\min}(\alpha)$.

Proposition 6. *Let α be a real number, $0 \leq \alpha < 1$, and k be the number from $\{1, \ldots, m\}$ such that $\gamma_k \leq \alpha < \gamma_{k-1}$. Then*

$$C_{\min}(\alpha) \geq \max\left\{(\gamma_i - \alpha)/(\gamma_i - \gamma_{i+1}) : i = k-1, \ldots, 0\right\} .$$

Proof. Let $i \in \{k-1, \ldots, 0\}$. Let $Q = \{B_{r_1}, \ldots, B_{r_t}\}$ be a subfamily of the family S such that $\gamma(Q) \leq \alpha$ and $t = C_{\min}(\alpha)$. Denote $D = B_{r_1} \cup \ldots \cup B_{r_t}$. Denote $B = B_1 \cup \ldots \cup B_i$ (if $i = 0$ then $B = \emptyset$). It is clear that $|B_{r_j} \setminus B| \leq |A|(\gamma_i - \gamma_{i+1})$ for $j = 1, \ldots, t$. Therefore $|D| \leq |B| + |A|(\gamma_i - \gamma_{i+1})t$. Since $\gamma(Q) \leq \alpha$, we have $1 - |D|/|A| \leq \alpha$ and $1 - \alpha \leq |D|/|A|$. Hence $1 - \alpha \leq |D|/|A| \leq |B|/|A| + (\gamma_i - \gamma_{i+1})t$. Since $\gamma_i = 1 - |B|/|A|$, we have $1 - \alpha \leq 1 - \gamma_i + (\gamma_i - \gamma_{i+1})t$. Therefore $t \geq (\gamma_i - \alpha)/(\gamma_i - \gamma_{i+1})$. $\square$

3   Greedy Algorithm for Partial Test Construction

A *decision table* is a rectangular table T with n columns labeled by attributes $f_1, \ldots, f_n$. Rows of T are labeled by decisions.

Denote by $P(T)$ the set of unordered pairs of different rows from T with different decisions. For $i = 1, \ldots, n$ denote by P_i the set of pairs from $P(T)$ such that rows from the considered pair are different in the column f_i. Denote $S(T) = \{P_1, \ldots, P_n\}$.

Denote $F(T) = \{f_1, \ldots, f_n\}$. A subset $U = \{f_{i(1)}, \ldots, f_{i(t)}\}$ of the set $F(T)$ will be called a *partial test* for the table T, and the number $\gamma(U) = 1 - |P_{i(1)} \cup \ldots \cup P_{i(t)}|/|P(T)|$ will be called the *inaccuracy* of this partial test. A partial test U for the table T will be called a *partial reduct* for the table T if for each subset V of the set U such that $V \neq U$ the inequality $\gamma(V) > \gamma(U)$ holds. It is clear that for each partial test U there exists a partial reduct V such that $V \subseteq U$ and $\gamma(V) = \gamma(U)$.

Let α be a real number and $0 \leq \alpha < 1$. Denote by $R_{\min}(\alpha)$ the minimal cardinality of a partial test which inaccuracy is at most α. It is clear that the number $R_{\min}(\alpha)$ coincides with the minimal cardinality of a partial reduct which inaccuracy is at most α.

We can use greedy algorithm, described in the previous section, for construction of partial tests. Let us apply greedy algorithm with the parameter α to the set cover problem defined by the set $P(T)$ and the family $S(T)$. Let $\{P_{i(1)}, \ldots, P_{i(t)}\}$ be the result of the considered algorithm work. Then $\{f_{i(1)}, \ldots, f_{i(t)}\}$ is a partial test for the table T which inaccuracy is at most α. Of course, by removal of some attributes from this partial test it is easy to obtain a partial reduct which inaccuracy is at most α.

Denote by $R_{\text{greedy}}(\alpha)$ the cardinality of the partial test constructed by the considered algorithm. The next statement follows immediately from Proposition 1.

Proposition 7. *Let α be a real number, $0 \leq \alpha < 1$ and $\lceil |S(T)|(1-\alpha) \rceil \geq 2$. Then*

$$R_{\text{greedy}}(\alpha) < R_{\min}(\alpha) \left(\ln \lceil |S(T)|(1-\alpha) \rceil - \ln \ln \lceil |S(T)|(1-\alpha) \rceil + 0.78 \right) .$$

From Proposition 2 the next statement follows.

Proposition 8. *Let β be a real number and $0 < \beta \leq \alpha < 1$. Then*

$$R_{\text{greedy}}(\alpha) \leq R_{\min}(\alpha - \beta) \ln \beta^{-1} + 1 .$$

We will use the considered algorithm not only for partial test construction but also for obtaining of lower and upper bounds on the value $R_{\min}(\alpha)$.

Let us apply the greedy algorithm for partial cover construction with parameter $\alpha = 0$ to the set $P(T)$ and the family $S(T)$. This algorithm will choose sequentially subsets $\{P_{i(1)}, \ldots, P_{i(m)}\}$ from $S(T)$ such that $\gamma(\{P_{i(1)}, \ldots, P_{i(m)}\}) = 0$. Denote $Q_0 = \emptyset$ and for $j = 1, \ldots, m$ denote $Q_j = \{P_{i(1)}, \ldots, P_{i(j)}\}$. For $j = 0, \ldots, m$ denote $\gamma_j = \gamma(Q_j)$. It is clear that

$$0 = \gamma_m < \gamma_{m-1} < \ldots < \gamma_0 = 1 .$$

The following statement is obvious.

Proposition 9. *Let α be a real number, $0 \leq \alpha < 1$, and k be the number from $\{1, \ldots, m\}$ such that $\gamma_k \leq \alpha < \gamma_{k-1}$. Then*

$$R_{\min}(\alpha) \leq k .$$

Next statement follows immediately from Proposition 4.

Proposition 10. *Let α be a real number, $0 \leq \alpha < 1$, $\lceil |S(T)|(1-\alpha) \rceil \geq 2$ and k be the number from $\{1, \ldots, m\}$ such that $\gamma_k \leq \alpha < \gamma_{k-1}$. Then*

$$R_{\min}(\alpha) > k/ \left(\ln \lceil |S(T)|(1-\alpha) \rceil - \ln \ln \lceil |S(T)|(1-\alpha) \rceil + 0.78 \right) .$$

Next statement follows immediately from Proposition 5.

Proposition 11. *Let α be a real number, $0 \le \alpha < 1$, k be the number from $\{1, \ldots, m\}$ such that $\gamma_k \le \alpha < \gamma_{k-1}$ and $k \ge 3$. Then*

$$R_{\min}(\alpha) \ge \max\left\{(j-1)/\ln(\gamma_j - \alpha)^{-1} : j = k-1, \ldots, 2\right\} \ .$$

Using Proposition 6 we obtain the following statement.

Proposition 12. *Let α be a real number, $0 \le \alpha < 1$, and k be the number from $\{1, \ldots, m\}$ such that $\gamma_k \le \alpha < \gamma_{k-1}$. Then*

$$R_{\min}(\alpha) \ge \max\left\{(\gamma_i - \alpha)/(\gamma_i - \gamma_{i+1}) : i = k-1, \ldots, 0\right\} \ .$$

4   Results of Experiments

In this section we consider results of some experiments with software in Java which implements greedy algorithm for partial test construction and allows to obtain upper and lower bounds on the value $R_{\min}(\alpha)$ mentioned in Propositions 9 – 12.

We performed experiments with artificial rough and crisp decision tables containing from 100 to 5000 objects (rows). Each table contains 30 conditional

Table 1. Cardinalities of partial tests for given inaccuracies and given number of rows

Number of rows	Inaccuracy								
	0.1			0.01			0.0		
	min	avg	max	min	avg	max	min	avg	max
100	4.0	4.0	4.0	6.0	6.55	7.0	9.0	9.6	11.0
500	4.0	4.0	4.0	7.0	7.0	7.0	13.0	14.2	15.0
1000	4.0	4.0	4.0	7.0	7.0	7.0	16.0	16.45	17.0
2500	4.0	4.0	4.0	7.0	7.0	7.0	19.0	19.35	20.0
5000	4.0	4.0	4.0	7.0	7.0	7.0	21.0	21.5	22.0

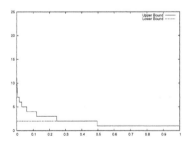

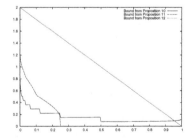

Fig. 1.   Upper and lower bounds on the value $R_{\min}(\alpha)$ for a table with 4000 rows

Fig. 2.   Three different lower bounds on the value $R_{\min}(\alpha)$ for a table with 4000 rows

attributes and one decision attribute. All conditional attributes have binary values. Decision attribute has 10 values. Each value is equally probable. For each number of rows we performed 20 experiments. In Table 1 we present minimal, average and maximal cardinalities of partial tests constructed by greedy algorithm with inaccuracies equal to 0.1, 0.01 and 0.

In Fig. 1 we show upper and lower bounds on minimal cardinality of partial tests and reducts for a decision table containing 4000 rows. For this table the cardinality of exact test (test with inaccuracy 0) constructed by greedy algorithm equals to 21. The value of lower bound is taken as function "⌈⌉" of highest of the three presented lower bound estimations.

In Fig. 2 we show three different lower bounds obtained for the same table.

5   Conclusion

In the paper a greedy algorithm for construction of partial tests is considered. This algorithm can be useful in such applications of rough set theory where we look at constructed partial tests and partial reducts as on a way of knowledge representation.

References

1. Moshkov, M.Ju.: Greedy algorithm for set cover in context of knowledge discovery problems. Proceedings of the International Workshop on Rough Sets in Knowledge Discovery and Soft Computing (ETAPS 2003 Satellite Event). Warsaw, Poland. Electronic Notes in Theoretical Computer Science **82**(4) (2003)
2. Moshkov, M.Ju.: On greedy algorithm for partial cover construction. Proceedings of the Fourteenth International Workshop Design and Complexity of Control Systems. Nizhny Novgorod, Russia (2003) 57 (in Russian)
3. Moshkov, M.Ju., Piliszczuk, M.: On construction of partial reducts and bounds on their complexity. Proceedings of the Conference Decision Support Systems. Zakopane, Poland (2004) (to appear)
4. Nguyen, H.S., Ślęzak, D.: Approximate reducts and association rules - correspondence and complexity results. Proceedings of the Seventh International Workshop on Rough Sets, Fuzzy Sets, Data Mining, and Granular-Soft Computing. Yamaguchi, Japan. Lecture Notes in Artificial Intelligence **1711**, Springer-Verlag (1999) 137–145
5. Pawlak, Z.: Rough set elements. Rough Sets in Knowledge Discovery **1**. Methodology and Applications (Studies in Fuzziness and Soft Computing **18**). Edited by L. Polkowski and A. Skowron. Phisica-Verlag (1998) 10–30
6. Skowron, A.: Rough sets in KDD. Proceedings of the 16-th World Computer Congress (IFIP'2000). Beijing, China (2000) 1–14
7. Slavík, P.: A tight analysis of the greedy algorithm for set cover. Proceedings of 28th Annual ACM Symposium on the Theory of Computing (1996) 435–439
8. Ślęzak, D.: Normalized decision functions and measures for inconsistent decision tables analysis. Fundamenta Informaticae **44** (2000) 291–319
9. Ślęzak, D.: Approximate entropy reducts. Fundamenta Informaticae **53** (2002) 365–390

The Second Attribute[*]

Suqing Han[1,2] and Jue Wang[1]

[1] Laboratory of Complex Systems and Intelligence Science,
Institute of Automation, Chinese Academy of Sciences,
Beijing 100080, P.R China
[2] Department of Mathematics, Taiyuan Normal College,
Taiyuan, China
{suqing.han, jue.wang}@mail.ia.ac.cn

Abstract. In practice, many datasets are shared among multiple users. However, different users may desire different knowledge from the datasets. It implies that we need to provide a specification which mines different solutions from the dataset according to the semantic of requirements. Attribute order is a better approach to describing the semantic. A *reduct* algorithm based on attribute order has been presented in [1]. Because of its completeness for *reduct* and its unique output for a given attribute order, this algorithm can be regarded as a mapping from the attribute orders set to the *reducts* set. This paper investigates the structure of attribute orders set for the *reduct*. The second attribute theorem, which can be used to determine the range of attribute orders with the same *reduct* for a given attribute order, has been proved in [2]. Consequently, key to use the second attribute theorem is how to find the second attributes with the largest subscript for application in an efficient way. This paper therefore presents a method based on the tree expression to fulfill the above task.

Keywords: reduct, attribute order, second attribute, discernibility matrix, tree expression.

1 Introduction

In practice, a dataset is often shared by many users with different requirement. It implies that we need to provide a specification on the semantic of users' requirements in order to mine the solutions that meet their requirements from the dataset. Attribute order is a better approach to describing semantics. A *reduct* algorithm based on attribute order has been presented in [1]. Due to its completeness for the *reduct* and its unique output for a given attribute order, this algorithm can be regarded as a mapping from the set of attribute orders to the set of *reducts*, namely, *R=reduct(S)* where *R* is the *reduct* for attribute order *S*. Since obviously it's not a one-to-one mapping, there rise questions such

---

[*] This work was supported in part by the National Basic Research Program of China under grant no. 2004CB318103.

D. Ślęzak et al. (Eds.): RSFDGrC 2005, LNAI 3641, pp. 156–165, 2005.

as whether its inverse mapping $S=reduct(R)$ can be formally expressed; which attribute orders respond to the same *reduct* and whether there is any criterion for judgment of two different orders with the same *reduct*. To clarify these questions, we analyzed the relation between *reducts* and attribute orders and then presented the notion second attribute and proved the second attribute theorem in [2].

The proof of the second attribute theorem was based on discernibility matrix [6], thus the algorithm it implied has a time complexity of $O(n^2 \times m)$. Since most information systems have more objects than attributes $(n \gg m)$, an algorithm of complexity $O(n \times m^2)$ was designed and proven equivalent with the second attribute algorithm implied by the second attribute theorem.

The aim of this paper is to present an integrated description for *second attribute* and its functions, so proof for the results obtained in [2] is omitted whereas proofs for some new results are given.

2 The Reduct Algorithm Based on Attribute Order [1]

Given an information system $\langle U, C \cup D \rangle$ (U is the universe and C is the condition attribute set), if $\prec$ is the total relation over C, $S : a_1 \prec a_2 \prec \cdots \prec a_m$ is called an *attribute order*. Let S, H be two attribute orders over C, for any attribute $a_j (a_j \in C)$ in S, there must be an attribute b_k in H such that $a_j = b_k$. It is obvious that there are many rules that can transform attribute order S into H within limited times.

Assume M be the discernibility matrix of a given information system $\langle U, C \cup D \rangle$, $Card(C) = m$ and S be an attribute order over C. $\forall \delta \in M$, the attributes of discernibility elements δ inherit attribute order S from left to right, i.e., $\delta = aB$, where $a \in C$ and $B \subset C - \{a\}$ ("a" is the first attribute of δ by S, called the label attribute of δ). Then the set below

$$\{\delta | \delta = aB, \delta \text{ inherit the attribute order } S \text{ from left to right}, \delta \in M\} \quad (1)$$

is an equivalent relation defined on discernibility matrix M for attribute order S. Denoted as $L(S)$, it partitions M into equivalence classes, namely $M/L(S) = \{[1]_S, [2]_S, \cdots, [k]_S\}$, where $[x]_S = \{\delta | \delta = a_x B, \delta \in M, \delta \text{ inherit attribute order} S \text{ from left to right}\}$ is the xth equivalence class of M in S.

Suppose N be the maximal subscript of non-empty equivalence classes in $M/L(S)$, $N \leq Card(C)$ and a_N is the label attribute of non-empty equivalence class $[N]_S = \{\delta | \delta = a_N B, \delta \in M\}$. The largest subscript can be expressed as $max\{[M/L(S)]\}$. Here $\{[M/L(S)]\}$ is the subscript set of the label attributes of all the non-empty equivalence classes in $M/L(S)$. The *reduct* algorithm based on attribute order is demonstrated as follows. At the beginning, $R = \emptyset$.

Algorithm 1
(1). Let a_N be a reduct attribute, $R = R \cup \{a_N\}$;
(2). $E = \{a | a \cap \{a_N\} = \emptyset, a \in M\}, M = E$;
(3). $N' = max\{[M/L(S)]\}, N = N'$;
(4). Repeat (1)-(3) until $M = \emptyset$.
Set R is a *reduct* of $\langle U, C \cup D \rangle$ for attribute order S.

As to Algorithm 1, we have proved in [1] that it is complete for *reduct* and its output is unique for the given attribute order.

Remark: If the solution an algorithm finds is a Pawlak *reduct* [5], this algorithm is called a complete algorithm for *reduct*.

3   Second Attribute Theorem [2]

Based on [1], we analyzed the relation between *reducts* and attributes orders and then proposed the notion second attribute and proved the second attribute theorem in [2]. Here we review them as follows.

3.1   Notation Conventions

PAO: a pair of attribute orders.

$x \rightarrow y$: attribute a_x is moved rightward from position x to y in a given attribute order.

$R_S(x)$: the functional expression of the *reduct* attribute at position x for attribute order S. $R_S(x) = \emptyset$ means that label attribute is a *non-reduct* attribute.

$R_S[x, y]$: the functional expression of the *reduct* attributes in interval $[x, y]$ for attribute order S.

$[x]_S^* = \{\delta | \delta \in [x]_S, \delta \cap R_S[x+1, m] = \emptyset, 1 \le x \le m\}$: the set of discernibility elements in $[x]_S$ that do not include any *reduct* attributes behind a_x.

3.2   The Second Attribute and the Second Attribute Theorem

Taking the effect produced by moving attributes in an attribute order into account, we can transform the computation of the *reducts* of different attribute orders into the inquiry about the second attributes of equivalence classes. As to the effect produced by moving a *reduct* attribute leftward, we have proved in [2] that any *reduct* attribute can be moved leftward to any position in S and the *reduct* remains unchanged. Then the second attribute theorem deal with the effect produced by moving a *reduct* attribute rightward.

Given an information system$\langle U, C \cup D \rangle$, $Card(C) = m$, S be an attribute order over C. Suppose N be the maximal subscript of non-empty equivalence classes in $M/L(S)$ and a_N be the label attribute of non-empty equivalence class $[N]_S$. According to algorithm 1, firstly, the label attribute a_N of the non-empty equivalence class $[N]_S$ is appointed a *reduct* attribute of the information system, denoted as $R_S(N)$; secondly, all discernibility elements including $R_S(N)$ are deleted from M, and then, the equivalence class $[N-1]_S$ in $M/L(S)$ is altered to $[N-1]_S^* = \{\delta | \delta \in [N]_S, \delta \cap R_S[N, m] = \emptyset\}$. As the algorithm runs iteratively, we use $[x]_S^* = \{\delta | \delta \in [x]_S, \delta \cap R_S[x+1, m] = \emptyset, 1 \le x \le m\}$ to denote the set of discernibility elements in $[x]_S$ that does not include any *reduct* attributes behind a_x, called the relative equivalence class of $[x]_S$. If $[x]_S^* \ne \emptyset$, its label attribute is a *reduct* attribute; otherwise it is a non-*reduct* attribute.

Let $a \in [x]_S^*$, if $a = a_x b_t B_t$, the second attribute is b_t; if $\alpha = a_x$, namely, α is a core attribute in $[x]_S^*$; or $[x]_S^* = \emptyset$, the second attribute of $[x]_S^*$ is appointed $\emptyset$.

For the sake of readability, we introduce the principle of the second attribute first, and then the second attribute theorem.

The principle of the second attribute

Assume S be a given attribute order over C, Δ_x be the set of the second attributes of discernibility elements in $[x]^*_S$, namely, $\Delta_x = \{b_t | \alpha = a_x b_t B_t, (B_t \subset C), \alpha \in [x]^*_S\}$, attribute order Q be obtained by moving attribute a_x by $x \to y$ in S.

If $y < min\{t | b_t \in \Delta_x\}$, Δ_x remains unchanged for Q and $reduct(S) = reduct(Q)$.

If $y \geq max\{t | b_t \in \Delta_x\}$, because discernibility elements in $[x]^*_S$ are assigned to the equivalence classes in interval $[x+1, y]$ when attribute a_x is moved by $x \to y$ in S, $\Delta_x = \emptyset$ for Q. In other words, the second attributes in Δ_x are turned into the label attributes for Q. It implies $[y]^*_Q = \emptyset$ and a_x is a non-*reduct* attribute for Q, consequently, $reduct(S) \neq reduct(Q)$.

If $min\{t | b_t \subset \Delta_x\} \leq y < max\{t | b_t \in \Delta_x\}$, it means that some discernibility elements in $[x]^*_S$ are assigned to the equivalence classes in interval $[x+1, y]$ when attribute a_x is moved by $x \to y$ in S. And yet at least one of them still remains, namely, $[y]^*_Q \neq \emptyset$, a_x still is a *reduct* attribute for Q and $reduct(S) = reduct(Q)$.

The second attribute theorem:

Given attribute order S, let attribute order Q be obtained by $x \to y$ in S and the maximal subscript of the second attribute in Δ_x be m, then $reduct(S) = reduct(Q)$ if and only if $y < m$.

The significance of this theorem is that it relies only on the second attribute of relative equivalence class of the current attribute order and can be used to determine the range of attribute orders with the same *reduct* for a given attribute order.

An interesting phenomenon is: if attribute orders H and G are obtained by $x \to y (y = m)$ and $x \to z (z > m)$ in S respectively (m be the maximal subscript of discernibility elements in Δ_x), $reduct(H) \neq reduct(S)$, $reduct(G) \neq reduct(S)$, and yet $reduct(H) = reduct(G)$. It shows that if $y \geq m$, all the attribute orders obtained by $x \to y$ will have the same *reduct*, no matter what position y is at.

Example. Let $M/L(S) = \{\{lw\}, \{fms, fw\}, \{em\}, \{mg\}, \{gw\}\}$ be the partition of the discernibility matrix M for attribute order $S : l \prec f \prec e \prec m \prec g \prec s \prec w \prec d$. The equivalence classes are $[1]_S = \{lw\}$, $[2]_S = \{fms, fw\}$, $[3]_S = \{em\}$, $[4]_S = \{mg\}$, $[5]_S = \{gw\}$; the relative equivalence classes are $[1]^*_S = \{lw\}$, $[2]^*_S = \{fms, fw\}$, $[3]^*_S = \{em\}$, $[4]^*_S = \emptyset$, $[5]^*_S = \{gw\}$.

According to the second attribute theorem, if the moving position of attributes g or f or l does not overrun that of w, and that of attribute e doesn't overrun that of m in S, for the obtained attribute order Q, $reduct(Q) = reduct(S)$. However, if the moving position of attributes g or f or l overruns that of w, or e overruns that of m in S, for the obtained attribute order Q, $reduct(Q) \neq reduct(S)$.

4   The Basic Decision Theorem

The second attribute theorem is applied to move only one *reduct* attribute right-ward at a time in a given attribute order. In this section, we try to move more than one attribute in S rightward in series, and then observe the changes of second attributes that occur when moving the *reduct* attributes in S rightward every time.

4.1   The Normal Attribute Order

Let's take into account a particular sort of attribute order, the normal attribute order, which is obtained by moving all the *reduct* attributes in a given attribute order to the left and all the non-*reduct* attributes to the right. Obviously, there are more than one normal attribute order on a given attribute order. In fact if we suppose S be an attribute order over C and the card of *reducts* be k, then the card of normal attribute orders is $k!(m-k)!$ and there rises a question: what is the relation between a given attribute order and its normal attribute orders? The following Proposition 1 proved in [2] provides the answer.

Proposition 1: Let S be a given attribute order and Q be its normal attribute order. Then $reduct(S) = reduct(Q)$.

Proposition 1 implies that all the normal attribute orders of a given attribute order have the same *reduct*. The following Proposition 2 reveals the relation between an attribute order and its normal attribute order obtained by moving *reduct* attributes leftward.

Proposition 2: Let H be an attribute order, S be a normal attribute order obtained by moving reduct attributes leftward in H. Then for $[y]_H^*(a_y \in C)$, $\exists [x]_S^*(a_x \in C)$ such that $[y]_H^* \subseteq [x]_S^*$, and the second attribute with the largest subscript of $[x]_S^*$ is equal to that of $[y]_H^*$.

Proof: Suppose a be a *reduct* attribute which is at position x in S and at position $y(x \leq y)$ in H. For $x \leq t \leq y$, since the discernibility elements including a in $[t]_H^*$ are absorbed into equivalence class $[x]_S^*$ in the process of moving *reduct* attribute a leftward in H, $[y]_H^* \subseteq [x]_S^*$. Furthermore, their second attributes with the largest subscript are the same, in that the label attributes of the absorbed discernibility elements are ahead of a and the second attributes are behind a in H And the sequence of non-*reduct* attributes remains unchanged in the process of moving attribute a. End of the proof.

4.2   Rules on Attribute Moving [2]

In paper [2], the judgment of the *reduct* on *PAO* has been altered to the judgment of the sequence of the *adjacent PAOs*. The process of altering the *PAO* to the *adjacent PAOs* involves the notion of the consistency of two attribute orders and the manner of attribute moving.

Assume S and H be two attribute orders over condition attributes set C. For $a, b \in C$, if $a \prec b$ comes into existence both in S and H, S is consistent with H in terms of a and b; Otherwise, S is inconsistent with H in terms of a and b.

Attribute a in S is proper for H if and only if S is consistent with H in terms of a and b for any attribute b behind a; otherwise, a is improper for H.

Grounded on the notions above, we presented and proved the following proposition and rule on attribute moving in [2].

Proposition 3: For any attribute a_x in S, there is a unique position y in S, such that in the new attribute order Q obtained by $x \to y$, a_x is proper for H.

Rule 1: For two given attribute orders S and H, if attribute a_x is improper for H, then select y and move a_x by $x \to y$ such that in the new attribute order Q, a_x is proper for H.

Proposition 3 shows that Rule 1 ensures attribute order S be transformed into attribute order H with each attribute in S being moved only once. In fact, any given attribute order S can be transformed into its normal attribute order by moving the attributes in S within limited times.

For a given attribute order S, suppose $\langle S, Q \rangle$ be an adjacent *PAO* obtained by $x \to y$ in S; $[t]_S^*$ and $[t']_Q^*$ are the relative equivalence classes of S and Q respectively. The change of the second attribute that occurs when moving attributes rightward is depicted by lemmas proved in [2] and listed below.

Lemma 1: Let $\langle S, Q \rangle$ be an adjacent PAO obtained by moving reduct attribute a_x by $x \to y$ in S. $reduct(S) = reduct(Q)$ if and only if $[t]_S^* = [t']_Q^*$ for all $t \neq x$, and $[t]_S^* \supseteq [t']_Q^*$ for $t = x$.

Lemma 2: Let $\langle S, Q \rangle$ be an adjacent PAO obtained by moving non-reduct attribute a_x by $x \to y$ in S, then $[t]_S^* \subseteq [t']_Q^*$ for all $t \neq x$, and $[t]_S^* \supseteq [t']_Q^*$ for $t = x$.

Lemma 1 and Lemma 2 show: if a *reduct* attribute is moved rightward, as long as $reduct(S) = reduct(Q)$, for $t \neq x$, the relative equivalence sets does not change; but if a non-*reduct* attribute is moved rightward, the relative equivalence sets might change. However, if all the attributes in $[x, y]$ are *reduct* attributes or non-*reduct* attributes, $\{[y]_Q^* | a_y \in C\} = \{[x]_S^* | a_x \in C\}$ holds. This implies that if we change a normal attribute order of S to another, their sets of relative equivalence classes remain unchanged, and if we do it by just moving the *reduct* attributes, their corresponding sets of second attributes are also unchanged.

Proposition 4: Let S and H be two normal attribute orders for a given attribute order Q. If their non-reduct attributes are arranged in the same sequence, they have the same relative equivalence classes, and their second attributes with the largest subscript are the same as well.

Based on the notion of normal attribute order, we propose the basic decision theorem to facilitate the direct judgment of whether two different attribute orders have the same *reduct*.

4.3   Basic Decision Theorem

Guided by the fact that any attribute order can be transformed into a given one within limited times; Rule 2 is designed as follows according to Lemma 1 and 2, which later are the foundation of the basic decision theorem [2].

Rule 2: Given attribute orders S and H, the sequence of adjacent PAOs: $\langle S, S^{(1)} \rangle, \langle S^{(1)}, S^{(2)} \rangle, \cdots, \langle S^{(m-1)}, H \rangle$ can be achieved in two steps:

(1). Select non-reduct attributes one by one and move them according to Rule 1.

(2). Select reduct attributes one by one and move them according to Rule 1

In order to judge whether $reduct(S^{(k-1)}) = reduct(S^{(k)})$ holds for all $k \in [1,m]$ $(S^{(m)} = H)$, the first question we face is: can Rule 2 ergode the whole attribute orders set? It is answered as follows by the Ergodic Lemma proved in [2].

Ergodic Lemma: Let $\langle S, H \rangle$ be a given PAO. Attribute order S can be transformed into H according to Rule2 and each attribute in S is only moved once.

Grounded on the above discussion, the basic criterion is obtained in [2]:

Decision theorem: Let $\langle S, H \rangle$ be a given PAO, S be a normal attribute order and $\langle S, S^{(1)} \rangle$, $\langle S^{(1)}, S^{(2)} \rangle$, $\cdots$,$\langle S^{(m-1)}, H \rangle$ be the sequence of adjacent PAOs of $\langle S, H \rangle$ according to Rule2. $reduct(H) = reduct(S)$ holds if and only if $reduct(S^{(j)})$
$= reduct(S)$ holds for every attribute order $S^{(j)}$ and $reduct(S^{(m-1)}) = reduct(H)$.

We'd like to point out that attribute moving has to be done in the manner of Rule 2; otherwise, the above decision theorem may not be true.

In addition to judging whether two different attribute orders have the same *reduct*, decision theorem can also be used for determining the range in the set of attribute orders in which all the attribute orders have the same *reduct*. We conclude as follows.

Proposition 5: Let J be the set of all the attribute orders with the same reduct, $S \in J$ and S be a normal attribute order. Then, $\forall H \in J$, based on the second attribute theorem, H can be obtained by moving attributes in S according to Rule 2.

Proof: Firstly, according to Rule 2, obtain the attribute order S' by moving all the non-*reduct* attributes in S such that the non-*reduct* attributes in S' are arranged in the same sequence as in H. Since the non-*reduct* attributes can be moved rightward freely while the *reduct* does not change, $reduct(S') = reduct(H)$. Consequently, H can be obtained by only moving *reduct* attributes in S'. By Proposition 2, we have $[y]_H^* \subseteq [x]_{S'}^*$ and their second attributes with the largest subscript are the same. Hence, for any *reduct* attribute a_x in S' that needs to be moved, there is a unique position y in S' which satisfies the second attribute theorem and makes the attribute order S'' obtained by $x \rightarrow y$ in S' consistent with H in terms of a_x and b for any attribute b behind a_x. Therefore, based on the second attribute theorem, H can be obtained by moving attributes in S according to Rule 2. End of the proof.

5   The Second Attribute Algorithm

The second attribute theorem is based on the discernibility matrix, hence the computation of the second attribute with the largest subscript is at least of order n^2 (n is the number of the objects in an information system) for time complexity. Based on the tree expression in information system [3], we present here an algorithm called the second attribute algorithm, which is linear in n for time complexity, to compute the second attribute with the largest subscript.

5.1 The Tree Expression [3]

Given an information system $\langle U, C \cup D \rangle$, let $S : a_1 \prec a_2 \prec \cdots \prec a_m$ be the attribute order over C. The tree expression of $\langle U, C \cup D \rangle$ for S, denoted by T, is a tree with each non-leaf node being assigned an attribute a_i in C, each link of non-leaf node a_i being attached with a value in the domain of a_i, and each node being associated with a subset E_{it} that belongs to $U/\{a_1, a_2, \cdots a_i\}$; leaf node being assigned a D-subtrees, denoted by $T(d_t)$, which is a tree composed of only two levels: a root node d_t and $\mathrm{Card}(E_{+t}/D)$ leaf nodes, where E_{+t} is the equivalence class attached to leaf node a_{+t}; each leaf node is attached with a different non-empty equivalence class belonging to E_{+t}/D.

If a condition attribute node a_i is linked directly to the decision attribute node in a tree expression, it is called a subtree expression and denoted as $T(a_i)$. A subtree is a dead one if its position range remains unchanged when it is pruned; otherwise, it is a live one.

The process of computing a *reduct* in an information system based on tree expression is equivalent to that of pruning from the tree expression.

If a tree expression is obtained by pruning all the dead subtrees from a given tree expression T, it is called the closed tree expression of T and denoted as T_C.

5.2 The Second Attribute Algorithm

Since the second attribute algorithm is closely related to discernibility matrix, relative equivalence classes $[x]_S^*(a_x \in C)$ and tree expression, we analyzed their characteristics and established the following rule to facilitate the designing of the second attribute algorithm.

Rule 3

1. If a pair of branches has the same value for their root nodes and for their decision attributes, leave out the comparing operation.

2. If there are more than one subtree at the same level, the comparing operation is restricted to each of these subtrees.

3. The comparing operation runs from top to bottom.

Given an information system $\langle U, C \cup D \rangle$ and a normal attribute order $S :$ $a_1 \prec a_2 \prec \cdots a_k \prec \cdots \prec a_m$. Let $a_1, a_2, \cdots, a_k$ be the *reduct* attributes, H be anyone attribute order over C and a_{i+1} be the successor attribute of a_i in H. Based on tree expression and normal attribute order, the second attribute algorithm is designed according to Rule 3 as follows.

Second attribute algorithm:

Suppose M' be the set of discernibility elements and each discernibility element in M' includes only the label attribute and the second attribute.

At the beginning, Let $H = S$, and $M' = \emptyset$.

(1). Generate closed tree expression T_C and subtree expression $T(a_k^i)(i = 1, 2, \cdots, s)$ for H;

(2). Fix on the range of the pairs of branche that need to be compared in subtrees $T(a_k^i)(i = 1, 2, \cdots, s)$ according to Rule 3.

(3). According to attribute order H and formulae $F = F - \{(x, y)|(x, y) \in F, a_j(x) \neq a_j(y)\}$£ñprune the pairs of branches with different values for attribute a_j. The algorithm ends when $F = \emptyset$ or the comparing operation goes to the tail of attribute order H.

If $F = \emptyset$ and the algorithm ends, let $M' = M' \cup \{a|a = a_k a_j\}$ and $H = a_k \prec a_1 \prec a_2 \prec \cdots \prec a_{k-1} \prec \cdots \prec a_m$; If $F \neq \emptyset$ and the algorithm ends, let $M' = M' \cup \{a|a = a_k\}$£ñ$H = a_k \prec a_1 \prec a_2 \prec \cdots \prec a_{k-1} \prec \cdots \prec a_m$;

(4). Repeat (1)-(3) until $H = S$.

Then we find that $\Omega = \{b_t|a = a_x b_t, a \in M'\}$ is the solution.

5.3   The Completeness of the Second Attribute Algorithm

If an algorithm ensures that each element in the solution it finds is the second attribute with the largest subscript in its corresponding second attributes set, this algorithm is called a complete algorithm for the second attribute with the largest subscript.

In section 5.2, Rule 3(1) is based on the definition of discernibility matrix; 3(2) ensures that the second attribute has the root node of subtree as its label attribute; 3(3) ensures that the second attribute of the output has the largest subscript in its corresponding second attributes set.

Proposition 6: The second attribute algorithm based on tree expression is complete for the second attribute with the largest subscript.

Proof: Suppose T be the tree expression for normal attribute order S. According to Proposition 4, we just need to prove that the algorithm is complete at the last level subtree of the closed tree expression of T. Let the last level subtree of the closed tree expression be $T(a_k)$, (x, y) denotes any pair of branches in the subtree expression. The algorithm runs iteratively from $j = k+1$ to m. According to the given normal attribute order S and the formula $F = F - \{(x, y)|(x, y) \in F, a_j(x) \neq a_j(y)\}$, the pairs of branches with the same attribute value are selected to be compared first. If for attribute a_j, $F = \emptyset$ and the algorithm ends, it implies that attribute a_j is the second attribute with the largest subscript in equivalence class $[k]_S$; if $F \neq \emptyset$ and the algorithm ends, it means that attribute a_k is a core attribute, whose second attribute is appointed $\emptyset$. Hence, for a given normal attribute order, the algorithm for subtree $T(a_k)$ is complete.

Since the algorithm goes through all the relative equivalence classes, it is complete for second attributes with the largest subscripts. End of the proof.

5.4   Computational Complexity

The process and the computational complexity of obtaining the second attribute with the maximal subscript based on discernibility matrix and on tree expression are shown below.

Discernibility matrix	Complexity	Tree expression	Complexity
Work out the discernibility matrix.	$O(m \times n^2)$	Work out a normal. attribute order	$O(m^2 \times n)$
The discernibility matrix is simplified by using the absorption law.	$O(n^4)$	Construct the subtree at its last level.	$O(k \times m \times n)$ Where k is a constant.
Partition M on equivalent relation $L(S)$.	$O(n^4)$	Fix on range F in which the pairs of branches need to be compared.	$O(n \times m)$
Work out the relative equivalence class $[a_x]_S^*$ for each equivalence class $[a_x]_S$ in $M/L(S)$ and work out the second attribute with the maximal subscript.	$O(n^2)$	Prune the pairs of branches with different attribute value according to the comparing rule and work out the second attribute with the maximal subscript.	$O(n \times m)$

It is obvious that the second attribute algorithm based on tree expression is linear in n for time complexity.

6 Conclusion

The most interesting conclusions we reach in this paper are: first, for a given attribute order S and its *reduct* R, by using the second attribute theorem we can (1) determine the range of attribute orders within which all the attribute orders have the same *reduct*; (2) present a criterion for the judgement of whether two different attribute orders have the same *reduct*. Second, By comparing with the obtaining of second attribute based on discernibility matrix, this paper presents an effective second attribute algorithm based on tree expression with both time and space complexity linear with n, which greatly facilitates the using of the second attribute theorem.

References

1. Wang, J., Wang, J.: *Reduct* Algorithms on Discernibility Matrix: The Ordered Attributes Method. J. Computer Science and Technology. **16(6)** (2001) 489-504
2. Han, S.Q., Wang, J.: Reduct and Attribute Order. J. Computer Science and Technology. **19(4)** (2004) 429-449
3. Zhao, M.: Data Description Based on Reduct Theory. PhD thesis, Institute of Automation, Chinese Academy of Sciences. (2004)
4. Pawlak, Z.: Rough sets. Int. J. Comput. Inform. Sci. **11(5)** (1982) 341-356
5. Skowron, A., Rauszer, C.: The discernibility matrices and functions in information systems. Intelligent Decision Support Handbook of Applications and Advance of the Rough sets Theory, Slowinski R (eds.). (1991) 331-362

Pairwise Cores in Information Systems

Jakub Wróblewski

Polish-Japanese Institute of Information Technology,
Koszykowa 86, 02-008 Warsaw, Poland
jakubw@pjwstk.edu.pl

Abstract. A core in information system is a set of attributes globally necessary to distinct objects from different decision classes (i.e., the intersection of all reducts of the information system). A notion of a pairwise core (2-core), which naturally extends the definition of a core into the case of pairs of attributes is presented. Some useful features concerned with the graph representation of pairwise cores are discussed.

The paper presents also practical application of the notion of 2-core. It is known that a core (if exists) may be used to improve the reduct finding methods, since there exist polynomial algorithms for core construction. The same may be proven for a 2-core, which may be also used for estimation of minimal reduct size.

Keywords: reducts, core, pairwise core, reduct finding algorithms.

1 Introduction

Rough set theory [7] provides the tools for extracting knowledge from incomplete data based information. The rough set approximations enable us to describe the decision classes, regarded as the sets of objects satisfying some predefined conditions, by means of indiscernibility relations grouping into classes the objects with the same values of the considered attributes. Rough set expert systems are based on the notion of *reduct* [7] [9], a minimal subset of attributes which is sufficient to discern between objects with different decision values. A set of reducts can be used to generate decision rules, thus the reduct finding algorithms are investigated intensively (cf. [9] [1] [4] [3]). The problem of optimal reducts generation (criteria include reduct length, the number of generated rules etc. [12]) is NP-hard, however, approximate algorithms (like the genetic one [10] [8]) can be used to obtain reducts in reasonable time.

The notion of a *core* of the information system, i.e., the intersection of all reducts can be used in searching for reducts [9] [6] [3]. Our work extends this notion to the *pairwise core* (*2-core*), i.e., the set of pairs of attributes such that at least one of the attribute in a pair is necessary to discern between decision classes. The next sections are devoted to the study of connections between 2-cores and some graph-theoretic features and algorithms, as well as reduct finding algorithms employing the new notions and theorems. Section 5 describes results of experiments on benchmark data sets.

D. Ślęzak et al. (Eds.): RSFDGrC 2005, LNAI 3641, pp. 166–175, 2005.

2   Cores and Reducts

In rough set theory [7] [9] a sample of data takes the form of an *information system* $\mathbb{A} = (U, A)$, where each attribute $a \in A$ is a function $a : U \rightarrow V_a$ into the set V_a of all possible values on a. Reasoning about data can be stated as, e.g., a classification problem, where the values of a distinguished decision attribute are to be predicted under information over conditional attributes. In this case, we consider a triple $\mathbb{A} = (U, A, d)$, called a *decision table*, where, for the decision attribute $d \notin A$, values $v_d \in V_d$ correspond to mutually disjoint decision classes of objects.

Definition 1. *Let* $\mathbb{A} = (U, A, d)$, *where* $A = \{a_1, \ldots, a_n\}$, *be given. For any* $B \subseteq A$, *the* B**-indiscernibility relation** *is the equivalence relation defined by*

$$IND_{\mathbb{A}}(B) = \{(u_1, u_2) \in U \times U : \forall_{a \in B}\, a(u_1) = a(u_2)\} \tag{1}$$

Each $u \in U$ *induces a* B**-indiscernibility class** *of the form*

$$[u]_B = \{u' \in U : (u, u') \in IND_{\mathbb{A}}(B)\} \tag{2}$$

Definition 2. *The decision table* $\mathbb{A} = (U, A, d)$ *is* **consistent** *iff* $IND_{\mathbb{A}}(A) \subseteq IND_{\mathbb{A}}(\{d\})$, *i.e., if there are no identical (wrt. A) objects with different decisions.*

We will assume further that our decision tables are consistent. Most of the features and notions described in this paper hold also for the case of non-decision problems (i.e., for information systems and general, not decision reducts) as well as for inconsistent tables (using a generalized decisions [9]); however, for the sake of simplicity of notation and proofs we will restrict ourselves to the less general case.

Indiscernibility relation enables us to express global dependencies as follows:

Definition 3. *Given* $\mathbb{A} = (U, A, d)$, *we say that* $B \subseteq A$ **defines** d *in* $\mathbb{A}$ *iff*

$$IND_{\mathbb{A}}(B) \subseteq IND_{\mathbb{A}}(\{d\}) \tag{3}$$

or, equivalently:

$$\forall_{u_1, u_2 \in U}\, d(u_1) \neq d(u_2) \implies \exists_{a \in B} a(u_1) \neq a(u_2) \tag{4}$$

Assume that $\mathbb{A}$ *is consistent. We say that* $B \subseteq A$ *is a* **decision reduct** *iff it defines* d *and none of its proper subsets does it. By* $\mathcal{R}_{\mathbb{A}}$ *we will denote the set of all decision reducts of* $\mathbb{A}$.

The following property is widely utilized by many reduct finding algorithms [1]:

Lemma 1. *Suppose that* $B \subseteq A$ *defines* d *(note that* B *does not need to be a reduct, because a reduct has to be locally minimal). There exists* $B' \subseteq B$ *such that* B' *is a reduct.*

Proof. If B is a reduct itself, then B′ = B. If B = ∅ then B is a reduct (because it is locally minimal).

Suppose that B ≠ ∅ and B is not a reduct. In this case there exists B″ ⊂ B such that B″ defines d. In this case there are two possibilities:

- *B″ is a reduct (thus B′ = B″) and the procedure stops,*
- *B″ is not a reduct (it is not minimal), thus the same procedure of reduction may be applied to B″.*

Since B is finite and each step of the above procedure will decrease the cardinality of involved subsets, the procedure of reduction must stop.

□

A reduct denotes a minimal set of attributes which are sufficient to define (e.g. using decision rules) the value of decisions for all objects. On the other hand, a *core* is used to denote attributes which are necessary for that.

Definition 4. *Let $\mathbb{A}$ and the family of its decision reducts $\mathcal{R}_\mathbb{A}$ be given. By a* **core** $C \subseteq A$ *of the decision table $\mathbb{A}$ we will denote:*

$$C = \bigcap_{R \in \mathcal{R}_\mathbb{A}} R \tag{5}$$

i.e., the intersection of all reducts. (To avoid confusion with the further notation, the core will be sometimes denoted by **1-core**).

The core may be empty. In fact, for many of real-world data it is empty (see Table 2). It is interesting to see that, although the problem of minimal reduct finding is NP-hard [9] and $|\mathcal{R}_\mathbb{A}|$ may be exponential, the core C is easy to be found.

Lemma 2. *For a consistent decision table $\mathbb{A}$ and its core C the following condition holds:*

$$a \in C \iff IND_\mathbb{A}(A \setminus \{a\}) \not\subseteq IND_\mathbb{A}(\{d\}) \tag{6}$$

i.e., C is a set of all attributes which are indispensable for discernibility of decision classes in $\mathbb{A}$.

Proof. Let $a \in C = \bigcap_{R \in \mathcal{R}_\mathbb{A}} R$. Suppose that $IND_\mathbb{A}(A \setminus \{a\}) \subseteq IND_\mathbb{A}(\{d\})$, i.e., $A \setminus \{a\}$ defines d. Thus, according to Lemma 1, there exists a reduct $R \subseteq A \setminus \{a\}$. This contradicts the assumption that a belongs to any reduct of $\mathbb{A}$.

What is left is to show that if $A \setminus \{a\}$ does not define d, then $a \in C$. It is evident, as (by definition) in this case neither $A \setminus \{a\}$ nor any of its subset may be a reduct, thus any $R \in \mathcal{R}_\mathbb{A}$ must contain a.

□

Let us extend the notion of a 1-core as follows:

Definition 5. *By the* **pairwise core** *or* **2-core** *of a decision table $\mathbb{A}$, denoted by C_p, we mean a set of (unordered) pairs of attributes $C_p \subseteq A \times A$ such that:*

1. $\{a_1, a_2\} \in C_p \Longrightarrow a_1 \notin C \wedge a_2 \notin C$, where C is a core of $\mathbb{A}$,
2. $\{a_1, a_2\} \in C_p \Longrightarrow \forall_{R \in \mathcal{R}_\mathbb{A}}\ a_1 \in R \vee a_2 \in R$,
3. C_p is the maximal set satisfying the above conditions.

The pairwise core is a set of pairs $\{a_1, a_2\}$ of attributes such that neither a_1 nor a_2 belongs to a core, but at least one of them is required for discernibility between decision classes (i.e., any reduct of $\mathbb{A}$ must contain at least one attribute from every pair).

Such notions as reducts or cores are often defined using *discernibility matrix* of decision table [9], i.e., the matrix of size $|U| \times |U|$ which for any pair of objects u_1, u_2 (from different decision classes) contains a set of attributes discerning u_1 and u_2. In this formulation a 1-core may be found by collecting all attributes present in the discernibility matrix as singletons. On the other hand, a 2-core is a collection of all two-attribute elements of the matrix (not containing core attributes).

As a natural extension of 1-core (i.e., a classical core) and 2-core one may define a notion of k-core, i.e., the set of k-element subsets of attributes, which do not contain elements of any lower l-core ($l < k$) and every reduct must contain at least one attribute from every element of the k-core. Alternatively, the k-core contain all k-element cells of indiscernibility table (not covered by any l-core, $l < k$). We will not consider k-cores for $k > 2$ because of two reasons: first, the most of the results presented in the next sections are not easily extendable to the k-cores, and second, the time of computation of k-core (see below) rises significantly.

As stated above, the problem of reduct finding is generally hard. In contrast, both core and 2-core can be calculated quickly, i.e., in polynomial time wrt. both the number of attributes and objects:

Fact 1 *(algorithm for finding cores). The following procedure may be applied to find both a core C and a pairwise core C_p of a consistent decision table $\mathbb{A} = (U, A, d)$:*

1. $C := \emptyset,\ C_p := \emptyset$
2. *For all $a \in A$ do*
3. $R := A \setminus \{a\}$
4.   *If R does not define d, then $C := C \cup \{a\}$*
5. *End For*
6. *For all $a_i, a_j \in A \setminus C,\ i < j,$ do*
7. $R := A \setminus \{a_i, a_j\}$
8.   *If R does not define d, then $C_p := C_p \cup \{\{a_i, a_j\}\}$*
9. *End For.*

To determine whether R defines d or not, one may use the following procedure, based on an algorithm for reduct finding [10] [1]:

1. *Sort the set of objects U according to values of attributes from R.*
2. *Determine the indiscernibility classes $[u]_R$, $u \in U$ (linear scan, as U is sorted).*
3. *If all $[u]_R$ have uniform values of decision d, then R defines d.*

Alternatively, the discernibility matrix can be used to obtain both 1-core and 2-core (refer to the discussion above). But the time and space complexity of indiscernibility matrix calculation is $O(m \times n^2)$ where $m = |A|$, $n = |U|$. For a large data set the factor of n^2 is too high. On the other hand, the algorithm described above is $O(m^2 \times n \log n)$ in a case of efficient implementation [1], which is much more acceptable. Note that the procedure may be easily extended to k-cores, but it will have the complexity of $O(m^k \times n \log n)$.

3   Pairwise Core Graph

The following notion allows us to use wide range of graph-theoretic tools and heuristics for efficient reduct finding:

Definition 6. *The **pairwise core graph** for a consistent decision table $\mathbb{A} = (U, A, d)$ is an undirected graph $G_\mathbb{A} = (V, E)$ such that:*

$$V = A, \qquad E = C_p$$

where C_p is a 2-core for $\mathbb{A}$.

The notion of pairwise core graph allows us to express connections between reducts and 2-cores as some graph-theoretic features of $G_\mathbb{A}$. One of the most interesting results is concerned with the *vertex covering* of graph $G_\mathbb{A}$ (i.e., finding a subset of vertices of $G_\mathbb{A}$ such that every edge connects at least one vertex).

Theorem 1. *Suppose that $G_\mathbb{A}$ is a pairwise core graph for a consistent decision table $\mathbb{A}$. Let $R \in \mathcal{R}_\mathbb{A}$ be a reduct. Then R is a vertex cover of $G_\mathbb{A}$.*

Proof. The proof is straightforward from Definitions 5 and 6, since for every edge (a_i, a_j) at least one of the attributes a_i, a_j must be contained by R.

$\square$

Unfortunately, the opposite property does not hold, i.e., not all vertex covers (even minimal ones) are reducts. The simplest example is a decision table for which $C_p = \emptyset$ thus the minimal cover is empty, whereas the table may still have nonempty reducts. Moreover, if $B \subseteq A$ is a vertex cover of $G_\mathbb{A}$, then B is not necessarily a subset of any reduct. For the decision table $\mathbb{A}$ presented below, we have $C_p = \{\{a_1, a_2\}, \{a_3, a_4\}, \{a_5, a_6\}\}$ and $B = \{a_1, a_3, a_5\}$; as we can see, B is a minimal vertex cover and is not a reduct (nor a subset of any of the 7 reducts of $\mathbb{A}$):

a_1	a_2	a_3	a_4	a_5	a_6	d
0	0	0	0	0	0	0
1	1	0	0	0	0	1
0	0	1	1	0	0	1
0	0	0	0	1	1	1
0	2	0	2	0	2	2

The following properties will be useful for reduct finding task:

Corollary 1. *Suppose that $G_\mathbb{A}$ contains a clique $K = \{a_{k_1}, ..., a_{k_i}\}$. Then any reduct $R \in \mathcal{R}_\mathbb{A}$ must contain at least $i - 1$ attributes from K.*

Corollary 2. *Suppose that $G_\mathbb{A}$ is a full graph: $G_\mathbb{A} = K_n$ where $n = |A|$. Then:*

$$\mathcal{R}_\mathbb{A} = \{A \setminus \{a_i\}, \quad i = 1, ..., n\}$$

Proof. It is immediate from Corollary 1. Note that the set A cannot be a reduct itself (because in this case $C - A$, thus $C_p = \emptyset$) and the only possible sets containing at least $n - 1$ attributes are defined as above.

□

Note that Theorem 1 provides a lower bound on the reduct size: every reduct must be at least as large as the minimal vertex covering of $G_\mathbb{A}$. Fortunately, we do not need to find the minimal covering (which is NP-hard [2]) to obtain a weaker lower bound:

Corollary 3. *Suppose that $G_\mathbb{A}$ may be divided into a set of disjoint cliques K_1, ... K_i. Let R be an arbitrary reduct of $\mathbb{A}$. Then:*

$$|R| \geq (|K_1| - 1) + \cdots + (|K_i| - 1) \tag{7}$$

It is interesting to see that a structure of 2-core may be very rich:

Theorem 2. *Let G be an arbitrary graph, $|E| \geq 1$. Then, there exists $\mathbb{A}$ such that $G_\mathbb{A} = G$*

Tabl

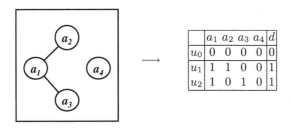

	a_1	a_2	a_3	a_4	d
u_0	0	0	0	0	0
u_1	1	1	0	0	1
u_2	1	0	1	0	1

Proof. Consider $G = (V, E)$. *Let* $\mathbb{A} = (U, A, d)$ *be defined such that* $A = V$, $a : U \to \{0, 1\}$ *for each* $a \in A$, *and* $U = \{u_0, u_1, ..., u_k\}$ *for* $k = |E|$, *and:*

$$\forall_i \qquad d(u_0) = 0 \wedge a_i(u_0) = 0$$

$$\forall_{e_j \in E} \ d(u_j) = 1 \wedge a_i(u_j) = \begin{cases} 1 & \text{where } e_j = (a_{k_1}, a_{k_2}), \ i = k_1 \vee i = k_2 \\ 0 & \text{otherwise} \end{cases}$$

In this decision table the 1-core is empty, because the decision table have exactly two "1"-s in each row u_j, $j > 0$ *and thus reduction of any single attribute is not enough to make* u_0 *and* u_j *indiscernible.*

On the other hand, any reduct R *of* $\mathbb{A}$ *must contain at least one attribute for all edges* $e_j = (a_{k_1}, a_{k_2})$. *If not, a pair* $\{u_0, u_j\}$ *(having opposite decision values) will be indiscernible by* R.

$\square$

An example presented in Table 1 illustrates the proof of Theorem 2.

4   Application of the Pairwise Cores for Reducts Finding

Finding a 1-core or a 2-core in an information system may lead to two kinds of profits. Firstly, an information about importance of attributes and their influence into decision value is stated, which may be interesting in descriptive data analysis. Secondly, due to the properties presented in Section 3, the 2-core graph may be very helpful in reduct finding task.

Let $\mathbb{A}$ be given, let C and C_p will be a 1-core and a 2-core of $\mathbb{A}$, respectively. Suppose we have a method for finding all reducts being supersets of a set $B \subseteq A$. One may use e.g. techniques adopted from [1] (i.e., reducing a subset of attributes until a reduct is found, omitting attributes from B), or Apriori-like algorithm [4] for all reducts finding. The following hints may be used for finding all reducts:

1. Let $B = C$, since all reducts must contain the core.
2. Divide $G_\mathbb{A}$ into a family of disjoint cliques $K_1, ... K_m$.
3. For each K_i omit exactly one attribute and add the rest of them into B. Then find all reducts being supersets of B.
4. Cycle through the above steps checking all possible combinations of omitted attributes.

Any reduct of $\mathbb{A}$ must contain at least $|K_i| - 1$ attributes from every clique K_i (Corollary 1). Thus, all reducts may be found by checking all supersets of sets generated by the above procedure.

The procedure in the worst case is exponential (as the number of reducts may be exponential, and the problem of finding maximal clique is NP-hard, and the number of all possible combinations checked in step 4 may be exponential). Nevertheless, the procedure may be treated as a heuristics which may highly restrict the search space. The main advantage of the pairwise core graphs is that they are in most cases considerably small. Even for large data sets (see Section

5) these graphs can be analyzed exhaustively. For larger graphs one may use e.g. greedy heuristics for decomposition into cliques: find the largest clique (by selecing a vertex with maximal rank and finding a clique around it), then remove it from the graph and iterate these steps until there is no clique (even a single edge) left. This heuristics may be extended in many ways, e.g. by randomization.

Another direction of searching for all reducts is to generate all locally minimal vertex covers of G_A and to analyze theirs supersets. This algorithm may be harder to use as it is much easier to find one decomposition into cliques than all minimal vertex covers.

5   Experimental Results

Several data sets were tested to find a 2-core and G_A (see Table 2). We have selected these decision tables because they are widely used as machine learning benchmarks [5] and in most cases they contain mainly nominal (not numerical) attributes which is preferable for reduct-based analysis of data. One of these tables may be regarded as a relatively large one (Covtype). Results presented in Table 2 show, that more than a half of these tables have nonempty 2-cores, whereas in only 5 out of 14 cases a 1-core was nonempty. It means that the notion of 2-core may be virtually more helpful for reduct finding tasks than the 1-core. For the largest decision table Covtype we found its 2-core in about 6 minutes (Celeron 1 GHz machine) which is still acceptable.

The variety of structures of pairwise core graphs of these decision tables is surprisingly rich, what can be seen in Figure 1. Note that these vertices, which are not present in any 2-core pair, were omitted in Figure 1.

Table 2. Experimental results: benchmark tables, the size of the core and the pairwise core, the estimated (basing on a core and 2-core graph) minimal size of reducts and actual minimal (or minimal known) size of reducts

Data set	Size (obj.×attr.)	Size of C	Size of C_p	Min. reduct estim./known
Australian credit	690×14	1	0	1/3
CoIL 2000	5822×85	9	9	18/22
Optical digits	3823×64	0	0	
Pen-based digits	7494×17	0	0	
DNA splices	2000×180	0	0	
German credit	1000×24	0	1	1/5
Letter	15000×16	3	14	7/10
Pima	768×8	0	0	
Shuttle	43500×9	1	0	1/4
Covtype	581012×54	0	4	2/4
Soybean	307×35	2	7	6/9
Tic-tac-toe	958×9	0	36	**8/8**
Mushroom	8124×22	0	1	1/4
Lymnography	148×18	0	1	1/6

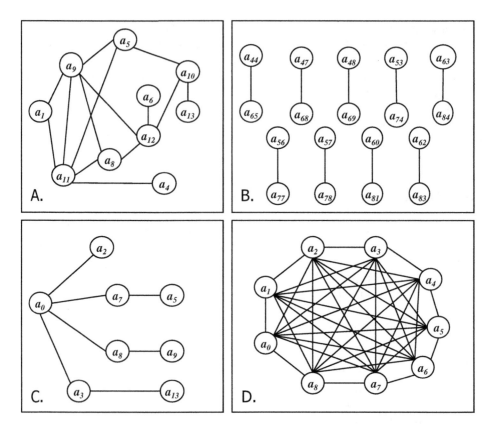

Fig. 1. The pairwise core graphs for benchmark data sets (numbering of attributes starts with 0). A. `Letter`, B. `CoIL'2000`, C. `Soybean`, D. `Tic-Tac-Toe`

Finally, the possibility of estimating the size of minimal reduct in the tables was analyzed. Note that even for very large data sets their pairwise core graphs are often relatively simple. For all analyzed data sets we may quickly perform decomposition into disjoint cliques (even manually) and obtain a lower bound of minimal reduct size due to Corollary 2. The results of these estimations are presented in Table 2. For `Tic-Tac-Toe` data set we have obtained a full graph, so we apply Corollary 2 directly and obtain the set of all reducts immediately. For the rest of data sets, we obtained a lower bound which in some cases (`CoIL 2000`, `Letter`, `Soybean`) are not far from actual minimal reduct size.

The usefulness of the pairwise core graphs may be justified by the following experiment. Suppose we have to check whether known 4-attribute reduct of `Cov-type` decision table is the minimal one. The straightforward method is to check all 3-attribute subsets, i.e., to perform 24804 sortings of more than half million objects of the table [1]. On the other hand, the pairwise core for this data set is $C_p = \{\{a_0, a_5\}, \{a_0, a_9\}, \{a_4, a_9\}, \{a_5, a_9\}\}$. It means that it is enough to check only 3-attribute supersets of all possible vertex covers of pairwise core graph, i.e., 52 supersets of $\{a_0, a_9\}$, 52 supersets of $\{a_5, a_9\}$ and the set $\{a_0, a_4, a_5\}$. We perform 105 sortings, which is 236 times faster than without use of the pairwise core graph.

6   Conclusions

The notion of pairwse core (2-core) was introduced and discussed. This notion may be interesting and helpful for reduct finding. One of the most interesting results of this paper is Theorem 1 and its corollaries concerning connections between reducts of decision tables and vertex covers of particular graph. The size of minimal reduct may also be estimated due to Corollary 3.

The efficient algorithms for generating all reducts needs further research. The algorithms may use a wide set of heuristics designed for clique finding and graph covering, adopted to the special case of reduct finding. Results of experiments on a set of benchmark tables (presented in Section 5) are very promising.

Acknowledgements. Supported by the Research Center of the Polish-Japanese Institute of Information Technology.

References

1. Bazan J., Nguyen H.S., Nguyen S.H., Synak P., Wróblewski J.: Rough Set Algorithms in Classification Problem. In: L. Polkowski, S. Tsumoto, T.Y. Lin (ed.): Rough Set Methods and Applications. Physica-Verlag, Heidelberg, New York (2000) 49–88.
2. Garey M.R., Johnson D.S.: Computers and Intractability, a Guide to the Theory of NP-Completeness. W.H. Freeman and Company, San Francisco (1979).
3. Hu X., Lin T. Y., Han J.: A New Rough Sets Model Based on Database Systems. Fundamenta Informaticae **59** (2,3), IOS Press (2004) 135–152.
4. Kryszkiewicz M., Cichon K.: Towards Scalable Algorithms for Discovering Rough Set Reducts. In: J.F. Peters et al. (eds.), Transaction on Rough Sets vol. I. Springer (LNCS 3100), Berlin, Heidelberg (2004) 120–143.
5. UCI Machine Learning Rep.: http://www.ics.uci.edu/~mlearn/MLRepository.html.
6. Miao D., Hou L.: An Application of Rough Sets to Monk's Problems Solving. Proc. of the RSFDGrC2003, Springer (LNAI 2639), Berlin, Heidelberg (2003) 138– 145.
7. Pawlak, Z.: Rough sets – Theoretical aspects of reasoning about data. Kluwer Academic Publishers, Dordrecht (1991).
8. RSES – Rough Set Exploration System: http://logic.mimuw.edu.pl/~rses/
9. Skowron A., Rauszer C.: The discernibility matrices and functions in information systems. W: R. Slowinski (ed.). Intelligent Decision Support. Handbook of Applications and Advances of the Rough Set Theory. Kluwer, Dordrecht (1992) 311–362.
10. Wróblewski J.: Finding minimal reducts using genetic algorithms. Proc. of the Second Annual Join Conference on Information Sciences, Wrightsville Beach, NC (1995) 186–189, http://www.mimuw.edu.pl/~jakubw/bib/
11. Wróblewski J.: Covering with reducts – a fast algorithm for rule generation. Proc. of RSCTC'98, Warsaw, Poland. Springer-Verlag (LNAI 1424), Berlin Heidelberg (1998) 402–407, http://www.mimuw.edu.pl/~jakubw/bib/
12. Wróblewski J.: Ensembles of classifiers based on approximate reducts. Fundamenta Informaticae **47** (3,4), IOS Press (2001) 351–360.

Data Preprocessing and Kappa Coefficient

Gaelle Legrand and Nicolas Nicoloyannis

Laboratory ERIC, University Lumière Lyon 2,
5 av. Pierre Mendès-France 69676 Bron, France

Abstract. Data preprocessing is an essential step of the KDD process. It makes it possible to extract useful information from data. We propose two coefficients which respectively study the informational contribution of initial data in supervised learning and the intrinsic structure of initial data in not supervised one. These coefficients are based on Kappa coefficient. The confrontation of these two coefficients enables us to determine if feature construction is useful. We can present a system allowing the optimization of preprocessing step : feature selection is applied in all cases; then the two coefficients are calculated for the selected features. With the comparison of the two coefficients, we can decide the importance of feature construction.

1   Introduction

In the Knowledge Discovery in Databases (KDD) process, the preprocessing step is very important. This step conditions the quality of the discovered patterns and makes it possible to find useful information from initial data. We can apply two different feature transformation: feature selection and feature construction.

Feature selection removes at the same time the noise generated by some features and redundant features. Thus, after feature selection, only relevant features are kept, and the effective number of features under consideration is reduced.

Feature construction changes the representation space thanks to the creation of synthetic features. Thus, after feature construction, the effective number of features under consideration increases.

We think that feature selection must be applied in all cases. Indeed, feature selection reduces the effective number of features under consideration and improves the learning accuracy or, in worst cases keeps it constant thanks to the suppression of noisy, redundant and/or irrelevant features. Moreover, if all features are relevant then feature selection won't remove any features.

However, the question is: when apply feature construction? The answer depends on data structure. It is possible to distinguish two different data structures:

1. The information necessary to discriminate endogenous feature is contained in the initial features set. But among these features, some are redundant or noisy. To eliminate these irrelevant features, feature selection is sufficient.
2. Some features discriminates the endogenous feature but they are not sufficient. In this case, feature construction and feature selection are necessary.

D. Ślęzak et al. (Eds.): RSFDGrC 2005, LNAI 3641, pp. 176–184, 2005.

To answer this question, we use the Cohen's Kappa coefficient, see [1], which quantifies the degree of agreement's quality between paired qualitative judgements. We use the Kappa coefficient in two ways: in supervised learning and in unsupervised one. So we obtain a double indicator:

1. Firstly, we want to obtain a "measurement" of the information bringing by exogenous features about the endogenous feature. So we answer the next question: The results provided by the learning algorithm are they in agreement with the endogenous feature?
2. Then, we want to assess the quality of the inherent structure of data. Without any information about the endogenous feature, can the classes induced by this feature be found?

2   Kappa Coefficient

The Kappa coefficient, κ, introduced by [1], is a measure of interrater agreement, see table 1:

$$\kappa = (P_o - P_e)/(1 - P_e) \tag{1}$$

with the observed agreements,

$$P_o = (\sum_{r=1}^{R} n_{rr})/n \tag{2}$$

and the chance agreement,

$$P_e = (\sum_{r=1}^{R} n_{r.} n_{.r})/n^2 \tag{3}$$

When the observed agreement exceeds the chance agreement, κ is positive, with its magnitude reflecting the strength of agreement.

It reaches its maximum value (i.e. 1) when $P_e = 0.5$ and $P_o = 1$. In this situation, the agreement between the two observers is maximum. The two observers have the same judgements.

Although this is unusual in practice, κ is negative when the observed agreement is less than the chance agreement.

The minimum value of κ is -1. It reaches its minimal value when $P_e = 0.5$ and $P_o = 0$. In this situation, the two observers are in complete disagreement. The two observers have opposite judgements.

Landis and Koch, in [2], propose threshold values for the Kappa coefficient. It is thus possible to qualify the agreement between the two judgements considered according to the value of the Kappa coefficient, (see table 2).

Table 1. Two-way frequency table of the judgements of two observers

	C'_1	...	C'_r	...	C'_R	Total
C_1	n_{11}	...	n_{1r}	...	n_{1R}	$n_{1.}$
...	...	...	...	...	...	...
C_r	n_{r1}	...	n_{rr}	...	n_{rR}	$n_{r.}$
...	...	...	...	...	...	...
C_R	n_{R1}	...	n_{Rr}	...	n_{RR}	$n_{R.}$
Total	$n_{.1}$	...	$n_{.r}$	...	$n_{.R}$	n

Table 2. Threshold values for the Kappa coefficient

κ Values	Agreement
$0.75 \leq \kappa \leq 1$	Perfect
$0.41 < \kappa < 75$	Good
$0 < \kappa \leq 0.41$	Weak
$\kappa = 0$	Independents judgements
$-1 < \kappa < 0$	Disagreement $>$ agreement
$\kappa = -1$	Disagreement

2.1 Supervised Kappa Coefficient

We want to know if, without feature construction, exogenous features can well discriminate the endogenous feature. The use's condition of Kappa coefficient is to be in presence of two paired samples. We will use the Kappa coefficient in the following way :

1. The observer 1 is represented by the values of the endogenous variable, (in table 2, C_r, in rows);
2. The observer 2 is represented by the values assigned by the learning algorithm, (in table 2, C'_r, in columns).

We are in presence of two paired sample. Indeed, the same sample is judged by two different observers: the endogenous feature and the learning algorithm. We can thus determine if the classification induced by the learning algorithm corresponds to the classification induced by the endogenous feature.

We will note κ_S the Kappa coefficient obtained in this situation and we will name it Supervised Kappa.

In order to calculate the value of κ_S, we must initially launch the learning algorithm. Then, it is necessary to build the two-way frequency table. Then, we can calculate κ_S.

2.2 Non-supervised Kappa Coefficient

In order to determine if data contains necessary and sufficient information to discriminate the endogenous feature, we compare the result of a non-supervised learning algorithm and the classification induced by the endogenous feature.

We choose to use the K-Modes, see [3], if there are quantitative features and we choose to use K-Means, see [4], if there are qualitative features.

Of course, we could use other method: these methods were adopted because they are known and give us the possibility of choosing the number of the classes of partition. We consider that the well classified objects are well classified in comparison with the endogenous feature.

We can thus use the Kappa coefficient in the following way:

1. The observer 1 is represented by the values of the endogenous feature, (in table 2, C_r, in rows);
2. The observer 2 is represented by the values assigned by the non supervised learning algorithm, (in table 2, C'_r, in columns).

We will note κ_{NS} the Kappa coefficient obtained in this situation and we will name it Non-Supervised Kappa.

In order to calculate the value of κ_{NS}, we must initially launch the learning algorithm. Then, it is necessary to build the two-way frequency table. Then, we can calculate κ_{NS}.

3   Choice Procedure

The choice of constructing new features will depend on the values of the two Kappa coefficients. The threshold values of Landis and Kosh are kept here.

Thus if the two values are strictly higher than 0.41 then feature construction (FC) is useless. On the other hand, if these values are lower or equal to 0, then feature construction is essential. In table 3, the "recommended" concept is stronger than the "advised" concept.

If the value of κ_{NS} or κ_S is lower than 0 or if the values of κ_{NS} and κ_S are between 0 to 0.41, feature construction is recommended.

If the value of κ_{NS} or κ_S is between 0 and 0.41 then feature construction is advised. In these cases, feature construction can or cannot improve the learning accuracy. However the decision must depend on :

1. The effective number of features : does the user want to reduce the effective number of features?
2. The learning accuracy : does the user want to improve the learning accuracy with-out taking account of the effective number of features?
3. The calculative cost.

Table 3. Decisional table

κ_{NS} κ_S	$]0.41; 1[$	$]0; 0.41[$	$] - 1; 0[$
$]0.41; 1[$	FC useless	FC advised	FC recommended
$]0; 0.41[$	FC advised	FC recommended	FC essential
$] - 1; 0[$	FC recommended	FC essential	FC essential

In order to obtain a visual representation, we can use a graph whose X-axis represents κ_S and the Y-axis represents κ_{NS}. Each data base is represented in the decisional graph by a point having for X-coordinate the value of κ_S and for Y-coordinate the value of κ_{NS}. According to the area in which the point is, the user can easily know if he must or not apply feature construction.

4   Preprocessing Step

We propose to structure the preprocessing step. Two cases can be met :

1. Applying feature selection only ;
2. Applying feature construction and feature selection.

All features are provided to the preprocessing step. We apply a feature selection method in order to remove the noisy, redundant and/or irrelevant features. The features subset is then subjected to the two Kappa coefficients. If these coefficients conclude that feature construction is essential then a method of feature construction is applied. If these coefficients conclude that the feature construction method is useless then the features subset is directly provided to the learning algorithm.

5   Experimentation

We study 9 data bases resulting from the collection of UCI, [5]. The quantitative features are discretized with Fusinter method, [6]. We use ID3, see [7]. The objects set is shared in two subsets, while keeping the initial distribution of classes. The first subset contains 30% of the objects set and will be used to apply feature selection, to calcul the two Kappa coefficients, and to apply feature construction if it's necessary. The second subset contains 70% of the objects set and will be used for the tests before and after the preprocessing step. The method of feature selection used is developed by [8] and the method of feature construction used is developed by [9]. On each data base, we first apply the method of feature selection. Then, we calculate the two Kappa coefficients.

Tables 4 and 5 present the values of κ_{NS} and κ_S:

1. Few bases do not require feature construction. Only bases Monks-3, Iono and Vehicle do not require this process.
2. Feature construction is essential for German base.
3. Feature construction is advised for Austra, Breast and CRX bases.
4. Feature construction is recommended for Pima and Tic Tac Toe bases.

We apply the feature construction method for all bases for which feature construction is advised, recommended or essential.

Tables 6 and 7 present the cost and the standard deviation for a 10-Fold-Cross-Validation and for a 5-Fold-Cross-Validation with ID3.

Table 4. κ_{NS}

	Austra	Breast	CRX	Iono	German	Monks-3	Pima	Tic Tac Toe	Vehicle
P_o	0,56	0,68	0,56	0,90	0,55	0,98	0,60	0,68	0,58
P_e	0,55	0,63	0,55	0,54	0,60	0,50	0,64	0,53	0,25
κ_{NS}	0,01	0,13	0,01	0,79	-0,11	0,96	-0,09	0,31	0,44

Table 5. κ_S

	Austra	Breast	CRX	Iono	German	Monks-3	Pima	Tic Tac Toe	Vehicle
P_o	0,87	0,96	0,91	0,98	0,76	0,99	0,79	0,65	0,72
P_e	0,50	0,55	0,50	0,54	0,62	0,50	0,53	0,54	0,25
κ_S	0,75	0,90	0,81	0,96	0,38	0,99	0,54	0,25	0,62

Table 6. ID3 and 10-Fold-Cross-Validation.$[Cost(\sigma)]$

	Without preprocessing	With preprocessing	Preprocessing step
Austra	16.6 (4.57)	15.72 (5.6)	Selection + Construction
Breast	5.95 (1.95)	4.29 (2.13)	Selection + Construction
CRX	14.73 (5.68)	14.06 (4.73)	Selection + Construction
German	31.86 (7.53)	25.57 (7.16)	Selection + Construction
Iono	21.37 (8.39)	11.73 (5.59)	Selection
Monks-3	1.28 (1.28)	3.88 (2.69)	Selection
Pima	26.11 (5.43)	25.45 (7.86)	Selection + Construction
Tic Tac Toe	33.43 (5)	23.08 (5.59)	Selection + Construction
Vehicle	34.24 (4.96)	28.75 (5.44)	Selection

Table 7. ID3 and 5-Fold-Cross-Validation.$[Cost(\sigma)]$

	Without preprocessing	With preprocessing	Preprocessing step
Austra	15,91 (2,58)	15,49 (4,63)	Selection + Construction
Breast	5,7 (1,89)	5,29 (0,99)	Selection + Construction
CRX	14,66 (2,43)	16,11 (2,36)	Selection + Construction
German	28,57 (4,58)	24,14 (2,23)	Selection + Construction
Iono	13,39 (3,62)	11,72 (2,91)	Selection
Monks-3	1,29 (0,81)	3,86 (3,34)	Selection
Pima	24,3 (2,48)	23,74 (5,22)	Selection + Construction
Tic Tac Toe	22,8 (3,94)	24,1 (2,2)	Selection + Construction
Vehicle	29,41 (3,49)	32,1 (2,78)	Selection

Table 8. Effective number of features under consideration

	Without preprocessing	With preprocessing
Austra	14	3
Breast	9	5
CRX	15	5
German	20	7
Iono	34	2
Monks-3	6	2
Pima	8	4
Tic Tac Toe	9	9
Vehicle	18	14

Table 9. Gap and relative gap(ID3 and 10-Fold-Cross-Validation)

	Gap	Relative Gap
Austra	-0,88	-0,05
Breast	-1,66	-0,28
CRX	-0,67	-0,05
German	-6,29	-0,20
Iono	-9,64	-0,45
Monks-3	2,60	2,03
Pima	-0,66	-0,03
Tic Tac Toe	-10,35	-0,31
Vehicle	-5,49	-0,16

Table 10. Gap and relative gap(ID3 and 5-Fold-Cross-Validation)

	Gap	Relative Gap
Austra	-0,42	-0,03
Breast	-0,41	-0,07
CRX	1,45	0,10
German	-4,43	-0,16
Iono	-1,67	-0,12
Monks-3	2,57	1,99
Pima	-0,56	-0,02
Tic Tac Toe	1,30	0,06
Vehicle	2,69	0,09

Table 8 presents the effective number of features under consideration before and after the preprocessing step.

Tables 9 and 10 present the gap and the relative gap between the learning cost without preprocessing and the learning cost with preprocessing.

The gap is: Learning cost with preprocessing - Learning cost without preprocessing. The relative gap is: (Learning cost with preprocessing - Learning cost without preprocessing)/Learnig cost without preprocessing.

In most cases, with the 10-Fold-Cross-Validation, the preprocessing step is followed by an improvement of the accuracy and a reduction of the effective number of features under consideration. We can note a reduction of the accuracy with Monks-3 : but This base doesn't need feature selection nor feature construction.

With the 5-Fold-Cross-Validation, we can note some reduction of the accuracy (bases CRX, Tic Tac Toe, Monks-3 and Vehicle) with a reduction of the effective number of features under consideration. So, in this case the user must arbitrate between the learning accuracy and the effective number of features under consideration.

6 Conclusion

We create a system allowing to manage and to optimize the preprocessing step. After the application of the feature selection process, we use two coefficients based on the Kappa coefficient. These two coefficients enable us to determine if feature construction is useful. The experiments show us that the feature construction process is not always essential. The learning accuracy is improved. The user can influence the decision related to the feature construction process according to his priorities.

It would be interesting to create a coefficient which can arbitrate between selection and construction. Four situations would be then possible:

1. Feature construction and feature selection are useful to improve the learning accuracy;
2. Feature selection is essential and feature construction is useless;
3. Feature construction is essential and feature selection is useless;
4. Feature construction and feature selection are useless.

Thus, the preprocessing step would then be preceded by the calculus of a coefficient which structure the preprocessing step.

References

1. Cohen, J.: "A coefficient of agreement for nominal scales." Educ. Psychol. Meas. **20**: 27-46 (1960).
2. Landis, J.R., Koch, G.G.: "The Measurement of Observer Agreement for Categorical Data." Biometrics **33**: 159-174 (1977).
3. Huang, Z.: "A fast clustering algorithm to cluster very large categorical data sets in data mining." Research Issues on Data Mining and Knowledge Discovery (1997).
4. MacQueen, J.B.: Some methods for classification and analysis of multivariate observations. Proc. of 5th Berkley Symposium on Mathematical Statistics and Probbility (1967).

5. Blake, C.L., Merz, C.J.: UCI Repository of machine learning databases, Irvine, CA: University of California, Department of Information and Computer Science (1998).
6. Zighed, D., Rabaseda, S., et al.: "FUSINTER: a method for discretization of continuous attributes for supervised learning." International Journal of Uncertainty, Fuziness and Knowledge-Based Systems (1998).
7. Quinlan, J.R.: Discovering rules from large collections of examples: a case study. Expert Systems in the Micro-electronic Age. D. Michie. Edinburgh, Edinburgh University Press: 168-201 (1979).
8. Legrand, G., Nicoloyannis, N.: Sélection de variables et agrégation d'opinions, Revue des nouvelles technologies de l'information, RNTI-C-1, Cépaduès, 89-101, ISBN 2.85428.667.7. (2004).
9. Legrand, G., Nicoloyannis, N.: Nouvelle méthode de construction de variables, Rencontres de la société française de classification, SFC04, Bordeaux (2004).

Incremental Attribute Reduction Based on Elementary Sets

Feng Hu, Guoyin Wang, Hai Huang, and Yu Wu

Institute of Computer Science and Technology,
Chongqing University of Posts and Telecommunications,
Chongqing 400065, P.R.China
wanggy@ieee.org

Abstract. In the research of knowledge acquisition based on rough sets theory, attribute reduction is a key problem. Many researchers proposed some algorithms for attribute reduction. Unfortunately, most of them are designed for static data processing. However, many real data are generated dynamically. In this paper, an incremental attribute reduction algorithm is proposed. When new objects are added into a decision information system, a new attribute reduction can be got by this method quickly.

1   Introduction

Rough Sets [1] (RS) is a valid mathematical theory to deal with imprecise, uncertain, and vague information. It has been applied in such fields as machine learning, data mining, intelligent data analyzing and control algorithm acquiring, etc, successfully since it was developed by Professor Z. Pawlak in 1982.

Attribute reduction [2] is a key problem in rough sets based knowledge acquisition, and many researchers proposed some algorithms for attribute reduction [3-5]. Unfortunately, most of them are designed for static data processing. However, many real data are generated dynamically. Thus, many researchers suggest that knowledge acquisition algorithms should better be incremental[6-8]. Some incremental rough sets based rule extraction algorithms [9-11] have been developed, but they don't consider attribute reduction problem. An incremental attribute reduction algorithm is developed in paper [12]. It can only process information systems without decision attribute. However, most of real information systems are decision information system. Incremental attribute reduction in decision information system would be more important. In paper [13-15], some methods are proposed for incremental attribute reduction in decision information system. In this paper, we develop an incremental attribute reduction algorithm. It can generate a new reduction result for a decision information system quickly after new objects are added. Now, we are comparing our algorithm with these methods developed in paper [13-15] and testing more difficult data.

The rest of this paper is organized as follows: In section 2, basic notions about rough sets theory are introduced. In section 3, we proposed the principle

D. Ślęzak et al. (Eds.): RSFDGrC 2005, LNAI 3641, pp. 185–193, 2005.

of incremental attribute reduction. In section 4, the incremental attribute reduction algorithm based on elementary set is developed. In section 5, the result of simulation experiments is discussed. At last, we conclude this paper in section 6.

2   Basic Notions in Rough Sets Theory

For the convenience of description, some basic notions of decision information systems are introduced here at first.

Definition 1. *(decision information systems [16-18]) A decision information system is defined as $S =< U, R, V, f >$, where U is a non-empty finite set of objects, called universe, R is a non-empty finite set of attributes, $R = C \bigcup D$, where C is the set of condition attributes and D is the set of decision attributes, $D \neq$. $V = \bigcup_{p \in R} V_p$, and V_p is the domain of the attribute p. $f : U \times R \to V$ is a total function such that $f(x_i, p) \in V_p$ for every $p \in R, x_i \in U$.*

Definition 2. *(indiscernibility relation [16-18]) Given a decision information system $S =< U, C \bigcup D, V, f >$, each subset $B \subseteq C$ of attribute determines an indiscernibility relation $IND(B)$ as follows: $IND(B) = \{(x, y) | (x, y) \in U \times U, \forall b \in B, (b(x) = b(y))\}$. Equivalent classes of the relation $IND(B)$ will be called B elementary sets in S, we denote it as E_i. The set of all elementary sets will be denoted by $U/IND(B)$.*

Definition 3. *(consistency and inconsistency of elementary sets) Given a decision information system $S =< U, C \bigcup D, V, f >$. An elementary set $E_i \in U/IND(B)$ $(B \subseteq C)$ is consistent iff all its objects have the same decision value. Otherwise, it is inconsistent.*

Definition 4. *(lower-approximation and upper-approximation [16-18]) Given an information system $S =< U, R, V, f >$, for any subset $X \subseteq U$ and indiscernibility relation $IND(B)$, the B lower-approximation and upper-approximation of X is defined as: $B\_(X) = \bigcup\{Y_i | Y_i \in U/IND(B) \land Y_i \subseteq X\}$, $B^-(X) = \bigcup\{Y_i | Y_i \in U/IND(B) \land Y_i \cap X \neq \}$.*

Definition 5. *(positive region [16-18]) Given a decision information system $S =< U, R, V, f >$, $P \subseteq R$ and $Q \subseteq R$, the P positive region of Q is defined as: $Pos_P(Q) = \bigcup_{X \in U/Q} P\_(X)$.*

3   Principle of Incremental Attribute Reduction

According to Definition 3, all elementary sets can be divided into two parts: positive elementary set and negative elementary set.

Definition 6. *(positive elementary set and negative elementary set): Given a decision information system $S =< U, C \bigcup D, V, f >$, $D=\{d\}$. All consistent C elementary sets in S construct a set Ps, that is, $\forall_{E_i \in Ps} \forall_{x, y \in E_i} (d(x) = d(y))$.*

Ps is called the positive elementary set. All inconsistent C elementary sets in S construct another set Ns, that is, $\forall_{E_i \in Ns} \exists_{x,y \in E_i}(d(x) \neq d(y))$ *, Ns is called the negative elementary set.*

Definition 7. *(collision elementary set): Given a decision information system* $S = < U, C \bigcup D, V, f >$, *C and D are its condition attribute set and decision attribute set respectively. Ps is its positive elementary set and Ns is its negative elementary set. Given an attribute subset* $B \subseteq C, \forall E_i \in Ps$, *if* E_i *can satisfy one of the following two conditions:*

(1) There is a elementary set $E_j \in Ps(E_i \neq E_j)$ *, E_i and E_j have the same values for the condition attribute subset B, and different values for the decision attribute set D.*

(2) There is a elementary set $E_j \in Ns$ *, E_i and E_j have the same values for the condition attribute subset B.*

Then E_i *is called a collision elementary set on attribute set B in Ps, otherwise* E_i *is called a non-collision elementary set on attribute set B in Ps.*

Proposition 1. *(monotony of collision element set): Assume E_i is a non-collision elementary set on attribute set* $B(B \subseteq C)$ *, for any attribute set* $A(B \subseteq A \subseteq C)$ *, E_i is also a non-collision elementary set on attribute A. On the contrary, assume E_i is a collision elementary set on attribute set* $B(B \subseteq C)$, *for any attribute set* $A(A \subseteq B \subseteq C)$, *$E_i$ a is also collision elementary set on attribute set A.*

Proof: according to Definition 7, it is obvious.

Proposition 2. *Given a decision information system* $S = < U, C \bigcup D, V, f >$, *for any attribute set* $B \subseteq C$, $Pos_B(D) = Pos_C(D)$ *iff there is no collision elementary set on B in its positive elementary set Ps.*

Proof: It is obvious according to the define of positive region.

In this paper, an incremental attribute reduction algorithm is developed based on Proposition 1 and Proposition 2.

4   Incremental Attribute Reduction Algorithm Based on Elementary Sets

Let *red* be an attribute reduction of a decision information system $S = < U, C \bigcup D, V, f >$, where $D=\{d\}$. Thus, $Pos_C(D) = Pos_{red}(D)$. According to Proposition 2, there is no collision elementary set on attribute set *red* in the positive elementary set Ps of S. When a new object (we denote it as $record_{new}$) is added into the decision information system, three different cases may happen.

1. $\exists_{E_i \in Ns}(record_{new} \in E_i)$. According to Definition 7, it is obvious that there is no collision element on *red* in Ps after $record_{new}$ is added into the decision information systems, thus $Pos_C(D) = Pos_{red}(D)$ still holds after $record_{new}$ is added.

2. $\exists_{E_i \in Ps}(record_{new} \in E_i)$. There will be the following two cases:

   2.1. $\forall_{x \in E_i}(d(x) = d(record_{new}))$. According to Definition 7, it is obvious that there is no collision elementary set on red in Ps after $record_{new}$ is added, thus $Pos_C(D) = Pos_{red}(D)$ still holds.

   2.2. $\forall_{x \in E_i}(d(x) \neq d(record_{new}))$. That is, the elementary set E_i will no longer belong to Ps after $record_{new}$ is added into E_i. Thus, $Ps = Ps - E_i, Ns = Ns \bigcup E_i$. It is obvious that there is no collision elementary set on red in Ps after $record_{new}$ is added, thus $Pos_C(D) = Pos_{red}(D)$ still holds.

3. $\forall_{E_i \in Ps \wedge E_i \in Ns} record_{new} \notin E_i$. Thus, a new elementary set E_{new} will be generated for $record_{new}$. E_{new} must belong to the positive elementary set, so $Ps = Ps \bigcup E_{new}$. We compare E_{new} with all other elementary sets in Ps and Ns:

   3.1. If E_{new} is a non-collision elementary set on red, it is obvious that there is no collision elementary set on red in Ps after $record_{new}$ is added, then $Pos_C(D) = Pos_{red}(D)$ still holds.

   3.2. If E_{new} is a collision elementary set on red, that is $Pos_C(D) \neq Pos_{red}(D)$ after $record_{new}$ is added into Ps. We might as well assume that E_{new} contradicts E_k on red. There must be some condition attributes in attribute set $C - red$ on which E_{new} and E_k have different values. Let $(c_1, c_2, ..., c_k \in (C - red)) \wedge \forall_{x \in E_{new}, y \in E_k}((c_1(x) \neq c_1(y)) \wedge (c_2(x) \neq c_2(y)) \wedge ... \wedge (c_k(x) \neq c_k(y)))$, according to Definition 7, it is obviously that E_{new} won't contradict E_k on $red \cup \{c_i\} (i = 1, ..., k)$. According to Proposition 1, those elementary sets that don't contradict E_{new} on red won't contradict on $red \cup \{c_i\} (i = 1, ..., k)$ also. Therefore, there is no collision elementary set on $red \cup \{c_i\}$ in Ps, that is $Pos_C(D) = Pos_{red \cup \{c_i\}}(D)$.

In step 3.2, in order to get the attribute reduction result with as less number of condition attributes as possible, we would not choose a condition attribute from $c_i, c_2, ..., c_k$ and add it into red immediately in our algorithm when more than 1 objects are added. We could generate a disjunctive formula for each of them, that is $b_j = c_i \vee c_2 \vee, ..., \vee c_k$. After all new objects are added into the original decision information system, we unite all these disjunctive formulas, let it be $F = b_1 \wedge b_2 \wedge ... \wedge b_m$ (Suppose m disjunctive formulas are generated). F is a conjunctive formal formula (CNF). We could transform F into a disjunctive normal formula (DNF), that is, $F = q_1 \vee q_2 \vee ... \vee q_i \vee ... \vee q_n (q_i = c_1 \wedge c_2 \wedge ... \wedge c_l)$. Suppose $q_i(q_i = c_1 \wedge c_2 \wedge ... \wedge c_l)$ is the smallest term in F, that is the number of attributes in q_i is less than all other terms in F. Let $A = \{c_1, c_2, ..., c_l\}$. It is obvious that there is no collision elementary set on $red \cup A$ in Ps, that is, $Pos_C(D) = Pos_{red \cup A}(D)$.

In the following, we can get the attribute reduction of the new decision information systems after getting rid of possible redundant attribute in $red \cup A$.

Algorithm1: Incremental attribute reduction algorithm based on element set.

Input: An original decision information system $S = < U, C \bigcup D, V, f >$, one of its attribute reduction red, its positive elementary set Ps and negative element set Ns, and a new object set Add to be added.

Output: the attribute reduction result Red of the new decision information system $S_1 =< U \bigcup Add, C \bigcup D, V_1, f_1 >$.

1. Choose the first object from Add and denote it as $record_{new}$, let $k=1$, $Add = Add - \{record_{new}\}$.
2. if $(\exists_{E_i \in Ns}(record_{new} \in E_i))$, go to Step 5.
3. if $(\exists_{E_i \in Ps}(record_{new} \in E_i))$,
    3.1. if $\forall_{x \in E_i}(d(x) = d(record_{new})$, go to Step5.
    3.2. if $\forall_{x \in E_i}(d(x) \neq d(record_{new})$, $Ps = Ps - E_i$, $Ns = Ns \bigcup E_i$, go to Step5.
4. Generate a new elementary set E_{new} for $record_{new}$.
    4.1. for $i=1$ to $|Ps|$ do
        4.1.1. Let E_i be the i-th elementary set in Ps.
        4.1.2. If E_{new} contradicts E_i on attribute set red, let $c_i, c_2, ..., c_j$ be the attributes in the attribute set $C - red$ on which E_{new} and E_i have different values, and $b_k = c_i \vee c_2 \vee, ..., \vee c_j$, $k = k + 1$.
    4.2. for $i=1$ to $|Ns|$ do
        4.2.1. (Let E_i be the i-th elementary set in Ns.
        4.2.2. If E_{new} contradicts E_i on attribute set red, just like Step 4.1, we can get $b_k = c_i \vee c_2 \vee, ..., \vee c_j$, $k = k + 1$.
        4.2.3. 4.3 $Ps = Ps \cup E_{new}$.
5. If $Add = \emptyset$, go to Step6. Otherwise, choose the next object from Add, and denote it as $record_{new}$, $Add = Add - \{record_{new}\}$, go to Step 2.
6. Let $F = b_1 \wedge b_2 \wedge ... \wedge b_{k-1}$ and transform F to a disjunctive formula $(F = q_1 \vee q_2 \vee ... \vee q_i \vee ... \vee q_n)$. Choose the smallest term $q_j (q_i = c_1 \wedge c_2 \wedge ... \wedge c_l)$ from F. $A = \{c_1, c_2, ..., c_l\}$.
7. $Red = red \cup A$.
8. for $i=1$ to $|Red|$ do
    8.1. $P = Red$;
    8.2. Let c_i be i-th attribute in Red;
    8.3. $P = P - \{c_i\}$;
    8.4. if $Pos_C(D) = Pos_P(D)$, then $Red = P$.
9. Return Red.

5   Experiment Results

In order to test the validity of the our algorithm, three classical algorithms for attribute reduction (attribute reduction algorithm based on information entropy, attribute reduction algorithm based on discernibility matrix, and attribute reduction algorithm based on character choice) in RIDAS system [19] are used. The configuration of the PC in our experiments is P4 2.66G(CPU), 512M(memory), windows2000 (operation system).

5.1   UCI Database Test

We use datasets Heart_c_ls, Pima_India, Crx_bq_ls, Liver_disorder and Abalone from UCI database (These data sets can be downloaded at http://www.ics.uci.edu) as test dataset. The parameters of these five data sets are shown in Table 1. 80% objects of these five data sets are used as the original decision information systems, and the other 20% are used as additive datasets respectively. The whole dataset are used as the new decision information systems. Firstly, we use the three classical algorithms to generate the attribute reductions for each original decision information system. Secondly, based on previous results, we use Algorithm 1 to generate the attribute reductions for each new decision information system. Finally, we use the three classical algorithms to generate the attribute reductions for each new decision information system, and compare them with the attribute reductions generating by Algorithm 1. The experiment results are shown in Table 2. Where, T is running time of algorithm, its unit is second. T=0 means that the running time is less than 1 millisecond. n is the number of condition attributes in reduction results.

From Table 2, we can find that the running time of our incremental algorithm is much less than non-incremental algorithms.

5.2   Test on Inconsistent Dataset

In order to test the validity of Algorithm 1 for processing inconsistent decision information systems, we construct five inconsistent datasets randomly. The

Table 1. Experiment Dataset

Dataset	Number of Condition Attributes	Number of Objects
Heart_c_ls	13	303
Pima_India	8	738
Crx_bq_ls	15	690
Liver_disorder	6	1260
Abalone	8	4177

Table 2. Experiment Results for UCI Databases

Dataset	Character choice				Information entropy				discernibility matrix			
	Non-incremental		incremental		Non-incremental		incremental		Non-incremental		incremental	
	T	n	T	n	T	n	T	n	T	n	T	n
Heart_c_ls	4.704	9	0	9	0.156	9	0	9	0.187	9	0.016	9
Pima_India	36.422	5	0	5	0.406	5	0.016	5	0.5	5	0.016	5
Crx_bq_ls	48.187	13	0.109	6	1.032	6	0.031	6	1.954	6	0.015	6
Liver_disorder	71.64	5	0	5	0.078	5	0.016	5	1.359	5	0	5
Abalone	118.406	7	1.266	6	17.234	6	0.594	6	41.875	6	0.578	6

Table 3. Experiment results of Intolerant Dataset

	Character choice				Information entropy				discernibility matrix			
Dataset	Non-increm ental		incremental		Non-increm ental		incremental		Non-increm ental		incremental	
	T	n	T	n	T	n	T	n	T	n	T	n
DataSet1	109.484	7	0.11	7	2.109	6	0.032	6	7.015	6	0.047	6
DataSet2	783.438	7	0.344	7	8.484	6	0.156	7	19.922	6	0.172	7
DataSet3	2598.39	7	0.875	7	19.219	6	0.453	7	42.875	7	0.484	7
DataSet4	6800.11	7	1.5	7	34.516	6	1.219	7	76.563	6	0.813	7
DataSet5	12727.11	8	1.375	8	54.625	7	1.5	7	122.06	7	1.719	7

number of objects of the five datasets are 1000, 2000, 3000, 4000 and 5000 respectively. The number of condition attributes and decision attribute are 15 and 1. For the former 80% objects, the values of their former 10 condition attributes and decision attribute are generated randomly from 0 to 9, and the other 5 condition attributes are all set to be 0. It is taken as the original decision information system. For the other 20% objects, the values of their former 10 condition attributes and decision attribute are generated randomly from 0 to 9, and the other 5 condition attributes are generated randomly from 0 to 1. It is taken as the dataset to be added. The whole dataset is taken as the new decision information system. Some conflict objects will be generated in this way. The test method is similar to 5.1. The experiment result is shown in Table 3.

From Table 3, we can find that the running time of our incremental algorithm is also much less than non-incremental algorithms when processing inconsistent decision information systems.

5.3 Continuous Incremental Learning Test

In order to simulate the incremental knowledge learning ability of a human brain, we construct another dataset randomly. The number of condition attributes and decision attribute are 15 and 1 respectively. The values of condition attributes and decision attribute are generated randomly from 0 to 9, the number of objects of this dataset is 1000 at first. We use the attribute reduction algorithm based on information entropy to generate its attribute reduction. Then, we add new objects into this dataset and use Algorithm 1 to generate the attribute reduction of the new decision information system continuously. The number of objects are 2000, 5000, 10,000, 20,000, 50,000, 100,000, 200,000, 500,000 and 1,000,000 respectively after new objects are added each time. The experiment result is shown in Table 4. Where, N is the number of objects in new decision information system, T is running time, h means hour, m means minute, s means second, and n is the number of condition attributes in the attribute reduction result.

From Table 4, we can find that continuous incremental attribute reduction could be conducted with Algorithm 1. It could simulate the incremental knowledge learning process of a human brain.

Table 4. Experiment Result of Continuous Incremental Test

N	2,000	5,000	10,000	20,000	50,000	100,000	200,000	500,000	1,000,000
T	0.328s	6s	22s	1m29s	12m34s	45m11s	2h20m42s	15h12m6s	71h46m40s
n	6	7	8	8	9	10	10	11	11

Based on above tests, we could have a conclusion that the Algorithm 1 can generate attribute reduction for dynamic decision information systems quickly.

6   Conclusion

Incremental learning is an important problem in AI research. Attribute reduction is a key problem for rough sets based knowledge acquisition. Some incremental rough sets based algorithms for rule extraction have been developed. Unfortunately, they don't consider the attribute reduction problem. In paper [13-15], some methods are proposed for incremental attribute reduction in decision information system. In this paper, an incremental attribute reduction algorithm based on elementary sets is proposed, it can generate attribute reduction for dynamic decision information systems quickly. Our experiment results illustrate that this algorithm is effective. Now, we are comparing our algorithm with these methods developed in paper [13-15] and testing more difficult data.

Acknowledgements. This paper is partially supported by Program for New Century Excellent Talents in University (NCET), National Natural Science Foundation of P. R. China (No.60373111), Application Science Foundation of Chongqing, and Science & Technology Research Program of the Municipal Education Committee of Chongqing of China (No.040505), Young Teacher Foundation of Chongqing University of Posts and Telecommunications (No. A2004-16).

References

1. Pawlak Z.: Rough Set. International Journal of Computer and Information Sciences, Vol.11 (1982) 341-356
2. Wang G.Y. (ed): Rough Set Theory and Knowledge Acquisition, Xi'an Jiaotong University Press, Xi'an (2001)
3. Bazan J.G.: Dynamic reducts and statistical inference, Sixth International Conference on Information Processing and Management of Uncertainty in Knowledge-based Systems (IPMU'96), Vol.III (1996) 1147–1152
4. Bazan J. G., Skowron A., Synak P.: Reducts as a tool for extracting laws from decision tables, International Symposium on Methodologies for Intelligent Systems (ISMIS), Charlotte, NC, series: Lecture Notes in Artificial Intelligence, Vol.869 (1994) 346-355
5. Wroblewski J.: Theoretical Foundations of Order-Based Genetic Algorithms, Fundamenta Informaticae, Vol.28(3-4) (1996) 423-430

6. Fayyad U.M., Shapiro L.P., Smyth P., Uthurusamy R.: Advances in Knowledge Discovery and Data Mining. Menlo Park (ed.), AAAI Press/The MIT Press, California (1996)
7. Cercone V., Tsuchiya M.: Luesy Editors Introdunction, IEEE Transactions on Knowledge and Data Engineering, Vol.5(6) (1993) 901-902
8. Shapiro L.P., Frawley W.J.: Knowledge Discovery in Database, Menlo Park (ed.), AAAI Press/The MIT Press, California (1991)
9. Zheng Z., Wang G.Y.: RRIA: A Rough Set and Rule Tree Based Incremental knowledge Acquisition Algorithm, Fundamenta Informaticae, Vol.59 (2004) 299-313
10. Synak P.: Adaptation of decomposition tree to extended data, Fifth World Multiconference on Systemics, Cybernetics and Informatics, Vol.VII (2001) 552-556
11. Li Y.L., Xu C.F., Gen W.D.: Incremental rule extraction algorithm based on improved discernibility matrix. Chinese Journal of Computer Science, Vol.30(5.A) (2003) 46-49
12. Liu Z.T.: An Incremental Arithmetic for the Smallest Reduction of Attributes, Chinese Journal of Electronics, Vol.27(11) (1999) 96-98
13. Orlowska M., Orlowski M.: Maintenance of Knowledge in Dynamic Information Systems, In: Slowinski R. (ed.), Intelligent Decision Support. Handbook of Applications and Advances of the Rough Set Theory, Kluwer Academic Publishers, Dordrecht (1992) 315-330
14. Susmaga R.: Experiments in Incremental Computation of Reducts, In: Skowron A., Polkowski L. (eds), Rough Sets in Data Mining and Knowledge Discovery, Springer-Verlag, Berlin (1998)
15. Ziarko W., Shan N.: Data-Based Acquisition and Incremental Modification of Classification Rules, Computational Intelligence, Vol.11(2) (1995) 357-370
16. Hu X.H. (ed), Knowledge Discovery in Databases: An Attribute-Oriented rough set approach, University of Regina Press, Regina (1996)
17. Pawlak Z.: Rough sets – Theoretical aspects of reasoning about data. Kluwer Academic Publishers (1991)
18. Polkowski L.: Rough Sets: Mathematical Foundations, Physica Verlag, Heidelberg (2002)
19. Wang G.Y., Zheng Z., Zhang Y.: RIDAS – A Rough Set Based Intelligent Data Analysis System. The First Int. Conf. on Machine Learning and Cybernetics (2002) 646-649

Finding Rough Set Reducts with SAT

Richard Jensen[1], Qiang Shen[1], and Andrew Tuson[2]

[1] Department of Computer Science,
The University of Wales, Aberystwyth
[2] Department of Computing, School of Informatics,
City University, London
{rkj, qqs}@aber.ed.ac.uk

Abstract. Feature selection refers to the problem of selecting those input features that are most predictive of a given outcome; a problem encountered in many areas such as machine learning, pattern recognition and signal processing. In particular, solution to this has found successful application in tasks that involve datasets containing huge numbers of features (in the order of tens of thousands), which would be impossible to process further. Recent examples include text processing and web content classification. Rough set theory has been used as such a dataset pre-processor with much success, but current methods are inadequate at finding *minimal* reductions, the smallest sets of features possible. This paper proposes a technique that considers this problem from a propositional satisfiability perspective. In this framework, minimal subsets can be located and verified. An initial experimental investigation is conducted, comparing the new method with a standard rough set-based feature selector.

1 Introduction

Many problems in machine learning involve high dimensional descriptions of input features. It is therefore not surprising that much research has been carried out on dimensionality reduction [4]. However, existing work tends to destroy the underlying semantics of the features after reduction or require additional information about the given data set for thresholding. A technique that can reduce dimensionality using information contained within the dataset and that preserves the meaning of the features (i.e. semantics-preserving) is clearly desirable. Rough set theory (RST) can be used as such a tool to discover data dependencies and to reduce the number of attributes contained in a dataset using the data alone, requiring no additional information [10,11].

Over the past ten years, RST has indeed become a topic of great interest to researchers and has been applied to many domains. Given a dataset with discretized attribute values, it is possible to find a subset (termed a *reduct*) of the original attributes using RST that are the most informative; all other attributes can be removed from the dataset with very little information loss. However, current methods such as heuristic and stochastic-based search are inadequate at finding minimal reductions. By reformulating the rough set reduction task

D. Ślęzak et al. (Eds.): RSFDGrC 2005, LNAI 3641, pp. 194–203, 2005.

in a propositional satisfiability (SAT) framework, solution techniques from SAT may be applied that should be able to discover such subsets, guaranteeing their minimality.

The rest of this paper is structured as follows. Section 2 details the main concepts involved in rough set feature selection, with an illustrative example. The third section introduces propositional satisfiability and how the problem of finding rough set reducts can be formulated in this way. The initial experimental results of the application of the new method is presented in section 4. Section 5 concludes the paper, with a discussion of some of the future work in this area.

2   Rough Set-Based Feature Selection

Rough set theory [10] is an extension of conventional set theory that supports approximations in decision making. The rough set itself is the approximation of a vague concept (set) by a pair of precise concepts, called lower and upper approximations, which are a classification of the domain of interest into disjoint categories. The lower approximation is a description of the domain objects which are known with certainty to belong to the subset of interest, whereas the upper approximation is a description of the objects which possibly belong to the subset.

There are two main approaches to finding rough set reducts: those that consider the degree of dependency and those that are concerned with the discernibility matrix. This section describes the fundamental ideas behind both approaches. To illustrate the operation of these, an example dataset (table 1) will be used.

Table 1. An example dataset

$x \in \mathbb{U}$	a	b	c	d	$\Rightarrow$ e
0	1	0	2	2	0
1	0	1	1	1	2
2	2	0	0	1	1
3	1	1	0	2	2
4	1	0	2	0	1
5	2	2	0	1	1
6	2	1	1	1	2
7	0	1	1	0	1

2.1   Rough Set Attribute Reduction

Central to Rough Set Attribute Reduction (RSAR) [3,7] is the concept of indiscernibility. Let $I = (\mathbb{U}, \mathbb{A})$ be an information system, where $\mathbb{U}$ is a non-empty set of finite objects (the universe) and $\mathbb{A}$ is a non-empty finite set of attributes such that $a : \mathbb{U} \to V_a$ for every $a \in \mathbb{A}$. V_a is the set of values that attribute a may take. With any $P \subseteq \mathbb{A}$ there is an associated equivalence relation $IND(P)$:

$$IND(P) = \{(x, y) \in \mathbb{U}^2 \mid \forall a \in P, \ a(x) = a(y)\} \tag{1}$$

The partition of $\mathbb{U}$, generated by $IND(P)$ is denoted $\mathbb{U}/IND(P)$ (or $\mathbb{U}/P$) and can be calculated as follows:

$$\mathbb{U}/IND(P) = \otimes\{a \in P : \mathbb{U}/IND(\{a\})\}, \tag{2}$$

where

$$A \otimes B = \{X \cap Y : \forall X \in A, \forall Y \in B, X \cap Y \neq \varnothing\} \tag{3}$$

If $(x, y) \in IND(P)$, then x and y are indiscernible by attributes from P. The equivalence classes of the P-indiscernibility relation are denoted $[x]_P$.

Let $X \subseteq \mathbb{U}$. X can be approximated using only the information contained within P by constructing the P-*lower* and P-*upper* approximations of X:

$$\underline{P}X = \{x \mid [x]_P \subseteq X\} \tag{4}$$

$$\overline{P}X = \{x \mid [x]_P \cap X \neq \varnothing\} \tag{5}$$

Let P and Q be equivalence relations over $\mathbb{U}$, then the positive region can be defined as:

$$POS_P(Q) = \bigcup_{X \in \mathbb{U}/Q} \underline{P}X \tag{6}$$

The positive region contains all objects of $\mathbb{U}$ that can be classified to classes of $\mathbb{U}/Q$ using the information in attributes P. For example, let $P = \{b,c\}$ and $Q = \{e\}$, then

$$POS_P(Q) = \bigcup\{\varnothing, \{2,5\}, \{3\}\} = \{2,3,5\}$$

Using this definition of the positive region, the rough set degree of dependency of a set of attributes Q on a set of attributes P is defined in the following way:

For P, $Q \subset A$, it is said that Q depends on P in a degree k $(0 \le k \le 1)$, denoted $P \Rightarrow_k Q$, if

$$k = \gamma_P(Q) = \frac{|POS_P(Q)|}{|\mathbb{U}|} \tag{7}$$

In the example, the degree of dependency of attribute $\{e\}$ from the attributes $\{b,c\}$ is:

$$\gamma_{\{b,c\}}(\{e\}) = \frac{|POS_{\{b,c\}}(\{e\})|}{|\mathbb{U}|}$$
$$= \frac{|\{2,3,5\}|}{|\{0,1,2,3,4,5,6,7\}|} = \frac{3}{8}$$

The reduction of attributes is achieved by comparing equivalence relations generated by sets of attributes. Attributes are removed so that the reduced set provides the same predictive capability of the decision feature as the original. A *reduct* is defined as a subset of minimal cardinality R_{min} of the conditional attribute set $\mathbb{C}$ such that $\gamma_R(\mathbb{D}) = \gamma_\mathbb{C}(\mathbb{D})$.

QUICKREDUCT($\mathbb{C}$,$\mathbb{D}$).
$\mathbb{C}$, the set of all conditional features;
$\mathbb{D}$, the set of decision features.

(1) $R \leftarrow \{\}$
(2) **do**
(3) $T \leftarrow R$
(4) $\forall x \in (\mathbb{C} - R)$
(5)   **if** $\gamma_{R \cup \{x\}}(\mathbb{D}) > \gamma_T(\mathbb{D})$
(6) $T \leftarrow R \cup \{x\}$
(7) $R \leftarrow T$
(8)   **until** $\gamma_R(\mathbb{D}) == \gamma_{\mathbb{C}}(\mathbb{D})$
(9)   **return** R

Fig. 1. The QUICKREDUCT Algorithm

The QUICKREDUCT algorithm given in figure 1, attempts to calculate a reduct without exhaustively generating all possible subsets. It starts off with an empty set and adds in turn, one at a time, those attributes that result in the greatest increase in the rough set dependency metric, until this produces its maximum possible value for the dataset.

According to the QUICKREDUCT algorithm, the dependency of each attribute is calculated, and the best candidate chosen. Attribute d generates the highest dependency degree, so that attribute is chosen and the sets $\{a, d\}$, $\{b, d\}$ and $\{c, d\}$ are evaluated. This process continues until the dependency of the reduct equals the consistency of the dataset (1 if the dataset is consistent). In the example, the algorithm terminates after evaluating the subset $\{b, d\}$. The generated reduct shows the way of reducing the dimensionality of the original dataset by eliminating those conditional attributes that do not appear in the set.

This, however, is not guaranteed to find a *minimal* subset. Using the dependency function to discriminate between candidates may lead the search down a non-minimal path. It is impossible to predict which combinations of attributes will lead to an optimal reduct based on changes in dependency with the addition or deletion of single attributes. It does result in a close-to-minimal subset, though, which is still useful in greatly reducing dataset dimensionality.

2.2 Discernibility Matrix-Based Selection

Many applications of rough sets to feature selection make use of discernibility matrices for finding reducts. A discernibility matrix [12] of a decision table $D = (\mathbb{U}, \mathbb{C} \cup \mathbb{D})$ is a symmetric $|\mathbb{U}| \times |\mathbb{U}|$ matrix with entries defined:

$$d_{ij} = \{a \in \mathbb{C} | a(x_i) \neq a(x_j)\} \ \ i, j = 1, ..., |\mathbb{U}| \tag{8}$$

Each d_{ij} contains those attributes that differ between objects i and j. For finding reducts, the decision-relative discernibility matrix is of more interest. This only

considers those object discernibilities that occur when the corresponding decision attributes differ. Returning to the example dataset, the decision-relative
discernibility matrix found in table 2 is produced. For example, it can be seen
from the table that objects 0 and 1 differ in each attribute. Although some attributes in objects 1 and 3 differ, their corresponding decisions are the same so
no entry appears in the decision-relative matrix. Grouping all entries containing
single attributes forms the core of the dataset (those attributes appearing in
every reduct). Here, the core of the dataset is $\{d\}$.

Table 2. The decision-relative discernibility matrix

$x \in \mathbb{U}$	0	1	2	3	4	5	6	7
0								
1	a,b,c,d							
2	a,c,d	a,b,c						
3	b,c		a,b,d					
4	d	a,b,c,d		b,c,d				
5	a,b,c,d	a,b,c		a,b,d				
6	a,b,c,d		b,c		a,b,c,d	b,c		
7	a,b,c,d	d		a,c,d			a,d	

From this, the discernibility function can be defined. This is a concise notation
of how each object within the dataset may be distinguished from the others. A
discernibility function f_D is a boolean function of m boolean variables $a_1^*, ..., a_m^*$
(corresponding to the attributes $a_1, ..., a_m$) defined as below:

$$f_D(a_1^*, ..., a_m^*) = \wedge\{\vee c_{ij}^* | 1 \leq j \leq i \leq |\mathbb{U}|, c_{ij} \neq \emptyset\} \tag{9}$$

where $c_{ij}^* = \{a^* | a \in c_{ij}\}$. By finding the set of all prime implicants of the dis-
cernibility function, all the minimal reducts of a system may be determined.
From table 2, the decision-relative discernibility function is (with duplicates removed):

$$f_D(a,b,c,d) = \{a \vee b \vee c \vee d\} \wedge \{a \vee c \vee d\} \wedge \{b \vee c\}$$
$$\wedge \{d\} \wedge \{a \vee b \vee c\} \wedge \{a \vee b \vee d\}$$
$$\wedge \{b \vee c \vee d\} \wedge \{a \vee d\}$$

Further simplification can be performed by removing those sets (clauses) that
are supersets of others:

$$f_D(a,b,c,d) = \{b \vee c\} \wedge \{d\}$$

The reducts of the dataset may be obtained by converting the above expression from conjunctive normal form to disjunctive normal form (without negations). Hence, the minimal reducts are $\{b,d\}$ and $\{c,d\}$. Although this is guaranteed to discover all minimal subsets, it is a costly operation rendering the
method impractical for even medium-sized datasets.

For most applications, a single minimal subset is required for data reduction. This has led to approaches that consider finding individual shortest prime implicants from the discernibility function. A common method is to incrementally add those attributes that occur with the most frequency in the function, removing any clauses containing the attributes, until all clauses are eliminated [9]. However, even this does not ensure that a minimal subset is found - the search can proceed down non-minimal paths.

3   RSAR-SAT

The Propositional Satisfiability (SAT) problem [5] is one of the most studied NP-complete problems because of its significance in both theoretical research and practical applications. Given a boolean formula (typically in conjunctive normal form (CNF)), the SAT problem requires an assignment of variables/features so that the formula evaluates to true, or a determination that no such assignment exists. In recent years search algorithms based on the well-known Davis-Logemann-Loveland algorithm (DPLL) [5] are emerging as some of the most efficient methods for complete SAT solvers. Such solvers can either find a solution or prove that no solution exists.

Stochastic techniques have also been developed in order to reach a solution quickly. These pick random locations in the space of possible assignments and perform limited local searches from them. However, as these techniques do not examine the entire search space, they are unable to prove unsatisfiability.

A CNF formula on n binary variables $x_1, ..., x_n$ is the conjunction of m clauses $C_1, ..., C_m$ each of which is the disjunction of one or more literals. A literal is the occurrence of a variable or its negation. A formula denotes a unique n-variable boolean function $f(x_1, ..., x_n)$. Clearly, a function f can be represented by many equivalent CNF formulas. The satisfiability problem is concerned with finding an assignment to the arguments of $f(x_1, ..., x_n)$ that makes the function equal to 1, signalling that it is satisfiable, or proving that the function is equal to 0 and hence unsatisfiable [14]. By viewing the selection problem as a variant of SAT, with a bound on true assignments, techniques from this field can be applied to reduct search.

3.1   Finding Rough Set Reducts

The problem of finding the smallest feature subsets using rough set theory can be formulated as a SAT problem. Rough sets allows the generation from datasets of clauses of features in conjunctive normal form. If after assigning truth values to all features appearing in the clauses the formula is satisfied, then those features set to true constitute a valid subset for the data. The task is to find the smallest number of such features so that the CNF formula is satisfied. In other words, the problem here concerns finding a minimal assignment to the arguments of $f(x_1, ..., x_n)$ that makes the function equal to 1. There will be at least one solution to the problem (i.e. all x_is set to 1) for consistent datasets. Preliminary work has been carried out in this area [1], though this does not adopt a DPLL-style approach to finding solutions.

The DPLL algorithm for finding minimal subsets can be found in figure 2, where a search is conducted in a depth-first manner. The key operation in this procedure is the unit propagation step, unitPropagate(F), in lines (6) and (7). Clauses in the formula that contain a single literal will only be satisfied if that literal is assigned the value 1 (for positive literals). These are called unit clauses. Unit propagation examines the current formula for unit clauses and automatically assigns the appropriate value to the literal they contain. The elimination of a literal can create new unit clauses, and thus unit propagation eliminates variables by repeated passes until there is no unit clause in the formula. The order of the unit clauses within the formula makes no difference to the results or the efficiency of the process.

Branching occurs at lines (9) to (12) via the function selectLiteral(F). Here, the next literal is chosen heuristically from the current formula, assigned the value 1, and the search continues. If this branch eventually results in unsatisfiability, the procedure will assign the value 0 to this literal instead and continue the search. The importance of choosing good branching literals is well known - different branching heuristics may produce drastically different sized search trees for the same basic algorithm, thus significantly affecting the efficiency of the solver. The heuristic currently used within RSAR-SAT is to select the variable that appears in the most clauses in the current set of clauses. Many other heuristics exist for this purpose [14], but are not considered here.

A degree of pruning can take place in the search by remembering the size of the currently considered subset and the smallest optimal subset encountered so far. If the number of variables currently assigned 1 equals the number of those in the presently optimal subset, and the satisfiability of F is still not known, then any further search down this branch will not result in a smaller optimal subset.

DPLL(F).
F, the formula containing the current set of clauses.

    (1)   **if** (F contains an empty clause)
    (2)   **return** unsatisfiable
    (3)   **if** (F is empty)
    (4)   **output** current assignment
    (5)   **return** satisfiable
    (6)   **if** (F contains a unit clause $\{l\}$)
    (7) $F' \leftarrow$ unitPropagate(F)
    (8)   **return** DPLL(F')
    (9) $x \leftarrow$ selectLiteral(F)
   (10) **if** (DPLL($F \cup \{x\}$) is satisfiable)
   (11)   **return** satisfiable
   (12) **else return** DPLL($F \cup \{-x\}$)

Fig. 2. The definition of the DPLL algorithm

Although stochastic methods have been applied to SAT problems [6], these are not applicable here as they provide no guarantee of solution minimality. The DPLL-based algorithm will always find the minimal optimal subset. However, this will come at the expense of time taken to find it.

3.2   Pre-processing Clauses

The discernibility function can be simplified by replacing those variables that are simultaneously either present or absent in all clauses by single representative variables. For instance, in the formula below, variables a and f can be replaced by a single variable.

$$\{a \vee b \vee c \vee f\} \wedge \{b \vee d\} \wedge \{a \vee d \vee e \vee f\} \wedge \{d \vee c\}$$

The first and third clauses may be considered to be $\{\{a \vee f\} \vee b \vee c\}$ and $\{\{a \vee f\} \vee d \vee e\}$ respectively. Replacing $\{a \vee f\}$ with g results in

$$\{g \vee b \vee c\} \wedge \{b \vee d\} \wedge \{g \vee d \vee e\} \wedge \{d \vee c\}$$

If a reduct resulting from this discernibility function contains the new variable g, then this variable may be replaced by either a or f. Here, $\{g, d\}$ is a reduct and so $\{a, d\}$ and $\{f, d\}$ are reducts of the original set of clauses. Hence, fewer attributes are considered in the reduct-determining process with no loss of information [13]. The complexity of this (optional) pre-processing step is $O(a * c + a^2)$, where a is the number of attributes and c is the number of clauses.

From the generation of the discernibility matrix, the core attributes are immediately determined (as discussed in section 2.2). These may then be removed from the discernibility function as they will appear in every rough set reduct. Hence, if the union of the core attributes for a dataset results in a reduct, no search is required as this will be the minimal subset.

4   Evaluation

Initial experimentation has been carried out using the algorithm outlined previously. The datasets have been obtained from [2]. Table 3 shows the average time taken for the preprocessing of each dataset. For RSAR, this involves constructing partitions for each attribute. For RSAR-SAT, the discernibility matrix is calculated and simplified. It can be seen from the table that RSAR-SAT requires more pre-processing time. Included in this table are the number of clauses appearing in the resultant discernibility function for the RSAR-SAT method.

The average times of the execution of these algorithms are also presented in table 3. The time taken for RSAR-SAT is split into two columns. The first indicates the average length of time taken to find the minimal subset, the second how long it takes to verify that this is indeed minimal. For RSAR, an asterisk next to the time indicates that it found a non-minimal reduct.

The results show that RSAR-SAT is comparable to RSAR in the time taken to find reducts. However, RSAR regularly fails to find the smallest optimal subset, being misled in the search process. For larger datasets, the time taken for

Table 3. Runtimes for RSAR and RSAR-SAT

Dataset	No. of clauses	No. of Features	RSAR setup (s)	SAT setup (s)	RSAR (s)	SAT: Minimal (s)	SAT: Full (s)
M-of-N	6	13	0.164	2.333	0.171*	0.001	0.007
Exactly	6	13	0.146	2.196	0.304*	0.001	0.008
Exactly2	10	13	0.136	1.898	0.823*	0.001	0.008
Heart	12	13	0.085	0.380	0.207*	0.002	0.009
Vote	12	16	0.076	0.333	0.170*	0.004	0.009
Credit	200	20	0.148	3.873	1.988*	0.077	0.094
LED	167	24	0.125	68.20	0.097*	0.041	0.051
Letters	57	25	0.019	0.074	0.067*	0.024	0.116
Derm	1126	34	0.187	11.31	0.758*	0.094	0.456
Derm2	1184	34	0.133	6.796	0.897*	0.104	0.878
WQ	6534	38	0.168	87.85	9.590*	0.205	116.1
Lung	171	56	0.032	0.125	0.059	0.023	0.786
DNA	3861	58	0.139	30.40	1.644*	0.227	53.81

RSAR-SAT verification exceeds that of RSAR. Note that the verification stage involves simple chronological backtracking. There are ways in which this can be made more effective and less time-consuming.

5   Conclusion

This paper has presented a new DPLL-based technique for locating and verifying minimal subsets in the rough set context. The initial experimentation has shown that the method performs well in comparison to RSAR, which often fails to find the smallest subsets. Additional investigations to be carried out here include evaluating the proposed work against further well established heuristic-based approaches to reduct finding other than RSAR. Typical methods can be found in [7,8,9,13].

DPLL resorts to chronological backtracking if the current assignment of variables results in the unsatisfiability of F. Much research has been carried out in developing solution techniques for SAT that draws on related work in solvers for constraint satisfaction problems (CSPs). Indeed the SAT problem can be translated to a CSP by retaining the set of boolean variables and their $\{0,1\}$ domains, and to translate the clauses into constraints. Each clause becomes a constraint over the variables in the constraint. Unit propagation can be seen to be a form of forward checking.

In CSPs, more intelligent ways of backtracking have been proposed such as backjumping, conflict-directed backjumping and dynamic backtracking. Many aspects of these have been adapted to the SAT problem solvers. In these solvers, whenever a conflict (dead-end) is reached, a new clause is recorded to prevent the occurrence of the same conflict again during the subsequent search. Non-chronological backtracking backs up the search tree to one of the identified causes of failure, skipping over irrelevant variable assignments.

With the addition of intelligent backtracking, RSAR-SAT should be able to handle datasets containing large numbers of features. As seen in the preliminary results, the bottleneck in the process is the verification stage - the time taken to confirm that the subset is indeed minimal. This requires an exhaustive search of all subtrees containing fewer variables than the current best solution. Much of this search could be avoided through the use of more intelligent backtracking. This would result in a selection method that can cope with many thousands of features, whilst guaranteeing resultant subset minimality - something that is particularly sought after in feature selection.

References

1. A.A. Bakar, M.N. Sulaiman, M. Othman, M.H. Selamat. IP algorithms in compact rough classification modeling. Intelligent Data Analysis, Vol. 5, No. 5, pp. 419–429. 2001.
2. C.L. Blake and C.J. Merz. UCI Repository of machine learning databases. Irvine, University of California. 1998. http://www.ics.uci.edu/~mlearn/.
3. A. Chouchoulas and Q. Shen. Rough set-aided keyword reduction for text categorisation. Applied Artificial Intelligence, Vol. 15, No. 9, pp. 843–873. 2001.
4. M. Dash and H. Liu. Feature Selection for Classification. Intelligent Data Analysis, Vol. 1, No. 3, pp. 131–156. 1997.
5. M. Davis, G. Logemann and D. Loveland. A machine program for theorem proving. Communications of the ACM, vol. 5, pp. 394–397, 1962.
6. H.H. Hoos and T. Stützle. Towards a Characterisation of the Behaviour of Stochastic Local Search Algorithms for SAT. Artificial Intelligence, Vol. 112, pp. 213–232. 1999.
7. R. Jensen and Q. Shen. Semantics-Preserving Dimensionality Reduction: Rough and Fuzzy-Rough Based Approaches. IEEE Transactions on Knowledge and Data Engineering, Vol. 16, No. 12, pp. 1457–1471. 2004.
8. M. Kryszkiewicz. Comparative Study of Alternative Types of Knowledge Reduction in Inconsistent Systems. International Journal of Intelligent Systems, Vol. 16, No. 1, pp. 105–120. 2001.
9. H.S. Nguyen and A. Skowron. Boolean Reasoning for Feature Extraction Problems. In Proceedings of the 10th International Symposium on Methodologies for Intelligent Systems, pp. 117–126. 1997.
10. Z. Pawlak. Rough Sets: Theoretical Aspects of Reasoning About Data. Kluwer Academic Publishing, Dordrecht. 1991.
11. L. Polkowski. Rough Sets: Mathematical Foundations. Advances in Soft Computing. Physica Verlag, Heidelberg, Germany. 2002.
12. A. Skowron and C. Rauszer. The discernibility matrices and functions in Information Systems. In: R. Slowinski (Ed.), Intelligent Decision Support, Kluwer Academic Publishers, Dordrecht, pp. 331–362. 1992.
13. J.A. Starzyk, D.E. Nelson, and K. Sturtz. Reduct Generation in Information Systems. Bulletin of the International Rough Set Society, Vol. 3, No. 1–2, pp. 19–22. 1999.
14. L. Zhang and S. Malik. The Quest for Efficient Boolean Satisfiability Solvers. In Proceedings of the 18th International Conference on Automated Deduction, pp. 295–313. 2002.

Feature Selection with Adjustable Criteria

JingTao Yao and Ming Zhang

Department of Computer Science, University of Regina,
Regina, Saskatchewan, Canada S4S 0A2
jtyao@cs.uregina.ca

Abstract. We present a study on a rough set based approach for feature selection. Instead of using significance or support, Parameterized Average Support Heuristic (PASH) considers the overall quality of the potential set of rules. It will produce a set of rules with balanced support distribution over all decision classes. Adjustable parameters of PASH can help users with different levels of approximation needs to extract predictive rules that may be ignored by other methods. This paper finetunes the PASH heuristic and provides experimental results to PASH.

1 Introduction

One of the main research challenges of information analyzing from large databases is how to reduce the complexity of the data. One faces two characteristics of complexity, namely, the curse of dimensionality and the peaking phenomenon. The curse of dimensionality refers to the fact that the complexity grows exponentially with the dimension. Therefore, the time required to generate rules will increase dramatically with the number of features [2]. The peaking phenomenon says that if the number of training instances is relatively smaller than the number of features, it will degrade the accuracy of prediction [14]. Feature selection techniques aim at simplifying complexity of data by reducing the number of unnecessary, irrelevant, or unimportant features. The additional benefits of doing feature selection include improving the learning efficiency and increasing predicative accuracy.

The ability to process insufficient and incomplete information makes rough set theory a good candidate for classification and feature selection [3]. In fact, rough set theory has a very close tie with feature selection. Similar to the concept of keys in database, the reduct represents the minimal set of non-redundant features that are capable of discerning objects in a information table. Another concept, the core, which is the intersection of all reducts, represents the set of indispensable features. Many researchers have presented their study on using rough set theory for feature selection [4,7,11,16,17]. Normally, the measures of necessity of the features are calculated by the functions of lower and upper approximations. These measures are employed as heuristics to guide the feature selection processes. For example, Hu proposes a heuristic in favors of significant features, i.e., features causing the faster increase of the positive region [7]. The heuristic of Zhong *et al.* considers the positive region as well as the support of

D. Ślęzak et al. (Eds.): RSFDGrC 2005, LNAI 3641, pp. 204–213, 2005.
© Springer-Verlag Berlin Heidelberg 2005

rules [17]. However, it may not be sufficient by considering only the significant or support factors. It may be useful to consider the overall quality of the set of potential rules. The new heuristic function called Average Support Heuristic is a study towards this direction [16]. To further develop this idea, 100% support may not be needed for all applications. Parameterized Average Support Heuristic (PASH) is the result of this improvement.

We will reformat and fine-tune the PASH heuristic in this paper. The experimental results will also be presented. The organization of this paper is as follows: Section 2 studies feature selection in brief term. Section 3 reviews rough set based feature selection methods. The PASH heuristic is presented in Section 4 and experimental results in Section 5. Finally, the paper ends with concluding remarks.

2   Brief of Feature Selection

Feature selection is considered as one of the important research topics of machine learning [6]. In many applications, especially in the age of an information explosion, one collects many features that are potentially useful. However, all of these features may not be useful or relevant to one's classification, forecasting, or clustering objects. Therefore, choosing a subset of the original features will often lead to better performance. Features may be classified as significant, relevant, dependent and useless according to their importance to the application. The goal of feature selection is to find the optimal subset of features that satisfy certain criteria. For instance, although there may be dozens of features (make, brand, year, weight, length, hight, engine size, transmission, colour, owner, price, etc.) available when one purchases a second hand vehicle, one may only read a handful of important features (e.g., make, year, engine, colour and price) that meet one's needs.

Studies show that there are at least four criteria to judge a feature selection method [5], such as,

- Find the minimal feature subset that is necessary and sufficient to decide the classes;
- Select a subset of M features from a set of N features, $M < N$, such that the value of a criterion function is optimized over all subsets of size M;
- Improve prediction accuracy or decrease the size of the feature subset without significantly decreasing prediction accuracy of the classifier built using only the selected features;
- Select a small subset such that the resulting class distribution, given only the values for the selected feature, is as close as possible to the original class distribution given all feature values.

It is observed that each of the criterion considers two parameters, namely, the size of the selected feature subset and the accuracy of the classifier induced using only the selected features. No matter what criterion is employed, one has to define an evaluation measure to express the chosen criterion. The evaluation measure must be able to reflect both of the parameters. From a machine learning point of view, the feature selection problem is in fact a search problem. The optimal feature subset is one that maximizes the value of an evaluation measure. Therefore, the general search principles apply to feature selection.

An exhaustive search of 2^n possible subsets for a feature set of size n is almost infeasible under most circumstances [6]. It could only be used in a domain where n is small. However, the needs for feature selection is limited in such cases. In random search, the candidate feature subset is generated randomly and each time the evaluation measure is applied to the generated feature subset to check whether it satisfies the criterion. This process repeats until one that satisfies the criterion is found. The process may stop when a predefined time period has elapsed or a predefined number of subsets have been tested. A random search algorithm worthwhile to mention is the LVF algorithm proposed by Liu and Setiono [12].

The third and most commonly used method is called the heuristic search, where a heuristic function is employed to guide the search [9,10]. The search is performed towards the direction that maximizes the value of a heuristic function. Heuristic search is an important search method used by the feature selection community. The rough set approaches for feature selection discussed in this article are heuristic search methods.

The exhaustive search is infeasible due to its high time complexity. The random and heuristic search reduce computational complexity by compromising performance. It is not guaranteed that an optical result can be achieved. They are not complete search techniques. However, if a heuristic function is monotonic, as the branch and bound method proposed by Narendra and Fukunaga, the optimal subset of features can be found muck quick than exhaustive search [13].

3   Evolution of Rough Sets Based Feature Selection

As we discussed above, reducts in a rough set represent sets with minimal number of features. These features are significant features. The most important features are those appearing in core, i.e., in every reduct. The measures of necessity of features are usually calculated based on the concept of lower and upper approximations. These measures are employed as heuristics to guide the feature selection process.

The concepts in the rough set theory can manifest the property of strong and weak relevance as defined in [8]. They can be used to define the necessity of features. There are at least three types of rough set based heuristics, namely the significance oriented method, the support oriented method, and average support heuristic appearing in literature. The heuristic in [7] favors significant features, i.e., features causing the faster increase of the positive region. Zhong's heuristic considers the positive region as well as the support of rules [17]. The Average Support Heuristic considers the overall quality of the potential set of rules rather than the support of the most significant rule [16].

3.1   Significance Oriented Methods

One of the simplest and earliest rough set based feature selection method is to use significance of features as the heuristic as studied by Hu [7]. The feature selection process selects the most significant feature at each step until the stop condition is satisfied. The most significant feature is the one that, by adding this feature, can cause the fastest increase of dependency between condition attributes and decision attribute, where the dependency reflects the relative size of positive region. In short, the significance oriented method always selects the feature that makes the positive region grow faster.

The significance oriented method is simple and the heuristic function can be computed with low time complexity. However, this method only considers one of the two factors in feature selection: the number of instances covered by the potential rules (the size of positive region). It ignores the second factor: the number of instances covered by each individual rule (the support of each rule.) Rules with very low support are usually of little use.

3.2   Support Oriented Methods

The support oriented method proposed Zhong *et al.* considers both factors [17]. This method selects features based on the composite metric: the size of consistent instance and the support of an individual rule. The heuristic function is defined as the product of the positive region and the support of the most significant rule, where the most significant rule is the one with the largest support. In the remaining part of the paper, we refer to Zhong's heuristic as the maximum support heuristic.

The maximum support heuristic is far from an ideal heuristic. It only considers the support of the most significant rule rather than the overall quality of the potential rules. Among the classes of the training instances, this method favors one of them. As a result, it will produce rules with a biased support distribution.

3.3   Average Support Heuristic

A newer heuristic function, called average support heuristic, was proposed recently [16]. The average support heuristic uses the average support of the rules to replace the highest support of the rule in the maximum support heuristic. The heuristic function is defined as the product of the positive region and the average support of the most significant rules over all decision classes, as follows:

$$F(R, a) = Card(POS_{R+\{a\}}(D)) \times \frac{1}{n} \sum_{i=1}^{n} S(R, a, d_i) \qquad (1)$$

where

$$S(R, a, d_i) = MAX Size(POS_{R+\{a\}}(D = d_i)/IND(R + \{a\}))$$

is the support of the most significant rule for decision class $\{D = d_i\}$ and D is the decision attribute. The domain of D is $\{d_1, d_2, \ldots, d_n\}$. We call the second factor $\frac{1}{n} \sum_{i=1}^{n} S(R, a, d_i)$ the overall quality of potential rules. As the heuristic considers all the decision classes, the biased support distribution can be avoided.

4   Parameterized Average Support Heuristic

Completely ignoring the inconsistent instances of the information table, as the above heuristic functions do, is not a good strategy when the size of the boundary region increases [16]. Some useful predictive rules obtained from the boundary region might be lost in the result. The predictive rules hold true with high probability but are not necessarily 100%.

All the above heuristics are defined on the basis of the traditional lower approximation, the union of which includes only the consistent instances. In order to include the predictive rules, we give a broader concept of lower approximation, upon which a parameterized average support heuristic is defined.

The decision-theoretic rough set model and variable precision rough set model are two examples of non-traditional lower approximation [15,18]. They consider the information in the boundary region. However, the a priori probability of each decision class required by these models is usually unknown in the real world application. Furthermore, the pair of lower and upper limit certainty threshold parameters confines these models to information tables with only a binary decision attribute.

Our new lower approximation does not require known a priori probabilities of the decision classes and it is applicable to multi-valued decision attribute. Suppose we have an information table T, in which the domain of decision attribute D, denoted by V_D, contains n values, such that $V_D = \{d_1, d_2, \ldots, d_n\}$. Here we consider two different situations: (1) the a priori probabilities are unknown; and (2) the a priori probabilities are known.

4.1   Lower Approximation with Unknown a Priori Probability

When the a priori probabilities are unknown, we assume they are equal, i.e. $P(D = d_1) = P(D = d_2) = \cdots P(D = d_n)$. In this case, we define the lower approximation of class $\{D = d_i\}$ as follows:

$$R_*(D = d_i) = \bigcup \{E_j \in U/IND(R) : P(D = d_i|E_j) > P(D \neq d_i|E_j)\}, \quad (2)$$

where $P(D \neq d_i|E_j) = \sum_{k=1, k\neq i}^{n} P(D = d_k|E_j)$. The lower approximation of class $\{D = d_i\}$ is the set of such objects E_j in U that, given E_j, the probability of $D = d_i$ is greater than the probability of $D \neq d_i$. In other words, E_j is predictive of concept $D = d_i$ from $D \neq d_i$.

Since $P(D \neq d_i|E_j) = 1 - P(D = d_i|E_j)$, we can rewrite Equation 2 to Equation 3:

$$R_*(D = d_i) = \bigcup \{E_j \in U/IND(R) : P(D = d_i|E_j) > 0.5\}, \quad (3)$$

where $P(D = d_i|E_j)$ could be estimated by taking the ratio of $Card(D = d_i \bigcap E_j)/Card(E_j)$.

When the decision attribute has fewer number of values, in the extreme case, the decision attribute is binary, that is, $|V_D| = 2$, Equation 2 may be too broad and degrade the performance. We can introduce a parameter $k(k \geq 1)$ to Equation 2 as follows:

$$R_*(D = d_i) = \bigcup\{E_j \in U/IND(R) : P(D = d_i|E_j) > k \times P(D \neq d_i|E_j)\}. \quad (4)$$

Equation 4 reflects that, given E_j, the concept $D = d_i$ is k times more probable than the concept $D \neq d_i$.

By replacing $P(D \neq d_i|E_j)$ with $1 - P(D = d_i|E_j)$, Equation 4 becomes

$$R_*(D = d_i) = \bigcup\{E_j \in U/IND(R) : P(D = d_i|E_j) > \tfrac{k}{k+1}\}. \quad (5)$$

As $k \geq 1 \Longrightarrow \tfrac{k}{k+1} \geq 0.5$, we can simplify Equation 5 as:

$$R_*(D = d_i) = \bigcup\{E_j \in U/IND(R) : P(D = d_i|E_j) > t(t \geq 0.5)\}. \quad (6)$$

Clearly, Equation 3 is a special case of Equation 6. Equation 6 guarantees that each object $E \in U$ is contained in at most one lower approximation, that is,

$$R_*(D = d_i) \bigcap R_*(D = d_j) = \phi, (i \neq j).$$

4.2   Lower Approximation with Known a Priori Probability

In the case that the a priori probabilities of decision classes are known, Equation 6 is too simple to be effective. Assume that the information table obtained from the training data can reflect the distribution of decision classes. The a priori probability of class $(D = d_i)$ could be estimated by

$$(D = d_i) = \frac{Card(D = d_1)}{Card(U)}.$$

We can modify Equation 6 to Equation 7:

$$R_*(D = d_i) = \bigcup \{E_j \in U/IND(R) :$$

$$\frac{P(D=d_i|E_j)}{P(D=d_i)} = MAX\{\frac{P(D=d_k|E_j)}{P(D=d_k)}, 1 \leq k \leq n\} \quad (7)$$

$$\text{and } P(D = d_i|E_j) > t(t \geq 0.5)\}.$$

Equation 7 ensures that the lower approximation of class $\{D = d_i\}$ contains such objects $E_j \in U$ that, given E_j, the probability of class $\{D = d_i\}$ increases faster than any other classes. Equation 7 also guarantees

$$R_*(D = d_i) \bigcap R_*(D = d_j) = \phi, (i \neq j).$$

Equation 6 is a special case of Equation 7.

4.3   PASH

Parameterized average support heuristic or PASH is defined the same as the average support heuristic in appearance. It is also a product of two factors: $Card(POS_{R+\{a\}}(D)) \times Q(R,a)$, where $Card(POS_{R+\{a\}}(D))$ is the cardinality of the positive region and $Q(R,a)$ is the overall quality of potential rules. The difference is that, in PASH, the positive region is the union of the new lower approximations and $Q(R,a)$ is also defined on the new lower approximations.

In summary, there are two cases to be considered when using PASH:

- When the a priori probabilities of decision classes are unknown, we assume they have equal a priori probability and use Equation 6.
- When the a priori probabilities of decision classes are known, we use Equation 7.

Average support heuristic and parameterized average support heuristic can be viewed as extensions to maximum support heuristic.

5   Experiments

We will give brief experiments and analysis of results in this section. We conducted a series of experiments with PASH using the mushroom data set obtained from the UC Irvine's machine learning repository [1]. Comparisons with results achieved with other methods running on the same data set were also performed. The mushroom data set has 8,124 instances with 22 condition attributes and 1 decision attribute. These algorithms are implemented in C language and executed on a PC with CPU 1.7GHz and 128MB RAM. There were three groups of experiments conducted.

5.1   Comparison of PASH with the Other Three Methods

We first tested PASH with the parameter value 1 under the stop condition $POS_R(D) = POS_C(D)$, that is, the program stops when one reduct is found. The execution time was around 15 minutes under this stop condition.

Table 1. Result of feature selection with stop condition $POS_R(D) = POS_C(D)$

Method	Selected features
Significance-oriented	5,20,8,12,3
Maximum support	5,10,17,6,8,16,18,13,12,11,22,4
Average support	5,10,17,6,8,16,18,13,12,11,4,7,19,20
PASH (parameter=1)	5,16,17,6,18,8,10,12,13,11,4,7,19,20

The comparison of the PASH result with results of significance-oriented method, maximum support method and average support method is presented

Table 2. Result of PASH with stop condition $POS_R(D) - POS_C(D)$

Parameter	Selected features
5	5,16,17,6,18,8,10,12,13,11,4,7,19,20
15	5,16,17,6,18,7,4,12,13,11,8,10,19,20
30	5,18,16,17,6,7,4,12,13,11,8,10,19,20
60	5,18,16,17,6,8,10,13,12,11,4,7,19,20
100	5,10,17,6,8,16,18,13,12,11,4,7,19,20

in Table 1. The left column indicates the method used and the right column lists the selected features in the order of selection. For example, the last row indicates that PASH selects the 5th feature as the most important feature, followed by the 16th feature, and then the 17th. The significance-oriented method obtained the smallest reduct which contains only five features. It may be concluded as the most time-efficient method. However, the features obtained from the significance-oriented method are not so important if they are evaluated by the criteria used in other methods. In other words, although a smaller and concise reduct is obtained, it may lose some important features. In fact, the significance-oriented method selected the 20th feature as the second most important feature whereas the maximum support method did not select it at all. The other two methods consider the 20th feature as the least important feature in the reducts. Another finding is that all three methods except the first one selected the 17th feature as the third important one but the significance-oriented method ignored it.

5.2 PASH with a Standard Stop Condition

The second set of experiments aimed to find out how the parameters value affect the feature selection results.

We tested PASH with random parameters under the same stop condition as the first set of experiments. The experimental results are shown in Table 2. The left column is the value of the parameter and the right column lists the selected features in the order of selection. It is suggested that the values of the parameter do not affect the size of reducts. However, the value of the parameter does influence the order of features in the reduct, i.e., the importance of the features. It is interesting that no matter what parameter value is used, the most important features (e.g. the 5th, the 17th) would be ordered in the first few steps and the least important ones would appear in the later parts of the reduct (e.g. the 19th, the 20th). In other words, PASH is not very sensitive to the parameter value and quite stable in feature selection.

5.3 Approximate Reducts with Different Parameter Levels

Finally, we tested PASH with different parameters under the stop condition $POS_R(D)/POS_C(D) > 85\%$. This allows the program to stop when an approximate reduct is obtained. 85% is an accuracy threshold.

Table 3. Results of the PASH with stop condition $POS_R(D)/POS_C(D) > 85\%$

Parameter	Selected features
5	5,16,17,6,18,8
15	5,16,17,6,18,7,4
30	5,18,16,17,6,7,4
60	5,18,16,17,6,8
100	5,10,17

In real world applications where the size of data set is large, we may not need to complete the computation of a reduct with PASH. If some of the most important features can be obtained in the first few steps, it may not need to compute the remaining less important features. The remaining part may cost a large part of the execution time. An approximate reduct which includes the most important features can be obtained with an accuracy threshold. In the test, we set the threshold as 85% and the program stops when the condition $POS_R(D)/POS_C(D) > 85\%$ is satisfied. Table 3 shows the result using PASH with different parameter values under this stop condition. It is shown that PASH stopped after selecting 3 to 7 features. Comparing with Table 2, PASH obtained an approximate reduct in much fewer steps. It is more efficient to use an approximate reduct with fewer features. It is suggested that when an appropriate parameter (e.g. parameter = 100) is given, PASH can produce satisfactory results efficiently. In fact, reducts with 3 features were obtain with parameter size over 100.

6   Concluding Remarks

We present a recently proposed rough set based feature selection method, parameterized average support heuristic, and report a set of experiments results based on PASH in this paper. PASH considers the overall quality of the potential rules and thus may produce a set of rules with balanced support distribution over all decision classes. PASH includes a parameter to adjust the level of approximation and keeps the predictive rules that are ignored by the existing methods. The experiment results suggest that the an approximate reduct can be obtained with adjustable criteria. Further experiments with different data sets and parameter values need to be conducted.

Acknowledgement

Financial support through a grant of NSERC, Canada is gratefully acknowledged. Gratitude is given to anonymous reviewers of RSFDGrC'05 and participants of NAFIPS'04 for their generous and constructive comments.

References

1. C.L. Blake and C.J. Merz, UCI Repository of machine learning databases. Available at http://www.ics.uci.edu/~mlearn/MLRepository.html, University of California, 1998.

2. R. Bellman, *Adaptive Control Processes: A Guided Tour*, Princeton University Press, 1961.

3. J. S. Deogun, V. V. Raghavan, and H. Sever, "Rough set based classification methods and extended decision tables", *Proc. of The Int. Workshop on Rough Sets and Soft Computing*, pp302-309, 1994.

4. J. S. Deogun, S. K. Choubey, V. V. Raghavan, and H. Sever, "On feature selection and effective classifiers", *Journal of American Society for Information Science*, 49(5), 423-434, 1998.

5. M. Dash, H. Liu, "Feature selection for classification," *Intelligence Data Analysis*, 1, 131-156, 1997.

6. J.G. Dy and C. E. Brodley, "Feature selection for unsupervised learning", *The Journal of Machine Learning Research archive*, 5, 845 - 889, 2004.

7. X. Hu, *Knowledge discovery in databases: an attribute-oriented rough set approach*, PhD thesis, University of Regina, Canada, 1995.

8. G. H. John, R. Kohavi and K. Pfleger, "Irrelevant features and the subset selection problem," *Proceedings of the 11th International Conference on Machine Learning*, pp121-129, 1994.

9. K. Kira, L. Rendell, "A practical approach to feature selection," *Proceedings of the 9th International Conference on Machine Learning*, pp249–256, 1992.

10. I. Kononenko, "Estimating attributes: analysis and extension of relief," *Proceedings of European Conference on Machine Learning*, pp171-182, 1994.

11. T. Y. Lin, "Attribute (Feature) completion- the theory of attributes from data mining prospect," *Proceedings of International Conference on Data Mining*, Maebashi, Japan, pp.282-289, 2002.

12. H. Liu and R. Setiono, "A probabilistic approach to feature selection - a filter solution," *Proceedings of the 13th International Conference on Machine Learning*, pp319-327, 1996.

13. P.M. Narendra and K. Fukunaga, "A branch and bound algorithm for feature subset selection", *IEEE Transactions on Computers*, C-26(9), 917-922, 1977.

14. G.V. Trunk, "A problem of dimensionality: a simple example," *IEEE Transactions on Pattern Analysis and Machine Intelligence*, 1(3), 306-307, 1979.

15. Y.Y. Yao and S.K.M. Wong, "A decision theoretic framework for approximating concepts," *International Journal of Man-machine Studies*, 37(6), 793-809, 1992.

16. M. Zhang and J.T. Yao, "A rough set approach to feature selection", *Proceedings of the 23rd International Conference of NAFIPS*, Canada, pp434-439, 2004.

17. N. Zhong, J.Z. Dong and S. Ohsuga, "Using rough sets with heuristics for feature selection," *Journal of Intelligent Information Systems*, 16, 199-214, 2001.

18. W. Ziarko, "Variable precision rough set model," *Journal of Computer and System Sciences*, 46, 39-59, 1993.

Feature Selection Based on Relative Attribute Dependency: An Experimental Study

Jianchao Han[1], Ricardo Sanchez[1], and Xiaohua Hu[2]

[1] Department of Computer Science, California State University Dominguez Hills,
1000 E. Vistoria Street, Carson, CA 90747
[2] College of Information Science and Technology, Drexel University,
3141 Chestnut Street, Philadelphia, PA 19104

Abstract. Most existing rough set-based feature selection algorithms suffer from intensive computation of either discernibility functions or positive regions to find attribute reduct. In this paper, we develop a new computation model based on relative attribute dependency that is defined as the proportion of the projection of the decision table on a subset of condition attributes to the projection of the decision table on the union of the subset of condition attributes and the set of decision attributes. To find an optimal reduct, we use information entropy conveyed by the attributes as the heuristic. A novel algorithm to find optimal reducts of condition attributes based on the relative attribute dependency is implemented using Java, and is experimented with 10 data sets from UCI Machine Learning Repository. We conduct the comparison of data classification using C4.5 with the original data sets and their reducts. The experiment results demonstrate the usefulness of our algorithm.

Keywords: Rough set theory, machine learning and data mining, classification, data reduction, feature selection.

1 Introduction

There are many factors affecting the performance of data analysis, and one prominent factor is the size of the data set. In the era of information, the availability of huge amounts of computerized data that many organizations possess about their business and/or scientific research attracts many researchers from different communities such as statistics, bioinformatics, databases, machine learning and data mining. Most data sets collected from real world applications contain noisy data, which may distract the analyst and mislead to nonsense conclusions. Thus the original data need to be cleaned in order to not only reduce the size of the dataset but also remove noise as well. This data cleaning is usually done by data reduction.

Feature selection has long been an active research topic within statistics, pattern recognition, machine learning and data mining. Most researchers have demonstrated the interest in designing new methods and improving the performance of their algorithms. These methods can be divided into two types:

D. Ślęzak et al. (Eds.): RSFDGrC 2005, LNAI 3641, pp. 214–223, 2005.

exhaustive or heuristic search. The exhaustive search probes all possible subsets chosen from the original features. This is prohibitive when the number of the original features is large. In practice, the heuristic search is the way out of this exponential computation and in general makes use of background information to approximately estimate the relevance of features. Although the heuristic search works reasonably well, it is certain that some features with high order correlation may be missed out.

Rough set theory has been used to develop feature selection algorithm by finding condition attribute reduct. Most existing rough set-based feature selection algorithms suffer from intensive computation of either discernibility functions or positive regions to find attribute reduct. In order to improve the efficiency, in this paper, we develop a new computation model based on relative attribute dependency. With this model, a novel algorithm to find optimal reducts of condition attributes based on the relative attribute dependency are proposed and implemented. The implemented algorithm is experimented with 10 data sets from UCI Machine Learning Repository. The experiment results demonstrate their usefulness and are analyzed for further research.

2   Rough Set Approach

Rough set theory was developed by Pawlak [12] in the early 1980's and has been used in data analysis, pattern recognition, and data mining and knowledge discovery [8], [15]. Recently, rough set theory has also been employed to select feature subset [4], [11], [12], [16], [18], [9], [20], [21]. In the rough set community, feature selection algorithms are attribute-reduct oriented, that is, finding optimal reduct of condition attributes of a given data set. Two main approaches to finding attribute reducts are recognized as discernibility function-based and attribute dependency-based [3], [12], [20], [21]. These algorithms, however, suffer from intensive computations of either discernibility functions for the former or positive regions for the latter, although some computation efficiency improvement has been made in some new developments.

In rough set theory, the data is collected in a table, called decision table. Rows of the decision table correspond to instances, and columns correspond to features (or attributes). All attributes are recognized into two groups: conditional attributes set C as input and decision attributes set D as output.

Assume $P \subseteq C \cup D$ and $Q \subseteq C \cup D$, the positive region of Q with respect to P, denoted $POS_P(Q)$, is defined as $POS_P(Q) =_{def} \sum_{X \in U/IND(Q)} \underline{P}X$, where $\underline{P}X$ is the lower approximation of X and $U/IND(Q)$ is the equivalent partition induced by Q. The positive region of Q with respect to P contains all objects in U that can be classified using the information contained in P. With this definition, the degree of dependency of Q from P, denoted $\gamma_P(Q)$, is defined as $\gamma_P(Q) =_{def} \frac{|POS_P(Q)|}{|U|}$, where $|X|$ denotes the cardinality of the set X.

The degree of attribute dependency provides a measure how an attributes subset is dependent on another attributes subset. $\gamma_P(Q) = 1$ means that Q totally depends on P, $\gamma_P(Q) = 0$ indicates that Q is totally independent from P, while $0 < \gamma_P(Q) < 1$ denotes a partially dependency of Q from P. Particularly, assume $P \subset C$, then $\gamma_P(D)$ can be used to measure the dependency of the decision attributes from a conditional attributes subset. The task of rough set attribute reduction is to find a subset of the conditional attributes set, which functions as the original conditional attributes set without loss of classification capability. This subset of the conditional attributes set is called *reduct*, and defined as follows [15].

$R \subseteq C$ is called a *reduct* of C, if and only if $POS_R(D) = POS_C(D)$, or equivalently, $\gamma_R(D) = \gamma_C(D)$. A reduct R of C is called a minimum reduct of C if, $\forall\, Q \subset R$, Q is not a reduct of C.

A reduct R of C has the same expressiveness of instances as C with respect to D. A decision table may have more than one reduct. Anyone of them can be used to replace the original condition attributes set. Finding all the reducts from a decision table, however, is NP-hard. Thus, a natural question is which reduct is the best. Without domain knowledge, the only source of information to select the reduct is the contents of the decision table. For example, the number of attributes can be used as the criteria and the best reduct is the one with the smallest number of attributes. Unfortunately, finding the reduct with the smallest number of attributes is also NP-hard. Some heuristic approaches to finding a *good* enough reduct have been proposed, which will be discussed in Section 6.

3   Relative Attribute Dependency Based on Rough Set Theory

In order to improve the efficiency of algorithms to finding optimal reducts of condition attributes, we proposed a new definition of attribute dependency, called *relative attribute dependency*, with which we showed a sufficient and necessary condition of the optimal reduct of conditional attributes [4]. The relative attribute dependency degree can be calculated by counting the distinct instances of the subset of the data set, instead of generating discernibility functions or positive regions. Thus the computation efficiency of finding minimum reducts is highly improved.

Most existing rough set-based attribute reduction algorithms suffer from intensive computation of either discernibility functions or positive regions. In the family of QuickReduct algorithms [19], in order to choose the next attribute to be added to the candidate reduct, one must compute the degree of dependency of all remaining conditional attributes from the decision attributes. This means that the positive regions $POS_{R \cup \{p\}}(D)$, $\forall\, p \in C - R$, must be computed. To improve the efficiency of the attribute reduction algorithms, we define a new concept, called the degree of relative attribute dependency. For this purpose, we assume that the decision table is consistent, that is, $\forall\, t, s \in U$, if $f_D(t) \neq f_D(s)$, then $\exists\, q \in C$ such that $f_q(t) \neq f_q(s)$. This assumption is not realistic in most real-life applications. Fortunately, any decision table can be uniquely decomposed into two decision tables, with one being consistent and the other the boundary area [15], and our method could be performed on the consistent one.

We first define the concept of projection and then define the relative attribute dependency. Let $P \subseteq C \cup D$. The projection of U on P, denoted as $\Pi_P(U)$, is a sub-table of U and constructed as follows: 1) eliminating attributes $C \cup D - P$ from U; and 2) merging all indiscernible tuples (rows) with respect to the remaining attributes.

Let $Q \subseteq C$. The degree of relative dependency, denoted $\chi_Q(D)$, of Q on D over U is defined as $\chi_Q(D) = \frac{|\Pi_Q(U)|}{|\Pi_{Q \cup D}(U)|}$, where $|\Pi_X(U)|$ is actually the number of equivalence classes in $U/IND(X)$.

The relative attribute dependency is the proportion of the projection of the decision table on a subset of condition attributes to the projection of the decision table on the union of the subset of condition attributes and the set of decision attributes. On the other hand, the regular attribute dependency is the proportion of the positive region of one subset of attributes with respect to another subset of attributes to the decision table. With the relative attribute dependency measure, we propose a new computation model to find a minimum reduct of condition attributes in a consistent decision table, which is described as follows.

The Computation Model Based on Relative Attribute Dependency (RAD):
Input:
   A decision table U, condition attributes set C and decision attributes set D
Output:
   A minimum reduct R of condition attributes set C with respect to D in U
Computation:
   Find a subset R of C such that $\chi_R(D) = 1$, and $\forall\, Q \subset R, \chi_Q(D) < 1$.

The following theory shows that our proposed computation model is equivalent to the traditional model. The correctness of our model is built on the following condition: a subset of condition attributes is a minimum reduct in the tradition model if and only if it is a minimum reduct of condition attributes in our new model [4].

Theorem 1. *Assume U is consistent. $R \subseteq C$ is a reduct of C with respect to D if and only if 1) $\chi_R(D) = \chi_C(D) = 1$; and 2) $\forall\, Q \subset R, \chi_Q(D) < \chi_C(D)$.*

The degree of relative attribute dependency provides a mechanism of finding a minimum reduct of the conditional attributes set of a decision table. This dependency measure can be more efficiently calculated than the traditional functional computation.

4   A Heuristic Algorithm for Finding Optimal Reducts

Some authors propose algorithms for constructing the best reduct, but what is the best depends on how to define the criteria, such as the number of attributes in the reduct. In the absence of criteria, the only source of information to select the reduct is the content of the data table. A common metric of data content is information entropy contained in the data items. In this section, we develop a heuristic algorithm to implement the proposed model based on the relative attribute dependency. The algorithm is based on the heuristic backward elimination in terms of the information entropy conveyed by condition attributes. The algorithm calculates the information entropy conveyed in each attribute and selects the one with the maximum information gain for elimination.

The goal of the algorithm is to find a subset R of the condition attributes set C such that R has the same classification power as C with respect to the given decision table. As our model suggests, such R is a minimum reduct of C with the total relative dependency on the decision attributes set D. To find such an R, we initialize R to containing all condition attributes in C, and then eliminate redundant attributes one by one.

Given the partition by D, $U/IND(D)$, of U, the entropy, or expected information based on the partition by $q \in C$, U/q, of U, is given by $E(q) = \sum_{Y \in U/q} \frac{|Y|}{|U|} I(q|Y)$, where $I(q|Y) = -\sum_{X \in U/IND(D)} \frac{|Y \cap X|}{|Y|} \log_2 \frac{|Y \cap X|}{|Y|}$. Thus, the entropy $E(q)$ can be represented as $E(q) = -\frac{1}{|U|} \sum_{X \in U/IND(D)} \sum_{Y \in U/q} |X \cap Y| \log_2 \frac{|X \cap Y|}{|Y|}$.

Algorithm A: *Attribute information entropy based backward elimination*
Input: Consistent decision table U, condition attributes set C, decision
       attributes set D
Output: R – a minimum reduct of condition attributes set C with respect
        to D in U
Procedure:
   1. $R \leftarrow C, Q \leftarrow \emptyset$
   2.   **For** each attribute $q \in C$ **Do**
   3.   Compute the entropy $E(q)$ of q
   4. $Q \leftarrow Q \cup \{< q, E(q) >\}$
   5.   **While** $Q \neq \emptyset$ **Do**
   6. $q \leftarrow \arg\max\{E(p)| < p, E(p) >\in Q\}$
   7. $Q \leftarrow Q - \{< q, E(q) >\}$
   8.   **If** $\chi_{R-\{q\}}(D) = 1$ **Then**
   9. $R \leftarrow R - \{q\}$
  10. Return R

The following theorem demonstrates the correctness of *Algorithm A* [4].

Theorem 2. *The outcome of Algorithm A is a minimum reduct of C with respect to D in U.*

Algorithm A has been implemented using the computer programming language Java. To calculate the information entropy of condition attributes and the relative dependency, the original data set is sorted using the Radix-Sort technique. One can easily see that the time complexity of *Algorithm A* is $O(|C||U|log_2|U|)$, where $|C|$ is the number of condition attributes, and $|U|$ is the number of tuples in the decision table.

5   Experiments

We select 10 data sets from UCI machine learning repository [2] to experiment our implemented algorithm, which are illustrated in Table 1. These data sets were carefully chosen to avoid numerical attributes and reflect diverse sizes. Since the current version of our approach only considers categorical attributes, numerical attributes need to be partitioned into non-intersected intervals. To verify our approach, we choose such data sets with small number of tuples and small number of attributes, small number of tuples and large number of attributes, large number of tuples and small number of attributes, as well as large number of tuples and large number of attributes. We also remove all inconsistent tuples from all data sets.

Table 1 describes each data set with the number of condition attributes and the number of rows. All data sets have only one decision attribute. Since some data sets such as *breast-cancer-wisconsin, dermatology, zoo*, and *audiology*, contain tuple identifiers as a column which provides no information for data analysis, we remove these *id* columns. Table 1 also shows our experiment results using *Algorithm A*, where the column *Number of Rows* under *Reducts* gives the number of distinct tuples in the reduced data set by projecting the original data set on the reduct that the algorithm found; the column *Number of Condition Attributes* shows the number of condition attributes contained in the reduct.

From Table 1, one can see that in the cases where reducts were smaller than the number of condition attributes in the original data set, the number of indiscernible rows was reduced very much.

To verify the effectiveness of the reducts discovered by *Algorithm A*, we run C4.5 [17] on both original data sets and the reudcts. The experiment results are listed in Table 2, which shows the classification accuracy by applying C4.5 on each original data set and its reduct found by our algorithm, recpectively.

Table 1. The 10 data sets excerpted from the UCI machine learning repository

Data Set	Original Data Sets		Reducts	
	Number of Rows	Number of Condition Attributes	Number of rows	Number of Condition Attributes
Adult+Stretch (AS)	20	4	4	2
Breast-Cancer-Wisconsin (BCW)	699	9	299	4
Dermatology (DER)	366	33	313	10
House-votes-84 (HV)	435	16	227	9
Lung-cancer (LC)	32	56	26	6
SPECT (SPE)	187	22	171	22
Yellow-small (YS)	20	4	4	2
Zoo (ZOO)	101	16	22	5
Audiology (AUD)	200	69	157	13
Soybean-large (SOY)	307	35	249	11

Table 2. Classification accuracy comparison using C4.5: Original data sets vs. reducts

Data Set	Original Data Sets	Reducts
Adult+Stretch (AS)	90.1	91.4
Breast-Cancer-Wisconsin (BCW)	92.5	92.3
Dermatology (DER)	96	97.2
House-votes-84 (HV)	86.7	89.3
Lung-cancer (LC)	97.5	98.2
SPECT (SPE)	93.2	94.3
Yellow-small (YS)	78.6	76.4
Zoo (ZOO)	82.4	84.5
Audiology (AUD)	92.2	94.6
Soybean-large (SOY)	94.8	95.3

From Table 2, one can see that, with C4.5, using the reducts that are discovered by **Algorithm A**, we can obtain almost the same good classifiers as using the original data sets in most situations.

Actually, only 2 of 10 data sets, namely, *Breast-Cancer-Wisconsin* and *Yellow-small*, C4.5 can find more accurate classifiers from the original data sets than from the reducts induced by our algorithm, and the difference is very small (92.5% vs. 92.3% for *Breast-Cancer-Wisconsin*, 78.6% vs. 78.4% for *Yellow-small*). This experimental results show us that *Algorithm A* is very useful and can be used to find optimal reducts for most application data sets to replace the original data sets. It is demonstrated that the reducts that the algorithm discovers have almost the same classification power as the original data sets, which is what feature selection research pursuits.

6   Related Work

Many feature subset selection algorithms have been proposed, and many approaches and algorithms to find classifiers based on rough set theory have been developed in the past decades. Grzymala-Busse [5], [6] developed a learning system LERS that applies two algorithms LEM1 and LEM2 based on rough sets to deal with non-numerical and numerical attributes, respectively. LERS finds a minimal description of a concept, which is a set of rules. The rough measure of the rules describing a concept X is defined as $\frac{|X \cap Y|}{|Y|}$, where Y is the set of all examples described by the rule. This definition is very similar to our relative attribute dependency, which is defined as $\frac{|\Pi_Q(U)|}{|\Pi_{Q \cup D}(U)|}$. Nguyen and Nguyen [12] developed an approach to first construct the discernibility relation by sorting the data tuples in the data table, the use the discernibility relation to build the lower and upper approximations, and finally apply the approximations to find a semi-minimal reduct. Our algorithm takes advantage of the Radix-sorting technique, and has the same running efficiency as theirs, but our algorithm does not need to maintain the discernibility relation, and lower and upper approximations. Recently, Lin and Yin [9] use the cardinality of distinct value of attributes as heuristics to guess a short reduct quickly and then extend to the best reduct. Zhang and Yao [21] proposes a greedy approach to find an "optimal" reduct. Zhang et al. [20] present an algorithm to generate the optimal reduct from the discernibility matrix, which uses the occurrence frequence of attributes as heuristics to speed up the selection process. An algorithm QuickReduct that is very close to ours was proposed by Shen and Chouchoulas [19] develop an algorithm, which is a filter approach of feature selection and a forward searching hill climber. QuickReduct initializes the candidate reduct R as an empty set, and attributes are added to R incrementally using the following heuristic: the next attribute to be added to R is the one with the highest significance to R with respect to the decision attributes. R is increased until it becomes a reduct. The basic idea behind this algorithm is that the degree of attribute dependency is monotonically increasing. There are two problems with this algorithm, however. First, it is not guaranteed to yield the best reduct with the smallest number of attributes. Second, to calculate the significance of attributes, the discernibility function and positive regions must be computed, which is inefficient and time-consuming. A variant of QuickReduct, called QuickReduct II is also a filter algorithm, but performs the backward elimination using the same heuristic [19].

Almuallim and Dietterich [1] proposed an exhaustive search algorithm, FO-CUS, in 1994. The algorithm starts with an empty feature set and carries out exhaustive search until it finds a minimal combination of features that are sufficient for the data analysis task. It works on binary, noise-free data and runs in time of $O(N^M)$, where N is the number of tuples, and M is the number of attributes. They also proposed three heuristic algorithms to speed up the search algorithm. Kira and Rendell [7] developed a heuristic algorithm, RELIEF, for data classification. RELIEF assigns a relevance weight to each feature, which is meant to denote the relevance of the feature to the task. RELIEF samples instances randomly from the given data set and updates the relevance values based on the difference between the selected values and the two nearest instances of the same and opposite classes. It assumes two-class classification problems and does not help with redundant features. If most of the given features are relevant to the task, it would select most of them even though only a fraction is necessary for the classification. Another heuristic feature selection algorithm, PRESET, was developed by Modrzejewski [3] in 1993, that heuristically ranks the features and assumes a noise-free binary domain. Chi2 is also a heuristic algorithm proposed by Liu and Setiono [10] in 1995, which automatically removes irrelevant continuous features based on the statistics and the inconsistency found in the data. Some other algorithms have been employed in data classification methods, such as C4.5 by Quinlan [17], FRINGE by Pagallo and Haussler [13].

7   Summary and Future Work

We proposed a novel definition relative attribute dependency, with which we developed a computational model for finding optimal reducts of conditional attributes. The relative attribute dependency degree can be calculated by counting the distinct instances of the subset of the data set, instead of generating discernibility functions or positive regions. Thus the computation efficiency of finding minimum reducts is highly improved. We implemented an algorithm using the object-oriented programming language Java, based on the backward elimination.

We experiment the implemented algorithm with 10 data sets from UCI Machine Learning Repository. These data sets are carefully excerpted to cover various situations with different number of features and tuples. Our experiment results show the algorithm significantly reduces the size of original data sets, and improves the prediction accuracy of the classifiers discovered by C4.5. It is demonstrated that the reducts yielded by our algorithm have all the same classification accuracy as the entire original data sets.

Our future work will focus on the following aspects: 1) Apply more existing classification algorithms besides C4.5 to the results of our algorithms to see whether the classifier can be improved. We expect the classifier discovered in the reducts is more accurate than the one discovered in the original data sets. 2) Extend the algorithms to be able to process other types of data, such as numerical data. 3) Attempt to develop novel classification algorithms based on our definition of relative attribute dependency.

References

1. Almuallim H., Dietterich, T. G., Learning Boolean concepts in the presence of many irrelevant features, Artificial Intelligence, Vol. 69(1-2), pp 279-305, 1994.
2. Blake, C. L. and Merz, C. J. (1998). UCI Repository of machine learning databases [http://www.ics.uci.edu/ mlearn/MLRepository.html]. Irvine, CA: University of California, Department of Information and Computer Science.
3. Han, J., Hu, X., and Lin T. Y., A New Computation Model for Rough Set Theory Based on Database Systems, 5th International Conference on Data Warehousing and Knowledge Discovery, Lecture Notes in Computer Science 2737, pp. 381 - 390, 2003.
4. Han, J., Hu, X., and Lin T. Y., Feature Subset Selection Based on Relative Dependency Between Attributes, 4th International Conference on Rough Sets and Current Trends in Computing, Lecture Notes in Computer Science 3066, pp. 176-185, Springer, 2004.
5. Grzymala-Busse, J. W., LERS - A system for learning from examples based on rough sets. In Intelligent Decision Support. Handbook of Applications and Advances of the Rough Sets Theory, ed. by R. Slowinski, Kluwer Academic Publishers, 3-18, 1992.
6. Grzymala-Busse, J. W., A Comparison of Three Strategies to Rule Induction, Proc. of the International Workshop on Rough Sets in Knowledge Discovery, Warsaw, Poland, April 5-13, pp.132-140, 2003.
7. Kira, K., Rendell, L.A., The Feature Selection Problem: Traditional Methods and a new Algorithm, 9th National Conference on Artificial Intelligence (AAAI), pp 129-134, 1992.
8. Lin, T.Y., Cercone, N., Applications of Rough Sets Theory and Data Mining, Kluwer Academic Publishers, 1997.
9. Lin, T. Y., Yin, P., Heuristically Fast Finding of the Shortest Reducts, Proc. of RSCTC, pp. 465-470, 2004.

10. Liu, H., Setiono, R., Chi2: Feature Selection and Discretization of Numeric Attributes, 7th IEEE International Conference on Tools with Artificial Intelligence, 1995.
11. Modrzejewski, M., Feature Selection Using Rough Sets Theory, European Conference on Machine Learning, pp.213-226, 1993.
12. Nguyen, H., Nguyen, S., Some efficient algorithms for rough set methods, IPMU, 1451-1456, 1996
13. Pagallo, G., Haussler, D., Boolean Feature Discovery in Empirical Learning, Machine Learning, Vol. 5, pp 71-99, 1990.
14. Pawlak, Z., Rough Sets, International Journal of Information and Computer Science, 11(5), pp.341-356, 1982.
15. Pawlak, Z., Rough Sets: Theoretical Aspects of Reasoning About Data, Kluwer Academic Publishers, 1991.
16. Quafafou, M., Boussouf, M., Generalized Rough Sets Based Feature Selection, Intelligent Data Analysis, Vol. 4, pp. 3-17, 2000.
17. Quinlan, J.R., C4.5: Programs for Machine Learning, Morgan Kaufmann, 1993.
18. Sever, H., Raghavan, V., Johnsten, D. T., The Status of Research on Rough Sets for Knowledge Discovery in Databases, 2nd International Conference on Nonlinear Problems in Aviation and Aerospace, Vol. 2, pp. 673-680, 1998.
19. Shen, Q., Chouchoulas A., A Rough-fuzzy Approach for Generating Classification Rules, Pattern Recognition, Vol. 35, pp. 2425-2438, 2002.
20. Zhang, J., Wang J., Li, D., He, H., Sun, J., A New Heuristic Reduct Algorithm Based on Rough Sets Theory, Proc. of 4th International Conf. on Web-Age Information Management, pp.247-253, 2003.
21. Zhang, M., Yao, J., A Rough Set based Approach ro Feature Selection, Proc. IEEE Annual Meeting of Fuzzy Information NAFIP, pp. 434-439, 2004.

On Consistent and Partially Consistent Extensions of Information Systems

Zbigniew Suraj, Krzysztof Pancerz, and Grzegorz Owsiany

Chair of Computer Science Foundations,
University of Information Technology and Management,
Sucharskiego Str. 2, 35-225 Rzeszów, Poland
{zsuraj, kpancerz, gowsiany}@wsiz.rzeszow.pl

Abstract. Consistent extensions of information systems have been earlier considered in the literature. Informally, a consistent extension of a
given information system includes only such objects corresponding to
known attribute values which are consistent with the whole knowledge
represented by rules extracted from the information system. This paper presents a new look at consistent extensions of information systems
focusing mainly on partially consistent extensions and broadening the approach proposed earlier by Z. Suraj. To this end, a notion of a partially
consistent extension of an information system is introduced. The meaning, properties and application examples of such extensions are given. In
the approach presented, we admit the situation that some objects in an
extension are consistent only with a part of the knowledge extracted from
the information system. We show how a factor of consistency with the
original knowledge for a given object from an extension can be computed.
Some coefficients concerning rules in information systems are defined to
compute a factor of consistency. The notions presented are crucial for
solving different problems. An example is given in the paper to show an
application of the proposed approach in modelling of concurrent systems
described by information systems.

1 Introduction

In the rough set theory introduced by Z. Pawlak, information systems are used
to represent knowledge about elements of a universe of discourse (cf. [1]). Any
information system can be represented as a data table, where columns are labeled by attributes, rows are labeled by objects, and entries of the table are
attribute values. The main idea of building an extension of a given information
system S is the following. An extension of S is created by adding to S new objects corresponding to known attribute values. The consistent extensions have
been earlier considered (see [2], [3]). In [3], a definition of the so-called maximal
consistent extension of an information system S is given as well as algorithms
for determining it are proposed. In [2], a new method of determining consistent
extensions of information systems is proposed. That paper also contains some
necessary and sufficient conditions for the existence of consistent extensions. In

D. Ślęzak et al. (Eds.): RSFDGrC 2005, LNAI 3641, pp. 224–233, 2005.

the case of consistent extensions, each new object added to S satisfies all true rules extracted from S. One of the interesting problems concerning consistent extensions is to find a maximal (with respect to the number of objects) consistent extension of a given information system S. Maximal consistent extensions are used, among others, in the modelling of concurrent systems described by information systems (see [4], [5]). If an information system S describes a concurrent system (i.e., includes all global states of the system observed or measured by us), then the maximal consistent extension of S represents the largest set of global states of the concurrent system consistent with all rules extracted from S. Rules represent some restrictions put on the local states of individual processes of a given concurrent system. In this paper, we introduce a notion of a partially consistent extension of an information system S. New objects added to the system S do not have to satisfy all rules true in S. An interesting thing is to determine a degree of consistency of a new added object with the original knowledge represented by the rules. In the approach proposed, we first search for all rules which are not true for a given object, next, we compute some level of significance of these rules in S. This level is expressed by the support or strength coefficient computed from a data table representing S. Obviously, the smaller the strength the greater is the consistency. It is worth noting that other approaches to computing a consistency degree are possible. The consistency factor can have the following interpretation. Its value can be interpreted as a degree of certainty to which the added object representing a global state can appear in the described system with respect to the knowledge possessed (in the original information system). Our approach to extensions of information systems presented here widens and generalizes that presented in [2] and [3]. The membership of objects to the consistent extensions of information systems does not have to be clear-cut like previously. Thanks to the introduction of the notion of a partially consistent extension, the transition from the belongingness to nonbelongingness of objects to the consistent extension is not abrupt. It is important that we admit that some requirements, restrictions, specification, etc. may be satisfied to a certain degree only. For example, in economic or financial systems, some states not satisfying less significant restrictions may be admit in the specific situations.

The rest of the paper is organized as follows. A brief review of the basic concepts underlying the rough set theory and information systems is given in Section 2. Basic definitions of consistent and partially consistent extensions of information systems are presented in Section 3. In Section 4, some approaches to generating maximal consistent extensions are cursorily described. Finally, concluding remarks are given in Section 5. The main idea of the approach proposed is illustrated by a practical example taken from economics.

2   Preliminaries

First, we recall basic concepts of the rough set theory [1] used in the paper.

An *information system* is a pair $S = (U, A)$, where U is a nonempty, finite set of objects, called the universe, A is a nonempty, finite set of attributes, i.e., $a : U \rightarrow V_a$ for $a \in A$, where V_a is called the value set of a. With every information system $S = (U, A)$ we associate a formal language $L(S)$. The alphabet of $L(S)$ consists of A (the set of attribute constants), $V = \bigcup_{a \in A} V_a$ (the set of attribute value constants) and the set $\{\neg, \vee, \wedge, \Rightarrow, \Leftrightarrow\}$ of propositional connectives, called negation, disjunction, conjunction, implication and equivalence, respectively. An expression of the form (a, v), where $a \in A$ and $v \in V_a$ is called an atomic (elementary) formula of $L(S)$. The set of formulas of $L(S)$ is the least set satisfying the following conditions: (1) (a, v) is a formula of $L(S)$, (2) if ϕ and ψ are formulas of $L(S)$, then so are $\neg\phi$, $\phi \vee \psi$, $\phi \wedge \psi$, $\phi \Rightarrow \psi$, and $\phi \Leftrightarrow \psi$.

The object $u \in U$ satisfies formula ϕ of $L(S)$, denoted by $u \models_S \phi$ (or in short $u \models \phi$), if and only if the following conditions are satisfied: $u \models (a, v)$ iff $a(u) = v$, $u \models \neg\phi$ iff not $u \models \phi$, $u \models \phi \vee \psi$ iff $u \models \phi$ or $u \models \psi$, $u \models \phi \wedge \psi$ iff $u \models \phi$ and $u \models \psi$, $u \models \phi \Rightarrow \psi$ iff $u \models \neg\phi \vee \psi$, $u \models \phi \Leftrightarrow \psi$ iff $u \models \phi \Rightarrow \psi$ and $u \models \psi \Rightarrow \phi$.

If ϕ is a formula of $L(S)$, then set $|\phi|_S = \{u \in U : u \models \phi\}$ is called the meaning of formula ϕ in S. For any formula ϕ of $L(S)$, set $|\phi|_S$ can be defined inductively as follows: $|(a, v)|_S = \{u \in U : a(u) = v\}$, $|\neg\phi|_S = U - |\phi|_S$, $|\phi \vee \psi|_S = |\phi|_S \cup |\psi|_S$, $|\phi \wedge \psi|_S = |\phi|_S \cap |\psi|_S$, $|\phi \Rightarrow \psi|_S = \neg|\phi|_S \cup |\psi|_S$, $|\phi \Leftrightarrow \psi|_S = (|\phi|_S \cap |\psi|_S) \cup (\neg|\phi|_S \cap \neg|\psi|_S)$.

A rule in the information system S is a formula of the form $\phi \Rightarrow \psi$, where ϕ and ψ are referred to as the predecessor and the successor of a rule, respectively. The rule $\phi \Rightarrow \psi$ is true in S if $|\phi|_S \subseteq |\psi|_S$. An inhibitor rule in the information system S is a formula of the form $\phi \Rightarrow \neg\psi$. In this paper, we consider only true rules for which ϕ is a conjunction of atomic formulas of $L(S)$ and ψ is an atomic formula of $L(S)$, i.e., each rule has the form $(a_1, v_1) \wedge \ldots \wedge (a_q, v_q) \Rightarrow (a_d, v_d)$. A rule is called minimal in S if and only if removing any atomic formula from the predecessor of a rule causes that a rule is not true in S. The set of all minimal rules true in S will be denoted by $RUL(S)$. A method for generating the minimal rules in an information system is given among others in [6], [5]. Each rule of the form $(a_1, v_1) \wedge \ldots \wedge (a_q, v_q) \Rightarrow (a_d, v_d)$ can be transformed into a set of inhibitor rules: $\{(a_1, v_1) \wedge \ldots \wedge (a_q, v_q) \Rightarrow \neg(a_d, v_{d_1}), \ldots, (a_1, v_1) \wedge \ldots \wedge (a_q, v_q) \Rightarrow \neg(a_d, v_{d_k})\}$, where $v_{d_1}, \ldots, v_{d_k} \in V_{a_d} - \{v_d\}$. The set of all minimal inhibitor rules true in S will be denoted by $\overline{RUL}(S)$.

3   Extensions of Information Systems

In this section, we recall some earlier and introduce new notions concerning extensions of information systems. Especially, we are interested in consistent and partially consistent extensions. An important thing is how to compute for each object from the extension of a given information system S, its consistency factor using the knowledge included in S.

Definition 1 (Extension of an information system). *Let $S = (U, A)$ be an information system. An information system $S^* = (U^*, A^*)$ is called an extension of S if and only if the following conditions are satisfied: (1) $U \subseteq U^*$, (2) $card(A) = card(A^*)$, (3) $\underset{a \in A}{\forall} \underset{a^* \in A^*}{\exists} V_{a^*} = V_a \wedge a^*(u) = a(u)$ for all $u \in U$.*

Each extension S^* of a given information system S includes the same number of attributes and only such objects whose attribute values appeared in the original table representing S. Moreover, the data table representing S is a part of the data table representing S^*, i.e., all objects which appear in S, also appear in S^*.

Remark 1. In the sequel, the sets A and A^* will be marked by the same letter A.

Example 1. Information systems can be applied as a tool for the description of concurrent systems (cf. [4], [7], [5]). Then, elements of U can be interpreted as global states of a given concurrent system and attributes from A can be interpreted as local processes in a given system. With every process $a \in A$, there is associated a finite set V_a of its local states. So, each row in the table includes record of local states of processes from A. Let us assume that we have observation of some economic processes like exchange rates (marked by *usd* and *euro*), a stock exchange index (marked by *wig*) and an oil price (marked by *oil*). All observed global states of an economic system are presented using an information system (see Table 1a). The meaning of local states of processes is the following: -5 - decrease of 5%, -1 - decrease of 1%, 0 - no change, 1 - increase of 1%, 2 - increase of 2%, 3 - increase of 3%, 5 - increase of 5%. Each row of a data table describes percentage changes of quotations on a given day with relation to the previous day. So, we have the set of global states $U = \{d_1, d_2, \ldots, d_{10}\}$, the set of attributes (local processes) $A = \{usd, euro, wig, oil\}$, and the value sets of attributes (the sets of local states of processes) $V_{usd} = V_{wig} = \{-1, 0, 1, 2\}$, $V_{euro} = \{-1, 0, 1\}$, $V_{oil} = \{-5, -1, 0, 1, 2, 3, 5\}$. Table 1b

Table 1. An information system S (a) and its extension S^* (b)

(a)

$U\backslash A$	usd	euro	wig	oil
d_1	0	0	1	-1
d_2	1	0	-1	2
d_3	0	0	-1	3
d_4	2	1	0	0
d_5	2	1	0	-5
d_6	-1	-1	0	2
d_7	0	0	0	1
d_8	-1	-1	1	5
d_9	-1	0	2	-1
d_{10}	1	0	0	2

(b)

$U\backslash A$	usd	euro	wig	oil
d_1	0	0	1	-1
d_2	1	0	-1	2
d_3	0	0	-1	3
d_4	2	1	0	0
d_5	2	1	0	-5
d_6	-1	-1	0	2
d_7	0	0	0	1
d_8	-1	-1	1	5
d_9	-1	0	2	-1
d_{10}	1	0	0	2
d_{11}	0	0	0	2
d_{12}	1	-1	0	3

represents some extension S^* of information system S. Objects d_{11} and d_{12} have been added. It is easy to check that system S^* satisfies all conditions given in Definition 1.

The number of extensions of a given information system $S = (U, A)$ is equal to $2^{n-k} - 1$ (see [3]), where $k = card(U)$, $A = \{a_1, a_2, \ldots, a_m\}$, $n = card(V_{a_1} \times V_{a_2} \times \ldots \times V_{a_m})$, and V_{a_i} is a value set of a_i for $i = 1, 2, \ldots, m$. By a nontrivial extension of a given information system $S = (U, A)$ we understand any extension $S^* = (U^*, A)$ of S such that $U \subset U^*$. The set of all extensions of a given information system S will be denoted by $EXT(S)$. This set may be partially ordered by a relation "$\leq$" defined as follows: $S_1^* \leq S_2^*$ if and only if $U_1^* \subseteq U_2^*$ for all $S_1^* = (U_1^*, A), S_2^* = (U_2^*, A) \in EXT(S)$. Maximal elements in $EXT(S)$ ordered by "$\leq$" are called maximal extensions of S. There exists exactly one maximal extension for every information system. It includes all objects generated by the cartesian product of attribute value sets (i.e., $V_{a_1} \times V_{a_2} \times \ldots \times V_{a_m}$). The maximal extension of a given information system S will be denoted by S_{MAX}.

Let $S = (U, A)$ be an information system, $S^* = (U^*, A)$ its extension, and $u \in U^*$. By $\widetilde{RUL}_u(S)$ we denote the set of all rules true in S, which are not true for object u from extension S^* of S, i.e.,

$$\widetilde{RUL}_u(S) = \{(\phi \Rightarrow \psi) \in RUL(S) : \neg u \models (\phi \Rightarrow \psi)\} \text{ for } u \in U^* \tag{1}$$

or, in other words:

$$\widetilde{RUL}_u(S) = \{(\phi \Rightarrow \psi) \in RUL(S) : u \models \phi \wedge \neg u \models \psi\} \text{ for } u \in U^*. \tag{2}$$

For a given set $RUL'(S) \subseteq RUL(S)$ of rules in S, we can compute some coefficients, like support and strength, defined below. These coefficients will be needed to compute consistency factors of objects from extensions.

Definition 2 (Support of a set of rules). *Let $RUL(S)$ be a set of all minimal rules true in an information system S and $RUL'(S) \subseteq RUL(S)$. The number $supp(RUL'(S))$ is called the support of $RUL'(S)$ and defined as*

$$supp(RUL'(S)) = card \left(\bigcup_{(\phi \Rightarrow \psi) \in RUL'(S)} |\phi \wedge \psi|_S \right). \tag{3}$$

The support of $RUL'(S)$ is equal to the number of objects in S satisfying simultaneously the predecessor and the successor of at least one rule from $RUL'(S)$. Obviously, $0 \leq supp(RUL'(S)) \leq card(U)$.

Definition 3 (Strength of a set of rules). *Let $RUL(S)$ be a set of all minimal rules true in an information system S and $RUL'(S) \subseteq RUL(S)$. The number $str(RUL'(S))$ is called the strength of $RUL'(S)$ and defined as*

$$str(RUL'(S)) = \frac{supp(RUL'(S))}{card(U)}. \tag{4}$$

The strength of $RUL'(S)$ is a relative measure of the support coefficient (with reference to the number of all objects in S). So, we have $0 \leq str(RUL'(S)) \leq 1$.

For any object u from extension S^* of a given information system S, we can define some coefficient called a consistency factor. This coefficient expresses a consistency degree of u with the knowledge included in the original information system S.

Definition 4 (Consistency factor of an object). *Let $S = (U, A)$ be an information system, $S^* = (U^*, A)$ its extension, and $u \in U^*$. The consistency factor of object u is the number defined as*

$$\xi_S(u) = 1 - str(\widetilde{RUL}_u(S)). \tag{5}$$

We have $0 \leq \xi_S(u) \leq 1$ for each $u \in U^*$. It is obvious that if $u \in U$, then $\xi_S(u) = 1$ because $\widetilde{RUL}_u(S) = \emptyset$ (the empty set).

Example 2. Let us consider the information system S and its extension S^* from Example 1. On the basis of the knowledge possessed (the information system S given in Table 1a), we would like to know what the consistency factor $\xi_S(d_{11})$ of object d_{11} from extension S^* is . The set $RUL(S)$ of all minimal rules true in S includes 49 rules and its presentation has been omitted here. The set of rules which are not satisfied by object d_{11} is shown in Table 2. Moreover, the table includes, for each rule, the objects from system S satisfying simultaneously both the predecessor formula and the successor formula of a rule. According to

Table 2. The set $\widetilde{RUL}_{d_{11}}(S)$

$\phi \Rightarrow \psi$	$\|\phi \wedge \psi\|_S$
$(oil, 2) \wedge (euro, 0) \Rightarrow (usd, 1)$	$\{d_2, d_{10}\}$
$(wig, 0) \wedge (usd, 0) \Rightarrow (oil, 1)$	$\{d_7\}$

formula (3), we obtain $supp(\widetilde{RUL}_{d_{11}}(S)) = card(\{d_2, d_7, d_{10}\}) = 3$. Because $card(U) = 10$, therefore from (4) we have $str(\widetilde{RUL}_{d_{11}}(S)) = 0.3$ and from (5) $\xi_S(d_{11}) = 0.7$. We can say that object d_{11} is consistent with the knowledge included in S to a degree of 0.7. On the other hand, we can say that the degree of certainty that global state d_{11} will appear in the modeled system is equal to 0.7.

Definition 5 (Consistent extension of an information system). *Let $S = (U, A)$ be an information system and $S^* = (U^*, A)$ its extension. S^* is called a consistent extension of an information system S if and only if $\xi_S(u) = 1$ for all $u \in U^*$.*

The set of all consistent extensions of a given information system S will be denoted by $\widehat{EXT}(S)$. This set may be partially ordered by a relation "$\leq$" defined as follows: $S_1^* \leq S_2^*$ if and only if $U_1^* \subseteq U_2^*$ for all $S_1^* = (U_1^*, A), S_2^* = (U_2^*, A) \in \widehat{EXT}(S)$. Maximal elements in $\widehat{EXT}(S)$ ordered by "$\leq$" are called maximal consistent extensions of S. There exists exactly one maximal consistent extension for every information system (see [2]). The maximal consistent extension of a given information system S will be denoted by $\widehat{S}_{MAX}$.

Let $S = (U, A)$ be an information system, $S_{MAX} = (U', A)$ its maximal extension, and $\widehat{S}_{MAX} = (U'', A)$ its maximal consistent extension. Then, we have $S \leq \widehat{S}_{MAX} \leq S_{MAX}$ (or, equivalently, $U \subseteq U'' \subseteq U'$).

Definition 6 (Partially consistent extension of an information system).
Let $S = (U, A)$ be an information system and $S^* = (U^*, A)$ its extension. S^* is called a partially consistent extension of an information system S if and only if there exists $u \in U^*$ such that $\xi_S(u) < 1$.

Definition 7 (Consistency factor of an extension). *Let $S = (U, A)$ be an information system and $S^* = (U^*, A)$ its extension. The consistency factor of extension S^* of S is the number defined as $\xi(S^*) = \min_{u \in U^*} \xi_S(u)$.*

Obviously, if $\xi(S^*) = 1$, then extension S^* is consistent, and if $\xi(S^*) < 1$, then extension S^* is partially consistent. It is worth mentioning that the consistent extension S^* of S includes the same knowledge as the original information system S. However, if we add to S a new object u such that $\xi_S(u) < 1$, then the knowledge included in S is modified. Since then some rules from $RUL(S)$ are not true in S^*, where S^* is the system arisen from S by adding u. We can also say this about a maximal partially consistent extension $\widehat{S}^{\beta}_{MAX}$ of a given information system S with the consistency factor equal to β. Such an extension consists of each object u from the maximal extension S_{MAX} of S for which $\xi_S(u) \geq \beta$.

For each information system S, we can compute the so-called consistency formula $\sigma(S)$ of S. $\sigma(S)$ is a formula in $L(S)$ language constructed on the basis of either the set $RUL(S)$ of all minimal rules true in S or the set $\overline{RUL}(S)$ of all minimal inhibitor rules true in S. For $RUL(S) = \{\phi_1 \Rightarrow \psi_1, \ldots, \phi_r \Rightarrow \psi_r\}$, we obtain $\sigma(S) = (\neg\phi_1 \vee \psi_1) \wedge \ldots \wedge (\neg\phi_r \vee \psi_r)$ using the logical law $(x \Rightarrow y) \Leftrightarrow (\neg x \vee y)$. This formula can be transformed into $\sigma(S) = \neg(\phi_1 \wedge \neg\psi_1) \wedge \ldots \wedge \neg(\phi_r \wedge \neg\psi_r)$, and next $\sigma(S) = \neg[(\phi_1 \wedge \neg\psi_1) \vee \ldots \vee (\phi_r \wedge \neg\psi_r)]$. Analogously, for $\overline{RUL}(S) = \{\phi_1 \Rightarrow \neg\psi'_1, \ldots, \phi_r \Rightarrow \neg\psi'_r\}$, where $\psi'_1 = \neg\psi_1, \ldots, \psi'_r = \neg\psi_r$ according to the construction of inhibitor rules, we obtain $\overline{\sigma}(S) = \neg(\phi_1 \wedge \psi'_1) \wedge \ldots \wedge \neg(\phi_r \wedge \psi'_r)$ using the logical law $(x \Rightarrow \neg y) \Leftrightarrow \neg(x \wedge y)$. This formula can be transformed into $\overline{\sigma}(S) = \neg[(\phi_1 \wedge \psi'_1) \vee \ldots \vee (\phi_r \wedge \psi'_r)]$. It is easy to see that formulas $\sigma(S)$ and $\overline{\sigma}(S)$ are equivalent, i.e., $|\sigma(S)|_S = |\overline{\sigma}(S)|_S$. So, for a given information system S, the sets $RUL(S)$ and $\overline{RUL}(S)$ are equivalent in the sense that they describe the same sets of objects belonging to the maximal consistent extension $\widehat{S}_{MAX}$ of S.

Corollary 1. *Let $S = (U, A)$ be an information system, $S_{MAX} = (U', A)$ be a maximal extension of S, and $\widehat{S}_{MAX} = (U'', A)$ be a maximal consistent extension of S. If $u \in U'$ and $u \models \sigma(S)$ (or, equivalently, $u \models \overline{\sigma}(S)$), then $u \in U''$.*

4 Generating Extensions of Information Systems

The maximal extension of a given information system $S = (U, A)$, where $A = \{a_1, a_2, \ldots, a_m\}$, includes all objects generated by the cartesian product of attribute value sets (i.e., $V_{a_1} \times V_{a_2} \times \ldots \times V_{a_m}$). Only a part of them belongs to the consistent extension of S. One of the problems is to find a maximal consistent extension of a given information system S. In [3], the algorithm for computing a maximal consistent extension has been given. That algorithm consists of two stages. At the first stage, all attribute value vectors (objects) determined by the cartesian product of attribute value sets, which do not appear in S, are fixed. At the second stage, each object u obtained in the first step is verified using the set $RUL(S)$ of all minimal rules true in S. If there exists a rule $(\phi \Rightarrow \psi) \in RUL(S)$ such that u does not satisfy $\phi \Rightarrow \psi$, then u does not belong to the maximal consistent extension.

In [4], [8], the methods for constructing concurrent models in the form of coloured Petri nets [9] from information systems have been described. Coloured Petri (CP) nets are used, among others, for modelling, specifying and designing concurrent systems. For a given information system S, the constructed model has the following property: the reachability set of markings (including all markings reachable from the initial marking) defines a maximal consistent extension of S. A block diagram in Figure 1 shows a computation path. The foregoing way is

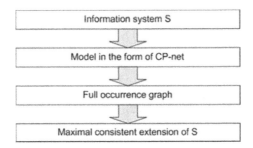

Fig. 1. Generating a maximal consistent extension

accessible from the computer tool called $ROSECON$ [10]. This system supports users in automated discovering of net models from data tables. For a given information system S, we can obtain its net model CPN_S in the form of a coloured Petri net; next, we can compute a full occurrence graph $OG(CPN_S)$ (a graph with a node for each reachable marking) [9] of this model. $OG(CPN_S)$ includes markings corresponding to all attribute value vectors (objects) from the maximal consistent extension of S.

Example 3. Let us consider the information system S from Example 1. We would like to find all global states in which the described system can hold apart from those observed by us, which are consistent with the whole knowledge included in the data table representing S. In order to do it we need to compute the maximal consistent extension $\widehat{S}_{MAX}$ of S. Using the $ROSECON$ system we obtain the maximal consistent extension shown in Table 3. It is easy to see that object d_{11} is new. It satisfies the consistency formula $\overline{\sigma}(S)$ of S, which has the form:
$\overline{\sigma}(S) = \neg\{[(usd, 2) \wedge (oil, 3)] \vee [(usd, 1) \wedge (oil, 3)] \vee [(usd, -1) \wedge (oil, 3)] \vee [(usd, 1) \wedge (euro, 1)] \vee [(usd, 0) \wedge (euro, 1)] \vee [(usd, -1) \wedge (euro, 1)] \vee [(usd, 1) \wedge (oil, 0)] \vee [(usd, 0) \wedge (oil, 0)] \vee [(usd, -1) \wedge (oil, 0)] \vee [(usd, 1) \wedge (oil, -5)] \vee [(usd, 0) \wedge (oil, -5)] \vee [(usd, -1) \wedge (oil, -5)] \vee [(usd, 2) \wedge (euro, -1)] \vee [(usd, 1) \wedge (euro, -1)] \vee [(usd, 0) \wedge (euro, -1)] \vee$

Table 3. A maximal consistent extension $\widehat{S}_{MAX}$ of S

$U\backslash A$	usd	euro	wig	oil	$U\backslash A$	usd	euro	wig	oil
d_1	0	0	1	-1	d_7	0	0	0	1
d_2	1	0	-1	2	d_8	-1	-1	1	5
d_3	0	0	-1	3	d_9	-1	0	2	-1
d_4	2	1	0	0	d_{10}	1	0	0	2
d_5	2	1	0	-5	d_{11}	2	1	0	2
d_6	-1	-1	0	2					

$[(usd, 2) \wedge (oil, 1)] \vee [(usd, 1) \wedge (oil, 1)] \vee [(usd, -1) \wedge (oil, 1)] \vee [(usd, 2) \wedge (oil, 5)] \vee [(usd, 1) \wedge (oil, 5)] \vee [(usd, 0) \wedge (oil, 5)] \vee [(usd, 2) \wedge (wig, 2)] \vee [(usd, 1) \wedge (wig, 2)] \vee [(usd, 0) \wedge (wig, 2)] \vee [(euro, 1) \wedge (oil, -1)] \vee [(euro, -1) \wedge (oil, -1)] \vee [(euro, 1) \wedge (wig, -1)] \vee [(euro, -1) \wedge (wig, -1)] \vee [(euro, 1) \wedge (oil, 3)] \vee [(euro, -1) \wedge (oil, 3)] \vee [(euro, 0) \wedge (usd, 2)] \vee [(euro, 0) \wedge (oil, 0)] \vee [(euro, -1) \wedge (oil, 0)] \vee [(euro, 0) \wedge (oil, -5)] \vee [(euro, -1) \wedge (oil, -5)] \vee [(euro, 1) \wedge (oil, 1)] \vee [(euro, -1) \wedge (oil, 1)] \vee [(euro, 1) \wedge (oil, 5)] \vee [(euro, 0) \wedge (oil, 5)] \vee [(euro, 1) \wedge (wig, 2)] \vee [(euro, -1) \wedge (wig, 2)] \vee [(wig, 2) \wedge (oil, 3)] \vee [(wig, 0) \wedge (oil, 3)] \vee [(wig, 1) \wedge (oil, 3)] \vee [(wig, 1) \wedge (usd, 2)] \vee [(wig, -1) \wedge (usd, 2)] \vee [(wig, 1) \wedge (euro, 1)] \vee [(wig, 2) \wedge (oil, 0)] \vee [(wig, 1) \wedge (oil, 0)] \vee [(wig, -1) \wedge (oil, 0)] \vee [(wig, 2) \wedge (oil, -5)] \vee [(wig, 1) \wedge (oil, -5)] \vee [(wig, -1) \wedge (oil, -5)] \vee [(wig, 2) \wedge (oil, 1)] \vee [(wig, 1) \wedge (oil, 1)] \vee [(wig, -1) \wedge (oil, 1)] \vee [(wig, 2) \wedge (oil, 5)] \vee [(wig, 0) \wedge (oil, 5)] \vee [(wig, -1) \wedge (oil, 5)] \vee [(oil, -1) \wedge (usd, 1)] \vee [(oil, 2) \wedge (wig, 2)] \vee [(usd, 0) \wedge (oil, 2) \wedge (euro, 0)] \vee [(wig, 1) \wedge (oil, 2) \wedge (usd, -1)] \vee [(wig, -1) \wedge (oil, 2) \wedge (usd, -1)] \vee [(wig, 1) \wedge (oil, 2) \wedge (euro, -1)] \vee [(euro, 0) \wedge (wig, 1) \wedge (usd, -1)] \vee [(usd, -1) \wedge (oil, 2) \wedge (euro, 0)] \vee [(wig, 0) \wedge (oil, -1) \wedge (usd, 0)] \vee [(wig, -1) \wedge (oil, -1) \wedge (usd, 0)] \vee [(wig, 0) \wedge (euro, 0) \wedge (usd, -1)] \vee [(wig, -1) \wedge (euro, 0) \wedge (usd, -1)] \vee [(wig, 0) \wedge (oil, -1) \wedge (usd, -1)] \vee [(wig, 1) \wedge (oil, -1) \wedge (usd, -1)] \vee [(wig, -1) \wedge (oil, -1) \wedge (usd, -1)] \vee [(oil, 2) \wedge (wig, 1) \wedge (usd, 0)] \vee [(oil, 2) \wedge (wig, 1) \wedge (euro, 0)] \vee [(usd, 0) \wedge (oil, 2) \wedge (wig, -1)] \vee [(usd, 1) \wedge (wig, 1) \wedge (euro, 0)] \vee [(oil, 2) \wedge (wig, 0) \wedge (usd, 0)]\}.$

In order to determine a maximal partially consistent extension $\widehat{S}^{\beta}_{MAX}$ (with a consistency factor equal to β) of a given information system S, we must compute a consistency factor $\xi_S(u)$ for each object u from the maximal extension S_{MAX} of S and we have to remove each u from S_{MAX} for which $\xi_S(u) < \beta$. This approach seems to be simple to realize, but its computational complexity is high. We must have the set $RUL(S)$ of minimal rules true in S. The problem of computing of $RUL(S)$ is NP-hard [11]. Thus, it is important to work out algorithms for generating maximal consistent extensions without the necessity of computing rules.

5   Conclusions

In this paper, we have defined a notion of a partially consistent extension of a given information system. In the approach considered in the paper we admit that some objects added to the original information system S are not consistent with the whole knowledge included in S, but with its part only. We have shown how to compute a consistency factor with this knowledge for any object from some extension of S. The approach presented generalizes that proposed earlier. Some important problems concerning extensions of information systems remain to be solved, among others: determining necessary and sufficient conditions for the existence of nontrivial consistent extensions of information systems, elaboration of efficient algorithms for generating maximal consistent extensions and maximal partially consistent extensions (with assumed consistency factors) of information systems, calculating consistency factors of objects without the necessity of computing rules.

Acknowledgements

This paper has been partially supported by the Ministry of Scientific Research and Information Technology of the Republic of Poland research grants 3 T11C 005 28 and 3 T11C 012 28.

References

1. Pawlak, Z.: Rough Sets - Theoretical Aspects of Reasoning About Data. Kluwer Academic Publishers, Dordrecht (1991)
2. Rząsa, W., Suraj, Z.: A new method for determining of extensions and restrictions of information systems. In Alpigini, J., Peters, J., Skowron, A., Zhong, N., eds.: Proceedings of the RSCTC'2002. Volume 2475 of Lecture Notes in Artificial Intelligence. Springer Verlag, Berlin Heidelberg (2002) 197–204
3. Suraj, Z.: Some remarks on extensions and restrictions of information systems. In Ziarko, W., Yao, Y., eds.: Rough Sets and Current Trends in Computing. Volume 2005 of Lecture Notes in Artificial Intelligence. Springer Verlag, Berlin Heidelberg (2001) 204–211
4. Pancerz, K., Suraj, Z.: Synthesis of Petri net models: A rough set approach. Fundamenta Informaticae **55** (2003) 149–165
5. Suraj, Z.: Rough set methods for the synthesis and analysis of concurrent processes. In Polkowski, L., Tsumoto, S., Lin, T.Y., eds.: Rough Set Methods and Applications. Springer Verlag, Berlin (2000) 379–488
6. Skowron, A.: Boolean reasoning for decision rules generation. In Komorowski, J., Ras, Z., eds.: Proceedings of the ISMIS'1993. Volume 689 of Lecture Notes in Artificial Intelligence. Springer Verlag, Berlin (1993) 295–305
7. Pawlak, Z.: Concurrent versus sequential - the rough sets perspective. Bull. of EATCS **48** (1992) 178–190
8. Suraj, Z., Pancerz, K.: A synthesis of concurrent systems: A rough set approach. In Wang, G., Liu, Q., Yao, Y., Skowron, A., eds.: Proceedings of the RSFDGrC'2003. Volume 2639 of Lecture Notes in Artificial Intelligence. Springer Verlag, Berlin Heidelberg (2003) 299–302
9. Jensen, K.: Coloured Petri Nets. Basic Concepts, Analysis Methods and Practical Use. Volume 1. Springer Verlag, Berlin (1997)
10. Pancerz, K., Suraj, Z.: Discovering concurrent models from data tables with the ROSECON system. Fundamenta Informaticae **60** (2004) 251–268
11. Skowron, A., Rauszer, C.: The discernibility matrices and functions in information systems. In Slowiński, R., ed.: Intelligent Decision Support. Handbook of Applications and Advances of the Rough Set Theory. Kluwer Academic Publishers, Dordrecht (1992) 331–362

A New Treatment and Viewpoint of Information Tables

Mineichi Kudo and Tetsuya Murai

Division of Computer Science,
Graduate School of Information Science and Technology,
Hokkaido University, Sapporo 060-0814, Japan
{mine, murahiko}@main.ist.hokudai.ac.jp
http://ips9.main.eng.hokudai.ac.jp

Abstract. According to the sizes of the attribute set and the information table, the information tables are categorized into three types of Rough Set problems, Pattern Recognition/Machine Learning problems, and Statistical Model Identification problems. In the first Rough Set situation, what we have seen is as follows: 1) The "granularity" should be taken so as to divide equally the unseen tuples out of the information table, 2) The traditional "Reduction" sense accords with the above insistence, and 3) The "stable" subsets of tuples, which are defined through a "Galois connection" between the subset and the corresponding attribute subset, may play an important role to capture some characteristics that can be read from the given information table. We show these with some illustrative examples.

1 Introduction

So far, an information table has been considered as a subset of the universe that is the product space of attributes. In addition, reflecting the difference of treatments, such a finite piece of information is called an "information table" in rough set community, "instances" in machine learning or data mining communities and "training samples" in pattern recognition community. An information table implies that we are given only part of full information of a finite size. An instance or a sample is the word related to finding a true model or a true rule, that is, learning, and often the size of full information is infinite. However, we are using these different terms to the same object. In this study, we start with classifying information tables from the viewpoint of the number of attributes and the number of tuples. This way gives us a piece of intuition and enables us to take different approaches depending on given information tables.

We consider also about so-called "reduction" in rough set or "feature selection" in pattern recognition, and "prime implicant" in machine learning. The goal is the same and is to find a minimum number of attributes/features/terms so as to keep a condition we require. However, it does not always work, because we need many attributes when the number of decision classes is large or when it requires

D. Ślęzak et al. (Eds.): RSFDGrC 2005, LNAI 3641, pp. 234–243, 2005.

essentially many attributes. We will discuss what removing an attribute in the entropy of division.

Last, we suggest to use the "stable" subsets to express any subset of tuples sharing a same property. Here, a subset is called "stable" when it is unchanged after mappings from a attribute subset to a tuple subset and the tuple subset to another attribute subset.

2   Categories of Information Tables

2.1   Information Table

Let us consider an information table. First we consider m different attributes as $A = \{A_1, A_2, \ldots, A_m\}$, $A_i = \mathbb{O}$ or $\mathbb{C}$, where $\mathbb{O}$ is a finite ordered set and $\mathbb{C}$ is a finite categorical set. Here, we identify the attributes with their domains as long as no confusion occurs. Therefore, A is of m different domains. Then the universe U is written as the product space of these: $U = U_A = A_1 \times A_2 \times \cdots \times A_m$. An information table $T = \{x^1, x^2, \ldots, x^n\}$ is given as a subset of U and denoted also by U_n for emphasizing the number of tuples.

2.2   Categories of Information Tables

First, we consider an information table shown in Fig. 1. We regard such an information as a limited piece of information or incomplete information. We are limited in two ways. First, the attribute set A may be incomplete compared to the full attribute set Φ, so that it can happen that we cannot discern each tuple in the current attribute set. However, this situation may be resolved by obtaining further evidence (attributes). Second, we have only a part U_n of full information U_A even in the current attribute set A. Therefore, we have to infer the remaining tuples that are possible to be represented in the same universe.

Next, on the basis of above considerations, let us classify such information tables into three categories according to the size of attribute set and the size

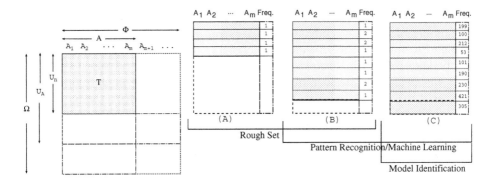

Fig. 1. An information table as part

Fig. 2. Three types of information tables

of information table. In Fig.2, due to the limitation of the universe size or the limitation of the tuple set size, we traverse among (A), (B) and (C). One useful viewpoint is as follows; (A) is typical in rough set problems in which the goal is to extract some characteristics among a given subset of tuples or to infer those over a full tuple set in the universe, (B) is typical in pattern recognition and in machine learning in which the goal is to identify a concept (a subset) from a limited number of instances (samples), and (C) is typical in statistics in which we want to know the probabilistic structure from a finite but reasonable number of instances.

Classification of information tables is important in the following sense. If we take the problem at hand as one in Type (A), we have to note that some characteristics extracted from a given information table also say something for the remaining unseen tuples. For example, if we specify a combination of attributes valid only for a certain subset of given tuples, e.g., tuples belonging to a same decision class, then there exist the other tuples satisfying the same relation. In the case of Type (B), the goal is identification of a concept (a subset over the universe). Under this goal, it is worth finding a compact representation of the concept. There are many ways to specify a same subset. Among these, it is convenient to find out some simple way to express such a concept. In decision rules, a conjunctive expression of conditional attributes is such an example. In the case of Type (C), it may be useful to take a histogram approach. In this situation, the goodness of the methodology is evaluated in the consistency (the identification in the limit) and the convergence rate to the true model.

As for traversing between (A) to (B) and (B) to (C), there are two viewpoints. As the number of the attributes decreases or the number of tuples increases, the problem goes to (A) to (B) and (B) to (C). That is, as the amount of information increases or as the possible worlds reduces, then we could know the nature of the problem more than before. We can interpret this also from the viewpoint of granularity. As the granule increases, we approach to (B) or to (C). That is, if we are satisfied with a more rough expression, we can have an easier problem. Reversely speaking, we should let the granule smaller if we want to investigate the information table in detail. Notifying this fact is important when we analyze a given information table. For example, we often face up to the problem where the number of tuples available is limited. Then we should find an appropriate "granule" to analyze such an information table. Excess granularity causes too specific knowledge, while too less granularity causes too general knowledge.

In this paper, we consider only Type (A). In this case, the main topic is how a characteristics extracted from a limited number of tuples affects the remaining unseen tuples. Therefore, throughout this paper, we assume all members are discernible, i.e., $x \neq y$ for distinct two elements $x, y \in T$.

2.3   Relations

A relation R is said to be "decomposable" if R can be written by

$$R = R_1 \times R_2 \times \cdots \times R_m,$$

where the following holds:

$$xRy \leftrightarrow (x, y) \in R \leftrightarrow (x_i, y_i) \in R_i \leftrightarrow x_i R_i y_i, \quad \forall i \in \{1, 2, \dots, m\}.$$

It is easy to confirm that when R is an equivalence relation (shortly, e.r.) and decomposable (shortly, d.e.r., from now on), then the partition derived from R,

$$P_R = U/R = \{[x]_R = \{y|(x, y) \in R\} \,|x \in U\}$$

is also decomposed as

$$P_R = P_{R_1} \times P_{R_2} \times \cdots \times P_{R_m} = A_1/R_1 \times A_2/R_2 \times \cdots \times A_m/R_m$$
$$= \{[x_1]_{R_1}\} \times \{[x_2]_{R_2}\} \times \cdots \times \{[x_m]_{R_m}\}.$$

We prepare two extreme relations $\underline{R}$ and $\bar{R}$ as

$$x\underline{R}y \Leftrightarrow x = y, \qquad x\bar{R}y \Leftrightarrow x, y \in U.$$

That is, any reflective relation R is found between $\underline{R}$ and $\bar{R}$. These two notations are defined on each R_i as well. It looks meaningless for $\bar{R}$, but it will play an important role later. It is also noted that both $\underline{R}$ and $\bar{R}$ are decomposable e.r.'s. Therefore, using these special relations, the universe U can be interpreted by

$$U/\underline{R} \leftrightarrow U = A_1 \times A_2 \times \cdots \times A_m \leftrightarrow A_1/\underline{R}_1 \times A_2/\underline{R}_2 \times \cdots \times A_m/\underline{R}_m$$

where $\leftrightarrow$ shows the one-to-one corresponding in which a set X or a member x corresponds to the set consisting only of X or x, respectively, such as

$$A_i = \{a_{i1}, a_{i2}, \dots, a_{ik_i}\} \leftrightarrow A_i/\underline{R}_i = \{\{a_{i1}\}, \{a_{i2}\}, \dots, \{a_{ik_i}\}\}.$$

In this way, the universe U is identified as $U/\underline{R} = \{\{x^1\}, \{x^2\}, \dots\}$. So, from now on, we identify these two expressions as the same, as long as no confusion occurs. In the "reduction" that will be discussed later, we have an option for the decomposable R and their R_i's as $R = \{\underline{R}_1 \text{ or } \bar{R}_1\} \times \{\underline{R}_2 \text{ or } \bar{R}_2\} \times \cdots \times \{\underline{R}_m \text{ or } \bar{R}_m\}$.

We may say that one extreme relation $\underline{R}$ causes a world consisting of individual tuples, while another extreme $\bar{R}$ cause a world consisting of a whole tuples. Using a decomposable e.r. R between these, we have a world consisting of several subsets mutually exclusive and covering U. Such an intuition is strongly related to the zooming theory proposed by Murai et al. [1,2] in which a sequence of logics or analyses goes to by zooming-in and zooming-out operations, which corresponds to choosing a larger R or a smaller R.

3   Representative Granularity

3.1   Granularity

A "granularity" is usually referred to as an e.r. R on U [3]. That gives a certain level of expression of any concept (subset) X. Indeed, as long as the available attributes are all finite, we have so-called "measurement granularity" $R^M = \underline{R}$ in the beginning [4]. Here we use a notation $\tilde{R}$ to distinguish a relation $\tilde{R}$ on U/R from a usual relation R' on U. We distinguish R and $\tilde{R}$ by calling R a "base granularity (base relation)" and $\tilde{R}$ a "representation granularity (representation relation)." As long as we use $\underline{R}$, it is identical to consider $\tilde{R}$ on $U/\underline{R}$ and a relation $\tilde{R}$ on U. However, this distinguishing gives an extension and flexible treatment as for granularity.

Example 1 *Let $A_1 = \{a, b, c\}$ and $A_2 = \{0, 1\}$. Take an e.r. $R \subseteq (A_1 \times A_2) \times (A_1 \times A_2)$. Then R is defined on $U = A_1 \times A_2 = \{x^1, x^2, \ldots, x^6\}$. On the other hand, consider the base relation $\underline{R}$ on U. Then we have*

$$U/\underline{R} = \{\{x^1 = (a, 0)\}, \{x^2 = (a, 1)\}, \ldots, \{x^6 = (c, 1)\}\}.$$

At this time, we see the one-to-one correspondence between R and $\tilde{R}$ through

$$(x, y) \in R \leftrightarrow (\{x\}, \{y\}) \in \tilde{R} \subseteq U/\underline{R} \times U/\underline{R}.$$

On the other hand, it is possible to think, as a base relation, another decomposable e.r. $R = \underline{R}_1 \times \bar{R}_2$ on U. Then $U/R = \{\{x^1, x^2\}, \{x^3, x^4\}, \{x^5, x^6\}\}$. This brings more rough granular. We can consider another d.e.r. $R = R_1 \times \bar{R}_2$ where $R_1 = \{(a, a), (b, b), (c, c), (a, b), (b, a)\}$ which gives a partition: $U/R = \{X_1 = \{x^1, x^2, x^3, x^4\}, X_2 = \{x^5, x^6\}\}$. In this case, the number of possible e.r. on U/R and the corresponding partitions are only two: $\{\{X_1\}, \{X_2\}\}, \{\{X_1, X_2\}\}$.

We adopt a d.e.r. R only as "granular" and consider a representation relation $\tilde{R}$ on U/R.

3.2   Discernibility and Reduction

A principle concept of Rough Sets is "discernibility." One of purposes of Rough Sets theory is to find the minimal subsets of attributes keeping some discernibility on a given T. Sometimes, a harder request is imposed to find the minimum number of attributes. This goal is refereed to as "reduction." In this section, we extend this concept in a natural way.

A granular R is said to keep the "individual discernibility" when it holds

$$T = \{[x]_R \cap T\}, \quad \text{where } T = \{x^1, x^2, \ldots, x^n\}.$$

Then we can regard T is a restriction of U such as

$$T = U|_T = U \cap T.$$

In addition, T derives a partition P_T and the corresponding equivalence relation R_T which is defined as

$$P_T = U/R_T = \{T^c, \{x^i\}(i = 1, 2, \ldots, n)\}.$$

We, then, can also consider T as a set of singleton sets as

$$T = \{\{x^i\}(i = 1, 2, \ldots, n)\}. \tag{1}$$

According to this double notation, we may write $P_T = T \cup \{T^c\}$.

Let us introduce one more notation. By $R|T$ we denote an e.r. when e.r. R is restricted on T and by $P_{R|T}$ the corresponding partition as

$$R|T = R \cap (T \times T), \qquad P_{R|T} = \{[x]_R \cap T\} = \{[x]_{R|T}\}$$

Then, the condition of granularity R and the corresponding partition P_R to keep individual discernibility is written as

$$R|T = R_T - (T^c \times T^c) \quad \text{and} \quad P_{R|T} = T. \tag{2}$$

That is, such a partition P_R is identical to T in the sense of Eq. (1) when it is restricted on T.

The point is that unlike U itself, T is a subset of U, which is a part of full information. So far, only T has been our main concern. However once we pay an attention to the remaining $U - T$, the problem becomes to evaluate how $U - T$ is partitioned by a granularity R keeping (2). We denote such a granularity by R^I. Here it should be noted that R^I is defined on $U/\underline{R}$. Then there are some criteria to think:

1. (Minimum Division Criterion) minimize $|P_R|$. This is the same as the requirement to take as large relation as possible.
2. (Maximum Entropy Criterion) maximize entropy

$$H(P_R) = -\sum^{|P_R|} |[x]_R|/|U| \log |[x]_R|/|U|.$$

This requires the granule to be as uniform as possible. Or equivalently, each world determined by d.e.r. R should be as same size as possible.

Usually it is better to use both criteria in some way; for example, take the minimum division criterion primly and the entropy criterion secondly. Such a criterion is given by $|P_R| + H(P_R)/\log |P_R|$. In the ordinal "reduction" we want to choose an attribute subset so as to have the smallest number of attributes as possible. In this case, the size of the partition becomes small so that the minimum division criterion is fairly satisfied. In addition, removing an attribute produces an equally-sized partition so that the entropy criterion is automatically satisfied. However, there is a big difference.

Example 2 *Let us consider Fig. 3. In Fig.3 (a), $A_1 = \{1, 2, 3, 4\}$ and $A_2 = \{1, 2, 3\}$ are both ordered finite sets. Thus, $U = \{(i, j) | i = 1, 2, 3, 4, j = 1, 2, 3\}$. Let us find an d.e.r. R distinguishing two tuples $x^4 = (4, 1)$ and $x^9 = (1, 3)$ for $T = \{x^4, x^9\}$. There are five such R's (Fig.3 (b)-(f)). They use only one attribute A_1 or A_2, and $|P_R| = 2$. So reduction is possible to be achieved. If we*

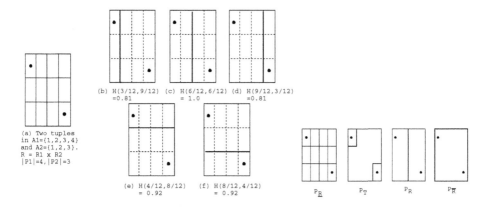

Fig. 3. A case of individually discernibility

Fig. 4. Relationship between partitions

further require the maximum entropy criterion to them, then (c) is chosen. The chosen (c) gives a d.e.r.

$$R = R_1 \times \bar{R}_2 \text{ ,or shortly, } R = R_1$$

and the corresponding partition P_R is

$$P_R = \left\{ X_1 = \{x^1, x^2, x^5, x^6, x^9, x^{10}\}, X_2 = \{x^3, x^4, x^7, x^8, x^{11}, x^{12}\} \right\}.$$

It is noted that in this granular R, two tuples x^4 and x^5 are identified as X_1 and X_2, respectively. This is our representation granularity R^I. The relationship between several relations defined so far are displayed in Fig. 4.

It seems to be natural to require the uniformness on each axis in addition to above two criteria. We call such a criterion 'the maximum component entropy criterion." However, it can be shown that this criterion is satisfied automatically due to the maximum entropy criterion when the partition size $|P_R|$ is the same.

Example 3 *Let us consider Fig. 5 under the maximum component entropy criterion.*

In Fig. 5(a), $A_1 = \{1, 2, \ldots, 6\}$ and $A_2 = \{1, 2, \ldots, 5\}$ that are both ordered finite sets. Thus, $U = \{(i, j) \mid i = 1, \ldots, 6, j = 1, \ldots, 5\}$. The three d.e.r. R's (Fig. 5(b)-(d)) satisfy the maximum component entropy criterion. Indeed these three produces an almost equally-spaced partition on each attribute. Among these three, (b) and (c) uses only one attribute A_1 or A_2. So they are best in the meaning of usual reduction. However, if we use the minimum division criterion, (d) is the best. The chosen (d) gives a d.e.r. $R = R_1 \times R_2$ connected to the partition

$$P_R = \{\{(1 - 3, 1, 2)\}, \{(4 - 6, 1, 2)\}, \{(1 - 3, 3 - 5)\}, \{(4 - 6, 3 - 5)\}\}.$$

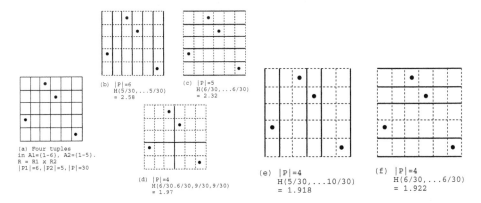

(a) Four tuples
in A1=(1-6), A2=(1-5).
R = R1 x R2
|P1|=6,|P2|=5,|P|=30

(b) |P|=6
H(5/30,...5/30)
= 2.58

(c) |P|=5
H(6/30,...6/30)
= 2.32

(d) |P|=4
H(6/30.6/30,9/30,9/30)
= 1.97

(e) |P|=4
H(5/30,...10/30)
= 1.918

(f) |P|=4
H(6/30,...6/30)
= 1.922

Fig. 5. Another case of individually discernibility

Fig. 6. Minimum division cases

If we do not impose the maximum component entropy criterion, we have two more candidates (Fig. 6(e),(f)). Even in this case, (d) becomes best in the entropy values.

As a result of previous discussions, we can say: "the 'Reduction' is a trial to find the maximum and equally-sized granule upon some discernibility. In other words, the set of worlds should be granularized equally and each world should be represented by one of tuples we can see." In many cases, this statement is consistent to the traditional "reduction" criterion of minimum number of attributes.

3.3   Galois Connection

Next, let us consider how to express a concept (a subset) X of the universe U. When a tuple x is given by $x = (x_1, x_2, \ldots, x_m)$, $x_i \in A_i$, we define an operator called "closure" of X as follows.

Definition 1 *(Closure)*

$$[X] \equiv \bigcup_{x \in X} x_1 \times \bigcup_{x \in X} x_2 \times \cdots \times \bigcup_{x \in X} x_m$$
$$\equiv [X_1] \times [X_2] \times \cdots [X_m]$$

Clearly, $[X]$ is a subset of U as well as X itself. We, thus, have some properties:

Property 1   1. $X \subseteq [X]$ 2. $[[X]] = [X]$

Furthermore, let us consider a sequence of attribute-value subsets derived from X as $A_X = ([X_1], [X_2], \ldots, [X_m])$, $[X]_i \subseteq A_i$. Then the following flow can be seen:

$$X \to A_X \to [X] \to A_{[X]} = A_X \to [X] \to \cdots. \tag{3}$$

Reversely, for any sequence of attribute-value subsets $B = (B_1, B_2, \ldots, B_m)$, $B_i \subseteq A_i$, and the product space of those $X_B = B_1 \times B_2 \times \ldots \times B_m$, we have

$$B \to X_B \to B \to X_B \to \cdots. \tag{4}$$

We, therefore, notice that

1. Triple arrow operator is identical to single arrow operator (see (3)).
2. Double arrow operator brings identity for any B and $[X]$. (see (3) and (4)).

Thus, if $X = [X]$ we have $X \leftrightarrow A_X$. This one-to-one corresponding is called a "Galois connection" between U and A. Here, a subset X such that $X = [X]$ is said to be "closed" in this paper.

3.4   Maximal Conjunctive Closed Subsets and Set Cover

As we have seen, a closed subset X is "stable" under the arrow operation, that is, $[X] = X$. This means that we may identify a closed subset X with its attribute-value set sequence A_X. Thus, it seems better to use only such closed subsets to express any subset. Indeed, this is possible as shown below.

Let us consider a special type of closed subsets called "conjunctive subsets" as follows. A subset X is said to be "conjunctive" when X is written as

$$X = B_1 \times B_2 \times \cdots \times B_m,$$
$$\text{where} \quad B_i \subseteq A_i, \ B_i = [l_i, L_i] \text{ for } B_i = \mathbb{O} (i = 1, 2, \ldots, m).$$

This conjunctive subsets are obviously closed from the form. To obtain an compact expression, we furthermore requite such conjunctive closed subsets to be maximal in the set inclusion relation. Then, it is easy to see that any subset X can be expressed by the union of maximal conjunctive closed subsets. A disjunctive normal form of a logical formula is such an example.

4   Discussion

We have defined a "representation granularity." Our motivation is described as follows. When an information table is given with a number of finite attributes, such a piece of information is already granularized. To indicate it, we defined the measurement granularity R^M. Next, to discern each tuple of the information table, we considered another granularity R^I on U/R^M. Obviously, R^I is more rough than R^M. If we move to keeping a class discernibility, we could find a more rough granularity R^D on U/R^I. It is possible to consider a sequence $U/\underline{R}, U/\underline{R}/R^I, U/\underline{R}/R^I/R^D, \ldots$ and simply $U/\underline{R}, U/R^I, U/R^D, \ldots$ if $\underline{R}, R^I, R^D, \ldots$ are refinements of their predecessors [4]. That is our way to consider several viewpoints to analyze a given information table. Under this viewpoint, a lower approximation and an upper approximation of a subset shows a gap between R^M and R^I.

We have also emphasized on the granularity bringing an almost equally division. This is because what we extracted from a given information table can affect to the remaining unseen tuples. Then, this criterion seems to give a good guideline. In this direction, we recommended to use the maximal conjunctive closed subsets for expressing any concept. This is a standpoint to make us be conscious to the remaining unseen tuples. As long as such a maximal conjunctive closed subset, every tuples in the set is explicitly considered through the corresponding d.e.r. relation.

All these things enable us to find useful knowledge efficiently and understandably. This is because a more rough granularity reduces to the size of representation space and a maximal conjunctive closed subset helps us to understand it due to its disjunctive form. As for the reduction of the complexity, we will show this in another paper in which a polynomial time learnability is shown w.r.t. the size of the information table.

5   Conclusion

We have insisted that the information tables should be specified as one of three categories according to the size of the attribute set and the size of available tuples. In addition, if we stand at the simplest Rough Set category, what should be considered is to divide the unseen tuples as equally as possible. The traditional "reduction" can be interpreted in the same sense. From this viewpoint, we justified that a "stable" subsets expression is best for capturing any concept. Although only finite attributes are considered in this paper, this framework is easily extended to continuous attributes.

References

1. Murai, T., Resconi, T., Nakata, M., Sato, M.: Operations of Zooming In and Out on Possible Worlds for Semantic Fields. *E.Damiani et al.(eds.), Knowledge-Based Intelligent Information Engineering Systems and Allied Technologies* IOS Press (2002) 1083–1087
2. Murai, T., Resconi, G., Nakata, M., Sato, Y.: Granular Reasoning Using Zooming In & Out: Part 1. Propositional Reasoning. *Proceedings of International Conference on Rough Sets, Fuzzy Sets, Data Mining, and Granular Computing* LNAI Springer (2003) 421-424
3. Pawlak, Z.: *Rough Sets: Theoretical Aspects of Reasoning about Data* Kluwer (1991)
4. Muto, Y., Kudo, M.: Discernibility Based Variable Granularity and its Relation to Kansei Representations. to appear in RSFDGrC 2005.

Incomplete Data and Generalization of Indiscernibility Relation, Definability, and Approximations

Jerzy W. Grzymala-Busse

Department of Electrical Engineering and Computer Science,
University of Kansas, Lawrence, KS 66045, USA
Institute of Computer Science,
Polish Academy of Sciences, 01-237 Warsaw, Poland
Jerzy@ku.edu
http://lightning.eecs.ku.edu/index.html

Abstract. In incomplete data missing attribute values may be universally interpreted in several ways. Four approaches to missing attribute values are discussed in this paper: lost values, "do not care" conditions, restricted "do not care" conditions, and attribute-concept values. Rough set ideas, such as attribute-value pair blocks, characteristic sets, characteristic relations and generalization of lower and upper approximations are used in these four approaches. A generalized rough set methodology, achieved in the process, may be used for other applications as well. Additionally, this generalized methodology is compared with other extensions of rough set concepts.

1   Introduction

Initially rough set theory was applied to complete data sets (with all attribute values specified). Recently rough set theory was extended to handle incomplete data sets (with missing attribute values) [1], [2]–[6], [7], [8], [13], and [14].

Development of appropriate methodology to incomplete data sets is crucial since many real-life data sets have missing attribute values. Mining incomplete data requires either a preprocessing (filling in missing attribute values before the main process of rule set induction, decision tree generation, etc.) or mining the data set taking into account that it is incomplete. In this paper we will use the latter approach.

We will distinguish four types of missing attribute values. The first type of missing attribute value will be called *lost*. A missing attribute value is lost when for some case (example, object) the corresponding attribute value was mistakenly erased or forgotten to enter into the data set. The original value existed but for a variety of reasons now it is not accessible.

The next three types of missing attribute values, called *"do not care" conditions*, *restricted "do not care" conditions* and *attribute-concept values* are based on an assumption that these values were initially, when the data set was created,

D. Ślęzak et al. (Eds.): RSFDGrC 2005, LNAI 3641, pp. 244–253, 2005.

irrelevant. For example, in a medical setup, patients were subjected to preliminary tests. Patients whose preliminary test results were negative were diagnosed as not affected by a disease. They were perfectly well diagnosed in spite of the fact that not all tests were conducted on them. Thus some test results are missing because these tests were redundant. In different words, a missing attribute value of this type may be potentially replaced by any value typical for that attribute. This type of a missing attribute value will be called a "do not care" condition. A special case of a "do not care" condition, called restricted "do not care" condition, has another interpretation: a restricted "do not care" condition may be replaced by any value typical for that attribute excluding lost values. Obviously, when the data set does not have any lost values, both "do not care" conditions, ordinary and restricted, are interpreted in the same way. On the other hand, we may have different expectations, for example, if a patient was diagnosed as not affected by a disease, we may want to replace the missing test (attribute) value by any typical value for that attribute but restricted to patients in the same class (concept), i.e., for other patients not affected by the disease. Such missing attribute value will be called attribute-concept value.

Note that all four types of discussed attribute values are universal (or standard), since they can be used for any incomplete data set. Obviously, if we are familiar with the reason why some attribute values are missing, we should apply the appropriate interpretation: lost value or one of the three types of "do not care" conditions.

For incomplete decision tables there are two special cases: in the first case, all missing attribute values are lost, in the second case, all missing attribute values are ordinary "do not care" conditions. Incomplete decision tables in which all attribute values are lost, from the viewpoint of rough set theory, were studied for the first time in [6], where two algorithms for rule induction, modified to handle lost attribute values, were presented. This approach was studied later, e.g., in [13] and [14], where the indiscernibility relation was generalized to describe such incomplete decision tables.

On the other hand, incomplete decision tables in which all missing attribute values are "do not care" conditions, from the view point of rough set theory, were studied for the first time in [2], where a method for rule induction was introduced in which each missing attribute value was replaced by all values from the domain of the attribute. Originally such values were replaced by all values from the entire domain of the attribute, later, by attribute values restricted to the same concept to which a case with a missing attribute value belongs. Such incomplete decision tables, with all missing attribute values being "do not care conditions", were extensively studied in [7], [8], including extending the idea of the indiscernibility relation to describe such incomplete decision tables.

In general, incomplete decision tables are described by characteristic relations, in a similar way as complete decision tables are described by indiscernibility relations [3], [4], and [5].

In rough set theory, one of the basic notions is the idea of lower and upper approximations. For complete decision tables, once the indiscernibility relation is fixed and the concept (a set of cases) is given, the lower and upper approximations are unique.

For incomplete decision tables, for a given characteristic relation and concept, there are three important and different possibilities to define lower and upper approximations, called singleton, subset, and concept approximations [3]. Singleton lower and upper approximations were studied in [7], [8], [12], [13], [14]. Note that similar three definitions of lower and upper approximations, though not for incomplete decision tables, were studied in [15]. In this paper we further discuss applications to data mining of all three kinds of approximations: singleton, subset and concept. As it was observed in [3], singleton lower and upper approximations are not applicable in data mining.

Note that some other rough-set approaches to missing attribute values were presented in [1] and [2] as well.

2   Blocks of Attribute-Value Pairs

We assume that the input data sets are presented in the form of a *decision table*. An example of a decision table is shown in Table 1. Rows of the decision

Table 1. An incomplete decision table

| Case | Attributes | | | Decision |
	Temperature	Headache	Nausea	Flu
1	high	–	no	yes
2	very_high	yes	yes	yes
3	?	no	no	no
4	high	yes	yes	yes
5	high	?	yes	no
6	+	yes	no	no
7	normal	no	yes	no
8	–	yes	*	yes

table represent *cases*, while columns are labeled by *variables*. The set of all cases will be denoted by U. In Table 1, $U = \{1, 2, ..., 8\}$. Independent variables are called *attributes* and a dependent variable is called a *decision* and is denoted by d. The set of all attributes will be denoted by A. In Table 1, $A = \{$ *Temperature, Headache, Nausea* $\}$. Any decision table defines a function ρ that maps the direct product of U and A into the set of all values. For example, in Table 1, $\rho(1, Temperature) = high$. Function ρ describing Table 1 is completely specified (total). A decision table with completely specified function ρ will be called *completely specified*, or, for the sake of simplicity, *complete*. In practice, input data for data mining are frequently affected by missing attribute values. In other words, the corresponding function ρ is incompletely specified (partial). A decision table with an incompletely specified function ρ will be called *incomplete*.

For the rest of the paper we will assume that all decision values are specified, i.e., they are not missing. Also, we will assume that lost values will be denoted by "?", "do not care" conditions by "*", restricted "do not care" conditions by "+", and attribute-concept values by "−". Additionally, we will assume that for each case at least one attribute value is specified.

Incomplete decision tables are described by characteristic relations instead of indiscernibility relations. Also, elementary blocks are replaced by characteristic sets [3]–[5].

An important tool to analyze complete decision tables is a block of the attribute-value pair. Let a be an attribute, i.e., $a \in A$ and let v be a value of a for some case. For complete decision tables if $t = (a, v)$ is an attribute-value pair then a *block* of t, denoted $[t]$, is a set of all cases from U that for attribute a have value v. For incomplete decision tables the definition of a block of an attribute-value pair must be modified in the following way:

- If for an attribute a there exists a case x such that $\rho(x, a) =?$, i.e., the corresponding value is lost, then the case x should not be included in any blocks$[(a, v)]$ for all values v of attribute a,
- If for an attribute a there exists a case x such that the corresponding value is a "do not care" condition or a restricted "do not care" condition, i.e., $\rho(x, a) = *$ or $\rho(x, a) = +$, then the case x should be included in blocks $[(a, v)]$ for all specified values v of attribute a,
- If for an attribute a there exists a case x such that the corresponding value is an attribute-concept value, i.e., $\rho(x, a) = -$, then the corresponding case x should be included in blocks $[(a, v)]$ for all specified values $v \in V(x, a)$ of attribute a, where

$$V(x, a) = \{\rho(y, a) \mid \rho(y, a) \text{ is specified}, y \in U, \rho(y, d) = \rho(x, d)\}.$$

These modifications of the definition of the block of attribute-value pair are consistent with the interpretation of missing attribute values: lost, "do not care" conditions, restricted "do not care" conditions, and attribute-concept values. Also, note that the attribute-concept value is the most universal, since if $V(x, a) = \emptyset$, the definition of the attribute-concept value is reduced to the lost value, and if $V(x, a)$ is the set of all values of an attribute a, the attribute-concept value becomes a "do not care" condition.

In Table 1, for case 1, $\rho(1, Headache) = -$, and $V(1, Headache) = \{yes\}$, so we add the case 1 to $[(Headache, yes)]$. For case 3, $\rho(3, Temperature) =?$, hence case 3 is not included in either of the following sets: $[(Temperature, high)]$, $[(Temperature, very\_high)]$, and $[(Temperature, normal)]$.

Similarly, $\rho(5, Headache) = ?$, so the case 5 is not included in $[(Headache, yes)]$ and $[(Headache, no)]$. For case 6, $\rho(6, Headache) = +$, so the case 6 is included in $[(Temperature, normal)]$, $[(Temperature, high)]$, and $[(Temperature, very\_high)]$. Also, $\rho(8, Temperature) = -$, and $V(8, Temperature) =$

{*high*, *very_high*}, so the case 8 is a member of both [(*Temperature*, *high*)] and [(*Temperature*, *very_high*)]. Finally, $\rho(8, Nausea) = *$, so the case 8 is included in both [(*Nausea*, *no*)] and [(*Nausea*, *yes*)]. Thus,

[(Temperature, high)] = {1, 4, 5, 6, 8},
[(Temperature, very_high)] = {2, 6, 8},
[(Temperature, normal)] = {6, 7},
[(Headache, yes)] = {1, 2, 4, 6, 8},
[(Headache, no)] = {3, 7},
[(Nausea, no)] = {1, 3, 6, 8},
[(Nausea, yes)] = {2, 4, 5, 7, 8}.

For a case $x \in U$ the *characteristic set* $K_B(x)$ is defined as the intersection of the sets $K(x, a)$, for all $a \in B$, where the set $K(x, a)$ is defined in the following way:

- If $\rho(x, a)$ is specified, then $K(x, a)$ is the block [$(a, \rho(x, a))$] of attribute a and its value $\rho(x, a)$,
- If $\rho(x, a) = ?$ or $\rho(x, a) = *$ then the set $K(x, a) = U$,
- If $\rho(x, a) = +$, then $K(x, a)$ is equal to the union of all blocks of (a, v), for all specified values v of attribute a,
- If $\rho(x, a) = -$, then the corresponding set $K(x, a)$ is equal to the union of all blocks of attribute-value pairs (a, v), where $v \in V(x, a)$ if $V(x, a)$ is nonempty. If $V(x, a)$ is empty, $K(x, a) = \{x\}$.

The way of computing characteristic sets needs a comment. For both lost values and "do not care" conditions the corresponding set $K(x, a)$ is equal to U because the corresponding attribute a does not restrict the set $K_B(x)$: if $\rho(x, a) = *$, the value of the attribute a is irrelevant; if $\rho(x, a) = ?$, only the existing values need to be checked. However, the case when $\rho(x, a) = -$ is different, since the attribute a restricts the set $K_B(x)$. Furthermore, the description of $K_B(x)$ should be consistent with other (but similar) possible approaches to missing attribute values, e.g., an approach in which each missing attribute value is replaced by the most common attribute value restricted to a concept. Here the set $V(x, a)$ contains a single element and the characteristic relation is an equivalence relation. Our definition is consistent with this special case in the sense that if we compute a characteristic relation for such a decision table using our definition or if we compute the indiscernibility relation as for complete decision tables using definitions from Section 2, the result will be the same. For Table 2 and $B = A$,

$K_A(1) = \{1, 4, 5, 6, 8\} \cap \{1, 2, 4, 6, 8\} \cap \{1, 3, 6, 8\} = \{1, 6, 8\}$,
$K_A(2) = \{2, 6, 8\} \cap \{1, 2, 4, 6, 8\} \cap \{2, 4, 5, 7, 8\} = \{2, 8\}$,
$K_A(3) = U \cap \{3, 7\} \cap \{1, 3, 6, 8\} = \{3\}$,
$K_A(4) = \{1, 4, 5, 6, 8\} \cap \{1, 2, 4, 6, 8\} \cap \{2, 4, 5, 7, 8\} = \{4, 8\}$,
$K_A(5) = \{1, 4, 5, 6, 8\} \cap U \cap \{2, 4, 5, 7, 8\} = \{4, 5, 8\}$,
$K_A(6) = (\{1, 4, 5, 6, 8\} \cup \{2, 6, 8\} \cup \{6, 7\}) \cap \{1, 2, 4, 6, 8\} \cap \{1, 3, 6, 8\} = \{1, 6, 8\}$,
$K_A(7) = \{6, 7\} \cap \{3, 7\} \cap \{2, 4, 5, 7, 8\} = \{7\}$, and
$K_A(8) = (\{1, 4, 5, 6, 8\} \cup \{2, 6, 8\}) \cap \{1, 2, 4, 6, 8\} \cap U = \{1, 2, 4, 6, 8\}$.

Characteristic set $K_B(x)$ may be interpreted as the set of cases that are indistinguishable from x using all attributes from B and using a given interpretation of missing attribute values. Thus, $K_A(x)$ is the set of all cases that cannot be distinguished from x using all attributes.

The characteristic relation $R(B)$ is a relation on U defined for $x, y \in U$ as follows

$$(x, y) \in R(B) \ \text{if and only if} \ y \in K_B(x).$$

Thus, the relation $R(B)$ may be defined by $(x, y) \in R(B)$ if and only if y is indistinguishable from x by all attributes from B. In [12] "y is indistinguishable from x" was phrased as "x is similar to y". Furthermore, in [12] the set $K_B(x)$ was denoted by $R^{-1}(x)$. The characteristic relation $R(B)$ is reflexive but—in general—does not need to be symmetric or transitive. Also, the characteristic relation $R(B)$ is known if we know characteristic sets $K(x)$ for all $x \in U$. In our example, $R(A) = \{(1, 1), (1, 6), (1, 8), (2, 2), (2, 8), (3, 3), (4, 4), (4, 8), (5, 4), (5, 5), (5, 8), (6, 1), (6, 6), (6, 8), (7, 7), (8, 1), (8, 2), (8, 4), (8, 6), (8, 8)\}$. The most convenient way is to define the characteristic relation through the characteristic sets.

For decision tables, in which all missing attribute values are lost, a special characteristic relation was defined in [13], see also, e.g., [14]. For decision tables where all missing attribute values are "do not care" conditions a special characteristic relation was defined in [7], see also, e.g., [8]. For a completely specified decision table, the characteristic relation $R(B)$ is reduced to the indiscernibility relation $IND(B)$.

3   Definability

For completely specified decision tables, any union of elementary sets of B is called a B-definable set [11]. Definability for completely specified decision tables should be modified to fit into incomplete decision tables. For incomplete decision tables, a union of some intersections of attribute-value pair blocks will be called B-*locally definable* sets. A union of characteristic sets $K_B(x)$, where $x \in X \subseteq U$ will be called a B-*globally definable* set. Any set X that is B-globally definable is B-locally definable, the converse is not true. For example, the set $\{6, 8\}$ is A-locally definable since $\{6, 8\} = [(Temperature, very\_high)] \cap [(Nausea, no)]$. However, the set $\{6, 8\}$ is not A-globally definable. Obviously, if a set is not B-locally definable then it cannot be expressed by rule sets using attributes from B. This is why it is so important to distinguish between B-locally definable sets and those that are not B-locally definable.

Note that definability, introduced in [12], differs from our definition. For example, the set $\{1, 2, 4, 6, 8\}$, A-globally definable according to our definition, is not definable in [12]. Additionally, sets that are definable in [12], are not even A-locally definable according to our definition.

4   Lower and Upper Approximations

For completely specified decision tables lower and upper approximations are defined on the basis of the indiscernibility relation. Let X be any subset of the set U of all cases. The set X is called a *concept* and is usually defined as the set of all cases defined by a specific value of the decision. In general, X is not a B-definable set. However, set X may be approximated by two B-definable sets, the first one is called a B-*lower approximation* of X, denoted by $\underline{B}X$ and defined as follows

$$\{x \in U \mid [x]_B \subseteq X\}.$$

The second set is called a B-*upper approximation* of X, denoted by $\overline{B}X$ and defined as follows

$$\{x \in U \mid [x]_B \cap X \neq \emptyset\}.$$

The above shown way of computing lower and upper approximations, by constructing these approximations from singletons x, will be called the *first method*. The B-lower approximation of X is the greatest B-definable set, contained in X. The B-upper approximation of X is the smallest B-definable set containing X.

As it was observed in [11], for complete decision tables we may use a *second method* to define the B-lower approximation of X, by the following formula

$$\cup\{[x]_B \mid x \in U, [x]_B \subseteq X\},$$

and the B-upper approximation of x may be defined, using the second method, by

$$\cup\{[x]_B \mid x \in U, [x]_B \cap X \neq \emptyset\}.$$

Obviously, for complete decision tables both methods result in the same respective sets, i.e., corresponding lower approximations are identical, and so are upper approximations.

For incomplete decision tables lower and upper approximations may be defined in a few different ways. In this paper we suggest three different definitions of lower and upper approximations for incomplete decision tables. Again, let X be a concept, let B be a subset of the set A of all attributes, and let $R(B)$ be the characteristic relation of the incomplete decision table with characteristic sets $K(x)$, where $x \in U$. Our first definition uses a similar idea as in the previous articles on incomplete decision tables [7], [8], [13], [14], i.e., lower and upper approximations are sets of singletons from the universe U satisfying some properties. Thus, lower and upper approximations are defined by analogy with the above first method, by constructing both sets from singletons. We will call these approximations *singleton*. A singleton B-lower approximation of X is defined as follows:

$$\underline{B}X = \{x \in U \mid K_B(x) \subseteq X\}.$$

A singleton B-upper approximation of X is

$$\overline{B}X = \{x \in U \mid K_B(x) \cap X \neq \emptyset\}.$$

In our example of the decision table presented in Table 2 let us say that $B = A$. Then the singleton A-lower and A-upper approximations of the two concepts: $\{1, 2, 4, 8\}$ and $\{3, 5, 6, 7\}$ are:

$$\underline{A}\{1, 2, 4, 8\} = \{2, 4\},$$

$$\underline{A}\{3, 5, 6, 7\} = \{3, 7\},$$

$$\overline{A}\{1, 2, 4, 8\} = \{1, 2, 4, 5, 6, 8\},$$

$$\overline{A}\{3, 5, 6, 7\} = \{1, 3, 5, 6, 7, 8\}.$$

We may easily observe that the set $\{2, 4\}$ is not A-locally definable since in all blocks of attribute-value pairs cases 2 and 8 are inseparable. Additionally, the set $\{1, 3, 5, 6, 7, 8\}$, by the same reason, is not A-locally definable. Thus, as it was observed in, e.g., [3]–[5], singleton approximations should not be used, in general, for data mining and, in particular, for rule induction.

The second method of defining lower and upper approximations for complete decision tables uses another idea: lower and upper approximations are unions of elementary sets, subsets of U. Therefore we may define lower and upper approximations for incomplete decision tables by analogy with the second method, using characteristic sets instead of elementary sets. There are two ways to do this. Using the first way, a *subset* B-lower approximation of X is defined as follows:

$$\underline{B}X = \cup\{K_B(x) \mid x \in U, K_B(x) \subseteq X\}.$$

A *subset* B-upper approximation of X is

$$\overline{B}X = \cup\{K_B(x) \mid x \in U, K_B(x) \cap X \neq \emptyset\}.$$

Since any characteristic relation $R(B)$ is reflexive, for any concept X, singleton B-lower and B-upper approximations of X are subsets of the subset B-lower and B-upper approximations of X, respectively. For the same decision table, presented in Table 2, the subset A-lower and A-upper approximations are

$$\underline{A}\{1, 2, 4, 8\} = \{2, 4, 8\},$$

$$\underline{A}\{3, 5, 6, 7\} = \{3, 7\},$$

$$\overline{A}\{1, 2, 4, 8\} = \{1, 2, 4, 5, 6, 8\},$$

$$\overline{A}\{3, 5, 6, 7\} = \{1, 2, 3, 4, 5, 6, 7, 8\} = U.$$

The second possibility is to modify the subset definition of lower and upper approximation by replacing the universe U from the subset definition by a concept X. A *concept* B-lower approximation of the concept X is defined as follows:

$$\underline{B}X = \cup\{K_B(x) \mid x \in X, K_B(x) \subseteq X\}.$$

Obviously, the subset B-lower approximation of X is the same set as the concept B-lower approximation of X. A concept B-upper approximation of the concept X is defined as follows:

$$\overline{B}X = \cup\{K_B(x) \mid x \in X, K_B(x) \cap X \neq \emptyset\} =$$
$$= \cup\{K_B(x) \mid x \in X\}.$$

The concept upper approximations were defined in [9] and [12] as well. The concept B-upper approximation of X is a subset of the subset B-upper approximation of X. Besides, the concept B-upper approximations are truly the smallest B-definable sets containing X. For the decision table presented in Table 2, the concept A-upper approximations are

$$\overline{A}\{1, 2, 4, 8\} = \{1, 2, 4, 6, 8\},$$
$$\overline{A}\{3, 5, 6, 7\} = \{1, 3, 4, 5, 6, 7, 8\}.$$

Definitions of lower approximations, numbered as (9) and (10) in [12], are different from any of the definitions of lower approximations from this paper. Sets defined by (9) and (10) in [12] are, in general, not even A-locally definable. Similarly, a set defined by yet another definition of upper approximation, numbered as (11) in [12] (and different from any of the three upper approximations defined in this paper this paper) does not need to be A-locally definable as well.

Note that for complete decision tables, all three definitions of lower approximations, singleton, subset and concept, coalesce to the same definition. Also, for complete decision tables, all three definitions of upper approximations coalesce to the same definition. This is not true for incomplete decision tables, as our example shows.

5   Conclusions

Four standard interpretations of missing attribute values are discussed in this paper. These interpretations may be applied to any kind of an incomplete data set. This paper shows how to compute blocks of attribute-value pairs for data sets with missing attribute values, how to compute characteristic sets (generalization of elementary sets), how to compute characteristic relation (i.e., generalization of an indiscernibility relation), and three types of approximations (reduced for ordinary approximations for complete data sets). Additionally, the idea of global and local definability for incomplete data sets is introduced. In general, sets computed as results of singleton approximations are not even A-locally definable. Thus they should not be used for data mining.

References

1. Greco, S., Matarazzo, B., and Slowinski, R.: Dealing with missing data in rough set analysis of multi-attribute and multi-criteria decision problems. In *Decision Making: Recent developments and Worldwide Applications*, ed. by S. H. Zanakis, G. Doukidis, and Z. Zopounidis, Kluwer Academic Publishers, Dordrecht, Boston, London, 2000, 295–316.

2. Grzymala-Busse, J.W.: On the unknown attribute values in learning from examples. Proc. of the ISMIS-91, 6th International Symposium on Methodologies for Intelligent Systems, Charlotte, North Carolina, October 16–19, 1991. Lecture Notes in Artificial Intelligence, vol. 542, Springer-Verlag, Berlin, Heidelberg, New York (1991) 368–377.

3. Grzymala-Busse, J.W.: Rough set strategies to data with missing attribute values. Workshop Notes, Foundations and New Directions of Data Mining, the 3-rd International Conference on Data Mining, Melbourne, FL, USA, November 19–22, 2003, 56–63.

4. Grzymala-Busse, J.W.: Data with missing attribute values: Generalization of idiscernibility relation and rule induction. *Transactions on Rough Sets*, Lecture Notes in Computer Science Journal Subline, Springer-Verlag, vol. **1** (2004) 78–95.

5. Grzymala-Busse, J.W.: Characteristic relations for incomplete data: A generalization of the indiscernibility relation. Proceedings of the RSCTC'2004, the Fourth International Conference on Rough Sets and Current Trends in Computing, Uppsala, Sweden, June 1–5, 2004. Lecture Notes in Artificial Intelligence 3066, Springer-Verlag 2004, 244 253.

6. Grzymala-Busse, J.W. and Wang A.Y.: Modified algorithms LEM1 and LEM2 for rule induction from data with missing attribute values. Proc. of the Fifth International Workshop on Rough Sets and Soft Computing (RSSC'97) at the Third Joint Conference on Information Sciences (JCIS'97), Research Triangle Park, NC, March 2–5, 1997, 69–72.

7. Kryszkiewicz, M.: Rough set approach to incomplete information systems. Proceedings of the Second Annual Joint Conference on Information Sciences, Wrightsville Beach, NC, September 28–October 1, 1995, 194–197.

8. Kryszkiewicz, M.: Rules in incomplete information systems. *Information Sciences* **113** (1999) 271–292.

9. Lin, T.Y.: Topological and fuzzy rough sets. In Intelligent Decision Support. Handbook of Applications and Advances of the Rough Sets Theory, ed. by R. Slowinski, Kluwer Academic Publishers, Dordrecht, Boston, London (1992) 287–304.

10. Pawlak, Z.: Rough Sets. *International Journal of Computer and Information Sciences* **11** (1982) 341–356.

11. Pawlak, Z.: Rough Sets. Theoretical Aspects of Reasoning about Data. Kluwer Academic Publishers, Dordrecht, Boston, London (1991).

12. Slowinski, R. and Vanderpooten, D.: A generalized definition of rough approximations based on similarity. *IEEE Transactions on Knowledge and Data Engineering* **12** (2000) 331–336.

13. Stefanowski, J. and Tsoukias, A.: On the extension of rough sets under incomplete information. Proceedings of the 7th International Workshop on New Directions in Rough Sets, Data Mining, and Granular-Soft Computing, RSFDGrC'1999, Ube, Yamaguchi, Japan, November 8–10, 1999, 73–81.

14. Stefanowski, J. and Tsoukias, A.: Incomplete information tables and rough classification. *Computational Intelligence* **17** (2001) 545–566.

15. Yao, Y.Y.: On the generalizing rough set theory. Proc. of the 9th Int. Conference on Rough Sets, Fuzzy Sets, Data Mining and Granular Computing (RSFDGrC'2003), Chongqing, China, October 19–22, 2003, 44–51.

Discernibility Functions and Minimal Rules in Non-deterministic Information Systems

Hiroshi Sakai[1] and Michinori Nakata[2]

[1] Department of Mathematics and Computer Aided Science,
Faculty of Engineering, Kyushu Institute of Technology,
Tobata, Kitakyushu 804, Japan
sakai@mns.kyutech.ac.jp
[2] Faculty of Management and Information Science,
Josai International University,
Gumyo, Togane, Chiba 283, Japan
nakatam@ieee.org

Abstract. Minimal rule generation in *Non-deterministic Information Systems* (*NISs*), which follows rough sets based rule generation in *Deterministic Information Systems* (*DISs*), is presented. According to *certain rules* and *possible rules* in *NISs*, *minimal certain rules* and *minimal possible rules* are defined. *Discernibility functions* are also introduced into *NISs* for generating minimal certain rules. Like minimal rule generation in *DISs*, the condition part of a minimal certain rule is given as a solution of an introduced discernibility function. As for generating minimal possible rules, there may be lots of discernibility functions to be solved. So, an algorithm based on an order of attributes is proposed. A tool, which generates minimal certain and minimal possible rules, has also been implemented.

Keywords: Rough sets, Non-deterministic information, Minimal rules, Discernibility functions, Tool for rule generation.

1 Introduction

Rough set theory is seen as a mathematical foundation of soft computing. This theory usually handles tables with deterministic information. Many applications of this theory to rule generation, machine learning and knowledge discovery have been presented [1,2,3,4].

We follow rule generation in *DISs* [1,2,3,4] and propose rule generation in *NISs*. *NISs* were proposed by Pawlak, Orłowska and Lipski in order to handle information incompleteness in *DISs*, like null values, unknown values, missing values. From the beginning of the research on incomplete information, *NISs* have been recognized to be the most important framework for handling information incompleteness [5,6]. Therefore, rule generation in *NISs* will also be an important framework for rule generation from incomplete information.

However, very few work deals with rule generation from incomplete information on computers. In [6], Lipski showed a question-answering system besides

D. Ślęzak et al. (Eds.): RSFDGrC 2005, LNAI 3641, pp. 254–264, 2005.

an axiomatization of logic. Grzymala-Busse developed a system named $LERS$, which depends upon $LEM1$ and $LEM2$ algorithms [7,8]. Kryszkiewicz proposed a framework of rules in incomplete information systems [9]. These are the most important work for handling incomplete information, especially missing values, on computers.

In this paper, we briefly survey rule generation in $DISs$ and propose rule generation in $NISs$.

2 Basic Definitions

A *Deterministic Information System* (DIS) is a quadruplet $(OB, AT, \{VAL_A|$ $A \in AT\}, f)$, where OB is a finite set whose elements are called *objects*, AT is a finite set whose elements are called *attributes*, VAL_A is a finite set whose elements are called *attribute values* and f is such a mapping that $f : OB \times AT \rightarrow \cup_{A \in AT} VAL_A$ which is called a *classification function*. If $f(x, A)=f(y, A)$ for every $A \in ATR \subset AT$, we see there is a relation between x and y for ATR. This relation is an equivalence relation over OB. Let $[x]_{ATR}$ denote an equivalence class $\{y \in OB|f(y, A)=f(x, A)$ for every $A \in ATR\}$.

Let us consider two sets $CON \subset AT$ which we call *condition attributes* and $DEC \subset AT$ which we call *decision attributes*. An object $x \in OB$ is *consistent* (with any distinct object $y \in OB$), if $f(x, A)=f(y, A)$ for every $A \in CON$ implies $f(x, A)=f(y, A)$ for every $A \in DEC$. For any $x \in OB$, let $imp(x, CON, DEC)$ denote a formula called *implication*: $\wedge_{A \in CON}[A, f(x, A)] \Rightarrow \wedge_{A \in DEC}[A, f(x, A)]$, where a formula $[A, f(x, A)]$ implies that $f(x, A)$ is the value of the attribute A. This is called a *descriptor*.

A *Non-deterministic Information System* (NIS) is also a quadruplet $(OB, AT, \{VAL_A|A \in AT\}, g)$, where $g : OB \times AT \rightarrow P(\cup_{A \in AT} VAL_A)$ (a power set of $\cup_{A \in AT} VAL_A$). Every set $g(x, A)$ is interpreted as that there is an actual value in this set but this value is not known.

Definition 1. Let us consider a $NIS=(OB, AT, \{VAL_A|A \in AT\}, g)$, a set $ATR \subset AT$ and a mapping $h : OB \times ATR \rightarrow \cup_{A \in ATR} VAL_A$ such that $h(x, A) \in g(x, A)$. We call a $DIS=(OB, ATR, \{VAL_A|A \in ATR\}, h)$ a *derived DIS (for ATR) from NIS*.

Definition 2. For a set $ATR=\{A_1, \cdots, A_n\} \subset AT$ and any $x \in OB$, let $PT(x, ATR)$ denote the Cartesian product $g(x, A_1) \times \cdots \times g(x, A_n)$. We name every element a *possible tuple (for ATR) of* x. For a possible tuple $\zeta=(\zeta_1, \cdots, \zeta_n) \in PT(x, ATR)$, let $[ATR, \zeta]$ denote a formula $\wedge_{1 \le i \le n}[A_i, \zeta_i]$.

Definition 3. Let $PI(x, CON, DEC)$ $(x \in OB)$ denote a set $\{[CON, \zeta] \Rightarrow [DEC, \eta]|\zeta \in PT(x, CON), \eta \in PT(x, DEC)\}$. We name an element of $PI(x, CON, DEC)$ a *possible implication (from CON to DEC) of* x.

Example 1. Let us consider NIS_1 in Table 1. There are 7346640384 derived $DISs$ for all attributes. For $CON=\{A, B\}$ and $DEC=\{C\}$, there are $216(=2^3 \times 3^3)$ derived $DISs$. Here, $PT(1, \{A, B\})=\{(3, 1), (3, 3), (3, 4)\}, PT(1, \{C\})=\{(3)\}$

Table 1. A Table of NIS_1

OB	A	B	C	D	E	F	G	H
1	{3}	{1,3,4}	{3}	{2}	{5}	{5}	{2,4}	{3}
2	{2}	{3,4}	{1,3,4}	{4}	{1,2}	{2,4,5}	{2}	{2}
3	{4,5}	{5}	{1,5}	{5}	{2}	{5}	{1,2,5}	{1}
4	{1}	{3}	{4}	{3}	{1,2,3}	{1}	{2,5}	{1,2}
5	{4}	{1}	{2,3,5}	{5}	{2,3,4}	{1,5}	{4}	{1}
6	{4}	{1}	{5}	{1}	{4}	{2,4,5}	{2}	{1,2,3}
7	{2}	{4}	{3}	{4}	{3}	{2,4,5}	{4}	{1,2,3}
8	{4}	{5}	{4}	{2,3,5}	{5}	{3}	{1,2,3}	{1,2,3}
9	{2}	{3}	{5}	{3}	{1,3,5}	{4}	{2}	{3}
10	{4}	{2}	{1}	{5}	{2}	{4,5}	{3}	{1}

and $PI(1, \{A, B\}, \{C\})$ consists of three possible implications $[A, 3] \wedge [B, 1] \Rightarrow [C, 3]$, $[A, 3] \wedge [B, 3] \Rightarrow [C, 3]$ and $[A, 3] \wedge [B, 4] \Rightarrow [C, 3]$. Since there exists no possible tuple $(3, \_) \in PT(x, \{A, B\})$ $(x \neq 1)$, each possible implication is consistent.

For $NISs$, we have proposed a framework of *Rough Non-deterministic Information Analysis* [10]. In this analysis, we apply the standard methods in rough set theory to every derived DIS, and we deal with the certainty and the possibility, or the worst case and the best case. An important problem is how to compute two modalities depending upon all derived $DISs$ from a NIS. A simple method, such that every definition is sequentially computed in all derived $DISs$ from a NIS, is not suitable. Because the number of derived $DISs$ from a NIS increases in exponential order. We have proposed *possible equivalence relations* and inf and sup information for solving this problem [10].

3 Theoretical Foundations of Rule Generation in NISs

Definition 4. For any $\tau \in PI(x, CON, DEC)$, let $DD(\tau, x, CON, DEC)$ denote a set $\{\varphi | \varphi$ is such a derived DIS for $CON \cup DEC$ that an implication $imp(x, CON, DEC)$ in φ is equal to $\tau\}$.

Definition 5. If $PI(x, CON, DEC)$ is a singleton set $\{\tau\}$, we say τ (from x) is *definite*. Otherwise we say τ (from x) is *indefinite*. If a set $\{\varphi \in DD(\tau, x, CON, DEC) | x$ is consistent in $\varphi\}$ is equal to $DD(\tau, x, CON, DEC)$, we say τ is *globally consistent* (GC). If this set is equal to $\emptyset$, we say τ is *globally inconsistent* (GI). Otherwise we say τ is *marginal* (MA). By combining two cases, i.e., '$D(efinite)$ or $I(ndefinite)$' and 'GC, MA or GI', we define six classes, $DGC, DMA, DGI, IGC, IMA, IGI$, for possible implications.

Table 2. Six classes of possible implications in NISs

	GC	MA	GI
Definite	DGC	DMA	DGI
Indefinite	IGC	IMA	IGI

A possible implication τ_1 belonging to DGC class is consistent in all derived $DISs$, and this τ_1 is not influenced by the information incompleteness, therefore we especially say τ_1 is a *certain rule*. A possible implication τ_2 (from object x) belonging to IGC class is consistent in every $\varphi \in DD(\tau_2, x, CON, DEC)$, too. However, one of $PI(x, CON, DEC)$ is the real implication with unknown truth attributes values, therefore we say τ_2 is a *possible rule*. A possible implication τ_3 belonging to MA class is consistent in some derived $DISs$. Because there may be a derived DIS with unknown truth attributes values, we also say τ_3 is a *possible rule*.

The definition of classes GC and MA is semantically the same as the definition in [9]. For handling the information incompleteness in $NISs$, we introduced possible implications. In [9], Kryszkiewicz proposed *generalized decision* $\partial_{AT}(x)$ for handling null values in $DISs$. In definite class, our definition and Kryszkiewicz's definition specify the same implications. However, there exists a difference [10]. Now, we give necessary and sufficient conditions for characterizing GC, MA and GI classes.

Definition 6. Let us consider a NIS and a set $ATR \subset AT$. For any $\zeta \in PT(x, ATR)$, we fix the tuple of x to ζ, and define (1) and (2) below.
(1) $inf(x, \zeta, ATR) = \{y \in OB | PT(y, ATR) = \{\zeta\}\}$,
(2) $sup(x, \zeta, ATR) = \{y \in OB | \zeta \in PT(y, ATR)\}$.

In Definition 6, $inf(x, \zeta, ATR)$ implies a set of objects whose tuples are ζ and definite. A set $sup(x, \zeta, ATR)$ implies a set of objects whose tuples may be ζ. In $DISs$, $[x]_{ATR} = inf(x, \zeta, ATR) = sup(x, \zeta, ATR)$ holds, and $\{x\} \subset inf(x, \zeta, ATR) \subset sup(x, \zeta, ATR)$ holds in $NISs$.

Theorem 1 [10]. For a NIS, let us consider a possible implication $\tau:[CON, \zeta] \Rightarrow [DEC, \eta] \in PI(x, CON, DEC)$. Then, the following holds.
(1) τ belongs to GC class if and only if $sup(x, \zeta, CON) \subset inf(x, \eta, DEC)$.
(2) τ belongs to MA class if and only if $inf(x, \zeta, CON) \subset sup(x, \eta, DEC)$.
(3) τ belongs to GI class if and only if $inf(x, \zeta, CON) \not\subset sup(x, \eta, DEC)$.

Corollary 2. Let us consider a possible implication whose decision part is $[DEC, \eta]$. Then, the following holds.
(1) For an object x, let $(AT\text{-}DEC)^*$ be a set of attributes $\{A \in AT\text{-}DEC \| PT(x, A)| = 1\}$. In this case, $PT(x, (AT\text{-}DEC)^*)$ consists of a possible tuple. Let ζ denote this tuple. It is possible to generate a certain rule from object x if and only if $sup(x, \zeta, (AT\text{-}DEC)^*) \subset inf(x, \eta, DEC)$ holds.
(2) It is possible to generate a possible rule from object x if and only if $inf(x, \zeta', (AT\text{-}DEC)) \subset sup(x, \eta, DEC)$ holds for a possible tuple $\zeta' \in PT(x, AT\text{-}DEC)$.

Proposition 3 [10]. For any NIS, let $ATR \subset AT$ be $\{A_1, \cdots, A_n\}$, and let a possible tuple $\zeta \in PT(x, ATR)$ be $(\zeta_1, \cdots, \zeta_n)$. Then, the following holds.
(1) $inf(x, \zeta, ATR) = \cap_i inf(x, (\zeta_i), \{A_i\})$.
(2) $sup(x, \zeta, ATR) = \cap_i sup(x, (\zeta_i), \{A_i\})$.

By means of Theorem 1 and Proposition 3, it is possible to decide a class of each possible implication. Namely, we first prepare $inf(x, (\zeta_{i,j}), \{A_i\})$ and $sup(x, (\zeta_{i,j}), \{A_i\})$ for any $x \in OB$, any $A_i \in AT$ and any $(\zeta_{i,j}) \in PT(x, \{A_i\})$.

Then, we produce $inf(x, \zeta, CON)$, $sup(x, \zeta, CON)$, $inf(x, \eta, DEC)$ and $sup(x, \eta, DEC)$ according to Proposition 3. Finally, we apply Theorem 1 to them. By means of Corollary 2, it is possible to decide whether certain or possible rules can be generated from an object x.

4   Certain Rules Based on an Order of Attributes

In [11], we introduced a total order, which is defined by the significance of attributes, over $(AT\text{-}DEC)$, and realized a tool for rule generation.

Algorithm 1 [11]. (Order-method)
(Step 1) Fix the decision part $[DEC, \eta]$ of the rule.
(Step 2) Translate data file into inf and sup information according to $[DEC, \eta]$.
(Step 3) Apply Corollary 2, and obtain a set $OB_{DGC}(DEC, \eta) = \{x \in OB|$ a certain rule, whose decision part is $[DEC, \eta]$, can be generated from $x\}$.
(Step 4) According to the order of attributes, generate $sup(x, \zeta, CON)$ for $(x \in OB_{DGC}(DEC, \eta))$, and apply Theorem 1.

Due to the order of attributes, it is easy to define attributes CON. Namely, CON is sequentially $\{A_1\}$, $\{A_1, A_2\}$, $\cdots$, $\{A_1, \cdots, A_n\}$ for the order A_1, A_2, $\cdots$, A_n of attributes. The following is the real execution of Step 4 in Table 1. Here, an attribute is identified with the ordinal number of the attribute.

```
?-step4.
Rs File:'data.rs'. /* Translated data file */
DECLIST:<inf=[3,5,10],sup=[3,4,5,6,7,8,10]>
■Certain Rules from object 3■
[2,5]&[5,2]=>[8,1][17496/17496(=324/324,54/54),Definite,GC]
■Certain Rules from object 5■
[1,4]&[2,1]&[4,5]=>[8,1][1944/1944(=36/36,54/54),Definite,GC]
■Certain Rules from object 10■
[1,4]&[2,2]=>[8,1][648/648(=12/12,54/54),Definite,GC]
EXEC_TIME=0.046(sec)
yes
```

However in this implementation, the minimality of a rule, which is defined in the next section, is not assured. In reality, a possible implication $[2,2]\Rightarrow[8,1]$ from object 10 is also a certain rule. The details of $order$-method and real execution time for some $NISs$ are in [11].

5   A Problem on Minimal Rule Generation in NISs

Now, let us consider minimal rules in $NISs$. According to the usual definition in $DISs$ [1,2,7], we give the definition of minimal rules in $NISs$.

Definition 7. Let us consider a possible implication $\tau : [CON, \zeta] \Rightarrow [DEC, \eta]$, which belongs to GC class. We say τ is a *minimal rule* in GC, if there is no proper non-empty subset $CON^* \subset CON$ such that $[CON^*, \zeta^*] \Rightarrow [DEC, \eta]$ (ζ^*

is a tuple restricted to CON^*) belongs to GC class. A *minimal rule* in MA class is similarly defined.

Problem 1. For a NIS, let DEC be decision attributes and let η be a tuple of decision attributes values for DEC. Then, find all minimal certain rules and minimal possible rules in the form of $[CON, \zeta] \Rightarrow [DEC, \eta]$.

This problem has already been investigated in $DISs$. To find a minimal reduct in a DIS is proved to be NP-hard [12]. Basically, it is necessary to examine each possible implication $[CON', \zeta'] \Rightarrow [DEC, \eta]$ for $(CON' \subset CON)$. In such a situation, a *discernibility function* in $DISs$ has been proposed [12]. Some algorithms including reduction of attributes were investigated by means of discernibility functions. We also introduce discernibility functions in $NISs$, and investigate a method to generate minimal rules in $NISs$.

6   Discernibility Functions and Minimal Certain Rules

Let us suppose $OB_{DGC}(DEC, \eta) \neq \emptyset$ in Algorithm 1. According to Theorem 1, the problem is to find such a minimal conjunction $[CON, \zeta]$ that $sup(x, \zeta, CON) \subset inf(x, \eta, DEC)$. Here, $sup(x, \zeta, CON) = \cap_i sup(x, (\zeta_i), \{A_i\})$ $(A_i \in CON, PT$ $(x, \{A_i\}) = \{\zeta_i\})$ holds. Therefore, a minimal set of definite descriptors, which discriminate every object in $OB\text{-}inf(x, \eta, DEC)$ from $inf(x, \eta, DEC)$, becomes a minimal conjunction $[CON, \zeta]$. According to this property, we give the following definitions.

Definition 8. Let us consider an object $x \in OB$. Any distinct $y \in OB$ is *discriminated from* x by a definite descriptor $[A_i, \zeta_i]$ $(A_i \in AT\text{-}DEC)$ in x, if $y \notin sup(x, (\zeta_i), \{A_i\})$ and $PT(x, A_i) = \{\zeta_i\}$. Let $DISC(x, y)$ denote a disjunction of such definite descriptors in x. We say $[A_i, \zeta_i]$ is a *core descriptor*, if $DISC(x, y) = [A_i, \zeta_i]$.

Definition 9. For every $x \in OB_{DGC}(DEC, \eta)$, we define
$DF_{DGC}(x) = \wedge_{y \in OB - inf(x, \eta, DEC)} DISC(x, y)$,
and we name $DF_{DGC}(x)$ a *discernibility function* of x (in DGC class).

Definition 10. For a discernibility function $DF_{DGC}(x)$, let us identify every descriptor in $DF_{DGC}(x)$ with a propositional variable. If a set SOL of descriptors assigns true to $DF_{DGC}(x)$, we say SOL *satisfies* $DF_{DGC}(x)$. Especially, if $OB\text{-}inf(x, \eta, DEC) = \emptyset$ holds, we define every descriptor satisfies $DF_{DGC}(x)$.

Example 2. In Table 1, let us consider possible implications $[CON, \zeta] \Rightarrow [H, 1]$. Since a definite descriptor $[H, 1]$ appears in objects 3, 5 and 10, it may be possible to generate certain rules from these three objects. The following shows a real execution to obtain $DF_{DGC}(3)$.

```
?-dfdgc(3).
DF=[[1,[2,5],[4,5],[5,2]],[2,[2,5],[4,5]],[4,[2,5],[4,5],[6,5]],
[6,[2,5],[4,5],[5,2]],[7,[2,5],[4,5],[5,2]],[8,[5,2],[6,5]],
[9,[2,5],[4,5],[5,2],[6,5]]]
EXEC_TIME=0.003(sec)
```

Since $DISC(3, y) \neq \emptyset$ holds for every $y \in OB\text{-}inf(3, (1), \{H\})$=$OB$-$\{3, 5, 10\}$= $\{1, 2, 4, 6, 7, 8, 9\}$, it is possible to generate a certain rule from object 3. Here, the first element [1,[2,5],[4,5],[5,2]] implies that each descriptor $[B, 5]$, $[D, 5]$ and $[E, 2]$ discriminates object 1 from object 3. The complexity of calculating $DF_{DGC}(x)$ depends upon $|AT\text{-}DEC| \times |OB\text{-}inf(x, \eta, DEC)|$. A set $\{[B, 5], [E, 2]\}$ satisfies this function, and neither $\{[B, 5]\}$ nor $\{[E, 2]\}$ satisfy this function. Thus, we obtain a minimal certain rule $[B, 5] \wedge [E, 2] \Rightarrow [H, 1]$.

Theorem 4. For a NIS, let us suppose $x \in OB_{DGC}(DEC, \eta) \neq \emptyset$ and $OB\text{-}$ $inf(x, \eta, DEC) \neq \emptyset$. Then, for a minimal solution SOL satisfying $DF_{DGC}(x)$, $\wedge_{DESC \in SOL} DESC \Rightarrow [DEC, \eta]$ is a minimal certain rule.

7   Minimal Certain Rule Generation in DGC Class

At first, we propose a simple method to obtain all minimal solutions of a discernibility function, which we name *enumeration method* (*e-method*). In this method, we enumerate every subset of all descriptors in $DF_{DGC}(x)$, then we sequentially examine the satisfiability of $DF_{DGC}(x)$.

Algorithm 2. (Enumeration method)
Input: An object $x \in OB_{DGC}(DEC, \eta) \neq \emptyset$.
Output: All minimal solutions of DF$_{DGC}$(x), and all minimal certain rules.
```
begin
    generate DF_DGC(x);
    enumerate every subset SUB of all descriptors in DF_DGC(x)
      according to the number of elements;
    repeat the following until there exists no SUB;
      if SUB satisfies DF_DGC(x), SUB is a minimal solution,
      (∧_DESC∈SUB DESC ⇒[DEC,η] is a minimal certain rule)
      and remove every SUB1 (SUB⊂SUB1);
end.
```

E-method can obtain all minimal solutions of $DF_{DGC}(x)$. However, there exist $2^{|ALL\_DESC|}$ kinds of subsets for a set ALL_DESC of all descriptors in $DF_{DGC}(x)$. Therefore, this method works well just for small size $NISs$.

Now, let us consider another method to obtain a minimal subset of descriptors, which satisfy $DF_{DGC}(x)$. Namely, we sequentially select a descriptor in $DF_{DGC}(x)$, and we reduce $DF_{DGC}(x)$ to new $DF'_{DGC}(x)$. By repeating this procedure, it is possible to obtain a set of descriptors satisfying $DF_{DGC}(x)$. We name this method an *interactive selection method* (*is-method*). However, we have to pay attention to this method. Let us consider the following example.

Example 3. Let a,b,c,d be descriptors in a NIS, and let us suppose DF=$(a \vee b) \wedge (b \vee c) \wedge (c \vee d)$ be a discernibility function for a class. If we select descriptor a in DF, DF is revised to DF'=$(b \vee c) \wedge (c \vee d)$. This *absorption law* is the key procedure to reduce DF. In [13], this absorption law takes an important role. Similarly if we select descriptor b in DF', DF' is revised to DF''=$(c \vee d)$.

Finally, we select descriptor c and we obtain a set $\{a, b, c\}$. This set satisfies DF, but this set is not minimal. Because, both sets $\{a, c\}$ and $\{b, c\}$ satisfy DF.

For solving the problem in Example 3, we combine is-method with e-method, and propose Algorithm 3. We name this method *interactive selection and enumeration method* with a *threshold value (isetv-method)*. In this method, at first we depend upon ise-method and we reduce $DF_{DGC}(x)$ to $DF'_{DGC}(x)$. Let SOL denote a set of currently selected descriptors, and let $LIST\_DESC$ denote a set of all distinct descriptors in $DF'_{DGC}(x)$. When the amount of selected descriptors and descriptors in $DF'_{DGC}(x)$ is less than a threshold value α, i.e., $|SOL| + |LIST\_DESC| \leq \alpha$, we employ e-method. A threshold value controls to obtain all minimal solutions in $DF_{DGC}(x)$. The property is as follows:

(Property 1) For large threshold values, less selections are necessary and most of all minimal solutions are generated. However, it takes much execution time in e-method. Because, there exist $2^{|ALL\_DESC|}$ kinds of subsets.

(Property 2) For small threshold values, more selections are necessary and minimal solutions depending upon selections are generated. In this case, it takes less execution time in e-method.

Algorithm 3.(Interactive selection and enumeration method with a threshold value)

Input: An object $x \in OB_{DGC}(DEC, \eta) \neq \emptyset$ and a threshold value α.
Output: Minimal solutions and minimal certain rules, which depend upon selections of descriptors.

```
begin
  Fix a value α; DF=DF_DGC(x); CORE=∅; SOL=∅;
  for (every descriptor DESC in DF) if (DESC is a core) CORE=
    CORE∪{DESC} and remove every disjunction with DESC from DF;
  if (DF==∅) CORE is a unique minimal solution,
    ∧_DESC∈CORE DESC ⇒[DEC,η] is a minimal certain rule and end;
  assign no to FINISH;
  while (DF ≠ ∅) do
    if (|SOL| + |LIST_DESC| ≤ α) assign SOL to SOL∪LIST_DESC,
      and exit while loop;
    assign the number of disjunctions in DF to NUM;
    find a set COMMON={DESC|DESC is in every disjunction in DF};
    if (COMMON ≠ ∅) CORE∪SOL∪{DESC'} (DESC' ∈ COMMON) is
      a solution of DF_DGC(x), apply E-method and obtain minimal
      solutions, remove every DESC' from DF, and assign the number of
      disjunctions in the revised DF to NUM'; else assign NUM'=NUM;
    if (NUM'! = NUM) there exist no solutions of DF_DGC(x),
      assign yes to FINISH and exit while loop;
    select a descriptor DESC in DF, SOL=SOL∪{DESC} and remove
      every disjunction with DESC from DF;
  end_while;
  if (FINISH==no) apply E-method to descriptors CORE∪SOL,
    and obtain minimal solutions of DF_DGC(x);
end.
```

8   A Real Execution of ISETV-Method in DGC Class

The following is a real execution of *isetv*-method for object 5 in Table 1. In non-interactive mode, solutions consisting of only core descriptors are handled. There exist no such solutions. Then, interactive mode starts. In Operation 2, the threshold value α is fixed to 3. In Operation 3, a descriptor $[2, 1]$ is selected, and a common descriptor $[4, 5]$ is found. For a set $\{[2, 1], [4, 5]\}$, *e*-method is applied and a minimal certain rule is generated. In order to obtain other minimal certain rules, the same procedure is applied to $DF = [[1, [1, 4]], [6, [7, 4]]]$ in Loop 2. In this case, $SOL = \{[2, 1]\}$ and $LIST\_DESC = \{[1, 4], [7, 4]\}$, so $|SOL| + |LIST\_DESC| \leq 3$ holds. *E*-method is applied to $\{[1, 4], [2, 1], [7, 4]\}$ again. The selected descriptor $[2,1]$ can be reduced, and a minimal certain rule is displayed.

```
?-isetv_method(5). [Operation 1]
===== NON-INTERACTIVE MODE =================
Core Descriptors:[]
EXEC_TIME=0.003(sec)
===== INTERACTIVE MODE ====================
Input a Threshold Value:3. [Operation 2]
[Loop:1]
    DF without Core:[[1,[1,4],[4,5]],[2,[1,4],[2,1],[4,5],[7,4]],
    [4,[1,4],[2,1],[4,5],[7,4]],[6,[4,5],[7,4]],[7,[1,4],[2,1],[4,5]],
    [8,[2,1],[7,4]],[9,[1,4],[2,1],[4,5],[7,4]]]
    Descriptors in DF:[[1,4],[2,1],[4,5],[7,4]]
    Select a Descriptor:[2,1]. [Operation 3]
    Revised DF without Core:[[1,[1,4],[4,5]],[6,[4,5],[7,4]]]
    Common Descriptors in Revised DF:[[4,5]]
    Execute E-method for {[2,1],[4,5]}
        [2,1]&[4,5]⇒[8,1][972/972(=18/18,54/54),Definite,GC]
        This rule covers objects [5],Coverage=0.333
        [(0.1,0.1),(1.0,1.0),(0.142,0.333)] /* Minimum and maximum of */
[Loop:2]                                   /* Support,Accuracy,Coverage */
    DF without Core:[[1,[1,4]],[6,[7,4]]]
    Descriptors in DF:[[1,4],[7,4]]
    Threshold Value Condition is Satisfied
    Execute E-method for {[1,4],[2,1],[7,4]}
        [1,4]&[7,4]⇒[8,1][3888/3888(=72/72,54/54),Definite,GC]
        This rule covers objects [5],Coverage=0.333
        [(0.1,0.1),(1.0,1.0),(0.142,0.333)]
yes
```

9   Minimal Possible Rule Generation in Other Classes

Minimal possible rule generation in DMA class is similar to that in DGC class. According to Theorem 1, the problem is to find such a minimal conjunction $[CON, \zeta]$ that $inf(x, \zeta, CON) \subset sup(x, \eta, DEC)$ and $PT(x, CON) = \{\zeta\}$.

In DGC, we employed $sup(x, \zeta, CON)$ and $inf(x, \eta, DEC)$, but in DMA we employ $inf(x, \zeta, CON)$ and $sup(x, \eta, DEC)$. Let $DISC_{DMA}(x, y)$ denote a disjunction of such definite descriptors in x that $y \notin inf(x, (\zeta), \{A\})$, and we define $DF_{DMA}(x) = \wedge_{y \in OB-sup(x,\eta,DEC)} DISC_{DMA}(x, y)$. In order to obtain all minimal solutions of $DF_{DMA}(x)$, we similarly apply $isetv$-method to $DF_{DMA}(x)$, and it is possible to generate all minimal possible rules in DMA class.

In IGC class, the problem is find such a minimal conjunction $[CON, \zeta]$ that $sup(x, \zeta, CON) \subset inf(x, \eta, DEC)$. Similarly in IMA class, the problem is find such a minimal conjunction $[CON, \zeta]$ that $inf(x, \zeta, CON) \subset sup(x, \eta, DEC)$. In both cases, $PT(x, CON)$ may not be a singleton set. This implies there exist $|\prod_{A \in CON} g(x, A)|$ kinds of possible tuples and there exist $|\prod_{A \in CON} g(x, A)|$ kinds of discernibility functions.

Since $isetv$-method depends upon a discernibility function, it is hard to handle $|\prod_{A \in CON} g(x, A)|$ kinds of discernibility functions. For this reason, we apply $order$-method in Section 4 to each possible tuple in $\prod_{A \in CON} g(x, A)$, and we finally apply e-method to an obtained set of attributes. In this way, we have implemented programs for minimal possible rules in IGC and IMA.

10   Concluding Remarks

A framework of Minimal rule generation in $NISs$ is presented. For assuring the minimality of rules, we introduced discernibility functions. The minimal condition part in a rule is obtained as a solution of a discernibility function. According to some experiments, the absorption law seems effective for reducing a discernibility function. So, $isetv$-method will be applicable to relatively large-scale $NISs$. It is necessary to investigate the complexity of each algorithm, too.

Acknowledgment. This work is partly supported by the Grant-in-Aid for Scientific Research (C) (No.16500176), Japan Society for the Promotion of Science.

References

1. Pawlak, Z.: Rough Sets. Kluwer Academic Publisher (1991)
2. Pawlak, Z.: Some Issues on Rough Sets. Transactions on Rough Sets, Vol.1. Springer-Verlag (2004) 1-58
3. Komorowski, J., Pawlak, Z., Polkowski, L., Skowron, A.: Rough Sets: a tutorial. Rough Fuzzy Hybridization. Springer (1999) 3-98
4. Rough Set Software. Bulletin of Int'l. Rough Set Society **2** (1998) 15-46
5. Orłowska, E. (ed.): Incomplete Information: Rough Set Analysis. Physica-Verlag (1998)
6. Lipski, W.: On Semantic Issues Connected with Incomplete Information Data Base. ACM Trans. DBS **4** (1979) 269-296
7. Grzymala-Busse, J., Werbrouck, P.: On the Best Search Method in the LEM1 and LEM2 Algorithms. Incomplete Information: Rough Set Analysis. Phisica-Verlag (1998) 75-91

8. Grzymala-Busse, J.: Data with Missing Attribute Values: Generalization of In-discernibility Relation and Rule Induction. Transactions on Rough Sets, Vol.1. Springer-Verlag (2004) 78-95
9. Kryszkiewicz, M.: Rules in Incomplete Information Systems. Information Sciences **113** (1999) 271-292
10. Sakai, H., Okuma, A.: Basic Algorithms and Tools for Rough Non-deterministic Information Analysis. Transactions on Rough Sets, Vol.1. Springer-Verlag (2004) 209-231
11. Sakai, H.: A Framework of Rough Sets based Rule Generation in Non-deterministic Information Systems. Lecture Notes in AI, Vol.2871. Springer-Verlag (2003) 143-151
12. Skowron, A., Rauszer, C.: The Discernibility Matrices and Functions in Information Systems. In Intelligent Decision Support - Handbook of Advances and Applications of the Rough Set Theory. Kluwer Academic Publishers (1992) 331-362
13. Kryszkiewicz, M., Rybinski, H.: Computation of Reducts of Composed Information Systems. Fundamenta Informaticae **27** (1996) 183-195

Studies on Rough Sets in Multiple Tables

R.S. Milton[1], V. Uma Maheswari[2], and Arul Siromoney[2]

[1] Department of Computer Science,
Madras Christian College, Chennai – 600 059, India
[2] Department of Computer Science and Engineering,
College of Engineering Guindy,
Anna University, Chennai – 600 025, India
`asiro@vsnl.com, umam@annauniv.edu`

Abstract. Rough Set Theory is a mathematical tool to deal with vagueness and uncertainty. Rough Set Theory uses a single information table. Relational Learning is the learning from multiple relations or tables. This paper studies the use of Rough Set Theory and Variable Precision Rough Sets in a multi-table information system (MTIS). The notion of approximation regions in the MTIS is defined in terms of those of the individual tables. This is used in classifying an example in the MTIS, based on the elementary sets in the individual tables to which the example belongs. Results of classification experiments in predictive toxicology based on this approach are presented.

Keywords: Rough Set Theory, Variable Precision Rough Sets, multi-table information system, relational learning, prediction.

1 Introduction

Rough set theory [1,2,3,4], introduced by Zdzislaw Pawlak in the early 1980s, is a mathematical tool to deal with vagueness and uncertainty. Rough set theory defines an indiscernibility relation that partitions the universe of examples into elementary sets. In other words, examples in an elementary set are indistinguishable. A concept is rough when it contains at least one elementary set that contains both positive and negative examples. The indiscernibility relation is defined based on a single table.

Relational Learning is based on multiple relations or tables. Inductive Logic Programming (ILP) [5,6] is one of the approaches to Relational Learning. A brief survey of research in Rough Sets and Relational Learning is presented in [7].

The authors' work is in the intersection of Rough Sets and ILP. The gRS–ILP model [8,9] introduces a rough setting in Inductive Logic Programming. It describes the situation where any induced logic program cannot distinguish between certain positive and negative examples. Any induced logic program will either cover both the positive and the negative examples in the group, or not cover the group at all, with both the positive and the negative examples in this group being left out.

D. Ślęzak et al. (Eds.): RSFDGrC 2005, LNAI 3641, pp. 265–274, 2005.

The Variable Precision Rough Set (VPRS) model [10] allows for a controlled degree of misclassification. The Variable Precision Rough Set Inductive Logic Programming (VPRSILP) model [11] is an extension of the gRS–ILP model using features of the VPRS model. The cVPRSILP approach [12] uses clauses as the attributes. Test cases are classified based on their proximity to significant elementary sets.

In this paper, a Multi–Table Information System is defined that extends the single information table of rough set theory to multiple information tables. Notions from the Variable Precision Rough Set model are then introduced and used for prediction. An illustrative experiment in toxicology is then presented.

2   Multi–table Information System

2.1   Definitions

Tables and Information Systems: Consider a universe U of elements. A table T is defined as $T = (U, A, V, \rho)$, where A is a finite set of *attributes*; $V = \bigcup_{a \in A} V_a$ is the set of *attribute values* of all attributes, where V_a is the *domain* (the set of possible values) of attribute a; and $\rho : U \times A \to V$ is an *information function* such that for every element $x \in U$, $\rho(x, a) \in V_a$ is the value of attribute a for element x. This definition is based on the definition of Rough Set Information System in [1].

Each element $x \in U$ can be pictured as corresponding to a row in a table of rows and columns, with each column corresponding to an attribute $a \in A$. $\rho(x, a)$ is the value in the table at the intersection of the row corresponding to x and the column corresponding to a.

We define a *Multi-Table Information System (MTIS)* as a finite set of tables denoted as $T = \{T_0, T_1, \ldots, T_n\}$, where each table $T_i, 1 \le i \le n$ is defined as above and is denoted as $T_i = (U_i, A_i, V_i, \rho_i)$. $T_0 = \{U_0, A_0, V_0, \rho_0\}$ is a decision table with one of the attributes $d \in A_0$, as a binary valued *decision attribute*. A similar definition is also found in [13]. We denote U_0 as U, the universe of examples, since A_0 has the decision attribute.

In every $T_i, 0 \le i \le n$, let $L_i \subset A_i$ consist of *link attributes* that are used to link different tables. These are attributes that are common between different tables.

Let $I_i = (U_i, B_i, V_i, \rho_i), 0 \le i \le n$, where $B_i = A_i - L_i$. We note that I_i corresponds to the classical rough set information system.

Elementary Sets: An equivalence relation R_i, called *indiscernibility relation*, is defined on the universe U_i of an information system $I_i, 0 \le i \le n$, as

$$R_i = \{(x, y) \in U_i \times U_i \mid \forall b \in B_i, \rho_i(x, b) = \rho_i(y, b)\}$$

In the information system I_i, the *elementary set* containing the element $x \in U_i$, with respect to the indiscernibility relation R_i, is

$$[x]_{R_i} = \{y \in U_i \mid y R_i x\}$$

We consider R to be the indiscernibility relation on U over the entire MTIS T. Two elements $x, y \in U$, are indiscernible, that is xRy, if they cannot be distinguished using the information available in all the tables of the MTIS T. The elementary set of x consists of all elements y such that xRy.

Positive, Negative and Boundary Regions: In general, let the *concept* X_i be defined as some subset of U_i, where $i = 0, 1, \ldots, n,$. The *concept* $X \subseteq U$ with respect to the universe of examples U are the elements of U that have a particular value (say, t) of the decision attribute d. That is, $X = \{x \in U \mid \rho_0(x, d) = t\}$.

The *lower approximation* of $X_i \subseteq U_i$, with respect to any universe of elements U_i and an equivalence relation R_i on U_i, is the union of the elementary sets of U_i with respect to R_i that are contained in X_i. The *upper approximation* of X_i is the union of the elementary sets of U_i with respect to R_i that have a non–zero intersection with X_i.

The *lower approximation* of $X_i \subseteq U_i$, denoted $\underline{R_i}X_i$, with respect to a universe of elements U_i and an equivalence relation $\overline{R_i}$, where $i = 0, 1, \ldots, n$. is defined as $\underline{R_i}X_i = \{x \mid [x]_{R_i} \subseteq X_i\}$. The *upper approximation* of X_i, denoted $\overline{R_i}X$, is defined as $\overline{R_i}X_i = \{x \mid [x]_{R_i} \cap X \neq \emptyset\}$. The *lower approximation* of X_i is also known as the *Positive region* of X_i.

The set $BN_{R_i}(X_i) = \overline{R_i}X_i - \underline{R_i}X_i$ is called the *Boundary region* of X_i. The set $U - \overline{R_i}X_i$ is called the *outside region* of X_i, or the *Negative region* of X_i.

The lower approximation, upper approximation, Boundary region and Negative region with respect to the entire MTIS are defined as above but with respect to the equivalence relation R.

β–positive and β–negative Regions: The conditional probability that an element x in an elementary set $[x]_{R_i}$ is positive is

$$P(+|[x]_{R_i}) = \frac{|[x]_{R_i} \cap X|}{|[x]_{R_i}|}$$

The conditional probability that the element x in the elementary set is negative is

$$P(-|[x]_{R_i}) = 1 - P(+|[x]_{R_i})$$

When the context is clear, the *conditional probability* of an elementary set is taken to be $P(+|[x]_{R_i})$.

The β_u–*positive region* is the union of the elementary sets whose conditional probability is greater than or equal to β_u, where $\beta_u \geq 0.5$. The β_l–*negative region* is the union of the elementary sets whose conditional probability is less than β_l where $\beta_l \leq 0.5$. These are based on the definitions in [14]. When $\beta_u = 1 - \beta_l$, we denote it as β, and note that $\beta_l = 1 - \beta$.

The β_u–*positive region with respect to the entire MTIS* is defined as the union of the elementary sets in which each element has a probability greater than or equal to β_u that it is positive $(P(+|[x]_R) \geq \beta_u)$, where $\beta_u \geq 0.5$. The β_l–*negative region with respect to the entire MTIS* is defined as the union of the elementary sets in which each element has a probability less than or equal to β_l that it is positive $(P(+|[x]_R) \leq \beta_l)$, where $\beta_l \leq 0.5$. We note that the ratio of the count of positive elements by the total count of elements is not specifically used in the definition.

2.2   Studies in the Propositional Case

A simple case is studied as a first step towards the study of the more complex cases. This case corresponds to a single table of classical rough set theory being broken up into several tables.

Tables and Information Systems: Consider a Multi-Table Information System (MTIS) as defined earlier, where the following hold: Every table has the same universe of elements. The same attribute is used as the link attribute in each table. The values of the link attribute in the table are unique. Other than the link attribute, no attribute occurs in more than one table.

Let T be an MTIS and denoted as $T = \{T_0, T_1, \ldots, T_n\}$, where the following hold: For each table T_i, $0 \leq i \leq n$,

(1) $U_i = U$,
(2) $L_i = \{l\}$, $l \in A_i$
(3) $\rho(x, l) \neq \rho(y, l)$, for every $x, y \in U$ such that $x \neq y$.
(4) $a_i \neq a_j$, $a_i \in B_i$, $a_j \in B_j$, $i \neq j$, $0 \leq i, j \leq n$.

Let T_C be a single table combining the individual tables. The attributes of the combined table are the union of the attributes of the individual tables. The set of values for each attribute is the same as the set of values of that attribute in the respective individual table. The mapping from an element attribute pair onto a value is the same as the mapping from that element attribute pair in the respective individual table.

Thus, the combined table T_C is defined as $T_C = \{U_C, A_C, V_C, \rho_C\}$, where $U_C = U$, $A_C = \bigcup_{0 \leq i \leq n} A_i$, $V_C = \bigcup_{0 \leq i \leq n} V_i$, $\rho_C : U_C \times A_C \rightarrow V_C$ such that for every element $x \in \bar{U}_C$, $\rho_C(x, a) = \rho_i(x, a)$ where $a \in A_i, 0 \leq i \leq n$.

Let the corresponding information system be $I_C = \{U_C, B_C, V_C, \rho_C\}$, where $B_C = A_C - \{l\}$.

As a simple illustration, consider $T = \{T_0, T_1\}$ as shown below.

Table T_0

drug	element	charge	decision
d1	c	-7	true
d2	n	5	true

Table T_1

drug	property	value
d1	salmonella	p
d2	chromaberr	n

Combining the two tables together, we get the following combined table T_C

Table T_C

drug	element	charge	property	value	decision
d1	c	-7	salmonella	p	true
d2	n	5	chromaberr	n	true

The classical rough set information systems I_0, I_1 and I_C are given below.
The classical rough set information systems I_0, I_1 and I_C are given below.

Table I_0

element	charge	decision
c	-7	true
n	5	true

Table I_1

property	value
salmonella	p
chromaberr	n

Table I_C

element	charge	property	value	decision
c	-7	salmonella	p	true
n	5	chromaberr	n	true

Elementary Sets: Let R_C be the indiscernibility relation on U_C. We note that in this propositional case, for any $x, y \in U_C$, xR_Cy iff $xR_0y \wedge xR_1y \wedge \ldots \wedge xR_ny$. That is, since $B_C = \bigcup_{0 \leq i \leq n} B_i$

$$[x]_{R_C} = \bigcap_{0 \leq i \leq n} [x]_{R_i}$$

In this case, we note that the equivalence relation R over the entire MTIS is the same as R_C.

Posterior Probability of an Example Being Positive: The probability that an example x is +ve is computed in terms of the conditional probabilities of the elementary sets of x in each table.

Since the elementary sets of element x in the information systems $I_i, 0 \leq i \leq n$ are denoted by $[x]_{R_i}$, the *posterior probability* that x is +ve, given its elementary sets in each table, is denoted by $P(+|[x]_{R_1}[x]_{R_2} \ldots [x]_{R_n})$. As defined earlier, $P(+|[x]_{R_1})$ denotes the conditional probability of the elementary set $[x]_{R_1}$. $P(+)$ and $P(-)$ denote the *prior probability* that an example is positive or negative. $P([x]_{R_1}[x]_{R_2} \ldots [x]_{R_n}|+)$ is the probability of a +ve example falling in the elementary sets $[x]_{R_1}, [x]_{R_2} \ldots [x]_{R_n}$.

Applying Bayes rule gives

$$P(+|[x]_{R_1}[x]_{R_2} \cdots [x]_{R_n}) = \frac{P([x]_{R_1}[x]_{R_2} \cdots [x]_{R_n}|+)P(+)}{P([x]_{R_1}[x]_{R_2} \cdots [x]_{R_n})}$$

A simplifying assumption that the event of an example falling in a particular elementary set in one information system is independent of the event of the example falling in a particular elementary set in another information system yields

$$P(+|[x]_{R_1}[x]_{R_2} \cdots [x]_{R_n}) =$$

$$\frac{1}{1 + \left(\frac{1}{P(+|[x]_{R_1})} - 1\right)\left(\frac{1}{P(+|[x]_{R_2})} - 1\right) \cdots \left(\frac{1}{P(+|[x]_{R_n})} - 1\right)\left(\frac{P(+)}{P(-)}\right)^{n-1}} \tag{1}$$

Positive, Negative and Boundary Regions: We now study the relationship between the Positive, Negative and Boundary Regions in individual information systems and those in the overall system, and note the following.

If an element is in the positive (negative) region in any one of the individual information systems, it is in the positive (negative) region of the overall system.

Even if an element is in the boundary region in all the individual information systems, it need not be in the boundary region of the overall system.

In other words, the positive (negative) region in any individual information system is a subset of the positive (negative) region of the system. The boundary region in any individual information system is a superset of the boundary region of the system.

β–Positive and β–Negative Regions: We now study the relationship between the β–positive, β–negative and β–boundary regions in individual information systems and those in the overall system, and note the following.

If an element is in the β–positive region in all the individual information systems, then it has atleast a β probability of being positive, that is, it is in the β–positive region of the overall system (by the definition of the β–positive region used in this paper).

(If the definition of β–positive region is taken as the union of elementary sets whose ratio of count of positive elements by the total count of elements is greater than β, we note the following: even if an element is in the β–positive region in all the individual information systems, it need not be in the β–positive region of the overall system.)

From equation 1, we note the following. Consider $\beta'_u > P(+)$. If an element is in the β_u–positive region in atleast one information system, and is in the β'_u–positive region in all the information systems, then it is in the β_u–positive region of the overall system. Similarly, consider $\beta'_l < P(+)$. If an element is in the β_l–negative region in atleast one information system, and is in the β'_l–negative region in all the information systems, then it is in the β_l–negative region of the overall system.

From equation 1, we also note the following. If an element is in more number of elementary sets in the β_u–positive region than the elementary sets in the β'_u negative region, and is not in any elementary set in the $(1 - \beta_u)$–negative region, then it is in the β_u–positive region of the overall system. Similarly, if an element is in more number of elementary sets in the β_l–negative region than the elementary sets in the β'_l positive region, and is not in any elementary set in the $(1 - \beta_l)$–positive region, then it is in the β_l–negative region of the overall system.

2.3   Studies in 'Multiple Rows Per Example' Case

These studies are in the case where multiple rows in a table could correspond to a single example. In each of U_1, U_2, $\ldots$, U_n several elements may map onto a single element in U.

As a simple illustration, consider $T = \{T_0, T_1, T_2\}$ as shown below.

Table T_0

drug	decision
d1	true
d2	true

Table T_1

drug	element	charge
d1	c	-7
d1	c	-2
d2	n	5
d2	n	8

Table T_2

drug	property	value
d1	salmonella	p
d1	cytogen	p
d2	salmonella	p
d2	chromaberr	n

Combining the three tables together, we get the following combined table T_C

Table T_C

drug	element	charge	property	value	decision
d1	c	-7	salmonella	p	true
d1	c	-7	cytogen	p	true
d1	c	-2	salmonella	p	true
d1	c	-2	cytogen	p	true
d2	n	5	salmonella	p	truc
d2	n	5	chromaberr	n	true
d2	n	8	salmonella	p	true
d2	n	8	chromaberr	n	true

The classical rough set information systems I_0, I_1, I_2 and I_C are given below.

Table I_0

drug	decision
d1	true
d2	true

Table I_1

element	charge
c	-7
c	-2
n	5
n	8

Table I_2

property	value
salmonella	p
cytogen	p
salmonella	p
chromaberr	n

Table I_C

element	charge	property	value	decision
c	-7	salmonella	p	true
c	-7	cytogen	p	true
c	-2	salmonella	p	true
c	-2	cytogen	p	true
n	5	salmonella	p	true
n	5	chromaberr	n	true
n	8	salmonella	p	true
n	8	chromaberr	n	true

We note that since every element in U_C maps onto a unique element in U, each element in U_C is associated with the value of the decision attribute of the corresponding element in U. Similarly, each element in U_1, U_2, ..., U_n is associated with the value of the decision attribute of the corresponding element in U.

The definitions and discussions in the simpler case discussed in the previous section follow in this case also. Equation 1 is valid under the restriction that more than one element in any particular elementary set in any information system does not map onto the same element in U. (Elements in different elementary sets can map onto the same element in U.)

3   Application to Predictive Toxicology

The rodent carcinogenicity tests conducted within the US National Toxicology Program by the National Institute of Environmental Health Sciences (NIEHS) has resulted in a large database of compounds classified as carcinogens or otherwise. The Predictive Toxicology Evaluation project of the NIEHS provided the opportunity to compare carcinogenicity predictions on previously untested chemicals. This presented a formidable challenge for programs concerned with knowledge discovery. The ILP system Progol [15] has been used in this Predictive Toxicology Evaluation Challenge [16,17]. The dataset used is the Predictive Toxicology Evaluation Challenge dataset found at http://web.comlab.ox.ac.uk/oucl/research/areas/machlearn/cancer.html. The predicates atm, bond and has_property are used.

Illustrative experiments were performed earlier by the authors and the details are available in [7], where the best average prediction accuracy was 63.33%, and in [18], where the best average prediction accuracy was 66%.

The dataset used in this experiment has four tables with the fields as follows: drugtab (drugid, decision), atomtab (drugid, atomid, element, number, charge), bondtab (drugid, atomid1, atomid2, number), and proptab (drugid, prop, value).

Continuous attributes are discretised. Three information systems are got from these tables as follow: atomtab (element, number, charge), bondtab (number) and proptab (prop, value). Elementary sets and the β_u–positive and β_l–negative regions are determined for these information systems.

The following procedure is used. The value of β'_u is taken to be $P(+)$ if $P(+) > 0.5$, or 0.5 otherwise. The value of β'_l is taken to be $P(+)$ if $P(+) < 0.5$, or 0.5 otherwise. Predict1 predicts an element as positive if it falls in more elementary sets in the β_u–positive region than in the elementary sets in the β'_u–negative region, and in no elementary sets in the $(1 - \beta_u)$–negative region. Predict1 predicts an element as negative if it falls in more elementary sets in the β_l–negative region than in the elementary sets in the β'_l–positive region, and in no elementary sets in the $(1 - \beta_l)$–positive region. If there is no element from the training set in the elementary set, that elementary set is ignored.

Predict1 is used with β_u as 0.7 and β_l as 0.3. If there is no prediction, then Predict1 is used with β_u as 0.6 and β_l as 0.4. If there is still no prediction, then Predict0 is used. The results follow.

$\beta_u = 0.7, \beta_l = 0.3$				$\beta_u = 0.6, \beta_l = 0.4$				Equation 1					Overall				
Pos		Neg		Acc	Pos		Neg		Acc	Pos		Neg		Acc	Pos		Neg		Acc
+	-	+	-		+	-	+	-		+	-	+	-		+	-	+	-	
3	0	0	0	1.00	2	0	2	1	0.60	11	2	4	8	0.76	16	2	6	9	0.76
2	0	0	0	1.00	4	0	0	2	1.00	10	2	6	7	0.68	16	2	6	9	0.76
4	0	0	0	1.00	6	0	2	0	0.75	7	1	8	5	0.57	17	1	10	5	0.67
3	0	1	0	0.75	3	0	1	1	0.80	10	2	8	4	0.58	16	2	10	5	0.64
3	0	0	0	1.00	2	1	1	1	0.60	7	5	8	5	0.48	12	6	9	6	0.55
1	0	0	0	1.00	3	0	0	2	1.00	14	0	2	11	0.93	18	0	2	13	0.94
0	0	1	1	0.50	3	1	0	1	0.80	11	3	6	6	0.65	14	4	7	8	0.67
0	0	1	0	0.00	3	0	0	1	1.00	12	3	7	6	0.64	15	3	8	7	0.67
3	0	0	0	1.00	4	0	2	0	0.67	11	0	5	8	0.79	18	0	7	8	0.79
1	0	0	1	1.00	7	0	0	1	1.00	8	2	8	5	0.57	16	2	8	7	0.70
20	0	3	2	0.88	37	2	8	10	0.82	101	20	62	65	0.67	158	22	73	77	0.71

The average prediction accuracy in the first table (Predict1 on the entire dataset, with β_u as 0.7 and β_l as 0.3) is 88 %, in the second table (Predict1 on the remaining elements, with β_u as 0.6 and β_l as 0.4) is 82 %, the third table (Predict0 on the remaining elements) is 67 %, and the overall average prediction accuracy is 71 %. The average prediction accuracy is seen to be higher than the corresponding value of β used.

4   Conclusions

This paper presents an approach to learning from a Multi–Table Information System, by using Rough Set Theory and Variable Precision Rough Sets, without converting the MTIS into a traditional single table Information System. The results of an illustrative example in toxicology are presented.

A brief theoretical basis is presented for the relation between the β_u–positive and β_l–negative regions of individual tables, and those in the overall system. It is also noted in the illustrative experiment using ten–fold cross–validation that this result is useful in the prediction accuracy of test cases. The average prediction accuracy is seen to be higher than the corresponding value of β used.

References

1. Pawlak, Z.: Rough sets. International Journal of Computer and Information Sciences **11** (1982) 341–356
2. Pawlak, Z.: Rough Sets — Theoretical Aspects of Reasoning about Data. Kluwer Academic Publishers, Dordrecht, The Netherlands (1991)
3. Pawlak, Z., Grzymala-Busse, J., Slowinski, R., Ziarko, W.: Rough sets. Communications of ACM **38** (1995) 89–95
4. Komorowski, J., Pawlak, Z., Polkowski, L., Skowron, A.: Rough sets: A tutorial. In Pal, S.K., Skowron, A., eds.: Rough Fuzzy Hybridization: A New Trend in Decision-Making. Springer-Verlag (1999) 3–98

5. Muggleton, S.: Inductive logic programming. New Generation Computing **8** (1991) 295–318
6. Muggleton, S.: Scientific knowledge discovery through inductive logic programming. Communications of the ACM **42** (1999) 43–46
7. Milton, R.S., Uma Maheswari, V., Siromoney, A.: Rough Sets and Relational Learning. LNCS Transactions on Rough Sets **Inaugural Volume** (2004)
8. Siromoney, A.: A rough set perspective of Inductive Logic Programming. In Raedt, L.D., Muggleton, S., eds.: Proceedings of the IJCAI-97 Workshop on Frontiers of Inductive Logic Programming, Nagoya, Japan (1997) 111–113
9. Siromoney, A., Inoue, K.: The generic Rough Set Inductive Logic Programming (gRS–ILP) model. In Lin, T.Y., Yao, Y.Y., Zadeh, L.A., eds.: Data Mining, Rough Sets and Granular Computing. Volume 95., Physica–Verlag (2002) 499–517
10. Ziarko, W.: Variable precision rough set model. Journal of Computer and System Sciences **46** (1993) 39–59
11. Uma Maheswari, V., Siromoney, A., Mehata, K.M., Inoue, K.: The Variable Precision Rough Set Inductive Logic Programming Model and Strings. Computational Intelligence **17** (2001) 460–471
12. Milton, R.S., Uma Maheswari, V., Siromoney, A.: The Variable Precision Rough Set Inductive Logic Programming model — a Statistical Relational Learning perspective. In: Workshop on Learning Statistical Models from Relational Data (SRL 2003), IJCAI-2003. (2003)
13. Wroblewski, J.: Analyzing relational databases using rough set based methods. In: Proceedings of IPMU 2000. Volume 1. (2000) 256–262
14. Ziarko, W.: Set approximation quality measures in the variable precision rough set model. In: Proc. of 2nd Intl. Conference on Hybrid Intelligent Systems, Santiago, Chile (2002)
15. Muggleton, S.: Inverse entailment and Progol. New Generation Computing **13** (1995) 245–286
16. Srinivasan, A., King, R., Muggleton, S., Sternberg, M.: The predictive toxicology evaluation challenge. In: Proceedings of the Fifteenth International Joint Conference Artificial Intelligence (IJCAI-97). Morgan-Kaufmann (1997) 1–6
17. Srinivasan, A., King, R., Muggleton, S., Sternberg, M.: Carcinogenesis predictions using ILP. In Lavrač, N., Džeroski, S., eds.: Proceedings of the Seventh International Workshop on Inductive Logic Programming. Springer-Verlag, Berlin (1997) 273–287 LNAI 1297.
18. Milton, R.S., Uma Maheswari, V., Siromoney, A.: Rough Relational Learning in Predictive Toxicology. In: International Workshop on Knowledge Discovery in BioMedicine (KDbM 2004), PRICAI-2004. (2004)

Normalization in a Rough Relational Database

Theresa Beaubouef[1], Frederick E. Petry[2], and Roy Ladner[2]

[1] Southeastern Louisiana University,
Computer Science Department, SLU 10506,
Hammond, LA 70402, USA
tbeaubouef@selu.edu
[2] U.S. Naval Research Laboratory,
Code 7400, Stennis Space Center, MS 39529, USA
{fpetry, rladner}@nrlssc.navy.mil

Abstract. The rough relational database model was developed for the management of uncertainty in relational databases. In this paper we discuss rough functional dependencies and the normalization process used with them. Normalization is an important part of the relational database design process and rough normalization provides similar benefits for the rough relational database model.

Keywords: normalization, functional dependency, rough sets, relational database, uncertainty.

1 Introduction

Databases are known for the ability to store and update data in an efficient manner, providing reliability and the elimination of data redundancy. The relational database model, in particular, has well-established mechanisms built into the model for properly designing the database and maintaining data consistency. Constraints and data dependencies are used in database normalization to realize these goals and minimize such problems as update anomalies, thereby providing greater integrity maintenance.

Several types of data dependencies exist, and constraints on data may be specified in advance by the database administrator. These identify key attributes that uniquely identify tuples and constrain the possible relation instance values for specified relation schemas. The most important of these for the design of relational schemas is the functional dependency. A functional dependency specifies constraints on the attributes of a relation schema R that hold for all instances of the database. These dependencies are used in the process of normalization, which creates well-designed databases. This process is inherent to database design with relational databases [1]. In [2], fuzzy functional dependencies and normalization applied to fuzzy relational databases is discussed.

Rough set theory, developed by Pawlak [3], [4] provides a mathematical framework for the representation of uncertainty. It has been used in various applications, most notably for representation of uncertainty in databases for data

D. Ślęzak et al. (Eds.): RSFDGrC 2005, LNAI 3641, pp. 275–282, 2005.
© Springer-Verlag Berlin Heidelberg 2005

mining and improved information retrieval [5], [6]. In previous research, we developed the rough relational database model [7], and in [8] we defined rough functional dependencies. In this paper we discuss the concept of normalization based on these rough functional dependencies in the rough relational database. This is important because while we make the database more flexible to support uncertainty management, we must retain the ability to specify constraints and manage updates based on these constraints so that our database remains consistent. The traditional relational database is a special case of the rough relational database, and examples of poor design and the importance of normalization found throughout the literature for relational databases also apply for the rough relational database.

2   Background: Rough Sets and Rough Relational Database

Rough sets [3], [4] have been established as a mechanism for uncertainty management for both data and queries in relational databases in several ways [5], [7], [9]. In rough sets an approximation space is defined on some universe U by imposing upon it some equivalence relation which partitions the universe into equivalence classes called elementary sets, based on some definition of 'equivalence' as it relates to the application domain. This partitioning can be adjusted to increase or decrease the granularity of a domain, to group items together that are considered indiscernible for a given purpose, or to "bin" ordered domains into range groups.

Any finite union of these elementary sets is called a definable set. A *rough set* $X \subseteq U$, however, can be defined in terms of the definable sets by its lower ($\underline{R}X$) and upper ($\overline{R}X$) approximation regions:

$$\underline{R}X = \{x \in U \mid [x]_R \subseteq X\}$$

and

$$\overline{R}X = \{x \in U \mid [x]_R \cap X \neq \varnothing\}.$$

$\underline{R}X$ is the positive region, $U - \overline{R}X$ is the negative region, and $\overline{R}X - \underline{R}X$ is the boundary or borderline region of the rough set X. The lower and upper approximation regions, then, allow the distinction between certain and possible inclusion in a rough set.

The rough relational database model is an extension of the standard relational database model of Codd [1]. It captures all the essential features of the theory of rough sets including the notion of indiscernibility of elements through the use of equivalence classes and the idea of denoting an undefinable set by its lower and upper approximation regions. Full details of the rough relational database model are found in [7]. We review only a few relevant definitions here.

The attribute domains in this model are partitioned by equivalence relations designated by the database designer or user. Within each domain, a group of values that are considered indiscernible form an equivalence class. The query mechanism uses class equivalence rather than value equality in retrievals. A user may not know the particular attribute value, but might be able to think of a value that is equivalent to the value required. For example, if the query requests "COLOR = 'BLUE'", the result will contain all colors that are defined as equivalent to BLUE, such as CERULEAN, INDIGO, or AZURE, making the exact wording of a query less critical.

The rough relational database has several features in common with the ordinary relational database. Both models represent data as a set of *relations* containing *tuples*. The relations themselves are also sets. The tuples of a relation are its elements, and like the elements of sets in general, are unordered and nonduplicated. A tuple t_i takes the form $(d_{i1}, d_{i2}, ..., d_{im})$, where d_{ij} is a *domain value* of a particular *domain set* D_j. In the ordinary relational database, $d_{ij} \in D_j$. In the rough relational database, however, as in other non-first normal form extensions to the relational model [10], [11], $d_{ij} \subseteq D_j$, and although it is not required that d_{ij} be a singleton, $d_{ij} \neq \varnothing$. Let $P(D_i)$ denote the powerset(D_i) - $\varnothing$.

Definition. A *rough relation R* is a subset of the set cross product
$$P(D_1) \times P(D_2) \times \cdots \times P(D_m).$$

A rough tuple **t** is any member of R, which implies that it is also a member of $P(D_1) \times P(D_2) \times \cdots \times P(D_m)$. If t_i is some arbitrary tuple, then $t_i = (d_{i1}, d_{i2}, ..., d_{im})$ where $d_{ij} \subseteq D_j$.

Definition. Tuples $t_i = (d_{i1}, d_{i2}, ..., d_{im})$ and $t_k = (d_{k1}, d_{k2}, ..., d_{km})$ are *redundant* if
$$[d_{ij}] = [d_{kj}] \text{ for all } j = 1,..., m.$$

Tuples are sets of attributes, so this definition can be modified to define redundant sets of attribute values or sub-tuples:

Definition. Two sub-tuples $\mathbf{X} = (d_{i1}, d_{i2}, ..., d_{im})$ and $\mathbf{Y} = (d_{k1}, d_{k2}, ..., d_{km})$
are *redundant* if $[d_{ij}] = [d_{kj}]$ for all $j = 1, ..., m$.

Note that the attributes themselves are not ordered, but that an attribute component of X has a corresponding component in Y. This definition is used in defining functional dependencies of lower approximation tuples. Recall that the rough relational database is in non-first normal form; there are some attribute values which are sets. The following definition, which applies to upper approximation tuples, is also necessary. This definition captures redundancy between elements of attribute values that are sets.

Definition. Two sub-tuples $\mathbf{X} = (d_{i1}, d_{i2}, ..., d_{im})$ and $\mathbf{Y} = (d_{k1}, d_{k2}, ..., d_{km})$
are *roughly-redundant* if for some $[p] \subseteq [d_{ij}]$ and $[q] \subseteq [d_{kj}]$,
$[p] = [q]$ for all $j = 1, ..., m$.

3   Rough Functional Dependencies

A functional dependency can be defined as in [12] through the use of a universal database relation concept. Let $R = \{A_1, A_2, ..., A_n\}$ be a universal relation schema describing a database having n attributes. Let X and Y be subsets of R. A functional dependency between the attributes of X and Y is denoted by $X \rightarrow Y$. This dependency specifies the constraint that for any two tuples of an instance r of R, if they agree on the X attribute(s) they must agree on their Y attributes(s): if $t_1[X] = t_2[X]$, then it must be true that $t_1[Y] = t_2[Y]$. Tuples that violate the constraint cannot belong in the database.

Functional dependencies are data dependencies that are functional in the same sense as functions in mathematics. Therefore, if the functional dependency $X \rightarrow Y$

holds, then the values of X functionally determine the values of Y; equivalently, Y is functionally dependent on X. The functional dependencies are used to specify constraints on tuple values based on the semantics of the relation attributes. Functional dependencies must hold for all instances of the database on which it is defined. With these constraints incorporated into the design of the database schema, it is possible to restrict the tuples that comprise relations. These constraints aid in the maintenance of data integrity and prevention of update anomalies.

The database designer may specify functional dependencies on relation schemas. These are typically based on the primary key. However, there are usually many additional functional dependencies that will also hold. These dependencies can be inferred from those specified through the use of inference axioms.

The rough functional dependency [8] is based on the rough relational database model. The classical notion of functional dependency for relational databases does not naturally apply to the rough relational database, since all the "roughness" would be lost. We review rough functional dependencies for the rough relational database model here as they are needed for our definitions of normal forms in a later section.

Definition. A *rough functional dependency*, X→Y, for a relation schema R exists if for all instances T(R),

(1) for any two tuples t, t′ ∈ $\underline{R}$T,
    $redundant(t(X), t'(X)) \Rightarrow redundant(t(Y), t'(Y))$

(2) for any two tuples s, s′ ∈ $\overline{R}$ T,
    $roughly\text{-}redundant(s(X), s'(X)) \Rightarrow roughly\text{-}redundant(s(Y), s'(Y))$.

Y is roughly functional dependent on X, or X roughly functionally determines Y, whenever the above definition holds. This implies that constraints can be imposed on a rough relational database schema in a rough manner that will aid in integrity maintenance and the reduction of update anomalies without limiting the expressiveness of the inherent rough set concepts. The classical functional dependency for the standard relational database is a special case of the rough functional dependency; indiscernibility reduces to simple equality and part (2) of the definition is unused since all tuples in relations in the standard relational model belong to the lower approximation region of a similar rough model.

The first part of the definition of rough functional dependency compares with that of fuzzy functional dependencies discussed in [13], where adherence to Armstrong's axioms was proven. The results apply directly in the case of rough functional dependencies when only the lower approximation regions are considered. Given a set of rough functional dependencies, the complete set of rough functional dependencies can be derived using Armstrong's axioms as shown in [8]. The rough functional dependency, therefore, is an important formalism for design in the rough relational database. The next step is rough database normalization.

4   Rough Normal Forms

Normalization [1], [12] of relational databases is a process of evaluating the functional dependencies in a relation, and determining whether the dependencies meet certain conditions, which will minimize redundancy in the database and reduce the insertion, deletion, and update anomalies that could occur. These normal forms are based on the traditional definitions of key, superkey, candidate key, and prime attribute, as can be found in [12]. In general, a key is an attribute upon which all other attributes are functionally dependent, and a prime attribute is one that is part of a key.

During the normalization process, if a relation schema does not meet the conditions for a particular normal form, then steps are taken to decompose relations in order to meet the specified criteria. Although normal forms range from first normal form (1NF), a basic structure of the standard relational model, through fifth normal form (5NF), typically 3NF or Boyce-Codd normal form, a stricter version of 3NF, is used. Each normal form is more restrictive than the previous one. For example, a relation in 3NF is also in 2NF, but the opposite is not necessarily true. In non-first normal form extensions [10], [11] to the relational model, such as the rough relational model [7] discussed here, we need not concern ourselves with the 1NF restriction.

4.1 Rough Second Normal Form

A rough relation schema is in rough 2NF if every non prime attribute is fully functionally dependent on the key. In this rough relation, there will be no partial dependencies.

Definition. *Let F be the set of rough functional dependencies for schema R, and let K be a key of R. Then R is in rough 2NF if and only if none of the nonprime attributes is partially roughly dependent on K.*

Consider, for example, a rough relation schema R(A, B, C, D, E) having rough functional dependencies B→A, BC→D and BC→E. Here BC is the key, D and E are fully roughly functionally dependent on BC, and A is partially roughly functionally dependent on BC.

In order to normalize R so that our database schema is in rough 2NF, we must do the following:

1. For each partial key form a new rough relation containing the partial key and all of the attributes that are fully roughly functionally dependent on it.
2. Remove those nonprime attributes from the original rough relation that are in this new rough relation.

Performing this procedure on the relation schema R above yields the following database schema: R(B, C, D, E), S(B, A). This is now in rough 2NF since every attribute of R is fully roughly functionally dependent on the key AB and every attribute of S is fully roughly functionally dependent on the key B.

4.2 Rough Third Normal Form

A rough relation schema is in rough 3NF if every non prime attribute is fully functionally dependent on the key and there exist no transitive dependencies. In such a rough relation schema, there will be no dependencies on attributes other than the key.

Definition. *Let F be the set of rough functional dependencies for schema R, and let K be a key of R. Then R is in rough 3NF if whenever some nontrivial dependency G→H holds in R, then either (a) G is a superkey or (b) H is a prime attribute.*

Consider, for example, a rough relation schema R(B, C, G, H) having rough functional dependencies B→C, B→G, B→H, and also G→H. Here B is the key, but notice that H is dependent on G, and G is dependent on B. This is a transitive dependency that prevents rough schema R from being in rough 3NF. G is not a superkey, and H is not a prime attribute.

In order to normalize our schema so that it will meet the requirements for 3NF, perform the following:

1. For each transitive dependency form a new rough relation containing the non prime attribute that functionally determines the others in the dependency (this becomes the key) and all of the attributes that are roughly functionally dependent on it.
2. Remove those attributes from the original rough relation that are non prime attributes in this new rough relation.

In order to normalize R(B, C, G, H) in the example above so that it is in rough 3NF, a new rough relation schema is created: R(B, C, G), S(G, H). Notice that no transitive dependencies exist.

It is important that decomposition into rough third normal form also results in additional desirable properties, *rough lossless join* and *rough dependency preservation*. The rough lossless join property insures that the original relations can be recovered from their decompositions and that spurious tuples are not generated when the decomposed relations are joined. Such spurious tuples represent erroneous information that is not part of the database.

A rough dependency preserving decomposition insures that all rough functional dependencies that exist before the decomposition remain after the decomposition. If this property does not hold, such that rough dependencies cannot be represented by individual rough relations, inefficient and unnecessary join operations would be required in order for constraints based on the dependency to be checked.

We can insure lossless join decomposition that preserves dependencies if the following steps are taken:

1. For the set of functional dependencies F for rough relation schema R, find a minimal cover G, with no partial functional dependencies.
2. Eliminate from R any attributes that are not included in G and place them in a separate rough relation schema.
3. For each X, left hand side, of dependencies in G, create new rough relation schema in the decomposition with attributes $\{X \cup \{A_1\} \cup ... \cup \{A_k\}\}$, where $X \rightarrow A_1, ... X \rightarrow A_k$ are the rough functional dependencies in G with X as the left hand side.
4. If no relation schema in the decomposition contain a key of R, then create an additional rough relation schema that contains attributes that form a key of R.

Each relation schema in the decomposition will be in rough 3NF, and it can be shown that the lossless join and dependency preservation properties hold. We address these concepts further in a subsequent paper.

4.3 Rough Boyce Codd Normal Form

In terms of reducing redundancy, rough BCNF is the most desirable to achieve. It is more strict than rough 3NF since it eliminates condition (b) from the definition. Some decompositions result in "losing" the functional dependency and we must be careful not to decompose the schema in such a way as to not generate spurious tuples from a join operation.

Definition. *Let F be the set of rough functional dependencies for schema R, and let K be a key of R. Then R is in rough BCNF if R is in rough 3NF and for any nontrivial dependency G→H in F, G is a superkey.*

Although more restrictive normal forms have been defined for relational databases, a database design in BCNF is often considered "good" with respect to functional dependencies. For the rough relational database, rough 3NF or rough BCNF is usually sufficient.

5 Conclusion

Functional dependencies and normalization play a significant role in relational database design. The functional dependencies defined on relation schemas determine allowable values for all database instances. When database schema are normalized, the design has many desirable properties. Redundancy is reduced and anomalies from insert, delete, and update operations will be minimized.

In this paper we introduced rough normalization for the rough relational database model. The normal forms are based on rough functional dependencies. We defined rough second, rough third, and rough Boyce-Codd normal forms (2NF, 3NF, and BCNF), and explained how the rough relational database schema can be placed in these rough normal forms. This is important since although rough sets and the rough relational database model offer great benefits and allow for the management of various types of uncertainty, we still expect to develop good designs in this model. The formalisms for rough functional dependencies and rough relational database normalization developed here provide techniques to insure this is the case.

Acknowledgements. The authors would like to thank the Naval Research Laboratory's Base Program, Program Element No. 0602435N for sponsoring this research.

References

1. Codd, E.: A relational model of data for large shared data banks. Communications of the ACM. 13 (1970) 377-387
2. Bahar, O., Yazici, A.: Normalization and Lossless Join Decomposition of Similarity-Based Fuzzy Relational Databases. Int. Journal of Intelligent Systems, 19 (2004) 885-918
3. Pawlak, Z.: Rough Sets. Int. Journal of Man-Machine Studies. 21 (1984) 127-134
4. Pawlak, Z.: Rough Sets: Theoretical Aspects of Reasoning About Data. Kluwer Academic Publishers, Norwell, MA (1991)

5. Beaubouef, T., Petry, F.: Rough Querying of Crisp Data in Relational Databases. Proc. Third Int. Workshop on Rough Sets and Soft Computing (RSSC'94), San Jose, November (1994) 368-375
6. Srinivasan, P.: The importance of rough approximations for information retrieval. International Journal of Man-Machine Studies. 34 (1991) 657-671
7. Beaubouef, T. Petry, F., Buckles, B.: Extension of the Relational Database and its Algebra with Rough Set Techniques. Computational Intelligence. 11 (1995) 233-245
8. Beaubouef, T., Petry, F.: Rough Functional Dependencies. 2004 Multiconferences: Int. Conf. on Information and Knowledge Engineering (IKE'04). Las Vegas, June 21-24, (2004) 175-179
9. Beaubouef, T., Petry, F.: Fuzzy Rough Set Techniques for Uncertainty Processing in a Relational Database. Int. Journal of Intelligent Systems. 15 (2000) 389-424
10. Makinouchi, A.: A Consideration on normal form of not-necessarily normalized relation in the relational data model. Proc. Third Int.. Conf. on Very Large Databases (1977) 447-453
11. Roth, M., Korth, H., Batory, D.: SQL/NF: A query language for non-1NF databases. Information Systems. 12 (1987) 99-114
12. Elmasri, R., Navathe, S.: Fundamentals of Database Systems. Addison Wesley (2004)
13. Shenoi, S., Melton, A., Fan, L.: Functional Dependencies and Normal Forms in the Fuzzy Relational Database Model. Information Sciences. 60 (1992) 1-28

Probabilistic Rough Sets

Wojciech Ziarko

Computer Science Department,
University of Regina,
Regina, Saskatchewan, S4S 0A2, Canada

Abstract. The article introduces the basic ideas and investigates the probabilistic version of rough set theory. It relies on both classification knowledge and probabilistic knowledge in analysis of rules and attributes. One-way and two-way inter-set dependency measures are proposed and adopted to probabilistic rule evaluation. A probabilistic dependency measure for attributes is also proposed and demonstrated to have the monotonicity property. This property makes it possible for the measure to be used to optimize and evaluate attribute based-representation through computation of attribute reduct, core and significance factors.

1 Introduction

The rough set theory introduced by Pawlak [5] is concerned with finite universes and finite set cardinality-based evaluative measures. It lays out the foundations of the inspiring idea of classification knowledge, in the form of the approximation space, and of the notion of rough set and its approximations. Typical application scenario involves a partially known universe, represented by a set of samples, based on which rough set-based analysis is performed. The results are then considered to apply to the whole universe. This kind of approach is common in probabilistic reasoning, with the probability function used to represent relations among sets (events). The probability function values can be estimated from different sources, including assumed distribution functions and set frequencies in a sample. The set frequency estimators of probability theory correspond to set cardinality-based evaluative measures of rough set theory. This correspondence was observed quite early in the development of rough set methodology, leading to a succession of probabilistic generalizations [5-9,13-15] of the original rough set theory. The rough set theory methodologies provide additional instruments, originally not present in the probability theory, to conduct deeper analysis of experimental data and to construct adaptive models of the relations existing in the universe. The probability theory, on the other hand, contributes the basic notion of probability and its estimation, distribution evaluative measures, the notion of probabilistic independence and Bayes's equations, which together help to enhance the rough set theory to make it more applicable to real-life problems.

In what follows, the probabilistic version of rough set theory is presented and investigated, partially based on prior results of related research [7][13][14][9]. In the presentation, clear distinction is being made between classification knowledge

D. Ślęzak et al. (Eds.): RSFDGrC 2005, LNAI 3641, pp. 283–293, 2005.

and probabilistic knowledge. These two kinds of knowledge are defined in section 2. The probabilistic notion of event independence is generalized in section 3, to introduce one-way and two-way measures of set dependencies. One of the measures, the absolute certainty gain, is adopted as a probabilistic rule evaluative parameter. The probabilistic rules, their evaluation and their computation are discussed in section 4. In section 5, computation of rules satisfying predefined certainty requirements is discussed. Elements of the Bayesian rough set model [7] are introduced in section 6, as a prerequisite to the investigation of probabilistic attribute dependencies in section 8. In section 9, the monotonicity of the introduced probabilistic attribute dependency measure, called λ-*dependency*, is discussed. This leads to the definition of probabilistic reduct, core and significance factors for attributes. The characterization of unrelated, or independent attributes is also provided. Due to space restrictions, the proofs of theorems are omitted.

2   Classification and Probabilistic Knowledge

The rough set approaches are developed within the context of a universe of objects of interest U such as, for example, the collection of patients, sounds, web pages etc. We will assume here that the universe is infinite in general, but that we have access to a finite sample $S \subseteq U$ expressed by accumulated observations about objects in S. The sample represents available information about the universe U. We will say that a subset $X \subseteq U$ *occurred* if $X \cap S \neq \emptyset$, where $X \cap S$ is a *set of occurrences* of X.

We will also assume the knowledge of an equivalence relation, called the *indiscernibility relation* on U[5], $IND \subseteq U \otimes U$ with finite number of equivalence classes called *elementary sets*. The pair (U, IND) is called the *approximation space*. The collection of elementary sets will be denoted by IND^*. The ability to form elementary sets reflects our *classification knowledge* about the universe U. In the context of this article, the classification knowledge means that each elementary set E is assigned a *description*, denoted as *des(E)*, which specifies a criterion distinguishing all elements of E from its complement. That is, $E = \{e \in U : des(e) = des(E)\}$. Any subset $X \subseteq U$ expressible as a union of some elementary sets is said to be *definable*. Otherwise, the set X is *undefinable*, or *rough*[5]. Any non-elementary definable set will be called a *composed set*. The classification knowledge is said to be *trivial* (and useless), if there is only one elementary set, corresponding to the whole universe U. The classification knowledge, in the framework of rough set theory, is normally used in the analysis of a *target set* $X \subseteq U$. The target set is usually undefinable. Typical objective of the rough-set analysis is to form an approximate definition of the target set in terms of some definable sets.

In the framework of the variable precision rough set model (VPRSM)[14], the classification knowledge is assumed to be supplemented with the *probabilistic knowledge*. It is assumed that all subsets $X \subseteq U$ under consideration in this article are measurable by a probabilistic measure function P with $0 < P(X) <$

1. That is, they are likely to occur but their occurrence is not certain. The probabilistic knowledge consists of three parts:

- For each equivalence class E of the relation IND, it is assumed that its probabilistic measure $P(E)$ is known;
- We assume that the conditional probability $P(X|E)$ of X, for each elementary set E, is also known;
- The *prior probability* $P(X)$ of the target set X is known.

All these probabilities can be estimated based on data in a standard way by taking ratios of cardinalities of sample data.

3   Probabilistic Dependencies Between Sets

In the presence of probabilistic knowledge, it is possible to evaluate the degree of dependencies between measurable subsets of the universe U. This is particularly of interest in context of evaluation of rules learned from data [12]. In what follows, we propose two kinds of measures to evaluate the degree of connection or dependency between any two sets. The measures can be seen as generalizations of the well-known notion of probabilistic independence of random events.

The first, *one-way dependency* measure is concerned with quantifying the degree of the one-way relation between sets, denoted as $Y \Rightarrow X$, where X and Y are arbitrary measurable subsets of U. For the one-way dependency measure, the use of function called *absolute certainty gain* (*gabs*), is proposed:

$$gabs(X|Y) = |P(X|Y) - P(X)|, \tag{1}$$

where $| * |$ denotes absolute value function. The one-way dependency represents the degree of change of the certainty of prediction of X as a result of the occurrence of the set Y. In an approximation space, if the set Y is definable then absolute certainty gain can be computed directly from the available probabilistic knowledge according to the following:

Proposition 1. *If Y is definable in the approximation space (U, IND), then the absolute certainty gain between sets X and Y is given by:*

$$gabs(X|Y) = \frac{|\sum_{E \subseteq Y} P(E)P(X|E) - P(X)\sum_{E \subseteq Y} P(E)|}{\sum_{E \subseteq Y} P(E)} \tag{2}$$

The values of the one-way dependency fall in the range $0 \leq gabs(X|Y) \leq max(P(\neg X), P(X)) < 1$. In addition, let us note that if sets X and Y are independent in probabilistic sense, that is if $P(X \cap Y) = P(X)P(Y)$ then $gabs(X|Y) = 0$. We may also note that $gabs(U|Y) = 0$ and $gabs(\phi|Y) = 0$, for any measurable subset Y such that $P(Y) > 0$.

The second, *two-way dependency* measure is concerned with measuring the degree of the two-way connection between sets, represented by $Y \Leftrightarrow X$, where X and Y are arbitrary measurable subsets. For the two-way measure, the function *dabs*, called *absolute dependency gain*, is suggested:

$$dabs(X, Y) = |P(X \cap Y) - P(X)P(Y)|. \tag{3}$$

The absolute dependency gain reflects the degree of probabilistic dependency between sets by quantifying the amount of deviation of $P(X \cap Y)$ from probabilistic independence between sets X and Y, as expressed by the product $P(X)P(Y)$. Similarly, $|P(\neg X \cap Y) - P(\neg X)P(Y)|$ is a degree of deviation of the $\neg X$ from total independence with Y. Since $P(\neg X \cap Y) - P(\neg X)P(Y) = -(P(X \cap Y) - P(X)P(Y))$, both target set X and its complement $\neg X$ are dependent in the same degree with any measurable set Y.

As in the case of one-way dependency, if the set Y is definable then the absolute dependency gain can be computed directly from the available probabilistic knowledge, according to the following:

Proposition 2. *If Y is definable in the approximation space (U, IND), then the absolute dependency gain between sets X and Y is given by:*

$$dabs(X, Y) = |\sum_{E \subseteq Y} P(E)P(X|E) - P(X) \sum_{E \subseteq Y} P(E)| \tag{4}$$

The one-way and two-way dependencies are connected by $dabs(X, Y) = P(Y)gabs(X|Y)$. It follows that the values of the two-way dependency fall in the range $0 \leq dabs(X, Y) \leq P(Y)max(P(\neg X), P(X)) < P(Y) < 1$. Also $0 \leq dabs(X, Y) \leq P(X)max(P(\neg Y), P(Y)) < P(X) < 1$ i.e. $0 \leq dabs(X, Y) < min(P(X), P(Y))$. In addition, let us note that if sets X and Y are independent in probabilistic sense, that is if $P(X \cap Y) = P(X)P(Y)$ then $dabs(X, Y) = 0$. We may also note that $dabs(U, Y) = 0$ and $dabs(\phi|Y) = 0$, for any arbitrary subset Y such that $P(Y) > 0$.

4   Probabilistic Rules

The inter-sets dependency measures introduced in previous section can be used to evaluate the quality of probabilistic rules [14][12]. In the context of probabilistic approach to rough set theory, probabilistic rules are formal linguistic expressions representing relationships between subsets of the universe U. For any definable subset Y and an arbitrary subset X of the universe U, the *probabilistic rule* is a statement $des(Y) \rightarrow s(X)$, denoted shortly by $r_{X|Y}$, where $s(X)$ is a string of characters used to refer the set X and $des(Y)$ is a description of the set Y. The set Y is referred to as *rule support set*. As opposed to the description of a set, $s(X)$ is just a *reference* to a possibly undefinable set, whose description might be unknown. Since rules of this kind are normally used to determine, or to guess, the membership of an object in the set X based on knowing that it belongs to the definable set Y, for obvious reason it does not make much sense dealing with rules in which X is definable. Consequently, we will assume that the conclusion part $s(X)$ of the rule $r_{X|Y}$ corresponds to an undefinable set X.

Traditionally, the probabilistic rules are assigned two probabilistic parameters characterizing the relation between sets X and Y:

- The rule $r_{X|Y}$ *certainty* parameter defined as the conditional probability $cert(r_{X|Y}) = P(X|Y)$;
- The rule $r_{X|Y}$ *generality* (also called *support*) parameter defined as the probability $gen(r_{X|Y}) = P(Y)$;

Certainty and generality parameters can be equivalently replaced by certainty and *strength* measures, where the strength is defined as $str(r_{X|Y}) = P(X \cap Y)$. However, rule certainty and generality, or the certainty and strength, do not completely capture the intuitive perception of rule quality. For example, a rule with high certainty $P(X|Y)$ may not be very useful if the prior probability of X is also high. On the other hand, if the prior probability of X is low, a high certainty rule will represent a significant increase in the ability to predict X. Intuitively, such a rule will be very valuable.

To properly represent the degree of *certainty increase* attributed to a probabilistic rule $r_{X|Y}$, relative to the prior probability $P(Y)$, the use of the absolute certainty gain parameter $gabs(r_{X|Y}) = gabs(X|Y)$ is proposed. The absolute certainty gain represents the degree of increase of the certainty of prediction of X, as a result of the occurrence of the set Y. As the absolute certainty gain cannot be derived from certainty and generality parameters, we propose that probabilistic rules be evaluated in terms of the following three parameters: generality (or strength), certainty and certainty gain instead of generality and certainty only.

Any elementary set $E \in IND^*$ corresponds to an *elementary rule* $des(E) \rightarrow s(X)$. The strength, certainty and the absolute certainty gain of elementary rules can be simply obtained from the available probabilistic knowledge. It was shown in the Proposition 1 that the absolute certainty gain can be computed from the probabilities associated with the elementary sets. The following Proposition 3 demonstrates that strength and certainty of any probabilistic rule $des(Y) \rightarrow s(X)$ can also be computed in similar way.

Proposition 3. *The strength, certainty and absolute certainty gain of the rule* $r = des(Y) \rightarrow s(X)$ *are respectively given by* $str(r_{X|Y}) = P(Y) = \sum_{E \subseteq Y} P(E)$ *and* $cert(r_{X|Y}) = P(X|Y) = \frac{\sum_{E \subseteq Y} P(E)P(X|E)}{\sum_{E \subseteq Y} P(E)}.$

The practical implication from the Propositions 1 and 3 is that once the basic probabilistic knowledge is estimated from data, there is no need to refer to the data set again to compute any kind of probabilistic rules and attribute dependencies.

5   Probabilistic Approximation Regions

In applications related to data mining and machine learning, a common objective is finding rules that meet predefined level of quality. We show in this section that rules computed within the context of VPRSM have the quality level in the form of the certainty gain level requirement imposed through settings of model parameters. In the VPRSM, the probabilistic knowledge represented by the probability estimates associated with elementary sets is used to construct generalized rough approximations of the target subset $X \subseteq U$. The defining criteria are expressed here in terms of conditional probabilities and of the prior probability $P(X)$ of the target set X. Two *certainty control* criteria parameters are used to control degree of required certainty gain in the lower approximations of the set X or its complement $\neg X$.

The first parameter, referred to as the *lower limit* l, satisfying the constraint $0 \le l < P(X) < 1$, represents the highest acceptable degree of the conditional probability $P(X|E)$ to include the elementary set E in the negative region of the set X, i.e. in the positive region of its complement $\neg X$.

The second parameter, referred to as the *upper limit* u, satisfying the constraint $0 < P(X) < u \le 1$, defines the *positive region* of the set X. The upper limit reflects the least acceptable degree of the conditional probability $P(X|E)$ to include the elementary set E in the positive region.

The VPRSM is called *symmetric* if $l = 1 - u$ [13][14]. In this case, with the precision control parameter denoted as $\beta = u = 1 - l$, the *negative* and *positive* regions of the set X, are defined respectively by $NEG_\beta(X) = \cup\{E : P(\neg X|E) \ge \beta\}$ and $POS_\beta(X) = \cup\{E : P(X|E) \ge \beta\}$. Because $\beta > P(X)$, then both positive and negative regions can be expressed in terms of absolute certainty gain: $NEG_\beta(X) = \cup\{E : gabs(\neg X|E) \ge \beta - P(X)\}$ and $POS_\beta(X) = \cup\{E : gabs(X|E) \ge \beta - P(X)\}$. Consequently, we can define the positive region $POS(X, \neg X) = NEG(X) \cup POS(X)$ of the classification $(X, \neg X)$ by a single formula as $POS_\beta(X, \neg X) = \cup\{E : gabs(X|E) \ge \beta - P(X)\}$

Clearly, the approximation regions for the *asymmetric* VPRSM [14] can be also expressed in terms of the absolute gain function. The positive region of the classification $(X, \neg X)$ represents the area of desired absolute certainty gain, as expressed by the parameter β. Based on the positive region, probabilistic rules can be computed using any lower approximation-based techniques [8][2][15]. All these rules will satisfy the imposed minimum absolute certainty gain requirement $\beta - P(X)$.

The boundary area is a definable subset of U where the minimum certainty gain requirement is not satisfied, that is: $BND_\beta(X, \neg X) = \cup\{E : gabs(X|E) < \beta - P(X)\}$ No probabilistic rule computed from $BND(X, \neg X)$ will meet the minimum absolute certainty gain threshold of $\beta - P(X)$.

The definable area of the universe U characterized by the total lack of relationship to the target set $X \subseteq U$ was identified in [14] as the *absolute boundary* region of the set X. In the absolute boundary region, every elementary set E is probabilistically independent from the set X, i.e. $P(X \cap E) = P(X)P(E)$. The boundary area can be expressed by using of the absolute dependency gain function as the criterion: $BND^*(X, \neg X) = \cup\{E : dabs(X|E) = 0\}$.

The area of the universe characterized by at least some probabilistic connection with the target set X is called the *absolute positive region* of the classification $(X, \neg X)$. It can be expressed as $POS^*(X, \neg X) = \cup\{E : dabs(X|E) > 0\}$. Because $dabs(X|E) > 0$ is equivalent to $P(X|E) > P(X)$ or $P(X|E) < P(X)$, the *absolute positive region of the classification* $(X, \neg X)$ can be broken down into *the*

absolute positive region of the set X, $POS^*(X) = \cup\{E : P(X|E) > P(X)\}$ and
the absolute negative region of the set X, $NEG^*(X) = \cup\{E : P(X|E) < P(X)\}$.

The absolute approximation regions form the basis of the Bayesian Rough Set Model investigated in [7]. They are also useful in the analysis of probabilistic dependencies between attributes, as demonstrated in the following sections.

6 Elementary, Composed and Binary Attributes

In many applications, the information about objects is expressed in terms of values of observations or measurements referred to as *features*. For the purpose of rough set-based analysis, the feature values are typically mapped into finite-valued numeric or symbolic domains to form composite mappings referred to as *attributes*. A common kind of mapping is dividing the range of values of a feature into a number of suitably chosen subranges via a discretisation procedure. Formally, an attribute a is a function $a : U \rightarrow a(U) \subseteq V_a$, where V_a is a finite set of values called the *domain* of the attribute a. The size of the domain of an attribute a, denoted as $com(a) = card(V_a)$, will be called a *theoretical complexity* of the attribute. The theoretical complexity reflects the maximum number of values an attribute can take. Each attribute defines a classifications of the universe U into classes corresponding to different values of the attribute. That is, each attribute value $v \in a(U)$, corresponds the set of objects $E_v^a = a^{-1}(v) = \{e \in U : a(e) = v\}$. The classes E_v^a, referred to as a-*elementary sets*, form a partition of U. The equivalence relation corresponding to this partition will be denoted as IND_a. We will divide the attributes into two categories:

- The initial, given collection of attributes A, elements of which $a \in A$ are referred to as *elementary attributes*;
- The *composed attributes*, which are formed by taking combinations of some elementary attributes.

The values of a composed attribute are combinations of values of component elementary attributes. Each composed attribute is a subset of A. For proper reference between an elementary attribute and its value, we will assume that composed attributes are ordered. For the sake of consistency, we will also treat elementary attributes a as single-element subsets of A, $\{a\} \subseteq A$, and the empty subset of A, $\{\}$ will be interpreted as a *trivial attribute*, i.e. with only one value corresponding to the whole universe U. In the context of this assumption, both elementary and composed attributes C will be perceived in two ways: as subsets $C \subseteq A$ and also as mappings $C : U \rightarrow C(U) \subseteq \otimes_{a \in C} V_a$, where $\otimes$ denotes Cartesian product operator of all domains of attributes in C, the domain of C. The theoretical complexity of a composed attribute is a product of theoretical complexities of all its elementary attribute domains, $com(C) = \prod_{a \in C} com(a)$. The theoretical complexity of a trivial attribute is one. In practical applications, the theoretical complexity estimates our ability to learn from example observations, or the *learnability* of a classification represented by an attribute. High theoretical complexity attributes lead to non-learnable classifications.

The lowest complexity, non-trivial attributes are binary-valued attributes. Every non-trivial and non-binary attribute can be replaced equivalently by a collection of binary attributes. The binary attributes are defined for each value v of the attribute a, by creating a new attribute a_v such that $a_v(e) = 1$ if $a(e) = v$ and $a_v(e) = 0$ if $a(v) \neq v$.

The composed attribute B_a consisting of the binary attributes is equivalent to the attribute a because it generates the same classification of U as the attribute a, that is, $IND_{B_a} = IND_a$. Using binary elementary attributes has a number of advantages, including the consistency of representation, ease of implementation and increased generality of minimal length rules computed by applying the idea of rough set theory value reduct [5]. Consequently, from now on in this article, we will assume that all elementary attributes are binary. The composed attributes are vectors of binary attributes. The theoretical complexity of a composed attribute containing n binary attributes can be simply calculated as 2^n. Therefore, the number of bits n can be used as an alternative complexity measure.

7 Probabilistic Dependencies Between Attributes

The presence of non-trivial classification of the universe may improve the degree of the decision certainty. We will assume in this section that the classification IND_C^* corresponds to a composed, in general, attribute $C \subseteq A$. The degree of improvement can be quantified using the expected value $egabs(X|C)$ of the absolute gain functions assigned elementary rules $r_{X|E}$, $E \in IND_C^*$:

$$egabs(X|C) = \sum_{E \in IND_C^*} P(E)gabs(r_{X|E}) \qquad (5)$$

The *expected gain function* defined by (5) measures the average degree of increase of the occurrence probability of X or $\neg X$, relative to its prior probability $P(X)$, as a result of presence of the classification knowledge, as represented by equivalence classes of the indiscernibility relation IND_C^* and the associated probabilities. The notion of the expected gain function stems from the idea of the *relative gain* function reported in [14].

The expected gain function $egabs$ can also be seen as the measure of the degree of probabilistic dependency between classification represented by the relation IND and the partition of the universe corresponding to the sets X and $\neg X$. This follows from the following proposition:

Proposition 4. *The expected gain function can be expressed as*

$$egabs(X|C) = \sum_{E \in IND_C^*} |P(X \cap E) - P(X)P(E)| = \sum_{E \in IND_C^*} dabs(X, E) \quad (6)$$

The measure can be also expressed in the form:

$$egabs(X|C) = P(X) \sum_{E \in IND_C^*} gabs(E|X). \qquad (7)$$

For the purpose of normalization of the expected gain function, the following Proposition 5 is useful.

Proposition 5. *The expected gain falls in the range* $0 \leq egabs(X|C) \leq 0.5$.

The target set X and the attribute C are *independent* if $egabs(X|C) = 0$. The independence can occur only if $P(X \cap E) = P(X)P(E)$, for all elementary sets $E \in IND_C^*$. That is, for the independence between X, or $\neg X$, and the partition IND_C^* to hold, the set X, or $\neg X$, must be independent with each element of the partition IND_C^*. Conversely, the strongest dependency occurs when X is definable and when $P(X) = 0.5$. This would suggest the use of the λ-dependency function $0 \leq \lambda(X|C) \leq 1$, defined by:

$$\lambda(X|C) = \frac{egabs(X|C)}{2P(X)(1 - P(X))}, \tag{8}$$

as a normalized measure of dependency between attribute C and the target classification $(X, \neg X)$. The function $\lambda(X|C) = 1$ only if X is definable in the approximation space (U, IND_C), that is if the dependency is deterministic (functional). In line with our initial assumption of $0 < P(X) < 1$, $\lambda(X|C)$ is undefined for $X = \phi$ and for $X = U$.

Finally, because elementary attributes are binary, the λ-dependency function can be used to evaluate the degree of probabilistic dependency between any composed attribute $C \subseteq A$ and an elementary attribute $a \in A$. Consequently, the dependency between elementary attribute a and composed attribute C will be denoted as $\lambda(a|C)$. To be consistent with this notation, we will use symbol d to denote the *decision attribute* representing the target classification $(X, \neg X)$.

8   Optimization and Evaluation of Attributes

One of the main advantages of rough set methodology is the ability to perform reduction of features or attributes used to represent objects. The application idea of *reduct*, introduced by Pawlak [5] allows for optimization of representation of classification knowledge by providing a systematic technique for removal of redundant attributes. It turns out that the idea of reduct is also applicable to the optimization of probabilistic knowledge representation, in particular with respect to the representation of the probabilistic dependency between a composed attribute and a binary attribute. The following theorem, based on [7], demonstrates that the probabilistic dependency measure between attributes is *monotonic*, which means that expanding a composed attribute $C \subset A$ by extra bits would never result in the decrease of dependency $\lambda(d|C)$ with the decision attribute d corresponding to the partition $(X, \neg X)$ of the universe U.

Theorem 1. *λ-dependency is monotonic, that is, for any composed attribute $C \subset A$ and an elementary attribute $a \in A$ the relation $\lambda(d|C) \leq \lambda(d|C \cup \{a\})$ holds.*

As a consequence of the Theorem 1, the notion of the *probabilistic reduct* of attributes $RED \subseteq C$ can be defined as a minimal subset of attributes preserving the dependency with the decision attribute d. That is, the reduct satisfies the following two properties:

- $\lambda(d|RED) = \lambda(d|C)$;
- for any attribute $a \in RED$: $\lambda(d|RED - \{a\}) < \lambda(d|RED)$.

The probabilistic reducts can be computed using any methods available for reduct computation in the framework of the original rough set approach. The reduct provides a method for computing fundamental factors in a probabilistic relationship.

An important question is to characterize attributes that are *neutral* with respect to the relation between attribute C and d. Such attributes will have no effect on dependency with the decision attribute and will be always eliminated from any reduct. The following Theorem 2 provides the answer to this question.

Theorem 2. *If an attribute a is independent with $C \cup \{d\}$ i.e. if $\lambda(a|C \cup \{d\}) = 0$, then $\lambda(d|C \cup \{a\}) = \lambda(d|C)$.*

The above theorem suggests that for a new attribute to possibly contribute to the increase of dependency $\lambda(C|d)$, it should be correlated either with d or C. We also note that the independence of the attribute a with $C \cup \{d\}$ is a two-way property, that is, $\lambda(C \cup \{d\}|a) = 0$ if and only if $\lambda(a|C \cup \{d\}) = 0$.

Elementary and composed attributes appearing in a reduct can be evaluated with respect to their contribution to the dependency with the target attribute by adopting the notion of a *significance factor*. The significance factor $sig_{RED}(B)$ of an attribute $B \subseteq A$ represents the relative decrease of the dependency $\lambda(d|RED)$ due to removal of B from the reduct:

$$sig_{RED}(B) = \frac{\lambda(d|RED) - \lambda(d|RED - B)}{\lambda(d|RED)} \qquad (9)$$

Finally, as in the original rough set approach, one can define the *core* set of elementary attributes as the ones which form the intersection of all reducts of C, if the intersection is not empty. After [5], any core attribute a satisfies the inequality $\lambda(d|C) > \lambda(d|C - \{a\})$, which leads to a simple method of core computation.

9   Conclusion

The article is an attempt to introduce a comprehensive probabilistic version of rough set theory by integrating ideas from Pawlak's classical rough set model, elements of probability theory with its notion of probabilistic independence, the variable precision model of rough sets and the Bayesian model. The novel aspects of the approach include the introduction of measures of inter-set dependencies, based on the notion of absolute certainty gain and probabilistic dependence, the adaptation of the absolute certainty gain to probabilistic rule evaluation, the introduction of the notion of a composed attribute and of the attribute dependency measure based on the idea of expected gain function and its application to attribute optimization and evaluation. The presented ideas seem to connect well with the general methodology of rough sets, hopefully leading to new applications and better understanding of fundamental issues of learning from data.

References

1. Beynon, M. The elucidation of an iterative procedure to β-reduct selection in the variable precision rough set model. Proc. RSCTC'2004, LNAI 1711, 412-417.
2. Grzymala-Busse, J. LERS-A System for learning from examples based on rough sets. Intelligent Decision Support, Kluwer, 1991, 3-18.
3. Greco, S. Matarazzo, B. Slowinski, R. Stefanowski, J. Variable consistency model of dominance-based rough set approach. Proc. RSCTC'2000, LNAI 2005, 170-179.
4. Murai, T. Sanada, M. Kudo, M. A note on Ziarko's variable precision rough set model in non-monotonic reasoning. Proc. RSCTC'2004, LNAI 1711, 103-108.
5. Pawlak, Z. Rough sets - Theoretical Aspects of Reasoning About Data. Kluwer, 1991.
6. Mieszkowicz, A. Rolka, L. Remarks on approximation quality in variable precision rough set model. Proc. RSCTC'2004, LNAI 1711, 402-411.
7. Slezak, D., Ziarko, W. Investigation of the Bayesian rough set model. Intl. Journal of Approximate Reasoning, vol. 40(1-2), 2005, 81-91.
8. Skowron, A. Rauszer C. The discernibility matrices and functions in information systems. ICS Report 1/91, Warsaw University of Technology, 1991.
9. Wong, M. Ziarko, W. Comparison of the probabilistic approximate classification and the fuzzy set model. Intl. Journal for Fuzzy Sets and Systems, vol. 21, 1986, 357-362.
10. Yao, Y., Wong, M. A decision theoretic framework for approximating concepts. Intl. Journal of Man-Machine Studies, 37, 1992, 793-809.
11. Yao, Y. Probabilistic approaches to rough sets. Expert Systems, vol. 20(5), 2003, 287-291.
12. Yao, Y. Zhong, N. An analysis of quantitative measures associated with rules. Proc. PAKDD'99, LNAI 1574, 479-488.
13. Ziarko, W. Variable precision rough sets model. Journal of Computer and Systems Sciences, vol. 46(1), 1993, 39-59.
14. Ziarko, W. Set approximation quality measures in the variable precision rough set model. Soft Computing Systems, Management and Applications, IOS Press, 2001, 442-452.
15. Ziarko, W. Shan, N. A method for computing all maximally general rules in attribute-value systems. Computational Intelligence, vol. 12(2), 1996, 223-234.

Variable Precision Bayesian Rough Set Model and Its Application to Human Evaluation Data

Tatsuo Nishino, Mitsuo Nagamachi, and Hideo Tanaka

Department of *Kansei* Information,
Faculty of Human and Social Environments,
Hiroshima International University
555-36 Kurose, Higashihiroshima, Hiroshima 724-0695, Japan
{t-nishi, m-nagama, h-tanaka}@he.hirokoku-u.ac.jp

Abstract. This paper focuses on a rough set method to analyze human evaluation data with much ambiguity such as sensory and feeling data. In order to handle totally ambiguous and probabilistic human evaluation data, we propose a probabilistic approximation based on information gains of equivalent classes. Furthermore, we propose a two-stage method to simply extract uncertain $if - then$ rules using decision functions of approximate regions. Finally, we applied the proposed method to practical human sensory evaluation data and examined the effectiveness of the proposed method. The result shown that our proposed rough set method is more applicable to human evaluation data.

1 Introduction

The original rough sets approach is restricted to the case where there exist the fully correct and certain classifications derived from the decision table. Unfortunately, we have many cases where there is no lower approximation of a classification. Furthermore, if there are only very few elements of lower approximation of some decision set, the $if - then$ rules extracted from these few elements might be unreliable. Thus, it is necessary to handle a huge decision table. Consequently, combining rough sets approaches and probability concept, many research papers [1,2,3,4,5] have been published.

On the other hand, we have applied rough set methods to *Kansei* Engineering (KE) problems [7]. One of the core technologies in KE is to identify the relational rules between design elements of products and human evaluation data such as sensory and feeling evaluation [8]. Recently, it has been shown that rough set approaches are very effective to extract human decision rules in KE [9].

Accordingly, the aim of this paper is to develop a rough set method suitable for analyzing human evaluation data with much ambiguity. If one considers the properties of the human evaluation data such as ambiguity and non-linearity, we have to construct a rough set method that can treat the case where there is no lower approximation of a classification, and the case where the decision class occurs with different prior probability. Thus, our approach inspired by VPBRS-models [3,4,5] is based on a new information gain to equivalent classes suitable

D. Ślęzak et al. (Eds.): RSFDGrC 2005, LNAI 3641, pp. 294–303, 2005.
© Springer-Verlag Berlin Heidelberg 2005

for handling totally ambiguous and probabilistic properties of human evaluation data. Moreover, we propose a two-stage method for simply extracting uncertain decision rules from probabilistic decision table using decision functions of approximated classes. We applied our method to extract uncertain decision rules from the data obtained by human sensory evaluation experiment in practical coffee manufacturing problem.

The rest of the paper is organized as follows: preliminaries and notations to describe a decision table for human evaluation data are introduced in Section 2; in Section 3, a concept of information gain and probabilistic approximations to properly handle human evaluation data is introduced; in Section 4, we introduce a two-stage method to extract uncertain decision rules using decision functions from an approximated decision table; we show an application of our method to practical human evaluation data in Section 5; finally, Section 6 is the conclusions and our future work.

2   Preliminaries and Notations

Let us start with a simple example of human evaluation data with respect to products shown in Table 1 where a set of products, a set of design attributes (conditional attributes) of products and human evaluation (decision attribute) to product are denoted as $E = \{E_1, E_2, E_3, E_4\}$, $A = \{a_1, a_2, a_3\}$ and d.

Table 1. An example of human evaluation data

Product (E)	Event (U)	a_1	a_2	a_3	Evaluation (d)
	x_{11}	0	1	1	0
	x_{21}	0	1	1	0
E_1	x_{31}	0	1	1	0
	x_{41}	0	1	1	1
	x_{51}	0	1	1	1
	x_{12}	1	0	1	1
	x_{22}	1	0	1	1
E_2	x_{32}	1	0	1	1
	x_{42}	1	0	1	0
	x_{52}	1	0	1	2
	x_{13}	0	1	0	1
	x_{23}	0	1	0	2
E_3	x_{33}	0	1	0	2
	x_{43}	0	1	0	2
	x_{53}	0	1	0	2
	x_{14}	1	1	1	0
	x_{24}	1	1	1	0
E_4	x_{34}	1	1	1	0
	x_{44}	1	1	1	0
	x_{54}	1	1	1	1

An evaluation event of $j - th$ evaluator to $i - th$ product is denoted as x_{ji}. There are four products and five human evaluators. E_i are equivalent classes because the same product has the same attribute values.

Any attribute of A has a domain of its design attribute values, $V_{a1} = \{0, 1\}$, $V_{a2} = \{0, 1\}$ and $V_{a3} = \{0, 1\}$, which may be color, shape and size of products. Human evaluation d has also a domain of its evaluation values $V_d = \{0, 1, 2\}$, which may be "very good ", "good " and " no good". A set of decision classes is $D = \{D_0, D_1, D_2\}$ where $D_j = \{x \mid d(x) = j\}$, $j = 0, 1, 2$.

It should be noted that there is no lower approximation to any decision class, and that decision classes of human evaluation are assumed to occur with different prior probability. Thus, we have to define an approximate lower approximation of decision class by introducing the information gain to positive region. Table 1 will be used to illustrate our approach with a numerical example.

Formally, we have $U = \{x_{11}, \ldots, x_{ji}, \ldots, x_{mn}\}$ for the universe denoted as a set of events of n-evaluators to m-products, $A = \{a_1, \ldots, a_k, \ldots, a_p\}$ for p-conditional attributes, $U/A = \{E_1, \ldots, E_i, \ldots, E_m\}$ for m-products, and $D = \{D_1, \ldots, D_j, \ldots, D_r\}$ for r-decision classes where $D_j = \{x \mid d(x) = j\}$. Any conditional attribute a_k is a mapping function $a_k(x) = v_k$ and has a set of its values V_{ak}. A decision attribute d is a mapping function $d(x) = v_d$ and has V_d.

These evaluation data include at least two important probabilistic aspects. One is the probability of decisions dependent on the conditional attributes of products and the other is the prior probability of decision. Such probabilities are experientially acceptable in human evaluation data. These probabilities are well known as the conditional and prior probability, respectively. According to many literatures such as [2,3,4,5,6], the following probabilities can be defined:

$$P(D_j|E_i) = \frac{card(D_j \cap E_i)}{card(E_i)} . \qquad (\text{the conditional probability})$$

$$P(D_j) = \frac{card(D_j)}{card(U)} . \qquad (\text{the prior probability})$$

In the example of Table 1, we have Table 2.

Table 2. The prior and conditional probabilities

$P(D_0)=0.40$	$P(D_0\mid E_1)=0.6$	$P(D_0\mid E_2)=0.2$	$P(D_0\mid E_3)=0.0$	$P(D_0\mid E_4)=0.8$
$P(D_1)=0.35$	$P(D_1\mid E_1)=0.4$	$P(D_1\mid E_2)=0.6$	$P(D_1\mid E_3)=0.2$	$P(D_1\mid E_4)=0.2$
$P(D_2)=0.25$	$P(D_2\mid E_1)=0.0$	$P(D_2\mid E_2)=0.2$	$P(D_2\mid E_3)=0.8$	$P(D_2\mid E_4)=0.0$

3   Rough Sets Approach Based on Information Gain

According to the parameterized version of Bayesian Rough Set (BRS) model [3], let us consider the difference between probabilities $P(D_j)$ and $P(D_j|E_i)$ as a kind of information gain. We define the information gain denoted as

$$g(i,j) = 1 - \frac{P(D_j)}{P(D_j|E_i)} \ , \tag{1}$$

which means that the larger the conditional probability is, the larger the information gain is. Since the information gain enables to evaluate the influence of the set of conditional attributes on decision class relative to its prior probability, our approach based on the information gain is applicable to the human evaluation data with different prior probability. The similar concept to (1) is used in market basket analysis [10] and the meaning of (1) would be clear. This information gain would be acceptable with the following numerical cases:

1) $P(D_j) = 0.6$ and $P(D_j|E_i) = 0.8 : g(i,j) = 0.25$,
2) $P(D_j) = 0.2$ and $P(D_j|E_i) = 0.4 : g(i,j) = 0.50$.

It follows from the above that the case 2) is more informative than the case 1), although the differences between $P(D_j)$ and $P(D_j|E_i)$ are the same. This fact can be acceptable for everyone. The definition of information gain by (1) corresponds with our intuition that the large increment of $P(D_j|E_i)$ being more than $P(D_j)$ should take larger information gain when $P(D_j)$ is low, while the same increment of $P(D_j|E_i)$ should take smaller information gain when $P(D_j)$ is high. The similar index can be considered in [3], which can be written as

$$g_*(i,j) = \frac{P(D_j|E_i) - P(D_j)}{1 - P(D_j)} \ . \tag{2}$$

Thus, using (2), we have $g_*(i,j) = 0.5$ in the case 1) and $g_*(i,j) = 0.25$ in the case 2). This result is contrary to one obtained by our information gain. Let us define the positive region by using the information gain with parameter β as

$$POS^\beta(D_j) = \bigcup \{F_i \mid g(i,j) \geq \beta\}$$
$$= \bigcup \left\{E_i \mid P(D_j|E_i) \geq \frac{P(D_j)}{1 - \beta}\right\} \ . \tag{3}$$

It should be noted that $\beta \leq 1 - P(D_j)$. In other words, β should be less than the residual of the prior probability $P(D_j)$.

Using the duality of rough sets $NEG^\beta(D_j) = POS^\beta(\neg D_j)$, the negative region can be automatically defined as

$$NEG^\beta(D_j) = \bigcup \left\{E_i \mid P(D_j|E_i) \leq \frac{P(D_j) - \beta}{1 - \beta}\right\} \ . \tag{4}$$

It should be noted that $\beta \leq P(D_j)$.

Then, since $0 \leq \frac{P(D_j) - \beta}{1 - \beta} \leq P(D_j) \leq \frac{P(D_j)}{1 - \beta}$, we have the following boundary region:

$$BND^\beta(D_j) = \bigcup \left\{E_i \mid P(D_j|E_i) \in \left(\frac{P(D_j) - \beta}{1 - \beta}, \frac{P(D_j)}{1 - \beta}\right)\right\} \ . \tag{5}$$

It should be noted that β is similar to $1-\epsilon$ in [3]. If we take $\beta = 0$, $POS^\beta(D_j)$, $NEG^\beta(D_j)$ and $BND^\beta(D_j)$ are characterized by $P(D_j|E_i) \geq P(D_j)$, $P(D_j|E_i) \leq P(D_j)$, and $P(D_j|E_i) = P(D_j)$, respectively. As the value of β increases up to $min(1 - P(D_j), P(D_j))$, the positive and negative regions decrease, and boundary region increases. Furthermore, as the value of β increases, the information associated with D_j is strongly relevant to E_i.

Lastly it follows that

$$U = POS^\beta(D_j) \cup NEG^\beta(D_j) \cup BND^\beta(D_j) .   \tag{6}$$

We can have decision rules with different certainty by changing the value of β. It should be noticed that there are orthogonal partitions with respect to decision classes $D = \{D_1, \ldots, D_r\}$.

In the example of Table 1, assuming $\beta = 0.2$, we have:

$$POS^{0.2}(D_0) = \bigcup \left\{ E_i \mid P(D_0|E_i) \geq \frac{P(D_0)}{0.8} = 0.5 \right\} = E_1 \cup E_4 ,$$

$$NEG^{0.2}(D_0) = \bigcup \left\{ E_i \mid P(D_0|E_i) \leq 0.25 \right\} = E_2 \cup E_3 ,$$

$$BND^{0.2}(D_0) = \emptyset .$$

4   Extraction Method of Decision Rules from Approximate Regions

We propose here a two-stage method to simply extract uncertain probabilistic decision rule. The first stage extracts certain decision rules by using relative decision functions[11] of approximation region classes. Then the second stage gives rule evaluation factors to the extracted rules.

First Stage. Since approximate regions are exclusive each other from (6). we have a consistent decision table with respect to each approximate region. Thus, we can construct a decision matrix relative to each approximate class. A decision matrix with respect to $POS^\beta(D_j)$ can be described as Table 3.

Table 3. A decision matrix with respect to approximate regions

		$NEG^\beta(D_j)$		$BND^\beta(D_j)$	
		$E_{N1} \ldots$	E_j	$E_{B1} \ldots$	E_{Bn}
$POS^\beta(D_j)$	E_{P1}				
	$\vdots$				
	E_i	$\ldots$ $\ldots$	$M_{ij}^\beta(D_j)$		
	$\vdots$				
	E_{Pm}				

Any element of the decision matrix is defined:

$$M_{ij}^{\beta}(D_j) = \left\{ \bigvee a_k = v_{ik} \mid a_k(E_i) \neq a_k(E_j), \forall a_k \in A \right\} , \qquad (7)$$

where $\bigvee a_k = v_{ik}$ is a disjunction of attribute elements to discern E_i and E_j.

From $POS^{\beta}(D_j)$, we can derive minimal decision rules in the form of if *condition* then *decision* using the following decision function.

$$POS^{\beta-rule}(D_j) = \bigvee_{E_i \in POS^{\beta}(D_j)} \bigwedge_{E_j \notin POS^{\beta}(D_j)} M_{ij}^{\beta}(D_j) . \qquad (8)$$

Similarly, we can derive rules from $NEG^{\beta}(D_j)$ or $BND^{\beta}(D_j)$. In the example of Table 1, we have the decision matrix with respect to $POS^{0.2}(D_0)$ shown in Table 4.

Table 4. The decision matrix with respect to $POS^{0.2}(D_0)$

| | | $NEG^{0.2}(D_0)$ | |
		E_2	E_3
$POS^{0.2}(D_0)$	E_1	$a_1 = 0 \vee a_2 = 1$	$a_3 = 1$
	E_4	$a_2 = 1$	$a_1 = 1 \vee a_3 = 1$

From Table 4, we can obtain the following rules.

$$\begin{aligned} &r_1 : if\ a_1 = 0\ and\ a_3 = 1, then\ d = 0 \quad \{E_1\} \\ &r_2 : if\ a_1 = 1\ and\ a_2 = 1, then\ d = 0 \quad \{E_4\} \qquad (9) \\ &r_3 : if\ a_2 = 1\ and\ a_3 = 1, then\ d = 0 \quad \{E_1, E_4\} \end{aligned}$$

The symbols at the end of each decision indicate the equivalence classes matching with the condition part of the rule. Notice that the condition part of the rule r_3 is matching with E_1 and E_4.

Second Stage. The second stage gives rule evaluation factors to the extracted rules. We can convert the above rule represented as certain deterministic one into uncertain probabilistic rule by giving rule evaluation factors.

With considering indexes in [2], we can define the following three evaluation factors in the context of our applications by using the number of evaluation to products $|E_i|$ and the effects of products on decision $P(D_j|E_i)$. The extracted rule $rule_k$ can be represented in the form of if $cond_k$ then D_j ($k = 1, \ldots, m$). Let $Cond_k$ be a set of the equivalence classes E_i matched with the condition part $cond_k$ of the extracted rule, and $| \bullet |$ denote cardinality.

The following *certainty factor* denoted as $ccr(Cond_k; D_j)$ means the ratio of the number of events satisfied with $if - then$ rule to the number of events satisfied with the condition part $cond_k$ of the rule.

$$cer(Cond_k; D_j) = \frac{|Cond_k \cap D_j|}{|Cond_k|}$$
$$= \frac{\sum_{E_i \in Cond_k} |E_i| \, P(D_j|E_i)}{\sum_{E_i \in Cond_k} |E_i|}, \quad (10)$$

where $|Cond_k \cap D_j|$ referred as *support* is the number of events matched with both $cond_k$ and $d = j$ which equals $\sum_{E_i \in Cond_k} |E_i| \, P(D_j|E_i)$, and $|Cond_k|$ is the number of events matched with $cond_k$ which equals $\sum_{E_i \in Cond_k} |E_i|$. This certainty factor shows the degree to which $cond_k \to D_j$ holds. It should be noted that we derive $if - then$ rules from $POS^\beta(D_j)$.

In our applications, we can use this factor as confidence degree of decision to predict the human evaluation from any product design elements. Inversely, when we have to estimate the attribute values of the product candidates from targeted human evaluation, the following *coverage factor* denoted as $cov(Cond_k; D_j)$ will be useful.

$$cov(Cond_k; D_j) = \frac{\sum_{E_i \in Cond_k} |E_i| \, P(D_j|E_i)}{|D_j|}, \quad (11)$$

which means the ratio of the number of events satisfied with constructed rule to the number of the events satisfied with D_j. This factor shows the degree to which $D_j \to cond_k$, i.e., the inverse of rule holds.

The following *strength factor* denoted as $\sigma(Cond_k; D_j)$ can be used to evaluate the set of decision rules.

$$\sigma(Cond_k; D_j) = \frac{\sum_{E_i \in Cond_k} |E_i| \, P(D_j|E_i)}{|U|}, \quad (12)$$

which means the ratio of the number of events satisfied with $if - then$ rule to all the events.

In similar way, we can associate $if - then$ rules from $NEG^\beta(D_j)$ or $BND^\beta(D_j)$ with three factors mentioned above.

For example, the rule r_1 in (9) has the following values of three factors. Since $Cond_1 = \{E_1\}$, we have:
$cer(E_1; D_0) = \frac{|E_1| P(D_0|E_1)}{|E_1|} = 0.6$,
$cov(E_1; D_0) = 0.375$,
$\sigma(E_1; D_0) = 0.15$.

In similar way, as for r_3 we have:
$Cond_3 = \{E_1, E_4\}$,
$cer(E_1, E_4; D_0) = \frac{|E_1| P(D_0|E_1) + |E_4| P(D_0|E_4)}{|E_1| + |E_4|} = 0.7$,
$cov(E_1, E_4; D_0) = 0.875$,
$\sigma(E_1, E_4; D_0) = 0.35$.

5   Applications to Human Sensory Evaluation Data

We carried out experiments to identify the hidden relations between the significant coffee manufacturing conditions and human sensory evaluations. The manufacturing conditions were combinations of two conditional attributes of raw beans (a_1) and its roast time (a_2). $V_{a1} = \{$*Colombia Excelsio, Brazil No2 s 17/18, Mocha Lekempti* $\}$, and $V_{a2} = \{$*Light, Medium, French* $\}$ which roast time was controlled by roast machine.

A coffee manufacturing expert made 9-sorts of coffee by combining V_{a1} and V_{a2}, and 10-evaluators evaluated them on 5-points semantic differential scale of 10-sensory words, such as "aroma", "fruity", and "want to buy". The evaluation scores were divided into two decision classes $D = \{D_0, D_1\}$, for example, $D = \{$*Good aroma, No good aroma*$\}$. We obtained the decision table of 90-evaluation data for every coffee taste word as shown in Table 5.

Apparently, in spite of much ambiguity of human sensory data, if-then rules were able to be extracted from decision table of every measured sensory word by using our proposed method. Although we can show every rules for each sensory word, for simplicity, we show only the following $if - then$ rules as for $D_0 = \{$*Good aroma*$\}$ which prior probability is 0.644 and relatively higher. The evaluation factors of these rules are shown in Table 6.

Table 5. Human evaluation decision table of aroma

Product (E)	Event (U)	Beans (a_1)	Roast (a_2)	Evaluation (d)
	x_{11}	Colombia	French	0
	x_{12}	Colombia	.French	0
E_1	$\vdots$	$\vdots$	$\vdots$	$\vdots$
	x_{19}	Colombia	French	0
	$x_{1,10}$	Colombia	French	1
	x_{21}	Colombia	Medium	0
E_2	$\vdots$	$\vdots$	$\vdots$	$\vdots$
	$x_{2,10}$	Colombia	Medium	1
$\vdots$	$\vdots$	$\vdots$	$\vdots$	$\vdots$
	x_{51}	Brazil	Medium	1
E_5	$\vdots$	$\vdots$	$\vdots$	$\vdots$
	$x_{5,10}$	Brazil	Medium	0
$\vdots$	$\vdots$	$\vdots$	$\vdots$	$\vdots$
	x_{91}	Mocha	Light	1
	x_{92}	Mocha	Light	1
E_9	$\vdots$	$\vdots$	$\vdots$	$\vdots$
	x_{99}	Mocha	Light	0
	$x_{9,10}$	Mocha	Light	1

Table 6. The rule evaluation factors of "aroma" rules: $\beta = 0.0$

	Certainty (cer)	Coverage (cov)	Strength (σ)
r_1	0.87	0.47	0.30
r_2	0.80	0.14	0.09
r_3	0.80	0.14	0.09
r_4	0.67	0.63	0.22
r_5	0.40	0.13	0.04

$r_1 : if\ Roast = french,$ $then\ Aroma = good$
$r_2 : if\ Roast = medium\ and\ Beans = Colombia,\ then\ Aroma = good$
$r_3 : if\ Roast = medium\ and\ Beans = Mocha,$ $then\ Aroma = good$
$r_4 : if\ Roast = light,$ $then\ Aroma = no\ good$
$r_5 : if\ Roast = medium\ and\ Beans = Brazil,$ $then\ Aroma = no\ good$

The rule r_1 means that french coffee has good aroma for 87% person and in-

versely 47% of good aroma coffee is french. Each sum of coverage values of positive (r_1, r_2, r_3) and negative (r_4, r_5) rules is 75 % and 76%.

When $\beta = 0.2$, we obtained the following rules with Table 7:

$r_6\ :if\ Roast = french,\ and\ Beans = Colombia,\ then\ Aroma = good$
$r_7\ :if\ Roast = french,\ and\ Beans = Brazil,$ $then\ Aroma = good$
$r_8\ :if\ Roast = light,$ $then\ Aroma = no\ good$
$r_9\ :if\ Roast = medium,$ $then\ Aroma = good\ or\ no$
$r_{10} : if\ Roast = french,\ and\ Beans = Mocha,$ $then\ Aroma = good\ or\ no$

There are two boundary rules (r_9, r_{10}). Although the average of certainties is higher than when $\beta = 0.0$, each sum of coverage values of positive (r_6, r_7) and negative (r_8) rules falls down to 32% and 63%.

In similar way, even when decision class' prior probability is lower, our proposed method was able to extract decision rules because of set approximation based on the information gain. As a result, we found that not only these ex-

Table 7. The rule evaluation factors of "aroma" rules: $\beta = 0.2$

	Certainty (cer)	Coverage (cov)	Strength (σ)
r_6	0.90	0.16	0.10
r_7	0.90	0.16	0.10
r_8	0.67	0.63	0.22
r_9	1.00	0.24	0.24
r_{10}	1.00	0.09	0.09

tracted decision rules corresponded with expert knowledge, but also these rules would be very useful for coffee manufacturing fitted to human taste.

6   Conclusions

We introduced a new information gain that better reflects the gain feature of human sensory and feeling evaluation data. Next, the probabilistic set approximations method was introduced based on the new definition of information gain. Moreover, we proposed the two-stage method to derive probabilistic decision rules using the decision functions of approximated decision classes. Finally, we applied our proposed method to extracting uncertain decision rules from practical human evaluation data of coffee taste.

We found out that our VPBRS based rough sets approach to extract decision rules from human evaluation data would be more applicable and powerful to the practical problems we face to now. For approaching our goals, however, for example, we need to handle tolerance relation between products as well as equivalence relation . In nearest future, we plan to apply rough set approach to larger data set of human evaluation.

References

1. Ziarko, W.: Variable precision rough set model, *Journal of Computer and System Sciences.* **46** (1993) 39-59.
2. Pawlak, Z.: Decision rules, Bayes' rule and rough sets, RSFDGrC 1999, LNAI 1711, Springer Verlag (1999), 1-9.
3. Ślęzak, D. and Ziarko, W.: Variable precision Bayesian rough set model, RSFDGrC 2003, LNAI 2639, Springer Verlag (2003), 312-315.
4. Ślęzak, D. and Ziarko, W.: The investigation of the Bayesian rough set model, *Int. J. of Approximate Reasoning*, in press.
5. Ślęzak, D.: The Rough Bayesian Model for Distributed Decision Systems, RSCTC 2004, LNAI 3066, Springer Verlag (2004), 384-393.
6. Tsumoto, S.: Discovery of rules about complication, RSFDGrC 1999, LNAI 1711, Springer Verlag (1999), 29-37.
7. Nishino, T. and Nagamachi, M.: Extraction of Design Rules for Basic Product Designing Using Rough Set Analysis, *Proceedings of 14-th Triennial Congress of the International Ergonomics Association*, **3** (2003), 515-518.
8. Nagamachi, M.: *Introduction to Kansei Engineering*, Japan Standard Association (in Japanese) (1996).
9. Mori, N., Tanaka, H., and Inoue, K. (Eds.): *Rough Sets and Kansei*, Kaibundo (in Japanese) (2004).
10. Hastie, T., Tibshirani R. and Friedman J.: *The Elements of Statistical Learning*, Springer Verlag (2001), 440-447.
11. Stepaniuk, J.: Knowledge Discovery by Application of Rough Set Models, In: L. Polkowski, S. Tsumoto and T.Y. Lin (Eds.), *Rough Set Methods and Applications*, Physica-Verlag (2000), 137-233.

Variable Precision Rough Set Approach to Multiple Decision Tables

Masahiro Inuiguchi[1] and Takuya Miyajima[2]

[1] Graduate School of Engineering Science, Osaka University,
Toyonaka, Osaka 560-8531, Japan
inuiguti@sys.es.osaka-u.ac.jp
[2] Graduate School of Engineering, Osaka University,
Suita, Osaka 565-0871, Japan
miyajima@sa.eie.eng.osaka-u.ac.jp

Abstract. In this paper, we study variable precision rough set models based on multiple decision tables. The models can control the admissible level of classification error in each table, the ratio of supporting decision tables to all decision tables and the ratio of opposing decision tables to all decision tables. As the classical rough set model plays a key role in analysis of decision tables such as reduction, rule induction, etc., the proposed variable precision rough set models will play a key role in analysis of multiple decision tables.

1 Introduction

Recently, the applicability and advantages of rough sets [1] have been demonstrated in the literatures. The rough set analysis has been developed under a single decision table. However, we may have multiple decision tables when the information comes from multiple information sources or when objects are evaluated by multiple decision makers. In such cases, it would be better for obtaining more robust and accurate results to analyze all information provided from multiple decision tables in a lump. When each decision table is obtained from a decision maker, it can be regarded as partial information about the opinion of the decision maker. Therefore, the analysis of multiple decision tables is important for the investigation of group opinion, agreement in the group and group preference. We focus on the case when multiple decision tables are obtained from many decision makers.

In order to know product designs which are preferred by many customers as decision rules, Enomoto et al. [2] discussed rule induction from multiple decision tables based on rough set analysis. To analyze multiple decision tables, they proposed *merging decision rules* which is originally proposed by Mori [4] in analysis of single decision tables. However, in their method, we should first enumerate all decision rules from each decision table and then merge decision rules obtained from different decision tables. This requires a formidable computational effort and will be inapplicable when each decision table becomes large. Moreover, it is reported that the results can be different by the order of decision

D. Ślęzak et al. (Eds.): RSFDGrC 2005, LNAI 3641, pp. 304–313, 2005.

rules to be merged [3]. They proposed a few heuristic methods to order decision rules to be merged [3]. Then this approach includes a brute force method in the enumeration of decision rules from each decision table and also some ad hoc and heuristic methods to order decision rules to be merged.

In order to treat the problem more theoretically, Inuiguchi et=al. [5] have discussed rule induction from two decision tables. They extended the discernibility matrix method [6] to the case of two decision tables. They showed that there are a lot of approaches to treat the problem even in two decision tables. However, some of their various approaches cannot be applicable in the real world because they require a lot of computational effort.

In this paper, we propose a new rough set approach to analysis of multiple decision tables. While the previous approaches have focused on induction of decision rules, the proposed approach focuses on the definition of a rough set, i.e., definitions of lower and upper approximations. Given a rough set, we may define a reduct, induce decision rules, and so on. Then a definition of rough set can play a key role in analysis of multiple decision tables.

In order to treat the error caused by human evaluation as well as to accommodate disagreements among decision tables, we introduce the variable precision rough set model. Sets of objects are not assumed to be common among decision tables but sets of attributes and their domains are. Under this assumption, an object can be absent in some decision tables. Depending on the treatment of the absent objects, two kinds of rough sets are proposed.

In the next section, we briefly introduce decision tables and variable precision rough sets. We reformulate the decision tables using condition attribute patterns. In Section 3, we define rough sets under multiple decision tables. First agreement ratios are defined in two ways. Then by the use of agreement ratios, rough sets under multiple decision tables are defined. Some properties are described. In Section 4, simple numerical example is given to demonstrate the differences between two kinds of rough sets and transition of rough sets by the change in values of parameters.

2   Variable Precision Rough Sets and Decision Tables

2.1   Decision Tables

Rough sets proposed by Pawlak [1] has been applied to analysis of decision tables. The rough set analysis utilizes indiscernibility relations tactfully. By the rough set analysis, we can obtain minimal set of condition attributes to classify objects correctly and induce decision rules from a given decision table.

A decision table is composed of a set of objects U, a set of condition attributes C and a decision attribute d. A decision table is denoted by $(U, C \cup \{d\})$. We regard each attribute $a \in C \cup \{d\}$ as a function from U to V_a, where V_a is the set of attribute values a takes. An example of a decision table is given in Table 1. In Table 1, we have $U = \{u_i,\ i = 1, 2, \ldots, 10\}$, $C = \{\text{Design}, \text{Function}, \text{Size}\}$ and $d = \text{Dec. (Decision)}$.

Table 1. An example of decision table

object	Design	Function	SizeSize	Dec.
u_1	classic	simple	compact	accept
u_2	classic	multiple	compact	accept
u_3	classic	multiple	normal	reject
u_4	modern	simple	compact	reject
u_5	modern	simple	normal	reject
u_6	classic	multiple	compact	accept
u_7	modern	multiple	normal	reject
u_8	classic	simple	compact	accept
u_9	classic	multiple	normal	accept
u_{10}	modern	multiple	normal	reject

Table 2. A decision table described by condition attribute patterns

pattern	Design	Function	Size	σ
w_1	classic	simple	compact	(2,0)
w_2	classic	multiple	compact	(2,0)
w_3	classic	multiple	normal	(1,1)
w_4	modern	simple	compact	(0,1)
w_5	modern	simple	normal	(0,1)
w_6	modern	multiple	normal	(0,2)

Given a decision table $(U, C \cup \{d\})$, we define the condition attribute pattern, or simply, pattern $Inf_C(u)$ of an object $u \in U$ by

$$Inf_C(u) = \bigcup_{a \in C} \{\langle a, a(u) \rangle\}, \tag{1}$$

where $a(u)$ shows the attribute value of u with respect to attribute $a \in C \cup \{d\}$. The set V_C^U of all patterns in the given decision table is defined by

$$V_C^U = \{Inf_C(u) \mid u \in U\}. \tag{2}$$

Let V_d be the set of decision attribute values. Then frequency function σ_C and rough membership function μ_C are defined as follows for $w \in V_C^U$ and $v_d \in V_d$,

$$\sigma_C(w, v_d) = |Inf_C^{-1}(w) \cap d^{-1}(v_d)|, \tag{3}$$

$$\mu_C(w, v_d) = \frac{|Inf_C^{-1}(w) \cap d^{-1}(v_d)|}{|Inf_C^{-1}(w)|}, \tag{4}$$

where Inf_C^{-1} and d^{-1} are inverse images of Inf_C and d, respectively, i.e., $Inf_C^{-1}(w) = \{u \in U \mid Inf_C(u) = w\}$ and $d^{-1}(v_d) = \{u \in U \mid d(u) = v_d\}$. $\sigma_C(w, v_d)$ shows the number of objects whose patterns are w and whose decision attribute values are v_d. $\mu_C(w, v_d)$ shows the ratio of objects which take decision attribute value v_d to all objects whose patterns are w. Given $\sigma_C(w, v_d)$ for every $v_d \in V_d$, we obtain $\mu_C(w, v_d)$ as

$$\mu_C(w, v_d) = \frac{\sigma_C(w, v_d)}{\sum_{v_d \in V_d} \sigma_C(w, v_d)}. \tag{5}$$

However $\sigma_C(w, v_d)$ cannot be obtained from $\mu_C(w, v_d)$ for every $v_d \in V_d$. We can rewrite a decision table described by patterns $w \in V_C^U$ and frequencies $\{\sigma_C(w, v_d) \mid v_d \in V_d\}$. For example, the decision table shown in Table 1 can be rewritten as a table shown in Table 2. In Table 2, each entry in column 'σ' shows a vector $(\sigma_C(w_j, \text{accept}), \sigma_C(w_j, \text{reject}))$. In rough set analysis, the order of objects appearing in a decision table does not affect the results of the analysis. Then having a decision table described by patterns $w \in V_C^U$ as in Table 2 is equivalent to having a usual decision table as in Table 1. From this fact, we assume that decision tables are given by using patterns in what follows.

2.2   Rough Sets and Variable Precision Rough Sets

In rough set analysis of decision tables, a decision class or a union of decision classes $\hat{X}$ is analyzed. Namely, associated with $\hat{X}$, there is a unique set $X \subseteq V_d$ of decision attribute values such that

$$\hat{X} = \{u \in U \mid d(u) \in X\}. \tag{6}$$

To a set $X \subseteq V_d$ of decision attribute values, a rough membership function μ_C of patterns $w \in V_C^U$ is defined as

$$\mu_C(w, X) = \frac{\displaystyle\sum_{v_d \in X} \sigma_C(w, v_d)}{\displaystyle\sum_{v_d \in V_d} \sigma_C(w, v_d)}. \tag{7}$$

Given a set of decision attribute values $X \subseteq V_d$, lower and upper approximations composing a rough set are defined as sets of patterns instead of objects by;

$$\underline{C}(X) = \{w_i \in V_C^U \mid \mu_C(w_i, X) = 1\}, \tag{8}$$
$$\overline{C}(X) = \{w_i \in V_C^U \mid \mu_C(w_i, X) > 0\}. \tag{9}$$

The relations of $\underline{C}(X)$ and $\overline{C}(X)$ with usual lower and upper approximations $C_*(\hat{X})$ and $C^*(\hat{X})$ are given as

$$C_*(\hat{X}) = Inf_C^{-1}(\underline{C}(d(\hat{X}))) = Inf_C^{-1}(\underline{C}(X)), \tag{10}$$
$$C^*(\hat{X}) = Inf_C^{-1}(\overline{C}(d(\hat{X}))) = Inf_C^{-1}(\overline{C}(X)). \tag{11}$$

A rough set of $\hat{X}$ is often defined by a pair $(C_*(\hat{X}), C^*(\hat{X}))$. In this paper, a pair $(\underline{C}(X), \overline{C}(X))$ is called a rough set of X.

In the rough set defined by a pair $(\underline{C}(X), \overline{C}(X))$, patterns w_i included in lower approximation $\underline{C}(X)$ satisfy $\mu_C(w_i, X) = 1$. This implies that all objects having a pattern w_i take a common decision attribute value in X. However, from the consideration of possible errors in observation, evaluation, and so on, this requirement to be a member of lower approximation $\underline{C}(X)$ is too rigorous especially when the size of the given decision table is large. With such errors, we may obtain an empty lower approximation which deteriorates the effectiveness of the rough set analysis. In order to overcome this inconvenience, variable precision rough sets [7] have been proposed by relaxing the requirement to be a member of the lower approximation.

Let $\varepsilon_1 \in [0, 0.5)$ be an admissible level of classification error, lower and upper approximations in a variable precision rough set (VPRS) of X is defined as a set of patterns by

$$\underline{C}_{\varepsilon_1}(X) = \{w_i \in V_C^U \mid \mu_C(w_i, X) \geq 1 - \varepsilon_1\}, \tag{12}$$

$$\overline{C}_{\varepsilon_1}(X) = \{w_i \in V_C^U \mid \mu_C(w_i, X) > \varepsilon_1\}. \tag{13}$$

A VPRS of X is defined by a pair $(\underline{C}_{\varepsilon_1}(X), \overline{C}_{\varepsilon_1}(X))$. As can be seen easily, we have $\underline{C}_{\varepsilon_1}(X) = \underline{C}(X)$ and $\overline{C}_{\varepsilon_1}(X) = \overline{C}(X)$ when $\varepsilon_1 = 0$. As ε_1 increases, $\underline{C}_{\varepsilon_1}(X)$ becomes larger and $\overline{C}_{\varepsilon_1}(X)$ becomes smaller.

The following properties hold:

$$\underline{C}_{\varepsilon_1}(X) \subseteq \overline{C}_{\varepsilon_1}(X), \tag{14}$$

$$\overline{C}_{\varepsilon_1}(X) = V_C^U - \underline{C}_{\varepsilon_1}(V_d - X). \tag{15}$$

In this paper, we propose rough sets under multiple decision tables each of which is obtained by human evaluations. In consideration of the error caused by human evaluation as well as the disagreements among decision tables, the VPRS model is applied to the definitions.

3 Rough Sets Under Multiple Decision Tables

3.1 Agreement Ratio

We assume n decision tables evaluated by n decision makers are given. Let $\mathbf{T}$ be a set of decision tables $T_i = (U_i, C \cup \{d\})$, $i = 1, 2, \ldots, n$, i.e., $\mathbf{T} = \{T_1, T_2, \ldots, T_n\}$. We assume that all decision tables T_i, $i = 1, 2, \ldots, n$ share a set C of condition attributes and the unique decision attribute d. On the other hand, sets of objects U_i, $i = 1, 2, \ldots, n$ can be different among decision tables. Therefore, sets of patterns, $V_C^{U_i} = \{Inf_C(u) \mid u \in U_i\}$, $i = 1, 2, \ldots, n$ can be also different among decision tables. We define $V_C = \bigcup_{i=1,2,\ldots,n} V_C^{U_i}$ for convenience.

The evaluation can be different among decision makers. Therefore, decision rules behind each decision table may conflict with those behind another decision table. To treat the disagreement among decision tables, we introduce an agreement ratio. The difficulty to define an agreement ratio is in the treatment of patterns absent in a decision table but appears in the other decision tables because of the difference among sets of objects U_i, $i = 1, 2, \ldots, n$.

One of conceivable approaches is to define an agreement ratio to each pattern by using decision tables including the pattern. Following this approach, we can define lower and upper agreement ratios to each pattern with respect to a set X of decision attribute values as

$$\underline{\tau}_{\varepsilon_1}(w_i, X) = \frac{|\{T_j \in \mathbf{T} \mid w_i \in \underline{C}_{\varepsilon_1}^{T_j}(X)\}|}{|\{T_j \in \mathbf{T} \mid w_i \in V_C^{U_j}\}|}, \tag{16}$$

$$\overline{\tau}_{\varepsilon_1}(w_i, X) = \frac{|\{T_j \in \mathbf{T} \mid w_i \in \overline{C}_{\varepsilon_1}^{T_j}(X)\}|}{|\{T_j \in \mathbf{T} \mid w_i \in V_C^{U_j}\}|}, \tag{17}$$

where $\underline{C}_{\varepsilon_1}^{T_j}(X)$ and $\overline{C}_{\varepsilon_1}^{T_j}(X)$ are ε_1-lower approximation and ε_1-upper approximation corresponding to decision table T_j. By (15), we have

$$\underline{\tau}_{\varepsilon_1}(w_i, X) \leq \overline{\tau}_{\varepsilon_1}(w_i, X), \tag{18}$$

$$\overline{\tau}_{\varepsilon_1}(w_i, X) = 1 - \underline{\tau}_{\varepsilon_1}(w_i, V_d - X). \tag{19}$$

Then we call $\underline{\tau}_{\varepsilon_1}(w_i, X)$ and $\overline{\tau}_{\varepsilon_1}(w_i, X)$ lower agreement ratio and upper agreement ratio, respectively.

3.2   Upper Estimation of a Rough Membership Value

When the number of decision tables including the pattern is small, the lower and upper agreement ratios defined by (16) and (17) possess lower reliability. To overcome this drawback, it is conceivable to use estimated decision attribute values to absent patterns so that all decision tables are used in calculation of agreement ratios to any pattern.

To make such estimation, we propose the upper estimations of rough membership values. Consider a decision table T_i and a pattern $w \notin V_C^{U_i}$. To a pattern $w_k \in V_C^{U_i}$, we define a set of $B_k(w)$ condition attributes by

$$B_k(w) = \{a \mid \exists v_a \in V_a, \langle a, v_a \rangle \in w \cap w_k\}. \tag{20}$$

Using $B_k(w)$, the restriction of w on B_k is defined by

$$w^{\downarrow B_k(w)} = \{\langle a, v_a \rangle \mid \langle a, v_a \rangle \in w \cap w_k\}. \tag{21}$$

We can define a rough membership value $\mu_{B_k(w)}^{T_i}(w^{\downarrow B_k(w)}, X)$ in decision table T_i in the same way as (7) with the exception of a case when $B_k(w) = \emptyset$. Namely,

$$\mu_{B_k(w)}^{T_i}(w^{\downarrow B_k(w)}, X) = \begin{cases} \dfrac{\displaystyle\sum_{v_d \in X} \sigma_{B_k(w)}^{T_i}(w^{\downarrow B_k(w)}, v_d)}{\displaystyle\sum_{v_d \in V_d} \sigma_{B_k(w)}^{T_i}(w^{\downarrow B_k(w)}, v_d)}, & \text{if } B_k(w) \neq \emptyset, \\[4mm] \dfrac{|\{u \in U_i \mid d(u) \in X\}|}{|U_i|}, & \text{if } B_k(w) = \emptyset, \end{cases} \tag{22}$$

where $\sigma_B^{T_i}$ is a frequency function of decision table T_i with respect to a set $B \subseteq C$ of condition attributes.

Then, the upper estimation of rough membership value of a pattern $w \notin V_C^{U_i}$ can be defined by

$$\hat{\mu}_C^{T_i}(w, X) = \begin{cases} \displaystyle\max_{w_k \in V_C^{U_i}} \mu_{B_k(w)}(w^{\downarrow B_k(w)}, X), & \text{if } w \notin V_C^{U_i}, \\[3mm] \mu_C^{T_i}(w, X), & \text{if } w \in V_C^{U_i}, \end{cases} \tag{23}$$

where $\mu_C^{T_i}$ is a rough membership function with respect to decision table T_i. We have $\sum_{v_d \in V_d} \hat{\mu}_C^{T_i}(w, \{v_d\}) \geq 1$. In this sense, we call $\hat{\mu}_C^{T_i}(w, X)$ an upper estimation of the rough membership value.

Note that when decision rule 'if an object u satisfies a pattern $w^{\downarrow B_k(w)}$ then u takes a decision attribute value in X' induced from decision table T_i, we have $\mu_{B_k(w)}(w^{\downarrow B_k(w)}, X) = 1$. Moreover, when decision rule 'if an object u satisfies a pattern $w^{\downarrow B_k(w)}$ then u takes a decision attribute value in X' is certain with degree $\alpha \in [0, 1]$ under decision table T_i, we have $\mu_{B_k(w)}(w^{\downarrow B_k(w)}, X) \geq \alpha$. Therefore the upper estimation $\hat{\mu}_C^{T_i}(w, X)$ shows to what extent we certainly infer that an object having a pattern w takes a decision attribute value in X.

3.3   Modified Approximations and Modified Agreement Ratios

Using the upper estimation of rough membership value, we can define $(\varepsilon_1, \varepsilon_2)$-lower approximation and $(\varepsilon_1, \varepsilon_2)$-upper approximation as modifications of ε_1-lower approximation and ε_2-upper approximation, respectively, by

$$\underline{C}_{\varepsilon_1, \varepsilon_2}^{T_i}(X) = \{w_i \in V_C \mid \hat{\mu}_C^{T_i}(w_i, X) \geq 1 - \varepsilon_1, \ \hat{\mu}_C^{T_i}(w_i, U - X) \leq \varepsilon_2\}, \quad (24)$$

$$\overline{C}_{\varepsilon_1, \varepsilon_2}^{T_i}(X) = \{w_i \in V_C \mid \hat{\mu}_C^{T_i}(w_i, X) > \varepsilon_1 \ \text{or} \ \hat{\mu}_C^{T_i}(w_i, U - X) < 1 - \varepsilon_2\}, \quad (25)$$

where we assume $\varepsilon_1 \leq \varepsilon_2 < 1 - \varepsilon_1$. From $\hat{\mu}_C^{T_i}(w_i, X) + \hat{\mu}_C^{T_i}(w_i, U - X) \geq 1$, it is possible to have $\hat{\mu}_C^{T_i}(w_i, X) \geq 1 - \varepsilon_1$ and $\hat{\mu}_C^{T_i}(w_i, U - X) > \varepsilon_1$ at the same time. If $\hat{\mu}_C^{T_i}(w_i, X) \geq 1 - \varepsilon_1$ and $\hat{\mu}_C^{T_i}(w_i, U - X) > \varepsilon_1$ are satisfied at the same, objects having pattern w_i may take a decision attribute value in X and simultaneously a decision attribute value in $U - X$ both with high estimated degrees $\hat{\mu}_C^{T_i}(w_i, U - X)$ and $\hat{\mu}_C^{T_i}(w_i, U - X)$. This is contradictory. In order to avoid such a contradiction, we exclude such a pattern w_i from lower approximation by adding condition $\hat{\mu}_C^{T_i}(U - X|w_i) \leq \varepsilon_2$. The definition of $(\varepsilon_1, \varepsilon_2)$-upper approximation also follows this idea.

$(\varepsilon_1, \varepsilon_2)$-lower approximation and $(\varepsilon_1, \varepsilon_2)$-upper approximation satisfy

$$\underline{C}_{\varepsilon_1, \varepsilon_2}^{T_i}(X) \supseteq \underline{C}_{\varepsilon_1}^{T_i}(X), \ \overline{C}_{\varepsilon_1, \varepsilon_2}^{T_i}(X) \supseteq \overline{C}_{\varepsilon_1}^{T_i}(X), \quad (26)$$

$$\underline{C}_{\varepsilon_1, \varepsilon_2}^{T_i}(X) \subseteq \overline{C}_{\varepsilon_1, \varepsilon_2}^{T_i}(X), \quad (27)$$

$$\overline{C}_{\varepsilon_1, \varepsilon_2}^{T_i}(X) = V_C - \underline{C}_{\varepsilon_1, \varepsilon_2}^{T_i}(V_d - X). \quad (28)$$

Note that $\underline{C}_{\varepsilon_1}^{T_i}(X)$ and $\overline{C}_{\varepsilon_1}^{T_i}(X)$ are defined under universe $V_C^{U_i}$ while $\underline{C}_{\varepsilon_1, \varepsilon_2}^{T_i}(X)$ and $\overline{C}_{\varepsilon_1, \varepsilon_2}^{T_i}(X)$ are defined under universe V_C. When $V_C = V_C^{U_i}$, we have $\underline{C}_{\varepsilon_1, \varepsilon_2}^{T_i}(X) = \underline{C}_{\varepsilon_1}^{T_i}(X)$ and $\overline{C}_{\varepsilon_1, \varepsilon_2}^{T_i}(X) = \overline{C}_{\varepsilon_1}^{T_i}(X)$.

Using $(\varepsilon_1, \varepsilon_2)$-lower approximation and $(\varepsilon_1, \varepsilon_2)$-upper approximation, for each $w_i \in V_C$ and for a set X of decision attribute values, we can defined the modified lower and upper agreement ratios as

$$\underline{\tau}_{\varepsilon_1, \varepsilon_2}(w_i, X) = \frac{|\{T_j \in \mathbf{T} \mid w_i \in \underline{C}_{\varepsilon_1, \varepsilon_2}^{T_j}(X)\}|}{|\mathbf{T}|}, \quad (29)$$

$$\overline{\tau}_{\varepsilon_1, \varepsilon_2}(w_i, X) = \frac{|\{T_j \in \mathbf{T} \mid w_i \in \overline{C}_{\varepsilon_1, \varepsilon_2}^{T_j}(X)\}|}{|\mathbf{T}|}. \quad (30)$$

From (28), we have

$$\overline{\tau}_{\varepsilon_1,\varepsilon_2}(w_i, X) = 1 - \underline{\tau}_{\varepsilon_1,\varepsilon_2}(w_i, V_d - X). \tag{31}$$

3.4   Rough Sets Under Multiple Decision Tables

Let a pair $(\underline{\tau}_{\mathcal{X}}, \overline{\tau}_{\mathcal{X}})$ represent a pair of lower and upper agreement ratios, $(\underline{\tau}_{\varepsilon_1}, \overline{\tau}_{\varepsilon_1})$ or a pair of modified lower and upper agreement ratios, $(\underline{\tau}_{\varepsilon_1,\varepsilon_2}, \overline{\tau}_{\varepsilon_1,\varepsilon_2})$. Then we can define $(\mathcal{X}, \delta_1, \delta_2)$-lower approximation and $(\mathcal{X}, \delta_1, \delta_2)$-upper approximation as

$$\underline{\mathbf{T}}_{\mathcal{X}}^{\delta_1,\delta_2}(X) = \{w_i \in V_C \mid \underline{\tau}_{\mathcal{X}}(w_i, X) \geq 1 - \delta_1, \ \overline{\tau}_{\mathcal{X}}(w_i, X) \geq 1 - \delta_2\}, \tag{32}$$

$$\overline{\mathbf{T}}_{\mathcal{X}}^{\delta_1,\delta_2}(X) = \{w_i \in V_C \mid \underline{\tau}_{\mathcal{X}}(w_i, X) > \delta_1, \ \text{or} \ \overline{\tau}_{\mathcal{X}}(w_i, X) > \delta_2\}, \tag{33}$$

where we assume $0 \leq \delta_2 \leq \delta_1 < 0.5$. A variable $\mathcal{X}$ takes ε_1 or $\{\varepsilon_1, \varepsilon_2\}$. From (19) and (31), we have $\underline{\tau}_{\varepsilon_1}(w_i, X) = 1 - \overline{\tau}_{\varepsilon_1}(w_i, X)$ and $\underline{\tau}_{\varepsilon_1,\varepsilon_2}(w_i, X) = 1 - \overline{\tau}_{\varepsilon_1,\varepsilon_2}(w_i, X)$. Therefore, δ_2 in (32) and (33) represents the admissible ratio of decision tables which support the opposite conclusion.

We easily obtain the following properties of $(\mathcal{X}, \delta_1, \delta_2)$-lower approximation and $(\mathcal{X}, \delta_1, \delta_2)$-upper approximation:

$$\underline{\mathbf{T}}_{\mathcal{X}}^{\delta_1,\delta_2}(X) \subseteq \overline{\mathbf{T}}_{\mathcal{X}}^{\delta_1,\delta_2}(X), \tag{34}$$

$$\overline{\mathbf{T}}_{\mathcal{X}}^{\delta_1,\delta_2}(X) = V_C - \underline{\mathbf{T}}_{\mathcal{X}}^{\delta_1,\delta_2}(V_d - X). \tag{35}$$

4   A Numerical Example

Consider 4 decision tables $T_1 \sim T_4$ given in Tables 3~6. Those decision tables show preferences of 4 hypothetical decision makers in evaluation of audio equipments. In those decision tables, we have $C = \{\text{Design,Function,Size}\}$, $d =$ Dec. (Decision) and $V_d = \{\text{accept}, \text{reject}\}$. The column of Dec. in each decision table shows vectors of frequencies, $(\sigma_C^{T_i}(w_k, \text{accept}), \sigma_C^{T_i}(w_k, \text{reject}))$. We calculate lower approximations of $\{\text{accept}\}$ and $\{\text{reject}\}$ under a set of decision tables, $\mathbf{T} = \{T_1, T_2, T_3, T_4\}$.

We calculate $(\varepsilon_1, \delta_1, \delta_2)$-lower approximations fixing $\delta_2 = 0$ but varying values of ε_1 and δ_1. As an example, we show the calculation process of $\underline{\mathbf{T}}_{0.2}^{0.3,0}(\{\text{accept}\})$. ε_1-lower approximation in each decision table is obtained as

$$\underline{C}_{0.2}^{T_1}(\{\text{accept}\}) = \{w_1, w_2, w_7\}, \quad \overline{C}_{0.2}^{T_1}(\{\text{accept}\}) = \{w_1, w_2, w_3, w_5, w_7\},$$

$$\underline{C}_{0.2}^{T_2}(\{\text{accept}\}) = \{w_1, w_7, w_8\}, \quad \overline{C}_{0.2}^{T_2}(\{\text{accept}\}) = \{w_1, w_3, w_5, w_7, w_8\},$$

$$\underline{C}_{0.2}^{T_3}(\{\text{accept}\}) = \{w_1, w_6, w_7, w_8\}, \overline{C}_{0.2}^{T_3}(\{\text{accept}\}) = \{w_1, w_2, w_3, w_6, w_7, w_8\},$$

$$\underline{C}_{0.2}^{T_4}(\{\text{accept}\}) = \{w_7, w_8\}, \quad \overline{C}_{0.2}^{T_4}(\{\text{accept}\}) = \{w_2, w_3, w_7, w_8\}.$$

Then agreement ratios are obtained as in Table 7. Hence, we obtain $\underline{\mathbf{T}}_{0.2}^{0.3,0}$ ($\{\text{accept}\}$) = $\{w_7, w_8\}$. We should note that w_1 is rejected because we have

Table 3. Decision table T_1

$V_C^{U_1}$	Design	Function	Size	Dec.
w_1	classic	simple	compact	$(6,1)$
w_2	classic	multiple	compact	$(6,0)$
w_3	classic	multiple	normal	$(1,2)$
w_4	modern	simple	compact	$(0,2)$
w_5	modern	simple	normal	$(1,2)$
w_6	modern	multiple	compact	$(0,1)$
w_7	modern	multiple	normal	$(8,0)$

Table 4. Decision table T_2

$V_C^{U_2}$	Design	Function	Size	Dec.
w_1	classic	simple	compact	$(5,0)$
w_2	classic	multiple	compact	$(0,1)$
w_3	classic	multiple	normal	$(3,3)$
w_5	modern	simple	normal	$(1,3)$
w_6	modern	multiple	compact	$(1,4)$
w_7	modern	multiple	normal	$(6,0)$
w_8	classic	simple	normal	$(9,1)$

Table 5. Decision table T_3

$V_C^{U_3}$	Design	Function	Size	Dec.
w_1	classic	simple	compact	$(3,0)$
w_2	classic	multiple	compact	$(1,3)$
w_3	classic	multiple	normal	$(2,3)$
w_4	modern	simple	compact	$(0,3)$
w_6	modern	multiple	compact	$(1,0)$
w_7	modern	multiple	normal	$(8,0)$
w_8	classic	simple	normal	$(2,0)$

Table 6. Decision table T_4

$V_C^{U_4}$	Design	Function	Size	Dec.
w_1	classic	simple	compact	$(1,4)$
w_2	classic	multiple	compact	$(1,3)$
w_3	classic	multiple	normal	$(1,3)$
w_5	modern	simple	normal	$(1,5)$
w_6	modern	multiple	compact	$(0,3)$
w_7	modern	multiple	normal	$(3,0)$
w_8	classic	simple	normal	$(6,0)$

Table 7. Lower and upper agreement ratios

pattern	w_1	w_2	w_3	w_4	w_5	w_6	w_7	w_8
$\underline{\tau}_{0.2}$	0.75	0.25	0	0	0	0.25	1	1
$\overline{\tau}_{0.2}$	0.75	0.75	1	0	0.667	0.25	1	1

Table 8. Upper estimations

table	pat.	$\hat{\mu}$	table	pat.	$\hat{\mu}$
T_1	w_8	$(\frac{6}{7}, \frac{5}{12})$	T_2	w_4	$(1, \frac{4}{5})$
T_3	w_5	$(1,1)$	T_4	w_4	$(\frac{8}{17}, 1)$

$\overline{\tau}_{0.2}(w_1, \{accept\}) = 0.75 < 1$. Varying values of ε_1 and δ_1, we obtain $\underline{\mathbf{T}}_{\varepsilon_1}^{\delta_1, 0}$ ($\{accept\}$) and $\underline{\mathbf{T}}_{\varepsilon_1}^{\delta_1, 0}(\{reject\})$ as in Table 9. In Table 9, the former is shown on the upper part of each cell and the latter on the lower part.

Now let us calculate $(\varepsilon_1, \varepsilon_2, \delta_1, \delta_2)$-lower approximations fixing $\varepsilon_2 = 0.5$ and $\delta_2 = 0$ but varying values of ε_1 and δ_1. To this end, we should calculate the upper estimations of rough membership values for missing patterns in each decision table. The missing pattern (pat.) and upper estimations $(\hat{\mu})$ are shown in Table 8. The column '$\hat{\mu}$' shows vectors of upper estimations, $(\hat{\mu}_C^{T_i}(w, \{accept\}), \hat{\mu}_C^{T_i}(w, \{reject\}))$. Varying values of ε_1 and δ_1, we obtain $\underline{\mathbf{T}}_{\varepsilon_1, 0.5}^{\delta_1, 0}$ ($\{accept\}$) and $\underline{\mathbf{T}}_{\varepsilon_1, 0.5}^{\delta_1, 0}(\{reject\})$ as shown in Table 10. In Table 10, the former is shown on the upper part of each box and the latter on the lower part. In Tables 9 and 10, we observe that lower approximations do not become larger as ε_1 increases because of condition $\overline{\tau}_\mathcal{X}(w_i, X) \geq 1 - \delta_2$ in their definitions.

Comparing Tables 9 and 10, we know rough sets using upper estimations of rough membership values are more restrictive. This is because few absent patterns become members of lower and upper approximations of each table, i.e., decision attribute values of absent patterns cannot be inferred from information of other patterns. In this example, upper estimations are not useful but will be effective when inference from other patterns works.

Table 9. $\underline{\mathbf{T}}_{\varepsilon_1}^{\delta_1,0}(\{\text{accept}\})$ and $\underline{\mathbf{T}}_{\varepsilon_1}^{\delta_1,0}(\{\text{reject}\})$

$\varepsilon_1\backslash\delta_1$	$[0,1/4)$	$[1/4,1/3)$	$[1/3,1/2)$
$\left[0,\dfrac{1}{10}\right)$	$\{w_7\}$ / $\{w_4\}$	$\{w_7\}$ / $\{w_4\}$	$\{w_7,w_8\}$ / $\{w_4\}$
$\left[\dfrac{1}{10},\dfrac{1}{7}\right)$	$\{w_7,w_8\}$ / $\{w_4\}$	$\{w_7,w_8\}$ / $\{w_4\}$	$\{w_7,w_8\}$ / $\{w_4\}$
$\left[\dfrac{1}{7},\dfrac{1}{5}\right)$	$\{w_7,w_8\}$ / $\{w_4\}$	$\{w_1,w_7,w_8\}$ / $\{w_4\}$	$\{w_1,w_7,w_8\}$ / $\{w_4\}$
$\left[\dfrac{1}{5},\dfrac{1}{4}\right)$	$\{w_7,w_8\}$ / $\{w_4\}$	$\{w_7,w_8\}$ / $\{w_4\}$	$\{w_7,w_8\}$ / $\{w_4\}$
$\left[\dfrac{1}{4},\dfrac{1}{3}\right)$	$\{w_7,w_8\}$ / $\{w_4\}$	$\{w_7,w_8\}$ / $\{w_4\}$	$\{w_7,w_8\}$ / $\{w_4,w_5\}$
$\left[\dfrac{1}{3},\dfrac{2}{5}\right)$	$\{w_7,w_8\}$ / $\{w_4,w_5\}$	$\{w_7,w_8\}$ / $\{w_4,w_5\}$	$\{w_7,w_8\}$ / $\{w_4,w_5\}$
$\left[\dfrac{2}{5},\dfrac{1}{2}\right)$	$\{w_7,w_8\}$ / $\{w_4,w_5\}$	$\{w_7,w_8\}$ / $\{w_3,w_4,w_5\}$	$\{w_7,w_8\}$ / $\{w_3,w_4,w_5\}$

Table 10. $\underline{\mathbf{T}}_{\varepsilon_1,0.5}^{\delta_1,0}(\{\text{accept}\})$ and $\underline{\mathbf{T}}_{\varepsilon_1,0.5}^{\delta_1,0}(\{\text{reject}\})$

$\varepsilon_1\backslash\delta_1$	$[0,1/4)$	$[1/4,1/2)$
$\left[0,\dfrac{1}{10}\right)$	$\{w_7\}$ / $\emptyset$	$\{w_7\}$ / $\{w_4\}$
$\left[\dfrac{1}{10},\dfrac{1}{7}\right)$	$\{w_7\}$ / $\emptyset$	$\{w_7,w_8\}$ / $\{w_4\}$
$\left[\dfrac{1}{7},\dfrac{1}{5}\right)$	$\{w_7,w_8\}$ / $\emptyset$	$\{w_1,w_7,w_8\}$ / $\{w_4\}$
$\left[\dfrac{1}{5},\dfrac{1}{3}\right)$	$\{w_7,w_8\}$ / $\emptyset$	$\{w_7,w_8\}$ / $\{w_4\}$
$\left[\dfrac{1}{3},\dfrac{2}{5}\right)$	$\{w_7,w_8\}$ / $\emptyset$	$\{w_7,w_8\}$ / $\{w_4,w_5\}$
$\left[\dfrac{2}{5},\dfrac{1}{2}\right)$	$\{w_7,w_8\}$ / $\emptyset$	$\{w_7,w_8\}$ / $\{w_3,w_4,w_5\}$

Finally, from Tables 9 and 10, we can observe that products of pattern w_7 are accepted by all decision makers while products having pattern w_4 are rejected. Then we can advise factories to increase the production of audio equipments of pattern w_7 and to reduce the production of audio equipments of pattern w_4. By rough sets under multiple decision tables, we can analyze what patterns are popular and what pattern are unpopular. The induction of simple rules inferring popular patterns and unpopular patterns is one of future research topics.

References

1. Pawlak, Z.: Rough Sets. *International Journal of Information Computer Science* **11**(5) (1982) 341–356
2. Enomoto, Y., Harada, T., Inoue, T., Mori, N.: Analysis of Choice for Audio Products Using Annexation Reduct System (in Japanese). *The Bulletin of Japanese Society for the Science of Design* **49**(5) (2003) 11–20
3. Itou, K., Enomoto, Y., Harada, T.: Influence of Annexation Order to Plural Annexation Condition Parts of Decision Rules (in Japanese). *Proceedings of 19th Fuzzy System Symposium* (2003) 529–532
4. Mori, N.: Rough Set and Kansei Engineering (in Japanese). *Journal of Japan Society for Fuzzy Theory and Systems,* **13**(6) (2001) 600–607
5. Inuiguchi, M., Suzuki, J., Miyajima, T.: Toward Rule Extraction from Multiple Decision Tables Based on Rough Set Theory. *Proceedings of 15th Mini-Euro Conference on Managing Uncertainty in Decision Support Models* (2004) CD-ROM
6. Shan, N., Ziarko, W.: Data-based Acquisition and Incremental Modification of Classification Rules. *Computational Intelligence* **11** (1995) 357–370
7. Ziarko, W.: Variable Precision Rough Set Model. *Journal of Computer and System Sciences* **46** (1993) 39–59.

Rough Membership and Bayesian Confirmation Measures for Parameterized Rough Sets[*]

Salvatore Greco[1], Benedetto Matarazzo[1], and Roman Słowiński[2]

[1] Faculty of Economics, University of Catania,
Corso Italia, 55, 95129 Catania, Italy
[2] Institute of Computing Science, Poznań University of Technology,
60-965 Poznań, and Institute for Systems Research,
Polish Academy of Sciences, 01-447 Warsaw, Poland

Abstract. A generalization of the original idea of rough sets and variable precision rough sets is introduced. This generalization is based on the concept of absolute and relative rough membership. Similarly to variable precision rough set model, the generalization called parameterized rough set model, is aimed at modeling data relationships expressed in terms of frequency distribution rather than in terms of a full inclusion relation used in the classical rough set approach. However, differently from variable precision rough set model, one or more parameters modeling the degree to which the condition attribute values confirm the decision attribute value, are considered. The properties of this extended model are investigated and compared to the classical rough set model and the variable precision rough set model.

1 Introduction

In the rough set approach (Pawlak 1982, 1991), classification of an object x from a universe U to a given set X is based on available data. For example, in medical diagnosis, the objects are patients, the given set X is a set of patients suffering from a disease, and the available data are results of medical tests. Objects described by the same data are indiscernible in view of data and form elementary sets called granules. An elementary set including object x is denoted by $[x]_R$ where R is the indiscernibility relation for which xRy means that x and y have the same description for given data. Thus $[x]_R$ is the set of patients having the same results of the tests. The classification involves three regions:

- the positive region, including patients for which the available data suggest a certain membership to the given set, i.e. all $x \in U$ such that $[x]_R \subseteq X$,
- the negative region, including patients for which the available data suggest a certain non-membership to the given set, i.e. all $x \in U$ such that $[x]_R \cap X \neq \emptyset$,

[*] The research of the first two authors has been supported by the Italian Ministry of Education, University and Scientific Research (MIUR). The third author wishes to acknowledge financial support from the State Committee for Scientific Research (KBN).

D. Ślęzak et al. (Eds.): RSFDGrC 2005, LNAI 3641, pp. 314–324, 2005.

- the boundary region, including patients for which the available data suggest neither a certain membership nor a certain non-membership to the given set, i.e. all $x \in U$ such that $[x]_R \cap X \neq \emptyset$ and $[x]_R \cap (U \setminus X) \neq \emptyset$.

The Variable Precision Rough Set (VPRS) model (Ziarko 1993, 1994) defines the positive region as an area where, on the basis of available data, the rough membership of objects to the given set is certain to some degree. The rough membership (Pawlak and Skowron 1994) is calculated from data as the ratio of objects from elementary set $[x]_R$ that belong to X:

$$\mu_X^R(x) = card\left([x]_R \cap X\right) / card\left([x]_R\right), \qquad 0 \leq \mu_X^R(x) \leq 1.$$

For example, in the medical diagnosis, the rough membership is calculated from data as the percentage of patients with the same results of the tests and suffering from the considered disease; the positive region includes patients whose rough membership to the set of patients suffering from the considered disease is not smaller than a given threshold $t > 0$.

Analogously, the negative region includes objects whose membership to set X is smaller than a given threshold $q < 1$, $q < t$. Finally, the boundary region includes objects whose membership is between q and t.

The rough membership used to define the above regions, can be considered as an *absolute rough membership* because it is relative to elementary set $[x]_R$ only and does not take into account the percentage of objects from X being outside the elementary set, i.e. in $U \setminus [x]_R$. Comparison of a percentage of objects from X being inside and outside the elementary set, respectively, needs a concept of *relative rough membership*. For example, the relative rough membership of x in X can be defined as

$$\hat{\mu}_X^R(x) = \frac{card\left([x]_R \cap X\right)}{card\left([x]_R\right)} - \frac{card\left((U \setminus [x]_R) \cap X\right)}{card\left(U \setminus [x]_R\right)}.$$

Consequently, the generalized VPRS model considered in this paper assumes that in order to include object x in the positive region of set X, it is not sufficient to have a minimum percentage of objects from X in $[x]_R$, but it is also necessary that the percentage of objects from X in $[x]_R$ is sufficiently greater than the percentage of objects from X outside $[x]_R$. In other words, it is necessary that both the absolute and the relative memberships of x in X are not smaller than given thresholds t and α, respectively.

Coming back to the example of medical diagnosis, let us suppose that 80% of patients positive to all tests suffer from the disease. This would seem to suggest that the positive result of all tests indicates the presence of the disease. Thus, if we used the VPRS model with, say $t = 0.75$, we would include all the patients positive to all the tests in the positive region. Suppose, moreover, that, on the other hand, 85% of patients not positive to at least one test are suffering from the disease. This means that passing from the set of patients with the positive result of all the tests to the set of patients not positive to at least one test, increases the percentage of patients suffering from the disease, instead of decreasing it.

This means that the tests are not determinant for the diagnosis of the disease. Therefore, in contrast to the previous conclusion from the VPRS model, we should not include the patients with positive result to all the tests in the positive region. Using our generalization of the VPRS model, this is possible with, say $t = 0.75$ and $\alpha = 0.2$. In fact, in this case we have that $\mu_X^R(x) > t$ but $\hat{\mu}_X^R(x) < \alpha$ for each patient x with positive result of all the tests.

The above definition of $\hat{\mu}_X^R(x)$ is one among many possible definitions because the relative rough membership is equivalent to an interestingness measure considered for decision rules in data mining (see, for example, (Hilderman and Hamilton 2001) and (Yao and Zhong 1999) for exhaustive reviews of the subject). For the sake of the simplicity, in this paper, we consider a class of interestingness measures related to the concept of Bayesian confirmation (Greco, Pawlak and Słowiński 2004).

Let us remark that the idea of using an interestingness measure for definition of variable precision rough approximations is not new (see e.g. Ziarko (2001), Ślęzak and Ziarko (2002), Ślęzak (2005)), however, it has been used in a single condition of membership. In this paper, we are considering for the first time two conditions of membership, corresponding to absolute and relative rough memberships, and representing two complementary aspects of rough approximation.

The article is organized as follows. Second section introduces confirmation measures and recalls some desirable properties of symmetry and asymmetry proposed by Eells and Fitelson (2002). Third section gives some basic notions concerning decision rules and decision algorithms within rough set approach. Fourth section introduces rough set confirmation measures. Fifth section introduces our model of rough set approximation. Final section presents conclusions.

2   Confirmation Measures

According to Fitelson (2001), measures of confirmation quantify the degree to which a piece of evidence E provides "evidence for or against" or "support for or against" a hypothesis H. Fitelson remarks, moreover, that measures of confirmation are supposed to capture the impact rather than the final result of the "absorption" of a piece of evidence.

Bayesian confirmation assume the existence of a probability Pr. In the following, given a proposition X, $Pr(X)$ is the probability of X. Given X and Y, $Pr(X|Y)$ represents the probability of X given Y, i.e.

$$Pr(X|Y) = Pr(X \wedge Y) / Pr(Y).$$

In this context, a measure of confirmation of a piece of evidence E with respect to a hypothesis H is denoted by $c(E, H)$. $c(E, H)$ is required to satisfy the following minimal property:

$$c(E, H) = \begin{cases} > 0 & \text{if } Pr(H|E) > Pr(H) \\ = 0 & \text{if } Pr(H|E) = Pr(H) \\ < 0 & \text{if } Pr(H|E) < Pr(H) \end{cases}$$

The most well known confirmation measures proposed in the literature are the following:

$$d(E, H) = Pr(H|E) - Pr(H)$$
$$r(E, H) = log\left[Pr\left(H\,|E\right) / Pr\left(H\right)\right]$$
$$l(E, H) = log\left[Pr\left(E\,|H\right) / Pr\left(E\,|\neg H\right)\right]$$
$$f(E, H) = \left[Pr\left(E|H\right) - Pr\left(E|\neg H\right)\right] / \left[Pr\left(E|H\right) + Pr\left(E|\neg H\right)\right]$$
$$s(E, H) = Pr(H|E) - Pr(H|\neg E)$$
$$b(E, H) = Pr(H \wedge E) - Pr(H)Pr(E)$$

For the sake of the simplicity we suppose that $Pr(E|H)$ and $Pr(E|\neg H)$, $Pr(H)$ are always different from zero and, therefore, the above measures (more precisely, $r(E, H)$, $l(E, H)$ and $f(E, H)$) are always well defined.

Many authors have considered, moreover, some more or less desirable properties of confirmation measures. Fitelson (2001) makes a comprehensive survey of these considerations. At the end of his retrospective, Fitelson concludes that the most convincing confirmation measures are $l(E, H)$ and $f(E, H)$. He also proves that $l(E, H)$ and $f(E, H)$ are ordinally equivalent, i.e. for all E, H and E', H', $l(E, H) \geq l(E', H')$ if and only if $f(E, H) \geq f(E', H')$.

Among the properties of confirmation measures reviewed by Fitelson (2001), there are properties of symmetry introduced by Carnap (1962) and investigated recently by Eells and Fitelson (2002). For all E and H, one can have:

- Evidence Symmetry (ES): $c(E, H) = -c(\neg E, H)$
- Commutativity Symmetry (CS): $c(E, H) = c(H, E)$
- Hypothesis Symmetry (HS): $c(E, H) = -c(E, \neg H)$
- Total Symmetry (TS): $c(E, H) = c(\neg E, \neg H)$

Eells and Fitelson (2002) remarked that given (CS), (ES) and (HS) are equivalent, and that (TS) follows from the conjunction of (ES) and (HS). Moreover, they advocate in favor of (HS) and against (ES), (CS) and (TS). The reason in favor of (HS) is that the significance of E with respect to H should be of the same strength, but of opposite sign, as the significance of E with respect to $\neg H$.

Eells and Fitelson (2002) prove that

1) s and b verify (ES), whereas d, r, l and f do not verify (ES),
2) d, s, b, f and l verify (HS), whereas r does not verify (HS),
3) r and b verify (CS), whereas d, s, f and l do not verify (CS),
4) s and b verify (TS), whereas d, r, f and l do not verify (TS).

Thus, assuming that (HS) is a desirable property, while (ES), (CS) and (TS) are not, Eells and Fitelson (2002) conclude that with respect to the property of symmetry, d, f and l are satisfactory confirmation measures while s, r and b are not satisfactory confirmation measures.

3   Decision Rules and Decision Algorithm

Let $S = (U, A)$ be an information table, where U and A are finite, non-empty sets called the *universe* and the set of *attributes*, respectively. If the set A is divided into two disjoint subsets of attributes, called *condition* and *decision attributes*, then the system is called a *decision table* and is denoted by $S = (U, C, D)$, where C and D are sets of condition and decision attributes, respectively. With every subset of attributes, one can associate a formal language of logical formulas $\boldsymbol{L}$ defined in a standard way and called the *decision language*. Formulas for a subset $B \subseteq A$ are build up from attribute-value pairs (a, v), where $a \in B$ and $v \in V_a$ (set V_a is a domain of a), by means of logical connectives $\wedge$ (*and*), $\vee$ (*or*), $\neg$ (*not*). We assume that the set of all formula sets in $\boldsymbol{L}$ is partitioned into two classes, called *condition* and *decision formulas*, respectively.

A *decision rule* induced from S and expressed in $\boldsymbol{L}$ is presented as $\Phi \rightarrow \Psi$, read "*if Φ, then Ψ*", where Φ and Ψ are condition and decision formulas in $\boldsymbol{L}$, called *premise* and *conclusion*, respectively. A decision rule $\Phi \rightarrow \Psi$ is also seen as a binary relation between premise and conclusion, called *consequence relation* (see critical discussion about interpretation of decision rules as logical implications in (Greco, Pawlak and Słowiński 2004)).

Let $\|\Phi\|$ denote the set of all objects from universe U, having the property Φ in S.

If $\Phi \rightarrow \Psi$ is a decision rule, then $supp_S(\Phi, \Psi) = card(\|\Phi \wedge \Psi\|)$ will be called the *support* of the decision rule and

$$\sigma_S(\Phi, \Psi) = supp_S(\Phi, \Psi) \, / \, card(U)$$

will be referred to as the *strength* of the decision rule.

With every decision rule $\Phi \rightarrow \Psi$ we associate *certainty* and *coverage factors*

$$cer_S(\Phi, \Psi) = supp_S(\Phi, \Psi) \, / \, card(\|\Phi\|),$$
$$cov_S(\Phi, \Psi) = supp_S(\Phi, \Psi) \, / \, card(\|\Psi\|).$$

If $cer_S(\Phi, \Psi) = 1$, then the decision rule $\Phi \rightarrow \Psi$ will be called *certain*, otherwise the decision rule will be referred to as *uncertain*.

A set of decision rules supported in total by the universe U constitutes a *decision algorithm* in S. Pawlak (2002) points out that every decision algorithm associated with S displays well-known probabilistic properties. In particular, it satisfies the total probability theorem and Bayes' theorem. As a decision algorithm can also be interpreted in terms of the rough set concept, these properties give a new look on Bayes' theorem from the rough set perspective. In consequence, one can draw conclusions from data without referring to prior and posterior probabilities, inherently associated with Bayesian reasoning. The revealed relationship can be used to invert decision rules, i.e., giving reasons (explanations) for decisions, which is useful in decision analysis.

4   Confirmation Measures and Decision Algorithms

In this section, we translate confirmation measures to the language of decision algorithms. A preliminary question that arises naturally in this context is the following: why a new measure is required for decision rules in addition to strength, certainty and coverage? In other words, what is the intuition behind the confirmation measure that motivates its use for characterization of decision rules?

To answer this question, it will be useful to recall the following example proposed by Popper (1959). Consider the possible result of rolling a die: 1,2,3,4,5,6. We can built a decision table, presented in Table 1, where the fact that the result is even or odd is the condition attribute, while the result itself is the decision attribute.

Table 1. Decision table

Condition attribute (result odd or even)	Decision attribute (result of rolling the die)
odd	1
even	2
odd	3
even	4
odd	5
even	6

Let us consider the cases Ψ="the result is 6" and $\neg\Psi$="the result is not 6". Let us also take into account the information Φ="the result is an even number (i.e. 2 or 4 or 6)". Therefore, we can consider the following two decision rules:

- $\Phi\rightarrow\Psi$ = "if the result is even, then the result is 6",
  with certainty $cer_S(\Phi,\Psi)=1/3$,
- $\Phi\rightarrow\neg\Psi$ = "if the result is even, then the result is not 6",
  with certainty $cer_S(\Phi,\neg\Psi)=2/3$.

Note that the rule $\Phi\rightarrow\Psi$ has a smaller certainty than the rule $\Phi\rightarrow\neg\Psi$. However, the probability that the result is 6 is 1/6, while the probability that the result is different from 6 is 5/6. Thus, the information Φ raises the probability of Ψ from 1/6 to 1/3, and decreases the probability of $\neg\Psi$ from 5/6 to 2/3. In conclusion, we can say that Φ confirms Ψ and disconfirms $\neg\Psi$, independently of the fact that the certainty of $\Phi\rightarrow\Psi$ is smaller than the certainty of $\Phi\rightarrow\neg\Psi$. From this simple example, one can see that certainty and confirmation are two completely different concepts, so it advocates for a new index expressing the latter type of information.

Given a decision rule $\Phi\rightarrow\Psi$, the confirmation measure we want to introduce should give the credibility of the proposition: Ψ **is satisfied more frequently when Φ is satisfied rather than when Φ is not satisfied**.

Differently from Bayesian confirmation, however, we start from a decision table rather than from a probability measure. In this context, the probability Pr of Φ is substituted by the relative frequency Fr in the considered data table S, i.e. $Fr_S(\Phi) = card\,(\|\Phi\|)/card\,(U)$.

Analogously, given Φ and Ψ, $Pr(\Psi|\Phi)$ – the probability of Ψ given Φ – is substituted by the certainty factor $cer_S(\Phi,\Psi)$ of the decision rule $\Phi\rightarrow\Psi$.

Therefore, a measure of confirmation of property Ψ by property Φ, denoted by $c(\Phi,\Psi)$, where Φ is a condition formula in L and Ψ is a decision formula in L, is required to satisfy the following minimal property

$$c(\Phi,\Psi) = \begin{cases} > 0 & \text{if } cer_S(\Phi,\Psi) > Fr_S(\Psi) \\ = 0 & \text{if } cer_S(\Phi,\Psi) = Fr_S(\Psi) \\ < 0 & \text{if } cer_S(\Phi,\Psi) < Fr_S(\Psi) \end{cases} \tag{i}$$

Definition (i) can be interpreted as follows:

- $c(\Phi,\Psi) > 0$ means that property Ψ is satisfied more frequently when Φ is satisfied (then, this frequency is $cer_S(\Phi,\Psi)$), rather than generically in the whole decision table (where this frequency is $Fr_S(\Psi)$),
- $c(\Phi,\Psi) = 0$ means that property Ψ is satisfied with the same frequency when Φ is satisfied and generically in the whole decision table,
- $c(\Phi,\Psi) < 0$ means that property Ψ is satisfied less frequently when Φ is satisfied, rather than generically in the whole decision table.

Observe that (i) can also be interpreted as follows:

- $c(\Phi,\Psi) > 0$ means that property Ψ is satisfied more frequently when Φ is satisfied rather than when Φ is not satisfied,
- $c(\Phi,\Psi) = 0$ means that property Ψ is satisfied with the same frequency when Φ is satisfied and when Φ is not satisfied,
- $c(\Phi,\Psi) < 0$ means that property Ψ is satisfied more frequently when Φ is not satisfied rather than when Φ is satisfied.

The specific confirmation measures recalled in section 2 can be rewritten in this context as follows:

$$d(\Phi,\Psi) = cer_S(\Phi,\Psi) - Fr_S(\Psi)$$
$$r(\Phi,\Psi) = log\left[cer_S(\Phi,\Psi) / Fr_S(\Psi)\right]$$
$$l(\Phi,\Psi) = log\left[cer_S(\Psi,\Phi) / cer_S(\neg\Psi,\Phi)\right]$$
$$f(\Phi,\Psi) = \left[cer_S(\Psi,\Phi) - cer_S(\neg\Psi,\Phi)\right] / \left[cer_S(\Psi,\Phi) + cer_S(\neg\Psi,\Phi)\right]$$
$$s(\Phi,\Psi) = cer_S(\Phi,\Psi) - cer_S(\neg\Phi,\Psi)$$
$$b(\Phi,\Psi) = cer_S(\Phi,\Psi) - Fr_S(\Phi)Fr_S(\Psi)$$

Clearly, all the results about confirmation measures obtained within Bayesian confirmation theory are valid for the confirmation measures defined in the context of decision algorithms considered within rough set theory.

In this context, moreover, a new monotonicity property introduced in (Greco, Pawlak and Słowiński 2004) is desirable for confirmation measures. The monotonicity says that the confirmation measure $c(\Phi,\Psi)$ must be non-decreasing with respect to $supp_S(\Phi,\Psi)$ and $supp_S(\neg\Phi,\neg\Psi)$, and non-increasing with respect to $supp_S(\neg\Phi,\Psi)$ and $supp_S(\Phi,\neg\Psi)$. The confirmation measures verifying monotonicity are $l(\Phi,\Psi)$, $f(\Phi,\Psi)$ and $s(\Phi,\Psi)$, whereas monotonicity does not hold for $d(\Phi,\Psi)$, $r(\Phi,\Psi)$ and $b(\Phi,\Psi)$ (Greco, Pawlak and Słowiński 2004). Therefore, the only confirmation measures which verify both symmetry/asymmetry properties of Eells and Fitelson and monotonicity property (M) are the two ordinally equivalent confirmation measures $l(\Phi,\Psi)$ and $f(\Phi,\Psi)$.

Below, we will use the confirmation measures as rough relative membership functions.

5   Parameterized Rough Sets

Suppose we are given a finite set $U \neq \emptyset$ (the universe) of objects we are interested in. If R is an equivalence relation over U, then by U/R we mean the family of all the equivalence classes of R and $[x]_R$ denotes the equivalence class of $x \in U$. Given a set $X \subseteq U$, the lower and the upper approximations of X in U are defined, respectively, as

$$\underline{R}(X) = \{x \in U : [x]_R \subseteq X\},$$
$$\overline{R}(X) = \{x \in U : [x]_R \cap X \neq \emptyset\}.$$

Set $BN_R(X) = \overline{R}(X) - \underline{R}(X)$ will be called the R-boundary of X.

Let t and q be two real parameters, called *lower limit* and *upper limit*, respectively, such that $0 \leq q \leq t \leq 1$. According to the VPRS model (Ziarko 1993, 1994), lower and upper approximations of X in U are defined, respectively, as

$$\underline{R}_t(X) = \{x \in U : \frac{card([x]_R \cap X)}{card([x]_R)} \geq t\},$$
$$\overline{R}_q(X) = \{x \in U : \frac{card([x]_R \cap X)}{card([x]_R)} > q\}.$$

Ślęzak (2005) proposed an alternative parameterized rough set model called rough Bayesian model, in which the lower and upper approximations of X are defined as follows, for $\varepsilon_t, \varepsilon_q \in [0, 1]$, such that $\varepsilon_t \geq \varepsilon_q$:

$$\underline{R}_{\varepsilon_t}(X) = \{x \in U : \frac{card([x]_R \cap X)}{card([x]_R)} \geq \varepsilon_t \frac{card(X)}{card(U)}\},$$
$$\overline{R}_{\varepsilon_q}(X) = \{x \in U : \frac{card([x]_R \cap X)}{card([x]_R)} > \varepsilon_q \frac{card(X)}{card(U)}\}$$

Let us consider now the relative rough membership functions $c(x, X)$ for $x \in U$ and $X \subseteq U$. $c(x, X)$ is defined as a measure of confirmation that evidence $y \in [x]_R$ gives to hypothesis $y \in X$. They clearly correspond to confirmation measures introduced in section 4, as follows:

$$d(x, X) = \frac{card([x]_R \cap X)}{card([x]_R)} - \frac{card(X)}{card(U)}$$

$$r(x, X) = log\left[\frac{card([x]_R \cap X)}{card([x]_R)} \Big/ \frac{card(X)}{card(U)}\right]$$

$$l(x, X) = log\left[\frac{card([x]_R \cap X)}{card(X)} \Big/ \frac{card([x]_R \cap (U \setminus X))}{card(U \setminus X)}\right]$$

$$f(x, X) = \left[\frac{card([x]_R \cap X)}{card(X)} - \frac{card([x]_R \cap (U \setminus X))}{card(U \setminus X)}\right] \Big/ \left[\frac{card([x]_R \cap X)}{card(X)} + \frac{card([x]_R \cap (U \setminus X))}{card(U \setminus X)}\right]$$

$$s(x, X) = \frac{card([x]_R \cap X)}{card([x]_R)} - \frac{card((U \setminus [x]_R) \cap X)}{card(U \setminus [x]_R)}$$

$$b(x, X) = \frac{card([x]_R \cap X)}{card(U)} - \frac{card([x]_R)}{card(U)} \frac{card(X)}{card(U)}$$

Let us remark that in the above definitions of relative rough membership functions, the *log* function takes the following extreme values: $log(0/a) = -\infty$ and

$log(a/0) = +\infty$, for all $a > 0$. Let also α and β, $\alpha \geq \beta$, be two real values in the range of variation of relative rough membership $c(x, X)$ (for example, if $c(x, X) = d(x, X)$, then $\alpha, \beta \in [-1,1]$).

The parameterized lower and upper approximations of X in U with respect to relative rough membership $c(x, X)$ are defined, respectively, as

$$\underline{R}_{t,\alpha}(X) = \{x \in U : \frac{card([x]_R \cap X)}{card([x]_R)} \geq t \text{ and } c(x, X) \geq \alpha\},$$

$$\overline{R}_{q,\beta}(X) = \{x \in U : \frac{card([x]_R \cap X)}{card([x]_R)} > q \text{ or } c(x, X) > \beta\}.$$

One can notice that above definitions boil down to the following special cases:

1. The classical rough set model (Pawlak 1982), when $t = 1$, $q = 0$, $\alpha = \beta = min\{c(x, X) : x \in U \text{ and } X \subseteq U\}$. This definition does not involve neither absolute nor relative rough membership
2. The VPRS model (Ziarko 1993, 1994), when $0 \leq q \leq t \leq 1$, $\alpha = \beta = min\{c(x, X) : x \in U \text{ and } X \subseteq U\}$. This definition involves an absolute rough membership only.
3. The rough Bayesian model (Ślęzak 2005), when $t = 1$, $q = 0$, $c(x, X) = l(x, X)$, and $\alpha = log\varepsilon_t$, $\beta = log\varepsilon_q$. This definition involves a relative rough membership only.

Our parameterized rough set model is the most general since it involves both absolute and relative rough membership, moreover, it can be generalized further by considering more than one relative rough membership.

Theorem 1. *The following properties hold:*

1). *For every relative rough membership $c(x, X)$, for every $X \subseteq U$, for every $q,t \in]0,1]$, with $q < t$, and for every α, β in the range of variation of relative rough membership $c(x, X)$, such that $\alpha > \beta$,*

$$\underline{R}_{t,\alpha}(X) \subseteq \overline{R}_{q,\beta}(X).$$

2). *If the relative rough membership $c(x, X)$ is one among $d(x, X)$, $l(x, X)$, $f(x, X)$, $s(x, X)$, $b(x, X)$, then for every $X \subseteq U$, for every $t \in]0,1]$, and for every α in the range of variation of relative rough membership $c(x, X)$*

$$\underline{R}_{t,\alpha}(X) = U \setminus \overline{R}_{1-t,\beta}(U \setminus X)$$

with $\beta = -\alpha$.

3). *If $c(x, X) = l(x, X)$ or $c(x, X) = f(x, X)$, for every $x \in U$ and $X \subseteq U$, for every $q,t \in [0, 1]$ and for every α, β in the range of variation of relative rough membership $c(x, X)$, then*

$$\underline{R}_{t,\alpha}(X) \supseteq \underline{R}(X), \qquad \overline{R}_{q,\beta}(X) \subseteq \overline{R}(X).$$

4). *If $c(x, X) = r(x, X)$, for every $x \in U$ and $X \subseteq U$, for every $q \in [0, 1]$ and for every β in the range of variation of $c(x, X)$, then*

$$\overline{R}_{q,\beta}(X) \subseteq \overline{R}(X). \qquad \qquad \square$$

Results of Theorem 1 correspond to very well known properties of the classical rough set model and the VPRS model. More precisely, 1) means that the lower approximation is always included in the upper approximation, and 2) represents complementarity property (given that some conditions are satisfied, the lower approximation is the complement of the upper approximation of the complement). 3) and 4) represent properties relating rough approximations of the classical model with rough approximations of our parameterized rough set model, which are also verified by the VPRS model.

Theorem 2. *The following properties <u>do not</u> hold:*

1). For relative rough membership functions $c(x, X)$ equal to $b(x, X)$, or $d(x, X)$, or $r(x, X)$, or $s(x, X)$, for every $x \in U$ and $X \subseteq U$, for every $t \in]0,1]$ and for every α in the range of variation of relative rough membership $c(x, X)$,

$$\underline{R}_{t,\alpha}(X) \supseteq \underline{R}(X).$$

2). For relative rough membership functions $c(x, X)$ equal to $b(x, X)$, or $d(x, X)$, or $s(x, X)$, for every $x \in U$ and $X \subseteq U$, for every $q \in]0,1]$ and for every β in the range of variation of relative rough membership $c(x, X)$,

$$\overline{R}_{q,\beta}(X) \subseteq \overline{R}(X).$$

3). For every relative rough membership $c(x, X)$, for every $X, Y \subseteq U$, for every $q, t \in]0, 1]$ and for every α, β in the range of variation of relative rough membership $c(x, X)$,

$\underline{R}_{t,\alpha}(X \cap Y) \subseteq \underline{R}_{t,\alpha}(X) \cap \underline{R}_{t,\alpha}(Y),$
$\underline{R}_{t,\alpha}(X \cup Y) \supseteq \underline{R}_{t,\alpha}(X) \cup \underline{R}_{t,\alpha}(Y),$
$\overline{R}_{q,\beta}(X \cap Y) \subseteq \overline{R}_{q,\beta}(X) \cap \overline{R}_{q,\beta}(Y),$
$\overline{R}_{q,\beta}(X \cup Y) \supseteq \overline{R}_{q,\beta}(X) \cup \overline{R}_{q,\beta}(Y).$ $\qquad\qquad\square$

The results of Theorem 2 are somehow surprising: they say that some very typical properties of rough sets do not hold in the context of the parameterized rough set approach. This is due to the behavior of some relative rough membership functions. However, even if consideration of a relative rough membership provokes violation of some typical properties of rough approximations, the parameterized rough set approach gives a much more complete and realistic perspective to data analysis. In fact, there is a tradeoff between the elegance of a mathematical model, typical for classical rough set model and VPRS model, on one side, and the rich formulation permitting to control many specific aspects of data analysis, typical for parameterized rough set model, on the other side.

Let us conclude this section with the remark that, since the above confirmation measures are related to different aspects of data analysis, the parameterized rough set model can be simply generalized by considering two or even more relative rough membership functions.

6   Conclusions

We presented a parameterized rough set model that is a generalization of the VPRS model. Differently from the VPRS model, however, we do not take into account the frequency distribution only but also some parameters modeling the degree to which the condition attribute values confirm the decision attribute value. Consequently, we propose to use two kinds of parameters corresponding to absolute and relative rough membership. This model gives a richer insight into data analysis, compared to competitive rough set models, and this compensates the violation of some properties that are typically verified by rough set models.

References

1. Eells, E., Fitelson, B. (2002), Symmetries and assymetries in evidential support. *Philosophical Studies*, 107, 129-142
2. Fitelson, B. (2001), *Studies in Bayesian Confirmation Theory*. Ph.D. thesis, University of Wisconsin-Madison
3. Greco, S., Pawlak, Z., Słowiński, R. (2004), Can Bayesian confirmation measures be useful for rough set decision rules? *Engineering Applications of Artificial Intelligence*, 17, 345-361
4. Hilderman, R.J., Hamilton, H.J. (2001), *Knowledge Discovery and Measures of Interest*, Kluwer Academic Publishers, Boston
5. Pawlak, Z. (1982), Rough Sets. *International Journal of Computer and Information Sciences*, 11, 341-356
6. Pawlak, Z. (1991), *Rough Sets*, Kluwer, Dordrecht
7. Pawlak, Z. (2002), Rough Sets, decision algorithms and Bayes' Theorem. *European Journal of Operational Research*, 136, 181-189
8. Pawlak, Z., Skowron, A. (1994), Rough membership functions. [In]: R. R. Yager, M. Fedrizzi and J. Kacprzyk (eds.), *Advances in the Dempster-Shafer Theory of Evidence*, Wiley, New York, pp. 251-271
9. Popper, K. R. (1959), *The Logic of Scientific Discovery*, Hutchinson, London
10. Ślęzak, D. (2005), Rough sets and Bayes factor. *Transactions on Rough Sets III*, LNCS 3400, 202-229
11. Ślęzak, D. Ziarko, W. (2002), Bayesian rough set model. [In]: *Proc. of Intl. Conference on Data Mining. Foundations of Data Mining and Knowledge Discovery Workshop*, Meabashi City, Japan, pp. 131-136
12. Yao, Y.Y., Zhong, N. (1999), An analysis of quantitative measures associated with rules. [In]: N. Zhong and L. Zhou (eds.), *Methodologies for Knowledge Discovery and Data Mining*. Lecture Notes in Artificial Intelligence, 1574, Springer-Verlag, Berlin, pp. 479-488
13. Ziarko, W. (1993), Variable precision Rough Sets Model, *Journal of Computer and System Science*, 46, 1, 39-59
14. Ziarko, W. (1994), Variable precision rough sets with asymmetric bounds. [In]: W. Ziarko (ed.), *Rough sets, Fuzzy sets and Knowledge Discovery*, Springer-Verlag, Berlin, pp. 167-177
15. Ziarko, W. (2001), Set approximation quality measures in the variable precision rough set model. [In]: *Soft Computing Systems, Management and Applications*, IOS Press, pp. 442-452

Rough Sets Handling Missing Values Probabilistically Interpreted

Michinori Nakata[1] and Hiroshi Sakai[2]

[1] Faculty of Management and Information Science,
Josai International University,
1 Gumyo, Togane, Chiba, 283-8555, Japan
nakatam@ieee.org
[2] Department of Mathematics and Computer Aided Sciences,
Faculty of Engineering, Kyushu Institute of Technology,
Tobata, Kitakyushu, 804-8550, Japan
sakai@mns.kyutech.ac.jp

Abstract. We examine methods of valued tolerance relations where the conventional methods based on rough sets are extended in order to handle incomplete information. The methods can deal with missing values probabilistically interpreted. We propose a correctness criterion to the extension of the conventional methods. And then we check whether or not the correctness criterion is satisfied in a method of valued tolerance relations. As a result, we conclude that the method does not satisfy the correctness criterion. Therefore, we show how to revise the method of valued tolerance relations so that the correctness criterion can be satisfied.

1 Introduction

Rough sets, proposed by Pawlak [10], give suitable methods to knowledge discovery from data. Usually, methods based on rough sets are applied to complete data not containing uncertainty and imprecision. However, there ubiquitously exist uncertainty and imprecision in the real world[9].

Researches handling uncertainty and imprecision are actively done on the field of databases [9], but are not so much on the field of knowledge discovery. Some pioneering work was done by Słowiński and Stefanowski [13] and Grzymala [3] to handle imprecise information by using rough sets. Recently, several investigations have been made on this topic.

Kryszkiewicz applies rough sets to a data table containing incomplete information by assuming a missing value expressing unknown as indiscernible with an arbitrary value[6,7,8]. An indiscernibility relation under the assumption is called a tolerance relation. The tolerance relation is reflexive, symmetric, but not always transitive. In this method an object in which some attribute values are missing values is indiscernible with every object for the attributes. Stefanowski and Tsoukiàs apply rough sets to a data table containing incomplete information by making an indiscernibility relation from the assumption that an object with an exact attribute value is similar to another object with the attribute value being missing, but the converse is not so[14,16]. They call the indiscernibility relation a similarity relation. The similarity relation is only reflexive. The above two methods handle incomplete information by deriving an indiscernibility relation from giving some assumptions to indiscernibility of missing values, and then by applying the conventional methods of rough sets to the indiscernibility

D. Ślęzak et al. (Eds.): RSFDGrC 2005, LNAI 3641, pp. 325–334, 2005.

relation. Thus, obtained results depend on the assumptions to indiscernibility of missing values.

Furthermore, Stefanowski and Tsoukiás propose a method without assumptions to indiscernibility of missing values. They make an indiscernibility relation by introducing the probabilistic degree that two objects cannot be discerned [14,15,16]. In their method, an attribute can equally take an arbitrary value in the corresponding domain when the attribute value is a missing value; in other words, the missing value is equal to an imprecise value expressed in a uniform probability distribution over the domain. Under no assumption to indiscernibility of missing values, indiscernibility degrees of objects are calculated, which are elements of an indiscernibility relation. The indiscernibility relation is called a valued tolerance relation and each element is a value in the interval $[0, 1]$. In the method, they use indiscernible sets and use implication operators in calculating an inclusion degree of two indiscernible sets.

On the other hand, a method based on possible worlds is proposed [11,12]. This method is to apply the conventional method based on rough sets to possible tables into which an incomplete table is divided, and then to aggregate the obtained results. The method does not use any assumptions to indiscernibility of missing values. We can obtain to what degree every possible rule probabilistically holds. This method is time-consuming, because the more the number of missing values increases, the more the number of possible tables increases exponentially. However, this method admits of no doubt for how to handle imprecise values.

Active researches are made into imprecise information in the field of databases [9]. Some extensions have to be made to operators in order to directly deal with imprecise information. In order to check whether or not the extended operators create correct results in query processing, a correctness criterion is used[1,4,5,17]. The correctness criterion is as follows:

Results obtained from applying an extended operator to imprecise relations are the same as ones obtained from applying the corresponding conventional operator to possible relations derived from those imprecise relations.

We adopt this criterion to rough-set-based methods and check whether extended methods satisfy the correctness criterion or not. Using the correctness criterion means obtaining methods directly handling imprecise information, not dividing an imprecise table into possible tables, under the method that admits of no doubt for how to handle imprecise information.

This paper is organized as follows. In Section 2, the outline of methods based on rough sets and the process of checking the correctness criterion are described. Section 3 is for methods of possible tables. Section 4 is for methods of valued tolerance relations. In section 5 we address how to revise methods of valued tolerance relations so that the correctness criterion can be satisfied. The last section addresses conclusions.

2   Methods Based on Rough Sets

In a data table t having a set $\mathcal{A}(= \{A_1, \ldots, A_n\})$ of attributes and consisting of objects, the indiscernibility relation $IND(X)$ for a subset $X \subseteq \mathcal{A}$ of attributes is

$$IND(X) = \{(o, o') \in t \times t \mid \forall A_i \in X \ \ o[A_i] = o'[A_i]\},$$

where $o[A_i]$ and $o'[A_i]$ are attribute values of objects o and o', respectively. We suppose that the family of all equivalence classes obtained from the indiscernibility relation $IND(X)$ is denoted by $\mathcal{E}(X) \ (= \{E(X)_1, \ldots, E(X)_m\})$, where

$E(X)_i$ is an equivalence class. When every value of attributes comprising X is exact, $E(X)_i \cap E(X)_j = \emptyset$ with $i \neq j$. Thus, the objects are uniquely partitioned. The indiscernible set $S(X)_o \in \mathcal{E}(X)$ of an object o for a set X of attributes is

$$S(X)_o = \{o' \in t \mid \forall A_i \in X \;\; o[A_i] = o'[A_i]\}.$$

The lower approximation $\underline{IND(Y, X)}$ and the upper approximation $\overline{IND(Y, X)}$ of $IND(Y)$ by $IND(X)$ are expressed by means of using indiscernible sets as follows:

$$\underline{IND(Y, X)} = \{o \in t \mid \exists o' S(X)_o \subseteq S(Y)_{o'}\},$$

$$\overline{IND(Y, X)} = \{o \in t \mid \exists o' S(X)_o \cap S(Y)_{o'} \neq \emptyset\}.$$

When an object o takes imprecise values for some attributes, it does not always take the same actual value as another object o', even if both objects have the same expression. To what degree the object o takes the same actual value as the object o' is obtained. The degree is an indiscernibility degree of the object o with the object o'. The indiscernible set $S(X)_o$ is replaced as follows:

$$S(X)_o = \{(o', \kappa(o[X] = o'[X])) \mid (\kappa(o[X] = o'[X]) \neq 0) \wedge (o \neq o')\} \cup \{(o, 1)\},$$

where $\kappa(o[X] = o'[X])$ is an indiscernibility degree of objects o and o' for a set X of attributes, and

$$\kappa(o[X] = o'[X]) = \bigotimes_{A_i \in X} \kappa(o[A_i] = o'[A_i]),$$

where the operator $\bigotimes$ depends on the properties of imprecise attribute values. When the imprecise attribute values are expressed in probability distributions, the operator is product. We have to extend the conventional methods to handle the indiscernible set. Although some authors propose how to extend the conventional methods, they do not address at all why their extension is correct. Thus, in order to check whether the extended methods are correct or not, we adopt the following correctness criterion:

Results obtained from directly applying an extended method to an imprecise table are the same as ones obtained from applying the corresponding conventional method to possible tables derived from that imprecise table.

This is formulated as follows:

Suppose that $rep(t)$ is a set of possible tables derived from a data table t containing imprecise values. Let q' be the conventional method applied to $rep(t)$, where q' corresponds to an extended method q directly applied to the data table t. The two results is the same; namely,

$$q(t) = q'(rep(t)).$$

When this is valid, the extended method q gives correct results.

In rough-set-based methods this correctness criterion is checked as follows:

- Derive a set of possible tables from a data table containing imprecise values.
- Aggregate the results obtained from applying the conventional method to each possible table.

– Compare the aggregated results with ones obtained from directly applying the extended method to the original data table.

When two results coincide, the correctness criterion is satisfied. In the next section, we address methods of possible tables. We focus on the lower approximation $IND(Y, X)$ in a data table, because the upper approximation $\overline{IND}(Y, X)$ is equal to the whole objects in the data table.

3   Methods of Possible Tables

We suppose that data table t containing missing values is given as follows:

$$
\begin{array}{c|c|c}
\multicolumn{3}{c}{t} \\
O & A & B \\
\hline
1 & x & a \\
2 & x & a \\
3 & @ & b \\
4 & @ & a \\
\end{array}
$$

Here, column O denotes the object identity and @ denotes a missing value that means *unknown*. Possible tables obtained from table t are those that every missing value @ is replaced by an element comprising the corresponding domain. Suppose that domains $dom(A)$ and $dom(B)$ of attributes A and B are $\{x, y\}$ and $\{a, b\}$, respectively. The following four possible tables are derived:

$$
\begin{array}{c|c|c}
\multicolumn{3}{c}{Poss(t)_1} \\
O & A & B \\
\hline
1 & x & a \\
2 & x & a \\
3 & x & b \\
4 & x & a \\
\end{array}
\qquad
\begin{array}{c|c|c}
\multicolumn{3}{c}{Poss(t)_2} \\
O & A & B \\
\hline
1 & x & a \\
2 & x & a \\
3 & x & b \\
4 & y & a \\
\end{array}
\qquad
\begin{array}{c|c|c}
\multicolumn{3}{c}{Poss(t)_3} \\
O & A & B \\
\hline
1 & x & a \\
2 & x & a \\
3 & y & b \\
4 & x & a \\
\end{array}
\qquad
\begin{array}{c|c|c}
\multicolumn{3}{c}{Poss(t)_4} \\
O & A & B \\
\hline
1 & x & a \\
2 & x & a \\
3 & y & b \\
4 & y & a \\
\end{array}
$$

We check which object contributes the lower approximation $\underline{IND(A, B)}$ in these possible tables. For $Poss(t)_1$, indiscernible sets of the objects for attribute A are,

$$
S(A)_{o_1} = S(A)_{o_2} = S(A)_{o_3} = S(A)_{o_4} = \{o_1, o_2, o_3, o_4\}.
$$

The indiscernible sets of the objects for attribute B are,

$$
S(B)_{o_1} = S(B)_{o_2} = S(B)_{o_4} = \{o_1, o_2, o_4\}, \quad S(B)_{o_3} = \{o_3\}.
$$

With what degree each object $o_i (i = 1, 4)$ belongs to $IND(B, A)$ is,

$$
\kappa(o_i \in \underline{IND(B, A)}) = \max_j \kappa(S(A)_{o_i} \subseteq S(B)_{o_j}) = 0.
$$

Thus, there exists no object that contributes to $\underline{IND(B, A)}$ in $Poss(t)_1$. Similarly, only the fourth object contributes to $\underline{IND(B, A)}$ in $Poss(t)_2$. All the objects contribute to $\underline{IND(B, A)}$ in $Poss(t)_3$. The first and second objects contribute to $\underline{IND(B, A)}$ in $Poss(t)_4$. Collectively speaking at every object, the first object contributes to $\underline{IND(B, A)}$ in $Poss(t)_3$ and $Poss(t)_4$; the second in $Poss(t)_3$ and $Poss(t)_4$; the third in $Poss(t)_3$; the fourth in $Poss(t)_2$ and

$Poss(t)_3$. One of the possible tables is the actual table, but it is unknown which table is the actual one. In this point, they can be regarded as probabilistically equal; namely, each of them has the same probabilistic degree $1/4$. Thus, with what degree each object o_i belongs to $IND(B, A)$ is as follows:

$$\kappa(o_1 \in IND(B, A)) = 0 \times 1/4 + 0 \times 1/4 + 1 \times 1/4 + 1 \times 1/4 = 1/2,$$
$$\kappa(o_2 \in IND(B, A)) = 0 \times 1/4 + 0 \times 1/4 + 1 \times 1/4 + 1 \times 1/4 = 1/2,$$
$$\kappa(o_3 \in IND(B, A)) = 0 \times 1/4 + 0 \times 1/4 + 1 \times 1/4 + 0 \times 1/4 = 1/4,$$
$$\kappa(o_4 \in IND(B, A)) = 0 \times 1/4 + 1 \times 1/4 + 1 \times 1/4 + 0 \times 1/4 = 1/2.$$

We examine whether or not the same value $\kappa(o_i \in IND(B, A))$ for each object o_i is obtained by means of using the extended method, a method of valued tolerance relations, in the following section.

4   Methods of Valued Tolerance Relations

Stefanowski and Tsoukiàs[14,15,16] take the interpretation that when an attribute value is a missing value, the actual value is one of elements in the domain of the attribute and which element is the actual value does not depend on an specified element; in other words, each element has the same probability for the element being the actual value. This means that every missing value is expressed in a uniform probability distribution over the domain. Indiscernibility degrees of every pair of objects are calculated, where any assumptions to indiscernibility of missing values are not used. An obtained indiscernibility relation is reflexive and symmetric, but consists of values in the interval $[0, 1]$. The indiscernibility relations $IND(A)$ and $IND(B)$ for attributes A and B in table t are, respectively,

$$IND(A) = \begin{pmatrix} 1 & 1 & 1/2 & 1/2 \\ 1 & 1 & 1/2 & 1/2 \\ 1/2 & 1/2 & 1 & 1/2 \\ 1/2 & 1/2 & 1/2 & 1 \end{pmatrix}, \quad IND(B) = \begin{pmatrix} 1 & 1 & 0 & 1 \\ 1 & 1 & 0 & 1 \\ 0 & 0 & 1 & 0 \\ 1 & 1 & 0 & 1 \end{pmatrix}.$$

The indiscernible sets of the objects for attribute A are,

$$S(A)_{o_1} = \{(o_1, 1), (o_2, 1), (o_3, 1/2), (o_4, 1/2)\},$$
$$S(A)_{o_2} = \{(o_1, 1), (o_2, 1), (o_3, 1/2), (o_4, 1/2)\},$$
$$S(A)_{o_3} = \{(o_1, 1/2), (o_2, 1/2), (o_3, 1), (o_4, 1/2)\},$$
$$S(A)_{o_4} = \{(o_1, 1/2), (o_2, 1/2), (o_3, 1/2), (o_4, 1)\}.$$

The indiscernible sets of the objects for attribute B are,

$$S(B)_{o_1} = S(B)_{o_2} = S(B)_{o_4} = \{(o_1, 1), (o_2, 1), (o_4, 1)\}, \quad S(B)_{o_3} = \{(o_3, 1)\}.$$

Suppose that an object o belongs to sets S and S' with probabilistic degrees $P_{o,S}$ and $P_{o,S'}$, respectively. The degree $\kappa(S \subseteq S')$ that the set S is included in another set S' is,

$$\kappa(S \subseteq S') = \prod_{o \in S} \kappa(o \in S \rightarrow o \in S') = \prod_{o \in S} (1 - P_{o,S} + P_{o,S} \times P_{o,S'}).$$

In this formula, the inclusion degree of two sets is calculated by means of using Reichenbach implication ($u \rightarrow v = 1 - u + u \times v$). Now, S and S' are $S(A)_{o_i}$ and $S(B)_{o_k}$, respectively, and $P_{o_i, S(A)_{o_i}}$ and $P_{o_i, S(B)_{o_k}}$ are $\kappa(o_i[A] = o_j[A])$ and $\kappa(o_k[B] = o_j[B])$, respectively. Thus, the degree with which the object o_1 belongs to $\underline{IND(B, A)}$ is as follows:

$$\kappa(o_1 \in \underline{IND(B, A)}) = \max_k \kappa(S(A)_{o_1} \subseteq S(B)_{o_k})$$
$$= \kappa(S(A)_{o_1} \subseteq S(B)_{o_1})$$
$$= 1 \times 1 \times (1 - 1/2 + 1/2 \times 0) \times (1 - 1/2 + 1/2 \times 1) = 1/2.$$

Similarly,

$$\kappa(o_2 \in \underline{IND(B, A)}) = \kappa(S(A)_{o_2} \subseteq S(B)_{o_2}) = 1/2,$$
$$\kappa(o_3 \in \underline{IND(B, A)}) = \kappa(S(A)_{o_3} \subseteq S(B)_{o_3})$$
$$= (1 - 1/2 + 1/2 \times 0) \times (1 - 1/2 + 1/2 \times 0)$$
$$\times 1 \times (1 - 1/2 + 1/2 \times 0) = 1/8,$$
$$\kappa(o_4 \in \underline{IND(B, A)}) = \kappa(S(A)_{o_4} \subseteq S(B)_{o_4})$$
$$= (1 - 1/2 + 1/2 \times 1) \times (1 - 1/2 + 1/2 \times 1)$$
$$\times (1 - 1/2 + 1/2 \times 0) \times 1 = 1/2.$$

Thus, the lower approximation $\underline{IND(B, A)}$ is

$$\underline{IND(B, A)} = \{(o_1, 1/2), (o_2, 1/2), (o_3, 1/8), (o_4, 1/2)\}.$$

The degree $\kappa(o_3 \in \underline{IND(B, A)})$ of the object o_3 is not equal to one obtained from possible tables.

5   Revising Methods of Valued Tolerance Relations

The method of valued tolerance relations, which is proposed by Stefanowski and Tsoukiàs[14,15,16], probabilistically handles missing values. We have to examine why this method of Stefanowski and Tsoukiàs cannot satisfy the correctness criterion. Stefanowski and Tsoukiàs calculates the inclusion degree of two sets to which each element belongs with a probabilistic degree as follows:

- Calculate with what probabilistic degree every element belonging to a set also belongs to another set by using Reichenbach implication.
- Multiply the obtained degrees together.

The process shows that the total inclusion degree is obtained through aggregating the inclusion degrees separately obtained for each element. This is valid under the condition that an inclusion degree for an element is determined independently of another element. Is this valid in the present situation?

In the previous section, the degree $\kappa(o_3 \in \underline{IND(B, A)})$ of the lower approximation $\underline{IND(B, A)}$ for the third object o_3 does not coincide with the degree obtained from using possible tables. This would be due to not taking into account the fact that when the third object is indiscernible with the first for attribute A, simultaneously it is indiscernible with the second; in other words, the first and the second objects have to be dealt with together. This strongly suggests that the condition described above is not valid in the present situation.

Furthermore in order to examine this, we go into issues for using implication operators. In Reichenbach implication, a probability $Prob(a \rightarrow b)$ of a sentence $a \rightarrow b$ is equal to $1 - Prob(a) + Prob(a) \times Prob(b)$, when probabilities that a sentence a is valid and that a sentence b is valid are given with $Prob(a)$ and $Prob(b)$, respectively. This comes from the following: when the sentence a is valid, $a \rightarrow b$ is valid with $Prob(a) \times Prob(b)$; when a is invalid, $a \rightarrow b$ is valid regardless of b; namely, $a \rightarrow b$ is valid with $1 - Prob(a)$ when a is invalid; thus, $Prob(a \rightarrow b)$ is $1 - Prob(a) + Prob(a) \times Prob(b)$ generally. Is it correct in the present situation that $a \rightarrow b$ is valid regardless of b when a is invalid?

The fact that an object o_j belongs to $S(X)_{o_i}$ with a probabilistic degree $\kappa(o_i[X] = o_j[X])$ means that o_j is equal to o_i for a set X of attributes with the degree $\kappa(o_i[X] = o_j[X])$. In the method of Stefanowski and Tsoukiàs using an implication, Reichenbach implication, the degree that $o_j \in S(X)_{o_i} \rightarrow o_j \in S(Y)_{o_i}$ is valid is $1 - \kappa(o_i[X] = o_j[X]) + \kappa(o_i[X] = o_j[X]) \times \kappa(o_i[Y] = o_j[Y])$, when o_j is equal to o_i for sets X and Y of attributes with probabilistic degrees $\kappa(o_i[X] = o_j[X])$ and $\kappa(o_i[Y] = o_j[Y])$, respectively. This calculation means that the object o_j unconditionally contributes $IND(Y, X)$ with a probabilistic degree $1 - \kappa(o_i[X] = o_j[X])$; namely, $\kappa(o_i[Y] = o_j[Y]) = 1$, when o_j is not equal to o_i for a set X of attributes with a probabilistic degree $1 - \kappa(o_i[X] = o_j[X])$. However, this is not correct if there exists another object o_k that is equal to o_j with a probabilistic degree for a set X of attributes, but that is not at all to o_i for X, as is shown in the following example.

We suppose that data table t' containing missing values is given as follows:

$$t'$$

O	A	B
1	x	a
2	y	a
3	@	b
4	@	a

In data table t' only the attribute value $o_2[A]$ is different from data table t in section 3. Notice there exists another object o_2 that is equal to o_3 with a probabilistic degree for attribute A, but that is not at all equal to o_1 for A. Results obtained from using possible tables are:

$$\kappa(o_1 \in \underline{IND(B, A)}) = 1/2,$$
$$\kappa(o_2 \in \underline{IND(B, A)}) = 1/2,$$
$$\kappa(o_3 \in \underline{IND(B, A)}) = 0,$$
$$\kappa(o_4 \in \underline{IND(B, A)}) = 1/2.$$

The indiscernibility relations $IND(A)$ for attribute A in table t' is as follows:

$$IND(A) = \begin{pmatrix} 1 & 0 & 1/2 & 1/2 \\ 0 & 1 & 1/2 & 1/2 \\ 1/2 & 1/2 & 1 & 1/2 \\ 1/2 & 1/2 & 1/2 & 1 \end{pmatrix}.$$

$IND(B)$ is the same as in table t. The indiscernible sets of the objects for attribute A are,

$$S(A)_{o_1} = \{(o_1, 1), (o_3, 1/2), (o_4, 1/2)\},$$
$$S(A)_{o_2} = \{(o_2, 1), (o_3, 1/2), (o_4, 1/2)\},$$
$$S(A)_{o_3} = \{(o_1, 1/2), (o_2, 1/2), (o_3, 1), (o_4, 1/2)\},$$
$$S(A)_{o_4} = \{(o_1, 1/2), (o_2, 1/2), (o_3, 1/2), (o_4, 1)\}.$$

The indiscernible sets of the objects for attribute B are the same as in table t. We focus on the degree with which the third object o_3 belongs to $IND(B, A)$.

$$\kappa(o_3 \in \underline{IND(B, A)}) = \kappa(S(A)_{o_3} \subseteq S(B)_{o_3})$$
$$= (1 - 1/2 + 1/2 \times 0) \times (1 - 1/2 + 1/2 \times 0) \times 1$$
$$\times (1 - 1/2 + 1/2 \times 0) = 1/8.$$

In the example, the contribution of the fact that o_3 is equal to o_1 for attribute A with a probabilistic degree $\kappa(o_3[A] = o_1[A])$ is calculated by means of $1 - \kappa(o_3[A] = o_1[A]) + \kappa(o_3[A] = o_1[A]) \times \kappa(o_3[B] = o_1[B])$. The fact that o_3 is not equal to o_1 for attribute A means that o_3 is equal to another object o_2 for attribute A, because the domain of A is comprised of two elements; namely, $\{x, y\}$. Thus, when o_3 is not equal to o_1 for attribute A with a probabilistic degree $1 - \kappa(o_3[A] = o_1[A])$, o_3 has to be unconditionally equal to o_2 for attribute B. However, this is not valid in table t'. In other words, we cannot separate the two facts that o_3 is equal to o_1 for an attribute A with a probabilistic degree $\kappa(o_3[A] = o_1[A])$ and o_3 is not equal to o_1 for attribute A with a probabilistic degree $1 - \kappa(o_3[A] = o_1[A])$; in other words, o_3 is equal to o_2 for attribute A with a probabilistic degree $1 - \kappa(o_3[A] = o_1[A])(=\kappa(o_3[A] = o_2[A]))$. These two facts link with each other disjunctively. We simultaneously have to deal with the two facts.

From considering the above viewpoint, we propose a new formula for calculating $\kappa(o_i \in IND(Y, X))$.

Let $SS(X)_{o_i}$ be the set of elements removed grades from $S(X)_{o_i}$. Let $ps(X)_{o_i, l}$ be an element of the power set $PS(X)_{o_i}$ of $SS(X)_{o_i} \setminus o_i$.

$$\kappa(o_i \in \underline{IND(Y, X)}) = \max_k \kappa(S(X)_{o_i} \subseteq S(Y)_{o_k})$$
$$= \max_k (\sum_l (\kappa(\wedge_{o' \in ps(X)_{o_i, l}} (o_i[X] = o'[X])$$
$$\wedge_{o' \notin ps(X)_{o_i, l}} (o_i[X] \neq o'[X]))$$
$$\times \kappa(\wedge_{o' \in ps(X)_{o_i, l}} (o_i[Y] = o'[Y])))$$
$$\times \kappa(ps(X)_{o_i, l} \subseteq SS(Y)_{o_k}),$$

where $\kappa(f)$ is a probabilistic degree that a formula f is valid and $\kappa(f) = 1$ when there is no f.

In this formula, all the elements in an indiscernible set are simultaneously handled. The first in the first term denotes a probabilistic degree with which some objects ($o' \in ps(X)_{o_i, l}$) are indiscernible and the others ($o' \notin ps(X)_{o_i, l}$) are discernible for a set X of attributes. The second in the first term denotes a probabilistic degree with which the objects ($o' \in ps(X)_{o_i, l}$) that are indiscernible for X are also indiscernible for a set Y of attributes. The other term is equal to 1 if $ps(X)_{o_{i,l}}$ is included in $SS(Y)_{o_k}$ otherwise 0.

Proposition
Using the new formula, the method of valued tolerance relations satisfies the correctness criterion for the lower approximation.

As an example, we calculate the degree of the lower approximation $\kappa(o_3 \in \underline{IND(B,A)})$ for the object o_3 in data table t.

$$\kappa(o_3 \in \underline{IND(B,A)}) = \max_k \kappa(S(A)_{o_3} \subseteq S(B)_{o_k}) = \kappa(S(A)_{o_3} \subseteq S(B)_{o_3}),$$

where the second equality comes from $\kappa(o_3[B] = o_j[B]) = 0$ for $j = 1, 2$, and 4. For the object o_3,

$$SS(A)_{o_3} \backslash o_3 = \{o_1, o_2, o_4\}.$$

For the power set $PS(A)_{o_3}$ of $SS(A)_{o_3} \backslash o_3$,

$$PS(A)_{o_3} = \{\{\emptyset\}, \{o_1\}, \{o_2\}, \{o_4\}, \{o_1, o_2\}, \{o_1, o_4\}, \{o_2, o_4\}, \{o_1, o_2, o_4\}\}.$$

We calculate only for the element $\{\emptyset\}$, because $\kappa(o_3[B] = o_j[B]) = 0$ for $j = 1, 2$, and 4. For the element $\{\emptyset\}$,

$$\kappa((o_3[A] \neq o_1[A]) \wedge (o_3[A] \neq o_2[A]) \wedge (o_3[A] \neq o_4[A])) = 1/4.$$

Thus,

$$\kappa(o_3 \in \underline{IND(B,A)}) = 1/4 \times 1 + 0 + 0 + 0 + 0 + 0 + 0 + 0 = 1/4.$$

This value is equal to one obtained from possible tables. Similarly, for each object o_i with $i = 1, 2, 4$, the same results are derived as in section 3. Thus, the obtained results coincide with ones from possible tables.

6   Conclusions

We have proposed the correctness criterion in which results obtained from applying an extended method to an imprecise table are the same as ones obtained from applying the corresponding conventional method to possible tables derived from that imprecise table. We have examined a method of tolerance relations under the probabilistically interpretation of missing values for whether it satisfies the correctness criterion or not. The method of valued tolerance relations does not simultaneously handle all the elements in an indiscernible set. By the example, it is shown that the method does not satisfy the correctness criterion. Therefore, we have proposed a new formula in which all the elements in an indiscernible set are simultaneously dealt with. Using the new formula, the method of valued tolerance relations satisfies the correctness criterion for the lower approximation.

Acknowledgment. This research has partially been supported by the Grant-in-Aid for Scientific Research (C), Japanese Ministry of Education, Science, Sports, and Culture, No. 16500176.

References

1. Abiteboul, S., Hull, R., and Vianu, V. [1995] Foundations of Databases, Addison-Wesley Publishing Company, 1995.
2. Gediga, G. and Düntsch, I. [2001] Rough Approximation Quality Revisited, Artificial Intelligence, **132**, 219-234.
3. Grzymala-Busse, J. W. [1991] On the Unknown Attribute Values in Learning from Examples, in Ras, M. Zemankova, (eds.), Methodology for Intelligent Systems, ISMIS '91, Lecture Notes in Artificial Intelligence 542, Springer-Verlag, 368-377.
4. Imielinski, T. [1989] Incomplete Information in Logical Databases, Data Engineering, **12**, 93-104.
5. Imielinski, T. and Lipski, W. [1984] Incomplete Information in Relational Databases, Journal of the ACM, **31**:4, 761-791.
6. Kryszkiewicz, M. [1998] Properties of Incomplete Information Systems in the framework of Rough Sets, in L. Polkowski and A. Skowron, (ed.), Rough Set in Knowledge Discovery 1: Methodology and Applications, Studies in Fuzziness and Soft Computing 18, Physica Verlag, 422-450.
7. Kryszkiewicz, M. [1999] Rules in Incomplete Information Systems, Information Sciences, **113**, 271-292.
8. Kryszkiewicz, M. and Rybiński, H. [2000] Data Mining in Incomplete Information Systems from Rough Set Perspective, in L. Polkowski, S. Tsumoto, and T. Y. Lin, (eds.), Rough Set Methods and Applications, Studies in Fuzziness and Soft Computing 56, Physica Verlag, 568-580.
9. Parsons, S. [1996] Current Approaches to Handling Imperfect Information in Data and Knowledge Bases, IEEE Transactions on Knowledge and Data Engineering, **83**, 353-372.
10. Pawlak, Z. [1991] Rough Sets: Theoretical Aspects of Reasoning about Data, Kluwer Academic Publishers 1991.
11. Sakai, H. [1998] Some Issues on Nondeterministic Knowledge Bases with Incomplete Information, in: Proceedings of RSCTC'98, Polkowski, L. and Skowron, A., eds., Lecture Notes in Artificial Intelligence Vol. 1424, Springer-Verlag 1998, pp. 424-431.
12. Sakai, H. [1999] An Algorithm for Finding Equivalence Relations from Table Nondeterministic Information, in N. Zhong, A. Skowron, S. Ohsuga, (eds.), New Directions in Rough Sets, Data Mining and Granular-Soft Computing, Lecture Notes in Artificial Intelligence 1711, pp. 64-72.
13. Słowiński, R. and Stefanowski, J. [1989] Rough Classification in Incomplete Information Systems, Mathematical and Computer Modelling, **12**:10/11, 1347-1357.
14. Stefanowski, J. and Tsoukiàs, A. [1999] On the Extension of Rough Sets under Incomplete Information, in N. Zhong, A. Skowron, S. Ohsuga, (eds.), New Directions in Rough Sets, Data Mining and Granular-Soft Computing, Lecture Notes in Artificial Intelligence 1711, pp. 73-81.
15. Stefanowski, J. and Tsoukiàs, A. [2000] Valued Tolerance and Decision Rules, in W. Ziarko and Y. Yao, (eds.), Rough Sets and Current Trends in Computing, Lecture Notes in Artificial Intelligence 2005, Springer-Verlag, pp. 212-219.
16. Stefanowski, J. and Tsoukiàs, A. [2001] Incomplete Information Tables and Rough Classification, Computational Intelligence, **17**:3, 545-566.
17. Zimányi, E. and Pirotte, A. [1997] Imperfect Information in Relational Databases, in Uncertainty Management in Information Systems: From Needs to Solutions, A. Motro and P. Smets, eds., Kluwer Academic Publishers, 1997, pp. 35-87.

The Computational Complexity of Inference Using Rough Set Flow Graphs

Cory J. Butz, Wen Yan, and Boting Yang

Department of Computer Science, University of Regina,
Regina, Canada, S4S 0A2
{butz, yanwe111, boting}@cs.uregina.ca

Abstract. Pawlak recently introduced *rough set flow graphs* (RSFGs) as a graphical framework for reasoning from data. Each rule is associated with three coefficients, which have been shown to satisfy Bayes' theorem. Thereby, RSFGs provide a new perspective on Bayesian inference methodology.

In this paper, we show that inference in RSFGs takes polynomial time with respect to the largest domain of the variables in the decision tables. Thereby, RSFGs provide an efficient tool for uncertainty management. On the other hand, our analysis also indicates that a RSFG is a special case of conventional Bayesian network and that RSFGs make implicit assumptions regarding the problem domain.

1 Introduction

Bayesian networks [10] are a semantic modelling tool for managing uncertainty in complex domains. For instance, Bayesian networks have been successfully applied in practice by NASA [4] and Microsoft [5]. A Bayesian network consists of a *directed acyclic graph* (DAG) and a corresponding set of *conditional probability tables* (CPTs). The *probabilistic conditional independencies* [13] encoded in the DAG indicate that the product of the CPTs is a unique joint probability distribution. Although Cooper [1] has shown that the complexity of inference is NP-hard, several approaches have been developed that seem to work quite well in practice. Some researchers, however, reject any framework making probabilistic conditional independence assumptions regarding the problem domain.

Rough sets, founded by Pawlak's pioneering work in [8,9], are another tool for managing uncertainty in complex domains. Unlike Bayesian networks, no assumptions are made regarding the problem domain under consideration. Instead, the inference process is governed solely by sample data. Very recently, Pawlak introduced *rough set flow graphs* (RSFGs) as a graphical framework for reasoning from data [6,7]. Each rule is associated with three coefficients, namely, *strength*, *certainty* and *coverage*, which have been shown to satisfy Bayes' theorem. Therefore, RSFGs provide a new perspective on Bayesian inference methodology.

In this paper, we study the fundamental issue of the complexity of inference in RSFGs. Our main result is that inference in RSFGs takes polynomial time with respect to the largest domain of the variables in the decision tables. Thereby,

D. Ślęzak et al. (Eds.): RSFDGrC 2005, LNAI 3641, pp. 335–344, 2005.

RSFGs provide an efficient framework for uncertainty management. On the other hand, our analysis also indicates that a RSFG is a special case of Bayesian network. Moreover, unlike traditional rough set research, implicit independency assumptions regarding the problem domain are made in RSFGs.

This paper is organized as follows. Section 2 reviews the pertinent notions of Bayesian networks and RSFGs. The complexity of inference in RSFGs is studied in Section 3. In Section 4, we make a note on RSFG independency assumptions. The conclusion is presented in Section 5.

2   Background Knowledge

In this section, we briefly review Bayesian networks and RSFGs.

2.1   Bayesian Networks

Let $U = \{v_1, v_2, \ldots, v_m\}$ be a finite set of variables. Each variable v_i has a finite domain, denoted $dom(v_i)$, representing the values that v_i can take on. For a subset $X = \{v_i, \ldots, v_j\}$ of U, we write $dom(X)$ for the Cartesian product of the domains of the individual variables in X, namely, $dom(X) = dom(v_i) \times \ldots \times dom(v_j)$. Each element $x \in dom(X)$ is called a *configuration* of X.

A *joint probability distribution* [12] on $dom(U)$ is a function p on $dom(U)$ such that the following two conditions both hold: (i) $0 \leq p(u) \leq 1$, for each configuration $u \in dom(U)$, and (ii) $\sum_{u \in dom(U)} p(u) = 1.0$. A *potential* on $dom(U)$ is a function ϕ on $dom(U)$ such that the following two conditions both hold: (i) $0 \leq \phi(u)$, for each configuration $u \in dom(U)$, and (ii) $\phi(u) > 0$, for at least one configuration $u \in dom(U)$. For brevity, we refer to ϕ as a potential on U rather than $dom(U)$, and we call U, not $dom(U)$, its domain [12].

Let ϕ be a potential on U and $x \subseteq U$. Then the *marginal* [12] of ϕ onto X, denoted $\phi(X)$ is defined as: for each configuration $x \in dom(X)$,

$$\phi(x) = \sum_{y \in dom(Y)} \phi(x, y), \tag{1}$$

where $Y = U - X$, and x, y is the configuration of U that we get by combining the configuration, x of X and y of Y. The marginalization of ϕ onto $X = x$ can be obtained from $\phi(X)$.

A *Bayesian network* [10] on U is a DAG on U together with a set of *conditional probability tables* (CPTs) $\{ p(v_i|P_i) \mid v_i \in U \}$, where P_i denotes the parent set of variable v_i in the DAG.

Example 1. One Bayesian network on $U = \{Manufacturer\ (M), Dealership\ (D), Age\ (A)\}$ is given in Figure 1.

We say X and Z are *conditionally independent* [13] given Y in a joint distribution $p(X, Y, Z, W)$, if

$$p(X, Y, Z) = \frac{p(X, Y) \cdot p(Y, Z)}{p(Y)}. \tag{2}$$

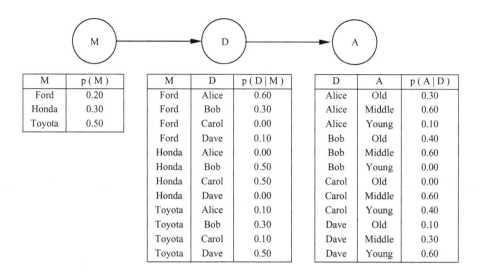

Fig. 1. A *Bayesian network* on $\{Manufacturer\ (M), Dealership\ (D), Age\ (A)\}$

The *independencies* [13] encoded in the DAG of a Bayesian network indicate that the product of the CPTs is a unique joint probability distribution.

Example 2. The independency $I(M, D, A)$ encoded in the DAG of Figure 1 indicates that

$$p(M, D, A) = p(M) \cdot p(D|M) \cdot p(A|D), \qquad (3)$$

where the joint probability distribution $p(M, D, A)$ is shown in Figure 2.

2.2   Rough Set Flow Graphs

Rough set flow graphs are built from decision tables. A *decision table* is a potential $\phi(C, D)$, where C is a set of conditioning attributes and D is a decision attribute. In [6], it is assumed that the decision tables are normalized, which we denote as $p(C, D)$.

Example 3. Consider the set $C = \{Manufacturer\ (M)\}$ of conditioning attributes and the decision attribute $Dealership\ (D)$. One decision table $\phi_1(M, D)$, normalized as $p_1(M, D)$, is shown in Figure 3 (left). Similarly, a decision table on $C = \{Dealership\ (D)\}$ and decision attribute $Age\ (A)$, normalized as $p_2(D, A)$, is depicted in Figure 3 (right).

Each decision table defines a binary flow graph. The set of nodes in the flow graph are $\{c_1, c_2, \ldots, c_k\} \cup \{d_1, d_2, \ldots, d_l\}$, where $c_1, c_2, \ldots, c_k$ and $d_1, d_2, \ldots, d_l$ are the values of C and D appearing in the decision table, respectively. For each row in the decision table, there is a directed edge (c_i, d_j) in the flow graph, where c_i is the value of C and d_j is the value of D. For example, given the decision tables in Figure 3, the respective binary flow graphs are illustrated in Figure 4.

M	D	A	p(M,D,A)
Ford	Alice	Old	0.036
Ford	Alice	Middle	0.072
Ford	Alice	Young	0.012
Ford	Bob	Old	0.024
Ford	Bob	Middle	0.036
Ford	Dave	Old	0.002
Ford	Dave	Middle	0.006
Ford	Dave	Young	0.012
Honda	Bob	Old	0.060
Honda	Bob	Middle	0.090
Honda	Carol	Middle	0.090
Honda	Carol	Young	0.060
Toyota	Alice	Old	0.015
Toyota	Alice	Middle	0.030
Toyota	Alice	Young	0.005
Toyota	Bob	Old	0.060
Toyota	Bob	Middle	0.090
Toyota	Carol	Middle	0.030
Toyota	Carol	Young	0.020
Toyota	Dave	Old	0.025
Toyota	Dave	Middle	0.075
Toyota	Dave	Young	0.150

Fig. 2. The *joint probability distribution* $p(M, D, A)$ defined by the Bayesian network in Figure 1

Each edge (c_i, d_j) is labelled with three coefficients: *strength* $p(c_i, d_j)$, *certainty* $p(d_j|c_i)$ and *coverage* $p(c_i|d_j)$. For instance, the strength, certainty and coverage of the edges of the flow graphs in Figure 4 are shown in Figure 5.

It should perhaps be emphasized here that *all* decision tables $\phi(C, D)$ define a *binary* flow graph regardless of the cardinality of C. Consider a row in $\phi(C, D)$, where c and d are the values of C and D, respectively. Then there is a directed edge from node c to node d. That is, the constructed flow graph treats the attributes of C as a whole, even when C is a non-singleton set of attributes. For instance, in Example 1 of [6], the decision table $\phi(C, D)$ is defined over conditioning attributes $C = \{M, D\}$ and decision attribute A. One row in this table has M = "Ford", D = "Alice" and A = "Middle". Nevertheless, the constructed flow graph has an edge from node c_1 to node "Middle", where $c_1 = (M = $ "Ford", $D = $ "Alice"). For simplified discussion, we will henceforth present all decision tables in which C is a singleton set.

In order to combine the collection of binary flow graphs into a general flow graph, Pawlak makes the *flow conservation* assumption [6]. This assumption means that the normalized decision tables are *pairwise consistent* [2,13].

M	D	ϕ_1 (M,D)	p_1 (M,D)
Ford	Alice	120	0.120
Ford	Bob	60	0.060
Ford	Dave	20	0.020
Honda	Bob	150	0.150
Honda	Carol	150	0.150
Toyota	Alice	50	0.050
Toyota	Bob	150	0.150
Toyota	Carol	50	0.050
Toyota	Dave	250	0.250

D	A	ϕ_2 (D,A)	p_2 (D,A)
Alice	Old	51	0.051
Alice	Middle	102	0.102
Alice	Young	17	0.017
Bob	Old	144	0.144
Bob	Middle	216	0.216
Carol	Middle	120	0.120
Carol	Young	80	0.080
Dave	Old	27	0.027
Dave	Middle	81	0.081
Dave	Young	162	0.162

Fig. 3. *Decision tables* $p_1(M, D)$ *and* $p_2(D, A)$, *respectively*

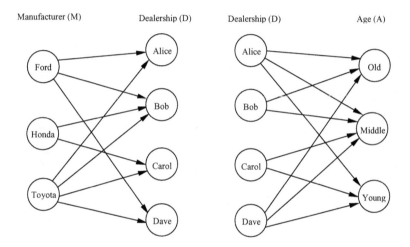

Fig. 4. The respective *binary* flow graphs for the decision tables in Figure 3, where the coefficients are given in Figure 5

Example 4. The two decision tables $p_1(M, D)$ and $p_2(D, A)$ in Figure 3 are pairwise consistent, since $p_1(D) = p_2(D)$. For instance, $p_1(D = \text{"Alice"}) = 0.170 = p_2(D = \text{"Alice"})$.

We now introduce the key notion of rough set flow graphs. A *rough set flow graph* (RSFG) [6,7] is a DAG, where each edge is associated with the strength, certainty and coverage coefficients. The task of inference is to compute $p(X = x|Y = y)$, where x and y are values of two distinct variables X and Y.

Example 5. The rough set flow graph for the two decision tables $p_1(M, D)$ and $p_2(D, A)$ in Figure 3 is the DAG in Figure 6 together with the appropriate strength, certainty and coverage coefficients in Figure 5. From these three coefficients, the query $p(M = \text{"Ford"}|A = \text{"Middle"})$, for instance, can be answered.

M	D	p₁(M,D)	p₁(D|M)	p₁(M|D)
Ford	Alice	0.12	0.60	0.71
Ford	Bob	0.06	0.30	0.16
Ford	Dave	0.02	0.10	0.07
Honda	Bob	0.15	0.50	0.42
Honda	Carol	0.15	0.50	0.75
Toyota	Alice	0.05	0.10	0.29
Toyota	Bob	0.15	0.30	0.42
Toyota	Carol	0.05	0.10	0.25
Toyota	Dave	0.25	0.50	0.93

D	A	p₂(D,A)	p₂(A|D)	p₂(D|A)
Alice	Old	0.05	0.30	0.23
Alice	Middle	0.10	0.60	0.19
Alice	Young	0.02	0.10	0.08
Bob	Old	0.14	0.40	0.63
Bob	Middle	0.22	0.60	0.42
Carol	Middle	0.12	0.60	0.23
Carol	Young	0.08	0.40	0.31
Dave	Old	0.03	0.10	0.14
Dave	Middle	0.08	0.30	0.15
Dave	Young	0.16	0.60	0.62

Fig. 5. The *strength* $p(a_i, a_j)$, *certainty* $p(a_j|a_i)$ and *coverage* $p(a_i|a_j)$ coefficients for the edges (a_i, a_j) in the two flow graphs in Figure 4, respectively

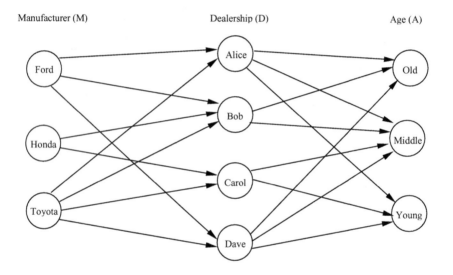

Fig. 6. The *rough set flow graph* (RSFG) for the two decision tables in Figure 3, where the strength, certainty and coverage coefficients can be found in Figure 5

3   The Complexity of Inference

In this section, we establish the complexity of inference in RSFGs by polynomially transforming a RSFG into a Bayesian network and then stating the known complexity of inference. That is, if the RSFG involves nodes $\{a_1, a_2, \ldots, a_k, b_1, b_2, \ldots, b_l, \ldots, k_1, k_2, \ldots, k_m\}$, then the corresponding Bayesian network involves variables $U = \{A, B, \ldots, K\}$, where $dom(A) = \{a_1, a_2, \ldots, a_k\}, dom(B) = \{b_1, b_2, \ldots, b_l\}, \ldots, dom(K) = \{k_1, k_2, \ldots, k_m\}$.

Let G be a RSFG for a collection of decision tables. It is straightforward to transform G into a Bayesian network by applying the definition of RSFGs.

We first show that the Bayesian network has exactly one root variable. Let a_i be a root node in G. The strength of a_i is denoted as $\phi(a_i)$. Let $a_1, a_2, \ldots, a_k$ be all of the root nodes in G, that is, $a_1, a_2, \ldots, a_k$ have no incoming edges in G. By the definition of throughflow in [6],

$$\sum_{i=1}^{k} \phi(a_i) = 1.0. \tag{4}$$

In other words, there is one variable A in U, such that $dom(A) = \{a_1, a_2, \ldots, a_k\}$. In the Bayesian network, A is the only root variable.

By definition, the outflow [6] from one node in G is 1.0. Let $\{b_1, b_2, \ldots, b_l\}$ be the set of all nodes in G such that each b_i, $1 \leq i \leq l$, has at least one incoming edge from a root node $a_1, a_2, \ldots, a_k$. By the definition of throughflow in [6],

$$\sum_{j=1}^{l} \phi(b_j) = 1.0. \tag{5}$$

This means there is a variable $B \in U$ such that $dom(B) = \{b_1, b_2, \ldots, b_l\}$. In the constructed Bayesian network of G, the root variable A has exactly one child B. This argument can be repeated to show that variable B has precisely one child, say C, and so on. The above discussion clearly indicates the structure of the Bayesian network constructed from G is a *chain*. In other words, there is only one root variable, and each variable except the last has exactly one child variable.

We now turn to the quantitative component of the constructed Bayesian network. For each variable v_i, a CPT $p(v_i|P_i)$ is required. Consider the root variable A. The CPT $p(A)$ is obtained from the strengths $\phi(a_1), \phi(a_2), \ldots, \phi(a_k)$. By Equation (4), $p(A)$ is a marginal distribution. We also require the CPT $p(B|A)$. Recall that every outgoing edge from nodes $a_1, a_2, \ldots, a_k$ must be an incoming edge for nodes $b_1, b_2, \ldots, b_l$. Moreover, let a_i be any node with at least one edge going to $b_1, b_2, \ldots, b_l$. Without loss of generality, assume a_i has edges to $b_1, b_2, \ldots, b_j$. This means we have edges $(a_i, b_1), (a_i, b_2), \ldots, (a_i, b_j) \in G$. By definition, the certainty is

$$\phi(B = b_j|A = a_i) = \frac{\phi(A = a_i, B = b_j)}{\phi(A = a_i)}. \tag{6}$$

Since every decision table is normalized, $\phi(A = a_i, B = b_j) = p(A = a_i, B = b_j)$. Therefore, the certainty in Equation (6) is, in fact,

$$p(B = b_j|A = a_i). \tag{7}$$

Hence,

$$\sum_{m=1}^{j} p(B = b_m|A = a_i) = 1.0. \tag{8}$$

Equation (8) holds for each value $a_1, a_2, \ldots, a_k$ of A. Therefore, the conditional probabilities for all edges from $a_1, a_2, \ldots, a_k$ into $b_1, b_2, \ldots, b_l$ define a single CPT $p(B|A)$. This argument can be repeated for the remaining variables in the Bayesian network. Therefore, given a RSFG, we can construct a corresponding Bayesian network in polynomial time.

Example 6. Given the RSFG in Figure 6, the corresponding Bayesian network is shown in Figure 1.

There are various classes of Bayesian networks [10]. A *chain* Bayesian network has exactly one root variable and each variable except the last has precisely one child variable. A *tree* Bayesian network has exactly one root variable and each non-root variable has exactly one parent variable. A *singly-connected* Bayesian network, also known as a *polytree*, has the property that there is exactly one (undirected) path between any two variables. A *multiply-connected* Bayesian network means that there exist two nodes with more than one (undirected) path between them. Probabilistic inference in Bayesian networks means computing $p(X = x|Y = y)$, where $X, Y \subseteq U$, $x \in dom(X)$ and $y \in dom(Y)$. While Cooper [1] has shown that the complexity of inference in multiply-connected Bayesian networks is NP-hard, the complexity of inference in tree Bayesian networks is polynomial. Inference, which involves additions and multiplications, is bounded by multiplications. For a m-ary tree Bayesian network with n values in the domain for each node, one needs to store $n^2 + mn + 2n$ real numbers and perform $2n^2 + mn + 2n$ multiplications for inference [11].

We can now establish the complexity of inference in RSFGs by utilizing the known complexity of inference in the constructed Bayesian network. In this section, we have shown that a RSFG can be polynomially transformed into a chain Bayesian network. A chain Bayesian network is a special case of tree Bayesian network, that is, where $m = 1$. By substitution, the complexity of inference in a chain Bayesian network is $O(n^2)$. Therefore, the complexity of inference in RSFGs is $O(m^2)$, where $m = max(|dom(v_i)|)$, $v_i \in U$. In other words, the complexity of inference is polynomial with respect to the largest domain of the variables in the decision tables. This means that RSFGs are an efficient tool for uncertainty management.

4   Other Remarks on Rough Set Flow Graphs

One salient feature of rough sets is that they serve as a tool for uncertainty management without making assumptions regarding the problem domain. On the contrary, we establish in this section that RSFGs, in fact, make implicit independency assumptions regarding the problem domain.

The assumption that decision tables $p_1(A_1, A_2)$, $p_2(A_2, A_3), \ldots, p_{m-1}(A_{m-1}, A_m)$ are pairwise consistent implies that the decision tables are marginals of a unique joint probability distribution $p(A_1, A_2, \ldots, A_m)$ defined as follows

$$p(A_1, A_2, \ldots, A_m) = \frac{p_1(A_1, A_2) \cdot p_2(A_2, A_3) \cdot \ldots \cdot p_{m-1}(A_{m-1}, A_m)}{p_1(A_2) \cdot \ldots \cdot p_{m-1}(A_{m-1})}. \quad (9)$$

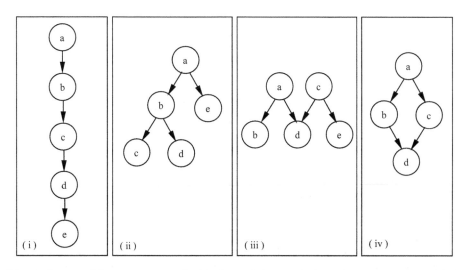

Fig. 7. Types of Bayesian network: (i) chain, (ii) tree, (iii) singly connected, and (iv) multiply-connected

Example 7. Assuming the two decision tables $p_1(M, D)$ and $p_2(D, A)$ in Figure 3 are pairwise consistent implies that they are marginals of the joint distribution,

$$p(M, D, A) = \frac{p_1(M, D) \cdot p_2(D, A)}{p_1(D)}, \tag{10}$$

where $p(M, D, A)$ is given in Figure 2.

Equation (9), however, indicates that the joint distribution $p(A_1, A_2, \ldots, A_m)$ satisfies $m - 2$ probabilistic independencies $I(A_1, A_2, A_3 \ldots A_m)$, $I(A_1 A_2, A_3, A_4 \ldots A_m)$, $\ldots$, $I(A_1 \ldots A_{m-2}, A_{m-1}, A_m)$. In Example 7, assuming $p_1(M, D)$ and $p_2(D, A)$ are pairwise consistent implies that the independence $I(M, D, A)$ holds in the problem domain $p(M, D, A)$.

The important point is that the flow conservation assumption [6] used in the construction of RSFGs implicitly implies probabilistic conditional independencies holding in the problem domain.

5   Conclusion

Pawlak [6,7] recently introduced the notion of rough set flow graph (RSFGs) as a graphical framework for reasoning from data. In this paper, we established that the computational complexity of inference using RSFGs is polynomial with respect to the largest domain of the variables in the decision tables. This result indicates that RSFGs provide an efficient framework for uncertainty management. At the same time, our study has revealed that RSFGs, unlike previous rough set research, makes implicit independency assumptions regarding the problem domain. Moreover, RSFGs are a special case of Bayesian networks. Future work will study the complexity of inference in generalized RSFGs [3].

References

1. Cooper, G.F.: The Computational Complexity of Probabilistic Inference Using Bayesian Belief Networks. Artificial Intelligence, Vol. 42, Issue 2-3, (1990) 393-405
2. Dawid, A.P. and Lauritzen, S.L.: Hyper Markov Laws in The Statistical Analysis of Decomposable Graphical Models. The Annals of Satistics, Vol. 21 (1993) 1272-1317
3. Greco, S., Pawlak, Z. and Slowinski, R.: Generalized Decision Algorithms, Rough Inference Rules and Flow Graphs. The Third International Conference on Rough Sets, and Current Trends in Computing (2002) 93-104
4. Horvitz, E. and Barry, E.M.: Display of Information for Time Critical Decision Making. Proceedings of Eleventh Conference on Uncertainty in Artificial Intelligence. Morgan Kaufmann, San Francisco (1995) 296-305
5. Horvitz, E., Breese, J., Heckerman, D., Hovel, D. and Rommelse, K.: The Lumiere Project: Bayesian User Modeling for Inferring the Goals and Needs of Software Users. Proceedings of the Fourteenth Conference on Uncertainty in Artificial Intelligence. Madison, WI (1998) 256-265
6. Pawlak, Z.: Flow Graphs and Decision Algorithms. The Ninth International Conference on Rough Sets, Fuzzy Sets, Data Mining, and Granular Computing (2003) 1-10
7. Pawlak, Z.: In Pursuit of Patterns in Data Reasoning from Data - The Rough Set Way. The Third International Conference on Rough Sets, and Current Trends in Computing (2002) 1-9
8. Pawlak, Z.: Rough Sets. International Journal of Computer and Information Sciences, Vol. 11, Issue 5 (1982) 341-356
9. Pawlak, Z.: Rough Sets: Theoretical Aspects of Reasoning about Data. Kluwer Academic (1991)
10. Pearl, J.: Probabilistic Reasoning in Intelligent Systems: Networks of Plausible Inference. Morgan Kaufmann, San Francisco, California (1988)
11. Pearl, J.: Reverend Bayes on Inference Engines: A Distributed Heirarchical Approach. AAAI (1982) 133-136
12. Shafer, G.: Probabilistic Expert Systems. Society for the Institute and Applied Mathematics, Philadelphia (1996)
13. Wong, S.K.M., Butz, C.J. and Wu, D.: On the Implication Problem for Probabilistic Conditional Independency, IEEE Transactions on Systems, Man, and Cybernetics, Part A: Systems and Humans, Vol. 30, Issue 6. (2000) 785-805

Upper and Lower Probabilities of Fuzzy Events Induced by a Fuzzy Set-Valued Mapping

Wei-Zhi Wu

Information College, Zhejiang Ocean University,
Zhoushan, Zhejiang, 316004, P.R. China
wuwz@zjou.net.cn

Abstract. In this paper, we study rough set approximations under fuzzy and random environments. A fuzzy set-valued mapping defines a pair of upper and lower fuzzy rough approximations. Properties of fuzzy approximation operators are examined and the crisp representations of fuzzy approximation operators are presented. A fuzzy random variable from a universe U to a universe W carries a probability measure defined over subsets of U into a system of upper and lower probabilities over subsets of W. The connections between fuzzy approximation spaces and fuzzy belief structures are also established.

1 Introduction

One of the main directions for the development of rough set theory is the extension of Pawlak rough approximation operators. In Pawlak's rough set model [11], an equivalence relation is a key and primitive notion. This equivalence relation, however, seems to be a very stringent condition that may limit the application domain of the rough set model. To solve this problem, several authors have generalized the notion of approximation operators by using nonequivalence binary relations [15], [16], [21], [24]. Rough set approximation operators can also be extended to fuzzy environment, the results are called rough fuzzy sets or fuzzy rough sets [1], [4], [8], [19], [21].

The classical rough-set data analysis uses only the internal knowledge, avoid external parameters and does not rely on prior model assumptions. It is well known, however, that in many real-world cases, available databases may be obtained by some random experiments. Thus the uncertainty due to randomness of the approximation spaces of rough set theory must be considered [6], [7], [17]. One important method used to deal with such uncertainty is the Dempster-Shafer theory of evidence (also called the theory of belief function). It was originated by Dempster's concept of lower and upper probabilities [2], and extended by Shafer [13] as a theory. The basic representational structure in this theory is a belief structure which consists of a family of subsets, called focal elements, with associated individual positive weights summing to one. The primitive numeric measures derived from the belief structure are a dual pair of belief and plausibility functions. A belief function can also be induced from a random set [10].

D. Ślęzak et al. (Eds.): RSFDGrC 2005, LNAI 3641, pp. 345–353, 2005.

The Dempster-Shafer theory can be generalized to the fuzzy environment [3], [5], [23], [26]. There are strong relationships between rough set theory and the Dempster-Shafer theory of evidence [14], [18], [25].

On the other hand, we often encounter random experiments whose outcomes are expressed in inexact linguistic terms. A possible way to handle the problem is to use the concept of fuzzy random variables introduced by Kwakernaak [9]. A fuzzy random variable is a random variable taking fuzzy sets as values. Kwakernaak's random variables take fuzzy numbers as values and later Puri and Ralescu [12] introduced the notion of a fuzzy random variable as a fuzzy set-valued function from a probability space to a set of fuzzy subsets of R^n subject to certain measurability conditions. Fuzzy random variables hence generalize random variables, random vectors, and random sets.

The present paper studies rough set approximations under fuzzy and random environment. Rough sets based on a fuzzy random variable, which include the mechanisms of numeric and non-numeric aspects of uncertain knowledge, are defined. The connections between fuzzy approximation spaces and fuzzy belief structures are discussed.

2   Fuzzy Plausibility and Belief Functions

Let U be a nonempty set. The class of all subsets (respectively, fuzzy subsets) of U will be denoted by $\mathcal{P}(U)$ (respectively, by $\mathcal{F}(U)$). The class of all normalized fuzzy sets of U will be denoted by $\mathcal{F}_0(U)$, that is, $\mathcal{F}_0(U) = \{A \in \mathcal{F}(U) : \exists x \in U \text{ such that } A(x) = 1\}$. For any $A \in \mathcal{F}(U)$, the α-level and the strong α-level of A will be denoted by A_α and $A_{\alpha+}$, respectively, that is, $A_\alpha = \{x \in U : A(x) \geq \alpha\}$ and $A_{\alpha+} = \{x \in U : A(x) > \alpha\}$, where $\alpha \in I = [0,1]$, the unit interval, $A_0 = U$, and $A_{1+} = \emptyset$. We denote by $\sim A$ the complement of A. The cardinality of a fuzzy set $A \in \mathcal{F}(U)$ is denoted by $|A| = \sum_{x \in U} A(x)$, and if P is a probability measure on U, then the probability of the fuzzy set A, denoted by $P(A)$, is defined, in the sense of Zadeh [27], by

$$P(A) = \sum_{x \in U} A(x)P(x). \tag{1}$$

Definition 1. *Let U be a nonempty finite universe of discourse. A fuzzy set function $m : \mathcal{F}(U) \to I = [0,1]$ is referred to as a fuzzy basic probability assignment if it satisfies*

$$\text{(FM1)} \ \ m(\emptyset) = 0, \qquad \text{(FM2)} \sum_{A \in \mathcal{F}(U)} m(A) = 1.$$

A fuzzy set $A \in \mathcal{F}(U)$ with $m(A) > 0$ is referred to as a focal element of m. Let $\mathcal{M} = \{A \in \mathcal{F}(U) : m(A) \neq 0\}$, then the pair $(\mathcal{M}, m)$ is called a fuzzy belief structure.

From a given fuzzy belief structure, a pair of fuzzy plausibility and fuzzy belief functions can be derived.

Definition 2. *A fuzzy set function Bel : $\mathcal{F}(U) \rightarrow I$ is called a fuzzy belief function iff (if and only if)*

$$Bel(X) = \sum_{A \in \mathcal{M}} m(A) \mathrm{N}_A(X), \quad \forall X \in \mathcal{F}(U), \tag{2}$$

and a fuzzy set function $Pl : \mathcal{F}(U) \rightarrow I$ is called a fuzzy plausibility function iff

$$Pl(X) = \sum_{A \in \mathcal{M}} m(A) \Pi_A(X), \quad \forall X \in \mathcal{F}(U), \tag{3}$$

where N_A and Π_A are the fuzzy necessity and fuzzy possibility measures generated by the fuzzy set A as follows:

$$\begin{aligned} \mathrm{N}_A(X) &= \bigwedge_{u \in U} (X(u) \vee (1 - A(u))), \forall X \in \mathcal{F}(U) \\ \Pi_A(X) &= \bigvee_{u \in U} (X(u) \wedge A(u)), \qquad \forall X \in \mathcal{F}(U). \end{aligned} \tag{4}$$

Remark 1. In Definition 2, if $X \in \mathcal{P}(U)$ and $A \in \mathcal{P}(U)$, then by Eq. (4) it can easily be checked that

$$\mathrm{N}_A(X) \neq 0 \Longleftrightarrow \mathrm{N}_A(X) = 1 \Longleftrightarrow A \subseteq X,$$

and

$$\Pi_A(X) \neq 0 \Longleftrightarrow \Pi_A(X) = 1 \Longleftrightarrow A \cap X \neq \emptyset.$$

Therefore, if $(\mathcal{M}, m)$ is a crisp belief structure, i.e.

$$(\mathrm{M1}) \ m(\emptyset) = 0, \qquad (\mathrm{M2}) \sum_{A \in \mathcal{P}(U)} m(A) = 1,$$

then we can deduce that

$$Bel(X) = \sum_{A \subseteq X} m(A), \tag{5}$$

and

$$Pl(X) = \sum_{A \cap X \neq \emptyset} m(A). \tag{6}$$

Thus a fuzzy belief (plausibility, respectively) function is indeed a generalization of a crisp belief (plausibility, respectively) function.

3   Fuzzy Rough Sets

Let U and W be two finite nonempty universes of discourse. Let $F : U \rightarrow \mathcal{F}_0(W)$ be a fuzzy set-valued mapping, such a fuzzy set-valued function can generate a normalized fuzzy binary relation R from U to W whose membership function is defined by

$$R(u, w) = F(u)(w), \quad \forall(u, w) \in U \times W.$$

Any normalized fuzzy binary relation R from U to W can derive a fuzzy mapping F from U to W defined by

$$F(u)(w) = R(u, w), \quad \forall (u, w) \in U \times W.$$

The triple (U, W, F) is referred to as a fuzzy approximation space.

Definition 3. *Let (U, W, F) be a fuzzy approximation space generated by a fuzzy set-valued mapping $F : U \to \mathcal{F}_0(W)$. For any $X \in \mathcal{F}(W)$, the upper and lower approximations of X, $\overline{F}(X)$ and $\underline{F}(X)$, with respect to the fuzzy approximation space (U, W, F) are fuzzy sets of U whose memberships are defined respectively by, for any $x \in U$,*

$$\overline{F}(X)(x) = \bigvee_{y \in W} (F(x)(y) \wedge X(y)),$$
$$\underline{F}(X)(x) = \bigwedge_{y \in W} ((1 - F(x)(y)) \vee X(y)). \tag{7}$$

The pair $(\underline{F}(X), \overline{F}(X))$ is referred to as a fuzzy rough set. The two fuzzy set operators from $\mathcal{F}(W)$ to $\mathcal{F}(U)$, $\overline{F}$ and $\underline{F}$, are called the upper and lower fuzzy rough approximation operators respectively.

Using the concepts of upper and lower fuzzy approximations, knowledge hidden in fuzzy information systems may be unraveled and expressed in the form of decision rules, see e.g. [22].

It can be verified that the upper and lower fuzzy rough approximation operators, $\overline{F}$ and $\underline{F}$, satisfy the properties: $\forall A, B \in \mathcal{F}(W)$, $\forall \alpha \in I$,

(FL1) $\underline{F}(A) = \sim \overline{F}(\sim A)$,   (FU1) $\overline{F}(A) = \sim \underline{F}(\sim A)$,

(FL2) $\underline{F}(A \cup \hat{\alpha}) = \underline{F}(A) \cup \hat{\alpha}$,   (FU2) $\overline{F}(A \cap \hat{\alpha}) = \overline{F}(A) \cap \hat{\alpha}$;

(FL3) $\underline{F}(A \cap B) = \underline{F}(A) \cap \underline{F}(B)$, (FU3) $\overline{F}(A \cup B) = \overline{F}(A) \cup \overline{F}(B)$;

(FL0) $\underline{F}(\hat{\alpha}) = \hat{\alpha}$,   (FU0) $\overline{F}(\hat{\alpha}) = \hat{\alpha}$,

(FLU0) $\underline{F}(A) \subseteq \overline{F}(A)$

where the set operations are defined in the sense of Zadeh [28], and $\hat{a}$ is the constant fuzzy set: $\hat{a}(x) = a$, for all x.

Remark 2. In Definition 3, if $F : U \to \mathcal{P}_0(W)$ is a crisp set-valued mapping, and $X \in \mathcal{P}(W)$ is a crisp subset of W, then it can easily be verified that

$$\overline{F}(X)(u) = 1 \iff F(u) \cap X \neq \emptyset,$$
$$\underline{F}(X)(u) = 1 \iff F(u) \subseteq X.$$

Thus the pair of upper and lower fuzzy rough approximation operators is indeed a generalization one of upper and lower crisp rough approximation operators, i.e.,

$$\overline{F}(X) = \{u \in U : F(u) \cap X \neq \emptyset\},$$
$$\underline{F}(X) = \{u \in U : F(u) \subseteq X\}. \tag{8}$$

On the other hand, the lower and upper fuzzy rough approximation operators defined by Eq.(7) can be represented by crisp approximation operators [21].

Theorem 1. *Let* (U, W, F) *be a fuzzy approximation space and* $A \in \mathcal{F}(W)$, *then*

$$(1) \ \overline{F}(A) = \bigvee_{\alpha \in I} [\alpha \wedge 1_{\overline{F_\alpha}(A_\alpha)}] = \bigvee_{\alpha \in I} [\alpha \wedge 1_{\overline{F_\alpha}(A_{\alpha+})}]$$

$$= \bigvee_{\alpha \in I} [\alpha \wedge 1_{\overline{F_{\alpha+}}(A_\alpha)}] = \bigvee_{\alpha \in I} [\alpha \wedge 1_{\overline{F_{\alpha+}}(A_{\alpha+})}],$$

$$(2) \ \underline{F}(A) = \bigvee_{\alpha \in I} [\alpha \wedge 1_{\underline{F_{1-\alpha}}(A_\alpha)}] = \bigvee_{\alpha \in I} [\alpha \wedge 1_{\underline{F_{1-\alpha}}(A_{\alpha+})}]$$

$$= \bigvee_{\alpha \in I} [\alpha \wedge 1_{\underline{F_{(1-\alpha)+}}(A_\alpha)}] = \bigvee_{\alpha \in I} [\alpha \wedge 1_{\underline{F_{(1-\alpha)+}}(A_{\alpha+})}],$$

and $\forall \alpha \in I$

$$(3) \ [\overline{F}(A)]_{\alpha+} \subseteq \overline{F_{\alpha+}}(A_{\alpha+}) \subseteq \overline{F_{\alpha+}}(A_\alpha) \subseteq \overline{F_\alpha}(A_\alpha) \subseteq [\overline{F}(A)]_\alpha,$$

$$(4) \ [\overline{F}(A)]_{\alpha+} \subseteq \overline{F_{\alpha+}}(A_{\alpha+}) \subseteq \overline{F_\alpha}(A_{\alpha+}) \subseteq \overline{F_\alpha}(A_\alpha) \subseteq [\overline{F}(A)]_\alpha,$$

$$(5) \ [\underline{F}(A)]_{\alpha+} \subseteq \underline{F_{1-\alpha}}(A_{\alpha+}) \subseteq \underline{F_{(1-\alpha)+}}(A_{\alpha+}) \subseteq \underline{F_{(1-\alpha)+}}(A_\alpha) \subseteq [\underline{F}(A)]_\alpha,$$

$$(6) \ [\underline{F}(A)]_{\alpha+} \subseteq \underline{F_{1-\alpha}}(A_{\alpha+}) \subseteq \underline{F_{1-\alpha}}(A_\alpha) \subseteq \underline{F_{(1-\alpha)+}}(A_\alpha) \subseteq [\underline{F}(A)]_\alpha.$$

Where the crisp upper and lower approximations are defined as Eq.(8).

4   Connections Between Fuzzy Approximation Spaces and Fuzzy Belief Structures

Let U and W be two finite nonempty universes of discourse. For simplicity, we treat a fuzzy set-valued function $F : (U, P) \to \mathcal{F}_0(W)$ with a probability distribution P on U such that $P(\{u\}) > 0$ for all $u \in U$ as a fuzzy random variable. Such a function is measurable with respect to the discrete measurability spaces $(U, \mathcal{P}(U))$ and $(W, \mathcal{P}(W))$. We can see that a fuzzy set-valued function $F : (U, P) \to \mathcal{F}_0(W)$ is a fuzzy random variable iff its α-level set function $F_\alpha : (U, P) \to \mathcal{P}(W)$, defined by $F_\alpha(u) = \{w \in W : F(u)(w) \geq \alpha\}$, is a random set for all $\alpha \in I$.

Assume that $F : (U, P) \to \mathcal{F}_0(W)$ is a fuzzy random variable, the quadruple $((U, P), W, F)$ is referred to as random fuzzy approximation space. For any $X \in \mathcal{F}(W)$, the probabilities of the upper and lower fuzzy approximations of X with respect to random fuzzy approximation space $((U, P), W, F)$, $P(\overline{F}(X))$ and $P(\underline{F}(X))$ generate two quantities $\overline{P}(X)$ and $\underline{P}(X)$ as follows:

$$\overline{P}(X) = P(\overline{F}(X)) = \sum_{x \in U} \overline{F}(X)(x)P(x),$$
$$\underline{P}(X) = P(\underline{F}(X)) = \sum_{x \in U} \underline{F}(X)(x)P(x), \tag{9}$$

The two quantities $\overline{P}(X)$ and $\underline{P}(X)$ are respectively called the upper and lower probabilities of X induced by the fuzzy random variable F.

Theorem 2. *The upper and lower probability functions,* $\overline{P}$ *and* $\underline{P}$, *induced by a fuzzy random variable* $F : (U, P) \to \mathcal{F}_0(W)$, *are fuzzy plausibility and fuzzy belief functions respectively, and the corresponding fuzzy basic probability assignment* is $m(A) = P(j(A))$, where $j(A) = \{u \in U : F(u) = A\}$, $A \in \mathcal{F}(W)$. Conversely, if Pl and Bel are a dual pair of fuzzy plausibility and fuzzy belief functions on W, that is,

$$Pl(X) = \sum_{A \in \mathcal{M}} m(A)\Pi_A(X), \quad \forall X \in \mathcal{F}(W),$$
$$Bel(X) = \sum_{A \in \mathcal{M}} m(A)\mathrm{N}_A(X), \quad \forall X \in \mathcal{F}(W), \tag{10}$$

where Π_A and N_A are the possibility and necessity measures generated by the fuzzy set A defined by Eq. (4), then there exists a random fuzzy approximation space $((U, P), W, F)$, i.e., there exists a finite universe of discourse U, a probability measure P on U, and a fuzzy random variable F from U to W, such that its induced upper and lower probabilities are respectively the fuzzy plausibility and fuzzy belief functions, i.e.,

$$\overline{P}(X) = Pl(X), \quad \underline{P}(X) = Bel(X), \quad \forall X \in \mathcal{F}(W). \tag{11}$$

Proof. Assume that $((U, P), W, F)$ is a fuzzy random approximation space, for $A \in \mathcal{F}(W)$, define

$$j(A) = \{u \in U : F(u) = A\}. \tag{12}$$

Obviously, j satisfies:

$$j(A) \cap j(B) = \emptyset \text{ for } A \neq B \text{ and } \bigcup_{A \in \mathcal{F}(W)} j(A) = U. \tag{13}$$

Let

$$m(A) = P(j(A)), \quad A \in \mathcal{F}(W).$$

Since $P(\{u\}) > 0$ for all $u \in U$, we have

$$m(A) > 0 \iff j(A) \neq \emptyset. \tag{14}$$

Thus, in terms of Eq. (13) and Eq. (14), we have, for all $X \in \mathcal{F}(W)$,

$$\overline{P}(X) = P(\overline{F}(X)) = \sum_{u \in U} \overline{F}(X)(u)P(\{u\})$$
$$= \sum_{u \in U} P(\{u\})\left(\bigvee_{y \in W} (F(u)(y) \wedge X(y)) \right)$$
$$= \sum_{A \in \mathcal{F}(W)} \sum_{u \in j(A)} P(\{u\})\left(\bigvee_{y \in W} (F(u)(y) \wedge X(y)) \right)$$
$$= \sum_{A \in \mathcal{F}(W)} \sum_{u \in j(A)} P(\{u\})\left(\bigvee_{y \in W} (A(y) \wedge X(y)) \right)$$
$$= \sum_{A \in \mathcal{M}} P(j(A)) \bigvee_{y \in W} (A(y) \wedge X(y)) = \sum_{A \in \mathcal{M}} m(A)\Pi_A(X).$$

Therefore $\overline{P} : \mathcal{F}(W) \to I$ is a fuzzy plausibility function.

Likewise we can conclude that

$$\underline{P}(X) = \sum_{A \in \mathcal{M}} m(A)\left(\bigwedge_{y \in W} (1 - A(y)) \vee X(y) \right) = \sum_{A \in \mathcal{M}} m(A)\mathrm{N}_A(X), \quad \forall X \in \mathcal{F}(W),$$

which implies that $\underline{P}$ is a fuzzy belief function.

Conversely, if Pl and Bel are a dual pair of fuzzy plausibility and fuzzy belief functions on W, let $\mathcal{M} = \{A_1, A_2, \ldots, A_k\}$ be the family of focal elements of m. Let $U = \{u_1, u_2, \ldots, u_k\}$ be a set having k elements, we define a set function $P : \mathcal{P}(U) \to I$ as

$$P(\{u_i\}) = m(A_i), \quad i = 1, 2, \ldots, k,$$
$$P(X) = \sum_{u \in X} P(\{u\}), \quad X \subseteq U.$$

It is easy to see that P is a probability measure on U.

We then define a fuzzy set-valued function $F : U \to \mathcal{F}(W)$ as

$$F(u_i) = A_i, \quad i = 1, 2, \ldots, k.$$

Since A_i is normalized for each $i = 1, 2, \ldots, k$ and P is a probability measure on U, F is a fuzzy random variable from (U, P) to $\mathcal{F}_0(W)$. It is clear that $j(A) = \{u_i\}$ for $A = A_i$ and $\emptyset$ otherwise. Then $m(A) = P(j(A)) > 0$ for $A \in \mathcal{M}$ and 0 otherwise. Therefore, for all $X \in \mathcal{F}(W)$, we have

$$P(\overline{F}(X)) = \sum_{u \in U} \overline{F}(X)(u)P(\{u\}) = \sum_{A \in \mathcal{M}} P(j(A)) \bigvee_{y \in W} (A(y) \wedge X(y))$$
$$= \sum_{A \in \mathcal{M}} m(A)\Pi_A(X) = Pl(X).$$

Similarly, we can conclude that

$$P(\underline{F}(X)) = \sum_{A \in \mathcal{M}} m(A)\mathrm{N}_A(X) = Bel(X).$$

Remark 3. This theorem shows that an arbitrary fuzzy belief structure $(\mathcal{M}, m)$ can be associated with a random fuzzy approximation space $((U, P), W, F)$ such that the induced dual pair of upper and lower fuzzy rough approximation operators from $\mathcal{F}(W)$ to $\mathcal{F}(U)$ may be used to interpret the dual pair of fuzzy plausibility and fuzzy belief functions induced by the fuzzy belief structure $(\mathcal{M}, m)$.

Remark 4. It should be noted that if there is no prior probability on U, the principle of indifference of the statistical model must be used in rough-set data analysis, i.e., we can take the probability on U as: $P(\{x\}) = 1/|U|$ for all $x \in U$, and thus the randomization methods are still applicable. The upper and lower probability functions, $\overline{P}$ and $\underline{P}$, are still fuzzy plausibility and fuzzy belief functions respectively. Conversely, if Pl and Bel are a dual pair of fuzzy plausibility and fuzzy belief functions on W with $m(A)$ being a rational number for each $A \in \mathcal{M}$, then there exists a random fuzzy approximation space $((U, P), W, F)$ with probability $P(\{x\}) = 1/|U|$ for all $x \in U$ such that its induced upper and lower probability functions are respectively the plausibility and belief functions, i.e., Eq. (11) holds.

5   Conclusion

We have developed a new rough set model defined by a fuzzy random variable which includes the mechanisms of numeric aspect (upper and lower probabilities of a fuzzy set) and non-numeric aspect (upper and lower approximations of a fuzzy set) of uncertain knowledge under fuzzy and random environment. We have also established relationships between fuzzy approximation spaces and fuzzy belief structures which shows that, though fuzzy rough set theory and the fuzzy evidence theory capture different aspects of uncertainty, they complement each other in analysis. The paper may be treated as a fuzzy generalization of Dempster [2] as well as Yao [25]. Further research is to study on properties of the fuzzy plausibility and fuzzy belief functions and their application to fuzzy information analysis.

Acknowledgement

This work was supported by a grant from the National Natural Science Foundation of China (No. 60373078)

References

1. Boixader, D., Jacas, J., Recasens, J.: Upper and lower approximations of fuzzy sets. International Journal of General Systems **29**(2000) 555–568
2. Dempster, A. P.: Upper and lower probabilities induced by a multivalued mapping. Annals of Mathematical Statistics **38**(1967) 325–339
3. Denoeux, T.: Modeling vague beliefs using fuzzy-valued belief structures. Fuzzy Sets and Systems **116**(2000) 167–199
4. Dubois, D., Prade, H.: Rough fuzzy sets and fuzzy rough sets. International Journal of General Systems **17**(1990) 191–209
5. Dubois, D., Prade, H,.: Evidence measures based on fuzzy information. Automatica **21(5)**(1985) 547–562
6. Düntsch, I., Gediga G.: Statistical evaluation of rough set dependency analysis. International Journal of Human-Computer Studies **46**(1997) 589–604
7. Düntsch I., Gediga G.: Uncertainty measures of rough set prediction. Artificial Intelligence **106**(1998) 109–137
8. Inuiguchi, M.: Generalizations of rough sets: from crisp to fuzzy cases. In: Tsumoto, S., Slowinski, R., Komorowski, J., Grzymala-Busse, J.W. (Eds.): RSCTC 2004, LNAI 3066, pp.26–37
9. Kwakernaak, H.: Fuzzy random variables-I: Definitions and theorems. Information Sciences **15**(1978) 1–29
10. Nguyen, H. T.: On random sets and belief functions. Journal of Mathematical Analysis and Applications **65**(1978) 531–542
11. Pawlak, Z.: Rough Sets: Theoretical Aspects of Reasoning about Data. Kluwer Academic Publishers, Boston, 1991
12. Puri, M. L., Ralescu, D. A.: Fuzzy random variables. Journal of Mathematical Analysis and Applications **114**(1986) 409–422
13. Shafer, G.: A Mathematical Theory of Evidence. Princeton University Press, Princeton, 1976
14. Skowron, A., Grzymala-Busse, J.: From rough set theory to evidence theory. In: Yager, R. R., Fedrizzi, M., Kacprzyk, J. (Eds.): Advances in the Dempster-Shafer Theory of Evidence, Wiley, New York, 1994, pp.193–236

15. Slowinski, R., Vanderpooten, D.: A generalized definition of rough approximations based on similarity. IEEE Transactions on knowledge and Data Engineering **12**(2000) 331–336
16. Stepaniuk, J.: Similarity based rough sets and learning. In: Tsumoto, S. et. al. (eds.): Proceedings of the Fourth International Workshop on Rough Sets, Fuzzy Sets, and Machine Discovery, The University of Tokyo, November 6-8, 1996, pp.18–22
17. Wong, S.K.M., Ziarko, W.: Comparison of the probabilistic approximate classification and the fuzzy set model. International Journal of Fuzzy Sets and Systems **21**(1986) 357–362
18. Wu W.-Z., Leung Y., Zhang W.-X.: Connections between rough set theory and Dempster-Shafer theory of evidence. International Journal of General Systems **31** (2002) 405–430
19. Wu W.-Z., Mi J.-S., Zhang W.-X.: Generalized fuzzy rough sets. Information Sciences **151**(2003) 263–282
20. Wu W.-Z., Zhang W.-X.: Neighborhood operator systems and approximations. Information Sciences **144**(2002) 201–217
21. Wu, W.-Z., Zhang, W.-X.: Constructive and axiomatic approaches of fuzzy approximation operators. Information Sciences **159**(2004) 233–254
22. Wu, W.-Z., Zhang, W.-X., Li, H.-Z.: Knowledge acquisition in incomplete fuzzy information systems via rough set approach. Expert Systems **20**(2003) 280–286
23. Yager, R. R.: Generalized probabilities of fuzzy events from fuzzy belief structures. Information Sciences **28**(1982) 45–62
24. Yao, Y. Y.: Generalized rough set models. In: Polkowski, L., Skowron, A. (Eds.): Rough Sets in Knowledge Discovery: 1. Methodology and Applications, Physica-Verlag, Heidelberg, 1998, pp.286–318
25. Yao, Y. Y.: Interpretations of belief functions in the theory of rough sets. Information Sciences **104**(1998) 81–106
26. Yen, J.: Generalizing the Dempster-Shafer theory to fuzzy sets. IEEE Transactions on Systems, Man and Cybernetics **20(3)**(1990) 559–570
27. Zadeh, L. A.: Probability measures of fuzzy events. Journal of Mathematical Analysis and Applications **23**(1968) 421–427
28. Zadeh, L. A.: Fuzzy sets. Information and Control **8** (1965) 338–353

Variable Precision Fuzzy Rough Sets Model in the Analysis of Process Data

Alicja Mieszkowicz-Rolka and Leszek Rolka

Department of Avionics and Control,
Rzeszów University of Technology,
ul. W. Pola 2, 35-959 Rzeszów, Poland
{alicjamr, leszekr}@prz.edu.pl

Abstract. This paper is concerned with describing and analyzing the control actions which are accomplished by a human operator, who controls a complex dynamic system. The decision model is expressed by means of a decision table with fuzzy attributes. Decision tables are generated by the fuzzification of crisp data, basing on a set of fuzzy linguistic values of the attributes. A T-similarity relation is chosen for comparing the elements of the universe. Fuzzy partitions of the universe with respect to condition and decision attributes are generated. The task of stabilization of the aircraft's altitude performed by a pilot is considered as an illustrative example. The limit-based and mean-based variable precision fuzzy rough approximations are determined. The measure of u-approximation quality is used for evaluating the consistency of the human operator's decision model, and assessing the importance of particular condition attributes in the control process.

1 Introduction

Uncertainty and vagueness are inherent features of data that are obtained from real processes controlled by an expert. The knowledge acquisition from such a kind of data is an interesting and important task especially in the area of engineering, expert systems and decision support systems.

In contrast to the classical approach of control theory, which treats the human operator as a controller, a new paradigm in form of the fuzzy sets theory was elaborated in the recent decades, which turned out to be suitable for modelling the expert's controlling behavior. The expert formulates his knowledge of proper control actions in the form of fuzzy decision rules. He defines the input and output variables and the membership functions of the linguistic values which are used in the rules. However, the experts can not always formulate the rule system explicitly. Hence, the decision system of the human operator has to be discovered, basing on the recorded process data. In such a case the rough sets theory can be successfully applied.

The use of the rough sets paradigm for modelling the human operator's control in industrial processes was initiated by Mrózek [12,13,14]. He utilized basically decision tables with crisp attributes. The intervals of the attributes values were coded as integers. Only static or slow processes were taken into account.

D. Ślęzak et al. (Eds.): RSFDGrC 2005, LNAI 3641, pp. 354–363, 2005.

Modelling dynamic processes using the crisp rough sets description was investigated in our former work [8,9]. It concerned the issue of generating and analyzing decision tables, which represented the control actions of a skilled military pilot, performing various flight tasks on a flight simulator. The obtained information systems were relatively large. The original rough sets approach is very sensitive to small changes in data. It can be especially observed in case of large decision tables. Therefore, we could effectively adopt the variable precision rough sets model (VPRS) introduced by Ziarko [6,17].

In this paper we consider some issues connected with application of the variable precision fuzzy rough sets model (VPFRS), proposed in [10,11], to modelling the human operator's decision system. This is a new contribution to our previous work, in which mainly theoretical aspects of the VPFRS model were considered. In particular, we discuss how to construct from process data decision tables with fuzzy attributes, choose an adequate fuzzy similarity relation, and analyze decision tables with the help of the VPFRS model. Additionally, we give a new definition of the upper variable precision fuzzy rough set approximation.

By using fuzzy sets one is able to introduce suitable linguistic values in the decision rules. In consequence, we obtain fuzzy decision tables, which are more adequate for describing the control actions of a human operator, because the human utilizes linguistic terms rather than numbers in his inference. The fuzzy rough sets extension is necessary for analyzing the obtained decision tables with fuzzy attributes. The variable precision fuzzy rough sets model is particularly advantageous in analysis of large fuzzy information systems, which are usually generated in case of dynamic processes.

2   Human Operator's Decision Model

2.1   Decision Tables with Fuzzy Attributes

Let us introduce the necessary description needed for construction of fuzzy decision tables. To this end we adopt an extension of Bodjanova's idea of fuzzy concepts [1], which was improved by Fernández Salido and Murakami in [4].

We have a finite universe U with N elements: $U = \{x_1, x_2, \ldots, x_N\}$. Each element x of the universe U is described with the help of fuzzy attributes, which are divided into a subset of n condition attributes $C = \{c_1, c_2, \ldots, c_n\}$, and a subset of m decision attributes $D = \{d_1, d_2, \ldots, d_m\}$.

For each fuzzy attribute a set of linguistic values can be given. We denote by $V_{i1}, V_{i2}, \ldots, V_{in_i}$ the linguistic values of the condition attribute c_i, and by $W_{j1}, W_{j2}, \ldots, W_{jm_j}$ the linguistic values of the decision attribute d_j, where n_i and m_j is the number of the linguistic values of the i-th condition and the j-th decision attribute respectively, $i = 1, 2, \ldots, n$ and $j = 1, 2, \ldots, m$.

For any element $x \in U$ its membership degrees in all linguistic values of the condition attribute c_i (or decision attribute d_j) have to be determined. It is done during the fuzzification stage, by utilizing the recorded crisp value of a particular attribute of x. When the linguistic values of an attribute have the

Table 1. Decision table with fuzzy attributes

	c_1	c_2	$\cdots$	c_n	d_1	d_2	$\cdots$	d_m
x_1	$V_1(x_1)$	$V_2(x_1)$	$\cdots$	$V_n(x_1)$	$W_1(x_1)$	$W_2(x_1)$	$\cdots$	$W_m(x_1)$
x_2	$V_1(x_2)$	$V_2(x_2)$	$\cdots$	$V_n(x_2)$	$W_1(x_2)$	$W_2(x_2)$	$\cdots$	$W_m(x_2)$
				$\cdots$				
x_N	$V_1(x_N)$	$V_2(x_N)$	$\cdots$	$V_n(x_N)$	$W_1(x_N)$	$W_2(x_N)$	$\cdots$	$W_m(x_N)$

form of singletons or disjoint intervals, with membership degree equal to 1 in the original domain of the attribute, then only one linguistic value can be assigned to that attribute. In that case we get a classical crisp decision table. In general, we obtain a non-zero membership of x to more than one linguistic value of an attribute. Moreover, we may say that the value of an attribute for a given element x is a fuzzy set in the domain of all linguistic values of that attribute. So, we denote by $V_i(x)$ the fuzzy value of the condition attribute c_i for any x, as a fuzzy set in the domain of the linguistic values of c_i:

$$V_i(x) = \{\mu_{V_{i1}}(x)/V_{i1},\, \mu_{V_{i2}}(x)/V_{i2},\, \ldots,\, \mu_{V_{in_i}}(x)/V_{in_i}\}\,.$$

$W_j(x)$ denotes the fuzzy value of the decision attribute d_j for any x, as a fuzzy set in the domain of the linguistic values of d_j:

$$W_j(x) = \{\mu_{W_{j1}}(x)/W_{j1},\, \mu_{W_{j2}}(x)/W_{j2},\, \ldots,\, \mu_{W_{jm_j}}(x)/W_{jm_j}\}\,.$$

2.2 Similarity Relations for Condition and Decision Attributes

The problem of comparing objects described by fuzzy sets has been widely studied in the literature [2,4]. Many different forms of similarity relation have been invented and investigated, e.g. Greco, Matarazzo and Słowiński proposed [5] approximation of fuzzy sets by means of fuzzy relations which are only reflexive. In our considerations, when we focus on the analysis of the recorded process data, the symmetry and some kind of transitivity of the fuzzy similarity relation should be assumed.

After fuzzification of real crisp numbers obtained from the control process, each row of the decision table (in a vector representation) contains the membership degrees of a particular element x in all possible linguistic values of the condition and decision attributes. We use further a symmetric, reflexive and T-transitive fuzzy similarity relation [2,4], which is defined by means of the distance between the compared elements. For the sake of brevity the following formulas will only be given for condition attributes.

If we want to compare any two elements x and y of the universe U with respect to the condition attribute c_i, then the similarity between x and y could be expressed as:

$$S_{c_i}(x, y) = 1 - \max_{k=1,n_i} |\mu_{V_{ik}}(x) - \mu_{V_{ik}}(y)|\,. \tag{1}$$

The above definition of $S_{c_i}(x, y)$ is one of many possible measures of similarity between the fuzzy sets $V_i(x)$ and $V_i(y)$. This is the case of T-similarity relation based on the Łukasiewicz T-norm [4].

In order to evaluate the similarity $S_C(x, y)$, with respect to condition attributes C, we have to aggregate the results obtained for all attributes c_i, $i = 1, 2, \ldots, n$. This can be done by using the T-norm operator min as follows:

$$S_C(x, y) = \min_{i=1,n} S_{c_i}(x, y) = \min_{i=1,n} \left(1 - \max_{k=1,n_i} |\mu_{V_{ik}}(x) - \mu_{V_{ik}}(y)|\right). \tag{2}$$

By the calculation of similarity for all pairs of elements of the universe U we obtain a symmetric similarity matrix. Every row of the similarity matrix forms a fuzzy set in the domain of U. If the value of similarity between the elements x and y is equal to 1, they do belong to the same similarity class. It means that two rows of the similarity matrix must be merged into one fuzzy set with the membership degrees equal to 1 for x and y. This way we obtain a family of fuzzy similarity classes $\tilde{C} = \{C_1, C_2, \ldots, C_{\tilde{n}}\}$ for the condition attributes C and a family of fuzzy similarity classes $\tilde{D} = \{D_1, D_2, \ldots, D_{\tilde{m}}\}$, for the decision attributes D.

The generated partitions $\tilde{C}$ and $\tilde{D}$ satisfy the property of covering U sufficiently and the property of disjointness [3]. For the partition $\tilde{C}$ with $\tilde{n}$ elements the properties of covering and disjointness are expressed as follows:

$$\inf_{x \in U} \max_{i=1,\tilde{n}} \mu_{C_i}(x) > 0, \tag{3}$$

$$\forall i, j \in \{1, 2, \ldots, \tilde{n}\} \ \wedge \ i \neq j, \quad \sup_{x \in U} \min(\mu_{C_i}(x), \mu_{C_j}(x)) < 1. \tag{4}$$

Now, we are able to calculate the approximations of $\tilde{D}$ by $\tilde{C}$. This will be done by using the VPFRS model.

2.3   Variable Precision Fuzzy Rough Approximations

We want to recall here our approach to VPFRS that bases on the use of fuzzy R-implication operators and extends the basic idea of inclusion error introduced by Ziarko [6,17].

Because every similarity class is a fuzzy set in the domain of U, calculating the approximations of particular members of the family $\tilde{D}$ by the family $\tilde{C}$ entails the problem of inclusion of one fuzzy set in another fuzzy set. Different measures of fuzzy sets inclusion were considered in the literature e.g. [1] and [7].

An important notion, on which our VPFRS model is based, is the inclusion degree of a fuzzy set A in a fuzzy set B with respect to particular elements of a set A. We construct a fuzzy set called the fuzzy inclusion set of A in B, denoted by A^B. We apply to this end an implication operator $\rightarrow$:

$$\mu_{A^B}(x) = \begin{cases} \mu_A(x) \rightarrow \mu_B(x) & \text{if } \mu_A(x) > 0, \\ 0 & \text{otherwise.} \end{cases} \tag{5}$$

Only the proper elements of A (support of A) are taken into account. In the definition (5) an implication operator $\rightarrow$ is used, with the aim of maintaining the compatibility (in limit cases) between the fuzzy rough sets model of Dubois and Prade [3] and our VPFRS model. This was stated in [10].

Furthermore, we require that the degree of inclusion with respect to x should be equal to 1, if the inequality $\mu_A(x) \leq \mu_B(x)$ for that x is satisfied:

$$\mu_A(x) \rightarrow \mu_B(x) = 1 \quad \text{if } \mu_A(x) \leq \mu_B(x) \,. \tag{6}$$

We can easy show that the requirement (6) is always satisfied by residual implicators (R-implicators) [15]. We have found out [10] that the most appropriate residual implicator for the VPFRS model is the Łukasiewicz R-implicator: $x \rightarrow y = \min(1, 1 - x + y)$.

In order to generalize the measure of inclusion error [10] introduced by Ziarko, we use a special interpretation of the VPRS approach. The determination of the lower approximation of a set in the (crisp or fuzzy) VPRS model can be interpreted as counting the indiscernibility classes into the lower approximation, basing on the "better" elements (concerning their membership in the set A^B) and disregarding the "worst" elements of the indiscernibility classes, provided that an admissible error is not exceeded. So, we must determine the error that would be made, when the "worst" elements of an approximating fuzzy set were discarded. We discard those elements by applying the notion of α-cut, defined for any fuzzy set $A \subseteq U$ and a level $\alpha \in [0, 1]$:

$$A_\alpha = \{x \in U : \ \mu_A(x) \geq \alpha\} \,. \tag{7}$$

The generalized measure of inclusion error of any nonempty fuzzy set A in a fuzzy set B is called the α-inclusion error $e_\alpha(A, B)$, and defined as:

$$e_\alpha(A, B) = 1 - \frac{\text{power}(A \cap A_\alpha^B)}{\text{power}(A)} \,, \tag{8}$$

where **power** denotes the cardinality of a fuzzy set.

An α value will be needed to express how many "bad" elements may be disregarded without violating the admissible error.

The admissible inclusion error will be expressed by using a lower limit l and an upper limit u for the required inclusion degree. The limits l and u were introduced in the extended version of VPRS by Katzberg and Ziarko [6], with

$$0 \leq l < u \leq 1 \,. \tag{9}$$

For a given decision table we approximate particular fuzzy similarity classes $D_j \in \tilde{D}$, $j = 1, 2, \ldots, \tilde{m}$, generated with respect to the decision attributes D, by all elements of the fuzzy partition $\tilde{C}$, generated with respect to the condition attributes C. According to the discussion given above we admit of some level of tolerance and take into account only the best elements of the approximating class. The u-lower approximation of a fuzzy set D_j by $\tilde{C}$ is a fuzzy set on the domain $\tilde{C}$ with the membership function expressed as follows:

$$\mu_{\tilde{\underline{C}}_u D_j}(C_i) = \begin{cases} f_{i_u} & \text{if } \exists \alpha_u = \sup\{\alpha \in (0, 1] : \ e_\alpha(C_i, D_j) \leq 1 - u\} \,, \\ 0 & \text{otherwise,} \end{cases} \tag{10}$$

where

$$f_{i_u} = \inf_{x \in S_{i_u}} \mu_{C_i}(x) \to \mu_{D_j}(x), \qquad S_{i_u} = \text{supp}(C_i \cap (C_i^{D_j})_{\alpha_u}),$$

and supp denotes the (crisp) support of a fuzzy set.

In the definition of the upper approximation we use only the best elements of the complement of the intersection of the approximating class C_i and the approximated set D_j. The l-upper approximation of the set D_j by $\tilde{C}$ is a fuzzy set on the domain $\tilde{C}$ with the membership function expressed by:

$$\mu_{\overline{\tilde{C}_l D_j}}(C_i) = \begin{cases} f_{i_l} & \text{if } \exists \alpha_l = \sup\{\alpha \in (0,1]: \ e'_{\alpha}(C_i, D_j) \leq l\}, \\ 1 & \text{otherwise,} \end{cases} \qquad (11)$$

where

$$f_{i_l} = \sup_{x \in \tilde{S}_{i_l}} \mu_{C_i}(x) * \mu_{D_j}(x), \qquad S_{i_l} = \text{supp}(C_i \cap (\overline{C_i \cap D_j})_{\alpha_l}),$$

$$e'_{\alpha}(C_i, D_j) = 1 - \frac{\text{power}(C_i \cap (\overline{C_i \cap D_j})_{\alpha})}{\text{power}(C_i)},$$

and $*$ denotes a fuzzy T-norm operator.

The limit-based fuzzy rough approximations are sensitive to small changes of data. An alternative definition of fuzzy rough approximations given in [10] bases on the mean value of membership (in the fuzzy inclusion set) for all used (not discarded) elements of the approximating class. Different importance of particular elements in the approximating classes is taken into account by determining the weighted mean membership in the inclusion set.

We define the weighted mean u-lower approximation of the set D_j by $\tilde{C}$ as a fuzzy set on the domain $\tilde{C}$ with the following membership function:

$$\mu_{\underline{\tilde{C}_u D_j}}(C_i) = \begin{cases} f_{i_u} & \text{if } \exists \alpha_u = \sup\{\alpha \in (0,1]: \ e_{\alpha}(C_i, D_j) \leq 1 - u\}, \\ 0 & \text{otherwise,} \end{cases} \qquad (12)$$

where

$$f_{i_u} = \frac{\text{power}((C_i^{D_j} \cap (C_i^{D_j})_{\alpha_u}) \cdot C_i)}{\text{card}((C_i^{D_j})_{\alpha_u})}. \qquad (13)$$

The membership function of the weighted mean l-upper approximation of the set D_j by $\tilde{C}$ is defined as follows:

$$\mu_{\overline{\tilde{C}_l D_j}}(C_i) = \begin{cases} f_{i_l} & \text{if } \exists \alpha_l = \sup\{\alpha \in (0,1]: \ e_{\alpha}(C_i, D_j) < 1 - l\}, \\ 0 & \text{otherwise,} \end{cases} \qquad (14)$$

where

$$f_{i_l} = \frac{\text{power}((C_i^{D_j} \cap (C_i^{D_j})_{\alpha_l}) \cdot C_i)}{\text{card}((C_i^{D_j})_{\alpha_l})}. \qquad (15)$$

The weighted mean value of inclusion degree of C_i in D_j is determined by using only those elements of C_i, which are included in D_j at least to a degree of α_u and

α_l and denoted by f_{i_u} and f_{i_l} respectively. The operator $\cdot$ used in (13) and (15) denotes the product of fuzzy sets, obtained by multiplication of the respective values of membership functions.

Furthermore, we can use a generalized measure of u-approximation quality in order to deal with fuzzy sets and fuzzy relations.

For the family $\tilde{D} = \{D_1, D_2, \ldots, D_{\tilde{m}}\}$ and the family $\tilde{C} = \{C_1, C_2, \ldots, C_{\tilde{n}}\}$ the u-approximation quality of $\tilde{D}$ by $\tilde{C}$ is defined as follows:

$$\gamma_{\tilde{C}_u}(\tilde{D}) = \frac{\text{power}(\text{Pos}_{\tilde{C}_u}(\tilde{D}))}{\text{card}(U)}, \tag{16}$$

where

$$\text{Pos}_{\tilde{C}_u}(\tilde{D}) = \bigcup_{D_j \in \tilde{D}} \omega(\underline{\tilde{C}}_u D_j) \cap D_j. \tag{17}$$

The fuzzy extension ω denotes a mapping from the domain $\tilde{C}$ into the domain of the universe U, which is expressed for any fuzzy set A by:

$$\mu_{\omega(A)}(x) = \mu_A(C_i) \quad \text{if} \quad \mu_{C_i}(x) = 1. \tag{18}$$

Note, that we use in (17) the notion of restricted positive region defined in [11] for any fuzzy set A and a similarity relation S as follows:

$$\text{Pos}_{S_u}(A) = A \cap \omega(\underline{S}_u A). \tag{19}$$

The u-approximation quality of $\tilde{D}$ by $\tilde{C}$ will be used as a measure of consistency of the human operator's decision model.

3   Example

We consider now the task of stabilization of the aircraft's altitude, performed by a pilot. Two condition attributes c_1 and c_2 were taken into account:

c_1 – altitude deviation from the required value
    (values: V_{11} – "Large Negative", V_{12} – "Small Negative", V_{13} – "Zero",
        V_{14} – "Small Positive", V_{15} – "Large Positive");
c_2 – rate of climb
    (values: V_{21} – "Negative", V_{22} – "Zero", V_{23} – "Positive").

One decision attribute d_1 was used:

d_1 – change of the rudder deflection angle,
    (values: W_{11} – "Negative (Decrease)", W_{12} – "Zero (No Change)",
        W_{13} – "Positive (Increase)").

The membership functions selected for all linguistic values of the attributes have a typical "trapezoidal" shape.

Table 2. Decision table with fuzzy attributes in vector representation

	c_1					c_2			d_1		
x_1	(0.0,	0.0,	1.0,	0.0,	0.0)	(0.0,	1.0,	0.0)	(0.0,	1.0,	0.0)
x_2	(0.0,	0.0,	1.0,	0.0,	0.0)	(0.1,	0.9,	0.0)	(0.0,	0.9,	0.1)
x_3	(0.0,	0.2,	0.8,	0.0,	0.0)	(0.8,	0.2,	0.0)	(0.0,	0.0,	1.0)
x_4	(0.0,	0.0,	0.0,	1.0,	0.0)	(0.0,	0.3,	0.7)	(0.9,	0.1,	0.0)
x_5	(0.0,	0.0,	0.9,	0.1,	0.0)	(1.0,	0.0,	0.0)	(0.0,	0.3,	0.7)
x_6	(0.0,	0.0,	0.0,	0.0,	1.0)	(0.0,	1.0,	0.0)	(1.0,	0.0,	0.0)
x_7	(0.0,	0.0,	0.0,	1.0,	0.0)	(0.8,	0.2,	0.0)	(0.0,	1.0,	0.0)
x_8	(0.0,	0.0,	1.0,	0.0,	0.0)	(0.0,	1.0,	0.0)	(0.0,	1.0,	0.0)
x_9	(0.0,	0.9,	0.1,	0.0,	0.0)	(1.0,	0.0,	0.0)	(0.0,	0.0,	1.0)
x_{10}	(0.1,	0.9,	0.0,	0.0,	0.0)	(0.0,	0.9,	0.1)	(0.0,	1.0,	0.0)
x_{11}	(0.0,	1.0,	0.0,	0.0,	0.0)	(1.0,	0.0,	0.0)	(0.0,	0.1,	0.9)
x_{12}	(0.9,	0.1,	0.0,	0.0,	0.0)	(0.0,	1.0,	0.0)	(0.0,	0.0,	1.0)
x_{13}	(0.0,	0.0,	1.0,	0.0,	0.0)	(0.0,	1.0,	0.0)	(0.0,	0.0,	1.0)
x_{14}	(0.0,	0.0,	1.0,	0.0,	0.0)	(0.1,	0.9,	0.0)	(0.0,	1.0,	0.0)
x_{15}	(0.0,	0.0,	1.0,	0.0,	0.0)	(0.0,	1.0,	0.0)	(0.0,	1.0,	0.0)

In reality, the process of altitude stabilization is more complicated, but a simplified description is sufficient for our considerations. The decision table with fuzzy attributes was generated from the control process by the fuzzification stage. In order to analyze the obtained decision table with the help of VPFRS the following steps were executed:

1. Determining the similarity matrix on the domain $U \times U$ with respect to all condition attributes and the similarity matrix with respect to all decision attributes, according to (2).
2. Determining the family of similarity classes $\tilde{C}$ and $\tilde{D}$.
3. Calculating the u-lower approximation of particular decision similarity classes by the family of condition similarity classes, in the domain of $\tilde{C}$, according to (10) and (12).
4. Determining the u-lower approximation of $\tilde{D}$ by $\tilde{C}$ in the domain of U, and calculating the u-approximation quality of $\tilde{D}$ by $\tilde{C}$, according to (16).
5. Evaluating the importance of each condition attribute for the human operator's decision model.

We obtained in the second step 11 similarity classes with respect to the condition attributes and 7 similarity classes with respect to the decision attribute. In the next step the Łukasiewicz implication operator was used in calculations. The last step consists in checking up the value of u-approximation quality of $\tilde{D}$ by $\tilde{C}$, after discarding particular condition attributes from the decision table. The omitted condition attribute is indispensable, when the value of u-approximation quality decreases. The results of u-approximation quality of $\tilde{D}$ by $\tilde{C}$ before and after removing of each condition attribute are given in Table 2.1. We see that even for a small universe the value of u-approximation quality increases, when we

Table 3. u-approximation quality for different values of required inclusion degree

Method	Removed attribute	$\gamma_{\tilde{C}_u}(\tilde{D})$				
		$u = 1$	$u = 0.9$	$u = 0.85$	$u = 0.8$	$u = 0.75$
L-inf	none	0.667	0.680	0.747	0.900	0.920
	c_1	0.207	0.233	0.347	0.447	0.467
	c_2	0.393	0.393	0.400	0.400	0.500
L-w.mean	none	0.885	0.887	0.901	0.946	0.948
	c_1	0.462	0.471	0.689	0.719	0.743
	c_2	0.705	0.705	0.742	0.742	0.782

use the VPFRS model with $u < 1$, especially for the limit-based method. Thus, the u-approximation quality is a good measure of consistency of the human operator's decision model. The analyzed pilot's decision system has a relatively high consistency. Calculations after discarding particular condition attributes lead to a conclusion that each of the condition attributes is important in the decision model.

4 Conclusions

In this paper we proposed to describe the human operator's decision model in the form of decision table with fuzzy attributes. The fuzzy character of attributes corresponds with the human ability to inference using linguistic concepts rather than numbers. The variable precision fuzzy rough sets model was recommended for analyzing this kind of decision tables. Particular steps of analysis were presented and discussed using a simple example. It was shown that relaxation of strong inclusion requirements of one fuzzy set in another fuzzy set (admitting of a certain misclassification level in the human operator's control) leads to an increase of the u-approximation quality of $\tilde{D}$ by $\tilde{C}$. The change of the u-approximation quality of $\tilde{D}$ by $\tilde{C}$, after omitting particular condition attribute in a decision table, is a good indicator of importance of that attribute in the human operator's decision system. The VPFRS model is an universal tool for analyzing decision tables with fuzzy or crisp attributes.

References

1. Bodjanova, S.: Approximation of Fuzzy Concepts in Decision Making. Fuzzy Sets and Systems **85** (1997) 23–29
2. Chen, S.M., Yeh, M.S., Hsiao, P.Y.: A Comparison of Similarity Measures of Fuzzy Values. Fuzzy Sets and Systems **72** (1995) 79–89
3. Dubois, D., Prade, H.: Putting Rough Sets and Fuzzy Sets Together. [16] 203–232
4. Fernández Salido, J.M., Murakami, S.: Rough Set Analysis of a General Type of Fuzzy Data Using Transitive Aggregations of Fuzzy Similarity Relations. Fuzzy Sets and Systems **139** (2003) 635–660

5. Greco, S., Matarazzo, B., Słowiński, R.: Rough Set Processing of Vague Information Using Fuzzy Similarity Relations. In: Calude, C.S., Paun, G., (eds.): Finite Versus Infinite — Contributions to an Eternal Dilemma. Springer-Verlag, Berlin Heidelberg New York (2000) 149–173

6. Katzberg, J.D., Ziarko, W.: Variable Precision Extension of Rough Sets. Fundamenta Informaticae **27** (1996) 155–168

7. Lin, T.Y.: Coping with Imprecision Information — Fuzzy Logic. Downsizing Expo, Santa Clara Convention Center (1993)

8. Mieszkowicz-Rolka, A., Rolka, L.: Variable Precision Rough Sets in Analysis of Inconsistent Decision Tables. In: Rutkowski, L., Kacprzyk, J., (eds.): Advances in Soft Computing. Physica-Verlag, Heidelberg (2003) 304–309

9. Mieszkowicz-Rolka, A., Rolka, L.: Variable Precision Rough Sets: Evaluation of Human Operator's Decision Model. In: Sołdek, J., Drobiazgiewicz, L., (eds.): Artificial Intelligence and Security in Computing Systems. Kluwer Academic Publishers, Boston Dordrecht London (2003) 33–40

10. Mieszkowicz-Rolka, A., Rolka, L.: Variable Precision Fuzzy Rough Sets. In: Peters, J.F., et al., (eds.): Transactions on Rough Sets I. Lecture Notes in Computer Science (Journal Subline), Vol. 3100. Springer-Verlag, Berlin Heidelberg New York (2004) 144–160

11. Mieszkowicz-Rolka, A., Rolka, L.: Remarks on Approximation Quality in Variable Precision Fuzzy Rough Sets Model. In: Tsumoto, S., et al., (eds.): Rough Sets and Current Trends in Computing. Lecture Notes in Artificial Intelligence, Vol. 3066. Springer-Verlag, Berlin Heidelberg New York (2004) 402–411

12. Mrózek, A.: Rough Sets in Computer Implementation of Rule-Based Control of Industrial Processes. [16] 19–31

13. Pawlak, Z.: AI and Inteligent Industrial Applications: The Rough Set Perspective. Cybernetics and Systems: An International Journal **31** (2000) 227–252

14. Peters, J.F., Skowron, A., Suraj, Z.: An Application of Rough Sets Methods in Control Design. Fundamenta Informaticae **43** (2000) 269–290

15. Radzikowska, A.M., Kerre, E.E.: A Comparative Study of Fuzzy Rough Sets. Fuzzy Sets and Systems **126** (2002) 137–155

16. Słowiński, R., (ed.): Intelligent Decision Support: Handbook of Applications and Advances of the Rough Sets Theory. Kluwer Academic Publishers, Boston Dordrecht London (1992)

17. Ziarko, W.: Variable Precision Rough Sets Model. Journal of Computer and System Sciences **46** (1993) 39–59

CRST: A Generalization of Rough Set Theory

Tian Hong[1,2], Zhao Pixi[1], and Wang Xiukun[1]

[1] Dalian University of Technology, Dalian, China
[2] Dalian Jiaotong University, Dalian, China
th@djtu.edu.cn

Abstract. Rough set theory is developed based on the notion of equivalence relation, but the property of equivalence has limited its application fields, which may not provide a realistic description of real-world relationships between elements. The paper presents a transition from the equivalence relation to the compatibility relation, called Compatibility Rough Set Theory or, in short, CRST. A specific type of fuzzy compatibility relations, called conditional probability relations, is discussed. All basic concepts or rough set theory are extended. Generalized rough set approximations are defined by using coverings of the universe induced by a fuzzy compatibility relation. Generalized rough membership functions are defined and their properties are examined.

Keywords: Rough Set Theory (RST), Compatibility Rough Set Theory (CRST), Compatibility Relation, Fuzzy Compatibility Relation.

1 Introduction

Rough set theory is a new mathematical approach to uncertain and vague data analysis. It plays an important role in many applications of data mining and knowledge discovery. The application of rough set theory for machine learning, knowledge discovery, decision analysis, expert system, decision support, classification, pattern recognition, fuzzy control and others have proved to be a very effective new mathematical approach [1]. It offers a mathematical model and tools for discovering hidden patterns in data, recognizing partial or total dependencies in data, removing redundant data, and many others [2, 3].

Rough set theory generalizes classical set theory by studying sets with imprecise boundaries. A rough set, characterized by a pair of lower and upper approximations, may be viewed as an approximate representation of a crisp set in terms of two subsets derived from a partition on the universe [4, 5].

The main objective of this paper is to generalize the standard rough sets by coverings of the universe induced by a fuzzy compatibility relation. The proposed rough sets may be considered as generalized fuzzy rough set [6, 7]. Rough membership functions are generalized and defined with respect to the covering, and their properties are investigated.

In this paper we present extensions of the basic concepts of rough set theory. Section 2 presents compatibility relations. Section 3 presents the Generalized

D. Ślęzak et al. (Eds.): RSFDGrC 2005, LNAI 3641, pp. 364–372, 2005.

Rough Set Approximations. Generalized Rough Membership Functions are defined in Section 4. An illustrative example is discussed in Section 5 and we conclude in Section 6.

2   Compatibility Relations

In general, relationships between elements may not necessarily be transitive for representing non-equivalence relationships between elements, conditional probability relations was introduced recently [8]. Conditional probability relations maybe considered as a generalization of compatibility relations and fuzzy compatibility relations.

The concept of conditional probability relations was introduced by Intan and Mukaidono in the context of fuzzy relational database [8]. It may be considered as a concrete example of fuzzy compatibility relation, which in turn is a special type of fuzzy binary relation.

The concept of compatibility relations are defined as follows:

Definition 1. *A compatibility relation is a mapping,$c : U \times U \longrightarrow [0,1]$, such that for any $x, y \in U$,*

$$Reflexivity : c(x,x) = 1 \tag{1}$$

$$Symmetry : c(x,y) = c(y,x) \tag{2}$$

Definition 2. *A fuzzy compatibility relation is a mapping, $C : U \times U \longrightarrow [0,1]$, such that for any $x, y \in U$,*

$$Reflexivity : C(x,x) = 1 \tag{3}$$

$$Symmetry : if \ \ C(x,y) > 0 \ \ then \ \ C(y,x) > 0 \tag{4}$$

Definition 3. *A conditional probability relation is a mapping, $R : U \times U \longrightarrow [0,1]$, such that for any $x, y \in U$,*

$$R(x,y) = P(y|x) \tag{5}$$

Where $R(x,y)$ means the degree x supports y or the degree x is similar to y.

When objects in U are represented by sets of features or attributes as in the case of binary information tables, we have a simple procedure for estimating the conditional probability relation. More specifically, we have:

$$R(x,y) = P(y|x) = \frac{|x \cap y|}{|x|} \tag{6}$$

Where $|.|$ denotes the cardinality of a set.

Definition 4. *Let μ_x and μ_y be two fuzzy sets over a set of attribute A for two elements x and y of a universe U . A fuzzy conditional probability relation is defined by:*

$$R(x,y) = \frac{\sum_{a \in A} min\{\mu_x(a), \mu_y(a)\}}{\sum_{a \in A} \mu_x(a)} \tag{7}$$

It can be easily verified that satisfies properties of a fuzzy compatibility relation. Additional properties of similarity as defined by conditional probability relations can be found in [8].

3   Generalized Rough Set Approximations

From fuzzy compatibility relations and conditional probability relations, coverings of the universe can be defined and interpreted. The concept of rough sets can be generalized based on coverings of universe.

Definition 5. *Let U be a non-empty universe , and C a fuzzy compatibility relation on U. For any element $x \in U$, $R_s^\alpha(x)$ and $R_p^\alpha(x)$ are defined as the set of elements that support x and the set of elements that are supported by x, respectively, to a degree of at least $\alpha \in [0,1]$, as follows:*

$$R_s^\alpha(x) = \{y \in U | C(x,y) \geq \alpha\} \tag{8}$$

$$R_p^\alpha(x) = \{y \in U | C(y,x) \geq \alpha\} \tag{9}$$

The set $R_p^\alpha(x)$ consists of elements that are similar to x, at least to a degree of α. The set $R_s^\alpha(x)$ consists of elements to which x is similar, at least to a degree of α. By the reflexivity, it follows that we can construct two covering of the universe, $\{R_p^\alpha(x)|x \in U\}$ and $\{R_s^\alpha(x)|x \in U\}$. By extending rough sets, we obtain two pairs of generalized rough set approximations.

Definition 6. *For a subset $X \subseteq U$, we define two pairs of generalized rough set approximations:*
(1) element-oriented generalization

$$\underline{apr}_e^\alpha(X) = \{x \in U | R_p^\alpha(x) \subseteq X\}$$
$$\overline{apr}_e^\alpha(X) = \{x \in U | R_p^\alpha(x) \cap X \neq \emptyset\}$$

(2) compatibility-class-oriented generalization

$$\underline{apr}_c^\alpha(X) = \bigcup\{R_p^\alpha(x) | R_p^\alpha(x) \subseteq X, x \in U\}$$
$$\overline{apr}_c^\alpha(X) = \bigcup\{R_p^\alpha(x) | R_p^\alpha(x) \cap X \neq \emptyset, x \in U\}$$

In Definition 6(1), the lower approximation consists of those elements in U whose similarity classes are contained in X. The upper approximation consists of those elements whose similarity classes overlap with X. In Definition 6(2), the lower approximation is the union of all similarity classes that are contained in X. The upper approximation is the union of all similarity classes that overlap with X. Relationships among these approximations can be represented by:

$$\underline{apr}_e^\alpha(X) \subseteq \underline{apr}_c^\alpha(X) \subseteq X \subseteq \overline{apr}_e^\alpha(X) \subseteq \overline{apr}_c^\alpha(X) \tag{10}$$

The difference between lower and upper approximations is the boundary region with respect to X:

$$BN_e^\alpha(X) = \overline{apr}_e^\alpha(X) - \underline{apr}_e^\alpha(X) \tag{11}$$

$$BN_c^\alpha(X) = \overline{apr}_c^\alpha(X) - \underline{apr}_c^\alpha(X) \tag{12}$$

Similarly, one can define rough set approximation based on the covering $\{R_s^\alpha(x) | x \in U\}$.

The pair $(\underline{apr}_e^\alpha, \overline{apr}_e^\alpha)$ gives rise to two unary set-theoretic operators. It is referred to as rough set approximation operators [9]. By combining with other set-theoretic operators such as $\sim, \cup,$ and $\cap$, we have the following results:

$$\underline{apr}_e^\alpha(X) = \sim \overline{apr}_e^\alpha(\sim X) \tag{13}$$

$$\overline{apr}_e^\alpha(X) = \sim \underline{apr}_e^\alpha(\sim X) \tag{14}$$

$$\underline{apr}_e^\alpha(X) \subseteq X \subseteq \overline{apr}_e^\alpha(X) \tag{15}$$

$$\underline{apr}_e^\alpha(\emptyset) = \overline{apr}_e^\alpha(\emptyset) = \emptyset \tag{16}$$

$$\underline{apr}_e^\alpha(U) = \overline{apr}_e^\alpha(U) = U \tag{17}$$

$$\underline{apr}_e^\alpha(X \cap Y) = \underline{apr}_e^\alpha(X) \cap \underline{apr}_e^\alpha(Y) \tag{18}$$

$$\overline{apr}_e^\alpha(X \cap Y) \subseteq \overline{apr}_e^\alpha(X) \cap \overline{apr}_e^\alpha(Y) \tag{19}$$

$$\underline{apr}_e^\alpha(X \cup Y) \supseteq \underline{apr}_e^\alpha(X) \cup \underline{apr}_e^\alpha(Y) \tag{20}$$

$$\overline{apr}_e^\alpha(X \cup Y) = \overline{apr}_e^\alpha(X) \cup \overline{apr}_e^\alpha(Y) \tag{21}$$

$$X \neq \emptyset \Longrightarrow \overline{apr}_e^0(X) = U \tag{22}$$

$$X \subset U \Longrightarrow \underline{apr}_e^0(X) = \emptyset \tag{23}$$

$$\alpha \leq \beta \Longrightarrow \overline{apr}_e^\beta(X) \subseteq \overline{apr}_e^\alpha(X) \tag{24}$$

$$\alpha \leq \beta \Longrightarrow \underline{apr}_e^\alpha(X) \subseteq \underline{apr}_e^\beta(X) \tag{25}$$

$$X \subseteq Y \Longrightarrow \underline{apr}_e^\alpha(X) \subseteq \underline{apr}_e^\alpha(Y) \tag{26}$$

$$X \subseteq Y \Longrightarrow \overline{apr}_e^\alpha(X) \subseteq \overline{apr}_e^\alpha(Y) \tag{27}$$

Property (13) and (14) show that lower and upper approximations are dual operators with respect to set complement $\sim$. Properties (16) and (17) provide two boundary conditions. Properties (18),(19),(20) and (21) may be considered as weak distributive and distributive over set intersection and union, respectively, when $\alpha = 0$, (22) and (23) show that lower and upper approximations of a non-empty set $X \subset U$ are equal to U and $\emptyset$, respectively. Property (24) and (25) show that if the value of α is larger then the lower approximation is also bigger, but the upper approximation is smaller. Property (26) and (27) indicate the monotonicity of approximation operators with respect to set inclusion.

Lower and upper approximations of Definition 6(2) satisfy the following properties:

$$\underline{apr}_c^\alpha(X) = \sim \overline{apr}_c^\alpha(\sim X) \tag{28}$$

$$\overline{apr}_c^\alpha(X) = \sim \underline{apr}_c^\alpha(\sim X) \tag{29}$$

$$\underline{apr}_c^\alpha(X) \subseteq X \subseteq \overline{apr}_c^\alpha(X) \tag{30}$$

$$\underline{apr}_c^\alpha(\emptyset) = \overline{apr}_c^\alpha(\emptyset) = \emptyset \tag{31}$$

$$\underline{apr}_c^\alpha(U) = \overline{apr}_c^\alpha(U) = U \tag{32}$$

$$\underline{apr}_c^\alpha(X \cap Y) = \underline{apr}_c^\alpha(X) \cap \underline{apr}_c^\alpha(Y) \tag{33}$$

$$\overline{apr}_c^\alpha(X \cap Y) \subseteq \overline{apr}_c^\alpha(X) \cap \overline{apr}_c^\alpha(Y) \tag{34}$$

$$\underline{apr}_c^\alpha(X \cup Y) \supseteq \underline{apr}_c^\alpha(X) \cup \underline{apr}_c^\alpha(Y) \tag{35}$$

$$\overline{apr}_c^\alpha(X \cup Y) = \overline{apr}_c^\alpha(X) \cup \overline{apr}_c^\alpha(Y) \tag{36}$$

$$X \neq \emptyset \Longrightarrow \overline{apr}_c^0(X) = U \tag{37}$$

$$X \subset U \Longrightarrow \underline{apr}_c^0(X) = \emptyset \tag{38}$$

$$\alpha \leq \beta \Longrightarrow \overline{apr}_c^\beta(X) \subseteq \overline{apr}_c^\alpha(X) \tag{39}$$

$$\alpha \leq \beta \Longrightarrow \underline{apr}_c^\alpha(X) \subseteq \underline{apr}_c^\beta(X) \tag{40}$$

$$X \subseteq Y \Longrightarrow \underline{apr}_c^\alpha(X) \subseteq \underline{apr}_c^\alpha(Y) \tag{41}$$

$$X \subseteq Y \Longrightarrow \overline{apr}_c^\alpha(X) \subseteq \overline{apr}_c^\alpha(Y) \tag{42}$$

It should be pointed out that they are not a pair of dual operators. Property (28) and (29) indicate that the results of iterative operations of both lower and upper approximation operators are the same a single application.

4   Generalized Rough Membership Functions

As pointed out in [5], there are at least two views which can be used to interpret the rough set theory, operator-oriented view and set-oriented view. The operator-oriented view discussed in previous section provides the generalization of lower and upper approximation operators. In this section, we provide a set-oriented view based on the notion of rough membership functions.

By using coverings of the universe in Definition 5, we extend rough membership function and obtain three values of generalized rough membership function.

Definition 7. *For a subset $X \subseteq U$, with respect to a value $\alpha \in (0, 1]$, we define the following three rough membership functions:*

$$\mu_X^m(y)^\alpha = min\left\{\frac{|R_p^\alpha(x) \cap X|}{|R_p^\alpha(x)|} \,\middle|\, x \in U, y \in R_p^\alpha(x)\right\} \tag{43}$$

$$\mu_X^M(y)^\alpha = max\left\{\frac{|R_p^\alpha(x) \cap X|}{|R_p^\alpha(x)|} \,\middle|\, x \in U, y \in R_p^\alpha(x)\right\} \tag{44}$$

$$\mu_X^*(y)^\alpha = avg\left\{\frac{|R_p^\alpha(x) \cap X|}{|R_p^\alpha(x)|} \,\middle|\, x \in U, y \in R_p^\alpha(x)\right\} \tag{45}$$

They are referred to as the minimum, maximum and average rough membership functions, respectively. Note: average function is interpreted as given example, $avg\{0.5, 0.5, 0.2\} = 0.4$.

The above definition generalizes the concept of rough membership functions proposed in [10]. It provides a concrete interpretation of coverings used to define the approximation operators [11]. The minimum, the maximum and the average equations may be assumed to be the most pessimistic, the most optimistic and the balanced view in defining rough membership function. The minimum rough membership function of y is determined by a set, $R_p^\alpha(x)$, which contains y and has the smallest relative overlap with X. The maximum rough membership function is determined by a set, $R_p^\alpha(x)$, which contains y and has the largest relative overlap with X. The average rough membership function depends on the average of all sets, $R_p^\alpha(x)$'s, that contains y.

The relationships of the three rough membership functions can be expressed by:

$$\mu_X^m(y)^\alpha \leq \mu_X^*(y)^\alpha \leq \mu_X^M(y)^\alpha \tag{46}$$

Depending on the value of α, we can define a family of rough membership functions. The minimum, maximum and average rough membership functions satisfy the properties: for $X, Y \subseteq U$,

$$\mu_U^m(x)^\alpha = \mu_U^*(x)^\alpha = \mu_U^M(x)^\alpha = 1 \tag{47}$$

$$\mu_\emptyset^m(x)^\alpha = \mu_\emptyset^*(X)^\alpha = \mu_\emptyset^M(x)^\alpha = 0 \tag{48}$$

$$[\forall x \in U, y \in R_p^\alpha(x) \Leftrightarrow z \in R_p^\alpha(x)] \Longrightarrow$$
$$\mu_X^m(y)^\alpha = \mu_X^m(z)^\alpha, \mu_X^*(y)^\alpha = \mu_X^*(z)^\alpha, \mu_X^M(y)^\alpha = \mu_X^M(z)^\alpha \tag{49}$$

$$\exists x \in U, y, z \in R_p^\alpha(x) \Longrightarrow$$
$$(\mu_X^m(y)^\alpha \neq 0 \Rightarrow \mu_X^m(z)^\alpha \neq 0), (\mu_X^m(y)^\alpha = 1 \Rightarrow \mu_X^m(z)^\alpha = 1) \tag{50}$$

$$y \in X \Longrightarrow \mu_X^m(y)^\alpha > 0 \tag{51}$$

$$\mu_X^M(y)^\alpha = 1 \Longrightarrow y \in X \tag{52}$$

$$X \subseteq Y \Longrightarrow [\mu_X^m(y)^\alpha \leq \mu_Y^m(y)^\alpha, \mu_X^*(y)^\alpha \leq \mu_Y^*(y)^\alpha, \mu_X^M(y)^\alpha \leq \mu_Y^M(y)^\alpha] \tag{53}$$

$$X \neq \emptyset \Longrightarrow \mu_X^m(x)^0 = \mu_X^*(x)^0 = \mu_X^M(x)^0 = \frac{|X|}{|U|} = P(X) \tag{54}$$

Properties (47) and (48) show the boundary conditions, namely, for U and $\emptyset$, the minimum, maximum and average membership functions have the same values for all elements, 1 and 0, respectively. Properties (49) and (50) indicate that two similar elements in a covering should have similar rough membership functions. Properties (51) and (52) show the constraints on the membership values of elements of X. Property (53) shows the monotonicity of approximation operators with respect to section inclusion. When α is set to be 0, the covering of the universe consists only of U. In this case, the rough membership values of elements in X equal to the probability of X, as shown by property (54).

With respect to set-theoretic operators, $\neg$,$\cup$, and$\cap$, rough membership functions satisfy the properties:

$$\mu_{\neg X}^m(x)^\alpha = 1 - \mu_X^M(x)^\alpha \tag{55}$$

$$\mu_{\neg X}^M(x)^\alpha = 1 - \mu_X^m(x)^\alpha \tag{56}$$

$$\mu_{\neg X}^*(x)^\alpha = 1 - \mu_X^*(x)^\alpha \tag{57}$$

$$max(0, \mu_X^m(x)^\alpha + \mu_Y^m(x)^\alpha - \mu_{X\cup Y}^M(x)^\alpha) \leq$$
$$\mu_{X\cap Y}^m(x)^\alpha) \leq min(\mu_X^m(x)^\alpha, \mu_Y^m(x)^\alpha) \tag{58}$$

$$max(\mu_X^M(x)^\alpha, \mu_Y^M(x)^\alpha) \leq \mu_{X\cup Y}^M(x)^\alpha) \leq$$
$$min(1, \mu_X^M(x)^\alpha + \mu_Y^M(x)^\alpha - \mu_{X\cap Y}^m(x)^\alpha) \tag{59}$$

$$\mu_{X\cup Y}^*(x)^\alpha = \mu_X^*(x)^\alpha + \mu_Y^*(x)^\alpha - \mu_{X\cap Y}^*(x)^\alpha \tag{60}$$

5   An Illustrative Example

Let us illustrate the above concepts by using binary information tables given by table1 £ňwhere the set of objects,$U = \{x_1, \ldots, x_{20}\}$, is described by a set of eight attributes,$A = \{a_1, \ldots, a_8\}$. Suppose α is chosen to be 0.7. By Definitions 3, 4 and 5, we obtain similarity classes of all elements in as follows:

Table 1. Binary Information Table

U/A	a_1	a_2	a_3	a_4	a_5	a_6	a_7	a_8	U/A	a_1	a_2	a_3	a_4	a_5	a_6	a_7	a_8
x_1	0	0	1	0	1	0	0	0	x_{11}	0	0	0	1	1	0	1	1
x_2	1	1	0	1	0	0	1	0	x_{12}	1	0	0	0	1	0	0	0
x_3	0	0	1	1	0	0	1	1	x_{13}	1	0	1	0	1	0	1	0
x_4	0	1	0	1	0	1	0	1	x_{14}	1	0	0	0	0	1	1	0
x_5	1	0	1	1	0	0	1	0	x_{15}	0	0	1	0	1	0	1	1
x_6	0	0	1	0	1	0	1	0	x_{16}	0	0	0	1	0	0	1	1
x_7	0	1	1	0	0	0	1	0	x_{17}	0	1	0	1	1	0	0	1
x_8	1	1	0	0	0	0	1	1	x_{18}	1	0	0	1	0	0	1	0
x_9	0	1	0	1	1	0	1	0	x_{19}	0	0	1	0	1	1	0	1
x_{10}	0	1	0	0	0	1	1	0	x_{20}	1	0	0	1	0	1	0	0

$R_p^{0.7}(x_1) = \{x_1\}$

$R_p^{0.7}(x_2) = \{x_2, x_5, x_8, x_9, x_{18}\}$

$R_p^{0.7}(x_3) = \{x_3, x_5, x_{11}, x_{15}, x_{16}\}$

$R_p^{0.7}(x_4) = \{x_4, x_{17}\}$

$R_p^{0.7}(x_5) = \{x_2, x_3, x_5, x_{13}\}$

$R_p^{0.7}(x_6) = \{x_1, x_6, x_{13}, x_{15}\}$

$R_p^{0.7}(x_7) = \{x_7\}$

$R_p^{0.7}(x_8) = \{x_2, x_8\}$

$R_p^{0.7}(x_9) = \{x_2, x_9, x_{11}, x_{17}\}$

$R_p^{0.7}(x_{10}) = \{x_{10}\}$

$R_p^{0.7}(x_{11}) = \{x_3, x_9, x_{11}, x_{13}, x_{15}\}$

$R_p^{0.7}(x_{12}) = \{x_{12}\}$

$R_p^{0.7}(x_{13}) = \{x_1, x_5, x_6, x_{12}, x_{13}, x_{15}\}$

$R_p^{0.7}(x_{14}) = \{x_{14}\}$

$R_p^{0.7}(x_{15}) = \{x_1, x_3, x_6, x_{11}, x_{13}, x_{15}, x_{19}\}$

$R_p^{0.7}(x_{16}) = \{x_3, x_{11}, x_{16}\}$

$R_p^{0.7}(x_{17}) = \{x_4, x_9, x_{11}, x_{17}\}$

$R_p^{0.7}(x_{18}) = \{x_2, x_5, x_{18}\}$

$R_p^{0.7}(x_{19}) = \{x_1, x_{15}, x_{19}\}$

$R_p^{0.7}(x_{20}) = \{x_{20}\}$

Consider the set of objects:

$$X = \{x_1, x_3, x_6, x_{10}, x_{14}, x_{15}, x_{19}\}$$

The rough set approximations of according to Definition6 are:

$\underline{apr}_e^{0.7}(X) = \{x_1, x_{10}, x_{14}, x_{19}\}$

$\overline{apr}_e^{0.7}(X) = \{x_1, x_3, x_5, x_6, x_{10}, x_{11}, x_{13}, x_{14}, x_{15}, x_{16}, x_{19}\}$

$\underline{apr}_c^{0.7}(X) = \{x_1, x_{10}, x_{14}, x_{15}, x_{19}\}$

$\overline{apr}_c^{0.7}(X) = \{x_1, x_2, x_3, x_5, x_6, x_9, x_{10}, x_{11}, x_{12}, x_{13}, x_{14}, x_{15}, x_{16}, x_{19}\}$

Rough boundaries of X are:

$BN_e^{0.7}(X) = \{x_3, x_5, x_6, x_{11}, x_{13}, x_{15}, x_{16}\}$

$BN_c^{0.7}(X) = \{x_2, x_3, x_5, x_6, x_9, x_{11}, x_{12}, x_{13}, x_{16}\}$

For the element x_{19} , it belongs to two similarity classes: $R_p^{0.7}(x_{15})$ and $R_p^{0.7}(x_{19})$. Moreover, we have:

$$\frac{|R_p^{0.7}(x_{15}) \cap X|}{|R_p^{0.7}(x_{15})|} = \frac{5}{7} \qquad \frac{|R_p^{0.7}(x_{19}) \cap X|}{|R_p^{0.7}(x_{19})|} = 1$$

By Definition 7, the minimum, maximum, and average rough membership values of x_{19} are given by:

$$\mu_X^m(x_{19})^{0.7} = min(1, \frac{5}{7}) = \frac{5}{7}$$

$$\mu_X^M(x_{19})^{0.7} = max(1, \frac{5}{7}) = 1$$

$$\mu_X^*(x_{19})^{0.7} = avg(1, \frac{5}{7}) = \frac{6}{7}$$

The above procedure can be applied to fuzzy information table. In this case, a fuzzy conditional probability relation as defined in Definition 4 can be used to construct $\alpha-$covering of the universe.

6   Conclusions

In general, relationship between elements may not necessarily be transitive. For representing non-equivalence relationships between elements, conditional probability relation was introduced recently [12]. Conditional probability relations may be considered as a generalization of compatibility relations. They can be considered as a special type of fuzzy compatibility relations [13].

In this paper, we introduce the notion of fuzzy compatibility relation. Conditional probability relations are suggested for the construction and interpretation of coverings of the universe. From the coverings induced by a fuzzy compatibility relation, we generalize the standard rough set approximations. Two pairs of lower and upper approximation operators are suggested and studied. Three rough membership functions, the minimum, maximum and average, are introduced and their properties are examined.

References

1. Pawlak, Z.: Rough sets – Theoretical aspects of reasoning about data. Kluwer Academic Publishers (1991).
2. Komorowski, J. Pawlak, Z. Polkowski, L. Skowron, A. Rough Sets: A Tutorial. (1999)
3. Polkowski, L. and Skowron, A. (Eds.): Rough Sets in Knowledge Discovery, **I,II,** Physica-Verlage, Heidelberg. (1998).
4. Klir, G.J. and Yuan, B. Fuzzy Sets and Fuzzy Logic: Theory and Applications, Prentice Hall, New Jersey. (1995)
5. Yao, Y.Y.: Two views of the theory of rough sets in finite universe, International Journal of Approximate Reasoning 15, (1996) pp. 291-317.
6. Yao, Y.Y.: Combination of rough and fuzzy sets based on $\alpha-$level sets,in: Rough Sets and Data Mining: Analysis for Imprecise Data, Lin, T.Y. andCercone, N. (Eds.), Kluwer Academic Publishers, Boston, (1997) pp. 227-242.
7. Yao, Y.Y.: Generalized rough set models, in: Rough Sets in Knowledge Discovery, Polkowski, L. and Skowron, A. (Eds.), Physica-Verlag, Heidelberg, (1998) pp. 286-318.
8. Intan, R. and Mukaidono, M. : Conditional probability relations in fuzzy relational database, Proceeding of RSCTC'00, (2000) pp. 213-222.
9. Yao, Y.Y.: A comparative study of fuzzy set and rough sets, International Journal of Information Science, **109**, (1998) pp. 227-242.
10. Pawlak, Z. Skowron, A.: Rough membership functions, Fuzzy Logic for the Management of Uncertainty (L. A. Zadeh and J. Kacprzyk, Eds.), (1994) pp. 251-271.
11. Yao, Y.Y. and Zhang, J. P.: Interpreting fuzzy membership functions in the theory of rough sets, Proceedings of RSCTC'00,(2000) pp. 50-57.
12. Intan, R. and Mukaidono, M.: Fuzzy functional dependency and its application to approximate querying', Proceedings of IDEAS'00, (2000) pp. 47-54.
13. Intan, R., Mukaidono, M., Yao, Y. Y.: Generalization of Rough Sets with a-coverings of the Universe Induced by Conditional Probability Relations', Proceedings of International Workshop on Rough Sets and Granular Computing,(2001), pp. 173-176.

An Extension of Rough Approximation Quality to Fuzzy Classification

Van-Nam Huynh[1], Tetsuya Murai[2], Tu-Bao Ho[1], and Yoshiteru Nakamori[1]

[1] Japan Advanced Institute of Science and Technology,
Ishikawa 923-1292, Japan
{huynh, bao, nakamori}@jaist.ac.jp
[2] Graduate School of Information Science and Engineering,
Hokkaido University, Sapporo 060-0814, Japan

Abstract. In this paper, to deal with practical situations where a fuzzy classification must be approximated by available knowledge expressed in terms of a Pawlak's approximation space, we investigate an extension of approximation quality measure to a fuzzy classification aimed at providing a numerical characteristic for such situations. Furthermore, extensions of related coefficients such as the precision measure and the significance measure are also discussed. A simple example is given to illustrate the proposed notions.

1 Introduction

Basically, while a fuzzy set introduced by Zadeh [18] models the ill-definition of the boundary of a concept often described linguistically, a rough set introduced by Pawlak [13] characterizes a concept by its lower and upper approximations due to indiscernibility between objects. Since their inception, both the theories of fuzzy sets and rough sets have been proving to be of substantial importance in many areas of application [12,14,19].

During the last decades, many attempts to establish the relationships between the two theories, and to hybridize them have been made, e.g. [7,12,15,16,17]. Recently, Banerjee and Pal [2] have proposed a roughness measure for fuzzy sets, making use of the concept of a rough fuzzy set [7]. In [10,11], the authors pointed out some undesired properties of Banerjee and Pal's roughness measure and, simultaneously, introduced an alternative roughness measure for fuzzy sets.

In rough-set-based data analysis, the so-called approximation quality measure is often used to evaluate the classification success of attributes in terms of a numerical evaluation of the dependency properties generated by these attributes. To deal with practical situations where a fuzzy classification must be approximated by available knowledge expressed in terms of a Pawlak's approximation space, we introduce in this paper an extension of approximation quality measure aimed at providing a numerical characteristic for such situations. Furthermore, extensions of related coefficients such as the precision measure and the significance measure are also discussed.

D. Ślęzak et al. (Eds.): RSFDGrC 2005, LNAI 3641, pp. 373–382, 2005.

2   Rough Sets and Approximation Quality

The rough set theory begins with the notion of an approximation space $\langle U, R \rangle$, where U be the universe of discourse and R an equivalence relation on U. Denote by U/R the quotient set of U by the relation R, and $U/R = \{X_1, X_2, \ldots, X_m\}$, where X_i is an equivalence class of R, $i = 1, 2, \ldots, m$.

Given an arbitrary set $X \in 2^U$, in general it may not be possible to describe X precisely in $\langle U, R \rangle$. One may characterize X by a pair of lower and upper approximations defined as follows [13]:

$$\underline{R}(X) = \underset{X_i \subseteq X}{\cup} X_i; \qquad \overline{R}(X) = \underset{X_i \cap X \neq \emptyset}{\cup} X_i$$

The pair $(\underline{R}(X), \overline{R}(X))$ is the representation of an ordinary set X in the approximation space $\langle U, R \rangle$ or simply called the rough set of X.

In [14], Pawlak introduces two numerical characterizations of imprecision of a subset X in the approximation space $\langle U, R \rangle$: *accuracy* and *roughness*. Accuracy of X, denoted by $\alpha_R(X)$, is defined as

$$\alpha_R(X) = \frac{|\underline{R}(X)|}{|\overline{R}(X)|} \tag{1}$$

where $| \cdot |$ denotes the cardinality of a set. Then the roughness of X, denoted by $\rho_R(X)$, is defined by subtracting the accuracy from 1: $\rho_R(X) = 1 - \alpha_R(X)$. Note that the lower the roughness of a subset, the better is its approximation.

In the rough set theory, the so-called approximation quality γ is often used to describe the degree of partial dependency between attributes. Assume now there is another equivalence relation P defined on U, which forms a partition (or, classification) U/P of U, say $U/P = \{Y_1, \ldots, Y_n\}$. Note that R and P may be induced respectively by sets of attributes applied to objects in U. Then the approximation quality of P by R, also called *degree of dependency*, is defined by

$$\gamma_R(P) = \frac{\sum_{i=1}^{n} |\underline{R}(Y_i)|}{|U|} \tag{2}$$

which is represented in terms of accuracy as follows [8]

$$\gamma_R(P) = \sum_{i=1}^{n} \frac{|\overline{R}(Y_i)|}{|U|} \alpha_R(Y_i) \tag{3}$$

3   Fuzzy Sets and Mass Assignment

Let U be a finite and non-empty set. A fuzzy set F of U is represented as a mapping $\mu_F : U \longrightarrow [0, 1]$, where for each $x \in U$ we call $\mu_F(x)$ the membership degree of x in F. Given a number $\alpha \in (0, 1]$, the α-cut, or α-level set, of F is defined as: $F_\alpha = \{x \in U | \mu_F(x) \geq \alpha\}$.

Viewing the membership function μ_F of a fuzzy set F as the possibility distribution of possible values of a variable, this distribution is easily related to the basic probability assignment of a consonant body of evidence [6], the family of its α-cuts forms a nested family of focal elements. Note that in this case the normalization assumption of F is imposed due to the body of evidence does not contain the empty set. In [9], a formal connection between fuzzy sets and random sets was also established. Interestingly, this view of fuzzy sets was used by Baldwin in [1] to introduce the so-called mass assignment of a fuzzy set with relaxing the normalization assumption of fuzzy sets, and to provide a probability based semantics for a fuzzy concept defined as a family of possible definitions of the concept. The mass assignment of a fuzzy set is defined as follows [1].

Let F be a fuzzy subset of a finite universe U such that the range of the membership function μ_F, denoted by $\mathrm{rng}(\mu_F)$, is $\mathrm{rng}(\mu_F) = \{\alpha_1, \ldots, \alpha_n\}$, where $\alpha_i > \alpha_{i+1} > 0$, for $i = 1, \ldots, n-1$. Let

$$F_i = \{x \in U | \mu_F(x) \geq \alpha_i\}$$

for $i = 1, \ldots, n$. Then the mass assignment of F, denoted by m_F, is a probability distribution on 2^U defined by

$$\begin{aligned} m_F(\emptyset) &= 1 - \alpha_1 \\ m_F(F_i) &= \alpha_i - \alpha_{i+1}, \text{ for } i = 1, \ldots, n, \end{aligned}$$

with $\alpha_{n+1} = 0$ by convention. The α-level sets F_i, $i = 1, \ldots, n$, (or $\{F_i\}_{i=1}^{n} \cup \{\emptyset\}$ if F is a subnormal fuzzy set) are referred to as the focal elements of m_F. From now on, unless stated otherwise we assume that fuzzy sets are always normal.

4   Roughness Measures of a Fuzzy Set

4.1   Rough Fuzzy Sets

Let a finite approximation space $\langle U, R \rangle$ be given. Let F be a fuzzy set in U with the membership function μ_F. The upper and lower approximations $\overline{R}(F)$ and $\underline{R}(F)$ of F by R are fuzzy sets in the quotient set U/R with membership functions defined [7] by

$$\mu_{\overline{R}(F)}(X_i) = \max_{x \in X_i}\{\mu_F(x)\}, \quad \mu_{\underline{R}(F)}(X_i) = \min_{x \in X_i}\{\mu_F(x)\} \tag{4}$$

for $i = 1, \ldots, m$. $(\underline{R}(F), \overline{R}(F))$ is called a rough fuzzy set.

The rough fuzzy set $(\underline{R}(F), \overline{R}(F))$ then induces two fuzzy sets F^* and F_* in U with membership functions defined respectively as follows

$$\mu_{F^*}(x) = \mu_{\overline{R}(F)}(X_i) \text{ and } \mu_{F_*}(x) = \mu_{\underline{R}(F)}(X_i)$$

if $x \in X_i$, for $i = 1, \ldots, m$. That is, F^* and F_* are fuzzy sets with constant membership degree on the equivalence classes of U by R, and for any $x \in U$,

$\mu_{F^*}(x)$ (respectively, $\mu_{F_*}(x)$) can be viewed as the degree to which x possibly (respectively, definitely) belongs to the fuzzy set F [2].

Under such a view, we now define the notion of a *definable fuzzy set* in $\langle U, R \rangle$. A fuzzy set F is called *definable* if $\underline{R}(F) = \overline{R}(F)$, i.e. there exists a fuzzy set $\mathcal{F}$ in U/R such that $\mu_F(x) = \mu_{\mathcal{F}}(X_i)$ if $x \in X_i$, $i = 1 \ldots, m$. Further, as defined in [2], fuzzy sets F and G in U are said to be *roughly equal*, denoted by $F \approx_R G$, if and only if $\underline{R}(F) = \underline{R}(G)$ and $\overline{R}(F) = \overline{R}(G)$.

4.2   Roughness Measures of Fuzzy Sets

In [2], Banerjee and Pal have proposed a roughness measure for fuzzy sets in a given approximation space. Essentially, their measure of roughness of a fuzzy set depends on parameters that are designed as thresholds of definiteness and possibility in membership of the objects in U to the fuzzy set.

Consider parameters α, β such that $0 < \beta \leq \alpha \leq 1$. The α-cut $(F_*)_\alpha$ and β-cut $(F^*)_\beta$ of fuzzy sets F_* and F^*, respectively, are called to be the α-*lower approximation*, the β-*upper approximation* of F in $\langle U, R \rangle$, respectively. Then a roughness measure of the fuzzy set F with respect to parameters α, β with $0 < \beta \leq \alpha \leq 1$, and the approximation space $\langle U, R \rangle$ is defined by

$$\rho_R^{\alpha, \beta}(F) = 1 - \frac{|(F_*)_\alpha|}{|(F^*)_\beta|} \tag{5}$$

It is obvious that this definition of roughness measure $\rho_R^{\alpha, \beta}(\cdot)$ strongly depends on parameters α and β.

As pointed out in [10], this measure of roughness has several undesirable properties. Simultaneously, the authors also introduce a parameter-free measure of roughness of a fuzzy set as follows.

Let F be a normal fuzzy set in U. Assume that the range of the membership function μ_F is $\{\alpha_1, \ldots, \alpha_n\}$, where $\alpha_i > \alpha_{i+1} > 0$, for $i = 1, \ldots, n - 1$, and $\alpha_1 = 1$. Let us denote m_F the mass assignment of F defined as in the preceding section and $F_i = \{x \in U | \mu_F(x) \geq \alpha_i\}$, for $i = 1, \ldots, n$.

With these notations, the roughness measure of F with respect to the approximation space $\langle U, R \rangle$ is defined by

$$\hat{\rho}_R(F) = \sum_{i=1}^{n} m_F(F_i)(1 - \frac{|\underline{R}(F_i)|}{|\overline{R}(F_i)|}) = \sum_{i=1}^{n} m_F(F_i)\rho_R(F_i) \tag{6}$$

That is, the roughness of a fuzzy set F is the weighted sum of the roughness measures of nested focal subsets which are considered as its possible definitions.

Observation 1.   – *Clearly, $0 \leq \hat{\rho}_R(F) \leq 1$.*
– *$\hat{\rho}_R(\cdot)$ is a natural extension of Pawlak's roughness measure for fuzzy sets.*
– *F is a definable fuzzy set if and only if $\hat{\rho}_R(F) = 0$.*

Let F^* and F_* be fuzzy sets induced from the rough fuzzy set $(\underline{R}(F), \overline{R}(F))$ as above. Denote

$$\mathrm{rng}(\mu_{F_*}) \cup \mathrm{rng}(\mu_{F^*}) = \{\omega_1, \ldots, \omega_p\}$$

such that $\omega_i > \omega_{i+1} > 0$ for $i = 1, \ldots, p-1$. Obviously, $\{\omega_1, \ldots, \omega_p\} \subseteq \text{rng}(\mu_F)$, and $\omega_1 = \alpha_1$ and $\omega_p \geq \alpha_n$. With this notation, we have

Proposition 1. *For any $1 \leq j \leq p$, if there exists $\alpha_i, \alpha_{i'} \in rng(\mu_F)$ such that $\omega_{j+1} < \alpha_i < \alpha_{i'} \leq \omega_j$ then we have $F_i \approx_R F_{i'}$, and so $\rho_R(F_i) = \rho_R(F_{i'})$.*

Further, we can represent the roughness $\hat{\rho}_R(F)$ in terms of level sets of fuzzy sets F_* and F^* in the following proposition.

Proposition 2. *We have*

$$\hat{\rho}_R(F) = \sum_{j=1}^{p} (\omega_j - \omega_{j+1})(1 - \frac{|(F_*)_{\omega_j}|}{|(F^*)_{\omega_j}|})$$

where $\omega_{p+1} = 0$, by convention.

More interestingly, we obtain the following.

Proposition 3. *If fuzzy sets F and G in U are roughly equal in $\langle U, R \rangle$, then we have $\hat{\rho}_R(F) = \hat{\rho}_R(G)$.*

5   Rough Approximation Quality of a Fuzzy Classification

As mentioned above, the roughness of a crisp set is defined as opposed to its accuracy. Note that we also have a similar correspondence between the roughness and accuracy of a fuzzy set. In particular, in the spirit of the preceding section, it is eligible to define the accuracy measure of a fuzzy set F by

$$\hat{\alpha}_R(F) = \sum_{i=1}^{n} m_F(F_i)\alpha_R(F_i) \tag{7}$$

and then we also have

$$\hat{\alpha}_R(F) = 1 - \hat{\rho}_R(F) \tag{8}$$

Before extending the the measure of rough dependency defined by (2) (or equivalently, (3)) for the case where P is a fuzzy classification of U instead of a crisp one, let us define the cardinality of a fuzzy set in the spirit of its probabilistic based semantics. That is, if $\{F_i\}_{i=1}^n$ could be interpreted as a family of possible definitions of the concept F, then $m_F(F_i)$ is the probability of the event "the concept is F_i", for each i. Under such an interpretation, the cardinality of F, also denoted by $|F|$, is defined as the expected cardinality by

$$|F| = \sum_{i=1}^{n} m_F(F_i)|F_i| \tag{9}$$

Quite interestingly, the following proposition [5] shows that the expected cardinality (9) is nothing but the Σ-count of the fuzzy set F as introduced by De Luca and Termini [4].

Proposition 4. *We have:* $|F| = \sum\limits_{i=1}^{n} m_F(F_i)|F_i| = \sum\limits_{x \in U} \mu_F(x)$

Let us return to an approximation space $\langle U, R \rangle$ and assume further a fuzzy partition, say $\mathcal{FC} = \{Y_1, \ldots, Y_k\}$, defined on U. This situation may come up in a natural way when a linguistic classification is defined on U and must be approximated in terms of already existing knowledge R.

In such a situation, with the spirit of the proposal described in the preceding section, one may define the approximation quality of $\mathcal{FC}$ by R as

$$\hat{\gamma}_R(\mathcal{FC}) = \frac{1}{|U|} \sum_{i=1}^{k} \sum_{j=1}^{n_i} m_{Y_i}(Y_{i,j})|\underline{R}(Y_{i,j})| \tag{10}$$

where for $i = 1, \ldots, k$, m_{Y_i} and $\{Y_{i,j}\}_{j=1}^{n_i}$ respectively stand for the mass assignment of Y_i and the family of its focal elements. Straightforwardly, it follows from Proposition 4 that

$$\hat{\gamma}_R(\mathcal{FC}) = \frac{1}{|U|} \sum_{i=1}^{k} |(Y_i)_*| \tag{11}$$

where $(Y_i)_*$, $i = 1, \ldots, k$, are fuzzy sets with constant membership degree on the equivalence classes of U by R as defined in Section 3. It is also interesting to note that the approximation quality of $\mathcal{FC}$ by R can be also extended via (3) as follows

$$\hat{\gamma}'_R(\mathcal{FC}) = \sum_{i=1}^{k} \frac{|\overline{R}(Y_i)|}{|U|} \hat{\alpha}_R(Y_i) \tag{12}$$

Furthermore, similar as mentioned in [14], the measure of rough dependency $\hat{\gamma}_R$ does not capture how this partial dependency is actually distributed among fuzzy classes of $\mathcal{FC}$. To capture this information we need also the so-called *precision measure* $\hat{\pi}_R(Y_i)$, for $i = 1, \ldots, k$, defined by

$$\hat{\pi}_R(Y_i) = \sum_{j=1}^{n_i} m_{Y_i}(Y_{i,j}) \frac{|R(Y_{i,j})|}{|Y_{i,j}|} \tag{13}$$

which may be considered as the expected relative number of elements in Y_i approximated by R. Clearly, we have $\hat{\pi}_R(Y_i) \geq \hat{\alpha}_R(Y_i)$, for any $i = 1, \ldots, k$. As such the two measures $\hat{\gamma}_R$ and $\hat{\pi}_R$ give us enough information about "classification power" of the knowledge R with respect to linguistic classification $\mathcal{FC}$.

In rough-set-based data analysis, R is naturally induced by a subset, say B, of the set of attributes imposed on objects being considered. Then as suggested in [14], we can also measure the significance of the subset of attributes $B' \subseteq B$ with respect to the linguistic classification $\mathcal{FC}$ by the difference

$$\hat{\gamma}_R(\mathcal{FC}) - \hat{\gamma}_{R'}(\mathcal{FC})$$

where R' denotes the equivalence relation induced by the subset of attributes $B \setminus B'$. This measure expresses how influence on the quality of approximation if we drop attributes in B' from B.

Table 1. A Relation and Induced Fuzzy Partition

(a) Relation in a Relational Database

(b) Induced Fuzzy Partition of U Based on **Salary**

ID	Degree	Experience (n)	Salary
1	Ph.D.	$6 < n \leq 8$	63K
2	Ph.D.	$0 < n \leq 2$	47K
3	M.S.	$6 < n \leq 8$	53K
4	B.S.	$0 < n \leq 2$	26K
5	B.S.	$2 < n \leq 4$	29K
6	Ph.D.	$0 < n \leq 2$	50K
7	B.S.	$2 < n \leq 4$	35K
8	M.S.	$2 < n \leq 4$	40K
9	M.S.	$2 < n \leq 4$	41K
10	M.S.	$8 < n \leq 10$	68K
11	M.S.	$6 < n \leq 8$	50K
12	B.S.	$0 < n \leq 2$	23K
13	M.S.	$6 < n \leq 8$	55K
14	M.S.	$6 < n \leq 8$	51K
15	Ph.D.	$6 < n \leq 8$	65K
16	M.S.	$8 < n \leq 10$	64K

U	μ_{Low}	μ_{Medium}	μ_{High}
1	0	0	1
2	0	0.87	0.13
3	0	0.47	0.53
4	1	0	0
5	1	0	0
6	0	0.67	0.33
7	0.67	0.33	0
8	0.33	0.67	0
9	0.27	0.73	0
10	0	0	1
11	0	0.67	0.33
12	1	0	0
13	0	0.33	0.67
14	0	0.6	0.4
15	0	0	1
16	0	0	1

6   An Illustration Example

Let us consider a relation in a relational database as shown in Table 1 (a) (this database is a variant of that found in [3]). Then by **Degree** and **Experience** we obtain an approximation space

$$\langle U, \text{ind}(\{\textbf{Degree}, \textbf{Experience}\})\rangle$$

where $U = \{1, \ldots, 16\}$, and the corresponding partition is

$$U/\text{ind}(\{\textbf{Deg.}, \textbf{Ex.}\}) = \{\{1, 15\}, \{2, 6\}, \{3, 11, 13, 14\}, \{4, 12\}, \{5, 7\}, \{8, 9\}, \{10, 16\}\}$$

Further, consider now for example a linguistic classification

$$\{Low, Medium, High\}$$

defined on the domain of attribute **Salary**, say [20K,70K], with membership functions of linguistic classes depicted graphically as in Fig. 1. Then the linguistic classification induces a fuzzy partition on U whose membership functions of fuzzy classes shown in Table 1 (b).

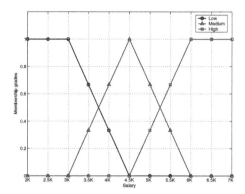

Fig. 1. A Linguistic Partition of **Salary** Attribute

Table 2. The approximations of the fuzzy partition based on **Salary**

X_i	$\{1,15\}$	$\{2,6\}$	$\{3,11,13,14\}$	$\{4,12\}$	$\{5,7\}$	$\{8,9\}$	$\{10,16\}$
μ_{High_*}	1	0.13	0.33	0	0	0	1
μ_{High^*}	1	0.33	0.67	0	0	0	1
μ_{Medium_*}	0	0.67	0.33	0	0	0.67	0
μ_{Medium^*}	0	0.87	0.67	0	0.33	0.73	0
μ_{Low_*}	0	0	0	1	0.67	0.27	0
μ_{Low^*}	0	0	0	1	1	0.33	0

Then approximations of the fuzzy partition induced by **Salary** in the approximation space defined by **Degree** and **Experience** are given in Table 2.

Using (11) we obtain

$$\hat{\gamma}_{\{\mathbf{Degree},\mathbf{Experience}\}}(\mathbf{Salary}) = \frac{13.46}{16} = 0.84$$

That is we have the following partial dependency in the database

$$\{\mathbf{Degree},\mathbf{Experience}\} \Rightarrow_{0.84} \mathbf{Salary} \tag{14}$$

To calculate the precision measure of fuzzy classes we need to obtain the mass assignment for each fuzzy class and approximations of its focal sets respectively. For example, the mass assignment of *Low* and approximations of its focal sets are shown in Table 3.

Then we have

$$\hat{\pi}_{\{\mathbf{Degree},\mathbf{Experience}\}}(Low) = 0.878$$

Similarly, we also obtain

$$\hat{\pi}_{\{\mathbf{Degree},\mathbf{Experience}\}}(Medium) = 0.646$$
$$\hat{\pi}_{\{\mathbf{Degree},\mathbf{Experience}\}}(High) \quad = 0.876$$

Table 3. Mass assignment for μ_{Low} and approximations of its focal sets

α	1	0.67	0.33	0.27
Low_α	$\{4,5,12\}$	$\{4,5,12,7\}$	$\{4,5,12,7,8\}$	$\{4,5,12,7,8,9\}$
$m_{Low}(Low_\alpha)$	0.33	0.34	0.06	0.27
$\underline{R}(Low_\alpha)$	$\{4,12\}$	$\{4,5,12,7\}$	$\{4,5,12,7\}$	$\{4,5,12,7,8,9\}$
$\overline{R}(Low_\alpha)$	$\{4,5,12,7\}$	$\{4,5,12,7\}$	$\{4,5,12,7,8,9\}$	$\{4,5,12,7,8,9\}$

Now in order to show how the influence of, for example, attribute **Experience** on the quality of approximation, let us consider the partition induced by the attribute **Degree** as follows.

$$U/\mathrm{ind}(\{\mathbf{Deg.}\}) = \{\{1,2,6,15\}, \{3,8,9,10,11,13,14,16\}, \{4,5,7,12\}\}$$

Then we obtain approximations of the fuzzy partition induced by **Salary** in the approximation space defined by **Degree** given in Table 4.

Table 4. The approximations of the fuzzy partition based on **Salary**

X_i	$\{1,2,6,15\}$	$\{3,8,9,10,11,13,14,16\}$	$\{4,5,7,12\}$
μ_{High_*}	0.13	0	0
μ_{High^*}	1	1	0
μ_{Medium_*}	0	0	0
μ_{Medium^*}	0.87	0.73	0.33
μ_{Low_*}	0	0	0.67
μ_{Low^*}	0	0.33	1

Thus we have

$$\hat{\gamma}_{\{\mathbf{Degree}\}}(\mathbf{Salary}) = \frac{3.2}{16} = 0.2$$

Similarly, we also easily obtain

$$\hat{\gamma}_{\{\mathbf{Experience}\}}(\mathbf{Salary}) = \frac{5.06}{16} = 0.316$$

As we can see, both attributes **Degree** and **Experience** are highly significant as without each of them the measure of approximation quality changes considerably. It would be worth noting that based on background knowledge one may infer a dependency between {**Degree**, **Experience**} and **Salary** which is often expressed linguistically, however such a dependency in general can not be described by traditional data dependencies.

7   Conclusions

In this paper we have extended the measure of rough dependency for fuzzy classification for dealing with practical situations where a fuzzy classification must be approximated by available knowledge expressed in terms of a classical approximation space. Such situations may come up naturally for example when we want to realize partial dependency between attributes which is inferred based on background knowledge; while such a dependency can not be expressed in terms of traditional data dependencies as described in Example.

References

1. J. F. Baldwin, The management of fuzzy and probabilistic uncertainties for knowledge based systems, in *The Encyclopaedia of AI*, S. A. Shapiro (Ed.), New York: Wiley, 1992, 528–537.
2. M. Banerjee, S. K. Pal, Roughness of a fuzzy set, *Infor. Sci.* **93** (1996) 235–246.
3. S. M. Chen, C. M. Huang, Generating weighted fuzzy rules from relational database systems for estimating null values using genetic algorithms, *IEEE Transactions on Fuzzy Systems*, **11** (2003) 495–506.
4. A. De Luca, S. Termini, A definition of a nonprobabilistic entropy in the setting of fuzzy set theory, *Information and Control* **20** (1972) 301–312.
5. D. Dubois, M.-C. Jaulent, A general approach to parameter evaluation in fuzzy digital pictures, *Pattern Recognition Letters* **6** (1987) 251–259.
6. D. Dubois, H. Prade, On several representations of an uncertain body of evidence, in *Fuzzy Information and Decision Processes*, M. M. Gupta and E. Sanchez, Eds., North-Holland, 1982, 167–181.
7. D. Dubois, H. Prade, Rough fuzzy sets and fuzzy rough sets, *Inter. J. of Gen. Sys.* **17** (1990) 191–209.
8. G. Gediga, I. Düntsch, Rough approximation quality revisited, *Artificial Intelligence* **132** (2001) 219–234.
9. I. R. Goodman, Fuzzy sets as equivalence classes of random sets, in *Fuzzy Set and Possibility Theory*, R. Yager, Ed., Oxford: Pergamon Press, 1982, 327–342.
10. V. N. Huynh, Y. Nakamori, An approach to roughness of fuzzy sets, *Proceedings of the FUZZ-IEEE 2004*.
11. V. N. Huynh, Y. Nakamori, A roughness measure for fuzzy sets, *Infor. Sci.*, 173 (2005) 255–275.
12. S. K. Pal, A. Skowron, Eds., *Rough Fuzzy Hybridization: New Trends in Decision Making*. Singapore: Springer Verlag, 1999.
13. Z. Pawlak, Rough sets, *Inter. J. of Comp. and Infor. Sci.* **11** (1982) 341–356.
14. Z. Pawlak, *Rough Sets: Theoretical Aspects of Reasoning about Data*. Boston, MA: Kluwer Academic Publishers, 1991.
15. M. Wygralak, Rough sets and fuzzy sets: some remarks on interrelations, *Fuzzy Sets and Systems* **29** (1989) 241–243.
16. Y. Y. Yao, Combination of rough and fuzzy sets based on alpha-level sets, in *Rough Sets and Data Mining: Analysis of Imprecise Data*, T. Y. Lin, N. Cercone, Eds., Boston/London/Dordrecht: Kluwer Academic Publishers, 1997, 301–321.
17. Y. Y. Yao, A comparative study of fuzzy sets and rough sets, *Infor. Sci.* **109** (1998) 227–242.
18. L. A. Zadeh, Fuzzy sets, *Information and Control* **8** (1965) 338–353.
19. H.-J. Zimmermann, *Fuzzy Set Theory and Its Applications*, second edition. Boston/Dordrecht/London: Kluwer Academic Publishers, 1991.

Fuzzy Rules Generation Method for Classification Problems Using Rough Sets and Genetic Algorithms*

Marek Sikora

Silesian University of Technology, Institute of Computer Sciences,
44-100 Gliwice, Poland
Marek.Sikora@polsl.pl

Abstract. A method of constructing a classifier that uses fuzzy reasoning is described in this paper. Rules for this classifier are obtained by means of algorithms relying on a tolerance rough sets model. Got rules are in so called sharp" form, a genetic algorithm is used for fuzzification of these rules. Presented results of experiments show that the proposed method allows getting a smaller rules set with similar (or better) classification abilities.

1 Introduction

An attempt of combining well defined techniques of decision rules induction with fuzzy classification, that allows to achieve good classification results in uncertainty situations with using of small rules number, is described in the paper. In the case of fuzzy classification, obtaining fuzzy rules set that will be used by classifier is still a current issue. Our proposition of getting fuzzy rules for classification consists in using decision rules induction algorithms for rules induction in so called "sharp" form, and then, by means of the genetic algorithm, fuzzification of the best rules in order to obtain classifier with both good describing and classification abilities. The rules fuzzification causes a transition from classification based on rules voting to constructive fuzzy reasoning [13].

The main purpose of the method we propose is rules set restriction with keeping its good classification abilities.

Algorithms used in decision rules induction and the process of fuzzy rules searching by means of the genetic algorithm are described in succeeding chapters. Results of experiments carried out for benchmark data and for data coming from industrial monitoring systems are also presented.

2 Induction of Decision Rules Based Upon Rough Sets Theory

Rough sets theory can be treated as a tool for data table analysis. Table data are representing as decision table $DT = (U, A \cup \{d\})$, where U is a set of objects,

---

* This research has been supported by the grant 5T12A00123 from Ministry of Scientific Research and Information Technology of the Republic of Poland.

D. Ślęzak et al. (Eds.): RSFDGrC 2005, LNAI 3641, pp. 383–391, 2005.

A is a set of features describing these objects called conditional attributes and d is a decision attribute, $d \notin A$. Each attribute can be treated as a function $a : U \rightarrow X_a$ ($d : U \rightarrow Y$), where X_a is a set of values of a attribute. For each decision attribute value $v \in Y$, set $C_v = \{x \in U : d(x) = v\}$ is called a decision class.

In rough sets theory rules of the following form are considered:

$$if \; a_1 \in V_{a_1} \; and \ldots and \, a_N \in V_{a_N} \; then \, d = v \qquad (1)$$

where: $\{a_1, .., a_N\} \subseteq A$, $\forall_{i \in \{1,...,N\}} V_{a_i} \subseteq D_{a_i}$. Each expression $a \in V_a$ is called a descriptor, especially in standard rough sets model [6] descriptors are in $a = v$ form, where $v \in V_a$.

The set of attributes occurred in conditional part of the rule consists of the attributes belonging to a relative reduct [6]. Depends on induction rules method it is the relative reduct for objects or the relative reduct for whole decision table.

Below we introduce the essential definitions that allow presenting our methods of decision rules generation.

With any subset of attributes $B \subseteq A$, an equivalence relation denoted by $IND(B)$ called the B-indiscernibility relation, can be associated and defined by $IND(B) = \{(x, y) \in U \times U : \forall_{a \in B} (a(x) = a(y))\}$. By $[x]_{IND(B)}$ we denote the equivalence class of $IND(B)$ defined by $x \in U$. For every $x \in U$, each minimal attribute set $B \subseteq A$ satisfying the condition $\{y \in [x]_{IND(B)} : d(x) \neq d(y)\} = \{y \in [x]_{IND(A)} : d(x) \neq d(y)\}$ is called the relative reduct for object x.

Application of rough set theory to data containing numerical attributes required their previous discretization [3] or tolerance based rough sets model use [12], in which the B-indiscernibility relation $IND(B)$ is replaced by tolerance relation $\tau(B)$ (equivalence classes $[x]_{IND(B)}$ are replaced by tolerance sets $I_{B(x)}$) in the following way:

$$\forall_{x,y \in U} (x, y) \in \tau(B) \Leftrightarrow \forall_{a_i \in B} [\delta_{a_i}(a_i(x), a_i(y)) \leq \varepsilon_{a_i}]) \qquad (2)$$

$$\forall_{y \in U} (y \in I_B(x) \Leftrightarrow (x, y) \in \tau(B)), \qquad (3)$$

where δ_{a_i} is a distance function (e.g. $\delta_{a_i}(a_i(x), a_i(y)) = \frac{|a(x) - a(y)|}{max \, D_a - min \, D_a}$), ε_{a_i} are fixed numbers called tolerance thresholds. The relative reducts set for object x can be determined based on analysis the corresponding row (column) in the discernibility matrix modulo d [10]. The discernibility matrix modulo d is a square matrix $[c_{xy}]_{x,y \in U}$ with the elements defined as follows:

$$c_{xy} = \begin{cases} a \in A : (y \neq I_a(x)) \wedge (d(x) \neq d(y)) \\ \emptyset : \qquad\qquad\quad d(x) = d(y) \end{cases} \qquad (4)$$

In consideration of their computational complexity, algorithms of generating object-related relative reducts using discernibility matrix can be employed for tables consisting of several thousand objects.

User is usually interested in getting the shortest rules, therefore in practical applications the shortest relative reducts are used. In [5], [12], the algorithms of finding the minimal relative reduct without using the discernibility matrix are presented.

We use the tolerance model of rough sets in our researches. Before rules calculation, we discretize the numerical data using the entropy method [3], then for some datasets (if cuts set get after discretization is big) we look for similarities between data that have been already discretized. We take a simple algorithm of finding the proper values of tolerance thresholds. We consider vectors of the form $(\varepsilon, \varepsilon, .., \varepsilon)$, where ε is increased 0.05 each step begin from $\varepsilon = 0$. From various tolerance threshold optimality criteria the most frequently we used the following formula:

$$\frac{\left(n_{R_d R_{IA}} n_{\neg R_d \neg R_{IA}} - n_{R_d \neg R_{IA}} n_{\neg R_d R_{IA}}\right)^2}{n_{R_{IA}} n_{\neg R_{IA}} n_{R_d} n_{\neg R_d}}, \tag{5}$$

where: n_{R_d} number of object pairs with the same value of the decision attribute; $n_{R_{IA}}$ number of object pairs staying in relation $\tau(A)$; $n_{R_d R_{IA}}$ number of object pairs with the same value of the decision attribute, staying in relation. The $n_{\neg R_d R_{IA}}, n_{R_d \neg R_{IA}}, n_{\neg R_d \neg R_{IA}}$ values we define analogously to $n_{R_d R_{IA}}$. Discussion of other methods tolerance threshold values searching one find, among others, in [7], [12].

Rough sets tolerance model application leads to approximate rules calculation. For calculation the quality of each rule, one compute the values of a rule quality evaluation measure [1]. We use the measures known as the Pearson, Gain or Michalski's measure [1] in our experiments. Usually, high accuracy and coverage are requirements of decision rules. Then, the probability that dependence representing by a rule is standing not only for analyzed table but also for objects from outside of the table increases.

We propose an approximate rule generation algorithm RMatrix [7]:

input: $\boldsymbol{DT} = (U, A \cup \{d\})$, the tolerance thresholds vector $(\varepsilon, \varepsilon, ..., \varepsilon)$, q - quality evaluation measure, x - object, rule generator, an order of conditional attributes $(a_{i_1}, a_{i_2}, ..., a_{i_{card(a)}})$ so as the attribute the most frequently appearing in c_x is the first (attribute appearing the most rarely is the last)
begin
create the rule r, which has the decision descriptor $d = d(x)$ only; $r_{best} := r$;
for every $j := 1, ..., card(A)$ add the descriptor $a_{i_j} \in V_{a_{i_j}}$ to conditional part of the rule r (where $V_{a_{i_j}} = \{a_{i_j}(y) \in X_{a_{i_j}} : y \in I_{a_{i_j}}(x)\}$)
if $q_p(r) > q_p(r_{best})$ **then** $r_{best} := r$
return r_{best}

The algorithm generates one rule for every object from U. Next descriptor adding causes an increasing of rule accuracy.

Another rule induction algorithm we used is the algorithm MODLEM [11], that generate rules of similar form as it was quoted in the first formula. MODLEM algorithm builds conditional descriptors occurring in rules premise differently (the algorithm does not require discretization).

If a is a symbolic attribute, the values range in the descriptor is a one-element set ($a \in \{v_a\}$, which is better to be written down as $a = v_a$). If attribute a is a numeric attribute, the range of V_a values can take one of the three forms: $(-\infty, v_a], [v_a, +\infty), [v_a^1, v_a^2]$, where $v_a^1, v_a^2, v_a \in V_a$.

Establishing points $v_a^1, v_a^2, v_a \in V_a$ (these points we call border points) in conditional attributes of each rule follows by minimizing of conditional entropy of sets of objects lying to the left ($U_1 \subseteq U$) and to the right ($U_2 \subseteq U$) of considered candidate for border point. An optimal is the candidate that minimizes a value of the below expression:

$$\frac{|U_1|}{|U|} Entr(U_1) + \frac{|U_2|}{|U|} Entr(U_2) \qquad (6)$$

The detailed description of the algorithm can be found in [11]. In a standard form the algorithm generates exact rules or so exact as analyzed rules set allows for (if the set is inconsistent, it is clear that some of generated rules will not be exact). Generating of exact rules in the case of industrial data analysis that are usually burdened with some uncertainty (for example, following from measure errors) leads to undesirable situations: generating of big number of rules that might be over-fitted to data. An introducing of rule quality evaluation measure in the algorithm, similarly as in RMatrix, is a possible modification of MODLEM algorithm [8].

As it was noticed during research [8], regardless of used evaluation measure, a quality of rule created by MODLEM increases so far as to gain a certain maximal value, and then decreases. This observation was used by us in a modification of stopping criterion for created rules. In the modified version of MODLEM algorithm, after next border point finding, there is also computed a value of the rule evaluation measure. An output rule is the rule with maximal value of used measure, and when this value starts to decrease, rule generation is finished.

3   Rules in Fuzzy Form

Conditional descriptors of obtained rules have "sharp" form, therefore a conditional part of a rule is a hypercube in a features space. In consequence, the space occupied by a given decision class can be approximated only by hypercubes. If a shape of the decision class is irregular then apart from strong rules that cover a big areas of the given class, it will exist rules covering edges of this class or atypical examples. Although voting classification is good for rules in "sharp" form, big rules number is characterized by small describing power (from data mining point of view). Moreover, algorithms of filtration or rules generalization not always allow significant limitation of the obtained rules set without decreasing classification abilities.

Fuzzification of the strongest from obtained rules should allow covering a whole examples described space by smaller rules number. Change of based on voting classification method for fuzzy one should not cause worsening of classification results.

Transposing the obtained rules set on base of fuzzy sets theory we deal with knowledge base composed of MISO rules in the following form:

$$R^{(k)} : \ if \ a_1 \ is \ A_1^{(k)} \ and \ a_2 \ is \ A_2^{(k)} \ and \ldots and \ a_N \ is \ A_N^{(k)} \ then \ d \ is \ B^{(k)} \quad (7)$$

where $A_1^{(k)}, A^{(k)}, \ldots, A_N^{(k)}$ denote the values of linguistic variables $a_1, a_2, \ldots, a_N$ of the antecedent defined in the following universes of discourse: $X_1, X_2, \ldots, X_N$, and $B^{(k)}$ stands for the value of linguistic variable d of the consequent in universe of discourse Y. Membership functions have initially a form of rectangle (fig. 2. the first graph). Rules fuzzification consists in replacing these membership functions with pseudo-trapezoidal ones. For fuzzy rules, constructive reasoning [13] is used.

4   The Genetic Algorithm Application for Rules Fuzzification

It's easy to observe that there are many possibilities of "sharp" rules fuzzification. For that reason the algorithm realizing fuzzification process must have a heuristic character. For realization and supervision rules fuzzification process the genetic algorithm was used.

In such approach to the subject one can say that rules induction is a model identification, while reduction and fuzzification process is parametric identification. Rules fuzzification process follows in order described below:

Step 1. Rules induction.

Step 2. Sorting of rules coming from each decision class according to their quality (established by selected evaluation measure q).

Step 3. Arbitrary selection of the best rules group from each decision class (in particular, the whole rules set can be subjected to fuzzification, it's also possible to add rules into classifier iteratively, beginning from the best rules in each decision class, as long as we will obtain the best classification results).

Step 4. Coding of rules selected in third step to the form acceptable by the genetic algorithm. Rules $r_1, \ldots, r_n$ are subjected to fuzzification. Thus, each specimen in population codes these n rules. Each rule consists of a certain number of descriptors $desc_{1\_i}, \ldots, desc_{m\_i}$, where i is the considered rule number (all conditional attributes needn't appear in the rule premise). Each descriptor can be coded by four numbers $p_1 \leq p_2 \leq p_3 \leq p_4$. These numbers are those values on attribute values axis which allow uniquely determining a pseudo-trapezoidal membership function (fig. 2).

Step 5. Creation of a first population. In some ordered way specimens are drawn into the first population. Firstly, in the first population lands a specimen representing "sharp" rules (fig. 2, the first graph). Secondly, in the first population lands also a specimen that represents a descriptor extended on a whole attribute domain (fig. 2, the central graph). And thirdly, in the first population lands also a specimen representing a triangle membership function (fig. 2, the third graph). Remaining specimens are created randomly. Decisions are coded as succeeding natural numbers. Each decision is extended for 0.5 on either side of a code given to this decision.

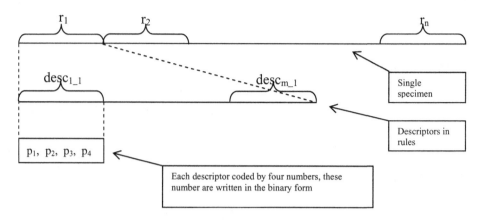

Fig. 1. Representation of a single specimen

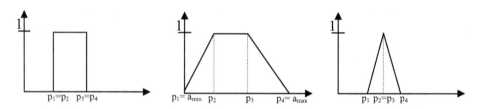

Fig. 2. Various forms of conditional descriptors in the first population

Step 6. Activation of the genetic algorithm. Used cross-over mechanism allows crossing all rules included in specimen at a time (thus we meet with n-positions cross-over, where n is a number of coded rules). A mutation consists on changing in description of one of descriptors occurring in a rule, one of values p_1, p_2, p_3 or p_4. Classification accuracy achieved by a specimen during objects tuning set classification is the function evaluating a specimen adaptation. The genetic algorithm succeeding populations and stopping criterion drawing takes place according to standard way [4]. The GaLib library made available by MIT was exploited in implementation.

5   Numerical Examples

In order to verify the proposed solution several benchmark data sets have been tested (we present results for Iris, and Diabetest-Statlog data), tests has been also carried out on data coming from coal-mine equipments monitoring systems.

The first of industrial data sets includes information about dewater pumps work in abyssal mining stations. Each pump's work cycle (from switch on till switch off) gave one record for analyzed set. Each record in the set was described by the following attributes: the pump temperature in the steady state T_U, the initial temperature T_0, power in the steady state P_U, delivery in the

Table 1. Results for benchmarks datasets

Iris data set			Diabetest-Statlog data set		
Algorithm	Classification accuracy	Rules number	Algorithm	Classification accuracy	Rules number
RMatrix	97%	7	RMatrix	74%	19
GA fuzzification of selected rules	95%	4	GA fuzzification of selected rules	76%	8

Table 2. Results for industrial datasets

Dewater pump's states classification			Total cutting energy classification		
Algorithm	Classification accuracy	Rules number	Algorithm	Classification accuracy	Rules number
MODLEM	95%	455	MODLEM	86%	91
MODLEM Modyf.	85%	16	MODLEM Modyf.	85%	35
GA fuzzification of selected rules	90%	9	GA fuzzification of selected rules	83%	9

steady state Q_U, the number L_i of the pump restarts the day before, times $t_{20-30}, t_{30-40}, t_{40-50}, t_{50-60}, t_{60-70}$ when the pump temperature changes for ten degrees. Two decision classes pointing at a number of weeks left to the pump repair needed for the sake of worsening technical parameters ("more then two weeks till repair", "less then two weeks till repair") were defined [9].

The second of data set includes parameters that were registered during rock cutting process. Each cut gave one record for analyzed set. Attributes described an individual record were: cutting scale, cutting depth, the geometric blade parameters (blade angle b, position angel d, revolution angle r), the rock type s. Determining of mentioned attributes' values influence on unit cutting energy Ec value was one of aims of the analysis. A range of variable Ec values was divided into three intervals, getting in this way three decision classes ("low energy", "average energy", "high energy").

For benchmark data sets the presented results have been obtained by the 10-fold cross validation methodology, for industrial data, by train and test method.

The genetic algorithm was started with cross-over probability 0.8, and mutation probability 0.1. During cross-over process there can appear such descriptors that doesn't satisfied the conditions $p_1 \leq p_2 \leq p_3 \leq p_4$, (thus descriptor interpretation in the context of membership function is impossible), then the cross-over isn't realized. This fact causes the high cross-over probability. In cases we have described a whole set of training data was used as a tuning set. The number of the best rules was established adaptively by maximizing classification accuracy obtained on trained set.

6 Conclusions

The algorithm of decision rules induction (RMatrix), some modification of known algorithm MODLEM and method of transition from classification that uses voting scheme to fuzzy classification have been presented in the paper. For rules fuzzification process supervising the genetic algorithm has been used.

Presented data sets analysis results confirm genetic algorithm usefulness for tuning of classifier that relies on fuzzy logic in order to limit a number of rules used in classification. Application of the genetic algorithm allowed getting better classification results then in the case of rules fuzzification according to the manually specified scheme [2]. A smaller number of rules can be easier interpreted by a user, thus these rules can be a source of a new, earlier unknown knowledge about a problem he is interested in. Improvement of classification abilities and significant limitation of rules quantity is obtained at the cost of more computation connected with genetic algorithm application.

Regarding classification abilities improvement one cannot draw explicit conclusions whether there are essential differences in obtained classifiers. For the present the conclusion is that based on voting classification is just as good as fuzzy classification. But there is no doubt about accuracy on training set to increase significantly after tuning. That is obvious because the genetic algorithm adjusts rules to data. It is possible for this property to prove undesirable because rules can over-fit to data.

Working out a procedure of the genetic algorithm stop while tuning rules become over-fit to data which makes worse classification results on tested data will be a matter of further works. Elaboration a better (faster) procedure of subjected to fuzzification rules selection will be also a matter of further search. In order to attain this, measures that allow determining degrees of area inclusion in a space of features covered by particular rules, will be used.

References

1. Bruha I.: Quality of Decision Rules: Definitions and Classification Schemes for Multiple Rules. In: Machine Learning and Statistics, The Interface, John Wiley and Sons, 1997
2. Drwal G., Sikora M.: Fuzzy Decision Support System with Rough Set Based Rules Generation Method. In:Rough Sets and Current Trends in Computing, LNAI 3006. Springer-Verlag (2004) 727-733
3. Fayad U. M., Irani K. B.: Multi-Interval Discretization of Continuous-Valued Attributes for Classification Learning. Proceedings of the 13th International Joint Conference on Artificial Intelligence. Morgan Kaufmann (1993) 1022-1027
4. Goldberg D. E.: Genetic Algorithms in Search, Optimization and Machine Learning. Addison-Wesley Publishing, 1989.
5. Nguyen H. S., Nguyen S. H.: Some Efficient Algorithms for Rough Set Methods. Proceedings of IPMU-96, Granada, Spain, **2** (1996) 1451-1456
6. Pawlak Z.: Rough Sets. International Journal of Information and Computer Sciences **11** (5), (1982) 341-356
7. Sikora M., Proksa P.: Algorithms for generation and filtration of approximate decision rules, using rule-related quality measures. Bulletin of IRSS **5** (1/2), (RSTGC-2001), 2001
8. Sikora M., Proksa P.: Induction of decision and association rules for knowledge discovery in industrial databases. ICDM-IEEE, Workshop of Alternative Techniques in Data Mining, Brighton, 2004

9. Sikora M., Widera D.: Identification of diagnostics states for dewater pumps working in abyssal mining pump stations. Proceedings of the XV International Conference on System Sciences, Wrocław, Poland, 2004
10. Skowron A., Rauszer C.: The Discernibility Matrices and Functions in Information systems. In: Słowiński R. (ed.) Intelligent Decision Support. Handbook of Applications and Advances of the Rough Sets Theory, Dordrecht: Kluwer (1992) 331-362
11. Stefanowski J.: Rough set based rule induction techniques for classification problems. Proc. of EUFIT-98, vol.1 Achen Sept. **7-10** (1998) 107-119
12. Stepaniuk J.: Knowledge Discovery by Application of Rough Set Models. Institute of Computer Sciences Polish Academy od Sciences, Report **887**, Warszawa, 1999
13. Yager R. R., Filev D. P.: Essential of Fuzzy Modelling and Control. John Wiley & Sons, Inc., 1994

Multilayer FLC Design Based on RST

Hongbo Guo, Fang Wang, and Yuxia Qiu

College of Information Engineering, Taiyuan University of Technology,
030024 Taiyuan, Shanxi, P.R. China
ghb666@sohu.com

Abstract. Based on the rough set theory, this paper introduces a multilayer rough-fuzzy rules design method to keep fuzzy rules dimension of every layer not more than three for consistency with man's thinking characteristics, advantageous for understanding, checking and correcting rules. For rationally reducing and integrating input variables, the paper presents a rapid fuzzy rules extraction algorithm based on RST, to discover knowledge from sample database. This algorithm improves C-D indiscernible matrix. It introduces the computation program for core attributes. The program for quasi-optimal attribute reduction is presented, in which information increment of decision D is used as heuristic information of attributes selection to accelerate selective velocity of optimal attributes set. This multilayer fuzzy controller is combined with conventional PID, applied in unit control system of power plant. The simulation results show that the control system has higher control qualities with high speed, small overshoot and strong robustness.

1 Introduction

Fuzzy logic control (FLC) has been applied in industrial process control systems broadly, since it was firstly used to boiler and steam engine control by Mamdani. But FLC design is still short of systematism. In most cases, cut-and-try methods are employed for selection of control rules, discourse universe, fuzzy membership functions and scaling factors. When the numbers of input variables and their linguistic terms rise for high-order and multi-input systems, controller dimension increases and fuzzy rules' number enhances exponentially. Fuzzy rules are mostly acquired by experts' experience and knowledge while man's logic thinking is usually not more than 3 dimensions. Thus, determination of fuzzy rules is hard to resolve.

Rough set theory (RST) is a kind of mathematical theory that deals with imprecise, conflicting and incomplete information and has far-reaching applications in data mining, speech recognition, pattern recognition, intelligent control and other fields [1,2,3]. Not needed any apriori knowledge, RST can reduce data on the premise of keeping essential information and acquire minimal representation; it can extract easy-confirmed rules from experiences. RST and fuzzy sets analyse two aspects of incomplete information and extend Cantor sets from different aspect. So they complete each other in real applications.

D. Ślęzak et al. (Eds.): RSFDGrC 2005, LNAI 3641, pp. 392–401, 2005.

This paper proposes a design method of fuzzy controller for MIMO (multi-input and multi-output) system according to the controller essence. The multilayer fuzzy rule design method is depicted in Section 2, whose main idea focus on reducing and integrating input variables. For rationally reducing and integrating input variables, Section 3 presents a RST-based rapid algorithm of fuzzy rule extraction to select the optimal attributes (fuzzy rule premise component) in the light of requests, simplify gradually control problem by information fusion and extract objective fuzzy rules from sample data, whose dimension number is no more than three for good understanding, examination and amendment. Section 4 gives a simulation experiment and the conclusion is depicts in Section 5.

2   FLC Design for MIMO System

The controller is a mapping transform of input and output variables, that is, $Y = F(X)$, in which, X and Y are input and output variable vector respectively, F is control algorithm. Thus, nesting multilayer strategies can be used in MIMO system, namely, $Y = f(g(X))$. Algorithm g deals primarily with input data, and algorithm f gives real controls according to the outputs of inner layer algorithm g. The work of algorithm f will be reduced if the dimension of output variable vector of algorithm g is smaller than that of X. Algorithm g, called reducing-dimension function, performs to integrate and mine problem information; algorithm f, called action function, reasons by those reducing ingredients and information. For the FLC, the functions g and f is corresponding to different rules. In this paper, the fuzzy rules adopt the multilayer form of IF-THEN, shown in Table1. Obviously, the key for the construction of functions g and f is how to establish multilayer fuzzy rules.

Taking the multi-input and single output system for example, knowledge represen-tation system is established by sample database, choosing properly N condition attributes, such as given instruction, error, error change, etc. The controller's output, namely, process control quality is adopted as decision attribute. After sample data discretization and normalization, fuzzy information representation system (FIRS) is established. Firstly, redundant rows are deleted. Then reduction attributes set is computed (How to compute will be presented in Section 3). Suppose reduction attributes set is consisted of condition attributes set $C = [C_1, C_2, \ldots, C_n]$ (n denotes attributes number) and decision attribute D. These condition and decision attributes are corresponding to premise and consequent components of fuzzy rules respectively. Reduction of condition attributes equals dimension decrease of FLC, thus the input number of FLC is reduced from N to n.

The most important attributes set $C_{p1} = [C_1, C_2, \ldots, C_{p1}]$ is calculated in fuzzy decision table, where $1 \leq p_1 \leq n$. Attribute important degrees are evaluated by heuristic function (HF) of attribute selection defined in Section 3. By these p_1 condition attributes and decision attribute D, FIRS is parted to two fuzzy decision sub-tables, consistent sub-table S_{11} and inconsistent sub-table S_{12}. The rules carried by table S_{11} are as follows.

Table 1. All multilayer fuzzy rules based on rough set theory

layer no	multilayer fuzzy rule form
first layer	Rule i: If C_1 is $A_{11i}, \ldots,$ and C_{p1} is A_{1p1i}, Then D is B_{1i} $\ldots$ Rule j: If C_1 is $A_{11i}, \ldots,$ and C_{p1} is A_{1p1i}, Then Y_1 is E_{1i} $\ldots$
second layer	Rule i: If Y_1 is E_{11i}, and C_{p1+1} is $A_{21i}, \ldots,$ and C_{p1+p2} is A_{2p2i}, Then D is B_{2i} $\ldots$ Rule j: If Y_1 is E_{11j}, and C_{p1+1} is $A_{21j}, \ldots,$ and C_{p1+p2} is A_{2p2j}, Then Y_2 is E_{2ij} $\ldots$
r-th layer	Rule i: If Y_{r-1} is E_{r-1i}, and $C_{\sum pn+1}$ is $A_{r1i}, \ldots,$ and C_n is A_{rpri}, Then D is B_{ri} $\ldots$ Rule j: If Y_{r-1} is E_{r-1j}, and $C_{\sum pn+1}$ is $A_{r1j}, \ldots,$ and C_n is A_{rprj}, Then D is B_{rj} $\ldots$

Rule i:If C_1 is $A_{11i}, \ldots,$ and C_{P1} is A_{1P1i}, Then D is B_{1i}

Where $C_k(k = 1, 2, \ldots, p_1)$ denotes the selected condition attributes. A_{mki} is the corresponding attribute value, in which m is the layer number (here $m = 1$); k indicates attribute serial number; i marks the fuzzy rule number. Confidence degrees of fuzzy rules, the weights, are defined by fuzzy membership degrees. In inconsistent sub-table S_{12}, these p_1 condition attributes divide objects into x_1 classes. Then x_1 rules are as follows.

Rule j:If C_1 is $A_{11j}, \ldots,$ and C_{P1} is A_{1P1j}, Then Y_1 is E_{11j}

In which, Y_1 is taken as temporary pre-decision of the first layer reducing-dimension function g_1 and E_{1j} ($j = 1, 2, \ldots, x_1$) is corresponding attribute value. The rules based on sub-tables S_{11} and S_{12} are corresponding to fuzzy inference function as first layer reducing-dimension function g_1. However, the function g_1 is not entirely same to reducing-dimension function because the rules from sub-table S_{11} can get conclusion directly without action function f.

Pre-decision Y_1 is used to denote attributes $[C_1, C_2, \ldots, C_{p1}]$ in inconsistent sub-table S_{12} where the value is $E_{1j}(j = 1, 2, \ldots, x1)$ and fuzzy membership degree is confidence degrees of fuzzy rule. For the new represented sub-table S_{12}, second selection of most important attributes $C_{p2} = [C_{p1+1}, C_{p1+2}, \ldots, C_{p1+p2}]$ is done according to attribute important degrees, in which $1 \leq p_1 + p_2 \leq n$. The attributes set $[Y_1, C_{p1+1}, C_{p1+2}, \ldots, C_{p1+p2}]$ distinguishes decision table as consistent sub-table S_{21} and inconsistent sub-table S_{22}. Same to above procedure, other fuzzy rules are acquired, that is, the second layer reduced-dimension function g_2.

By analogy, all reduction attributes $[C_1, C_2, \ldots, C_n]$ are calculated. The last-layer's rules are corresponding to action function f. The rules from the last layer may be inconsistent, whose confidence degrees are appointed by fuzzy membership degrees. In fact, the existence of inconsistent rules accords to practical conflict phenomena. The existence shows the objectivity and soundness of conclusion of RST-based reduced algorithm.

Set fuzzy control inference function F has p_r layers, then mapping relation of input and output variables is:

$$u = F(X) = f[g_{pr-1}(g_{pr-2}(\ldots g_1(X)))] \tag{1}$$

This method not only decreases total dimension of FLC, but also discovers multilayer fuzzy inference function. In every layer, fuzzy rules have small dimensions. According to man's thinking character that dimension is not more than 3, $p_1, \ldots, p_r$ are set as 2 or 1. That makes all rules easy to be understood, suitable to thinking characters, favor of comparison with experts' knowledge and rules amendment.

In the above procedure, attributes reduction and attribute important degrees are very important for multilayer fuzzy rules establishment. The essence of this idea is using input variables' integration to simplify control rules design. Only rational reduction and combination of fuzzy premise components can assure rational controller simplification. Using the RST-based rapid algorithm of fuzzy rules extraction, described as follows, can solve this key problem. The algorithm can calculate the important degrees of condition attributes, reduce the unnecessary attributes, integrate the premise components of fuzzy rules and extract the fuzzy rules.

3   RST-Based Rapid Algorithm of Fuzzy Rules Extraction

The key of fuzzy rules extraction by RST depends on rough set reduction. However, it has been proved that minimal or optimal reduction problem is NP-hard [4]. Thus, heuristic approach is employed to calculate quasi-minimal or quasi-optimal reduction, which can satisfy requirements and enhance the computing speed.

The first three steps depict the establishment process of the fuzzy decision table. Step 4 improves the C-D indiscernible matrix [5]. By analyzing the matrix, a computation program for core attributes is given. The program can avoid computing matrix. Step 5 presents the concrete program for the quasi-optimal reduction of attributes. Information increment of decision is used as heuristic information of attribution selection to accelerate the algorithm speed. The last two steps attain the multilayer fuzzy rules. The details are shown as follows.

Step 1: The condition attributes (input variables) and decision attributes (output variables) are properly selected by the measured data of inputs and outputs, then the decision table is made out.

The data of every sample time is an object of decision table. Because the response of the system has the transition period, any sample-time output is related to previous sample-time inputs and output. So the condition attributes should include input variable vectors $X(t)$, $X(t-kT)$ and output variable vector

$Y(t - kT)$, in which T denotes sample time and $k = 1, 2, \ldots$ decided by system order.

Step 2: The redundant rows are deleted. The consistent degree of decision table is computed. IF it isn't satisfied, turn back to step 1; otherwise, continue.

Step 3: The measured data is normalized by discrete fuzzy normalization algorithm [6], and the knowledge representation system of fuzzy information is established.

Step 4: The core attributes $CORE_D$ of decision D for decision table is calculated.

In the view of making decision, the knowledge representation system S consists of consistent and inconsistent subsystems S_1, S_2. The core attributes needn't be reckoned for inconsistent data. Therefore, this paper improves C-D indiscernible matrix as follows to avoid unnecessary computation between inconsistent data.

$$b_{ij} = \begin{cases} \{a \in C : a(x_i) \neq a(x_j)\} & D(x_i) \neq D(x_j) \text{ and } (x_i \text{ or } x_j \in S_1) \\ \Phi & D(x_i) = D(x_j) \text{ or } (x_i \text{ and } x_j \in S_2) \\ & i, j = 1, 2, \ldots, n; i \neq j \end{cases} \quad (2)$$

If $|b_{ij}| = 1$, the attribute included in b_{ij} is just the core attribute. What's more, if this attribute is expunged from the whole decision table, object x_i and object x_j would be inconsistent at least and the inconsistent object number would increase more than 1. If $|b_{ij}| > 1$ and any one of attributes included in bij is omitted, x_i and x_j are still consistent. If $|b_{ij}| = 0$, then x_i, x_j are surely consistent when they belong to the same decision class; the existence of any attribute is vain and there is no change of the inconsistent object number with the deletion of any attributes when x_i and x_j are both elements of inconsistent subsystem. In short, if any attributes is taken off from the decision table and the inconsistent object number rises, that belongs to the core attributes $CORE_D$ of D, otherwise, that doesn't belong to $CORE_D$ surely. So the core attributes can be directly computed by inconsistent objects number change to simplify the program complexity and decrease computing time. Delete any attribute from the decision table, then check the inconsistent object number change, at last if the number increases, add the attribute to $CORE_D$, otherwise, don't add. By this analysis, the core computation program can be presented as Figure 1.

The program computes the core attributes directly. It needn't calculate the indiscernible matrix to improve computation speed.

Step 5: The core attributes $CORE_D$, or adding some important attributes according to apriori knowledge, are employed as the starting-point of calculation. The most important attribute is chosen at a time by heuristic information until the selected attributes set satisfies the request, which is $RED_D(C)$ generally.

Information increment $\Delta I_D(r, R)$ of decision D shows the classification ability of attributes, defined as:

$$\Delta I_D(r, R) = I(r \cup R/D) - I(R/D) \quad (3)$$

Where $I(/D)$ indicates information quantity with respect to decision D and it is often used as heuristic information of attribute importance. It can be used

1) Set $X = \Phi, Y = C$

2) Compute num;

    //num indicates the inconsistent object number

3) $\forall a \in Y$, check numa change;

    //numa denotes the inconsisten object

    //number after deletion of attribute a

4) if numa > num, then $X = X \cup \{a\}$ and $Y = Y - \{a\}$;

5) if $Y \neq \phi$, turn back to 3);

6) CORED=X;

7) End

Fig. 1. The program for the core attributes CORE$_D$ of decision D

1) Set $X = \text{CORE}_D$, $Y = C - \text{CORE}_D$;

2) Compute $TF(C, D)$ of decision table,

3) Compute $TF(X, D)$,

4) if $TF(X, D) = TF(C, D)$, turn to 10),

5) For all $r \in Y$, compute $HF(r, X, D)$,

6) select r' with greatest value of $HF(a, R, D)$;

7) $X = X \cup \{r'\}$, $Y = Y - \{r'\}$;

8) Compute $TF(X, D)$,

9) if $TF(X, D) = TF(C, D)$, turn to 10), otherwise turn to 5),

10) RED$_D = X$,

11) End.

Fig. 2. The program for the quasi-optimal attributes reduction of RED$_D$ of decision D

as heuristic information of attribute selection, that is, heuristic function (HF) is defined: $HF(r, R, D) = \Delta I_D(r, R)$, where $HF(r, R, D)$ represents the classification ability increment after addition of attributer r to attribute set R. Obviously, the more great $HF(r, R, D)$ is, the more important attribute r is and the more classification ability r increases for R.. The terminal function (TF) of evaluation is defined as $TF(R, D) = I_D(R)$. If $TF(R, D)$ equals to that of original decision table, the calculation is end and R is just the quasi-optimal reduction of attributes. The concrete algorithm is as Figure 2.

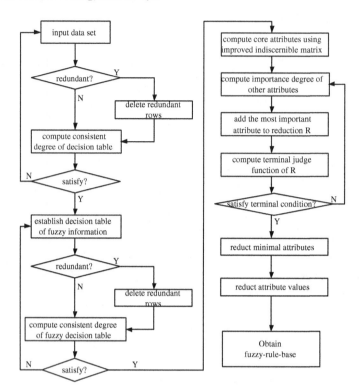

Fig. 3. Flow-diagram of multilayer rough-fuzzy rules extraction algorithm

Step 6: The decision table of fuzzy information is reduced and at the same time the existence of inconsistent rules is permitted.

The fuzzy membership degree is used as the credit degree of fuzzy rules, the rules weight, which is the key for dealing with inconsistent rules. Obviously, it is not hopeful that the existence of inconsistent decision rules in the real rule-base, which is related to the quantity and quality of sample data. But this kind of results is objective, which actually shows the objectivity and soundness of conclusion of RST-based reduced algorithm. The same rules with different credit degrees can be consolidated by the maximum or average credit degree.

Step 7: The reduced fuzzy rules with formal IF-THEN are attained.

By heuristic information of attributes selection, the attributes are chosen gradually to get multilayer fuzzy rules. Fuzzy con-troller function is described by these IF-THEN rules.

The multilayer rough-fuzzy rules extraction algorithm is shown in Figure 3.

4   Simulation Research

In thermal power plant, the electric generating unit, as the controlled plant of the load control system, is a multi-variable coupling plant, which is composed of boiler and turbine-generator whose dynamic characters are totally different. During load control process for unit, energy balance of supply and demand must be properly kept, considering load response performances and operation parameters stability.

In view of control task based on the characteristics of large change range of load, N_0, p_0, N_E, p_T are selected as controller's input variables; μ_t and μ_B are adopted as controller's output variables, where N_0, p_0, N_E, p_T, μ_t and μ_B denote load instruction, main steam pressure setting value, steam turbine's real power and main steam pressure, the opening degree of turbine's main throttle and the fuel volume of boiler respectively. FLC can improve distinctly control dynamic performance where far from working point and have strong robustness for controlled plant's parameters change compared with traditional PID. But FLC is generally difficult to eliminate error in small range. So the whole control system adopts the hybrid intelligent control (IC) of multilayer rough-fuzzy controller and PID controller and takes full use of their advantages. The rough-fuzzy controller operates mainly in large error range while PID controller runs primarily in small error range.

A certain mathematic model of electric generating unit is studied for simulation experiments. Set the transform function is:

$$\begin{bmatrix} p_r \\ N_E \end{bmatrix} = \begin{bmatrix} \frac{2.194}{(1+80s)^2} & -2.194(0.064 + \frac{0.093}{1+124s}) \\ \frac{1}{(1+80s)^2} & \frac{68.81s}{(1+12s)(1+82s)} \end{bmatrix} \begin{bmatrix} \mu_B \\ \mu_T \end{bmatrix} \tag{4}$$

Figure 4 presents p_T and N_E response curves under load instruction from 43.3% to 90% respectively. In these Figure s, the left cures are p_T response curves; the right curves are N_E response curves; curves 1 show simulation results of hybrid control of multilayer rough-fuzzy controller and PID controller; curves 2 are conventional PID control responds that employ the mode of boiler following turbine for unit load control. For p_T control, the hybrid control has high rising speed, small overshoot than PID control. For N_E control, the hybrid control also has high rising speed, but the overshoot is a little larger than PID control. The dynamic process of the hybrid intelligent control has relatively greater fluctuation than PID control. The main reason is that FLC is corresponding to nonlinear PD control. When the error is larger, rough-fuzzy control runs chiefly with rapid response speed and relatively larger fluctuation.

The dynamic characteristics and parameters alter because of operating conditions changes of unit or the slow effect of aging, wearing etc. Given different time constant as Formula (5).

$$\begin{bmatrix} p_r \\ N_E \end{bmatrix} = \begin{bmatrix} \frac{2.194}{(1+65s)^2} & -2.194(0.064 + \frac{0.093}{1+150s}) \\ \frac{1}{(1+90s)^2} & \frac{68.81s}{(1+10s)(1+100s)} \end{bmatrix} \begin{bmatrix} \mu_B \\ \mu_T \end{bmatrix} \tag{5}$$

After the parameters variation, Figure 5 illuminates p_T and N_E response curves under load instruction from 43.3% to 90% respectively. The left cures are p_T response curves and the right curves are N_E response curves. The curves 1 show simulation results of hybrid control and curves 2 are conventional PID

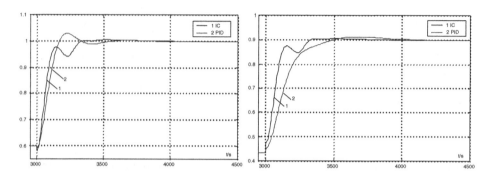

Fig. 4. p_T and N_E response curves under load instruction from 43.3% to 90% respectively

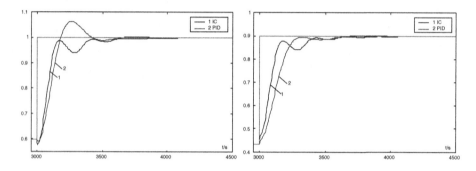

Fig. 5. p_T and N_E response curves under load instruction from 43.3% to 90% after parameters variation respectively

control responds. Accordingly, hybrid control has high rising speed and strong robustness owing to FLC.

5   Conclusion

Aiming at MIMO system, this paper proposes a multilayer fuzzy rules design method based on rough set theory. According to man's thinking logic characteristics, this method may select the dimension number of every layer fuzzy rules no more than 3, advantageous for understanding, checking and correcting rules. The key work, reducing and integrating input variables, is done by a rapid fuzzy rules extraction algorithm based on RST. In this algorithm, an improved C-D indiscernible matrix is proposed and analyzed. Then a computing core attributes method is given. The main programs and algorithm flow is shown in Figure 1-3. The multilayer rough-fuzzy controller is combined with conventional PID controller, applied in unit control system of power plant in this paper. The simulation results show that the control system has better control quality, such as high speed, small overshoot and strong robustness.

Acknowledgements

This research was funded by Chinese Nation Nature Science Foundation (60374029).

References

1. Xie, K.M., Liu, D.L.: A Fuzzy-Logic-Based Traffic Light Control System. 10th International Symposium on Integrated Circuits, Devices & Systems (2004) Suntec, Singapore
2. Francis, E.H., Taya, Shen, L.X.: Fault Diagnosis Based on Rough Set Theory. Engineering Applications of Artificial Intelligence. Vol.16 (2003): 39–43
3. Wang, F., Xie, G., Xie, K.M.: Reduced-Dimension Multilayer FLC Based on Rough Set The-ory. The 5th World Congress on Intelligent Control and Automation, WCICA, (2004) Hangzhou, China, 2686–2689
4. Wong, S. K. M., Ziavko, W.Cn.: Optimal Decision Rules in Decision Tables. Bulletin of Polish Academy of Sciences, (1985) Vol.33: 693–696
5. Skowron, A., Rauszer, C. : The Discernibility Matrices and Functions in Information Systems. In Intelligent Decision Support. Handbook of Application and Advances of The Rough Set Theory. (ed.) R. Slowinski, Kluwer, Dordrecht (1992) 331–362
6. Mohamed, Quafafou: α-RST: A Generalization of Rough Set Theory. Information Sciences. (2000) Vol.124: 301–316

Interpretable Rule Extraction and Function Approximation from Numerical Input/Output Data Using the Modified Fuzzy TSK Model, TaSe Model

L. J. Herrera, H. Pomares, I. Rojas, A. Guilén, M. Awad, and J. González

University of Granada, Department of Computer Architecture and Technology,
E.T.S. Computer Engineering, 18071 Granada, Spain
http://atc.ugr.es

Abstract. The fuzzy Takagi-Sugeno-Kang model and the inference system proposed by these authors is a very powerful tool for function approximation problems due to its capability of expressing a complex nonlinear system using a set of simple linear rules. Nevertheless, during the learning and optimization process, usually a trade-off has to be carried out among global system accuracy and sub-models (rules) interpretability. In this paper we review the TaSe model [8] for function approximation (for Grid-Based Fuzzy Systems and extend it to consider Clustering-Based Fuzzy Systems) that is learned from an I/O numerical data set and that will allow us to extract strong interpretable rules, whose consequents are the Taylor Series Expansion of the model output around the rule centres. This TaSe model provides full interpretability to the local models with high accuracy in the global approximation. The rule extraction process using the TaSe model and its properties will be reviewed using a significant example.

1 Introduction

Rule extraction is a crucial problem in many scientific, engineering and economic areas. Several paradigms have been applied for this topic and a huge number of works can be found in the literature. More specifically, when dealing with a modelling problem from a continuous data set with samples of the form

$$\{(\boldsymbol{x}^m; z^m) \; ; m = 1, 2, \ldots, M; \; \text{with} \; z^m = f(\boldsymbol{x}^m) \in \mathbb{R}, \; \text{and} \; \boldsymbol{x}^m \in \mathbb{R}^n\} \quad (1)$$

soft-computing techniques such as Neural Networks(NN) and Fuzzy Systems(FS) have been applied. Typically, NN provide a good approximation for the modelling problem, but the models obtained suffer from the lack of interpretability. In opposite, FS provide a good interpretable model from which rules can be easily extracted. Both paradigms are frequently mixed in the so-called neuro-fuzzy modelling techniques.

The Takagi-Sugeno-Kang (TSK) [1] neuro-fuzzy model has been widely used for function modelling due to its capacity of obtaining a highly interpretable

D. Ślęzak et al. (Eds.): RSFDGrC 2005, LNAI 3641, pp. 402–411, 2005.

model with high accuracy in the approximation, using a relatively low number of simple rules. Nevertheless, during the modelling process from a set of I/O data using a TSK model, some aspects of the intrinsic interpretability of that can be lost. The transparency of the input space partitioning, the number of rules of the obtained system [2] and the interpretability of the local models [3] are three crucial issues in the modelling of I/O data using TSK systems from the interpretability point of view.

In general, in Fuzzy Systems two types of partitioning of the input space can be carried out. On the one hand Grid-Based Fuzzy Systems (GBFSs) [6] perform a thorough coverage of the input space, they are highly interpretable since every rule make use of the the same group of fuzzy sets in each input variable, but, nevertheless, they notoriously suffer from the curse of dimensionality [8] in the number of rules. On the otherhand, Clustering-Based Fuzzy Systems (CBFSs) [7] place the rules in the zones of the input space in which they are needed, they are usually seen as less interpretable than GBFS [2], but the number of rules is not an exponential function of the number of input variables and the number of membership functions (MFs) per variable as in GBFSs.

In relation to both types of partitioning in TSK models, with respect to the transparency of the model, some approaches try to use similarity measures among the fuzzy sets obtained in the optimization of the TSK system process [4], but for GBFSs, a "partition-like" [8] MF distribution avoids a strong overlapping among the fuzzy sets. For CBFSs we will introduce now an equivalent approach to that of "partition" in section 3. With respect to the number of rules, higher-order consequent TSK rules can reduce drastically the number of rules needed to perform the approximation [5]; nevertheless, high-order TSK rules have always been seen as non-interpretable. The TaSe model, as we will review, allows such interpretability [8]. And finally with respect to the interpretability of the local sub-models some approaches have tried to overcome this problem [9,3]. Here we present the TaSe model as a rule extractor that provides fully TSK interpretable rules with respect to the rule centres both for GBFSs and CBFSs.

2   Interpretable Rule Extraction from I/O Data Using Grid Partitioning

Typically, the structure of a multiple-input single-output (MISO) TSK system and its associated fuzzy inference method comprises a set of K IF-THEN rules in the form

$$Rule^k : \text{IF } x_1 \text{ is } \mu_1^k \text{ AND } \ldots \text{ AND } x_n \text{ is } \mu_n^k \text{ THEN } y = R^k \qquad (2)$$

where the μ_i^k are fuzzy sets characterized by membership functions $\mu_i^k(x_i)$ in universes of discourse U_i (in which variables x_i take their values), and where R^k are the consequents of the rules.

The output of a fuzzy system with rules in the form shown in *eq.* 2 can be expressed (using weighted average aggregation) as

$$F(x) = \frac{\sum\limits_{k=1}^{K} \mu^k(x)R^k}{\sum\limits_{k=1}^{K} \mu^k(x)} \tag{3}$$

provided that $\mu^k(x)$ is the activation value for the antecedent of the rule k, which can be expressed as

$$\mu^k(x) = \mu_1^k(x_1)\mu_2^k(x_2)\ldots\mu_n^k(x_n) \tag{4}$$

As we have mentioned before, TSK fuzzy systems are often used to deal with function approximation problems, due to it's ability to explain non-linear relations using a relatively low number of simple rules. We must recall that the problem of function approximation deals with estimating an unknown function f from samples of the form 1, and is a crucial problem for a number of scientific and engineering areas. The main goal is thus to learn an unknown functional mapping between the input vectors and their corresponding continuous output values, using a set of known training samples. Later, this generated mapping will be used to obtain the expected output given any new input data.

For the case of GBFS, the TaSe model was presented in [8]; we will now review the main topics surrounding this methodology.

The TaSe model obtains *rules whose consequents can be interpreted as the Taylor Series Expansion of the model output around the rule centres*. This result is possible thanks to two main characteristics of the TaSe TSK model:

1. Rule consequents that have a general polynomial form that admits the Taylor Theorem that states that: "if a function $f(x)$ defined in an interval has derivatives of all orders, it can be approximates near a point $x = a$ as its Taylor Series Expansion around that point:

$$f(x) = f(a) + (x - a)^T \left[\frac{\partial f}{\partial x_i}(a)\right]_{i=1\ldots n} + \frac{1}{2}(x - a)^T W(x - a)$$

$$+ \ldots + \frac{1}{(l+1)!}f^{(l+1)}(c)(x - a)^{l+1} \tag{5}$$

where in each case, c is a point between x and a, and where W is a triangular matrix of dimensions $l \times l$ ". Taylor series opens a door for the approximation of any function through polynomials, that is, through the addition of a number of simple functions. It is therefore a fundamental key in the field of Function Approximation Theory and Mathematical Analysis. Using the general formulation of the TSK model, we can use rule consequents R^k (in *eq.* 2) that have the truncated form of *eq.* 5.

2. Rule antecedent structure that allows such interpretability, i.e. that allows the model output to be continuous and differentiable, and such that in each rule centre only its respective rule consequent has influence in the output. In the case of GBFS, the Orderly Local Membership Function (OLMF) bases [10] allow such interpretability. The most important characteristics of the OLMF bases are:

- all MFs are local (i.e. non-negative and vanishing with the distance), defined in a delimited domain and of the same type
- every MF extreme point coincides with the centre of the adjacent MF (they form a partition, thus avoiding uncontrolled overlapping of the MFs)
- all MFs are p times differentiable and the p-th derivative of the MF is continuous in all its domain
- the p-th derivative of the MF vanishes at its centre and at its boundaries
- the basis must accomplish the addition-to-unity property

Given a system with such two characteristics, and using Least Squares (LSE)

$$J = \sum_{m=1..M} (f(\boldsymbol{x}^m) - z^m)^2 \tag{6}$$

for obtaining the rule consequent coefficients [11] from a I/O data set, leads to a good approximator system with interpretable sub-models (rules) [8].

3   Interpretable Rule Extraction from I/O Data Using Clustering Partitioning

As we have seen, for GBFS, Bikdash in [10] presented a modified Membership Function (MF) type, the OLMF bases that allowed local models (rules) interpretability, and Herrera in [11] and [8], this approach was expanded to be used in function approximation problems from a I/O data set (TaSe model) and was endowed with a complete GBFS learning algorithm (TaSe learning algorithm). Nevertheless, for CBFS this problem is more tricky. For CBFSs, that in some cases are equivalent to Radial Basis Function Networks, we can have rules with the same truncated Taylor Series form, but in principle it's not so easy to have an input partition that satisfies the requirement that in each rule centre only its respective rule consequent has influence in the output, neither exists a Membership Function type that carry out such property in CBFSs.

As expounded in the introduction, for CBFSs as was for GBFSs, the problems of lack of transparency of the input space partition, an excessive number of rules, and the obtention of sub-models that don't reflect properly the model output in the area they have influence on, are three main issues that appear when dealing with fuzzy rule extraction in I/O data modelling from the interpretability point of view. Usually most of the neuro-fuzzy approaches (including RBF networks [12]) are centred in reducing the global error function, but don't deal with the natural posterior process of rule extraction and interpretability of the obtained model.

As we have mentioned, for CBFS it's impossible to have MFs that carry out the two desired properties in the input space partition. The non-grid input space partition organization avoids this possibility. Consider Gaussian-type MFs and suppose the simplest case in which we have a one-dimensional input space with domain $[0,1]$ and two MFs (thus two rules) centred in $c^1 = 0.3$ and $c^2 = 0.7$ with $\sigma = 0.3$. In this case there is a strong overlap among both MFs in both rule centres. To avoid this overlap we will allow the domain of the first MF $\mu^1(x)$ to be limited by the function $1 - \mu^2(x)$, i.e., when the activation value of the other rule is 1, the activation value of the first rule will be forced to be 0. More specifically the activation value for the first rule $\mu^1(x)$ will be limited by

$$1 - \mu'^2(x); \quad \mu'^2(x) = \begin{cases} \mu^2(x) & \text{if} \quad x < c_2 \\ 1 & \text{if} \quad x \geq c_2 \end{cases} \tag{7}$$

and on the other hand, the activation value for the first rule $\mu^1(x)$ will be limited by

$$1 - \mu'^1(x); \quad \mu'^1(x) = \begin{cases} \mu^1(x) & \text{if} \quad x > c_1 \\ 1 & \text{if} \quad x \leq c_1 \end{cases} \tag{8}$$

i.e. the final activation value of any point for the each rule will be

$$\mu^{k*}(x) = \mu^k(x) \prod_{j=1}^{\substack{j=n; \\ j \neq k}} \left(1 - \mu'^j(x)\right) \tag{9}$$

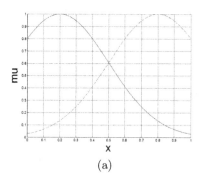
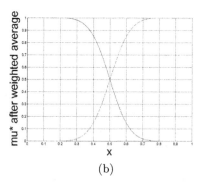

(a)   (b)

Fig. 1. a) Original MFs for a one-dimensional example. b) Activations using the modified Aggregation Operator.

Thus, generalizing to the n-dimensional case with any number of rules K, the general expression for the output of the TSK system, using weighted average (to force each activation value of each rule at the same rule centre to be 1) can be calculated as

$$F(x) = \frac{\sum\limits_{k=1}^{K} \mu^{k*}(x)R^k}{\sum\limits_{k=1}^{K} \mu^{k*}(x)} = \frac{\sum\limits_{k=1}^{K} \left(\mu^k(x) \prod\limits_{\substack{j=1}}^{\substack{j=n; \\ j \neq k}} \left(1 - \mu'^j(x)\right) \right) R^k}{\sum\limits_{k=1}^{K} \left(\mu^k(x) \prod\limits_{\substack{j=1}}^{\substack{j=n; \\ j \neq k}} \left(1 - \mu'^j(x)\right) \right)} \qquad (10)$$

where the $\mu'^j(x)$ has the form

$$\mu'^j(x) = \mu_1'^j(x_1)\mu_2'^j(x_2)\dots\mu_n'^j(x_n) \qquad (11)$$

in which each $\mu_i'^j(x_i)$ has the form shown in *eq.* 7 or 8 depending on the relative position of the centres c_i^j and c_i^k.

This new formulation of the system output in *eq.* 10 is simply a modified aggregation operator with weighted averaging behavior. *Fig.* 1 shows the unidimensional toy example with two MFs cited previously, with the original MFs $\mu^1(x)$ and $\mu^2(x)$ and the final effective MFs $\mu^{1*}(x)$ and $\mu^{2*}(x)$.

4   Example of Interpretable Rule Extraction Using the TaSe Model

Consider the example function

$$y_4(x_1, x_2) = \frac{1}{1 + exp(10(x_1 - x_2))} \qquad x_1, x_2 \in [0, 1] \qquad (12)$$

presented for comparisons in [13]. From this function example we will extract 400 equidistributed samples as our I/O data set, from which we will perform our interpretable rule extraction methodology using the TaSe model, both for clustering and grid-based fuzzy systems. For the two models we will perform rule extraction using 9 second order polynomial consequent rules. Thus we will obtain 9 interpretable rules that will define the shape of the model output around the rule centres, that are placed in a grid form in the case of GBFSs and that will be scattered in the case of CBFSs.

First consider the use of GBFSs. Using the learning methodology presented in [8], the optimal variable rule centres in the two variables (3 MFs per variable implies one variable rule centre for each variable, considering fixed the other two MF centres, one at each extreme of the domain) for this example (see *eq.* 12) are placed approximately in the middle of the variables domain (around 0.5). Thus the 9 rules are centred in $\{0, 0.5, 1\}$ for variable x_1 and again in $\{0, 0.5, 1\}$ for variable x_2. *Fig.* 2 shows the original function y_4 (see eq. 12) and the approximation obtained using these 9 rules obtained using the Grid-Based TaSe model. Our approach as we can see obtains a very good approximation of this function using only 9 rules (the NRMSE [6] obtained is 0.02).

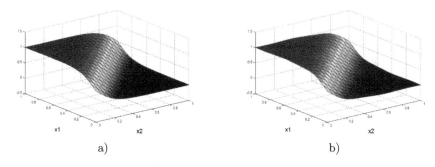

a)   b)

Fig. 2. a) Original function y_4. b) Approximation obtained by the Grid-Based TaSe model using 9 rules.

The nine rules obtained by the TaSe GBFS learning methodology are

IF x_1 is 0 and x_2 is 0 THEN $y = 4.30x_1^2 + 0.0x_1x_2$
$-4.30x_2^2 - 2.56x_1 + 2.56x_2 + 0.50$
IF x_1 is 0 and x_2 is 0.5 THEN $y = -3.43x_1^2 - 3.74x_1(x_2 - 0.5)$
$+0.78(x_2 - 0.5)^2 - 0.06x_1 + 0.25(x_2 - 0.5) + 1.00$
IF x_1 is 0 and x_2 is 1 THEN $y = -1.19x_1^2 - 4.06x_1(x_2 - 1)$
$-1.19(x_2 - 1)^2 - 0.12x_1 + 0.12(x_2 - 1) + 1.00$
IF x_1 is 0.5 and x_2 is 0 THEN $y = -0.78(x_1 - 0.5)^2 + 3.74(x_1 - 0.5)x_2$
$+3.43x_2^2 - 0.25(x_1 - 0.5) + 0.06x_2 + 0.0$
IF x_1 is 0.5 and x_2 is 0.5 THEN $y = 0.0(x_1 - 0.5)^2 + 0.0(x_1 - 0.5)(x_2 - 0.5)$
$+0.0(x_2 - 0.5)^2 - 2.28(x_1 - 0.5) + 2.28(x_2 - 0.5) + 0.50$
IF x_1 is 0.5 and x_2 is 1 THEN $y = 0.78(x_1 - 0.5)^2 - 3.74(x_1 - 0.5)(x_2 - 1)$
$-3.43(x_2 - 1)^2 - 0.25(x_1 - 0.5) + 0.06(x_2 - 1) + 1.00$
IF x_1 is 1 and x_2 is 0 THEN $y = 1.19(x_1 - 1)^2 + 4.06(x_1 - 1)x_2$
$+1.19x_2^2 - 0.12(x_1 - 1) + 0.12x_2 - 0.0$
IF x_1 is 1 and x_2 is 0.5 THEN $y = 3.43(x_1 - 1)^2 + 3.74(x_1 - 1)(x_2 - 0.5)$
$-0.78(x_2 - 0.5)^2 - 0.06(x_1 - 1) + 0.25(x_2 - 0.5) + 0.0$
IF x_1 is 1 and x_2 is 1 THEN $y = -4.30(x_1 - 1)^2 + 0.0(x_1 - 1)(x_2 - 1)$
$+4.30(x_2 - 1)^2 - 2.56(x_1 - 1) + 2.56(x_2 - 1) + 0.50$

Now, *fig.* 3 shows the approximation obtained plus the representation of the local models, identified by the consequent polynomials centred in their respective centres, and a representation of the local models themselves. We can clearly see how the TaSe model for GBFSs obtains rules whose consequent representation highly resembles the output of the model in the vicinity of the rule centres.

Now consider the use of CBFSs for the same problem. In this case, we have placed the rule centres according to the CFA clustering algorithm presented in [12], and afterwards we have used LSE to obtain the optimal consequent coefficients together with a gradient descent approach to obtain the optimal rule centres. *Fig.* 4 shows the effective activation values for each rule of the resulting CBFS TaSe model, and also the activation values for each of the rules in the previous case when we used the GBFS TaSe model.

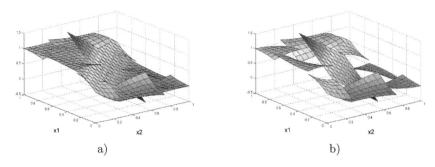

a)   b)

Fig. 3. a) Original function y_4. b) Approximation obtained by the Grid-Based TaSe model using 9 rules.

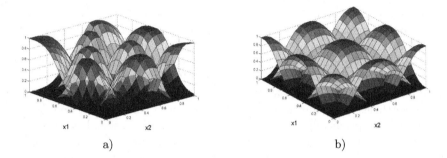

a)   b)

Fig. 4. a) Activation functions $\mu^{k*}(\boldsymbol{x})$ for the nine rules in the TaSe CBFS. b) Activation functions for the nine rules in the TaSe GBFS.

The rule centres for the TaSe CBFS model, after the gradient descent procedure for optimization of the rule centres (the sigmas are automatically calculated using the nearest centre criteria as in [14]), are placed in [0.71, 1], [0.43, 0.02], [0.83, 0.02], [0.54, 0.82],[0.02, 0.27], [0.61, 0.38], [0.91, 0.50], [0,1.00], [0.23, 0.48]. This approach obtains again a very good approximation to function y_4 using only 9 rules (the NRMSE obtained is 0.007, that is even better than the previous NRMSE = 0.02 obtained by the TaSe GBFS)

Fig. 5 shows the approximation obtained plus the representation of the local models, identified by the consequent polynomials centred in their respective centres, and a representation of the local models themselves. We can clearly see how the TaSe model for CBFSs also obtains rules whose consequent representation highly resembles the output of the model in the vicinity of the rule centres. Note that in this case the rule centres are not grid distributed along the domain but according to the optimal position found in the gradient descent approach. Nevertheless, the rule centres could be forced to be placed at any specific points without using any optimization method for centres placing, and the interpretability properties of the rules would be kept (the accuracy could be lower then).

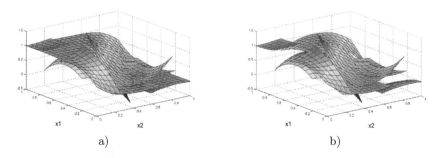

Fig. 5. a) Original function y_4. b) Approximation obtained by the Clustering-Based TaSe model using 9 rules (see also *fig.* 4.b to remind where the centres were localized).

Thus, we have seen that it is possible to obtain highly interpretable neuro-fuzzy systems using the TaSe methodology. We have a low number of rules, spread in a transparent input space partitioning, and that together provide a very good representation of the whole I/O data but also alone are a good representation of the input space area they represent (thanks to the Taylor Series Expansion). Specifically for the case of the CBFS, they have been seen as low interpretable systems due to the fact that they use different fuzzy sets in each rule. Nevertheless with our approach for input space partitioning, we can claim that each rule specifically defines a region in the n-dimensional space without a strong overlapping with the rest of the rules in all the input dimensions. For the given example, the TaSe CBFS has provided a better global approximation (0.006 NRMSE) than the TaSe GBFS (0.02 NRMSE) but obviously due to the higher flexibility inherent to the clustering-based neuro-fuzzy models (we had 9 free parameters in opposite to the 2 free parameters -centres- in the GBFS).

5 Conclusions

We have reviewed the TaSe model as an interpretable rule extractor, that can get rid of the loss of interpretability inherent to most of the learning and optimization techniques for TSK fuzzy systems when dealing with I/O data modelling. Also we have presented a modified TaSe model for CBFSs that allows interpretable rule extraction, thanks to an input space partitioning that resembles that of "partition-like" in GBFSs. Finally a comparison has been made among both approaches from the interpretability point of view using an example. The TaSe model for CBFS overcomes partially the reputation of low interpretable systems because of the fact that they use different MFs per rule, thanks to the partition-like input space partitioning expounded in section 3. The TaSe model for I/O data modelling both for GBFS and for CBFS, provides full interpretability to the local models with high accuracy in the global approximation.

Acknowledgements

This work has been partially supported by the Spanish CICYT Project TIN2004-01419.

References

1. Takagi, T., Sugeno, M.: Fuzzy identification of systems and its applications to modelling and control. IEEE Trans. Syst. Man and Cyber. **15** (1985) 116–132
2. Guillaume, S.: Designing fuzzy inference systems from data: an interpretability-oriented review, IEEE Trans. Fuz. Syst. **9** (2001) 426-Ű443.
3. Johansen, T.A., Babuska, R.: Multiobjective Identification of Takagi-Sugeno Fuzzy Models. IEEE Trans. Fuz. Syst. **11(6)** (2003) 847–860
4. Paiva, R.P., Dourado, A.: Interpretability and learning in neuro-fuzzy systems, Fuzzy Sets and Systems, **147** (2004) 17-Ű38
5. Herrera, L.J., Pomares, H., Rojas, Guillén, A., Awad, M.: Analysis of the TaSe-II TSK-type Fuzzy System for function approximation. Lecture Notes in Computer Science. ECSQARU'2005. Accepted
6. Pomares, H., Rojas, I., Ortega, J., Prieto, A.: A systematic approach to a self-generating fuzzy rule-table for function approximation. IEEE Trans. Syst., Man, Cybern. **30** (2000) 431–447
7. Chiu, S.: Fuzzy Model Identification Based on Cluster Estimation. Journal of Intelligent and Fuzzy Systems, **2(3)** (1994)
8. Herrera, L.J., Pomares, H., Rojas, I., Valenzuela, O., Prieto, A.: TaSe, a Taylor Series Based Fuzzy System Model that Combines Interpretability and Accuracy. Fuzzy Sets and Systems. *Accepted*
9. Zhou, S.M., Gan, J.Q.: Improving the interpretability of Takagi-Sugeno fuzzy model by using linguistic modifiers and a multiple objective learning scheme. Int. Joint Conf. on Neural Networks IJCNN (2004) 2385–2390
10. Bikdash, M.: A Highly Interpretable Form of Sugeno Inference Systems. IEEE Trans. Fuz. Syst. **7(6)** (1999) 686–696
11. Herrera, L.J., Pomares, H., Rojas, I., Gonález, J., Valenzuela, O.: Function Approximation through Fuzzy Systems Using Taylor Series Expansion-Based Rules: Interpretability and Parameter Tuning. Lecture Notes in Computer Science. New York: Springer-Verlag, **2972** 252–261
12. González, J., Rojas, I., Pomares, H., Ortega, J., Prieto, A.: A new Clustering Technique for Function Aproximation. IEEE Transactions on Neural Networks, **13(1)**(2002) 132Ű-142
13. Rovatti, R., Guerrieri, R.: Fuzzy Sets of Rules for System Identification, IEEE Trans. Fuz. Syst. **4(2)** (1996) 89–102
14. Moody, J., Darken, C.J.: Fast learning in networks of locally-tuned processing units. Neural Computation **1(2)** (1989) 281-294

A New Feature Weighted Fuzzy Clustering Algorithm*

Jie Li, Xinbo Gao, and Licheng Jiao

School of Electronic Engineering,
Xidian Univ., Xi'an 710071, P.R. China

Abstract. In the field of cluster analysis, the fuzzy k-means, k-modes and k-prototypes algorithms were designed for numerical, categorical and mixed data sets respectively. However, all the above algorithms assume that each feature of the samples plays an uniform contribution for cluster analysis. To consider the particular contributions of different features, a novel feature weighted fuzzy clustering algorithm is proposed in this paper, in which the ReliefF algorithm is used to assign the weights for every feature. By weighting the features of samples, the above three clustering algorithms can be unified, and better classification results can be also achieved. The experimental results with various real data sets illustrate the effectiveness of the proposed algorithm.

1 Introduction

Cluster analysis is one of multivariate statistical analysis methods and an important branch of unsupervised pattern classification in statistical pattern recognition [1]. The goal of cluster analysis is to partition an unlabeled sample set into some subsets so that the homogenous samples can be classified into the same subset and the inhomogeneous samples can be classified into different subsets. So, it can be used to investigate the closeness among the objects in quantity and to obtain the validate classification.

Fuzzy k-means (FKMe) algorithm is one of effective cluster analysis methods, which has been widely used in unsupervised pattern recognition and fuzzy control and other fields. Unfortunately, the FKMe algorithm can only deal with the numerical data set. In practice, both the numerical data and categorical data, even mixed data may be encountered. Since the categorical domain is disorder, it does not always work to convert the categorical values to numerical values. For this purpose, the k-modes and k-prototypes algorithms are presented for processing the categorical data set and the mixed data set respectively [2,3].

In the k-means and k-modes algorithms, contributions of all the features of samples are considered uniformly for classification. Even the k-prototypes algorithm only employs a weight to balance the numerical features and categorical features. In fact, since the feature values come from different measuring sensors,

---

* This work was supported by National Natural Science Foundation of China (No.60202004) and the Key Project of Chinese Ministry of Education (No.104173).

D. Ślęzak et al. (Eds.): RSFDGrC 2005, LNAI 3641, pp. 412–420, 2005.

there exist different dimensions, accuracy and reliability. In the other hand, not all the extracted features are suitable for pattern classification with the same degree. So, the above three clustering algorithms have some certain limitations in practical applications.

To consider the different contributions of features for classification, a novel feature weighted fuzzy clustering algorithm is presented in this paper. In this new method, the feature selection technique [4], the ReliefF algorithm is used to assign the weight for each feature. In this way, the fuzzy k-means, k-modes and k-prototypes algorithms can be unified, and better classification performance can be achieved. In the other hand, the contribution amounts of all the features can also be obtained.

The rest of this paper is organized as follows. In next section, the feature selection technique, the ReliefF algorithm is briefly introduced. Section 3 presents the feature weighted clustering algorithm. The experimental results are given in Section 4 with performance comparison among the proposed algorithm and the available k-means, k-modes and k-prototypes algorithms. The final section concludes this paper and points out the research topics in the future work.

2   The ReliefF Algorithm

Feature selection has been widely applied in the fields of data mining, image processing and pattern recognition, which is often used to assign a weight for each feature according to its contribution and to find the most effective features. The basic Relief algorithm is proposed by Kira and Rendell in 1992 [5], which is fit for the classification problem with two classes. In 1994, Kononenko extended the Relief algorithm to ReliefF algorithm so that it can be suitable for classification problem with multiple classes.

Let $X = \{x_1, x_2, \cdots, x_n\}$ be a given set of objects to be clustering processed, in which $x_i = [x_{i1}, x_{i2}, \cdots, x_{iN}]^T$ denotes the N features of the i-th object (sample). Let λ be a matrix with order of $1 \times N$, which assigns the weight for each feature. For any a sample x_i, R nearest-neighbor samples are first found out from the class of x_i, denoted as $h_j, j = 1, 2, \cdots, R$. Then R nearest-neighbor samples are found out from other classes respectively, denoted as $m_{lj}, j = 1, 2, \cdots, R, l \neq class(x_i)$. Let $diff\_hit$ be a matrix with order of $N \times 1$, which denotes the difference between h_j and x_i in features.

$$diff\_hit = \sum_{j=1}^{R} \frac{|x_i - h_j|}{\max(X) - \min(X)} \tag{1}$$

Let $diff\_miss$ be a matrix with order of $N \times 1$, which represents the difference between m_{lj} and x_i in features.

$$diff\_miss = \sum_{l \neq class(x_i)} \frac{p(l)}{1 - p(class(x_i))} \sum_{j=1}^{R} \frac{|x_i - m_{lj}|}{\max(X) - \min(X)} \tag{2}$$

where, $p(l)$ indicates the priori probability of the l-th class, which equals to the ratio of total number of samples in the l-th class to the total number of samples in data set. In ReliefF algorithm, the λ is updated as follows.

$$\lambda = \lambda - \frac{diff\_hit}{R} + \frac{diff\_miss}{R} \qquad (3)$$

Repeating the above steps several times, the appropriate weight of each feature will be achieved.

3 The Feature Weighted Clustering Algorithm

Let $X = \{x_1, x_2, \cdots, x_n\}$ be a set of objects to be clustering processed, and $x_j = [x_j^r, x_j^c]^T, j = 1, 2, \cdots, n$, denote the m features of the j-th samples, in which $x_j^r = [x_{j1}^r, \cdots, x_{jt}^r]$ indicates the numerical features and $x_j^c = [x_{j,t+1}^c, \cdots, x_{jm}^c]$ stands for the categorical features. Let $P = [p_1, p_2, \cdots, p_k]$, and $p_i = [p_{i1}^r, \cdots, p_{it}^r, p_{i,t+1}^c, \cdots, p_{im}^c]^T, i = 1, 2, \cdots, k$ represent the prototype of the i-th class. In the k-prototypes algorithm, the objective function is defined as follows.

$$J(P) = \sum_{i=1}^{k} \left(\sum_{j=1}^{n} \sum_{l=1}^{t} |x_{jl}^r - p_{il}^r|^2 + \lambda \sum_{j=1}^{n} \sum_{l=t+1}^{m} \delta(x_{jl}^c, p_{il}^c) \right) \qquad (4)$$

In the right hand of (4), the first term is the squared Euclidean distance in numerical feature space, and the second term is a simple dissimilarity matching measurement. Here $\delta(\cdot)$ is defined as

$$\delta(a, b) = \begin{cases} 0 & a = b \\ 1 & a \neq b \end{cases} \qquad (5)$$

The weight λ is used to balance the two kinds of features. From (4), it can be found that although the k-prototypes algorithm employs a parameter λ to control the proportion between the numerical and categorical feature sets, within the numerical or categorical feature sets, the contributions of each feature is assumed uniform for classification.

First, we extend the crisp k-partition to fuzzy k-partition. For the fuzzy k-prototypes clustering, the objective function is modified as

$$J(W, P) = \sum_{i=1}^{k} \left(\sum_{j=1}^{n} w_{ij}^2 \sum_{l=1}^{t} |x_{jl}^r - p_{il}^r|^2 + \lambda \sum_{j=1}^{n} w_{ij}^2 \sum_{l=t+1}^{m} \delta(x_{jl}^c, p_{il}^c) \right), \qquad (6)$$

where $w_{ij} \in [0, 1]$ indicates the membership degree of sample x_j to the i-th cluster. Note that we weight a exponential 2 for w_{ij} to guarantee the extension from crisp partition to fuzzy partition not trivial [6].

Furthermore, we extend the fuzzy k-prototypes algorithm by weighting every feature. The corresponding weight for each feature can be obtained with the

ReliefF algorithm. Let $\lambda^r = [\lambda_1^r, \cdots, \lambda_t^r]^T$ denote the weights for the numerical features and $\lambda^c = [\lambda_{t+1}^c, \cdots, \lambda_m^c]^T$ stand for the weights for the categorical features. Then the clustering objective function is rewritten as

$$J(W, P) = \sum_{i=1}^{k} \left(\sum_{j=1}^{n} w_{ij}^2 \sum_{l=1}^{t} \lambda_l^r |x_{jl}^r - p_{il}^r|^2 + \sum_{j=1}^{n} w_{ij}^2 \sum_{l=t+1}^{m} \lambda_l^c \delta(x_{jl}^c, p_{il}^c) \right) \quad (7)$$

By minimizing the objective function $J(W, P)$, the optimal clustering result can be achieved. Note that since all the weights can be classified into two groups, one for numerical features and another for categorical features, the two groups weights will be updated with ReliefF algorithm respectively. The weights for numerical features are updated as Eq.(8).

$$\lambda^r = \lambda^r - \frac{diff\_hit^r}{R} + \frac{diff\_miss^r}{R}, \quad (8)$$

where both the $diff\_hit^r$ and $diff\_miss^r$ are matrices with order of $t \times 1$ defined in Eq.(1) and Eq.(2), which denote the difference of numerical features.

Both the $diff\_hit^c$ and $diff\_miss^c$ are matrices with order of $(m-t+1) \times 1$ and indicate the difference of categorical features, which are defined as Eq.(9) and Eq.(10).

$$diff\_hit^c = \sum_{j=1}^{R} \delta(h_i^c, x_i^c) \quad (9)$$

$$diff\_miss^c = \sum_{l \neq class(x_i)} \frac{p(l)}{1 - p(class(x_i))} \sum_{j=1}^{R} \delta(m_i^c, x_i^c) \quad (10)$$

Then, the weights for categorical features will be updated as Eq.(11).

$$\lambda^c = \lambda^c - \frac{diff\_hit^c}{R} + \frac{diff\_miss^c}{R} \quad (11)$$

In this way, according to Eq.(8) and Eq.(11), the ReliefF algorithm can be used to obtain the weights for numerical and categorical features. Note that in the ReliefF algorithm to obtain the nearest neighbor, the distance function of each object-pair (x_i, x_j) is defined as

$$D(x_i, x_j) = \sum_{l=1}^{t} \lambda_l^r |x_{il} - x_{jl}| + \sum_{l=t+1}^{m} \lambda_l^c \delta(x_{il}^c, x_{jl}^c), \quad (12)$$

in which λ_l^r and λ_l^c are the current weights for numerical features and the categorical features respectively. In this algorithm, the λ_l^r and λ_l^c is initalized as $\frac{1}{m}$, and then they are updated with Eq.(8) and Eq.(11).

In addition, the ReliefF algorithm is initially proposed for supervised classification. In that application, each training sample has a determined class label. While, the processed samples are unlabeled in cluster analysis. To this end, we first employ the clustering result to label the samples. Then the ReliefF algorithm will be able to obtain the proper weight for each feature. By several times of iterations, the proposed new clustering algorithm will achieve the final optimal clustering result.

Although the proposed feature weighted clustering algorithm is constructed based on the fuzzy k-prototypes algorithm, it can also be used to modify the fuzzy k-means and k-modes algorithms. It is obvious that *when $\lambda^c = 0$, the new algorithm corresponds to the feature weighted fuzzy k-means algorithm, and when $\lambda^r = 0$, the new algorithm corresponds to the feature weighted fuzzy k-modes algorithm.* That is to say, the proposed feature weighted clustering algorithm unifies the k-means, k-modes and the k-prototype algorithms.

4   Experimental Results

To verify the effectiveness of the proposed feature weighted clustering algorithm, we conduct several test experiments with various data sets. By comparing with the traditional fuzzy k-means, k-modes and k-prototypes algorithms, the feasibleness and effectiveness of the new algorithm is demonstrated.

To evaluate the performance of the proposed algorithm objectively, here we select three labeled data sets as testbed. In the experiments, it is assumed that the class label of each sample is not available, and the different clustering algorithms are performed on the data set to assign the class label for each sample. Finally, by relabeling algorithm one can obtain the corresponding relationship between the real class labels and the assigned labels by clustering algorithm, and the classification performance will be able to achieved easily.

4.1   Experiment with Numerical Data Set

To test the classification performance of the proposed algorithm for the numerical data set, we adopt the famous IRIS data set as testbed [7].

The IRIS data set contains 150 samples in 4-dimensional feature space, and the 4 components of each sample represent the *petal length, petal width, sepal length* and *sepal width* of IRIS respectively. The whole data set is often divided into 3 categories, *i.e.*, *Setosa, Versicolor* and *Virginica*, each of which is composed of 50 samples. In feature space, the sample distribution of the Setosa are separated from the other 2 categories, while there exists overlapping between the Versicolor and the Virginica categories.

We employ the traditional fuzzy k-means algorithm (FKMe) and the proposed feature weighted FKMe algorithm to classify the IRIS data set. By relabeling the assigned class labels and the real labels of the 150 samples, the wrong classified number (WCN) of samples and the wrong classification rate (WCR) are computed as criteria for comparing the classification performance of the 2 clustering algorithms.

For the data set of IRIS, Hathaway provided the real cluster centers of the above 3 categories in 1995 [8].

$$p_1 = (5.00, 3.42, 1.46, 0.24),$$
$$p_2 = (5.93, 2.77, 4.26, 1.32),$$
$$p_3 = (6.58, 2.97, 5.55, 2.02).$$

Naturally, the sum of the squared error (SSE) between the obtained cluster centers by the algorithm and the real centers can also be used as criteria to evaluate the performance of the different clustering algorithms.

The clustering results of the FKMe algorithm and the feature weighted FKMe (FWFKMe) algorithm are presented in Table 1. It is obvious that the FWFKMe algorithm achieves not only the smaller wrong classification rate but also the more accuracy cluster centers than the traditional FKMe algorithm. The obtain weight matrix is $\lambda^r = [3.9720, 2.6880, 9.4350, 14.4810]$, which implies that the forth feature has the biggest contribution and the second feature has the smallest contribution for classification of these 3 categories.

Table 1. The comparison of performance between the FKMe and FWFKMe algorithms on the IRIS data set

Algorithms	WCN	WCR	The obtained cluster centers	SSE
FKMe	16	10.67%	$p_1 = (5.0062, 3.4242, 1.4684, 0.2492)$ $p_2 = (5.8946, 2.7460, 4.4154, 1.4273)$ $p_3 = (6.8484, 3.0750, 5.7283, 2.0741)$	0.1554
FWFKMe	6	4%	$p_1 = (5.0060, 3.4276, 1.4626, 0.2463)$ $p_2 = (5.9082, 2.7490, 4.2671, 1.3313)$ $p_3 = (6.6459, 3.0050, 5.5923, 2.0462)$	0.0125

4.2   Experiment with Categorical Data Set

To verify the classification performance of the proposed feature weighted clustering algorithm for the categorical data set, we employ the real data set of *bean diseases* as testbed [9]. The bean disease data set contains 47 recorders, and each of which is described with 35 features. Each recorder is labeled as one of the following 4 kinds of diseases, *i.e.*, *Diaporthe stem canker*, *Charcoal rot*, *Rhizoctonia root rot*, and *Phytophthora rot*. Except the Phytophthora rot with 17 recorders, all the other categories have 10 recorders.

The traditional k-modes (KMo) and the proposed feature weighted k-mode (FWKMo) algorithms are used to classify the data set of bean disease. The classification result is shown in Table 2, in which D,C,R,P denote one of disease types respectively. The FWKMo algorithm obtains a completely correct classification, which illustrates its effectiveness.

Fig.1 shows the obtained weights for features of bean disease data set by the proposed algorithm. It can be found that the weights of the 11-th, from the13-th to the 19-th and from the 29-th to the 34-th features are zeros, which

Table 2. The comparison of performance between the KMo and FWKMo algorithms on the *bean disease* data set

Clustering algorithms	D	C	R	P	WCN	WCR
FWKMo	10	10	10	17	0	0%
KMo	13	10	10	14	9	20%

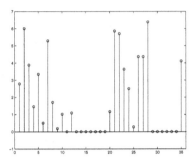

Fig. 1. The obtained weights for features of the *bean disease* data set

implies these 14 features having no contribution for classification of the above 4 categories. By checking the original data set, all the recorders have the same values in the 14 features. It proves that the proposed algorithm can not only improve the classification performance but also be used for feature optimal choice in pattern recognition.

4.3   Experiment with Mixed Data Set

As well known, the mixed data sets with numerical and categorical attributes are often encountered in data mining and other applications. To test the performance of the proposed algorithm to such mixed data set, we select the real data set of *zoo* as testbed [10], which contains 101 recorders, and each recorder including 15 categorical attributes and 1 numerical attribute.

The k-prototypes (KP) and the feature weighted KP (FWKP) algorithms are adopted to classify the data set of zoo. The traditional k-prototypes algorithm makes 19 mistakes in classification, while the FWKP algorithm makes 3 mistakes. The classification result of FWKP algorithm is shown in Table 3, in which the number with "*" denotes the amount of the wrong classified samples. Since the number of mammals is greater than others, it is partitioned into 2 classes falsely, *i.e.*, class 1 and class 7. The crawlers and amphibians are merged into one class. The other classes are achieved correct classification.

Fig.2 shows the obtained weights for categorical features of *zoo* data set. It is obvious that the forth feature has the biggest weight, which implies the biggest contribution in this feature. In fact the forth feature is the key attribute for distinguishing the mammals from others. The fourteenth feature has the smallest weight. In addition, the weight for the numerical attribute is $\lambda^r = 46.1842$.

Table 3. The classification result of the FWKP algorithms on the data set of *zoo*

Standard Categories	Class 1 (31)	Class 2 (20)	Class 3 (14)	Class 4 (10)	Class 5 (8)	Class 6 (8)	Class 7 (10)
Mammals (41)	31						10*
Birds (20)		20					
Fish (13)			13				
Insectology (8)				8			
Molluscs (10)				2*	8		
Crawlers (5)			1*			4	
Amphibians (4)						4	

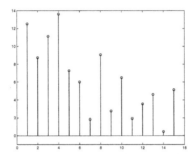

Fig. 2. The obtained weights for categorical features of the *zoo* data set

The above experimental results with various data sets demonstrate that the proposed feature weighted clustering algorithm is reasonable and effective.

5   Conclusions

This paper presents a novel feature weighted clustering algorithm. On the one hand, the proposed algorithm unifies the traditional k-means, k-modes and k-prototypes algorithms by introducing weights for each dimensional feature. On the other hand, it can obtain better classification performance than traditional clustering algorithms. In addition, the new algorithm can be used to analyze the different contributions among the features for classification, which is suitable for feature optimal choice in pattern recognition.

Of course, since the weights for features should be optimized by iterative ReliefF algorithm, the good performance of the proposed feature weighted clustering algorithm is at a cost of more CPU times. In addition, to employ the ReliefF algorithm, one have to specify a value for the number of nearest neighbors, R. However, how to choice an optimal value of R is an open problem, which is remained for future work.

References

1. He, Q.: Advance of the theory and application of fuzzy clustering analysis, Fuzzy System and Fuzzy Mathematics, **12(2)** (1998) 89–94. (In Chinese)
2. Huang, Z., Ng, M.K.: A fuzzy k-modes algorithm for clustering categorical data. IEEE Trans. on Fuzzy Systems, August, **7(4)** (1999) 446–452.
3. Huang, Z.: A fast clustering algorithm to cluster very large categorical data sets in data Mining. Proceedings of the SIGMOD Workshop on Research Issues on Data Mining and Knowledge Discovery, Dept. of Computer Science, The University of British Columbia, Canada (1997) 1–8.
4. Kononenko, I.: Estimating attributes: Analysis and extensions of Relief. Proceedings of the 7th European Conference on Machine Learning. Berlin: Springer (1994) 171–182.
5. Kira, K., Rendell, L.A.: A practical approach to feature selection, Proceedings of the 9th International Workshop on Machine Leaning, San Francisco (1992) 249–256.
6. Li, J., Gao, X., Jiao, L.: A CSA-Based Clustering Algorithm for Large Data Sets With Mixed Numeric and Categorical Values, Acta Electronica Sinica, **32(3)** (2004) 357–362.
7. Duda, R.O., Hart, P.E.: Pattern classification and scene analysis, New York (1973).
8. Hathaway, R.J., Bezdek, J.C.: Nerf C-means: Non-Euclidean relation fuzzy clustering, Pattern recognition, **27(3)** (1994) 429–437.
9. Michalski, R.S., Stepp, R.E.: Automated construction of classifications: Conceptual clustering versus numerical taxonomy, IEEE Trans. on PAMI, **(5)** (1983) 396–410.
10. Jollois, F.X., Nadif, M.: Clustering large categorical data. Advances in Knowedge Discovery and Data Mining, Heidelberg: Springer-Verlag (2002) 257–263.

User-Driven Fuzzy Clustering: On the Road to Semantic Classification

Andres Dorado[1], Witold Pedrycz[2], and Ebroul Izquierdo[1]

[1] Dept. of Electronic Engineering, Queen Mary,
University of London, Mile End Road, London E1 4NS, UK
{andres.dorado, ebroul.izquierdo}@elec.qmul.ac.uk
[2] Dept. of Electrical & Computer Engineering, University of Alberta,
9107 116 Street, Edmonton, AB, T6G 2V4, Canada
pedrycz@ee.ualberta.ca

Abstract. The work leading to this paper is semantic image classification. The aim is to evaluate contributions of clustering mechanisms to organize low-level features into semantically meaningful groups whose interpretation may relate to some description task pertaining to the image content. Cluster assignment reveals underlying structures in the data sets without requiring prior information. The semantic component indicates that some domain knowledge about the classification problem is available and can be used as part of the training procedures. Besides, data structural analysis can be applied to determine proximity and overlapping between classes, which leads to misclassification problems. This information is used to guide the algorithms towards a desired partition of the feature space and establish links between visual primitives and classes. It derives into partially supervised learning modes. Experimental studies are addressed to evaluate how unsupervised and partially supervised fuzzy clustering boost semantic-based classification capabilities.

1 Introduction

The objective of this paper is to evaluate contributions of clustering mechanisms to the first instance of the semantic problem in large-scale image databases: classification using generic semantic descriptions. The challenge relates to the automatic classification of visual information.

In order to reduce the complexity of the classification process and improve its accuracy, the image database is partitioned into classes according to the properties of the extracted low-level descriptors. The database is clustered by applying Fuzzy C-Means algorithm (ref [1][2]) on the descriptor space as presented in Sect. 2.

As presented in [3], three problems are found in clustering algorithms: (1) determining the optimal number of clusters to partition the data space, (2) the clusters do not match the expected groups, and (3) the cluster populations are equalized.

Since the number of classes in the underlying classification problem can be predetermined, the optimal number of clusters to partition the data space can be

D. Ślęzak et al. (Eds.): RSFDGrC 2005, LNAI 3641, pp. 421–430, 2005.
© Springer-Verlag Berlin Heidelberg 2005

computed in function of the class set cardinality. Subsequently, validity functions (cf. [4][5]) such as *the fuzziness performance index* [6] or *the compactness and separation* [7] can be used.

Furthermore, it can be assumed that an expert user has classified a small set of images per class in the database. Sect. 3 shows how this type of information can be used to perform structural analysis of the descriptor space.

The second problem can be tackled using the classified images (labeled data) to guide the clustering algorithm towards a desired partition of the descriptor space[8]. However, the nature of the problem demands an extension to deal with the subjectivity and fuzziness of the human interpretation [9]. Consequently, a fuzzy clustering method with partial supervision is proposed in Sect. 4.

Shape and size regularization methods have been proposed (cf. [10]) to handle the third problem, which occurs in response of the tendency presented in c-means clustering algorithms when grouping data within (hyper-) spherical or (hyper-) ellipsoid spaces based on the similarity to the cluster prototypes. Besides, as indicated in [11] the objective function being selected in advance predefines the shapes that want to be found in the data set. Accordingly, the method presented in Sect. 4 uses an objective function to modify the shape of the clusters .

Sect. 5 presents an experimental study in which clustering mechanisms have been applied to improve performance of semantic classifiers. Concluding remarks are given in Sect. 6.

2   Unsupervised Fuzzy Partition of the Feature Space

Clustering methods help to organize low-level features into groups which interpretation may relate to some classification or description task pertaining to the image content. Thus, feature vectors are clustered according to similarities among them [12]. Such a similarity between vectors is quantified or measured using a proximity metric.

Fuzzy clustering applies a partitioning-optimization technique based on minimization of an objective function that measures the desirability of partitions [13].

The criterion function is a scalar index that indicates the quality of the partition and has the form

$$J(X, \mathbf{V}, \mathbf{U}) = \sum_{i=1}^{N} \sum_{j=1}^{c} u_{ij}^m d^2(\mathbf{x}_i, \mathbf{v}_j) \ , \tag{1}$$

where X is a data space consisting of N p-dimension feature vectors to cluster, $\mathbf{V}$ is a set of $c(2 \le c \le N)$ cluster prototypes – centers, and $\mathbf{U}$ is a matrix belonging to the set of all possible fuzzy partitions defined by

$$\Im = \left\{ \mathbf{U} \in \Re_{Nc} \Big| \underset{\substack{1 \le i \le N \\ 1 \le j \le c}}{\forall} u_{ij} \in [0,1], \ \sum_{j=1}^{c} u_{ij} = 1, \ 0 < \sum_{i=1}^{N} u_{ij} < N \right\} \ , \tag{2}$$

where u_{ij} is the degree of membership of vector $\mathbf{x}_i$ in the cluster j, $\mathbf{v}_j$ is the p-dimension prototype of the cluster, $d^2(\cdot)$ is any distance norm expressing the

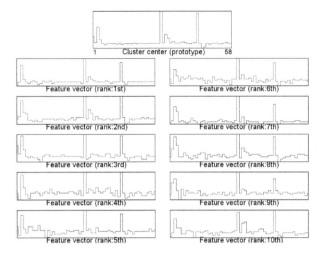

(a) Features vectors ranked by membership degree in the cluster

(b) Images used to extract the low-level vectors

Fig. 1. Sample of clustering results resembling semantic grouping (e.g. Outdoor or City view)

similarity between any feature vector and the prototype, and $m(1 < m < \infty)$ is a fuzzy exponent which determines the degree of overlap of fuzzy clusters.

Fig. 1 presents clustering results after applying fuzzy c-means onto a two-class classification problem using color descriptions. In this case feature similarity can be used to ascribe images to a common semantic class.

If clusters are manually labeled as a representative of a class with an identifying string, e.g. "skyline", then the problem may appear to have been finessed. However, the adequacy of such a solution depends on human interaction, which is completely subjective.

Besides, it is intuitive that two objects can be similar in their visual primitives but semantically different to a human observer. This is a drawback to classify images using only low-level vision and the foundation of the critical paradigm of "bridging the semantic gap"[14].

Alternatively, if clusters are described by an equivalence class

$$[\mathbf{v}_j]_E \doteq \{\mathbf{x}_i : \mathbf{x}_i \in X, E(\mathbf{v}_j) = 1\} \ , \tag{3}$$

where $\mathbf{v}_j (1 \leq j \leq c)$ is a cluster center (or prototype) and $\mathbf{x}_i (1 \leq i \leq N)$ is a feature vector associated with the i-th image in the data set X. Then, the set of equivalence classes

$$X/E \doteq \{[\mathbf{v}_j]_E\} \tag{4}$$

called a quotient set forms a partition of the feature space. The clustering outcome can be used as a pre-processing classification procedure based on the map from X onto X/E is defined by

$$\phi : X \mapsto X/E \ . \tag{5}$$

Information provided by this pre-classification step along with hints given by an expert user regarding to the problem domain knowledge are quite useful to design the semantic classifier and subsequently improve its accuracy.

3   Structural Data Analysis

As the image classifier is designed on the space formed with low-level visual primitives, it is worth to take another look at images by running cluster analysis and visualizing the relationships between the clusters and classes as well as linkages formed between the clusters themselves.

The first type of analysis provides an interesting insight as to the geometry and complexity of classes, homogeneity of clusters and proximity between the classes. Anticipating the possible complex geometry of individual classes, usually the number of cluster is kept higher than the number of categories of images.

As we are concerned with unsupervised learning, it is very likely that the cluster is not completely homogeneous and could comprise also some other patterns coming from remaining classes.

The first and second classes with higher percentage of patterns within the cluster are marked as *dominant classes*. Accepting the notation in which a size of dots corresponds to the percentage of the dominant class forming the cluster and a thickness of line originating from the cluster characterizes its linkages with other classes, we can succinctly portray the essential relationships between clusters, classes, and their geometry.

As illustrated in Fig. 2, clusters can be predominantly associated with a class with practically no linkages (associations) with other classes (e.g. $c_1 : \omega_3$). Others are very much a mixture of classes with very limited dominance of the most frequent class ($c_2 : \omega_1, \omega_2, \omega_3$). There is a weaker linkage between classes ω_1 and ω_3 than the one presented by classes ω_2 and ω_3.

Fig. 3 presents cluster-class relationships after applying fuzzy c-means onto a multi-class classification problem. The descriptor space is grouped into five semantic classes namely animal, building, city view, landscape, and vegetation.

The entries (bubble size) correspond to percentage of feature vectors (patterns) from each class assigned to the cluster.

Occurrence of several dominant classes contributes to higher values of the confusion rate coming with the specific cluster. Furthermore, ranking the frequent *class pairs* presenting higher levels of association helps to determine classes in which their abstractions are leading to misclassification. Tab. 1 summarizes this observation on a basis of the class-cluster dependencies.

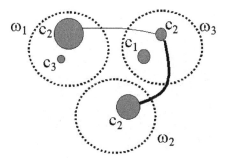

Fig. 2. Graphical visualization of clusters (c_1, c_2, c_3) and related classes $(\omega_1, \omega_2, \omega_3)$ along with the "classification" content of the clusters

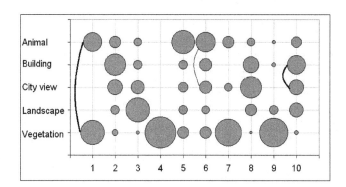

Fig. 3. Cluster-class dependencies (5×10). Class linkages are indicated by connecting lines. E.g. semantic relation between animal-vegetation (cluster 1) and building-city view (cluster 10) is stronger than animal-city view (cluster 6)

Looking at pair classes, vegetation-animal presents the highest confusion. This semantic overlapping can be observed at cluster and image level. One sample of the latter is given in Fig. 4 in which an animal image satisfies also criteria of vegetation.

Table 1. Ranking of frequent class pairs presenting higher levels of association leading to misclassification

Rank	Pair of classes
1	Vegetation - Animal
2	Building - City view
3	Vegetation - Landscape
4	Landscape - City view
5	Building - Animal

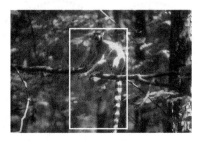

Fig. 4. Semantic overlapping: image categorized as "animal" with strong content of "vegetation"

4 Partially Supervised Clustering for Semantic Classification

Semantic-based image classification combines low and high-level numerical interpretations of the visual content. The built-in knowledge of descriptions enables systems to perform more "intelligent" processing on large-scale image databases.

The training data set is denoted by

$$X = \left\{ \underbrace{\mathbf{x}_1^1, \ldots \mathbf{x}_{n_1}^1}_{labeled\ 1} \cdots \underbrace{\mathbf{x}_1^c, \ldots, \mathbf{x}_{n_c}^c}_{labeled\ c} \underbrace{\mathbf{x}_1^u, \ldots, \mathbf{x}_{n_u}^u}_{unlabeled} \right\} = X^d \cup X^u \ , \qquad (6)$$

where superscripts $1, \ldots, c$ indicate the class label for design data and u for unlabeled data. It leads to a partition matrix with the form

$$\underbrace{\mathbf{U}}_{N \times c} = \left[\underbrace{\mathbf{U}^d}_{c \times N_d} \underbrace{\mathbf{U}^u}_{c \times N_u} \right]^T . \qquad (7)$$

Information concerning design data can also be provided using additional structures [11]. A binary vector to indicate whether the data is or is not labeled.

$$\mathbf{b} = [b_i], \ i = 1, 2, \ldots, N$$

$$b_i = \begin{cases} 1, & \mathbf{x}_i \in X^d \\ 0, & \mathbf{x}_i \in X^u \end{cases} \qquad (8)$$

and a matrix containing degrees of memberships for the known data

$$\mathbf{F} = [f_{ij}], \ i = 1, 2, \ldots, N; \ j = 1, 2, \ldots, c \ . \tag{9}$$

The partially supervised method, based on [3][11], defines the objective function as follows

$$J(X, \mathbf{V}, \mathbf{U}) = \sum_{i=1}^{N} \sum_{j=1}^{c} (1 - b_i + \alpha f_{ij} b_i)^m u_{ij}^m d^2(\mathbf{x}_i, \mathbf{v}_j) \ , \tag{10}$$

where the binary vector $\mathbf{b}$ and matrix $\mathbf{F}$ are defined by Eq. 8 and Eq. 9, respectively. $\alpha(\alpha \le 0)$ denotes a scaling factor to keep a balance between the supervised and unsupervided components within the minimization-optimization mechanism [11]. As studied in [8], the fuzzy exponent m is set up to 2. The value of α is suggested to be proportional to the rate N/N_d where N_d indicates the number of labeled data.

The necessary conditions for minimization of Eq. 10 can be obtained using the Lagrange multipliers technique with the constraints established at Eq. 2.

The distance matrix is calculated as

$$d_{ij}^2 \doteq \|\mathbf{x}_i - \mathbf{v}_j\|_{\mathbf{A}}^2 = (\mathbf{x}_i - \mathbf{v}_j)^T \mathbf{A}_j (\mathbf{x}_i - \mathbf{v}_j) \ , \tag{11}$$

where $\mathbf{A}_j$ is the identity matrix for Euclidean distance and inverse of fuzzy variance-covariance matrix for Mahalanobis distance [11]. The latter is computed as follows

$$\mathbf{A}_j^{-1} = \left[\frac{1}{\rho_j det(\mathbf{P}_j)} \right]^{\frac{1}{n}} \mathbf{P}_j \ , \tag{12}$$

where typically $\rho_j = 1$, $j = 1, \ldots, c$, and

$$\mathbf{P}_j = \frac{\sum_{i=1}^{N} u_{ij}^2 (\mathbf{x}_i - \mathbf{v}_j)(\mathbf{x}_i - \mathbf{v}_j)^T}{\sum_{i=1}^{N} u_{ij}^2} \ . \tag{13}$$

Cluster prototypes are defined by

$$v_j = \frac{\sum_{i=1}^{N} (1 - b_i + \alpha f_{ij} b_i)^2 u_{ij}^2 \mathbf{x}_i}{\sum_{i=1}^{N} (1 - b_i + \alpha f_{ij} b_i)^2 u_{ij}^2} \tag{14}$$

and the membership degrees are computed by

$$u_{ij} = \begin{cases} f_{ij}, & b_i = 1 \\ \left[\sum_{k=1}^{c} \left(\frac{d_{ij}}{d_{ik}} \right)^2 \right]^{-1}, & b_i = 0 \end{cases} \ . \tag{15}$$

The complete algorithm is summarized in Tab. 2

Table 2. Partially supervised clustering algorithm

Given	$X = X^d \cup X^u$, `data space containing labeled and unlabeled data`
	$N = N_d + N_u$, `number of feature vectors`
	c, `number of clusters`
	$\mathbf{b}$, `indicator vector`
	$\mathbf{F}$, `known membership matrix`
	δ, `criterion used in the Picard Iteration`
	E, `maximum number of epochs (optional stop condition)`
Step 1	`Initialize the partition matrix randomly,` $\mathbf{U}_{(0)}$ `including` $\mathbf{F}$
Step 2	`Calculate cluster centers using Eq. 14`
Step 3	`Compute the distance matrix applying Eq. 11`
Step 4	`Update the partition matrix using Eq. 15`
Step 5	`Compare` $\mathbf{U}_{(t+1)}$ `to` $\mathbf{U}_{(t)}$. `If` $\|\mathbf{U}_{(t+1)} - \mathbf{U}_{(t)}\| < \delta$ `or` $t > E$ `then STOP`
	`Otherwise return to step 2 with` $\mathbf{U}_{(t)} = \mathbf{U}_{(t+1)}$

5 Experimental Results

Fig. 5 depicts a two-class synthetic data set presented in [3], which is used to evaluate clustering results applying the unsupervised (left) and partially supervised
(right) algorithms presented above.

Several experiments were conducted using a feature space built with color
and texture descriptions extracted from 1000 images. Pictures were categorized

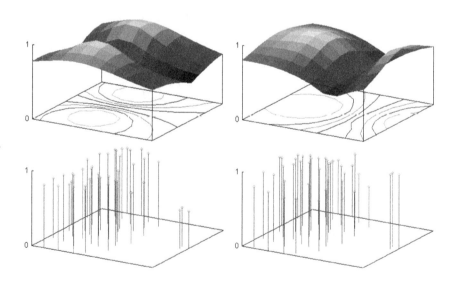

Fig. 5. Space partition, membership degrees, cluster centers, and shapes obtained by
unsupervised clustering (left) do not match the expected solution as does its counterpart the partially supervised algorithm (right) using few labeled data

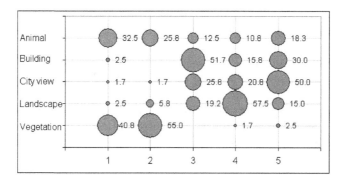

(a) Unsupervised feature space partition

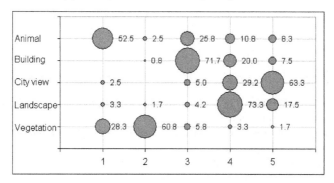

(b) Partially supervised feature space partition

Fig. 6. Cluster-class dependencies (5×5) Values next to the bubbles indicate percentage of patterns within the cluster. Pre-classification accuracy is improved from 49% to 64.3% by labeling 17% of training data

into a certain class (animal, building, city view, landscape, and vegetation), if the camera was focused in an object satisfying the name of the class.

As is observed in Fig. 6, partially supervised clustering achieves more optimal grouping and reduces mixture of classes within clusters. The new clusters are more accurate in terms of semantic categorization.

6   Conclusions

Information obtained through clustering algorithms (prototypes, space partition) and analysis (class-cluster dependencies, ranking of overlapped categories) provides a better insight of the image abstractions, refine the classifier design, and improve classification performance. More specific "user-driven" information is incorporated by tagging global and local annotations, e.g. region-oriented labels, and creating a keyword profile for each cluster.

Ranking of dominant classes along with information given by pair classes and the strength of their linkage are useful to perform either individual feature selection or feature weighting in order to minimize the average within-cluster dispersion and maximizes the average between-cluster dispersion.

Clustering outcomes can be used to learn support vectors and subsequently define an optimal decision hyperplane to classify new patterns. Alternatively, cluster prototypes can be used in the design of a radial basis function type of classifier. Thus, partially supervised clustering equipped with an objective function establishes a solid base to build a more accurate semantic categorization.

Acknowledgements

Support from the Natural Sciences and Engineering Research Council (NSERC) and Canada Research Chair (W. Pedrycz) is gratefully acknowledged.

References

1. Dunn, J.: A fuzzy relative of the isodata process and its use in detecting compact well-separated clusters. Journal of Cybernetics **3** (1973) 32–57
2. Bezdek, J.: Pattern recognition with fuzzy objective function algorithms. Plenum Press, New York (1981)
3. Bensaid, A., Hall, L., Bezdek, J., Clarke, L.P.: Partially supervised clustering for image segmentation. Pattern Recognition **29** (1996) 859–871
4. Pedrycz, W.: Knowledge-based clustering: from data to information granules. Wiley, US (2005)
5. Halkidi, M., Batistakis, Y., Vazirgiannis, M.: On clustering validation techniques. J. Intell. Inf. Syst. **17** (2001) 107–145
6. Roubens, M.: Fuzzy clustering algorithms and their cluster validity. European Journal of Operational Research **10** (1982) 294–301
7. Xie, X., Beni, G.: A validity measure for fuzzy clustering. IEEE Trans. on Pattern Analysis and Machine Learning **13** (1991) 841–847
8. Pedrycz, W.: Algorithms of fuzzy clustering with partial supervision. Pattern Recognition Letter **13** (1985) 13–20
9. Pedrycz, W.: Fuzzy sets in pattern recognition: methodology and methods. Pattern Recognition **23** (1990) 121–146
10. Borgelt, C., Kruse, R.: Shape and size regularization in expectation maximization and fuzzy clustering. In: Proc. 8th European Conf. on Principles and Practice of Knowledge Discovery in Databases, Germany, Springer (2004) 52–62
11. Pedrycz, W., Waletzky, J.: Fuzzy clustering with partial supervision. IEEE Trans. on Systems, Man, and Cybernetics–Part B: Cybernetics **27** (1997) 787–795
12. Jain, A.K., Murty, M.N., Flynn, P.J.: Data clustering: a review. ACM Computing Surveys **31** (1999) 264–323
13. Bezdek, J.: A convergence theorem for the isodata clustering algorithms. IEEE Trans. on Pattern Analysis and Machine Intelligence **2** (1980) 1–8
14. Dorai, C., Venkatesh, S.: Bridging the semantic gap with computational media aesthetics. IEEE Multimedia **10** (2003) 15–17

Research on Clone Mind Evolution Algorithm

Gang Xie, Hongbo Guo, Keming Xie, and Wenjing Zhao

College of Information Engineering, Taiyuan University of Technology,
030024 Taiyuan, Shanxi, P.R. China
xiegangtut@yahoo.com.cn

Abstract. A new algorithm of evolutionary computing, which combines clone selective algorithm involved in artificial immunity system theory and mind evolution algorithm (MEA) proposed in reference [4], is presented in this paper. Based on similartaxis which is the one of MEA operators, some operators borne by the new algorithm including clone mutation, clone crossover, clone selection, is also introduced. Then the clone mind evolution algorithm (CMEA) is developed by using the diversity principle of antigen-antibody. The simulating results of the representative evaluation function show that the problem of degeneration phenomenon existing in GA and MEA can be perfectly solved, and the rapidity of convergence is evidently improved by CMEA studied in the paper. In the example of the solution to the numerical problem, the search range of solution is expanded and the possibility of finding the optimal solution is increased.

1 Introduction

In the research field which modern information science and life science overlap and interpenetrate to form into, artificial immune system (AIS) is an other research focus subsequently following cranial nerves (e.g. neural network) and evolutionary computing (e.g. GA), which is inspired by the biological immune system (BIS). BIS mechanics based research on computing model is concentrated on two main aspects: network model of AIS and immune learning algorithm. The former aims to construct various computing model, based on the clone selective theory of Bernet [1] and the unique network adjusting theory of Jernet [2], to imitate or explain immune phenomena by simulation experiments. The latter is focused on computing methods with stronger intentness or implement strategies based on existed system models. Clonal selection algorithm [3] that is presented by Castro, Kim, Du, etc. is one of outstanding achievement. The characteristics of memory, learning and evolution are utilized to implement the task such as machine learning or pattern recognition. Mind evolution algorithm (MEA) [4] that is a kind of evolution computing method has been applied in the field of intelligent control [5]. In this paper, how to utilize practicable clone selective behavior to design suitable clone selective optimal method in order to improving the optimal result of MEA is studied.

D. Ślęzak et al. (Eds.): RSFDGrC 2005, LNAI 3641, pp. 431–440, 2005.

2 Philosophy of MEA

The nature evolution of biology depends on inheritance and nature selection. The evolutionary process will experience thousands of years. Comparatively, the evolutionary process of the human's mind is short. The reason is that human being cannot only adapts actively the change of the nature environment but studies knowledge and experience from predecessor and other people selfconsciously. This phenomenon is called similartaxis. During the recent years, with the development of the exchange way of the information, the development of human's mind is accelerating. At the same time, many innovations have been acquired by human. This phenomenon is called dissimilation. Depending on the similartaxis and dissimilation, people develop science and technology.

MEA is a new type of evolutional computing method that simulates evolutional process of people's thought. It uses the concept 'population' of GA, but is radically different from it. "Similartaxis" and "dissimilation" operators are presented. Since memory function and directional study mechanism are introduced and population optimization replaces the individual optimization, the intelligence of the algorithm is improved and the search efficiency is also enhanced.

2.1 Population and Group

The set of all individuals is called a population. The population is divided into several groups, and there are two main classes of groups: the winner groups and the temporary groups.

2.2 Billboard

The billboards, which record the information of the individuals or the groups including theirs serial number, operation and score, provide the environment of information communication among the individuals or the groups. There are two kinds of billboards: one is the local billboard which is used to record information of individuals in each group; another is the global billboard which is used to record information of each group in the whole population.

2.3 Similartaxis and Dissimilation

"Similartaxis" performs local competition inside subpopulations among individuals and produces local optimal points. At first N individuals are distributed normally around one "winner" with the variance δ and then the scores of them are computed and the one with highest score is the "winner" that will take part in the global competition delegating the subpopulation in the following dissimilation.

"Dissimilation" performs global competition. The "winners" of subpopulations from "similartaxis" compete with each other and those having high score are kept to next round but the others are eliminated and are replaced by new individuals distributed in the solution space. This makes the evolution of the population heads toward the optimal point and gets there finally.

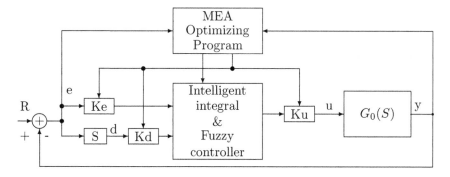

Fig. 1. Schematic diagram of an optimal fuzzy controller based MEA

2.4 Convergence

It can be proved by means of Markov chains that population of discrete state executed by similartaxis operator is convergent at the global optimal state with total probability. But because of localness of similartaxis, there is little probability that the local optimal state transfers to the global optimal state. In order to this transfer probability, it is necessary to introduce dissimilation operator [6].

2.5 The Application of MEA

MEA has been successfully applied to intelligent control. The principium of an optimal fuzzy controller OFC design method based on MEA is showed in figure 1. At first the system and the controller are constructed and the membership functions are built with conventional method. Then the fuzzy rules and quantified factors and proportional factors are optimized by use of MEA. During the optimizing process, the universe of the parameters (including the fuzzy control rules and quantified factors and proportional factors) is divided into different subspaces according to their own solution range and then MEA searches the best solutions in each subspace and forms a number of parameter groups and evaluates each group synthetically with one criterion. The optimization is along the direction that the criterion value reduces. The criterion is selected by designers practically to meet the demand of system performance.

When the parameters that make the criterion value least are found, so is the optimal operation condition.

The design procedures are shown as following:

1. Decide controller structure.
2. Select appropriate membership functions, fuzzy variables and universe.
3. Set the solution spaces of parameters.
4. Make optimizing program and optimize the parameters.
5. End of design.

It is convenient to complete this method by software and easy to generalize it. Once it is completed, the program can be used to design any fuzzy controller and what the designer need to do is to reset a number of parameters and membership functions.

3   Mechanism of Clone Selection

Nowadays, most of researches on the intelligent systems revolve around the mechanism of inspiring and learning of person brain. Over the last few years, there has been an ever increasing interest in the area of artificial immune systems (AIS) and their applications.The ability of the immune system to respond to an antigen exists before it ever encounters that antigen.

The immune system relies on the prior formation of an incredibly diverse population of B cells and T cells.When an animal is exposed to an antigen, some subpopulation of its bone marrow derived cells (B lymphocytes) respond by producing antibodies (Ab). Each cell secretes only one kind of antibody, which is relatively specific for the antigen. By binding to these antibodies (receptors), and with a second signal from accessory cells, such as the T-helper cell, the antigen stimulates the B cell to proliferate (divide) and mature into terminal (non-dividing) antibody secreting cells, called plasma cells. The various cell divisions (mitosis) generate a clone, i.e., a set of cells that are the progeny of a single cell. While plasma cells are the most active antibody secretors, large B lymphocytes, which divide rapidly, also secrete Ab, albeit at a lower rate. While B cells secrete Ab, T cells play a central role in the regulation of the B cell response and are preeminent in cell mediated immune responses. Lymphocytes, in addition to proliferating and/or differentiating into plasma cells, can differentiate into long-lived B memory cells. Memory cells circulate through the blood, lymph and tissues, and when exposed to a second antigenic stimulus commence to differentiate into large lymphocytes capable of producing high affinity antibodies, pre-selected for the specific antigen that had stimulated the primary response [7]. The clou of reference [8] is that antibody in cell surface as offspring of natural exists in the form of receptor, and can selectively react to antigen. The reaction, which takes place between antigen and receptor, can cause to clonal breeding of cell. So the great number of clonal cell owns the identical specificity of antibody. Some of these clonal cells in which some cells differentiate to a generation of antibody cell, and others form immunity memory cell so as to attend the second immunity reaction later. Clone selective theory acts as an important enlightenment role for improving the performance of MEA, because of the clone selective course of antibody possesses learning, memory development, diversity of antibody, selfadaptive adjustment and such performance, so as to prevent the phenomenon of "prematurity" well, efficiently improve the rapidity of optimization and advance the quality of optimization result.

4   Clone Mind Evolutionary Algorithm (CMEA)

In general, the following steps of CMEA are made up of 6 key steps illustrated in figure 2. It is well known that antigen, antibody, affinity of antigen-antibody is respectively corresponded to the object function, optimal solution, and match degree of solution to the object function.

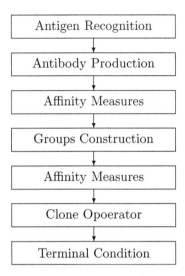

Fig. 2. Diagram of CMEA

1. **step1: antigen recognition** Choose the target function and various constraints as the antigen of CMEA, then the immune system confirms that the antigen invades;
2. **step2: initial antibody production** While iterating at the first time, the antibody is produced at random in the whole solution space, or by means of activating memory cells. At the same time, the foregone antigen is removed, and M individuals from the database including the optimal antibody (optimal solution) are choose to produce initial antibody groups;
3. **step3: affinity calculation** Separately calculates the affinity between antigen and antibody, and the affinity between antibody and antibody;
4. **step4: groups' construction** N individuals with supreme affinity are arranged in an order. For every individual with supreme affinity, k-1 individuals are randomly choosed among the remaining individuals, and are constructed to a group (the size of group is k). Thus N groups are produced by the identical operation to the N individual of supreme affinity;
5. **step5:** Calculate every individual affinity in each group again;
6. **step6:** According to clone operators, produce new group with the following steps:
   (a) **clone:** Choose A(m) individuals that own higher antibody-antigen affinity and lower antibody- antibody affinity, then regard them as cloned individuals and add clonal results to new groups.
   (b) **clone mutation:** Carry out clone mutation operation on the groups after completing clone operator. In order to reserve the original information of antibody population, do not operate mutation to A(m) individuals.

(c) **clone crossover:** Choose A(n) individuals that have higher antibody-antibody affinity and lower antigen-antibody affinity, and uniformly code them. Then, execute crossover operator.

(d) **clone selection:** Select M new individuals owning the highest affinity to form a new generation of population in order to keep the number of individuals. Meanwhile, other rejected individuals are deleted from groups.

7. **step7: Terminal condition** Repeat step5 and step6, until satisfy termination condition (convergence criterion), optimal course end. In this paper, limited iteration times are adopted as termination condition. Choose the optimal individual as the result of algorithm.

5 Convergence Analysis of CMEA

In generally speaking, we consider maximum problem in this paper, to find solution for an optimal problem $\varphi : \prod_{i=1}^{m} [d_i, u_i \to R(d_i \prec u_i)]$, where m is the number of the optimized variables, i.e. $X = \{x_1, x_2, \ldots, x_m\}$. The antigen $\varphi : R^m \to R$ is the optimized function. Real number code is adopted in this paper.

Antibody group $\bar{A} = \{A_1, A_2, \ldots, A_n\}$ is an nth multi group; it is a point in the Antibody population space S^n[9].

Definition 1. $M = \{\bar{A}| \max(f(\bar{A})) = f^*, \forall \bar{A} \in S^n\}$ *is called satisfied population set, that is, any initial antibody population in M at least contains a best solution.*

The mathematic model of CMEA can be described as: after real number coded, CEMA process is a memorized stochastic walk form one state to another state, which can be described by a Markov Chain process.

In the antibody population space S^n, antibody group transferred from the state $\bar{A}(k) = \{A_1(k), A_2(k) \ldots A_n(k)\}$ to a new one $\bar{A}(k+1) = \{A_1(k+1), A_2(k+2) \ldots A_n(k+1)\}$ after the CMEA operation and this process is expressed by: $\bar{A}(k+1) = T(\bar{A}(k)) = T_d^c \circ T_s^c \circ T_r^c \circ T_c^c(\bar{A}(k))$

Where, T_d^c is clone operator, T_s^c is clone selection operator, T_r^c is clone recombination operator, and T_c^c is clone mutation operator.

Mark $\bar{A}(k) = X, \bar{A}(k+1) = Y$ then the transition probability $p_{xy}(k) = p\{\bar{A}(k+1) = Y|\bar{A}(k) = X\}$

When $X \neq Y$:

$$p_{xy}(k) = \begin{cases} 0 & i \in M, j \notin M \\ \prod_{j=1}^{n} p_d p_s^k \left(\sum_{i=1}^{q_j-1} (p_m^i)^{d(X,Y)} (1 - p_m^i)^{l-d(X,Y)} \right) & other \end{cases} \tag{1}$$

when $X = Y$:

$$p_{xy}(k) = \begin{cases} 1 - \sum\limits_{L \neq Y}^{|M|} \prod\limits_{j=1}^{n} p_d p_s^k \left(\sum\limits_{i=1}^{q_j-1} \left(p_m^{i^{d(X,Y)}} (1-p_m^i)^{l-d(X,Y)} \right) \right) & i \in M, j \in M \\ 1 - \sum\limits_{L \neq Y}^{|S^n|-|M|} \prod\limits_{j=1}^{n} p_d p_s^k \left(\sum\limits_{i=1}^{q_j-1} (p_m^i)^{d(X,L)} (1-p_m^i)^{l-d(X,L)} \right) & i \notin M, j \notin M \end{cases} \tag{2}$$

Equation (1), (2) are the main model of the CMEA.

Theorem 1. *The antibody population series of the CMEA algorithm is $\{\bar{A}, k \geq 0\}$, and it is a finite nonhomogeneous reducible Markow chain.*

Proof. Any antibody in an antibody population $\bar{A} = \{A_1, A_2 \ldots A_n\}$ is a limited real number in a limited population, so its state variable is changing in a limited state space S^n, for p_s^k has relation with population state in time k, so does $p_{xy}(k)$, so it is nonhomogeneous.

From the definition of M , M is a closed set, because:

1. If $X, Y \in M$, then $p_{xy}(k) > 0, p_{xy}(k) > 0$ i.e.$X \leftrightarrow Y$
2. If $X \in M$ and $Y \notin M$, then $p_{xy}(k) = 0$, i.e. $X \nrightarrow Y$

So $\{\bar{A}(k), k \geq 0\}$ is reducible.
Thus, the theorem 1 is proved.

Theorem 2. *The antibody population series $\{\bar{A}(k), k \geq 0\}$ of the CMEA algorithm is convergent to satisfied population set with probably 1. That is, to any initial state $\bar{A}_0$*

$$\lim_{k \to \infty} P\{\bar{A}(k) \in M | \bar{A}(0) = \bar{A}_0\} = 1 \tag{3}$$

Proof. Without loss of generality, suppose $f(A)$ has only one maximum, mark: $F(A(k)) = \max\{f(A(k)_i), i = 1, 2, \ldots n\}$,

$$P(k) = p\{\bar{A}(k+1) = Y | \bar{A}(k) = X; X, Y \in S^n\} = (p_{xy}(k); X, Y \in S^n) \tag{4}$$

Equation 4 is called the state transfer matrix.
To selection operator, there exist:

$$p_s^k = \begin{cases} 0 & F(X) > F(Y) \\ 1 & F(X) \leq F(Y) \end{cases} \tag{5}$$

Then for $F(Y) \geq F(X)$, we have: $p_{xy}(k) = p\{T_d^c \circ T_s^c \circ T_r^c \circ T_c^c = Y\} > 0$ if $F(Y) < F(X)$ we have: $p_{xy}(k) = 0$,Mark:

$$P(\infty) = \lim_{k \to \infty} P(k) = (P_\infty(X,Y); X, Y \in S^n) \tag{6}$$

Then:

$$P_\infty(X,Y) = \begin{cases} > 0 & F(X) \geq F(Y) \\ = 0 & F(Y) < F(X) \end{cases} \tag{7}$$

Obviously: $P(\infty)$ is a stochastic matrix, and $\{\bar{A}(k), k \geq 0$ is strong ergodic. To any initial state $\bar{A}_0$, we have:

$$\lim_{k \to \infty} P\{\bar{A}(k) = Y|\bar{A}(0) = \bar{A}_0\} = \pi_\infty(Y) \tag{8}$$

And $\sum\limits_{\gamma \in M}^{k \to \infty} \pi_\infty(Y) = 1$, so:

$$\lim_{k \to \infty} P\{\bar{A}(k) = Y|\bar{A}(0) = \bar{A}_0| = \sum_{Y \in M} \pi_\infty(Y) = 1 \tag{9}$$

This completes the proof of Theorem 2.

6   Research Example

In order to verify the preceding analysis, numerical experimentation employing MEA, CMEA and GA are studied by the following classical testing functions.

1. $fit_1 = \sum\limits_{i=1}^{3} x_i^2 \; x_i \in [-5,5]$

   The function is adopted for testing rapidity of convergence, the global minimum $f(0,0,0) = 0$.
2. $fit_2 = 100(x_1^2 - x_2)^2 + (1 - x_1)^2 \; x_i \in [-5,5]$

   The minimum point (0, 0) of this function locates at curved surface with a long and narrow paraboloid, so it is difficult to find the minimum. The function is used to test immaturity convergence.
3. $fit_3 = 0.5 + [\sin^2(x_1^2 + x_2^2)^{1/2} - 0.5]/[1 + 0.001(x_1^2 + x_2^2)]^2$

Minimum of this function is fit3(0,0)=0. Within scope of 3.14 around (0, 0), there are many protuberant department that is the global suboptimal points. The function characteristic that is properties of strong oscillation and the global optimal point surrounded by the suboptimal global points make it is very difficult to find the global optimal solution. In experiments, let M=200, there kinds of algorithms are respectively examined 100 times with evaluation function. But if the optimal solution is not improved within 10 times, then the calculating is terminal in advance. In every operation cycle, if the value of fitness is smaller than the threshold 0.0001, the algorithm is regarded as success, otherwise failure. The number of successful optimization is denoted as NTS, and the number of failure is denoted as NTF, where NTS+NTF=100. The sum of all successful iteration times divided by the successes times is the mean successful iteration times denoted as NMIS. Table 1 shows test data.

Showed from experiment results, the searching and optimization ability of CMEA is greater than of MEA and GA. Especially, when the extreme point is surrounded by the local subextreme points, more embody the superiority ofCMEA. Function fit3 optimization result shows, in 100 times operations, MEA succeeds four only, and CMEA have 100% rate of success. The optimization result of CMEA is 10e-9 times more accurate than that of MEA.

Table 1. Optimization Result

Evaluation function	Algorithm	Threshold	N_{TS}	N_{TF}	N_{MIS}	Optimal evaluation value
fit_1	MEA		100	0	20.24	5.252053e-5
	CMEA		100	0	19.27	2.225179e-14
	Ga		99	1	69.20	6.628564e-6
fit_2	MEA		84	16	79.37	1.864154e-4
	CMEA	0.0001	100	0	8.11	1.272805e-7
	GA		100	0	98.75	3.464789e-5
fit_3	MEA		4	96	77	9.172560e-5
	CMEA		100	0	11.86	2.947642e-14
	GA		82	18	42.63	1.096471e-6

7   Conclusion

Both CMEA and MEA belong to group search strategy, and emphasize the information exchanging among the individuals of population. So there are similarities between CMEA and MEA.

Firstly on the structure, both of them circularly proceed with a course that is "initial population production → dividing into smaller groups → calculating evaluation function → exchanging information among individuals of groups → producing a new generation of population". Population is divided into several groups to prevent information exchange among groups. So it is helpful for the population differentiation, for the maintenance of diversity and for the prevention of prematurity, eventually the optimal solution is obtained with greater probability; Secondly on the property, both of them inhere parallelism in essence so as to make it difficult to fall into the local minimum in searching process.

On the other hand, due to the introduced operators such as antigen recognition, clone, clone mutation, clone crossover, and clone selection etc., there are some difference between them as follows:

1. clone mutation operator does not affect on the optimal solution which is held in memory units. Thus it ensures to converge fast the global optimal solution;
2. The considerable calculation is caused by affinity measure, including the affinity of the antibody-antigen and the affinity of antibody-antibody. But it do not influence the rapidity of convergence;
3. By promoting or restraining the antibody production, the function of self-regulation is achieved, and the diversity of individuals is guaranteed. Considering both the local and global search ability, it is especially suitable to optimize the multimodal function;
4. Mutation operator of MEA is replaced by clone crossover and clone mutation, thus it is sure to extend the search region and to ensure the convergence to the global optimal solution.

Acknowledgements

This work was financed by Chinese Nation Nature Science Foundation (60374029), and Visiting Scholar Foundation of Shanxi Province, P. R. China (2004-18).

References

1. Burnet, F. M.: The Clonal Selection Theory of Acquired Immunity.Cambridge University Press (1958)
2. Jerne, N. K.: The immune system. Scientific American, Vol.229(1) (1973) 52–60
3. Castro, L. N. D., Zuben, F. J. V.: An evolutionary immune system for data clustering. Proceedings of Sixth Brazlilian Symulation on Neural Network (2000) 84–89
4. Sun, C.Y., Xie, K.M., Cheng, M.Q.: Mind-Evolution-Based Machine Learning Framework and New Development. Journal of Taiyuan University of Technology, Vol.30(5) (1999) 453–457
5. Xie, K.M., Du, Y.G., Sun, C.Y.: Application of the mind-evolution-based machine learning in mixture-ratio calculation of raw materials cement. Proceedings of the World Congress on Intelligent Control and Automation (WCICA), Vol.1 (2000) 132–134
6. Wang, C.L., Xie, K.M., Sun, C.Y.: A Study of convergence of mind evolution based machine learning. Journal of computer research and development, Vol.37(7) (2000) 838–842
7. Castro, L. N. D., Zuben, F. J. V.: The Clonal Selection Algorithm with Engineering Applications. Proc. of GECCO'00, Workshop on Artificial Immune Systems and Their Applications, Nevada (2000) 36–37
8. Zhou, G.Y.: Principles of Immunology. Shanghai Press of Science and Technology Literature (2000)
9. Jiao, L.C.: Intelligent Signal and Image Process. Xidian University Intelligent Information Process Institute (2003) 282–283

A Study on the Global Convergence Time Complexity of Estimation of Distribution Algorithms

R. Rastegar and M.R. Meybodi

Computer Engineering Department, Amirkabir University, Tehran, Iran
{rrastegar, meybodi}@ce.aut.ac.ir

Abstract. The Estimation of Distribution Algorithm is a new class of population based search methods in that a probabilistic model of individuals are estimated based on the high quality individuals and used to generate the new individuals. In this paper we compute 1) some upper bounds on the number of iterations required for global convergence of EDA 2) the exact number of iterations needed for EDA to converge to global optima.

1 Introduction

Genetic Algorithms (GAs) are a class of optimization algorithm motivated from the theory of natural selection and genetic recombination. It tries to find better solution by selection and recombination of promising solution. It works well in wide verities of problem domains. The poor behaviors of genetic algorithms in some problems, in which the designed operators of crossover and mutation do not guarantee that the building block hypothesis is preserved, have led to the development of other type of algorithms. The search for techniques to preserve building blocks has led to the emergence of new class of algorithm called Probabilistic Model Building Genetic Algorithm (PMBGA) also known as Estimation of Distribution Algorithm (EDA). The principle concept in this new technique is to prevent disruption of partial solutions contained in an individual by giving them high probability of being presented in the child individual. It can be achieved by building a probabilistic model to represent correlation between variables in individual and build model to generate next population.

The EDAs are classified into three classes based on the interdependencies between variables in individuals [9]. Instances of EDAs algorithm include Population-based Incremental Learning (PBIL) [1], Univariate Marginal Distribution Algorithm (UMDA) [10], Learning Automata-based Estimation of Distribution Algorithm (LAEDA) [14], Compact Genetic Algorithm (cGA) [7] for no dependencies model, Mutual Information Maximization for Input Clustering (MIMIC) [3], Combining Optimizer with Mutual Information Trees (COMIT) [2] for bivariate dependencies model, and Factorized Distribution Algorithm (FDA) [11], Bayesian Evolutionary Algorithm (BOA) [13] for multiple dependencies model, to name a few.

Some researchers have studied the working mechanism of EDAs. Mühlenbein [10], González et al [4][5], Höhfeld and Rudolph [6] have studied the behavior of UMDA and PBIL. Mühlenbein and Mahnig [12] discussed the convergence of FDA for

D. Ślęzak et al. (Eds.): RSFDGrC 2005, LNAI 3641, pp. 441–450, 2005.
© Springer-Verlag Berlin Heidelberg 2005

separable additively decomposable functions. In [15], Zhang and Mühlenbein proved that EDAs with infinite population size globally converge. Despite the fact that working mechanisms of EDAs has been studied, the time complexity and the speed of convergence of EDAs algorithm are not known. In this paper we propose some results on the number of iterations needed for EDAs to converge globally when population size is infinite. Our approach is proposed in two sections. At first some upper bounds on the number of iterations required for global convergence of EDA are calculated and then in the second section the exact number of iterations needed for EDA to converge to global optima is calculated.

The rest of paper is organized as follows. Section 2 briefly presents the EDA algorithm and its modeling when EDA uses an infinite population size. Section 3 and 4 demonstrate some theorems about time complexity of EDAs. Conclusion is given in final section.

2   Estimation of Distribution Algorithm with Infinite Population Size

Given a search space D and a positive and continuous function $f(\mathbf{x})$: $D \rightarrow \mathfrak{R}^{\geq 0}$, find

$$\max\{f(\mathbf{x}); \mathbf{x} \in D\} \ . \tag{1}$$

Let D^* be a set of all points at which function f reaches its maximum value f_{max}. The steps of the EDA algorithm for solving such an optimization problem are described below.

1-**Initialization**: generate an initial population, $\xi(0)$, of N individuals.
2-**Selection**: choose Se $(Se<N)$ individuals from population $\xi(n)$ (i.e. population in iteration n) to form the parent population $\xi^S(n)$ using a selection schema such as truncation, tournament or proportional selection schema.
3-**Updating**: perform updating operations on individuals of parent population at iteration n, $\xi^S(n)$, and generate new individuals to form the new population at time n, $\xi(n+1)$, e.g. $\xi(n+1)=\xi^S(n)$.
4- If $E\{f(\mathbf{X})| \xi(n+1)\}=f_{max}$ then stop else go to step 2 .

Condition of step 4 of the above algorithm is met when every individual in the population is an optimal solution, that is, the EDA has globally converged.

Let the underlying probability distribution functions for the individuals of $\xi(n)$ and $\xi^S(n)$ be $P(\mathbf{X}|\xi(n))$ and $P(\mathbf{X}| \xi^S(n))$, respectively. By the famous Glivenko-Canteli theorem [17], the empirical probability density functions induced by individuals in $\xi(n)$ and $\xi^S(n)$ will converge to $P(\mathbf{X}|\xi(n))$ and $P(\mathbf{X}| \xi^S(n))$ respectively, as the sizes of $\xi(n)$ and $\xi^S(n)$ tend to infinity. Therefore $P(\mathbf{X}|\xi(n))$ and $P(\mathbf{X}| \xi^S(n))$ can be thought of as the population and the parent population at iteration n in EDA with infinite population [15]. Below we describe the selection schemes used in this paper.

The Truncation Selection Schema: Truncation selection ranks all the individuals in population $\xi(n)$ according to their fitness and selects the best ones as the set of parents $\xi^S(n)$. In truncation selection with threshold $0<\mu<1$ only the $100\mu\%$ of best individuals are selected to become the parents for the next generation. When the population size is infinite, it can be modeled as [15]:

$$P(\mathbf{X} = \mathbf{x} \mid \xi^S(n)) = \begin{cases} \dfrac{P(\mathbf{X} = \mathbf{x} \mid \xi(n))}{\mu} & f(\mathbf{x}) \geq \beta(n) \\ 0 & otherwise \end{cases} \qquad (2)$$

Where:

$$\mu = \int_{f(\mathbf{x}) \geq \beta(n)} P(\mathbf{X} = \mathbf{x} \mid \xi(n)) .$$

The Two-Tournament Selection Schema: In the two-tournament selection model, 2 individuals are chosen from the current population $\xi(n)$ and the best individual is selected to be a parent. This selection must be repeated Se times to generate the set of parents $\xi^S(n)$. When the population size is infinite then this schema can be modeled as [15][16],

$$P(\mathbf{X} = \mathbf{x} \mid \xi^S(n)) = 2P(\mathbf{X} = \mathbf{x} \mid \xi(n)) \int_{f(\mathbf{y}) \leq f(\mathbf{x})} P(\mathbf{X} = \mathbf{y} \mid \xi(n)) . \qquad (3)$$

Remark 1. In [15] Zhang and Mühlenbein have proved that EDA with truncation, or two-tournament selection schema, when using infinite population size, will globally converge.

Let $d(\xi)$ be the ratio of the number of individuals in population ξ, that do not belong to D^*, to the size of ξ. The sequence $\{d(\xi(n)); n=0,1,2,...\}$ generated by EDA is a random sequence in general. If $d(\xi)$ is 0, then all individuals of population ξ, are members of D^*. If the population size tends to infinity, then according to Glivenko-Canteli theorem [17] $d(\xi(n))$ can be computed as follows,

$$d(\xi(n)) = \sum_{x \in D - D^*} P(\mathbf{X} = \mathbf{x} \mid \xi(n)) = 1 - \sum_{x \in D^*} P(\mathbf{X} = \mathbf{x} \mid \xi(n)) . \qquad (4)$$

Define the global convergence stopping time of EDA as $\tau = min\{n \mid E\{f(X) \mid \xi(n)\} = f_{max}\}$ where for every $\tau \lesssim t$ $E\{f(X) \mid \xi(t)\} = f_{max}$, According to the definition of it, τ is the first time that EDA globally converges. τ can be infinite or finite. In the same manner, we define τ' as $min\{n \mid d(\xi(n)) = 0\}$. In the following we state two lemmas to show the relationship between τ' and τ.

Lemma 1. The global convergence stopping time of EDA, τ, is equal to $\tau' = min\{n \mid d(\xi(n)) = 0\}$.

Proof. We prove this lemma by contradiction. First assume that $\tau < \tau'$, by the definition of τ' we have $d(\xi(\tau)) > 0$ i.e. there exists at least one $\mathbf{y} \in \xi(\tau)$ that doesn't belong to D^* (i.e. $f(\mathbf{y}) < f_{max}$) and $P(\mathbf{X} = \mathbf{y} \mid \xi(\tau)) = b > 0$. Thus we have

$$E\{f(\mathbf{X}) \mid \xi(\tau)\} = \sum_{x \in D} f(\mathbf{x}) P(\mathbf{X} = \mathbf{x} \mid \xi(\tau)) \leq bf(\mathbf{y}) + f_{max}(1 - b) . \qquad (5)$$

Using (5) and the fact that $E\{f(\mathbf{X}) \mid \xi(\tau)\} = f_{max}$ we can conclude that $f_{max} \leq f(\mathbf{y})$ and hence a contradiction. Second, assume that $\tau > \tau'$. Using definitions of τ and τ', and (4) we have

$$d(\xi(\tau')) = \sum_{x \in D-D^*} P(\mathbf{X} = \mathbf{x} \mid \xi(\tau')) = 0 . \tag{6}$$

Using (6) and $0 \le P(\mathbf{X} = \mathbf{x} \mid \xi(\tau')) \le 1$, we have,

$$P(\mathbf{X} = \mathbf{x} \mid \xi(\tau')) = 0 \quad if \quad \mathbf{x} \in D - D^* . \tag{7}$$

By definition of $E\{f(X) \mid \xi(\tau')\}$ we can write

$$E\{f(\mathbf{X}) \mid \xi(\tau')\} = \sum_{x \in D} f(\mathbf{x}) P(\mathbf{X} = \mathbf{x} \mid \xi(\tau')) =$$

$$\sum_{x \in D^*} \underbrace{f(\mathbf{x})}_{f_{max}} P(\mathbf{X} = \mathbf{x} \mid \xi(\tau')) + \sum_{x \in D-D^*} f(\mathbf{x}) P(\mathbf{X} = \mathbf{x} \mid \xi(\tau')) . \tag{8}$$

Using (7) and (8) we have

$$E\{f(\mathbf{X}) \mid \xi(\tau')\} = f_{max}(1) + \sum_{x \in D-D^*} 0 \times f(\mathbf{x}) = f_{max} .$$

Which contradicts the assumption that $\tau > \tau'$ and hence the proof. **Q.E.D.**

Lemma 2. If $\tau' = min\{n \mid d(\xi(n)) = 0\}$, then for every $\tau' \le t, \ d(\xi(t)) = 0$.

Proof. Proof is done by contradiction. Assume that $d(\xi(t)) \ne 0$, then there exists at least one $y \in \xi(t)$ that doesn't belong to D^* (i.e. $f(\mathbf{y}) < f_{max}$) and $P(\mathbf{X}=\mathbf{y} \mid \xi(t)) = b > 0$. So we have,

$$E\{f(\mathbf{X}) \mid \xi(t)\} = \sum_{x \in D} f(\mathbf{x}) P(\mathbf{X} = \mathbf{x} \mid \xi(t)) \le bf(\mathbf{y}) + f_{max}(1-b) . \tag{9}$$

Using (9) and $E\{f(\mathbf{X}) \mid \xi(t)\} = f_{max}$ (By lemma 1), we have $f_{max} \le f(\mathbf{y})$ and hence a contradiction. **Q.E.D.**

Lemma 1 indicates that $\tau = \tau'$ and Lemma 2 and Remark 1 state that τ' is the stopping time of $\{d(\xi(n)); n=0,1,2,...\}$. That is the stopping time of $\{E\{f(\mathbf{X}) \mid \xi(n)\}; n=0,1,2,...\}$ is the same as the stopping time of $\{d(\xi(n)); n=0,1,2,...\}$ and for this reason in the rest of the paper we study the time complexity of $d(\xi(n))$ rather than the time complexity of $\{E\{f(\mathbf{X}) \mid \xi(n)\}; n=0,1,2,...\}$.

Using above notations and lemmas the EDA algorithm can be described as follows.

1- **Initialization**: $P(\mathbf{X} = \mathbf{x} \mid \xi(0)) > 0$ for all $\mathbf{x}$ (That is $P(\mathbf{X}=\mathbf{x} \mid \xi(0)) = p$ for all $\mathbf{x}$ where $0<p<1$).
2- **Selection**: generate $P(\mathbf{X} \mid \xi^S(n))$ from $P(\mathbf{X} \mid \xi(n))$ according to a selection schema.
3- **Updating**: $P(\mathbf{X} \mid \xi(n+1))$ is set to $P(\mathbf{X} \mid \xi^S(n))$.
4- if $d(\xi(n+1)) = 0$ then stop; otherwise go to step 2.

3 Upper Bounds on Time Complexity of Global Convergence

The Results for upper bounds on time complexity of global convergence of EDA reported in this paper can be summarized by the following two theorems.

Theorem 1. If an EDA with infinite population size and truncation selection schema is used for optimizing function f, then the termination condition is met at most after $(\mu d(\xi(0))/((1-\mu)(1-d(\xi(0)))))+1$ iterations.

It is obvious that $0<\mu<1$ is an important parameter for the stopping time of EDA when EDA use truncation selection schema. Lower values for μ will impose a lower upper bound on the stopping time and higher values for μ will exert a higher upper bound on the stopping time of EDA.

Theorem 2. If an EDA using infinite population size and 2-tournament selection schema is considered for optimizing f, at most after $(d(\xi(0))/(1- d(\xi(0))))+1$ iterations the termination condition is met.

Before we give the proofs of the above two theorems we state one useful lemma.

Lemma 3. If $d(\xi) \le h_0$, $h_0 > 0$, for any given population ξ and $\{E\{d(\xi(n)) - d(\xi(n+1))| d(\xi(n)) > 0\} \ge (1 / h_1)\}$ then starting from any initial population $\xi(0)$ with $d(\xi(0)) > 0$,

$$E\{\tau \mid d(\xi(0)) > 0\} \le h_0 h_1 . \tag{10}$$

Proof[1]. Since $\{E\{d(\xi(n)) - d(\xi(n+1)) \mid d(\xi(n)) > 0\} \ge (1/h_1)\}$ we have $\{d(\xi(n)); n=0,1,2,\dots\}$ as a super-martingale. Since $h_0 \ge d(\xi(n)) \ge 0$, it ultimately converges, that is

$$\lim_{n \to \infty} E\{d(\xi(n)) \mid d(\xi(0)) > 0\} = 0 .$$

From the definition of stopping time τ, we have $d(\xi(\tau)) = 0$. Therefore,

$$E\{d(\xi(\tau)) \mid d(\xi(0)) > 0\} = 0 .$$

For $n \ge 1$, we have

$$E\{d(\xi(n)) \mid d(\xi(0)) > 0\} =$$
$$E\{E\{d(\xi(n-1)) + d(\xi(n)) - d(\xi(n-1)) \mid \xi(n-1)\} \mid d(\xi(0)) > 0\} .$$

Since $E\{d(\xi(n)) - d(\xi(n+1)) \mid d(\xi(n)) > 0\} \ge (1/h_1)\}$, for $n-1 < \tau$, we have

$$E\{d(\xi(n-1)) + d(\xi(n)) - d(\xi(n-1)) \mid \xi(n-1)\} \le d(\xi(n-1)) - \frac{1}{h_1} . \tag{11}$$

From (11) we can write

$$E\{d(\xi(n)) \mid d(\xi(0) > 0\} \le E\{d(\xi(n-1)) - \frac{1}{h_1} \mid d(\xi(0)) > 0\} . \tag{12}$$

Using (12) and by induction on n, we can get

$$E\{d(\xi(n)) \mid d(\xi(0)) > 0\} \le E\{d(\xi(0)) - \frac{n}{h_1} \mid d(\xi(0)) > 0\} \; and$$
$$0 = E\{d(\xi(\tau)) \mid d(\xi(0)) > 0\} \le E\{d(\xi(0))\} - \frac{1}{h_1} E\{\tau \mid d(\xi(0)) > 0\} \tag{13}$$

From (13) and $d(\xi) \le h_0$, we have

$$E\{\tau \mid d(\xi(0)) > 0\} \le E\{d(\xi(0))\}h_1 \le h_0 h_1 ,$$

and hence the proof. **Q.E.D.**

---

[1] The idea of the proof is borrowed from [8].

Now we are ready to prove theorems 1 and 2. To do this we first prove that conditions of lemma 3 stand and then using lemma 3 we conclude the theorems.

Proof of theorem 1: We first show that conditions of lemma 3 hold and then use lemma 3 to conclude the theorem.

Using the definition of $d(\xi(n))$ and steps 2 and 3 of EDA algorithm we can write

$$E\{d(\xi(n)) - d(\xi(n+1)) \mid d(\xi(n)) > 0\} = E\{\sum_{x \in D^*} P(X = x \mid \xi(n+1)) -$$

$$\sum_{x \in D^*} P(X = x \mid \xi(n)) \mid d(\xi(n)) > 0\} = \tag{14}$$

$$E\{\sum_{x \in D^*} P(X = x \mid \xi^S(n)) - \sum_{x \in D^*} P(X = x \mid \xi(n)) \mid d(\xi(n)) > 0\}$$

Using (2) and the fact that for all $x \in D^*$ we have $f(x) = f_{max} \geq \beta(n)$, (14) can be rewritten as

$$E\{\sum_{x \in D^*} \frac{P(X = x \mid \xi(n))}{\mu} - \sum_{x \in D^*} P(X = x \mid \xi(n)) \mid d(\xi(n)) > 0\} =$$

$$\tag{15}$$

$$E\{(\frac{1}{\mu} - 1) \sum_{x \in D^*} P(X = x \mid \xi(n)) \mid d(\xi(n)) > 0\} = (\frac{1}{\mu} - 1)(1 - d(\xi(n)))$$

Using (15) and induction on n we have

$$d(\xi(n)) \leq d(\xi(0)) = h_0 . \tag{16}$$

From (16) we have,

$$E\{d(\xi(n)) - d(\xi(n+1)) \mid d(\xi(n)) > 0\} \geq (\frac{1}{\mu} - 1)(1 - d(\xi(0))) =$$

$$\frac{1}{\dfrac{1}{\mu}} = \frac{1}{h_1} \tag{17}$$
$$\frac{}{(1 - \mu)(1 - d(\xi(0)))}$$

From (16) and (17) we conclude that conditions of Lemma 3 are satisfied and therefore we can write,

$$E\{\tau \mid d(\xi(0)) > 0\} \leq h_0 h_1 = \frac{\mu \, d(\xi(0))}{(1 - \mu)(1 - d(\xi(0)))} .$$

Hence the proof. **Q.E.D.**

Proof theorem 2: Using the definition of $d(\xi(n))$ and steps 2 and 3 of EDA algorithm, we can write,

$$E\{d(\xi(n)) - d(\xi(n+1)) \mid \xi(n)\} = E\{\sum_{x \in D^*} P(X = x \mid \xi(n+1)) -$$

$$\sum_{x \in D^*} P(X = x \mid \xi(n)) \mid \xi(n)\} = E\{\sum_{x \in D^*} P(X = x \mid \xi^S(n)) - \sum_{x \in D^*} P(X = x \mid \xi(n)) \mid \xi(n)\} \tag{18}$$

Using (3) and the fact that for all $y \in D$ we have $f_{max} \geq f(y)$, we can rewrite (18) as

$$E\{\sum_{x \in D^*}\{2P(\mathbf{X} = \mathbf{x} \mid \xi(n))\underbrace{\int_{f_{max}=f(\mathbf{x}) \geq f(\mathbf{y})}P(\mathbf{X} = \mathbf{y} \mid \xi(n))\}}_{1} - \sum_{x \in D^*}P(\mathbf{X} = \mathbf{x} \mid \xi(n)) \mid \xi(n)\}$$

(19)

$$E\{\sum_{x \in D^*}P(\mathbf{X} = \mathbf{x} \mid \xi(n)) \mid \xi(n)\} = (1 - d(\xi(n)))$$

Using (19) and induction on n we can write

$$d(\xi(n)) \leq d(\xi(0)) = h_0 .$$

(20)

Using the (18), (19) and (20) we have

$$E\{d(\xi(n)) - d(\xi(n+1)) \mid \xi(n)\} \geq (1 - d(\xi(0))) = \frac{1}{h_1} .$$

Since conditions of Lemma 3 are satisfied and we have,

$$E\{\tau \mid d(\xi(0)) > 0\} \leq h_0 h_1 = \frac{d(\xi(0))}{1 - d(\xi(0))} ,$$

Hence the theorem. **Q.E.D.**

4   Computation of Global Convergence Stopping Time

In this section, some strong results about the convergence of EDA are derived. As stated before $\{d(\xi(n)); \ n=0,1,2,...\}$ is a random sequence in general and when population size tends to infinity this sequence becomes a deterministic sequence. In other words by knowing $d(\xi(n-1))$ we can compute the exact value of $d(\xi(n))$. We can use these properties to derive some strong results about the convergence of EDA.

Definition 1. (Convergence Rate). Let $\{a_n; \ n=0,1,2,...\}$ be a sequence that converges to a^*. If we have

$$\lim_{n \to \infty} \frac{\mid a_{n+1} - a^* \mid}{\mid a_n - a^* \mid} = \beta$$

then $\{a_n; \ n=0,1,2,...\}$ converges to a^* with convergence rate β.

The results for the exact number of iterations needed for EDA to converge to global optima reported in this paper can be summarized by the following two theorems

Theorem 3. If we use an EDA with infinite population size and truncation selection method having threshold μ then a) After $1+(log(1-d(\xi(0)))/log \ \mu)$ iterations the condition of termination is met. b) $\{d(\xi(n)); \ n=0,1,2,...\}$ converges to 0 with convergence rate $1/\mu$.

Theorem 4. If we use an EDA with infinite population size and 2-tornumant selection method, then a) After $1+(log(1-d(\xi(0)))/log \ 0.5)$ iterations the condition of termination is met. b) $\{d(\xi(n)); n=0,1,2,...\}$ converges to 0 with convergence rate 2.

Before we give the proofs of theorems 3 and 4, we state two lemmas for the computation of $d(\xi(n))$.

Lemma 4. For EDA algorithm with infinite population size and truncation selection method $d(\xi(n))$ can be computed as follows,

$$d(\xi(n)) = 1 - (1 - d(\xi(0)))(\frac{1}{\mu})^n,$$

where $0 < \mu < 1$ is the selection threshold.

Proof. We the definition $d(\xi(n))$ and (2) we have,

$$d(\xi(n+1)) = 1 - \sum_{x \in D^*} P(X = x \mid \xi(n+1)) = 1 - \sum_{x \in D^*} P(X = x \mid \xi^S(n))$$

$$= 1 - \frac{1}{\mu} \sum_{x \in D^*} P(X = x \mid \xi(n)) = 1 - \frac{1}{\mu}(1 - d(\xi(n))) \qquad (21)$$

From (21) we have

$$d(\xi(n+1)) - \frac{1}{\mu} d(\xi(n)) = (1 - \frac{1}{\mu}) . \qquad (22)$$

Characteristic equation of (22) is,

$$r^2 - (\frac{1}{\mu} + 1)r + \frac{1}{\mu} = 0 . \qquad (23)$$

By solving (23) we have

$$d(\xi(n)) = 1 - (1 - d(\xi(0)))(\frac{1}{\mu})^n .$$

Q.E.D.

Lemma 5. For EDA algorithm with infinite population size and tournament selection method we have

$$d(\xi(n)) = 1 - (1 - d(\xi(0)))2^n .$$

Proof. By the definition of $d(\xi(n))$.and (3) we have,

$$d(\xi(n+1)) - 2d(\xi(n)) + 1 = 0 . \qquad (24)$$

The characteristic equation of (24) is,

$$r^2 - 3r + 2 = 0 . \qquad (25)$$

By solving (24) we have

$$d(\xi(n)) = 1 - (1 - d(\xi(0)))2^n .$$

Q.E.D.

Now we use Lemmas 4 and 5 and prove theorems 3 and 4.

Proof of theorem 3. (a) By definition of stopping time and Lemma 4 we have

$$d(\xi(\tau)) = 1 - (1 - d(\xi(0)))(\frac{1}{\mu})^\tau = 0 . \qquad (26)$$

Using (26) we conclude,

$$\tau = \log(1 - d(\xi(0))) / \log \mu \; . \tag{27}$$

By (27) after $1+(log(1-d(\xi(0)))/log\ \mu)$ iterations the condition of termination is met.
(b) By lemma 4, we have

$$\lim_{n \to \infty} \frac{|d(\xi(n+1)) - 0|}{|d(\xi(n)) - 0|} = \frac{1}{\mu} \; .$$

From definition 1, $\{d(\xi(n)); n=0,1,2,\ldots\}$ converges to 0 with convergence rate $1/\mu$.
Q.E.D.

Proof of theorem 4: (a) By definition of stopping time and lemma 5 we have

$$d(\xi(\tau)) = 1 - (1 - d(\xi(0)))2^{\tau} = 0 \; . \tag{28}$$

Using (28) we have,

$$\tau = \log(1 - d(\xi(0))) / \log(0.5) \; . \tag{29}$$

By (29) after $1+(log(1-d(\xi(0)))/log\ 0.5)$ iterations the condition of termination is met.
(b) By lemma 5, we conclude that

$$\lim_{n \to \infty} \frac{|d(\xi(n+1)) - 0|}{|d(\xi(n)) - 0|} = 2 \; .$$

According to definition 1, $\{d(\xi(n)); n=0,1,2,\ldots\}$ converges to 0 with convergence rate
2. **Q.E.D.**

5 Conclusion

This paper presented some new results for global convergence computation time for
EDA algorithms. The following quantities were computed: 1) some upper bounds on
the number of iterations required for global convergence of EDA 2) the exact number
of iterations needed for EDA to converge to global optima.

References

1. Baluja, S.: Population Based Incremental Learning: A Method for Integrating Genetic
   Search Based Function Optimization and Competitive Learning. Technical Report,
   Carnegie Mellon University (1994)
2. Baluja, S., Davis, S.: Fast Probabilistic Modeling for Combinatorial Optimization. In: The
   15th National Conference on Artificial Intelligence, Madison, Wisconsin, AAAI Press,
   (1998) 469-476
3. Bonet, D., Isbell, J.S., Viola, P.: MIMIC: Finding Optima by Estimation Probability
   Densities. Advances in Neural Information Processing Systems, Vol. 9, MIT Press,
   Cambridge (1997) 424-431
4. González, C., Lozano, J.A., Larrañaga, P.: The Convergence Behavior of the PBIL
   Algorithm: A Preliminary Approach. In: The 5th International Conference on Artificial
   Neural Networks and Genetic Algorithms (2001)
5. González, C., Lozano, J.A., Larrañaga, P.: Analyzing the PBIL Algorithm by Means of
   Discrete Dynamical Systems. Complex Systems, Vol. 12, (2000) 465-479

6. Höhfeld, M., Rudolph, G.: Towards A Theory of Population Based Incremental Learning. In: The 4th IEEE Conferences on Evolutionary Computation, Indianapolis, IEEE Press, (1997) 1-5

7. Harik, G.R., Lobo, F.G., Goldberg, D.E.: The Compact Genetic Algorithm. IEEE Transactions on Evolutionary Computation, Vol. 3, No. 4 (1999) 287-297

8. He. J., Yao, X.: Drift Analysis and Average Time Complexity of Evolutionary Computation. Artificial Intelligence, Vol. 127, (2001) 57-85

9. Larrañaga, P., Lozano, J.A.: Estimation of Distribution Algorithms. A New tools for Evolutionary Computation. Kluwer Academic Publishers (2001)

10. Mühlenbein, H.: The Equation for Response to Selection and Its Use for Prediction. Evolutionary Computation, Vol. 5, (1998) 303-346

11. Mühlenbein, H., Mahnig, T., Rodriguez, A.O.: Schemata, Distributions and Graphical Models in Evolutionary Optimization. Journal of Heuristics, Vol. 5, (1999) 215-247

12. Mühlenbein, H., Mahnig, T.: Evolutionary Computation and Wright's Equation. Theoretical Computer Science (in press)

13. Pelikan, M., Goldberg D.E., Cantz Paz, E.: BOA: the Bayesian Optimization Algorithm. In: the Genetic and Evolutionary Computation Conference, Morgan Kaufmann Publishers, (1999) 525-532

14. Rastegar, R., Meybodi, M.R.: LAEDA, A New Evolutionary Algorithm using Learning Automata. In: The 9th Annual International Computer Society of Iran Computer Conference CSICC2004, Tehran, Iran, (2004) 456-464

15. Zhang, Q., Mühlenbein, H.: On the Convergence of a Class of Estimation of Distribution Algorithms. IEEE Transactions on Evolutionary Computation, Vol. 8, No. 2 (2004)

16. Blickle, T., Thiele, L.: A Mathematical Analysis of Tournament selection. In: The 6th International Conference of Genetic Algorithms, Morgan Kaufmann Publishers, San Francisco, CA (1995) 9-16

17. Devroye, L., Gyorfi, L., Lugosi, G.: A Probabilistic Theory of Pattern Recognition. Springer Verlag, Berlin (1996)

Finding Minimal Rough Set Reducts with Particle Swarm Optimization

Xiangyang Wang, Jie Yang, Ningsong Peng, and Xiaolong Teng

Inst. of Image Processing & Pattern Recognition, Jiaotong University,
Shanghai, 200030, P.R. China
wangxiangyang@sjtu.edu.cn

Abstract. We propose a new algorithm to find minimal rough set reducts by using Particle Swarm Optimization (PSO). Like Genetic Algorithm, PSO is also a type of evolutionary algorithm. But compared with GA, PSO does not need complex operators as crossover and mutation that GA does, it requires only primitive and simple mathematical operators, and is computationally inexpensive in terms of both memory and times. The experiments on some UCI data compare our algorithm with GA-based, and other deterministic rough set reduction algorithms. The results show that PSO is efficient to minimal rough set reduction.

1 Introduction

Rough set reduction method has been used for feature selection [1,2]. It is worth to find minimal reducts, with which we can generate more general decision rules and better classification quality of new samples. However, the problem of finding a minimal reduct is NP-hard [3]. So some heuristic or approximation algorithms have to be considered.

X.Hu gives a rough set reduction algorithm using positive region based attribute significance as heuristics [4]. G. Y. Wang develops a conditional information entropy reduction algorithm [5]. These hill-climbing methods, however, do not guarantee to find a global optimal or minimal reducts. Using the attribute significance discriminate between candidates may lead the search down a non-minimal path.

Wroblewski and Bazan et al. [6,8] use genetic algorithms to find minimal reducts. One of their methods uses classical genetic algorithm with individuals represented by bit strings to short reducts finding. This method, sometimes fails to find the global optimum. Another is the hybrid algorithm that exploits advantages of both genetic and heuristic algorithms. Genetic algorithm is used to produce proper attributes order, and heuristic algorithm finds the minimal reducts. Although this method is much better, it increases the computation complexity [6]. One of the most widely used hybrid algorithm is the order-based genetic algorithm [7]. Slezak and Wroblewski [10] extend it to search approximate entropy reducts.

We propose a new algorithm to find minimal rough set reducts with Particle Swarm Optimization (PSO). PSO is a new evolutionary computation technique

D. Ślęzak et al. (Eds.): RSFDGrC 2005, LNAI 3641, pp. 451–460, 2005.

[12], in which each potential solution is seen as a particle with certain velocity flying through the problem space. Each particle adjusts its flying according to its own flying experience and its companions'. The Particle Swarms find optimal regions of complex search spaces through the interaction of individuals in population. PSO has been successfully applied to a large number of difficult combinatorial optimal problems. In general, it exceeds Genetic Algorithms [13].

In this paper, like classical genetic algorithm, the particle's position is binary representation for subsets of the set of attributes. The compared genetic algorithm for rough set reduction is also classical.

2 Related Rough Set Concepts

First we briefly review the basic concepts of the rough set theory [5,8].

Let $I = (U, A)$ be an information system, where U is the universe with non-empty set of finite objects. A is a non-empty finite set of attributes. For $\forall a \in A$ determines a function $f_a : U \to V_a$. If $P \subseteq A$, there is an associated equivalence relation:

$$IND(P) = \{(x, y) \in U \times U | \forall a \in P, f_a(x) = f_a(y)\} \tag{1}$$

The partition of U, generated by $IND(P)$ is denoted U/P. If $(x, y) \in IND(p)$, then x and y are indiscernible by attributes from P. The equivalence classes of the P-indiscernibility relation are denoted $[x]_p$. Let $X \subseteq U$, the P-lower approximation $\underline{P}X$ and P-upper approximation $\overline{P}X$ of set X can be defined as:

$$\underline{P}X = \{x \in U | [x]_p \subseteq X\} \tag{2}$$

$$\overline{P}X = \{x \in U | [x]_p \cap X \neq \phi\} \tag{3}$$

Let $P, Q \subseteq A$ be equivalence relations over U, then the positive, negative and boundary regions can be defined as:

$$POS_p(Q) = \bigcup_{X \in U/Q} \underline{P}X \tag{4}$$

$$NEG_p(Q) = U - \bigcup_{X \in U/Q} \overline{P}X \tag{5}$$

$$BND_p(Q) = \bigcup_{X \in U/Q} \overline{P}X - \bigcup_{X \in U/Q} \underline{P}X \tag{6}$$

The positive region of the partition U/Q with respect to P, $POS_p(Q)$, is the set of all objects of U that can be certainly classified to blocks of the partition U/Q by means of P. Q depends on P in a degree $k \in [0, 1]$, denoted $P \Rightarrow_k Q$

$$k = \gamma_p(Q) = \frac{|POS_p(Q)|}{|U|} \tag{7}$$

If $k = 1$, Q depends totally on P, if $0 < k < 1$, Q depends partially on P, and if $k = 0$ then Q does not depend on P. When P is a set of condition attributes and Q is the decision, $\gamma_p(Q)$ is the quality of classification.

The attribute reduction is to remove some redundant attributes so that the reduced set provides the same quality of classification as the original one. A reduct is defined as:

$$Red = \{R \subseteq C | \gamma_R(D) = \gamma_C(D), \forall B \subset R, \gamma_B(D) \neq \gamma_C(D)\} \qquad (8)$$

A dataset may have many attribute reducts. The minimal cardinality reduct is:

$$Red_{min} = \{R \in Red | \forall R^{'} \in Red, |R| \leq |R^{'}|\} \qquad (9)$$

The intersection of all reducts is called core, the elements of which are those attributes that cannot be eliminated. The core is defined as:

$$Core(C) = \cap Red \qquad (10)$$

3   PSO for Rough Set Reduction

Since PSO has been used widely to solve combination optimization problems. In this paper we apply PSO to find minimal rough set reducts. Particle swarm optimization (PSO) is an evolutionary computation technique developed by Kennedy and Eberhart [12]. The original intent was to graphically simulate the choreography of a bird flock. Shi.Y introduced inertia weight into the particle swarm optimizer to produce the standard PSO algorithm [14,15].

3.1   Standard PSO Algorithm

PSO is initialized with a population of particles. Each particle is treated as a point in a S-dimensional space. The ith particle is represented as $X_i = (x_{i1}, x_{i2}, \ldots, x_{iS})$. The best previous position (pbest, the position giving the best fitness value) of any particle is $P = (p_{i1}, p_{i2}, \ldots, p_{iS})$. The index of the global best particle is represented by 'gbest'. The velocity for particle i is $V_i = (v_{i1}, v_{i2}, \ldots, v_{iS})$. The particles are manipulated according to the following equations:

$$v_{id} = w * v_{id} + c_1 * rand() * (p_{id} - x_{id}) + c_2 * Rand() * (p_{gd} - x_{id}) \qquad (11)$$

$$x_{id} = x_{id} + v_{id} \qquad (12)$$

Where w is the inertia weight, it is a positive linear function of time changing according to the generation iteration. Suitable selection of the inertia weight provides a balance between the global and local exploration. The acceleration constants $c1$ and $c2$ in equation (11) represent the weighting of the stochastic acceleration terms that pull each particle toward pbest and gbest positions. Low values allow particles to roam far from target regions before being tugged back, while high values result in abrupt movement toward, or past, target regions.

$rand()$ and $Rand()$ are two random functions in the range [0,1]. Particle's velocities on each dimension are limited to a maximum velocity $Vmax$. If $Vmax$ is too small, particles may not explore sufficiently beyond locally good regions. If $Vmax$ is too high particles might fly past good solutions.

The first part of equation (11) makes the "flying particles" has memory capability and exploring new search space. The second part is the "cognition" part, which represents the private thinking of the particle itself. The third part is the "social" part, which represents the collaboration among the particles. The equation (11) is used to update the particle's velocity. Then the particle flies toward a new position according to equation (12). The performance of each particle is measured according to a pre-defined fitness function.

The process for implementing the PSO algorithm is as follows:

1) Initialize a population of particles with random positions and velocities on S dimensions in the problem space.
2) For each particle, evaluate the desired optimization fitness function in d variables.
3) Compare particle's fitness evaluation with particle's pbest. If current value is better than pbest, then set pbest value equal to the current value, and the pbest location equal to the current location in d dimensional space.
4) Compare fitness evaluation with the population's overall previous best. If current value is better than gbest, then reset gbest to the current particle's array index and value.
5) Change the velocity and position of the particle according to formulas (11) and (12).
6) Loop to 2) until a criterion is met, usually a sufficiently good fitness or a maximum number of iterations (generations).

3.2 Encoding

To apply PSO to rough set reduction, we represent the particle's position as binary bit strings of length N, where N is the total attribute number. Every bit represents an attribute, the value '1' means the corresponding attribute is selected while '0' not selected. Each position is an attribute subset.

3.3 Representation of Velocity

Each particle's velocity is represented as a positive integer varying between 1 and $Vmax$. It implies that at one time how many of the particle's bit should be changed to as the same as that of the global best position, i.e. the velocity of the particle flying toward the best position. The number of different bits between two particles relates to the difference between their positions. See Fig.1 is for the principle of velocity updating.

For example, $Pgbest = [1, 0, 1, 1, 1, 0, 1, 0, 0, 1]$ and $X_i = [0, 1, 0, 0, 1, 1, 0, 1, 0, 1]$. The difference between gbest and the particle's current position is $Pgbest - P_i = [1, -1, 1, 1, 0, -1, 1, -1, 0, 0]$. '1' means that, by being compared with the best position, this bit (feature) should be selected but not, which will decrease

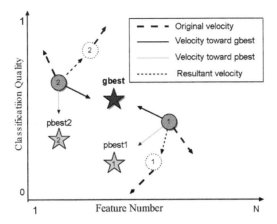

Fig. 1. The principle of velocity updating. Individual particles (1 and 2) are accelerated toward the location of the best solution, gbest, and the location of their own personal best, pbest, in the two dimension problem space

classification quality. On the other hand, '-1' means that, by being compared with the best position, this bit should not be selected but it does. Redundant features will make the length of the subset longer. Both cases will lead to lower fitness value. Assume that the number of '1' is a and that of '-1' is b. The value of $(a - b)$ is the distance between two positions. $(a - b)$ may be positive or negative, such a variety makes particles possess 'exploration ability' in solution space. In this example, $(a - b) = 4 - 3 = 1$, so $P_g - X_i = 1$.

3.4   Position Update Strategies

After updating velocity, particle's position will be updated by the new velocity. If the new velocity is V, the number of different bits between the current particle and *gbest* is x_g, there exists two cases while updating the position:

1) $V \leq x_g$. In this case, randomly change V bits of the particle, which are different from that of *gbest*. The particle moves toward the global best while keeping itself 'searching ability'.
2) $V > x_g$. In this case, besides changing all the different bits to be same as that of *gbest*, we should further randomly ('random' implies 'exploration ability') change $(V - x_g)$ bits outside the different bits between particle and *gbest*. So after the particle reaching to the global best position, it keep on moving some distance toward other directions, which gives it further searching ability.

3.5   Velocity Limitation (Maximum Velocity, Vmax)

In our experiment, first we limit the particles' velocity in the region of $[1, N]$. But we notice that in some cases after some generations, the swarms find out a global best (but not the real optimal one) solution, and in the following generations the *gbest* keeps freezing. It can only find the sub-optimal solution. This indicates that the maximum velocity is too high and particles often 'fly past' the optimal solution.

We set $Vmax = (1/3) * N$ and limit the velocity in $[1, (1/3) * N]$, which prevents velocity to be too large. By limiting the maximum velocity, particles cannot fly too far away from the optimal solution. Once finding a global best position, other particles will adjust their velocities and positions, searching around the best position. If $V < 1$, then $V = 1$. If $V > (1/3) * N$, $V = (1/3) * N$. PSO can often find the optimal reducts quickly under such a limit.

3.6   Fitness Function

We use the fitness function as given in equation (13):

$$Fitness = \alpha * \gamma_R(D) + \beta * \frac{|C| - |R|}{|C|} \qquad (13)$$

Where $\gamma_R(D)$ is the classification quality of condition attribute set R relative to decision D, $|R|$ is the length of selected feature subset. $|C|$ is the total number of features. α and β are two parameters corresponding to the importance of classification quality and subset length. $\alpha \in [0, 1]$ and $\beta = 1 - \alpha$. In our experiments we set $\alpha = 0.9$, $\beta = 0.1$. The high α assures that the best position is at least a real rough set reduct. Our goal is to maximize fitness values.

3.7   Setting Parameters

In our algorithm, the inertia weight decreases along with the iterations according to the equation (14).

$$W = W_{max} - \frac{W_{max} - W_{min}}{iter_{max}} * iter \qquad (14)$$

Where W_{max} is the initial value of weighting coefficient. W_{min} is the final value of weighting coefficient. $iter_{max}$ is the maximum number of iterations or generation. $iter$ is the current iteration or generation number.

4   Experiments

We compare the rough set attribute reduction algorithm with Particle Swarms Optimization (PSORSFS) and other rough set reduction algorithms on some discrete UCI datasets [16]. Comparison algorithms include positive region (POSAR), conditional entropy (CEAR), and the GA-based attribute reduction algorithm (GAAR). The parameter settings for GAAR and PSORSFS are in Table 1. The experimental results are listed in Table 2.

From the results, it can be seen that in some cases hill-climbing methods can find out the optimal solution. For example, POSAR find exclusive optimal

Table 1. PSORSFS&GAAR parameter settings

	Population size	Maximum Generation	Crossover Probability	Mutation Probability	c1	c2	weight weight	Max Velocity
GA	100	100	0.6	0.4	-	-	-	-
PSO	20	100	-	-	2.0	2.0	1.4~0.4	$(1/3)*N$

Table 2. Reduct size found by Reduction algorithms (∗ Optimal solution)

Data	Features	Instances	POSAR	CEAR	GAAR	PSORSFS
Breastcancer	9	699	4	4	4	4
M-of-N	13	1000	7	7	6	6
Exactly	13	1000	8	8	6	6
Exactly2	13	1000	10	11	11	10∗
Vote	16	300	9	11	9	8∗
Zoo	16	101	5∗	10	6	5∗
Lymphography	18	148	6∗	8	8	7
Mushroom	22	8124	5	5	5	4∗
Led	24	2000	6	12	8	5∗
Soybean-small	35	47	2	2	6	2
Lung	56	32	4∗	5	6	4∗

Table 3. Classification results with different reducts 1: Number of rules; 2: Classification accuracy

Data	POSAR		CEAR		GAAR		PSORSFS	
	1	2	1	2	1	2	1	2
Breastcancer	67	95.94	75	94.20	64	95.65	64	95.80
M-of-N	35	100	35	100	35	100	35	100
Exactly	50	100	50	100	50	100	50	100
Exactly2	217	83.7	178	69.6	200	80.8	217	83.7
Vote	25	94.33	25	92.33	25	94.0	25	95.33
Zoo	13	96.0	13	94.0	13	92.0	10	96.0
Lymphography	32	85.71	42	72.14	38	70.00	39	75.71
Mushroom	19	100	61	90.83	19	100	23	99.70
Led	10	100	228	83.10	10	100	10	100
Soybean-small	5	100	4	100	4	97.50	4	100
Lung	11	86.67	13	73.33	12	70.0	8	90.0

solution on dataset Exactly2 and Lymphography. But on other datasets, what they find is always not optimal. CEAR often contains more redundant features than POSAR. As for stochastic searching algorithms, GAAR and PSORSFS, PSORSFS successfully find the optimal reducts on most of these datasets. For instance, PSORSFS finds an optimal reduct on Mushroom, and finds the exclusive optimal reduct on Exactly2, Vote and Led.

Table 4. PSO searching process on data Exactly2

Iter	Best Solution	Fitness Value	Feature Subset Length
1	1,2, 4, 5, 7, 8, 9, 10, 11, 12, 13	0.8272	11
2	1,2, 4, 5, 6, 7, 8, 9, 10, 11, 13	0.8362	11
3	1,2, 4, 5, 6, 7, 8, 9, 10, 11, 13	0.8362	11
4-11	1,2, 4, 5, 6, 7, 8, 9, 10, 11, 12, 13	0.8663	12
12	1, 2, 3, 4, 5, 6, 7, 8, 9, 10, 13	0.9154	11
13	1, 2, 3, 4, 5, 6, 7, 8, 9, 10	0.9231	10

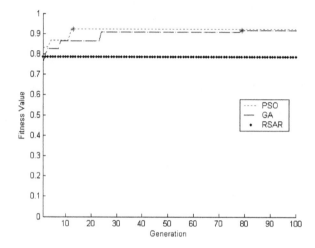

Fig. 2. Evolution process of the global best on data Exactly2

Compared with GA, PSO is more faster in finding out the optimal solution (Table 4 and Fig.2). Since PSO only requires primitive and simple mathematical operators, it is computationally inexpensive and asks for less memory. Most of its time is cost on basic rough set computation. GA is affected greatly by problem dimension. It needs more time for generations with the increasing of feature number. This is due to its complex crossover and mutation operations.

The comparison of the number of decision rules and the classification accuracy with different reducts are shown in Table 3. We use the LEM2 algorithm [11] to extract rules from the data and the global strength [8,9] for rule negotiation in classification. We apply the ten-fold cross validation method to estimate the classification accuracy. Most of the reducts found by PSO can generate rather minimal rules and higher classification accuracy.

5 Conclusions

This paper proposes a new method to find minimal rough set reducts with Particle Swarm Optimization. Experimental results demonstrate competitive performance. PSO has a strong search capability in problem space and can efficiently find minimal reducts. It is a promising method for rough set reduction.

More experiments and further investigation into this technique may be required. In this paper, we apply PSO to find minimal size of reducts and like classical genetic algorithm, the particle's position is binary representation for attributes subsets. We will go further to select a reduct due to the number of decision rules it generates rather than its length. If a reduct generates fewer rules, it means that the rules are more general and they should better recognize new objects [8]. We should also extend to hybrid algorithm, order-based PSO for searching approximate entropy reducts [10], where the particle's position is a permutation of attributes and PSO is use to find the proper order. Such reducts are much better applicable in practice. These will be our future works.

References

1. Swiniarski, R.W., Skowron, A.: Rough set methods in feature selection and recognition. Pattern Recognition Letters 24 (2003) 833-849
2. Chouchoulas, A., Shen, Q.: Rough set-aided keyword reduction for text categorization. Applied Artificial Intelligence, 15(9) (2001) 843-873
3. Skowron, A., Rauszer, C.: The discernibility matrices and functions in information systems. In: Swiniarski, R. (ed.): Intelligent Decision Support–Handbook of Applications and Advances of the Rough Sets Theory, Kluwer Academic Publishers, Dordrecht (1992) 311-362
4. Hu, X.: Knowledge discovery in databases: An attribute-oriented rough set approach. Ph.D thesis, Regina university (1995)
5. Wang, G.Y. et al.: Theoretical Study on Attribute Reduction of Rough Set Theory: Comparison of Algebra and Information Views. In: Proceedings of the Third IEEE International Conference on Cognitive Informatics (2004)
6. Wroblewski, J.: Finding minimal reducts using genetic algorithms. In: Proc. of the Second Annual Join Conference on Information Sciences. Wrightsville Beach, NC, September 28-October 1 (1995) 186-189
7. Wroblewski, J.: Theoretical Foundations of Order-Based Genetic Algorithms. Fundamenta Informaticae. IOS Press, 28(3-4) (1996) 423-430
8. Bazan, J., Nguyen, H.S. et al.: Rough set algorithms in classification problems. In: Polkowski, L., Lin, T.Y., Tsumoto, S. (eds): Rough Set Methods and Applications: New Developments in Knowledge Discovery in Information Systems. Studies in Fuzziness and Soft Computing, vol. 56. Physica-Verlag, Heidelberg, Germany (2000) 49-88
9. Bazan, J.: A Comparison of Dynamic and non-Dynamic Rough Set Methods for Extracting Laws from Decision Table. In: Polkowski, L., Skowron, A. (eds.): Rough Sets in Knowledge Discovery. Heidelberg: Physica-Verlag (1998) 321-365.
10. Slezak, D., Wroblewski, J.: Order based genetic algorithms for the search of approximate entropy reducts. In: Wang, G.Y. et al. (eds.): RSFDGrC. LNAI, Vol. 2693. Chongqing, China (2003) 308-311
11. Stefanowski, J.: On rough set based approaches to induction of decision rules. In: Skowron, A., Polkowski, L. (eds.): Rough Sets in Knowledge Discovery, Vol. 1. Physica Verlag, Heidelberg (1998) 500-529

12. Kennedy, J., Eberhart, R.: Particle Swarm Optimization. In: Proc IEEE Int. Conf. On Neural Networks. Perth (1995) 1942-1948
13. Kennedy, J., Spears, W.M.: Matching Algorithms to Problems: An Experimental Test of the Particle Swarm and Some Genetic Algorithms on the Multimodal Problem Generator. In: Proceedings of the IEEE Int'l Conference on Evolutionary Computation, (1998)
14. Shi, Y., Eberhart, R.: A modified particle swarm optimizer. In: Proc. IEEE Int. Conf. On Evolutionary Computation. Anchorage, AK, USA (1998) 69-73
15. Eberhart, R., Shi, Y.: Particle swarm optimization: Developments, applications and resources. In: Proc. IEEE Int. Conf. On Evolutionary Computation. Seoul (2001) 81-86
16. Blake, C., Keogh, E. et al.: UCI repository of machine learning databases. Tech. rep. Department of Information and Computer Science, University of California, Irvine, CA. (1998) http://www.ics.uci.edu/mlearn/MLRepository.htm

MEA Based Nonlinearity Correction Algorithm for the VCO of LFMCW Radar Level Gauge

Gaowei Yan, Gang Xie, Yuxia Qiu, and Zehua Chen

College of Information Engineering, Taiyuan University of Technology Taiyuan,
Shanxi, P.R.China, 030024
firstygw@yahoo.com.cn

Abstract. In this paper, Mind Evolutionary Algorithm (MEA) is introduced to correct the nonlinearity of voltage-controlled oscillator (VCO)
in linear frequency modulation continuous wave (LFMCW) radar level
gauge. Firstly, the frequency modulation (FM) voltage is divided into several subsections. By using fast Fourier transform (FFT) analysis for the
beat frequency signals and distilling the characteristic of the spectrum,
an evaluation function is constructed. Then MEA is applied to optimize
the end coordinates of the subsections to achieve the nonlinear curve of
FM voltage so as to compensate for the nonlinearity of VCO. Experiments show that the proposed method has good correction performance
with no requirement of additional hardware and measuring equipment
and is easy to apply.

1 Introduction

Linear frequency modulation continuous wave (LFMCW) radar level gauge has
advantages of non-touch, high resolution, and good media adaptability. It has
been widely used in diverse level measurements. However, the nonlinearity of
the voltage-controlled oscillator (VCO) in LFMCW will cause nonlinearity in the
final frequency output, which is modulated by linear voltage. The beat frequency
signal being mixed is no longer the idea single frequency signal due to frequency
and phase variation and the spectrum width being broadened. The resolution of
the LFMCW and the S/N ratio are then being affected, and thus degraded the
computation accuracy [1]. The open loop and closed loop correction methods are
usually taken to eliminate this kind of nonlinearity with hardware and software
[2,3,4,5,6,7], but there are difficulties and problems in getting high correction
accuracy with low cost. So we need a new method.

Mind evolutionary algorithm (MEA) is a new type of evolutional computing
method that simulates evolutional process of people's thoughts. It uses the concept 'population' of genetic algorithm (GA), but is radically different from it.
"Similartaxis" and "dissimilation" operators are presented. Since memory function and directional study mechanism are introduced and population optimization replaces the individual optimization, the intelligence of the algorithm is improved and the search efficiency is also enhanced. MEA has successfully solved

D. Ślęzak et al. (Eds.): RSFDGrC 2005, LNAI 3641, pp. 461–470, 2005.

the problems of precocity and slowness of convergence [8,9,10]. It has been successfully applied to solve concrete compound [11] and other problems.

This paper analyzes the effect of the frequency modulation(FM) nonlinearities of VCO to the range resolution, based on which a new subsection correction
method of the VCO voltage control signal is proposed.

2   Influence on LFMCW Radar of Nonlinearities of VCO

LFMCW radar adopts periodic modulation voltage to control VCO to generate continuous wave signal $s(t)$, at the same time receives the echo signal $r(t)$
reflected from target after a delay τ ($\tau=R/C$, where R is distance from radar
to target and C is light velocity). Fig. 1(a) shows the block diagram of homodyne LFMCW radar. Fig. 1(b) shows the transmitted and received signals as
functions of time; dashed line is ideal and solid line is the actual situation. The
instantaneous difference in frequency between transmitted and received signal is
beat frequency, which is obtained by mixing the target return signal $r(t)$ with
the transmitted signal $s(t)$. The beat frequency reflects the target's distance.
Therefore the information of the objective's distance can be gained by analyzing
the spectrum of the beat frequency in one cycle and getting the frequency at the
point with the maximum amplitude value.

Suppose the initial control voltage $V(t)$ is a sawtooth wave with period T,
$V(t) = V_0 + V_m t/T$ within $[V_0, V_0 + V_m]$ to control VCO generating a transmitted
signal $s(t)$ with period T and bandwidth B. In the effective processed bandwidth
$T_0(T_0=T-\tau, \tau \ll T)$, the beat frequency signal $S_b(t)$ is single-frequency signal. Its
bandwidth δf_b is $1/T_0$. Samuel O.Piper [12] gave the range resolution equation
of LFMCW radar as follows:

$$\Delta R = TC/(2B) \times \delta f_b \tag{1}$$

For $\tau \ll T$, the relation $T_0 \approx T$ can be obtained and the limit resolution of LFMCW
radar is $\Delta R \approx C/(2B)$. When the transmitted signal is a non-ideal frequency

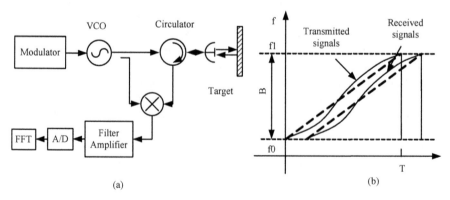

Fig. 1. (a) Diagram of LFMCW radar system   (b) Transmitted and received signals

modulation signal, the spectrum of beat signal is spread leading to the decline of the range resolution. Reference [13] analyzed the approximate relation between frequency modulation linearity and range resolution. As the result of the non-linearity of VCO, the transmitted signal produced with control voltage can be described as:

$$f(t) = F[V(t)] = F_0 + KV_0 + \frac{KV_m t}{T} + E[V(t)] \triangleq f_0 + Bt/T + e(t) \quad (2)$$

where $e(t)$ is the error function of frequency characteristic. Linearity function and linearity are respectively defined as:

$$\begin{cases} L(t) = e(t)/B \\ L = |L(t)|_{\max} \end{cases} \quad (3)$$

It is non-ideal linear frequency modulation when $e(t) \neq 0$. Suppose the beat signal is $S_b(t)$ and target delay is τ, then the corresponding beat frequency is

$$g(t) = f(t) - f(t - \tau) = B\tau/T + e(t) - e(t - \tau) \quad (4)$$

where $B\tau/T$ determines the spectrum center of $S_b(t)$, denoting target range, and $e(t) - e(t-\tau)$ determines the spectrum width of $S_b(t)$. For a very small τ, the variety of $e(t)$ is also small. Thus the beat frequency can be approximated by

$$g(t) = f(t) - f(t - \tau) = B\tau/T + e'(t)\tau \quad (5)$$

If the change of amplitude is not considered, $S_b(t)$ can be denoted as

$$S_b(t) = A\cos[2\pi B\tau\, t/T + 2\pi e(t)\tau + \phi_0] \quad (6)$$

According to the signal modulation theory, the 20dB spectral bandwidth of $S_b(t)$ is

$$\Delta f \approx 4\pi |e(t)|_{\max} \tau F_m \quad (7)$$

F_m is the maximal frequency of the signal components contained in $e(t)$ and can be denoted by $F_m = a/T$, where a is the parameter relational to the shape of $e(t)$ and the variety of speed. With a view to $|e(t)|_{\max} = LB$, the above equation can be rewritten as

$$\Delta f \approx 4\pi a LB\tau/T \quad (8)$$

Compared with that with ideal linear frequency modulation, the spectrum of $S_b(t)$ has changed. The ratio is

$$\Delta n = \Delta f/\delta f = 4\pi a LB\tau \quad (9)$$

It can be seen that the spectrum of beat signals will be broadened and the beat frequency spectral width is broadened Δn times. The result of spectral analysis will take up many spectral bins, which worsen the range resolution. Simultaneously the nonlinearity and the phase noise produced by it might induce several fake peaks appearing beside the main peak in the spectrum gained by

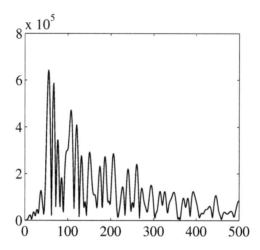

Fig. 2. Spectrum of the beat signal with nonlinear frequency modulation

fast Fourier transform (FFT). It will influence the judgments of the main peak in practical measurement with great difference. Fig. 2 shows the spectrum of the measurement of a metal flat placed three meters before the radar level gauge. It can be seen that there are a series of fake peaks on the right side of the main peak.

To eliminate $e(t)$ from equation (2), a nonlinear frequency modulation voltage can be used to compensate the nonlinearity of VCO. But it is impossible to find a universal function to realize the compensation because the specialty of each VCO is different. Using the correction method of nonlinearity in analog circuits as reference, this paper uses MEA to acquire the nonlinear frequency modulation voltage and then perform the subsection correction of the nonlinearity of VCO.

3   The Correction of Linearity Based on MEA

3.1   Brief Introduction of MEA

The concepts of 'population' and 'evolution' are introduced into MEA. Evolutionary objectives include N_S "superior" subpopulations, N_T "temporary" subpopulations and a global information board. Each subpopulation is composed of S_G individuals and a local information board. "Similartaxis" and "dissimilation" operators execute the virtual evolutionary process. "Similartaxis" performs the local competition inside the subpopulations and the individuals in same subpopulation exchange information and learn from each other. "Dissimilation" performs the global competition and the subpopulations exchange information and learn from each other. MEA has strong ability to search for the global optimum and has advantages in convergence ability and calculative efficiency against GA. Please see reference [8,9] for the detailed description. The brief introduction on MEA is as follows:

At the beginning of "study", M individuals are scattered in solution space evenly and randomly. Then the score of each individual is calculated and those with highest scores are selected as "winners", the seeds of future subpopulations.

"Similartaxis" performs local competition inside subpopulations among individuals and produces local optimal points. At first N individuals are distributed normally around one "winner" with the variance δ and then their scores are computed. The highest one is the winner, and will take part in the global competition in the following dissimilation.

"Dissimilation" completes global competition. The "winners" of subpopulations from "similartaxis" compete with each other and those with high score are kept to next round but the rest are eliminated and replaced by new individuals distributed in the solution space. This makes the population evolves toward the global optimum. Thus the "similartaxis" and "dissimilation" are repeated in turn until the stop conditions are met.

3.2 The Conception of the Subsection Nonlinearity Correction Method Based on MEA

The nonlinear voltage can be used to eliminate the nonlinearity of VCO. The frequency modulation curve is divided into several subsections and each end of the subsections varies in a limited area. Thereby the problem of correction is transformed to the optimization of the coordinates of these ends. It is MEA that performs the task. Then, the curve of optimal nonlinear voltage is gained by joining the ends optimized by MEA. As shown in Fig. 3, if the FM curve is departed into M segments, there are $M+1$ ends—original spot, terminal spot and $M-1$ mid spots. Whereas the original and terminal spots are invariable, the mid ones are alterable. Suppose the coordinate of the ith mid spot is denoted by (x_i, y_i) and it is subjected to $x_i \in [x_l, x_h]$, $y_i \in [y_l, y_h]$, then the confine where the point varies is described as following:

$$\begin{cases} x_l = i \times N/M - 0.5\delta \\ x_h = i \times N/M + 0.5\delta \\ y_l = i \times N/M - 0.5\delta \\ y_h = i \times N/M + 0.5\delta \end{cases} \quad i = 1, 2 \cdots, M-1 \tag{10}$$

Where δ is the length of area, i.e. the variety range of coordinate x_i and y_i; N is the length of the digital sequence output from D/A converter; M is the number of segments.

There are totally $M-1$ points, i.e. $2(M\text{-}1)$ coordinates to be optimized. Thus each individual in MEA includes $2(M-1)$ variables. Because a 16-bit fixed point digital signal processor(DSP) is employed in the experiment, to exert the superiority of the processor and enhance the calculative efficiency, 16-bit binary code method is adopted. In the evolutionary process, the schema characteristic of excellent individuals is distilled and the schema information is used to instruct the learning among the individuals in "similartaxis" and "dissimilation" operation [14].

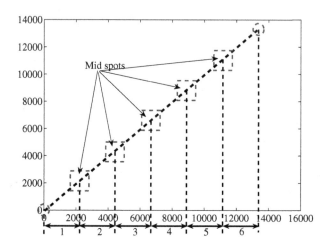

Fig. 3. The sketch map for FM voltage curve subsections. In this figure, FM voltage curve is divided into six subsections and the area of dashed square is alterable space of mid point

3.3   Structure for Fitness Function

For optimal algorithms, a proper fitness is a key factor for global optimal. The purpose of this paper is to reduce the spectral spread brought by VCO FM nonlinearities and restrain the fake peaks arose by nonlinearity and phrase noise. Accordingly the fitness function employed in this paper has the form of:

$$Fit = \alpha Fit_1 + \beta Fit_2 \qquad (11)$$

$$Fit_1 = \begin{cases} L_{initial} - l_n & L_{initial} \geq l_n \\ 0 & L_{initial} < l_n \end{cases} \qquad (12)$$

$$Fit_2 = \frac{P_{\max}}{P_1} + \frac{P_{\max}}{P_2} \qquad (13)$$

Where α and β are evaluating coefficients. Fit_1 denotes the evaluation to spectral spread. As limited with the dashed square in Fig. 4, the number of the spectrum bins over 1/2 peak magnitude is used to evaluate the extended spectrum, L_{intial} is the number before corrected. l_n is the number during the evolution. Considering some changeable ends randomly generated in initial stages of evolution might worsen the linearity, let $Fit_1 = 0$ when $L_{initial} < l_n$.

Fit_2 is the evaluation to the restrain effect of the fake peaks to the sides of the main peak. P_{max} is the amplitude value of the main peak after spectrum analyzed. P_1 and P_2 respectively denotes the amplitude values of the two fake peaks closest to the main peak which is marked with square in Fig. 5.

An individual during the evolution is a series of numbers in [0 65535]. Firstly, they are transformed into the practical coordinates and linked as a voltage curve.

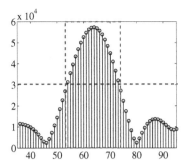

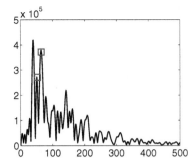

Fig. 4. The implication of Fit_1 **Fig. 5.** The implication of Fit_2

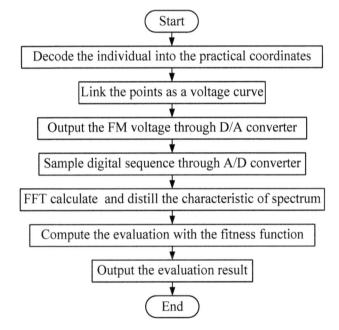

Fig. 6. The flow chart of the evaluation to the individual

Then the voltage curve is output through D/A converter to control VCO to generate frequency signals .Fig. 6 is the flow chart of the evaluation to the individual.

4   Experiment Results

For the LFMCW radar level gauge employed in this paper, the center frequency is 9.5GHz, FM bandwidth is 0.7GHz, FM period is 0.75ms, the 16-bit fixed point DSP processor is TMS320VC5509, and the frequency of the system clock is 120MHz. In the experiment, a metal flat is placed three meters before the

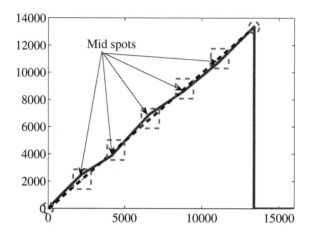

Fig. 7. FM voltage curve after nonlinearity correction. Dashed line is the line of linear FM voltage, solid curve is the result by the proposed method.

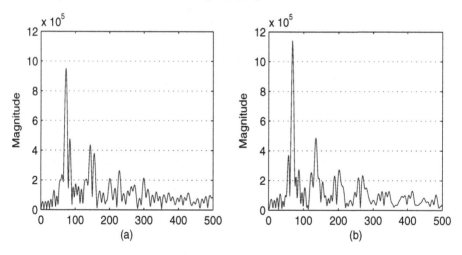

Fig. 8. The spectrum before and after correction. (a) is before correction and (b) is after correction.

LFMCW radar level gauge as the target, the new method proposed above is applied to correct the nonlinearity of VCO. The corrected nonlinear voltage curve is shown in Fig. 7. Fig. 8 shows the same position spectrum comparison between before and after correction which is obtained by 4096 points FFT with 1024 points sample padded zeros. After corrected, the value of the main peak is improved notably and the fake peaks beside it are restrained efficiently. Fig. 9 is the main peak bins of Fig. 8. It shows the spectrum spread narrowed. For MEA algorithm, the maximum iterative times is set as 100. During the experiment,

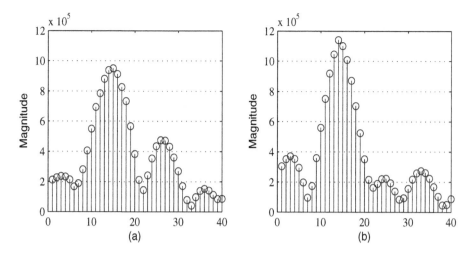

Fig. 9. The bins figure before and after correction. (a) is before correction and (b) is after correction.

the average iterative times for the optimal solution is 29. The results show that the new method is valid and the level measurement is notably improved.

5   Conclusion

MEA based nonlinear correction algorithm for the VCO in LFMCW radar level gauge is proposed in this paper. The frequency modulation voltage is firstly divided into several subsections, and then MEA is used to optimize the end coordinates of the subsections to get nonlinear frequency modulation voltage curve, so as to compensate for the nonlinearity of VCO. Good linear frequency modulation signal can be obtained without measuring the frequency or phase of the high frequency signals. And at the same time, its high accuracy is guaranteed. The proposed algorithm is suited for diverse level measurements due to its low cost, simplicity and good performance with no additional correction circuit.

Acknowledgements

This paper is financed by Chinese National Natural Science Foundations Project (60374029), Shanxi Province Tackle Projects in Science and Technology (001043).

References

1. Chen, Z.M., Ding, Y.Y., Xiang, J.C.: The Effects of Nonlinearity in Frequency Sweep on the Range Precision and Range Resolution of LFMCW Radar. Acta Electronica Sinica (1999) Vol.27(9) 103-104

2. Shen, T., Sun, Z.L.: Design of a highly Linearized 35GHz VCO. Journal of Southeast University (1996) Vol.26(1) 14-18
3. Huang, R.X., ZONG, C.G.: Research into the Method of the Nonlinear Compensation for VCO. Control and Instruments in Chemical Industry (2004) Vol.31(3) 50-51
4. Wang, X.G., Feng, J.X., Xiang, J.C.: Linearity Correction for linear FM Sweep Signals. Acta Electronica Sinica (1996) Vol.24(10) 120-122
5. Jing, Y.Q., He, G.Y., Xu, D.: Suppression of Sweeping Nonlinearity Based on Resampling Technique. Journal of Microwaves (2003) Vol.19(4) 92-95
6. Chen, Z.M., Ding, Y.Y., Xiang, J.C.: A Method on Nonlinear Correction of Broadband LFMCW Signal Utilizing Its Relative Sweep Nonlinear Error. Systems Engineering and Electronics (2001) Vol.23(2) 16-18
7. Wang, X.G., Feng, J.X., Xiang, J.C., Yuan, X.H.: An Iterative Algorithm of Sweep Linearity Correction for FMCW Signals. Systems Engineering and Electronics (1997) vol.7 23-26
8. Xie, K.M., Mou, C.H., Xie, G.: A MEA-based adaptive fuzzy logic controller. 2000 IEEE International Conference on Industrial Electronics, Control and Instrumentation (2000) 1492-1496
9. Xie, K.M., Mou, C.H., Xie, G.: The multi-parameter combination mind-evolutionary-based machine learning and its application. Proceedings of 2000 IEEE International Conference on Systems, Man, and Cybernetics (SMC2000) (2000) 183-187
10. Hao, X.L., Xie, K.M.: Design of a Fuzzy PID Controller Employed Multilevel Mind Evolution Algorithm. Journal of Taiyuan University of Technology (2004) Vol.35(2) 130-133
11. Xie, K.M., Du, Y.G., Sun, C.Y.: Application of the mind-evolution-based machine learning in mixture-ratio calculation of raw materials cement. Proceedings of the World Congress on Intelligent Control and Automation (WCICA) (2000) Vol.1 132-134
12. Piper, S.O.: Homodyne FMCW Radar Range Resolution Effects with Sinusiodal Nonlinearity in the Frequency Sweep. IEEE International Radar Conference (1995) 563-567
13. Wang, X.G., Yuan, X.H., Xiang, J.C., Feng, J.X.: Sweep Linearity Effect on Linear FMCW Radar Range Resolution.Systems Engineering and Electronics (1995) Vol.10 19-23
14. Zeng, J.C., Sun, C.Y.: A Mind-Evolution Method with Binary-Code. Aeronautical Computer Technique (1999) Vol.29(4) 43-45

On Degree of Dependence
Based on Contingency Matrix

Shusaku Tsumoto and Shoji Hirano

Department of Medical Informatics,
Shimane University, School of Medicine,
Enya-cho Izumo City, Shimane 693-8501 Japan
tsumoto@computer.org, hirano@ieee.org

Abstract. This paper discusses the degree of granularity and dependence of contingency tables from the viewpoint of linear algebra. From the results of determinantal divisors, it seems that the devisors provide information on the degree of dependencies between the matrix of the whole elements and its submatrices and the increase of the degree of granularity may lead to that of dependence. However, this paper shows that a constraint on the sample size of a contingency table is very strong, which leads to the evaluation formula where the increase of degree of granularity gives the decrease of dependency.

1 Introduction

Independence (dependence) is a very important concept in data mining, especially for feature selection. In rough sets [1], if two attribute-value pairs, say $[c = 0]$ and $[d = 0]$ are independent, their supporting sets, denoted by C and D do not have a overlapping region ($C \cap D = \phi$), which means that one attribute independent to a given target concept may not appear in the classification rule for the concept.

This idea is also frequently used in other rule discovery methods: let us consider deterministic rules, described as *if-then* rules, which can be viewed as classic propositions ($C \rightarrow D$). From the set-theoretical point of view, a set of examples supporting the conditional part of a deterministic rule, denoted by C, is a subset of a set whose examples belong to the consequence part, denoted by D. That is, the relation $C \subseteq D$ holds and deterministic rules are supported only by positive examples in a dataset [2].

When such a subset relation is not satisfied, indeterministic rules can be defined as if-then rules with probabilistic information [3]. From the set-theoretical point of view, C is not a subset, but closely overlapped with D. That is, the relations $C \cap D \neq \phi$ and $|C \cap D|/|C| \geq \delta$ will hold in this case.[1] Thus, probabilistic rules are supported by a large number of positive examples and a small number of negative examples.

---

[1] The threshold δ is the degree of the closeness of overlapping sets, which will be given by domain experts. For more information, please refer to Section 3.

D. Ślęzak et al. (Eds.): RSFDGrC 2005, LNAI 3641, pp. 471–480, 2005.

On the other hand, in a probabilistic context, independence of two attributes means that one attribute (a_1) will not influence the occurrence of the other attribute (a_2), which is formulated as $p(a_2|a_1) = p(a_2)$.

Although independence is a very important concept, it has not been fully and formally investigated as a relation between two attributes. Tsumoto introduces linear algebra into formal analysis of a contingency table [4]. The results give the following interesting results. First, a contingency table can be viewed as comparison between two attributes with respect to information granularity. Second, algebra is a key point of analysis of this table. A contingency table can be viewed as a matrix and several operations and ideas of matrix theory are introduced into the analysis of the contingency table. Especially, The degree of independence, rank plays a very important role in extracting a probabilistic model from a given contingency table.

This paper gives a further investigation on the degree of independence of contingency matrix.

Intuitively and empirically, when two attributes has many values, the dependence between these two attributes becomes low. However, from the results of determinantal divisors, it seems that the devisors provide information on the degree of dependencies between the matrix of the whole elements and its submatrices and the increase of the degree of granularity may lead to that of dependence. The key of the resolution of these conflicts is to consider the constraint on the sample size.

In this paper we show that a constraint on the sample size of a contingency table is very strong, which leads to the evaluation formula where the increase of degree of granularity gives the decrease of dependency.

2   Contingency Table from Rough Sets

2.1   Notations

In the subsequent sections, the following notations is adopted, which is introduced in [5]. Let U denote a nonempty, finite set called the universe and A denote a nonempty, finite set of attributes, i.e., $a : U \rightarrow V_a$ for $a \in A$, where V_a is called the domain of a, respectively. Then, a decision table is defined as an information system, $A = (U, A \cup \{\mathcal{D}\})$, where $\{\mathcal{D}\}$ is a set of given decision attributes. The atomic formulas over $B \subseteq A \cup \{\mathcal{D}\}$ and V are expressions of the form $[a = v]$, called descriptors over B, where $a \in B$ and $v \in V_a$. The set $F(B, V)$ of formulas over B is the least set containing all atomic formulas over B and closed with respect to disjunction, conjunction and negation. For each $f \in F(B, V)$, f_A denote the meaning of f in A, i.e., the set of all objects in U with property f, defined inductively as follows.

1. If f is of the form $[a = v]$ then, $f_A = \{s \in U | a(s) = v\}$
2. $(f \wedge g)_A = f_A \cap g_A; (f \vee g)_A = f_A \vee g_A; (\neg f)_A = U - f_a$

Table 1. Contingency Table ($n \times m$)

	A_1	A_2	$\cdots$	A_n	Sum
B_1	x_{11}	x_{12}	$\cdots$	x_{1n}	$x_{1\cdot}$
B_2	x_{21}	x_{22}	$\cdots$	x_{2n}	$x_{2\cdot}$
$\cdots$	$\cdots$	$\cdots$	$\cdots$	$\cdots$	$\cdots$
B_m	x_{m1}	x_{m2}	$\cdots$	x_{mn}	$x_{m\cdot}$
Sum	$x_{\cdot 1}$	$x_{\cdot 2}$	$\cdots$	$x_{\cdot n}$	$x_{\cdot\cdot} = |U| = N$

2.2 Multi-way Contingency Table

Two-way contingency table can be extended into a contingency table for multi-nominal attributes.

Definition 1. *Let R_1 and R_2 denote multinominal attributes in an attribute space A which have m and n values. A contingency tables is a table of a set of the meaning of the following formulas: $|[R_1 = A_j]_A|$, $|[R_2 = B_i]_A|$, $|[R_1 = A_j \wedge R_2 = B_i]_A|$, $|[R_1 = A_1 \wedge R_1 = A_2 \wedge \cdots \wedge R_1 = A_m]_A|$, $|[R_2 = B_1 \wedge R_2 = A_2 \wedge \cdots \wedge R_2 = A_n]_A|$ and $|U|$ ($i = 1, 2, 3, \cdots, n$ and $j = 1, 2, 3, \cdots, m$). This table is arranged into the form shown in Table 1, where: $|[R_1 = A_j]_A| = \sum_{i=1}^{m} x_{1i} = x_{\cdot j}$, $|[R_2 = B_i]_A| = \sum_{j=1}^{n} x_{ji} = x_{i\cdot}$, $|[R_1 = A_j \wedge R_2 = B_i]_A| = x_{ij}$, $|U| = N = x_{\cdot\cdot}$ ($i = 1, 2, 3, \cdots, n$ and $j = 1, 2, 3, \cdots, m$).*

3 Rank of Contingency Table (Multi-way)

The relation between rank and independence in a multi-way contingency table is obtained.

Theorem 1. *Let the corresponding matrix of a given contingency table be a square $n \times n$ matrix. If the rank of the corresponding matrix is 1, then two attributes in a given contingency table are statistically independent. If the rank of the corresponding matrix is n, then two attributes in a given contingency table are dependent. Otherwise, two attributes are contextual dependent, which means that several conditional probabilities can be represented by a linear combination of conditional probabilities. Thus,*

$$
rank = \begin{cases} n & dependent \\ 2, \cdots, n-1 & contextual\ independent \\ 1 & statistical\ independent \end{cases} \qquad \square
$$

This theorem can be generalized into $m \times n$ matrix. If the corresponding matrix of a given contingency table is not square and of the form $m \times n$, then its rank is at most $\min(m, n)$.

Theorem 2. *Let the corresponding matrix of a given contingency table be a $m \times n$ matrix. The rank of this matrix is less than $\min(m, n)$. If the rank of the* *corresponding matrix is 1, then two attributes in a given contingency table are statistically independent. If the rank of the corresponding matrix is n , then two attributes in a given contingency table are dependent. Otherwise, two attributes are contextual dependent, which means that several conditional probabilities can be represented by a linear combination of conditional probabilities. Thus,*

$$
rank = \begin{cases} \min(m,n) & dependent \\ 2, \cdots, & \\ \quad \min(m,n) - 1 & contextual\ independent \\ 1 & statistical\ independent \end{cases} \qquad \square
$$

In the cases of $m \neq n$, we need a discussion on submatrix and subderminant in the next section.

4   Rank and Degree of Dependence

4.1   Submatrix and Subdeterminant

The next interest is the structure of a corresponding matrix with $1 \leq rank \leq n - 1$. First, let us define a submatrix (a subtable) and subdeterminant.

Definition 2. *Let A denote a corresponding matrix of a given contigency table $(m \times n)$. A corresponding submatrix $A_{j_1 j_2 \cdots j_s}^{i_1 i_2 \cdots i_r}$ is defined as a matrix which is given by an intersection of r rows and s columns of A ($i_1 < i_2 < \cdots < i_r, j_1 < j_2 < \cdots < j_r$).*

Definition 3. *A subdeterminant of A is defined as a determinant of a submatrix $A_{j_1 j_2 \cdots j_s}^{i_1 i_2 \cdots i_r}$, which is denoted by $det(A_{j_1 j_2 \cdots j_s}^{i_1 i_2 \cdots i_r})$.*

Let us consider the contingency table given as Table 1. Then, a subtable for $A_{j_1 j_2 \cdots j_s}^{i_1 i_2 \cdots i_r}$ is given as Table 2.

4.2   Rank and Subdeterminant

Let δ_{ij} denote a co-factor of a_{ij} in a square corresponding matrix of A. Then,

$$
\Delta_{ij} = (-1)^{i+j} det(A_{1,2,\cdots,j-1,j+1,\cdots,n}^{1,2,\cdots,i-1,i+1,\cdots,n}).
$$

Table 2. A subtable ($r \times s$)

	A_{j_1}	A_{j_2}	$\cdots$	A_{j_r}	Sum
B_{i_1}	$x_{i_1 j_1}$	$x_{i_1 j_2}$	$\cdots$	$x_{i_1 j_r}$	$x_{i_1 \cdot}$
B_{i_2}	$x_{i_2 j_1}$	$x_{i_2 j_2}$	$\cdots$	$x_{i_2 j_r}$	$x_{i_2 \cdot}$
$\cdots$	$\cdots$	$\cdots$	$\cdots$	$\cdots$	$\cdots$
B_{i_r}	$x_{i_r j_1}$	$x_{i_r j_2}$	$\cdots$	$x_{i_r j_n}$	$x_{i_r \cdot}$
Sum	$x_{\cdot 1}$	$x_{\cdot 2}$	$\cdots$	$x_{\cdot n}$	$x_{\cdot \cdot} = |U| = N$

It is notable that a co-factor is a special type of submatrix, where only ith-row and j-column are removed from a original matrix. By the use of co-factors, the determinant of A is defined as:

$$det(A) = \sum_{j=1}^{n} a_{ij}\Delta_{ij},$$

which is called *Laplace expansion*.

From this representation, if $det(A)$ is not equal to 0, then $\Delta_{ij} \neq 0$ for $\{a_{i1}, a_{i2}, \cdots, a_{in}\}$ which are not equal to 0. Thus, the following proposition is obtained.

Proposition 1. *If $det(A)$ is not equal to 0 if at least one co-factor of $a_{ij}(\neq 0)$, Δ_{ij} is not equal to 0.*

It is notable that the above definition of a determinant gives the relation between a original matrix A and submatrices (co-factors). Since cofactors gives a square matrix of size $n - 1$, the above proposition gives the relation between a matrix of size n and submatrices of size $n - 1$. In the same way, we can discuss the relation between a corresponding matrix of size n and submatrices of size $r(1 \leq r < n - 1)$.

4.3   Rank and Submatrix

Let us assume that corresponding matrix and submatrix are square ($n \times n$ and $r \times r$, respectively).

Theorem 3. *If the rank of a corresponding matrix of size $n \times n$ is equal to r, at least the determinant of one submatrix of size $r \times r$ is not equal to 0. That is, there exists a submatrix $A_{j_1 j_2 \cdots j_r}^{i_1 i_2 \cdots i_r}$, which satisfies $det(A_{j_1 j_2 \cdots j_r}^{i_1 i_2 \cdots i_r}) \neq 0$*

Corollary 1. *If the rank of a corresponding matrix of size $n \times n$ is equal to r, all the determinants of the submatrices whose number of columns and rows are larger than $r + 1(\leq n)$ are equal to 0.*   □

Thus, one attribute-value pair is statistically dependent on other two pairs, statistically independent of the other attribute. In other words, if two pairs are fixed, the remaining one attribute-value pair will be statistically independently determined.

4.4   Determinantal Divisors

From the subdeterminants of all the submatrices of size 2, all the subdeterminants of a corresponding matrix has the greatest common divisor, equal to 3.

From the recursive definition of the determinants, it is show that the subdeterminants of size $r + 1$ will have the greatest common divisor of the subdeterminants of size r as a divisor. Thus,

Theorem 4. *Let $d_k(A)$ denote the greatest common divisor of all the subdeterminants of size k, $det(A_{j_1 j_2 \cdots j_r}^{i_1 i_2 \cdots i_k})$. $d_1(A), d_2(A), \cdots, d_n(A)$ are called determinantal divisors. From the definition of Laplace expansion,*

$$d_k(A)|d_{k+1}(A). \qquad \square$$

It is notable that a simple change of a corresponding matrix gives a significant change to the determinant, which suggests a change of structure in dependence/independence.

The relation between $d_k(A)$ gives a interesting constraint.

Proposition 2. *Since $d_k(A)|d_{k+1}(A)$, the sequence of the devisiors is monotonically increasing one:*

$$d_1(A) \le d_2(A) \cdots \le d_r(A),$$

where r denotes the rank of A.

The sequence of B illustrates this: $1 < 3 < 18$.

Let us define a ratio of $d_k(A)$ to $d_{k-1}(A)$, called *elementary divisors*, where C denotes a corresponding matrix and $k \le rankA$:

$$e_k(C) = \frac{d_k(C)}{d_{k-1}(C)} (d_0(C) = 0).$$

The elementary divisors may give the increase of dependency between two attributes. For example, $e_1(B) = 1$, $e_2(B) = 3$, and $e_3(B) = 6$. Thus, a transition from 2×2 to 3×3 have a higher impact on the dependency of two attributes.

It is trivial to see that $det(B) = e_1 e_2 e_3$, which can be viewed as a decomposition of the determinant of a corresponindg matrix.

4.5   Divisors and Degree of Dependence

Since the determinant can be viewed as the degree of dependence, this result is very important. If values of all the subdeterminants (size r) are very small (nearly equal to 0) and $d_r(A) \simeq 1$, then the values of the subdeterminants (size $r + 1$) are very small. This property may hold until the r reaches the rank of the corresponding matrix. Thus, the sequence of the divisiors of a corresponding matrix gives a hidden structure of a contingency table.

Also, this results show that $d_1(A)$ and $d_2(A)$ are very important to estimate the rank of a corresponding matrix. Since $d_1(A)$ is only given by the greatest common divisor of all the elements of A, $d_2(A)$ are much more important components. This also intuitively suggests that the subdeterminants of A with size 2 are principal components of a corresponding matrix from the viewpoint of statistical dependence.

Recall that statistical independence of two attributes is equivalent to a corresponding matrix with rank being 1. A matrix with rank being 2 gives a context-dependent independence, which means three values of two attributes are independent, but two values of two attributes are dependent.

4.6 Elementary Divisors and Elementary Transformation

Let us define the following three elementary (row/column)transformations of a corresponding matrix:

1. Exchange two rows (columns), i_0 and j_0 $(P(i_0, j_0))$.
2. Multiply -1 to a row (column) i_0 $(T(i_0; -1))$.
3. Multiply t to a row (column) j_0 (i_0) and add it to a row i_0 (j_0). $(W(i_0, j_0, t))$.

Then, three transformations have several interesting characteristics.

Proposition 3. *Matrices corresponding to three elementary transformations are regular.*

Proposition 4. *Three elementary transformations do not change the rank of a corresponding matrix.*

Proposition 5. *Let $\tilde{A}$ denote a matrix transformed by finite steps of three operations. Then,*

$$rank\tilde{A} = rankA, \quad d_r(\tilde{A}) = d_r(A),$$

where r denotes the rank of matrix A.

Then, from the results of linear algebra, the following interesting result is obtained.

Theorem 5. *With the finite steps of elementary transformations, a given corresponding matrix is transformed into*

$$
\tilde{A} = \begin{pmatrix}
e_1 & & & & \\
 & e_2 & & & O \\
 & & \ddots & & \\
 & & & e_r & \\
\hline
 & O & & & O
\end{pmatrix},
$$

where $e_j = \frac{d_j(A)}{d_{j-1}(A)}$ $(d_0(A) = 1)$ and r denotes the rank of a corresponding matrix. Then, the determinant is decomposed into the product of e_j.

$$d_r(\tilde{A}) = d_r(A) = e_1 e_2 \cdots e_r. \qquad \Box$$

5 Degree of Granularity and Dependence

From Theorem 5, it seems that the increase of the degree of granularity gives that of the dependence between two attributes.

However, our empirical observations are different from the above intuitive analysis. Thus, there should be a strong constraint which suppress the above effects on the degree of granularity.

Let us assume that the determinant of a give contingency matrix gives the degree of the dependence of the matrix. Then, from the results of linear algebra, we obtain the following theorem.

Theorem 6. *Let A denote a* $n \times n$ *contingency matrix, which includes N samples. If the rank of A is equal to n, then there exists a matrix B* $(n \times n)$ *which satisfies*

$$BA = \begin{pmatrix} \rho_1 & & & \\ & \rho_2 & & O \\ & & \ddots & \\ O & & & \rho_n \end{pmatrix} = P,$$

where $\rho_1 + \rho_2 + \cdots + \rho_n = N$.

It is notable that the value of determinants of P is larger than A:

$$det A \leq det P \qquad \qquad \square$$

It is easy to see that the tranformed matrix P has a very nice property to calculate the determinant.

Proposition 6. *The determinant of the transformed matrix P is equal to the multiplication of* ρ_1 *to* ρ_n. *That is,*

$$det P = \rho_1 \rho_2 \cdots \rho_n \qquad \qquad \square$$

Then, the following constraint will be have the special meaning:

$$\rho_1 + \rho_2 + \cdots + \rho_n = N, \tag{1}$$

because the following inequality holds in general:

$$\frac{\rho_1 + \rho_2 + \cdots + \rho_n}{n} \geq \sqrt[n]{\rho_1 \rho_2 \cdots \rho_n}, \tag{2}$$

where the equality holds when $\rho_1 = \rho_2 = \cdots = \rho_n$. Since the above inequality can be transformed into:

$$\rho_1 \rho_2 \cdots \rho_n \leq \left(\frac{\rho_1 + \rho_2 + \cdots + \rho_n}{n} \right)^n,$$

the following inequality is obtained:

$$det P = \rho_1 \rho_2 \cdots \rho_n \leq \left(\frac{\rho_1 + \rho_2 + \cdots + \rho_n}{n} \right)^n, \tag{3}$$

where the equality holds when $\rho_1 = \rho_2 = \cdots = \rho_n$. From the theorem 6 and equation 1, the following theorem is obtained.

Theorem 7. *When a contingency matrix A holds* $AB = P$, *where P is a diagonal matrix, the following inequality holds:*

$$det A \leq \left(\frac{N}{n} \right)^n,$$

Proof.

$$det A = det(PB^{-1})$$
$$\leq det P$$
$$= \rho_1 \rho_2 \cdots \rho_n$$
$$\leq \left(\frac{\rho_1 + \rho_2 + \cdots + \rho_n}{n} \right)^n = \left(\frac{N}{n} \right)^n, \tag{4}$$

where the former equality holds when $det B^{-1} = det B = 1$ and the latter equality holds when $\rho_1 = \rho_2 = \cdots = \rho_n = \frac{N}{n}$.

Thus, the maximum value of the determinant of A is at most $\left(\frac{N}{n} \right)^n$. Since N is constant for the given matrix A, the degree of dependence will decrease very rapidly when n becomes very large. That is,

$$det A \sim n^{-n}.$$

Thus,

Corollary 2. *The determinant of A will converge into 0 when n increases into infinity.*

$$\lim_{n \to \infty} det A = 0. \qquad \square$$

This results suggest that when the degree of granularity becomes higher, the degree of dependence will become lower, due to the constraints on the sample size.

However, it is notable that N/n is very important. If N is very large, the rapid decrease will be observed N is close to n. For the behavior of $(N/n)^n$, we can apply the technique of real analysis, which will our future work.

6   Conclusion

In this paper, a contingency table is interpreted from the viewpoint of granular computing and statistical independence. Matrix algebra is a key point of the analysis of a contingency table and the degree of independence, rank plays a very important role in extracting a probabilistic model. From the correspondence between contingency table and matrix, the following results are obtained: First, the value of determinants gives the degree of of dependency between attribute-value pairs for a set of submatrices with the same size. Second, from the characteristics of the determinants, the larger rank a corresponding matrix has, the higher the two attributes are dependent. This results is shown by a monotonicity of a sequence of determinantal divisors. Third, elementary divisors give a decomposition of the determinant of a corresponding matrix. Finally, the constraint on the sample size of a contingency table is very strong, which leads to the evaluation formula where the increase of degree of granularity gives the decrease of dependency.

Acknowledgement

This work was supported by the Grant-in-Aid for Scientific Research (13131208) on Priority Areas (No.759) "Implementation of Active Mining in the Era of Information Flood" by the Ministry of Education, Science, Culture, Sports, Science and Technology of Japan.

References

1. Pawlak, Z.: Rough Sets. Kluwer Academic Publishers, Dordrecht (1991)
2. Tsumoto, S.: Knowledge discovery in clinical databases and evaluation of discovered knowledge in outpatient clinic. Information Sciences (2000) 125–137
3. Tsumoto, S., Tanaka, H.: Automated discovery of medical expert system rules from clinical databases based on rough sets. In: Proceedings of the Second International Conference on Knowledge Discovery and Data Mining 96, Palo Alto, AAAI Press (1996) 63–69
4. Tsumoto, S.: Statistical independence as linear independence. In Skowron, A., Szczuka, M., eds.: Electronic Notes in Theoretical Computer Science. Volume 82., Elsevier (2003)
5. Skowron, A., Grzymala-Busse, J.: From rough set theory to evidence theory. In Yager, R., Fedrizzi, M., Kacprzyk, J., eds.: Advances in the Dempster-Shafer Theory of Evidence. John Wiley & Sons, New York (1994) 193–236

Model Selection and Assessment for Classification Using Validation

Wojciech Jaworski

Faculty of Mathematics, Informatics and Mechanics,
Warsaw University, Banacha 2, 02-097 Warsaw, Poland
wjaworski@mimuw.edu.pl

Abstract. We address the problem of determination of the size of the test set which can can guarantee statistically significant results in classifier error estimation and in selection of the best classifier from a given set. We focus on the case of the 0-1 valued loss function and we provide one and two sides optimal bounds for Validation (known also as Hold-Out Estimate and Train-and-Test Method). We also calculate the smallest sample size, necessary for obtaining the bound for given estimation accuracy and reliability of estimation, and we present the results in tables. Finally, we propose strategies for classifier design using the bounds derived.

Keywords: Computational learning theory, Model Selection, Model Assessment, Hold-Out Estimate, Train-and-Test, Validation.

1 Introduction

The ability to act properly in a partially unknown environment is one of the most important properties of an intelligent system. In the case of classification, this 'proper act' is a generalization ability — an ability to classify new samples correctly.

In a classifier design cycle, there are two aspects which concern the classifier behaviour on new samples: Model Selection and Model Assessment. During the Model Selection process, we try to choose the best classifier from a given set. For example, in a rough set theory, this phrase refers to choosing the minimal support for decision rules. During the Model Assessment, we estimate the generalization ability of the classifier.

There are several methods for performing Model Selection and Assessment. However, we restrict ourselves to the analysis of Validation (also known as Train-and-Test Method or Hold-Out Estimate). The reason is that the quality of Validation estimation is independent from the classifying algorithm. Hence, an efficient universal bound can be obtained.

We derive optimal bounds in a probabilistic model of a learning process, based on independence of samples. In this model, we restrict ourselves to the case of the 0-1 valued loss function. Since the 0-1 valued loss function is the one used most often in pattern recognition, this case has multiple applications.

D. Ślęzak et al. (Eds.): RSFDGrC 2005, LNAI 3641, pp. 481–490, 2005.

Using the bounds, the smallest number of samples, needed for performing of the model selection and assessment with statistically significant results, can be determined. The 'optimality' of bound assures that the size of a testing sample, assessed by it, is necessary and it cannot be decreased.

We describe the model and give a formal definition of Validation in Sect. 2. In Sect. 3 we present results concerning the classifier error estimation using Validation. We also provide the tables, where the smallest sample size necessary for obtaining the bound for given estimation accuracy and reliability of estimation is calculated. We discuss the bound in the case of testing many classifiers with the same sample. In Sect. 4, we present the Model Selection and Assessment strategies based on the bounds.

2   The Problem of Learning from the Statistical Point of View

In this section, the fundamental concepts of the learning theory are introduced.

Let X be the **set of examples (attribute value vectors)**, Y be the **set of decisions (labels)**, and ρ be a Borel probability measure on $Z = X \times Y$. ρ plays an important role in sampling as it describes the probability of getting a given sample as well as distribution of decision for any example. Unfortunately, ρ is unknown to us.

We are given a finite sequence $\mathbf{z} = \big((x_1, y_1), \ldots, (x_m, y_m)\big)$, where x_i is an example and y_i – a decision for $i = 1, \ldots, m$. The sequence $\mathbf{z}$ will be called a **sample** of the length m; $\mathbf{z}$ is randomly got by m independent draws according to the probability measure ρ; $\mathbf{z}$ describes all our knowledge about ρ.

An algorithm $A_m : Z^m \to (X \to Y)$ is also such that for each sample $\mathbf{z}$ of the length m, A_m yields a **classifier** (i.e., a function) $f_{\mathbf{z}} : X \to Y$.

Having a classifier, we want to evaluate its quality. The quality of a classifier f is determined by its **generalization error** defined by

$$\mathcal{E}(f) - \int_Z V\big(y, f(x)\big) d\rho(x, y),$$

where $V : Y \times Y \to \mathbb{R}_+$ is called the **loss function**. For example, the loss function can be defined by:

$$V\big(y, f(x)\big) = (y - f(x))^2,$$

$$V\big(y, f(x)\big) = |y - f(x)|,$$

or

$$V\big(y, f(x)\big) = \begin{cases} 0 & \text{if } y = f(x) \\ 1 & \text{if } y \neq f(x). \end{cases}$$

For a finite set of decisions $Y = \{d_1, d_2, \ldots, d_l\}$, the last case may be generalized to

$$V\big(d_i, d_j\big) = a_{i,j}$$

where $a_{i,i} = 0$ and $0 \leq a_{i,j} \leq 1$. Such a loss function allows us to express the fact that we prefer one type of the classifier error to another. In this paper, we concern only with the 0-1 valued loss function, i.e., we assume that

$$V : Y \times Y \rightarrow \{0, 1\}.$$

We want to estimate $\mathcal{E}(f_{\mathbf{z}})$, which cannot be calculated directly. To this end, we use the generalization error evaluators such as Validation.

The idea of **Validation** is to divide a given sample $\mathbf{z}$ into two distinct parts $\mathbf{z}_1, \mathbf{z}_2$. The sample $\mathbf{z}_1$ will be used to learn the classifier and the sample $\mathbf{z}_2 = \big((x'_1, y'_1), \dots, (x'_{m'}, y'_{m'}) \big)$ to test it by calculation of

$$\mathcal{E}_{\mathbf{z}_2}(f_{\mathbf{z}_1}) = \frac{1}{m'} \sum_{i=1}^{m'} V\big(y'_i, f_{\mathbf{z}_1}(x'_i) \big).$$

$\mathcal{E}_{\mathbf{z}}(f)$ is called the **empirical error** of the function f on the sample $\mathbf{z}$. Having calculated $\mathcal{E}_{\mathbf{z}_2}(f_{\mathbf{z}_1})$, we claim that its value is similar to the value of the **generalization error** of $f_{\mathbf{z}_1}$.

$$\mathcal{E}_{\mathbf{z}_2}(f_{\mathbf{z}_1}) \sim \mathcal{E}(f_{\mathbf{z}_1})$$

In the next sections, we will try to express this similarity by numeric means.

3   Bounds for Classifier Error Estimation

The simplest way to obtain the quality of estimation is to assess

$$|\mathcal{E}_{\mathbf{z}_2}(f_{\mathbf{z}_1}) - \mathcal{E}(f_{\mathbf{z}_1})|$$

or at least

$$\mathcal{E}(f_{\mathbf{z}_1}) - \mathcal{E}_{\mathbf{z}_2}(f_{\mathbf{z}_1})$$

if we are interested only in how bad the estimation can be.

According to [8], we may use the following inequalities:

Theorem 1. *Let m denote the size of $\mathbf{z}_2$, and let $\varepsilon > 0$. If $V\big(f_{\mathbf{z}_1}(x), y \big) \in \{0, 1\}$, then the least δ such that*

$$P\big(\mathcal{E}(f_{\mathbf{z}_1}) - \mathcal{E}_{\mathbf{z}_2}(f_{\mathbf{z}_1}) > \varepsilon \big) < \delta \tag{1}$$

has the value

$$\delta = \max_{k < (1-\varepsilon)m} \sum_{i=0}^{k} \binom{m}{i} \left(\varepsilon + \frac{k}{m} \right)^i \left(1 - \varepsilon - \frac{k}{m} \right)^{m-i}.$$

The behaviour of the bound is shown in Table 1.

Table 1. Number of samples needed for inequality (1) to hold for given ε and δ

$\varepsilon\backslash\delta$	0.1000	0.0500	0.0200	0.0100	0.0050	0.0020	0.0010	0.0005	0.0002	0.0001
0.005	16624	27255	42379	54319	66549	83038	95695	108475	125522	138510
0.010	4206	6864	10645	13630	16687	20809	23974	27169	31430	34677
0.015	1891	3073	4753	6080	7439	9271	10677	12097	13991	15434
0.020	1076	1741	2686	3432	4197	5227	6018	6817	7882	8694
0.025	697	1122	1727	2205	2694	3353	3860	4371	5053	5572
0.030	489	785	1205	1537	1876	2334	2686	3041	3514	3875
0.035	364	581	889	1133	1383	1719	1977	2238	2586	2851
0.040	281	448	684	871	1062	1319	1517	1717	1983	2186
0.045	225	356	543	690	841	1045	1201	1359	1569	1729
0.050	184	291	442	561	683	848	975	1103	1273	1403
0.055	154	242	367	465	566	703	807	913	1054	1161
0.060	131	205	310	392	477	592	680	768	887	977
0.065	112	175	265	336	408	505	580	656	757	833
0.070	98	152	230	290	353	437	501	566	653	720
0.075	86	134	201	254	308	381	438	494	570	628
0.080	77	118	177	224	272	336	385	435	502	552
0.085	69	105	158	199	241	298	342	386	445	490
0.090	62	95	141	178	216	267	306	345	398	438
0.095	56	86	127	160	194	240	275	310	357	393
0.100	51	78	115	145	176	217	249	280	323	355
0.105	47	71	105	132	160	197	226	255	293	323
0.110	43	65	96	121	146	180	206	233	268	294
0.115	40	60	88	111	134	165	189	213	245	270
0.120	37	55	82	102	123	152	174	196	226	248
0.125	34	51	76	95	114	140	161	181	208	229
0.130	32	48	70	88	106	130	149	168	193	212
0.135	30	45	65	82	98	121	138	156	179	197
0.140	28	42	61	76	92	113	129	145	167	183
0.145	26	39	57	71	86	105	120	135	156	171
0.150	25	37	54	67	80	99	113	127	146	160
0.155	24	35	50	63	75	93	106	119	137	150
0.160	22	33	48	59	71	87	99	112	128	141
0.165	21	31	45	56	67	82	94	105	121	133
0.170	20	29	42	53	63	77	88	99	114	125
0.175	19	28	40	50	60	73	84	94	108	118
0.180	18	27	38	47	57	69	79	89	102	112
0.185	17	25	36	45	54	66	75	84	97	106
0.190	17	24	35	43	51	63	71	80	92	101
0.195	16	23	33	41	49	60	68	76	87	96
0.200	15	22	31	39	46	57	65	72	83	91

Theorem 2. *Let $\varepsilon > 0$ and m be such that $\frac{1}{4\varepsilon^2} + 1 \leq m$. The least δ such that*

$$\mathrm{P}\big(|\mathcal{E}(f_{\mathbf{z}_1}) - \mathcal{E}_{\mathbf{z}_2}(f_{\mathbf{z}_1})| > \varepsilon\big) < \delta \tag{2}$$

satisfies

$$\delta = \max_{0 \le k < m(1-\varepsilon)} \sum_{i=0}^{k} \binom{m}{i} \left(\varepsilon + \frac{k}{m} \right)^i \left(1 - \varepsilon - \frac{k}{m} \right)^{m-i} +$$

$$+ \sum_{i=k+\lfloor 2m\varepsilon \rfloor + 1}^{m} \binom{m}{i} \left(\varepsilon + \frac{k}{m} \right)^i \left(1 - \varepsilon - \frac{k}{m} \right)^{m-i}.$$

The behaviour of the bound is shown in Table 2 As we can see, the necessary number of samples for the two side bound is only slightly greater that the number of samples for the one side bound for small δ.

Observe that Theorem 1 provides us with the optimal $\delta_{m,\varepsilon}$ for the following inequality:

$$P(\mathcal{E}(f) - \mathcal{E}_\mathbf{z}(f) > \varepsilon) \le \delta_{m,\varepsilon}.$$

Now, we will look for the optimal bound, considering inequalities of the form

$$P(\mathcal{E}(f) > g(\mathcal{E}_\mathbf{z}(f))) \le \delta,$$

where $g : \{\frac{0}{m}, \frac{1}{m}, \dots, \frac{m}{m}\} \to [0, 1]$ is monotonically increasing and $g(1) = 1$. Let

$$\mathcal{G}_{m,\delta} = \{ g : \{\frac{1}{m}, \frac{2}{m}, \dots, \frac{m}{m}\} \to [0, 1] \mid P(\mathcal{E}(f) > g(\mathcal{E}_\mathbf{z}(f))) \le \delta \wedge$$

$$\wedge \forall_{x,y}\ x < y \Rightarrow g(x) \le g(y) \wedge g(1) = 1 \}.$$

In order to compare the quality of inequalities, we introduce a partial order on $\mathcal{G}_{m,\delta}$. For any $g_1, g_2 \in \mathcal{G}_{m,\delta}$, let

$$g_1 \preceq g_2 \text{ iff } \forall_x\ g_1(x) \le g_2(x).$$

$g_1 \preceq g_2$ means that the bound estimated using g_1 is better than the one estimated by g_2. The optimal bound is the one corresponding to the $\preceq$-least element.

Definition 1. *Let $k < m$ and $g_{m,\delta}(\frac{k}{m}) = p$ be such that*

$$\sum_{i=0}^{k} \binom{m}{i} p^i (1 - p)^{m-i} = \delta$$

and $g_{m,\delta}(1) = 1$.

Since $\sum_{i=0}^{k} \binom{m}{i} p^i (1 - p)^{m-i}$ is strictly monotonically decreasing with growing p, $g_{m,\delta}$ is well-defined.

Theorem 3. *Let $0 < \delta < 1$, $m \in \mathbb{N}$. $g_{m,\delta}$ is the $\preceq$-least element of $\mathcal{G}_{m,\delta}$, i.e.,*

$$P(\mathcal{E}(f) > g_{m,\delta}(\mathcal{E}_\mathbf{z}(f))) < \delta$$

is the optimal bound.

Table 2. Number of samples needed for inequality (2) to hold for given ε and δ

ε\δ	0.1000	0.0500	0.0200	0.0100	0.0050	0.0020	0.0010	0.0005	0.0002	0.0001
0.005	27100	38500	54200	66400	78800	95500	108300	121200	138400	151400
0.010	6800	9650	13550	16600	19700	23900	27100	30300	34600	37850
0.015	3034	4300	6034	7400	8767	10634	12034	13467	15400	16834
0.020	1700	2425	3400	4150	4925	5975	6775	7575	8650	9475
0.025	1100	1540	2180	2660	3160	3820	4340	4860	5540	6060
0.030	767	1084	1517	1850	2200	2667	3017	3367	3850	4217
0.035	558	786	1115	1358	1615	1958	2215	2486	2829	3100
0.040	425	613	850	1038	1238	1500	1700	1900	2163	2375
0.045	345	478	678	823	978	1189	1345	1500	1712	1878
0.050	280	390	550	670	790	960	1090	1220	1390	1520
0.055	228	328	455	555	655	791	900	1010	1146	1255
0.060	192	275	384	467	550	667	759	842	967	1050
0.065	162	231	324	400	470	570	647	724	824	900
0.070	143	200	279	343	408	493	558	622	708	772
0.075	127	174	247	300	354	427	487	540	620	674
0.080	113	157	213	263	313	375	425	475	544	594
0.085	100	136	189	236	277	336	377	424	483	524
0.090	89	123	173	206	245	300	339	378	428	467
0.095	79	111	153	190	222	269	300	337	385	422
0.100	70	100	140	170	200	240	275	305	345	380
0.105	67	91	124	153	181	220	248	277	315	343
0.110	60	82	114	141	164	200	228	250	287	314
0.115	57	74	105	127	153	183	209	231	261	287
0.120	50	71	96	117	138	167	192	213	242	263
0.125	44	64	88	108	128	156	176	196	224	244
0.130	43	58	81	100	120	143	162	181	204	227
0.135	41	56	78	93	112	134	152	167	189	208
0.140	36	50	72	86	104	125	140	158	179	193
0.145	35	49	66	80	97	114	132	145	166	180
0.150	34	47	64	77	90	107	120	137	154	170
0.155	33	42	59	71	84	100	113	126	146	159
0.160	29	41	57	66	79	94	107	119	135	147
0.165	28	37	52	64	73	88	100	113	128	140
0.170	27	36	50	59	71	86	95	106	121	133
0.175	23	35	46	58	66	80	89	100	115	123
0.180	23	31	45	53	62	75	84	95	109	117
0.185	22	30	41	52	60	71	82	90	103	111
0.190	22	29	40	48	56	69	77	85	98	106
0.195	21	29	36	47	54	65	72	80	93	100
0.200	20	25	35	43	50	60	68	75	88	95

Proof. First, we prove that $g_{m,\delta} \in \mathcal{G}_{m,\delta}$. It is obvious that $g_{m,\delta}(\frac{k}{m}) \leq g_{m,\delta}(\frac{k+1}{m})$. Let $g_{m,\delta}(\frac{-1}{m}) = 0$. We show that the inequality holds.

$$P(\mathcal{E}(f) > g(\mathcal{E}_{\mathbf{z}}(f))) = \sum_{i=0}^{m} P(\mathcal{E}_{\mathbf{z}}(f) = \frac{i}{m}) P(\mathcal{E}(f) > g(\mathcal{E}_{\mathbf{z}}(f)) | \mathcal{E}_{\mathbf{z}}(f) = \frac{i}{m}) =$$

$$= \sum_{i=0}^{m} \binom{m}{i} \mathcal{E}(f)^i (1 - \mathcal{E}(f))^{m-i} P(\mathcal{E}(f) > g_{m,\delta}(\frac{i}{m})) \leq$$

$$\leq \max_{k\in\{-1,0,\ldots,m-1\}} \sup_{p\in(g_{m,\delta}(\frac{k}{m}),g_{m,\delta}(\frac{k+1}{m})]} \sum_{i=0}^{m} \binom{m}{i} p^i (1-p)^{m-i} P(p > g_{m,\delta}(\frac{i}{m})) =$$

$$= \max_{k\in\{-1,0,\ldots,m-1\}} \sup_{p\in(g_{m,\delta}(\frac{k}{m}),g_{m,\delta}(\frac{k+1}{m})]} \sum_{i=0}^{k} \binom{m}{i} p^i (1-p)^{m-i} < \delta$$

Now, we show that $g_{m,\delta}$ is the smallest in $\mathcal{G}_{m,\delta}$. Let $g \in \mathcal{G}_{m,\delta}$. Assume that $\mathcal{E}(f) = g(\frac{k}{m}) + \varepsilon$. Then,

$$\lim_{\varepsilon\to 0^+} P(\mathcal{E}(f) > g(\mathcal{E}_{\mathbf{z}}(f))) = \lim_{\varepsilon\to 0^+} \sum_{i=0}^{k} \binom{m}{i} \mathcal{E}(f)^i (1 - \mathcal{E}(f))^{m-i} =$$

$$= \sum_{i=0}^{k} \binom{m}{i} g(\frac{k}{m})^i (1 - g(\frac{k}{m}))^{m-i}.$$

Since $g \in \mathcal{G}_{m,\delta}$,

$$\sum_{i=0}^{k} \binom{m}{i} g(\frac{k}{m})^i (1 - g(\frac{k}{m}))^{m-i} \leq \delta.$$

Thus, from monotonicity of $\sum_{i=0}^{k} \binom{m}{i} p^i (1-p)^{m-i}$,

$$g(\frac{k}{m}) \geq g_{m,\delta}(\frac{k}{m}).$$

Using Theorem 3, we derive an efficient algorithm for that approximation of $g_{m,\delta}$ for given m and δ. Let k_p be the largest k such that

$$\sum_{i=0}^{k} \binom{m}{i} p^i (1-p)^{m-i} \leq \delta$$

and $n \in \mathbb{N}$. We calculate $k_{\frac{j}{n}}$ for $j \in \{0,1,\ldots,n\}$. Values $g_{m,\delta}$ satisfy following inequality:

$$\min\{\frac{j}{n} : k_{\frac{j}{n}} \geq k\} - \frac{1}{n} < g_{m,\delta}(\frac{k}{m}) \leq \min\{\frac{j}{n} : k_{\frac{j}{n}} \geq k\}.$$

Function $g(\frac{k}{m}) = \min\{\frac{j}{n} : k_{\frac{j}{n}} \geq k\}$ generates a bound that is worse than the best one less than $\frac{1}{n}$.

Table 3 illustrates the behaviour of the bound.

Remark 1. If we consider function $g(\frac{k}{m}) = g_{m,\delta}(\frac{k-1}{m})$, where $p_{-1} = -1$, than we will obtain the inequality

$$P(\mathcal{E}(f) > g(\mathcal{E}_{\mathbf{z}}(f))) \geq \delta.$$

As $\sum_{i=0}^{m} p_k - p_{k-1} = 1$, the average distance between lower and upper bounds is $\frac{1}{m}$.

Table 3. Values of $g_{m,\delta}(\frac{k}{m})$ for a chosen values of k and $m = 1000$ (In sup row are the maximum values)

$\frac{k}{m}\backslash\delta$	0.1000	0.0500	0.0200	0.0100	0.0050	0.0020	0.0010	0.0005	0.0002	0.0001
0.01	0.0054	0.0070	0.0088	0.0101	0.0113	0.0129	0.0140	0.0151	0.0165	0.0176
0.02	0.0070	0.0090	0.0113	0.0129	0.0145	0.0164	0.0177	0.0191	0.0208	0.0220
0.05	0.0101	0.0129	0.0162	0.0185	0.0206	0.0231	0.0250	0.0268	0.0290	0.0307
0.10	0.0133	0.0170	0.0213	0.0242	0.0269	0.0302	0.0326	0.0348	0.0376	0.0397
0.15	0.0155	0.0199	0.0249	0.0282	0.0313	0.0351	0.0378	0.0403	0.0435	0.0458
0.20	0.0172	0.0220	0.0275	0.0311	0.0345	0.0387	0.0416	0.0444	0.0479	0.0504
sup	0.0208	0.0266	0.0330	0.0373	0.0413	0.0460	0.0494	0.0526	0.0565	0.0593

We construct a two sides bound, combining the one side ones:

Theorem 4. *Let* $0 < \delta < 1$ *and* $m \in \mathbb{N}$.

$$P(\mathcal{E}(f) > g_{m,\delta}(\mathcal{E}_{\mathbf{z}}(f)) \cup \mathcal{E}(f) < 1 - g_{m,\delta}(1 - \mathcal{E}_{\mathbf{z}}(f))) < 2\delta.$$

As Remark 1 is valid for the two sides inequality, we see that it is quite strict.

Now, we deal with another important question: What does it happen, when one uses the same test sample for testing many classifiers?

Assume that we have k classifiers $f_1, \ldots, f_k$ and we want to estimate probability that $\mathcal{E}(f_i) \in G(\mathcal{E}_{\mathbf{z}}(f_i))$ for each of them, i.e.,

$$P(\mathcal{E}(f_1) \in G(\mathcal{E}_{\mathbf{z}}(f_1)) \wedge \cdots \wedge \mathcal{E}(f_k) \in G(\mathcal{E}_{\mathbf{z}}(f_k))).$$

The trivial bound uses the fact that $P(A \vee B) \leq P(A) + P(B)$ for any random events A and B:

$$P(\mathcal{E}(f_1) \in G(\mathcal{E}_{\mathbf{z}}(f_1)) \wedge \cdots \wedge \mathcal{E}(f_k) \in G(\mathcal{E}_{\mathbf{z}}(f_k))) \geq$$

$$1 - k + \sum_{i=0}^{k} P(\mathcal{E}(f_i) \in G(\mathcal{E}_{\mathbf{z}}(f_i))) \tag{3}$$

On the other hand, if $\mathcal{E}_{\mathbf{z}}(f_1), \ldots, \mathcal{E}_{\mathbf{z}}(f_k)$ are independent, then

$$P(\mathcal{E}(f_1) \in G(\mathcal{E}_{\mathbf{z}}(f_1)) \wedge \cdots \wedge \mathcal{E}(f_k) \in G(\mathcal{E}_{\mathbf{z}}(f_k))) = \prod_{i=0}^{k} P(\mathcal{E}(f_i) \in G(\mathcal{E}_{\mathbf{z}}(f_i))).$$

Note that unseemingly, the independence of $\mathcal{E}_{\mathbf{z}}(f_1), \ldots, \mathcal{E}_{\mathbf{z}}(f_k)$ is possible when $\mathcal{E}(f_i)$ is small, whereas the classifiers $f_1, \ldots, f_k$ are similar.

If we assume $P(\mathcal{E}(f_i) \in G(\mathcal{E}_{\mathbf{z}}(f_i))) = 1 - \delta$, we can easily calculate the difference between the trivial bound and the case of independence.

$$\prod_{i=0}^{k} P(\mathcal{E}(f_i) \in G(\mathcal{E}_{\mathbf{z}}(f_i))) - 1 + k - \sum_{i=0}^{k} P(\mathcal{E}(f_i) \in G(\mathcal{E}_{\mathbf{z}}(f_i))) =$$

$$= (1 - \delta)^k - 1 + k\delta \leq \frac{1}{2}(k\delta)^2$$

As we can see, there is no big difference between the both cases, so the trivial bound is near to the optimal one in the interesting cases.

4   Model Selection and Assessment

In order to assess the model, we simply need to estimate its generalization error, using one of the bounds presented above. The procedure is the following:

- Divide the data given into the training sample and the test sample. Choose the size of the test sample, m, according to Table 1 or 2, and the total number of samples.
- Generate the classifier f using training sample.
- Test f using the test sample and the bound from Theorem 3 or 4.

To assure the bound to hold true, it has to be chosen before the testing process starts. The test may be performed only once. Any repetition, especially the one performed in order to choose the best bound, causes a rapid decrease in reliability.

While selecting a classifier from a given set, we are interested in its behaviour in comparison to the other ones. We select the classifier which has the smallest empirical error. The question is: How many samples do we need to know that the classifier which has the smallest empirical error is the one that has the smallest generalization error?

When classifiers have very similar generalization errors, they are almost indistinguishable. Fortunately, in this case, it is not really important which one we choose. It is enough to consider the differences bigger than ε.

The most straightforward way is to use Theorem 4 for every classifier from the set. Testing multiple classifiers on the same data will decrease the reliability, as shown in (3). So we will obtain the bound

$$P(\mathcal{E}(f_1) \in G(\mathcal{E}_\mathbf{z}(f_1)) \wedge \cdots \wedge \mathcal{E}(f_k) \in G(\mathcal{E}_\mathbf{z}(f_k))) \geq 1 - k\delta, \qquad (4)$$

where

$$G(\mathcal{E}_\mathbf{z}(f_i)) = [1 - g_{m,\delta}(1 - \mathcal{E}_\mathbf{z}(f_i)), g_{m,\delta}(\mathcal{E}_\mathbf{z}(f_i))].$$

If $G(\mathcal{E}_\mathbf{z}(f_i)) \cap G(\mathcal{E}_\mathbf{z}(f_j)) = \emptyset$, then we can decide which one is better with probability $\geq 1 - k\delta$. The procedure is the following:

- Divide the data given into the training sample and the validation sample. Choose the validation sample size, m, according to Table 2, the number of classifiers to be constructed and total number of samples.
- Generate classifiers $f_1, \ldots, f_k$ using the training sample.
- Select the best classifier that has the smallest empirical error on the validation sample. The relation between the generalization errors of classifiers is described by the inequality (4).

As we can see in Table 2, in order to estimate the error of 100 classifiers with the reliability 95%, one needs to have aproximately 4 times the number of samples that is needed to estimate the error of one classifier. The advantage is that all classifiers are already assessed after the selection process. We may combine the model selection and the model assessment and we may use the same sample for both of them. As a consequence, the sample is bigger and the bound is tighter.

Acknowledgment. The research has been supported by the grant 3 T11C 002 26 from Ministry of Scientific Research and Information Technology of the Republic of Poland.

References

1. F. Cucker and S. Smale, *On the mathematical foundations of learning*, Bulletin of AMS, 39:1-49, 2001.
2. R. Duda, P. Hart, D. Stock, *Pattern Classification*, John Wiley & Sons, Inc. 2001
3. J. H. Friedman, T. Hastie, R. Tibshirani, *Statistical Learning: Data Mining, Inference, and Prediction*, Springer-Verlag, Heidelberg, 2001
4. K. Fukunaga, R. R. Hayes, *Effects of Sample Size in Classifier Design* IEEE Transactions on Pattern Analysis and Machine Intelligence, 11(8):873-885, 1989
5. K. Fukunaga, R. R. Hayes, *Estimation of Classifier Performance*, IEEE Transactions on Pattern Analysis and Machine Intelligence, 11(10):1087-1101, 1989
6. I. Guyon, J. Makhoul, R. Schwartz, V. Vapnik, *What size test set gives good error rate estimates?*, IEEE Pattern Analysis and Machine Intelligence, 20:52-64, 1998
7. W. Hoeffding, *Probability Inequalities for Sums of Bounded Random Variables*, JASA 58, 13-30
8. W. Jaworski, *Bounds for Validation*, Fundamenta Informaticae (to appear)
9. D. Michie, D. Spiegelhalter, C. Taylor (Eds.), *Machine Learning, Neural and Statistical Classification*, John Wiley & Sons, Inc. 2001
10. V. N. Vapnik, *Statistical Learning Theory*, Wiley, New York, 1998.

Dependency Bagging

Yuan Jiang[1], Jin-Jiang Ling[1], Gang Li[2], Honghua Dai[2], and Zhi-Hua Zhou[1]

[1] National Laboratory for Novel Software Technology,
Nanjing University, Nanjing 210093, China
[2] School of Information Technology,
Deakin University, Burwood, Vic3125, Australia
{jiangy, lingjj, zhouzh}@lamda.nju.edu.cn
{gang.li, hdai}@deakin.edu.au

Abstract. In this paper, a new variant of Bagging named *DepenBag* is proposed. This algorithm obtains bootstrap samples at first. Then, it employs a causal discoverer to induce from each sample a dependency model expressed as a Directed Acyclic Graph (DAG). The attributes without connections to the class attribute in all the DAGs are then removed. Finally, a component learner is trained from each of the resulted samples to constitute the ensemble. Empirical study shows that DepenBag is effective in building ensembles of nearest neighbor classifiers.

1 Introduction

Ensemble learning methods train multiple component learners and then combine their predictions. Since the generalization ability of an ensemble could be significantly better than that of a single learner, ensemble learning has been a hot topic during the past years [9].

Bagging [4] is one of the most famous ensemble learning algorithms, which utilizes *bootstrap sampling* [10] to generate multiple training sets from the original training set and then trains a learner from each generated training set. This algorithm has achieved great success in building ensembles of decision trees and neural networks. A recent empirical study [11] on ensembles of C4.5 decision trees disclosed that although many ensemble learning algorithms where component learners could be trained in parallel have been developed, few of them significantly outperforms Bagging. However, as Breiman indicated [4], although Bagging could work well on unstable base learners such as decision trees and neural networks, it could hardly work on stable base learners such as nearest neighbor classifiers. Since nearest neighbor classifiers are very useful in real-world applications [1][8], it will be desirable if the powerful Bagging algorithm can be adapted to such local learners.

Recently, there are many works devoted to adapting Bagging to k-nearest neighbor classifiers [2][22]. In this paper, a new variant of Bagging is proposed with the help of graphical models [20]. For a given data set, the proposed method generates many samples from the training set via bootstrap sampling. Then, it employs a causal discoverer to induce a dependency model expressed as a Directed Acyclic Graph (DAG) from each sample. If a node has neither direct nor

D. Ślęzak et al. (Eds.): RSFDGrC 2005, LNAI 3641, pp. 491–500, 2005.

indirect connections to the class node in all the DAGs, then the corresponding attribute is removed. Finally, a component learner is trained from each sample and their predictions are combined via *majority voting*. Since the proposed method introducing dependency into Bagging, it is called as *DepenBag* (abbreviated from *Dependency Bagging*). Empirical study shows that DepenBag is effective on building ensembles of nearest neighbor classifiers.

The rest of this paper is organized as follows. Section 2 briefly introduces causal discovery with graphical models. Section 3 presents the DepenBag algorithm. Section 4 reports on the empirical study and explores why DepenBag works. Finally, Section 5 concludes and raises several issues for future work.

2   Causal Discovery with Graphical Models

Graphical model is a succinct and efficient way to represent dependency relations among a set of attributes [20]. Roughly speaking, a graphical model contains two parts, i.e. *structure* that qualitatively describes the relation among different attributes, and *parameter* that quantitatively describe the relation between an attribute and its parents. When the structure of a graphical model is a Directed Acyclic Graph (DAG), it is often referred to as *directed graphical model*, which is very popular in expert systems. Its semantics lend it to what is sometimes loosely referred to as *causal model* [20], which represents the causal relation among different attributes and constitutes an efficient tool to perform probabilistic inference. If such a model is induced from a data sample, it can be called as *dependency model* which reflects the (in)dependency relation occurred in the corresponding sample.

According to the nature of the attributes concerned, there exist two different kinds of causal models, i.e. *linear causal model* and *Bayesian network*. The former is also referred to as *Gaussian network*. In a linear causal model, all the attributes are continuous, and the local parameters are given by the coefficients of the linear function between each node and its parents. In a Bayesian network, all the attributes are categorical, and the parameters are often represented as a set of conditional probability tables.

During the past decade, learning causal models, especially the Bayesian network, has become an active topic and many algorithms have been developed. Roughly speaking, there are two fundamentally different paradigms, i.e. the *statistic test* paradigm and the *evaluation+search* paradigm. Algorithms belonging to the first paradigm try to get some conditional independence relations between some subset of attributes, and use these independence relations to infer the structure of model. Algorithms belonging to the second paradigm use some metrics to evaluate the goodness of fit of a structure to the data set, transform the structure learning problem into an optimization problem, and then solve the problem by search. Since the statistic test paradigm usually requires an exponential number of conditional independence tests and many of these tests involve with large condition set, the evaluation+search paradigm is more popularly used.

For a given data set, the number of possible directed graphical model structures that may fit the data is exponential in the number of attributes [21]. The huge search space poses a great challenge, but also gives a good chance of using diverse heuristic search strategies. Through comparing a number of different search strategies, Heckerman et al. [12] recognized that greedy search is the best choice when the quality of results and the computational efficiency are both concerned. Cooper and Herskovits [6] proposed an algorithm that employs greedy search to find the structure with the best BDe metric. Given the total ordering on the nodes, it begins by assuming that a node has no parents, and then repeatedly adds the parent whose addition will improve the BDe metric. The process terminates when the metric cannot be increased through adding any parent. On the learning of linear causal models, greedy search based algorithms have also been presented [7], which can be used even when the total ordering on the nodes is not available. Note that greedy search usually fails to find the global optima. A common augmenting strategy is hill-climbing search with random restarts [5].

Almost all the algorithms in causal discovery suffer from the problem that, even given infinite data, they can only identify the model up to Markov equivalence, i.e. members in the same Markov equivalence class can not be distinguished from each other using statistical data. Therefore, although the real causal model should be fixed for a concrete domain, due to the Markov equivalence class and heuristic nature of the evaluation+search algorithms, it is usually difficult to find the exact causal model. Instead, different models may be induced from different samples of the domain, which can be referred as dependency models because they reflect the (in)dependency relation occurred in corresponding samples. Such kind of models are employed by the DepenBag algorithm to help generate accurate but diverse component k-NN classifiers.

3   DepenBag

Krogh and Vedelsby [14] have derived a famous equation $E = \bar{E} - \bar{A}$, where E is the generalization error of an ensemble, while $\bar{E}$ and $\bar{A}$ are the average generalization error and average ambiguity of the component learners, respectively. This equation discloses that the more accurate and the more diverse the component learners are, the better the ensemble is. Unfortunately, it is difficult to manipulate the diversity directly because as a recent study [16] reveals, although there are many measures of diversity, their usefulness in ensemble construction is very limited. In fact, the study on how to effectively measure and exploit diversity is very active and many problems remain unsolved [15]. Nevertheless, methods that could help generate accurate but diverse component learners are very desirable in building strong ensembles.

In Bagging, for a given data set D, T samples $D_1, D_2, \ldots, D_T$ are generated by the bootstrap sampling process. Note that the data distribution held by a sample, say D_i, is usually different from that of D. Assume that D is described by n attributes, i.e. $\{A_1, A_2, \ldots, A_n\}$ where A_n is the class attribute. It is evident that these T samples are also described by the same set of attributes. Previous research ignores the phenomenon that on D_i some attribute, say $A_i(i \neq n)$, may become irrelevant to A_n. This is the fact even though A_i may be relevant to A_n on D. For an extreme example, suppose A_i is a binary attribute whose value is 0 or 1, and 0 is the dominant value of A_i on D, that is, only a small fraction of instances in D hold the value 1 on A_i. Since statistically only about 63.2% instances in D will appear in the sample D_i [4], on D_i there are chances that all the instances hold the value 1 on A_i so that A_i conveys no information of A_n. In other words, A_i becomes an irrelevant attribute which is useless in predicting the value of A_n. It is obvious that if A_i is useless on all of these T samples, it should be removed because intuitively, such a removal might help reduce the degree of overlapping of the samples therefore help increase the diversity of the component learners. Moreover, since A_i is irrelevant to the learning objective on the samples, removing it might help increase the accuracy and/or the learning efficiency because the existence of irrelevant attributes might interfere the learning on relevant attributes.

Causal discovery provides a feasible way to identify these irrelevant attributes. Suppose a dependency model expressed as a DAG is induced on D_i, and let DM_i denote this model, as shown in Figure 1. It is evident that the class attribute A_8 won't be impacted by the attributes A_5, A_6 and A_7 because they have neither direct nor indirect connections to A_8. In other words, A_5, A_6 and A_7 are irrelevant attributes to A_8 on D_i. These attributes can be easily identified from DM_i through tracing the paths leading to or from the class attribute. If such a process is performed on all the bootstrap samples, i.e. $D_1, D_2, \ldots, D_T$, then the irrelevant attributes shared by the samples can be found out. Thus, component learners can be trained on the samples where the shared irrelevant attributes are removed. Such a routine leads to the DepenBag algorithm whose pseudo-code is shown in Table 1, where x is an instance to be predicted and Y is the set of values that A_n can take.

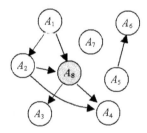

Fig. 1. A dependency model involving eight attributes

Intuitively, an alternative routine may be to induce a dependency model on the original data set, identify and remove attributes irrelevant to the class attribute, then perform bootstrap sampling and train a component learner on each sample. Unfortunately, such a routine overlooks the fact that irrelevant

Table 1. The DepenBag algorithm

Input: Data set D, base learner L, causal discoverer C, trials T
Output: Ensemble L^*
Process:
    $Irrelevant = \{A_1, A_2, \ldots, A_{n-1}\}$
    for $t = 1$ to T {
        D_t = bootstrap sample from D
        if $Irrelevant \neq \emptyset$
            $DM_t = C(D_t)$
            $Irrelevant_t$ = irrelevant attributes identified on DM_t
            $Irrelevant = Irrelevant \cap Irrelevant_t$
    }
    for $t = 1$ to T {
        if $Irrelevant \neq \emptyset$
            remove attributes in $Irrelevant$ from D_t
        $L_t = L(D_t)$
    }
    $L^*(x) = \arg\max_{y \in Y} \sum_{t:\, L_t(x)=y} 1$

attributes on the original data set may become relevant to the class attribute on some sample. The reason is the same as what has been used to explain the phenomenon that relevant attributes may become irrelevant after bootstrap sampling, that is, the distribution held by a sample is rarely the same as that of the original data set. In fact, these originally irrelevant attributes might provide extra resource for increasing the diversity of the component learners, and only the irrelevant attributes shared by the samples are useless. So, DepenBag induces a suite of dependency models on the samples instead of only one model on the original data set. This also distinguishes DepenBag from routines that perform feature selection at first and then run Bagging to generate an ensemble.

From a Bayesian view, given its ancestors in conditional dependence, the class attribute won't be impacted by any other attributes. For example, for the dependency model shown in Figure 1, the value of the class attribute A_8 could be fully determined by the value of its ancestors, i.e. A_1 and A_2. So it seems that A_3 and A_4 can also be removed. However, in the absence of time order a causal discoverer is usually only able to find an equivalence class of models. Hence it is not clear which attributes are real ancestors. So, in the DepenBag algorithm these attributes are not removed.

4   Empirical Study

Ten data sets from the UCI Machine Learning Repository [3] are used in the empirical study. The number of instances, number of categorical attributes, and number of continuous attributes of these data sets are tabulated in Table 2. In

Table 2. Experimental data sets

Data set	Size	Categorical	Continuous
wpbc	194	0	33
sonar	208	0	60
liver	345	0	6
ionosphere	351	0	33
vote	435	16	0
credit	653	9	6
diabetes	768	0	8
tic	958	9	0
german	1,000	0	24
sick	2,643	16	6

the experiments 3-NN classifiers are used, other k values will be investigated in the future. Note that all the data sets are with binary classes, therefore tie won't occur in the predictions made by single k-NN ($k = 3$) classifiers.

Almost any algorithm that could induce directed graphical model can be used to instantiate the causal discoverer C in Table 1. Here the MLGS algorithm [7] is used, which uses the MML criterion and could discover dependency models expressed as DAGs even without prior knowledge of total ordering among attributes. The algorithm was implemented under the BNT package [19]. Since this causal discoverer can deal with only categorical attributes (as mentioned in Section 2, current causal discoverers can deal with only categorical attributes or only continuous attributes), continuous attributes are discretized with the Chi2 algorithm [18] before the induction of the dependency models. After the removal of irrelevant attributes, these discretized attributes are recovered to their original continuous values for the training of the component learners. In the empirical study, each ensemble built by DepenBag comprises 10 k-NN ($k = 3$) classifiers.

Besides Bagging, considering that the working mechanism of DepenBag looks like performing feature selection on each bootstrap samples, another algorithm named *ReliefF-Bag* is designed and compared. This algorithm employs the famous feature selection algorithm ReliefF [13] to select 75% attributes on each sample, and then builds a component learner from each sample. Note that even when the causal discovery process in DepenBag is viewed as only a specific feature selection process, it has an apparent advantage to most feature selection schemes, that is, it does not require the pre-specification of the number of attributes to be selected. In the empirical study, each ensemble built by ReliefF-Bag is constituted of 100 k-NN ($k = 3$) classifiers.

4.1   Comparison on Generalization Error

Ten times 10-fold cross validation is performed on each data set listed in Table 2. In detail, each data set is partitioned into ten subsets with similar sizes and distributions. Then, the union of nine subsets is used as the training set while

Table 3. Comparison on generalization error

Data set	Single	Bagging	ReliefF-Bag	DepenBag
wpbc	.2633 ± .0097	.2685 ± .0091	.3312 ± .0085	**.1907 ± .0053**
sonar	**.1587 ± .0068**	.1925 ± .0088	.1918 ± .0061	.2849 ± .0124
liver	.3684 ± .0099	.4265 ± .0086	**.3240 ± .0064**	.3703 ± .0101
ionosphere	.1451 ± .0063	.1533 ± .0072	**.1394 ± .0040**	.1422 ± .0058
vote	**.0437 ± .0036**	.0498 ± .0028	**.0400 ± .0041**	.0435 ± .0026
credit	.1505 ± .0045	.1643 ± .0049	.1598 ± .0041	**.1391 ± .0029**
diabetes	.2605 ± .0039	.2840 ± .0054	.3451 ± .0024	**.2357 ± .0064**
tic	.1805 ± .0022	.1733 ± .0016	.2161 ± .0043	**.1473 ± .0041**
german	.2940 ± .0031	.3350 ± .0039	.3540 ± .0050	**.2780 ± .0031**
sick	.0519 ± .0011	.0545 ± .0011	.0954 ± .0009	**.0280 ± .0007**

the remaining subset is used as the test set, which is repeated for ten times such that every subset has been used as the test set once. The average test result is regarded as the result of the 10-fold cross validation. The whole above process is repeated for 10 times with randomly partitions of the ten subsets, and the average results are recorded as the final results.

The generalization error of the compared algorithms are presented in Table 3, where "Single" denotes single k-NN classifier. The table entries show the average error and standard deviations (the values following '±'). Pairwise two-tailed t-tests with .05 significance level are performed on each data set, and the result of the algorithm which is significantly better than others are boldfaced.

Table 3 shows that Bagging is almost always worse than single k-NN classifier except on *tic*, which confirms that Bagging can be hardly used in building ensembles of nearest neighbor classifiers [4]. ReliefF-Bag is better than single k-NN classifier on three data sets too, i.e. *liver*, *ionosphere*, and *vote* (on *vote* the difference is not statistically significant), which suggests that the enhancement contributed by pure feature selection to Bagging is limited. In contrast to these ensemble algorithms, DepenBag is only worse than single k-NN classifier on *sonar* and *liver* (on *liver* the difference is not statistically significant). It is evident that DepenBag is with the best performance in the empirical study.

4.2   Error-Ambiguity Decomposition

In order to explore why DepenBag works well, the error-ambiguity decomposition [14] is performed on the experimental results presented in Table 3. In detail, the errors of the ensembles presented in Table 3 are regarded as E, while the average errors of the component learners constituting the ensembles are regarded as $\bar{E}$, then $\bar{A}$, the average ambiguity, can be obtained from $\bar{E} - E$ since $E = \bar{E} - \bar{A}$ [14]. The decomposition results are shown in Table 4 (the zero $\bar{A}$s are caused by round truncation), where on each data set, the smallest $\bar{E}$ and the biggest $\bar{A}$ are boldfaced (without statistical significance test).

Table 4 shows that on six data sets, i.e. *wpbc*, *ionosphere*, *diabetes*, *tic*, *german*, and *sick*, the $\bar{E}$ of DepenBag is the smallest among that of all of the

Table 4. Error-ambiguity decomposition of the experimental results

Data set	Bagging		ReliefF-Bag		DepenBag	
	$\bar{E}$	$\bar{A}$	$\bar{E}$	$\bar{A}$	$\bar{E}$	$\bar{A}$
wpbc	.2953	**.0268**	.3312	.0000	**.2079**	.0172
sonar	**.1859**	-.0066	.1918	**.0000**	.2588	-.0261
liver	.3977	-.0288	**.3240**	.0000	.4254	**.0551**
ionosphere	.1567	**.0034**	.1394	.0000	**.1283**	-.0139
vote	**.0448**	-.0050	.0468	.0068	.0518	**.0083**
credit	.1749	.0106	**.1603**	.0005	.1738	**.0347**
diabetes	.2956	**.0116**	.3451	.0000	**.2409**	.0052
tic	.2701	**.0968**	.2430	.0269	**.2184**	.0711
german	.3280	-.0070	.3540	.0000	**.2842**	**.0062**
sick	.0563	.0018	.0939	-.0015	**.0386**	**.0106**

compared ensemble algorithms, while on *liver, vote, credit, german*, and *sick* the $\bar{A}$ of DepenBag is the biggest. Through comparing the table entries belonging to Bagging and DepenBag, it can be found that DepenBag can decrease $\bar{E}$ as on *wpbc, ionosphere, credit, diabetes, tic, german*, and *sick*, while it can also increase $\bar{A}$ as on *liver, vote, credit, german*, and *sick*. It is evident that both the decrease of $\bar{E}$ and the increase of $\bar{A}$ owe much to the causal discovery process employed by DepenBag. It can also be found that on different data sets where DepenBag is effective, its success may be caused by either small $\bar{E}$, or big $\bar{A}$, or both. Table 4 also shows ReliefF-Bag can generate accurate component nearest neighbor classifiers in some cases, but since these classifiers are not diverse, the overall performance of ReliefF-Bag is not so good as that of DepenBag. In summary, the success of DepenBag owes much to the fact that the causal discovery process employed by DepenBag can help generate accurate but diverse component nearest neighbor classifiers.

5   Conclusion

In this paper, the DepenBag algorithm is proposed. After bootstrap sampling, this algorithm discovers a dependency model on each sample, then identifies and removes irrelevant attributes shared by the samples, and finally combines the component learners trained from each of the samples via majority voting. Empirical study shows that this algorithm is effective in building ensembles of k-NN classifiers, and its success owes much to the fact that it could generate accurate but diverse component k-NN classifiers.

A weakness of DepenBag is that the cost of building an ensemble is burdened by the discovery of a dependency model on each sample. However, obtaining a stronger ensemble may be worthy of the extra cost in many applications, especially when considering that the causal discovery process can be executed off-line and therefore the predictive process of an ensemble built by DepenBag might be more efficient than that of an ensemble built by Bagging because usually fewer attributes are involved in identifying the nearest neighbors.

The strategy for removing attributes adopted by DepenBag is quite conservative. This is because an attribute is removed only when it is irrelevant to the class attribute on all the bootstrap samples. It may be possible to explore variants of DepenBag that removes irrelevant attributes shared by several instead of all samples, or even removes irrelevant attributes for a sample based on only its own dependency model. This is an interesting issue for future work.

Moreover, although this paper shows that DepenBag is effective in building ensembles of nearest neighbor classifiers, it is not clear whether it is also effective on other kinds of stable base learners such as naive Bayes classifier, or even effective on unstable base learners such as decision trees and neural networks. This is left to be investigated in the future.

Furthermore, the role of causal discovery in DepenBag is in fact a specific scheme for perturbing the input attributes to introduce more diversity. Previous work has shown that incorporating such perturbation is beneficial to Bagging in building decision tree ensembles [17], while DepenBag shows that it is also helpful in building nearest neighbor classifier ensembles. Exploring other efficient and effective schemes for perturbing the input attributes for Bagging is another interesting issue for future work.

Acknowledgement

The comments and suggestions from the anonymous reviewers greatly improved this paper. This work was supported by the National Outstanding Youth Foundation of China under the Grant No. 60325207, the Fok Ying Tung Education Foundation under the Grant No. 91067, and the Excellent Young Teachers Program of MOE of China.

References

1. Aha, D.W.: Lazy learning: special issue editorial. Artificial Intelligence Review **11** (1997) 7–10
2. Alkoot, F.M., Kittler, J.: Moderating k-NN classifiers. Pattern Analysis & Applications **5** (2002) 326–332
3. Blake, C., Keogh, E., Merz, C.J.: UCI repository of machine learning databases [http://www.ics.uci.edu/~mlearn/MLRepository.html], Department of Information and Computer Science, University of California, Irvine, CA (1998)
4. Breiman, L.: Bagging predictors. Machine Learning **24** (1996) 123–140
5. Chickering, M.: Learning equivalence classes of bayesian networks structures. In: Proceedings of the 12th International Conference on Uncertainty in Artificial Intelligence, Portland, OR (1996) 150–157
6. Cooper, G.F., Herskovits, E.: A bayesian method for the induction of probabilistic networks from data. Machine Learning **9** (1992) 309–347
7. Dai, H., Li, G.: An improved approach for the discovery of causal models via MML. In: Proceedings of the 6th Pacific-Asia Conference on Knowledge Discovery and Data Mining, Taipei, Taiwan (2002) 304–315

8. Dasarathy, B.V.: Nearest Neighbor Norms: NN Pattern Classification Techniques. IEEE Computer Society Press, Los Alamitos, CA (1991)

9. Dietterich, T.G.: Ensemble learning. In: Arbib, M.A. (ed.): The Handbook of Brain Theory and Neural Networks, 2nd edition. MIT Press, Cambridge, MA (2002)

10. Efron, B., Tibshirani, R.: An Introduction to the Bootstrap. Chapman & Hall, New York (1993)

11. Hall, L.O., Bowyer, K.W., Banfield, R.E., Bhadoria, D., Eschrich, S.: Comparing pure parallel ensemble creation techniques against bagging. In: Proceedings of the 3rd IEEE International Conference on Data Mining, Melbourne, FL (2003) 533–536

12. Heckerman, D., Geiger, D., Chickering, D.M.: Learning bayesian networks: the combination of knowledge and statistical data. Machine Learning **20** (1995) 197–243

13. Kononenko, I.,: Estimating attributes: analysis and extensions of relief. In: Proceedings of the 7th European Conference on Machine Learning, Catania, Italy (1994) 171–182

14. Krogh, A., Vedelsby, J.: Neural network ensembles, cross validation, and active learning. In: Tesauro, G., Touretzky, D.S., Leen, T.K. (eds.): Advances in Neural Information Processing Systems, Vol. 7. MIT Press, Cambridge, MA (1995) 231–238

15. Kuncheva, L.I.: Diversity in multiple classifier systems: special issue editorial. Information Fusion **6** (2005) 3–4

16. Kuncheva, L.I., Whitaker, C.J.: Measures of diversity in classifier ensembles. Machine Learning **51** (2003) 181–207

17. Latinne, P., Debeir, O., Decaestecker, C.: Mixing bagging and multiple feature subsets to improve classification accuracy of decision tree combination. In: Proceedings of the 10th Belgian-Dutch Conference on Machine Learning, Tilburg, The Netherlands (2000)

18. Liu, H., Setiono, R.: Chi2: feature selection and discretization of numeric attributes. In: Proceedings of the 7th IEEE International Conference on Tools with Artificial Intelligence, Washington, DC (1995) 388–391

19. Murphy, K.: The bayes net toolbox for matlab. Computing Science and Statistics **33** (2001) 331–351

20. Pearl, J.: Probabilistic Reasoning in Intelligent Systems: Networks of Plausible Inference. Morgan Kaufmann, San Mateo, CA (1988)

21. Robinson, R.W.: Counting unlabelled acyclic digraphs. In: Proceedings of the 5th Australian Conference on Combinatorial Mathematics, Melbourne, Australia (1976) 28–43

22. Zhou, Z.-H., Yu, Y.: Adapt bagging to nearest neighbor classifiers. Journal of Computer Science and Technology **20** (2005) 48–54

Combination of Metric-Based and Rule-Based Classification

Arkadiusz Wojna

Institute of Informatics, Warsaw University,
Banacha 2, 02-097, Warsaw, Poland
wojna@mimuw.edu.pl

Abstract. We consider two classification approaches. The metric-based approach induces the distance measure between objects and classifies new objects on the basis of their nearest neighbors in the training set. The rule-based approach extracts rules from the training set and uses them to classify new objects. In the paper we present a model that combines both approaches. In the combined model the notions of rule, rule minimality and rule consistency are generalized to metric-dependent form.

An effective polynomial algorithm implementing the classification model based on minimal consistent rules has been proposed in [2]. We show that this algorithm preserves its properties in application to the metric-based rules. This allows us to combine this rule-based algorithm with the k nearest neighbor (k-nn) classification method. In the combined approach the rule-based algorithm takes the role of nearest neighbor voting model. The presented experiments with real data sets show that the combined classification model have the accuracy higher than single models.

1 Introduction

Empirical comparison of rule-based systems [2] and metric-based methods [1] shows that each approach is more accurate than the other one for some classification problems but not for all. Therefore a lot of work has been done to construct hybrid classifiers that take the advantages of both approaches [4,6,8].

All these methods focus on how to use distance measure or the nearest neighbors of an object to be classified to improve the selection of rules for classification. However, in classification problems with many attributes the space of possible rules is enormous and searching for accurate rules is a very hard task. Therefore for many such problems the k nearest neighbors (k-nn) method is more accurate than rule-based systems and the approach where one uses rules to improve k-nn can be more effective than using k-nn to improve rule-based classification.

In the paper we propose the general hybridization framework where the notion of rules is generalized to a metric-dependent form and the rules generated from a training set are used to verify and improve selection of nearest neighbors in the k-nn. We apply this framework to the case where minimal consistent rules [9] are used to improve the k-nn. The idea of improving k-nn by rule induction

D. Ślęzak et al. (Eds.): RSFDGrC 2005, LNAI 3641, pp. 501–511, 2005.
© Springer-Verlag Berlin Heidelberg 2005

was used in [7]. However, the rules in [7] have specific, non-uniform conditions and do not correspond to the metric-based model presented in the paper.

2 Metric Based Generalization of Minimal Consistent Rules

We assume that a finite set of training examples U_{trn} is provided. Each training example $x \in U_{trn}$ is decribed by a vector of attribute values $(x_1, \ldots, x_n)$ corressponding to a fixed set of n attributes $A = \{a_1, \ldots, a_n\}$, and by its decision value $dec(x)$ from a discrete and finite set $V_{dec} = \{d_1, \ldots d_m\}$.

Originally the notions of rule minimality and consistency [9] were introduced for rules with equality conditions: $a_{i_1} = v_1 \wedge \ldots \wedge a_{i_p} = v_p \Rightarrow dec = d_j$. We generalize this approach to a metric-dependent form. We assume only that the metric ρ is an l_p-combination of metrics for particular attributes $(p \geq 1)$:

$$\rho(x, y) = \left(\sum_{i=1}^{n} w_i \cdot \rho_i(x_i, y_i)^p \right)^{\frac{1}{p}} . \tag{1}$$

The equality $a_{i_j} = v_j$ as the condition in the premise of a rule represents selection of attribute values, in this case always a single value. We replace equality conditions with a more general metric based form of conditions. This form allows us to select more than one attribute value in a single attribute condition, and thus, to obtain more general rules.

Definition 1. *A generalized rule consists of a premise and a consequent:*

$$\rho_{i_1}(v_1, *) \leq r_1 \wedge \ldots \wedge \rho_{i_p}(v_p, *) < r_p \Rightarrow dec = d_j.$$

Each condition $\rho_{i_q}(v_q, *) \leq r_q$ or $\rho_{i_q}(v_q, *) < r_q$ in the premise of the generalized rule represents the range of acceptable values of a given attribute a_{i_q} around a given value v_q. The range is specified by the distance function ρ_{i_q} that is the component of the total distance ρ and by the threshold r_q.

The definition of rule consistency with a training set for the generalized rules is analogous to the equality-based rules. This describes the rules that classify correctly all the covered objects in a given training set:

Definition 2. *A generalized rule $\alpha \Rightarrow dec = d_j$ is consistent with a training set U_{trn} if for each object $x \in U_{trn}$ matching the rule the decision of the rule is correct, i.e., $dec(x) = d_j$.*

Next, we generalize the notion of rule minimality.

Definition 3. *A consistent generalized rule $\rho_{i_1}(v_1, *) < r_1 \wedge \ldots \wedge \rho_{i_p}(v_p, *) < r_p \Rightarrow dec = d_j$ is minimal in a training set U_{trn} if for each attribute $a_{i_q} \in \{a_{i_1}, \ldots, a_{i_p}\}$ occurring in the premise of the generalized rule the rule $\rho_{i_1}(v_1, *) < r_1 \wedge \ldots \wedge \rho_{i_q}(v_q, *) \leq r_q \wedge \ldots \wedge \rho_{i_p}(v_p, *) < r_p \Rightarrow dec = d_j$ with the enlarged range of acceptable values on this attribute (obtained by replacing $<$ by $\leq$ in the condition of the original rule) is inconsistent with the training set U_{trn}.*

Algorithm 1. Algorithm $decision_{local-rules}(x)$ classifying a given test object x based on lazy induction of local rules.

```
for each d_j ∈ V_dec  support[d_j] := ∅
for each y ∈ U_trn
    if r_local(x,y) is consistent with U_trn then
        support[dec(y)] := support[dec(y)] ∪ {y}
return arg max_{d_j∈V_dec} |support[d_j]|
```

Observe, that each condition in the premise of a minimal consistent generalized rule is always a strict inequality. It results from the assumption that a training set U_{trn} is finite.

Both the metric and the metric-based rules can be used to define tolerance relations which are used in construction of generalized approximation spaces [10].

3   Effective Classification by Minimal Consistent Rules

In this section we recall the classification model based on all minimal consistent rules in the original equality-based form [2]. The complete set of all minimal consistent rules has good theoretical properties: it corresponds to the set of all rules generated from all local reducts of a given training set [12]. The original version of the classification model [2] uses the notion of rule support:

Definition 4. *The support of a rule* $a_{i_1} = v_1 \wedge \ldots \wedge a_{i_p} = v_p \Rightarrow dec = d_j$ *in a training set* U_{trn} *is the set of all the objects from* U_{trn} *matching the rule and with the same decision* d_j:

$$support(a_{i_1} = v_1 \wedge \ldots \wedge a_{i_p} = v_p \Rightarrow dec - d_j) =$$
$$\{x = (x_1, \ldots, x_n) \in U_{trn} : x_{i_1} = v_1 \wedge \ldots \wedge x_{i_p} = v_p \wedge dec(x) = d_j\}.$$

The rule support based models compute the support set for each rule $r \in R$ covering a test object x from a given set of rules R and then they select the decision with the greatest total number of the supporting objects:

$$dec_{rules}(x, R) := \arg \max_{d_j \in V_{dec}} \left| \bigcup_{\alpha \Rightarrow dec=d_j \in R:\, x \text{ satisfies } \alpha} support(\alpha \Rightarrow dec = d_j) \right|.$$
$$(2)$$

The classification model proposed in [2] is the rule support model where R is assumed to be the set of all minimal consistent rules.

The number of all minimal consistent rules can be exponential. Therefore Bazan [2] proposed Algorithm 1 that classifies objects on the basis of the set of all minimal consistent rules without computing them explicitly. It simulates the rule support based classifier dec_{rules} by lazy induction of local rules.

Definition 5. *The* local rule *for a given pair of a test object x and a training object $y \in U_{trn}$ is the rule $r_{local}(x, y)$ defined by*

$$\bigwedge_{a_i \in A:\, y_i = x_i} a_i = y_i \Rightarrow dec = dec(y).$$

The conditions in the premise of the local rule $r_{local}(x, y)$ are chosen in such a way that both the test object x and the training object y match the rule and the rule is maximally specific relative to the matching condition. The following relation holds between minimal consistent rules and local rules:

Fact 6. *[2] The premise of a local rule $r_{local}(x, y)$ implies the premise of a certain minimal consistent rule if and only if the local rule $r_{local}(x, y)$ is consistent with the training set U_{trn}.*

This property made it possible to prove that Algorithm 1 simulates correctly the classifier based on all minimal consistent rules:

Corollary 7. *[2] The classification result of the rule support based classifier from Equation 2 with the set R of all minimal consistent rules and the lazy local rule induction classifier (Algorithm 1) is the same for each test object x:*

$$dec_{rules}(x, R) = decision_{local-rules}(x).$$

The consistency checking of a local rule $r_{local}(x, y)$ can be made in $O(|U_{trn}||A|)$ time. Hence, the classification of a single object by Algorithm 1 has the polynomial time complexity $O(|U_{trn}|^2 |A|)$.

4   Metric Based Generalization of Classification by Minimal Consistent Rules

The original version of Algorithm 1 was proposed for data with nominal attributes only and it uses equality as the only form of conditions on attributes in the premise of a rule. We generalize this approach to the metric-dependent form of rules introduced in Section 2. This allows us to apply the algorithm to data both with nominal and with numerical attributes.

For the generalized version of the classifier based on the set of all generalized minimal consistent rules we use the notion of generalized rule center.

Definition 8. *An object $(x_1, \ldots, x_n)$ is the* center *of the generalized rule from Definition 1 if for each attribute condition $\rho_{i_q}(v_q, *) < r_q$ (or $\rho_{i_q}(v_q, *) \leq r_q$) occuring in its premise we have $x_{i_q} = v_q$.*

For a given set of generalized rules R and an object x by $R(x)$ we denote the set of all rules in R centered at x. Observe, that a rule can have many centers if there are attributes that do not occur in the premise of the rule.

In the generalized rule support based classification model the support set for a test object x is counted using all generalized minimal consistent rules centered at x:

$$decision_{gen-rules}(x, R) := \arg \max_{d_j \in V_{dec}} \left| \bigcup_{r \in R(x)} support(r) \right| \qquad (3)$$

where R contains all generalized minimal consistent rules. Although in the generalized version we consider only minimal consistent rules centered at a test object the number of these rules can be exponential as in the non-generalized version.

Since it is impossible to enumerate all generalized minimal consistent rules in practice, we propose to simulate the generalized rule support based classification model from Equation 3 by analogy to Algorithm 1. First, we introduce the definition of a generalized local rule analogous to Definition 5. The conditions in generalized local rule are chosen in such a way that both the test and the training object match the rule and the conditions are maximally specific.

Definition 9. *The generalized local rule for a given pair of a test object x and a training object $y \in U_{trn}$ is the rule $r_{gen-local}(x, y)$:*

$$\bigwedge_{a_i \in A} \rho_i(x_i, *) \leq \rho_i(x_i, y_i) \Rightarrow dec = dec(y).$$

First, we identify the relation between the original and the generalized notion of local rule. Let us consider the case where to define the generalized rules the Hamming metric is used for all the attributes:

$$\rho_i(x_i, y_i) = \begin{cases} 1 \text{ if } x_i \neq y_i \\ 0 \text{ if } x_i = y_i. \end{cases}$$

It is easy to check that:

Fact 10. *For the Hamming metric the generalized local rule $r_{gen-local}(x, y)$ in Definition 9 is equivalent to the local rule $r_{local}(x, y)$ in Definition 5.*

The most important property of the generalization is the relation between generalized minimal consistent rules and generalized local rules analogous to Fact 6.

Theorem 11. *The premise of the generalized local rule $r_{gen-local}(x, y)$ implies the premise of a certain generalized minimal consistent rule centered at x if and only if the generalized local rule $r_{gen-local}(x, y)$ is consistent with U_{trn}.*

Proof. First, we show that each generalized local rule $r_{gen-local}(x, y)$ consistent with U_{trn} extends to the generalized minimal rule centered at x. We define the sequence of rules $r^0, \ldots, r^n$. The first rule is the local rule $r^0 = r_{gen-local}(x, y)$. To define each next rule r_i we assume that the previous rule r_{i-1}:

$$\bigwedge_{1 \leq j < i} \rho_j(x_j, *) < M_j \bigwedge_{i \leq j \leq n} \rho_j(x_j, *) \leq \rho_j(x_j, y_j) \Rightarrow dec = dec(y).$$

is consistent with the training set U_{trn} and the first $i-1$ conditions of the rule r_{i-1} are maximally general, i.e., replacing any strong inequality $\rho_j(x_j, *) < M_j$ for $j < i$ by the weak makes this rule inconsistent. Let S_i be the set of all the object that satisfy the premise of the rule r_{i-1} with the condition on the attribute a_i removed:

$$S_i = \{z \in U_{trn} : z \text{ satisfies} \bigwedge_{1 \le j < i} \rho_j(x_j, *) < M_j \bigwedge_{i < j \le n} \rho_j(x_j, *) \le \rho_j(x_j, y_j)\}.$$

In the rule r_i the i-th condition is maximally extended in such way that the rule remains consistent. It means that the range of acceptable values for the attribute a_i in the rule r_i has to be equal or less than the attribute distance from x to any object in S_i with a decision different from $dec(y)$. If S_i does not contain an object with a decision different from $dec(y)$ the range remains unlimited:

$$M_i = \begin{cases} \infty & \text{if } \forall z \in S_i \, dec(z) = dec(y) \\ \min\{\rho_i(x_i, z_i) : z \in S_i \wedge dec(z) \ne dec(y)\} & \text{otherwise.} \end{cases}$$

By limiting the range of values on the attribute a_i in the rule r_i to M_i:

$$\bigwedge_{1 \le j < i} \rho_j(x_j, *) < M_j \wedge \rho_i(x_i, *) < M_i \bigwedge_{i < j \le n} \rho_j(x_j, *) \le \rho_j(x_j, y_j) \Rightarrow dec = dec(y)$$

we ensure that the rule r_i remains consistent. On the other hand, the value M_i is maximal: replacing the strong inequality by the weak inequality or replacing M_i by a larger value makes an inconsistent object $z \in S_i$ match the rule r_i.

Since r_{i-1} was consistent the range M_i is greater than the range for the attribute a_i in the rule r_{i-1}: $M_i > \rho(x_i, y_i)$. Hence, the ranges for the previous attributes $M_1, \ldots, M_{i-1}$ remain maximal in the rule r_i: widening of one of these ranges in the rule r_{i-1} makes an inconsistent object match r_{i-1} and the same happens for the rule r_i.

By induction the last rule $r_n : \bigwedge_{1 \le j \le n} \rho_j(x_j, *) < M_j \Rightarrow dec = dec(y)$ in the defined sequence is consistent too and all the conditions are maximally general. Then r_n is consistent and minimal. Since the premise of each rule r_{i-1} implies the premise of the next rule r_i in the sequence and the relation of implication is transitive the first rule r_0 that is the generalized local rule $r_{gen-local}(x, y)$ of the objects x, y implies the last rule r_n that is a minimal consistent rule. Thus we have proved the theorem for the case when the generalized local rule is consistent.

In case where the generalized local rule $r_{gen-local}(x, y)$ is inconsistent with the training set each rule centered at x implied by $r_{gen-local}(x, y)$ covers all objects covered by $r_{gen-local}(x, y)$, in particular it covers an object causing inconsistency. Hence, each rule implied by $r_{gen-local}(x, y)$ is inconsistent too.   □

Consider the classifier $decision_{gen-local-rules}(x)$ defined by Algorithm 1 with a single change: the generalized local rules $r_{gen-local}(x, y)$ are used instead of original local rules $r_{local}(x, y)$. Theorem 11 ensures that for each object x this algorithm counts all and only those objects that are covered by a certain generalized minimal consistent rule centered at x. Hence, we obtain the final conclusion.

Corollary 12. *The classification result of the generalized rule support based classifier from Equation 3 with the set R of all the generalized minimal consistent rules and Algorithm 1 used with the generalized local rules is the same for each test object x:*

$$decision_{gen-rules}(x, R) = decision_{gen-local-rules}(x).$$

The time complexity of the generalized lazy rule induction algorithm is the same as the complexity of the non-generalized version: $O(|U_{trn}|^2 |A|)$.

5   Combination of k Nearest Neighbors with Generalized Rule Induction

To classify an object x the k-nn classifier finds the set $NN(x, k)$ of k nearest neighbors of x and it assigns the most frequent decision in $NN(x, k)$ to x:

$$decision_{knn}(x) := \arg \max_{d_j \in V_{dec}} |\{y \in NN(x, k) : dec(y) = d_j\}|. \qquad (4)$$

The k-nn model implements the lazy learning approach: the k nearest neighbors of a test object x are searched during the classification. The previous approaches [4,6,8] combining k-nn with rule induction do not preserve the laziness of learning. We propose the algorithm that preserves lazy learning, i.e., rules are constructed in lazy way at the moment of classification. The proposed combination uses the metric based generalization of rules described in Section 4.

For each test object x Algorithm 1 looks over all the training examples $y \in U_{trn}$ during construction of the support sets $support[d_j]$. Instead of that we can limit the set of the considered examples to the set of the k nearest neighbors of x. The intuition is that training examples far from the object x are less relevant for classification than closer objects. Therefore in the combined method we use the modified definition of the rule support, depending on the object x:

Definition 13. *The k-support of the generalized rule $\alpha \Rightarrow dec = d_j$ for a test object x is the set:*

$$k - support(x, \alpha \Rightarrow dec = d_j) = \{y \in NN(x, k) : y \text{ matches } \alpha \wedge dec(y) = d_j\}.$$

The k-support of the rule contains only those objects from the original support set that belong to the set of the k nearest neighbors.

Now, we define the classification model that combines the k-nn method with rule induction by using the k-supports of the rules:

$$decision_{knn-rules}(x, R) := \arg \max_{d_j \in V_{dec}} \left| \bigcup_{r \in R(x)} k - support(x, r) \right|. \qquad (5)$$

where R is the set of all generalized minimal consistent rules. The classifier $decision_{knn-rules}(x, R)$ can be defined by the equivalent formula:

$$\arg\max_{d_j \in V_{dec}} |\{y \in NN(x, k) : \exists r \in R(x) \text{ supported by } y \wedge dec(y) = d_j\}| .$$

This formula shows that the combined classifier can be viewed as the k-nn classifier with the specific rule based zero-one voting model.

As for the generalized rule support classifier we propose an effective algorithm simulating the combined classifier $decision_{knn-rules}$ based on the generalized local rules. The operation of consistency checking for a single local rule in Algorithm 1 takes $O(|U_{trn}||A|)$ time. We can use the following fact to accelerate this consistency checking operation in the generalized algorithm:

Fact 14. *For each training object $z \in U_{trn}$ matching a generalized local rule $r_{gen-local}(x, y)$ based on the distance ρ from Equation 1 the distance between the objects x and z is not greater than the distance between the objects x and y:*

$$\rho(x, z) \le \rho(x, y).$$

Proof. The generalized local rule $r_{gen-local}(x, y)$ for a test object $x = (x_1, \ldots, x_n)$ and a training object $y = (y_1, \ldots, y_n)$ has the form

$$\bigwedge_{a_i \in A} \rho_i(x_i, *) \le \rho_i(x_i, y_i) \Rightarrow dec = dec(y).$$

If $z = (z_1, \ldots, z_n)$ matches the rule then it satisfies the premise of this rule. It means that for each attribute $a_i \in A$ the attribute value z_i satisfies the following condition: $\rho_i(x_i, z_i) \le \rho_i(x_i, y_i)$. Hence, we obtain that the distance between the objects x and z is not greater than the distance between the objects x and y:

$$\rho(x, z) = \left(\sum_{a_i \in A} w_i \rho_i(x_i, z_i)^p \right)^{\frac{1}{p}} \le \left(\sum_{a_i \in A} w_i \rho_i(x_i, y_i)^p \right)^{\frac{1}{p}} = \rho(x, y). \qquad \square$$

The above fact proves that to check consistency of a local rule $r_{gen-local}(x, y)$ with a training set U_{trn} it is enough to check only those objects from the training set U_{trn} that are closer to x than the object y.

Algorithm 2 is the lazy simulation of the classifier $decision_{knn-rules}(x, R)$ combining the k nearest neighbors method with rule induction. The algorithm follows the scheme of Algorithm 1. There are two differences. First, only the k nearest neighbors of a test object x are allowed to vote for decisions. Second, the consistency checking operation for each local rule $r_{gen-local}(x, y)$ checks only those objects from the training set U_{trn} that are closer to x than the object y. Thus the time complexity of the consistency checking operation for a single neighbor is $O(k|A|)$. Hence, the cost of consistency checking in the whole procedure testing a single object is $O(k^2|A|)$. In practice, consistency checking takes less time than searching for the k nearest neighbors. Thus addition of the rule induction to the k nearest neighbors algorithm does not lengthen significantly the performance time of the k-nn method.

Algorithm 2. Algorithm $decision_{knn-local-rules}(x)$ simulating the classifier $decision_{knn-rules}(x, R)$ with lazy induction of the generalized local rules.

```
for each d_j ∈ V_dec support[d_j] := ∅
neighbor_1, ..., neighbor_k := the k nearest neighbors of x
            sorted from the nearest to the farthest object
for each i := 1 to k
    if r_gen-local(x, neighbor_i) is consistent
    with neighbor_1, ..., neighbor_{i-1} then
        support[dec(neighbor_i)] := support[dec(neighbor_i)]∪{neighbor_i}
return arg max_{d_j ∈ V_dec} |support[d_j]|
```

---

6   Experimental Results

In this section we compare the performance of the classical k-nn with the combined model described in Section 5. To compare classification accuracy we used the 8 large data sets from the repository of University of California at Irvine [3]: *segment* (19 attr, 2310 obj), *splice-DNA* (60 attr, 2000 train, 1186 test obj), *chess* (36 attr, 3196 obj), *satimage* (36 attr, 4435 train, 2000 test obj), *pendigits* (16 attr, 7494 train, 3498 test obj), *nursery* (8 attr, 12960 obj), *letter* (16 attr, 15000 train, 5000 test obj) and *census94* (13 attr, 30160 train, 15062 test obj). The data provided originally as a single set (*segment, chess, nursery*) were randomly split into a training and a test part with the split ratio 2 to 1.

For each of these 8 data sets the classical k-nn and the combined model were trained and tested 5 times for the same partition of the data set and the average classification error was calculated for comparison. In each test of a given classification method, first, the metric defined by the City-VDM metric [4] was induced from the training set with $p = 1$ and attribute weighting [11], then the optimal value of k was estimated from the training set with the procedure [7] in

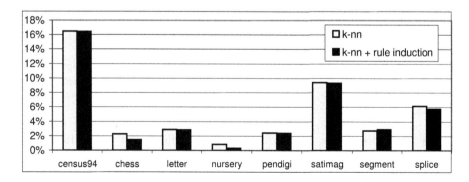

Fig. 1. The average classification error of the classical k-nn and the method combining k-nn with rule induction

the range $1 \leq k \leq 100$, and finally, the test part of a data set was tested with the previously estimated value of k.

Since distance-based voting by the k nearest neighbors outperforms majority voting [5], both in the k-nn and in the combined model we assigned the inverse squre distance weights $\frac{1}{\rho(x,y)^2}$ to the neighbors $y \in NN(x,k)$ instead of equal weights (used in Equations 4 and 5) while classifying a test object x.

Figure 1 shows that the method combining the k-nn with rule based induction is for all the data sets at least equally accurate as the k-nn alone, and sometimes it improves significantly the k-nn accuracy. For example, for *nursery* the combined model gives the 0.3% error in comparison to the 0.82% error of the pure k-nn and for *chess* the combined model gives the 1.46% error in comparison to the 2.24% error of the k-nn. Investigating lack of improvement for some data we observed that very few neighbors are rejected. For future we consider to apply rules that are more specific and selective than the local rules proposed.

7   Conclusions

In the paper we have introduced the new hybrid classification model that combines the rule based classification with the k nearest neighbors method. An important property of the combined model is that by adding rule based component we do not change essentially the performance time of the k nearest neighbors method. In this model the nearest neighbors of a test object are verified and filtered by the rule based-component. This gives more certainty that these neighbors are appropriate for decision making. The experiments confirm that the combined model can provide more accurate classification than the k-nn alone.

Acknowledgements. The research has been supported by the grants 4 T11C 040 24 and 3 T11C 002 26 from Ministry of Scientific Research and Information Technology of the Republic of Poland.

References

1. D. W. Aha, D. Kibler, and M. K. Albert. Instance-based learning algorithms. *Machine Learning*, 6:37–66, 1991.
2. J. G. Bazan. Discovery of decision rules by matching new objects against data tables. In *Proceedings of the First International Conference on Rough Sets and Current Trends in Computing*, volume 1424 of *Lectures Notes in Artificial Intelligence*, pages 521–528, Warsaw, Poland, 1998. Springer-Verlag.
3. C. L. Blake and C. J. Merz. UCI repository of machine learning databases. http://www.ics.uci.edu/~mlearn/MLRepository.html, Department of Information and Computer Science, University of California, Irvine, CA, 1998.
4. P. Domingos. Unifying instance-based and rule-based induction. *Machine Learning*, 24(2):141–168, 1996.
5. S. Dudani. The distance-weighted k-nearest-neighbor rule. *IEEE Transactions on Systems, Man and Cybernetics*, 6:325–327, 1976.

6. A. R. Golding and P. S. Rosenbloom. Improving accuracy by combining rule-based and case-based reasoning. *Artificial Intelligence*, 87(1-2):215–254, 1996.
7. G. Góra and A. G. Wojna. RIONA: a new classification system combining rule induction and instance-based learning. *Fundamenta Informaticae*, 51(4):369–390, 2002.
8. J. Li, K. Ramamohanarao, and G. Dong. Combining the strength of pattern frequency and distance for classification. In *Proc. of the 5th Pacific-Asia Conference on Knowledge Discovery and Data Mining*, pages 455–466, Hong Kong, 2001.
9. A. Skowron and C. Rauszer. The discernibility matrices and functions in information systems. In R. Slowinski, editor, *Intelligent Decision Support, Handbook of Applications and Advances of the Rough Sets Theory*, pages 331–362. Kluwer Academic Publishers, Dordrecht, 1992.
10. A. Skowron and J. Stepaniuk. Tolerance approximation spaces. *Fundamenta Informaticae*, 27(2-3):245–253, 1996.
11. A. G. Wojna. Center-based indexing in vector and metric spaces. *Fundamenta Informaticae*, 56(3):285–310, 2003.
12. J. Wróblewski. Covering with reducts - a fast algorithm for rule generation. In *Proceedings of the First International Conference on Rough Sets and Current Trends in Computing*, volume 1424 of *Lectures Notes in Artificial Intelligence*, pages 402–407, Warsaw, Poland, 1998. Springer-Verlag.

Combining Classifiers Based on OWA Operators with an Application to Word Sense Disambiguation

Cuong Anh Le[1], Van-Nam Huynh[2], Hieu-Chi Dam[2], and Akira Shimazu[1]

[1] School of Information Science
[2] School of Knowledge Science,
Japan Advanced Institute of Science and Technology,
Tatsunokuchi, Ishikawa, 923-1292, Japan
{cuonganh, huynh, dam, shimazu}@jaist.ac.jp

Abstract. This paper proposes a framework for combining classifiers based on OWA operators in which each individual classifier uses a distinct representation of objects to be classified. It is shown that this framework yields several commonly used decision rules but without some strong assumptions made in the work by Kittler et al. [7]. As an application, we apply the proposed framework of classifier combination to the problem of word sense disambiguation (shortly, WSD). To this end, we experimentally design a set of individual classifiers, each of which corresponds to a distinct representation type of context considered in the WSD literature, and then the proposed combination strategies are experimentally tested on the datasets for four polysemous words, namely *interest*, *line*, *serve*, and *hard*, and compared to previous studies.

Keywords: Computational linguistics, Classifier combination, Word sense disambiguation, OWA operator.

1 Introduction

The automatic disambiguation of word senses has been an interest and concern since the 1950s. Roughly speaking, word sense disambiguation involves the association of a given word in a text or discourse with a particular sense among numerous potential senses of that word. As mentioned in [5], this is an "intermediate task" necessarily to accomplish most natural language processing tasks. It is obviously essential for language understanding applications, while also at least helpful for other applications whose aim is not language understanding such as machine translation, information retrieval, among others. Since its inception, many methods involving WSD have been developed in the literature (see, e.g., [5] for a survey). During the last decade, many supervised machine learning algorithms have been used for this task, including Naïve Bayesian (NB) model, decision trees, exemplar-based model, SVM, maximum entropy, etc. As observed

D. Ślęzak et al. (Eds.): RSFDGrC 2005, LNAI 3641, pp. 512–521, 2005.

in studies of machine learning systems, although one could choose one of learning systems available to achieve the best performance for a given pattern recognition problem, the set of patterns misclassified by the different classification systems would not necessarily overlap [7]. This means that different classifiers may potentially offer complementary information about patterns to be classified. In other words, features and classifiers of different types complement one another in classification performance. This observation highly motivated the interest in combining classifiers during the recent years. Especially, classifier combination for WSD has been unsurprisingly received much attention recently from the community as well, e.g., [6,4,13,8,2,14].

As is well-known, there are basically two classifier combination scenarios. In the first scenario, all classifiers use the same representation of the input pattern. In the context of WSD, the work by Kilgarriff and Rosenxweig [6], Klein et al. [8], and Florian and Yarowsky [2] could be grouped into this first scenario. In the second scenario, each classifier uses its own representation of the input pattern. An important application of combining classifiers in this scenario is the possibility to integrate physically different types of features. In this sense, the work by Pedersen [13] can be considered as belonging to this scenario, although the difference of representations here is only in terms of size of context windows. Further, an important issue in combining classifiers is the combination strategy used to derive a consensus decision.

In this paper, we focus on classifier combination for WSD in the second scenario mentioned above. Particularly, we first consider various ways of using context in WSD as distinct representations of a polysemous word under consideration, then all these representations are used jointly to identify the meaning of the target word. By considering each representation of the context as an information inspired by a semantical or syntactical criterion for the purpose of word sense identification, we can apply OWA operators for aggregating multi-criteria to form an overall decision function considered as the fuzzy majority based voting strategy [9]. Interestingly, this approach also yields several commonly used decision rules for WSD. It would be worth noting that in [7], the authors proposed a theoretical framework for combining classifiers which also leads to many commonly used decision rules used in practice. However, to derive these decision rules, this framework adopts several assumptions imposed on individual classifiers (for more details, see [7]) which, to our opinion, are difficult to be accepted and verified in text-related applications.

This paper is organized as follows. In Section 2, it is necessary to briefly recall the notion of OWA operators. After reformulating the WSD problem in terms of a pattern recognition problem with multi-representation of patterns, Section 3 discusses two strategies of combining classifiers for WSD based on the Bayesian approach and OWA operators respectively. In Section 4, we describe our method of feature selection for WSD problem. Then Section 5 presents experimented results and some comparison with previous known results on the same test datasets. Finally, some conclusions are presented in Section 6.

2   OWA Operators

The notion of OWA operators was first introduced in [15] regarding the problem of aggregating multi-criteria to form an overall decision function. A mapping

$$F : [0,1]^n \to [0,1]$$

is called an OWA operator of dimension n if it is associated with a weighting vector $W = [w_1, \ldots, w_n]$, such that 1) $w_i \in [0,1]$ and 2) $\sum_i w_i = 1$, and

$$F(a_1, \ldots, a_n) = \sum_{i=1}^{n} w_i b_i$$

where b_i is the i-th largest element in the collection $a_1, \ldots, a_n$.

OWA operators provide a type of aggregation operators which lay between the "and" and the "or" aggregation. As suggested by Yager [15], there exist at least two methods for obtaining weights w_i's. The first approach is to use some kind of learning mechanism. That is, we use some sample data, arguments and associated aggregated values and try to fit the weights to this collection of sample data. The second approach is to give some semantics or meaning to the weights. Then, based on these semantics we can directly provide the values for the weights. In the following we use the semantics based on fuzzy linguistic quantifiers for the weights.

The fuzzy linguistic quantifiers were introduced by Zadeh in [16]. According to Zadeh, there are basically two types of quantifiers: absolute, and relative. Here we focus on the relative quantifiers typified by terms such as *most, at least half, as many as possible*. A relative quantifier Q is defined as a mapping $Q : [0,1] \to [0,1]$ verifying $Q(0) = 0$, there exists $r \in [0,1]$ such that $Q(r) = 1$, and Q is a non-decreasing function. For example, the membership function of relative quantifiers can be defined [3] as

$$Q(r) = \begin{cases} 0 & \text{if } r < a \\ \frac{r-a}{b-a} & \text{if } a \leq r \leq b \\ 1 & \text{if } r > b \end{cases} \tag{1}$$

with parameters $a, b \in [0,1]$.

Then, Yager [15] proposed to compute the weights w_i's based on the linguistic quantifier represented by Q as follows:

$$w_i = Q(\frac{i}{n}) - Q(\frac{(i-1)}{n}), \text{ for } i = 1, \ldots, n. \tag{2}$$

3   Classifier Combination for WSD

In this section, after reformulating the WSD problem in terms of a pattern recognition problem with multi-representation of patterns, the Bayesian approach to combining classifiers for the WSD problem is reviewed. Then, a framework of classifier fusion strategies in WSD based on OWA operators is developed.

3.1 WSD with Multi-representation of Context

As is well-known, in WSD problem, context plays an essentially important role and is the only means to identify the meaning of a polysemous work. Given an ambiguous word w, which may have m possible senses (classes): $c_1, c_2, \ldots, c_m$, in a context C, the task is to determine the most appropriate sense of w.

Generally, context C can be used in two ways [5]: in the *bag-of-words approach*, the context is considered as words in some window surrounding the target word w; in the *relational information based approach*, the context is considered in terms of some relation to the target such as distance from the target, syntactic relations, selectional preferences, phrasal collocation, semantic categories, etc. As such, for a target word w, we may have different representations of context C corresponding to different views of context. Assume we have such R representations of C, say $\mathbf{f}_1, \ldots, \mathbf{f}_R$, serving for the aim of identifying the right sense of the target w. Clearly, each $\mathbf{f}_i$ can be also considered as a semantical representation of w. Each representation $\mathbf{f}_i$ of context has its own type depending on which way context is used. In the sequent, we can use a set of features and a representation interchangeably without danger of confusion.

3.2 Bayesian Combination Strategy

Assume that the set of features $\mathbf{f}_i$, which is considered as a representation of context C of the target w, is used by the i-th classifier. Due to the interpretation of $\mathbf{f}_i$'s and the role of context in WSD, we shall assume that the classification models are mutually exclusive, i.e. that only one model can be associated with each target w.

Under such a mutually exclusive assumption, given representations $\mathbf{f}_i$ ($i = 1, \ldots, R$), the Bayesian theory suggests that the word w should be assigned to class c_j provided the a posteriori probability of that class is maximum, namely

$$j = \arg\max_k P(c_k | \mathbf{f}_1, \ldots, \mathbf{f}_R) \tag{3}$$

That is, in order to utilize all the available information to reach a decision, it is essential to consider all the representations of the target simultaneously.

The decision rule (3) can be rewritten using Bayes theorem as follows:

$$j = \arg\max_k \frac{P(\mathbf{f}_1, \ldots, \mathbf{f}_R | c_k) P(c_k)}{P(\mathbf{f}_1, \ldots, \mathbf{f}_R)}$$

Because the value of $P(\mathbf{f}_1, \ldots, \mathbf{f}_R)$ is unchanged with variance of c_k, we have

$$j = \arg\max_k P(\mathbf{f}_1, \ldots, \mathbf{f}_R | c_k) P(c_k) \tag{4}$$

As we see, $P(\mathbf{f}_1, \ldots, \mathbf{f}_r | c_k)$ represents the joint probability distribution of the representations extracted by the classifiers. Assume that the representations used are conditional independent, so that (4) can be rewritten as follows:

$$j = \arg\max_k P(c_k) \prod_{i=1}^{R} P(\mathbf{f}_i | c_k) \tag{5}$$

According to Bayes rule, we have:

$$P(\mathbf{f}_i|c_k) = \frac{P(c_k|\mathbf{f}_i)P(\mathbf{f}_i)}{P(c_k)} \qquad (6)$$

Substituting (6) into (5), we obtain:

$$j = \arg\max_k P(c_k) \prod_{i=1}^{R} \frac{P(c_k|\mathbf{f}_i)P(\mathbf{f}_i)}{P(c_k)} = \arg\max_k [P(c_k)]^{-(R-1)} \prod_{i=1}^{R} P(c_k|\mathbf{f}_i) \qquad (7)$$

The decision rule (7) quantifies the likelihood of a hypothesis by combining the a posteriori probabilities generated by the individual classifiers by means of a product rule.

3.3   The Combination Strategy Based on OWA Operators

As mentioned in Introduction, each representation $\mathbf{f}_i$ of the context C can be considered as providing the information inspired by a semantical or syntactical criterion for the purpose of word sense identification. Under such a consideration, let us assume that we have R classifiers corresponding to R representations $\mathbf{f}_i$ of the context, each of which provides a soft decision for identifying the right sense of the target word w in the form of a posterior probability $P(c_k|\mathbf{f}_i)$, for $i = 1, \ldots, R$.

Now, we can define an overall decision function D, with the help of an OWA operator F of dimension R, which combines individual opinions to derive a consensus decision as follows:

$$D(c_k) = F(P(c_k|\mathbf{f}_1), \ldots, P(c_k|\mathbf{f}_R)) = \sum_{i=1}^{R} w_i p_i \qquad (8)$$

where p_i is the i-th largest element in the collection $P(c_k|\mathbf{f}_1), \ldots, P(c_k|\mathbf{f}_R)$, and $W = [w_1, \ldots, w_R]$ is a weighting vector semantically associated with a fuzzy linguistic quantifier.

Then, the fuzzy majority based voting strategy suggests that the target word w should be assigned to class c_j provided that $D(c_j)$ is maximum, namely

$$j = \arg\max_k D(c_k) \qquad (9)$$

It should be worth mentioning that the use of OWA operators in classifier combination has been studied, for example, in [9]. In this work we use OWA operators for classifier fusion in their semantic relation to linguistic quantifiers so that we could provide a framework for combining classifiers, which also yields several commonly used decision rules but without some strong assumptions made in the work by Kittler et al. [7].

As studied in [15], using Zadeh's concept of linguistic quantifiers and Yager's idea of associating their semantics to various weighting vectors W, we can obtain many commonly used decision rules as following.

Max Rule. First let us use the quantifier *there exists* which can be relatively represented as a fuzzy set Q of $[0,1]$ such that $Q(r) = 0$, for $r < 1/R$ and $Q(r) = 1$, for $r \geq 1/R$. We then obtain from (2) the weighting vector $W = [1, 0, \ldots, 0]$, which yields from (8) and (9) the Max Decision Rule as

$$j = \arg\max_k \left[\max_i P(c_k | \mathbf{f}_i) \right] \tag{10}$$

Min Rule. Similarly, if we use the quantifier *for all* which can be defined as a fuzzy set Q of $[0,1]$ such that $Q(1) = 1$ and $Q(r) = 0$, for $r \neq 1$ [15]. We then obtain from (2) the weighting vector $W = [0, \ldots, 0, 1]$, which yields from (8) and (9) the Min Decision Rule as

$$j = \arg\max_k \left[\min_i P(c_k | \mathbf{f}_i) \right] \tag{11}$$

Median Rule. In order to have the Median decision rule, we use the absolute quantifier *at least one* which can be equivalently represented as a relative quantifier with the parameter pair $(0,1)$ for the membership function Q in (1). Then we obtain from (2) the weighting vector $W = [1/R, \ldots, 1/R]$, which from (8) and (9) leads to the median decision rule as:

$$j = \arg\max_k \left[\frac{1}{R} \sum_{i=1}^{R} P(c_k | \mathbf{f}_i) \right] \tag{12}$$

Fuzzy Majority Voting Rules. We now use the relative quantifier *at least half* with the parameter pair $(0, 0.5)$ for the membership function Q in (1). Then, depending on a particular value of R, we can obtain from (2) the corresponding weighting vector $W = [w_1, \ldots, w_R]$ for the decision rule, denoted by FM1, as:

$$j = \arg\max_k \left[\sum_{i=1}^{R} w_i p_i \right] \tag{13}$$

where p_i is the i-th largest element in the collection $P(c_k | \mathbf{f}_1), \ldots, P(c_k | \mathbf{f}_R)$.

Similarly, we can also use the relative quantifier *as many as possible* with the parameter pair $(0.5, 1)$ for the membership function Q in (1) to obtain the corresponding decision rule, denoted by FM2.

Interestingly also, from the following relation

$$\prod_{i=1}^{R} P(c_k | \mathbf{f}_i) \leq \min_{i=1}^{R} P(c_k | \mathbf{f}_i) \leq \sum_{i=1}^{R} w_i p_i \leq \max_{i=1}^{R} P(c_k | \mathbf{f}_i) \leq \sum_{i=1}^{R} P(c_k | \mathbf{f}_i) \tag{14}$$

it suggests that the Max and Min decision rules can be approximated by the upper or lower bounds appropriately. Especially, under the assumption of equal priors, the decision rule (7) simplifies to the Product rule, which is a lower approximation of the Min rule, while approximating Max rule by the upper bound yields the Sum rule.

In addition, from the classical voting strategy, we can also obtain the following decision rule.

Majority Vote Rule. Majority voting follows a simple rule as: it will vote for the class which is chosen by maximum number of individual classifiers. This can be done by hardening the a posteriori probabilities $P(c_k|\mathbf{f}_i)$ in terms of functions Δ_{ki} defined as follows:

$$\Delta_{ki} = \begin{cases} 1, & \text{if } P(c_k|\mathbf{f}_i) = \max_j P(c_j|\mathbf{f}_i) \\ 0, & \text{otherwise} \end{cases}$$

then the right class (sense) c_j is determined as follows:

$$j = \arg\max_k \sum_i \Delta_{ki} \tag{15}$$

3.4   Multi-representation of Context for WSD

It is worth to emphasize that, as mentioned above, two of the most important kinds of information for determining the sense of a polysemous word are the topic of the context and relational information representing the structural relations between the target word and the surrounding words in a local context. A bag of unordered words in the context can determine the topic of the context and collocation can determine grammatical information. Ordered words in a local context are also an important resource for relational information. We did not use syntactical relations such as verb-object, which are used by Ng and Lee in [12], because this information can be found in collocation features and a syntactic parser does not always output a correct result. More particularly, we use five kinds of representations corresponding to five classifiers. Each representation is a set of features organized as following:

- $\mathbf{f}_1$ is a set of unordered words in the large context, namely

$$\mathbf{f}_1 = \{w_{-n_1}, \ldots, w_{-2}, w_{-1}, w_1, w_2, \ldots, w_{n_1}\}$$

- $\mathbf{f}_2$ is a set of words assigned with their positions in the local context, namely

$$\mathbf{f}_2 = \{(w_{-n_2}, -n_2), \ldots, (w_{-2}, -2), (w_{-1}, -1), (w_1, 1), (w_2, 2), \ldots, (w_{n_2}, n_2)\}$$

- $\mathbf{f}_3$ is a set of part-of-speech tags assigned with their positions in the local context, namely

$$\mathbf{f}_3 = \{(p_{-n_3}, -n_3), \ldots, (p_{-2}, -2), (p_{-1}, -1), (p_1, 1), (p_2, 2), \ldots, (p_{n_3}, n_3)\}$$

- $\mathbf{f}_4$ is a set of collocations of words, namely

$$\mathbf{f}_4 = \{w_{-l} \cdots w_{-1} w w_1 \cdots w_r | + r \leq n_4\}$$

- $\mathbf{f}_5$ is a set of collocations of part-of-speech tags, namely

$$\mathbf{f}_5 = \{p_{-l} \cdots p_{-1} w p_1 \cdots p_r | l + r \leq n_5\}$$

Where w_i is the word at position i in the context of the ambiguous word w and p_i be the part-of-speech tag of w_i, with the convention that the target word w appears precisely at position 0 and i will be negative (positive) if w_i appears on the left (right) of w.

In the experiment, we design the window size of topic context (for both left and right windows) as 50 for the representation f_1, i.e. $n_1 = 50$, while the window size of local context as 3 for remaining representations, i.e. $n_i = 3$, for $i = 2, 3, 4, 5$. Our representations for the individual classifiers are richer than the representation that just uses words in the context because the features containing richer information about structural relations are also used. Even that the unordered words in a local context may also contain structure information, but collocations and words and part-of-speech tags assigned with their positions of course will bring richer information.

4   Experiments

4.1   Data

We tested on the datasets for four words, namely *interest, line, serve,* and *hard,* which are used in numerous comparative studies of word sense disambiguation methodologies such as Pedersen [13], Ng and Lee [12], Bruce & Wiebe [1], and Leacock and Chodorow [10]. We have obtained those data from Pedersen's homepage [1]. There are 2369 instances of *interest* with 6 senses, 4143 instances of *line* with 6 senses, 4378 instances of *serve* with 4 senses, and 4342 instances of *hard* with 3 senses.

4.2   Experimental Results

In the experiment, we obtain the results that are the average of 5 results from 10-folds cross validation. Data included four datasets corresponding to four polysemous words *interest, line, hard,* and *serve,* were tested based on multi-representation of context as defined in the preceding section. Table 1 shows the experimental results obtained by using various strategies of classifier combination developed in Section 3 and the best results obtained by individual classifiers respectively. It is of interest to note that Majority Voting, which is widely used in many studies of combining classifiers, may not be a good choice for classifier combination in WSD.

Table 2 shows the comparison of results from the best classifier combination with previous WSD studies, which were also tested on the four words. It is shown that the best classifier combination based on multi-representation of context gives the highest accuracy on all the four words.

---

[1] http://www.d.umn.edu/~tpederse/data.html

Table 1. Experimental Results

	Best individual classifier (%)	Product (%)	Sum (%)	Max (%)	Min (%)	Median (%)	Majority Voting (%)	FM1 (%)	FM2 (%)
interest	86.8	**91.4**	89.2	90.0	89.9	90.2	88.7	91.0	90.2
line	82.8	**89.4**	81.4	86.6	87.0	83.9	79.8	84.3	83.1
hard	90.2	89.5	85.2	89.8	89.2	91.0	90.4	**91.2**	91.0
serve	84.4	**89.6**	86.9	87.5	87.9	88.6	85.4	88.9	88.6

Table 2. The comparison with previous studies

(%)	BW^2	M	NL	LC	P	Best combined classifiers
interest	78	–	87	–	89	**91.4**
line	–	72	–	84	88	**89.4**
hard	–	–	–	83	–	**91.2**
serve	–	–	–	83	–	**89.6**

5   Conclusion

In this paper we have argued that various ways of using context in WSD can be considered as distinct representations of a polysemous word under consideration, then all these representations are used jointly to identify the meaning of the target word. This consideration allowed us to develop a framework for combining classifiers based on Bayesian approach and the notion of OWA operators with the help of fuzzy majorities. Interestingly, this framework also yields many commonly used decision rules for WSD, without assumptions imposed on individual classifiers as done in [7]. We also experimentally explored all developed combination strategies on the datasets for four polysemous words, namely *interest, line, serve*, and *hard*, which are used in numerous comparative studies of word sense disambiguation methodologies. It has been also shown that multi-representation of context significantly improves the accuracy of WSD by combining classifiers, as individual classifiers corresponding to different types of representation suitably offer complementary information about the target to be assigned a sense, this consequently helps to make more correct decisions.

Acknowledgement. This research is partly conducted as a program for the "Fostering Talent in Emergent Research Fields" in Special Coordination Funds for Promoting Science and Technology by the Japanese Ministry of Education, Culture, Sports, Science and Technology.

---

[2] In the table, BW, M, NL, LC, and P respectively abbreviate for Bruce & Wiebe [1], Mooney [11], Ng & Lee [12], Leacock & Chodorow [10], and Pedersen [13].

References

1. Bruce, R., Wiebe, J.: Word-Sense Disambiguation using Decomposable Models. In: *Proc. of the 32nd Annual Meeting of the Association for Computational Linguistics (ACL)* (1994) 139–145
2. Florian, R., Yarowsky, D.: Modeling consensus: Classifier combination for Word Sense Disambiguation. In: *Proc. of EMNLP 2002* (2002) 25–32
3. Herrera, F., Verdegay, J.L.: A linguistic decision process in group decision making. *Group Decision Negotiation* **5** (1996) 165–176
4. Hoste, V., Hendrickx, I., Daelemans, W., van den Bosch, A.: Parameter optimization for machine-learning of word sense disambiguation. *Natural Language Engineering* **8** (3) (2002) 311–325
5. Ide, N., Véronis, J.: Introduction to the Special Issue on Word Sense Disambiguation: The State of the Art. *Computational Linguistics* **24** (1998) 1–40
6. Kilgarriff, A., Rosenzweig, J.: Framework and results for English SENSEVAL. *Computers and the Humanities* **36** (2000) 15–48
7. Kittler, J., Hatef, M., Duin, R.P.W., Matas, J.: On combining classifiers. *IEEE Transactions on Pattern Analysis and Machine Intelligence* **20** (3) (1998) 226–239
8. Klein, D., Toutanova, K., Ilhan, H.T., Kamvar, S.D., Manning, C.D.: Combining heterogeneous classifiers for Word-Sense Disambiguation. In: *Proc. of ACL WSD Workshop* (2002) 74–80
9. Kuncheva, L.I.: Combining classifiers: Soft computing solutions. In: S. K. Pal, A. Pal (eds) *Pattern Recognition: From Classical to Modern Approaches.* World Scientific (2001) 427–451
10. Leacock, C., Chodorow, M., Miller, G.: Using corpus statistics and WordNet relations for Sense Identification. *Computational Linguistics* (1998) 147–165
11. Mooney, R.J.: Comparative experiments on Disambiguating Word Senses: An illustration of the role of bias in machine learning. In: *Proc. of the Conference on Empirical Methods in Natural Language Processing (EMNLP)* (1996) 82–91
12. Ng, H.T., Lee, H.B.: Integrating multiple knowledge sources to Disambiguate Word Sense: An exemplar-based approach. In: *Proc. of the 34th Annual Meeting of the Society for Computational Linguistics (ACL)* (1996) 40–47
13. Pedersen, T.: A simple approach to building ensembles of Naive Bayesian classifiers for Word Sense Disambiguation. In: *Proc. of the North American Chapter of the Association for Computational Linguistics (NAACL)* (2000) 63–69
14. Wang, X.J., Matsumoto, Y.: Trajectory based word sense disambiguation. In: *Proc. of the 20th International Conference on Computational Linguistics.* Geneva (2004) 903–909
15. Yager, R.R.: On ordered weighted averaging aggregation operators in multicriteria decision making. *IEEE Transactions on Systems, Man, and Cybernetics* **18** (1988) 183–190
16. Zadeh, L.A.: A computational approach to fuzzy quantifiers in natural languages. *Computers and Mathematics with Applications* **9** (1983) 149–184

System Health Prognostic Model Using Rough Sets

Zbigniew M. Wojcik

OnBoard Software Inc.,
12621 Silicon Drive, San Antonio, TX 78249

Abstract. A new rough sets data fusion model is presented fusing measured health degradation levels and influences on these degradations. The data fusion model is a system of matrix inequalities of the rough sets covariances. Rough sets variance allows to explicitly assess only health degradations assuring increased signal-to-noise ratio, thus high accuracy of processing. The matrices of inequalities fuse measured health degradation levels and influences on these degradations. Adaptations mechanisms are by a new machine learning approach determining weights of the terms of the inequalities at the time of key events found in the historical data. Prognostic is always time-sequenced, therefore methods based on time sequences are incorporated, e.g. a new data fusion model exploiting time-dependency of events, assuring high quality of prediction. Deterministic prognostic is by estimating the pattern of health degradation in question, finding the match with degradation pattern in historical data, and then tracing this historical degradation pattern up to its conclusion. The model is hierarchical: the right sides of the data fusion expressions substitute for endogenous variables of higher-level expressions.

1 Introduction

Rough sets approach [3] incorporates a conceptual and mathematical information model that splits data into: (a) data that is CERTAIN and HEALTHY, and (b) all other related data that is AMBIGUOUS or UNHEALTHY, and builds relationships on the above two groups of data. The rough sets approach is significant for health degradation data analysis, because of: (1) Setting the focus on the split of all data into the two parts: on completely healthy and on partly degraded of different levels of degradation; (2) Providing tools to measure level of health ambiguity and level of health degradation; (3) Intelligent data mining, because considering relationships between unambiguous and ambiguous data is known from the psychology of human perception as INTELLIGENT.

Our rough sets approach incorporates the Universe (or data) U of degradation signals (called test points) and a set R of equivalence relations. Examples of test points: (a) trf, the set of measurements of turbine fan vibration level over time, (b) tit, the set of Turbine Inlet Temperatures over time. Each test point $u \in U$ has its own equivalence relation $r \in R$. Each first level equivalence relation r for each test point u describes the equivalence class of the

D. Ślęzak et al. (Eds.): RSFDGrC 2005, LNAI 3641, pp. 522–531, 2005.
© Springer-Verlag Berlin Heidelberg 2005

measurements *'in healthy condition'* not looked for, because the focus is on health degradation. Health degradation of a part described by the test point u is represented by the complement of u/r in u. Diagnostics of a health problem is frequently based on a specific non-empty intersection of the equivalence relations *'in degraded condition'*. For instance, a disintegration of an engine is likely to happen when: $TRF/degraded \cap TIT/degraded \neq \phi$, where *degraded* $\equiv$ *'in degraded condition'*. Engine *disintegration* is thus representable by non-empty indiscernibility relation [3] over two or more specific equivalence relations, e.g.: *disintegration* $\Leftarrow IND\{trf\_degraded, tit\_degraded\} = trf/degraded \cap tit/degraded$ executed on paired elements that occur at the same time. Unhealthy situations are detected by rough sets variance. Rough sets variance prevents obscuration of degradation information by measuring distance to healthy interval. Statistical population variance of variable X: $Var(X) = 1/N \sum (x - \overline{x})(x - \overline{x})$ where $(x - \overline{x})$ is a measure of deviation of the values x from their mean. The statistical variance obscures degradation information, because it collects into the sum also healthy measurements. There may be no significant difference between: (a) a signal of a few unhealthy measurements accompanied with a large number of small deviations from the mean and (b) a signal of no unhealthy measurements accompanied with a large number of slightly higher (but still normal) deviations from the mean. Rough sets variance of variable X for N measurements is:

$$rsVar(X) = Median|x - L(X)| \tag{1}$$

where: $L(X)$ is the value of the healthy range of X, nearest to x; the x must be outside of the healthy range, otherwise $x - L(X)=0$ and is rejected from considering to the median. Only non-zero degradations count. Rough sets variance is non-linear. For a large number of elements the rough sets variance may also be expressed by: $rsVa(X) = 1/N \sum (x - L(X))(x - L(X))$, or by $rsVm(X) = 1/N \sum |x - L(X)|$

Statistical covariance between variables X and Y: $Cov(X,Y) = 1/N \sum (x - \overline{x})(y - \overline{y})$. Rough sets covariance (compare [6]) between variables X and Y for N measurements is as follow:

$$rsCov(X,Y) = Median(x - L(X))(y - L(Y)) \tag{2}$$

Also rough sets covariance provides very high signal-to-noise ratio, as opposed to the statistical covariance which incorporates the mean. For a large number of elements the rough sets variance may also be expressed by $rsVa(X) = 1/N \sum (x - L(X))(y - L(Y))$.

In the context of the mining to health degradation data, selected differences between rough sets approach and statistics can be stressed as follow: 1. Statistics focuses on deviations from the mean, sampling, distributions, probabilities; 2. Rough sets focus on relationships between (a) unambiguous / healthy and (b) ambiguous / unhealthy data. Parameters of relationships are used instead of distribution parameters and probabilities. Data *AS IS* are analyzed without sampling.

The equivalence class of measurements x taken at test point$X$ of a part represented by the equivalence relation $r = $ *in degraded condition* equals:

$$x/r = \bigcap \{x \in X : |x| > rsVar(X)\} \tag{3}$$

where $|x| > rsVar(X) \equiv r \equiv$ *'degraded'*. The $\bigcap$ means that $r \equiv$ *'degraded'* is the indiscernibility relation over all historical data of the test point X.

With the approximate knowledge $k=(X, 'degraded')$, the degraded health at test point$X$ can be approximated by two subsets [3]:

$$\underline{x}r = \bigcup \{x \in x/r : x \subseteq X\} \tag{4}$$

$$\overline{x}r = \bigcup \{x \in x/r : x \bigcap X \neq \emptyset\} \tag{5}$$

called the lower and upper approximations of health degradation represented by the test point X.

Any health degradation issues are time - sequenced and inter-related with many degradation problems which also are time dependent. Health degradations detected by rough sets variance must be related, around times when they occur, with other health degradations, e.g. with the aid of the rough sets covariance. All these other health degradations can be predicted: by using historical data and rough sets covariances they can be discovered as inherently co-occurring with the health degradations detected with the aid of the rough sets variance. Health degradations are quite deterministic in nature: if a symptom occurs, a number of specific degradations are likely to follow, and if two or more symptoms occur simultaneously, then a severe specific health degradation is almost imminent.

The basic rough set model introduced by Pawlak [3] and the Variable Precision Rough Set Model (VPRSM) [8,1,2,4] are concerned with implicit static-like data (i.e. not necessarily sequenced by time) and rather probabilistic type of events. The IF-THEN rules generated from this type of data are probabilistic in nature. The rough sets model proposed in this paper considers only data sequenced by time. The time makes data mining deterministic in the domain of health degradations. Predictions are more accurate when data is deterministic, or much less amount of data is needed for the same quality predictions. E.g., an imminent problem is very likely for only a few specific symptoms occurring almost simultaneously in time. This way the proposed method is to significantly improve the quality of prediction. Time attribute can be used in the basic Pawlak's rough set model or the VPRSM to make predictions deterministic and then to develop a more deterministic classifications. The conditional probabilities of VPRSM are suitable to do time-related classifications by introducing time moment, estimating overlap of events with that time moment and sequencing all time moments.

This article attacks the classification of time-sequenced events by rough sets covariances of co-occurring degradation features, by new data fusion model and a new neural net based on this data fusion model. The proposed system analyzes data recorded from interrelated system components and makes predictions using the degradation levels of these components and health status measurements from historical data. Statistical failure time does not predict failure of a particular item based on its specific level of degradation, but on statistics of a large number of items. Without the deterministic knowledge of the degradation level and influences on degradations no other health status can be determined except the probability of survival for the item being measured. This assumption is true e.g. when material fatigue leads to failure. Application of the proposed model needs knowledge of events co-existing in time and properties of changes of observations over time. All this knowledge can be acquired from historical databases. The proposed approach makes sense of knowledge databases.

The proposed model is a data fusion system similar to [6], in which terms are the products of ratios of degradation and the ratios of influences on the degradations. The degradation data fusion system presented here is deterministic for data sequenced by time. It exploits available degradation signals and gets optimized by removal of insignificant terms. The model is hierarchical and does not limit the object's complexity. Reasoning is deterministic and rule-like chaining is applicable. Determinism of time sequences allows using simple inequalities with weights learned at the time of major events such as failure times, near-failures or major repairs. Patterns of degradation are created from historical data at times of known failures or major repairs. Predictions are made by: (i) matching current object conditions with the patterns of degradation learned through historical data, and (ii) computing and applying the increments of degradations and of the influences on the degradations learned from the patterns matched, minute-by-minute, to see when possible failures could happen. A method is offered for computing elementary increments to extrapolate the actual and predicted patterns of degradation to the points of predicted failures and repairs. The system avoids obscuration of rare degradation measurements by healthy measurements by using rough sets: any healthy status is immediately considered irrelevant. Logistics operations can be optimized by accurately preparing to predicted repairs. Influences of environmental degradations that start to affect system at the earliest stages can be traced back. The existing structural modelling and regression models are equalities, not inequalities. New proposed reasoning technology is based on testing the inequality $' >'$ in each modelling record, making a rule that fires an alarm if the measurement data implies a significant level of degradation. Records of lower-level components are listed and executed first, and whenever inequality is true, using its right side as an operand of one of the inequalities that is listed later as a higher-level component. Coefficients are not computed as in structural modelling by minimizing an error, but by a new machine learning from time-sequenced events.

The state-of-the-art machine learning methods do not adapt to the time of an event but to the event itself: this prediction of time of fault or time of repair is not direct and therefore incurs inaccuracies. A near-deterministic approach proposed allows making predictions based on degradation patterns gathered automatically for different applications and at the time moments of failures. Prediction of failures and the health status takes place by deterministic application of these increments to the actual patterns of degradation matched. Statistical (and not deterministic) predictions would require more cases, which are not always available.

The above new concepts are presented below with more details, and with results of predicting disintegration of a C-5 aircraft engine.

2   Fusion of Degradation Factors Sequenced by Time

The proposed prognostic tool balances the messages of positive performance with the messages of negative performance by applying some weights over a time period. When a failure status is approached, the positive performance reports will decrease and at the same time the negative reports will substantially increase. The parameters are collected in a similar way as performance is measured for computing systems [7]. Latent variables describing object's health degradation over some recent time periods are collected into matrices. The object is in good health if each record of the following matrix inequalities is true (compare [6]):

$$[p] > [D][n] + [G][x] \tag{6}$$

where: $[p]$ is the column matrix of M health endogenous variables, i.e. health variables influenced by other health variables. The $[p]$ on the left side of (6) are positive performance ratios. E.g., the value of each specific element $p1$ of $[p]$ equals to the ratio of the number of estimates when the propulsion health on *object*1 was at least good, to the number of all the health estimates during the same time in question. The ratio $t = $ *(time over which a part was working over the last 3 years) / (3 years)* can be used as $p2$.

$[G]$ is the matrix of rough sets compound covariances representing degradation influences of all health exogenous variables x on the endogenous variables p:

$$G_{pk} = (1/K) \sum_{k=1}^{K} |(p_k - \|p\|) \prod_{i=1}^{I} (x_{ki} - \|x_i\|)| \tag{7}$$

where: $\|x_i\|$ it is not the mean or median, but it is the upper or lower bound of the range of healthy measurements of exogenous variable x_i, a concept of the rough sets representing a set of elements indiscernible by equivalence relation *'in healthy condition'*. The difference $x_{ki} - \|x_i\|$ denotes the difference of current measured value x_{ki} from the whole healthy range $\|x_i\|$ of x_i, i.e. from the upper or lower value of x_i. Term with the measurement value x_{ki} in the healthy range is set to 0. E.g., in some cases pressure should not be higher, and in some cases lower than a limit; k is the time moment of taking sample; $\|p\|$ is the upper bound of the set of the measurements of endogenous variable p, indiscernible by the equivalence relation *'in healthy condition'*, and the difference $p_k - \|p\|$ on the right side of (6) denotes the degradation of p - the difference of current measurement p_k of p from the whole healthy range $\|p\|$ of p; K is the normalization factor over the number of all elements summed, making G_{px} a ratio; k is the measurement index.

Eq.(7) computes the product of measures of degradations of I exogenous variables and one endogenous variable at each time moment k, and sums it over total time K. The above rough sets compound covariance is the measure of non-obscured degradation relationship between the I exogenous variables on the endogenous variable p working together in a compound system with possible multiple mutual influences. Most measurements of the health status may be in the healthy state and only several deviations may be symptomatic to a health problem. The state-of-the-art statistical covariance incorporating the deviation from the mean would obscure a small number of significant deviations, which make insignificant contribution to a sum compared to thousands of small deviations in the healthy range. The rough sets covariance may incorporate more that one exogenous variable and is non-linear: it ignores small deviations in the healthy range.

EXAMPLE: When the endogenous variable p is binary, e.g. of two values $\{working, not\ working\} \equiv \{1, 0\}$, then $\|p\| = 0$. When each measured status of p is $working$, then $p_k - \|p\| = 1$ for all k making degradations observable in exogenous variables. Then $G_{px} > 0$ because $p \equiv working$ and thus exogenous variables x_i have observed influence on p. More values of p allow to observe growing degradation of p.

[n] and [x] are the column matrices of weights of endogenous and exogenous variables initially set to 1, so that at the beginning of data analysis, instead of (6) the following is assumed: $[p] > [D] + [G]$;

[D] is the matrix of rough sets covariances [6] representing degradation influences of all health status endogenous variables on the endogenous variables:

$$D_{pv} = (1/M) \sum_{k=1}^{M} |(p_k - \|p\|)(v_k - \|v\|)| \qquad (8)$$

where: $\|p\|$ and $\|v\|$ are the bounds of the set of the measurements k of endogenous variables p and v indiscernible by the equivalence relation 'in degraded condition'. Endogenous variable can affect any other endogenous variable except itself: the diagonal of $[D]$ is set to 0 to prevent each endogenous variable from having a direct degradation influence on itself: $D_{pv} = 0$ for $v = p$. Normalization by M makes D_{pv} a ratio. Only degradation levels are considered in rough sets covariance.

By incorporating the above rough sets degradation covariances, the proposed tool directly rejects obscuration by all measurements indiscernible by healthy status, automatically sets to 0 all influences of no impact on the system degradation, and retains only critical influences degrading the system. By this the proposed system correctly assesses the critical factors for prediction. Relating health status measurement to the equivalence class of the rough sets representing the healthy ranges and not to the mean or to median is the key difference with respect to statistics [6]. Note, that matrices $[p]$, $[D]$, and $[G]$ are not the values of the variables as commonly used in statistics, they are the ratios directly representing health problem level. The proposed tool can manipulate the bound level to trace details of the early stages of the degradation, whereas the fault code threshold is basically fixed.

3   Machine Learning in Time-Sequenced Data Fusion Model

Machine learning, in general, adapts weights for classification purposes. The goal here is to discriminate precisely between the degraded and the healthy system by using weights that are learned in a changing environment. Fast and reliable determination of the weights, with the aid of the original machine learning is proposed, instead of using a slow, multiple step convergence to the weights.

Inequalities (6) have no weights yet adapting the values of the upper bounds of the proposed degradation covariances to the actual health problems on the object: smaller bounds would set Ineq.(6) to false quicker than higher bounds. The solution is to first set the bounds $\|p\|$ and $\|v\|$ of the set of the measurements indiscernible by the equivalence relation 'in healthy condition' to some reasonable levels, and then to adapt them to actual (degraded) health conditions in a machine learning process by introducing a weight Wx for each dependent variable p. The weight Wx which is the same at each independent variable x is computed at the minimum problem needing repair when the object is no longer ready for application, by read-out of all the values p, $[D]$, $[G]$ in:

$$p = [D]n + [G]x = [D] + [G]Wx \tag{9}$$

where $n = 1$ and $x = Wx$, and simply determining the Wx from (9) as the unknown. Any further increase of any of influences of $[D]$ or $[G]$ will keep Ineq.(6) false: the degradation ratios and the degradation influences only grow once they start to exist. Because the fault or significant degradation needing repair must be detected even at zero influences from the other endogenous variables, $[D] = 0$ to determine weight Wx. For instance, for the dependent variable p representing the propulsion health degradation on $object1$, the weights Wx_i are determined from:

$$[p] = [G][Wx] \tag{10}$$

by investigating each problem i in propulsion system on $object1$ in the past and finding the maximum of Wx_i for all the health problems in exogenous variables:

$$Wx = max_i(Wx_i) \tag{11}$$

After each weight Wx_i is determined, the system health decision inequalities become as (6) with [x]=[Wx]. Finding the maximum of the weights Wx_i for all the system health problems i for the endogenous variable p sets the Ineq.(6) to false quite easily for any problem considered in (9, 10, 11) even when the object with that problem would still be in working conditions. The maximum weight Wx determines the upper approximation of all faults and system conditions close to faults. To find the range of health ambiguity issues, the lower approximation is found for the minimum of weights Wx_i for each problem i:

$$Wx = mini(Wx_i) \tag{12}$$

The conditions of the system in between the lower and upper approximations are worthy maintenance care, and at least data should be examined. The system belonging to the lower approximation certainly does not fit for the application, however, when using only the minimum of weights Wx_i there is a risk of not spotting a real health problem that would be detected for a Wx located in between its minimum and maximum. The table composed of all weights Wx_i made for all problems i is the solution, telling exactly when the object is not ready for the application. The lower and upper approximations are still useful to estimate the level to which maintenance is needed on a compound system. Each group of problems should have its own sub-set of records in (6) and its own weight Wx_i. Similarly, adjusting the degradation weights $[Wn]$ in: $p = [D][Wn] + [G][Wx]$ makes system accurately sensitive to degradations caused by endogenous variables: at $[G] = 0$ the weights Wn_j are determined for all problems j.

The advantages of the proposed machine learning that computes each weight as unknown from the equations are: (i) high precision of classification; (ii) high speed of accurate machine learning even from one example to classify one class of degradation cases; and (iii) simplicity, by adjusting weights directly on the level of dichotomization concepts and by this easiness to interpret the machine learning process.

4   Example of Predicting Jet Engine Disintegration

To deterministically predict C-5 jet engine disintegration, DB tables were created to collect rs statistics on the following jet engine degradations: 1. Rapid ramp in Compressor Fan Vibration (crf) level; 2. Highest tit (Turbine Inlet Temperature); and 3. High n1rpm/n2rpm (the ratio of turbine fan speed [revolutions per minute] to compressor fan speed). DB Table 1 (a file) collects ramp type degradation information $vibration\_ramp = \{x \in X : SIZE > rsVar(X\_ramp) \}$, where $X=crf$; $SIZE$ is the length of the vertical component of each ascending ramp detected in X; rough sets variance $rsVar(X\_ramp) = Median \mid SIZE - 1.2 \mid$ with healthy vibration ramp interval=1.2; $LEVEL$ is the percent of the ramp length [mil] over a threshold=1.2; $BEGIN$ and END are the times of $vibration\_ramp$ beginning and end. DB Table 2 collects degradation information in: (a) test point tit, and (b) ratio of $n1$ rpm to $n2$ rpm only if the $vibration\_ramp$ degradation was detected. The $highest\_tit = \{x \in X : SIZE > rsVar(X) \cap tit = max\{all\_tit\}\}$, where all_tit is the set of tit of all 4 C-5 engines: $all\_tit = \{ Eng1\_tit, Eng2\_tit, Eng13\_tit, Eng4\_tit \}$; $high\_n1/n2 = \{x \in X : SIZE > rsVar(X) \cap n1/n2 > Average\{all\_n1/n2\} \}$.

DB Table 1: Vibration ramp-degradation in Engine 3 crf fan signal:

```
PART SIGNAL DEGRADATION SIZE LEVEL% BEGIN END
Eng3 crf vibration_ramp 3.84 320 0 10
Eng3 crf vibration_ramp 1.92 160 42 50
Eng3 crf vibration_ramp 1.6 133 159 177
```

DB Table 2: Range degradations in Engine 3 tit and $n1/n2$ signals:

```
PART SIGNAL DEGRADATION SIZE LEVEL% BEGIN END
Eng3 tit highest 23.5 2.79 0 10
Eng3 n1/n2 high 0.0113 1.1682 0 10
Eng3 tit highest 26.7 3.26 42 50
Eng3 n1/n2 high 0.0113 1.1115 42 50
Eng3 tit highest 26.6 3.29 159 177
Eng3 n1/n2 high 0.011 1.0707 159 177
```

Engine *disintegration* $\equiv DISINTEGRATION\_soon$ is predicted at the first intersection of *vibration_ramp* and *highest_tit* and *high_n1/n2*. These intersections are computed by applying data from the intermediate DB Tables 1 and 2 to the rough sets compound covariance (7) instead of operating on the level of signal. The intermediate DB tables collecting degradation features at separate test points assure very fast evaluation of the rough sets compound covariances. DB Tables 3 and 4 list the results of this prediction. In fact, a complete jet engine disintegration happened at the third ramp of crf: the engine should be shut-off at the first ramp.

The endogenous variable p of (7) is initially with two values {*working, disintegrated*} $\equiv \{1,0\}$ and with $\|p\| = 0$. At the time of each disintegration ramp, each measured status of $p = p + 1$ on right side of (7), so that Ineq.(6) turns to false to shut-off the engine. Several cases of engine disintegration are analyzed now to determine accurate value of the weight Wx.

DB Table 3: Disintegration after ramp-degradation in Engine 3 crf fan signal combined with range degradations in Engine 3 tit and n1 / n2 signals:

```
PART SIGNAL DEGRADATION SIZE LEVEL% BEGIN END}
Eng3 crf DISINTEGRATION_vibr_ramp 3.84 320 0 10
Eng3 crf DISINTEGRATION_vibr_ramp 1.92 160 42 50
Eng3 crf DISINTEGRATION_vibr_ramp 1.6 133 159 177
```

DB Table 4: Disintegration after ramp-degradation in Engine 3 crf3 fan signal combined with range degradations in Engine 3 tit and n1 / n2 signals:

```
PART SIGNAL DEGRADATION SIZE LEVEL% BEGIN END
Eng3 tit DISINTEGRATION_soon 23.5 2.79 0 10
Eng3 n1/n2 DISINTEGRATION_soon 0.0113 1.1682 0 10
Eng3 tit DISINTEGRATION_soon 26.7 3.26 42 50
Eng3 n1/n2 DISINTEGRATION_soon 0.0113 1.1115 42 50
Eng3 tit DISINTEGRATION_soon 26.6 3.29 159 177
Eng3 n1/n2 DISINTEGRATION_soon 0.011 1.0707 159 177
```

5   Conclusion

The paper uncovers very large areas of applications for rough sets, including predictions of health problems, diagnostics, mission readiness evaluation, equipment maintenance, optimization of logistics operations, avoidance of unnecessary repairs and data fusion for decision making. The paper defines and proves usefulness of the rough sets approaches for the tasks like real-time prediction of equipment disintegration.

New tools were developed and used for accurate data mining and prediction, such as rough sets variance, rough sets covariances, time-sequenced data fusion model, and deterministic machine learning. The rough sets compound covariance proved successful to mine and detect engine disintegration, and new time-sequenced data fusion model to predict it in real-time. Determinism of these new tools assure higher accuracy of predictions and increased precision of mining in historical data.

Prognostic is always time-sequenced, therefore should incorporate methods based on time sequences. Focus on time-sequenced knowledge is implied to make progress in data mining.

Machine learning is commonly understood as a slow adjustment of weights, and not just by setting the weights using knowledge. Rough sets variance and covariance provide accurate values and weights for the terms of the new deterministic data fusion model, which constitute knowledge model for time-sequenced prognostic. This deterministic knowledge acquisition is advantageous: is faster and more accurate compared to statistical or stochastic adjustment of weights.

Acknowledgments. The data for the practical results were selected by Carlos Villarreal [5] and Mark Warren, the employees of OnBoard Software Inc., and the charge codes were found by Hector Pena. I would like to express deep gratitude to my manager Bruce Mather and the CEO David Spencer whose supports were crucial for the successful completion of this paper.

References

1. Grzymala-Busse, J.: LERS-A System for Learning from Examples Based on Rough Sets. In: Slowinski, R. (ed.) Intelligent Decision Support: Handbook of Applications and Advances of Rough Sets Theory. Kluwer Academic Publishers (1991) pp. 3-18.
2. Grzymala-Busse, J., Ziarko, W.: Data mining based on rough sets. Data Mining: Opportunities and Challenges. IDEA Group Publishing (2003) pp. 142-173.
3. Pawlak, Z.: Rough sets - Theoretical aspects of reasoning about data. Kluwer Academic Publishers (1991).
4. Ślęzak, D., Ziarko, W.: Bayesian Rough Set Model. In: Proc. of FDM'2002. December 9, Maebashi, Japan (2002) pp. 131-135.
5. Villarreal, C., Cicek, I.: Automated Troubleshooting Tools for Minimizing Downtime And Reducing the Labor and Material Costs of C-5 Aircraft, IEEE Autotestcon 2004, September 19-23, San Antonio, Texas (2004).
6. Wojcik, Z.M., Wojcik, B.E.: Structural Modeling Using Rough Sets, Proc. Fifth IEEE intern Confr on Fuzzy Systems FUZZ-IEEE'96, September 8-11, New Orleans, LA (1996) pp. 761-766.
7. Wojcik, Z.M., Wojcik, B.E.: Rough Grammar For Efficient and Fault-Tolerant Computing on a Distributed System, IEEE Trans. On Software Engineering, vol.17, no.7 (1991) pp. 652-668.
8. Ziarko, W.: Probabilistic Decision Tables in the Variable Precision Rough Set Model. Computational Intelligence: an International Journal, vol.17, no.3 (2001) pp. 593-603.

Live Logic^{TM}: Method for Approximate Knowledge Discovery and Decision Making

Marina Sapir, David Verbel, Angeliki Kotsianti, and Olivier Saidi

Aureon Biosciences, 28 Wells ave Yonkers NY 10701
marina.sapir@aureon.com

Abstract. Live Logic is an integrated approach for support of the learning and decision making in conditions of uncertainty. The approach covers both induction of probabilistic logical hypotheses from known examples and deduction of the plausible solution for an unknown case based on the inducted hypotheses.

The induction method generalizes empirical data, discovering statistical patterns, expressed in logical language. The deduction method uses multidimensional ranking to reconcile contradictory patterns exhibited by a particular case.

The method was applied on clinical data of the patients with prostate cancer who underwent prostatectomy. The goal was to predict biochemical failure based on the pre- and post- operative status of the patient. The patterns found by the method proved to be insightful from the pathologist's point of view. Most of them had been confirmed on the control dataset.

In our experiments, the predictive accuracy of the Live Logic^{TM} was also higher than that of other tested methods.

1 Introduction

Live Logic^{TM} induction method is developed for learning with inconclusive, inconsistent, noisy data. We assume, the dataset of known observations represents only small part of the general population, and the used descriptors are not enough to distinguish the concepts under study completely. The problem is further complicated by requirement for the decision rule to be transparent for the persons who supply the data. This is a very common situation for medical problems, for example.

Traditional approaches building logical rules (such as decision trees [6], Logical analysis of data [13], induction logic programming [7]) build deterministic rules which do not capture the uncertain nature of the problem.

Currently, there are two major ways expressing uncertainty and building the decision systems from inconclusive data: fuzzy systems, and rough sets systems.

D. Ślęzak et al. (Eds.): RSFDGrC 2005, LNAI 3641, pp. 532–540, 2005.
© Springer-Verlag Berlin Heidelberg 2005

Fuzzy systems build rules which infer fuzzy conclusions from fuzzy premises [4]. The main source of uncertainty taken into account in the fuzzy approach is uncertainty of the descriptions of the training data. Yet, in most of applications, data contain crisp numeric features. Fuzzy systems have to use some external knowledge to introduce the membership functions artificially.

The classic rough sets classifiers work with decision space granulated by indiscernibility relationship introduced prior the analysis. In this approach, each example is considered as a decision rule, which infers its class (decision) from the conditions [5]. If all examples with indiscernible conditions have the same class, the rule is considered to be deterministic. Otherwise, the rule is said to describe a borderline case.

Both traditional approaches tend to produce large amount of rules. The finer is the granulation of the decision space, the more rules will be produced, and the smaller is support of each rule, since the size of the available training set is always limited. It leads to poor predictive ability and poor interpretability [4]. It can be seen, for example, in the application of the rough sets to predict metastases in breast cancer patients [18].

Various precision rough sets [19] approach addresses this problem by introducing probabilistic membership function. The concept of tolerance approximation spaces (see [11] and [12]) further extends possibilities of inductive learning by considering similarity relations, more general than indiscernibility relationship. Another way of increasing the power and predictive ability of the decision rules was introduced in [2] with approximate rules, with relaxed requirement on conditional probability of the correct decision.

Several other approaches are proposed to find coarse homogeneous granules in information space based on data itself, to take into account the association between the values of attributes and the decisions. For example, in the same work [2] authors propose methods of discretization for attributes with large number of values. In in [12], some methods for finding similarity relationships in data are introduced. In all the mentioned works, the coarse granules in information space are built upon indiscernibility relationship by combining fine homogeneous granules.

In this paper, we propose an alternative way to build interpretable and statistically justified decision rules with uncertain data. We discover information granules not by combining elementary homogeneous granules but by eliminating external parts of heterogeneous multidimensional blocks in attribute space, until the necessary homogeneity will be achieved.

Live Logic^{TM} builds all the most general rules, sufficiently supported by data. The approach allows us to work with continuous attributes, without prior discretization or finding similarity relationship on each variable.

To make the decisions for new instances using these uncertain rules, we propose a novel deduction procedure, which involves preliminary classification of instances by all the rules and multidimensional ranking of these decision vectors.

2   Induction Method

2.1   Definitions

The induction procedure finds maximal sufficiently homogeneous granules in the feature space as patterns. The theoretical aspects of the proposed induction method are investigated in [10].

The procedure works with data in the form $[X, Y]$, where $X = \{x_{i,j}\}$, $i = 1, \ldots, m$, $j = 1, \ldots, n$ is matrix with description of n observations (cases) by m features; $Y = \{y_1, \ldots, y_n\}$ is a binary outcome vector, assigning a class to each observation. For $j \in [1, n]$, if $y_j = c$, $(c \in \{1, 2\})$, we say that the j-th observation x_j belongs to the class c. Denote C_1, C_2 all the observations from the classes 1, 2, respectively.

The dataset may have features of various types, such as continuous, nominal or ordinal. For a feature p_i, $i \in [1, m]$, denote $[\alpha_i, \beta_i]$ its range in the dataset.

The procedure induces rules of the type:

$$\text{``}MostLikely\text{''}\, I(p_1, a_1, b_1)\& \ldots \& I(p_m, a_m, b_m) \Rightarrow (y = c), \tag{1}$$

where, for every $i \in \{1, \ldots, m\}$, p_i is a feature, a_i, b_i are arbitrary numbers, $I(p_i, a_i, b_i)$ is an interval predicate of the form $a_i \leq p_i \leq b_i$, y is the class variable.

If both $a_i = \alpha_i$, $b_i = \beta_i$, the predicate $I(p_i, a_i, b_i)$ is true for all possible values of the variable p_i, and it is called **trivial**. The premises in the rule above will be called **clause**. The set $X(B)$ of the observations satisfying the clause B is called **block** of the clause B.

We assume, each feature has its own admissible set of interval predicates. Consider a case of "oriented" [16] feature, which naturally correlates with outcome. For example, the condition "degree of cancer" correlates with the "prognosis". Then an interpretable rule may associate "small" or "large" values of the feature with the decision, not "middle" values. For such a feature, only predicates

$$I(p_i, \alpha_i, c) = (p \leq c), I(p_i, c, \beta_i) = (p \geq c),$$

including ends of the domain are pragmatically justified and admissible.

For a nominal feature, the only meaningful non-trivial predicates are equalities

$$I(p, c, c) = (p = c).$$

The trivial interval is admissible for each feature.

Also, we may want to restrict the number of the nontrivial predicates in the clauses, because complex patterns are often difficult to understand and use. Denote $\mathbf{B}(k)$ all clauses with not more than k non-trivial admissible statements.

Suppose, B is a clause in $\mathbf{B}(k)$, where all predicates are admissible. Clause B is a (h, g)-**interesting** in $\mathbf{B}(k)$ for the class C, if it satisfies the next two requirements:

1. The block $X(B)$ is h-**homogeneous:** The proportion of the cases of the class C, among all the cases $X(B)$ is above the threshold h:

$$\frac{\|X(B) \bigcap C\|}{\|X(B)\|} \geq h.$$

2. The block $X(B)$ is g-**representative** : The proportion of the all cases of the class C in X, which belong to $X(B)$, is above the threshold g:

$$\frac{\|X(B) \bigcap C\|}{\|C\|} \geq g.$$

The requirements on the interesting clause interpret the quantifier "most likely" in (1).

The goal of the induction step of the Live Logic^{TM} is to find all (h, g)-patterns for given values h, g.

One may notice here that the concept of h-homogeneous block may be interpreted as an approximate rule from [2]. However, here it is only auxiliary concept, used to define (h, g)-interesting rules. Unlike approximate rules, the rules we build here are required to be not only sufficiently consistent, but also representative, describe enough of known examples.

An (h, g)-interesting clause for the class C is a (h, g)-**pattern** for the class C, if it is the most general among (h, g)-interesting clauses. If an observation satisfies the conditions of the pattern we will say that it **exhibits** the pattern.

One can notice the parallel and difference between Live Logic^{TM} and association rules method (see [1] and[3]), since the definition of interesting clause closely resemble requirements on support and confidence of the interesting association rules.

The most important difference between Live Logic^{TM} and association rules method, in our view, is that the goal of learning step in our method is patterns, which are the most general among interesting rules, not all interesting rules. The most general, representative rules are the most robust ones, because they are supported by maximum number of cases; and they are the most parsimonious and understandable, since they do not contain excessive conditions and unnecessary terms.

The discovered patterns describe the maximal sufficiently homogeneous granules in the feature space, which can be used to classify new instances.

2.2   The Block Algorithm

The algorithm, mostly, follows one presented in [8] and [9].

Since we have descriptions of only n cases, every feature has not more than n different values in the dataset. Therefore, it is sufficient to search patterns only among blocks with limits a_i, b_i in their interval statements taken among actual values of the feature in the dataset. We further decrease the search space by considering only clauses form $\mathbf{B}(k)$ with admissible interval statements for each feature. The algorithm uses "smart" search among all admissible clauses to find the patterns.

First, describe the convenient way of coding clauses. We code the interval statement $a \leq p_j \leq b$ by the pair $\langle L_j(a), R_j(b) \rangle$, where $L_j(t), R_j(t)$ are the numbers of the values of the feature j, which are less and higher than t, respectively. Notice that the trivial interval statement for any feature will be coded by the pair $\langle 0, 0 \rangle$. A block $B = I_1 \& \ldots \& I_m$ is coded by the sequence $\langle d_1, \ldots, d_{2m} \rangle$, where d_{2i-1}, d_{2i} is a pair, coding i-th interval statement I_i.

Let us define the order on the set of all clauses. For clauses $B_1 = \langle d_1, \ldots, d_{2m} \rangle$, $B_2 = \langle q_1, \ldots q_{2m} \rangle$, $B_1 \prec B_2$ if there exists i such that $d_j = q_j$ for all $j < i$ and $q_i > d_i$. The first clause in this order is the clause with all trivial intervals.

For a clause B, denote $Nxt(B, k)$ the very next after B clause in $\mathbf{B}(k)$ in the order $\prec$; $NxtOut(B, k)$ the very next after B block in $\mathbf{B}(k)$ in the order $\prec$ which is not included in B.

The current clause in the algorithm is denoted by W. The algorithm starts search with the trivial clause $W = \langle 0, \ldots, 0 \rangle$. Let the set M be the current set of found patterns, empty at the start of the algorithm. The parameters h, g, k from the definition of a pattern and class C are selected upfront.

Let $R(B, g)$ denote the condition that the clause B is g-representative, $H(B, h)$ the condition that the clause B is h-homogeneous. By definition, a pattern is the most general clause $B \in \mathbf{B}(k)$ satisfying the conditions $R(B, g) \& H(B, h)$. Then the algorithm [8] may be presented the next way:

- **Case 1: If $R(W, g)$ is not true, $W := NxtOut(W, k)$,**
- **Case 2: If $R(W, g)$ and $H(W, h)$ are true,**
    1. **if M does not contain any clause $C : C \Rightarrow W$, then $M := M \cup \{W\}$;**
    2. **$W := NxtOut(W, k)$;**
- **Case 3: If $R(W, g)$ is true, but $H(W, h)$ is false, $W := Nxt(W, k)$.**

In the first case, the current clause is not a pattern, and there are no patterns among the clauses, less general than the current one. Therefore, we skip all less general clauses in the order and find the next one not included in W.

In the second case, the current clause is a pattern, if it is not less general than any pattern in the set M. In this case, we put it in the set of the patterns M. Since no clause less general than the current one can be a pattern, we skip all next less general clauses in the order $\prec$.

In the third case, the clause is not a pattern. But some less general clause may be a pattern. Therefore, we proceed to test the very next clause in the order $\prec$.

The algorithm repeats this conditional operator in a loop until the procedure $Nxt(W, k)$ or $NxtOut(W, k)$ required on the current step is impossible.

The paper [8] contains proof that the algorithm above finds all patterns for the given class.

The algorithm avoids looking over many possible clauses because, when the current clause is not representative or is a pattern, we skip the less general clause, following in the order. The order is designed to maximize this advantage.

3   Deduction and Decision Making Apparatus

3.1   Decision Vectors

Below we assume that the dataset has only two classes. By definition, patterns for a certain class describe mostly cases of this class. A pattern of a class C may be considered as a classifier: if the case exhibits the pattern, it is classified as a case of the class C. If the case does not exhibit the pattern, the classifier does not give any answer.

If each observation exhibits patterns of only one class, the final conclusion is obvious. Most of time, this is not the case. Therefore, we need a reconciliation procedure.

Suppose, we discovered k_1 patterns of the first class, and k_2 patterns of the second class. Then each case may be coded by a decision vector r of the length $k_1 + k_2$, using the next procedure:

- if the case exhibits the pattern i of the first class, $r_i = 1$, otherwise $r_i = 0$;
- if the case exhibits the pattern j of the second class, $r_{k_1+j} = -1$, otherwise $r_{k_1+j} = 0$.

As result of this procedure, we will have dataset R with binary features, where each entry is a decision vector for an instance in the dataset X.

3.2   Multidimensional U-Scoring

Having decision vectors, one now needs to compare evidence provided for each instance to belong to one class over the other. Thus, some scoring method and threshold needs to be chosen.

A traditional approach is voting: a score assigned to a vector with values 1, -1 and 0 is the sum of its values. This approach may be generalized as a "weighted voting" system, where the score is a weighted sum of the classifiers' values. The weights need to take into account mutual correlation of the features and their relative importance for the decision process.

To overcome the need for subjective weights, we use a multidimensional U-score (mU-score) proposed by K. Wittkowski [15]. The dataset R meets the requirement for mU-scoring: each classifier is "oriented" (positively correlated with the outcome). The mU-scores of decision vectors are built upon a partial order [14] on them. In this order, instances classified by different classifiers are deemed incomparable. The order is defined as follows: for any two vectors $r_1, r_2 \in R$, $r_1 < r_2$ iff for every coordinate i, $r_{1i} \leq r_{2i}$ and $r_1 \neq r_2$.

Then, for each $d \in R$

$$mUScore(d) = \sum_{r \in R} I(d > r) - \sum_{r \in R} I(r > d),$$

where $I(a)$ equals 1, if a is true and is equal 0 otherwise. In another words, the score of the decision vector d is number of vectors in R which are smaller that d minus number of vectors which are larger than d in the described partial order.

The proper threshold for the separation of the classes by the mU-score may be found by optimization of a chosen criterion for sensitivity and specificity of classification.

4 Application of the Method

The method was applied on a dataset from Baylor College of Medicine of the patients with prostate cancer after prostatectomy. The patients were characterized by 15 clinical features. For each patient, either his known time of the biochemical failure or the last observation is present in the data. The goal was to learn to predict biochemical failure within 5 years after the surgery. For this purpose, only the patients with known time of failure and patients with observations after 5 years were selected. The dataset consists of two parts, separated by historical reasons: one part includes 171 cases, out of them 35 are failures. The second dataset contains 282 cases, with 52 failures. Thus, in each dataset, only about 20% of cases belong to the first class. Traditional machine learning methods designed to maximize accuracy of the decision (as SVM, for example) produce the rule, which classifies all or almost all cases as low risk, which is not acceptable. The goal was to develop a decision rule, having high **min(sensitivity, specificity)**, because both sensitivity and specificity are important in this case.

The induction step of the Live Logic^{TM} had its own control. First, each pattern, obtained on one dataset, was tested on another dataset. Second, pathologist, specializing in the prostate cancer, analyzed the patterns to evaluate their consistency with current medical knowledge. Generally, the features were coded in such a way, that the higher value of the feature, the higher is the risk. The found patterns, mostly, follow this rule. One exception is the feature "uicc", which characterizes the degree of the spread of primary tumor over prostate. The patterns for low and high risk contain conditions for high levels of spread only. The reason is that for small tumors cancer aggressiveness is difficult to recognize and the prognosis can not be certain. Below are the examples of the found patterns.

Table 1. Examples of patterns of high and low risk of failure

High Risk	Train %	Test %	Low Risk	Train %	Test %
tnm = 5	92	100	uicc < 4 ggtot ≤ 7 tnm ≤ 3	97.3	86.7
gg1 > 3 tnm > 3	83	87	uicc > 4 gg1 ≤ 3 tnm ≤ 4	97.1	83.3
ln =1 uicc > 4 tnm > 3	92 90	100 100	uicc > 4 svi = 0 ggtot ≤ 7 tnm ≤ 4	97.3	86.7
prepsa > 11.4 gg1 > 3 tnm > 2	86.7	88.9			

In the tables above, *tnm* stands for "TNM stage", *ggtot* means "Prostatectomy Gleason Grade", *gg1* means "Prostatectomy Gleason Score 1", *svi* means "Seminal Vesical Invasion", *ln* is "Lymph Node Status", *prepsa* is "Preoperative PSA".

In the next table, we compare sensitivity and specificity of the decision rules obtained on one set and tested on another set. For comparison we use SVRc^{TM} method which uses some adjustment of the support vector regression method for the censored data [17].

Comparing Sensitivity and Specificity of Live Logic^{TM} and SVRc^{TM}

Datasets		Sensitivity		Specificity	
Training	Testing	LL	SVRc^{TM}	LL	SVRc^{TM}
Set 1	Set 2	0.79	0.5	0.77	0.87
Set 2	Set 2	0.8	0.65	0.66	0.81

As we see from this table, sensitivity of Live Logic^{TM} is consistently higher, while the specificity is lower than that of SVRc^{TM}. For the practical purposes, the results of the Live Logic^{TM} are preferable, since low sensitivity means that large cohort of the high risk patients will not get a necessary treatment. The results of Live Logic^{TM} are preferable from the ***min(sensitivity, specificity)*** criterion as well.

5   Conclusions

The main contribution of this paper is a general approach to the problem of learning under uncertainty, where the resulting rules need to be understandable. The learning and decision making methods for this problem are presented. The learning method finds all strongest and sufficiently consistent decision rules. The decision making method is based on multidimensional partial ordering and calculation of U-score. We demonstrate the advantages of the approach in application to the problem of prognosis of clinical failure for patients with prostate cancer after prostatectomy.

References

1. Agraval, R., Mannila, H. , Srikant, R. Toivonen, H. Verkamo, A.: Fast discovery of association rules. Advances in Knowledge Discovery and data Mining. AAAI/MIT Press, Cambridge, MA. (1995)
2. Bazan, J., Nguyen, H.S., Nguyen, S.H., Synak, P., Wróblewski, J.: Rough set algorithms in classification problems. In: Polkowski, L., Lin, T. Y., Tsumoto, S. (eds.): Rough Set Methods and Applications: New Developments in Knowledge Discovery in Information Systems. **56** Physica-Verlag, Heidelberg, Germany (2000) 49 – 88.
3. Borgelt, C. and Kruse, R.: Induction of Association Rules: Apriori Implementation. 15th Conference on Computational Statistics (Compstat 2002, Berlin, Germany) Physica Verlag, Heidelberg, Germany (2002).

4. Klose, A. , Nurnberger, A. and Nauck, D.: Some Approaches to Improve the Inter-pretability of Neuro-Fuzzy Classifiers. Proc. 6th European Congress on Intelligent Techniques and Soft Computing (EUFIT'98), Aachen (1998) 629 – 633.

5. Pawlak, Z.: Some Issues on Rough Sets. Transactions on Rough Sets I. Lecture notes in computer science 3100 Springer-Verlag, Berlin Heidelberg New York (2004) 375 – 391.

6. Quinlan, J.: Induction of decision trees. Machine Learning, 1 (1986) 81 – 106.

7. Quinlan, J.: Learning logical definitions from relations. Machine Learning **5**(3) (1990).

8. Sapir, M.: Constructing plausible hypothesis for diverse attributes. Automat. Re-mote control, No 11 (1993) 134 – 142.

9. Sapir, M., Sherman, S.: A toolkit for automated search for the most general and easily interpretable hypotheses in first order logic systems. International Conference on Integration of Knowledge Intensive Multi-Agent Systems. KIMAS'03 (2003) 318 – 323.

10. Sapir, M.: Formalization of Induction Logic in Biomedical Research. 4th Interna-tional Symposium on Robotics and Automation ISRA'2004: 1 – 8.

11. Skowron, A., Stepaniuk, J. Tolerance approximation spaces. Fundamenta Infor-maticae. **27** (1996) 245 – 253.

12. Stefanowski, J.: On rough set based approaches to induction of decision rules. In: Skowron, A., Polkowski L. (eds.): Rough sets in knowledge discovery. **1**, Physica Verlag, Heidelberg (1998) 500 – 529.

13. Triantaphyllou, E., Kovalerchuk, B., Deshpande, A.: Some recent developments of using logical analysis for inferring a Boolean function with few clauses. In: Barr, R., Helgason, R., Kennington, L. (eds.): Interfaces in Computer Science and Operations Research Series, **7**, Kluwer (1997) 215 – 236.

14. Wittkowski, K.M.: An extension to Wittkowski. J Am Statist Assoc (1992) 87 – 258.

15. Wittkowski, K.M., Lee, E, Nussbaum, R., Chamian, F.N., Krueger, J.G.: Combin-ing several ordinal measures in clinical studies. Stat Med, 23 (2004) 1579 – 1592.

16. Wittkowski, K.M.: Novel Methods for Multivariate Ordinal Data applied to Genetic Diplotypes, Genomic Pathways, Risk Profiles, and Pattern Similarity. Computing Science and Statistics **35** (2003) 626 – 46

17. Yan, L., Verbel, D., Saidi, O.: Predicting prostate cancer recurrence via maximizing the concordance index. ACM SIGKDD Conference Proceedings (2004)

18. Zaluski, J., Szoszkiewisz, R., Krisinski, J., Stefanowski, J.: Rough Set Theory and Decison Rules in Data Analysis of Breast Cancer Patients. Transactions on Rough Sets I. Lecture notes in computer science Vol 3100 Springer-Verlag, Berlin Heidel-berg New York (2004) 1 – 58.

19. Ziarko, W.: Variable precision rough sets model. Journal of Computer and Systems Sciences. **46** no. 1 (1993) 39 – 59.

Similarity, Approximations and Vagueness*

Patrick Doherty[1], Witold Łukaszewicz[2], and Andrzej Szałas[1,2]

[1] Department of Computer Science, University of Linköping, Sweden
[2] The College of Economics and Computer Science, Olsztyn, Poland
{patdo, witlu, andsz}@ida.liu.se

Abstract. The relation of similarity is essential in understanding and developing frameworks for reasoning with vague and approximate concepts. There is a wide spectrum of choice as to what properties we associate with similarity and such choices determine the nature of vague and approximate concepts defined in terms of these relations. Additionally, robotic systems naturally have to deal with vague and approximate concepts due to the limitations in reasoning and sensor capabilities. Halpern [1] introduces the use of subjective and objective states in a modal logic formalizing vagueness and distinctions in transitivity when an agent reasons in the context of sensory and other limitations. He also relates these ideas to a solution to the Sorites and other paradoxes. In this paper, we generalize and apply the idea of similarity and tolerance spaces [2,3,4,5], a means of constructing approximate and vague concepts from such spaces and an explicit way to distinguish between an agent's objective and subjective states. We also show how some of the intuitions from Halpern can be used with similarity spaces to formalize the above-mentioned Sorites and other paradoxes.

1 Introduction and Preliminaries

1.1 Introduction

In a recent paper, Halpern [1] points out the tight correlation between similarity notions on individuals and their relation to vague predicates. He also considers a distinction between the subjective and objective realities of agent systems and how standard properties of similarity such as transitivity do not necessarily make sense when taking into account epistemic and subjective states of agent systems. Objectively, viewing similarity as an equivalence relation may make sense, but when taking into account capabilities of agents to discern, or their subjective psychological states, it may not make sense to view similarity as a transitive relation. One can also find other examples where intransitivity may hold at the objective level, but not at the subjective level.

When viewing similarity and vagueness in this respect, it turns out that a number of interesting reasoning paradoxes such as the *Sorites Paradox*, can be explained in a matter both satisfactory in the formal sense and also in the pragmatic sense, where agents would have to represent and reason about such concepts as heaps. In attacking these problems, [1] proposes a modal logic which semantically represents both the subjective

---

* Supported in part by a WITAS UAV project grant under the Wallenberg Foundation, Sweden and an NFFP03 grant (COMPAS).

D. Ślęzak et al. (Eds.): RSFDGrC 2005, LNAI 3641, pp. 541–550, 2005.

and objective states accessible by an agent and also allows for the ability to distinguish between *perception reports* and what an agent may definitely know about its objective state. This is done by introducing two modal operators.

Rather than going the modal route, we introduce a general method for modeling similarity relations, approximate sets, and vague predicates. We show how this formal framework can be used to model scenarios associated with an agent, its objective and subjective realities, similarity relations contributing to the definition of vague or approximate predicates, and the sensory limitations essentially defining what it formally means for an agent to have a subjective view of reality as observed through its sensory filters. The basis for this representational capability are *similarity spaces, neighborhoods of individuals* derived from such spaces and *approximate or vague predicates* defined using such neighborhoods. We also show that when restricted to finite domains in a relational database framework, inference associated with the approach is tractable.

Before providing the formal framework, we describe an intuitive scenario from [1]. Relative predicates associated with the sensing modalities are often difficult to represent and define due to the subjective nature of the concepts involved. For example, given samples of beverages and the task of stating which one is sweeter than which, it is difficult to characterize a comparative component of the definition while keeping it consistent with the objective sensor data from which it is grounded.

On the one hand, similarity of sweetness is transitive relative to the number of grains of sugar in beverages, but at a more subjective level, transitivity breaks down. We often experience such comparative situations where beverage A's sweetness is indistinguishable from beverage B, and B's sweetness is indistinguishable from beverage C, but A's sweetness is in fact quite distinguishable from C. Distinguishability at this level is qualitatively different from that at the granular level where a beverage with n grains of sugar is indistinguishable from that with $n+1$ grains of sugar and so on and so forth.

It is obvious to see how the Sorites Paradox is related to this issue. At an objective level, heaps are simply piles of sand with a certain number of grains in them. At the subjective level they are based on subjective perception reports which do not necessarily reflect transitive nature of the sensor data, but should still remain consistent with it.

The literature on similarity is vast and it is often the case that different properties of the associated relation are played off against the other, such as transitivity versus intransitivity, symmetry versus anti-symmetry, etc. One can relax the requirement of a tradeoff in many ways. Some such relaxations are introduced in Section 1.3 and used throughout the paper. In summary, our main goal is to introduce a general framework for representing similarity structures, which permits the definition of vague sets/relations in a meaningful and intuitive way. This will be partly verified by modeling some of the interesting scenarios presented in [1]. The starting point for the approach we propose was initiated by [6], but substantially generalized and applied in [2,3,4,5].

1.2   Paper Structure

In the remainder of this section, we provide some preliminary definitions. In Section 2, we consider the objective and subjective levels of an agent system interfacing with sensors to an external environment. We then relate these levels to vague concepts. In Section 3, we introduce similarity spaces which are the formal vehicle for making distinctions between objective and subjective perceptual descriptions and formalizing vagueness using approximate sets constructed from similarity-based neighborhoods. In Section 5, we formalize a number of examples including those already mentioned. In Section 6, we state some results on the complexity of the approach. In Section 7, we refer to some of the related literature and conclude the paper.

1.3 Preliminaries

Below we assume that $[0, 1]$ is the closed interval of all real numbers between 0 and 1, ordered by the standard ordering on reals $\leq$. We shall also use value Υ, meaning "unknown", which is not in $[0, 1]$ and is incomparable wrt $\leq$ with any number of $[0, 1]$. Let U be a set, $\sigma : U \times U \longrightarrow [0, 1] \cup \{\Upsilon\}$ be a binary function on U and $p \in [0, 1]$ be a given real number. Then, σ is called

- *p-serial* iff for any $x \in U$ there is $y \in U$ such that $\sigma(x, y) \geq p$
- *p-reflexive* iff for any $x \in U$, $\sigma(x, x) \geq p$ (note: p-reflexivity implies p-seriality)
- *p-symmetric* iff for any $x, y \in U$, $\sigma(x, y) \geq p$ implies $\sigma(y, x) \geq p$
- *p-transitive* iff for any $x, y, z \in U$, $\sigma(x, y) \geq p$ and $\sigma(y, z) \geq p$ implies $\sigma(x, z) \geq p$

One can also relax transitivity, as is often done in the fuzzy set area (cf. [7]).

2 Objectiveness, Subjectiveness and Vagueness

It is often the case that an intelligent system interfaces to external environment through the use of real sensors as in the robotics domain or through virtual sensors as in the software agent domain. Already, at this sensor interface level, there is a gap between what the world is actually like and what the robot or software agent is capable of perceiving given a particular sensor suite. For example, a red car may often be perceived by a robot to be brown in color due to special lighting conditions. There is an additional gap between raw sensor data and additional qualitative structures derived via the raw data and additional data fusion and knowledge construction processes. For example, a vehicle which is objectively on a road may be perceived by sensors to be both on and off the road due to sensor noise and inaccuracies, but at a qualitative level, a normative decision has been made to view the vehicle as being completely on the road.

In order to make these distinctions clear, we assume the existence of an *objective reality* independent of any agent's particular perceptive capabilities and the existence of a *subjective reality* specific to an agent. Each agent may or may not have different subjective realities and one agent may in fact have several subjective realities based on its particular configuration and context. Assuming the distinction between objective and subjective realities of an agent, we can refer to an agent's objective state in addition to its subjective states. This distinction is central to Halpern's approach [1] and we will show how our framework can clearly model this distinction in a highly flexible manner. We also use the term *subjective perception* to refer to perceptual activity which results in the generation of perception reports associated with the subjective state(s) of an agent.

In addition to perception reports regarding properties and relations between objects, perception reports about objects themselves and their similarity or lack thereof is equally important as input to reasoning processes. Subjective perception often cannot distinguish objects which are different at the objective level. In some situations this leads to *borderline cases*, where the observer cannot classify objects relative to a given concept. For example, we may not be able to state unequivocally that a vehicle is too close to another or that it is moving too fast relative to a specified speed limit.

According to the literature (see, e.g., [8]), a concept is vague when it has borderline cases, i.e., some objects cannot be classified to the concept or to its complement with certainty. In this paper vagueness is modelled by introducing similarity-based approximations of concepts. More specifically, the lower approximation of a concept consists of objects that are known to belong to the concept and the upper approximation of the concept consists of objects that might belong to the concept.

Observe that even the properties of similarity notion might be substantially different at the objective and subjective level, as illustrated by the following examples.

Example 2.1. Consider a robot equipped with a camera. Assume that the camera's field of view does not allow the robot to fully observe itself, which is a very strong perceptual limitation. In this case the similarity relation on the objective level is reflexive, while on the robot's subjective level it does not have to be reflexive, since the robot cannot observe itself (but might be p-reflexive and/or p-serial, for some p).   □

Example 2.2. Assume that in a given application one considers a similarity relation, $\sim$, between children and parents. On the objective level, it is defined to satisfy $x \sim y$ iff $[Child(x,y) \wedge Sex(x) = Sex(y)]$. Then $\sim$ is not symmetric.[1] Now, suppose that on the subjective level one cannot recognize whether $Child(x,y)$ holds. In this case similarity is defined as $x \sim_s y$ iff $[\Upsilon \wedge Sex(x) = Sex(y)]$, which is symmetric.   □

Example 2.3. Consider the similarity between persons in the set $\{P_1, P_2, P_3\}$. This relation, on the objective level, does not have to be transitive, since similarities between persons P_1 and P_2 as well as between P_2 and P_3 do not have to imply the similarity between P_1 and P_3. On the other hand, subjectively, a robot might not be able to distinguish between P_1, P_2 and P_3, which makes the similarity relation transitive.   □

3   Similarity Spaces

Similarity spaces are used as the formal mechanism for representing the indistinguishability of individuals in a specific domain of discourse. Similarity spaces are quite versatile in use. They are also used as a basis for defining approximate sets and vague predicates in addition to modeling the sensory limitations of agents and provide a formal basis for constructing and analyzing subjective state.

Similarity spaces [2] generalize tolerance spaces as defined in [3]. Comparing the current approach to the approaches of [2,3], we assume that the similarity function can return the value Υ, since the similarity between some objects might be unknown. Also, as argued in [2], and advocated in Examples 2.1 and 2.2, we also relax the requirements that similarity has to be symmetric or reflexive. However, in order to make approximations intuitively meaningful, we will require the seriality of similarity spaces.

---

[1] In fact, one usually compares children to parents, not vice versa and it might be desirable that computer reflects this human behavior.

Definition 3.1. *By a* similarity function *on a set U we mean any function $\sigma : U \times U \longrightarrow$ $[0,1] \cup \{\Upsilon\}$. A similarity function σ is called a* total similarity function *if, for any $x, y \in U$, $\sigma(x, y) \in [0,1]$. For $p \in [0,1]$, by a* similarity relation to a degree at least p, *based on σ, we mean the relation $\sigma^p = \{\langle x, y \rangle \mid \sigma(x, y) \geq p\}$. Such defined σ^p is also simply called the* similarity relation. □

A similarity relation is used to construct similarity neighborhoods for individuals.

Definition 3.2. *By a* neighborhood *of u wrt σ^p we mean the pair of sets $n^{\sigma^p}(u) = \langle n_+^{\sigma^p}(u), n_\oplus^{\sigma^p}(u) \rangle$, where $n_+^{\sigma^p}(u) = \{u' \in U \mid \sigma^p(u, u') \text{ holds}\}$ is called the* lower approximation *of the neighborhood, and $n_\oplus^{\sigma^p}(u) = n_+^{\sigma^p}(u) \cup \{y \mid \sigma(u, y) = \Upsilon\}$ is called the* upper approximation *of the neighborhood.* □

The lower approximation $n_+^{\sigma^p}(u)$ consists of elements which, in the context of available knowledge, are surely similar enough to u, while the upper approximation $n_\oplus^{\sigma^p}(u)$ consists additionally of elements that might be similar to u due to the unknown status of the similarity function. Note that in the case when σ is a total similarity function, we have that $n_+^{\sigma^p}(u) = n_\oplus^{\sigma^p}(u)$, thus the neighborhood can be considered as a single crisp set rather than pair of approximations.

Definition 3.3. *A* similarity space *is defined as tuple $\Sigma = \langle U, \sigma, p \rangle$, consisting of*

- *a nonempty set U, called the* domain *of Σ*
- *a similarity function σ*
- *a* similarity threshold *$p \in [0,1]$.*

If σ is a total similarity function, then Σ is called total. *If σ is p-serial (p-reflexive, p-symmetric, p-transitive) then Σ is called* serial (reflexive, symmetric, transitive). □

Tolerance spaces, as defined in [3], are total reflexive and symmetric similarity spaces (cf. [9]). Since reflexivity implies seriality, tolerance spaces are serial similarity spaces.

4   Approximations and Vagueness

Let us define the notions of approximation and vagueness as understood in this paper.

Definition 4.1. *Let $\Sigma = \langle U, \sigma, p \rangle$ be a serial similarity space and let $S \subseteq U$. The lower and upper approximation of S wrt Σ, denoted respectively by $S_{\Sigma+}$ and $S_{\Sigma\oplus}$, are defined by $S_{\Sigma+} \overset{\text{def}}{=} \{u \in U : n_+^{\sigma^p}(u) \subseteq S\}$ and $S_{\Sigma\oplus} \overset{\text{def}}{=} \{u \in U : n_\oplus^{\sigma^p}(u) \cap S \neq \emptyset\}$.* □

By $S_{\Sigma-}$ and $S_{\Sigma\ominus}$ we denote the complement of $S_\oplus$ and of S_+, respectively. The *boundary region* of S, denoted by $S_{\Sigma\pm}$, is defined as $(S_{\Sigma\oplus} - S_{\Sigma+})$.

Intuition behind Definition 4.1 is depicted in Fig.1. The element marked by $\triangledown$ is in the lower approximation of S – its whole lower approximation neighborhood is included in S. The element marked by $\square$ is in the boundary region – its upper approximation neighborhood contains elements which are in S and elements outside S. Finally, the element marked by $\triangle$ is outside of the upper approximation – its whole upper approximation neighborhood is outside S. Given a particular similarity space, one can be sure that $\triangledown$ is in S, $\triangle$ is outside S. The membership of $\square$ in S cannot be determined.

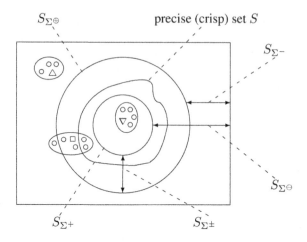

Fig. 1. Approximations of set S wrt a similarity space Σ

We observe[2] that the following proposition holds.

Proposition 4.2. *For any serial $\Sigma = \langle U, \sigma, p \rangle$ and $S \subseteq U$, we have $S_{\Sigma+} \subseteq S_{\Sigma\oplus}$.*   □

If Σ is not serial, then, in general, the above inclusion does not hold. Without this property, the intuitive idea of an approximate set being bound set theoretically from below and above would not hold.

Definition 4.3. *Given a similarity space $\Sigma = \langle U, \sigma, p \rangle$, by a* vague *set over Σ or simply a* vague *set[3] (when Σ is known from context), we shall understand a pair $\langle S_{\Sigma+}, S_{\Sigma\oplus} \rangle$, where $S \subseteq U$. $\langle S_{\Sigma+}, S_{\Sigma\oplus} \rangle$ is called a* crisp *set over Σ (or simply a* crisp *set, when Σ is known), when $S_{\Sigma+} = S_{\Sigma\oplus}$. Then we write $S_{\Sigma+}$ rather than the whole pair.*   □

Observe that in the definition above, boundary regions model borderline cases. Moreover, the parameter p of Σ may vary when perceptual capabilities of an observer change. Consequently, for a given concept its boundary region is not definitely fixed but contextual. Note also that relations are sets of tuples and can be approximated given a similarity space on tuples of the corresponding type.

We assume that the objective level is specified by means of crisp or vague relations, e.g., stored in a relational or deductive database, or defined by means of formulas of a given logic with underlying relational semantics. We also assume that any serial similarity space Σ reflects perceptual limitations of an observer's subjective level:

Definition 4.4. *Assume $\Sigma = \langle U, \sigma, p \rangle$ is a serial similarity space and let $Z = \langle X, Y \rangle$ be a vague set over U. Then a* perception report *of Z wrt $\Sigma_1 = \langle U_1, \sigma_1, p_1 \rangle$ is defined as the vague set $\langle X_{\Sigma_1+}, Y_{\Sigma_1\oplus} \rangle$.*   □

---

[2] E.g., by a slight generalization of the corresponding argument given in [2].

[3] We sometimes use the term *approximate set* as a synonym for "vague set". We also deal with *vague predicates* to mean that their extensions are vague sets (of tuples of respective arity).

Definition 4.4 allows one to model perception reports pertaining to both the objective and subjective levels of different agents. For example, in agent communication, a receiving agent may view the sending agent's knowledge as objective and then apply a perceptual filter in terms of its current perceptual limitations. The resulting interpretation of knowledge is that perceived subjectively by the receiver and it is different from that perceived "objectively" by the sender. For example, the vague set Z can be provided by an agent with some perceptual limitations modelled by Σ. Receiver approximates Z using its own filter Σ_1. These ideas are developed, in the context of tolerance spaces, in [4,5], and can easily be generalized onto arbitrary serial similarity spaces.

We also have the following theorem about the unfalsifiability of perception in the case of serial similarity spaces. It essentially states that once an element is surely perceived to be in a set under observation, it cannot be further classified not to be in the set, even when the similarity threshold is arbitrarily changed (without violating seriality). Similarly, once it is surely perceived to be outside the set, it cannot be further classified to be in the set no matter what the similarity threshold is (again, retaining seriality).

Theorem 4.5. *Let* $\Sigma = \langle U, \sigma, p \rangle$ *and* $\Sigma_1 = \langle U, \sigma, q \rangle$ *be any serial similarity spaces.*[4] *Then, for any vague set* $Z = \langle X, Y \rangle$ *over* U, *we have:*

1. *if* $s \in X_{\Sigma^+}$ *then* $s \in X_{\Sigma_1^\oplus}$
2. *if* $s \in Y_{\Sigma^-}$ *then* $s \in Y_{\Sigma_1^\ominus}$

Proof. We prove the first part. The second is symmetric. Consider the following cases:

$q \leq p$: then $n_\oplus^{\sigma^p}(s) \subseteq n_\oplus^{\sigma^q}(s)$. If $s \in X_{\Sigma^+}$ then, by seriality of Σ, $s \in X_{\Sigma^\oplus}$. Thus $n_\oplus^{\sigma^p}(s) \cap X \neq \emptyset$, i.e., $n_\oplus^{\sigma^q}(s) \cap X \neq \emptyset$, i.e., $s \in X_{\Sigma_1^\oplus}$

$q > p$: then $n_+^{\sigma^q}(s) \subseteq n_+^{\sigma^p}(s)$. Thus, if $s \in X_{\Sigma^+}$ then $n_+^{\sigma^q}(s) \subseteq n_+^{\sigma^p}(s) \subseteq X$. By seriality of Σ_1, $n_+^{\sigma^q}(s) \neq \emptyset$. Thus $n_+^{\sigma^q}(s) \cap X \neq \emptyset$. By definition, $n_+^{\sigma^q}(s) \subseteq n_\oplus^{\sigma^q}(s)$, hence $n_\oplus^{\sigma^q}(s) \cap X \neq \emptyset$, i.e., $s \in X_{\Sigma_1^\oplus}$.   □

In the non-serial case the above theorem does not hold, as is shown in Example 5.1.

5   Examples

The first example provides a counter-example to Theorem 4.5 in the case of non-seriality of the underlying similarity spaces.

Example 5.1. Let us go back to Example 2.1. Assume that there are two objects: Ob and the robot Ro, and that the robot determines similarity $\sigma(Ob, Ob) = 1.0$, $\sigma(Ob, Ro) = \sigma(Ro, Ob) = 0.8$ and $\sigma(Ro, Ro) = 0.6$. Consider similarity spaces $\Sigma = \langle \{Ob, Ro\}, \sigma, 0.8 \rangle$ and $\Sigma_1 = \langle \{Ob, Ro\}, \sigma, 1.0 \rangle$. Σ is serial while Σ_1 is not. We have: $\{Ob\}_{\Sigma^+} = \{Ro\}$ and $\{Ob\}_{\Sigma_1^\oplus} = \{Ob\}$. Thus Ro is in $\{Ob\}_{\Sigma^+}$ but not in $\{Ob\}_{\Sigma_1^\oplus}$ which, in the non-serial case, falsifies Theorem 4.5 with $X = \{Ob\}$.   □

Consider the heap example and the Sorites Paradox, widely discussed, also in [1].

---

[4] Thus, it is sufficient to require that σ is $(\max\{p, q\})$-serial.

Example 5.2. Let *Heap*(n) be a predicate, denoting that n grains of sand make a heap. Assume that an agent is asked to recognize heaps, provided that the objective level definition of *Heap* is *Heap*(n) $= n \geq 100$. Assume further that the agent's subjective reality is modeled in terms of a perception filter given by the similarity space $\langle N, \sigma, 0.8\rangle$, where N is the set of natural numbers and

$$\sigma(k, m) = 1 - \frac{\mid k - m \mid}{\max\{1, k, m\}} \cdot \quad [5]$$

Since σ is total, we have that $n_+^{\sigma^{0.8}}(i) = n_\oplus^{\sigma^{0.8}}(i) = \{j \mid \sigma(i,j) \geq 0.8\}$. We now calculate approximations of $[100, +\infty]$ which is the set of natural numbers satisfying the predicate *Heap*. Using Definition 4.1, we get *Heap*$_{\Sigma+} = [125, +\infty)$ and *Heap*$_{\Sigma\oplus} = [80, +\infty)$. Consequently, we can put *Heap*$_{\Sigma-} = N - $*Heap*$_{\Sigma\oplus} = [0, 79]$ and *Heap*$_{\Sigma\pm} = $*Heap*$_{\Sigma\oplus} - $*Heap*$_{\Sigma+} = [80, 125)$. *Heap*$_{\Sigma+}(n)$ implies *Heap*$_{\Sigma+}(n+1)$, but the converse implication is satisfied only when n is greater than or equal to a certain natural number, in our case, $n = 125$. Similarly, *Heap*$_{\Sigma\oplus}(n + 1)$ implies *Heap*$_{\Sigma\oplus}(n)$ for $n \geq 80$.

The above induction is related to the Sorites Paradox. We share the opinion that the paradox results from mixing the objective and subjective levels. Quantitative measurements on the objective level are often not reflected by a qualitative change on the subjective level. One cannot expect a relatively small change, that cannot be observed due to perceptual limitations, to cause qualitative change at the agent's subjective level. "Grains of sand" are too small to register a qualitative change from non-heap to heap.

To be more specific, consider similarity $\sigma(1000, 1001) = 1 - 1/1001 = 0.999$ between 999 and 1000 grains of sand. Given particular perceptual limitations, say $p = 0.99$, we have that 999 and 1000 grains are indiscriminately different. One grain is too small "particle" to be recognized in this context and to make a qualitative change.   □

In Example 5.2 we computed the subjective perception of *Heap* wrt the considered similarity space. One can additionally solve two other related tasks, where the subjective perception of *Heap* is understood according to Definition 4.4:

- given a subjective perception of *Heap* and a similarity space Σ, determine the objective level definition of *Heap*
- given an objective level definition of *Heap*, a subjective perception of *Heap* and a similarity space σ, determine the similarity threshold p of Σ,

Example 5.3. Assume that we compare the sweetness of coffee cups by comparing the number of sugar grains in each cup. Suppose further that objectively two cups containing k and m grains of sugar, respectively, are of the same sweetness, denoted by $k \sim n$, when for some natural number i, both k and m are in the same interval $[i*10, i*10+9]$. Clearly, $\sim$ is transitive. Suppose, a robot is given the task to measure sweetness, but has some subjective limitations pertaining to its sensors. Limitations are represented as the similarity space $\Sigma = \langle \{0, 1, 2, \ldots\}, \sigma, 0.6\rangle$, where σ is defined as in Example 5.2. Now, $\sigma(2, 3) = 2/3 \geq 0.6$, $\sigma(3, 5) = 0.6 \geq 0.6$ and $\sigma(2, 5) = 0.4 \ngeq 0.6$, i.e., 2, 3 and 3, 5 are of the same sweetness wrt Σ, whereas 2, 5 are not. Thus, on the subjective level, transitivity does not apply.   □

---

[5] This similarity function is just an example. However, it reflects the intuition that heaps, say, of 1000 and 1001 grains are more similar than heaps of, e.g., 100 and 101 grains.

Example 5.4. Let $Fast(c)$ be a predicate denoting that a car c's speed is very high. We assume here that each car is characterized by its speed, measured by a radar.[6] The speed of a car c is given by a function $S(c)$, whose value is in $[0, 200] \cup \Upsilon$. Assume that an agent is asked to identify fast cars, provided that the objective level definition of $Fast$, given particular road conditions, is $Fast(c) \equiv [S(c) \geq 80]$.

Suppose that the agent's subjective perceptual capability is modelled by a similarity space $\Sigma = \langle C, \sigma, 0.9 \rangle$, where C is the set of considered cars and

$$\sigma(c_1, c_2) \overset{\text{def}}{=} \begin{cases} 1 - |S(c_1) - S(c_2)| / 200 & \text{when } S(c_1), S(c_2) \neq \Upsilon \\ 1 & \text{when } S(c_1) = S(c_2) = \Upsilon \\ \Upsilon & \text{otherwise.} \end{cases}$$

We have $n_+^{\sigma^{0.9}}(c) = \{c' \mid \sigma(S(c), S(c')) \geq 0.9\}$. In the same way we have $n_\oplus^{\sigma^{0.9}}(c) = n_+^{\sigma^{0.9}}(c) \cup \{c' \mid \sigma(S(c), S(c')) = \Upsilon\}$. We now compute approximations of the set $FC = \{c \in C \mid S(c) \geq 80\}$. Using Definition 4.1, we finally obtain that $FC_{\Sigma+} = \{c \in C \mid S(c) \geq 100\}$ and $FC_{\Sigma\oplus} = \{c \in C \mid S(c) \geq 60 \text{ or } S(c) = \Upsilon\}$. □

6 Complexity of the Approach

The approach we propose is tractable in the case of finite domains, as shown below.

Definition 6.1. *A similarity space $\Sigma = \langle U, \sigma, p \rangle$ is tractable, if U is finite and, for all $a, b \in U$, $\sigma(a, b)$ can be computed in deterministic polynomial time in the size of U.* □

Assume the considered relations are stored in relational or deductive databases tractable intensional part (e.g., expressed by the classical first-order rules or fixpoint calculus – see, e.g., [10]). Under such assumptions, we have the following proposition.

Proposition 6.2. *Let $\Sigma = \langle U, \sigma, p \rangle$ be a tractable similarity space. Then, for any set $S \subseteq U$, approximations $S_{\Sigma+}$ and $S_{\Sigma\oplus}$ are computable in deterministic polynomial time in the size of U.* □

In consequence, any query referring to $R_{\Sigma+}$ and $R_{\Sigma\oplus}$, where R is a relation on U, are computable in deterministic polynomial time in the size of U.

7 Relation to Other Approaches and Conclusion

The use of similarity spaces is a generalization of Pawlak's [6] pioneering work with rough sets where indiscernibility among individuals is modeled in terms of equivalence classes on feature/value pairs. In this paper, we also extend the results in [2,3,4,5]. The incentive for this generalization is due to the novel manner in which Halpern [1] approaches problems of intransitivity and vagueness. Fuzzy sets [11,12,13] provide another means of modeling vagueness and [14,15] provide insights into how one can formally translate between fuzzy and rough sets. These techniques can also be applied to our generalizations. There is also some relevant work outside the soft computing genre which attempts to provide methods and techniques for reasoning with approximate relations of which ([16,17,18,19,20]) are representative.

---

[6] Note that a radar may not be able to measure the speed of some cars.

References

1. Halpern, J.: Intransitivity and vagueness. In Dubois, D., Welty, C., Williams, M.A., eds.: Proc. of 9th Int. Conf. KR'2004, AAAI Press (2004) 121–129
2. Doherty, P., Szałas, A.: On the correspondence between approximations and similarity. In Tsumoto, S., Slowinski, R., Komorowski, J., Grzymala-Busse, J., eds.: Proc. of 4th Int. Conf. RSCTC'2004. Volume 3066 of LNAI., Springer-Verlag (2004) 143–152
3. Doherty, P., Łukaszewicz, W., Szałas, A.: Tolerance spaces and approximative representational structures. In Günter, A., Kruse, R., Neumann, B., eds.: Proc. 26th German Conf. on AI. Volume 2821 of LNAI., Springer-Verlag (2003) 475–489
4. Doherty, P., Łukaszewicz, W., Szałas, A.: Approximate databases and query techniques for agents with heterogenous perceptual capabilities. In: Proc. of the 7th Int. Conf. on Information Fusion, FUSION'2004. (2004) 175–182
5. Doherty, P., Łukaszewicz, W., Szałas, A.: Approximative query techniques for agents with heterogeneous ontologies and perceptive capabilities. In Dubois, D., Welty, C., Williams, M.A., eds.: Proc. of the 9th Int. Conf. KR'2004, AAAI Press (2004) 459–468
6. Pawlak, Z.: Rough Sets. Theoretical Aspects of Reasoning about Data. Kluwer Academic Publishers, Dordrecht (1991)
7. Klir, G., Folger, T.: Fuzzy Sets, Uncertainty, and Information. Prentice Hall (1988)
8. Williamson, T.: Vagueness. Routledge (1994)
9. Skowron, A., Stepaniuk, J.: Tolerance approximation spaces. Fundamenta Informaticae **27** (1996) 245–253
10. Abiteboul, S., Hull, R., Vianu, V.: Foundations of Databases. Addison-Wesley (1996)
11. Zadeh, L.: Fuzzy sets. Information and Control **8** (1965) 333–353
12. Zadeh, L.: A new direction in AI: Toward a computational theory of perceptions. AI Magazine **22** (2001) 73–84
13. Murai, T., Kanemitsu, H., Shimbo, M.: Fuzzy sets and binary-proximity-based rough sets. Information Sciences **104** (1998) 49–80
14. Dubois, D., Prade, H.: Rough fuzzy sets and fuzzy rough sets. International Journal of General Systems **17** (1990) 191–209
15. Dubois, D., Prade, H.: Putting rough sets and fuzzy sets together. In Slowinski, R., ed.: Intelligent Decision Support: Handbook of Applications and Advances of the Rough Sets Theory, Kluwer (1992) 204–232
16. McCarthy, J.: Approximate objects and approximate theories. In Cohn, A., Giunchiglia, F., Selman, B., eds.: Proc. 7th Int. Conf. KR'2000, San Francisco, Ca., Morgan Kaufmann Pub., Inc. (2000) 519–526
17. Kautz, H., Selman, B.: Knowledge compilation and theory approximation. Journal of the ACM **43** (1996) 193–224
18. Lin, F.: On strongest necessary and weakest sufficient conditions. In Cohn, A., Giunchiglia, F., Selman, B., eds.: Proc. 7th Int. Conf. KR'2000, Morgan Kaufmann (2000) 167–175
19. Cadoli, M.: Tractable Reasoning in Artificial Intelligence. Volume 941 of LNAI. Springer-Verlag, Berlin Heidelberg (1995)
20. Doherty, P., Łukaszewicz, W., Szałas, A.: Computing strongest necessary and weakest sufficient conditions of first-order formulas. Proc. IJCAI'2001 (2001) 145 – 151

Decision Theory = Performance Measure Theory + Uncertainty Theory*

Eugene Eberbach

Comp. and Inf. Science Dept., University of Massachusetts,
North Dartmouth, MA 02747-2300, USA
eeberbach@umassd.edu

Abstract. The decision theory is defined typically as the combination of utility theory and probability theory. In this paper we generalize the decision theory as the performance measure theory and uncertainty theory. Intelligent agents look for approximate optimal decisions under bounded resources and uncertainty. The $-calculus process algebra for problem solving applies the cost performance measures to converge to optimal solutions with minimal problem solving costs, and allows to incorporate probabilities, fuzzy sets and rough sets to deal with uncertainty and incompleteness.

Keywords: resource-bounded reasoning, problem solving, decision theory, process algebra, uncertainty.

1 Introduction

In 1944 von Neumann and Morgenstern [9] gave the foundations of the decision theory using utilities and probabilities. In 1995 Russell and Norvig [7] in the most popular AI textbook argued that the decision theory = utility theory + probability theory. In this paper, we generalize the utility theory to allow to use various performance measures, including utilities, costs and fitness, and probability theory we extend to uncertainty theory, including probabilities, fuzzy sets and rough sets.

AI typically deals with dynamic, incomplete and uncertain domains where conventional algorithms do not perform well because of intractability or even undecidability. If so, the need for the new computational theory serving better new real-world applications and not hampered by computational explosion is obvious. Simply, in the solution of computational problems, the complexity of the reasoning process/search should be taken into account. Resource-based reasoning [4,7], called also anytime algorithms, trading off the quality of solutions for the amount of resources used, seems to be particularly well suited for the solution of hard computational problems in real time and under uncertainty. Additionally, new superTuring models of computation [2,3] trying to provide nonalgorithmic solutions to the TM undecidable problems, can and should be useful for solutions

* Research supported in part by ONR under grant N00014-03-1-0421.

D. Ślęzak et al. (Eds.): RSFDGrC 2005, LNAI 3641, pp. 551–560, 2005.

of real-world problems. On the other hand, process algebras [5] are currently the most mature approach to concurrent and distributed systems, and seem to be the appropriate way to formalize multiagent systems.

The $-calculus, presented in this paper (section 3), belongs to superTuring models of computation and provides a support to handle intractability and undecidability in problem solving. Technically, this is a process algebra derived from Milner's π-calculus [5] extended by von Neumann/Morgenstern's costs/utilities [9] and a very general search method, called the $k\Omega$-optimization. This novel search method allows to simulate many other search algorithms (of course, not all), including A*, minimax, expectiminimax, hill climbing, dynamic programming, evolutionary algorithms, neural networks. The search tree can be infinite - this in the limit allows to solve nonalgorithmically some undecidable problems (for instance, the halting problem of the Universal Turing Machines, or to approximate a nonexisting universal search algorithm). For solutions of intractable problems the total optimization is utilized to provide an automatic way to deal with intractability by optimizing together the quality of solutions and search costs. In this paper we present the solution of the total optimization problem (section 3.4) in the context of uncertain dynamic environments using either probabilities, or fuzzy sets or rough sets membership functions.

2   Measuring Problem Solving Performance: Optimization Under Bounded Resources

The performance of search algorithms (intelligence of an agent) can be evaluated in four ways (see e.g. [7]) capturing whether a solution has been found, its quality and the amount of resources used to find it.

Definition 1. On completeness, optimality, search optimality, and total optimality *We say that the search algorithm is*

- **Complete** *if it guarantees reaching a terminal state/solution if there is one.*
- **Optimal** *if the solution is found with the optimal value of its objective function.*
- **Search Optimal** *if the solution is found with the minimal amount of resources used (e.g., the time and space complexity).*
- **Totally Optimal** *if the solution is found both with the optimal value of its objective function and with the minimal amount of resources used.*

Definition 2. On problem solving as a multiobjective minimization problem *Given an objective function $f : A \times X \to R$, where A is an algorithm space with its input domain X and codomain in the set of real numbers, R, problem solving can be considered as a multiobjective minimization problem to find $a^* \in A_F$ and $x^* \in X_F$, where $A_F \subseteq A$ are terminal states of the algorithm space A, and $X_F \subseteq X$ are terminal states of X such that*

$$f(a^*, x^*) = min\{f_1(f_2(a), f_3(x)), a \in A, x \in X\}$$

where f_3 is a problem-specific objective function, f_2 is a search algorithm objective function, and f_1 is an aggregating function combining f_2 and f_3.

Without losing generality, it is sufficient to consider only minimization problems. An objective function f_3 can be expanded to multiple objective funtions if the problem considered has several objectives. The aggregating function f_1 can be arbitrary (e.g., additive, multiplicative, a linear weighted sum). The only requirement is that it captures properly the dependence between several objectives. In particular, if f_1 becomes an identity function, we obtain the Pareto optimality

$$f(a^*, x^*) = min\{(f_2(a), f_3(x)), a \in A, x \in X\}$$

Using Pareto optimality is simpler, however we lose an explicit dependence between several objectives (we keep a vector of objectives ignoring any priorities, on the other hand, we do not have problems combining objectives if they are measured in different "units", for example, an energy used and satisfaction of users). For fixed f_2 we consider an optimization problem - looking for minimum of f_3, and for fixed f_3 we look for minimum of search costs - search optimum of f_2.

Objective functions allow capturing convergence and the convergence rate of construction of solutions much better than symbolic goals. Obviously every symbolic goal/termination condition can be expressed as an objective function. For example, a very simple objective function can be the following: if the goal is satisfied the objective is set to 1, and if not to 0. Typically, much more complex objective functions are used to better express evolutions of solutions.

Let (A^*, X^*) denotes the set of totally optimal solutions. In particular X^* denotes the set of optimal solutions, and A^* the optimal search algorithms.

Let Y be a metric space, where for every pair of its elements x, y there is assigned the real number $D(x, y) \geq 0$, called *distance*, satisfying three conditions:

1. $D(x, x) = 0$,
2. $D(x, y) = D(y, x)$
3. $D(x, y) + D(y, z) \geq D(x, z)$

The distance function can be defined in different ways, e.g., as the Hamming distance, Euclidean distance, $D(x) = 0$ if x satisfies termination condition and $D(x) = 1$ otherwise. To keep it independent from representation, and to allow to compare different solving algorithms, we will fix the distance function to the absolute value of difference of the objective functions $D(x, y) = |f(x) - f(y)|$. We extend the definition of the distance from the pairs of points to the distance between a point and the set of points $D(x, Y) = min\{|f(x) - f(y)|; y \in Y\}$

In problem solving, we will be interested in the distance to the set of optimal solutions Y^*, i.e., in the distance $D((a, x), (A^*, X^*))$, and in particular $D(x, X^*), D(a, A^*)$, where $x \in X$ is the solution of the given problem instance, and $a \in A$ is the algorithm producing that solution.

Definition 3. On solution convergence *For any given problem instance, its solution evolved in the discrete time $t = 0, 1, 2, ...$, will be said to be*

– convergent *to the total optimum iff there exists such τ that for every $t > \tau$*
   $D((a[t], x[t]), (A^*, X^*)) = 0$,
– asymptotically convergent *to the total optimum iff for every ε, $\infty > \varepsilon > 0$,
   there exists such τ that for every $t > \tau$ $D((a[t], x[t]), (A^*, X^*)) < \varepsilon$,*
– convergent with an error ε *to the total optimum, where $\infty > \varepsilon > 0$ iff there
   exists such τ that for every $t > \tau$ $D((a[t], x[t]), (A^*, X^*)) \leq \varepsilon$,*
– divergent, *otherwise.*

If solution is convergent and τ is fixed, then the convergence is algorithmic, otherwise it is nonalgorithmic. Asymptotic convergence is nonalgorithmic (the time is unbounded).

Search can involve single or multiple agents. For multiple agents search can be *cooperative, competitive*, or *random*. In cooperative search other agents help to find an optimum, in competitive search - they distract to reach an optimum, and in random search other agents do not care about helping or distracting to reach an optimum. Search algorithms can be *online*, where action execution and computation are interleaved, and *offline*, where the complete solution is computed first and executed after without any perception.

3   The $-Calculus Algebra of Bounded Rational Agents

The $-calculus is a mathematical model of processes capturing both the final outcome of problem solving as well as the interactive incremental way how the problems are solved. The $-calculus is a process algebra of Bounded Rational Agents for interactive problem solving targeting intractable and undecidable problems. It has been introduced in the late of 1990s [1,2,3,8]. The $-calculus (pronounced COST calculus) is a formalization of resource-bounded computation (also called anytime algorithms), proposed by Dean, Horvitz, Zilberstein and Russell in the late 1980s and early 1990s [4,7]. Anytime algorithms are guaranteed to produce better results if more resources (e.g., time, memory) become available. The standard representative of process algebras, the π-calculus [5] is believed to be the most mature approach for concurrent systems.

The $-calculus rests upon the primitive notion of *cost* in a similar way as the π-calculus was built around a central concept of *interaction*. Cost and interaction concepts are interrelated in the sense that cost captures the quality of an agent interaction with its environment. The unique feature of the $-calculus is that it provides a support for problem solving by incrementally searching for solutions and using cost to direct its search. The basic $-calculus search method used for problem solving is called $k\Omega$-optimization. The $k\Omega$-optimization represents this "impossible" to construct, but "possible to approximate indefinitely" universal algorithm. It is a very general search method, allowing the simulation of many other search algorithms, including A*, minimax, dynamic programming, tabu search, or evolutionary algorithms. Each agent has its own Ω search space and its own limited horizon of deliberation with depth k and width b. Agents can cooperate by selecting actions with minimal costs, can compete if some of them minimize and some maximize costs, and be impartial (irrational or probabilistic) if they do not attempt optimize (evolve, learn) from the point of view of the observer. It can be understood as another step in the never ending dream of universal problem solving methods recurring throughout all computer science history. The $-calculus is applicable to robotics, software agents, neural nets, and evolutionary computation. Potentially it could be used for design of cost languages, cellular evolvable cost-driven hardware, DNA-based computing and molecular biology, electronic commerce, and quantum computing. The $-calculus leads to a new programming paradigm *cost languages* and a new class of computer architectures *cost-driven computers.*

3.1   The $-Calculus Syntax

In $-calculus everything is a cost expression: agents, environment, communication, interaction links, inference engines, modified structures, data, code, and meta-code. $-expressions can be simple or composite. Simple $-expressions α are considered to be executed in one atomic indivisible step. Composite $-expressions P consist of distinguished components (simple or composite ones) and can be interrupted.

Definition 4. The $-calculus *The set $\mathcal{P}$ of $-calculus process expressions consists of simple $-expressions α and composite $-expressions P, and is defined by the following syntax:*

$$\alpha ::= (\$_{i\in I} \; P_i) \qquad cost$$
$$| \quad (\rightarrow_{i\in I} \; c \; P_i) \;\; send \; P_i \; with \; evaluation \; through \; channel \; c$$
$$| \quad (\leftarrow_{i\in I} \; c \; X_i) \;\; receive \; X_i \; from \; channel \; c$$
$$| \quad ('_{i\in I} \; P_i) \qquad suppress \; evaluation \; of \; P_i$$
$$| \quad (a_{i\in I} \; P_i) \qquad defined \; call \; of \; simple \; \$\text{-}expr. \; a \; with \; parameters \; P_i$$
$$| \quad (\bar{a}_{i\in I} \; P_i) \qquad negation \; of \; defined \; call \; of \; simple \; \$\text{-}expression \; a$$

$$P ::= (\circ_{i\in I} \; \alpha \; P_i) \;\; sequential \; composition$$
$$| \quad (\parallel_{i\in I} \; P_i) \quad parallel \; composition$$
$$| \quad (\cup_{i\in I} \; P_i) \quad cost \; choice$$
$$| \quad (\uplus_{i\in I} \; P_i) \quad adversary \; choice$$
$$| \quad (\sqcup_{i\in I} \; P_i) \quad general \; choice$$
$$| \quad (f_{i\in I} \; P_i) \qquad defined \; process \; call \; f \; with \; parameters \; P_i, \; and \; its$$
$$associated \; definition \; (:= \; (f_{i\in I} \; X_i) \; R) \; with \; body \; R$$

The indexing set I is a possibly countably infinite. In the case when I is empty, we write empty parallel composition, general, cost and adversary choices as $\perp$ (blocking), and empty sequential composition (I empty and $\alpha = \varepsilon$) as ε (invisible transparent action, which is used to mask, make invisible parts of $-expressions). Adaptation (evolution/upgrade) is an essential part of $-calculus, and all $-calculus operators are infinite (an indexing set I is unbounded). The $-calculus agents interact through send-receive pair as the essential primitives of the model.

Sequential composition is used when $-expressions are evaluated in a textual order. Parallel composition is used when expressions run in parallel and it picks a subset of non-blocked elements at random. Cost choice is used to select the cheapest alternative according to a cost metric. Adversary choice is used to select the most expensive alternative according to a cost metric. General choice picks one non-blocked element at random. General choice is different from cost and adversary choices. It uses guards satisfiability. Cost and adversary choices are based on cost functions. Call and definition encapsulate expressions in a more complex form (like procedure or function definitions in programming languages). In particular, they specify recursive or iterative repetition of $-expressions.

Simple cost expressions execute in one atomic step. Cost functions are used for optimization and adaptation. The user is free to define his/her own cost metrics. Send and receive perform handshaking message-passing communication, and inferencing. The suppression operator suppresses evaluation of the underlying $-expressions. Additionally, a user is free to define her/his own simple $-expressions, which may or may not be negated.

3.2   The $-Calculus Semantics: The $k\Omega$-Search

In this section we define the operational semantics of the $-calculus using the $k\Omega$-search that captures the dynamic nature and incomplete knowledge associated with the construction of the problem solving tree.

The basic $-calculus problem solving method, the $k\Omega$-optimization, is a very general search method providing meta-control, and allowing to simulate many other search algorithms, including A*, minimax, dynamic programming, tabu search, or evolutionary algorithms [7]. The problem solving works iteratively: through select, examine and execute phases. In the select phase the tree of possible solutions is generated up to k steps ahead, and agent identifies its alphabet of interest for optimization Ω. This means that the tree of solutions may be incomplete in width and depth (to deal with complexity). However, incomplete (missing) parts of the tree are modeled by silent $-expressions ε, and their cost estimated (i.e., not all information is lost). The above means that $k\Omega$-optimization may be if some conditions are satisfied to be complete and optimal. In the examine phase the trees of possible solutions are pruned minimizing cost of solutions, and in the execute phase up to n instructions are executed. Moreover, because the $ operator may capture not only the cost of solutions, but the cost of resources used to find a solution, we obtain a powerful tool to avoid methods that are too costly, i.e., the $-calculus directly minimizes search cost. This basic feature, inherited from anytime algorithms, is needed to tackle directly hard optimization problems, and allows to solve total optimization problems (the best quality solutions with minimal search costs). The variable k refers to the limited horizon for optimization, necessary due to the unpredictable dynamic nature of the environment. The variable Ω refers to a reduced alphabet of information. No agent ever has reliable information about all factors that influence all agents behavior. To compensate for this, we mask factors where information is not available from consideration; reducing the alphabet of variables used by the

$-function. By using the $k\Omega$-optimization to find the strategy with the lowest $-function, meta-system finds a satisficing solution, and sometimes the optimal one. This avoids wasting time trying to optimize behavior beyond the foreseeable future. It also limits consideration to those issues where relevant information is available. Thus the $k\Omega$ optimization provides a flexible approach to local and/or global optimization in time or space. Technically this is done by replacing parts of $-expressions with invisible $-expressions ε, which remove part of the world from consideration (however, they are not ignored entirely - the cost of invisible actions is estimated).

3.3   Probabilistic, Fuzzy Sets and Rough Sets Performance Measure

The domain of the cost function is a problem-solving derivation tree constructed by the $k\Omega$-optimization meta-procedure. The derivation tree consists of nodes S and edges E. Both $k\Omega_i[t]$ and $x_i[t]$ $-expressions form own trees, where $k\Omega_i[t]$ tree is responsible for generation, pruning and evaluation of $x_i[t]$ tree representing a problem solution. To avoid the complexity to analyze and synchronize two trees for total optimization, both trees can be compressed/collapsed into a single tree, where $k\Omega_i[t]$ can be represented as nodes, and $x_i[t]$ as edges of the combined tree, or, alternatively, $k\Omega_i[t]$ can form edges, and $x_i[t]$ nodes of the tree. In such a way, a problem-solving tree will capture both solutions and the search process. The cost function $\$_3$ measures the quality of solutions (costs of $x_i[t]$), the cost function $\$_2$ measures the costs of search (costs of $k\Omega_i[t]$), and $\$_1$ aggregating function combines costs of solutions and search.

Let us define costs of nodes and edges as $\$_2 : \mathcal{S} \to \mathcal{R}^\infty$ and $\$_3 : \mathcal{E} \to \mathcal{R}^\infty$ (or alternatively, as $\$_3 : \mathcal{S} \to \mathcal{R}^\infty$ and $\$_2 : \mathcal{E} \to \mathcal{R}^\infty$, depending whether $k\Omega$ and x have been associated with nodes or edges of the tree).

Then the cost of the problem-solving trees $\mathcal{T}$ as combining costs of the search and the solution quality can be defined as $\$: \mathcal{T} \to \mathcal{R}^\infty$, i.e.,

$$\$(k\Omega_i[t], x_i[t]) = \$_1(\$_2(k\Omega_i[t]), \$_3(x_i[t])),$$

where $\$_1$ is an aggregating cost function, $\$_2$ is a search cost function, and $\$_3$ is the problem-specific cost function.

In this paper, both $\$_1$, $\$_2$, and $\$_3$ will take the same uniform form of the standard cost function defined below. In other words, both trees, edges and nodes will form the $-expressions, and then it is sufficient to define how to compute the costs of $-expressions.

Let $v : \mathcal{A}^\varepsilon \to \mathcal{R}^\infty$ be costs of simple cost expressions, including a silent expression. They are context dependent, i.e., they depend on states. In particular, cost of ε may depend which cost expression is made invisible by ε. Technically, $\$ is defined on the problem-solving tree, consisting of nodes and edges expressed by $-expressions, as the function mapping the tree to a real number: $\$_i : \mathcal{P} \to \mathcal{R}^\infty, i = 2, 3$. Thus it is sufficient to define costs of $-expressions P. Note that the value of the cost function (or its estimate) can change after each loop iteration (evaluation of a simple cost expression).

Definition 5. A Standard Cost Function For every $-expression P its cost $(\$_i \, P), i = 1, 2, 3$ is defined as below:

1. $(\$_i \perp) = +\infty$

2. $(\$_i \, \varepsilon) = \begin{cases} 0 & \text{for observation congruence} \\ (v \, \varepsilon) & \text{for strong congruence} \end{cases}$

3. $(\$_i \, \alpha) = c_\alpha + (v \, \alpha)$, where $c_\alpha = \begin{cases} 0 & \alpha \text{ does not block} \\ +\infty & \alpha \text{ blocks} \end{cases}$

   $(\$_i \, \bar{\alpha}) = \frac{1}{c_\alpha} + (v \, \bar{\alpha})$

4. $(\$_i \, (\sqcup_{i \in I} \, P_i)) = \begin{cases} \Sigma_{i \in I} \, (p_i * (\$_i \, P_i)) & \text{for probability-based cost function} \\ \max_{i \in I} \, (m_i * (\$_i \, P_i)) & \text{for fuzzy sets-based cost function} \\ \max_{i \in I} \, (\mu_i * (\$_i \, P_i)) & \text{for rough sets-based cost function} \end{cases}$

   where p_i is the probability of choice of the i-th branch, m_i is a fuzzy set membership function of choice of the i-th branch, and μ_i is a rough sets membership function of the i-th branch choice

5. $(\$_i \, (\cup_{i \in I} \, P_i)) = (min_{i \in I} \, (\$_i \, P_i))$

6. $(\$_i \, (\uplus_{i \in I} \, P_i)) = (max_{i \in I} \, (\$_i \, P_i))$

7. $(\$_i \, (\circ_{i \in I} \, \alpha \, P_i)) = (\$_i \, \alpha) + \Sigma_{i \in I} \, (\$_i \, P_i')$

   where P_i' represents a possible change of P_i by receive or return value by α

8. $(\$_i \, \| \, _{i \in I} P_i)) = \begin{cases} \Sigma_{J \subseteq I} \, p_J * ((\$_i \, \{\alpha_j\}_{j \in J}) + (\$_i \, (\, \| \, _{i \in I-J, j \in J} \, P_i \, P_j'))) & \text{for} \\ \text{probability-based standard cost function} \\ max_{J \subseteq I} \, m_J * ((\$_i \, \{\alpha_j\}_{j \in J}) + (\$_i \, (\, \| \, _{i \in I-J, j \in J} \, P_i \, P_j'))) \text{ for} \\ \text{fuzzy sets-based standard cost function} \\ max_{J \subseteq I} \, \mu_J * ((\$_i \, \{\alpha_j\}_{j \in J}) + (\$_i \, (\, \| \, _{i \in I-J, j \in J} \, P_i \, P_j'))) \text{ for} \\ \text{rough sets-based standard cost function} \end{cases}$

   where p_J is the probability of choice of the J-th multiset, m_i is a fuzzy set membership function of choice of the J-th multiset, and μ_i is a rough sets membership function of the J-th multiset choice

9. $(\$_i \, (f_{i \in I} \, Q_i)) = (\$_i \, P\{Q_i/X_i\})$ where $(:= \, (f_{i \in I} \, X_i) \, P)$.

Cost choice calculates costs as the minimum of costs of its components. Adversary choice cost is defined as the cost of its most expensive component. General choice cost has been defined as the average component cost if to use probabilities to represent uncertainty, or the maximum if to use fuzzy sets [10] or rough sets [6]. Sequential composition cost adds costs of its components. Parallel composition cost selects a nonempty multiset that does not block. It has been defined as the average component cost. Alternatively, parallel composition could select a specific multiset to be executed, e.g., the maxium subset that does not block (for the maximum concurrency semantics), or the subset with the minimal costs (probably the most interesting alternative, on the other hand, increasing costs of the $k\Omega$-search). However, both these alternatives we will leave as viable choices for the user who can overwrite the cost of parallel composition definition if it is preferable. Cost of the recursive (user defined) function call is calculated as the cost of its body.

3.4   The $-Calculus Support for Intractability: Optimization Under Bounded Resources and Total Optimality

Definition 6. (On elitist selection of the $-calculus search) *The $-calculus search will use an* elitist *strategy if states selected for expansion in the next loop iteration of the $k\Omega$-optimization will contain states with the most promising (i.e., minimal) costs.*

Using elitism will allow to expand the most promising parts of the tree only.

Definition 7. (On admissibility of the $-calculus search) *The $-calculus search will be* admissible *if the costs of silent $-expressions are not overestimated.*

The admissibility requirement will prohibit to stop prematurely search if a non-optimal goal is found that may look a more promising than the optimal goal. Note that elitist selection concept is typical for evolutionary algorithms, and admissibility for heuristic search, e.g., the A* algorithm.

A total optimality provides a direct and elegant method to deal with intractability of problem solving search. It will use a power of evolution to avoid expensive search methods. In other words, both the solutions and algorithms producing the solutions will be evolved (but for the price that perhaps the quality of solutions found would be worse compared to solutions where we ignore search costs, i.e., total optima in most cases are different than problem-specific optima).

Definition 8. (On total optimality of the $-calculus search) *The $-calculus search of the i-th agent is* totally optimal *if the $k\Omega$-optimization has its goal condition set to the optimum of the cost function $\$_i(k\Omega_i[t], x_i[t])$ and $\$_i(k\Omega_i[t], x_i[t])$ is convergent/asymptotically convergent to the set of optimal solutions $(k\Omega_i^*, X_i^*)$.*

Theorem 1. (On total optimality of the $-calculus search) *For a given $k\Omega$-optimization procedure $k\Omega_i[0]$ with an initial problem solution $x_i[0]$, if the $-calculus search of the i-th agent satisfies four conditions*

1. *the goal condition is set to the optimum of the search algorithm cost function $\$_i(k\Omega_i[t], x_i[t])$ with the optimum $\$_i^*$,*
2. *search is complete,*
3. *elitist selection is used, and*
4. *search is admissible,*

then the $k\Omega$-optimization will find and maintain the optimum $(k\Omega_i^*, x_i^*)$ of $\$_i(k\Omega_i[t], x_i[t])$ in $t = 0, 1, 2, ...$ iterations.

Proof: By completeness, the $k\Omega$-search reaches (perhaps in an infinite number of loop iterations) a goal state that is equivalent to the optimal state. By elitism, the found optimum will not be lost even for cases where the verification of finding the optimum will be very difficult or impossible (e.g., a very complex or not precisely defined analytically fitness function). By admissibility the premature stopping *in a local optimum will be prevented, because an optimal state will be always looking as a more promising. Always the most promising node (the cheapest one, according to the $\$_i$ metric) will be in the group of nodes selected for expansion in a new iteration, because the $k\Omega$-optimization expands all nodes in order of increasing $\$_i$ values, thus it must eventually expand the optimal (reachable) goal state. Both conditions imply that the $k\Omega$-optimization will eventually converge (asymptotically converge), perhaps requiring an infinite number of generations, to the total optimum $(k\Omega_i^*, x_i^*)$ of $\$_i$, i.e., the best quality solution with minimal resources used.*

The possible scenario to test the total optimality could be a robot navigating from the starting to the terminal point, where the trajectory of the robot is a subject to uncertainty (wheels are slippery, sensors measurements are imprecise). Thus we can interpret that the robot, instead of the desired point/state, may reach several points/states measured either with some probablity, or fuzzy, or rough membership function. The robot tries to find both the shortest path, and to minimize the time spent on the trajectory computation at the same time.

4   Conclusions

In the paper the solution of the total optimization problem under uncertainty has been presented. The extension of this work could be twofold: a new axiomatization of the utility theory allowing to incorporate fuzzy sets and rough sets instead of probabilities, and the standardization of the cost performance measures that may lead to a new cost paradigm languages.

References

1. Eberbach E., $-Calculus Bounded Rationality = Process Algebra + Anytime Algorithms, in: (ed.J.C.Misra) Applicable Mathematics: Its Perspectives and Challenges, Narosa Publishing House, New Delhi, Mumbai, Calcutta, 2001, 213-220.
2. Eberbach E., Wegner P., Beyond Turing Machines, The Bulletin of the European Association for Theoretical Computer Science (EATCS Bulletin), 81, Oct. 2003, 279-304.
3. Eberbach E., Goldin D., Wegner P., Turing's Ideas and Models of Computation, in: (ed. Ch.Teuscher) Alan Turing: Life and Legacy of a Great Thinker, Springer-Verlag, 2004, 159-194.
4. Horvitz, E., Zilberstein, S. (eds), Computational Tradeoffs under Bounded Resources, Artificial Intelligence 126, 2001, 1-196.
5. Milner R., Parrow J., Walker D., A Calculus of Mobile Processes, I & II, Information and Computation 100, 1992, 1-77.
6. Pawlak Z., Rough Sets, Int. J. Computer and Information Sci., 11, 1982, 341-356.
7. Russell S., Norvig P., Artificial Intelligence: A Modern Approach, Prentice-Hall, 1995 (2nd ed. 2003).
8. Wegner P., Eberbach E., New Models of Computation, The Computer Journal, 47(1), 2004, 4-9.
9. Von Neumann J., Morgenstern O., Theory of Games and Economic Behavior, Princeton University Press, 1944.
10. Zadeh L.A., Fuzzy Sets, Information and Control, 12, 1965, 338-353.

The Graph-Theoretical Properties of Partitions and Information Entropy[*]

Cungen Cao[1], Yuefei Sui[1], and Youming Xia[2]

[1] Key Laboratory of Intelligent Information Processing,
Institute of Computing Technology, Chinese Academy of Sciences,
Beijing 100080, China
cgcao@ict.ac.cn, suiyyff@hotmail.com
[2] Department of Computer Science, Yunnan Normal University,
Kunming 650092, Yunnan, China
xyouming@ynmail.com

Abstract. The information entropy, as a measurement of the average amount of information contained in an information system, is used in the classification of objects and the analysis of information systems. The information entropy of a partition is non-increasing when the partition is refined, and is related to rough sets by Wong and Ziarko. The partitions and information entropy have some graph-theoretical properties. Given a non-empty universe U, all the partitions G on U are taken as nodes, and a relation V between partitions are defined and taken as edges. The graph obtained is denoted by (G, V), which represents the connections between partitions on U. According to the values of the information entropy of partitions, a directed graph $(G, \overrightarrow{V})$ is defined on (G, V). It will be proved that there is a set of partitions with the minimal entropy; and a set of partitions with the maximal entropy; and the entropy is non-decreasing on any directed pathes in $(G, \overrightarrow{V})$ from a partition with the minimal entropy to one of the partitions with the maximal entropy. Hence, in $(G, \overrightarrow{V})$, the information entropy of partitions is represented in a clearly structured way.

Keywords: Information systems, information entropy, classification, partitions.

1   Introduction

Entropy as a basic notion of science was introduced by Clausius to summarize thermal behavior of systems in equilibrium or changing in reversible fashion in the second principle of thermodynamics. The second principle of thermodynamics says that in a spontaneous evolution of closed system not in equilibrium,

---

[*] The work is supported by the National NSF of China (60373042, 60273019 and 60073017), the National 973 Project of China (G1999032701), Ministry of Science and Technology (2001CCA03000). The second author was partially supported by the Yunnan Provincial NSF grant 2000F0049M and 2001F0006Z.

D. Ślęzak et al. (Eds.): RSFDGrC 2005, LNAI 3641, pp. 561–570, 2005.

the entropy always increases and attains its maximum value for the state of equilibrium.

The physical entropy used in thermodynamics is more or less closely related to the concept of information as used in communication theory (see [5]). If so, then what is the state of equilibrium of an information system? Information systems are used to represent objects in the real worlds. When the information entropy of an information system is not equal to zero, it means that the knowledge or the language (the set of attributes in the information system) is not expressible enough to distinguish objects from each other ([1],[9]). An information system is taken as an approximation of information about objects in the real world. As we know better about these objects, the information system should be refined. Hence, we can define that an information system (U, A) is in the state of equilibrium, if for any $x, y \in U$, if $x \neq y$ then there is at least one $a \in A$ such that $x(a) \neq y(a)$. Define θ to be an equivalence relation on U such that for any $x, y \in U$, $x\theta y$ iff for every $a \in A, x(a) = y(a)$. Let $\{X_1, ..., X_k\}$ be the equivalence classes of θ. We define the information entropy of information system (U, A) by

$$E(U, A) = \frac{1}{n} \sum_{i=1}^{k} |X_i| \log_a |X_i|,$$

where $n = |U|$, and $a = 2, e,$ or 10, and a is omitted below. Hence, an information system is in the state of equilibrium if and only if the information entropy of the system is equal to 0.

Using information entropy to measure the uncertainty of rough set prediction is a competing way for predicting a decision variable. Let Q be a set of conditional attributes, and d a decision attribute such that $A = Q \cup \{d\}$. Assume that the partition of U given by Q is $X_1, ..., X_t$, and the partition of U given by d is $Y_1, ..., Y_s$; and assume that $c \leq t$ is such that for every $i \leq c, X_i \subseteq Y_j$ for some j. Wong and Ziarko ([6]) firstly studied the connection between entropy and rough set analysis, and claimed the following

Claim. *Suppose that for each $c < i \leq t, | X_i \cap Y_j |= d_i$ for all $j \leq s$. Then*

$$H^{\mathrm{loc}}(d \mid Q) = \frac{| \overline{Y_j}^Q - \underline{Y_j}_Q |}{n}$$

for all $j \leq s$.

Düntsch and Gediga ([2]) gave three models for predicting a decision variable, defined by different entropy, and gave a counterexample to the claim by Wong and Ziarko. A modified version of the claim has an affirmative answer (Sui, et al.[5]).

As a measurement of the average amount of information, the entropy $E(\theta)$ is known to be minimal (0) when θ is the identity relation θ_0 on U, i.e., θ is the finest equivalence relation on U; and maximal ($\log n$) when θ is the trivial relation θ_1 on U, i.e., θ is the coarsest equivalence relation on U. Except that $E(\theta)$ is non-increasing when θ is refined, little is known about $E(\theta)$ for any equivalence relation θ on U which is finer than θ_1 and coarser than θ_2. In this paper we shall discuss $E(\theta)$ for any equivalence relation θ on U, and describe the value distribution of $E(\theta)$ for different θ's. Given an equivalence relation θ on U, let $\{X_1, ..., X_k\}$ be the partition induced by θ, and $x_i = |X_i|$. Then, $n = \sum_{i=1}^{k} x_i$. We call such a k-dimensional vector $(x_1, ..., x_k)$ a k-partition of n.

Given natural numbers n and k with $n > k$, we define a graph $(G, V)_{n,k}$ such that every node in G denotes a k-partition of n, i.e., a k-dimensional vector $(x_1, ..., x_k)$ such that $\sum_{i=1}^{k} x_k = n$; and two nodes $(x_1, ..., x_k)$ and $(y_1, ..., y_k)$ have an edge iff there are $i, j \leq k$ such that $x_i = y_i + 1$ and $x_j = y_j - 1$, and for any $i' \neq i, j, x_{i'} = y_{j'}$, where $y_i = \min\{y_1, ..., y_k\}$ and $y_j = \max\{y_1, ..., y_k\}$. By introducing the information entropy of partitions, graph $(G, V)_{n,k}$ is transformed into a directed graph $(G, \overrightarrow{V})_{n,k}$ such that $(\boldsymbol{x}, \boldsymbol{y}) \in \overrightarrow{V}$ if and only if $E(\boldsymbol{x}) \leq E(\boldsymbol{y})$. In the middle of $(G, \overrightarrow{V})_{n,k}$ there is a circle on which the entropy of every node is minimal, and the entropy of nodes is increasing when nodes leave the circle.

The paper is arranged as follows: in the next section we give the basic definitions and properties of information entropy; in the third section we give the basic properties of the entropy of k-partitions and two examples to show basic ideas about the value distribution of the entropy of k-partitions; in the fourth section for any pair (n, k) satisfying $n \geq k$, we define one undirected graph $(G, V)_{n,k}$ and one directed graph $(G, \overrightarrow{V})_{n,k}$ and prove that the entropy of nodes in $(G, V)_{n,k}$ is non-decreasing when the nodes leave the middle of the graphes; and the last section concludes the paper.

2   The Preliminaries

Given an information system (context, approximation space) (U, A), where U is a nonempty universe and A is a set of attributes, we have an equivalence relation θ, where θ is defined on U as follows: for any $x, y \in U$, $x\theta y$ iff for all $a \in A, x(a) = y(a)$. For $X \subseteq U$, we say that $\underline{X}_A = \bigcup\{\theta x : \theta x \subseteq X\}$ is the *lower approximation* or *positive region* of X, and $\overline{X}^A = \bigcup\{\theta x : x \in X\}$ is the *upper approximation* or *possible region* of X, where θx is the equivalence class of θ containing x.

Given a partition $P = \{X_i : i \leq k\}$ of U, we define the *entropy* of P by

$$H(P) = \sum_{i=1}^{k} \frac{|X_i|}{n} \log \left(\frac{n}{|X_i|} \right) = \log n - \frac{1}{n} \sum_{i=1}^{k} |X_i| \log |X_i|,$$

where $n = |U|$. If P_θ is the partition induced by θ we denote $H(P_\theta)$ by $H(\theta)$ or $H(A)$. To simplify the discussion in the next section, we shall use

$$E(\theta) = \frac{1}{n} \sum_{i=1}^{k} |X_i| \log |X_i|,$$

instead of $H(\theta)$. When θ is the identity relation θ_0 on U, $E(\theta) = 0$; and when θ is the coarsest relation θ_1 on U, that is, for any $x, y \in U, x\theta y$, $E(\theta) = \log n$.

Proposition 2.1. *Given two equivalence relations θ_1 and θ_2 on universe U, if θ_1 is a refinement of θ_2 then*

$$E(\theta_1) \le E(\theta_2),$$

equivalently, $H(\theta_1) \ge H(\theta_2)$.

□

Düntsch and Gediga ([2]) defined the conditional entropy as follows. Let Q be a set of conditional attributes, d a decision attribute such that $A = Q \cup \{d\}$. Assume that the partition given by Q is $X_1, ..., X_t$, the partition given by d is $Y_1, ..., Y_s$. Assume that $c \le t$ is such that for every $i \le c, X_i \subseteq Y_j$ for some j. For every $1 \le i \le t$ and $1 \le j \le s$, define

$$\hat{\pi}_i = \frac{|X_i|}{n}; \qquad \hat{\eta}_{i,j} = \frac{|X_i \cap Y_j|}{|X_i|}.$$

The *conditional entropy* of d given Q is defined as

$$H^{\mathrm{loc}}(d \mid Q) = \sum_{i=c+1}^{t} \hat{\pi}_i \sum_{j \le s} \hat{\eta}_{i,j} \log(\frac{1}{\hat{\eta}_{i,j}}).$$

Then, $H^{\mathrm{loc}}(d \mid Q) = H(Q \to d) - H(Q)$.

Sui, et al. ([5]) proved the following theorem and refuted Wong and Ziarko's claim.

Theorem 2.2. *Suppose that for each $c < i \le t, | X_i \cap Y_j | = d_i$ for all $j \le s$. Then*

$$H^{\mathrm{loc}}(d \mid Q) = \log(s+1)\frac{| \overline{Y_j}^Q - Y_{j_Q} |}{n}$$

for all $j \le s$.

□

Düntsch and Gediga [2] gave a counterexample to the claim and a proposition to show that the value of $H^{\mathrm{loc}}(d \mid Q)$ does not depend so much on γ as it does on the number of classes of θ_d which is not Q-definable, where $\gamma = \frac{1}{n}\sum_{i=1}^{c}|X_i|$. It is easy to show that the counterexample and the proposition follow directly from theorem 2.2.

3 The Entropy and Partitions

As for the entropy $E(\theta)$, we know that (3.1) the maximal value of $E(\theta)$ is $\log n$; (3.2) the minimal value is 0; and (3.3) $E(\theta)$ is non-increasing if θ is refined. We know little about the entropy of partitions between the finest and coarsest partitions. In the following we discuss the connection between entropy and partitions in a graph-theoretical way. To simplify the discuss we shall use x_i to denote $|X_i|$, so that a partition is denoted by a vector $(x_1, ..., x_k)$ such that $\sum_{i=1}^{k} x_i = n$.

Given a k-dimensional vector $(x_1, ..., x_k)$, we say that $(x_1, ..., x_k)$ is a k-partition of n, if $\sum_{i=1}^{k} x_i = n$. We denote a k-partition $(x_1, ..., x_k)$ of n by $\boldsymbol{x}$. Given a k-partition $\boldsymbol{x}$ of n, define the *information entropy* of $\boldsymbol{x}$ by

$$E(\boldsymbol{x}) = \frac{1}{n} \sum_{i=1}^{k} x_i \log x_i.$$

Proposition 3.1. *Assume that* $n = kd + r$. *Given a k-partition $\boldsymbol{x}$ of n, if there is a $C \subseteq \{1, ..., k\}$ such that*
   (1) $|C| = r$;
   (2) *for every* $i \in C$, $x_i = d + 1$; *and*
   (3) *for every* $i \notin C, x_i = d$,
then $E(\boldsymbol{x})$ is minimal.

Proof. First of all, for any natural numbers x, y, we have that

$$(x + y)^{x+y} \geq x^x \cdot y^y;$$
$$(x + 1)^{x+1} \cdot (x - 1)^{x-1} \geq x^x \cdot x^x;$$

and

$$(x + y) \log(x + y) \geq x \log x + y \log y;$$
$$(x + 1) \log(x + 1) + (x - 1) \log(x - 1) \geq x \log x + x \log x.$$

To prove that $E(\boldsymbol{x})$ is minimal, we prove by induction on k that for any $\boldsymbol{m} = (m_1, m_2, ..., m_k)$,

$$(d + 1)^{(d+1)r} \cdot d^{d(k-r)} \leq m_1^{m_1} \cdot m_2^{m_2} \cdots m_k^{m_k}.$$

Hence, $E(\boldsymbol{x}) = \log((d + 1)^{(d+1)r} \cdot d^{d(k-r)}) \leq \log(m_1^{m_1} \cdot m_2^{m_2} \cdots m_k^{m_k}) = E(\boldsymbol{m})$.
   Assume the claim holds for $k - 1$. Without loss of generality, assume that $m_k > d + 1$. By the induction assumption, we have that if $r \geq 1$ then

$$(d + 1)^{(d+1)(r-1)} \cdot d^{d(k-r+1)} \leq m_1^{m_1} \cdot m_2^{m_2} \cdots (m_k - 1)^{m_k - 1};$$

and if $r = 0$ then

$$d^{d(k-1)} \cdot (d - 1)^{(d-1)} \leq m_1^{m_1} \cdot m_2^{m_2} \cdots (m_k - 1)^{m_k - 1}.$$

Assume $r \geq 1$. Then,

$$(d + 1)^{(d+1)r} \cdot d^{d(k-r)} = (d + 1)^{(d+1)(r-1)} \cdot (d + 1)^{(d+1)} \cdot d^{d(k-r+1)} \cdot d^{-d}$$
$$\leq m_1^{m_1} \cdot m_2^{m_2} \cdots \cdot (m_k - 1)^{m_k - 1} \frac{(d + 1)^{(d+1)}}{d^d}$$
$$\leq m_1^{m_1} \cdot m_2^{m_2} \cdots \cdot m_k^{m_k},$$

because, $(m_k - 1)^{(m_k-1)} \dfrac{(d + 1)^{(d+1)}}{d^d} \leq m_k^{m_k}$ when $m_k > d + 1$.
   Similar to prove the case when $r = 0$. $\square$

Example 3.2. Let $k = 2$. n has 2-partitions:

$$(0, n), (1, n - 1), ..., (n - 1, 1), (n, 0).$$

$E((0, n))$ and $E((n, 0))$ are maximal.

If n is even then $E\left(\left(\frac{n}{2}, \frac{n}{2}\right)\right)$ is minimal; for any $i \leq \frac{n}{2}$, $E((i - 1, n - i + 1)) > E((i, n - i))$, and for any $i > \frac{n}{2}$, $E((i - 1, n - i + 1)) < E((i, n - i))$, we denoted by

$$(0, n) \leftarrow (1, n - 1) \leftarrow \cdots \left(\frac{n}{2}, \frac{n}{2}\right) \rightarrow \cdots \rightarrow (n - 1, 1) \rightarrow (n, 0);$$

If n is odd then $E\left(\left(\frac{n-1}{2}, \frac{n+1}{2}\right)\right)$ and $E\left(\left(\frac{n+1}{2}, \frac{n-1}{2}\right)\right)$ are minimal and equal; for any $i \leq \frac{n-1}{2}$, $E((i - 1, n - i + 1)) > E((i, n - i))$, and for any $i > \frac{n+1}{2}$, $E((i - 1, n - i + 1)) < E((i, n - i))$, and, we denoted by

$$(0, n) \leftarrow \cdots \leftarrow \left(\frac{n-1}{2}, \frac{n+1}{2}\right) = \left(\frac{n+1}{2}, \frac{n-1}{2}\right) \rightarrow \cdots \rightarrow (n, 0).$$

$\square$

Example 3.3. Let $k = 3$ and $n = 3$. Define $(G, V)_{3,3}$ such that G is the set of all the 3-partitions of 3, and V is defined as follows: $((x_1, x_2, x_3), (y_1, y_2, y_3)) \in V$ iff either

(1) $x_1 = y_1, x_2 = y_2 - 1, y_2 = \max\{y_1, y_2\}$, or
(2) $x_1 = y_1 - 1, x_2 = y_2, y_1 = \max\{y_1, y_2\}$, or
(3) $x_1 = y_1 - 1, x_2 = y_2 + 1, y_1 = \max\{y_1, y_2\}, y_2 = \min\{y_1, y_2\}$.

We have graph $(G, V)_{3,3}$ as in Fig. 1.

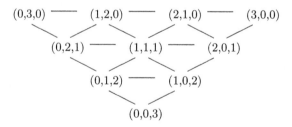

Fig. 1. $(G, V)_{3,3}$

$E((1, 1, 1))$ is minimal;
$E((0, 0, 3)), E((0, 3, 0)), E((3, 0, 0))$ are maximal.
$E((0, 2, 1)) = E((1, 2, 0)) = E((2, 1, 0)) = E((0, 1, 2)) = E((1, 0, 2))$;
$E((0, 2, 1)) > E((1, 1, 1)) < E((2, 0, 1))$.

In Fig. 1, if $(1, 1, 1) \rightarrow (2, 0, 1)$ denotes $E((1, 1, 1)) < E((2, 0, 1))$; $(1, 1, 1) = (2, 1, 0)$ denotes $E((1, 1, 1)) = E((2, 1, 0))$, then we get the following directed graph in Fig. 2, denoted by $(G, \overrightarrow{V})_{3,3}$.

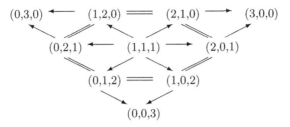

Fig. 2. $(G, \overrightarrow{V})_{3,3}$

Example 3.4. Let $k = 3$ and $n = 4$. We have that

$E((1, 1, 2)) = E((1, 2, 1)) = E((2, 1, 1))$ is minimal;

$E((0, 0, 4)), E((0, 4, 0)), E((4, 0, 0))$ are maximal.

$E((0, 3, 1)) = E((1, 3, 1)) = E((3, 1, 1)) = E((3, 0, 1)) = E((0, 1, 3)) = E((1, 0, 3))$;

$E((0, 2, 2)) > E((1, 1, 2)) < E((2, 0, 2))$.

Similarly we have graph $(G, V)_{4,3}$ in Fig. 3 and $(G, \overrightarrow{V})_{4,3}$ in Fig. 4.

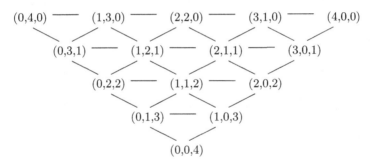

Fig. 3. $(G, V)_{4,3}$

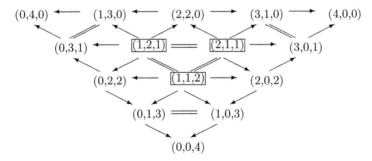

Fig. 4. $(G, \overrightarrow{V})_{4,3}$

4   The Graph-Theoretical Representation of Partitions and Entropy

In this section we give the definition of the undirected graph (G, V) and directed graph $(G, \vec{V})$.

Definition 4.1. Fix n and k such that $n \geq k$. We define a graph $(G, V)_{n,k}$ (simply denoted by (G, V)) such that

(a) $G = \{(x_1, ..., x_k) : \sum_{i=1}^{k} x_i = n\}$; and

(b) given $\boldsymbol{x} = (x_1, ..., x_k), \boldsymbol{y} = (y_1, ..., y_k) \in G$, $(\boldsymbol{x}, \boldsymbol{y}) \in V$ if and only if there are $i, j \leq k$ such that

(b1) $x_i = y_i + 1$, $x_j = y_j - 1$, $y_i = \min\{y_1, ..., y_k\}$, $y_j = \max\{y_1, ..., y_k\}$; and

(b2) for any $i' \leq k$ such that $i' \neq i, j$, $x_{i'} = y_{i'}$.

Let

$$\boldsymbol{z}_1 = (n, 0, ..., 0), \boldsymbol{z}_2 = (0, n, ..., 0), ..., \boldsymbol{z}_k = (0, 0, ..., n).$$

Let $n = kd + r$. Define a subset W of G as follows: for any vector $\boldsymbol{x} \in G$, $\boldsymbol{x} \in W$ iff there is a set $C \subseteq \{1, ..., k\}$ such that $|C| = r$; for any $i \in C, x_i = d + 1$; and for any $i \notin C, x_i = d$.

By (3.1) and Proposition 3.1, we have the following

Proposition 4.2. (i) For any $1 \leq i \leq k$, $E(\boldsymbol{z}_i)$ is maximal among $\{E(\boldsymbol{x}) : \boldsymbol{x} \in G\}$;

(ii) For any $\boldsymbol{w} \in W$, $E(\boldsymbol{w})$ is minimal among $\{E(\boldsymbol{x}) : \boldsymbol{x} \in G\}$.

$\square$

Lemma 4.3. Let ρ be the graph-theoretical distance on (G, V). For any $\boldsymbol{x}, \boldsymbol{y} \in G$ with $(\boldsymbol{x}, \boldsymbol{y}) \in V$, if

$$\min\{\rho(\boldsymbol{x}, \boldsymbol{z}_i) : 1 \leq i \leq k\} < \min\{\rho(\boldsymbol{y}, \boldsymbol{z}_i) : 1 \leq i \leq k\}$$

then there are $i, j \leq k$ such that $x_i = y_i + 1, x_j = y_j - 1, y_i = \min\{y_1, ..., y_k\}, y_j = \max\{y_1, ..., y_k\}$, and for any $i' \leq k$ such that $i' \neq i, j$, $x_{i'} = y_{i'}$.

Proof. Directly from the definition of (G, V).

$\square$

Theorem 4.4. For any $\boldsymbol{x}, \boldsymbol{y} \in G$ with $(\boldsymbol{x}, \boldsymbol{y}) \in V$,

(i) if $\min\{\rho(\boldsymbol{x}, \boldsymbol{z}_i) : 1 \leq i \leq k\} = \min\{\rho(\boldsymbol{y}, \boldsymbol{z}_i) : 1 \leq i \leq k\}$ then $E(\boldsymbol{x}) = E(\boldsymbol{y})$;

(ii) if $\min\{\rho(\boldsymbol{x}, \boldsymbol{z}_i) : 1 \leq i \leq k\} < \min\{\rho(\boldsymbol{y}, \boldsymbol{z}_i) : 1 \leq i \leq k\}$ then $E(\boldsymbol{x}) > E(\boldsymbol{y})$;

(iii) if $\min\{\rho(\boldsymbol{x}, \boldsymbol{z}_i) : 1 \leq i \leq k\} > \min\{\rho(\boldsymbol{y}, \boldsymbol{z}_i) : 1 \leq i \leq k\}$ then $E(\boldsymbol{x}) < E(\boldsymbol{y})$.

Proof. We prove (ii) only, and it is similar to prove (i) and (iii).

(ii) By lemma 4.3, there are $i, j \leq k$ satisfying (b1) and (b2). Hence,

$$E(\boldsymbol{x}) - E(\boldsymbol{y}) = \frac{1}{n} \left(x_i \log x_i + x_j \log x_j - y_i \log y_i - y_j \log y_j \right).$$

Because $x_i + x_j = y_i + y_j$ and $x_j < y_j \leq \dfrac{x_i + x_j}{2}$, we have that

$$\frac{1}{x_i + x_j} \left(x_i \log x_i + x_j \log x_j \right) > \frac{1}{y_i + y_j} \left(y_i \log y_i + y_j \log y_j \right).$$

Therefore, $E(\boldsymbol{x}) - E(\boldsymbol{y}) > 0$, i.e., $E(\boldsymbol{x}) > E(\boldsymbol{y})$.

□

We define a directed graph $(G, \overrightarrow{V})$ as follows. Label (G, V) in the following way:

- mark every $\boldsymbol{w} \in W$ with □;
- for any $\boldsymbol{x}, \boldsymbol{y} \in G$ with $(\boldsymbol{x}, \boldsymbol{y}) \in V$, if

$$\min\{\rho(\boldsymbol{x}, \boldsymbol{z}_i) : 1 \leq i \leq k\} = \min\{\rho(\boldsymbol{y}, \boldsymbol{z}_i) : 1 \leq i \leq k\}$$

then mark edge $(\boldsymbol{x}, \boldsymbol{y})$ with $=$; if

$$\min\{\rho(\boldsymbol{x}, \boldsymbol{z}_i) : 1 \leq i \leq k\} < \min\{\rho(\boldsymbol{y}, \boldsymbol{z}_i) : 1 \leq i \leq k\}$$

then mark edge $(\boldsymbol{x}, \boldsymbol{y})$ with $\leftarrow$; if

$$\min\{\rho(\boldsymbol{x}, \boldsymbol{z}_i) : 1 \leq i \leq k\} > \min\{\rho(\boldsymbol{y}, \boldsymbol{z}_i) : 1 \leq i \leq k\}$$

then mark edge $(\boldsymbol{x}, \boldsymbol{y})$ with $\rightarrow$.

After labelling, we have a directed graph, denoted by $(G, \overrightarrow{V})$. In Example 3.4, after being labelled, Fig. 3 becomes Fig. 4.

Corollary 4.5. *For any $\boldsymbol{x}, \boldsymbol{y} \in G$ with $(\boldsymbol{x}, \boldsymbol{y}) \in V$, $(\boldsymbol{x}, \boldsymbol{y}) \in \overrightarrow{V}$ (i.e., $\boldsymbol{x} \rightarrow \boldsymbol{y}$) if and only if $E(\boldsymbol{x}) \leq E(\boldsymbol{y})$.*

Proof. From theorem 4.4.

□

Corollary 4.6. *Given $\boldsymbol{x}, \boldsymbol{y} \in G$, if there is a directed path from $\boldsymbol{x}$ to $\boldsymbol{y}$ in $(G, \overrightarrow{V})$ then there is a $\boldsymbol{z}_i$ such that*

$$\rho(\boldsymbol{x}, \boldsymbol{z}_i) > \rho(\boldsymbol{y}, \boldsymbol{z}_i).$$

Hence, if there is a directed path from $\boldsymbol{x}$ to $\boldsymbol{y}$ in $(G, \overrightarrow{V})$ then $E(\boldsymbol{x}) < E(\boldsymbol{y})$.

□

5   Conclusions

We discussed and compared the entropy of different partitions, and built a graph $(G, V)_{n,k}$ for any natural numbers n and k with $n \geq k$. It is proved that there is a set of partitions with the minimal entropy; and a set of partitions with the maximal entropy; and the entropy is non-decreasing on any directed pathes in $(G, \overrightarrow{V})_{n,k}$ from a partition with the minimal entropy to one of the partitions with the maximal entropy.

On the graph $(G, \overrightarrow{V})_{3,3}$ there are two circles of the equal entropy: the first one consists of only one vector $(1, 1, 1)$; the second one consists of six vectors $(1, 2, 0), (2, 1, 0), (2, 0, 1), (1, 0, 2), (0, 1, 2), (0, 2, 1)$ such that

$$E((1,2,0)) = E((2,1,0)) = E((2,0,1)) = E((1,0,2)) = E((0,1,2)) = E((0,2,1));$$

and on the graph $(G, \overrightarrow{V})_{4,3}$, there are two circles of the equal entropy: the first one consists of only three vectors $(1, 1, 2), (1, 2, 1), (2, 1, 1)$, and

$$E((1,1,2)) = E((1,2,1)) = E((2,1,1));$$

the second one consists of six vectors $(0,3,1)$, $(1,3,0)$, $(3,1,0)$, $(3,0,1)$, $(1,0,3)$, $(0,1,3)$ such that

$$E((0,3,1)) = E((1,3,0)) = E((3,1,0)) = E((3,0,1)) = E((1,0,3)) = E((0,1,3)),$$

and this circle is disconnected.

The same situation occurs when $k > 3$, where the circle becomes a hyper-ball. We conjecture that given any pair (n, k) with $n \geq k$, there is a set of hyper-balls in $(G, \overrightarrow{V})_{n,k}$ such that for any two consecutive hyper-balls, any node on one hyper-ball is connected directly with a node on another hyper-ball.

References

1. Beaubouef, T., Petry, F. E. and Arora, G., Information-theoretic measures of uncertainty for rough sets and rough relational databases, J. Information Sciences **109**(1998) 185–195.
2. Düntsch, I. and Gediga, G., Uncertainty measures of rough set prediction, Artificial Intelligence **106**(1998) 109–137.
3. Hu, X., Lin, T. Y. and Han, J., A new rough sets model based on database systems, Fundamenta Informaticae **59**(2004), 135–152.
4. Pawlak, Z., Rough sets - theoretical aspects of reasoning about data, Kluwer Academic Publishers, Dordrecht, 1991.
5. Shannon, C. E., A mathematical theory of communication, The Bell system Technical Journal **27**(1948) 379–423, 623–656.
6. Pawlak, Z., Rough sets - theoretical aspects of reasoning about data, Kluwer Academic Publishers, Dordrecht, 1991.
7. Sui, Y., Wang, J. and Jiang, Y., Formalization of the conditional entropy in rough set theory, J. of Software **12**(2001) 23–25.
8. Wong, S. K. M. and Ziarko, W., On optimal rules in decision tables, Bull. of the Polish Academy of Sciences, Math. **33**(1985) 693–696.
9. Yao, Y. Y., Probabilistic approaches to rough sets, Expert Systems **20**(2003) 287–297.

A Comparative Evaluation of Rough Sets and Probabilistic Network Algorithms on Learning Pseudo-independent Domains

Jae-Hyuck Lee

Department of Computing and Information Science,
University of Guelph, Guelph, Ontario, Canada N1G 2W1
jaehyuck@cis.uoguelph.ca

Abstract. This study provides a comparison between the rough sets and probabilistic network algorithms in application to learning a *pseudo-independent (PI) model*, a type of probabilistic models hard to learn by common probabilistic learning algorithms based on search heuristics called *single-link lookahead*. The experimental result from this study shows that the rough sets algorithm outperforms the common probabilistic network method in learning a PI model. This indicates that the rough sets algorithm can apply to learning PI domains.

1   Introduction

Inductive machine learning is a process by which dependency relations among attributes of a dataset are automatically discovered. The rough sets [14] and probabilistic networks (PNs) [15] are both widely applied for dealing with vagueness and uncertainty in inductive learning and reasoning. The rough sets method is based on a pair of sets, called lower- and upper-approximation, and PN methods are founded on graphical models in which the probability distribution on the problem domains are encoded. Depending on the learning method used, the learned result varies in form: a set of decision rules by the rough sets method and a graphical model by the PN methods.

PN learning algorithms typically consist of a search through a space of candidate structures and a scoring measure by which the structures are evaluated and the best one is selected. However, the exhaustive search is NP-hard [3], and the learning algorithms, therefore, uses a heuristic search method. The common search heuristics is the *single-link lookahead* [27] which generates network structures that differ only by a single link at each level of search. The problem with this heuristics is that it cannot learn a special type of domains called *pseudo-independent(PI)* domains [27] where a group of marginally independent attributes show *collective dependency*, a special type of dependency that holds only in the scope of a group and not in any subsets of it. Thornton [20] showed that the parity mapping, which is a type of PI models, cannot be learned by many popular learning algorithms that rely on a probabilistic or statistical method, which include the perceptron learning algorithm, the neural network backpropagation algorithm, the CART family [2], and the ID3 [16] due to the statistical neutrality of the mapping. On the more general type of PI models, Xiang et al. [27] proved that all major

D. Ślęzak et al. (Eds.): RSFDGrC 2005, LNAI 3641, pp. 571–580, 2005.
© Springer-Verlag Berlin Heidelberg 2005

PN learning algorithms such as the Kutato [5], the Lam-Bacchus [10], the PC [19], and the K2 [4] algorithm fail to recover any PI models.

Note that the learnability of a learning algorithm on PI domains is not related to its scoring function or noise threshold level but to its scope of search. Although weak collective dependency can be approximated to independency, according to the PI model theory collective dependency can be of any strength including the degree of strength that cannot be approximated to independency. Incorrectly learned models introduce silent errors when used for classification, inference or decision making. Therefore, it is practically important to correctly recover PI models especially when learned models are to be used for critical tasks. About practicalness of PI models, an empirical study [23] with a real-world dataset showed a learned PI model reached the ultimate predictive accuracy, but caused only slight increase in inference complexity.

To learn PI models, the more sophisticated search method called *multi-link lookahead* [28] is needed, and it was implemented in a learning algorithm called *RML* [23]. The algorithm is equipped with the Kullback-Leibler cross entropy as its scoring measure for the goodness-of-fit to data. Regardless of either the common single-link or the multi-link method, however, the probabilistic learning method in general has some known disadvantages such as its large sample size required for obtaining probability distribution (relative frequencies) and its output graphical form that is less friendly to the human and less expressive than a set of rules. Therefore, it is meaningful to explore the learnability of algorithms from different approaches, and yet no other algorithms except the multi-link method have been known so far to learn PI models.

Table 1. The mixed PI model [21]

$(X_1, \ldots, X_5)$	$P(.)$	$(X_1, \ldots, X_5)$	$P(.)$	$(X_1, \ldots, X_5)$	$P(.)$	$(X_1, \ldots, X_5)$	$P(.)$
$(0,0,0,0,0)$	0.0000	$(0,1,0,0,0)$	0.0018	$(1,0,0,0,0)$	0.0080	$(1,1,0,0,0)$	0.0004
$(0,0,0,0,1)$	0.0000	$(0,1,0,0,1)$	0.0162	$(1,0,0,0,1)$	0.0720	$(1,1,0,0,1)$	0.0036
$(0,0,0,1,0)$	0.0000	$(0,1,0,1,0)$	0.0072	$(1,0,0,1,0)$	0.0120	$(1,1,0,1,0)$	0.0006
$(0,0,0,1,1)$	0.0000	$(0,1,0,1,1)$	0.0648	$(1,0,1,0,0)$	0.0704	$(1,1,0,1,1)$	0.0054
$(0,0,1,0,1)$	0.0072	$(0,1,1,0,1)$	0.0012	$(1,0,1,0,1)$	0.0176	$(1,1,1,0,1)$	0.0216
$(0,0,1,1,0)$	0.1152	$(0,1,1,1,0)$	0.0192	$(1,0,1,1,0)$	0.1056	$(1,1,1,1,0)$	0.1296
$(0,0,1,1,1)$	0.0288	$(0,1,1,1,1)$	0.0048	$(1,0,1,1,1)$	0.0264	$(1,1,1,1,1)$	0.0324

The purpose of this study is to investigate the performance of the rough sets algorithm on a PI domain in comparison with two PN learning algorithms: one with the single-link and the other the multi-link search method. The single-link search method represents the common PN learning algorithms, and the multi-link method serves for the learning algorithm with the best known accuracy so far on PI domains. This study uses a reclassification method for the performance evaluation, which divides a set of sample data into a training set and a test set, and obtains an output classifier learned from the training set by an algorithm, followed by testing the performance of the classifier by reclassifying the test set.

2   Methodology

2.1   Algorithm and Software Selection

ROSETTA [8] [13] was chosen for representing the rough sets method for this experiment. ROSETTA uses the *Rough Set Exploration System (RSES)* [1] library. For the procedures of the experiment, the following specific methods are used: *Johnson's algorithm* [7] for computing object-related reducts, and *the standard voting* [6] for reclassifying the test set. Johnson's algorithm which is implemented as *JohnsonReducer* [6] in ROSETTA uses a greedy algorithm for computing a single reduct. The standard voting is an algorithm for classifying each object into the class that maximizes the support (or any other measures) of a rule.

WEBWEAVR-III [22] was selected for both PN methods: the single-link and multi-link learning. By setting the number of lookahead links to one, the algorithm can represent the single-link method and to any number greater than one it can do the multi-link method [28]. WEBWEAVR-III employs *the Kullback-Leibler cross entropy* [9] as its scoring metric for measuring the goodness-of-fit of candidate structures to data and a user-provided threshold value as the stopping condition that defines the minimum entropy decrement for continuing the search. The detailed description of the algorithm is found in [23].

2.2   Data Preparation

This experiment requires a dataset of a PI domain. There are three different types of PI domains, that is, *full* [27], *partial* [23], and *mixed* [12] PI models. Collective dependency of PI models means an extra constraint over domain attributes. Because full or partial PI models have the stronger constraint than mixed PI models that the distribution over the domain must satisfy, real-world PI domains are expected to be found more likely in the form of a mixed type. In this experiment, hence, the mixed type of PI models was chosen for the type of a PI domain to be experimented with.

The dataset should be prepared for being isolated of any factors that may give a bias in performance evaluation on an algorithm under test. Such factors include incompleteness, noise and inaccuracy in data. For this reason, a synthetic dataset was used. It was created from the joint probability distribution over a mixed PI domain of five binary attributes shown in Table 1. Such a domain, especially a PI subdomain, of a small dimension (or the size of the joint space of attribute dimensions) is best suited to the primary aim of this experiment, that is, to test the learnability of the rough sets algorithm on a PI domain. Furthermore, domains of a small dimension help relax the computational time and space requirement for learning and, especially, for the multi-link method although the multi-link and the single-link method have the same order of the worst-case computational complexity [28].

Figure 1 depicts the graphical representation of the mixed PI model shown in Table 1 which is the structural learning target for this experiment. The multi-link method can recover this structure correctly. On the other hand, the single-link method will return an incorrectly learned structure such as Figure 2 where the links $\langle X_1, X_2 \rangle$ and $\langle X_1, X_3 \rangle$ are missing since the single-link method cannot discover the collective dependency among the PI subdomain $\{X_1, X_2, X_3\}$.

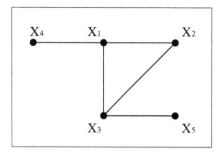

Fig. 1. The graphical representation for the mixed PI model shown in Table 1

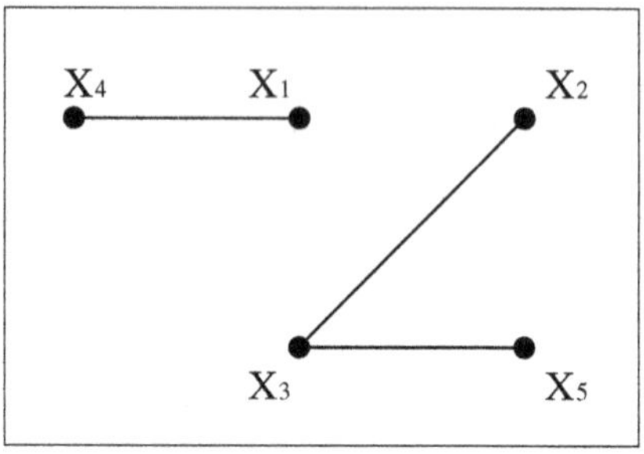

Fig. 2. The learned result on the same domain by the single-link method

2.3   Method for Comparison

The measures popularly used for comparing algorithms include the predictive accuracy, complexity and comprehensibility of the learned classifier, and the learning time and the sample size required for the learning. In this experiment, accuracy was chosen for the only quantitative measure for evaluation because the other measures are not suitable for the instrument of "cross-comparison" among the incompatible algorithms. For example, consider the learning time measure. It judges the performance of algorithms under comparison in terms of computational time complexity on condition that each algorithm does not require its input and/or output to be processed by pre- and/or post-processing programs. Learning time cannot be a fair measure if algorithms with a different format of input or output are compared by learning time since extra steps for "normalizing" the different input or output to the same format would likely require different computation time for each format. As a qualitative supplement to the quantitative analysis based on accuracy, pattern comparison between the rule structures and network structures of high predictive accuracy was made.

The predictive accuracy measures how close the learned classifier is to the "true" classifier. Various metrics such as entropy have been proposed to measure this distance which represents the error rate. In this experiment, *confusion matrices* were used for representing the measured accuracy of the classifiers. As shown in Table 9 or 10, a confusion matrix is a square matrix of which rows correspond to the true classification and columns correspond to the predictive classification done by a classifier.

Since this experiment uses a synthetic dataset whose true classifier is known, estimation on the true classification is not needed. However, the sole measure of accuracy may lead a possible over-fitting problem. Methods that tackle the problem based on *the minimum description length (MDL)* [17] approach include *the approximate reducts* [18] in the field of the rough sets method and the MDL-based learning method [10] in the field of the single-link method. For the multi-link method, the current research in this direction is still in progress [25] [26] [12] [11] that intends to provide explicit trade-off [24] between accuracy and complexity. For this experiment, a reasonable level of model complexity giving the best accuracy was pursued by using measures such as support, accuracy and coverage for the rough sets method and by adjusting the threshold value for the PN learning methods.

To evaluate the predictive accuracy of a learned classifier, this experiment employed a reclassification method which divides the input dataset into a training set and a test set, and obtains an output classifier learned from the training set by an algorithm, followed by testing the performance of the classifier by reclassifying the test set. Both the training set and the test set were made of the size larger than the sample complexity of each learning.

2.4 Experiment Setup

Procedure 1 (Rough sets method) (i) *Compute object-related reducts from the training set. Johnson's greedy search algorithm is used for this.*

(ii) *Generate decision rules on each attribute by using the reducts from Step (i). Compute the quality (the strength) of the generated rules, and, based on this, control the number of rules to a reasonable size.*

(iii) *Classify the objects in the test set by using the rules from Step (ii). The standard voting algorithm is used for this classification. Measure the classification performance by producing the confusion matrix on each decision attribute.*

All tasks listed above can be done by ROSETTA that uses the RSES library.

Procedure 2 (PN methods) (i) *Tune the entropy decrement threshold based on the optimum parameter approach for the maximum performance. Since the optimum values are not the same between the single-link and the multi-link method, they should be tuned separately.*

(ii) *Build a probabilistic network from the training set by the single-link method (or the multi-link method) with the optimum threshold setting.*

(iii) *On each object in the test set, randomly select a decision attribute and mask the value. Take the value of each attribute in the object, except the decision attribute, and input it as an evidence to the network built from Step (ii), followed by classifying the object by inference using the network. Check whether the classification is correct and record the score. Repeat this step until all objects in the test set are classified.*

(iv) *On each decision attribute, create a confusion matrix on the classification scores from Step (iii) and measure the performance of the network.*

3   Experimental Result

Table 2 shows the object-related reducts acquired by the rough sets method with setting the decision attribute on X_1. The reducts are good enough to capture all the dependency and conditional independency/dependency relation involving X_1. The attribute X_5 is redundant and is correctly removed from this set of reducts. This removal is, in terms of probabilistic relation, due to X_1 being conditionally independent of X_5 given X_3, which can be represented by $P(X_1 \mid X_3, X_5) = P(X_1 \mid X_3)$. The collective dependency is expressed by the generated decision rules shown in Table 7, which are $X_2(0)\ AND\ X_3(0) \implies X_1(1)$ and $X_2(0)\ AND\ X_3(0) \implies X_1(0)\ OR\ X_1(1)$. This rule shows 100 % accuracy in the data. This is a surprising result since this rule

Table 2. The reducts setting the decision attribute on X_1

Reduct	Support	Length
$\{X_3, X_4\}$	100	2
$\{X_2, X_3\}$	100	2
$\{X_2, X_3, X_4\}$	100	3

Table 3. The reducts setting the decision attribute on X_2

Reduct	Support	Length
$\{X_3\}$	100	1
$\{X_1, X_3\}$	100	2

Table 5. The reducts setting the decision attribute on X_4

Reduct	Support	Length
$\{\}$	1	0

Table 4. The reducts setting the decision attribute on X_3

Reduct	Support	Length
$\{X_1, X_5\}$	100	2
$\{X_1, X_2\}$	100	2
$\{X_1, X_2, X_4\}$	100	3
$\{X_1, X_2, X_4, X_5\}$	100	4
$\{X_1, X_2, X_5\}$	100	3

Table 6. The reducts setting the decision attribute on X_5

Reduct	Support	Length
$\{X_2\}$	100	1
$\{X_1\}$	100	1
$\{X_3\}$	100	1
$\{X_2, X_3\}$	100	2

describes (collective) dependency among X_1, X_2, X_3 which would not be recovered by any probabilistic algorithms equipped with the single-link lookahead search. For example, the result from the single-link method is depicted by Figure 2 where the links $\langle X_1, X_2 \rangle$ and $\langle X_1, X_3 \rangle$ are missing. The classification accuracy on the decision attribute X_1 is shown in the confusion matrix on the top left of Table 9 that shows the accuracy of the rough sets classifier on X_1 is 0.7755, close to 0.7945 from the multi-link, while the accuracy of the single-link reaches only 0.6975 shown in Table 10. This means the rough sets classifier outperforms the single-link on X_1 by 10 % in accuracy.

The object-related reducts on X_2 are shown in Table 3, which accord with collective dependency among $\{X_1, X_2, X_3\}$. This is also supported by the rules in Table 8. The accuracy of the rough set classifier outperforms the single-link by 15 %, which is shown on the top right of Table 9 and 10 .

The reducts on X_3 in Table 4 contain an error of including X_4 which is conditionally independent of X_3 given X_1. This error is propagated to the generated rules, causing a deterioration in predictive accuracy resulting 0.866 shown in Table 9 but is still 3.5 % better accuracy than the single-link classifier shown in Table 10.

X_4 and X_5 are the attributes irrelevant to collective dependency. For this reason, both the single-link and the multi-link classifier give the same accuracy as shown in Figure 3. On those attributes, the rough sets classifier performs only as good as the single-link, which is the case of X_4, or even worse in the case of X_5. Conversely, this strongly suggests that the good performance made on X_1, X_2 and X_3 by the rough sets comes from its recognition of the collective dependency, not from its overall good capability in learning regardless of dependency patterns.

Table 7. The rule output with the decision attribute on X_1

Decision Rule	LHS Support	RHS Support	RHS Accuracy	LHS Coverage	RHS Coverage
$X_3(1) \wedge X_4(1) \Longrightarrow X_1(1) \vee X_1(0)$	3717	2372, 1345	0.638, 0.362	0.465	0.465, 0.556
$X_2(0) \wedge X_3(1) \Longrightarrow X_1(0) \vee X_1(1)$	3219	1411, 1808	0.438, 0.562	0.402	0.584, 0.324
$X_2(0) \wedge X_3(0) \Longrightarrow X_1(1)$	1589	1589	1.0	0.199	0.285
$X_2(1) \wedge X_3(1) \wedge X_4(0) \Longrightarrow X_1(1) \vee X_1(0)$	903	846, 57	0.937, 0.063	0.113	0.152, 0.024
$X_2(1) \wedge X_3(0) \wedge X_4(1) \Longrightarrow X_1(0) \vee X_1(1)$	664	615, 49	0.926, 0.074	0.083	0.254, 0.009
$X_2(1) \wedge X_3(0) \wedge X_4(0) \Longrightarrow X_1(0) \vee X_1(1)$	164	134, 30	0.817, 0.183	0.021	0.055, 0.005

Table 8. The rule output with the decision attribute on X_2

Decision Rule	LHS Support	RHS Support	RHS Accuracy	LHS Coverage	RHS Coverage
$X_3(1) \Longrightarrow X_2(1) \vee X_2(0)$	5583	2364, 3219	0.423, 0.577	0.698	0.741, 0.670
$X_1(1) \wedge X_3(0) \Longrightarrow X_2(0) \vee X_2(1)$	1668	1589, 79	0.953, 0.047	0.209	0.330, 0.025
$X_1(0) \wedge X_3(0) \Longrightarrow X_2(1)$	749	749	1.0	0.094	0.235

Table 9. The confusion matrices from the rough sets algorithm

	Predicted		
Values	0	1	Ratio
0	177	428	0.293
Actual 1	21	1374	0.985
Ratio	0.894	0.762	0.776

The decision attribute on X_1

	Predicted		
Values	0	1	Ratio
0	1201	0	1.0
Actual 1	622	177	0.222
Ratio	0.659	1.0	0.689

The decision attribute on X_2

	Predicted		
Values	0	1	Ratio
0	523	48	0.916
Actual 1	220	1209	0.846
Ratio	0.704	0.962	0.866

The decision attribute on X_3

	Predicted		
Values	0	1	Ratio
0	0	685	0.000
Actual 1	0	1315	1.000
Ratio	Undef.	0.658	0.658

The decision attribute on X_4

	Predicted		
Values	0	1	Ratio
0	1159	37	0.969
Actual 1	468	336	0.418
Ratio	0.712	0.901	0.748

The decision attribute on X_5

Table 10. The confusion matrices from the single-link method

		Predicted		
	Values	0	1	Ratio
	0	0	605	0.000
Actual	1	0	1395	1.000
	Ratio	Undef.	0.698	0.698

The decision attribute on X_1

		Predicted		
	Values	0	1	Ratio
	0	1201	0	1.000
Actual	1	799	0	0.000
	Ratio	0.601	Undef.	0.601

The decision attribute on X_2

		Predicted		
	Values	0	1	Ratio
	0	523	48	0.916
Actual	1	281	1148	0.803
	Ratio	0.650	0.960	0.836

The decision attribute on X_3

		Predicted		
	Values	0	1	Ratio
	0	0	685	0.000
Actual	1	0	1315	1.000
	Ratio	Undef.	0.658	0.658

The decision attribute on X_4

		Predicted		
	Values	0	1	Ratio
	0	1148	48	0.960
Actual	1	281	523	0.650
	Ratio	0.803	0.916	0.836

The decision attribute on X_5

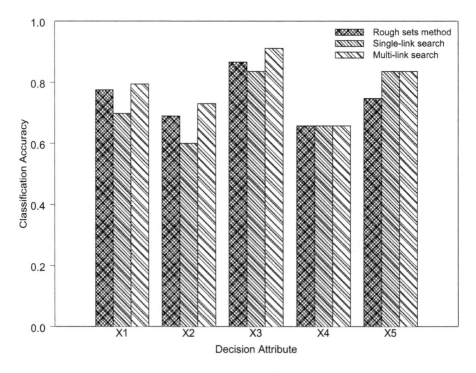

Fig. 3. Comparison of classification performance of the three algorithms on decision attributes X_1 to X_5

4   Discussion

This study empirically showed that the rough sets algorithm can be applied to learning a PI domain and can achieve the better result than common PN learning algorithms. This result is significant for the problem of learning PI domains since, generally, the rough sets method has the lower sample complexity for learning a classifier than PN methods and its classifier has the more expressive power. A possible explanation for the better performance by the rough sets classifier is that unlike the common PN learning, the rough sets algorithm is not based on any probabilistic/statistical methods of which learning depends on the search scope. Instead, it is based on symbolic logic and algebra to learn relevant relations among attributes. Although the rough sets classifier was out-performed by the multi-link, it could be rather due to the dataset artificially generated from a probabilistic domain model; only a conjecture that needs to be confirmed with further tests with different experimental setting.

Further studies can be made on the following directions: trying with other methods for computing reducts and generating rules, followed by comparing the results; repeating the same experiment on real-world datasets with the larger number of attributes and comparing the performance between the rough sets and the multi-link method; implementing trade-off between accuracy and model complexity in the three algorithms and repeating the experiment; and developing the method for measuring the normalized computation time for the incompatible algorithms on comparison.

Acknowledgments. The author is grateful to the anonymous reviewers for their comments on this work, and especially thanks Dominik Ślęzak for many helpful comments on formatting this final camera-ready paper.

References

1. J.G. Bazan, M.S. Szczuka, and J. Wróblewski. A new version of rough set exploration system. In J.J. Alpigini, J.F. Peters, A. Skowron, and N. Zhong, editors, *Lecture Notes in Artificial Intelligenence*, pages 397–404. Springer, 2002.
2. L. Breiman, J. Friedman, R. Olshen, and C. Stone. *Classification and Regression Trees*. Wadsworth, 1984.
3. D. Chickering, D. Geiger, and D. Heckerman. Learning Bayesian networks: search methods and experimental results. In *Proceedings of 5th Conference on Artificial Intelligence and Statistics*, pages 112–128, Ft. Lauderdale, 1995.
4. G.F. Cooper and E. Herskovits. A Bayesian method for the induction of probabilistic networks from data. *Machine Learning*, 9:309–347, 1992.
5. E.H. Herskovits and G.F. Cooper. Kutato: an entropy-driven system for construction of probabilistic expert systems from database. In *Proceedings of 6th Conference on Uncertainty in Artificial Intelligence*, pages 54–62, Cambridge,, 1990.
6. A. Øhrn. ROSETTA – Technical Reference Manual, 1999.
7. D.S. Johnson. Approximation algorithms for combinatorial problems. *Journal of Computer and System Science*, 9:256–278, 1974.
8. J. Komorowski, , A. Øhrn, and A. Skowron. The ROSETTA rough set software system. In W. Klösgen and J. Zytkow, editors, *Handbook of Data Mining and Knowledge Discovery*. Oxford University Press, 2002.

9. S. Kullback and R.A. Leibler. On information and sufficiency. *Annals of Mathematical Statistics*, 22:79–86, 1951.

10. W. Lam and F. Bacchus. Learning Bayesian networks: an approach based on the MDL principle. *Computational Intelligence*, 10(3):269–293, 1994.

11. J. Lee. Foundation for the new algorithm learning pseudo-independent models. In *Proceedings of 8th European Conference on Symbolic and Quantitative Approaches on Reasoning with Uncertainty*, Barcelona, 2005.

12. J. Lee and Y. Xiang. Model complexity of pseudo-independent models. In *Proceedings of 16th Florida Artificial Intelligence Research Society Conference*, Clearwater, 2005.

13. A. Øhrn. ROSETTA, Computer Software. Available via World Wide Web site, URL is http://rosetta.lcb.uu.se/, 1997.

14. Z. Pawlak. *Rough Sets – Theoretical Aspects of Reasoning about Data*. Kluwer Academic Publishers, Dordrecht, 1991.

15. J. Pearl. *Probabilistic Reasoning in Intelligent Systems: Networks of Plausible Inference*. Morgan Kaufmann, San Mateo, California, 1988.

16. J.R. Quinlan. Induction of decision trees. *Machine Learning*, 1:81–106, 1986.

17. J. Rissanen. Universal coding, information, prediction, and estimation. *IEEE Transactions on Information Theory*, IT-30(4):629–636, 1984.

18. D. Slezak and J. Wróblewski. Order based genetic algorithms for the search of approximate entropy reducts. In *Proceedings of the 9th International Conference on Rough Sets, Fuzzy Sets, Data Mining, and Granular Computing*, pages 308–311, Chongqing, China, 2003.

19. P. Spirtes and C. Glymour. An algorithm for fast recovery of sparse causal graphs. *Social Science Computer Review*, 9(1):62–73, 1991.

20. C. Thornton. Parity: the problem that won't go away. In G. McCalla, editor, *Advances in Artificial Intelligence*, pages 362–374. Springer, 1996.

21. Y. Xiang. Towards understanding of pseudo-independent domains. In *Poster Proceedings of 10th International Symposium on Methodologies for Intelligent Systems*, Charlotte, 1997.

22. Y. Xiang. WEBWEAVR-III, Computer Software. Available via World Wide Web site, URL is http://www.cis.uoguelph.ca/ yxiang/, 1998.

23. Y. Xiang, J. Hu, N. Cercone, and H. Hamilton. Learning pseudo-independent models: analytical and experimental results. In H. Hamilton, editor, *Advances in Artificial Intelligence*, pages 227–239. Springer, 2000.

24. Y. Xiang and J. Lee. Local score computation in learning belief networks. In E. Stroulia and S. Matwin, editors, *Advances in Artificial Intelligence*, pages 152–161. Springer, 2001.

25. Y. Xiang, J. Lee, and N. Cercone. Parameterization of pseudo-independent models. In *Proceedings of 16th Florida Artificial Intelligence Research Society Conference*, pages 521–525, St. Augustine, 2003.

26. Y. Xiang, J. Lee, and N. Cercone. Towards better scoring metrics for pseudo-independent models. *International Journal of Intelligent Systems*, 20, 2004.

27. Y. Xiang, S.K.M. Wong, and N. Cercone. Critical remarks on single link search in learning belief networks. In *Proceedings of 12th Conference on Uncertainty in Artificial Intelligence*, pages 564–571, Portland, 1996.

28. Y. Xiang, S.K.M. Wong, and N. Cercone. A 'microscopic' study of minimum entropy search in learning decomposable Markov networks. *Machine Learning*, 26(1):65–92, 1997.

On the Complexity of Probabilistic Inference in Singly Connected Bayesian Networks

Dan Wu[1] and Cory Butz[2]

[1] School of Computer Science, University of Windsor,
Windsor Ontario, Canada N9B 3P4
[2] Department of Computer Science, University of Regina,
Regina Saskatchewan, Canada S4S 0A3

Abstract. In this paper, we revisit the consensus of computational complexity on exact inference in Bayesian networks. We point out that even in singly connected Bayesian networks, which conventionally are believed to have efficient inference algorithms, the computational complexity is still NP-hard.

1 Introduction

Bayesian networks (BNs) have gained popularity in the last decade as a successful framework for processing uncertainty using probability. A Bayesian network [7] consists of two components: a *directed acyclic graph* (DAG) and a set of *conditional probability distributions* (CPDs). The product of these CPDs defines a *joint probability distribution* (JPD). One of the most important tasks for a BN is to perform *probabilistic inference*, which simply means computing the posterior probability distribution for a set of variables given the evidence that some other variables in the network are taking specific values. There are two kinds of probabilistic inference that can be performed, namely, *exact* inference and *approximate* inference. Exact inference means computing the exact posterior probability distribution. Approximate inference produces an inexact, bounded solution, but guarantees that the exact solution is within those bounds. In this paper, we will only comment on the computational complexity of exact inference.

During the development of various probabilistic inference algorithms, the following statements regarding computational complexity of exact inference in BNs are made. Singly connected BNs have linear time algorithm in the number of nodes in a network or the size of the network for exact inference. On the other hand, multiply connected Bayesian networks do not admit efficient algorithms for exact inference in the worst case. Finally, exact probabilistic inference in the general case is NP-hard because it was proved that exact inference in multiply connected BNs is NP-hard [1] [1]. Based on the above remarks, it has come to the consensus that the singly connected BNs are favorable and tractable while the

---

[1] It is perhaps worth mentioning that approximate inference in BNs was also proved NP-hard [8].

D. Ślęzak et al. (Eds.): RSFDGrC 2005, LNAI 3641, pp. 581–590, 2005.

multiply connected BNs are intractable (at least in the worst case) and should be blamed for causing the exact inference in BNs to be NP-hard.

In this paper, we revisit the consensus of computational complexity on exact inference in BNs. It seems that the consensus is somewhat misleading. Our main argument is that inference in a singly connected BN can be exponential in the worst case. More specifically, we adapt the proof in [1] to demonstrate that exact inference in singly connected BNs can also be NP-hard. That is to say, the hardness of exact inference in BNs should have nothing to do with the topological structure of the DAG of a BN.

The paper is organized as follows. In Section 2, we introduce pertinent background material and notation. We review the current consensus on exact inference in BNs in Section 3. In Section 4, we point out an inconsistency in the consensus. We investigate the inconsistency in Section 5. We discuss the implication of our investigation and conclude the paper in Section 6.

2   Background

We use $R = \{x_1, \ldots, x_n\}$ to represent a set of discrete variables. Each x_i takes value from a finite domain denoted V_{x_i}. We use capital letters such as X to represent a subset of R and its domain is denoted by V_X. By XY we mean $X \cup Y$. We write $x_i = \alpha$, where $\alpha \in V_{x_i}$, to indicate that the variable x_i is instantiated to the value α. Similarly, we write $X = \beta$, where $\beta \in V_X$, to indicate that X is instantiated to the value β. For convenience, we write $p(x_i)$ to represent $p(x_i = \alpha)$ for all $\alpha \in V_{x_i}$. Similarly, we write $p(X)$ to represent $p(X = \beta)$ for all $\beta \in V_X$.

Definition 1. Let $R = \{x_1, \ldots, x_n\}$ be a set of discrete variables. A Bayesian network (BN) defined over R consists of two components:(i) a *directed acyclic graph* (DAG) $\mathcal{D}$ whose nodes correspond one-to-one to the variables in R, and (ii) a set $\{p(x_i|\pi_{x_i}) \mid 1 \leq i \leq n\}$ of CPDs where π_{x_i} denotes the parents of x_i in $\mathcal{D}$. The product of the CPDs define a unique joint distribution $p(R)$ as: $p(R) = \prod_{1 \leq i \leq n} p(x_i|\pi_{x_i})$.

BNs are usually classified into three categories, according to the topological structures of their respective DAGs.

Definition 2. A BN is called a *tree structure* BN if for each node in the DAG of the BN except the root, there is only one parent node.

Definition 3. A BN is called a *singly connected* BN (also known as *polytree*) if there exists at most one (undirected) path between any two nodes in the DAG of the BN. Obviously, tree structure BNs are special cases of singly connected BNs.

Definition 4. A BN is called a *multiply connected* BN if there exists more than one (undirected) path between at least two nodes in the DAG of the BN.

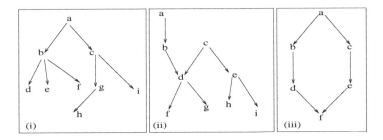

Fig. 1. (i) The DAG of a tree structure BN. (ii) The DAG of a singly connected BN. (iii) The DAG of a multiply connected BN.

Example 1. By definition, the BN in Fig. 1(i) is a tree structure BN. The BN in Fig. 1(ii) is a singly connected BN. The BN in Fig. 1(iii) is a multiply connected BN.

The classification of tree structure, singly connected, and multiply connected BNs, resulted to some extent from the historical development of different algorithms for exact inference, which are discussed in the next section.

3   Computational Complexity of Exact Inference: The Consensus

The key problem in BNs is to perform *probabilistic inference*, which means computing $p(X)$ or $p(X|Y = \beta)$, where $X \cap Y = \emptyset$, and $\beta \in V_Y$. The fact that Y is instantiated to β, i.e., $Y = \beta$, is called the *evidence*.

Algorithms for tree structure BNs and singly connected BNs were designed first. In 1982, Pearl first developed an algorithm featuring message passing for carrying out probabilistic inference in tree structure BNs. The following year Kim and Pearl extended the algorithm to singly connected BNs. These results were summarized in [6]. For tree structure BNs, Pearl gave a complexity result for exact inference in [6]. For an m-ary tree with n values in the domain for each node in the tree structure BN, one needs to store $n^2 + mn + 2n$ real numbers and perform $2n^2 + mn + 2n$ multiplications per update for inference. Obviously, both storage and computation are efficient in tree structure BNs. For singly connected BNs, it is commonly written that the time and space complexity of exact inference in singly connected BNs is linear in the size of the networks. Here, the size is defined as the number of CPD entries. Further more, if the number of parents of each node is *bounded* by a constant, then the complexity will also be linear in the number of nodes [8].

For multiply connected BNs, the algorithms developed for singly connected BNs can be adapted to process multiply connected BNs through conditioning [8]. Nevertheless, the predominant algorithm so far is the so-called local computation method [5].

The local computation method first transforms the DAG of a BN into a secondary structure called *junction tree* through the moralization and triangulation procedures. A formal treatment on triangulation and building junction trees can be found in [8]. After constructing the junction tree, a potential (a nonnegative function) $\phi(C_i)$ is formed for each clique C_i in the junction tree. We say the size of a clique C_i is the cardinality of its domain, that is, $|V_{C_i}|$. It is easy to see that the bigger the size of a clique, the more expensive the computation will be whenever $\phi(C_i)$ is engaged in the computation for inference.

Exact inference in multiply connected BNs was developed as follows. Lauritzen and Spiegelhalter [4] first proposed the local computation method for exact inference on junction trees (also called clustering method) and showed that their method can be implemented in a computationally *feasible* manner in some real-life expert systems. The authors were concerned with the size of the clique in the junction tree (transformed from the DAG of a BN), and they realized that their method would not be computational *feasible* if a large clique is present in the junction tree. Different architectures were developed to implement the local computation method. Jensen et al. [3] provided an object-oriented version of the computational scheme in [4]. This extension forms the core of the renowned Hugin architecture. Consequently, the Hugin architecture has the same concern as the Lauritzen-Spiegelhalter architecture, namely, the size of the clique in a junction tree. The Shafer-Shenoy architecture [9] used a different propagation scheme and used hypertree and Markov tree (junction tree) to describe the architecture. In [9], it was repeatedly emphasized that the efficiency and feasibility of their architecture depends on the size of the clique in a junction tree. Cooper formally confirmed these concerns by showing that exact probabilistic inference in BNs is NP-hard [1].

To summarize, the above discussion gives rise to the consensus that singly connected BNs have efficient inference, while multiply connected BNs do not. Thus, multiply connected BNs are the core of the inference problem.

4   Inconsistency in the Consensus

Although the local computation method was originally developed with the intention to solve the problem of exact inference in multiply connected BNs, it is important to realize that it is also applicable to singly connected BNs. In other words, given a singly connected BN, besides the specifically designed algorithms in [6], one can also apply the local computation architecture to solve the inference problem in a given singly connected BN. Regarding inference in singly connected BNs, an inconsistency arises when we compare the *specifically designed algorithms* [6] with the *local computation method* [5].

Consider an application involving a singly connected BN. On one hand, if one applies the specifically designed algorithms [6], results will be returned in time *linear* to the size of the network [8]. On the other hand, if one applies the local computation architecture, one has to be cautious that the size of the cliques in the constructed junction tree should be feasible. If a large clique is present in the junction tree and the size of the clique is not feasible, then the task of inference would *not* be computational feasible even given a singly connected BN.

In other words, there are then two different claims regarding inference in a singly connected BN. One is very positive and says this is definitely efficient in time linear to the size of the network. The other is rather conservative and says this may not be computational feasible if the junction tree transformed from the given *singly connected* BN contains a large clique. These two claims are seemingly inconsistent and are more carefully examined in the next section.

5   Exploring the Inconsistency

The concern of the local computation architecture pertains to the presence of a large clique size in the junction tree, which renders the local computations intractable. When transforming a singly connected BN into a junction tree, is it possible to create a large clique? The answer is definitely yes as the following example shows.

Example 2. Consider the singly connected DAG $\mathcal{D}$ in Fig. 2 (i). Note that the node x in $\mathcal{D}$ has n parents, i.e., y_1, ..., y_n. The junction tree constructed from $\mathcal{D}$ is shown in Fig. 2 (ii). As one may notice that one of the cliques contains variables x, y_1, ..., y_n. If n is large, even assuming all the variables are binary, storing the potential $\phi(x, y_1, ..., y_n)$ or engaging it in any computation will not be feasible as the storage and computation will be exponential with respect to the number of variables involved.

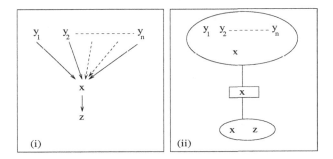

Fig. 2. (i) A singly connected DAG $\mathcal{D}$, where variable x has a large number of parents. (ii) The constructed junction tree has a large clique.

Example 2 explicitly demonstrates that a node in a singly connected BN with a large number of parent nodes must result in a large clique in the transformed junction tree. That is, it is entirely possible for a singly connected BN to have a large size clique. The presence of a large size clique will cause not only a storage problem for the corresponding CPD $p(x|y_1, ..., y_n)$, but also the problem of engaging $p(x|y_1, ..., y_n)$ in any computation during inference.

The exponential computational complexity entailed by large size cliques occurring in a junction tree hints that exact inference might be NP-hard. Cooper [1] successfully proved that the exact inference is NP-hard by transforming a well known NP-complete problem, namely, the *3SAT* problem [2], into a decision problem version of exact inference in multiply connected BNs. Since a singly connected BN, as demonstrated in Example 2, may also induce large cliques, it is thus worth exploring whether exact inference in a singly connected BN is also NP-complete.

In the following, we first demonstrate that a variant of the 3SAT problem is itself also a NP-complete problem. We then further show that this variant can be transformed into a *singly connected* BN in order to show that exact inference in singly connected BNs is also NP-hard.

5.1   A Variant of the 3SAT Problem

The 3SAT problem includes a collection $C = \{c_1, c_2, \ldots, c_m\}$ of clauses on a finite set U of n Boolean variables. If u is a variable in U, then u and $\neg u$ are *literals* over U. Each clause c_i contains a disjunction of three literals over U, for example, $(\neg u_2 \vee u_6 \vee \neg u_8)$. A *truth assignment* for U is an assignment which assigns either T (true) or F (false) to each variable in U. The literal u is true if and only if the variable u is assigned T. The literal $\neg u$ is false if and only if the variable u is assigned F. Given a truth assignment, a clause is satisfied (or evaluated true) if at least one literal is true. The clause $(\neg u_2 \vee u_6 \vee \neg u_8)$ is satisfied (i.e., true) unless $u_2 = T$, $u_6 = F$ and $u_8 = T$. A collection C of clauses over U is satisfiable if and only if there exists some truth assignment for U that simultaneously satisfies all of the clauses in C. The 3SAT decision problem involves determining whether there is a truth assignment for U that satisfies all of the clauses in C. We denote an instance of the 3SAT problem as $I = (U, \ C)$.

Example 3. Consider an instance $I = (U, \ C)$ of the problem 3SAT in which $U = \{u_1, u_2, u_3, u_4\}$ and $C = \{(u_1 \vee u_2 \vee u_3), (\neg u_1 \vee \neg u_2 \vee u_3), (u_2 \vee \neg u_3 \vee u_4)\}$. One satisfying truth assignment is given by $u_1 = T$, $u_2 = F$, $u_3 = F$ and $u_4 = T$. Thus, this instance of 3SAT decision problem has the answer "yes" in this example. This example will be called $3SAT_{ex}$.

We now introduce a variant of the 3SAT problem, which will be referred to as the 3SATV problem. We then prove that the 3SATV problem is NP-complete.

Very much similar to the 3SAT problem, the 3SATV problem also includes a collection C' of clauses on a finite set U' of n Boolean variables. The only difference between 3SAT and 3SATV is that each variable in U' is denoted u_i^j with not only the subscript i but also a superscript j. The 3SATV decision problem involves determining whether there is a truth assignment for U' that satisfies all of the clauses in C' and all the variables in U' with the same subscript are assigned the same truth value. We denote an instance of the 3SATV problem as $I' = (U', \ C')$.

Example 4. Consider an instance $I' = (U', C')$ of the 3SATV problem, where
$U' = \{u_1^1, u_1^2, u_2^1, u_2^2, u_3^3, u_3^1, u_3^2, u_3^3, u_4^1\}$ and $C' = \{(u_1^1 \vee u_2^1 \vee u_3^1), (\neg u_1^2 \vee \neg u_2^2 \vee u_3^2), (u_2^3 \vee \neg u_3^3 \vee u_4^1)\}$. We want to determine whether there exists an truth
assignment for U' that satisfies all of the clauses in C', furthermore, we require
that variables u_1^1, u_1^2, u_1^3 are assigned the same truth value; variable u_2^1, u_2^2, u_2^3
are assigned the same truth value; u_3^1, u_3^2, u_3^3 are assigned the same truth value.
One satisfying truth assignment is given by $u_1^j = T$ where $j = 1, 2, 3, u_2^j = F$
where $j = 1, 2, 3, u_3^j = F$ where $j = 1, 2, 3$ and $u_4^1 = T$. Thus, this instance of
the 3SATV decision problem has the answer "yes". This example will be called
$3SATV_{ex}$.

In the following, we will prove that the 3SATV problem is also NP-complete.
We first demonstrate how one can polynomially transform any instance of a
known NP-complete problem, for example, the 3SAT problem, to an instance of
the 3SATV problem. We use an example to illustrate this transformation.
Consider the instance $I = (U, C)$ in $3SAT_{ex}$ in Example 3 and the instance
$I' = (U', C')$ in $3SATV_{ex}$ in Example 4. We demonstrate how one can transform
$I = (U, C)$ into $I' = (U', C')$. If we rewrite the clause set C from $3SAT_{ex}$ and
the clause set C' from $3SATV_{ex}$ together below, one may immediately realize
that the transformation is straightforward.

$$C = \{(u_1 \vee u_2 \vee u_3), (\neg u_1 \vee \neg u_2 \vee u_3), (u_2 \vee \neg u_3 \vee u_4)\},$$
$$C' = \{(u_1^1 \vee u_2^1 \vee u_3^1), (\neg u_1^2 \vee \neg u_2^2 \vee u_3^2), (u_2^3 \vee \neg u_3^3 \vee u_4^1)\}.$$

The clause set C' is obtained by transforming each clause in C to a clause in
C'. More specifically, we transform one-to-one a clause c (in C) to a clause c'
(in C') by adding a superscript j to each variable u_i occurring in the clause c
to obtain the variable u_i^j which will appear in the transformed clause c'. The
superscript j indicates that the original variable u_i appears for the jth time
in the clause set C. For example, consider the clause $(\neg u_1 \vee \neg u_2 \vee u_3)$ in C
above. When transforming this clause to a corresponding clause in C', we add
superscript to each variable occurring in it, namely, $u_1, u_2,$ and u_3. Since u_1 now
appears for the second time (variable u_1 appears for the first time in the clause
$(u_1 \vee u_2 \vee u_3)$), it is then transformed into the variable u_1^2. Similarly, u_2 and u_3
are transformed into u_2^2 and u_3^2, respectively. Once we obtain the transformed
clause set C', the set of Boolean variable U' is just the union of all the variables
occurring in each clause in C'. Obviously, this process can be generalized to be
applied to any instance of the 3SAT problem in polynomial time.
Besides showing that one can transform polynomially any instance of the
3SAT problem to an instance of the 3SATV problem, in order to prove that the
3SATV problem is NP-complete, we also need to show that any instance I of
the 3SAT problem is satisfiable if and only if the transformed instance I' of the
3SATV problem is also satisfiable.
Suppose instance I is satisfiable, that means there exists a truth assignment
to the variables in U such that all the clauses in C are evaluated true. For the
instance I', we now demonstrate a truth assignment to the variables in U' such

that all the clauses in C' are evaluated true as well. For each variable u_i in U, there are variables u_i^j in U' which are constructed from the multiple occurrence of the variable u_i among the clauses in C. We assign the same truth value of u_i to those variables u_i^j in U'. In other words, it u_i is assigned T(F), then u_i^j are all assigned T(F). For any clause c in C consisting of variables u_i, u_j, and u_k, according to the construction process of I', there is a corresponding clause c' in C' consisting of variable u_i^l, u_j^m, and u_k^n. Since u_i^l, u_j^m, and u_k^n are assigned the same truth values as those of u_i, u_j, and u_k, respectively, and clause c is satisfiable, it then follows that the clause c' is also satisfiable. Therefore, every clause in C' is satisfiable.

Suppose the instance I' is satisfiable, we now need to show that there exists a truth assignment to the variables in U under which every clause in C is satisfiable. Consider a truth assignment to the variables in U' such that each clause c' in C' is satisfiable. For variables u_i^j in U', they are all assigned the same truth value, we then assign the same truth value assigned to u_i^j to the variable u_i in U. We thus obtain a truth assignment to every variable in U. Suppose the clause c' in C' consists of variable u_i^l, u_j^m, and u_k^n. According to the construction process described early, there is a corresponding clause c in C consisting of variables u_i, u_j, and u_k. Since u_i, u_j, and u_k are assigned the same truth values as those of u_i^l, u_j^m, and u_k^n, respectively, it then follows that the clause c in C is satisfiable. Therefore, every clause c in C is satisfiable.

The above discussion in fact proves the following theorem.

Theorem 1. The 3SATV problem is NP-complete.

5.2   The Complexity of Exact Inference in Singly Connected BNs

To prove that a problem Q' is NP-hard, it is sufficient to transform a known NP-complete problem Q to Q' and to show that this transformation can be done in time that is polynomial in the size of Q. In this subsection, we transform the 3SATV problem to a decision-problem version of probabilistic inference using singly connected BNs (*PISBND*). The transformation from the PISBND decision problem to the probabilistic inference problem, called *PISBN*, will be straightforward. Therefore, we will show that PISBN is NP-hard.

We first show how to polynomially transform 3SATV into PISBND, a decision problem that determines whether $p(Y = T) > 0$ in a given singly connected BN. PISBN returns "yes," if $p(Y = T) > 0$; it returns "no," otherwise.

Let $I' = (U', C')$ be any instance of the 3SATV problem. We seek to construct a singly connected BN on $U'C'Y$ from any instance of 3SATV in polynomially time, where Y is a new variable, such that $p(Y = T) > 0$ if and only if C' is satisfiable.

The nodes in the constructed singly connected BN are $U' \cup C' \cup \{Y\}$. Each variable $u_i^j \in U'$ is represented as a node u_i in the singly connected BN. Each clause $c_i \in C'$ is represented as a node c_i in the singly connected BN. For each clause $c_i \in C'$, let the three literals in c_i be denoted w_i^1, w_i^2 and w_i^3. For instance, given clause $c_2 = (\neg u_1 \vee \neg u_2 \vee u_3)$, then $w_2^1 = u_1$, $w_2^2 = u_2$, $w_2^3 = u_3$. The edges

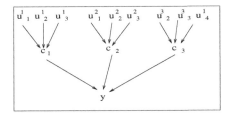

Fig. 3. A singly connected BN transformed from $3SATV_{ex}$

can now be defined as follows. For each node $c_i \in C'$, there is a directed edge from each of the three literals w_i^1, w_i^2 and w_i^3 to c_i. Finally, there are directed edges from each $c_i \in C'$ to variable Y.

Example 5. Given the example $3SATV_{ex}$, the DAG of the constructed singly connected BN is shown in Figure 3.

The CPDs for the singly connected BN are now constructed. For each of the root nodes $u_i^j \in U'$, the CPD $p(u_i^j)$ is $p(u_i^j = T) = 1/2$. For each of the clause nodes $c_j \in C'$, the CPD $p(c_j | w_j^1, w_j^2, w_j^3)$ is defined as follows. If clause c_j is T, then $p(c_j = T | w_j^1, w_j^2, w_j^3) = 1$; otherwise, if clause c_j is F, then $p(c_j = T | w_j^1, w_j^2, w_j^3) = 0$. The last CPD to construct is $p(Y | c_1, c_2, \ldots, c_m)$. If $c_1 = T$, and $c_2 = T$, $\ldots$, and $c_m = T$, then $p(Y = T | c_1, c_2, \ldots, c_m) = 1$; otherwise, $p(Y = T | c_1, c_2, \ldots, c_m) = 0$. That is, if at least one clause $c_i = F$, then $p(Y = T | c_1, c_2, \ldots, c_m) = 0$. We now show the claim in the next result.

Theorem 2. Let $I' - (U', C')$ be any instance of the 3SATV problem. Consider the singly connected BN on $U'C'Y$ constructed as above. Then C' is satisfiable if and only if $p(Y = T) > 0$ in the constructed singly connected BN. [2]

Thus, we have shown that any instance of 3SATV can be polynomially transformed to PISBND. This result implies that PISBN is NP-hard.

6   Concluding Remarks

Our analysis raises the question as to why inference in singly connected BNs is considered to be efficient. The complexity of exact inference in singly connected BNs was written as $O(N \cdot q^e)$ in [6], where N is the number of variables in the BN, q denotes the cardinality of the domain of each variable, and the number of parents for each variable in the BN is bounded by e. Obviously, if e is bounded and q is fixed, q^e is the coefficient of N and $O(Nq^e)$ could be considered linear and not exponential. However, if the number of parents for each variable in the BN is not bounded by e, then as N grows bigger, e may also grow bigger (e can

---

[2] Due to page limit, the proof will appear in an extended version of this paper.

be as large as $N - 1$), then the complexity $O(Nq^e)$ perhaps can not be simply considered as linear(or polynomial) anymore.

Our investigation in the previous sections has showed that the feasibility of exact inference lies with whether the DAG of a BN contains a node with a large number of parent nodes (which causes exponential storage and computation). The presence of a node with a large number of parents can occur in both singly connected and multiply connected BNs. Therefore, in both singly and multiply connected BNs, the computation for exact inference will be exponential in the worst case. On the contrary, the computational cost in tree structure BNs is efficient as characterized by Pearl in [6]. This is a result of the fact that, by definition, every node in a tree structure BN has at most one parent node. Subsequently every clique in the constructed junction tree will contain only two nodes, i.e., no large size clique will ever be created.

References

[1] G.F. Cooper. The computational complexity of probabilistic inference using bayesian belief networks. *Artificial Intelligence*, 42(2-3):393–405, 1990.

[2] M.R. Garey and D.D. Johnson. *Computers and Intractability: A Guide to the Theory of NP-Completeness*. W.H. Freeman and Company, New York, 1979.

[3] F.V. Jensen, S.L. Lauritzen, and K.G. Olesen. Bayesian updating in causal probabilistic networks by local computation. *Computational Statistics Quarterly*, 4:269–282, 1990.

[4] S.L. Lauritzen and D.J. Spiegelhalter. Local computation with probabilities on graphical structures and their application to expert systems. *Journal of the Royal Statistical Society*, 50:157–244, 1988.

[5] V. Lepar and P.P. Shenoy. A comparison of Lauritzen-Spiegelhalter, Hugin, and Shenoy-Shafer architectures for computing marginals of probability distributions. In Gregory F. Cooper and Serafín Moral, editors, *Proceedings of the 14th Conference on Uncertainty in Artificial Intelligence (UAI-98)*, pages 328–337, San Francisco, July 24–26 1998. Morgan Kaufmann.

[6] J. Pearl. Fusion, propagation, and structuring in belief networks. *Artificial Intelligence*, 29:241–288, 1986.

[7] J. Pearl. *Probabilistic Reasoning in Intelligent Systems: Networks of Plausible Inference*. Morgan Kaufmann Publishers, San Francisco, California, 1988.

[8] S. Russell and P. Norvig. *Artificial Intelligence: A Modern Approach (2nd edition)*. Prentice Hall, Englewood Cliffs, New Jersey, 2003.

[9] G. Shafer. *Probabilistic Expert Systems*. Society for Industrial and Applied Mathematics, 1996.

Representing the Process Semantics in the Situation Calculus

Chunping Li

School of Software, Tsinghua University, Peking 100084, China
`cli@tsinghua.edu.cn`

Abstract. This paper presents a formal method based on the high-level semantics of processes to reason about continuous change. With a case study we show how the semantics of processes can be integrated with the situation calculus. The soundness and completeness of situation calculus with respect to the process semantics are proven. Furthermore, the logical programming is implemented to support the semantics of processes with the situation calculus.

1 Introduction

In the real world, a vast variety of applications need logical reasoning about physical properties in continuous systems, e.g., specifying and describing physical systems with continuous actions and changes. The early research work on this aspect was encouraged to address the problem of representing continuous change in a temporal reasoning formalism. The research standpoint concentrated on specialized logical formalisms, typically of the situation calculus and its extensions [7,9,6].

Whereas these previously described formalisms have directly focused on creating new or extending already existing specialized logical formalisms, the other research direction consists in the development of an appropriate semantics as the basis for a general theory of action and change, and applied to concrete calculi [10,1,11,12,2].

In this paper, we present a formal method of integrating the semantics of processes with the situation calculus to reason about continuous change. With a case study we show how the semantics of processes can be integrated with the situation calculus to reason about continuous change. In Section 2, the semantics of processes is described briefly. In Section 3, an example domain is introduced, and a conventional mathematical model is constructed. Section 4 shows the method how to represent the semantics of processes in the situation calculus. In Section 5, the soundness and the completeness of the situation calculus with respect to the semantics of processes are proven. In Section 6, the logical programming is implemented to support the semantics of processes with the situation calculus. In Section 7, we have the concluding remarks for this work.

D. Ślęzak et al. (Eds.): RSFDGrC 2005, LNAI 3641, pp. 591–600, 2005.

2   The Semantics of Processes

In this section, we introduce the high-level semantics of processes [3] for reasoning about continuous processes, their interaction in the course of time, and their manipulation.

Definition 2.1. A process scheme is a pair $\langle C, F \rangle$ where C is a finite, ordered set of symbols of size $l > 0$ and F is a finite set functions f: $I\!R^{l+1} \rightarrow I\!R$.

Definition 2.2. Let N be a set of symbols (called names). A process is a 4-tuple $\langle n, \tau, t_0, \boldsymbol{p} \rangle$ where

1. $n \in N$;
2. $\tau = \langle C, F \rangle$ is a process scheme where C is of size m;
3. $t_0 \in I\!R$; and
4. $\boldsymbol{p} = (p_1, \ldots, p_m) \in I\!R^m$ is an m-dimensional vector over $I\!R$.

Definition 2.3. A situation is a pair $\langle S, t_s \rangle$ where S is a set of processes and t_s is a time-point which denotes the time when S started.

Definition 2.4. An event is a triple $\langle P_1, t, P_2 \rangle$ where P_1 (the precondition) and P_2 (the effect) are finite sets of processes and $t \in I\!R$ is the time at which the event is expected to occur.

Definition 2.5. An event $\langle P_1, t, P_2 \rangle$ is potentially applicable in a situation $\langle S, t_s \rangle$ iff $P_1 \subseteq S$ and $t > t_s$.

Definition 2.6. Let ε be a set of events and $\langle S, t_s \rangle$ a situation, then the successor situation $\varPhi(\langle S, t_s \rangle)$ is defined as follows.

1. If no applicable event exists in ε, then $\varPhi(\langle S, t_s \rangle) = \langle S, \infty \rangle$;
2. if $\langle P_1, t, P_2 \rangle \in \varepsilon$ is the only applicable event, then $\varPhi(\langle S, t_s \rangle) = \langle S', t_s \rangle$, where $S' = (S \setminus P_1) \cup P_2$ and $t_{s'} = t$;
3. Otherwise $\varPhi(\langle S, t_s \rangle)$ is undefined, i.e., events here are not allowed to occur simultaneously.

Definition 2.7. An observation is an expression of the form $[t] \propto (n) = r$ where

1. $t \in I\!R$ is the time of the observation;
2. $\propto$ is either a symbol in C or the name of a function in F for some process scheme $\langle C, F \rangle$;
3. n is a symbol denoting a process name; and
4. $r \in I\!R$ is the observed value.

Definition 2.8. A model for a set of observations $\varPsi$ (under given sets of names $\mathcal{N}$ and events $\mathcal{E}$) is a system development $\langle S_0, t_0 \rangle, \varPhi(\langle S_0, t_0 \rangle), \varPhi^2(\langle S_0, t_0 \rangle), \ldots$ which satisfies all elements of $\varPsi$. Such a set $\varPsi$ *entails* an (additional) observation ψ iff ψ is true in all models of $\varPsi$.

3   An Example: Pendulum and Balls Scenario

We illustrate how an example, the interaction between a pendulum and balls that travel along a 1-dimension space, can be formalized. As described in Figure 1, a pendulum collides at angle $\varphi = 0$ with a ball being at position $y = y_c$ at the same time. We need to find appropriate equations describing various possible movements and interactions. Supposing the damping factor is neglected, the motion of the pendulum can be described by the following differential equation.

$$m \cdot l^2 \cdot \frac{d^2\varphi}{dt^2} = -m \cdot g \cdot l \cdot \sin\varphi - l^2 \cdot \frac{d\varphi}{dt}$$

where l is the length of the pendulum, m is the mass of the pendulum, and g is $9.8\frac{m}{s^2}$. Solving the differential equation results in the angle of the pendulum φ, the angular velocity φ' and the angular acceleration φ''. φ_{max} denotes the maximum angle of the motion of the pendulum, T_{P0} the starting time of the motion of the pendulum, and γ the time constant of the pendulum.

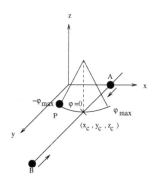

Fig. 1. Pendulum and balls A and B in positions

Here we define two different types of events. The first is the collision of two balls A and B, caused by identical locations at a certain time. The second type of event is the collision between one of the balls and the pendulum P, defined by the angle of the pendulum being zero while the ball's position is at the y-axis position of the pendulum y_c, at the same time. The pendulum is assumed to be of much larger mass than the balls, such that the collision will simply be an elastic impact with one of the balls (reflection into opposite direction) while the pendulum keeps moving continuously.

For ball A and ball B moving along the y-axis, we use the process scheme $\tau_{move} = \langle C, F \rangle$, namely, $C = \{y_0, v\}$ and $F = \{y = y_0 + v \cdot (t - t_0)\}$. As the process scheme for the motion of the pendulum we obtain $\tau_{pendulum} = \langle C', F' \rangle$ where $C' = \{\varphi_{max}, \gamma, y_c\}$ and $F' = \{\varphi, \varphi', \varphi''\}$.

4 Representing the Process Semantics in the Situation Calculus

4.1 Situation Calculus with the Branch Time

The situation calculus is the most popular formalism designed to represent theories of action and change [5]. The situation calculus does not yet provide a very rich temporal ontology. Pinto and Reiter proposed the concept of a time line to extend the original situation calculus by incorporating the basic elements of a linear temporal logic [8,9]. For reasoning about time in the situation calculus, a predicate *actual* is incorporated.

A new sort is incorporated into the situation calculus, interpreted as a continuous time line. The sort is considered isomorphic to the non-negative real. Intuitively, each situation has a starting time and an ending time. Actions occur at the ending time of situations. This is captured by the following axioms.

$(\forall s, a)\ end\,(s, a) = start\,(do\,(a, s))$.
$(\forall s, a)\ start\,(s) < start\,(do\,(a, s))$.
$start\,(S_0) = 0$.

The predicate *occurs* is introduced as describing a relation between action types and situations.

$occurs\,(a, s)\ \equiv\ actual\,(do\,(a, s))$.

To establish the relation between actions that occur and the time at which they occur, the predicate $occurs_T$ is defined as

$occurs_T(a, t)\ \equiv\ (\exists s)\ occurs\,(a, s) \wedge start\,(do\,(a, s)) = t$.

Similarly, a relation $holds_T$ between fluents and time points and a relation *during* between time points and situations are defined as

$holds_T(f, t)\ \equiv\ (\exists s)\ actual\,(s) \wedge during\,(t, s) \wedge holds\,(f, s)$.

$during\,(t, s)\ \equiv\ actual\,(s) \wedge start\,(s) < t \wedge (\forall a)\ [occurs\,(a, s) \rightarrow end\,(s, a) \geq t]$.

4.2 An Axiomatization of Pendulum and Balls Scenario

In the pendulum and balls scenario, we suppose that two balls move toward each other along the y-axis. A pendulum maybe collides at its suspension point with one of balls. The successor state axioms and action precondition axioms are suitable for formalizing the motion processes of the balls and the events. We have the following successor state axioms:

$Poss\,(a, s) \rightarrow\ holds\,(moving\,(ball, \tau_{move}, T, (l, v)), do\,(a, s)) \equiv$
$(a = impetus\,(ball, (l, v))\ \wedge occurs_T(a, T)$
$\wedge f = F(l, v, t, T)) \vee\ (holds\,(moving\,(ball, \tau_{move}, T, (l, v)), s) \wedge$
$\neg(a = impetus\,(ball, (l, v))))$.

$Poss\,(a, s) \rightarrow\ holds\,(sway\,(Pendulum, \tau_{pendulum}, T_{P0}, (\varphi_{max}, \gamma, y_c)), do\,(a, s))$
$\equiv (a = starting\,(Pendulum, (\varphi_{max}, \gamma, y_c)) \wedge$
$occurs_T\,(a, T_{P0}) \wedge \varphi = -\varphi_{max} \cdot \cos(\frac{2\pi}{\gamma} \cdot (t - t_{P0})))$
$\vee\ (holds\,(sway\,(Pendulum, \tau_{pendulum}, T_{P0}, (\varphi_{max}, \gamma, y_c)), s)$
$\wedge \neg(a = starting\,(Pendulum, (\varphi_{max}, \gamma, y_c)))).$

We formalize the actions with the action precondition axioms as follows.

$Poss\,(starting\,(ball, (l, v)), s)\ \equiv$
$occurs_T\,(impetus\,(ball, (l, v)), T) \wedge start\,(s) < T.$

$Poss\,(starting\,(Pendulum, (\varphi_{max}, \gamma, y_c)), s)\ \equiv$
$occurs_T\,(starting\,(Pendulum, (\varphi_{max}, \gamma, y_c)), T_{P0}) \wedge start\,(s) < T_{P0}.$

$Poss\,(collide\,((Pendulum, ball), ((\varphi_{max}, \gamma, y_c), (l_{new}, v_{new})), t), s)\ \equiv$
$holds\,(sway\,(Pendulum, \tau_{pendulum}, T_{P0}, (\varphi_{max}, \gamma, y_c)), s) \wedge$
$holds\,(moving\,(ball, \tau_{move}, t, (l_{old}, v_{old})), s) \wedge t = \frac{y_c - l_{old}}{v_{old}} + t_0$
$\wedge\ l_{new} = y_c \ \wedge\ v_{new} = -v_{old} \wedge\ v_{old} \neq 0.$

$Poss\,(collision\,((ballA, ballB), ((l'_{A0}, v'_{A0}), (l'_{B0}, v'_{B0})), t), s)\ \equiv$
$holds\,(moving\,(ballA, \tau_{move}, T_{A0}, (l_{A0}, v_A)), s) \wedge$
$holds\,(moving\,(ballB, \tau_{move}, T_{B0}, (l_{B0}, v_B)), s) \wedge$
$t = (l_{B0} - l_{A0} + v_A \cdot T_{A0} - v_B \cdot T_{B0})/(v_A + v_B)$
$\wedge\ l'_{A0} = l'_{B0} = l_{A0} + v_A \cdot (t - T_{A0}) \wedge$
$v'_{A0} = v'_{B0} = v_A + v_B \ \wedge\ start\,(s) < t.$

There are two natural actions (events) that may occur in this scenario:

$natural\,(a) \equiv a = collide\,((Pendulum, ball), ((\varphi_{max}, \gamma, y_c), (l_{new}, v_{new})), t) \vee$
$a = collision\,((ballA, ballB), ((l'_{A0}, v'_{A0}), (l'_{B0}, v'_{B0})), t).$

Suppose that ball A starts from position 0m at time 2sec to move with speed 0.4m/sec, while ball B starts from position 4m at time 4sec with speed -0.3m/sec. If there is no other event to occur, the two balls A and B which move toward each other along y-axis would have a collision at time 10sec. We start the pendulum with suspension point $x_c = 1$m, $y_c = 0.3$m, $z_c = 0$, time constant $\gamma = 1$ and starting angle $\varphi_{max} = 10$ at time $T_{P0} = 1$. The natural action (event) of the collision between the pendulum and ball A will occur at time $t = (y_c - y_{A0})/v_A + t_{A0} = 2.75$ sec.

This nearest event results in the pendulum moving unchanged while the ball A moves into the opposition direction, and avoids the collision possibility of the balls A and B. Here we describe the initial facts and equality constraints as follows.

$$F : y = y_0 + v \cdot (t - t_0); \ F' : \varphi = -\varphi_{max} \cdot \cos(\tfrac{2\pi}{\gamma} \cdot (t - t_{P0}))$$

Furthermore, the occurrence axiom can be described as follows.

$occurs(starting(Pendulum, (\varphi_{max}, \gamma, y_c)), S_1) \wedge$
$occurs(impetus(ballA, (y_{A0}, v_A)), S_2) \wedge occurs(impetus(ballB, (y_{B0}, v_B)), S_3)$

where $start(S_1) = 1sec \wedge start(S_2) = 2sec \wedge start(S_3) = 4sec$, $S_0 < S_1 < S_2 < S_3$.

Let $AXIOMS$ be the axioms given in Subsection 4.1 with the action precondition and the successor state axioms. It is easy to see that for any model $\mathcal{M}$ of $AXIOMS$ it holds that $\mathcal{M} \models S_1 = do(starting(Pendulum, (\varphi_{max}, \gamma, y_c)), S_0)$ $\wedge S_2 = do(impetus(ballA, (y_{A0}, v_A)), S_1) \wedge S_3 = do(impetus(ballB, (l_{B0}, v_B)), S_2)$.

From the occurrence axiom and the ordering statement, we infer that $\mathcal{M}$ satisfies $occurs_T(impetus(ballA, (y_{A0}, v_A)), t_{A0}) \wedge occurs_T(impetus(ballB, (y_{B0}, v_B)), t_{B0}) \wedge occurs_T(starting(Pendulum, (\varphi_{max}, \gamma, y_c)), t_{P0})$ and $t_{P0} < t_{A0} < t_{B0}$.

The natural action $collide$ will occur in the time t for which the equation $t = (y_c - y_{old})/v_{A0} + t_{A0} \wedge y_{newA} = y_c \wedge v_{newA} = -v_B$ will be true.

Thus, $occurs_T(collide((Pendulum, ballA), ((\varphi_{max}, \gamma, y_c), (y_{newA}, v_{newA})), t))$ will hold in the model $\mathcal{M}$. By using the successor state axiom for $sway$ and the action precondition axioms, we obtain $\mathcal{M} \models$

$S_4 = do(collide((Pendulum, ballA), ((\varphi_{max}, \gamma, y_c), (y_{newA}, v_{newA})), t), S_3) \wedge$
$holds(sway(Pendulum, \tau_{pendulum}, T_{P0}, (\varphi_{max}, \gamma, y_c)), S_4) \wedge$
$holds(moving(ballA, \tau_{move}, T_{A0}, (y_{newA}, v_{newA})), S_4)$.

5   Soundness and Completeness Theorem

Definition 5.1. Let Σ_{proc} be a theory of action with occurrences and continuous processes. It should include:

- basic axioms of the situation calculus;
- axioms based on the actual time line;
- successor state axioms and action precondition axioms.

The problem of reasoning about actions and continuous processes is: given an incomplete description of the actions that occur in time, what are the actions that actually will occur, especially in regard of the implicit events in the process semantics? Here we choose models that contain minimal sets of occurring actions and events. This can be formalized using circumscription. In order to simplify the presentation of circumscription, we consider the predicates $occurs$, $holds_T$, $during$ and the function end to be abbreviations.

The circumscription policy is as follows.

$$CIRC(\Sigma_{proc}; occurs_T; actual, start)$$

We select the models that satisfy Σ_{proc} with a minimal extension for the predicate $occurs_T$. The predicate $actual$ and the function $start$ are variable elements in circumscription. Clearly, these elements need to vary since $occurs_T$ is defined in terms of them. Notice that the situation tree is fixed except for the elements that determine what the actual line looks like. A property of this policy is that if we know all the actions that occur, and if it is consistent to believe that they are all that occurred, then the circumscription will select those models in which the actual line of situation contains all and only those actions.

Based on Lifschitz's results [4], we present the model-theoretic meaning of the above circumscription.

Let $\mathcal{D} = (\mathcal{P}, \mathcal{E})$ be a consistent domain description for the process semantics, where $\mathcal{P}$ is a set of initial processes and $\mathcal{E}$ is a set of events. We write $\mathcal{P} = (p_1, p_2, \ldots, p_m)$ and $\mathcal{E} = (e_1, e_2, \ldots, e_n)$.

Let π denote the translation from the domain description of the process semantics into the formalism of the situation calculus. The following symbols are used: situation variables $s, s', \ldots$, time variables $t, t', \ldots$, action (event) variables $a, a', \ldots$, fluent representing process $P(n, F, R, C)$, action $A(n, C)$ and event $E(\hat{n}, \hat{C}, t)$. Furthermore, let $OBS(P, \alpha, t_s)$ denote an observation of the process with name n at time t_s in the process semantics, where α is a symbol in C or R for some process scheme (C, F) and $\alpha = r$ (r is an observed value). In the situation calculus we describe an observation in the form

$$holds_T(P(n, F, R, C), t_s) \wedge \alpha = r$$

where α is a variable name in R or C.

Lemma 1. Let $\mathcal{D}$ be a domain description for the process semantics. For any process P from $\mathcal{D}$, if $CIRC[\pi\mathcal{D} \wedge \Sigma_{proc}] \models holds_T(P(n, F, R, C), t_s) \wedge \alpha \in (R \cup C) \wedge \alpha = r$, then $\mathcal{D}$ entails $OBS(P, \alpha, t_s) \wedge \alpha = r$.

Proof. Assume that a process $P(n, F, R, C)$ in $CIRC[\pi\mathcal{D} \wedge \Sigma_{proc}]$ holds at time t_s. For some parameter α and $\alpha \in R \cup C$, there exists an observed value which we denote by r. Since $CIRC[\pi\mathcal{D} \wedge \Sigma_{proc}] \models holds_T(P(n, F, R, C), t_s)$, there must exist the actual occurrences of a set of actions and events in some order such that the process $holds_T(P(n, F, R, C), t_s)$ holds at time t_s. Σ_{proc} is a theory in which the set $\mathcal{T}_{occ}$ contains an axiom of the form

$$(\exists s_1, \ldots, s_n) \; occurs(A_1, s_1) \wedge \ldots \wedge occurs(A_n, s_n) \wedge \mathcal{O}_<(s_1, \ldots, s_n) \equiv$$
$$(\exists t_1, \ldots, t_n) \; occurs_T(A_1, t_1) \wedge \ldots \wedge occurs_T(A_n, t_n) \wedge \mathcal{O}_<(t_1, \ldots, t_n)$$

where $\mathcal{O}_<$ is an ordering formula.

Thus, every model in $CIRC[\pi\mathcal{D} \wedge \Sigma_{proc}]$ satisfies

$occurs(a, s) \equiv (a = A_1 \wedge s = S_1) \vee \ldots \vee (a = A_n \wedge s = S_n)$, correspondingly,

$occurs_T(a, t) \equiv (a = A_1 \wedge t = T_1) \vee \ldots \vee (a = A_n \wedge t = T_n)$, where $T_1 < \ldots < T_n < t_s$. Then, every model of $CIRC[\pi\mathcal{D} \wedge \Sigma_{proc}]$ also will satisfy

$S_n = do(A_{n-1}, S_{n-1}) \wedge \ldots \wedge S_2 = do(A_1, S_1) \wedge S_1 = S_0$.

$t_n = start(do(A_{n-1}, S_{n-1})) \wedge \ldots \wedge t_2 = start(do(A_1, S_1)) \wedge t_1 = start(S_0)$.

Thus, for all models in $CIRC[\pi\mathcal{D} \wedge \Sigma_{proc}]$, there must exists time points t_i and t_{i+1} where $1 \leq i < n$, so that the process $P(n, F, R, C)$ holds in the time period $[t_i, t_{i+1}]$, and it is concluded that for $t_s \in [t_i, t_{i+1}]$, $\alpha \in (R \cup C) \wedge \alpha = r$ must be true.

We need to prove that $\mathcal{D} \models OBS(P, \alpha, t_s) \wedge \alpha = r$ under the condition mentioned above. We prove this by contradiction. Suppose that the observation of the process $OBS(P, \alpha, t_s)$ with the observation value $\alpha = r$ is not entailed from the domain description $\mathcal{D}$. Then there exists a model of $\mathcal{D}$, in which the value of the observation $\alpha = r$ is false. Thus, a corresponding system development of this model (under the domain description $\mathcal{D}$ with initial processes and events) satisfies that the observation $OBS(P, \alpha, t_s)$ which its value $\alpha = r$ is false. In the process semantics, since a system development $\langle S_0, t_0 \rangle$, $\Phi(\langle S_0, t_0 \rangle)$, $\Phi^2(\langle S_0, t_0 \rangle)$, ... is regarded as an infinite sequence of situations which are transformed by the events and actions, the state of the system at the particular time-point t_s can be described by the collection of processes S where $\langle S, t_i \rangle = \Phi^i(\langle S_0, t_0 \rangle)$ and $\langle S', t_{i+1} \rangle = \Phi^{i+1}(\langle S_0, t_0 \rangle)$ such that $t_i \leq t_s < t_{i+1}$. Corresponding to the situation calculus paradigm, it follows that the observation where its value $\alpha = r$ for $OBS(P, \alpha, t_s)$ at the time t_s does not hold. In this case, the contradiction between this assumption and the premise takes place. Thus, it follows that $\mathcal{D}$ entails the observation $OBS(P, \alpha, t_s) \wedge \alpha = r$.

Theorem 1. [Soundness Theorem] Let $\mathcal{D}$ be a domain description for process semantics, for any process P if $\pi\mathcal{D}$ entails πP, then $\mathcal{D}$ entails P.

Proof. By Lemma 1, an observation $OBS(P, \alpha, t_s) \wedge \alpha = r$ is entailed by $\mathcal{D}$, if $CIRC[\pi\mathcal{D} \wedge \Sigma_{proc}] \models \pi OBS$. Suppose that $\pi\mathcal{D}$ entails πP, since the observation is made during a development of the system being modelled and involved in some concrete process at time t_s, the observed process holds under the development of the system (given the set of initial processes and the set of events), if $holds_T(P(n, F, R, C), t_s)$ is true in all the models of $CIRC[\pi\mathcal{D} \wedge \Sigma_{proc}]$. It follows that $\mathcal{D}$ entails P.

Theorem 2. [Completeness Theorem] Let $\mathcal{D}$ be a domain description for process semantics, for any process P if $\mathcal{D}$ entails P, then $\pi\mathcal{D}$ entails πP.

Proof. Given a process P and let $\mathcal{D}$ entail P. Then in the process semantics, there must be a system development satisfying a set of observations Ψ for the process P under $\mathcal{D}$. We assume that a model for the observations Ψ is represented as a system development $\langle S_0, t_0 \rangle, \ldots, \langle S_n, t_n \rangle$ which satisfies all elements of Ψ (where $\langle S_i, t_i \rangle$ is defined as a *situation* at the start time t_i, and there exists a successor situation function Φ such that we can yield an infinite sequence of situation: $\langle S_{i+1}, t_{i+1} \rangle = \Phi(\langle S_i, t_i \rangle)$ see [3]). Let $OBS(P, \alpha, t_s)$ represent an observation for the process P at time t_s and the observed value $\alpha = r$. Then $OBS(P, \alpha, t_s) \in \Psi$ and $OBS(P, \alpha, t_s)$ is true in all models of Ψ.

By the definition of the system development, it is consistent to assume that all the events (actions) are only those that occur during the system development and the events (actions) are totally ordered. Let $\mathcal{M}$ be a model for $OBS(P, \alpha, t_s)$. Thus, there is a corresponding model $\pi\mathcal{M}$ of the theory Σ_{proc} in the situation calculus that satisfies

$$occurs\,(a, s) \equiv (a = A_1 \wedge s = S_1) \vee \ldots \vee (a = A_n \wedge s = S_n),$$

and also

$$occurs_T\,(a, t) \equiv (a = A_1 \wedge t = T_1) \vee \ldots \vee (a = A_n \wedge t = T_n).$$

Since Σ_{proc} is a theory in which $\mathcal{T}_{occ}$ takes the form

$$occurs\,(A_1, S_1) \wedge \ldots \wedge occurs\,(A_n, S_n) \wedge \mathcal{O}_<(S_1, \ldots, S_n)$$

where $\mathcal{O}_<$ is an ordering formula, therefore, $\pi\mathcal{M}$ is a model of $CIRC[\pi\mathcal{D}\wedge\Sigma_{proc}]$. Thus, $holds_T\,(P\,(n,\ F,\ R,\ C)) \wedge \alpha \in (R \cup C) \wedge \alpha = r$ is true in all models of $CIRC[\pi\mathcal{D} \wedge \Sigma_{proc}]$. It follows that $\pi\mathcal{D}$ entails πP.

6   Implementation

We have implemented a logic programming system supporting the process semantics based on the situation calculus in Prolog under the environment of Eclipse, which incorporates a number of subroutines and additional features.

The logical program for the example of balls and pendulum is shown partially as follows. Because of space restrictions we here omit the clauses specifying the functions of the manipulation of situation and process set.

```
%%% Primitive actions %%%
action(impetus(ball(a), pos(a, Y), v(a, Y), t(a,T))).
action(impetus(ball(b), pos(a, Y), v(a, Y), t(a, T))).
%%% Initial situation %%%
initial_proc([ball(a), ball(b), pendulum(p), pos(a,0), pos(b,4),
v(a,0),v(b,0), v(p,0), last_Tdc(0), t(a, 0), t(b, 0), t(p,0)]).
%%% Preconditions for primitive actions %%%
poss(impetus(ball(a), pos(a, Y), v(a, Y), t(a, T)), S) :-
   T=2, V=0.4 , initial_state(I, S0),occurs(T, action(impetus(ball(a),
   pos(a, Y), v(a, Y), t(a, T)))).
poss(impetus(ball(b), pos(b, Y), v(b, Y), t(b, T)), S) :-
   T=4, V=-0.3, initial_state(I, S0),occurs(T, action(impetus(ball(b),
   pos(b, Y), v(b, Y), t(b, T)))).
poss(natural(a), S, Tdc):-
   proc_match([ball(X), pendulum(p), v(X,VX), var(p, VY), pos(X, X0),
   pos(p, Y0), t(X, TX), t(p, TV)],S,_), Tdc is   TX+(Y0-X0)*VX.
%%% Successor state axioms for primitive fluent %%%
holds(moving(ball(X), pos(X,Y), v(X,V), t(X,Tdc), _), do(a,S)):-
   holds(moving(ball(X), pos(X,Y), v(X,V), t(X,Tdc), _),S),
   poss(natural(a), S, Tdc), next_state(I,S), Tdc>0.
holds(moving(ball(X), pos(X,Y), v(X,V), t(X,Tdc), _),S):-
   poss(impetus(ball(X), pos(X, Y), v(X, Y), t(X, T)),S),
   next_state(I,S), Tdc>0.
%%% specifying process and state transition %%%
holdsAt(sway(pendulum(p),pos(p, Y), var(p, V), t(p, Tdc),L),TT):-
   holds(sway(pendulum(p), pos(p, Y), var(p, V), t(p, Tdc), L),S),
   proc_match([ball(X), pendulum(p), v(X, VX), var(p, VY), pos(X,X0),
   pos(p,Y0),t(X,TX),t(p,TV)],S,_),TT>Tdc, L is -10*cos(2*3.14*(TT-T)).
```

7 Concluding Remarks

This paper presents a formal method based on the high-level semantics of processes to reason about continuous change. With a case study we show how to integrate the semantics of processes with the situation calculus for reasoning about continuous changes. Our method carries on some important properties of Pinto and Reiter's temporal situation calculus, and implements the automated reasoning about continuous change in the logical programming framework. The main difference is that we adopt a more general concept of the process, which is more appropriate to the semantic description in the case of continuous change. We have proven the soundness and completeness of the situation calculus with respect to the process semantics. Furthermore, the logical programming is implemented to support the semantics of processes with the situation calculus.

Acknowledgments. This work was supported by Chinese 973 Research Project under grant No. 2004CB719401.

References

1. Gelfond, M., Lifschitz, V.: Representing action and change by logic programs. Journal of Logic Programming **17** (1993) 301–321
2. Grosskreutz, H., Lakemeyer, G.: ccGolog: A logical language dealing with continuous change. Logical Journal of IGPL **11 (2)** (2003) 179–221
3. Herrmann, C., Thielscher, M.: Reasoning about continuous change. In Proc. of AAAI, Portland, U.S.A. (1996) 639–644
4. Lifschitz, V.: Circumscription. The Handbook of Logic in Artificial Intelligence and Logic Programming, Vol.3: Nonmonotonic Reasoning and Uncertain Reasoning, Oxford Science Publications (1994) 297–352
5. McCarthy, J., Hayes, P.: Some philosophical problems from the standpoint of artificial intelligence. Machine Intelligence **4**, Edinburgh University Press (1969) 463–502
6. Miller, R.: A case study in reasoning about action and continuous change. In Proc. ECAI, Budapest, Hungary (1996) 624–628
7. Levesque, H., Reiter, R., Lin, F., Scherl. R.: GOLOG: a logic programming language for dynamic domains, Journal of Logic Programming **31** (1997) 59–84
8. Pinto, J., Reiter, R.: Reasoning about time in the situation calculus. Annals of Mathematics and Artificial Intelligence 14 (1995) 251–268
9. Reiter, R.: Natural actions, concurrency and continuous time in the situation calculus. In Proceedings of the 5th International Conference on Principles of Knowledge Representation and Reasoning. Cambridge, Massachusetts, U.S. (1996) 2–13
10. Sandewall, E.: The range of applicability and non-monotonic logics for the inertia problem. In Proc. International Joint Conference on Artificial Intelligence, France (1993) 738–743
11. Thielscher, M.: The logic of dynamic system. In Proc. International Joint Conference on Artificial Intelligence, Montreal, Canada (1995) 639–644
12. Thielscher, M.: A Concurrent, Continuous Fluent Calculus. Studia Logica **67(3)** (2001) 315–331

Modeling and Refining Directional Relations Based on Fuzzy Mathematical Morphology

Haibin Sun and Wenhui Li

Key Laboratory of Symbol Computation and Knowledge Engineering
of the Ministry of Education, College of Computer Science and Technology,
Jilin University, Changchun 130012, China
Offer_sun@hotmail.com

Abstract. In this paper, we investigate the deficiency of Goyal and Egenhofer's method for modeling cardinal directional relations between simple regions and provide the computational model based on the concept of mathematical morphology, which can be a complement and refinement of Goyal and Egenhofer's model for crisp regions. Based on fuzzy set theory, we extend Goyal and Egenhofer's model to handle fuzziness and provide a computational model based on alpha-morphology, which combines fuzzy set theory and mathematical morphology, to refine the fuzzy cardinal directional relations. Then the computational problems are investigated. We also give an example of spatial configuration in 2-dimensional discrete space. The experiment results confirm the cognitive plausibility of our computational models.

1 Introduction

Goyal and Egenhofer's model [1] represents the cardinal direction relation between simple spatial regions. This model considers the effect of the region's shape on their directional relations, but the reference region is still approximated by the minimum bounding rectangle, which leads to some anomalous instances.

Our work is based on the dilation operation in mathematical morphology, by which a region is dilated by a structuring element (a ray with an angle). We consider the intersection of the dilated reference region with the target region to define the cardinal direction between them. We find that this method is cognitively plausible.

The importance of modeling for vague regions has been realized by more and more researchers. Generally the vagueness is captured by a broad boundary. The vagueness can be classified as uncertainty and fuzziness. In this paper, we will focus on fuzziness. Cicerone and Felice [14] has investigated the cardinal relations between regions with a broad boundary qualitatively. We present the computational model for cardinal direction between fuzzy regions after we introduce the concept of fuzzy set and fuzzy morphology and present the previous works on modeling directions. A fuzzy region can be regarded as a set of α-cut level regions (crisp regions), on which the computational method for cardinal direction relation between crisp regions can be applied.

D. Ślęzak et al. (Eds.): RSFDGrC 2005, LNAI 3641, pp. 601–611, 2005.

This paper could be useful as a basis for discussion on navigation, e.g. storm front or wildfire (fuzzy set) is approaching and individual motorists need an alert telling them which direction to go to avoid the storm. We can combine the direction of the approaching front with road network information to suggest a route.

In this paper, the crisp regions are regular, connected and non-empty closed point sets in the Euclidean space $\Re^2$. Accordingly the fuzzy regions are regular, connected and non-empty closed fuzzy point sets in the Euclidean space $\Re^2$. Schneider [11] has given the definition of fuzzy region based on the framework of fuzzy set theory and fuzzy topology. In the next section, we present Goyal and Egenhofer's model and point out its deficiency. The mathematical morphological model for refining cardinal directional relations between crisp regions is introduced in section 3. Section 4 presents the extended Goyal and Egenhofer's model to handle fuzziness and combines the fuzzy set theory with mathematical morphology to produce the computational model for refining cardinal directional relations between fuzzy regions. An example is given to examine the properties of the models in section 5. Some conclusions are given in the last section.

2   Goyal and Egenhofer's Model

Goyal and Egenhofer [1] introduced a direction-relation model for extended spatial objects that considers the influence of the objects' shapes. It uses the projection-based direction partitions and an extrinsic reference system, and considers the exact representation of the target object with respect to the reference frame. The reference frame with a polygon as reference object has nine direction tiles: North(N_A), NorthEast(NE_A), East(E_A), SouthEast(SE_A), South(S_A), SouthWest(SW_A),West(W_A), NorthWest(NW_A), and Same(O_A). The cardinal direction from the reference object to a target is described by recording those tiles into which at least one part of the target object falls (Fig. 1). From Fig. 1, we can see that B lies to the North(N), NorthEast(NE) and East(E) of A.

At a finer level of granularity, the model of Goyal and Egenhofer [1] also offers the option to record how much of a region falls into each tile. Such re-

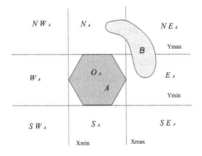

Fig. 1. Capturing the cardinal direction relation between two polygons, A and B, through the projection-based partitions around A as the reference object

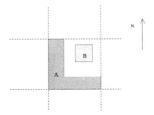

Fig. 2. Illustration for anomalous cardinal direction relation defined by Goyal and Egenhofer's model

lations are called cardinal direction relations with percentages and can be represented with cardinal direction matrices with percentages. Goyal and Egenhofer's model can more precisely describe the cardinal direction relations between regions than the model approximating regions (reference and target regions) by their Minimum Bounding Rectangles (MBRs)(formed by broken lines X_{min}, X_{max}, Y_{min} and Y_{max}, where X_{min}(respectively Y_{min}) is the minimum x-coordinate(respectively y-coordinate), and X_{max}(respectively Y_{max}) is the maximum x-coordinate(respectively y-coordinate) of the region, as shown in Fig. 1). But the model still approximates the reference region with its MBR, which leads to some anomalous instances. Figure 2 is taken as an example for illustration. According to the above model the cardinal direction relation between the target region B and the reference region A is O, i.e., the location of B is the Same as the MBR of A. Obviously we can see that B is North of, East of and NorthEast of A, i.e. B is partially surrounded by A. Namely, the real direction relation between region A and B is not captured by Goyal and Egenhofer's model.

3   Mathematical Morphological Model

Mathematical morphology is a well-known body of methods and theories, which has been proven valuable in many image analysis applications. Recently it has been used to represent spatial relationship knowledge [2,3]. The major part of morphological operations can be defined as a combination of two basic operations, dilation and erosion, and non-morphological operations like difference, sum, maximum or minimum of two sets. The operation of interest in this paper is mainly dilation.

The dilation and erosion of a set X by a structuring element B in a space $\mathcal{S}$ (n-dimensional continuous or discrete space) are described respectively by $D_B(X)$ (or $X \oplus B$) and $E_B(X)$ (or $X \ominus B$) as follows:

$$D_B(X) = \{x \in S | \check{B}_x \cap X \neq \emptyset\} \ , \tag{1}$$

$$E_B(X) = \{x \in \mathcal{S} | B_x \subseteq X\} \ , \tag{2}$$

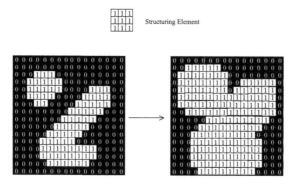

Fig. 3. Illustration of effect of dilation using a 3 × 3 square structuring element

where B_x denotes the translation of B at point x, and $\check{B}_x$ denotes the reflection of B_x about its origin. Dilation, in general, causes objects to dilate or grow in size; erosion causes objects to shrink. To illustrate the dilation operation, we take the greyscale dilation for binary images as an example. Suppose that the structuring element is a 3 × 3 square, with the origin at its center as shown in Fig. 3. Note that in the figure, foreground pixels are represented by 1's and background pixels by 0's. The input image is in the leftmost corner of Fig. 3, and the dilated image in the rightmost corner.

To compute the dilation of a binary input image by this structuring element, we consider each of the background pixels in the input image in turn. For each background pixel (which we will call the input pixel) we superimpose the structuring element on top of the input image so that the origin of the structuring element coincides with the input pixel position. Here, the reflection of B_x about its origin is identical with B_x (i.e. $\check{B}_x = B_x$). If at least one pixel in the structuring element coincides with a foreground pixel in the image underneath, then the input pixel is set to the foreground value. If all the corresponding pixels in the image are background however, the input pixel is left at the background value. The result is shown in Fig. 3.

To define the cardinal directional relations using the dilation operator in mathematical morphology, of particular interest to us is the class of structuring elements that we refer to as "rays". In the continuous case, they are line segments with one end at the origin. Let Θ denote the angle between a ray and the horizontal line. We will refer to these rays as $ray(r, \theta)$ (Fig. 4). In the discrete case, we must use an appropriate digitization of a line segment. If a direction is defined as an angle interval, the structuring element is a sector.

Before we use these rays as structuring elements to define the cardinal directional relationships, we should introduce the concept of Hausdorff Distance (HD) metric first. For two non-empty, closed sets X and Y in space $\mathcal{S}$, let S_r denote a closed (super) sphere (a sphere in 3-dimensional space or a circle in 2-dimentional space) centered at origin and whose radius is r. The Hausdorff Distance between X and Y: $HD(X, Y)$ is defined as follows:

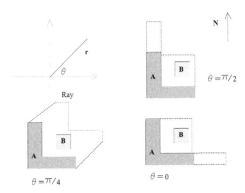

Fig. 4. Example of cardinal direction evaluation through dilation operation by the structuring element ray with different angles (the broken line segments constitute the new boundary part of the region induced by dilation operation)

$$HD(X,Y) = inf\{r|X \subseteq D_{S_r}(Y) \cap Y \subseteq D_{S_r}(X)\} \qquad (3)$$

By considering the degree of intersection of a region A dilated by $ray(r,\theta)(r \geq HD(A,B))$ with another region B, we can derive the degree of the relationship B is in the direction Θ relative to A. The degree of intersection can be defined as

$$Area\left(D_{ray(r,\theta)}(A) \cap B\right)/Area(B) \ . \qquad (4)$$

From Fig. 4, we can see that the region B is completely included in the dilated region A by a ray with $\theta = \pi/2$, i.e. the region B is completely North of A. If we want to know the degree to which region B is East of A, we can dilate A by a ray with $\theta = 0$ and consider their intersection. If we want to know the degree to which region B is rightly NorthEast of region A (assuming we consider the right NorthEast corresponding to $\theta = \pi/4$), we can dilate A by a ray with $\theta = \pi/4$ and consider their intersection (see Fig. 4). Other direction relations of interest can be defined similarly.

Goyal and Egenhofer's model describes a complete partition of the whole space and defines the cardinal direction relationships more precisely than previous models (e.g. model based on MBRs). But it is rough when compared to the morphological method. These relations can be described as a hierarchy. Considering the regular cardinal directional relations, i.e. N, E, S and W, the morphological model can lead to the same results as Goyal and Egenhofer's model. But when the diagonal cardinal directional relations (i.e. NW, NE, SE, SW) are examined, Goyal and Egenhofer's model presents the rough partition and cannot represent detailed information, which can be computed using the morphological model. For example, we can not differentiate between the cardinal directional relations of C relative to A and of B relative to A (see Fig. 5) by Goyal and Egenhofer's model, which are all NE, but we can know that the cardinal directional relation of B relative to A is right NE but it is a little bit NE for C relative to A(i.e. with less degree when compared to B)when the morphological model is used.

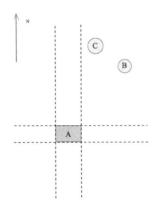

Fig. 5. Example for cardinal directional relations that Goyal and Egenhofer's model regards as identical, but the morphological model can differentiate

4 Modeling Cardinal Directional Relationships Between Fuzzy Regions

So far, spatial data modeling implicitly assumes that the extent and hence the boundary of spatial objects is precisely determined and universally recognized. This leads exclusively to determinate spatial models. Increasingly, researchers are beginning to realize that there are many spatial objects in reality which do not have sharp boundaries or whose boundaries cannot be precisely determined. Erig and Schneider [4] has identified two kinds of vagueness or indeterminacy concerning spatial objects: uncertainty and fuzziness. In this paper, the fuzzy region is based on a finite-valued (multi-valued) logic, i.e. it is associated to an n-valued membership function for representing a wide range of belonging of a point to a fuzzy region, where $n > 3$.

4.1 Fuzzy Set Theory

Fuzzy set theory [5] is an extension and generalization of Boolean set theory. Let X denote the set of objects, called the universe of discourse (it is 2-dimensional space in this paper), and $\widetilde{A}$ denote a fuzzy subset.

The set $\widetilde{A} = \{(x, \mu_{\widetilde{A}}(x)) \,|\, x \in X\}$ is called a fuzzy set in X. From structured point of view, a fuzzy region can be described in terms of nested α-level sets. The α-cut level region of a fuzzy region $\widetilde{A}$ is defined by

$$A_\alpha = \{x \in X | \mu_{\widetilde{A}}(x) \geq \alpha \cap 0 \leq \alpha \leq 1\} \ ,$$

and the strict α-cut level region of a fuzzy region $\widetilde{A}$ is defined by

$$A_\alpha^* = \{x \in X | \mu_{\widetilde{A}}(x) > \alpha \cap 0 \leq \alpha < 1\} \ .$$

Clearly, A_α is a crisp region whose boundary is defined by all points with membership value α. The strict α-cut level region for $\alpha{=}0$ is called the support of $\widetilde{A}$, i.e., $supp(\widetilde{A}) = A_0^*$. The α-cut level regions of a fuzzy region are nested, i.e., for membership values $1 = \alpha_1 > \alpha_2 > \cdots > \alpha_n > \alpha_{n+1} = 0$, one has $A_{\alpha_1} \subseteq A_{\alpha_2} \subseteq \cdots A_{\alpha_n} \subseteq A_{\alpha_{n+1}}$.

α-cuts give a very convenient way for linking fuzzy concepts and crisp concepts. By using α-cuts, all standard operations of fuzzy sets can be derived from their crisp counterparts. Alpha-Morphology can be derived by combining mathematical morphology and fuzzy set theory. Based on the proposed morphological model for cardinal directional relationships between crisp regions and Alpha-Morphology, we can handle the refinement of cardinal directional relationships between fuzzy regions.

4.2   Modeling and Refining Cardinal Directional Relationships Between Fuzzy Regions

In Alpha-Morphology, for two fuzzy sets U and V, the fuzzy dilation of U by fuzzy structuring element V is defined as [6]:

$$(U \oplus V)_\alpha = U_\alpha \oplus V_\alpha \ , \tag{5}$$

where $\oplus$ is the dilation operator. This definition is from the field of image processing. The resulting fuzzy set can be obtained using an aggregation schema (see [6], page 9). Bloch and Maitre [7] presented a formula to compute the result image in a comprehensive way as follows:

$$(U \oplus V)(x) = \sup_{y \in X} \min[U(x - y), V(y)] \ . \tag{6}$$

Koppen et al. [6] proved the two formulae (5) and (6) were equal for image processing, i.e. when applied, they can produce the same result(see [6],page 10). Gader [8] defined fuzzy spatial direction relations between two crisp images based on fuzzy morphology, and the experiments showed that this fuzzy morphology method was more cognitively correct than previous methods(for details, see [8]). Based on these results, we extend the computational model in [8] to handle our case, i.e. cardinal directional relations between fuzzy regions.

For simplicity, we consider the structuring elements to be crisp ones, i.e. $ray(r, \theta)(\theta=0, \pi/4, \pi/2, 3\pi/4, \pi, -3\pi/4, -\pi/2$ and $-\pi/4$, corresponding to East, NorthEast, North, NorthWest, West, SouthWest, South and SouthEast, respectively). For a fuzzy region A and a crisp structuring element B, the formula (5) can be modified as:

$$(A \oplus B)_\alpha = A_\alpha \oplus B \ . \tag{7}$$

To allow for the computation of the area of a fuzzy region, we adopt the definition in [9], where the area of a fuzzy region F is defined as the scalar cardinality of F, i.e.,

$$Area(F) = \sum_{x \in X} \mu_F(x) \ . \tag{8}$$

To aggregate the α-cut level regions and use the aggregated measurements to determine binary cardinal directional relations between two fuzzy regions, we adopt the concept of basic probability assignment in [15], which has also been applied in [10] to handle fuzzy regions in images and in [13] to calculate the topological relations between fuzzy regions. A basic probability assignment $m(A_{\alpha_i})$ can be attached to each α-cut level region A_{α_i}. $m(A_{\alpha_i})$ can be interpreted as the probability that A_{α_i} is the "true" representative of A. The value of $m(A_{\alpha_i})$ is defined as follows:

$$m(A_{\alpha_i}) = \alpha_i - \alpha_{i+1} \ , \tag{9}$$

which satisfies $\sum m(A_{\alpha_i}) = \alpha_1 - \alpha_{n+1} = 1 - 0 = 1$.

Then, the degree to which fuzzy region $\widetilde{B}$ is located in the direction θ relative to fuzzy region $\widetilde{A}$ can be defined as follows:

$$\mu_\theta\left(\widetilde{A}, \widetilde{B}\right) = \left(\sum_{i=1}^{n} m(A_{\alpha_i})\left(\frac{Area((A_{\alpha_i} \oplus ray(r, \theta)) \cap B)}{Area(B)}\right)^p\right)^{1/p} , \tag{10}$$

where i enumerates all the levels $\alpha \in [0, 1]$ that represent distinct α-cuts of a given fuzzy set $\widetilde{A}$, $\mu_\theta\left(\widetilde{A}, \widetilde{B}\right)$ is the generalized mean value and p is used to suit the required degree of optimism or pessimism (in this paper, we set $p=1$), and $\alpha_i > 0$.

Our method is based on operations on regions instead of points. It is applicable to regions both in continuous space and discrete space, and the computational cost is cheap while the fuzziness of both the reference region and target region is considered. Moreover if A and B are crisp regions and $p=1$, the formula is the same as the formula (4), so our model provides a unified framework for modelling cardinal directional relations between regions. When the structuring element $ray(r, \theta)$ is fuzzy like in [8], we can apply formula (6) to the item $A_{\alpha_i} \oplus ray(r, \theta)$ and the intersection operation in formula (10) becomes a fuzzy one, which has been discussed in fuzzy set theory.

To enable Goyal and Egenhofer's model to handle fuzziness, we can easily define the following formula similar to [13] to compute the degree to which $\widetilde{B}$ is in the direction C relative to $\widetilde{A}$:

$$\mu_C\left(\widetilde{A}, \widetilde{B}\right) = \sum_{i=1}^{n} m(A_{\alpha_i})\mu_C(A_{\alpha_i}, B) , \tag{11}$$

where $\mu_C(A_{\alpha_i}, B)$ denotes the percentage of cardinal directional relation C between B and A_{α_i} computed by Goyal and Egenhofer's model, and the area of B is computed using formula (8), and i enumerates all the levels $\alpha \in [0, 1]$ that represent distinct α-cuts of a given fuzzy set $\widetilde{A}$, and $\alpha_i > 0$.

4.3   Computational Problems

In this paper, we regard the reference point set as a region, because the point set is conceptually unitary. This kind of point set can be represented by its convex hull. Formally, the convex hull is the smallest convex set containing the points; Informally, it is a rubber band wrapped around the "outside" points. For a point set X, we use $CH(X)$ to denote its convex hull. The algorithm for computing $CH(X)$ has been well studied in computational geometry, and many fast algorithms have been put forward (for example in [12]). In this paper considering directional relations between two regions, the convex hull of the reference region can give the same result as the reference region, so we replace the reference region with its convex hull, which can simplify the computation. Then the formula (10) can be reformulated as

$$\mu_\theta \left(\widetilde{A}, \widetilde{B} \right) = \left(\sum_{i=1}^{n} m(A_{\alpha_i}) \left(\frac{Area\left((CH(A_{\alpha_i}) \oplus ray(r, \theta)) \cap B\right)}{Area(B)} \right)^p \right)^{1/p} . \quad (12)$$

To this end, we just need to compute the dilation of the convex hull of the reference region, which leads to a convex region. When the convex region is dilated by a ray, the resulting region is still a convex region whose boundary is the convex hull of the new vertexes resulting from the translating of the original vertexes along the ray plus the original vertexes. So we just need to compute the new vertexes and combine them with the original vertexes to form the resulting region. Obviously the new vertexes are computed from the original vertexes and some may become the inner point of the new region while others form the new vertexes of the new region. An original vertex that leads to inner points when translating along the ray can be decided by checking if the ray going through it intersects with the original region at any other point. So the computation can be further simplified by only considering part of the original vertexes.

We then consider the intersection between two regions, i.e., the intersection between the dilated reference region and the target region (point set). When the target region is based on vector model, the intersection of these two regions can be seen as the intersection of two polygons, which has been investigated widely in computational geometry. When the target region is based on raster model (e.g., in our experiment), we only need to consider the points that fall into the dilated reference region, which is also a well-studied computational geometry problem.

5   Simulation Experiment

To examine the properties of the presented computational model of cardinal directional relations between fuzzy regions, we give an example of spatial configuration in 2-dimensional discrete space (see Fig. 6), which can be a special case of 2-dimensional Euclidean space. In this kind of space, a non-trivial boundary of a point set S is a directed line l_α with the direction α such that at least two points lie in l_α and all other points of S lie in the right half-plane of l_α. A region can be defined by the convex closure, which is formed by a set of non-trivial boundaries. There are three discretized regions A, B and C, which are fuzzy point sets composed of many points labeled with the degree to which they belong to regions A, B and C, respectively. The points that have no labels definitely belong to their regions.

In this example, we use $p=1$. The cardinal direction relations RNE, RSE, RSW and RNW denote right NorthEast, right SouthEast, right SouthWest and right NorthWest, respectively. We postulate they correspond to $\theta =$

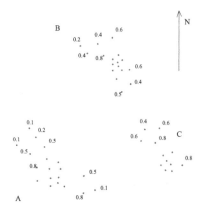

Fig. 6. An example for evaluating our computational model

$\pi/4, -\pi/4, -3\pi/4$ and $3\pi/4$. We first use formula (11) to compute the eight cardinal directional relations, and then use formula (12) to refine the results considering RNE, RSE, RSW and RNW. The results of computing the cardinal directional relations between regions A, B and C are listed in table 1. As expected, the results computed using our model are optimistic and conform to human perception and the mathematical model can refine the direction relation to a finer level. For example, the degree to which the fuzzy region C is located SouthEast relative to the fuzzy region B is 1, which means that region C is definitely SouthEast of region B regardless of their fuzziness, and the degree to which the fuzzy region C is located rightly SouthEast of the fuzzy region B is 0.19, which means that the possibility of region C being right SouthEast of B is small. It can also be seen that our model measures the cardinal directional relationships quantitatively by taking into account of the fuzziness of regions.

Table 1. Computation results using our model for Fig. 6

$\mu_\theta(X,Y)$ θ	N	NE/RNE	E	SE/RSE	S	SW/RSW	W	NW/RNW
$\mu_\theta(A,B)$	0.22	0.98/0.40	0	0	0	0	0	0
$\mu_\theta(A,C)$	0	0.30/0	0.70	0	0	0	0	0
$\mu_\theta(B,A)$	0	0	0	0	0.02	0.98/0.48	0	0
$\mu_\theta(B,C)$	0	0	0	1/0.19	0	0	0	0
$\mu_\theta(C,B)$	0	0	0	0	0	0	0	1/0.18
$\mu_\theta(C,A)$	0	0	0	0	0	0.54/0	0.43	0.03/0

6   Conclusions

Computational models for computing and refining cardinal directional relation between fuzzy regions have been put forward and their usefulness is shown by the results in the experiment. We show that the two models are also compatible with the crisp ones. The morphological model can be a refinement of the conventional model to distinguish more detailed information and avoid some anomalies. The two models are very useful in modeling knowledge in GIS, content-based image retrieval system and computer vision, etc. More experiments will be carried out to evaluate our computational models. The application of this technique to one of these systems is the future research.

References

1. R. Goyal and M. Egenhofer: Similarity of Direction Relations. In: C. Jensen et al.(Eds): Seventh International Symposium on Spatial and Temporal Databases, Los Angeles, CA , July 2001, LNCS 2121, (2001)36-55
2. I. Bloch: Fuzzy Spatial Relationships from Mathematical Morphology for Model-based Pattern Recognition and Spatial Reasoning. In: I.Nystrom et al.(Eds): DGCI 2003, LNCS 2886, (2003)16-33
3. I. Bloch: Unifying Quantitative, Semi-quantitative and Qualitative Spatial Relation knowledge Representation Using Mathematical Morphology. In: T.Asano et al.(Eds): Geometry, Morphology, and Computational Imaging, 11th International Workshop on Theoretical Foundations of Computer Vision Dagstuhl Castle, Germany, April 7-12, 2002, LNCS, 2616, (2003)153-164
4. M. Erig and M. Schneider: Vague Regions. In: 5th Int. Symp. On Advances in Spatial Databases (SSD'97), LNCS 1262, (1997)298-320
5. L.A. Zadeh: Fuzzy Sets. Information and Control, (1965)8: 338-353
6. M. Koppen, K. Franke and O. Unold: A Tutorial on Fuzzy Morphology. http:// visionic.fhg.de/ipk/publikationen/pdf/fmorph.pdf
7. I. Bloch and H. Maitre: Fuzzy Mathematical Morphologies: A Comparative Study. Pattern Recognition, (1995)28(9): 1341-1387
8. P.D. Gader: Fuzzy Spatial Relations Based on Fuzzy Morphology. In: FUZZ-IEEE 1997 (IEEE Int. Conf. on Fuzzy Systems), Barcelona, Spain, (1997) 2: 1179-1183
9. A. Rosenfeld: Fuzzy geometry: An overview. In: Proceedings of First IEEE Conference in Fuzzy Systems (San Diego), March, (1992)113-118
10. D. Dubois and M.C. Jaulent: A general approach to parameter evaluation in fuzzy digital pictures. Pattern Recognition Lett, 6, (1987)251-259
11. M. Schneider: Uncertainty Management for Spatial Data in Databases: Fuzzy Spatial Data Types. In: R.H.Guting, et al. (Eds.): SSD'99, LNCS 1651, (1999)330-351
12. R.L. Graham: An Efficient Algorithm for determining the Convex Hull of a Finite Planar Set. Information Processing Letters, vol. 1 (1972) 73-82
13. F.B. Zhan: Approximate analysis of binary topological relations between geographic regions with indeterminate boundaries. Soft Computing 2, Springer-Verlag (1998) 28-34
14. S. Cicerone and P. Di Felice: Cardinal Relations Between Regions with a Broad Boundary. 8th ACM Symposium on GIS, (2000) 15-20
15. G. Shafer: A Mathematical Theory of Evidence. Princeton University Press. 1976.

A Clustering Method for Spatio-temporal Data and Its Application to Soccer Game Records

Shoji Hirano and Shusaku Tsumoto

Department of Medical Informatics, Shimane University, School of Medicine,
89-1 Enya-cho, Izumo, Shimane 693-8501, Japan
hirano@ieee.org, tsumoto@computer.org

Abstract. This paper presents a novel method for finding interesting patterns from spatio-temporal data. First, we perform a pairwise comparison of spatio-temporal sequences using the multiscale matching, taking into account the requirements for multiscale observation. Next, we construct the clusters of sequences using rough-set based clustering technique. Experimental results on real soccer game records demonstrated that the method could discover some interesting pass patterns that may be associated with successful goals.

1 Introduction

Clustering of spatio-temporal data provides a new, data-oriented way of discovering interesting knowledge about the movement of targets. It has been receiving much attention in various fields such as crime research, meteorology and sports data analysis, as a tool for revealing common behavioral characteristics of the targets. For example, in soccer game, by clustering spatio-temporal data about the pass sequence, one may obtain interesting knowledge about the strategy of a team like 'frequent use of right-side attack'.

This paper presents a novel method for visualizing interesting patterns hidden in the spatio-temporal data. As a tangible data we employ soccer game records, as they involve the most important problems in spatio-temporal data mining – the temporal irregularity of data points. Especially, we focus on discovering the features of pass transactions, which resulted in successful goals, and representing the difference of strategies of a team by the pass strategies.

There are two points that should be technically solved. First, the length of a sequence, number of data points constituting a sequence, and intervals between data points in a sequence are all irregular. A pass sequence is formed by concatenating contiguous pass events; since the distance of each pass, the number of players translating the contiguous passes are by nature difference, the data should be treated as irregular sampled time-series data. Second, multiscale observation and comparison of pass sequences are required. This is because a pass sequence represents both global and local strategies of a team. For example, as a global strategy, a team may frequently use side-attacks than counter-attacks. As a local strategy, the team may frequently use one-two pass. Both levels of

D. Ślęzak et al. (Eds.): RSFDGrC 2005, LNAI 3641, pp. 612–621, 2005.

strategies can be found even in one pass sequence; one can naturally recognize it from the fact that a video camera does zoom-up and zoom-out of a game scene. In order to solve these problems, we employed multiscale matching [1], [2], a pattern recognition based contour comparison method. And we employed rough clustering [3], which are suitable of handing relative dissimilarity produced by multiscale matching.

The rest of this paper is organized as follows. Section 2 describes the data structure and preprocessing. Section 3 describes multiscale matching. Section 4 describes rough clustering. Section 5 shows experimental results on the FIFA world cup 2002 data and Section 6 concludes the results.

2   Data Structure and Preprocessing

2.1   Data Structure

We used the high-quality, value-added commercial game records of soccer games provided by Data Stadium Inc., Japan. The current states of pattern recognition technique may enable us to automatically recognize the positions of ball and players [4], [5], [6], however, we did not use automatic scene analysis techniques because it is still hard to correctly recognize each action of the players.

The data consisted of the records of all 64 games of the FIFA world cup 2002, including both heats and finals, held during May-June, 2002. For each action in a game, the following information was recorded: time, location, names(number) of the player, the type of event (pass, trap, shoot etc.), etc. All the information was generated from the real-time manual interpretation of video images by a well-trained soccer player, and manually stored in the database. Table 1 shows an example of the data. In Table 1, 'Ser' denotes the series number, where a series

Table 1. An example of the soccer data record

Ser	Time	Action	T_1	P_1	T_2	P_2	X_1	Y_1	X_2	Y_2
1	20:28:12	KICK OFF	Senegal	10			0	-33		
1	20:28:12	PASS	Senegal	10	Senegal	19	0	-50	-175	50
1	20:28:12	TRAP	Senegal	19			-175	50		
1	20:28:12	PASS	Senegal	19	Senegal	14	-122	117	3004	451
1	20:28:14	TRAP	Senegal	14			3004	451		
⋮				⋮						
169	22:18:42	P END	France	15			1440	-685		

denotes a set of contiguous events marked manually by expert. The remaining fields respectively represent the time of event occurrence ('Time'), the type of event ('Action'), the team ID ('T_1') and player ID ('P_1') of one acting player 1, the team ID ('T_2') and player ID ('P_2') of another acting player 2, spatial

position of player 1 (’X_1’, ’Y_1’), and spatial position of player 2 (’X_1’, ’Y_1’),
Player 1 represents the player who mainly performed the action. As for pass
action, player 1 represents the sender of a pass, and player 2 represents the
receiver of the pass. Axis X corresponds to the long side of the soccer field, and
axis Y corresponds to the short side. The origin is the center of the soccer field.
For example, the second line in Table 1 can be interpreted as: Player no. 10 of
Senegal, locating at (0,-50), sent a pass to Player 19, locating at (-175,50).

2.2   Target Series Selection

We selected the series that contains important PASS actions that resulted in
goals as follows.

1. Select a series containing an IN GOAL action.
2. Select a contiguous PASS event. In order not to divide the sequence into
   too many subsequences, we regarded some other events as contiguous events
   to the PASS event; for example, TRAP, DRIBBLE, CENTERING, CLEAR,
   BLOCK. Intercept is represented as a PASS event in which the sender's team
   and receiver's team are different. However, we included an intercept into the
   contiguous PASS events for simplicity.
3. From the Selected contiguous PASS event, we extract the locations of Player
   1, X_1 and Y_1, and make a time series of locations $p(t) = \{(X_1(t), Y_1(t))|1 \leq t \leq T\}$ by concatenating them. For simplicity, we denote $X_1(t)$ and $Y_1(t)$ by
   x(t) and y(t) respectively.

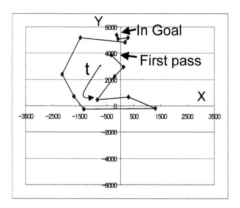

Fig. 1. Spatial representation of a PASS sequences

Figure 1 shows an example of spatial representation of a PASS sequence
generated by the above process. Table 2 provides an additional information, the
raw data that correspond to Figure 1. In Figure 1 the vertical line represents the
axis connecting the goals of both teams. Near the upper end (+5500) is the goal

of France, and near the lower end is the goal of Senegal. This example PASS sequence represents the following scene: Player no. 16 of France, locating at (-333,3877), send a pass to player 18. Senegal cuts the pass at near the center of the field, and started attack from the left side. Finally, Player no. 11 of Senegal made a CENTERING, and after several block actions of France, Player no. 19 of Senegal made a goal.

Table 2. Raw data corresponding the sequence in Figure 1

Ser	Time	Action	T_1	P_1	T_2	P_2	X_1	Y_1	X_2	Y_2
47	20:57:07	PASS	France	16	France	18	-333	3877	122	-2958
47	20:57:08	PASS	France	18	France	17	122	2958	-210	-2223
47	20:57:10	DRIBBLE	France	17			-210	2223	-843	-434
47	20:57:14	PASS	France	17	France	4	-843	434	298	-685
47	20:57:16	PASS	France	4	France	6	298	685	1300	217
47	20:57:17	TRAP	France	6			1300	217		
47	20:57:19	CUT	Senegal	6			-1352	-267		
47	20:57:19	TRAP	Senegal	6			-1352	-267		
47	20:57:20	PASS	Senegal	6	Senegal	11	-1704	702	-2143	2390
47	20:57:21	DRIBBLE	Senegal	11			-2143	2390	-1475	5164
47	20:57:26	CENTERING	Senegal	11			-1475	5164		
47	20:57:27	CLEAR	France	17			175	4830		
47	20:57:27	BLOCK	France	16			281	5181		
47	20:57:27	CLEAR	France	16			281	5181		
47	20:57:28	SHOT	Senegal	19			-87	5081		
47	20:57:28	IN GOAL	Senegal	19			-140	5365		

By applying the above preprocess to all the IN GOAL series, we obtained N sequences of passes $P = \{p_i | 1 \leq i \leq N\}$ that correspond to N goals, where i of p_i denote the i-th goal.

2.3   Data Cleansing and Interpretation

Continuous actions occurred at the same location should be considered as a single action. For example, in Table 2, the 7th and 8th actions consisting of CUT and TRAP should be treated as a single action, because their interaction does not actually involve any movement of a ball on the field. The 13rd and 14th actions consisting of BLOCK and CLEAR should be similarly treated as a single action. In such a case, we employed only the first action and removed other redundant actions.

We here do not use the time information provided in the data for each action, because the time resolution is insufficient for calculating the moving speed of a ball. Instead, with a fixed interval we performed re-sampling of a trajectory of ball between two successive actions. In this experiment we linearly interpolated the location data at every 55 locational unit (Field length / 200).

3   Multiscale Comparison of Pass Sequences

For every pair of PASS sequences $\{(p_i, p_j) \in P | 1 \leq i < N, i < j \leq N\}$, we apply multiscale matching to compare their dissimilarity. Based on the resultant dissimilarity matrix, we perform grouping of the sequences using rough clustering [3].

Multiscale Matching is a method to compare two planar curves by partly changing observation scales. We here briefly explain the basic of multiscale matching. Details of matching procedure are available in [2].

Let us denote two input sequences to be compared, p_i and p_j, by A and B. First, let us consider a sequence $x(t)$ containing X_1 values of A. Multiscale representation of $x(t)$ at scale σ, $X(t, \sigma)$ can be obtained as a convolution of $x(t)$ and a Gaussian function with scale factor σ as follows.

$$X(t, \sigma) = \int_{-\infty}^{+\infty} x(u) \frac{1}{\sigma\sqrt{2\pi}} e^{-(t-u)^2/2\sigma^2} du \tag{1}$$

where the gauss function represents the distribution of weights for adding the neighbors. It is obvious that a small σ means high weights for close neighbors, while a large σ means rather flat weights for both close and far neighbors. A sequence will become more flat as σ increases, namely, the number of inflection points decreases. Multiscale representation of $y(t)$, $Y(t, \sigma)$ is obtained similarly. The m-th order derivative of $X(t, \sigma)$, $X^{(m)}(t, \sigma)$, is derived as follows.

$$X^{(m)}(t, \sigma) = \frac{\partial^m X(t, \sigma)}{\partial t^m} = x(t) \otimes g^{(m)}(t, \sigma). \tag{2}$$

According to the Lindeberg's notions [7], it is preferable to use the modified Bessel function instead of Gaussian function as a convolution kernel for discrete signals. Below we formalize the necessary functions:

$$X(t, \sigma) = \sum_{n=-\infty}^{\infty} e^{-\sigma} I_n(\sigma) x(t - n) \tag{3}$$

where $I_n(\sigma)$ denotes the modified Bessel function of n-th order. The first- and second-order derivatives of $X(t, \sigma)$ are given as follows.

$$X'(t, \sigma) = \sum_{n=-\infty}^{\infty} -\frac{n}{\sigma} e^{-\sigma} I_n(\sigma) x(t - n) \tag{4}$$

$$X''(t, \sigma) = \sum_{n=-\infty}^{\infty} \frac{1}{\sigma} (\frac{n^2}{\sigma} - 1) e^{-\sigma} I_n(\sigma) x(t - n) \tag{5}$$

The curvature of point t at scale σ is obtained as follows.

$$K(t, \sigma) = \frac{X'Y'' - X''Y'}{(X'^2 + Y'^2)^{3/2}}, \tag{6}$$

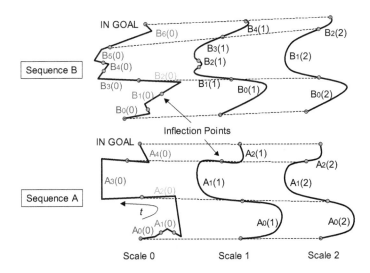

Fig. 2. An illustrative example of multiscale description and matching

where X', X'', Y' and Y'' denote the first- and second-order derivatives of $X(t, \sigma)$ and $Y(t, \sigma)$ by t, respectively.

Next, we divide the sequence $K(t, \sigma)$ into a set of convex/concave subsequences called segments based on the place of inflection points. A segment is a subsequence whose ends correspond to the two adjacent inflection points, and can be regarded as a unit representing substructure of a sequence.

Let us assume that a pass sequence $A^{(k)}$ at scale k is composed of R segments. Then $A^{(k)}$ is represented by

$$A^{(k)} = \left\{ a_i^{(k)} \mid i = 1, 2, \cdots, R^{(k)} \right\}, \tag{7}$$

where $a_i^{(k)}$ denotes the i-th segment of $A^{(k)}$ at scale $\sigma^{(k)}$. By applying the same process to another input sequence B, we obtain the segment-based representation of B as follows.

$$B^{(h)} = \left\{ b_j^{(h)} \mid j = 1, 2, \cdots, S^{(h)} \right\} \tag{8}$$

where $\sigma^{(h)}$ denote the observation scale of B and $S^{(h)}$ denote the number of segments at scale $\sigma^{(h)}$.

After that, we trace the hierarchy of inflection points from the top scale to bottom scale based on the proximity of inflection points. This trace is important to capture the hierarchy of segment replacement and to guarantee the connectivity of segments represented at at different scales.

The main procedure of multiscale matching is to find the best set of segment pairs that minimizes the total segment difference. The search is performed throughout all the scales. Figure 2 illustrates the process. For example, three contiguous segments $B_3^{(0)}$, $B_4^{(0)}$ and $B_5^{(0)}$ of sequence B at scale 0 have no similar segments of sequence A at scale 0. However, at a global scale, they can be represented (merged) as a single segment $B_1^{(2)}$ at scale 2, whose shape is similar to $A_1^{(1)}$ or $A_1^{(2)}$ of sequence A at scales 1 or 2. As their origin is $A_3^{(0)}$, we can conclude that the set of segments $B_3^{(0)}$, $B_4^{(0)}$ and $B_5^{(0)}$ are structurally similar to segment $A_3^{(0)}$. On the contrary, segments such as $B_0^{(0)}$ and $B_1^{(0)}$ have locally similar segments $A_0^{(0)}$ and $A_1^{(0)}$ respectively. In this way, we can compare the structural similarity of sequences by changing the observation scales.

There are two restrictions in determining the best set of the segments. First, the resultant set of the matched segment pairs must not be redundant or insufficient to represent the original sequences. Namely, by concatenating all the segments in the set, the original sequence must be completely reconstructed without any partial intervals or overlaps.

Second, the segment dissimilarities accumulated over all matched pairs must be minimized. Dissimilarity $d(a_i^{(k)}, b_j^{(h)})$ of two segments $a_i^{(k)}$ and $b_i^{(h)}$ is defined as follows.

$$d(a_i^{(k)}, b_j^{(h)}) = \frac{\mid \theta_{a_i}^{(k)} - \theta_{b_j}^{(h)} \mid}{\theta_{a_i}^{(k)} + \theta_{b_j}^{(h)}} \left| \frac{l_{a_i}^{(k)}}{L_A^{(k)}} - \frac{l_{b_j}^{(h)}}{L_B^{(h)}} \right| \tag{9}$$

where $\theta_{a_i}^{(k)}$ and $\theta_{b_j}^{(h)}$ denote rotation angles of tangent vectors along segments $a_i^{(k)}$ and $b_j^{(h)}$, $l_{a_i}^{(k)}$ and $l_{b_j}^{(h)}$ denote the length of segments, $L_A^{(k)}$ and $L_B^{(h)}$ denote the total length of sequences A and B at scales $\sigma^{(k)}$ and $\sigma^{(h)}$, respectively.

The total difference between sequences A and B is defied as a sum of the dissimilarities of all the matched segment pairs as

$$D(A, B) = \sum_{p=1}^{P} d(a_p^{(0)}, b_p^{(0)}), \tag{10}$$

where P denotes the number of matched segment pairs. The matching process can be fasten by implementing dynamic programming scheme [2].

4   Grouping of Sequences by Rough Clustering

One of the important issues in multiscale matching is treatment of 'no-match' sequences. Theoretically, any pairs of sequences can be matched because a sequence will become single segment at enough high scales. However, this is not a realistic approach because the use of many scales results in the unacceptable increase of computational time. If the upper bound of the scales is too low, the method may possibly fail to find the appropriate pairs of subsequences. For example, suppose we have two sequences, one is a short sequence containing only one segment and another is a long sequence containing hundreds of segments. The segments of the latter sequence will not be integrated into one segment until the scale becomes considerably high. If the range of scales we use does not cover such a high scale, the two sequences will never be matched. In this case, the method should return infinite dissimilarity, or a special number that identifies the failed matching. This property prevents conventional agglomerative hierarchical clusterings (AHCs) [8] from working correctly. Complete-linkage (CL-) AHC will never merge two clusters if any pair of 'no-match' sequences exist between them. Average-linkage (AL-) AHC fails to calculate average dissimilarity between two clusters.

In order to handle the 'no-match' problem, we employed rough clustering [3], that can handle relatively defined dissimilarity. This method is based on iterative refinement of N binary classifications, where N denotes the number of objects. First, an equivalence relation, that classifies all the other objects into two classes, is assigned to each of N objects by referring to the relative proximity. Next, for each pair of objects, the number of binary classifications in which the pair is included in the same class is counted. This number is termed the indiscernibility degree. If the indiscernibility degree of a pair is larger than a user-defined threshold value, the equivalence relations may be modified so that all of the equivalence relations commonly classify the pair into the same class. This process is repeated until class assignment becomes stable. Consequently, we may obtain the clustering result that follows a given level of granularity, without using geometric measures.

5   Experimental Results

We applied the proposed method to the action records of 64 games in the FIFA world cup 2002 described in Section 2. First let us summarize the procedure of experiments.

1. Select all IN GOAL series from original data.
2. For each IN GOAL series, generate a time-series sequence containing contiguous PASS events. In our data, there was in total 168 IN GOAL series excluding own goals. Therefore, we had 168 time-series sequences, each of which contains the sequence of spatial positions $(x(t), y(t))$.
3. For each pair of the 168 sequences, compute dissimilarity of the sequence pair by multiscale matching. Then construct a 168×168 dissimilarity matrix.
4. Perform cluster analysis using the induced dissimilarity matrix and rough clustering method.

The following parameters were used in multiscale matching: the number of scales $= 100$, scale interval $= 0.5$, start scale $= 0.5$, cost weight for segment replacement $= 20.0$. We used the following parameters for rough clustering: $\sigma = 2.0, T_h = 0.3$. These parameters were determined through preparatory experiments.

Out of 14,196 comparisons, 7,839 (55.2%) resulted in 'matching failure' for which we assigned a special value of '-1' as their dissimilarity. For this highly disturbed dissimilarity matrix, rough clustering produced a total of 12 clusters, each of which contains 4, 87, 27, 17, ... sequences respectively. Figures 3 - 6 respectively show examples of sequences grouped into the four major clusters: cluster 2 (87 cases), 3 (24 cases), 4 (17 cases), 6 (16 cases). Cluster 2 contained remarkably short sequences. They represented special events such as free kicks,

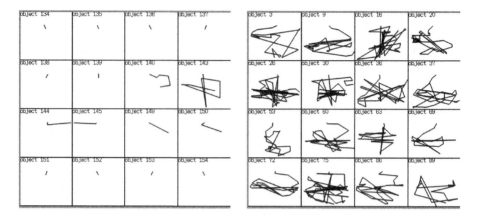

Fig. 3. Sequences in cluster 2 (87 cases).   **Fig. 4.** Sequences in cluster 3 (24 cases).

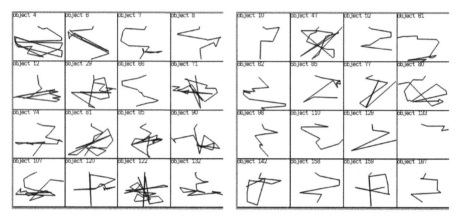

Fig. 5. Sequences in cluster 4 (17 cases).   **Fig. 6.** Sequences in cluster 6 (16 cases).

penalty kicks and corner kicks, that made goals after one or a few touches. On the contrary, cluster 3 contained complex sequences, each of which contained many segments and often included loops. These sequences represented that the goals were succeeded after long, many steps of pass actions, including some changes of the ball-owner team. Clusters 4 and 6 contained rather simple sequences, most of which contained only several segments. These sequences represented that the goals were obtained after interaction of a few players. These observations demonstrate that the sequences were clustered according to the structural complexity of the pass routes.

6   Conclusions

In this paper, we have presented a new method for cluster analysis of spatio-temporal data with an application to finding interesting pass patterns from time-series soccer game records. Taking two characteristics of the pass sequence – irregularity of data and requirements of multiscale observation – into account, we developed a cluster analysis method based on multiscale matching and rough clustering, which may build a new scheme of sports data mining. Although the experiments are in the preliminary stage and subject to further quantitative evaluation, the proposed method demonstrated its potential for finding interesting patterns in real soccer data. The future work will include the use of ball speed, use of other feature points than inflection points, and optimization of segment difference parameters.

Acknowledgments

The authors would like to express their sincere appreciation to Data Stadium Inc. for providing the valuable dataset. This research was supported in part by the Ministry of Education, Science, Sports and Culture, Grant-in-Aid for Young Scientists (B), #16700144, 2004.

References

1. Mokhtarian, F., Mackworth, A.K.: Scale-based Description and Recognition of planar Curves and Two Dimensional Shapes. IEEE Transactions on Pattern Analysis and Machine Intelligence, PAMI-8(1) (1986) 24-43
2. Ueda, N., Suzuki, S.: A Matching Algorithm of Deformed Planar Curves Using Multiscale Convex/Concave Structures. IEICE Transactions on Information and Systems, J73-D-II(7) (1990) 992-1000
3. Hirano, S., Tsumoto, S.: An Indiscernibility-Based Clustering Method with Iterative Refinement of Equivalence Relations - Rough Clustering. Journal of Advanced Computational Intelligence and Intelligent Informatics, 7(2) (2003) 169-177
4. Yamada, A., Shirai, Y., Miura, J.: Tracking Players and a Ball in Video Image Sequence and Estimating Camera Parameters for 3D Interpretation of Soccer Games. In: Proc. the 16th International Conference on Pattern Recognition (2002) 1, 303-306
5. Gong, Y., Sin, L.T., Chuan, C.H., Zhang, H., Sakauchi, M.: Automatic Parsing of TV Soccer Programs. Proceedings of the International Conference on Multimedia Computing and Systems (1995) 167-174
6. Taki, T., Hasegawa, J.: Visualization of Dominant Region in Team Games and Its Application to Teamwork Analysis. Computer Graphics International (2000) 227-238
7. Lindeberg, T.: Scale-Space for Discrete Signals. Transactions on Pattern Analysis and Machine Intelligence, PAMI-12(3) (1990) 234-254
8. Everitt, B.S., Landau, S., Leese, M.: Cluster Analysis Fourth Edition. Arnold Publishers (2001)

Hierarchical Information Maps

Andrzej Skowron[1] and Piotr Synak[2]

[1] Institute of Mathematics, Warsaw University,
Banacha 2, 02-097 Warsaw, Poland
[2] Polish-Japanese Institute of Information Technology,
Koszykowa 86, 02-008 Warsaw, Poland

Abstract. We discuss the problems of spatio-temporal reasoning in the context of hierarchical information maps and approximate reasoning networks (AR networks). Hierarchical information maps are used for representation of domain knowledge about objects, their parts, and their dynamical changes. They are constructed out of information maps connected by some spatial relations. Each map describes changes (e.g., in time) of states corresponding to some parts of complex objects. We discuss the details of defining relations between levels of hierarchical information maps as well as between parts satisfying some additional constraints, e.g. spatial ones.

1 Introduction

One of the forms of data representation is an information system, where each investigated object is described by means of some attributes (features). Once some reflexive binary relation on a set of objects is given (e.g., a neighbourhood relation), one can consider new information systems with more complex objects that are clusters (clumps) of objects determined by this relation. In this case, the attributes reflect some more general properties of objects, i.e., properties of sets of objects. This approach is typical for time series analysis, where attributes (features) are defined on the basis of relevant windows [10]. The chosen neighbourhoods and their properties should make it possible to induce the high quality approximations of a given concept. Observe that there are two problems in this approach: discovery of relevant neighbourhoods of objects and their properties. These are key problems of spatio-temporal data mining [3].[1]

In this paper, we extend this approach to the case of information maps and hierarchical information maps, where unstructured objects are substituted by more complex information granules corresponding to structured objects evolving in time. The paper is a continuation of [15,16,7].

We emphasise that in the case of modelling of structured objects the information granulation, in passing from a lower level of a hierarchy (defined by the structure of an object) to a higher one, may be performed, e.g., by indiscernibility or similarity relation. Hierarchical information maps make it possible to model information granules relevant for the target tasks by taking into account the functionality that the information granules should possess.

---

[1] See [11] for recent issues on modelling of spatio-temporal data.

D. Ślęzak et al. (Eds.): RSFDGrC 2005, LNAI 3641, pp. 622–631, 2005.

2   Preliminaries

In the paper, we use the notation of rough set theory [6,4]. In particular, by $\mathbb{A} = (U, A)$ we denote an *information system* with the universe U of *objects* and the attribute set A. Each *attribute* $a \in A$ is a function $a : U \to V_a$, where V_a is the *value set* of a. For a given set of attributes $B \subseteq A$, we define the *indiscernibility relation* $IND(B)$ on the universe U that partitions U into classes of indiscernible objects. We say that objects x and y are *indiscernible* with respect to B if and only if $a(x) = a(y)$ for each $a \in B$.

Decision tables are denoted by $\mathbb{A} = (U, A, d)$, where $d \notin A$ is the *decision* attribute. The decision attribute d defines partition of the universe U into *decision classes*. An object x is *inconsistent* if there exists an object y such that $xIND(A)y$, but x and y belong to different decision classes, i.e., $d(x) \neq d(y)$. The *positive region* of a decision table $\mathbb{A}$ (denoted by $POS(\mathbb{A})$) is the set of all consistent objects.

Any pair $(\mathbb{A}, \mathbb{R})$, where $\mathbb{A} = (U, A, d)$ is a decision table and $\mathbb{R}$ is a set of binary and reflexive relations over $U \times U$, is called a *relational decision table*. For any $R \in \mathbb{R}$ by $R(x)$ we denote the *neighbourhood* of an object x, i.e., the set $\{y \in U : xRy\}$. One can consider a new decision table $\mathbb{A}_R = (U_R, A_R, d_R)$ obtained from $(\mathbb{A}, \mathbb{R})$, where $U_R = \{(x, R(x)) : x \in U\}$ is a family of object neighbourhoods, A_R is a set of attributes describing properties of objects and their neighbourhoods, and, e.g., $d_R((x, R(x))) = d(x)$. In this way, one can consider attributes whose values depend on the context in which objects occur, i.e., on neighbourhoods of objects rather than on objects only. This approach is typical for time series analysis, where attributes (features) are defined on the basis of relevant windows [2,1,10]. It is also used in multi-criteria decision making (see, e.g., [17]). The chosen neighbourhoods and their properties should make it possible to induce high quality approximations of a given target concept. Observe that there are two problems in this approach: discovery of relevant neighbourhoods of objects and properties of such neighbourhoods defined by means of some new attributes. The former problem is related to the selection of $\mathbb{R}$ as well as $R \in \mathbb{R}$ for any object, whereas the latter is based on discovery of a relevant language of formulas expressing properties of neighbourhoods and next on the selection of relevant formulas from this language. Discovery of relevant neighbourhoods and their properties for proper object approximation is a key problem of spatio-temporal data mining [3]. From such a decision table there can be derived concept approximation classifiers by using strategies developed in rough sets or other areas like machine learning and pattern recognition.

3   Information Maps

3.1   Basic Definitions

Information maps [14,16] are usually generated from experimental data (e.g., information systems or decision tables) and are defined by some binary (transition) relations on the set of states. In this context a state consists of an information

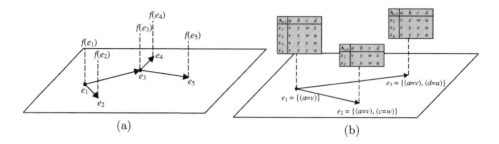

Fig. 1. (a) An information map; (b) An information map of an information system

label and the corresponding information extracted from a given data set. This kind of structure provides basic models over which one can search for relevant patterns for many data mining problems [14,16].

An *information map* $\mathcal{A}$ is a quadruple

$$\mathcal{A} = (E, \leq, I, f), \tag{1}$$

where E is a finite set of *information labels*, $\leq \, \subseteq E \times E$ is a binary *transition relation* on information labels, I is an *information set* and $f : E \rightarrow I$ is an *information function* associating any information label with the corresponding information. In Fig. 1a, we present an example of information map, where $E = \{e_1, e_2, e_3, e_4, e_5\}$, $I = \{f(e_1), f(e_2), f(e_3), f(e_4), f(e_5)\}$, and the transition relation $\leq$ is a partial order on E.

A *state* is any pair $(e, f(e))$, where $e \in E$. The set $\{(e, f(e)) : e \in E\}$ of all states of $\mathcal{A}$ is denoted by $S_{\mathcal{A}}$. The transition relation on information labels can be extended to the relation on states, e.g., in the following way: $(e_1, i_1) \leq (e_2, i_2)$ if and only if $e_1 \leq e_2$. A *path* in $\mathcal{A}$ is any sequence $s_0 s_1 s_2 \ldots$ of states such that $s_i \leq s_{i+1}$ for every $i \geq 0$, and if $s_i \leq s \leq s_{i+1}$ then $s = s_i$ or $s = s_{i+1}$.

3.2   Information Maps of Data Tables

Any information system $\mathbb{A} = (U, A)$ defines its information map as a graph consisting of nodes that are elementary patterns generated by $\mathbb{A}$, where an *elementary pattern* (or *information signature*) $Inf_B(x)$ is a set $\{(a, a(x)) : a \in B\}$ of attribute-value pairs over $B \subseteq A$ consistent with a given object $x \in U$. Thus, the set of labels E is equal to the set $INF(A) = \{Inf_B(x) : x \in U, B \subseteq A\}$ of all elementary patterns of $\mathbb{A}$. The relation $\leq$ is defined in a straightforward way, i.e., for $e_1, e_2 \in INF(A)$, $e_1 \leq e_2$ if and only if $e_1 \subseteq e_2$. Hence, relation $\leq$ is a partial order on E. Finally, the information set I is equal to $\{\mathbb{A}_e : e \in INF(A)\}$, where $\mathbb{A}_e$ is a sub-system of $\mathbb{A}$ with the universe U_e equal to the set $\{x \in U : \forall (a, t) \in e \; a(x) = t\}$. Attributes in $\mathbb{A}_e$ are attributes from $\mathbb{A}$ restricted to U_e. The information function f mapping $INF(A)$ into I is defined by $f(e) = \mathbb{A}_e$ for any $e \in INF(A)$ (see Fig. 1b).

One can consider other information functions for information maps over data tables. Such a function can be a kind of "view" of dependencies in the data table.

Then, for example, $f(e)$ can be equal to the set of all dependencies in $\mathbb{A}_e$ that have sufficient support and confidence.

3.3 Decision Tables over Information Maps

One of the typical schemes of object classification is based on the analysis of decision tables. From the given information about an object (object pattern), we try to classify it relative to a proper decision class. In many cases this scheme needs to be extended because the context of the information should be considered together with the information itself. This means that instead of a single information signature relative to the investigated object x, we also have to examine some other objects that are in some relation to x. Properties of those objects can be important in order to extend information about x by information about the context in which x occurs. In a more complex case, we can consider states of objects and relations between such states. Temporal relations between states, in the case of objects changing in time, provide another possible source of information about the context in which objects occur.

Thus, the scheme of object classification can be as follows. We are given a decision table. Next, it can be extended by some relations on objects (or values of attributes) to a relational decision table defining some neighbourhoods of objects (possibly overlapping each other). Thus, we construct a new decision table, where objects are pairs (*object, object_neighbourhood*), and attributes describe properties of the objects in the context of their neighbourhoods.

In the case of information maps, the above idea is generalised to more complex information granules that are pairs (*state, state_neighbourhood*), where *state* is a state of a given information map $\mathcal{A}$ and *state_neighbourhood* is the neighbourhood of this state in $\mathcal{A}$. A state can be identified by some information about an object and it determines some set of objects (a sub-table), e.g., set of objects indiscernible by means of some attributes. Thus, *state_neighbourhood* is a much more complex structure than *object_neighbourhood* in the previous case, because it is a set (defined by transition relation) of sub-tables satisfying some constraints. Also the attributes of the constructed decision table are more complex because they express properties of complex neighbourhoods. The decision attribute is complex as well because it classifies a state, which is a complex object (in our example – a sub-table). Thus, for a given state s, we can consider, e.g., the distribution of objects corresponding to s in decision classes as the value of decision for s.

4 Hierarchical Information Maps

4.1 Spatio-temporal Modelling of Objects

Let us discuss in more detail the possibilities of modelling of objects evaluated over time. In the simplest case, we can consider separate series of observations: one series corresponds to one object (see Fig. 2a). Each of the series of observations can be modelled, e.g., by an information map (see Section 3), where labels

x_1
x_2

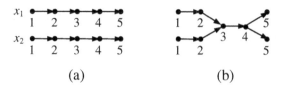

(a)   (b)

Fig. 2. States of objects evaluating in time

correspond to time indices and information to object signatures (for details see [16]). To make the modelling more general, one can combine different series to one more complex information map by joining those states that carry the same information. In this case, we lose some information about the observed objects, however, the model is more general, hopefully still relevant, and applicable to a potentially larger number of cases (see Fig. 2b).

Another possibility is to construct an information map where states denote all the possible states of observed objects (defined by means of some properties, e.g., "moving car", "stopped car") and the transition relation describes the possible next (previous) states if some temporal relation is additionally satisfied. The main difference here is that the states are not labelled by time indices but by some properties of objects. Thus, the space of states can potentially be reduced to a significant degree.

Yet another case of perceiving objects is when we consider their structure. Structured (complex) objects can consist of some parts constrained by some relations of different nature, e.g., spatial relations. The parts can be built from some simpler parts and therefore the structure can be hierarchical with many different levels. The relation object-part corresponds in most cases to some spatial relation. These problems are considered in rough-mereological approach [9].

The combination of the last two cases, i.e., structured objects evaluating in time, gives spatio-temporal objects. For modelling of such objects we can use hierarchical information maps. Each level of such a map models temporal behaviour of the corresponding parts. The levels are connected by spatial relation, e.g., object-part relation relative to the actual context (state of a complex object and states of its parts) (see Fig. 3). The hierarchical information maps are presented in more detail in the following section.

Especially interesting in modelling of object changes are rules that describe how changes of some features (attributes) influence changes of some other ones. Let us consider an example related to information maps. Assume that with any label e there is associated an information $f(e)$ which is a pair $(T_1(e), T_2(e))$ of theories representing some view on knowledge represented in $\mathbb{A}_e$ consisting of the set of dependencies between conditional and decision attributes in the data table $\mathbb{A}_e$, respectively. Such a view can consist of association rules with sufficient support and confidence. Assume that e' is another label (e.g., an extension of e). Then, one can consider rules making it possible to predict differences between $T_2(e)$ and $T_2(e')$ on the basis of differences between $T_1(e)$ and $T_1(e')$. Such rules are interesting on different levels of hierarchical modelling for spatio-temporal

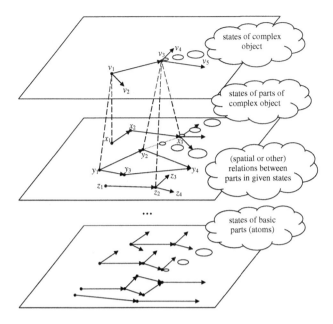

Fig. 3. An example of hierarchical information map

reasoning. Moreover, the laws for predicting changes in decisions quite often require to discover relevant trends of conditional attribute changes (e.g., over some period of time) from data. We plan to develop algorithmic tools for discovery of such laws (dependencies) supported by hierarchical modelling. Observe that in searching for these laws one should, in particular, discover relevant "views" of sets of dependencies and measures of differences.

4.2   Hierarchical Information Maps

One possibility of modelling structured objects evaluated over time is to use some multi-level relational structure. A hierarchical information map is an example of such a structure. It consists of several levels, each modelling temporal behaviour of parts from the same level of the object's structure. Every part of a complex (structured) object defines its own space of states together with the corresponding transitions. Thus, on each level we keep several graphs – one graph for one part. The edges of these graphs are labelled with some temporal relations, however, they are defined for particular parts. The lowest level of the map corresponds to elementary (atomic) parts.

We connect the nodes of graphs from adjacent levels by some spatial relation, defining schemes of constructing a more complex object in a given state from its parts (which are also in some states). An example is presented in Fig. 3. A complex object in state v_1 consists of two parts that are in states x_1 and y_1. The same object in state v_3 consists of three parts in states x_3, y_2, and z_2, respectively. With each non-atomic part in some state x_i at any level, we can associate a decision table containing, e.g., information about historical observations of this part in x_i. The rows (objects) of such a system correspond to different observations.

In a more general case, there can be also given some other relations defined between parts from the same level, e.g., spatial or temporal, reflecting some constraints which should be satisfied by parts in given states in order to reason about more complex object (see Fig. 3). For example, the state of an object can change from safe to unsafe if its parts are in some particular states and, additionally, if they are too close each other. Thus, while modelling complex objects we have to also take into account such relations.

We propose to use labelling of relations linking levels of hierarchical information maps. A label can reflect the fact that some parts satisfy some additional constraint R, or do not satisfy R, or, e.g., do not satisfy any additional constraint at all. In Fig. 4 we can see a part of hierarchical information map where two parts x and y constitute a more complex object $x \oplus y$. There are two additional constraints defined: relations R and S, denoted by dashed and dotted line respectively. From the map it follows that the state of the complex object $x \oplus y$ can depend on the states of parts x and y as well as satisfaction of R or S.

A very important problem is how to check that some complex relation is satisfied or not. Some simple constrains can be checked directly by using some predefined formulas. For example, we can consider a spatial relation "too close" reflecting the fact that two cars are too close each other. Assuming that measurements include location of the cars, we can directly compute the distance and check whether the relation is satisfied or not.

In a more general case we are unable to check satisfiability of relations directly and have to learn it from historical observations of objects. For this purpose, we propose to construct relevant decision tables and to induce classifiers. Let $A = (a_1, \ldots, a_n)$, $B = (b_1, \ldots, b_m)$ be sets of attributes describing parts x and y respectively, and let R be a binary relation that we want to learn. We can construct a decision table $\mathbb{A}_R = (X \times Y, A \cup B, d_R)$, where X and Y are all historical observations of parts x and y respectively; each pair of observations $(x_i, y_j) \in X \times Y$ is described by a vector $(a_1(x_i), \ldots, a_n(x_i), b_1(y_j), \ldots, b_m(y_j))$; and d_R is a binary decision attribute taking value 1 if given observation of

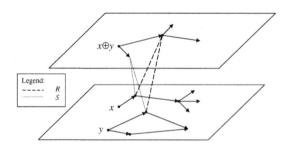

Fig. 4. Satisfaction of spatial or spatio-temporal constraints R and S

parts x and y satisfies the relation R, and 0 otherwise. One can also consider extraction of new features from $A \cup B$ to make the approximation of R more precise. Therefore, for each non-trivial constraint related to parts on a certain level of information map we need to build separate classifier.

In the case of spatio-temporal constraints we may be required to define more complex decision tables for classifier's induction. First of all, we may need to observe a particular object in time, e.g., in some time window. Then, the set of attributes has to be extended by features describing dynamical properties of observed objects. Secondly, new features may have to be extracted. For example, basing on positions of two parts we can extract a new feature describing distance between them by using some specialised metric.

The presented structure – multi-level hierarchical information maps – consists of several information maps that are linked together by some relations on the sets of states. It is important to note that in modelling of such maps we express properties of states and relations between them using the language of domain knowledge (e.g., a simplified natural language). Next, using hierarchical information maps and experimental data one can search for AR networks (see [15,16]), representing relevant patterns for approximation of complex concepts that appear on different levels of maps. Such AR networks are constructed along the derivations performed in domain knowledge using the representation in hierarchical information maps.

4.3   Constructing Higher Levels of Hierarchical Maps by Information Granulation

In this section we discuss an important role which the relational structure granulation [13,8] plays in searching for relevant patterns in approximate reasoning, e.g., approximation patterns (see Fig. 5). For any object x, there is defined a neighbourhood $I(x)$ specified by the value of the uncertainty function from an approximation space (see [12]). From these neighbourhoods some other, more relevant ones (e.g., for the considered concept approximation), should be found. Such neighbourhoods can be extracted by searching in a space of neighbourhoods generated from values of the uncertainty function by applying to them some operations like generalisation operations, set theoretical operations (union, intersection), clustering, and operations on neighbourhoods defined by functions and relations in the underlying relational structure.[2] Fig. 5 illustrates an exemplary scheme of searching for neighbourhoods (patterns, clusters) relevant for concept approximation. In this example f denotes a function with two arguments from the underlying relational structure. Due to the uncertainty, we cannot perceive objects exactly but only by using available neighbourhoods defined by the uncertainty function from an approximation space. Hence, instead of the value $f(x, y)$ for a given pair of objects (x, y), one should consider a family of neighbourhoods $\mathcal{F} = \{I(f(x', y')) : (x', y') \in I(x) \times I(y)\}$. From this family $\mathcal{F}$, a subfamily $\mathcal{F}'$ of neighbourhoods can be chosen which consists of neighbourhoods

---

[2] Relations from such a structure may define relations between objects or their parts.

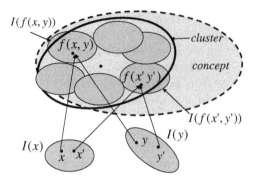

Fig. 5. Relational structure granulation

with some properties relevant for approximation. Next, a subfamily $\mathcal{F}'$ can be, e.g., generalised to clusters that are relevant for the concept approximation, i.e., clusters sufficiently included into the approximated concept (see Fig. 5). The inclusion degrees can be measured by granulation of the inclusion function from the relational structure.

Using information granulation one can construct from a given information map a new one at the higher level which is simpler (more compact) but still sufficient for approximation of complex concepts with a satisfactory quality.

5   Conclusions

In the paper, we have discussed some problems related to hierarchical approximation of spatio-temporal knowledge by means of hierarchical information maps. They can help to discover AR networks representing relevant spatio-temporal patterns from data and soft domain knowledge.

The levels of hierarchical information maps are connected by some spatial or spatio-temporal relations. Satisfaction of different constraints may lead to connecting of the same states from one level to different state in the upper level. We have also discussed the problem of learning such constraints.

Acknowledgements. The research has been supported by the grant 3 T11C 002 26 from Ministry of Scientific Research and Information Technology of the Republic of Poland, and by the Research Center at the Polish-Japanese Institute of Information Technology, Warsaw, Poland.

References

1. J. P. Caraça-Valente and I. López-Chavarrías.   Discovering similar patterns in time series. In R. Ramakrishnan, S. Stolfo, R. Bayardo, and I. Parsa, editors, *Sixth ACM SIGKDD International Conference on Knowledge Discovery and Data Mining KDD*, pp. 497–505, Boston, MA, August 20-23 2000. ACM Press.

2. G. Das, K.-I. Lin, H. Mannila, G. Renganathan, and P. Smyth. Rule discovery from time series. In R. Agrawal, P. E. Stolorz, and G. Piatetsky-Shapiro, editors, *Fourth International Conference on Knowledge Discovery and Data Mining KDD*, pp. 16–22, New York, NY, August 27-31 1998. AAAI Press.

3. W. Kloesgen and J. Żytkow, editors. *Handbook of Knowledge Discovery and Data Mining*. Oxford University Press, 2002.

4. J. Komorowski, L. Polkowski, and A. Skowron. Rough sets: A tutorial. In S. K. Pal and A. Skowron, editors, *Rough Fuzzy Hybridization: A New Trend in Decision-Making*, pp. 3–98. Springer-Verlag, Singapore, 1999.

5. S. K. Pal, L. Polkowski, and A. Skowron, editors. *Rough-Neural Computing: Techniques for Computing with Words*. Cognitive Technologies. Springer Verlag, Heidelberg, Germany, 2004.

6. Z. Pawlak. Rough sets. *International Journal of Computer and Information Sciences*, 11:341–356, 1982.

7. J. F. Peters, A. Skowron, J. Stepaniuk, and S. Ramanna. Towards an ontology of approximate reason. *Fundamenta Informaticae*, 51(1-2):157–173, 2002.

8. J. F. Peters, A. Skowron, P. Synak, and S. Ramanna. Rough sets and information granulation. In T. Bilgic, D. Baets, and O. Kaynak, eds., *LNAI* 2715, pp. 370–377, 2003. Springer-Verlag.

9. L. Polkowski and A. Skowron. Rough mereology: A new paradigm for approximate reasoning. *International Journal of Approximate Reasoning*, 15(4):333–365, 1996.

10. J. F. Roddick, K. Hornsby, and M. Spiliopoulou. YABTSSTDMR - yet another bibliography of temporal, spatial and spatio-temporal data mining research. In K. P. Unnikrishnan and R. Uthurusamy, editors, *SIGKDD Temporal Data Mining Workshop*, pp. 167–175, San Francisco, CA, 2001. ACM Press.

11. J. F. Roddick, E. Hoel, M. J. Egenhofer, D. Papadias, and B. Salzberg. Spatial, Temporal and Spatio-Temporal Databases - Hot Issues and Directions for PhD Research. *ACM SIGMOD Record*, 33(2):126–131, 2004.

12. A. Skowron and J. Stepaniuk. Tolerance approximation spaces. *Fundamenta Informaticae*, 27(2-3):245–253, 1996.

13. A. Skowron and J. Stepaniuk. Information granules and rough-neural computing. In Pal et al. [5], pp. 43–84.

14. A. Skowron and P. Synak. Patterns in information maps. In J. Alpigini, J. Peters, A. Skowron, and N. Zhong, eds., *LNAI* 2475, pp. 453–460, 2002. Springer-Verlag.

15. A. Skowron and P. Synak. Complex patterns. *Fundamenta Informaticae*, 60(1-4):351–366, 2004.

16. A. Skowron and P. Synak. Reasoning in information maps. *Fundamenta Informaticae*, 59(2-3):241–259, 2004.

17. R. Słowiński, S. Greco, and B. Matarazzo. Rough set analysis of preference-ordered data. In J. Alpigini, J. Peters, A. Skowron, and N. Zhong, eds., *LNAI* 2475, pp. 44–59, 2002. Springer-Verlag.

Ordered Belief Fusion in Possibilistic Logic

Churn-Jung Liau

Institute of Information Science,
Academia Sinica, Taipei, 115, Taiwan
liaucj@iis.sinica.edu.tw

Abstract. In this paper, we propose a logical framework for reasoning about uncertain belief fusion. The framework is a combination of multi-agent epistemic logic and possibilistic logic. We use graded epistemic operators to represent agents' uncertain beliefs, and the operators are interpreted in accordance with possibilistic semantics. Ordered fusion can resolve the inconsistency caused by direct fusion. We consider two strategies to merge uncertain beliefs. In the first strategy, called level cutting fusion, if inconsistency occurs at some level, then all beliefs at the lower levels are discarded simultaneously. In the second, called level skipping fusion, only the level at which the inconsistency occurs is skipped. We present the formal semantics and axiomatic systems for these two strategies.

Keywords: Belief fusion, database merging, epistemic logic, multi-agent systems, possibilistic logic.

1 Introduction

The development of epistemic logic has been stimulated by the philosophical analysis of knowledge and belief [7]. This kind of logic has attracted the attention of researchers from diverse fields, such as artificial intelligence (AI), economics, linguistics, and theoretical computer science. Among them, AI researchers and computer scientists have developed some technically sophisticated formalisms and applied them to the analysis of distributed and multi-agent systems [6,13].

The application of epistemic logic to AI and computer science emphasizes the interaction of agents, from which multi-agent epistemic logic has been developed. One representative example of such logic is proposed by Fagin et al. [6]. The term "knowledge" is used in a broad sense in [6] to cover cases of belief and information[1]. The most novel feature of their logic is its consideration of common knowledge and distributed knowledge among a group of agents. Distributed knowledge is that which can be deduced by pooling everyone's knowledge. In this paper, the distributed knowledge operator is also called the *direct fusion* operator. While it is essential that proper knowledge must be true, the belief of

---

[1] More precisely, the logic for belief is called doxastic logic. However, here we use the three terms knowledge, belief, and information interchangeably, so epistemic logic is assumed to cover all these notions.

D. Ślęzak et al. (Eds.): RSFDGrC 2005, LNAI 3641, pp. 632–641, 2005.

an agent may be wrong. Therefore, in general, there will be conflict between the beliefs to be merged. In this case, everything can be deduced from the distributed belief due to the notorious omniscience property of epistemic logic, so the merged result will be useless for further reasoning. To resolve the inconsistency of merged belief, *ordered fusion* operators are incorporated into multi-agent epistemic logic. This has resulted in the development of fusion logics [3,4,8,9], in which the reliability ordering of agents is taken into account when their beliefs are merged.

While multi-agent epistemic logic does not consider the uncertainty of beliefs, a quantitative modal logic (QML) has been proposed for reasoning about such beliefs [10,11,12]. The direct fusion of uncertain beliefs is also considered in possibilistic logic, $\mathbf{PL}_n^\otimes$, which extends QML with distributed belief operators [1]. The inconsistency problem in the direct fusion of beliefs also arises in the direct> fusion of uncertain beliefs. Therefore, in this paper, we propose the ordered fusion of uncertain beliefs to resolve the problem.

2   Review of Previous Approaches

In this section, we review some logics for distributed belief fusion. For brevity, we only sketch the syntax and semantics of these logics, and omit their proof methods.

2.1   Direct Fusion in Epistemic Logic

In [6], some variants of epistemic logic systems are presented. Using the naming convention in [2], the most basic system with distributed beliefs is called K_n^D, with n being the number of agents and D denoting the distributed belief operators. In this system, logical omniscience is the only property imposed on agents' beliefs. Nevertheless, we further require that the belief of each individual agent should be consistent, even though the agents' collective beliefs may be in conflict. Thus, we actually use the logic KD_n^D in [6], where an axiom D is used to guarantee the consistency of each agent's belief.

The alphabet of KD_n^D consists of the following symbols: a countable set $\Phi_0 = \{p, q, r, \ldots\}$ of atomic propositions; the propositional constants $\bot$ (falsum or falsity constant) and $\top$ (verum or truth constant); the binary Boolean operator $\vee$ (or) and the unary Boolean operator $\neg$ (not); a set $Ag = \{1, 2, \ldots, n\}$ of agents; the modal operator-forming symbols "[" and "]"; and the left and right parentheses " (" and ")".

The set of well-formed formulas (wffs)is defined as the smallest set containing $\Phi_0 \cup \{\bot, \top\}$ and is closed under Boolean operators and the following rule[2]:

– if φ is a wff, then $[G]\varphi$ is a wff for any nonempty $G \subseteq Ag$.

The intuitive meaning of $[G]\varphi$ is "The group of agents G has distributed belief φ"

---

[2] We change the syntactic notation of epistemic logic in [6] slightly.

As usual, other classical Boolean connectives, such as $\wedge$ (and), $\supset$ (implication), and $\equiv$ (equivalence) can be defined as abbreviations. Also, we write $\langle G \rangle \varphi$ as an abbreviation of $\neg[G]\neg\varphi$. When G is a singleton $\{i\}$, we write $[i]\varphi$ instead of $[\{i\}]\varphi$, so $[i]\varphi$ means that agent i knows φ.

For the semantics, a possible world model for KD_n^D is a triple

$$(W, (\mathcal{R}_i)_{1 \leq i \leq n}, V),$$

where

- W is a set of possible worlds,
- $\mathcal{R}_i \subseteq W \times W$ is a serial binary relation[3] over W for $1 \leq i \leq n$,
- $V : \Phi_0 \rightarrow 2^W$ is a truth assignment mapping each atomic proposition to the set of worlds in which it is true.

From the binary relations, $\mathcal{R}_i$'s, we can define a derived relation, $\mathcal{R}_G$, for each nonempty $G \subseteq Ag$:

$$\mathcal{R}_G = \cap_{i \in G} \mathcal{R}_i.$$

Note that the seriality of $\mathcal{R}_i$ guarantees the consistency of each agent's belief state. However, $\mathcal{R}_G$ may be not serial.

Informally, $\mathcal{R}_i(w)$ is the set of worlds that agent i considers possible under w according to his belief, so $\mathcal{R}_G(w)$ is the set of worlds that are considered possible under w according to the direct fusion of agents' beliefs. This informal intuition is reflected in the definition of the satisfaction relation. Let $M = (W, (\mathcal{R}_i)_{1 \leq i \leq n}, V)$ be a model and $\mathcal{L}$ be the set of wffs for KD_n^D. The satisfaction relation $\models_M \subseteq W \times \mathcal{L}$ is then defined by the following inductive rules (we use the infix notation for the relation and omit the subscript M for convenience):

1. $w \models p$ iff $w \in V(p)$, for each $p \in \Phi_0$,
2. $w \not\models \bot$ and $w \models \top$,
3. $w \models \neg\varphi$ iff $w \not\models \varphi$,
4. $w \models \varphi \vee \psi$ iff $w \models \varphi$ or $w \models \psi$,
5. $w \models [G]\varphi$ iff for all $u \in \mathcal{R}_G(w)$, $u \models \varphi$.

2.2   Ordered Fusion in Epistemic Logic

To encode the degrees of reliability of n agents, we use ordering relations over any subset of $\{1, \ldots, n\}$. Let $\mathcal{TO}_n$ denote the set of all possible strict total orders over any non-empty subset of $\{1, \ldots, n\}$; then we can associate a unique syntactic notation with each total order in $\mathcal{TO}_n$. Let $X = \{i_1, i_2, \ldots, i_m\}$ be a non-empty subset of $\{1, \ldots, n\}$ and $>$ be a strict total order such that $i_j > i_k$ iff $j < k$ for all $1 \leq, j, k \leq m$; then the syntactic notation for $(X, >)$ is the string

$$i_1 > i_2 > \cdots > i_m.$$

In this paper, the capital letter O is used to denote meta-variables ranging over such notations. Let O be the string $i_1 > i_2 > \cdots > i_m$; then the set

---

[3] A binary relation $\mathcal{R}$ is serial if $\forall w \exists u. \mathcal{R}(w, u)$.

$\{i_1, i_2, \ldots, i_m\}$ is called the domain of O and denoted by $\delta(O)$. In this case, $O > i_{m+1}$ denotes $i_1 > i_2 > \cdots > i_m > i_{m+1}$ if $i_{m+1} \notin \delta(O)$. As the syntactic notation is unique for each total order, we can also identify the notation with the total order itself, so we can write $O \in \mathcal{TO}_n$. Furthermore, the upper-case Greek letter Ω is used to denote meta-variables ranging over nonempty subsets of $\mathcal{TO}_n$.

In [9], two logics for ordered distributed belief fusion are proposed. The first, DBF_n^c, is based on a level cutting strategy. The set of DBF_n^c wffs is defined by the rules for KD_n^D and the following rule:

- if φ is a wff, then $[O]\varphi$ is a wff for any $O \in \mathcal{TO}_n$.

Intuitively, $[O]\varphi$ means that φ is derivable from the merged beliefs of agents in $\delta(O)$ according to the specific order of O.

For the semantics, a DBF_n^c model is a possible world model $(W, (\mathcal{R}_i)_{1 \le i \le n}, V)$ for KD_n^D. For each $O \in \mathcal{TO}_n$, a derived relation, $\mathcal{R}_O^c$, is defined inductively as follows:

$$\mathcal{R}_{O>i}^c(w) = \begin{cases} \mathcal{R}_O^c(w) & \text{if } \bigcap_{j \in \delta(O>i)} \mathcal{R}_j(w) = \emptyset, \\ \mathcal{R}_O^c(w) \cap \mathcal{R}_i(w) & \text{otherwise,} \end{cases}$$

for any $w \in W$. The superscript c denotes level cutting fusion and can usually be omitted when the context is clear. The following satisfaction condition is then added to those of epistemic logic:

$$w \models [O]\varphi \text{ iff for all } u \in \mathcal{R}_O(w), u \models \varphi.$$

Let $O = i_1 > i_2 > \cdots > i_m$. Also, define $G_j = \{i_1, i_2 \ldots, i_j\}$ for $1 \le j \le m$ and assume k is the largest j such that $\bigcap_{i \in G_j} \mathcal{R}_i(w) \ne \emptyset$; then we have

$$\mathcal{R}_O(w) = \bigcap_{i \in G_k} \mathcal{R}_i(w).$$

In other words, beliefs from agents below level k are completely discarded from the merged result. Our rationale is that if a belief in level $k+1$ is unacceptable, then any belief in a less reliable level is also unacceptable.

The second logic, DBF_n^s, is based on a level skipping strategy, which only skips the agent causing the inconsistency and continues to consider the next level. This strategy corresponds to the suspicious attitude of multi-source reasoning [3], and has also been used in belief revision by Nebel [14]. The set of DBF_n^s is the smallest set containing $\Phi_0 \cup \{\perp, \top\}$, and is closed under Boolean operators and the following rule:

- if φ is a wff, so is $[\Omega]\varphi$ for any nonempty $\Omega \subseteq \mathcal{TO}_n$.

When Ω is a singleton $\{O\}$, we write $[O]\varphi$ instead of $[\{O\}]\varphi$. If $\Omega = \{O_1, \ldots, O_m\}$ such that $|\delta(O_i)| = 1$ for all $1 \le i \le m$, then $[\Omega]$ is the distributed belief operator among ordinary agents. Therefore, the language is more general than that of DBF_n^c.

For the semantics, DBF_n^s model is still a possible world model $(W, (\mathcal{R}_i)_{1 \leq i \leq n}, V)$ for KD_n^D. Therefore, we can define $\mathcal{R}_O^s$ inductively as follows:

$$\mathcal{R}_{O>i}^s(w) = \begin{cases} \mathcal{R}_O^s(w) & \text{if } \mathcal{R}_O^s(w) \cap \mathcal{R}_i(w) = \emptyset, \\ \mathcal{R}_O^s(w) \cap \mathcal{R}_i(w) & \text{otherwise,} \end{cases}$$

for any $w \in W$. As in the case of $\mathcal{R}_O^c$, the superscript s denotes the level skipping strategy and can be omitted when the context is clear. We further define

$$\mathcal{R}_\Omega = \bigcap_{O \in \Omega} \mathcal{R}_O.$$

Then, the following clause is used to define the satisfaction of modal formulas in DBF_n^s.

- $w \models [\Omega]\varphi$ iff for all $u \in \mathcal{R}_\Omega(w), u \models \varphi$.

2.3   Direct Fusion in Possibilistic Logic

In [1], a logic $\mathbf{PL}_n^\otimes$ is proposed for reasoning about distributed belief fusion with a *continuous T-norm* $\otimes^4$. The set of $\mathbf{PL}_n^\otimes$ wffs is the smallest set containing $\Phi_0 \cup \{\bot, \top\}$, and is closed under Boolean operators and the following rule:

- if φ is a wff, so are $B_a^i \varphi$ and $D_a \varphi$ for any $1 \leq i \leq n$ and rational number $a \in [0, 1]$.

The intuitive meaning of $B_a^i \varphi$ is that agent i believes φ with strength (at least) a, and the modal operator, D_a, represents the distributed beliefs of all agents with strength (at least) a.

Formally, the semantics of $\mathbf{PL}_n^\otimes$ is based on possibility theory [15]. A $\Pi_n^\otimes$-structure is a tuple $(W, (\pi_i)_{0 \leq i \leq n}, V)$ such that W is a set of possible worlds; each π_i maps each world w to a possibility distribution $\pi_{i,w} : W \rightarrow [0, 1]$ over W; V maps elements in Φ_0 to subsets of W; and, for any $w \in W$,

$$\pi_{0,w} \leq \bigotimes_{i=1}^n \pi_{i,w}.$$

In possibility theory, each possibility distribution π can derive the associated possibility measure $\Pi : 2^W \rightarrow [0, 1]$ and necessity measure $N : 2^W \rightarrow [0, 1]$ as

$$\Pi(X) = \sup_{x \in X} \pi(x)$$

$$N(X) = 1 - \sup_{x \notin X} \pi(x).$$

Then, the satisfaction relation $\models$ for $\Pi_n^\otimes$-structures are defined as

- $w \models B_a^i \varphi$ iff $N_{i,w}(|\varphi|) \geq a$,
- $w \models D_a \varphi$ iff $N_{0,w}(|\varphi|) \geq a$,

where $|\varphi| = \{x \in W \mid x \models \varphi\}$ is the truth set of φ in the model, and $N_{i,w}$ is the necessity measure associated to $\pi_{i,w}$ for $0 \leq i \leq n$ and $w \in W$.

---

[4] A T-norm is any binary operation on [0,1] that is commutative, associative, and non-decreasing in each argument, and has 1 as its unit.

3 Ordered Fusion in Possibilistic Logic

To resolve the inconsistency problem in $\mathbf{PL}_n^{\otimes}$, we combine DBF_n^c (resp. DBF_n^s) with $\mathbf{PL}_n^{\otimes}$. Since possibilistic logic is inconsistency-tolerant [5], we introduce a parameter, ϵ, to denote the degree of inconsistency tolerance. Recall that a possibility distribution $\pi : X \rightarrow [0,1]$ is normalized if $\Pi(X) = \sup_{x \in X} \pi(x) = 1$. A normalized possibility distribution represents a consistent belief state. If π is not normalized, i.e., $\sup_{x \in X} \pi(x) < 1$, π represents a partially inconsistent belief state. $1 - \sup_{x \in X} \pi(x)$ is called the *inconsistency degree* of π, and denoted by $\iota(\pi)$.

3.1 Level Cutting Fusion in Possibilistic Logic

In this subsection, we present a logic for reasoning about possibilistic belief fusion based on a level cutting strategy. The logic is called $\mathrm{CFPL}_n^{\otimes,\epsilon}$, where ϵ is the inconsistency tolerance degree of the logic. The set of $\mathrm{CFPL}_n^{\otimes,\epsilon}$ wffs is defined as the smallest set containing $\Phi_0 \cup \{\bot, \top\}$, and is closed under Boolean operators and the following rule:

- if φ is a wff, then $[G]_a\varphi, [O]_a\varphi, [G]_a^+\varphi$, and $[O]_a^+\varphi$ are wffs for any nonempty $G \subseteq Ag$, any $O \in \mathcal{TO}_n$, and any rational number $a \in [0,1]$.

As in epistemic logic, we use $[i]$ instead of $[\{i\}]$ when $\{i\}$ is a singleton. The intuitive meanings of $[i]_a\varphi$ and $[Ag]_a\varphi$ are respectively the same as those of $B_a^i\varphi$ and $D_a\varphi$ in $\mathbf{PL}_n^{\otimes}$. However, we not only consider a single agent and the set of all agents, but also any nonempty subset of agents. $[G]_a^+\varphi$ is similar to $[G]_a\varphi$, except that the former means the strength of belief is greater than a. Additionally, we have modal operators corresponding to the ordered fusion of uncertain beliefs. $[O]_a\varphi$ (resp. $[O]_a^+\varphi$) means that an agent merging distributed beliefs in accordance with the ordering O will believe φ with a strength of at least (resp. more than) a.

For the semantics, a $\mathrm{CFPL}_n^{\otimes,\epsilon}$-model is a tuple $M = (W, (\pi_i)_{1 \leq i \leq n}, V)$ such that W is a set of possible worlds; each π_i maps each world w to a possibility distribution $\pi_{i,w} : W \rightarrow [0,1]$ over W such that $\iota(\pi_{i,w}) \leq \epsilon$; and V maps elements in Φ_0 to subsets of W. Note that we require the inconsistency degree of the belief state of each single agent to be no more than ϵ. This is the inconsistency tolerance degree of the logic. Any belief with inconsistency beyond this degree must be discarded. Let us now define derived possibility distributions $\pi_{G,w}$ and $\pi_{O,w}$ from $\{\pi_i \mid 1 \leq i \leq n\}$ for each nonempty subset $G \subseteq Ag$, $O \in \mathcal{TO}_n$, and $w \in W$ as follows:

$$\pi_{G,w} = \bigotimes_{i \in G} \pi_{i,w}$$

$$\pi_{O>i,w} = \begin{cases} \pi_{O,w} & \text{if } \iota(\bigotimes_{j \in \delta(O>i)} \pi_{j,w}) > \epsilon, \\ \pi_{O,w} \otimes \pi_{i,w} & \text{otherwise,} \end{cases}$$

Then, the satisfaction relation $\models$ for the $\mathrm{CFPL}_n^{\otimes,\epsilon}$-model is defined as

$- \ w \models [G]_a \varphi$ iff $N_{G,w}(|\varphi|) \geq a$,
$- \ w \models [G]_a^+ \varphi$ iff $N_{G,w}(|\varphi|) > a$,
$- \ w \models [O]_a \varphi$ iff $N_{O,w}(|\varphi|) \geq a$,
$- \ w \models [O]_a^+ \varphi$ iff $N_{O,w}(|\varphi|) > a$,

where $|\varphi|$ is the truth set of φ in the model, and $N_{G,w}$ (resp. $N_{O,w}$) is the necessity measure associated with $\pi_{G,w}$ (resp. $\pi_{O,w}$) for $G \subseteq Ag$ (resp. $O \in \mathcal{TO}_n$) and $w \in W$.

A set of wffs Σ is satisfied in a world w, written as $w \models \Sigma$, if $w \models \varphi$ for all $\varphi \in \Sigma$. We write $\Sigma \models_M \varphi$ if for each possible world w in M, $w \models \Sigma$ implies $w \models \varphi$, and $\Sigma \models_{\mathrm{CFPL}_n^{\otimes,\epsilon}} \varphi$ if $\Sigma \models_M \varphi$ for each $\mathrm{CFPL}_n^{\otimes,\epsilon}$-model M. A wff φ is valid in M if $\emptyset \models_M \varphi$. Σ can be omitted when it is empty. Thus, $\models_M \varphi$ and $\models_{\mathrm{CFPL}_n^{\otimes,\epsilon}} \varphi$ are the abbreviations of $\emptyset \models_M \varphi$ and $\emptyset \models_{\mathrm{CFPL}_n^{\otimes,\epsilon}} \varphi$ respectively. The subscript is also usually omitted if it is clear from the context.

An axiomatic system for $\mathrm{CFPL}_n^{\otimes,\epsilon}$ is presented in Figure 1. The system was developed by generalizing KD_n^D to QML [10,11,12]. However, the consistency of each individual agent's belief is replaced by $(1 - \epsilon)$-consistency, which means that the inconsistency degree of each agent's belief state is at most ϵ. Axiom G2 enforces this requirement. The axioms governing modal operators $[O]_a$ and $[O]_a^+$ are generalized from those of DBF_n^c. Also, the symbol $\oplus$ in axiom G3 denotes a T-conorm corresponding to $\otimes$, which is defined by $a \oplus b = 1 - (1 - a) \otimes (1 - b)$.

A wff φ is derivable from the system $\mathrm{CFPL}_n^{\otimes,\epsilon}$, or simply, φ is a *theorem* of $\mathrm{CFPL}_n^{\otimes,\epsilon}$, if there is a finite sequence $\varphi_1, \ldots, \varphi_m$ such that $\varphi = \varphi_m$ and every φ_i is an instance of an axiom schema, or obtained from earlier φ_j's by the application of an inference rule. It is written as $\vdash_{\mathrm{CFPL}_n^{\otimes,\epsilon}} \varphi$ if φ is a theorem of $\mathrm{CFPL}_n^{\otimes,\epsilon}$. Let $\Sigma \cup \{\varphi\}$ be a subset of wffs, then φ is derivable from Σ in the system $\mathrm{CFPL}_n^{\otimes,\epsilon}$, written as $\Sigma \vdash_{\mathrm{CFPL}_n^{\otimes,\epsilon}} \varphi$, if there is a finite subset Σ' of Σ such that $\vdash_{\mathrm{CFPL}_n^{\otimes,\epsilon}} \bigwedge \Sigma' \supset \varphi$. We drop the subscript when no confusion occurs.

We now have the soundness and completeness results for the system $\mathrm{CFPL}_n^{\otimes,\epsilon}$.

Theorem 1. *For any wff of $CFPL_n^{\otimes,\epsilon}$, $\models \varphi$ iff $\vdash \varphi$.*

3.2   Level Skipping Fusion in Possibilistic Logic

In this subsection, we present a logic for reasoning about possibilistic belief fusion based on a level skipping strategy. The logic is called $\mathrm{SFPL}_n^{\otimes,\epsilon}$, where ϵ is the inconsistency tolerance degree of the logic. The set of $\mathrm{SFPL}_n^{\otimes,\epsilon}$ wffs is defined as the smallest set containing $\Phi_0 \cup \{\bot, \top\}$, and is closed under Boolean operators and the following rule:

$-$ if φ is a wff, then $[\Omega]_a \varphi$ and $[\Omega]_a^+ \varphi$ are wffs for any nonempty $\Omega \subseteq \mathcal{TO}_n$ and any rational number $a \in [0, 1]$.

Semantically, an $\mathrm{SFPL}_n^{\otimes,\epsilon}$-structure is the same as a $\mathrm{CFPL}_n^{\otimes,\epsilon}$-structure. However, we redefine $\pi_{O,w}$ for each $O \in \mathcal{TO}_n$ and $w \in W$ as follows:

$$\pi_{O>i,w} = \begin{cases} \pi_{O,w} & \text{if } \iota(\pi_{O,w} \otimes \pi_{i,w}) > \epsilon, \\ \pi_{O,w} \otimes \pi_{i,w} & \text{otherwise.} \end{cases}$$

- Axioms:
  1. P: all tautologies of propositional calculus
  2. Bookkeeping ($\square$ denotes either $[G]$ or $[O]$):
     (a) $\square_c\varphi \supset \square_d^+\varphi$ if $c > d$
     (b) $\square_c^+\varphi \supset \square_c\varphi$
     (c) $\square_0\varphi$
     (d) $\neg\square_1^+\varphi$
  3. G1:
     (a) $([G]_a\varphi \wedge [G]_a(\varphi \supset \psi)) \supset [G]_a\psi$
     (b) $([G]_a^+\varphi \wedge [G]_a^+(\varphi \supset \psi)) \supset [G]_a^+\psi$
  4. G2: $\neg[i]_\epsilon^+\bot$
  5. G3: if $G_1 \cap G_2 = \emptyset$, then
     (a) $([G_1]_a\varphi \wedge [G_2]_b\varphi) \supset [G_1 \cup G_2]_{a\oplus b}\varphi$
     (b) $([G_1]_a^+\varphi \wedge [G_2]_b^+\varphi) \supset [G_1 \cup G_2]_{a\oplus b}^+\varphi$
  6. O1:
     (a) $\neg[\delta(O > i)]_\epsilon^+\bot \supset ([O > i]_a\varphi \equiv [\delta(O > i)]_a\varphi)$
     (b) $\neg[\delta(O > i)]_\epsilon^+\bot \supset ([O > i]_a^+\varphi \equiv [\delta(O > i)]_a^+\varphi)$
  7. O2:
     (a) $[\delta(O > i)]_\epsilon^+\bot \supset ([O > i]_a\varphi \equiv [O]_a\varphi)$
     (b) $[\delta(O > i)]_\epsilon^+\bot \supset ([O > i]_a^+\varphi \equiv [O]_a^+\varphi)$
- Rules of Inference:
  1. R1 (Modus ponens, MP):

$$\frac{\varphi \quad \varphi \supset \psi}{\psi}$$

  2. R2 (Generalization, Gen):

$$\frac{\varphi}{[G]_1\varphi}$$

Fig. 1. The axiomatic system for $\text{CFPL}_n^{\otimes,\epsilon}$

Furthermore, we also define $\pi_{\Omega,w}$ for each $\Omega \subseteq \mathcal{TO}_n$ and $w \in W$ as

$$\pi_{\Omega,w} = \bigotimes_{O\in\Omega} \pi_{O,w}.$$

Then, the satisfaction relation $\models$ for the $\text{SFPL}_n^{\otimes,\epsilon}$-model is defined as

- $w \models [\Omega]_a\varphi$ iff $N_{\Omega,w}(|\varphi|) \geq a$,
- $w \models [\Omega]_a^+\varphi$ iff $N_{\Omega,w}(|\varphi|) > a$,

where $|\varphi|$ is the truth set of φ in the model, and $N_{\Omega,w}$ is the necessity measure associated with $\pi_{\Omega,w}$. The definition of the validity and consequence relation is the same as above.

An axiomatic system can be also developed for $\text{SFPL}_n^{\otimes,\epsilon}$ by generalizing the corresponding axioms in DBF_n^s, as shown in Figure 2.

- Axioms:
    1. P: all tautologies of propositional calculus
    2. Bookkeeping:
        (a) $[\Omega]_c\varphi \supset [\Omega]_d^+\varphi$ if $c > d$
        (b) $[\Omega]_c^+\varphi \supset [\Omega]_c\varphi$
        (c) $[\Omega]_0\varphi$
        (d) $\neg[\Omega]_1^+\varphi$
    3. V1:
        (a) $([\Omega]_a\varphi \wedge [\Omega]_a(\varphi \supset \psi)) \supset [\Omega]_a\psi$
        (b) $([\Omega]_a^+\varphi \wedge [\Omega]_a^+(\varphi \supset \psi)) \supset [\Omega]_a^+\psi$
    4. V2: $\neg[i]_\epsilon^+\bot$
    5. V3: if $\Omega_1 \cap \Omega_2 = \emptyset$, then
        (a) $([\Omega_1]_a\varphi \wedge [\Omega_2]_b\varphi) \supset [\Omega_1 \cup \Omega_2]_{a\oplus b}\varphi$
        (b) $([\Omega_1]_a^+\varphi \wedge [\Omega_2]_b^+\varphi) \supset [\Omega_1 \cup \Omega_2]_{a\oplus b}^+\varphi$
    6. O1:
        (a) $\neg[\{O,i\}]_\epsilon^+\bot \supset ([\Omega \cup \{O > i\}]_a\varphi \equiv [\Omega \cup \{O,i\}]_a\varphi)$
        (b) $\neg[\{O,i\}]_\epsilon^+\bot \supset ([\Omega \cup \{O > i\}]_a^+\varphi \equiv [\Omega \cup \{O,i\}]_a^+\varphi)$
    7. O2:
        (a) $[\{O,i\}]_\epsilon^+\bot \supset ([\Omega \cup \{O > i\}]_a\varphi \equiv [\Omega \cup \{O\}]_a\varphi)$
        (b) $[\{O,i\}]_\epsilon^+\bot \supset ([\Omega \cup \{O > i\}]_a^+\varphi \equiv [\Omega \cup \{O\}]_a^+\varphi)$
- Rules of Inference:
    1. R1 (Modus ponens, MP):
    $$\frac{\varphi \quad \varphi \supset \psi}{\psi}$$
    2. R2 (Generalization, Gen):
    $$\frac{\varphi}{[\Omega]_1\varphi}$$

Fig. 2. The axiomatic system for $SFPL_n^{\otimes,\epsilon}$

The definition of derivability and theoremhood in the $SFPL_n^{\otimes,\epsilon}$ system is the same as above. We now have the soundness and completeness theorem for $SFPL_n^{\otimes,\epsilon}$.

Theorem 2. *For any wff of $SFPL_n^{\otimes,\epsilon}$, $\models \varphi$ iff $\vdash \varphi$.*

4   Concluding Remarks

In this paper, we present two logics for reasoning about ordered possibilistic belief fusion. Direct fusion and ordered fusion in epistemic logic, as well as direct fusion in possibilistic logic have been proposed in the previous literature. Therefore, the results in this paper fill a gap in the previous work. We believe that the logics, which are summarized in Table 1, are applicable to reasoning in multi-agent systems.

Table 1. Logics for belief fusion

	without uncertainty	with uncertainty
direct fusion	KD_n^D	$\mathbf{PL}_n^{\otimes}$
ordered fusion	DBF_n^c /DBF_n^s	$\mathrm{CFPL}_n^{\otimes,\epsilon}$/$\mathrm{SFPL}_n^{\otimes,\epsilon}$

References

1. L. Boldrin and A. Saffiotti. A modal logic for merging partial belief of multiple reasoners. *Journal of Logic and Computation*, 9(1):81–103, 1999.
2. B.F. Chellas. *Modal Logic: An Introduction*. Cambridge University Press, 1980.
3. L. Cholvy. A logical approach to multi-souces reasoning. In M. Masuch and L. Pólos, editors, *Knowledge Representation and Reasoning under Uncertainty*, LNCS 808, pages 183–196. Springer-Verlag, 1994.
4. L. Cholvy. Reasoning about data provided by federated deductive databases. *Journal of Intelligent Information Systems*, 10:49–80, 1998.
5. D. Dubois, J. Lang, and H. Prade. Possibilistic logic. In D.M. Gabbay, C.J. Hogger, and J.A. Robinson, editors, *Handbook of Logic in Artificial Intelligence and Logic Programming, Vol 3 : Nonmonotonic Reasoning and Uncertain Reasoning*, pages 439–513. Clarendon Press - Oxford, 1994.
6. R. Fagin, J.Y. Halpern, Y. Moses, and M.Y. Vardi. *Reasoning about Knowledge*. MIT Press, 1996.
7. J. Hintikka. *Knowledge and Belief*. Cornell University Press, 1962.
8. C. J. Liau. A conservative approach to distributed belief fusion. In *Proc. of the Third International Conference on Information Fusion*, pages MoD4–1, 2000.
9. C.J. Liau. A modal logic framework for multi-agent belief fusion. *ACM Transactions on Computational Logic*, 6(1):124–174, 2005.
10. C.J. Liau and I.P. Lin. Quantitative modal logic and possibilistic reasoning. In B. Neumann, editor, *Proceedings of the 10th ECAI*, pages 43–47. John Wiley & Sons. Ltd, 1992.
11. C.J. Liau and I.P. Lin. Proof methods for reasoning about possibility and necessity. *International Journal of Approximate Reasoning*, 9(4):327–364, 1993.
12. C.J. Liau and I.P. Lin. Possibilistic reasoning—a mini-survey and uniform semantics. *Artificial Intelligence*, 88:163–193, 1996.
13. J.-J. Ch. Meyer and W. van der Hoek. *Epistemic Logic for AI and Computer Science*. Cambridge University Press, 1995.
14. B. Nebel. Base revision operator and schemes: semantics representation and complexity. In *Proceedings of the 11th European Conference on Artificial Intelligence*, pages 341–345. John Wiley & Sons, 1994.
15. L.A. Zadeh. Fuzzy sets as a basis for a theory of possibility. *Fuzzy Sets and Systems*, 1(1):3–28, 1978.

Description of Fuzzy First-Order Modal Logic Based on Constant Domain Semantics*

Zaiyue Zhang[1], Yuefei Sui[2] and Cungen Cao[2]

[1] Department of Computer Science,
Jiangsu University of Science and Technology, Zhenjiang,
Jiangsu 212003, China
njzzy@yzcn.net
[2] Key Laboratory of Intelligent Information Processing,
Institute of Computing Technology, Chinese Academy of Sciences,
Beijing 100080, China
suiyyff@hotmail.com, cgcao@ict.ac.cn

Abstract. As an extension of the traditional modal logic, the fuzzy first-order modal logic is discussed in this paper. A description of fuzzy first-order modal logic based on constant domain semantics is given, and a formal system of fuzzy reasoning based on the semantic information of models of first-order modal logic is established. It is also introduced in this paper the notion of the satisfiability of the reasoning system and some properties associated with the satisfiability are proved.

Keywords: modal logic, fuzzy reasoning system, rough set.

1 Introduction

Modal logic is an important logic branch developed firstly in the category of non-classical logics ([1]), and has been now widely used as a formalism for knowledge representation in artificial intelligence and an analysis tool in computer science ([2],[3]). Along with the study of the modal logics, it has been found that the modal logic has a close relationship with many other knowledge representation theories. The most well-known result is the connection of the possible world semantics for the modal epistemic logic S_5 with the approximation space in rough set theory (see [4]), where the system S_5 has been shown to be useful in the analysis of knowledge in various areas (see [5]). As a fragment of the first order logic, modal logics are limited to deal with crisp assertions, as its possible world semantics is crisp. That is, assertions about whether a formal proposition holds are yes-no questions. More often than not, the assertions encountered in the real world are not precise and thus cannot be treated simply by using the yes-no questions. Fuzzy logic directly deals with the notion of vagueness and imprecision, and has been used in many research areas such as interval mathematics ([6]), possibility theory ([7]), rough set theory ([14]) or artificial neural networks.

* The work is supported by the National NSF of China (60373042, 60273019 and 60073017), the National 973 Project of China (G1999032701), Ministry of Science and Technology (2001CCA03000).

D. Ślęzak et al. (Eds.): RSFDGrC 2005, LNAI 3641, pp. 642–650, 2005.

By combining with fuzzy logic, traditional modal logic has been extended. For example, Hájek ([8]) provided a complete axiomatization of fuzzy S_5 system where the accessibility relation is the universal relation; Godo and Rodríguez ([9],[10]) gave a complete axiomatic system for an extension of Hájek's logic with another modality corresponding to a fuzzy similarity relation; Zhang, et al. ([11],[12]) established a formal system of fuzzy reasoning based on propositional modal and discussed the soundness and completeness of the system. The work in this paper is an extensive study of the fuzzy propositional modal logic. We shall discuss the properties of the fuzzy first-order modal logic based on constant domain semantics, introduce a fuzzy reasoning formal system based on fuzzy first-order modal logic, and study the satisfiability of the reasoning procedure.

2   A Quick Overview of First-Order Modal Logic

In general, first-order modal logic will have its alphabet of symbols: a set of variable symbols, denoted by $VS = \{x_1, x_2, ...\}$; a set of relation symbols, denoted by $PS = \{P_i^n : n, i = 1, 2, ...\}$, where P_i^n is the ith n-place relation symbol; the logical symbols, $\neg$ (negation), $\wedge$ (and), $\vee$ (or), $\supset$ (material implication); quantifiers $\forall$ (for all) and $\exists$ (exists); the modal operator symbols $\square$ (necessity operator) and $\Diamond$ (possibility operator).

Definition 1. *An atomic formula of first-order modal logic is any expression of the form $P(x_1, ..., x_n)$, where P is an n-place relation symbol and $x_1, ..., x_n$ are variables.*

Definition 2. *The set of first-order formulas of first-order modal logic is the smallest set satisfying the following conditions: Every atomic formula is a formula; if φ is a formula, so are $\neg\varphi$, $\square\varphi$, $\Diamond\varphi$, $\forall x\varphi$ and $\exists x\varphi$; if φ and ψ are formulas and $\circ$ is a binary connective, then $\varphi \circ \psi$ is a formula.*

To establish the formal systems of modal logics, it is convenient to take $\neg$, $\supset$ and $\square$ as primitive, and the other connectives and modal operator as defined. For quantifiers we take $\forall$ as primitive, and treat $\exists$ as defined. Hence, the modal logic formal system contains following axioms and inference rules:

- *Axioms*: A_p1 $(\varphi \supset (\psi \supset \varphi))$;
  A_p2 $((\varphi \supset (\psi \supset \gamma)) \supset ((\varphi \supset \psi) \supset (\varphi \supset \gamma)))$;
  A_p3 $((\neg\varphi \supset \neg\psi) \supset (\psi \supset \varphi))$;
  A_p4 $(\forall x\varphi(x) \supset \varphi(y))$, where y is any variable free for x in $\varphi(x)$;
  A_p5 $(\forall x(\varphi \supset \psi) \supset (\forall x\varphi \supset \forall x\psi))$;
  $\mathbf{K}$ $(\square(\varphi \supset \psi) \supset (\square\varphi \supset \square\psi))$;
  $\mathbf{T}$ $(\square\varphi \supset \varphi)$;
  $\mathbf{E}$ $(\neg\square\neg\varphi \supset \square\neg\square\neg\varphi)$.
- *Inference rules:* N(necessity rule) if $\vdash \varphi$ then $\vdash \square\varphi$;
  UG(universal generalization) if $\vdash \varphi$ then $\vdash \forall x\varphi$;
  MP (modus ponens) if $\vdash \varphi \supset \psi$ and $\vdash \varphi$ then $\vdash \psi$.

A *constant domain semantics* (or *model*) for first-order modal logic is a structure $M = \langle W, R, D, I \rangle$ where W is a set of possible worlds, R is a relation on W, D is a non-empty set called the *domain* of the frame $\langle W, R \rangle$, I is an *interpretation* of the frame $\langle W, R, D \rangle$, which assigns to each n-place relation symbol P and to each possible world $w \in W$, some n-place relation on the domain D. Thus, $I(P, w)$ is an n-place relation on D, and so each n-tuple $\langle d_1, ..., d_n \rangle$ of members of D either is in the relation $I(P, w)$ or is not. Notice that in the constant domain semantics, the domain of quantification is the same from possible world to possible world.

Remark 1. Different modal logics are characterized by the different classes of frames which rely on the properties of the relations defined between possible worlds. Without loss of generality, we shall consider the logic which is characterized by the class of reflexive, symmetric and transitive frames.

Let $M = \langle W, R, D, I \rangle$ be a model. A *valuation* in model M is a mapping v that assigns to each free variable x some member $v(x)$ of domain D.

Definition 3. *Let M be a model and φ be a formula. For each $w \in W$ and each valuation v in M, the notion that φ is true at possible world w of model M with respect to valuation v, denoted by $M, w \models_v \varphi$, is defined as follows:*

(1) If φ is an atomic formula $P(x_1, ...x_t)$, then $M, w \models_v P(x_1, ...x_t)$ provided $\langle v(x_1), ..., v(x_t) \rangle \in I(P, w)$.
(2) $M, w \models_v \neg\varphi \Leftrightarrow M, w \not\models_v \varphi$.
(3) $M, w \models_v \varphi \supset \psi \Leftrightarrow M, w \models_v \neg\varphi$ or $M, w \models_v \psi$.
(4) $M, w \models_v \Box\varphi \Leftrightarrow$ for every $w' \in W$, if wRw' then $M, w' \models_v \varphi$.
(5) $M, w \models_v \forall x\varphi \Leftrightarrow$ for every x-variant v' of v in M, $M, w \models_{v'} \varphi$, where v' is an x-variant of v, i.e. v' and v agree on all variables except possibly variable x.

Definition 4. *Let M be a model and φ be a formula. For each $w \in W$, we say that φ is true at possible world w of model M, denoted by $M, w \models \varphi$, if $M, w \models_v \varphi$ for every valuation v in M; we say that φ is true in model M, denoted by $M \models \varphi$, if $M, w \models \varphi$ for every possible world w of M.*

Typically, first-order modal logics are limited to deal with crisp concepts. However, many useful concepts encountered in the real world do not have a precisely defined criteria of membership. To cope with this, we shall introduce a fuzzy first-order modal logic system based on *believable degrees*.

3   Fuzzy First-Order Modal Logic with Believable Degrees

Our fuzzy first-order modal system will have the same alphabet of symbols and the set of formulas as in the first-order modal logic mentioned in section 2. In order to deal with the vagueness and imprecision notions, we extend the first-order modal logics by using expressions of form $\langle \varphi(x_1, ...x_t), \varepsilon \rangle$ with intended meaning that *the believable degree of the individuals expressed by variables $x_1, ..., x_t$ having the relation expressed by formula φ is at least ε*, where $\varphi(x_1, ...x_t)$ is a formula of the first-order modal logic and $\varepsilon \in [0, 1]$. An expression of the form $\langle \varphi, \varepsilon \rangle$ is also called a *fuzzy assertion*.

Definition 5. *A constant domain semantics (or model) for the fuzzy first-order modal logic is a structure* $\mathcal{M} = \langle \mathcal{W}, \mathcal{R}, \mathcal{D}, \mathcal{I} \rangle$, *where* $\mathcal{W}$ *is a set of possible worlds,* $\mathcal{R}$ *is a binary relation on* $\mathcal{W}$, $\mathcal{D}$ *is a non-empty set called domain of the frame* $\langle \mathcal{W}, \mathcal{R} \rangle$, $\mathcal{I}$ *is interpretation of the frame* $\langle \mathcal{W}, \mathcal{R}, \mathcal{D} \rangle$, *which assigns to each formula* $\varphi(x_1, ..., x_t)$ *with free variables* $x_1, ..., x_t$ *and to each possible world* $w \in \mathcal{W}$, *some t-place function on* $\mathcal{D}$ *such that following conditions are satisfied:*
(1) If φ *is an atomic formula* $\mathcal{P}(x_1, ..., x_t)$ *then for each t-tuple* $(d_1, ..., d_t)$ *of* $\mathcal{D}$,
    $\mathcal{I}(\mathcal{P}, w)(d_1, ..., d_t) \in [0, 1]$.
(2) $\mathcal{I}(\neg \varphi, w)(d_1, ..., d_t) = 1 - \mathcal{I}(\varphi, w)(d_1, ..., d_t)$.
(3) $\mathcal{I}(\varphi \supset \psi, w)(d_1, ..., d_t) = \max\{1 - \mathcal{I}(\varphi, w)(d_1, ..., d_t), \mathcal{I}(\psi, w)(d_1, ..., d_t)\}$.
(4) $\mathcal{I}(\Box \varphi, w)(d_1, ..., d_t) = \inf\{\mathcal{I}(\varphi, w')(d_1, ..., d_t) : w \mathcal{R} w'\}$.
(5) For any $\varphi(x, x_1, ... x_t)$ *and any t-tuple* $\langle d_1, ..., d_t \rangle$ *of members of* $\mathcal{D}$,
    $\mathcal{I}(\forall x \varphi, w)(d_1, ..., d_t) = \inf\{\mathcal{I}(\varphi, w)(d, d_1, ..., d_t) : d \in \mathcal{D}\}$.
Let $\mathcal{M} = \langle \mathcal{W}, \mathcal{R}, \mathcal{D}, \mathcal{I} \rangle$ *be a model. A valuation in* $\mathcal{M}$ *is a mapping* v *that assigns to each free variable* x *some member* $v(x)$ *of domain* $\mathcal{D}$.

Definition 6. *Let* $\mathcal{M}$ *be a model and* φ *be a formula with free variables* $x_1, ..., x_t$. *For each* $w \in \mathcal{W}$ *and each valuation* v *in* $\mathcal{M}$, *a fuzzy assertion* $\langle \varphi, \varepsilon \rangle$ *is true at possible world* w *of model* $\mathcal{M}$ *with respect to valuation* v, *denoted by* $\mathcal{M}, w \models_v \langle \varphi, \varepsilon \rangle$, *if* $\mathcal{I}(\varphi, w)(v(x_1), ..., v(x_t)) \geq \varepsilon$.

Proposition 1. *Let* $\mathcal{M}$ *be a model and* φ *be a formula. Then for each* $w \in \mathcal{W}$ *and each valuation* v *in* $\mathcal{M}$, *following properties hold.*
(1) If φ *is an atomic formula* $P(x_1, ... x_t)$, *then* $\mathcal{M}, w \models_v \langle P(x_1, ... x_t), \varepsilon \rangle$ *provided* $\mathcal{I}(P, w)(v(x_1), ..., v(x_t)) \geq \varepsilon$.
(2) If $\mathcal{M}, w \models_v \langle \neg \varphi, \varepsilon \rangle$ *then* $\mathcal{I}(\varphi, w)(v(x_1), ..., v(x_t)) \leq 1 - \varepsilon$.
(3) $\mathcal{M}, w \models_v \langle \varphi \supset \psi, \varepsilon \rangle \Leftrightarrow \mathcal{M}, w \models_v \langle \neg \varphi, \varepsilon \rangle$ *or* $\mathcal{M}, w \models_v \langle \psi, \varepsilon \rangle$.
(4) $\mathcal{M}, w \models_v \langle \Box \varphi, \varepsilon \rangle \Leftrightarrow$ *for every* $w' \in \mathcal{W}$, *if* $w \mathcal{R} w'$ *then* $\mathcal{M}, w' \models_v \langle \varphi, \varepsilon \rangle$.
(5) $\mathcal{M}, w \models_v \langle \forall x \varphi, \varepsilon \rangle \leftrightarrow$ *for every x-variant* v' *of* v *in* $\mathcal{M}$, $\mathcal{M}, w \models_{v'} \langle \varphi, \varepsilon \rangle$. $\Box$

Definition 7. *Let* $\mathcal{M}$ *be a model and* $\langle \varphi, \varepsilon \rangle$ *be a formula. For each* $w \in \mathcal{W}$, *we say that* $\langle \varphi, \varepsilon \rangle$ *is true at possible world* w *of model* $\mathcal{M}$, *denoted by* $\mathcal{M}, w \models \langle \varphi, \varepsilon \rangle$, *if* $\mathcal{M}, w \models_v \langle \varphi, \varepsilon \rangle$ *for every valuation* v *in* $\mathcal{M}$; *we say that* $\langle \varphi, \varepsilon \rangle$ *is true in model* $\mathcal{M}$, *denoted by* $\mathcal{M} \models \langle \varphi, \varepsilon \rangle$, *if* $\mathcal{M}, w \models \langle \varphi, \varepsilon \rangle$ *for every possible world* w *of* $\mathcal{M}$.

Proposition 2. *Let* $\mathcal{M}$ *be a model and* $\varphi(x)$ *be a formula in which* x *is free, and let* y *be any variable which is free for* x *in* $\varphi(x)$. *Suppose* v *and* v' *are valuations in* $\mathcal{M}$ *such that* v' *is x-variant of* v *and has* $v'(x) = v(y)$. *Then for any* $\varepsilon \in [0, 1]$ *and any possible world* w, $\mathcal{M}, w \models_v \langle \varphi(y), \varepsilon \rangle$ *if and only if* $\mathcal{M}, w \models_{v'} \langle \varphi(x), \varepsilon \rangle$.

Proof. The proposition is proved by induction on the length of the formula $\varphi(x)$. For basic step, assume $\varphi(x)$ is an atomic formula, say $P(x, x_1, ..., x_t)$ where x and x_i are free variables and $x_i \neq x$ for all $i = 1, ..., t$. Since v' is x-variant of v, we have $v(x_i) = v'(x_i)$ for all $i = 1, ..., t$, by the assumption that $v(y) = v'(x)$ we have $\mathcal{I}(P, w)(v(y), v(x_1), ..., v(x_t)) = \mathcal{I}(P, w)(v'(x), v'(x_1), ..., v'(x_t))$, which implies that $\mathcal{M}, w \models_v \langle P(y, x_1, ..., x_t), \varepsilon \rangle$ holds iff $\mathcal{M}, w \models_{v'} \langle P(x, x_1, ..., x_t), \varepsilon \rangle$.

    In the induction step, the cases that $\varphi(x)$ is $\neg \psi(x)$, or is $\psi(x) \supset \xi(x)$, or is $\Box \psi(x)$ can be easily verified. Now we consider the case that $\varphi(x)$ is $\forall z \psi(x)$, where

$z \neq x$. Suppose that $\mathcal{M}, w \not\models_v \langle \forall z \psi(y), \varepsilon \rangle$. We show that $\mathcal{M}, w \not\models_{v'} \langle \forall z \psi(x), \varepsilon \rangle$. Let u be a z-variant of v and $\mathcal{M}, w \not\models_u \langle \psi(y), \varepsilon \rangle$. Define valuation u' by setting $u'(x) = u(y)$ and $u'(x') = u(x')$ for all x' such that $x' \neq x$. Then, u' is x-variant of u, and by the induction hypothesis applied to $\psi(x)$, we have $\mathcal{M}, w \not\models_{u'} \langle \psi(x), \varepsilon \rangle$. Now y is free for x in $\forall z \psi(x)$, so $z \neq y$. For any x', if $x' \neq z$ and $x' \neq x$ then $u'(x') = u(x') = v(x') = v'(x')$, notice that $u'(x) = u(y) = v(y) = v'(x)$, thus u' is z-variant of v'. Since $\mathcal{M}, w \not\models_{u'} \langle \psi(x), \varepsilon \rangle$, then, $\mathcal{M}, w \not\models_{v'} \langle \forall z \psi(x), \varepsilon \rangle$. The converse can be verified by a similar argument. □

Proposition 3. *Let* $\mathcal{M} = \langle \mathcal{W}, \mathcal{R}, \mathcal{D}, \mathcal{I} \rangle$ *be any model such that* $\mathcal{R}$ *is an equivalence relation on* $\mathcal{W}$*. Then,*

(a) $\mathcal{M} \models \langle A_p 1, 0.5 \rangle$*;*
(b) $\mathcal{M} \models \langle A_p 2, 0.5 \rangle$*;*
(c) $\mathcal{M} \models \langle A_p 3, 0.5 \rangle$*;*
(d) $\mathcal{M} \models \langle A_p 4, 0.5 \rangle$*;*
(e) $\mathcal{M} \models \langle A_p 5, 0.5 \rangle$*;*
(f) $\mathcal{M} \models \langle \mathbf{K}, 0.5 \rangle$*;*
(g) $\mathcal{M} \models \langle \mathbf{T}, 0.5 \rangle$*;*
(h) $\mathcal{M} \models \langle \mathbf{E}, 0.5 \rangle$*.*

Proof. We prove (d) and (e) as examples. Now, let w be any possible world and v be any valuation in $\mathcal{M}$. For (d), we prove that $\mathcal{M}, w \models_v \langle \forall x \varphi(x) \supset \varphi(y), 0.5 \rangle$, i.e. $\mathcal{I}(\forall x \varphi(x) \supset \varphi(y), w)(v(y)) \geq 0.5$, where y is free for x in $\varphi(x)$. Notice that $\mathcal{I}(\forall x \varphi(x) \supset \varphi(y), w)(v(y)) = \max\{1 - \mathcal{I}(\forall x \varphi(x), w)(v(y)), \mathcal{I}(\varphi(y), w)(v(y))\}$, it is sufficient to show that either $\mathcal{I}(\forall x \varphi(x), w)(v(y)) \leq 0.5$ or $\mathcal{I}(\varphi(y), w)(v(y)) \geq 0.5$. If $\mathcal{I}(\forall x \varphi(x), w)(v(y)) > 0.5$ then $\mathcal{M}, w \models_v \langle \forall x \varphi(x), 0.5 \rangle$. Define valuation v' in $\mathcal{I}$ by setting $v'(x) = v(y)$ and $v'(x') = v(x')$ for all x' such that $x' \neq x$, then v' is x-variant of v, and thus $\mathcal{M}, w \models_{v'} \langle \varphi(x), 0.5 \rangle$. By Proposition 2, we have that $\mathcal{M}, w \models_v \langle \varphi(y), 0.5 \rangle$, i.e. $\mathcal{I}(\varphi(y), w)(v(y)) \geq 0.5$.

For (e), let y be a free variable in $\forall x(\varphi \supset \psi) \supset (\forall x \varphi \supset \forall x \psi)$, let $\alpha(d) = \mathcal{I}(\varphi, w)(d, v(y))$ and $\beta(d) = \mathcal{I}(\psi, w)(d, v(y))$. We have $\mathcal{I}((\forall x(\varphi \supset \psi) \supset (\forall x \varphi \supset \forall x \psi)), w)(v(y)) = \max\{1 - \mathcal{I}(\forall x(\varphi \supset \psi), w)(v(y)), \mathcal{I}((\forall x \varphi \supset \forall x \psi), w)(v(y))\}$, where $1 - \mathcal{I}((\forall x(\varphi \supset \psi)), w)(v(y)) = 1 - \inf\{\mathcal{I}((\varphi \supset \psi), w)(d, v(y)) : d \in \mathcal{D}\} = 1 - \inf\{\max\{1 - \alpha(d), \beta(d)\} : d \in \mathcal{D}\}$, and where $\mathcal{I}((\forall x \varphi \supset \forall x \psi), w)(v(y)) = \max\{1 - \mathcal{I}(\forall x \varphi)(v(y)), \mathcal{I}(\forall x \psi, w)(v(y))\} = \max\{1 - \inf\{\alpha(d) : d \in \mathcal{D}\}, \inf\{\beta(d) : d \in \mathcal{D}\}\}$. If $\max\{1 - \inf\{\alpha(d) : d \in \mathcal{D}\}, \inf\{\beta(d) : d \in \mathcal{D}\}\} < 0.5$ then there exists $d' \in \mathcal{D}$, $\alpha(d') > 0.5$ and $\beta(d') < 0.5$, thus $\inf\{\max\{1 - \alpha(d), \beta(d)\} : d \in \mathcal{D}\} < 0.5$. Therefore, we have that $1 - \inf\{\max\{1 - \alpha(d), \beta(d)\} : d \in \mathcal{D}\} > 0.5$, which implies that $\mathcal{I}((\forall x(\varphi \supset \psi) \supset (\forall x \varphi \supset \forall x \psi)), w)(v(y)) \geq 0.5$. □

Proposition 4. *Let* $\mathcal{M}$ *be any fuzzy modal model. If* $\mathcal{M} \models \langle \varphi, \varepsilon \rangle$ *then* $\mathcal{M} \models \langle \Box \varphi, \varepsilon \rangle$*.* □

Proposition 5. *If* $\mathcal{M} \models \langle \varphi \supset \psi, \varepsilon \rangle$ *and* $\mathcal{M} \models \langle \varphi, \varepsilon' \rangle$ *then* $\mathcal{M} \models \langle \psi, \varepsilon \rangle$*, where* $\varepsilon, \varepsilon' \in [0, 1]$ *such that* $\varepsilon > 1 - \varepsilon'$*.* □

Proposition 6. *If* $\mathcal{M} \models \langle \varphi, \varepsilon \rangle$ *then* $\mathcal{M} \models \langle \forall x \varphi, \varepsilon \rangle$*.* □

There is a close relationship between modal logics and the theory of rough set ([13]). The notion of rough set was introduced by Pawlak, and has been widely used in the areas of data mining and knowledge representation and reasoning ([14],[15]). The basic ingredients in the rough set theory are the lower and upper approximation. More precisely, let (U, R) be an information system, where U is a non-empty universe and R is an equivalence relation on U. For any subset X of U, the lower and upper approximations of X are defined respectively by

$$\underline{R}X = \{y \in U : [y]_R \subseteq X\}$$
$$\overline{R}X = \{y \in U : [y]_R \cap X \neq \emptyset\}$$

X is *definable* (or *exact*) if it is the union of R-equivalence classes, and is *rough* otherwise. Now in the fuzzy first-order modal logic, let $\mathcal{M} = \langle \mathcal{W}, \mathcal{R}, \mathcal{D}, \mathcal{I} \rangle$ be a fuzzy modal model, where $\mathcal{R}$ is an equivalence relation on $\mathcal{W}$, and

$$\| \langle \varphi, \varepsilon \rangle \| = \{w \in \mathcal{W} : \mathcal{M}, w \models \langle \varphi, \varepsilon \rangle\}.$$

Below we show relationship between rough sets and fuzzy modal logic.

Proposition 7. *We have equality* $\|\langle \Box\varphi, \varepsilon \rangle\| = \underline{\mathcal{R}} \, \|\langle \varphi, \varepsilon \rangle\|$, *as well as inclusion* $\|\langle \Diamond\varphi, \varepsilon \rangle\| \supseteq \overline{\mathcal{R}} \, \|\langle \varphi, \varepsilon \rangle\|$. *Moreover, if the domain of the possible worlds is finite then* $\supseteq$ *can be replaced by* $=$. □

4   Fuzzy Reasoning and Satisfiability

Let Σ be a set of fuzzy assertions and $\langle \varphi, \varepsilon \rangle$ be a fuzzy assertion. We say that $\langle \varphi, \varepsilon \rangle$ is a *logical consequence* of Σ, denoted by $\Sigma \models \langle \varphi, \varepsilon \rangle$, if every model of Σ is a model of $\langle \varphi, \varepsilon \rangle$. The process of deciding whether $\Sigma \models \langle \varphi, \varepsilon \rangle$ or not is called a *fuzzy reasoning procedure based on fuzzy first-order modal logics*. To verify that $\Sigma \models \langle \varphi, \varepsilon \rangle$, one has to verify that every model of Σ is a model of $\langle \varphi, \varepsilon \rangle$, which is not convenient in practical applications. To cope with it, we attempt to find a method which can be used to decide whether $\Sigma \models \langle \varphi, \varepsilon \rangle$ or not effectively. The associated work about fuzzy propositional modal logic has been discussed in [11] and [12]. In the following, we shall extend the work from propositional modal logic to first-order modal logic and establish a fuzzy reasoning formal system based on fuzzy first-order modal logic.

The basic idea is to syntactize the semantic information. In detail, we extend the logical langauge for the fuzzy first-order modal logic in such a way that there are infinite many possible world symbols **w** and a binary relation symbol **R**. Under an extended interpretation $\mathcal{I}$, **w** is interpreted to be a possible world, and **R** to be R, the accessibility relation in the frame of interpretation $\mathcal{I}$.

Definition 8. *In addition to the basic symbols of the first-order modal logic, the fuzzy reasoning formal system also contains a set of possible worlds symbols* $\mathbf{w}_1, \mathbf{w}_2, ...$, *a set of relation symbols* $\{<, \leq, >, \geq\}$ *and a binary relation symbol* **R**. *The basic expression, called fuzzy constraint, in the system is in the form of* $\langle \mathbf{w} : \varphi \ rel \ \varepsilon \rangle$, *where* φ *is any formula in the first-order modal logic,* $\varepsilon \in [0, 1]$ *and* $rel \in \{<, \leq, >, \geq\}$.

Definition 9. *An interpretation $\mathcal{I}$ of the system contains a model $(\mathcal{W}_\mathcal{I}, \mathcal{R}, \mathcal{D}_\mathcal{I}, \mathcal{I})$, where for any $\mathbf{w}$, $\mathbf{w}^\mathcal{I} \in \mathcal{W}_\mathcal{I}$ is a possible world, $\mathbf{R}^\mathcal{I} = R$. Also for any $\mathbf{w}$ and any formula $\varphi(x_1, ..., x_t)$ with free variables $x_1, ..., x_t$, $(\varphi^\mathcal{I}, \mathbf{w}^\mathcal{I})$ (simply denoted by $\mathcal{I}(\varphi, \mathbf{w})$) ia a t-place function on $\mathcal{D}_\mathcal{I}$ such that the properties (1)-(5) in Definition 5 are satisfied. For any two possible world symbols $\mathbf{w}$ and $\mathbf{w}'$, $\mathbf{w}'$ is said to be accessible from $\mathbf{w}$ if $\mathbf{w}^\mathcal{I} \mathbf{R}^\mathcal{I} \mathbf{w}'^\mathcal{I}$.*

Definition 10. *A fuzzy constraint $\langle \mathbf{w} : \varphi \text{ rel } \varepsilon \rangle$, where φ is a formula with free variables $x_1, ..., x_t$, is said to be satisfiable in $\mathcal{I}$ if there exists a valuation v such that $\mathcal{I}(\varphi, \mathbf{w})(v(x_1), ..., v(x_t))$ rel ε. A set S of fuzzy constraints is said to be uniformly satisfiable in an interpretation $\mathcal{I}$ if there exists a valuation v such that every fuzzy constraint of S is satisfiable in $\mathcal{I}$ with respect to v.*

Proposition 8. *Let S be a set of fuzzy constraints and $\langle \mathbf{w} : \Box\varphi \geq \varepsilon \rangle \in S$. If S is satisfiable in $\mathcal{I}$ then $S \cup \{\langle \mathbf{w}' : \varphi \geq \varepsilon \rangle\}$ is satisfiable in $\mathcal{I}$ for any $\mathbf{w}'$ such that $\mathbf{w}'$ is accessible from $\mathbf{w}$.*

Proof. Let v be the valuation in $\mathcal{I}$ such that S is satisfiable in $\mathcal{I}$ with respect to v. Then we have that $\mathcal{I}(\Box\varphi, \mathbf{w})(v(x_1), ..., v(x_t)) \geq \varepsilon$. Let us notice that we have $\mathcal{I}(\Box\varphi, \mathbf{w})(v(x_1), ..., v(x_t)) = \inf\{\mathcal{I}(\varphi, \mathbf{w}')(v(x_1), ..., v(x_t)) : \mathbf{w}^\mathcal{I}\mathbf{R}^\mathcal{I}\mathbf{w}'^\mathcal{I}\}$. Thus we have $\mathcal{I}(\varphi, \mathbf{w}')(v(x_1), ..., v(x_t)) \geq \varepsilon$ for any $\mathbf{w}'$ such that $\mathbf{w}^\mathcal{I}\mathbf{R}^\mathcal{I}\mathbf{w}'^\mathcal{I}$, i.e., for any $\mathbf{w}'$ accessible from $\mathbf{w}$, $\langle \mathbf{w}' : \varphi \geq \varepsilon \rangle$ is satisfied in $\mathcal{I}$ by valuation v. $\qquad\square$

Proposition 8 is also correct if $\geq$ is replaced by $>$. As for the constraints with the form $\langle \mathbf{w} : \Box\varphi \leq \varepsilon \rangle$, the condition of the associated proposition should be modified slightly. This is due to the simple fact that $\inf S \leq \varepsilon$ does not necessarily imply the existence of an element in S that is less than or equal to ε.

Proposition 9. *Let S be a set of fuzzy constraints and $\langle \mathbf{w} : \Box\varphi < \varepsilon \rangle \in S$. If S is satisfiable in $\mathcal{I}$ then $S \cup \{\langle \mathbf{w}' : \varphi < \varepsilon \rangle\}$ is satisfiable in $\mathcal{I}$ for some $\mathbf{w}'$ such that $\mathbf{w}'$ is accessible from $\mathbf{w}$. Moreover, if $\langle \mathbf{w} : \Box\varphi \leq \varepsilon \rangle \in S$ and S is satisfiable in $\mathcal{I}$ with the condition such that $\mathcal{W}_\mathcal{I}$ is finite, then $S \cup \{\langle \mathbf{w}' : \varphi \leq \varepsilon \rangle\}$ is satisfiable in $\mathcal{I}$ for some $\mathbf{w}'$ such that $\mathbf{w}'$ is accessible from $\mathbf{w}$.*

Proof. The proof of the former part is similar to that of Proposition 8 with the property that $\inf\{\mathcal{I}(\varphi, \mathbf{w}')(v(x_1), ..., v(x_t)) : \mathbf{w}^\mathcal{I}\mathbf{R}^\mathcal{I}\mathbf{w}'^\mathcal{I}\} < \varepsilon$. The proof of the latter part is based on the fact that $\inf\{\mathcal{I}(\varphi, \mathbf{w}')(v(x_1), ..., v(x_t)) : \mathbf{w}^\mathcal{I}\mathbf{R}^\mathcal{I}\mathbf{w}'^\mathcal{I}\} \leq \varepsilon$ and that $\mathcal{W}_\mathcal{I}$ is finite. $\qquad\square$

Proposition 10. *If S is satisfiable in an interpretation $\mathcal{I}$ and $\langle \mathbf{w} : \neg\varphi \text{ rel } n \rangle \in S$, then $S \cup \{\langle \mathbf{w} : \varphi \text{ rel}^* 1 - \varepsilon \rangle\}$ is satisfiable in $\mathcal{I}$. Where rel $\in \{\geq, \leq, >, <\}$ and rel* is the converse of rel.*

Proof. Let v be the valuation in $\mathcal{I}$ such that S is satisfiable in $\mathcal{I}$ with respect to v. Then we have that $\mathcal{I}(\neg\varphi, \mathbf{w})(v(x_1), ..., v(x_t))$ rel ε. Since $\mathcal{I}(\neg\varphi, \mathbf{w})(v(x_1), ..., v(x_t)) = 1 - \mathcal{I}(\varphi, \mathbf{w})(v(x_1), ..., v(x_t))$, we have that $\mathcal{I}(\varphi, \mathbf{w})(v(x_1), ..., v(x_t))$ rel* $1 - \varepsilon$, i.e., $\langle \mathbf{w} : \varphi \text{ rel}^* 1 - \varepsilon \rangle$ is also satisfied by the valuation v. $\qquad\square$

Proposition 11. *If S is satisfiable in $\mathcal{I}$ and $\langle \mathbf{w} : \varphi \supset \psi \leq \varepsilon \rangle \in S$, then $S \cup \{\langle \mathbf{w} : \varphi \geq 1 - \varepsilon \rangle, \langle \mathbf{w} : \psi \leq \varepsilon \rangle\}$ is satisfiable in $\mathcal{I}$.*

Proof. Let v be the valuation in $\mathcal{I}$ such that S is satisfiable in $\mathcal{I}$ with respect to v. Then the proposition can be easily proved by the fact that $\mathcal{I}(\varphi \supset \psi, \mathbf{w})(v(x_1), ..., v(x_t)) \leq \varepsilon$ if and only if $\mathcal{I}(\varphi, \mathbf{w})(v(x_1), ..., v(x_t)) \geq 1 - \varepsilon$ and $\mathcal{I}(\psi, \mathbf{w})(v(x_1), ..., v(x_t)) \leq \varepsilon$. □

Proposition 12. *If S is satisfiable in $\mathcal{I}$ and $\langle \mathbf{w} : \varphi \supset \psi \geq \varepsilon \rangle \in S$, then at least one of the sets $S \cup \{\langle \mathbf{w} : \varphi \leq 1 - \varepsilon \rangle\}$ and $S \cup \{\langle \mathbf{w} : \psi \geq \varepsilon \rangle\}$ is satisfiable in $\mathcal{I}$.*

Proof. This is simply because that if $\mathcal{I}(\varphi \supset \psi, \mathbf{w})(v(x_1), ..., v(x_t)) \geq \varepsilon$ then we have either $\mathcal{I}(\varphi, \mathbf{w})(v(x_1), ..., v(x_t)) \leq 1 - \varepsilon$ or $\mathcal{I}(\psi, \mathbf{w})(v(x_1), ..., v(x_t)) \geq \varepsilon$. □

Proposition 13. *If S is satisfiable in $\mathcal{I}$ and $\langle \mathbf{w} : \forall x \varphi(x) \geq \varepsilon \rangle \in S$, then $S \cup \{\langle \mathbf{w} : \varphi(y) \geq \varepsilon \rangle\}$ is satisfiable in $\mathcal{I}$, given any variable y free for x in $\varphi(x)$.*

Proof. Let v be the valuation such that $\mathcal{I}(\forall x \varphi(x), \mathbf{w})(v(x_1), ..., v(x_t)) \geq \varepsilon$. Then for any v', if v' is x-variant of v then $\mathcal{I}(\varphi, \mathbf{w})(v'(x), v'(x_1), ..., v'(x_t)) \geq \varepsilon$. Now let u be the valuation such that $u(x) = v(y)$ and $u(x') = v(x')$ for any $x' \neq x$. Then we have that u is x-variant of v, thus by Proposition 2 we have that $\mathcal{I}(\varphi(y), \mathbf{w})(v(y), v(x_1), ..., v(x_t)) \geq \varepsilon$ since y is free for x in $\varphi(x)$, therefore the constraint $\langle \mathbf{w} : \varphi(y) \geq \varepsilon \rangle$ is also satisfied by v in $\mathcal{I}$. □

Proposition 13 also holds if the symbol $\geq$ is replaced by $>$. For the constraint with the form $\langle \mathbf{w} : \forall x \varphi(x) \leq \varepsilon \rangle$, the condition of the associated proposition should also be modified slightly just like that in Proposition 9. But at this time, the interpretation domain $\mathcal{D}_{\mathcal{I}}$ will be considered.

Proposition 14. *If S is satisfiable in $\mathcal{I}$ and $\langle \mathbf{w} : \forall x \varphi(x) < \varepsilon \rangle \in S$, where x dose not occur free in any formula of the constraint in S, then $S \cup \{\langle \mathbf{w} : \varphi(x) < \varepsilon \rangle\}$ is satisfiable in $\mathcal{I}$. Moreover, If $\langle \mathbf{w} : \forall x \varphi(x) \leq \varepsilon \rangle \in S$, where x dose not occur free in any formula of the constraint in S, and S is satisfiable in $\mathcal{I}$ with the condition that $\mathcal{D}_{\mathcal{I}}$ is finite , then $S \cup \{\langle \mathbf{w} : \varphi(x) \leq \varepsilon \rangle\}$ is satisfiable in $\mathcal{I}$.*

Proof. Let v be the valuation such that $\mathcal{I}(\forall x \varphi(x), \mathbf{w})(v(x_1), ..., v(x_t)) < \varepsilon$. Then there exists a valuation v' such that v' is x-variant of v and $\mathcal{I}(\varphi, \mathbf{w})(v'(x), v'(x_1), ..., v'(x_t)) < \varepsilon$ i.e., the fuzzy constraint $\langle \mathbf{w} : \varphi(x) < \varepsilon \rangle$ is satisfied by v' in $\mathcal{I}$. Suppose $\langle \mathbf{w} : \psi \ rel \ \varepsilon' \rangle$ is any fuzzy constraint in S, and $x_1, ..., x_t$ are free variables in ψ. Since x is not free in ψ and v' is x-variant of v, we have that $\mathcal{I}(\psi, \mathbf{w})(v'(x_1), ..., v'(x_t)) = \mathcal{I}(\psi, \mathbf{w})(v(x_1), ..., v(x_t))$. Thus the fuzzy constraint $\langle \mathbf{w} : \psi \ rel \ \varepsilon' \rangle$ is also satisfied by v' in $\mathcal{I}$. When consider the fuzzy constraint with the form $\langle \mathbf{w} : \forall x \varphi(x) \leq \varepsilon \rangle$, the valuation v' also exists simply because that $\mathcal{D}_{\mathcal{I}}$ is finite. □

5   Conclusion and Further Works

In this paper we discussed the properties of the fuzzy first-order modal logic, and introduce a fuzzy reasoning formal system based on the first-order modal logic, and studied the properties about the satisfiability of the reasoning procedure. Our further work is to discuss the soundness and completeness of the fuzzy reasoning system and build a reasoning mechanism which can be used to decide whether $\Sigma \models \langle \varphi, \varepsilon \rangle$ or not efficiently.

Acknowledgement: The authors are grateful to the anonymous referee of the RSFDGrC 2005 for the useful suggestion.

References

1. Melvin, F. and Richard, L. M., First-Order Modal Logic, Kluwer Academic Publishers, 1998.
2. Gabbay, D. M., Hogger, C. J. and Robinson, J. A. (eds.), Handbook of Logic in Artificial Intelligence and Logic Programming, Vol.1-4, Clarendon Press-Oxford, 1994.
3. Abramsky, S., Gabbay, D. M. and Maibaum, T. S. E. (eds.), Handbook of Logic in Computer Science, Vol.1-3, Clarendon Press-Oxford, 1992.
4. Orłowska, E., Kripke semantics for knowledge representation logics, Studia Logica XLIX(1990), 255–272.
5. Fagin, R. F., Halpern, J. Y., Moses, Y. and Vardi, M. Y., Reasoning about Knowledge, MIT press, 1996.
6. Alefeld, G. and Herzberger, J., Introduction to Interval Computations, Academic Press, New York, 1983.
7. Dubois, D. and Prade, H., Possibility Theory: An Approach to Computerized Processing of Uncertainty, Plenum Press, New York, 1988.
8. Hájek, P. and Harmancová, D., A many-valued modal logics, in: Proceedings of IPMU'96, 1021–1024, 1996.
9. Rodríguez, R., Garcia, P. and Godo, L., Using fuzzy similarity relations to revise and update a knowledge base, Mathware and Soft Computing **3**(1996), 357–370.
10. Godo, L. and Rodríguez, R., Graded similarity based semantics for nonmonotonic inference, Annals of Mathematics and Artificial Intelligence **34**(2002), 89–105, 2002.
11. Zhang Z Y, Sui Y F, Cao C G. Fuzzy reasoning based on propositional modal logic, in: Proceedings of the 4th International Conference on Rough Sets and Current Trends in Computing (RSCTC2004), LNCS 3066, 109–115, 2004.
12. Zhang, Z. Y., Sui, Y. F. and Cao, C. G., Formal reasoning system based on fuzzy propositional modal logic, to appear in Journal of Software, 2005.
13. Yao, Y. Y., A comparative study of fuzzy sets and rough sets, Information Science **109**(1998), 227–242.
14. Pawlak, Z., Rough sets, International Journal of Computer and Information Science **11**(1982), 341–356.
15. Pawlak, Z., Rough Sets – Theoretical Aspects of Reasoning about Data, Kluwer Academic Publishers, 1991.

Arrow Decision Logic

Tuan-Fang Fan[1,2], Duen-Ren Liu[3], and Gwo-Hshiung Tzeng[4]

[1] Institute of Information Management
National Chiao-Tung University, Hsinchu 300, Taiwan
tffan.iim92g@nctu.edu.tw
[2] Department of Information Engineering,
National Penghu Institute of Technology, Penghu, Taiwan.
dffan@npit.edu.tw
[3] Institute of Information Management
National Chiao-Tung University, Hsinchu 300, Taiwan
dliu@iim.nctu.edu.tw
[4] Institute of Management of Technology
National Chiao-Tung University, Hsinchu 300, Taiwan
ghtzeng@cc.nctu.edu.tw

Abstract. In this paper, we propose arrow decision logic (ADL), which combines the main features of decision logic and arrow logic. Decision logic represents and reasons about knowledge extracted from decision tables based on rough set theory, while arrow logic is the basic modal logic of arrows. The semantic models of ADL are pairwise comparison tables, which are useful in rough set-based multicriteria analysis. Consequently, ADL can represent preference knowledge induced from multicriteria decision tables.

Keywords: Arrow logic, decision logic, multicriteria decision analysis, rough sets.

1 Introduction

The rough set theory proposed by Pawlak [16] provides an effective tool for extracting knowledge from data tables. To represent and reason about extracted knowledge, a decision logic (DL) is proposed in [17]. The semantics of the logic is defined in a Tarskian style through the notions of models and satisfaction. While DL can be considered as an instance of classical logic in the context of data tables, different generalizations of DL corresponding to some non-classical logics are also desirable from the knowledge representation viewpoint. For example, to deal with uncertain or incomplete information, some generalized decision logics have been proposed [2,13,14,20,21].

When rough set theory is applied to multi-criteria decision analysis (MCDA), it is crucial to deal with preference-ordered attribute domains and decision classes [4,5,6,7,8,9,10,18]. The original rough set theory cannot handle inconsistencies arising from violation of the dominance principle due to its use of the indiscernibility relation. In the above-mentioned works, the relation is replaced by a

D. Ślęzak et al. (Eds.): RSFDGrC 2005, LNAI 3641, pp. 651–659, 2005.

dominance relation for solving the multi-criteria sorting problem, and the data table is replaced by a pairwise comparison table (PCT) for solving multi-criteria choice and ranking problems. This approach is called the dominance-based rough set approach (DRSA). For MCDA problems, DRSA can induce a set of decision rules from exemplary decisions provided by decision-makers. The induced decision rules play the role of a comprehensive preference model and can provide recommendations in a new decision-making environment. DL has also been generalized to represent such kinds of decision rules[3].

In this paper, we propose arrow decision logic (ADL), which combines the main features of DL and arrow logic to represent the decision rules induced from PCT. The atomic formulas of ADL are descriptors the same as those in DL; while the formulas of ADL are interpreted with respect to each pair of objects, just as in the pair frames of arrow logic[15,19]. The semantic model of ADL is PCT; thus, ADL can represent preference knowledge induced from multicriteria decision tables.

The remainder of this paper is organized as follows. In Section 2, we review DL and arrow logic. In Section 3 we present the syntax and semantics of ADL, and define some quantitative measures for the rules of ADL. Finally, we present our conclusions in Section 4.

2　Decision Logic and Arrow Logic

2.1　Decision Logic

In data mining problems, data is usually provided in the form of a data table (DT). A formal definition of a data table is given in [17].

Definition 1. *A data table[1] is a quadruple*

$$T = (U, A, \{V_i \mid i \in A\}, \{f_i \mid i \in A\}),$$

where U is a nonempty finite set, called the universe; A is a nonempty finite set of primitive attributes; for each $i \in A$, V_i is the domain of values for i; and for each $i \in A$, $f_i : U \to V_i$ is a total function.

In [17], a decision logic (DL) is proposed to represent the knowledge discovered from data tables. It is called decision logic because it is particularly useful in a special kind of data tables, called *decision tables*. A decision table is a data table $T = (U, A, \{V_i \mid iA\}, \{f_i \mid i \in A\})$ such that A can be partitioned into two sets, called condition attributes and decision attributes. By data analysis, decision rules relating the condition and the decision attributes can be derived from the table. A rule is then represented as an implication between formulas of the logic.

The basic alphabet of a DL consists of a finite set of attribute symbols, A, and for $i \in$ A, a finite set of value symbols, V_i. An atomic formula of DL is a

---

[1] Also called knowledge representation systems, information systems, or attribute-value systems.

descriptor, (i, v), where $i \in A$ and $v \in V_i$. The set of DL well-formed formulas (wff) is the smallest set containing the atomic formulas and is closed under the Boolean connectives $\neg$ and $\vee$. If φ and ψ are wffs of DL, then $\varphi \longrightarrow \psi$ is a rule in DL, where φ is called the antecedent of the rule and ψ the consequent. As usual, we use standard Boolean connectives $\wedge, \supset, \equiv$ as abbreviations.

A data table $T = (U, A, \{V_i \mid i \in A\}, \{f_i \mid i \in A\})$ is a model for a given DL if there is a bijection $\tau : A \rightarrow A$ such that for every $a \in A$, $V_{\tau(a)} = V_a$. Thus, by somewhat abusing the notation, we usually denote an atomic formula as (i, v), where $i \in A$ and $v \in V_i$, if the data tables are clear from the context. Intuitively, each element in the universe of a data table corresponds to a data record, and an atomic formula, which is in fact an attribute-value pair, describes the value of some attribute in data record. Thus, the atomic formulas (and therefore the wffs) can be verified or falsified in each data record. This gives rise to a satisfaction relation between the universe and the set of wffs.

Definition 2. *Given a DL and a data table $T = (U, A, \{V_i \mid i \in A\}, \{f_i \mid i \in A\})$ for it, the satisfaction relation $\models_T$ between U and the wffs of DL is defined inductively as follows (the subscript T is omitted for brevity).*

1. *$x \models (i, v)$ iff $f_i(x) = v$,*
2. *$x \models \neg\varphi$ iff $x \not\models \varphi$,*
3. *$x \models \varphi \vee \psi$ iff $x \models \varphi$ or $x \models \psi$.*

If φ is a DL wff, the set $m_T(\varphi)$ defined by

$$m_T(\varphi) = \{x \in U \mid x \models \varphi\} \tag{1}$$

is called the meaning set of the formula φ in T. If T is understood, we simply write $m(\varphi)$.

A formula φ is said to be valid in a data table, T, if and only if $m(\varphi) = U$. That is, φ is satisfied by all individuals in the universe. We usually write $\models \varphi$ instead of $\models_T \varphi$, when T is clear from the context.

2.2   Arrow Logic

Arrow logic is the basic modal logic of arrows [15,19]. An arrow can represent a state transition in program execution, a morphism in category theory, an edge in a directed graph, etc. In arrow logic, an arrow is an abstract entity; however, we can usually interpret it as a concrete relationship between two objects, which results in a pair-frame model[15,19]. Below, we present the basic syntax and semantics of arrow logic.

The basic alphabet of arrow logic consists of a countable set of propositional symbols, the Boolean connectives $\neg$ and $\vee$, the modal constant δ, the unary modal operator $\otimes$, and the binary modal operator $\circ$. The set of arrow logic wffs is the smallest set containing the propositional symbols and δ, closed under the Boolean connectives $\neg$ and $\vee$, and satisfying

- if φ is a wff, then $\otimes\varphi$ is a wff, too.
- if φ and ψ are wffs, so is $\varphi \circ \psi$.

Semantically, these wffs are interpreted in arrow models.

Definition 3
1. *An arrow frame is a quadruple $\mathfrak{F} = (W, C, R, I)$ such that $C \subseteq W \times W \times W$, $R \subseteq W \times W$ and $I \subseteq W$.*
2. *An arrow model is a pair $\mathfrak{M} = (\mathfrak{F}, \pi)$, where $\mathfrak{F} = (W, C, R, I)$ is an arrow frame and π is a valuation that maps propositional symbols to subsets of W. An element in W is called an arrow in the model $\mathfrak{M}$.*
3. *The satisfaction of a wff φ at an arrow w of $\mathfrak{M}$, denoted by $w \models_{\mathfrak{M}} \varphi$ (as usual, the subscript $\mathfrak{M}$ can be omitted), is inductively defined as follows:*
   (a) $w \models p$ iff $w \in \pi(p)$, for any propositional symbol p,
   (b) $w \models \delta$ iff $w \in I$,
   (c) $w \models \neg\varphi$ iff $w \not\models \varphi$,
   (d) $w \models \varphi \vee \psi$ iff $w \models \varphi$ or $x \models \psi$,
   (e) $w \models \varphi \circ \psi$ iff there are s, t with $(w, s, t) \in C$, $s \models \varphi$, and $t \models \psi$,
   (f) $w \models \otimes\varphi$ iff there is a t with $(w, t) \in R$ and $t \models \varphi$.

Intuitively, an arrow frame (W, C, R, I) can be seen as a set of edges, W, in a directed graph. An arrow is in I if it forms an edge from a node to itself; $(w, s) \in R$ if s is a reversed arrow of w; and $(w, s, t) \in C$ if w is a composed arrow of s and t. This intuition is reflected in the definition of pair frames.

Definition 4. *An arrow frame $\mathfrak{F} = (W, C, R, I)$ is a pair frame if there exists a set U such that $W \subseteq U \times U$ and*

1. *for $x, y \in U$, if $(x, y) \in I$ then $x = y$,*
2. *for $x_1, x_2, y_1, y_2 \in U$, if $((x_1, y_1), (x_2, y_2)) \in R$, then $x_1 = y_2$ and $y_1 = x_2$,*
3. *for $x_1, x_2, x_3, y_1, y_2, y_3 \in U$, if $((x_1, y_1), (x_2, y_2), (x_3, y_3)) \in C$, then $x_1 = x_2$, $y_2 = x_3$, and $y_1 = y_3$.*

3   Arrow Decision Logic

3.1   Pairwise Comparison Table

In [4,5,6], pairwise comparison tables (PCT) are proposed for dealing with multicriteria choice or ranking problems. In PCT, the strength of the preference between objects, instead of the evaluation scores of the objects, are given with respect to each criterion. Formally, a PCT is a quadruple

$$T = (U, A, \{H_i \mid i \in A\}, \{f_i \mid i \in A\}),$$

where U and A are the same as in the definition of data tables; for each $i \in A$, H_i is a finite set of integers, and $f_i : U \times U \rightarrow H_i$ encodes the preferential information[2]. Each H_i denotes a set of different grades of preference (such as "very weak", "weak", "strong", etc.) with respect to the criterion i. If $f_i(x, y) = h > 0$, then x is preferred to y by degree h with respect to the criterion i. If $f_i(x, y) = h < 0$, then x is inferior to y by degree h with respect to the criterion i. If $f_i(x, y) = 0$, then x is similar to y with respect to the criterion i. A PCT is *coherent* if for each $i \in A$ and $x, y \in U$, $f_i(x, y) > 0$ implies $f_i(y, x) \leq 0$ and $f_i(x, y) < 0$ implies $f_i(y, x) \geq 0$. In this paper, we only consider coherent PCT.

---

[2] Without loss of generality, we have changed the original definition in [4,5,6] slightly.

3.2   Formulas and Semantics of ADL

To represent rules induced from a PCT, we propose arrow decision logic (ADL). An atomic formula of ADL is a descriptor of the form $(i, \geq_h)$ or $(i, \leq_h)$, where $i \in A$ and $h \in H_i$. In addition, the wffs of ADL are defined by the formation rules for arrow logic. Also, we define a rule of ADL as $\varphi \longrightarrow \psi$, where φ and ψ are wffs of ADL, called the antecedent and the consequent of the rule respectively.

A PCT can be seen as a pair frame for arrow logic. Thus, the wffs of ADL are evaluated with respect to a pair of objects. More precisely, the satisfaction of a wff with respect to a pair of objects (x, y) is defined as follows:

1. $(x, y) \models (i, \geq_h)$ iff $f_i(x, y) \geq h$,
2. $(x, y) \models (i, \leq_h)$ iff $f_i(x, y) \leq h$,
3. $(x, y) \models \delta$ iff $x = y$,
4. $(x, y) \models \neg\varphi$ iff $(x, y) \not\models \varphi$,
5. $(x, y) \models \varphi \vee \psi$ iff $(x, y) \models \varphi$ or $(x, y) \models \psi$,
6. $(x, y) \models \otimes\varphi$ iff $(y, x) \models \varphi$,
7. $(x, y) \models \varphi \circ \psi$ iff there exists z such that $(x, z) \models \varphi$ and $(z, y) \models \psi$.

If φ is an ADL wff and T is a PCT, the set $m_T(\varphi)$ defined by

$$m_T(\varphi) = \{(x, y) \in U \times U \mid (x, y) \models \varphi\} \tag{2}$$

is called the meaning set of the formula φ in T. If T is understood, we simply write $m(\varphi)$. A formula φ is valid in T if $m(\varphi) = U$. Some quantitative measures that are useful in data mining can be redefined for ADL rules.

Definition 5. *Let Φ be the set of all ADL rules and $T = (U, A, \{H_i \mid i \in A\}, \{f_i \mid i \in A\})$ be a PCT, then*

1. *the rule $\varphi \longrightarrow \psi$ is valid in T iff $m_T(\varphi) \subseteq m_T(\psi)$*
2. *the absolute support function $\alpha_T : \Phi \to \mathbb{N}$ is*

$$\alpha_T(\varphi \longrightarrow \psi) = |m_T(\varphi \wedge \psi)|$$

3. *the relative support function $\rho_T : \Phi \to [0, 1]$ is*

$$\rho_T(\varphi \longrightarrow \psi) = \frac{|m_T(\varphi \wedge \psi)|}{|U|^2}$$

4. *the confidence function $\gamma_T : \Phi \to [0, 1]$ is*

$$\gamma_T(\varphi \longrightarrow \psi) = \frac{|m_T(\varphi \wedge \psi)|}{|m_T(\varphi)|}.$$

Without loss of generality, we can assume that the elements of U are natural numbers from 0 to $|U| - 1$. Each wff can then be seen as a $|U| \times |U|$ Boolean matrix, called its *characteristic matrix*. Thus, we can employ matrix algebra to test the validity of a rule and calculate its support and confidence in an analogous way to that proposed in [11,12]. This is based on the intimate connection between arrow logic and relation algebra[15,19].

By using ADL, three main types of decision rules mentioned in [8] can be represented as follows:

1. $D_{\geq}$-decision rules:

$$\bigwedge_{i \in B} (i, \geq_{h_i}) \longrightarrow (d, \geq_1),$$

2. $D_{\leq}$-decision rules:

$$\bigwedge_{i \in B} (i, \leq_{h_i}) \longrightarrow (d, \leq_0),$$

3. $D_{\geq\leq}$-decision rules:

$$\bigwedge_{i \in B_1} (i, \geq_{h_i}) \wedge \bigwedge_{i \in B_2} (i, \leq_{h_i}) \longrightarrow (d, \geq_1) \vee (d, \leq_0),$$

where B, B_1, and $B_2 \subseteq A$ are sets of criteria and $d \in A$ is the decision attribute. We assume that $\{0, 1\} \subseteq H_d$ so that $f_d(x, y) = 1$ means that x outranks y, and $f_d(x, y) = 0$ means that x does not outrank y.

Furthermore, the modal formulas of ADL allow us to represent some properties of preference relations. For example,

1. reflexivity: $\delta \longrightarrow (i, \geq_0) \wedge (i, \leq_0)$,
2. anti-symmetry: $\otimes(i, \geq_h) \longrightarrow (i, \leq_{-h})$, and
3. transitivity: $(i, \geq_{h_1}) \circ (i, \geq_{h_2}) \longrightarrow (i, \geq_{h_1+h_2})$.

Reflexivity means that each object is similar to itself in any attribute; anti-symmetry means that if x is preferred to y by degree (at least) h, then y is inferior to x by degree (at least) h; and transitivity denotes the additivity of preference degrees. The measures α, ρ, and γ can be used to assess the degree of reflexivity, anti-symmetry, and transitivity of an induced preference relation.

3.3   An Example

We now illustrate ADL by example. Assume that Table 1 is the summary of the reviews of ten papers submitted to a journal. The papers are rated according to four criteria:

Table 1. A data table of the reviews of 10 papers

$U \setminus A$	o	p	t	d
1	4	4	3	4
2	3	2	3	3
3	4	3	2	3
4	2	2	2	2
5	2	1	2	1
6	3	1	2	1
7	3	2	2	2
8	4	1	2	2
9	3	3	2	3
10	4	3	3	3

- o: originality,
- p: presentation,
- t: technical soundness, and
- d: the overall evaluation (the decision attribute)

Let us further assume that each V_i $(i = o, p, t, d)$ is endowed with a weak preference relation $\succeq_i$ such that $4 \succeq_i 3 \succeq_i 2 \succeq_i 1$. Then a PCT from the data table is defined as

$$(U, A, \{H_i \mid i \in A\}, \{f_i \mid i \in A\}),$$

where $U = \{1, 2, 3, 4, 5, 6, 7, 8, 9, 10\}$; $A = \{o, p, t, d\}$; $H_i = \{-3, -2, -1, 0, 1, 2, 3\}$; and f_i is defined as $f_i(x, y) = i(x) - i(y)$ for all $x, y \in U$ and $i \in A$, where $i(x)$ is the value of criterion i of x in the original data table. As examples, let us consider the following two rules:

$$r_1 = (o, \geq_2) \longrightarrow (d, \geq_1),$$

$$r_2 = (p, \leq_{-2}) \longrightarrow (d, \leq_0),$$

then we have

	α	ρ	γ
r_1	7	0.07	0.875
r_2	15	0.15	1

Note that rule r_2 is valid though it only has a support value of 0.15. Furthermore, since in this example $m((d, \geq_1) \vee (d, \leq_0)) = U \times U$ holds, the $D_{\geq\leq}$-decision rules are always valid and have confidence value 1. Also, we note that the anti-symmetry rule $\otimes(i, \geq_h) \longrightarrow (i, \leq_{-h})$ is valid in this PCT, which means that the preference relation is anti-symmetrical.

4   Conclusions

In this paper, we present arrow decision logic, which is useful for representing rules induced from preference-ordered data tables that are commonly used in MCDA. The main advantage of using arrow decision logic is its precision in syntax and semantics. As DL is a precise way to represent decision rules induced from classical data tables, we use ADL to reformulate the decision rules induced from PCT in DRSA.

While this paper is primarily concerned with the syntax and declarative semantics of ADL, efficient algorithms for data mining based on logical representation are also important. One of our future research directions is to develop such algorithms.

In addition to decision logics, another kind of logic arising from data tables is called information logic [1], the semantics of which is the Kripke semantics for modal logics. We believe that it would also be interesting to explore information logics with respect to dominance relations.

References

1. P. Balbiani and E. Orlowska. A hierarchy of modal logics with relative accessibility relations. *Journal of Applied Non-Classical Logics*, 9(2-3):303–348, 1999.
2. T.F. Fan, W.C. Hu, and C.J. Liau. Decision logics for knowledge representation in data mining. In *Proceedings of the 25th Annual International Computer Software and Applications Conference*, pages 626–631. IEEE Press, 2001.
3. T.F. Fan, D.R. Liu, and G.H. Tzeng. Rough set-based logics for multicriteria decision analysis. In *Proceedings of the 34th International Conference on Computers and Industrial Engineering*, 2004.
4. S. Greco, B. Matarazzo, and R. Slowinski. Rough set approach to multi-attribute choice and ranking problems. In *Proceedings of the 12th International Conference on Multiple Criteria Decision Making*, pages 318–329, 1997.
5. S. Greco, B. Matarazzo, and R. Slowinski. Rough approximation of a preference relation in a pairwise comparison table. In L. Polkowski and A. Skowron, editors, *Rough Sets in Data Mining and Knowledge Discovery*, pages 13–36. Physica-Verlag, 1998.
6. S. Greco, B. Matarazzo, and R. Slowinski. Rough approximation of a preference relation by dominance relations. *European Journal of Operational Research*, 117(1):63–83, 1999.
7. S. Greco, B. Matarazzo, and R. Slowinski. Extension of the rough set approach to multicriteria decision support. *INFOR Journal: Information Systems & Operational Research*, 38(3):161–195, 2000.
8. S. Greco, B. Matarazzo, and R. Slowinski. Rough set theory for multicriteria decision analysis. *European Journal of Operational Research*, 129(1):1–47, 2001.
9. S. Greco, B. Matarazzo, and R. Slowinski. Rough sets methodology for sorting problems in presence of multiple attributes and criteria. *European Journal of Operational Research*, 138(2):247–259, 2002.
10. S. Greco, B. Matarazzo, and R. Slowinski. Axiomatic characterization of a general utility function and its particular cases in terms of conjoint measurement and rough-set decision rules. *European Journal of Operational Research*, 158(2):271–292, 2004.
11. C.J. Liau. Belief reasoning, revision and fusion by matrix algebra. In J. Komorowski and S. Tsumoto, editors, *Fourth International Conference on Rough Sets and Current Trends in Computing*, LNAI 3066, pages 133–142. Springer-Verlag, 2004.
12. C.J. Liau. Matrix representation of belief states: An algebraic semantics for belief logics. *International Journal of Uncertainty, Fuzziness and Knowledge-based Systems*, 12(5), 2004.
13. C.J. Liau and D.R. Liu. A logical approach to fuzzy data analysis. In J.M. Zytkow and J. Rauch, editors, *Proceedings of the Third European Conference on Principles of Data Mining and Knowledge Discovery*, LNAI 1704, pages 412–417. Springer-Verlag, 1999.
14. C.J. Liau and D.R. Liu. A possibilistic decision logic with applications. *Fundamenta Informaticae*, 46(3):199–217, 2001.
15. M. Marx and Y. Venema. *Multi-Dimensional Modal Logic*. Kluwer Academic Publishers, 1997.
16. Z. Pawlak. Rough sets. *International Journal of Computer and Information Sciences*, 11(15):341–356, 1982.
17. Z. Pawlak. *Rough Sets–Theoretical Aspects of Reasoning about Data*. Kluwer Academic Publishers, 1991.

18. R. Slowinski, S. Greco, and B. Matarazzo. Rough set analysis of preference-ordered data. In J.J. Alpigini, J.F. Peters, A. Skowron, and N. Zhong, editors, *Proceedings of the 3rd International Conference on Rough Sets and Current Trends in Computing*, LNAI 2475, pages 44–59. Springer-Verlag, 2002.

19. Y. Venema. A crash course in arrow logic. In M. Marx, L. P'olos, and M. Masuch, editors, *Arrow Logic and Multi-Modal Logic*, pages 3–34. CSLI Publications, 1996.

20. Y.Y. Yao and C.J. Liau. A generalized decision logic language for granular computing. In *Proceedings of the 11th IEEE International Conference on Fuzzy Systems*. IEEE Press, 2002.

21. Y.Y. Yao and Q. Liu. A generalized decision logic in interval-set-valued information tables. In N. Zhong, A. Skowron, and S. Ohsuga, editors, *New Directions in Rough Sets, Data Mining, and Granular-Soft Computing*, LNAI 1711, pages 285–293. Springer-Verlag, 1999.

Transforming Information Systems

Piero Pagliani

Research Group on Knowledge and Communication Models,
Via Imperia, 6 - 00161 Rome, Italy
p.pagliani@agora.stm.it

Abstract. In different fields data are presented under the form of Property Systems or Attribute Systems (i. e. Information Systems). In order to collect items linked together by attributes or properties we can use a number of techniques whose results range from exact classifications to different kinds of approximations. This range depends on the collecting operators and the characteristics of the Information System at hand. In this paper we discuss how to transform Information Systems in order to apply a well-funded set of operators and to improve their precision.

1 Introduction

Structures in which objects (entities, items) are connected with properties, "Property Systems" or structures evaluating attributes of given objects, "Attribute Systems", have been widely investigated in Computer Science. We shall refer to both types of structures as to Information Systems. In [5] we have showed how Information Systems can be transformed into relational systems $\langle G, R \rangle$, called "I-Quantum Relational Systems", where $R \subseteq G \times G$ is a preorder, so that Pawlak's Approximation Spaces (see [6]) are instances of I-Quantum Relational Systems. In the present paper we want to show how Attribute Systems may be transformed into Property Systems and Property Systems into systems fulfilling particular nice properties for classification purposes (strictly speaking this transform is an instance of what in Formal Concept Analysis is called a "conceptual scaling" - see [9]). In the present paper we shall show how the transformed systems are equivalent under an intuitive, although not exclusive, notion of an "informational equivalence". This way we can:

- uniformly treat Attribute Systems and Property System using operators from relational modal logic,
- use adjoint relationships between modal operators to define topological operators on transformed Information Systems,
- exhibit when and how topological and operational patterns change when these operators are applied to informationally equivalent (with respect to the notion we have chosen) Information Systems.

D. Ślęzak et al. (Eds.): RSFDGrC 2005, LNAI 3641, pp. 660–670, 2005.

2   Property Systems and Attribute Systems

A basic way to represent observation systems is to arrange them into structures composed by: (a) a set G of 'objects', (b) a set M of 'observable properties' and (c) a fulfillment relation, $\Vdash$, between G and M. Moreover we assume that a property which is not fulfilled by any element is a "non-property" and that an object g does not manifest any property is a "non-object" from an observational point of view so that we start from the following definition:

Definition 1. *A triple $\langle G, M, \Vdash \rangle$ where G and M are finite sets, $\Vdash \subseteq G \times M$ is a relation such that for all $g \in G$ there is $m \in M$ such that $g \Vdash m$, and vice-versa, is called a* property system *or a* P-system.

Among *P-systems* we distinguish:
a) *Functional systems*, or *FP-systems*, where $\Vdash$ is functional in the sense that for any element $g \in G$, $g \Vdash m$ and $g \Vdash m'$ implies $m = m'$.
b) *Dichotomic systems* or *DP-systems*, if for all $p \in M$ there is $\overline{p} \in M$ such that for all $g \in G$, $g \Vdash p$ if and only if $g \nVdash \overline{p}$.
A more complex way to structure observations is given by Attribute Systems:

Definition 2. *A triple $\langle G, At, \{V_a\}_{a \in At}, \rangle$, where G, At and V_a are sets (of objects, attributes and, resp., attribute-values) and for all $a \in At$, $a : G \longmapsto At_a$ is a function, is called a* deterministic Attribute System *or an* A-system.

From now on we assume that **P** always denotes a *Property System* $\langle G, M, \Vdash \rangle$ and that **A** denotes an *Attribute System* $\langle G, At, \{V_a\}_{a \in At} \rangle$.

3   *P-Systems*, Classification and Approximation

If $\langle G, M, \Vdash \rangle$ is an *FP-system*, by pulling back $\Vdash$ along itself we obtain the kernel $k_{\Vdash}$ which is an equivalence relation, so that any element of G is associated one and only one equivalence class modulo $k_{\Vdash}$. On the contrary, if we deal with generic *P-systems*, we cannot directly obtain sharp classifications by means of the above maneuver, but we need a mathematical machinery based on the notion of an "approximation".

To this end we have to notice that since the only relationships between objects are induced by the fulfillment relation $\Vdash$ and such relationships are grouping relations, we can compare subsets of objects but not, directly, objects. Therefore, the result of such an activity is a "type" not a "token". It follows that we shall lift from the level of pure *P-systems* $\langle G, M, \Vdash \rangle$ to that of *Perception systems* $\langle \wp(G), \wp(M), \{\phi_i\}_{i \in I} \rangle$ where ϕ_i is a map $\wp(G) \longmapsto \wp(M)$ or $\wp(M) \longmapsto \wp(G)$.

In [5] we have introduced some approximating operators derived from investigations presented in [9], [7], [1], [2] and [3]. The starting point is the definition of formal operators linking sets of objects with sets of properties:

Definition 3 (Formal operators). *Let* $\mathbf{P} = \langle G, M, \Vdash \rangle$ *be a P-system. Then:*
- $\langle \Vdash \rangle : \wp(M) \longmapsto \wp(G)$; $\langle \Vdash \rangle(Y) = \{g \in G : \exists m (m \in Y \ \& \ g \Vdash m)\}$;
- $[\Vdash] : \wp(M) \longmapsto \wp(G)$; $[\Vdash](Y) = \{g \in G : \forall m (g \Vdash m \Longrightarrow m \in Y)\}$;

- $[[\Vdash]] : \wp(M) \longmapsto \wp(G); [[\Vdash]](Y) = \{g \in G : \forall m(m \in Y \Longrightarrow g \Vdash m)\};$
- $\langle\Vdash^{\smile}\rangle : \wp(G) \longmapsto \wp(M); \langle\Vdash^{\smile}\rangle(X) = \{m \in M : \exists g(g \in X \ \& \ g \Vdash m)\}$
- $[\Vdash^{\smile}] : \wp(G) \longmapsto \wp(M); [\Vdash^{\smile}](X) = \{m \in M : \forall g(g \Vdash m \Longrightarrow g \in X)\};$
- $[[\Vdash^{\smile}]] : \wp(G) \longmapsto \wp(M); [[\Vdash^{\smile}]](X) = \{m \in M : \forall g(g \in X \Longrightarrow g \Vdash m)\}.$

NOTE: From now on, if an operator, say Op, is applied to a singleton $\{x\}$ we shall also write $Op(x)$ instead of the correct $Op(\{x\})$, if there is no risk of confusion.

Then we can prove that the following adjointness relationships hold (see [5]):

$$\mathbf{M} \dashv^{\langle\Vdash\rangle,[\Vdash^{\smile}]} \mathbf{G}; \ \mathbf{G} \dashv^{\langle\Vdash^{\smile}\rangle,[\Vdash]} \mathbf{M}; \ \mathbf{M} \dashv^{[[\Vdash]],[[\Vdash^{\smile}]]} \mathbf{G}^{\mathbf{op}}; \ \mathbf{G} \dashv^{[[\Vdash^{\smile}]],[[\Vdash]]} \mathbf{M}^{\mathbf{op}},$$

where $\mathbf{M} = <\wp(M), \subseteq>$, $\mathbf{G} = <\wp(G), \subseteq>$ and given two partial orders $\mathbf{O}$ and $\mathbf{O'}$ and two maps $\sigma : \mathbf{O} \longmapsto \mathbf{O'}$ and $\iota : \mathbf{O'} \longmapsto \mathbf{O}$, $\mathbf{O'} \dashv^{\iota,\sigma} \mathbf{O}$ if and only if $\forall p \in O, \forall p' \in O', \iota(p') \leq p \Longleftrightarrow p' \leq' \sigma(p)$. In this case we say that ι and σ fulfill an *adjointness relation* or that $\langle\sigma, \iota\rangle$ is an "axiality" or a *Galois adjunction*. If the right structure is reversed upside-down we say that $\langle\sigma, \iota\rangle$ is a "polarity" or a *Galois connection*. From this general fact (plus a few others derivable from our assumptions on the relation $\Vdash$) a number of consequences follows (see [1] and [7] for definitions and details in two comparable frameworks). Let ρ be $\Vdash$ or $\Vdash^{\smile}$. Then: (a) $[\rho]$ is a *necessity* operator, (b) $\langle\rho\rangle$ is a *possibility* operator, (c) $[[\rho]]$ is a *sufficiency* operator. By combining them we can prove that: (d) $int(X) = \langle\Vdash\rangle[\Vdash^{\smile}](X)$ is an interior operator on $\mathbf{G}$; (e) $cl(X) = [\Vdash]\langle\Vdash^{\smile}\rangle(X)$ is a closure operator on $\mathbf{G}$; (f) $\mathcal{A}(Y) = [\Vdash^{\smile}]\langle\Vdash\rangle(Y)$ is a closure operator on $\mathbf{M}$; (g) $\mathcal{C}(Y) = \langle\Vdash^{\smile}\rangle[\Vdash](Y)$ is an interior operator on $\mathbf{M}$; (h) $est(X) = [[\Vdash]][[\Vdash^{\smile}]](X)$ and $\mathcal{ITS}(Y) = [[\Vdash^{\smile}]][[\Vdash]](Y)$ are the two closure operators on $\mathbf{G}$ and, resp., $\mathbf{M}$, used in Concept Lattices.

NOTE: If needed, operators will be decorated by superscripts denoting the systems they refer to.

Particularly, adjointness relations make the following hold:

$$cl(X) \subseteq X \subseteq int(X), \quad \forall X \subseteq G \tag{3.1}$$

We can interpret the above relationships by saying that

- cl is an *upper approximation* of the identity map on $\wp(G)$;
- int is a *lower approximation* of the identity map on $\wp(G)$.

More precisely, because of the adjunction properties, one can prove that $\langle\Vdash^{\smile}\rangle(X) = min([\Vdash^{\smile}]^{\leftarrow}(\uparrow X)) = min\{X' \subseteq G : [\Vdash](X') \supseteq X\}$, so that $cl(X)$ - i. e. $[\Vdash]\langle\Vdash^{\smile}\rangle(X)$ - is the *best approximation from above* to X via function $[\Vdash]$. Dually, $[\Vdash^{\smile}](X) = max(\langle\Vdash\rangle^{\leftarrow}(\downarrow X)) = max\{X' \subseteq G : \langle\Vdash\rangle(X') \subseteq X\}$. Hence $int(X)$ is the *best approximation from below* to X, via function $\langle\Vdash\rangle$[1].

---

[1] If $\langle\Vdash^{\smile}\rangle$ is injective ($[\Vdash]$ is surjective), then we can exactly reach X from above by means of $[\Vdash]$. The element that must be mapped is, indeed, $\langle\Vdash^{\smile}\rangle(X)$. Dually, if $[\Vdash^{\smile}]$ is injective ($\langle\Vdash\rangle$ is surjective), then we can exactly reach X from below by means of $\langle\Vdash\rangle$ applied to $[\Vdash^{\smile}](X)$.

Therefore, we have introduced the notion of a *Multi-agent pre-topological Approximation Space* over two sets G and M as a structure

$$\langle G, M, \{\mathbf{pG^{P_k}}\}_{k \in K} \rangle \text{ or, shortly, } \langle G, \{\mathbf{pG^{P_k}}\}_{k \in K} \rangle$$

where any $\mathbf{P}_k$ is an Information System on the same set of objects G (not necessarily the same set of properties M) and $\mathbf{pG^{P_k}} = \{int^{\mathbf{P}_k}, cl^{\mathbf{P}_k}, est^{\mathbf{P}_k}\}$. This generalisation makes it possible to manipulate sets of objects by subsequently applying informational criteria induced by different *P-systems*.

In particular we called $\langle G, G, int, cl \rangle$ a *Basic pre-topological Approximation Space*.

Now we have to solve some problems: a) For one cannot apply the above operators to *A-systems*, is it possible to transform *A-systems* into *P-systems* in order to be able to apply that formal machinery? b) Generally cl is not a topological closure operator, since in general it is not additive and int is not a topological interior operator since in general it is not multiplicative; is it possible to transform *P-systems* in order to make these operators topological? c) What are the connections (if any) between these transforms? d) How to define a notion of "informational equivalence" which makes it possible to control them?

4 From Information Systems to Information Quantum Relational System

In [5] we have given a solution to d) and b) based on the notion of an *Information Quantum*, or *i-quantum*. In this paper we aim at building the solution of a) and c) on it. An i-quantum is a way to collect together objects that fulfill *at least* the same properties as a given object.

Definition 4 (Information Quantum - or I-Quantum)

1. Let $\langle G, At, \{V_a\}_{a \in At} \rangle$ be an *Attribute System*. For all $g \in G$ let us define:
   $Q_g = \{g' : \forall a \in At, \forall x \in V_a((a(g) = x) \Longrightarrow (a(g') = x))\}$.
2. Let $\langle G, M, \Vdash \rangle$ be a *Property System*. Then for all $g \in G$ let us define:
   $Q_g = \{g' : \forall p \in M(g \Vdash p \Longrightarrow g' \Vdash p)\}$.

The set Q_g is called the *i-quantum at* g and we can extend the operator Q to subsets X of G by setting $Q_X = \bigcup_{x \in X} Q_x$. After that we can introduce the notion of an I-Quantum Relational System:

Definition 5. *Let* $\mathbf{S}$ *be an Information System. Let us define a binary relation* $R_{\mathbf{S}}$ *on* G *as follows:*

$$\langle g, g' \rangle \in R_{\mathbf{S}} \text{ iff } g' \in Q_g, \text{ for all } g, g' \in G.$$

We call $R_{\mathbf{S}}$ *the i-quantum relation induced by* $\mathbf{S}$. *Moreover,* $\mathbf{Q}(\mathbf{S})$ *will denote the relational system* $\langle G, G, R_{\mathbf{S}} \rangle$, *called the* I-Quantum Relational System - IQRS, *induced by* $\mathbf{S}$.

It is immediate to verify that i-quantum relations are preorders[2].

This way we have actually transformed an Information System $\mathbf{S}$ into a *P-system* $\mathbf{Q(S)}$ where $R_{\mathbf{S}}$ plays the role of a fulfillment relation. Thus, by means of the adjointness relations together with fact that i-quanta relations are preorders, one can prove what follows (see [5]):

Proposition 1. *Let* $\mathbf{S}$ *be an Information System. Then:*

1. *If* $\mathbf{S}$ *is an A-system, an FP or a DP system, then* $R_{\mathbf{S}}$ *is an equivalence relation and* Im_Q *equipped with the set theoretical operations is a Boolean algebra.*
2. *If* $\mathbf{S}$ *is an FP-system then* (a) $R_{\mathbf{S}} = k_{|\vdash}$; (b) *cl and int are topological closure, respectively, interior operators.*
3. $cl^{\mathbf{Q(S)}} = [R_{\mathbf{S}}^{\smile}]\langle R_{\mathbf{S}}\rangle = \langle R_{\mathbf{S}}\rangle$ *and both* $\langle R_{\mathbf{S}}\rangle$ *and* Q *are a topological closure operators, whose images are closed under intersections (and symmetrically by reversing the relations).*
4. $int^{\mathbf{Q(S)}} = \langle R_{\mathbf{S}}^{\smile}\rangle[R_{\mathbf{S}}] = [R_{\mathbf{S}}]$ *and* $[R_{\mathbf{S}}]$ *is a topological interior operator, whose image is closed under unions (and symmetrically by reversing the relations).*

On this basis any boxed operator induced by an IQRS is a topological lower approximation and any diamond-like operator is a topological upper approximation of subsets of G.

5 Comparing Information Systems

The notion of an i-quantum makes it possible to compare Information Systems. First of all we should ask whether it is possible to compare two quanta of information Q_g and $Q_{g'}$. At first sight we would say that Q_g is finer than $Q_{g'}$ if $Q_g \subseteq Q_{g'}$. However, this intuition works for *P-systems*, but not for *A-systems* because from *Proposition* 1.(1) if $Q_g \subseteq Q_{g'}$ then $Q_{g'} \subseteq Q_g$. Thus non trivial comparisons of quanta of information in *A-systems* require a specialised notion of an i-quantum, which, in any case, is useful for *P-systems* too.

Definition 6 (Relativised quanta of information)
- Let $\mathbf{A}$ be an *A-system*. The *quantum of information of g relative to a subset* $A \subseteq At$ is defined as: $Q_g \upharpoonright A = \{g' \in G : \forall a \in A, \forall x \in V_a((a(g) = x) \Longrightarrow (a(g') = x))\}$.
- Let $\mathbf{P}$ be a *P-system*. The *quantum of information of g with respect to a subset* $A \subseteq M$ is defined as: $Q_g \upharpoonright A = \{g' \in G : \forall a \in A(g \Vdash a \Longrightarrow g' \Vdash a)\}$.

Definition 7 (I-quantum dependence). *Let* $\mathbf{S}$ *be an Information System. Let* $A, A' \subseteq At$ *(or* $A, A' \subseteq M$*),* $g \in G$.

1. *We say that* A' *functionally depends on* A *at* g, *in symbols* $A \mapsto_g A'$, *if for all* $g' \in G$, $g' \in Q_g \upharpoonright A \Longrightarrow g' \in Q_g \upharpoonright A'$ *(that is, if* $Q_g \upharpoonright A \subseteq Q_g \upharpoonright A'$*).*

---

[2] With different names, these notions were introduced in [2] to analyse the topological features of *P-systems*.

2. *We say that A' functionally depends on A, in symbols $A \mapsto A'$, if for all $g \in G$, $A \mapsto_g A'$.*
3. *If $A \mapsto A'$ and $A' \mapsto A$, we say that A and A' are informationally equivalent, $A \cong_I A'$ (thus, $A \cong_I A'$ if for all $g \in G$, $Q_g \upharpoonright A = Q_g \upharpoonright A'$).*

So, a set of attributes (properties) A' functionally depends on a set of attributes (properties) A if A has a higher discriminatory capability than A'[3].

From now on, if $\Vdash\upharpoonright X$ denotes the relation $\Vdash$ with co-domain restricted to X then with $\mathbf{S} \upharpoonright X$ we shall denote the subsystem $\langle G, X, \Vdash\upharpoonright X\rangle$. If $\mathbf{S}$ is an A-*system* and $X \subseteq At$, with $\mathbf{S} \upharpoonright X$ we shall denote the subsystem $\langle G, X, \{V_a\}_{a \in X}\rangle$.

The following statement formalises the above intuitions with respect to i-quantum relations:

Proposition 2. *Let $\mathbf{S}$ be an Information System. Let $A, A' \subseteq At$ $(A, A' \subseteq M)$ such that $A \mapsto A'$. Then $R_{(\mathbf{A}\upharpoonright A)} \subseteq R_{(\mathbf{A}\upharpoonright A')}$.*

Proof. The proof is immediate. Suppose $A \mapsto A'$. Then for all $g \in G$, $Q_g \upharpoonright A \subseteq Q_g \upharpoonright A'$, so that $\langle g, g'\rangle \in R_{(\mathbf{A}\upharpoonright A)}$ implies $\langle g, g'\rangle \in R_{(\mathbf{A}\upharpoonright A')}$. QED

It follows that we can naturally extend the notion of a functional dependence in order to compare two sets X and X' of properties or attributes from two distinct (property or attribute) systems $\mathbf{S}$ and $\mathbf{S}'$ over the same set of points G. Thus, we can extend the notion of "informational equivalence" to entire systems:

Definition 8. *Let $\mathbf{S}$ and $\mathbf{S}'$ be Information Systems over the same set of points G. Let S and S' be the sets of attributes (properties) of $\mathbf{S}$ and, respectively, $\mathbf{S}'$. We say that $\mathbf{S}$ and $\mathbf{S}'$ are informationally equivalent, in symbols $\mathbf{S} \cong_I \mathbf{S}'$, if and only if for any $g \in G, Q_g \upharpoonright S = Q_g \upharpoonright S'$.*

Informational equivalence tells something about the behaviour of cl and int:

Proposition 3. *Let it be $\mathbf{P} \cong_I \mathbf{P}'$. Then for all $x \in G$, $cl^{\mathbf{P}}(x) = cl^{\mathbf{P}'}(x)$. If both $cl^{\mathbf{P}}$ and $cl^{\mathbf{P}'}$ are topological, then $cl^{\mathbf{P}}(X) = cl^{\mathbf{P}'}(X)$ and $int^{\mathbf{P}}(X) = int^{\mathbf{P}'}(X)$, for any $X \subseteq G$.*

Proof. Suppose $cl^{\mathbf{P}}(x) \neq cl^{\mathbf{P}'}(x)$. Then there is $g \in G$ such that, say, $g \in cl^{\mathbf{P}}(x)$ and $g \notin cl^{\mathbf{P}'}(x)$. It follows that $\langle \Vdash^{\smile}\rangle(g) \subseteq \langle \Vdash^{\smile}\rangle(x)$ but $\langle \Vdash'^{\smile}\rangle(g) \nsubseteq \langle \Vdash'^{\smile}\rangle(x)$. Thus $x \in Q^{\mathbf{P}}(g)$ and $x \notin Q^{\mathbf{P}'}(g)$, so that $\mathbf{P} \ncong_I \mathbf{P}'$. If both closure operators are additive, then by easy induction we obtain that $cl^{\mathbf{P}}(X) = cl^{\mathbf{P}'}(X)$ for any $X \subseteq G$. Moreover, suppose $int^{\mathbf{P}}(X) \neq int^{\mathbf{P}'}(X)$. Then $-int^{\mathbf{P}}(X) \neq -int^{\mathbf{P}'}(X)$, so that $cl^{\mathbf{P}}(-X) \neq cl^{\mathbf{P}'}(-X)$ - contradiction. QED

The above reasoning for generic subsets does not hold if either $cl^{\mathbf{P}}$ or $cl^{\mathbf{P}'}$ is not topological because in this case the equality between $cl^{\mathbf{P}}$ and $cl^{\mathbf{P}'}$ is guaranteed just for singletons so that $cl^{\mathbf{P}}(-X) \neq cl^{\mathbf{P}'}(-X)$ is not a contradiction. Notice that we can have $\mathbf{P}$ and $\mathbf{P}'$ such that $int^{\mathbf{P}}(x) \neq int^{\mathbf{P}'}(x)$ but still $\mathbf{P} \cong_I \mathbf{P}'$. Therefore, the relation $\cong_I$ is far to be considered the "best" way to compare Information Systems, though very useful to our purposes.

---

[3] If $\mathbf{S}$ is an A-*system* then the notion of an i-quantum dependence relation turns into the usual notion of a *functional dependence*.

Now we want to stress the fact that we can compare not only the informational behaviour of the same point g with respect two different sets of properties (attributes) X and X', but we can also compare the behaviours of two different points g and g' with respect to the same set of properties (attributes) P.

Definition 9. *Let* **S** *be an Information System,* $X \subseteq M$ *(or* $X \subseteq At$*) and* $g, g' \in G$.

1. *We say that* g *is an* X*-specialisation of* g' *(or that* g' *is an* X*-approximation of* g*), in symbols* $g' \preccurlyeq_X g$*, if and only if the following condition holds:*

$$\forall x \in G(g' \in Q_x \upharpoonright X \Longrightarrow g \in Q_x \upharpoonright X).$$

2. *We say that* g *is a specialisation of* g'*,* $g' \preccurlyeq g$*, if and only if* $g' \preccurlyeq_M g$.

Since for q-reflexivity $x \in Q_x$, any $x \in G$, if $g' \preccurlyeq_X g$ then $g \in Q_{g'} \upharpoonright X$, so that $g' \preccurlyeq_X g$ says that g fulfills at least all the properties from X that are fulfilled by g'. Therefore, $g' \preccurlyeq g$ implies $\langle g', g \rangle \in R_{\mathbf{S}}$. Conversely, if $\langle g', g \rangle \in R_{\mathbf{S}}$ then $g \in Q_{g'}$. Hence $g' \in Q_x$ implies $g \in Q_x$, any $x \in G$, from transitivity of $R_{\mathbf{S}}$. It follows that the two relations $\preccurlyeq$ and $R_{\mathbf{S}}$ coincide. In fact they are the same instance of the usual topological notion of a *specialisation preorder*. Indeed in view of *Proposition* 1.(3) we can construct a topological space $\langle G, Im_Q \rangle$ on G whose specialisation preorder is indeed $\preccurlyeq$ (that is, $R_{\mathbf{S}}$).

6   Transforming Perception Systems

Now we are equipped with a sufficient machinery in order to compare transformed systems.

Let **A** be an *A-system*. To get a *P-system* out of **A**, the basic step derives from the observation that any attribute a is actually a set of properties, namely the possible attribute values for a. Thus we start associating each attribute a with the family $\mathcal{N}(a) = \{a_v\}_{v \in V_a}$. We set $\mathcal{N}(At) = \bigcup_{a \in At} \mathcal{N}(a)$. For each value v, a_v is the property "taking value v for attribute a". This transform is usually called a "scale nominalisation". Now let us set a relation $\Vdash^{\mathcal{N}}$ as:

$$g \Vdash^{\mathcal{N}} a_v \text{ if and only if } a(g) = v, \text{ all } g \in G, a \in At, v \in V_a.$$

We call the resulting system, $\mathcal{N}(\mathbf{A}) = \langle G, \mathcal{N}(At), \Vdash^{\mathcal{N}} \rangle$, the "*nominalisation of* **A**". $\mathcal{N}(\mathbf{A})$ will be called a *nominal A-system* or *NA-system*.

Proposition 4. *Let* **A** *be an A-system. Then:* (a) $\mathcal{N}(\mathbf{A})$ *is a P-system;* (b) $\mathcal{N}(\mathbf{A}) \cong_I \mathbf{A}$.

Proof. (a) is obvious. (b) Let us prove that for any $g \in G$, $Q_g \upharpoonright At = Q_g \upharpoonright \mathcal{N}(At)$. Indeed, if $g' \in Q_g \upharpoonright At$, then $a(g) = x$ if and only if $a(g') = x$, all $a \in At$. Therefore for any $x \in \mathcal{N}(a)$, $g \Vdash a_x$ if and only if $g' \Vdash a_x$, whence $g' \in Q_g \upharpoonright \mathcal{N}(a)$. Finally, $g' \nVdash a_{x'}$ for any other $x' \neq x$, so we have the reverse implication. QED

Moreover, if we formally consider *P-systems* as binary *A-systems*, we can also nominalise *P-systems*. But in this case we have a further property:

Proposition 5. *Let* **P** *be a P-system. Then* $\mathcal{N}(\mathbf{P})$ *is a dichotomic system.*

Proof. This is obvious, because for any property p, the nominalisation $\mathcal{N}(p) = \{p_1, p_0\}$ forms a pair of complementary properties, since for all $g \in G$, $g \Vdash^{\mathcal{N}} p_1$ if and only if $g \Vdash p$ and $g \Vdash^{\mathcal{N}} p_0$ if and only if $g \nVdash p$. QED

Nominalisation of dichotomic or functional systems does not give rise to any further result.

Proposition 6. *If* **P** *is a DP system or an FP system, then* $\mathcal{N}(\mathbf{P}) \cong_I \mathbf{P}$.

Proof. If **P** is dichotomic let $\langle p, \bar{p} \rangle$ be a pair of complementary properties. After nominalisation we shall obtain two pairs $\mathcal{N}(p) = \{p_1, p_0\}$ and $\mathcal{N}(\bar{p}) = \{\bar{p_1}, \bar{p_0}\}$. Clearly, for any $g \in G$, $g \Vdash p$ in **P** if and only if $g \Vdash^{\mathcal{N}} p_1$ in $\mathcal{N}(\mathbf{P})$. But $g \Vdash^{\mathcal{N}} p_1$ if and only if $g \nVdash^{\mathcal{N}} p_0$ if and only if $g \Vdash^{\mathcal{N}} \bar{p_0}$. Conversely, $g \Vdash \bar{p}$ if and only if $g \Vdash^{\mathcal{N}} p_0$ if and only if $g \nVdash^{\mathcal{N}} p_1$ if and only if $g \Vdash^{\mathcal{N}} \bar{p_1}$. If **P** is functional and $g' \in Q_g \upharpoonright M$ then $g \Vdash m$ if and only if $g' \Vdash m$, since $\langle \Vdash^{\smile} \rangle(g) = \langle \Vdash^{\smile} \rangle(g') = m$. Thus the proof runs as in *Proposition 4.(b)*. QED

For $\mathcal{N}(\mathbf{A})$ is not only a *P-system* but it is still an *A-system* with $At = \{0, 1\}$, we obtain the following corollary:

Corollary 1. *Let* **S** *be an Information System. Then* $\mathcal{N}(\mathbf{S}) \cong_I \mathcal{N}(\mathcal{N}(\mathbf{S}))$.

Proof. If **S** is a *P-system* then $\mathcal{N}(\mathbf{S})$ is a dichotomic systems so that from *Proposition 6* $\mathcal{N}(\mathcal{N}(\mathbf{S})) \cong_I \mathcal{N}(\mathbf{S})$. If **S** is an *A-system* then $\mathcal{N}(\mathbf{S})$ is a binary *A-system* and from *Proposition 4.(b)* $\mathcal{N}(\mathbf{S}) \cong_I \mathcal{N}(\mathcal{N}(\mathbf{S}))$. QED

Corollary 2. *If* **A** *is an A-system then there is a dichotomic system* **D** *such that* $\mathbf{D} \cong_I \mathbf{A}$.

Proof. : Since $\mathcal{N}(\mathbf{A})$ is a *P-system*, from *Proposition 5* $\mathcal{N}(\mathcal{N}(\mathbf{A}))$ is dichotomic. But from *Proposition 4.(b)* and *Corollary 1* $\mathbf{A} \cong_I \mathcal{N}(\mathbf{A}) \cong_I \mathcal{N}(\mathcal{N}(\mathbf{A}))$. QED

As a side result we again obtain *Proposition 1.(1)*. Notice that this *Proposition*, as well as *Corollary 1*, relies on the fact that we are dealing with deterministic Information Systems so that either two objects converge on the same attribute-value, or they diverge, but not both.

6.1 Example

Here are some examples: a *P-system* $\mathbf{P} = \langle G, M, \Vdash \rangle$, an *FP-system* $\mathbf{F} = \langle G, M', \hat{f} \rangle$ and an *A-system* $\mathbf{A} = \langle G, At, V \rangle$ over the same set G:

$\Vdash$	b	b'	b''	b'''	$\hat{f}$	m	m'	m''			A	A'	A''
a	1	1	0	0	a	1	0	0		a	1	b	α
a'	0	1	0	1	a'	0	1	0		a'	0	c	α
a''	0	1	1	1	a''	1	0	0		a''	1	b	α
a'''	0	0	0	1	a'''	0	0	1		a'''	3	f	δ

Considering the system $\mathbf{P}$ let $A = \{b, b'\}$ and $B = \{b'', b'''\}$. Then $Q_{a''} \restriction A = \{a, a', a''\}$ while $Q_{a''} \restriction B = \{a''\}$. It follows that $B \mapsto_{a''} A$. On the contrary, $Q_{a'} \restriction A = \{a, a', a''\}$ and $Q_{a'} \restriction B = \{a', a'', a'''\}$ are not comparable. Hence $B \mapsto A$ does not hold. If we compare the above systems we notice what follows:
a) $\mathbf{A} \not\cong_I \mathbf{P}$ because $Q^{\mathbf{A}}_a = \{a, a''\}$ while $Q^{\mathbf{P}}_a = \{a\}$. Neither $\mathbf{P} \mapsto \mathbf{A}$ because $Q^{\mathbf{P}}_{a'} = \{a', a''\}$ while $Q^{\mathbf{A}}_{a'} = \{a'\}$. b) $\mathbf{F} \cong_I \mathbf{A}$, because for all $g \in G, Q^{\mathbf{A}}_g = Q^{\mathbf{F}}_g$.
Let us now nominalise the Information Systems $\mathbf{A}$ and $\mathbf{P}$:

$\Vdash^{\mathcal{N}}_{\mathbf{A}}$	A_0	A_1	A_3	A'_b	A'_d	A'_f	A''_α	A''_δ	$\Vdash^{\mathcal{N}}_{\mathbf{P}}$	b_1	b_0	b'_1	b'_0	b''_1	b''_0	b'''_1	b'''_0
a	0	1	0	1	0	0	1	0	a	1	0	1	0	0	1	0	1
a'	1	0	0	0	1	0	1	0	a'	0	1	1	0	0	1	1	0
a''	0	1	0	1	0	0	1	0	a''	0	1	1	0	1	0	1	0
a'''	0	0	1	0	0	1	0	1	a'''	0	1	0	1	0	1	1	0

Thus $\mathcal{N}(A) = \{A_0, A_1, A_3\}$, $\mathcal{N}(b) = \{b_1, b_0\}$ and so on. It is evident that, for instance, $a \in Q^{\mathcal{N}(\mathbf{A})}_{a''}$ and $a'' \in Q^{\mathcal{N}(\mathbf{A})}_a$. But the same happens already in $\mathbf{A}$. Indeed, $Q^{\mathbf{A}}_a = \{a, a''\} = Q^{\mathbf{A}}_{a''}$. On the contrary, $Q^{\mathbf{P}}_{a'} = \{a', a''\}$ but $Q^{\mathcal{N}(\mathbf{P})}_{a'} = \{a'\}$. In fact $a'' \in Q^{\mathbf{P}}_{a'}$ because it fulfills all the properties fulfilled by a' (i. e. b' and b''') plus the additional property b''. But in $\mathcal{N}(\mathbf{P})$ this latter fact prevents a''' from belonging to $Q^{\mathcal{N}(\mathbf{P})}_{a'}$, because property b'' splits into the pair $\langle b''_0, b''_1 \rangle$ and $a' \Vdash^{\mathcal{N}}_{\mathbf{P}} b''_0$ while $a'' \Vdash^{\mathcal{N}}_{\mathbf{P}} b''_1$, what are mutually exclusive possibilities. If we further nominalise $\mathcal{N}(\mathbf{P})$ and split, for instance, $\langle b''_0, b''_1 \rangle$ into $\langle b''_{0_1}, b''_{0_0}, b''_{1_1}, b''_{1_0} \rangle$, it is obvious that the pairs $\langle b''_{0_1}, b''_{1_0} \rangle$ and $\langle b''_{0_0}, b''_{1_1} \rangle$ give the same information as b''_0 and, respectively, b''_1. It is not difficult to verify that $R_{\mathcal{N}(\mathbf{A})} = R_{\mathbf{A}}$ so that $\mathcal{N}(\mathbf{A}) \cong_I \mathbf{Q}(\mathbf{A})$.

6.2   Dichotomic, Functional and Nominal Systems

First notice that the reverse of *Proposition* 1.(1) does not hold. For instance, if $\mathbf{P}'$ is such that $G = \{1, 2, 3, 4\}, M = \{A, B, C\}$ and $\Vdash (1) = \{A, B\}, \Vdash (2) = \{A, B\}, \Vdash (3) = \{B, C\}$ and $\Vdash (4) = \{B, C\}$, Q_g is an equivalence class, any $g \in G$ though $\mathbf{P}'$ is neither dichotomic nor functional. Also, if $\mathbf{A}$ is an A-*system*, then $\mathcal{N}(\mathbf{A})$ is not necessarily dichotomic. However $\mathcal{N}(\mathbf{A}) \cong_I \mathcal{N}(\mathcal{N}(\mathbf{A}))$ which is dichotomic (see *Corollary* 1). Indeed, notice that $\mathcal{N}(\mathcal{N}(\mathbf{A}))$ is informationally equivalent to the system defined as follows:

1) For each a_v in $\mathcal{N}(\mathbf{A})$, if V_a is not a singleton set $\neg a_v = \{a_{v'}\}_{v' \neq v, v' \in V_a}$, while if $V_a = \{v\}$ then set $\neg a_v = \{a_{v'}\}$. We set $P = \{a_v\}_{v \in V_a} \cup \{\neg a_v\}_{v \in V_a}$.
2) For each $g \in G$ set $g \Vdash^* \neg a_v$ if and only if $g \not\Vdash a_v$ and $g \Vdash^* a_v$ if and only if $g \Vdash a_v$. Clearly $\neg a_v$ is the complementary copy of a_v. Thus, 3) set $\mathbf{S} = \langle G, P, \Vdash^* \rangle$. We can easily verify that $\mathbf{S}$ is a dichotomic system and that $\mathbf{S} \cong_I \mathcal{N}(\mathbf{A})$.

In reversal, since for any P-*system* $\mathbf{P}$, $\mathcal{N}(\mathbf{P})$ induces an equivalence relation, we can ask whether $\mathcal{N}(\mathbf{P})$ itself "is", in some form, an A-*system*. Indeed it is trivially an A-*system* with set of attributes values $V = \{0, 1\}$ and such that $m_1(g) = 1$ iff $g \Vdash m_1$ iff $g \not\Vdash m_0$ iff $m_0(g) = 0$ and $m_1(g) = 0$ iff $g \Vdash m_0$ iff $g \not\Vdash m_1$ iff $m_0(g) = 1$, all $m \in M$ and by trivial inspection one can verify that $\langle G, \mathcal{N}(M), \{0, 1\} \rangle \cong_I \mathcal{N}(\mathbf{P})$.

Finally we discuss another natural equivalence. We know that if $\mathbf{S}$ is an A-*system*, or a DP or a FP *system* then $R_{\mathbf{S}}$ is an equivalence relation (see *Proposition 1*). Thus a question arises as how to define a functional system $F(\mathbf{S})$ informationally equivalent to a given A or DP *system* $\mathbf{S}$. The answer is simple. If $\mathbf{S}$ is a P-*system* consider it as an A-*system*. Any tuple $t \in \prod_{a \in At} V_a$ is a combination of attribute-values and has the form $\langle a_{1_m}, \ldots, a_{j_n} \rangle$. We set $g \Vdash^* t$ only if $a_1(g) = a_{i_m}$ for any $a_i \in At$ and $a_{i_m} \in t$. The resulting system $\langle G, \prod_{a \in At} V_a, \Vdash^* \rangle$ is the required $F(\mathbf{S})$. Indeed $\Vdash^*$ is a map because no $g \in G$ can satisfy different tuples. Thus $R_{F(\mathbf{S})}$ is an equivalence relation such that $\langle g, g' \rangle \in R_{F(\mathbf{S})}$ only if $a(g) = a(g')$ for all $a \in At$ (or in M). It follows that $\mathcal{N}(\mathbf{S}) \cong_I F(\mathbf{S})$ so that if $\mathbf{S}$ is dichotomic or it is an A-*system* then $R_{\mathbf{S}} = R_{F(\mathbf{S})}$ and $\mathbf{S} \cong_I F(\mathbf{S})$.

7   Conclusions

We have seen how to make different kinds of Information Systems into a uniform theoretical framework, *via* the notion of a *quantum of information* and control these manipulations by means of a particular notion of an "informational equivalence". This has practical consequences too. Indeed, the relational modal or/and topological operators that we have defined over P-*systems* may be directly translated into extremely simple constructs of functional languages such as LISP or APL (see [3]), thus providing a sound implementation. Finally, this approach directly links the logical interpretation of approximation operators to the manipulation of concrete data structures for it coherently embeds the concrete operations on Boolean matrices into a very general logical framework (the same relational interpretation of a modal operator applies to any sort of binary Kripke frame).

References

1. I. Düntsch & E. Orłowska, "Mixing modal and sufficiency operators". *Bulletin of the Section of Logic, Polish Academy of Sciences*, 28, 1999, pp.99-106.
2. P. Pagliani, "From Concept Lattices to Approximation spaces: Algebraic Structures of some Spaces of Partial Objects". Fund. Informaticae, 18 (1), 1993, pp. 1-25.
3. P. Pagliani, "Modalizing Relations by means of Relations: a general framework for two basic approaches to Knowledge Discovery in Database". In: Proc. of the International Conference on Information Processing and Management of Uncertainty in Knowledge-Based Systems. IPMU 98, July, 6-10, 1998. "La Sorbonne", Paris, France, pp. 1175-1182.
4. P. Pagliani, "A practical introduction to the modal relational approach to Approximation Spaces". In A. Skowron (Ed.): Rough Sets in Knowledge Discovery. Physica-Verlag, 1998, pp. 209-232.
5. P. Pagliani & M. Chakraborty, "Information Quanta and Approximation Spaces. I: Non-classical approximation operators - II: Generalised approximation operators". To appear in Proc. of the IEEE Int. Conf. on Granular Computing, Beijing, R. P. China 2005.

6. Z. Pawlak, Rough Sets: A Theoretical Approach to Reasoning about Data. Kluwer, 1991.
7. G. Sambin, S. Gebellato: "A Preview of the Basic Picture: A New Perspective on Formal Topology". TYPES 1998, pp. 194-207.
8. D. Vakarelov, "Information systems, similarity relations and modal logics". In E. Orlowska (Ed.) Incomplete Information - Rough Set Analysis Physica-Verlag, 1997, pp. 492-550.
9. R. Wille, "Restructuring Lattice Theory". In I. Rival (Ed.) *Ordered Sets*, NATO ASI Series 83, Reidel, 1982, pp. 445-470.

A Discrete Event Control Based on EVALPSN Stable Model Computation

Kazumi Nakamatsu[1], Sheng-Luen Chung[2], Hayato Komaba[3], and Atsuyuki Suzuki[3]

[1] School of H.S.E., University of Hyogo, Himeji 670-0092 Japan
`nakamatu@shse.u-hyogo.ac.jp`
[2] Dept. Electrical Eng., NTUST, Taipei 106, Taiwan
`slchung@mail.ntust.edu.tw`
[3] Dept. Information, Shizuoka University, Hamamatsu 432-8011 Japan
`{cs0038, suzuki}@cs.inf.shizuoka.ac.jp`

Abstract. In this paper, we introduce a discrete event control for Cat and Mouse example based on a paraconsistent logic program EVALPSN stable model computation. Predicting and avoiding control deadlock states are crucial problems in discrete event control systems. We show that the EVALPSN control can deal with prediction and avoidance of control dadlock states in the Cat and Mouse by defining general rules to represent the deadlock states in EVALPSN, and is much more flexible than the previous version of EVALPSN Cat and Mouse control. We also show how to translate the control properties of the Cat and Mouse into EVALPSN.

Keywords: discrete event control, EVALPSN(Extended Vector Annotated Logic Program with Strong Negation), stable model, control deadlock, paraconsistent logic program.

1 Introduction

We have proposed a paraconsistent logic program called EVALPSN (Extended Vector Annotated Logic Program with Strong Nagation) in order to deal with defeasible deontic reasoning and inconsistency [7,8], and already applied EVALPSN to various kinds of safety verification and control such as railway interlocking verification, traffic light control, and pipeline valve control [9,10,11,12]. We have a basic discrete event control example called Cat and Mouse [14] to which EVALPSN defeasible deontic control has been already applied, and a EVALPSN control for the Cat and Mouse [13]. The Cat and Mouse is a basic discrete event control example in which a cat and a mouse travel safely in a maze with doorway open-close control. Generally, an automaton model is used for controlling the Cat and Mouse doorways. However, the automaton model control is not flexible, that is to say, if the allocation of rooms and doorways in the Cat and Mouse maze has a minor change, the automaton model has to be reconstructed according to the new maze architecture. Moreover, the construction method of

D. Ślęzak et al. (Eds.): RSFDGrC 2005, LNAI 3641, pp. 671–681, 2005.

the automaton model is complicated, and the automaton model is not so adequate for computation and implementation. On the other hand, the EVALPSN control for the Cat and Mouse is adequate for computation and implementation compared to the automaton model one, because it is a logic program consisting of only 16 EVALPSN clauses, and can be computed and implemented easily. It is an inevitable problem for discrete event control to predict and avoid control deadlock. In the Cat and Mouse, such a deadlock state is defined as a state in which neither the cat nor the mouse can move to any other rooms. A control method in EVALPSN clauses to avoid the deadlock state has been previously implemented in the EVALPSN control. Therefore, even if the allocation of rooms and doorways in the maze is changed a little, the EVALPSN control has to be reconstructed as well as the automaton model control.

In this paper, we introduce a much more flexible EVALPSN control for the Cat and Mouse than the previous one. In the new EVALPSN control, the control deadlock is defined as EVALPSN clauses, and it is easy to predict and avoid it. Moreover, the control properties for the Cat and Mouse are represented more commonly in the new EVALPSN control, and the EVALPSN can meet a change of the allocation of rooms and doorways. In fact, the control properties are translated into six general rules and into EVALPSN. Although the new EVALPSN control is flexible, it requires stable model computation to predict and avoid deadlock states in each stage of the Cat and Mouse. It takes long time to compute stable models, which is a fatal problem for control. In order to realize prompt control, we restrict the deadlock prediction in the new EVALPSN control to predicting only one stage ahead.

This paper is organized as follows: first, we review EVALPSN briefly and introduce the Cat and Mouse; next, we show how to interpret the control properties in the six control rules and EVALPSN; last, we describe how the Cat and Mouse is controlled by the EVALPSN.

2   EVALPSN

2.1   EVALPSN Overview

Generally, a truth value called an *annotation* is explicitly attached to each literal in annotated logic programs [1]. For example, let p be a literal, μ an annotation, then $p : \mu$ is called an *annotated literal*. The set of annotations constitutes a complete lattice [2]. An annotation in VALPSN (Vector Annotated Logic Program with Strong Negation) [6] which can deal with defeasible reasoning is a 2-dimensional vector called a *vector annotation* such that each component is a non-negative integer and the complete lattice $\mathcal{T}_v$ of vector annotations is defined as:

$$\mathcal{T}_v = \{ (x, y) | 0 \le x \le n, 0 \le y \le n, x, y \text{ and } n \text{ are integers} \}.$$

The ordering of the lattice $\mathcal{T}_v$ is denoted by a symbol $\preceq_v$ and defined: let $\boldsymbol{v_1} = (x_1, y_1) \in \mathcal{T}_v$ and $\boldsymbol{v_2} = (x_2, y_2) \in \mathcal{T}_v$,

$$\boldsymbol{v_1} \preceq_v \boldsymbol{v_2} \quad \textit{iff} \quad x_1 \le x_2 \quad \text{and} \quad y_1 \le y_2.$$

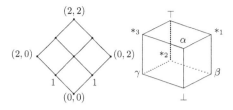

Fig. 1. Lattice $\mathcal{T}_v(n=2)$ and Lattice $\mathcal{T}_d$

For each vector annotated literal $p : (i, j)$, the first component i of the vector annotation denotes the amount of positive information to support the literal p and the second one j denotes that of negative information. For example, a vector annotated literal $p : (2, 1)$ can be intuitively interpreted that the literal p is known to be true of strength 2 and false of strength 1. In order to deal with defeasible deontic reasoning we have extended VALPSN to EVALPSN. An annotation in EVALPSN called an *extended vector annotation* has a form of $[(i, j), \mu]$ such that the first component (i, j) is a 2-dimentional vector as well as a vector annotation in VALPSN and the second one,

$$\mu \in \mathcal{T}_d = \{\bot, \alpha, \beta, \gamma, *_1, *_2, *_3, \top\},$$

is an index representing deontic notion or some kinds of inconsistency. The ordering of the lattice $\mathcal{T}_d$ is denoted by a symbol $\preceq_d$ and described by the Hasse's diagrams in **Fig. 1**. The intuitive meaning of each member in the lattice $\mathcal{T}_d$ is ; $\bot$ (unknown), α (fact), β (obligation), γ (non-obligation), $*_1$ (both fact and obligation), $*_2$ (both obligation and non-obligation), $*_3$ (both fact and non-obligation) and $\top$ (inconsistent). Therefore, EVALPSN can deal with not only inconsistency between usual truth values but also between permission and forbiddance, obligation and forbiddance, and fact and forbiddance. The complete lattice $\mathcal{T}_e$ of extended vector annotations is defined as the product $\mathcal{T}_v \times \mathcal{T}_d$. The ordering over the lattice $\mathcal{T}_e$ is denoted by a symbol $\preceq$ and defined as : let $[(i_1, j_1), \mu_1]$ and $[(i_2, j_2), \mu_2]$ be extended vector annotations,

$$[(i_1, j_1), \mu_1] \preceq [(i_2, j_2), \mu_2] \quad \textit{iff} \quad (i_1, j_1) \preceq_v (i_2, j_2) \text{ and } \mu_1 \preceq_d \mu_2.$$

There are two kinds of epistemic negations $\neg_1$ and $\neg_2$ in EVALPSN, which are defined as mappings over $\mathcal{T}_v$ and $\mathcal{T}_d$, respectively.

Definition 1. *(Epistemic Negations, $\neg_1$ and $\neg_2$)*

$$\neg_1([(i, j), \mu]) = [(j, i), \mu], \forall \mu \in \mathcal{T}_d,$$
$$\neg_2([(i, j), \bot]) = [(i, j), \bot], \quad \neg_2([(i, j), \alpha]) = [(i, j), \alpha],$$
$$\neg_2([(i, j), \beta]) = [(i, j), \gamma], \quad \neg_2([(i, j), \gamma]) = [(i, j), \beta],$$
$$\neg_2([(i, j), *_1]) = [(i, j), *_3], \quad \neg_2([(i, j), *_2]) = [(i, j), *_2],$$
$$\neg_2([(i, j), *_3]) = [(i, j), *_1], \quad \neg_2([(i, j), \top]) = [(i, j), \top].$$

These epistemic negations, $\neg_1$ and $\neg_2$, can be eliminated by the above syntactic operation. On the other hand, the strong negation (ontological negation $\sim$) in EVALPSN can be defined by the epistemic negations, $\neg_1$ or $\neg_2$, and interpreted as classical negation [2].

Definition 2. *(Strong Negation)*

$$\sim F =_{def} F \to ((F \to F) \wedge \neg(F \to F)),$$

where F be a formula and $\neg$ be $\neg_1$ or $\neg_2$, and $\to$ indicates a material implication.

Definition 3. *(well extended vector annotated literal)*
Let p be a literal. $p : [(i, 0), \mu]$ and $p : [(0, j), \mu]$ are called well extended vector annotated literals *(weva-literals for short), where $i, j \in \{1, 2\}$, and $\mu \in \{\alpha, \beta, \gamma\}$.*

Definition 4. *(EVALPSN)*
If $L_0, \cdots, L_n$ are weva-literals,

$$L_1 \wedge \cdots \wedge L_i \wedge \sim L_{i+1} \wedge \cdots \wedge \sim L_n \to L_0$$

is called an Extended Vector Annotated Logic Program clause with Strong Negation *(EVALPSN clause for short). If it does not include the strong negation, it is called an EVALP clause for short. An* Extended Vector Annotated Logic Program with Strong Negation *is a finite set of EVALPSN clauses.*

Deontic notions and fact are represented by extended vector annotations as follows:

"fact" is annotated as an annotation $[(m, 0), \alpha]$;
"obligation" is annotated as an annotation $[(m, 0), \beta]$;
"forbiddance" is annotated as an annotation $[(0, m), \beta]$;
"permission" is annotated as an annotation $[(0, m), \gamma]$;

where m is a positive integer. For example, a weva-literal $p : [(2, 0), \alpha]$ can be intuitively interpreted as "it is known that the literal p is a fact of strength 2", and a weva-literal $q : [(0, 1), \beta]$ can be intuitively interpreted as "the literal q is forbidden of strength 1".

2.2   EVALPSN Stable Model

The stable model semantics for EVALPSN is defined in [3,5].

Definition 5. *(Gelfond-Lifschitz transformation) [3]*
Let I be any interpretation for an EVALPSN P, P^I, the Gelfond-Lifschitz(G-L) transformation of the EVALPSN P with respect to the interpretation I is an EVALP obtained from the EVALPSN P by deleting

- *each EVALPSN clause that has a literal $\sim (C : \mu)$ in its body with $I \models C : \mu$, and*
- *all strongly negated weva-literals in the bodies of the remaining EVALPSN clauses.*

Since the EVALP P^I obtained by the G-L transformation has no strong negation, it has the unique least model given by $T_{P^I} \uparrow \omega$ [4].

Definition 6. *(Stable Model for EVALPSN)*
Let I be an interpretation for an EVALPSN P.

The interpretation I is called the stable model of the EVALPSN P
iff
$$I = T_{P^I} \uparrow \omega.$$

Generally, logic programs with strong negation may have more than two stable models or no stable model. Let us show an example.

Example 1. Let P be the EVALPSN:

$$\{ Q(n):[(2,0),\alpha], \quad R(n):[(2,0),\alpha],$$
$$Q(n):[(1,0),\alpha]\wedge \sim P(n):[(0,2),\beta] \rightarrow P(n):[(2,0),\beta],$$
$$R(n):[(1,0),\alpha]\wedge \sim P(n):[(2,0),\beta] \rightarrow P(n):[(0,2),\beta] \},$$

and

$$I_1 = \{ Q(n):[(2,0),\alpha], \; R(n):[(2,0),\beta], \; P(n):[(2,0),\beta] \}.$$

Then

$$P^{I_1} = \{ Q(n):[(2,0),\alpha], \; R(n):[(2,0),\beta], \; Q(n):[(1,0),\alpha] \rightarrow P(n):[(2,0),\beta] \}$$

and the interpretation I_1 is a stable model of the EVALPSN P. Moreover, let

$$I_2 = \{ Q(n):[(2,0),\alpha], \; R(n):[(2,0),\beta], \; P(n):[(0,2),\beta] \}.$$

Then the interpretation I_2 is also a stable model of the EVALPSN P.

3   EVALPSN Control for Cat and Mouse

3.1   Cat and Mouse Example

CAT AND MOUSE [14]   A cat and a mouse are placed in the maze shown in **Fig. 2**. Each doorway in the maze is either for the exclusive use of the cat, or for the exclusive use of the mouse. The doorways c_i ($i = 1, 2, \ldots, 7$) and $m_j (j = 1, 2, \ldots, 6)$ are for the cat and mouse, respectively. It is also assumed that each doorway, with the exception of c_7, can be opened or closed as required in order to control the movement of the cat and the mouse. The objective is to find the control schema that permits the cat and the mouse the greatest possible freedom of movement, but which also guarantees the following two properties:

1. the cat and the mouse never occupy the same room simultaneously, and
2. it is always possible for the cat and the mouse to return to the initial state, i.e., the state in which the cat is in room 2, and the mouse in the room 4.

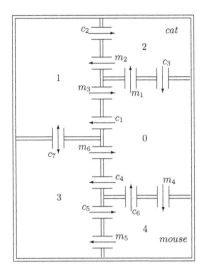

Fig. 2. Cat and Mouse Maze

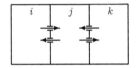

Fig. 3. Rooms

Taking the second property *2* into account, we consider states such that neither the cat nor the mouse can move to any other rooms. Suppose that the cat and mouse are in the rooms 0 and 3, respectively. As the doorway c_7 for the cat cannot be controlled to be closed, all the available doorways c_1, c_4, and m_6 must be closed. Then, both the cat and mouse are isolated. We call such a state *deadlock*.

3.2   Cat and Mouse Control in EVALPSN

We have already introduced an EVALPSN control for the Cat and Mouse [13], which is specified for the allocation of rooms and doorways in the maze. Therefore, if the maze has a minor change, the EVALPSN control does not work well. We provide a more flexible EVALPSN control with the prediction and avoidance of deadlock for the Cat and Mouse. In order to realize the flexible control, we make the following logical assumtions for the maze:

- there exist doorways between any two rooms, and even if we have no doorway between the two rooms in fact, a *strongly* (uncontrollably) closed doorway is supposed to exist;
- there also exist doorways for both the cat and mouse any room to itself, which are assumed to be strongly open;
- a broken doorway being always open is treated as a *strongly* open doorway, for example, the broken doorway C_7 for the cat is treated as a strongly open doorway;
- we call a state transition from a state to the following one a *step*.

In order to formalize the control in EVALPSN, we interpret the properties *1* and *2* as six general control rules, and translate them into EVALPSN. We introduce some annotated predicates used in the EVALPSN control.

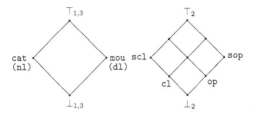

Fig. 4. Lattices $\mathcal{T}_{vn}(n = 1, 2, 3)$ of Annotations

$occu(i, t) : [\mathtt{ani}, \mu]$ the room i is occupied by an animal($\mathtt{ani}$) at the t-th step, where the cat($\mathtt{cat}$) and mouse($\mathtt{mou}$) are represented as conflicting annotations such that $\mathtt{ani} \in \mathcal{T}_{v1} = \{\perp_1, \mathtt{cat}, \mathtt{mou}, \top_1\}$ in **Fig. 4**, and $\mu \in \mathcal{T}_d$; for example, a weva-literal $occu(i, t) : [\mathtt{cat}, \beta]$ represents both bligation for the cat occupying the room i and forbiddance from the mouse ($\neg_1 \mathtt{cat}$) occupying the room i.

$door(i, j, ani, t) : [\mathtt{dst}, \mu]$ the doorway for the animal ani from the room i to the room j is controlled to be in a state($\mathtt{dst}$) at the t-th step. The four doorway states, "strongly open"($\mathtt{sop}$), "open"($\mathtt{op}$), "closed"($\mathtt{cl}$) and "strongly closed"($\mathtt{scl}$) of doorways are considered as conflicting annotations such that $\mathtt{dst} \in \mathcal{T}_{v2} = \{\perp_2, \mathtt{cl}, \mathtt{scl}, \cdots, \mathtt{op}, \mathtt{sop}, \top_2\}$ in **Fig. 4**, and $\mu \in \mathcal{T}_d$;

$circum(i, j, t) : [\mathtt{st}, \mu]$ circumstance in which the cat and mouse are in the rooms i and j at the t-th step, respectively, is a deadlock state or not, where the states "deadlock"($\mathtt{dl}$) and "normal"($\mathtt{nl}$) are also considered as conflicting annotations such that $\mathtt{st} \in \mathcal{T}_{v3} = \{\perp_3, \mathtt{nl}, \mathtt{dl}, \top_3\}$ in **Fig. 4**, and $\mu \in \mathcal{T}_d$.

The properties *1* and *2* can be interpreted in the following six rules and translated into EVALPSN.

CONTROL RULES

Rule 1.   If the animals ani and $eani$ are in the rooms i and j in **Fig. 3**, respectively, and there is a controllable doorway for the animal ani from the room i to the room j at the t-th step, then the doorway must be closed, that is to say, it is forbidden to control the doorway open. This rule is translated into

$$occu(i, t) : [ani, \alpha] \wedge occu(j, t) : [eani, \alpha] \wedge$$
$$\sim door(i, j, ani, t) : [\mathtt{sop}, \alpha] \wedge \sim door(i, j, ani, t) : [\mathtt{scl}, \alpha]$$
$$\rightarrow door(i, j, ani, t) : [\mathtt{cl}, \beta], \tag{1}$$
$$\text{where} \quad i \neq j, \quad ani, eani \in \{cat, mou\}, \quad t = u, u + 1,$$

and the expression $\sim door(i, j, ani, t) : [\mathtt{sop}, \alpha] \wedge \sim door(i, j, ani, t) : [\mathtt{scl}, \alpha]$ represents that there is a controllable doorway for the animal ani between the rooms i and j.

Rule 2.   If the doorway for the animal *ani* from the room *i* to the room *j* in **Fig. 3** is strongly closed or open at the *t*-th step, then the doorway must be closed or open, respectively. This rule is translated into

$$door(i, j, ani, t) : [\text{scl}, \alpha] \rightarrow door(i, j, ani, t) : [\text{cl}, \beta], \tag{2}$$

$$door(i, j, ani, t) : [\text{sop}, \alpha] \rightarrow door(i, j, ani, t) : [\text{op}, \beta], \tag{3}$$

$$\text{where} \quad i \neq j, \quad ani \in \{cat, mou\}, \quad t = u, u + 1.$$

Rule 3.   If there is a controllable doorway for the animal *ani* from the room *i* to the room *j* in **Fig. 3** at the *t*-th step, and no forbiddance from the doorway being open, then the doorway must be open. This rule is translated into

$$\sim door(i, j, ani, t) : [\text{sop}, \alpha] \wedge \sim door(i, j, ani, t) : [\text{scl}, \alpha] \wedge$$
$$\sim door(i, j, ani, t) : [\text{cl}, \beta] \rightarrow door(i, j, ani, t) : [\text{op}, \beta], \tag{4}$$
$$\text{where} \quad i \neq j, \quad ani \in \{cat, mou\}, \quad t = u, u + 1.$$

Rule 4.   If the animals *ani* and *eani* are in the rooms *i* and *j* in **Fig. 3**, and all the doorways from the rooms *i* and *j* must be closed at the *t*-th step, then such circumstance is defined as deadlock in EVALPSN :

$$occu(i, t) : [ani, \alpha] \wedge occu(j, t) : [eani, \alpha] \wedge$$
$$\bigwedge_{l=0}^{4} door(i, l, ani, t) : [\text{cl}, \beta] \wedge \bigwedge_{m=0}^{4} door(j, m, eani, t) : [\text{cl}, \beta]$$
$$\rightarrow circum(i, j, t) : [\text{dl}, \alpha], \tag{5}$$
$$\text{where} \quad l \neq i, \quad i \neq j, \quad m \neq j, \quad \text{and} \quad ani, eani \in \{cat, mou\}, \quad t = u + 1.$$

Rule 5.   If the animals *ani* and *eani* are in the rooms *i* and *k* in **Fig. 3**, respectively, there is a controllable doorway for the animal *ani* from the room *j* to the room *k* at the *t*-th step, and the next state in which the animals *ani* and *eani* are in the room *i* and the room *j* is a deadlock state, then the doorway for the animal *eani* from the room *k* to the room *j* must be closed. This rule is translated into

$$occu(i, t) : [ani, \alpha] \wedge occu(k, t) : [eani, \alpha] \wedge$$
$$\sim door(k, j, eani, t) : [\text{sop}, \alpha] \wedge \sim door(k, j, eani, t) : [\text{scl}, \alpha] \wedge$$
$$circum(i, j, t + 1) : [\text{dl}, \alpha] \rightarrow door(k, j, eani, t) : [\text{cl}, \beta], \tag{6}$$
$$\text{where} \quad i \neq j, \quad j \neq k, \quad k \neq i, \quad \text{and} \quad ani, eani \in \{cat, mou\}, \quad t = u.$$

Rule 6.   If the animals *ani* and *eani* are in the rooms *i* and *k* in **Fig. 3**, respectively, there is a controllable doorways for the animal *eani* from the room *k* to the room *j*, and the doorway for the animal *eani* from the room *j* to the room *i* (or the doorway for the animal *ani* from the room *i* to the room *j*) are strongly open at the *t*-th step, then the doorway for the animal *eani* from the room *k* to the room *j* must be closed. This rule is translated into

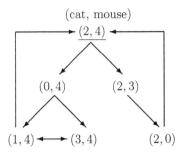

Fig. 5. State Transition in Cat and Mouse

$$occu(i,t):[ani,\alpha] \wedge occu(k,t):[eani,\alpha] \wedge$$
$$\sim door(k,j,eani,t):[\texttt{sop},\alpha] \wedge \sim door(k,j,eani,t):[\texttt{scl},\alpha] \wedge$$
$$door(j,i,eani,t):[\texttt{sop},\alpha] \rightarrow door(k,j,eani,t):[\texttt{cl},\beta], \qquad (7)$$

$$occu(i,t):[ani,\alpha] \wedge occu(k,t):[eani,\alpha] \wedge$$
$$\sim door(k,j,eani,t):[\texttt{sop},\alpha] \wedge \sim door(k,j,eani,t):[\texttt{scl},\alpha] \wedge$$
$$door(i,j,ani,t):[\texttt{sop},\alpha] \rightarrow door(k,j,eani,t):[\texttt{cl},\beta], \qquad (8)$$
$$\text{where} \quad i \neq j, \quad j \neq k, \quad k \neq i, \quad \text{and} \quad ani, eani \in \{cat, mou\}, \quad t = u, u+1.$$

In order to detect the deadlock states, all traveling routes for the cat and mouse are checked in the EVALPSN stable model computation. The EVALPSN $\{(1), \cdots, (5)\}$ have infinite stable model computation, if they have no restriction on the step number t.

In **Fig. 5**, an ordered pair (i,j) shows that the cat and mouse are in the rooms i and j, respectively, and in fact it contains infinite state transition chains such as $\{(2,4) \Rightarrow (0,4) \Rightarrow (3,4) \Rightarrow (1,4) \Rightarrow \cdots (2,4) \Rightarrow \cdots\}$. In order to avoid such eternal computation, we restrict the EVALPSN computation with the present step $t = u$ and the next step $t = u+1$, which makes the EVALPSN stable model computation much easier, although the prediction of deadlock states is restricted to until one step ahead.

3.3   Examples

Initial Stage   Suppose that the cat and mouse are appeared in the rooms 2 and 4 initially. Then, each doorway open-close state is computed by the EVALPSN P_0 consisting of all ground instances of EVALPSN clauses, $(1), \cdots, (5)$, with $u = 0$ as follows. First, EVALP clauses representing the locations of the cat and mouse,

$$occu(2,0):[\texttt{cat},\alpha] \quad \text{and} \quad occu(4,0):[\texttt{mou},\alpha],$$

are input to the EVALPSN P_0; next, EVALP clauses representing all doorways that are strongly closed or open such as $door(1,4,mou,0):[\texttt{scl},\alpha]$ and

$door(1, 3, cat, 0) : [\mathrm{sop}, \alpha]$ are also input to the EVALPSN P_0; lastly, two stable models of the EVALPSN P_0 that predict the two routes, the initial state $(2, 4)$ to the state $(0, 4)$ and the initial state $(2, 4)$ to the state $(2, 3)$ in **Fig. 5**, are computed, where it is verified that neither the states $(0, 4)$ nor $(2, 3)$ are deadlock states; then both of them include the weva-literals,

$$door(0, 1, cat, 0) : [\mathrm{op}, \beta], \quad door(0, 3, cat, 0) : [\mathrm{op}, \beta],$$
$$door(1, 2, cat, 0) : [\mathrm{op}, \beta], \quad door(2, 0, cat, 0) : [\mathrm{op}, \beta],$$
$$door(3, 4, cat, 0) : [\mathrm{op}, \beta], \quad door(4, 0, cat, 0) : [\mathrm{op}, \beta],$$
$$door(0, 2, mou, 0) : [\mathrm{op}, \beta], \quad door(0, 4, mou, 0) : [\mathrm{op}, \beta],$$
$$door(1, 0, mou, 0) : [\mathrm{op}, \beta], \quad door(2, 1, mou, 0) : [\mathrm{op}, \beta],$$
$$door(3, 0, mou, 0) : [\mathrm{op}, \beta], \quad door(4, 3, mou, 0) : [\mathrm{op}, \beta],$$

which indicate the doorway control at the initial stage($t = 0$) as obligation (all doorways must be open).

2nd Stage   Suppose that only the cat has moved to the room 0. Then, each doorway open-close state is computed by the EVALPSN P_1 consisting of all ground instances of EVALPSN clauses (1),$\cdots$,(5) with $u = 1$ as well as the initial stage. First, EVALP clauses representing the locations of the cat and mouse,

$$occu(0, 1) : [\mathrm{cat}, \alpha] \quad \text{and} \quad occu(4, 1) : [\mathrm{mou}, \alpha],$$

are input to the EVALPSN P_1; next, EVALP clauses representing all door-ways that are strongly closed or open such as $door(1, 4, mou, 1) : [\mathrm{scl}, \alpha]$ and $door(1, 3, cat, 1) : [\mathrm{sop}, \alpha]$ are also input to the EVALPSN P_1; lastly, two stable models of the EVALPSN P_1 that predict the two routes, the states $(0, 4)$ to $(1, 4)$ and the states $(0, 4)$ to $(3, 4)$ in **Fig. 5**, are computed, where it is verified that neither the states $(1, 4)$ nor $(3, 4)$ are deadlock states; then both of them include the weva-literals,

$$door(0, 1, cat, 1) : [\mathrm{op}, \beta], \quad door(0, 3, cat, 1) : [\mathrm{op}, \beta],$$
$$door(1, 2, cat, 1) : [\mathrm{op}, \beta], \quad door(2, 0, cat, 1) : [\mathrm{op}, \beta],$$
$$door(3, 4, cat, 1) : [\mathrm{op}, \beta], \quad door(4, 0, cat, 1) : [\mathrm{op}, \beta],$$
$$door(0, 2, mou, 1) : [\mathrm{op}, \beta], \quad door(0, 4, mou, 1) : [\mathrm{op}, \beta],$$
$$door(1, 0, mou, 1) : [\mathrm{op}, \beta], \quad door(2, 1, mou, 1) : [\mathrm{op}, \beta],$$
$$door(3, 0, mou, 1) : [\mathrm{op}, \beta], \quad door(4, 3, mou, 1) : [\mathrm{cl}, \beta],$$

which indicate the doorway control at the second stage($t = 1$) as obligation (the doorway for the mouse from the room 4 to the room 3 must be closed and the other doorways must be open).

4   Conclusion

In this paper, we have introduced a more flexible EVALPSN control for the Cat and Mouse, which contains deadlock state prediction and avoidance. The idea of the deadlock prediction and avoidance would be applicable to other discrete event control systems suffering from dealing with deadlock.

We have already implemented a simulation system for the EVALPSN cat and mouse control realizing prompt computation.

References

1. Blair, H.A., Subrahmanian, V.S.: Paraconsistent Logic Programming. *Theoretical Computer Science* **68** (1989) 135–154
2. da Costa, N.C.A., Subrahmanian, V.S., Vago, C.: The Paraconsistent Logics P$\mathcal{T}$. *Zeitschrift für Mathematische Logic und Grundlangen der Mathematik* **37** (1991) 139–148
3. Gelfond, M., Lifschitz, V.: The Stable Model Semantics for Logic Programming. In: *Proc. 5th IEEE Int'l Conf. and Symp. Logic Programming* (1989) 1070–1080
4. Lloyd, J.W.: Foundations of Logic Programming. Springer-Verlag (1987)
5. Nakamatsu, K., Suzuki, A.: Annotated Semantics for Default Reasoning. In: *Proc. 3rd Pacific Rim Int'l Conf. AI*, Academic Press (1994) 180–186
6. Nakamatsu, K., Abe, J.M., Suzuki, A.: Defeasible Reasoning Between Conflicting Agents Based on VALPSN. In: *Proc. AAAI Workshop Agents' Conflicts*, AAAI Press (1999) 20–27
7. Nakamatsu, K., Abe, J.M., Suzuki, A.: A Defeasible Deontic Reasoning System Based on Annotated Logic Programming. In: *Proc. the Fourth Int'l Conf. Computing Anticipatory Systems*, AIP Conf. Proc. **573**, AIP Press (2001) 609–620
8. Nakamatsu, K., Abe, J.M., Suzuki, A.: Annotated Semantics for Defeasible Deontic Reasoning. In: *Proc. the Second Int'l Conf. Rough Sets and Current Trends in Computing*, LNAI **2005**, Springer-Verlag (2001) 432–440
9. Nakamatsu, K., Abe, J.M., Suzuki, A.: Defeasible Deontic Robot Control Based on Extended Vector Annotated Logic Programming. In: *Proc. the Fifth International Conference on Computing Anticipatory Systems*, AIP Conference Proceedings **627**, American Institute of Physics (2002) 490–500
10. Nakamatsu, K., Suito, H., Abe, J.M., Suzuki, A.: Paraconsistent Logic Program Based Safety Verification for Air Traffic Control. In: *Proc. 2002 IEEE International Conference on Systems, Man and Cybernetics* (CD-ROM), IEEE (2002)
11. Nakamatsu, K., Abe, J.M., Suzuki, A.: A Railway Interlocking Safety Verification System Based on Abductive Paraconsistent Logic Programming. In: *Soft Computing Systems*, Frontiers in AI Applications, **87**, IOS Press (2002) 775–784
12. Nakamatsu, K., Seno, T., Abe, J.M., Suzuki, A.: Intelligent Real-time Traffic Signal Control Based on a Paraconsistent Logic Program EVALP. In: *Proc. the 9th International Conference on Rough Sets, Fuzzy Sets, Data Mining and Granular Computing*, LNCS **2639**, Springer-Verlag (2003) 719–723
13. Nakamatsu, K., Komaba, H., Suzuki, A.: Defeasible Deontic Control for Discrete Events Based on EVALPSN. In: *Proc. the Fourth International Conference on Rough Sets and Current Trends in Computing*, LNAI **3066**, Springer-Verlag (2004) 310–315
14. Ramadge, J.G.P., Wonham, W.M.: The Control of Discrete Event Systems. In: *Proc. IEEE*, **77**, No.1, (1989) 81–98

Tolerance Relation Based Granular Space*

Zheng Zheng[1,2], Hong Hu[1], and Zhongzhi Shi[1]

[1] Key Laboratory of Intelligent Information Processing, Institute of Computing
Technology, Chinese Academy of Sciences, 100080, Beijing, China
{zhengz, huhong, shizz}@ics.ict.ac.cn
[2] Graduate School of the Chinese Academy of Sciences, 100039, Beijing, China

Abstract. Granular computing as an enabling technology and as such
it cuts across a broad spectrum of disciplines and becomes important to
many areas of applications. In this paper, the notions of tolerance relation
based information granular space are introduced and formalized mathematically. It is a uniform model to study problems in model recognition
and machine learning. The key strength of the model is the capability of
granulating knowledge in both consecutive and discrete attribute space
based on tolerance relation. Such capability is reestablished in granulation and an application in information classification is illustrated. Simulation results show the model is effective and efficient.

1 Introduction

Information granules, as the name itself stipulates, are collections of entities,
usually originating at the numeric level, that are arranged together due to their
similarity, functional adjacency, indistinguishability, coherency or alike [1]. The
entities on data layer usually belong to two types: discrete or consecutive. Many
models and methods of granular computing [2][3][4][5][11][12] have been proposed
and studied, however, most of them discuss discrete and consecutive data respectively. In their theories, discretization features are represented by attributes,
which is calculated by the methods such as feature extraction, feature reduction
and classification or only discretization. That means the features of one type can
be generated from the other. So, it is time to construct a uniform model to study
some important problems in pattern recognition and machine learning, such as
feature extraction, feature reduction, discretization and classification.

Nowadays, many researchers study the equivalence relation based granular
computing theory, such as Zhang B. and Y.Y. Yao [3][6] indicate that granule
is closely related to quotient space. In reality, tolerance relation is a more broad
relation. So, this paper discuss mainly about the tolerance relation based granular computing theory. There are a lot of papers on tolerance based rough set
approaches [13][14][15], but this approaches don't uses the multi-level framework
for granular computing and discuss mainly discretization features.

---

* This paper is supported by National Natural Science Foundation of China No.
60435010 and National Basic Research Priorities Programme No. 2003CB317004.

D. Ślęzak et al. (Eds.): RSFDGrC 2005, LNAI 3641, pp. 682–691, 2005.

2   Model of Tolerance Relation Based Granular Space

In 1962, Zeeman proposed that cognitive activities can be viewed as some kind tolerance spaces in function spaces. The tolerance spaces, which are constructed by tolerance relations based on distance functions, is used for stability analysis of dynamic system by Zeeman. In this paper, a tolerance spaces based on distance functions are developed for the analysis of information granulation, which is defined as tolerance relation granulation in the following parts.

2.1   Tolerance Relation Based Granular Space

The aim of describing a problem at different granularities is to enable the computer to solve the same problem at different granule size hierarchically. Suppose the triplet $(\boldsymbol{OS}, \boldsymbol{TR}, \boldsymbol{NTC})$ describes a tolerance relation based granular space $\boldsymbol{TG}$, where

$\boldsymbol{OS}$ denotes an object set system, which is illustrated by definitions 2.1-2.2;

$\boldsymbol{TR}$ denotes a tolerance relation system, which is illustrated by definitions 2.3-2.7;

$\boldsymbol{NTC}$ denotes a nested tolerance covering system, which is illustrated by definitions 2.8-2.13.

2.2   Object Set System

Object set system is composed by the objects at difference levels. $\boldsymbol{OS}_k$ represents an object at level $\boldsymbol{k}$.

Definition 2.1. $\boldsymbol{OS}_0$, called an original object vector, is a vector of $\boldsymbol{R}^n$, where $\boldsymbol{R}$ is the real number set.

Definition 2.2. $\boldsymbol{OS}_1$, called a subset object of level 1, is a set of original object vectors. Generally speaking, $\boldsymbol{OS}_{k+1}$ is a set of level $\boldsymbol{k}$ subset objects, $\boldsymbol{OS}_k$.

For example, in image processing, $\boldsymbol{OS}_0$ can be viewed as a pixel of an image, $\boldsymbol{OS}_1$ can be viewed as an image and $\boldsymbol{OS}_2$ can be viewed as a set of frames in video stream.

2.3   Tolerance Relation System

Tolerance relation system is a (parameterized) relation structure, and it is composed by a set of tolerance relations.

Definition 2.3. A tolerance relation $\boldsymbol{sn}$, $\boldsymbol{sn} \subseteq \boldsymbol{X} \times \boldsymbol{X}$, is a reflexive and symmetrical binary relation, where $\boldsymbol{X}$ is the original space of object vector and $\boldsymbol{X} \subseteq \mathbf{R}_n$.

Suppose α and β are two $\boldsymbol{n}$ dimensional vectors of $\boldsymbol{X}$, and $\boldsymbol{dis}(\alpha, \beta|\omega)$ is a distance function, where the dimensional weight $\omega = (\omega_0, \omega_1, !, \omega_{n-1})$ and $\omega_i \geq 0$.

Definition 2.4. $\boldsymbol{sp}(\alpha, \beta|\boldsymbol{dis}, \boldsymbol{d})$, called a simple tolerance proposition, is defined as

$$\boldsymbol{sp}(\alpha, \beta|\boldsymbol{dis}, \boldsymbol{d}) \Leftrightarrow \boldsymbol{dis}(\alpha, \beta|\omega) \leq \boldsymbol{d}, \tag{1}$$

where $\boldsymbol{d} \geq 0$ is a real number, called the radius of $\boldsymbol{sp}(\alpha, \beta|\boldsymbol{dis}, \boldsymbol{d})$.

Definition 2.5. A compound tolerance proposition $P(\alpha, \beta | D)$, where $D = \{d_1, d_2, \cdots, d_k\}$ and d_i is the radius of $sp_i(\alpha, \beta | dis_i, d_i)$, is a Boolean function composed by a group of $sp_i(\alpha, \beta | dis_i, d_i)$ related with "$\wedge$" , "$\vee$" and "$\neg$" operators and $0 \leq i \leq k$. For simplicity, the dimensional weight ω_i in $sp_i(\alpha, \beta | dis_i, d_i)$ is same.

In the case that $P(\alpha, \beta | D)$ contains the negative operator "$\neg$", $P(\alpha, \beta | D)$ may not be reflexive, and for $sp(\alpha, \beta | dis, d) \Leftrightarrow dis(\alpha, \beta | \omega) \geq d$ is not a tolerance relation, so it can't be used in compound tolerance proposition. In this case, $P(\alpha, \beta | D)$ can be recomposed by extending it to $P(\alpha, \beta | D) \vee (dis(\alpha, \beta | \omega) \leq d)$, where $d_0 \leq d$.

Definition 2.6. The tolerance relation $sn(P, \omega, DIS, D)$ induced by $P(\alpha, \beta | D)$ is defined as $(\alpha, \beta) \in sn(P, \omega, DIS, D) \Leftrightarrow P(\alpha, \beta | D)$, where $DIS = \{dis_1, dis_2, \cdots, dis_k\}$.

Proposition P, weight vector ω, distance function vector DIS and radius vector D are the four important elements in a tolerance relation. Tolerance relation system is composed by a set of tolerance relations and many space areas can be described by tolerance relation system.

2.4   The Nested Tolerance Covering System

The nested tolerance covering system is a (parameterized) granule structure, which denotes different levels granules and the granulation process based on above object system and tolerance relation system. The nested tolerance covering on OS_k can be constructed as follows.

The Nested Tolerance Covering on OS_1
In this subpart, the definitions of granules, tolerance covering and nested tolerance covering are presented. Besides, with definition 2.8 and definition 2.9, the granulation process on OS_1 is illustrated. Here, we focus on the extension of a granule, that is, how to use the objects to construct granules.

Definition 2.8. A small granule over OS_1 is a set

$$G_0(a \,|\omega_0) = \{x \,|(x, a) \in sn(P, \omega_0, DIS, D) \wedge x \in OS_1\}, \qquad (2)$$

where $Grid \subseteq OS_1$ and $a=(a')$, $a' \in Grid$. a' can be viewed as the location of $G_0(a|\omega_0)$. $Grid$ is the set of all possible locations and defined as grid point set. ω_0 is the coordinate.

Definition 2.9. A nested tolerance covering over OS_1 is defined as follows:

(1) A level 0 granule $G_0(a|\omega_0)$ is a subset of OS_1 under coordinate $L_0 = \omega_0$ and a is the location of $G_0(a|\omega_0)$ in OS_1. The set of all level 0 granules, $\{G_0(a|\omega_0)\}$, under L_0, a grid point set $Grid_0$ and a tolerance relation set $sn(L_0, Grid_0)$ is defined as $C_1(0)$.

(2) Suppose $G_k(\eta_k|\omega_k)$ is a level k granule and a level $k+1$ granule

$$G_{k+1}(\eta_{k+1}|\omega_{k+1}) = \{x \,|((x, \eta_{(k+1)(k+1)}) \in sn(P, \omega_{k+1}, DIS, D)) \wedge x \in G_k(\eta_k|\omega_k)\}$$
$$(3)$$

where $\eta_i=(\eta_{i0}\ \eta_{i1},\ \cdots,\ \eta_{ii})$. η_i is the location set of all ancestor granules of $G_i(\eta_i|\omega_i)$. η_{ip} is the location of $G_i(\eta_i|\omega_i)$'s ancestor $G_p(\eta_p|\omega_p)$ in its father granule $G_{p-1}(\eta_{p-1}|\omega_{p-1})$. For $G_0(\eta_0|\omega_0)$, $\eta_0 = a$. $\eta_{(k+1)(k+1)}$ is the location of $G_{k+1}(\eta_{k+1}|\omega_{k+1})$ in its father granule $G_k(\eta_k|\omega_k)$. If $G_{k+1}(\eta_{k+1}|\omega_{k+1})=G_k(\eta_k|\omega_k)$, the set of all small level $k+1$ granule $G_{k+1}(\eta_{k+1}|\omega_{k+1})$ is defined as tolerance covering $GW_{k+1}(\eta_{k+1}|\omega_{k+1})$ on $G_k(\eta_k|\omega_k)$, which is based on the coordinate system $L_{k+1} = (\omega_0,\cdots,\omega_{k+1})$, a grid point set $Grid_{k+1}\subseteq G_k(\eta_k|\omega_k)$, and a tolerance relation set $sn(L_{k+1}, Grid_{k+1})$.

Based on above, suppose $C_1(0)=GW_0(\eta_0|\omega_0)$, $C_1(k)=\{GW_k(\eta_k|\omega_k)\}$, and $\bigcup GW_k(\eta_k|\omega_k)= OS_1$, then

$$\bigcup_{k=0,1,\cdots} TC_1 = (C_1(k)) \tag{4}$$

is the nested tolerance covering over OS_1.

The Adjoint Nested Tolerance Covering System on Level k Granules
In this subpart, the definition of adjoint subset object are presented, which can be viewed as the intension of a granule. Two ways to generate the adjoint subset object are developed as follows.

Definition 2.10. An adjoint subset object at level k over a nested tolerance covering of OS_1 is a new feature vector set. Each new feature vector belongs to a level k granule $G_k(\eta_k|\omega_k)$, and can be generated from nested smaller granules by two ways:

(1) Computing a new vector directly over all original object vectors OS_0 (Def.2.1) belong to $G_k(\eta_k|\omega_k)$. For example, the vector can be the centroid vector of $G_k(\eta_k|\omega_k)$, or a new long vector constructed by arranging all vectors of $G_k(\eta_k|\omega_k)$ in a row, which is a prevalent method in image module matching algorithms.

(2) Computing a new vector through nested granules in $C_1(k)$. According to above defined nested structure, a level k granule is larger than a level $k+1$ granule, so new vectors at level k can be calculated from new vectors of level $k+1$, each object vector OS_0 in OS_1 can be viewed as the highest level new vectors, and OS_1 itself can be viewed as a level 0 granule and assigned a new feature vector. After assigning every level k granule of OS_1 a new feature vector, all level k granules can be viewed as a new subset object.

The first kind is called as a usual adjoint subset object and the second is called as a nested subset object. Based on adjoint subset objects, adjoint nested tolerance covering system can be created as:

Definition 2.11. After assigning a new feature vector V to every OS_1, a nested tolerance covering

$$TC_2 = (\bigcup_{k=0,1,\cdots} C_2(k)) \tag{5}$$

on OS_2 can be constructed using the method constructing TC_1 in OS_1. A granule of TC_2 can be viewed as a classification of OS_1 and an integral class label c can be assigned to OS_1. If we divide every dimension of feature vectors V into regions marked by $n \in \{0,1,2,\cdots, N\}$, then a new discretized feature vector V' can be created by adding the classification label c to it. Such kind of new feature vectors are denoted as decision objects, $\boldsymbol{Iobject}$.

Similarly, we can define $\boldsymbol{TC}_k$ on $\boldsymbol{OS}_k$ and decision objects on $\boldsymbol{OS}_k$. The tolerance relation based granular space is so versatile that it includes all classification processes using distance functions and most of the multi-scale feature extraction processes in pattern recognition. For the sake of pages, we only focus on the knowledge discovery of lattice sub space of above granular space.

3   The Lattice Sub Space in Granular Space

Lattice is a simple but important sub space structure included by above granular space.

Definition 3.1. A level 1 granule $\boldsymbol{G}_l(\eta | \omega)$ on a subset object $\boldsymbol{OS_p}$ is a set of $\boldsymbol{OS}_{p-1}$, so in some cases, there are lattices $\boldsymbol{L} \subseteq \boldsymbol{TC}_p$, where $\boldsymbol{TC}_p = \bigcup(\boldsymbol{C}_p(\boldsymbol{k}))$ is a nested tolerance covering on $\boldsymbol{OS}_p$. These lattices are based on inclusion relation "$\subset$" and operators "$\cup$" and "$\cap$". In the lattice case, there must be some overlapped granules in $\boldsymbol{C}_p(\boldsymbol{l})$. If none of granules in $\boldsymbol{TC}_p$ are overlapped, granules in $\boldsymbol{C}_p(\boldsymbol{l})$ can be viewed as equivalent classes, so the granular theory based on equivalent relation is a special case.

Many problems can be described by the lattice space. In the following pages, we illustrate an example of lattice space, which is based on decision objects. Our object is to classify new decision objects according to the knowledge extracted from old classified objects. The information lattice space, based on a nested tolerance relation based granular space, can be used to model problems and describe problem solving algorithms. We also take a lot of experiments to test our theory's validity and ability to this problem.

3.1   The Construction of Tolerance Relation Based Granular Space

First, we define the object set system. Here $\boldsymbol{OS}_0 \in \boldsymbol{OS}_1$ can be viewed as a decision object $\boldsymbol{Iobject} = (v_0, v_1, \cdots, v_{n-1}, v_n)$, where v_i is a discretized feature and $v_n = c$ is the class label of this decision object. $\boldsymbol{OS}_1$ can also be viewed as a decision table (**Def.3.7**) composed by decision objects.

Second, we define the tolerance relation system. The distance function $\boldsymbol{dis}(\alpha, \beta | \omega_i)$ and the tolerance proposition $\boldsymbol{P}(\alpha, \beta | \boldsymbol{D})$ can be defined by the following definition.

Definition 3.2. $\boldsymbol{P}(\alpha, \beta | \boldsymbol{D}) = \boldsymbol{dis}(\alpha, \beta | \omega) \leq 0$, where

$$\boldsymbol{dis}(\alpha, \beta | \omega_i) = \sum_{j=0}^{n} \omega_{ij}(\alpha_j \oplus \beta_j), \tag{6}$$

$\alpha = (\alpha_0, \alpha_1, \cdots, \alpha_n), \beta = (\beta_0, \beta_1, \cdots, \beta_n)$, and

$$\alpha_j \oplus \beta_j = \begin{cases} 0 & \text{if } \alpha_j = \beta_j \\ 1 & \text{else} \end{cases} \tag{7}$$

According to above definition, the tolerance relation is generated as $(\alpha, \beta) \in sn(P, \omega, DIS, D) \Leftrightarrow P(\alpha, \beta | D)$. $\omega_i = (\omega_{i0}, \omega_{i1}, \cdots, \omega_{in})$ is a coordinate and $\omega_{ij} = 1$ or 0.

Third, we define the nested tolerance covering system. The following definition presents the method generating a new granule and its adjoint vector. With different forms of coordinate ω, different new granules are generated. The last element of ω is always "1" because the granules without the same decision cannot be combined.

Definition 3.3. A nested tolerance covering $TC_1 = (\bigcup_{k=0,1,\ldots} C_1(k))$ on OS_1 can be constructed using the method defined in section 2.4.1, where

$$C_1(i) = \{G_i(Obj_j | \omega_i) | G_i(Obj_j | \omega_i) = \{Ob_l | dis(Ob_l, Ob_j | \omega_i) \leq 0, Ob_j \in OS_1\}\}, \tag{8}$$

where $Ob_j = (v_{j0}, v_{j1}, \cdots, v_{jn})$. $G_i(Ob_j | \omega_i)$ is a level i granule and $i = \Sigma_{j=0,\cdots,n-1} \omega_{ij}$. A new vector $VG_{ij} = (VG_{ij0}, VG_{ij1}, \cdots, VG_{ij(n-1)}, VG_{ijn})$, denoted as decision rule (Def.3.9), is assigned to it, where if ω_p is equal to 1 then $vg_{ijp} = v_{jp}$, else $vg_{ijp} = "*"$. If $dis(Ob_l, Ob_j | \omega_i) \leq 0$, then $G_i(Ob_l | \omega_i) = G_i(Ob_j | \omega_i)$.

For example, if $Ob_1 = (f_1, r_1, e_1, s_1)$, $Ob_2 = (f_1, r_1, e_2, s_1)$, $r = 3$, and $\omega = (1, 1, 0, 1)$, then $G_2(Ob_2) = (f_1, r_1, *, s_1)$, and the level of the granule is $i = 2$.

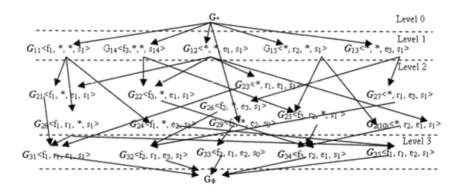

Fig. 1. Decision Granular Lattice of Table 1

In our algorithm, VG_{ij} is computed from $VG_{(i+1)l}$ with method 2 in definition 2.10 and the following definition is more detailed one. **Definition 3.4.** Suppose $C_1(i) = \{G_{i1}, G_{i2}, \cdots, G_{iq}\}$ is a level i tolerance covering over $G_{(i-1)p} \subseteq OS_1$. By Proposition 3.2, $q = 2$ and $dis(VG_{i1}, VG_{i2} | \omega) \leq 1$, where $\omega = \{1, 1, \cdots, 1\}$. Then $VG_{(i-1)p} = \{vg_{(i-1)p0}, vg_{(i-1)p1}, \cdots, vg_{(i-1)pn}\}$ of $G_{(i-1)p}$ can be calculated by: if $vg_{i1} \oplus vg_{i2} = 0$, $vg_{(i-1)pj} = vg_{i1j}$, else $vg_{(i-1)pj} = "*"$.

In granular space, each granule has only one feature vector VG_{ij}, so VG_{ij} can be viewed as the key of G_{ij}. This viewpoint is ensured by Proposition 3.2.

3.2   Decision Table and Decision Rule

In above description of problem, we mention that OS_1 is a decision table and the adjoint vector of each granule can be viewed as a decision rule. For the convenience of description, we define the two concepts clearly.

Definition 3.5. A decision table is defined as $S = <U, C, D, V, f>$. The details can be found in Ref. [8].

Definition 3.6. Let $S = <U, C, D, V, f>$ be a decision table, and let $B \subseteq C$. Then the rule set F generated from S and B consists of all rules of the form

$$\wedge (a, v) : a \in B \text{ and } v \in V_a \cup \{*\} \rightarrow d = v_d, \tag{9}$$

where $v_d \in V_a$. The symbol $*$ means that the value of the corresponding attribute is irrelevant for the rule, i.e., in conjunction we are not considering the descriptor for this attribute a. The length of the rule is the number of attribute values in precondition that not equal to "*", denoted as $|| \cdot ||$.

For example, in a decision system with 5 condition attributes $(a_1, \cdots, a_5)$, $(a_1 = 1) \wedge (a_2 = *) \wedge (a_3 = 1) \wedge (a_4 = 1) \wedge (a_5 = *) \rightarrow d = 4$ is a rule according to definition 3.6. In this paper, we describe a rule as a vector and the above decision rule is described as $(1, *, 1, 1, *, 4)$, and the length of the rule is 3.

3.3   Decision Granule

Now, we choose some granules from the constructed granular space to solve our problem, called decision granules.

Definition 3.7. Let S be a decision table and G_{ij} describes a granule. G_{ij} is a decision granule, iff G_{ij} satisfies the following conditions:
(1) The objects in G_{ij} satisfy a tolerance proposition(Def 2.4-2.5) ;
(2) VG_{ij} (Def. 3.6) is a decision rule defined at definition 3.6;
(3) There isn't any object in S satisfying the condition of VG_{ij}, but not satisfying the decision of VG_{ij}.

Definition 3.8. Let S be an decision table, then G_* denotes the maximal decision granule, where VG_* is the rule covered all objects; G_Φ denotes the minimal decision granule, where VG_Φ is the rule covered none objects.

3.4   Decision Granular Lattice

Definition 3.9. Suppose G_{ij} and G_{kp} are two decision granules, where $k \geq i$. Then, we denote that $G_{ij} \subseteq G_{kp}$, iff $dis(VG_{ij}, VG_{kp}|\omega) = 0$ and $|| VG_{ij} || \geq || VG_{kp} ||$. Here, we call G_{ij} is the child granule of G_{kp}, and VG_{kp} is the ancestral granule of VG_{ij}. If $|| VG_{ij} || = || VG_{kp} || + 1$, we call VG_{ij} is the son granule of VG_{kp}, and VG_{kp} is the father granule of VG_{ij}.

Proposition 3.1. The relation "$\subseteq$"(**Def.3.6**) is a partial ordering relation.

Proposition 3.2. Let $S = <U, C, D, V, f>$ be a decision table, GS is the set of all decision granules generated from S (including G_* and G_Φ) and "$\subseteq$" is the relation defined by definition 3.9, then $< GS, \subseteq >$ is a lattice, called decision granular lattice.

For the sake of pages, we aren't proving these propositions here.

Definition 3.10. Suppose G_{ij} and G_{pg} are two decision granules, G_{ij} is conflict with G_{pg}, iff

$$\sum_{k=0}^{1} \omega_j(vg_{ijk} \oplus vg_{pqk}) = 0 \tag{10}$$

and the decisions of VG_{ij} and VG_{pq} are different.

Definition 3.11. Suppose G_{ij} and VG_{pq} are two decision granules, G_{ij} is equal to G_{pg}, iff $dis(VG_{ij}, VG_{pq}|\omega)=0$.

Now, we present a simple algorithm generating granular lattice from decision table S. Suppose m is the number of condition attributes and n is the number of objects in S, $object_i$ is the ith object in S.

Algorithm 1 Decision Granular Lattice Construction Algorithm (DGLC)
Input: Decision table S;
Output: Granular Lattice GL;
Step 1(Initialization):
    FOR$(i = 1; i \le n; i + +)$
    {Generate G_i, where $VG_i = object_i$;
     Add G_i to GL; }
    $Number\_of\_granules = n$;
    //In the following, we call G_i is the ith granule in GL if the granule is the ith granule added to GL.
Step 2(Generating granules and establish relationships):
$Start=1$; $End=n$;
While ($Start \le End$)
    {FOR $(i= Start; i \le End - 1; i + +)$ {
    FOR $(j=i+1; j \le End; j + +)$ {
    Suppose G_i is the ith granule and G_i is the jth;
    Generate G and VG from G_i and G_j according to Def. 3.7;
    If G exist and there isn't any conflict granule with G, then {
        If there isn't any granule equal to G
        {Add G to GL; Connect G to G_i and G_j;
         $Number\_of\_granules++$;}
        else Connect granule G' that is equal to G (Def. 3.11) to G_i and G_j;}}}}
    $Start=n+1$; $End=Number\_of\_granules$;}
Step 3(Establishing the remaining relationships)
    Connect the maximal decision granule to the granules without father;
    Connect the granules without son to the minimal decision granule.
                                                                    End

Example 1: Table 1 is a decision table and the last attribute is the decision attribute. Input table 1 to **DGLC** algorithm and **Fig. 1** is the resulted decision granular lattice.

Table 1. A Decision Table

Object	F	R	E	S
X_1	f_1	r_1	e_1	s_1
X_2	f_2	r_1	e_3	s_1
X_3	f_2	r_1	e_2	s_0
X_4	f_3	r_2	e_1	s_1
X_5	f_1	r_1	e_2	s_1

3.5   Decision Granular Lattice Based Classification Algorithm

We can use decision granular lattice to classify new decision objects and the following is the decision granular lattice based classification algorithm (DGLC).

Definition 3.12. The matching degree of object **object** to a decision granule **G** is defined as Match(**object, G**), and Match(**object, G**)=max{**level**| **level** is the level number of **G** or **G**'s child granule G_{ij}, where object satisfy **VG** or VG_{ij}}.

Algorithm 2 Decision Granular Lattice Based Classification Algorithm (DGLBC)
Input: Testing table **S**, decision granular lattice **GL**;
Output: Classification Result
FOR $(i=1; i \leq n; i++)//n$ is the object number of **S**
{ **Max** = 0; **MatchGranule** = Φ;
    FOR (each son granule **G** of G_* (Def.3.11))
    { If **VG** cover **object**$_i$,
      Y= Match (**object**$_i$, **G**);
      If (**Y** > **Max**) **Max**=**Y**; **MatchGranule**= **G**;}}}
Decision of **object**$_i$=the decision of the adjoint vector of **MatchGranule**;}

From the experiment results, we conclude that decision granular lattice can classify data with higher correct rate than most of other algorithms. In specially, decision granular lattice has very high classification correct rate when the training set is small. It is because decision granular lattice is a granulation knowledge structure, which not only includes the knowledge of the final results but includes the granulated knowledge with different granularities.

4   Conclusion

We basically construct a more uniform granulation model, which is established on both consecutive space and discrete attribute space and based on tolerance relation.

(1) A tolerance relation based granular space **TG**, which is described as (**OS**, **TR**, **NTC**), are modeled and constructed.
(2) An illustration of how to use the tolerance relation based granular space to represent and solve problems is presented.

(3) A decision granular lattice is developed. The lattice is a granulation knowledge structure, which not only includes the knowledge of the final results but includes the granulated knowledge at different granularities.

References

1. Bargiela A., Pedrycz W., Granular Computing: An Introduction. Kluwer Academic Publishers, Dordrecht, Boston, London, 2003.
2. Pal S.K., Polkowski L., Skowron A., Rough-Neural Computing: Techniques for Computing with Words. Springer Publishers, 2004.
3. Zhang B., Zhang L., Theory and Application of Problem Solving. Elsevier Science Publishers, North-Holland, 1992.
4. Zadeh L., Towards a theory of fuzzy information granulation and its centrality in human reasoning and fuzzy logic. Fuzzy Sets and Systems, 19: 111-127, 1997.
5. Pawlak Z., Rough Sets Theoretical Aspects of Reasoning about Data. Kluwer Academic Publishers, Dordrecht, Boston, London, 1991.
6. Yao Y.Y., Zhong N., Granular Computing Using Information Table. In T.Y. Lin, Y.Y Yao, and L. A. Zadeh (editors) Data Miming, Rough Sets and Granular Computing, Physica-Verlag, 102-124, 2000.
7. Hu X.H., Cercone N., Learning in relational database: a rough set approach. Computational Intelligence, 11(2): 323-338, 1995.
8. Wang G.Y., Rough set theory and knowledge acquisition, XI'an Jiaotong University Press, Xi'an, 2001.
9. Mollestad T., Skowron A., A rough set framework for data mining of propositional default rules. In Foundations of Intelligent Systems of the 9th International Symposium, pages 448-457, Springer-Verlag, 1996..
10. Wang G.Y., He X., A Self-Learning Model under Uncertain Condition, Chinese Journal of SoftWare, 14(6):1096-1102, 2003.
11. Yao, Y.Y., A partition model of granular computing, LNCS Transactions on Rough Sets, 1:232-253, 2004.
12. Yao, Y.Y., Granular computing, the 4th Chinese National Conference on Rough Sets and Soft Computing, 4-10, 2004.
13. Polkowski L., Skowron A., Zytkow J., Tolerance based rough sets. In Soft Computing: Rough Sets, Fuzzy Logic, Neural Networks, Uncertainty Management, edited by T. Lin and A. Wildberger, 55ÍC58, (San Diego: Simulation Councils), 1995.
14. Marcus S., Tolerance Rough Sets, Cech Topologies, Learning Processes, Bulletin of the Polish Academy of Sciences, Technical Sciences, 42(3):471-487, 1994.
15. Skowron A., Stepaniuk J., Tolerance Approximation Spaces, Fundamenta Informaticae, 27:245-253, 1996.

Discernibility-Based Variable Granularity and Kansei Representations

Yuji Muto and Mineichi Kudo

Division of Computer Science,
Graduate school of Information Science and Technology,
Hokkaido University, Sapporo 060-0814, Japan
{muto, mine}@main.ist.hokudai.ac.jp

Abstract. In this paper, we discuss the most suitable "representation granularity", keeping several types of discernibility including individually discernibility and class discernibility. In the traditional "reduction" sense, the goal is to find the smallest number of attributes such that they enable us to discern each tuple or each decision class. However, once we pay attention to the number of attribute values too, that is, the size of each attribute, another criterion is needed. Indeed, we should ask ourselves about which one is better in the following two situations: 1) we can discern them with a single attribute of size ten, and 2) we can do this with two attributes of size five. This study answers this question with some criteria. Especially, we deal with continuous attributes. If we evaluate this difference in the light of understandability, we may prefer the latter, because they give more simple descriptions. Such a combination of simple nominal description helps us as a language or as a Kansei representation. To do this, we propose some criteria and algorithms to find near-optimal solutions for those criteria. In addition, we show some results for some databases in UCI Machine Learning Repository.

1 Introduction

When we recognize objects (faces, fruits, books, feelings and so on), we do not always pay attention to all attributes/features of those objects. Especially, it is well known that an "expert" in a problem domain often choose some of features and sometimes enhance them to distinguish an object from the others. If we consider this situation well, it is noticed that we usually discern each object by enumerating its distinctive features in an appropriate roundness (a granularity) of description. We call such a roundness and its linguistic representation "Kansei" representation. "Kansei" is a Japanese word which refers to the psychological image evoked by the competing sensations of external stimuli, and affected by emotions and personal sense of values. Generally, this word is often used in the field of "Kansei Engineering". Kansei Engineering is proposed by Nagamachi [1], which is used to translate the feeling (Kansei) of the customer of a product to its physical design elements. Now, Kansei Engineering is applied to various fields Such as Kansei Information Processing, Kansei Information Retrieval, Kansei

D. Ślęzak et al. (Eds.): RSFDGrC 2005, LNAI 3641, pp. 692–700, 2005.

mining, and so on [2,3,4,5,6]. This study is a little different from such approaches in the following sense. In the previous Kansei-related studies, some nominal values are given such as those in a questionnaire. In such a case, the size of attribute values is already given according to a subjective point of view. In our study, when an ordered attribute or a continuous attribute is given, we try to find an appropriate size of attribute values (the number of equally-spaced intervals) , while keeping the potential or the expression ability. If we have a small number of intervals, it might be possible to give them Kansei-like expressions. As a result, with a set of Kansei representation words such as "bad", "normal" and "medium", we can share a same feeling about distinctive characteristic specifying the object. According to this direction, let us consider how to obtain Kansei representation, to specify an object among many objects as a help for people. Obviously, too rough description is not enough for distinguishing that object from the others. While, too fine description is redundant. That is, it is desired to find an appropriate roundness of representation on that problem domain. Such a trial is "reduction" in Rough Sets. We seek the minimum number of attributes enough for discern each object. However, such a "reduction" trial is not sufficient in finding an appropriate roundness. To have Kansei representation, each attribute has to be described in a few words.

To achieve this goal, we consider "representation granularity" according to several criteria on the basis of discernibility. A continuous attribute does not give us an appropriate roundness, because a statement such as '$x = 2.3$' does not resort to our feeling. Rather, Kansei representation such as 'x is medium' is hoped. To do this, we quantize a continuous feature by a few number of intervals and translate them to nominal values. This quantization can be seen as an extension of the traditional "reduction" in Rough Sets, as will be described later. We show some results of this approach in some databases of UCI Machine Learning Repository.

2   Reduction and Partition

A principal concept of Rough Sets [7, 8, 9] is "discernibility". One of purposes of Rough Sets theory is to find the minimal subsets of attributes keeping some discernibility on a given information/decision table T. This goal is referred to as "reduction". However, the number of attribute values, not the number of attributes, has not been considered so far. Therefore, it can happen that the number of attributes is small but those attributes are described in a very fine way, that is, the number of the attribute values is too many. Such a fine description is not useful in the light of understandability. Here, let us consider m different attributes and denote their domains by $C_1, C_2, \ldots, C_m$. In addition, by $U = C_1 \times C_2 \times \cdots \times C_m$, we denote the universe. An information table T is given as a subset of U. First let us see an example as follow.

Example 1. Let us consider Fig. 1. In Fig. 1 (a), $C_1 = C_2 = \{1, 2, \ldots, 8\}$ are both ordered finite sets. Thus, $U = \{(i, j) | i = 1, 2, \ldots, 8, j = 1, 2, \ldots, 8\}$. Let us find an equivalence relation R distinguishing two classes ∘ and ×. In the traditional "reduction" sense, we choose (b). The corresponding partition is described by $P_R = \{\{(1, 1 - 8), (2, 1 - 8), \ldots, (8, 1 - 8)\}\}$ of size 8. It is noted that only the first attribute is chosen from the two attributes. However, we need a fine granular in the attribute. While, it is obvious that we can do this by only two attribute values such as "low" and "high", or "small" and "large", in Kansei representation (Fig. 1 (c)). This example shows that we can sometimes obtain

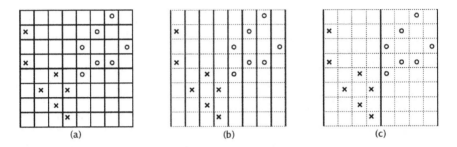

Fig. 1. "Further reduction" by unifying some values: (a) Base partition, (b) Reduction, and (c) The simplest partition

"further reduction" by unifying some attribute values in addition to attribute selection ("usual reduction"). Next, let us consider another example.

Example 2. Let us consider Fig. 2. Where the attributes and the universe are those of the same as the first example. Let us find an equivalence relation R distinguishing two class ∘ and ×. In the traditional "reduction" sense, we choose (b), because only one attribute is needed. In that way we cannot unify the attribute values. However, we can also find a 2×2 granularity (c), though it needs two attributes. The latter is advantageous in Kansei representation.

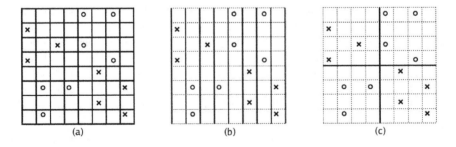

Fig. 2. "Reduction" vs. "Kansei Partition": (a) Base partition, (b) Reduction, and (c) The simplest partition

3   Variable Granularity

In this section, let us describe formally above discussion. A "granularity" is usually referred to as an equivalence relation R on U. That gives a certain level of expression of any concept. In Rough Sets theory, a "base" granularity along with the attributes is given as a tool for describing the objects in an information table (or a decision table). However, in the case when all the attributes are enough, especially when continuous attributes are considered, we need a finite granularity because the information table is finite. Let us call this granularity "measurement granularity." In fact, this is possible by finding the largest granule enough for separating the closest pair. Then, such a granularity becomes finite from the nature. Next, we proceed to find the largest granularity enough for discerning each object/record/tuple. We call such a granularity "individually discernible granularity". We also furthermore can proceed to "class discernible granularity".

3.1   Representation Granularity

First, we put the first priority on the uniformity that is related to equally-sized granules and evenly-divided resolution. Then, we divide a continuous attribute into some equally-spaced intervals. The both ends are determined by the maximal and minimal values of available objects on that attribute. We define several "representation granularities" on a set of m different attributes $C_1, C_2, \ldots, C_m$ as

$$G = (g_1, g_2, \ldots, g_m),$$
$$g_i = 2^{-d_i}, \quad (i = 1, 2, \ldots, m)$$

where d_i is a non-negative integer. That is, we divide a whole interval into 2^{d_i} small intervals. Here, the jth attribute with $d_j = 0$ is automatically removed, that is, "reduction" is automatically carried out.

3.2   Measurement Granularity

First, we call the granularity of given data itself "measurement granularity." We give it on account of the measurement precision, the description precision of the attribute, and data expression on memory. Here we assume that the measurement is fine enough for discerning individuals. However, it is possible that the measurement granularity is not enough for this goal. Then we need a finer granularity in measurements.

3.3   Discernible Granularity

Next, we define two kinds of granularity on the basis of two kinds of discernibility. In the following, we identify a representation granularity with its equivalence relation. In addition, we will use the word "largest"in granularity as for the size of the partition or the number of equivalence classes.

1) Individually Discernible Granularity R_I:
   The largest equivalence relation R_I such that $x \neq y \Rightarrow [x]_{R_I} \neq [y]_{R_I}$, where $[x]_{R_I}$ is an equivalence class of $x \in U$ in R_I.
2) Class Discernible Granularity R_D:
   The largest equivalence relation R_D such that $D(x) \neq D(y) \Rightarrow [x]_{R_D} \neq [y]_{R_D}$, where $D(x)$ is the decision class of $x \in U$.

We can consider one more granularity by loosening the class discernibility:

3) Class Discernible Granularity with a Grade R_G:
   The largest granularity with a "class-purity parameter" θ $(0 < \theta \leq 1)$ such that

$$\forall i, \ \max_j \frac{n_{ij}}{n_i} \geq \theta,$$

where n_i is the number of the objects contained in the ith equivalence class, n_{ij} is the number of the objects belonging to decision class j in the ith equivalence class.

We show an example of those granularities in Fig. 3.

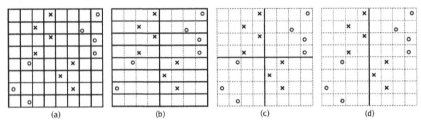

(a)   (b)   (c)   (d)

Fig. 3. Several kinds of granularity: (a) Measurement granularity, (b) Individually discernible granularity, (c) Class discernible granularity and (d) Class Discernible Granularity with a grade. (the class-purity is 0.571 in the both sides that is over $\theta = 0.55$)

3.4   Evaluation of Granularity

So far, we used the word "largest" without an exact definition. Here we give it. There are some possible definitions as for a given equivalence relation or the corresponding partition. Let us consider a representation granularity $G = (2^{-d_1}, 2^{-d_2}, \ldots, 2^{-d_m})$. Then, we define the two following criteria.

$$J_1(G) = d = \log_2 \prod_{i=1}^{m} 2^{d_i} = \sum_{i=1}^{m} d_i,$$

$$J_2(G) = d - H\left(\frac{d_1}{d}, \frac{d_2}{d}, \ldots, \frac{d_m}{d}\right) / \log m,$$

$$\text{where} \quad H\left(\frac{d_1}{d}, \frac{d_2}{d}, \ldots, \frac{d_m}{d}\right) = -\sum_{i=1}^{m} \frac{d_i}{d} \log \frac{d_i}{d}.$$

We say that a granularity is the "largest" when it minimizes one of these two. The first criterion J_1 requires the number of equivalence classes to be minimum.

So, it gives the smallest partition. However, this criterion does not consider an unbalance of granularity of each attribute, so that it cannot distinguish (a) and (b) in Fig. 4. Therefore, we recommend J_2 (Fig. 4 (b)), because it is advantageous in Kansei representation. It requires the entropy of the granularity of each attribute to be minimum in addition to J_1. So, it is expected to have a simpler granularity with a combination of attributes.

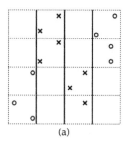 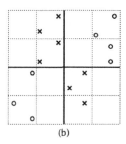

(a)   (b)

Fig. 4. Two granularities in two criteria of J_1 and J_2: (a) $J_1(G_a) = 0 + 2 = 2$ and $J_2(G_a) = 2 - 0 = 2$, (b) $J_1(G_b) = 1 + 1 = 2$ and $J_2(G_b) = 2 - 1 = 1$

3.5   Algorithms

We used a genetic algorithm (GA) to have the granularities satisfying J_1 and J_2. We encoded the integer value of d_i in a gene and an m-tuple $(d_1, d_2, \ldots, d_m)$ in a chromosome. In the following experiments, the population size (the number of chromosomes) is 101, the crossover probability is 1.0, and the mutation probability is 0.01. We used a roulette selection and elite strategy, and terminated the iteration when the evaluation for the elite converges for successive 10 generations.

4   Experiments

We dealt with two datasets of Iris and Wine from the UCI Machine Learning Repository [10] to evaluate the performance of the proposed method. Table 1 shows the characteristics of those two datasets, i.e., the number of objects, the number of attributes and the number of classes. Here, all the attributes are continuous. First, we found in order the measurement granularity, the individually

Table 1. Characteristic of Two Datasets

dataset	#objects	#attributes	#classes
Iris	150 (50,50,50)	4	3
Wine	178 (59,71,48)	13	3

discernible granularity and the class discernible granularity. Next, we translated the attribute values to a small number of Kansei words to help us to understand the attribute.

Table 2. Granularities of Iris

Attribute	Granularity 2^{d_i}		
	R_M	R_I	R_D
Sepal Length	64	32	1
Sepal Width	32	32	8
Petal Length	64	16	8
Petal Width	32	32	16

Table 3. Kansei Representation of Iris: '−' means "do not care".

(a) Some records of Iris data

x	S.L.	S.W.	P.L.	P.W.	Class
x_1	5.7	3.8	1.7	0.3	1
x_2	5.1	3.7	1.5	0.4	1
x_3	6.1	2.8	4.0	1.3	2
x_4	6.4	3.2	4.5	1.5	2
x_5	7.6	3.0	6.6	2.1	3
x_6	6.3	2.7	4.9	1.8	3

(b) Kansei representation

$[x]_{R_D}$	S.L.	S.W.	P.L.	P.W.	Class
$[x_1]_{R_D}$	−	3/8	1/8	1/16	1
$[x_2]_{R_D}$	−	3/8	1/8	2/16	1
$[x_3]_{R_D}$	−	2/8	3/8	5/16	2
$[x_4]_{R_D}$	−	3/8	3/8	5/16	2
$[x_5]_{R_D}$	−	2/8	4/8	7/16	3
$[x_6]_{R_D}$	−	2/8	4/8	7/16	3

Table 4. Granularities of Wine

Attribute	Granularity 2^{d_i}		
	R_M	R_I	R_D
Alcohol	512	1	2
Malic acid	512	2	2
Ash	256	2	2
Alcalinity of ash	256	1	2
Magnesium	128	4	1
Total phenols	32	4	1
Flavanoids	512	2	1
Nonflavanoid phenols	64	4	1
Proanthocyanins	512	2	1
Color intensity	2048	2	4
Hue	256	2	1
OD280/OD315 of d.w	512	8	2
Proline	2048	4	4

The results are shown in Tables 2 − 5. In the both discernible granularities we succeeded to reduce the attribute size largely from their original size in the measurement granularity especially in Wine. In addition, those sizes were further reduced in the class discernibility. In Iris, one attribute was removed (Table 2). As a result, some records of Iris data (Table 3 (a)) are translated into 8-level or 16-level representations (Table 3 (b)). It is hard to describe them linguistically, but 8 or 16 is rough enough.

In Wine, six attributes were removed in the class discernible granularity (Table 4). As a result, some records of Wine data (Table 5 (a)) are translated into a rough-level description which brings us Kansei representations (Table 5 (b)). Here we described them in two words ("small" or "large") or four words ("small", "rather small", "rather large" or "large"). These representations could indicate the distinctive features or more sharply compared with the original description of the records.

Table 5. Kansei Representation of Wine

(a) Some records of Wine data

x	Alco	M.A.	As	Alca	Mag	T.P.	Fla	N.P.	Proa	C.I.	Hue	OD	Prol	Class
x_1	14.23	1.71	2.43	15.6	127	2.8	3.06	0.28	2.29	5.64	1.04	3.92	1065	1
x_2	14.37	1.95	2.5	16.8	113	3.85	3.49	0.24	2.18	7.8	0.86	3.45	1480	1
x_3	12.08	1.13	2.51	24.0	78	2.0	1.58	0.4	1.4	2.2	1.31	2.72	630	2
x_4	12.34	2.45	2.46	21.0	98	2.56	2.11	0.34	1.31	2.8	0.8	3.38	438	2
x_5	12.53	5.51	2.64	25.0	96	1.79	0.6	0.63	1.1	5.0	0.82	1.69	515	3
x_6	13.45	3.7	2.6	23.0	111	1.7	0.92	0.43	1.46	10.68	0.85	1.56	695	3

(b) Kansei representation

$[x]_{R_D}$	Alco	M.A.	Ash	Alca	C.I.	OD	Prol	Class
$[x_1]_{R_D}$	large	small	large	small	rather small	large	rather large	1
$[x_2]_{R_D}$	large	small	large	small	rather large	large	large	1
$[x_3]_{R_D}$	small	small	large	large	small	large	rather small	2
$[x_4]_{R_D}$	small	small	large	large	small	large	small	2
$[x_5]_{R_D}$	small	large	large	large	rather small	small	small	3
$[x_6]_{R_D}$	large	large	large	large	large	small	rather small	3

5   Conclusion

In this paper, we have discussed the appropriate roughness of description using "representation granularity", as a tool for obtaining "Kansei" representation. We have thought that the given granularity (the measurement granularity) is usually too fine, and makes it hard to understand the records. This is the same even when reduction (removal of some attributes) is carried out. Especially, such a problem occurs when we deal with continuous attributes. However, we sometimes can have more rough granularity enough for discerning each record or each class. We have analyzed such granularities. We defined some granularities on the basis of some discernibility criteria, and proposed an algorithm to find the near-optimal solution for them. As a result, it was shown that we can have a granularity that enables us to understand each record in a friendly "Kansei" manner. This representation also gives us an insight about "how fine we should describe the attributes" or "which attributes have to be emphasized". We will extend "representation granularity" to categorical attributes in the future.

In this paper, we only have considered on equally-spaced division as a granularity. This is because we put the first priority on the uniformity that is related to equally-sized granules. It is natural to assume such uniformity in the first stepof analysis. If another criterion is considered for different goals such as information reduction goal, then variable-length intervals or more general discretization would be important. However, our uniformity releases us from specification of reasoning and brings the easiness for understanding. Such an equally-spaced division is the first step in our future work, although the second step is now under consideration. In the first step, we could have an appropriate size of equally-sized granules and we could couple some granules in the second step. Such a two-stage process would help us understand 1) to what degree of granularity is appropriate under the current (limited) knowledge and 2) what kind of coupling is possible on the appropriately chosen granularity to have Kansei-like expressions. In addition, we will compare our proposed method with Rough Set methods applying discretization and knowledge reduction in the future.

References

1. Nagamachi, M.: Kansei Engineering: A new ergonomic consumer-oriented technology for product development. International Journal of Industrial Ergonomics Vol. 15. (1995) 3–11
2. Suzuki, K., Hashimoto, S.: A Quantification of Kansei Information using Neural Network. IEICE Transaction on Information and System Vol. J82-DII. (1999) 677–684
3. Tsutsumi, K., Ito, N., Hashimoto, H.: A Development of the Building Kansei Information Retrieval System. Proceedings of International Conference on Computing in Civil and Building Engineering 10. (2004)
4. Camurri, A., et al.,: Towards Kansei information processing in music/dance interactive multi modal environments. Proceedings of the AIMI International Workshop. (1997) 74–78
5. Bianchi-Berthouze, N., Hayashi, T.: Subjective Interpretation of Complex Data: Requirements for Supporting Kansei Mining Process. Revised Papers from MDM/KDD and PAKDD/KDMCD. (2002) 1–17
6. Yanagisawa, H., Fukuda, S.: Interactive Reduct Evolutional Computation for Aesthetic Design, Journal of Computing and Information Science in Engneering Vol. 5. (2005)
7. Pawlak, Z.: Rough Sets: Theoretical Aspects of Reasoning about Data. Kluwer Academic Publishers, Dordrecht, The Netherlands (1991)
8. Pawlak, Z.: Rough classification. International Journal of Human-Computer Studies Vol. 51. (1999) 369–383
9. Ziarko, W.: Variable Precision Rough Set Model. Journal of Computer and System Sciences Vol. 46. (1993) 39–59
10. Blake, C.L., Merz, C.J.: UCI Repository of machine learning databases. [http://www.ics.uci.edu/~mlearn/MLRepository.html].

Rough Set Approximation
Based on Dynamic Granulation

Jiye Liang[1], Yuhua Qian[1], Chengyuan Chu[2], Deyu Li[1], and Junhong Wang[1]

[1] School of Computer and Information Technology, Shanxi University,
Taiyuan, 030006, People's Republic of China
[2] Institute of Computing Technology, the Chinese Academy of Sciences,
Beijing, 100080, People's Republic of China
ljy@sxu.edu.cn, jinchengqyh@126.com

Abstract. In this paper, the concept of a granulation order is proposed in an information system. The positive approximation of a set under a granulation order is defined. Some properties of positive approximation are obtained. For a set of the universe in an information system, its approximation accuracy is monotonously increasing under a granulation order. This means that a proper family of granulations can be chosen for a target concept approximation according to the user requirements. An algorithm based on positive approximation is designed for decision rule mining, and its application is illustrated by an example.

1 Introduction

Granular computing is a new active area of current research in artificial intelligence, and a new concept and computing formula for information processing. It has been widely applied to branches of artificial intelligence such as problem solving, knowledge discovery, image processing, semantic Web services, etc.

In 1979, the problem of fuzzy information granule was introduced by L.A. Zadeh in [1]. Then, in [2-4] he introduced the concept of granular computing, as a term with many meanings, covering all the research of theory, methods, techniques and tools related to granulation. A general model based on fuzzy set theory was proposed, and granules were defined and constructed basing on the concept of generalized constraints in [3]. Relationships among granules were represented in terms of fuzzy graphs or fuzzy if-then rules. Z. Pawlak [5] proposed that each equivalence class may be viewed as a granule consisting of indistinguishable elements, also referred to as to an equivalence granule. Some basic problems and methods such as logic framework, concept approximation, and consistent classification for granular computing were outlined by Y.Y. Yao in [6]. The structure, modeling, and applications of granular computing under some binary relations were discussed, and the granular computing methods based on fuzzy sets and rough sets were proposed by T.Y. Lin in [7]. Quotient space theory was extended to fuzzy quotient space theory based on fuzzy equivalence relation by L. Zhang and B. Zhang in [8], providing a powerful mathematical model and tools for granular computing. By using similarity between granules, some basic

D. Ślęzak et al. (Eds.): RSFDGrC 2005, LNAI 3641, pp. 701–708, 2005.

issues on granular computing were discussed by G.J. Klir in [9]. Several measures in information systems closely associated with granular computing, such as granulation measure, information and rough entropy, as well as knowledge granulation, were discussed by J.Y. Liang in [10, 11]. Decision rule granules and a granular language for logical reasoning based on rough set theory were studied by Q. Liu in [12].

In the view of granular computing, a general concept described by a set is always characterized via the so-called upper and lower approximations under static granulation in rough set theory, and a static boundary region of the concept is induced by the upper and lower approximations. However a general concept described by using positive approximation is characterized via the variational upper and lower approximations under dynamic granulation, which is an aspect of people's comprehensive solving ability at some different granulation space. The positive approximation extend classical rough set, enrich rough set theory and its application. The paper is organized as follows: in section 2, the concepts of a granulation order and the positive approximation under it are proposed. For any general concept of the universe, its boundary region is changeable and the approximation accuracy measure is monotonously increasing under a granulation order. This means that a proper family of granulations can be chosen for a target concept approximation according to the requirements of users; in section 3, an algorithm based on positive approximation is designed for decision rule mining, The algorithm will be helping for understanding the idea of positive approximation; in section 4, we show how the algorithm MABPA works by the example.

2   Positive Approximation

Let $S = (U, A)$ be an information system, $P, Q \in 2^A$ two attribute subsets. By $IND(P)$ and $IND(Q)$, we denote the indiscernible relation induced by P and Q. we define a partial relation $\preceq$ on 2^A as follows: $P \preceq Q$ $(Q \succeq P)$ if and only if, for every $P_i \in U/IND(P)$, there exists $Q_j \in U/IND(Q)$ such that $P_i \subseteq Q_j$, where $U/IND(P) = \{P_1, P_2, ..., P_m\}$ and $U/IND(Q) = \{Q_1, Q_2, ..., Q_n\}$ are partitions induced by $IND(P)$ and $IND(Q)$.

Let $S = (U, A)$ be an information system, X a subset of U and $P \subseteq A$ an attribute set. In rough set theory, X is characterized by $\overline{P}(X)$ and $\underline{P}(X)$, where

$$\underline{P}(X) = \bigcup \{Y \in U/IND(P) | Y \subseteq X\}, \tag{1}$$

$$\overline{P}(X) = \bigcup \{Y \in U/IND(P) | Y \bigcap X \neq \emptyset \}. \tag{2}$$

In an information system, a partition $U/IND(R)$ of U induced by the equivalence relation $IND(R)$, $R \in 2^A$, provides a granulation world for describing a concept X. So a sequence of attribute sets $R_i \in 2^A$ $(i = 1, 2, ..., n$) with $R_1 \succeq R_2 \succeq ... \succeq R_n$ can determine a sequence of granulation worlds, from the most rough to the most fine one. We define the upper and lower approximations of a concept under a granulation order.

Definition 1. *Let $S = (U, A)$ be an information system, X a subset of U and $P = \{R_1, R_2, ..., R_n\}$ a family of attribute sets with $R_1 \succeq R_2 \succeq ... \succeq R_n$ ($R_i \in 2^A$), we define P-upper approximation $\overline{P}X$ and P-lower approximation $\underline{P}X$ of X as follows:*

$$\overline{P}X = \overline{R_n}X, \tag{3}$$

$$\underline{P}X = \bigcup_{i=1}^{n} \underline{R_i}X_i, \tag{4}$$

where $X_1 = X$ and $X_i = X - \bigcup_{k=1}^{i-1} \underline{R_k}X_k$, for $i = 2, ..., n$.

$bn_P(X) = \overline{P}X - \underline{P}X$ is called P-boundary region of X, $pos_P(X) = \underline{P}X$ is called P-positive region of X, and $neg_P(X) = U - \overline{P}X$ is called P-negative region of X. Obviously, we have $\overline{P}X = pos_P(X) \cup bn_P(X)$.

Definition 1 shows that a target concept is approached by the change of the lower approximation $\underline{P}X$ and the upper approximation $\overline{P}X$.

Theorem 1. *Let $S = (U, A)$ be an information system, X a subset of U and $P = \{R_1, R_2, ..., R_n\}$ a family of attribute sets with $R_1 \succeq R_2 \succeq ... \succeq R_n$ ($R_i \in 2^A$). Let $P_i = \{R_1, R_2, ..., R_i\}$. Then for $\forall P_i$ ($i = 1, 2, ..., n$), we have*

$$\underline{P_i}(X) \subseteq X \subseteq \overline{P_i}(X), \tag{5}$$

$$\underline{P_1}(X) \subseteq \underline{P_2}(X) \subseteq ... \subseteq \underline{P_n}(X). \tag{6}$$

Proof. The proof follows directly from Definition 1.

Theorem 1 states that the lower approximation enlarges as the granulation order become longer through adding equivalence relation, which help to describe exactly the target concept.

In [14], the approximation measure $\alpha_R(X)$ was originally introduced by Z. Pawlak for classical lower and upper approximation, where $\alpha_R(X) = \frac{|\underline{R}X|}{|\overline{R}X|}(X \neq$). Here we introduce the concept to the positive approximation in order to describe the uncertainty of concept under a granulation order.

Definition 2. *Let $S = (U, A)$ be an information system, X a subset of U and $P = \{R_1, R_2, ..., R_n\}$ a family of attribute sets with $R_1 \succeq R_2 \succeq ... \succeq R_n$ ($R_i \in 2^A$). The approximation measure $\alpha_P(X)$ is defined as*

$$\alpha_P(X) = \frac{|\underline{P}X|}{|\overline{P}X|}, \tag{7}$$

where $X \neq$.

Theorem 2. *Let $S = (U, A)$ be an information system, X a subset of U and $P = \{R_1, R_2, ..., R_n\}$ a family of attribute sets with $R_1 \succeq R_2 \succeq ... \succeq R_n$ ($R_i \in 2^A$). Let $P_i = \{R_1, R_2, ..., R_i\}$. Then for $\forall P_i$ ($i = 1, 2, ..., n$), we have*

$$\alpha_{P_1}(X) \leq \alpha_{P_2}(X) \leq ... \leq \alpha_{P_n}(X). \tag{8}$$

Proof. The proof follows directly from Theorem 1 and Definition 2.

Theorem 2 states that the approximation measure $\alpha_P(X)$ increases as the granulation order become longer through adding equivalence relation.

3   Application

We apply rough set methods for decision rule mining from decision tables. It is not always possible to extract general laws from experimental data by computing first all reducts of a decision table and next decision rules on the basis of these reducts [15, 16].

In this section, we proposed an algorithm for decision rule mining in consistent decision tables by using positive approximation. The application will be helping for understanding the idea of positive approximation proposed in the paper.

Let $S = (U, C \cup D)$ be a consistent decision table [13], where C and D are condition and decision attribute sets respectively, and $C \cap D = $. The positive region of D with respect to C is defined as follows

$$pos_C(D) = \bigcup_{X \in U/D} \underline{C}X. \tag{9}$$

In a decision table $S = (U, C \cup D)$, the significance of $c \in C$ with respect to D is defined as follows [13]:

$$sig^D_{C-\{c\}}(c) = \gamma_C(D) - \gamma_{C-\{c\}}(D), \tag{10}$$

where $\gamma_C(D) = \frac{|pos_C(D)|}{|U|}$.

In a decision table $S = (U, C \cup D)$, the significance of $c \in C - C'$ ($C' \subseteq C$) with respect to D is defined as follows

$$sig^D_{C'}(c) = \gamma_{C' \cup \{c\}}(D) - \gamma_{C'}(D), \tag{11}$$

where $\gamma_C(D) = \frac{|pos_{C'}(D)|}{|U|}$.

Algorithm MABPA (mining rules in a consistent decision table)

Input: consistent decision table $S = (U, C \cup D)$;
Output: decision rules *Rule*.

(1) For $\forall c \in C$, compute the significance and relative core

$$core_D(C) = \{c \in C | sig^D_{C-c}(c) > 0\};$$

(2) If $core_D(C) \neq $, let $P_1 = core_D(C)$; else, for $\forall c \in C$, compute the dependence $\gamma_c(D)$ of D to c; let $\gamma_{c_1}(D) = \max\{\gamma_c(D) | c \in C\}$ and $P_1 = c_1$;

(3) Compute $U/D = \{Y_1, Y_2, ..., Y_d\}$;

(4) Let $P = \{P_1\}$, $i = 1$, $U^* = U$, $\Gamma = $, $Rule = $;

(5) Compute $U^*/IND(P_i) = \{X_{i1}, X_{i2}, ..., X_{is_i}\}$;

(6) Let $\Gamma' = \{X_k \in U^*/IND(P_i \mid X_k \subseteq Y_j (Y_j \in U/D, j = \{1, 2, ..., d\})\}$. Let $Rule' = $, for $\forall X_k \in \Gamma'$, put $des_{P_i}(X_k) \longrightarrow des_D(Y_j)(Y_j \in U/D, Y_j \supseteq X_k)$ into $Rule'$. Let $Rule = Rule \cup Rule'$, $\Gamma = \Gamma \cup \Gamma'$;

(7) If $\bigcup_{x \in \Gamma} x = U$, go to (8); else, $U^* = U^* - \bigcup_{x \in \Gamma} x$, for $\forall c \in C - P_i$, compute $sig_{P_i}^D(c)$, let $sig_{P_i}^D(c_2) = max\{sig_{P_i}^D(c), c \in C - P_i\}$, $P_{i+1} = P_i \cup \{c_2\}$, let $P = P \cup \{P_{i+1}\}$, $i = i + 1$, go to (5);

(8) Output $Rule$.

Obviously, generation of decision rules is not based on a reduct of a decision table, but P (a granulation order) and U^* in the MABPA. By using MABPA algorithm, the time complexity to extract rules is polynomial. At the first step, we need to compute $core_D(C)$, i.e., compute $sig_{C-c}^D(c)$ for all $c \in C$. The time complexity for computing $core_D(C)$ is $O(|C||U|^2)$. At step 3, the time complexity for computing U/D is $O(|U|^2)$. At step 5, the time complexity for computing $U^*/IND(P_i)$ is $O(|U|^2)$. At step 7, the time complexity for computing all $sig_{P_i}^D(c)$ is $O(|C - P_i||C||U|^2)$; the time complexity to choose maximum for significance of attribute is $|C - P_i|$. From step 5 to step 7, $|C| - 1$ is the maximum value for the circle times. Therefore, the time complexity is

$$\sum_{i=1}^{|C|-1} (O(|U|^2) + O(|C - P_i||C||U|^2) + O(|C - P_i|)) = O(|C|^3|U|^2).$$

Other steps will not be considered because that their time complexity are all const. Thus the time complexity of the algorithm MABPA is as follows

$$O(|C||U|^2) + O(|U|^2) + O(|U|^2) + O(|C|^3|U|^2) = O(|C|^3|U|^2).$$

In next section, we show how the algorithm MABPA works using an example.

4   Case Study

A consistent decision table $S = (U, C \cup D)$ is given by Table 1, where $C = \{a, b, c, d, e\}$ is condition attribute set and $D = \{f\}$ is decision attribute set. By the algorithm MABPA, we can extract decision rules from Table 1. We have:

$$U/C = \{\{1\}, \{2\}, \{3, 11\}, \{4\}, \{5\}, \{6\}, \{7, 12\}, \{8\}, \{9\}, \{10\}\},$$

$$U/D = \{\{1, 2, 3, 4, 5, 11\}, \{6, 7, 8, 9, 10, 12\}\}.$$

According to the formula $sig_{C-\{c\}}^D(c) = \gamma_C(D) - \gamma_{C-\{c\}}(D)$, we have

$$sig_{C-\{a\}}^D(a) = sig_{C-\{b\}}^D(b) = sig_{C-\{c\}}^D(c) = sig_{C-\{d\}}^D(d) = sig_{C-\{e\}}^D(e) = 0$$

So we get $core_D(C) = $.

Table 1. Example of a consistent decision table

U	attributes					
	a	b	c	d	e	f
1	3	2	3	0	2	1
2	2	2	3	0	2	1
3	1	0	2	0	1	1
4	3	1	3	0	2	1
5	2	0	3	0	2	1
6	0	0	1	0	0	0
7	3	2	0	1	1	0
8	1	0	1	0	0	0
9	2	0	2	1	1	0
10	1	1	3	1	0	0
11	1	0	2	0	1	1
12	3	2	0	1	1	0

By the formula $\gamma_{C'}(D) = |pos_{C'}(D)|/|U|(C' \subseteq C)$, we have

$$\gamma_{\{a\}}(D) = 1/12, \gamma_{\{b\}} = 0, \gamma_{\{c\}}(D) = 4/12, \gamma_{\{d\}}(D) = 4/12, \gamma_{\{e\}}(D) = 7/12$$

Hence, $P_1 = \{e\}$ and $P = \{P_1\}$. For

$$U/IND(P_1) = \{\{1, 2, 4, 5\}\}, \{3, 7, 9, 11, 12\}, \{6, 8, 10\}\}$$

we get

$$\Gamma = \{\{1, 2, 4, 5\}, \{6, 8, 10\}\},$$

and

$$Rule = \{r_1 : des_{\{e\}}(\{1, 2, 4, 5\}) \rightarrow des_D(\{1, 2, 3, 4, 5, 11\}),$$
$$r_2 : des_{\{e\}}(6, 8, 10) \rightarrow des_D(\{6, 7, 8, 9, 10, 12\})\}.$$

For

$$\bigcup_{x \in \Gamma} x = \{1, 2, 4, 5, 6, 8, 10\} \neq U,$$

we need to compute significance of the rest of attributes a, b, c, d with respect to D. By the formula for $sig_{C'}^D(c)$, we obtain

$$sig_{\{a\}\cup\{e\}}^D(a) = \gamma_{\{a\}\cup\{e\}}(D) - \gamma_{\{e\}}(D) = 5/12,$$

$$sig_{\{b\}\cup\{e\}}^D(b) = \gamma_{\{b\}\cup\{e\}}(D) - \gamma_{\{e\}}(D) = 2/12,$$

$$sig_{\{c\}\cup\{e\}}^D(c) = \gamma_{\{c\}\cup\{e\}}(D) - \gamma_{\{e\}}(D) = 2/12,$$

$$sig_{\{d\}\cup\{e\}}^D(d) = \gamma_{\{d\}\cup\{e\}}(D) - \gamma_{\{e\}}(D) = 5/12.$$

So we can choose a as c_2 (see the step (7) in the algorithm MABPA). Then, we have $P_2 = \{a, e\}, P = \{P_1, P_2\}$ and $U^* = \{3, 7, 9, 11, 12\}$. For

$$U^*/IND(P_2) = \{\{3, 11\}, \{7, 12\}, \{9\}\},$$

we get
$$\Gamma = \{\{1,2,4,5\},\{3,11\},\{6,8,10\},\{7,12\},\{9\}\}$$
and
$$Rule = \{r_1 : des_{\{e\}}(\{1,2,4,5\}) \rightarrow des_D(\{1,2,3,4,5,11\}),$$
$$r_2 : des_{\{e\}}(\{6,8,10\}) \rightarrow des_D(\{6,7,8,9,10,12\}),$$
$$r_3 : des_{\{a,e\}}(\{3,11\}) \rightarrow des_D(\{1,2,3,4,5,11\}),$$
$$r_4 : des_{\{a,e\}}(\{7,12\}) \rightarrow des_D(\{6,7,8,9,10,12\}),$$
$$r_5 : des_{\{a,e\}}(\{9\}) \rightarrow des_D(\{6,7,8,9,10,12\})\}.$$

It is easy to see $\bigcup_{x \in \Gamma} x = U$. So the algorithm MABPA is ended, and $Rule$ is obtained. For intuition, the five decision rules obtained by MABPA from the decision table S are listed in Table 2.

Table 2. Rules obtained for the decision table S

$Rule$	attributes		
	a	e	f
r_1		2	1
r_2	1	1	1
r_3		0	0
r_4	3	1	0
r_5	2	1	0

This example shows the mechanism of the decision rule mining algorithm based on positive approximation.

5   Conclusions

In this paper, we extend rough set approximation under static granulation to rough set approximation under dynamic granulation, the positive approximation is defined and its some properties are obtained. A target concept can be approached by the change of the positive approximation. An algorithm based on positive approximation for decision rule mining is given, and its application is illustrated by an illustrative example. The results obtained in this paper will play an important role in further research on rough set approximation and granular computing.

Acknowledgements. This work was supported by the national 863 plan project of China (No. 2004AA115460), the national natural science foundation of China (No. 70471003, No. 60275019), the natural science foundation of Shanxi, China (No. 20031036, No. 20041040) and the top scholar foundation of Shanxi, China.

References

1. Zadeh, L.A.: Fuzzy Sets and Information Granularity. In: Gupta, M., Ragade, R., Yager, R. (Eds.): Advances in Fuzzy Set Theory and Application, North-Holland, Amsterdam (1979) 3-18
2. Zadeh, L.A.: Fuzzy logic=computing with words. IEEE Transactions on Fuzzy Systems, 4(1) (1996) 103-111
3. Zadeh, L.A.: Toward a theory of fuzzy information granulation and its centrality in human reasoning and fuzzy logic. Fuzzy Sets and Systems, 90 (1997) 111-127
4. Zadeh, L.A.: Some reflections on soft computing, granular computing and their roles in the conception, design and utilization of information / intelligent systems. Soft Computing, 2(1) (1998) 23-25
5. Pawlak, Z.: Granularity of knowledge, indiscernibility and rough sets. In: Proceedings of 1998 IEEE International Conference on Fuzzy Systems (1998) 106-110
6. Yao, Y.Y.: Granular computing: basic issues and possible solutions. In: Proceedings of the Fifth International Conference on Computing and Information, I (2000) 186-189
7. Lin, T.Y.: Granular computing on binary relations I: Data mining and neighborhood systems, II: Rough sets representations and belief functions. In: Polkowski, L., Skowron, A. (Eds.): Rough Sets in Knowledge Discovery 1. Physica-Verlag, Heidelberg (1998) 107-140
8. Zhang, L., Zhang, B.: Theory of fuzzy quotient space (methods of fuzzy granular computing). Journal of Software (in Chinese), 14(4) (2003) 770-776
9. Klir, G.J.: Basic issues of computing with granular computing. In: Proceedings of 1998 IEEE International Conference on Fuzzy Systems (1998) 101-105
10. Liang, J.Y., Shi, Z.Z.: The information entropy, rough entropy and knowledge granulation in rough set theory. International Journal of Uncertainty, Fuzziness and Knowledge-Based Systems, 12(1) (2004) 37-46
11. Liang, J.Y., Shi, Z.Z., Li, D.Y.: The information entropy, rough entropy and knowledge granulation in incomplete information systems. International Journal of General Systems (to appear)
12. Liu, Q.: Granules and applications of granular computing in logical reasoning. Journal of Computer Research and Development (in Chinese), 41(4) (2004) 546-551
13. Zhang, W.X., Wu, W.Z., Liang, J.Y., Li, D.Y.: Theory and method of rough sets (in Chinese). Beijing, Science Press (2001)
14. Pawlak, Z.: Rough sets. Theoretical aspects of reasoning about data. Kluwer Academic Publishers, Dordrecht (1991)
15. Bazan, J., Nguyen, H. S., Skowron, A.: Rough set methods in approximation of hierarchical concepts. In: S. Tsumoto et al. (Eds.): Rough Sets and Current Trends in Computing RSCTC 2004, Lecture Notes in Computer Science 3066 (2004) 342-351.
16. Bazan, J., Nguyen, H. S., Skowron, A., Szczuka, M.: A view on rough set concept approximations, In: Wang, G., Liu, Q., Yao, Y.Y., Skowron, A.: Proceedings of the Ninth International Conference on Rough Sets, Fuzzy Sets, Data Mining and Granular Computing RSFDGrC (2003), Chongqing, China, May 26-29, 2003, Lecture Notes in Artificial Intelligence, Springer-Verlag, Heidelberg, 2639 (2003) 181-188.

Granular Logic with Closeness Relation " $\sim_\lambda$ " and Its Reasoning

Qing Liu[1] and Qianying Wang[2]

[1] Department of Computer Science,
Nanchang University, Nanchang, Jiangxi 330029, China
[2] Department of Information Science,
Nanchang University, Nanchang, Jiangxi 330047, China

Abstract. Significance of granular logic, including the operational rules, studying background, is presented in this paper. This closeness relation " $\sim_\lambda$ " is quoted in granular logic,and the closeness relation " $\sim_\lambda$ " quoted in granular logic is defined via logical truth values. Hence, we induce several new relative properties and inference rules in the granular logic with the closeness relation. The granular logical reasoning systems with the closeness relation " $\sim_\lambda$ " are also established. And this paper proves a few real examples by deductive reasoning in the systems. Significance of granular logic with closeness relation $\sim_\lambda$ is also described in the paper.

Keywords: Closeness relation, Granular logic, closeness degree, Deductive Reasoning.

1 Introduction

The idea of this paper is derived from granular computing approaches and rough logic with rough equality relation $=_R$. Hence, we present a short review of these approaches. Zadeh in 1979 published a paper on "Fuzzy sets and Granularity" ,which is probably the first granular computing that is outside of partition theory [1]. Granular computing is proposed based on Zadeh's granular mathematics, which is T.Y.Lin's contribution [2]. Lin proposed the word of Granular Computing and developed a wide range of theories [17,18,26,27]; And Zadeh emphasized the studying on granular logic in his papers [2,3]. He thinks that Granular Logic is a subset of Fuzzy Logic, and to be the better theoretical tools of describing global granulation decomposed, local granules amalgamated and causation relation between granules.

Next we turn to granular logic with closeness relation $\sim_\lambda$. Equal relation " $=$ " is a very important and frequently using relation, which is reflexive, symmetric and transitive. So we may do the substitute between two objects of having equal relation. The equal relation " $=$ " is quoted into classical logic, such that the logical reasoning in the classical logic with equal relation is convenient by using it, such as, paramodulation reasoning is the substitute. By two modal operators, Banarjee and Chakraborty quoted a new relation " $\approx$ " in S_5 of

D. Ślęzak et al. (Eds.): RSFDGrC 2005, LNAI 3641, pp. 709–717, 2005.

modal logic [4], that is, $\alpha \approx \beta$ iff $(L\alpha \leftrightarrow L\beta) \wedge (M\alpha \leftrightarrow M\beta)$, where α and β are logical formulas, L and M are necessary and possible operators in the modal logic respectively. Thus which had many new results in modal logic, not only enrich the content and theory of modal logic, but also provide the convenience for theorem proof in modal logic. In rough set theory, by lower and upper approximations Pawlak defined the rough equal relation of two sets [5], namely $X =_R Y$ iff $R_*(X) = R_*(Y) \wedge R^*(X) = R^*(Y)$, where X and Y are the sets on universal U, $R_*(S)$ and $R^*(S)$ are the lower and upper approximations of R with respect to S respectively, which deducted many new properties for rough set theory. Stepaniuk proposed an approximate first-order logic $\sigma = (IND, R_1, \cdots, R_m, =)$ by using an equal relation " $=$ ", such that first-order logic with equal relation $=$ is approximated. He established the approximate reasoning systems in the logic [8]. The author defined a λ-level rough equality for two objects by λ-level rough equality relation " $=_{\lambda R}$ ", namely, $x_1 =_{\lambda R} x_2$ iff $\mid f(a, x_1) - f(a, x_2) \mid < \epsilon$, where x_1, x_2 are arbitrary objects on U of discourse universe, f is an information function on an information system $S = (U, A, V, f)$. $a \in A$ is an attribute, $f(a, x) \in V$ is the attribute value of object x with respect to attribute a. ϵ is any small positive real number or a given threshold by experts [9]. Thereby, we deduct many new results for rough logic, to enrich the theory in rough logic and produce the λ-level rough paramodulation reasoning. In the paper, we will quote the closeness relation in granular logic, having a granular logic system with closeness relation predicate $\sim_\lambda$. We will do the deductive reasoning and other approximate proof in the granular logical system with the $\sim_\lambda$. We define the closeness relation " $\sim_\lambda$ " in granular logic [6], that is, for $\forall G, G', G \sim_\lambda G'$ iff $\mid T_{I_\lambda u_\lambda}(\varphi) - T_{I_\lambda u_\lambda}(\varphi') \mid < \epsilon \wedge \epsilon = 1 - \lambda \wedge (m(\varphi) \subseteq_\lambda m(\varphi')) \wedge (m(\varphi') \subseteq_\lambda m(\varphi))$, where $G = (\varphi, m(\varphi))$ and $G' = (\varphi', m(\varphi'))$ are granular formulas in granular logic [6,20-22], $T_{I_\lambda u_\lambda}(F)$ is the truth value of assignment to formula F in rough logic, $T_{I_\lambda u\lambda}$ is the joining assignment symbol [7].

We will further extend the studies of granular logic [6] in the paper, that is, to quote the closeness relation $\sim_\lambda$ in granular logic, and construct an approximate reasoning system of granular logic with closeness relation. In the logical systems, we may prove many relative theorems, so as to offer many convenience for approximate reasoning in the logic.

Rest of the paper is organized as follows: Section 2 defines a granular logic with closeness relation $\sim_\lambda$. Section 3 describes several relative properties in the logic. Section 4 proves many theorems of granular computing with deductive reasoning. The last section concludes the paper.

2   A Granular Logic with Closeness Relation $\sim_\lambda$

Zadeh in 1979 defined that data granules are characterized by propositions [1], formally, denoted by

$$g = x \text{ is } G \text{ is } \lambda$$

or written by set

$$g = \{e \in U : u_\lambda(x) = e \wedge e \in_\lambda G \subseteq_\lambda U\}$$

Table 1. Information Table

U	a	b	c	d
1	5	4	0	1
2	3	4	0	0
3	3	4	0	2
4	0	2	0	1
5	3	2	1	2
6	5	2	0	1

where u_λ is the assignment symbol on U, G is a fuzzy subset on U. Obviously, $0 \le \lambda \le 1$. By the viewpoint of fuzzy set, $\in_\lambda (e) = \lambda$ or $\mu_G(e) = \lambda$, namely λ is the value of fuzzy function μ_G with respect to entity e; By viewpoint of fuzzy logic, λ is the truth value of fuzzy proposition g. So, Zadeh's idea is the granular propositional logic. We studied a granular logic based on Zadeh's idea [6]. In the granular logic, a granule is defined as a pair $(F, m(F))$, where F is an assertion, or logical formula or predicate. The logical formula F may be a classical logical formula, rough logical formula or any non-standard logical formula. $m(F)$ is the meaning set corresponding to F. Because the pair is both logical formula and set, hence we call the pair granular logical formula [6,20-22]. In fact, this should be a generalization of granular propositional logic defined by Zadeh. For example, in the following information table $IS = (U, A)$, assertion F is taken as an elementary conjunction form $CF_B(x)$, where $B \subseteq A$ is the subset of attribute set A, $x \in U$ is individual variable on U. If $B = \{a, b\}$, $F = CF_B(x) = a_5 \wedge b_4$, then the granule of F is the meaning set of F, denoted by:

$$(F, m(F)) = (a_5 \wedge b_4, m(a_5 \wedge b_4)) = (a_5 \wedge b_4, m(a_5) \cap m(b_4))$$

We quote further the closeness relation $\sim_\lambda$ into the granular logic in the paper, which is also constructed the granular logical system with closeness relation $\sim_\lambda$. Its syntax is denoted by

$$\Gamma = \{QUA, ENT, VAR, FUN, WFG, OPE, PAR, \sim_\lambda\},$$

where

- $QUA = \{\forall\}$ is a set of the universal quantifier. And the $\forall$ is dual with exist quantifier $\exists$, hence $\exists$ may be got from $\forall$ and negative symbol $\neg$.
- $ENT = \{e_1, \cdots, e_m\}$ is the set of constant symbols, which is interpreted as the entity on U;
- $VAR = \{x_1, \cdots, x_n\}$ is a set of variables, which are viewed as variational measure on U. The assignment to them has the entity on U;
- $FUN = \{f, g, \cdots\}$ is the set of function symbols, to be called as term on GL;
- $WFG = \{\Xi, \Omega, R, p, q, \cdots, G_1, G_2, \cdots\}$ is called the set of granular logical functions on information system $IS = (U, A)$, where R is interpreted as $B \subseteq A$ and it is the indiscernibility relation on IS, to be viewed as a special predicate; $p, q, \cdots$ are interpreted as the attributes on A, to be also called as

predicate;$G_1, G_2, \cdots$ are the well-formed formulas in granular logic, to be the structure of pair $(F, m(F))$;

- $OPE = \{\neg, \oplus, \otimes, \odot, \ominus\}$ is the set of operation symbols in granular logical formula on IS. They are similar as usual operation symbol in logic, to be called negative, disjunctive, conjunctive, implication and equalization respectively;
- $PAR = \{(,)\}$ is the set of parenthesis.

3   Closeness Relation $\sim_\lambda$ and Its Relative Properties

The closeness relation $\sim_\lambda$ of two granular logical formulas is defined as follows:

Definition 1. For $G, G' \subset GL$, $G \sim_\lambda G'$ iff G is close to G' to degree at least λ iff $| T_{I_\lambda u_\lambda}(\varphi) - T_{I_\lambda u_\lambda}(\psi') | < \epsilon \wedge m(\varphi) \subseteq_\lambda m(\psi) \wedge m(\psi) \subseteq_\lambda m(\varphi)$, where $G = (\varphi, m(\varphi))$, $G' = (\psi, m(\psi))$. $\sim_\lambda$ is called closeness relation to degree at least λ.

The closeness relation $\sim_\lambda$ is quoted in granular logic,to have several new results about closeness concept. For discernment, the following derivable symbol $\vdash$ in classical logic is substituted by $|\sim$.

Property 1. $\forall G \in WFG$,if $\alpha \sim_\lambda \beta$, then $G(\alpha) \sim_\lambda G(\beta)$,where α and β are the terms included in G.

Property 2. $\forall G, G' \in WFG$, $|\sim G \sim_\lambda G' \rightarrow |\sim m(\varphi) \sim_\lambda m(\psi)$, where φ is the assert in G, ψ is the assert in G'.

Property 3. $\forall G, G' \in WFG$, $|\sim G \sim_\lambda G' \rightarrow m_*(\varphi) \sim_\lambda m_*(\psi)$.

Property 4. $\forall G, G' \in WFG$, $|\sim G \sim_\lambda G' \rightarrow m^*(\varphi) \sim_\lambda m^*(\psi))$.

Property 5. $\forall G, G' \in WFG$, $|\sim G \sim_\lambda G' \rightarrow m(\varphi \wedge \gamma) \sim_\lambda m(\psi \wedge \gamma))$.

Property 6. $\forall G, G' \in WFG$, $|\sim G \sim_\lambda G' \rightarrow m_*(\varphi \wedge \gamma) \sim_\lambda m_*(\psi \wedge \gamma))$.

Property 7. $\forall G, G' \in WFG$,$|\sim G \sim_\lambda G' \rightarrow m^*(\varphi \wedge \gamma) \sim_\lambda m^*(\psi \wedge \gamma))$.

Property 8. $\forall G, G' \in WFG$, $|\sim G \sim_\lambda G' \rightarrow |\sim \neg G' \sim_\lambda \neg G$.

Property 9. $\forall G, G' \in WFG$, if $|\sim G \sim_\lambda G' \wedge |\sim G$,then $|\sim G'$.

Property 10. $\forall G, G' \in WFG$, if $|\sim G \sim_\lambda G'$ then $|\sim (U - m(\varphi)) \sim_\lambda (U - m(\psi))$.

Property 11. $\forall G, G' \in WFG$, if $|\sim G \sim_\lambda G'$ then $|\sim (\varphi \rightarrow_\lambda \psi) \wedge (\psi \rightarrow_\lambda \varphi) \wedge (m(\varphi) \subseteq_\lambda m(\psi)) \wedge (m(\psi) \subseteq_\lambda m(\varphi))$.

Where $m_*(F)$ and $m^*(F)$ are the lower and upper approximations of meaning set of assert F respectively, γ is any assert in usually logic. Here, we proved the property 5. The proof of rest properties is similar.Property 5 is proved as follows:

Proof: $m(\varphi \wedge \gamma) = \{x \in U : x |\approx \varphi \wedge \gamma\} = \{x \in U : x |\approx \varphi \wedge x |\approx \gamma\} = \{x \in U : x |\approx \varphi\} \cap \{x \in U : x |\approx \gamma\} = m(\varphi) \cap m(\gamma)$.

For the same reason, $m(\psi \wedge \gamma) = m(\psi) \cap m(\gamma)$.

Suppose, $m(\varphi \wedge \gamma)\neg \sim_\lambda m(\psi \wedge \gamma)$,then $\exists x \in U$, $[x] \subseteq_\lambda m(\varphi \wedge \gamma)$ and $[x]\neg \subseteq_\lambda m(\psi \wedge \gamma)$,that is, $[x] \subseteq_\lambda m(\varphi) \cap m(\gamma)$,but $[x]\neg \subseteq_\lambda m(\psi) \cap m(\gamma)$.Because $[x] \subseteq_\lambda m(\varphi) \cap m(\gamma)$ so $[x] \subseteq_\lambda m(\varphi)$ and $[x] \subseteq_\lambda m(\gamma)$.Because $[x]\neg \subseteq_\lambda m(\psi) \cap m(\gamma)$

so $[x]\neg \subseteq_\lambda m(\psi)$,that is, $x\neg \in_\lambda m(\psi)$,but $[x] \subseteq_\lambda m(\varphi)$, so $x \in_\lambda m(\varphi)$. So $m(\varphi)\neg \sim_\lambda m(\psi)$, this is contrary to $G \sim_\lambda G'$,hence $m(\varphi \wedge \gamma) \sim_\lambda m(\psi \wedge \gamma)$.

Definition 2. Let $G_1 = (\varphi, m(\varphi))$ and $G_2 = (\psi, m(\psi))$ be two granules. The computing rules of them with respect to granular connectives: $\neg$(negative), $\oplus$(disjunctive), $\otimes$(conjunctive), $\odot$(implicative) and $\ominus$(equivalent) are defined as follows respectively:

(1) $\neg(\varphi, m(\varphi)) = (\neg\varphi, U - m(\varphi))$;
(2) $(\varphi, m(\varphi)) \oplus (\psi, m(\psi)) = (\varphi \vee \psi, m(\varphi) \cup m(\psi))$;
(3) $(\varphi, m(\varphi)) \otimes (\psi, m(\psi)) = (\varphi \wedge \psi, m(\varphi) \cap m(\psi))$;
(4) $(\varphi, m(\varphi)) \odot (\psi, m(\psi)) = (\varphi \rightarrow \psi, m(\varphi) \subseteq m(\psi))$;
(5) $(\varphi, m(\varphi)) \ominus (\psi, m(\psi)) = (\varphi \leftrightarrow \psi, (m(\varphi) \subseteq m(\psi) \wedge m(\psi) \subseteq m(\varphi))$.

We see that the calculus of granules in the logic are the operations of pairs called granule, where the first element of the pair is a logical formula and the second element is a meaning set corresponding to the formula. Because the pair is an entirety consisting of both syntax and semantics, hence the pair is both logic and set theory. So we can use both logical method and set theory method in approximate reasoning or other uncertainty reasoning. This is the superiority to approximate reasoning using information granulating and granular computing. The superiority of reasoning is illustrated with real examples for problem solving in artificial intelligence and deductive reasoning in rough logic respectively [6,14,17].

3.1   Axiom Schema in Granular Logic with Closeness Relation $\sim_\lambda$

GA_1 Each axiom schema in classical logic is one of granular logical axiom schema£ż
The closeness relation $\sim_\lambda$ is quoted in granular logic,which will be used as a new predicate,to have several special axioms:
GA_2 Identity $T_{I_\lambda u_\lambda}(\alpha \sim_\lambda \alpha) \geq \lambda$;
GA_3 Symmetry $T_{I_\lambda u_\lambda}(\alpha \sim_\lambda \beta) \geq \lambda \rightarrow T_{I_\lambda u_\lambda}(\beta \sim_\lambda \alpha) \geq \lambda$;
GA_4 Transitive $T_{I_\lambda u_\lambda}(\alpha \sim_\lambda \beta) \geq \lambda \wedge T_{I_\lambda u_\lambda}(\beta \sim_\lambda \chi) \geq \lambda \rightarrow T_{I_\lambda u_\lambda}(\alpha \sim_\lambda \chi) \geq \lambda$;
GA_5 Substitute $T_{I_\lambda u_\lambda}(\alpha \sim_\lambda \beta) \geq \lambda \rightarrow T_{I_\lambda u_\lambda}(P(\cdots\alpha\cdots) \sim_\lambda P(\cdots\beta\cdots)) \geq \lambda$;

Where α,β,χ may be terms or well-formed formulas, P is a well-formed formula of including term α or β or χ. We see that closeness relation $\sim_\lambda$ can be used in approximate reasoning from the special axioms.

3.2   Reasoning Rules

$G-R_1$ G-Modus Ponens(G-MP):If $|\sim (\varphi, m(\varphi)) \odot (\psi, m(\psi))$ and $|\sim (\varphi, m(\varphi))$, then $|\sim (\psi, m(\psi))$,where $|\sim (\varphi, m(\varphi))$ means that logical formula φ is true or rough true,semantic set $m(\varphi)$ of φ is universal U or $m(\varphi) \sim_\lambda U$. So, truth value of granular logical formula $(\varphi, m(\varphi))$ is the semantics in both logic and set theory, namely rough logical formula φ is true or rough true to degree at least λ in rough logic [10,11,12,13,14].

$G-R_2$ G-Universal Generalized(G-UG): $|\sim (\varphi, m(\varphi))$,then $|\sim ((\forall x)\varphi, m(\varphi))$, namely for $\forall x \in VAR$, to have $u_\lambda \in VAL$, $u_\lambda(x) = e \in U$, that $|\sim (\varphi, m(\varphi(e)))$ holds, where $m(\varphi(e))$ is universal or $m(\varphi) \sim_\lambda U$, $m(\varphi)$ is close to U to degree at least λ, and truth value of φ is 1 or > 0.5.

3.3   Semantics of the Logical Formulas

The semantics of granular logical formulas is the 6-tuple£ž

$$M = (U, A, I_G, VAL, m, \sim_\lambda).$$

Where U is a set of the entities;A is a set of the attributes.Its subset $B \subseteq A$ is an indiscernibility relation on U;$I_G = \{I_{G_1}, \cdots, I_{G_h}\}$ is a set of all interpretations on U; $VAL = \{u_{G_1}, \cdots, u_{G_t}\}$ is a set of all assignment symbols on U, $u_G \in VAL$ is different from meaning function symbol m. For $\forall \varphi \in WFF$, lower and upper satisfiability with respect to $I_G \in I_G$ and $u_G \in VAL$ in the model M are denoted respectively:

$$M, u_G \models_{L\varphi} (\varphi, m(\varphi)),\ M, u_G \models_{H\varphi} (\varphi, m(\varphi))\ \text{and}\ M, u_G \approx_{m\varphi} (\varphi, m(\varphi))$$

Where L and H is rough lower and upper approximate operators with respect to indiscernibility relation $B \in A$, for convenience, B_* and B^* is denoted by L and H respectively.

4   Reasoning in Granular Logic with Closeness Relation $\sim_\lambda$

The reasoning systems are consisted of five axioms $GA_1 - GA_5$ and two rules, $GR_1 - GR_2$. We can prove many theorems with closeness relation in the systems. For convenience, L and H is denoted by lower and upper approximations in operator rough logic respectively [6,9,14].

Theorems
(A_1) $(LL\varphi, m(LL\varphi)) \sim_\lambda (HL\varphi, m(HL\varphi))$;
(A_2) $(LH\varphi, m(LH\varphi)) \sim_\lambda (H\varphi, m(H\varphi))$;
(A_3) $(HH\varphi, m(HH\varphi)) \sim_\lambda (LH\varphi, m(LH\varphi))$;
(A_4) $(HH\varphi, m(HH\varphi)) \sim_\lambda (H\varphi, m(H\varphi))$.

We prove the theorem A_2. The proof needs only to show:

$$(LH\varphi \sim_\lambda H\varphi) \wedge (m(LH\varphi) \sim_\lambda m(H\varphi)).$$

Proof
(1) $(L\neg\varphi \rightarrow_\lambda \neg\varphi) \wedge (m(L\neg\varphi) \subseteq_\lambda m(\neg\varphi)))$,
Definition of operator L [14]
(2) $(\varphi \rightarrow_\lambda H\varphi) \wedge (m(\varphi) \subseteq_\lambda m(H\varphi))$,
Property 8 in (1) and dual of L and H [14,15].

(3) $(L\varphi \rightarrow_\lambda HL\varphi) \wedge (m(L\varphi) \subseteq_\lambda m(HL\varphi))$,
φ is substituted by $L\varphi$ in (2).
(4) $(HL\varphi \rightarrow_\lambda L\varphi) \wedge (m(HL\varphi) \subseteq_\lambda m(L\varphi))$,
Properties of operators L and H [5,14,17].
(5) $(HL\varphi \sim_\lambda L\varphi) \wedge (m(HL\varphi) \sim_\lambda m(L\varphi)))$,
By the definition of $\sim_\lambda$ in (3) and (4).
(6) $(HLH\varphi \sim_\lambda LH\varphi) \wedge (m(HLH\varphi) \sim_\lambda m(LH\varphi))$,
φ is substituted by $H\varphi$ in (5).
(7) $((LH\varphi \sim_\lambda HH\varphi) \wedge (m(LH\varphi) \sim_\lambda m(HH\varphi))$,
Properties of operators L and H [5,6,14].
(8) $(HH\varphi \sim_\lambda H\varphi) \wedge (m(HH\varphi) \sim_\lambda m(H\varphi))$,
Properties of operators L and H [5,6,14].
(9) $(LH\varphi \sim_\lambda H\varphi) \wedge (m(LH\varphi) \sim_\lambda m(H\varphi))$,
To quote "Hypothetical Syllogism" [6,14-16] in (7) and (8).

Similarly, we can prove (A_1), (A_3) and (A_4) in the theorems.

5 Conclusion

Closeness relation $\sim_\lambda$ is quoted in granular logic ,which have many new re-sults,such as,the reasoning rule of paramodulation in classical logic can be quoted in approximate reasoning of granular logic.The special axioms provided by $\sim_\lambda$ will be widely applied in approximate reasoning.And the real example of the applications in the paper has explained to be convenient and efficacious based on the reasoning of closeness relation $\sim_\lambda$.

The study of granular logic with closeness relation $\sim_\lambda$ brings a new path for applications of classical logic. The logic provides the better theoretical tool for treating irregular knowledge. The operation of the logic involves the decom-position of global granulation and the amalgamation of local granules, thus it provides the new idea for problem solving in AI. The logic is also a new gener-alization of Rough Logic. It extends a new predicate $\sim_\lambda$.Truth concept and its operations of the logic are different from classical logic and other non-standard logic. The logic is both logic and set theory. Thus it may use the logical methods when treating truth values,and it may use the set theory approach when treating including and closeness degree.

Further study is the spatial-temporal granular logic, namely spatial-temporal change function π , temporal operators U and s will be added into granular logic. The knowledge described has the properties of space and time, hence treat-ment for irregular knowledge may be different along with different of space and time.

Acknowledgement. This study is supported by the Natural Science Founda-tion of China (NSFC-#60173054) and the Natural Science Foundation of Jiangxi province (JXPNSF- 0311101) in China.

References

1. Zadeh, L.A.: Fuzzy Sets and Information Granularity. In: M. Gupta, R. Ragade, and R. Yager (eds), Advances in Fuzzy Set Theory and Applications, North-Holland, Amsterdam (1979) 3-18
2. Zadeh, L.A.: Some reflections on soft computing, granular computing and their roles in the conception, design and utilization of information/intelligent systems. Soft Computing 2, Springer, Berlin (1998) 23-25
3. Zadeh, L.A.: Toward a theory of fuzzy information granulation and its centrality in hunan reasoning and fuzzy logic. Fuzzy Sets and Systems 90 (1997) 111-127
4. Chakraborty, M.K., Banerjee, M.: Rough logic with rough quantifiers. Warsaw University of Technology, ICS Research Report 49/93 (1993)
5. Pawlak, Z.: Rough sets – Theoretical aspects of reasoning about data. Dordrecht, Kluwer Academic Publishers (1991)
6. Liu, Q., Huang, Z.H.: G-Logic and Its Resolution Reasoning. Chinese Journal of Computer (In Chinese), 27(7) (2004) 865-873
7. Liu, Q.: The OI-resolution of operator rough logic. In: L. Polkowski and A. Skowron (eds), Proc. of RSCTC'98, LNCS 1424, Springer (1998)
8. Stepaniuk, J.: Rough Relations and Logics. In: L. Polkowski and A. Skowron (eds), Rough Sets in Knowledge Discovery I, Physica-Verlag, Heideberg (1998) 248-260
9. Liu, Q.: λ-Level Rough Equality Relation and the Inference of Rough Paramodulation. In: W. Ziarko and Y.Y. Yao (eds), Proc. of RSCTC'2000, LNAI 2005, Springer, Berlin (2001) 462-469
10. Skowron, A.: Toward intelligent systems: Calculi of information granules. In: Proc. of RSTGC'2001, Bulletin of International Rough Set Society, Vol.5, No.1/2, Japan (2001) 9-30
11. Skowron, A., Stepaniuk, J.: Extracting patterns using information granules. In: Proc. of RSTGC'2001, Bulletin of International Rough Set Society, Vol.5, No.1/2, Japan (2001) 135-142
12. Liu, Q., Liu, S.H., Zheng, F.: Rough logic and its applications in data mining. Journal of Software, 12(3) (2001) 415-419
13. Rasiowa, H., Skowron, A.: Rough concepts logic. In: A. Skowron (ed.), Computation Theory, LNCS 208 (1985) 288-297
14. Lin, T.Y., Liu, Q.: First-order rough logic I: Approximate reasoning via rough sets. Fundamenta Informaticae, Vol.27, No.2-3 (1996) 137-154
15. Wang, X.J.: Introduction for mathematical logic. Press of Beijing Uni., Beijing (1982)
16. Hamilton, A.G.: Logic For Mathematicians. Cambridge Uni. Press, London (1978)
17. Lin, T.Y.: Granular Computing on Binary Relations II: Rough Set Representations and Belief Functions. In: A. Skowron and L. Polkowski (eds), Rough Sets In Knowledge Discovery, Physica-Verlag, Berlin (1998) 121-140
18. Lin, T.Y.: Granular Computing: Fuzzy Logic and Rough Sets. In: L.A. Zadeh, J. Kacprzyk (eds), Computing with Words, Information   Intelligent Systems 1, Springer, Berlin (1999) 183-200
19. Yao, Y.Y., Yao, J.T.: Granular Computing as a Basis for Consistent Classification Problems. In: Proc. of PAKDD'02 Workshop on Foundations of Data Mining, CIICM, Taiwan, 5 (2002) 101-106
20. Liu, Q., Liu, Q.: Approximate Reasoning Based on Granular Computing in Granular Logic. In: Proc. of IEEE ICMLS'2002 (2002)
21. Liu, Q.: Granular Language and Its Reasoning, Data Mining and Knowledge Discovery: Theory, Tools, and Technology V. In: Proc. of SPIE'2003 (2003) 279-287

22. Liu, Q., Liu, Q.: Granules and Applications of Granular Computing in Logical Reasoning (In Chinese). Journal of Computer Research and Development, Vol.41, No.4 (2004) 546-551
23. Liu, Q.: Temporal Rough Logic and Its Application in Data Analysis. Journal of Fudan University (Natural Science) (In Chinese), Vol.43, No.5 (2005) 852-855
24. Orlowska, E.: A Logic of Indiscernibility Relation. In: A. Skowron(ed.), Computational Theory, LNCS 208, Springer (1985) 177-186
25. Yao, Y.Y., Liu, Q.: A Generalized Decision Logic in Interval-Set-Valued Information Table. LNAI 1711, Springer (1999) 285-294
26. Lin, T.Y.: Granular Computing on Binary Relations-Analysis of Conflict and Chinese Wall Security Policy. In: Proc. of RSCTC'2002, LNAI 2475, Springer, Berlin (2002) 296-299
27. Lin, T.Y.: Granular Computing on Binary Relations I: Data Mining and Neighborhood Systems. In: A. Skowron and L. Polkowski (eds), Rough Sets In Knowledge Discovery, Physica-Verlag, Berlin (1998) 107-121
28. Zhang, L., Zhang, B.: The Quotient Space Theory of Problem Solving. In: Guoyin Wang, Qing Liu, Yiyu Yao and Andrzej Skowron (eds), Proc. of RSFDGrC'2003, LNAI 2639, Springer, Berlin (2003) 11-15
29. Yao, Y.Y.: Information granulation and Rough Set Approximation. International Journal of Intelligence Systems 16 (2001) 87-104
30. Yao, Y.Y., Yao, J.T.: Granular Computing as a Basis for Consistent Classification Problems. In: Proc. of PAKDD'02 Workshop on Foundations of Data Mining, CIICM, Taiwan, (2002) 101-106
31. Yao, Y.Y., Zhong, N.: Granular Computing Using Information Tables. In: T.Y. Lin, Y.Y. Yao and L.A. Zadeh (eds), Data Mining, Rough Sets and Granular Computing, Physica-Verlag, Berlin (2002) 102-124
32. Yao, J.T., Yao, Y.Y.: Induction of Classification Rules by Granular Computing. In: James J. Alpigini, James F. Peters, Andrzej Skowron and Ning Zhong (eds), Proc. of RSCTC'2002, LNAI 2475, Springer, Berlin (2002) 175-182
33. Peters, J.F., Skowron, A., Suraj, Z., Borkowski, M., Rzasa, W.: Measures of Inclusion and closeness of Information Granules: A Rough Set Approach. In: James J. Alpigini, James F. Peters, Andrzej Skowron and Ning Zhong (eds), Proc. of RSCTC'2002, LNAI 2475, Springer, Berlin (2002) 300-307
34. Liau, C.-J.: Belief Reasoning, Revision and Fusion by Matrix Algebra. In: Shususaku Tsumoto, Roman Slowinski, Jan Komorowski, Jerzy W. Grzymala-Busse (eds), Proc. of RSCTC'2004, LNAI 3066, Springer, Berlin (2004) 133-142
35. Liu, Q.: Granules and Reasoning Based on Granular Computing. In: Paul W.H. Chung, Chris Hinde and Moonis Ali (eds), Proc. of IEA/AIE2003, LNAI 2718, Springer, Berlin (2003) 516-526
36. Liau, C.-J.: Many-Valued Dynamic Logic for Qualitative Decision Theory. In: Ning Zhong, Andrzaj Skowron and Setsuo Ohsuga (eds), Proc. of RSFDGrC'99, LNAI 1711, Springer, Berlin (1999) 294-303
37. Doherty, P., Lukaszewicz, W., Szalas, A.: Information Granules for Intelligent Knowledge Structures. In: Guoyin Wang, Qing Liu, Yiyu Yao and Andrzej Skowron (eds), Proc. of RSFDGrC'2003, LNAI 2639, Springer, Berlin (2003) 405-412
38. Skowron, A., Stepaniuk, J., Peters, J.F.: Approximation of Information Granule Sets. In: Wojciech Ziarko and Yiyu Yao (eds), Proc. of RSCTC'2000, LNAI 2005, Springer, Berlin (2000) 65-72
39. Zadeh, L.A.: Information Granulation and Its Centrality. In: Lech Polkowski and Andrzej Skowron (eds), Proc. of RSCTC'98, LNAI 1424, Springer, Berlin (1998) 35-36

Ontological Framework for Approximation

Jarosław Stepaniuk[1] and Andrzej Skowron[2]

[1] Department of Computer Science, Białystok University of Technology,
Wiejska 45a, 15-351 Białystok, Poland
jstepan@ii.pb.bialystok.pl
[2] Institute of Mathematics, Warsaw University,
Banacha 2, 02-097 Warsaw, Poland
skowron@mimuw.edu.pl

Abstract. We discuss an ontological framework for approximation, i.e., to approximation of concepts and vague dependencies specified in a given ontology. The presented approach is based on different information granule calculi. We outline the rough–fuzzy approach for approximation of concepts and vague dependencies.

1 Introduction

We discuss the ontology for approximation in a granular computing framework. One of the main task in granular computing is to develop calculi of information granules [12,23,14,16]. Such calculi are aiming at constructing from elementary granules some target granules satisfying a given specification to a satisfactory degree. Hence, together with operations for construction of information granules one should define relevant measures of inclusion (to a degree) and closeness (to a degree) of granules. This idea has been presented and developed in the rough–mereological framework (see, e.g., [11,12]). Observe, that constructions of granules are often described by multilevel schemes and the final construction of the target information granule is obtained by a relevant composition of local schemes.

Vague dependencies have vague concepts in premises and conclusions. The approach to approximation of vague dependencies based only on degrees of closeness of concepts from dependencies and their approximations (classifiers) is not satisfactory for approximate reasoning. Hence, more advanced approach should be developed. Approximation of any vague dependency is a method which allows for any object to compute the arguments "for" and "against" its membership to the dependency conclusion on the basis of the analogous arguments relative to the dependency premises. Any argument is a compound information granule (compound pattern). Arguments are fused by local schemes (production rules) discovered from data. Further fusions are possible through composition of local schemes, called approximate reasoning schemes (AR schemes) (see, e.g., [2,12,10]). To estimate the degree to which (at least) an object belongs to concepts from ontology the arguments "for" and "against" those concepts are collected and next a conflict resolution strategy is applied to them to predict the degree.

D. Ślęzak et al. (Eds.): RSFDGrC 2005, LNAI 3641, pp. 718–727, 2005.

Several information granule calculi are involved in solving the problem of ontology approximation. Information granules in such calculi are represented by compound patterns.

By granulation of the discovered patterns to layers of vague concepts one can obtain more relevant approximations of dependencies. We outline the rough–fuzzy approach based on granulation.

The paper is organized as follows. In Section 2 we recall the basic concepts on approximation spaces. Rough information granule calculi based on the so called transducers are discussed in Section 3. In Section 4 we outline the approach to approximation of concepts and vague dependencies.

2   Approximation Spaces

In this section we recall a general definition of an approximation space [13,21]. Several known approaches to concept approximations can be covered using such spaces, e.g., the approach given in [9], approximations based on the variable precision rough set model [26] or tolerance (similarity) rough set approximations (see, e.g., [13,21] and references in [13,21]).

For every non-empty set U, let $P(U)$ denote the set of all subsets of U.

Definition 1. *[13,21] A parameterized approximation space is a system* $AS_{\#,\$} = (U, I_{\#}, \nu_{\$})$, *where*
  - *U is a non-empty set of objects,*
  - *$I_{\#} : U \to P(U)$ is an uncertainty function,*
  - *$\nu_{\$} : P(U) \times P(U) \to [0, 1]$ is a rough inclusion function,*

and $\#, \$$ denote vectors of parameters.

The uncertainty function defines for every object x, a set of objects described similarly. The set $I(x)$ is called the neighborhood of x (see, e.g., [9,7]). A set $X \subseteq U$ is *definable in* $AS_{\#,\$}$ if and only if it is a union of some values of the uncertainty function. The rough inclusion function defines the degree of inclusion of any $X \subseteq U$ in $Y \subseteq U$. In the simplest case it can be defined by (see, e.g., [13], [21]):

$$\nu_{SRI}(X, Y) = \begin{cases} \frac{card(X \cap Y)}{card(X)} & \text{if } X \neq \emptyset \\ 1 & \text{if } X = \emptyset. \end{cases}$$

This measure is widely used by the data mining and rough set communities. It is worth mentioning that Jan Łukasiewicz [8] was the first one who used this idea to estimate the probability of implications. However, rough inclusion can have a much more general form than inclusion of sets to a degree (see, e.g., [11,16,20]).

The lower and the upper approximations of subsets of U are defined as follows.

Definition 2. *For an approximation space $AS_{\#,\$} = (U, I_{\#}, \nu_{\$})$ and any subset $X \subseteq U$, the lower and upper approximations are defined by*
  $LOW(AS_{\#,\$}, X) = \{x \in U : \nu_{\$}(I_{\#}(x), X) = 1\}$,
  $UPP(AS_{\#,\$}, X) = \{x \in U : \nu_{\$}(I_{\#}(x), X) > 0\}$, *respectively.*

The lower approximation of a set X with respect to an approximation space $AS_{\#,\$}$ is the set of all objects, which can be classified with certainty as objects of X with respect to $AS_{\#,\$}$. The upper approximation of a set X with respect to an approximation space $AS_{\#,\$}$ is the set of all objects which can be possibly classified as objects of X with respect to $AS_{\#,\$}$.

The approximation spaces defined above have been generalized in [20]) to approximation spaces consisting of information granules. Approximation spaces themselves can be treated as special information granules. Granulation of approximation spaces, defined by operations of granulation and extension of relational structures, are studied, e.g., in [20]. For simplicity of considerations, we use in the paper the simple model of approximation space that has been recalled above.

3   Rough Information Granules and Transducers

Rough information granules are rough sets represented by some tuples of crisp sets (selected from lower and upper approximations, boundary regions, or complement of upper approximations). Then operations on such information granules transform rough sets into rough sets. Local schemes, called transducers [4], are used to represent operations for computing the lower and upper approximations of the target concept from the lower and upper approximations of arguments representing more elementary concepts. Multilevel schemes are representing compositions of such local schemes.

In [4], the authors study approximation transducers, devices that convert input approximate relations into output approximate ones by means of first-order theories. Different rough set techniques are applied to produce approximations of relations. In defining approximate transducers, methods of relational databases are invoked.

One can try to extend this approach to rough sets corresponding to approximations of concepts constructed using different operations such as transitive closure of relations, projections of sets, sets defined by formulas of modal logic, fixed point of some operators, etc. However, it is necessary to remember that the estimation of approximations of such concepts, obtained from approximations of concepts from which they are generated, can be of poor quality. The reason is the same as in the case of set theoretical operations, i.e., the approximation operations are not distributive with respect to such operations. Hence, the approximation quality can drop quickly with increasing of operation complexity. For example, if the only available information for approximation of the transitive closure R^* of relation R is the approximation of R then, usually, the received approximation will be of poor quality compared with the approximation that can be obtained by direct approximation of R^*, i.e., by using examples and counter examples of tuples satisfying R^*.

The conclusion is that, unfortunately, the approximation of more compound concepts has to be constructed gradually using more specific information, e.g., on patterns (information granules) discovered in construction of classifiers for some simpler concepts. In general, the high quality approximation of a concept dependent on some simpler concepts can not be derived from approximations of these simpler concepts only. In the next section we propose a step toward solution of this problem.

4 Approximation of Concepts and Dependencies from Ontology

In this section we discuss an approach to approximation of concepts and vague dependencies specified in a given concept ontology [15]. In the ontology concepts and local dependencies between them are specified. Global dependencies can be derived from local dependencies. Such derivations can be used as hints in searching for relevant compound patterns (information granules) in approximation of more compound concepts from the ontology.

The ontology approximation problem is one of the fundamental problems related to approximate reasoning in distributed environments. One should construct (in a given language that is different from the ontology specification language) not only approximations of concepts from ontology but also vague dependencies specified in the ontology. It is worthwhile to mention that an ontology approximation should be induced on the basis of incomplete information about concepts and dependencies specified in the ontology. Information granule calculi based on rough sets have been proposed as tools making it possible to solve this problem.

One can distinguish local and global dependencies between vague concepts specified in a given ontology. By a local dependency we mean a dependency consisting of concepts in premises in a sense "close" to the concept in the conclusion so that the process of inducing of classifiers and approximation of the dependency can be performed automatically from the partial information available about the concepts. If one would like to approximate a "global" dependency in which the vague concepts on the left hand side of dependency are "far" from concept on the right hand side then one should use additional information to bound the search for relevant patterns for concept approximation and dependency approximation. The solution in this case can be based on hierarchical learning (see, e.g., [22,2,3,5]).

Any concept from the left hand side of a given vague dependency is called its premise and the dependency conclusion is the concept from the right hand side of the dependency. By approximation of a given vague dependency we understood a method which allows for any object to compute the arguments "for" and "against" its membership to the dependency conclusion on the basis of analogous arguments relative to the dependency premises. Any argument "for" or "against" is a compound information granule (pattern) consisting of a pattern together with a degree to which (at least) this pattern is included to the concept and a degree to which (at least) the analyzed object is included to the pattern. Any local scheme (production rule) (see, e.g., [16]) or rough mereological connective (see, e.g., [12]) yields the fusion result of arguments for premises that is next taken as the argument for the dependency conclusion. By composition of local schemes more advanced fusion schemes are obtained, called approximate reasoning schemes (AR schemes) (see, e.g., [2,16,12,19]). They show how the arguments from premisses of dependencies are fused to arguments for more compound concepts derived in a given ontology from premisses. AR schemes can correspond to different parts of complex spatio-temporal objects. Hence, there is a need for composing AR schemes for parts into AR schemes for objects composed from these parts [19].

We assume that there are distinguished some primitive concepts in a given ontology for which it is possible to derive arguments "for" and "against" from experimental data tables (e.g., with sensory attributes). To estimate the degree to which a given object belongs (at least) to a given concept C from ontology there are collected arguments "for" and "against" by using appropriate AR schemes for this concept C and next is used a conflict resolution strategy for predicting the degree.

Observe also that the discovered information granules (patterns) can be used to specify different regions of the object universe on which different "parts" of approximation of a given vague dependency can be expressed in a more relevant way.

Now, we present more details on approximation of concepts and dependencies.

Patterns for a more complex concept C can be constructed along derivation of C from C_1, C_2 using the existing dependencies in ontology. The derivation helps gradually to construct patterns for more compound concepts in the derivation from less compound concepts (closer to C_1, C_2).

Let us now consider as an example of the dependency:

$$\text{If } C_1 \text{ and } C_2 \text{ then } C, \tag{1}$$

where C_1, C_2, C are vague concepts. We assume that examples of positive and negative cases for such concepts are given. We also assume that the condition attributes for C_1, C_2 are specified. To approximate the target concept C relevant patterns should be derived. The main idea is presented in Figure 1. We assume that basic information granules (basic patterns) used for approximation of concepts C_1, C_2 can be induced for C_1, C_2. Such patterns can be defined, e.g., by left hand sides of decision rules with decisions corresponding to the concepts C_1, C_2 and to their complements. For such basic granules, one can define operations of construction of more complex patterns relevant for approximation of the target concept C. The relevant patterns can be obtained by tuning parameters of the operations. One of the most important kind of such operations is defined by the constrained sums of information systems specified by patterns [18]. These operations filter objects satisfying the constraint from objects satisfying basic patterns.

For discovered patterns the degrees of their inclusion into the considered concepts are estimated.

Next, some rules are derived that make it possible to predict the degrees of inclusion of objects to target patterns (i.e., discovered for the dependency

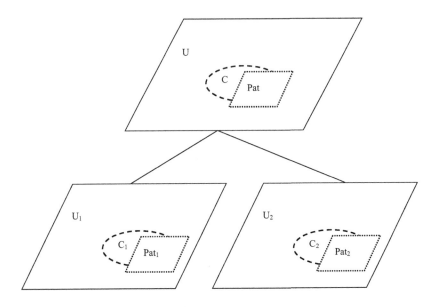

Fig. 1. Vague Concepts in U_1, U_2, U and Patterns

conclusion) from degrees of inclusion to source patterns (i.e., discovered for the dependency premisses) used for construction of the target patterns. Such rules are of the following form:

If the degree of inclusion of x in Pat_i is at least deg_i for $i = 1, 2$

then the degree of inclusion of x in Pat is at least deg

where Pat is a pattern constructed from Pat_1 and Pat_2 and deg_1, deg_2, deg, are the degrees of inclusion of x in patterns Pat_1, Pat_2, Pat, respectively, and Pat_1, Pat_2, Pat are relevant patterns discovered for approximation of concepts $C_1, , C_2, C$, respectively (for the details, the reader is referred to [14]).

The discovered patterns with their degrees of inclusion into concepts are used in the construction of classifiers. The degrees of inclusion of patterns in the concepts and objects in patterns are used by a conflict resolution strategy to predict the decision, i.e., to decide if the analyzed concept belongs to a concept or not. This is the standard procedure for construction of classifiers. In our example, the procedure of a classifier construction is performed for concepts C_1, C_2, C. In such a construction of classifiers inductive reasoning is used.

One can take into account some concordance conditions between strategies for conflict resolution in the constructed classifiers for C_1, C_2 and C. By tuning such conditions one can optimize the approximation of vague dependency on different object regions. This idea is depicted in Figure 2 (see also [5,3] for an application of weights defined by rule votes in extracting relevant patterns).

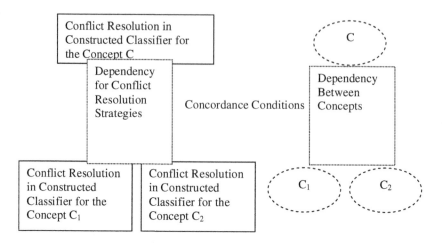

Fig. 2. Dependencies and Concordance Conditions

By granulation of discovered local schemes (production rules) more compound local schemes (production rules) can be discovered for approximation of concepts and dependencies. Such local schemes can represent dependencies between different layers of vague concepts. In this case one can use an approach based on the rough–fuzzy approach. To explain this idea we outline the approach using rough–fuzzy granules. These granules make it possible to derive a family of dependencies approximating a given dependency between vague concepts. The family consists of dependencies corresponding to different layers of the vague concepts.

Let us now discuss shortly an example of rough–fuzzy granules. Let $DT = (U, A, d)$ be a decision table with a binary decision $d : U \longrightarrow \{0, 1\}$, i.e., d is the characteristic function of some $X \subseteq U$. If the decision table is inconsistent [9], then one can define a new decision deg such that $deg(x) \in [0, 1]$ for any $x \in U$, may be interpreted as a degree to which x belongs to X [9,16]. Let us consider such a new decision table $DT' = (U, A, deg)$.

For given reals $0 < c_1 < \ldots < c_k$, where $c_i \in (0, 1]$ for $i = 1, \ldots, k$, we define c_i-cut by $X_i = \{x \in U : \nu(x) \geq c_i\}$. Assume that $X_0 = U$ and $X_{k+1} = X_{k+2} = \emptyset$. Any $B \subseteq A$ satisfying the following condition:

$$UPP(AS_B, (X_i - X_{i+1})) \subseteq (X_{i-1} - X_{i+2}), \text{ for } i = 1, \ldots, k, \qquad (2)$$

is called relevant for approximation of cuts $0 < c_1 < \ldots < c_k$ in DT'.

The condition (2) expresses the fact that the boundary region of the set between any two successive cuts is included into the union of this set and two adjacent to it such sets.

The language $\mathcal{L}_{rf}$ of rough–fuzzy patterns for DT' consists of tuples $(B, c_1, \ldots, c_k)$ defining approximations of regions between cuts, i.e.,

$$(LOW(AS_B, (X_i - X_{i+1})), UPP(AS_B, (X_i - X_{i+1}))), \text{ for } i = 0, \ldots, k, \qquad (3)$$

where we assume that B is relevant for approximation of cuts $0 < c_1 < \ldots < c_k$ in DT'.

Observe that searching for relevant patterns describing regions between cuts is related to tuning parameters $(B, c_1, \ldots, c_k)$ to obtain relevant patterns for the target concept approximation.

From a concept description in DT' (on a sample U) one can induce the concept approximation on an extension $U^* \supseteq U$. We consider, in a sense, richer classifiers, i.e., the classifiers that make it possible to predict different degrees to which the concept is satisfied. Such degrees can correspond to linguistic terms (e.g., low, medium, high) linearly ordered and to the boundary regions between successive degrees.

Any local scheme corresponding to a local dependency between vague concepts can be considered as a family of transducers satisfying a monotonicity property with respect to the linear order of linguistic degrees. This property can be expressed as follows:

if the granule corresponds to a linguistic membership degree deg of the dependency conclusion and it is constructed by the local scheme from some more elementary granules corresponding to some membership degrees $(deg_1, \ldots, deg_n)$

then this local scheme will yield a granule corresponding to deg at least from granules corresponding to $(deg_1', \ldots, deg_n')$ satisfying $deg_i' \geq deg_i$ for $i = 1, \ldots, n$, where $\geq$ denotes the linear order between linguistic degrees.

There are several problems to be solved to construct relevant layers of vague concepts for the approximation of dependencies between vague concepts. Among them are:

1. the problem of inducing relevant layers for the concepts;
2. the problem of inducing classifiers for the layers;
3. the monotonicity problem (the family of dependencies should satisfy the monotonicity property).

The discovered layers should make it possible to represent dependencies between vague concepts on the regions corresponding to the layers. We have developed strategies discovering such dependencies. Here, one can find an analogy to a neuron but a much more advanced neuron than that used in artificial neural networks [10].

We can conclude that taking fuzzy sets as models for vague concepts one can use rough sets for their constructive approximation. Then information granules we are searching for are families of approximations of different layers of concepts and dependencies between such approximated layers.

Observe that the family of dependencies discussed above may also be used in reasoning about changes. A linear order between layers corresponding to linguistic degrees of concept membership makes it possible to predict the degree of inclusion of a given object x to C on the basis of changes of degrees to which x is included in C_1, C_2.

Conclusions

We have discussed an ontological approach to the approximation problem. This approach covers the approximation of vague concepts and dependencies specified in a given ontology. Our ontology is presented in the framework of information granule calculi. The outlined methods for hierarchical construction of patterns, classifiers and vague dependency approximation create the basic step in our current project aiming at developing approximate reasoning methods in distributed or multiagent systems.

Acknowledgements

The authors gratefully acknowledge the suggestions made by Jim Peters concerning this paper. The research has been supported by the grants 3 T11C 002 26 and 4 T11C 014 25 from Ministry of Scientific Research and Information Technology of the Republic of Poland.

References

1. Barwise, J., Seligman, J.: *Information Flow: The Logic of Distributed Systems.* Cambridge University Press Tracts in Theoretical Computer Science 44, 1997.
2. Bazan, J., Skowron, A.: Classifiers based on approximate reasoning schemes. In: Dunin-Keplicz, B., Jankowski A., Skowron A., and Szczuka M., (Eds.), *Monitoring, Security, and Rescue Tasks in Multiagent Systems MSRAS*, Advances in Soft Computing. Springer, Heidelberg, 2005, 191–202.
3. Bazan, J., Nguyen, S. Hoa, Nguyen, H. Son, Skowron, A.: Rough set methods in approximation of hierarchical concepts. *Proc. of RSCTC'2004*, LNAI **3066**, Springer, Heidelberg, 2004, 346–355.
4. Doherty, P., Łukaszewicz, W., Skowron, A., Szałas, A.: Approximation transducers and trees: A technique for combining rough and crisp knowledge. In: [10], 189–218.
5. Nguyen, S. Hoa, Bazan, J., Skowron, A., Nguyen, H. Son: Layered learning for concept synthesis. *Transactions on Rough Sets I: LNCS Journal Subline*, LNCS **3100**, Springer, Heidelberg, 2004, 187–208,
6. Kloesgen, W., Żytkow, J. (eds.): *Handbook of Knowledge Discovery and Data Mining.* Oxford University Press, Oxford, 2002.
7. Lin, T.Y.: Granular computing and binary relations I & II. In: Skowron A. and Polkowski L. (Eds.), *Rough Sets in Knowledge Discovery* **1-2**, Physica-Verlag, Heidelberg, 1998, 107–120 and 121–140.
8. Łukasiewicz, J.: Die logischen Grundlagen der Wahrscheinilchkeitsrechnung, Kraków 1913. In: Borkowski, L. (ed.), *Jan Łukasiewicz - Selected Works.* North Holland, Amsterdam, Polish Scientific Publishers, Warsaw, 1970.
9. Pawlak, Z.: *Rough Sets. Theoretical Aspects of Reasoning about Data.* Kluwer Academic Publishers, Dordrecht, 1991.
10. Pal, S.K., Polkowski, L., Skowron, A. (Eds.): *Rough-Neural Computing: Techniques for Computing with Words.* Springer-Verlag, Berlin, 2004.
11. Polkowski, L., Skowron, A.: Rough mereology: A new paradigm for approximate reasoning. *Journal of Approximate Reasoning* **15**(4), 1996, 333–365.

12. Polkowski, L., Skowron, A.: Towards adaptive calculus of granules. In: [24], 201–227.
13. Skowron, A., Stepaniuk, J.: Tolerance approximation spaces. *Fundamenta Informaticae* **27**, 1996, 245–253.
14. Skowron, A., Stepaniuk, J.: Information granules: Towards foundations of granular omputing. *International Journal of Intelligent Systems* **16**(1), 2001, 57–86.
15. Staab, S., Studer, R., (Eds.): *Handbook on Ontologies*. International Handbooks on Information Systems, Springer, Heidelberg, 2004.
16. Skowron, A., Stepaniuk, J.: Information granules and rough-neural computing. In [10], 43–84.
17. Skowron, A., Stepaniuk, J., Peters, J.F.: Rough sets and infomorphisms: Towards approximation of relations in distributed environments. *Fundamenta Informaticae* **54**(1-2), 2003, 263–277.
18. Skowron, A., Stepaniuk, J.: Constrained sums of information systems. In: *Proc. RSCTC 2004*, LNCS **3066**, Springer , Heidelberg, 2004, 300–309.
19. Skowron, A., Synak, P.: Complex patterns. *Fundamenta Informaticae* **60**(1-4), 2004, 351–366.
20. Skowron, A., Swiniarski, R., Synak, P.: Approximation spaces and information granulation. *Transactions on Rough Sets III: LNCS Journal Subline*, LNCS **3400**, Springer, Heidelberg, 2005, 175–189.
21. Stepaniuk, J.: Knowledge discovery by application of rough set models. In: L. Polkowski, S. Tsumoto, T.Y. Lin (Eds.), *Rough Set Methods and Applications. New Developments in Knowledge Discovery in Information Systems*, Physica–Verlag, Heidelberg, 2000, 137–233.
22. Stone, P.: *Layered Learning in Multi-Agent Systems: A Winning Approach to Robotic Soccer*. MIT Press, Cambridge, MA, 2000.
23. Zadeh, L.A.: Toward a theory of fuzzy information granulation and its certainty in human reasoning and fuzzy logic. *Fuzzy Sets and Systems* **90** (1997) 111–127.
24. Zadeh, L.A., Kacprzyk, J. (eds.): *Computing with Words in Information/Intelligent Systems* **1-2**, Physica-Verlag, Heidelberg, 1999.
25. Zadeh, L.A.: A new direction in AI: Toward a computational theory of perceptions. *AI Magazine* **22**(1), 2001, 73–84.
26. Ziarko, W.: Variable precision rough set model, *Journal of Computer and System Sciences* **46**, 1993, 39–59.

Table Representations of Granulations Revisited
Pre-topological Information Tables

I-Jen Chiang[1], Tsau Young Lin[2], and Yong Liu[3]

[1] Graduate Institute of Medical Informatics, Taipei Medical University,
205 Wu-Hsien Street, Taipei, Taiwan 110
ijchiang@tmu.edu.tw
[2] Department of Computer Science, San Jose State University,
San Jose, California 95192, USA
tylin@cs.sjsu.edu
[3] College of Computer Science, Zhejiang University,
Hangzhou 310027, China
cckaffe@yahoo.com.cn

Abstract. This paper examines the knowledge representation theory of granulations. The key strengths of rough set theory are its capabilities in representing and processing knowledge in table format. For general granulation such capabilities are unknown. For single level granulation, two initial theories have been proposed previously by one of the authors. In this paper, the theories are re-visited, a new and deeper analysis is presented: Granular information table is an incomplete representation, so computing with words is the main method of knowledge processing. However for symmetrical granulation, the pre-topological information table is a complete representation, so the knowledge processing can be formal.

1 Introduction

Relational database theory is designed to model the real world of a long duration [10]. For each instance the interactions among entities can be very different from the other instance. So the relational model takes the common denominator and ignores the interactions among entities. So it assumes the universe of all entities and various attribute domains are Cantor sets, in which no interactions among elements are modeled. However, in data mining or data analysis the modeling is instance based. So the assumption that the underlying structure of the universe of entities is a classical set is an over simplified one.

1.1 Models of Real World Entities

A more realistic modeling is needed. What should be the proper model of real world entities? There are two views available. The first one is from the model theory of first order logic, where a model is a Cantor set together with the relational structure. The second one is from granulation.

D. Ślęzak et al. (Eds.): RSFDGrC 2005, LNAI 3641, pp. 728–737, 2005.

2   Granulation and Relational Structure

Let us revise our arguments in [14]. According to Lotfi Zadeh [20]:

- "*information granulation involves partitioning a class of objects (points) into granules, with a granule being a clump of objects (points), which are drawn together by indistinguishability, similarity or functionality.*"
- The phrase "drawn together by indistinguishability, similarity or functionality," in general, can be expressed mathematically by relations.

If the group of drawn together consists of n objects, then the relation is n-ary; we may refer to such structure as n-ary granulation. In general, for every n, there may be several, even infinitely many, n-ary relations. In granular computing, n can be any cardinal number. In relational structure of the model theory, they are all finite; first order logic does not use predicates of non-finite places. In real life, we go seldom beyond initial few n, taking topological space into consideration, n = 2 is adequate.

2.1   Basic Granulation and Relational Structure

As a first step, we have considered the simplest granulation or the simplest relational structure (of first order logic). In other words, the underlying structure is a binary granulation or equivalently binary relational structure [14], [10], [7], [6]. In this paper, we take a deeper and new view on its representation theory.

"Drawn together," in the binary cases, implies certain level of symmetry. If p is drawn towards q, then q is also drawn towards p. Such symmetry, we believe, is imposed by impreciseness of natural language. To avoid such implications, we will rephrase it to "drawn towards an object p," so that it is clear the reverse may or may not be true.

In binary relation, "drawn together" can be viewed as a special case of "drawn towards p," since p may vary through every object of a granule. So for each p, we will use $B(p)$ to denote the group of objects that are drawn toward p. Now we have a localized version of Zadeh's word:

Definition 1. *By a binary granulation we mean the association of an object $p \in V$ with a granule $B(p) \subseteq V$ (neighborhood), where p varies through all objects of the universe V. This association is a mapping $V \longrightarrow 2^V$, called a basic or binary granulation (BG).*

2.2   Geometric and Algebraic Views

It will be helpful to visualize the granulation, for this goal, we will use geometric terminology. We will refer to a granule as a neighborhood of p, and the collection,

$$\{B(p) \mid p \text{ varies through } V\}$$

is called the basic (binary) neighborhood system (BNS) of V. Note that it is possible that $B(p)$ is an empty set. In this case we will simply say p has no neighborhood by abuse of language; to be very correct, we should say p has an empty neighborhood.

Also we should note that many different points, $p, q, \ldots$ may have the same neighborhood (granule) $B(p) = B(q)$. The set of all q such that $B(q)$ is equal to $B(p)$, is called the center set $C(p)$ of the granule $B(p)$; each element in $C(p)$ is called a center. The collection of the center sets forms a partition on V.

To help us manipulating the granulation, we also reformulate it algebraically:

$$R = \{(p, v) \mid v \in B(p) \text{ and } p \in V\}$$

is a binary relation (BR) defined by BG.

Proposition 1. *A basic (binary) neighborhood system (BNS), a basic (binary) granulation (BG), and a binary relation (BR) are equivalent.*

3   Knowledge Representations

First we setup a convention.

Convention: A symbol is a string of "bits and bytes." Regardless of whether that symbol may or may not have the intended real world meaning, no real world meaning participates in the formal processing. A symbol is termed a word, if the intended real world meaning *participates* in the formal processing.

Please note that "symbol" here is equivalent to the "word" in group theory.

The main idea here is to extend representation theory of rough sets to granular computing, in which granules have overlapping semantics. Real world granulation often cannot be expressed by equivalence relations. For example, the notions of "near","similar", and "conflict" are not equivalence relations. The granulation of human body by body, leg and head, and etc is not a partition. So there are intrinsic needs to generalize the knowledge representation theory of partition (rough set theory) to more general settings (granular computing).

We will re-interpret and refine some earlier works; see the latest overview in [7]. Here are the three main topics:

1. Relational Table: This is the classical rough set representation of partitions. The basic idea is to assign a meaningful name to each equivalence class of an equivalence relation (partition). These names are independent from each other, since equivalence classes are mutually disjoint. The representation, in rough set theory, has been called an information system, a knowledge representation system, an information table, or a data table. In the relational database theory, it is called a *bag relation*.
2. Granular Table: This is the first representation theory of granulation observed [12], [15], [14]. The basic idea is to assign a meaningful name to each granule of a granulation (binary relation.) These names are not independent from each other, since granules may overlap; in other words, these names have non-trivial interactions. We capture these interactions partially. We represent it by the binary relation of the intersections of granules.

3. Topological Table: The representation is similar, but deeper than granular table. In this representation, we also consider the induced partition. Each equivalence class, called the center set, is uniquely associated with a granule. Hence, we assign a meaningful name to each granule, as well as equivalence class; so we have a granular table and a partition table. They are algebraically isomorphic [11]. In the partition table, we capture the interactions of granules by a pre-topology [7], [8], [9]. If the granulation (binary relation) is symmetric, the representation is complete in the sense we can recapture the binary relations from the pre-topological table.

4   Relational Tables - Representations of Partitions

A *partition* is a collection of pairwise disjoint subsets whose union is V. The corresponding algebraic concept is an equivalence relation. So each subset is called an equivalence class in mathematics; to synchronize with granulation, we may call it granule. It is the simplest kind of granulation.

Pawlak (1982) [18] and Tony Lee (1983)[5] observed that a relational table is a knowledge representation of a universe of entities. Each column induces an equivalence relation (partition) on the universe; n columns induce n partitions. More generally, they observed:

Proposition 2. *A subset B of attributes of a relational table K, in particular a single attribute, induces an equivalence relation Q^B on V.*

To do the knowledge representation, we will explore the converse. We shall recall some of the analysis in [12], [13], [15], [14].

Definition 2. *The pair (V, Q) is a granular data model (GDM), if V is a classical set of entities, and Q is a finite family of equivalence relations on V.*

Pawlak called it a knowledge base. As the latter one often has different meaning, we will use GDM. By reversing Pawlak and Tony Lee's observation, we assign a word (meaningful to human) to each equivalence class. Such an assignment can be expressed in a table format. We will illustrate the idea by example.

Let $U = \{id_1, id_2, \ldots, id_9\}$ be a set of nine balls with two partitions:

1. $\{\{id_1, id_2, id_3\}, \{id_4, id_5\}, \{id_6, id_7, id_8, id_9\}\}$
2. $\{\{id_1, id_2\}, \{id_3\}, \{id_4, id_5\}, \{id_6, id_7, id_8, id_9\}\}$

We label the first partition COLOR and the second WEIGHT. They are the best summarizations of the given partitions from the view of human. Next, we will name each equivalence class by its real world characteristic: We name the first equivalence class Red, because each ball of this group has red color (appears to human). Note that this name reflects human's view and human only. For example, physical characteristics, such as wave length are *not* implemented and stored in the system. In AI, such terms, COLOR and Red, are called semantic primitive [1]. They are primitives (undefined terms) from the view of computer systems, but they do have the intent to represent human perceived semantics. We will summarize the previous analysis as follows:

1. $id_1 \longrightarrow (\{id_1, id_2, id_3\}) \longrightarrow$ Red
   The first $\longrightarrow$ says that id_1 belongs to the equivalence class $[id_1]$ and
   the second $\longrightarrow$ says that the equivalence class has been named Red.
2. $id_2 \longrightarrow (\{id_1, id_2, id_3\}) \longrightarrow$ Red
   . . .
4. $id_4 \longrightarrow (\{id_4, id_5\}) \longrightarrow$ Orange
   . . .
9. $id_9 \longrightarrow (\{id_6, id_7, id_8, id_9\}) \longrightarrow$ Yellow

Similarly, we have names for all WEIGHT-classes. We have constructed Table 1:

Table 1. Constructing a relational table by naming each granule

U	COLOR	WEIGHT
id_1	Red	W1
id_2	Red	W1
id_3	Red	W2
id_4	Orange	W3
id_5	Orange	W3
id_6	Yellow	W4
id_7	Yellow	W4
id_8	Yellow	W4
id_9	Yellow	W4

Note that each word represents an equivalence class of a partition. So the words
within a column have no overlapping semantics; Each word is independent from
each other. So these words can be treated as symbols. In the table processing of
rough set theory, they have been regarded as symbols. Their intended semantics
can only be carried out in the presence of human operators.

4.1   Granular Tables

The representation of a partition is rested on two properties:

1. Each object p belongs to an equivalence class (the union of equivalence class
   covers the whole universe)
2. No objects belong to more than one equivalence class (equivalence classes
   are pairwise disjoint)

We need a similar property in binary granulation: Let B be a binary granulation

1. Each object, $p \in V$, is assigned to one and only one B-granule
2. No objects are assigned to more than one granule. Note that we are *not*
   using the memberships; we are considering the binary granulation, that is,
   the association between object and its granule.

Next we assign each B-granule a unique meaningful name. Such an association
allows us to represent *a finite set of binary granulations* by a "relational table",
called a *granular table*.

Let us recall the illustration in [15]. In binary granulation, each p is associated with a unique binary neighborhood B_p, which consists of balls that have certain color component:

1. $B_{id_1} = B_{id_2} = B_{id_3} = \{id_1, id_2, id_3, id_4, id_5\}$ is the set of all balls that have red color component in their color coating.
2. $B_{id_4} = B_{id_5} = \{id_1, id_2, id_3, id_4, id_5, id_6, id_7, id_8, id_9\}$ is the set of all balls that have red or yellow color components in their color coating.
3. $B_{id_6} = B_{id_7} = B_{id_8} = B_{id_9} = \{id_4, id_5, id_6, id_7, id_8, id_9\}$ is the set of all balls that have yellow color components in their color coating.

Then to each binary granule (neighborhood), we assign a word (not a symbol).

1. Having-RED $=$ Name$(B_{id_1}) = \ldots =$ Name(B_{id_3}); The name indicates that all the balls in this granule has red color component in its coating.
2. Having-RED+YELLOW $=$ Name$(B_{id_4}) =$ Name(B_{id_5}); The name indicates that all the balls in this granule has red and yellow color component(orange color is a mixture of red and yellow)
3. Having-YELLOW $=$ Name$(B_{id_6}) = \ldots =$Name(B_{id_9})

These words have human-perceived semantics attached and will participate in formal processing. The non-empty intersections among granules imply that there are non-trivial logical interactions among these words; and such interactions will be respected during data processing. By considering the following map:

- Entities $\rightarrow$ Granules $\rightarrow$ Words, we have
    1. $id_1 \rightarrow B_{id_1} \rightarrow$ Having-RED
       $\ldots$
    4. $id_4 \rightarrow B_{id_4} \rightarrow$ Having-RED+YELLOW
    5. $id_5 \rightarrow B_{id_4} \rightarrow$ Having-RED+YELLOW
       $\ldots$
    9. $id_9 \rightarrow B_{id_1} \rightarrow$ Having-YELLOW
    $\ldots$ similar statements for WEIGHT

They are summarized in granular table Table 2. To process such a table, we need computing with words (respecting the semantics). In Table 3, we express the binary relation, called granular binary relation, among these words. The binary relation only partially captures the interactions among words (in a column). Note that this binary relation reflects the non-empty intersection of granules: For example (Having-Red, Having-Red+Yellow) $\in B_{COLOR}$ if and only if the two granules have non-empty intersection.

Perhaps, we should stress again that attribute values have overlapping semantics; so the interactions among these words have to be properly handled.

Definition 3. *The name of a granule is binary related to the name of another granule, if they have non-empty intersection.*

Such a binary relation is described in Table 3; but we need to stress that the binary relation does not adequately describe the relationships among granules. We need computing with words to deal with the information on semantic level.

Table 2. Granular Table: There are interactions among the words

BALLs	Granulation 1	Granulation 2
id_1	Having-RED	W1
id_2	Having-RED	W1
id_3	Having-RED	W2
id_4	Having-RED+YELLOW	W3
id_5	Having-RED+YELLOW	W3
id_6	Having-YELLOW	W4
id_7	Having-YELLOW	W4
id_8	Having-YELLOW	W4
id_9	Having-YELLOW	W4

Table 3. A Symmetric Binary Relation for Color Attributes

Having-RED	Having-RED
Having-RED	Having-RED
Having-RED	Having-RED+YELLOW
Having-RED+YELLOW	Having-RED
Having-RED+YELLOW	Having-RED+YELLOW
Having-RED+YELLOW	Having-YELLOW
Having-YELLOW	Having-RED+YELLOW
Having-YELLOW	Having-YELLOW

5   Topological Tables

Note that the binary granulation $B : V \rightarrow 2^U; p \mapsto B(p)$ is a map whose inverse images $C(p) = B^{-1}(B(p))$ induce an equivalence relation E_B on V. The equivalence class is called the center set of $B(p)$. Let the center set be:

$$C_w = B^{-1}(B_p), \tag{1}$$

where w=Name(B_p). Verbally, C_w consists of all objects that have the same B-granule B_p. We use the granule's names to index the family of the center sets

$$C_{\text{Having-RED}} \equiv \text{Center of } B_{id_1} = \text{Center of } B_{id_2}$$
$$= \text{Center of } B_{id_3} = \{id_1, id_2, id_3\}$$
$$C_{\text{Having-RED+YELLOW}} \equiv \text{Center of } B_{id_4} = \text{Center of } B_{id_5}$$
$$= \{id_4, id_5\}$$
$$C_{\text{Having-YELLOW}} \equiv \text{Center of } B_{id_6} = \ldots = \text{Center of } B_{id_9}$$
$$= \{id_6, id_7, id_8, id_9\}$$

For $B(p) = \emptyset$, $C(p) = \{x \mid B(x) = \emptyset\}$. We call the collection of $\{C(p) \mid p \in V\}$ topological partition with the understanding that there is a neighborhood $B(p)$ for each equivalence class $C(p)$. The neighborhoods capture the interaction among equivalence classes. Such a family $\{C(p)\}$ is a partition in BNS-spaces. Now, we will define the topological binary relation.

Definition 4. *The name of a granule is topologically binary related to the name of another granule, if the first granule has non-empty intersection with the center set of second granule. We regard the name of the second granule as a member of the neighborhood of the name of first granule.*

Thus, for example to define the topological binary relation B_{COLOR} we have

$$(\text{Having} - \text{RED}, \text{Having} - \text{RED} + \text{YELLOW}) \in B_{\text{COLOR}}$$

if $B_{id_1} \cap C_{\text{Having-RED+YELLOW}} \neq \emptyset$ and $id_i \in C_{\text{Having-RED}}$ etc. Note that the B-granule is definable by the induced partition, if B is symmetric [8], [9].

Proposition 3. *If $B \subseteq V \times V$ is a symmetric binary relation, and E_B its induced equivalence relation, then each B-binary neighborhood is a union of E_B-equivalence classes.*

So B is definable on attribute domain (a quotient set of V) that consists of all center sets. So Table 4 and Table 5 completely defined by B and vice versa.

   Note that such a binary structure cannot be deduced from the table structure. We are ready to introduce the notion of semantic property.

Definition 5. *A property is said to be semantic if it is not implied by the table structure. A property is said to be syntactic if it is implied by the table structure.*

The binary relation (Table 3) is not derived from the table structure (of Table 2) so it is a semantic property. This type of tables has been studied in [17,16] for approximate retrievals; and is called topological relations or tables. Formally:

Definition 6. *A relational table (e.g. Table 4) whose attributes are equipped with topological binary relations (e.g. Table 5 for COLOR attribute) is called a (pre-) topological relation.*

By replacing the names of binary granules with the center sets, Table 2 is transformed to Table 4; they are isomorphic. However, the topologies are different: Table 5 provides the topology of Table 4. Table 3 provides that of Table 2.

Table 4. Topological Table

BALLs	Granulation 1	Granulation 2
id_1	$C_{\text{Having-RED}}$	W1
...	...	...
id_3	$C_{\text{Having-RED}}$	W2
id_4	$C_{\text{Having-RED+YELLOW}}$	W3
...	...	...
id_9	$C_{\text{Having-YELLOW}}$	W4

Table 5. A Topological Binary Relation on the Center sets of COLOR

$C_{\text{Having-RED}}$	$C_{\text{Having-RED}}$
$C_{\text{Having-RED}}$	$C_{\text{Having-RED+YELLOW}}$
$C_{\text{Having-RED+YELLOW}}$	$C_{\text{Having-RED}}$
$C_{\text{Having-RED+YELLOW}}$	$C_{\text{Having-RED+YELLOW}}$
$C_{\text{Having-RED+YELLOW}}$	$C_{\text{Having-YELLOW}}$
$C_{\text{Having-YELLOW}}$	$C_{\text{Having-RED+YELLOW}}$
$C_{\text{Having-YELLOW}}$	$C_{\text{Having-YELLOW}}$

Table 6. Topological Table

BALLs	Granulation 1	Granulation 2
id_1	NAME($C_{\text{Having-RED}}$)	NAME(W1)
...	...	...
id_4	NAME($C_{\text{Having-RED+YELLOW}}$)	NAME(W3)
...	...	...
id_9	NAME($C_{\text{Having-YELLOW}}$)	NAME(W4)

Theorem 1. *Given a finite set of binary relations B, a finite set of equivalence relations E_B can be induced. The knowledge representation of B is a topological representation of E_B.*

Proof. (A Sketchy) As we have illustrated before, the knowledge representations of B and E_B are accomplished by giving meaningful names to the granules and its center sets respectively. Note that Table 4 is a table of equivalence classes of E_B and its knowledge representation in Table 6 is a table with symbolic names replacing the equivalence classes. By replacing the names of binary granules with those of the center sets we will have Table 2 transformed to Table 6. Therefore, syntactically, the knowledge representation of B and E_B is the same (isomorphic). We can directly impose an isomorphic binary relation on Table 6. Note that Table 5 and the imposed relation provide the same pre-topology. In other words, the isomorphism becomes a topological isomorphism;   □

6   Conclusions

In the series of our papers, we have literally taken Zadeh's intuitive description of clumps as a formal mathematical notion of granulation. It is essentially a mild generalization of binary relations and neighborhood systems in (pre-)topological spaces [19], [17], [16], [14], [15], [7], [6]. By giving a (meaningful) name to each granule, we have a representation theory. The processing of this kind of representations has to be relied on computing with words; there are unformalized interactions among the attributes values (names of overlapping granules); the interactions need further investigation. However, the topological view, in the case of symmetric binary relational structure, does capture the representation quite "completely" in the sense that the interactions among granules can be specified formally by binary relations (of center sets which are equivalence classes).

References

1. Barr, A., Feigenbaum, E.A.: The handbook of Artificial Intelligence, Willam Kaufmann (1981)
2. Birkhoff, G., MacLane, S.: A Survey of Modern Algebra, Macmillan (1977)
3. Brualdi, R.A.: Introductory Combinatorics, Prentice Hall (1992)
4. Cai, Y.D., Cercone, N., Han, J.: Attribute-oriented induction in relational databases. In: Knowledge Discovery in Databases. AAAI/MIT Press, Cambridge, MA (1991) 213–228
5. Lee, T.T.: Algebraic Theory of Relational Databases. The Bell System Technical Journal, 62(10), December (1983) 3159–3204
6. Lin, T.Y., Liau, C.J.: Granular Computing and rough sets: An Incremental Development. In: Data Mining and Knowledge Discovery Handbook, Springer, to appear (2005)
7. Lin, T.Y.: Granular Computing from Rough Set Prospect. IEEE Computational intelligence Society Newsletter, November (2004)
8. Lin, T.Y.: Chinese Wall Security Policy Models: Information Flows and Confining Trojan Horses. In: Data and Applications Security XVII: Status and Prospects, Kluwer Academic Publishers (2003) 275–297
9. Lin, T.Y.: Granular Computing on Binary Relations-Analysis of Conflict and Chinese Wall Security Policy. In : Proceedings of RSCTC'2002. LNAI 2475, Springer (2002) 296–299
10. Lin, T.Y., Louie, E.: Modeling the Real World for Data Mining: Granular Computing Approach. In: Proceedings of Joint 9th IFSA World Congress and 20th NAFIPS International Conference (2001) 3044–3049
11. Lin, T.Y.: Generating Concept Hierarchies/Networks: Mining Additional Semantics in Relational Data. In: Advances in Knowledge Discovery and Data Mining. LNAI 2035, Springer (2001) 174–185
12. Lin, , T.Y.: Data Mining and Machine Oriented Modeling: A Granular Computing Approach. Journal of Applied Intelligence 13(2), Kluwer, (2000) 113–124
13. Lin, T.Y.: Granular Computing: Fuzzy Logic and Rough Sets. In: Computing with words in information/intelligent systems, Springer-Verlag (1999) 183–200
14. Lin, T.Y.: Granular Computing on Binary Relations I: Data Mining and Neighborhood Systems. In: Rough Sets In Knowledge Discovery, Springer-Verlag (1998) 107–121
15. Lin, T.Y.: Granular Computing on Binary Relations II: Rough Set Representations and Belief Functions. In: Rough Sets In Knowledge Discovery, Springer-Verlag (1998) 121–140
16. Lin, T.Y.: Neighborhood systems and approximation in database and knowledge base systems. In: Proceedings of the Fourth International Symposium on Methodologies of Intelligent Systems (1989) 75–86
17. Lin, T.Y.: Neighborhood Systems and Relational Database. In: Proceedings of 1988 ACM Sixteen Annual Computer Science Conference, February 23-25 (1988) 725
18. Pawlak, Z.: Rough sets. Theoretical Aspects of Reasoning about Data. Kluwer Academic Publishers (1991)
19. Sierpinski, W., Krieger, C.: General Topology. University of Toronto Press (1956)
20. Zadeh, L.: The Key Roles of Information Granulation and Fuzzy Logic in Human Reasoning. In: 1996 IEEE International Conference on Fuzzy Systems, September 8-11, 1 (1996)

Author Index

Lecture Notes in Artificial Intelligence (LNAI)